THE ENCYCLOPEDIA OF COLONIAL AND REVOLUTIONARY AMERICA

THE ENCYCLOPEDIA OF COLONIAL AND REVOLUTIONARY AMERICA

General Editor

John Mack Faragher

DA CAPO PRESS • NEW YORK

Library of Congress Cataloging in Publication Data

The encyclopedia of colonial and revolutionary America / general edi-
   tor, John Mack Faragher.
      p.   cm.
   Originally published: New York: Facts on File, 1990.
   Includes index.
   ISBN 0-306-80687-8 (alk. paper)
   1. United States—History—Colonial period, ca. 1600–1775—Encyclo-
pedias. 2. United States—History—Revolution, 1775–1783—Encyclope-
dias. 3. Great Britain—Colonies—America—Encyclopedias. 4.
Canada—History—To 1763 (New France)—Encyclopedias. I. Faragher,
John Mack, 1945–   .
[E188.E63   1996]   95-43888
973.2′03—dc20   CIP

First Da Capo Press edition 1996

This Da Capo Press paperback edition of *The Encyclopedia of
Colonial and Revolutionary America* is an unabridged republication of
the edition first published in New York in 1990. It is reprinted by
arrangement with Facts On File.

Published by Da Capo Press, Inc.
A Subsidiary of Plenum Publishing Corporation
233 Spring Street, New York, N.Y. 10013

Contents

To Josh and Jesse Hoffnung Garskof
My two sons

INTRODUCTION

This encyclopedia has been designed as a quick reference to topics in the history of Colonial and Revolutionary America. The entries are thoroughly cross referenced with *See also* citations at the end of most articles. By using the *See also* references and the more extensive Topic Guides the reader can follow a trail from the specific to the general, or vice versa. Moreover, the bibliographies that accompany the major entries allow this encyclopedia to be used as a guide to basic sources and further reading.

The Topic Guides, which accompany major articles, show the encyclopedia's coverage in broad fields in more detail than possible in *See also* references. The Topic Guides are as follows:

Afro-Americans	Indians, North American
Agriculture	Indian Wars
British Empire	Mercantilism
Colonial Government	Religion
Exploration	Revolutionary War
French Colonies	Spanish Colonies
Frontier	War
Geography and Culture	Women

Assisting in the construction of the master list of entries were four editorial consultants with distinguished reputations in the field: Joseph J. Ellis, Professor of History at Mount Holyoke College; Edwin S. Gaustad, Professor of History at the University of California at Riverside; Gary B. Nash, Professor of History at the University of California at Los Angeles; and Mary Beth Norton, Professor of History at Cornell University. Together we have made every effort to include not only the basic and traditional topics, but those suggested as well by the new work in the ethnohistory of American Indians, in African American history, women's history, social history, economic history, and demography. In addition, this encyclopedia includes not only the colonies of British America, but those areas of French and Spanish America that would later become territories of the United States. The entries were written not only by persons with the experience represented by the editorial consultants, but by a number of younger historians who are well-acquainted with the most recent work in the history of Colonial and Revolutionary America.

John Mack Faragher
Mt. Carmel, Connecticut
January, 1989

List of Contributors

Ackerman, Rebecca

Arnold, Douglas M., The Papers of Benjamin Franklin

Balesi, Charles J., The French Colonial Historical Society

Benson, Barbara E., Historical Society of Delaware

Breslaw, Elaine G., Morgan State University

Burke, Suzanne Stone

Carpenter, Rachel H., Rhode Island College

Cashin, Edward J., Augusta College

Chapelle, Suzanne Greene, Morgan State University

Chase, John Terry

Chase, Sara Hannum

Conley, Patrick T., Providence College

Cooper, James F., Jr., University of Connecticut

Cooper, Laura, University of Connecticut

Cortés, Carlos E., University of California, Riverside

Crane, Elaine Forman, Fordham University

Crosthwaite, Jane F., Mount Holyoke College

Crumpacker, Laurie T., Simmons College

Curry, Vanessa Jo

Duffy, Dan, Circle Repertory Company

Faragher, John Mack, Mount Holyoke College

Forster, Cornelius P., O.P., Providence College

Gaustad, Edwin S., University of California, Riverside

Gest, Maureen A., Yale University

Gitlin, Jay, Yale University

Haan, Richard L., Hartwick College

Halko, Henry J., Simmons College

Hall, Robert L., Northeastern University

Henderson, Rodger C., Pennsylvania State University, Fayette Campus

Hermes, Katherine A., Yale University

Ifkovic, John W., Westfield State College

Janson, Dena M., Rhode Island College

Karlsen, Carol F., University of Michigan, Ann Arbor

Lurie, Maxine N., Rutgers University

McCaffrey, Donna Thérèse, Providence College

Miles, George, Beinecke Rare Book Library, Yale University

Minkema, Kenneth P., University of Connecticut

Morgan, Lynda J., Mount Holyoke College

Moynihan, Ruth B., University of Connecticut

Nobles, Gregory H., Georgia Institute of Technology

Prioleau, Brian

Richman, Allen, Stephen F. Austin State University

Riforgiato, Leonard R., Pennsylvania State University, Shenango Valley Campus

Rink, Oliver A., California State College, Bakersfield

Ritchie, Robert C., University of California, San Diego

Roth, Leland M., University of Oregon

Saillant, John, Brown University

Salisbury, Neal, Smith College

Salmon, Marylynn, University of Maryland, Baltimore County

Selby, John E., College of William and Mary

Shatzman, Aaron M., Emory University

Silberman, Neil Asher

Sinclair, Peter

Somerville, James K., State University College, Geneseo, New York

Thompson, Thomas C., University of California, Riverside

Tripp, Wendell, New York State Historical Association

Wallace, R. Stuart, New Hampshire Division of Historical Research

Watson, Alan D., University of North Carolina at Wilmington

Wood, Peter H., Duke University

Wright, Robert K., U.S. Army Center of Military History

Zola, Gary P., Hebrew Union College–Jewish Institute of Religion

THE ENCYCLOPEDIA OF
COLONIAL
AND
REVOLUTIONARY
AMERICA

A

ABORTION   According to English tradition, it was only after the "quickening," the first perception of fetal movement by the mother, that abortion raised legal or ethical problems. Indeed, without any medical means of confirming pregnancy before the quickening, actions to "unblock" menstrual flow were tantamount to an abortion. In colonial America there was widespread knowledge and use of many herbal abortifacients as well as other folk practices, some dangerous, that might induce an abortion. Moreover, midwives and regular doctors frequently employed intrusive procedures. If not common, abortions were not rare, being employed not as a method of family limitation but as a way of terminating illegitimate pregnancies. Antiabortion legislation was not passed until the 19th century.

ABRAHAM, PLAINS OF   Located north and slightly west of Quebec, the field known as the Plains of Abraham was the site of an important British victory in the French and Indian War. After years of suffering defeats, the British forces were placed under the new command of Jeffrey Amherst and James Wolfe. Successes at Crown Point and Ticonderoga climaxed when, on September 13, 1759, General Wolfe led his army against Marquis Louis Joseph de Montcalm de Saint-Veran, commander of the French forces in defense of the Plains. Wolfe's victory at the Plains of Abraham set the stage for the British conquest of Montreal the following year.
See also French and Indian War; Montcalm, Marquis de; Wolfe, James.

ACT OF FRAUDS (1662)   Passed by Parliament on the recommendation of the Lords of Trade and Plantations, the Act of Frauds served to strengthen enforcement of the 1660 Navigation Act, which specified that all trade to and from English colonies in America, Asia, and Africa must be carried in English-owned vessels. A significant number of merchants had, however, been fraudulently transferring ownership of foreign trade vessels to English firms to facilitate otherwise illegal trade. The Act of Frauds made this evasive "reflagging" of vessels more difficult by requiring that all vessels trading with the colonies be English-built as well as English-owned.
See also Navigation Acts.

ACTS OF TRADE AND NAVIGATION   A reflection of England's mercantilist policy, the acts of trade and navigation were parliamentary statutes designed to control and regulate colonial trade for the benefit of the mother country, to secure colonial dependence, to encourage English and colonial shipping, to make England an entrepôt for colonial goods, and to advance English domestic industry. The principles of the acts of trade and navigation were not entirely novel, for the commercial regulations of the Tudor and early Stuart monarchs foreshadowed much of the later legislation.

First Acts   The Navigation Act of 1651 (presaged by legislation in 1650), the first comprehensive parliamentary statute to define English commercial policy, contained the following provisions: goods of the growth and manufacture of Asia, Africa, or America might be imported into England and English colonies only in ships of which the proprietor, master, and majority of sailors were English; goods of European growth or production might be imported into England or English dominions only in English ships or ships of the country in which the goods were grown or produced; goods of foreign growth or manufacture might only be brought into England from the place of growth or manufacture, or from those ports from which the goods were ordinarily shipped. The 1651 statute was aimed at the competition offered by the Dutch carrying trade and did not greatly restrict English colonial commerce.
Upon the restoration of the monarchy in 1660, legislation in that year (confirmed in 1661 and further defined in 1662) reiterated the provisions of the previous statutes with

the added stipulation that ships carrying goods to and from England must have been built in England or in the English colonies. The same statute also instituted the policy of "enumerated goods," articles of colonial growth, production, or manufacture that were required to be shipped first to England, Ireland, Wales, or Berwick-on-Tweed. Legislation in the 18th century constantly enlarged the list of enumerated goods so that by 1766-67, significant direct colonial trade with northern European countries except Great Britain was virtually eliminated.

By statute in 1663, England sought to monopolize the handling of colonial imports. High duties prohibited the importation of European goods into the colonies unless brought via England, Wales, or Berwick-on-Tweed in English or English-colonial vessels. Parliament allowed the following exceptions: salt for the Newfoundland and New England fisheries (and later for Pennsylvania, New York, Nova Scotia, and Quebec); servants, horses, anUd provisions from Scotland and Ireland (and later linen from Ireland); and wines from Madeira and the Azores.

Stricter Enforcement. Evasion of the 1660 and 1663 statutes occasioned legislation in 1673 and 1696 designed for the better enforcement of the laws. The 1673 law required the payment of an impost (which became known as a "plantation duty") on enumerated goods at their port of departure equal to the import tax levied on the goods in England if shipmasters had not first secured a surety bond in England. The law attempted to render unprofitable an illicit trade with Europe in enumerated goods; its object was regulation, not revenue. The 1696 law, a result mainly of the efforts of Edward Randolph, long-time English customs official in America, established an effective ship registry, required colonial governors to take oaths to obey faithfully the navigation laws, made customs officers in America directly responsible to the commissioners of customs in England, authorized the use of writs of assistance, and allowed violations of the laws to be tried in vice- admiralty courts.

The 1696 law marked the completion of the statutory regulations governing trade. Later decisions, rulings, legislation, and agencies merely supplemented the established policy. Lax enforcement, particularly in the case of the Molasses Act of 1733, and the proclivity of colonial commerce to follow the prescribed routes without coercion mitigated the economic burden of the navigation laws. Until 1760 the "Old Colonial System," by which England defined an empire and sought maritime supremacy among the western European nations, worked reasonably well. After that date, stricter enforcement of the acts of trade and the British perversion of the laws to obtain revenue engendered colonial resistance.

See also Enumerated Goods; Mercantilism; Molasses Act.

Bibliography: Andrews, Charles M., *The Colonial Period of American History*, 4 vols. (Yale Univ. Press, 1934-38); Harper, Lawrence A., *The English Navigation Laws: A Seventeenth-Century Experiment in Social Engineering* (Columbia Univ. Press, 1939).

Alan D. Watson
University of North Carolina at Wilmington

ADAIR, JAMES (?1709-83?) Trader to the Southern Indians, Irish-born Adair came to North America in the 1730s and soon began his work on the frontier. His History of the American Indians (1775), a distillation of his experiences, was one of the first accounts to express the views of the frontiersman and provided a valuable account of the language and customs of the Chickasaw and other tribes. It remains one of the best early ethnologies, despite his thesis that the Indians were remnants of the lost tribes of Israel.

Abigail Adams both supported and shared her husband John's interests. *(National Portrait Gallery)*

ADAMS, ABIGAIL (1744-1818) Abigail Adams, the wife of John Adams, second president of the United States, was born in Weymouth, Massachusetts. Despite a poor education and delicate health, she became a prolific writer and had much influence on the social and political life of her time. She married John Adams in 1764. Abigail shared her husband's interests in the American Revolution, and supported his efforts to construct the Declaration of Independence. While John spent much of his time in Philadelphia during the Revolution, Abigail managed John's affairs at home and tended to the farm. The many letters to her husband paint a vivid picture of the times. Between 1789 and 1801, while John was the vice president and president, she lived a simple life in Washington. She died of typhoid fever at Braintree (now Quincy), Massachusets.

ADAMS, JOHN (1735-1826)   Born in Braintree (now Quincy) Massachusetts, Adams graduated from Harvard College in 1755 and practiced law in Boston. In December 1765, he gave a speech before the government arguing the Stamp Act invalid because Massachusetts was not represented in Parliament. He became active in patriot issues during the early 1770s, especially after the governor refused him his seat on the Governor's Council because of partisanship (1773). Adams became a member of the First (1774) and Second (1775-78) Continental Congresses, and he nominated George Washington for commander-in-chief of the army. In June 1776, Adams was appointed to a committee to draft the Declaration of Independence.

Adams joined Benjamin Franklin and John Jay in France in 1778 to negotiate with European powers on behalf of the government. As a diplomat, he also helped negotiate peace with Britain in 1783 and served as the first U.S. minister to Great Britain (1785-88). In 1788, Adams was elected the nation's first vice president, serving under George Washington until 1797. Adams became the first leader of the Federalist Party in 1796 and was elected president the same year. During his administration (1797-1801), he tried unsuccessfully to avoid partisan politics.

See also Paris, Treaty of.

Bibliography: Hutson, James H., *John Adams and the Diplomacy of the American Revolution* (Kentucky, 1980).

ADAMS, SAMUEL (1722-1803)   The second cousin of John Adams, Samuel Adams is best known for his role in demanding American independence. In 1765, he was elected to the Massachusetts legislature and served until 1774. During this time, he became a leader of the radicals and helped organize the Sons of Liberty. In 1765, Adams led demonstrations in Boston against the Stamp Act. He organized the Nonimportation Association in 1768 in reaction to the Townshend Acts. Adams continuously spoke out against the British in newspapers between 1770 and 1773, and American independence became his major pursuit. He instigated the formation of the Committee of Correspondence (1772) to publicize the colonists' demands and grievances.

In 1773, Adams managed the famous Boston Tea Party in protest to the Tea Act. He was a leader of the resistance to the Coercive Acts that followed the tea party and supported the Suffolk Resolves. Adams was a member of the First and Second Continental Congresses (1774-81), during which time he signed the Declaration of Independence, and worked for the ratification of the U.S. Constitution. Adams later served as the governor of Massachusetts (1794-97) and died in Boston on October 2, 1803.

See also Boston Tea Party; Suffolk Resolves; Townshend Acts.

A renowned orator, Samuel Adams achieved his greatest fame in leading the Boston Tea Party. *(Library of Congress)*

ADOBE   Adobe is a dark, heavy soil high in clay content. When mixed with straw or grass, adobe is fashioned into sun-dried bricks, the primary building material of the sedentary Indians of Arizona and New Mexico. The large adobe structures built by these Indians were designed as communal homes known as pueblos. Named for their village dwellings, the Pueblo Indians would add rooms as space was needed, gradually creating contiguous buildings similar in appearance to modern apartment houses. Examples of this type of building found at Mesa Verde, Colorado, and Chaco Canyon, New Mexico, were built with sandstone blocks cemented by adobe mortar. When the Spanish came to the area they confined their adobe buildings to the traditional style of one story surrounding a central court. These buildings served as fortresses as well as homes.

See also Cibola, Seven Cities of; Pueblo.

AFRICA   Within the context of slavery and the Americas during the colonial era, sub-Saharan Africa in general and West Africa in particular were the most critical areas of the continent because the great majority of Afro-Americans in the colonies traced their ancestry there. The Atlantic slave trade with Africa spanned four centuries, from the 15th to the 18th, but it did not signify the first contact between Africans and Europeans. For centuries previously, long-distance trade across the Sahara had brought the two continents together. Commodities included slaves, but more important were olive oil, gold, nuts, spices, and fruits. Only with the rise of the Plantation System, also called the South Atlantic System, did the Atlantic slave trade escalate and restructure the relationship between Africans and Europeans.

Africans from a mélange of cultures became enmeshed in the Plantation System. Political systems varied from the so-called stateless societies, to village states, to the centralized kingdoms of Ghana, Mali, and Songhai. Local authority and loyalties predominated. Economic organization ranged from nomadic to sedentary agricultural societies and included artisanal, commercial, and industrial pursuits. Slavery could be found in many societies, but it differed considerably from American slavery and is generally considered a far milder variety. Kinship ties were especially strong, and families exercised considerable control. Descent was both matrilineal and patrilineal, and marriages were polygamous, polyandrous, and monogamous. Religion often involved ancestor worship and thus was connected intimately to kinship. Islam was also present, particularly among commercial elites. Hundreds of languages existed, and oral cultures and traditions prevailed. Painting, sculpture, carving, music, and dance were integral components of most African societies.

Afro-Americans thus came from heterogeneous social, political, and economic backgrounds. In the Americas, slaves melded their ancestries with European and native American cultures to produce distinct cultures whose African reverberations were particularly strong in the colonial period.

See also Afro-Americans; Plantation System; Slavery.

Lynda J. Morgan
Mount Holyoke College

AFRICAN-INDIAN CONTACT   From the time Africans were first brought to the Caribbean in the early 16th century to replace the Indian slaves so vulnerable to Old World diseases, there were extensive relations between Africans and Indians. The slave Estevanico, a dark-skinned North African, one of the survivors who wandered through the American Southwest with the shipwrecked Spaniard Cabeza de Vaca in 1528-36, became a skilled translator and respected medicine man among the Indians, yet later was murdered by the Zuni when he led a Spanish exploring mission to their pueblo.

At the Shawnee siege of Boonesboro in 1777, the slave London died fighting with the settlers, and the runaway slave Pompey was killed while sniping at settlers from Indian lines. In the Southeast, white officials deliberately set Indians and slaves upon each other, employing Indians as slave catchers and African slaves as Indian fighters in a classic example of the colonial strategy of divide and rule. By the late 18th century Indians of such "civilized" Southern tribes as the Cherokee had become slave owners themselves.

On the other hand, runaway black slaves often found refuge among Indian communities, especially in the Southeast among the Creek and the Seminole, where by the 1730s, the Spanish sponsored the creation of free black communities as buffers against the expansion of English settlement. These Florida communities were incorporated into the Seminole nation, where they gained great influence, playing instrumental roles in resisting American expansion in the first half of the 19th century.

Elsewhere along the Atlantic coast, runaway and free blacks lived among the defeated remnants of the Algonquin nations, where they found an acceptance that they could not hope to match among the whites. By the end of the 18th century blacks were intermixed, for example, with the Mashpee and Gay Head Indians of Massachusetts, the Montauk of Long Island, and the Pamunkey and Mattapony of Virginia. There are many cases of mixed-race peoples—the Melungeons of Tennessee, the Lumbee of North Carolina, and others—who undoubtedly originated in mixed communities of Indians, blacks, and possibly whites as well.

See also Slavery.

Bibliography: Craven, Wesley Frank, *White, Red, and Black: The Seventeenth-Century Virginian* (Univ. Press of Virginia, 1971); Johnston, James Hugo, "Documentary Evidence of the Relations of Negros and Indians," *Journal of Negro History 14* (1929): 21-43; Nash, Gary B., *Red, White and Black* (Prentice-Hall, 1982); Willis, William S., "Divide and Rule: Red, White, and Black in the Southeast," *Journal of Negro History 48* (1963): 157-76.

John Mack Faragher
Mount Holyoke College

AFRO-AMERICANS As a demographic term, Afro-American refers to native-born peoples of African descent, or creoles, in the Americas who reproduced through natural increase rather than forced importations. The word also refers to the distinct syncretic cultures that Afro-Americans developed. Usually, the isolation of specific times and places at which a naturally reproducing Afro-American population appeared indicated the emergence of Afro-American cultures. These cultures were defined chiefly by kinship, religion, and patterns of resistance.

Afro-American cultures varied according to time, work patterns, white and African population densities, white class structures, the status of the Atlantic slave trade, plantation size, and especially crop region. This complex and multifaceted process of institution-building is known as creolization. By transforming African, European, and native American cultures to suit their needs, free and enslaved Afro-Americans created cultures that acted as survival mechanisms designed to thwart total control by masters and to help withstand the oppressions of slavery and racism.

Three broad regional Afro-American cultures had appeared by 1789, each related to particular economic and demographic patterns and constructed over a period of 150 years. A predominantly nonplantation system developed in the North, whereas plantation regimes characterized the Chesapeake, and the Carolina and Georgia lowcountry.

Northern Characteristics. In the North, blacks formed a small fraction of the total population. Northern agriculture was small-scale, produced chiefly cereals and livestock, and had little demand for slave labor. Most blacks lived in the countryside, but many inhabited developing commercial centers, such as New York and Boston. There they labored chiefly as servants or skilled workers; many of the latter worked as hired slaves. Before the mid-18th century, most came from the mainland or the West Indies, rather than directly from Africa. They were therefore familiar with the preponderant Euro-American culture. Natural increase occurred easily, and a distinct Afro-American community appeared by the early 18th century. In the 1740s, the Atlantic slave trade accelerated

and reacquainted northern Afro-Americans with their African heritage. Creolization in the North therefore involved a distinct black minority, familiarity with Euro-American culture, nonplantation labor, and an infusion of African culture at midcentury.

Lowcountry Characteristics. By 1789 two varieties of Afro-American culture characterized the lowcountry, where creolization occurred more slowly and sporadically. A substantial creole population established itself in the 17th and early 18th centuries, but an active slave trade kept the proportion of Africans consistently high. Imports were composed of male majorities; labor was harsh and mortality high. Most Africans worked on large plantations, often under absentee ownership, producing substantial exports of naval stores, indigo, and rice for the world market. Among these peoples, natural increases did not occur until the eve of the American Revolution.

By 1708, the heavy demand for slave labor had resulted in a black majority. Imported Africans tended to be concentrated on large plantations, whereas creoles, often skilled and more experienced with Euro-American cultures, became an urban group. Because Africans on plantations lived distantly from both white and creole societies, they retained much of their African heritage. They spoke Gullah, and dressed and ate in African fashion. Because work was often organized through the task system, they could sometimes enhance their cultural autonomy.

Many 17th-century Chesapeake slaves came from the West Indies. They lived with resident planters on small plantations where they grew tobacco under the gang system. The heaviest importations occurred in the mid-18th century and coincided with early creolization. Distinctions between Africans and creoles were not pronounced, and because Chesapeake slavery evolved slowly over a period of nearly a century, a small but significant free black caste inhabited this region. By 1789 these factors had produced yet another Afro-American community.

Cultural Transformation. By the Revolution, most blacks in America had made the cultural transformation from African to Afro-American. They had been living in America for over a century and a half. During that time, they had adopted useful parts of European and native American cultures while enriching each with African traditions. These patterns established in the colonial period greatly influenced the nature of mature 19th-century slave systems. Slave cultures on the eve of the Civil War unfolded from foundations laid by their colonial forebears.

See also Plantation System; Slavery.

Bibliography: Kulikoff, Allan, *Tobacco and Slaves: The Development of Southern Cultures in the Chesapeake, 1680-1800* (Univ. of North Carolina, 1986); Wood, Peter H., *Black*

Majority: Negroes in Colonial South Carolina from 1670 through the Stono Rebellion (Norton, 1974).

Lynda J. Morgan
Mount Holyoke College

AFRO-AMERICANS AND THE AMERICAN REVOLUTION Afro-Americans, both slaves and free men, participated actively in all phases of the American Revolution and, like all people in the former colonies, were greatly affected by the American victory and independence. A few Afro-Americans joined the colonial protests of the early 1770s. Best known is Crispus Attucks, a mulatto runaway slave who fell before British gunfire at the Boston Massacre in March 1770.

Black soldiers had served in the colonial militias during the French and Indian War and continued to do so when hostilities broke out in 1775. Afro-Americans in the companies of minutemen at Lexington and Concord in April 1775 included Peter Salem, whose owners freed him so he could enlist, and Prince Estabrook, who died in battle.

AFRO-AMERICANS: TOPIC GUIDE

GENERAL

Africa
African-Indian Contact
Afro-Americans and the American Revolution
Free Blacks
Miscegenation
  Mulattoes
Race and Racism
  Negro Plot of 1741
Slavery (see **Topic Guide**)
  Antislavery
  Asiento
  Plantation System
  Race and Racism
  Royal African Company
  Slave Codes
  Slave Resistance
    Stono Rebellion (1739)
  Slave Trade

BIOGRAPHIES

Attucks, Crispus
Banneker, Benjamin
Benezet, Anthony
Estevanico
Pastorius, Francis Daniel
Wheatley, Phillis
Woolman, John

Salem Poor's bravery at Bunker Hill was cited by Massachusetts officers. Free black William Flore was the last sentinel to leave his post as the British approached for the Battle of Great Bridge, near Norfolk, Virginia, in December 1775. Despite their valuable contributions to the early fighting, Afro-Americans, slave and free, were soon excluded from enlisting by most colonies. Whites in a nation that allowed slavery feared the results of black men bearing arms.

Recruitment of Blacks. Exclusion of Afro-Americans did not continue long for several reasons. When the British governor of Virginia, Lord Dunmore, in November 1775, offered slaves freedom in exchange for military service, some 700-800 joined his forces. Americans responded by gradually reopening enlistment to free blacks and later to slaves. All colonies except South Carolina and Georgia encouraged Afro-American enlistments before the war's end. Approximately 5,000 blacks served in the American armies; many as infantry soldiers; a few in the artillery and cavalry; and many in wagon, commissary, and forage services. Black seamen were numerous. Afro-Americans sailed as pilots on ships in Chesapeake Bay and off the Carolina coast, and as privateers. By the war's end, some slaves had won their freedom and other black veterans had earned bounties in the form of money or land.

Responding to promises of freedom, around 1,000 Afro-Americans bore arms for the British. Many of these, and perhaps as many as 15,000 others who had come behind British lines during the war, were evacuated with the British in 1781. Some evacuees went to the British West Indies, others to Canada. From Canada, several traveled to Africa's west coast, where they established a colony in Sierra Leone.

The Revolutionary War brought freedom to many other former slaves. Thousands took advantage of the confusion to escape. After the war's end, northern states, recognizing the inconsistency between the revolutionary ideals and slavery, passed laws providing for gradual emancipation.

Bibliography: Quarles, Benjamin, *The Negro in the American Revolution* (1961; reprinted, Norton 1973).

Suzanne Greene Chapelle
Morgan State University

AGRICULTURE One of the most common generalizations about agriculture in colonial North America is the assumption that the Indians were nomadic hunters. Yet from the Southwest to the Mississippi Valley, from the Gulf Coast to the St. Lawrence, the first Europeans to encounter natives invariably found them living in settled communities and cultivating the soil. Indeed, during their first few years in America, the pioneers of Jamestown and

Plymouth depended for their survival on the purchase or plunder of Indian stores of corn, beans, and squash.

Indian Agriculture. There were important differences, however, between the farming traditions of America and of Europe. Indians did not practice agriculture proper, defined as the use of the plow to achieve the deep aeration of permanently cropped fields; but rather a variety of horticulture, in which the natural vegetation was burned, crops planted among the ashes, fields finally allowed to return to their original state after several seasons of use, and cultivation shifted to other newly-burned plots. Indian notions of property corresponded to this strategy of shifting cultivation. Productive resources such as fields, hunting territories, and fishing sites were not privately owned but held in common, their use allocated to families for specified periods of time.

Moreover, there were critical distinctions between the European and Indian sexual division of labor; Indian women were typically responsible for field work—considered a man's labor in Europe—while Indian men were assigned the duties of clearing and burning, as well as hunting, fishing, and trading. Lacking any intellectual notion of cultural relativity, Europeans interpreted these differences as signs of the Indians' technological, legal, and social inferiority. In fact, recent studies suggest that Indian horticulture produced crop yields as good or better than those of English agriculture; and although the substantial tracts kept in natural reserve by the technology of shifting cultivation held Indian populations to significantly lower levels than would European agriculture, cultivation supported a continental pre-Columbian population of 18-20,000,000 Indians.

Early Colonial Agriculture. Early European settlers attempted to transplant the entirety of their agricultural systems, but that was a difficult and often hazardous task. Traditional European cereal varieties, for example, often failed to survive both harsh northeastern and tropical southern winters, so after several "starving" seasons, settlers throughout North America learned to rely on locally adapted varieties of corn as their staple crop. In fact, colonists adopted the methods of planting, storing, and using a wide variety of New World crops from the Indians, mixing with this reservoir of continental knowledge the accoutrement of their agriculture.

The European tool collection—spades, plows, harrows, hayrakes, forks, and scythes; grindstones, saws, files, axes, adzes, and augurs; lumber and grist mills; spinning wheels, looms, and needles— little changed since the Middle Ages, and essentially unchanging until the 19th century, represented an era of transformation in America. Even more profound was the introduction of livestock—fowl, sheep, swine; and most especially horses, cattle, and oxen, which provided draft for plows, wagons, and mills. The clearing, plowing, and damming made possible by their tools and draft animals enabled the Europeans to create a familiar fixed landscape of field and pasture, transforming old ecological relationships and establishing new ones in the process.

Patterns of Cultivation. Because of its distinctive mixture of elements, the North American agricultural complex depended upon precise local combinations of indigenous patterns, settler traditions, climate, and geography. On the arid northern frontiers of Mexico, a ranching economy developed that drew directly upon Iberian traditions as well as upon the well-established irrigation and dry-land farming of the Indians. In the north, the French habitants of the St. Lawrence Valley, three-quarters of the population of New France, were cultivating some 250,000 acres of wheat and maize by the 1760s and exporting an average of 100,000 bushels annually. The Canadian diet differed from the French chiefly in the prominent place of the Indian components—corn, beans, squash, potatoes, and game, all liberally sweetened with local maple sugar. Along the Atlantic coast, after nearly two centuries of English colonization, the first federal census of 1790 revealed that a mere seven percent of the population resided in cities and towns. Farming, in other words, absorbed the energies of virtually all the colonists, and the distinctive agricultural history of each of the major regions is essential to an understanding of colonial life.

In the Chesapeake coastal plain, after an initial decade of impending disaster, the successful cultivation and marketing of tobacco in the 1610s transformed the first English settlements into highly profitable enterprises. As the tobacco habit took root in the Old World and demand grew, Virginia and Maryland life focused almost exclusively on tobacco production; plantations were narrowly strung out along the river highways to the Atlantic and England. A labor- intensive crop, tobacco dictated a search for cheap and exploitable labor, first through indentured servitude, then slavery, both critical to the development of the plantation system. By the end of the 17th century, Virginia, Maryland, and Delaware planters were annually exporting over 30,000,000 pounds of tobacco; by the Revolution, exports had risen to over 80,000,000 pounds.

The Lower South. The founding of English settlements in the lower South was similarly motivated by the desire to establish profitable plantation economies. South Carolina was first sustained by cattle grazing but soon turned to rice, thanks in part to the skill of slaves imported from the Rice Coast of Africa. The nearly 2,000,000 pounds exported in 1710 rose to 18,000,000 in 1730 and continued to rise before the Revolution. After the 1740s rice production was supplemented with indigo, the two commodities becoming by 1750 the third and fifth most valuable commodities exported from the mainland colonies.

Because wealthier planters occupied the best sites below the Fall Line on the main rivers throughout the South, poorer farmers as well as men who had worked out their indentures, had to settle for land in the interior, where they were distant from markets and exposed to attacks by the Indians upon whose lands they were encroaching. Bacon's Rebellion (1676) in Virginia, and later conflicts with the regulators in the Carolinas, were incidents in a developing antagonism between tidewater and backcountry farmers. Georgia was planned as a haven for such self-sufficient settlers, but the 1752 repeal of the original slavery prohibition opened the way for plantation development; and wealthy slave owners came to control the rice regions along the coast, while in the interior the vast majority of whites carried on small-scale, diversified farming. Throughout the colonial period, on the other hand, North Carolina remained a colony of small farmers, producing mostly for local consumption.

Self-Sufficient Production.   From the perspective of English mercantilism, colonies were enterprises for the production of foodstuffs and raw materials, but subsistence production was the first concern of most farmers. Self-sufficiency not only required raising crops for family consumption but also producing the family's clothing, utensils, and furniture. Complete self-sufficiency was rare, found only in isolated regions, and most farmers sought a marketable product, not only to exchange for such indispensable articles as ammunition and salt, but to better their standards of living.

Agriculture in New England, because of the harsh climate and poor soil, was characterized by autonomous family production. The precise character of New England farming communities depended upon the local tradition and geography; but before the mid-18th century the typical farmer lived in a clustered village, with a commons for grazing. A family's lots were often scattered, with some of the outlying fields, meadows, and woodlands near the township, and others several miles distant. The leaders of the New England colonies, no less interested in exports than their Southern counterparts, looked to other enterprises in order to generate foreign exchange, among the most important being fisheries, lumbering, shipbuilding, and shipping. Thus, more mere subsistence farming took place in the North, yet the diversification of economic activity stimulated multifaceted development. Meanwhile, successful Southern monoculture inhibited the growth of banking and credit facilities, of manufacturing and industry, as well as of cities and towns. By the Revolution, the South was still dependent on more highly developed economies for its capital, trading services, technology, manufactured goods, and in some cases even

food, while New England stood on the verge of industrial transformation.

The Middle Colonies.   The colonies of the mid-Atlantic incorporated the best features of its northern and southern neighboring regions, combining extensive commercial activity with staple crop production, and by 1750 becoming the most economically dynamic region of all British North America. In the mid-18th century, in the fertile coastal and valley plains of southeastern Pennsylvania, New Jersey, and New York's Hudson and Mohawk valleys, the food supply exceeded the needs of the local population by as much as 50 percent, surpluses unmatched anywhere else in North America; and Middle Colony farmers became the suppliers of the bread to feed West Indies slaves as well as the growing hungry population of Europe. The international demand for grain stimulated farmers in Maryland and Virginia to turn to corn and wheat production, a diversification that strengthened the upper South. Mid-Atlantic farmers kept their production diversified and did not fall into the trap of monoculture, just as merchants diversified their commerce. Philadelphia, the center of all this economic development, was, by the time of the Revolution, the world's second largest English city.

See also Household Industries; New World Crops; Plantation System; Self-sufficient and Market Farming.

Bibliography: Bidwell, Percy W. and Falconer, John I., *History of Agriculture in the Northern United States, 1620-1860* (1925; reprint, Kelly); Gray, Lewis C., *History of Agriculture in the Southern United States to 1860* (1933; reprint, Kelly); McCusker, John J., and Menard, Russel R., *The Economy of British America*, 1607-1789 (Univ. of N.C. Press, 1985).

John Mack Faragher
Mount Holyoke College

AGUAYO, JOSEF DE AZLOR Y VIRTO DE VERA, MARQUIS DE (1677-1734) The Spanish colonial officer Aguayo is best remembered for his action in 1719, during the War of the Spanish Succession, after French forces captured Pensacola, Florida, and pushed on into Texas. With the frontier in a panic, the Marquis de Aguayo, the governor of the combined provinces of Coahuila and Texas, led the Spanish forces sent to expel the French from Texas. Aguayo immediately sent reinforcements to the presidio at San Antonio, but when his main force met the French in July 1721, he was told that France and Spain were no longer at war. Nevertheless, Aguayo strengthened several Spanish positions, built new missions, and generally secured the province for Spain. In 1722 he returned to Coahuila, where he was allowed to retire.

AIX-LA-CHAPELLE, TREATY OF (1748) A document serving more as a respite than a final peace, the Treaty of Aix-La-Chapelle, signed October 18, 1748, concluded the War of the Austrian Succession (1740-48), known in the American colonies as King George's War. The treaty essentially restored all conquered territory, although it recognized Frederick of Prussia's annexation of Silesia from Austria. It confirmed the succession of Maria Theresa to the Austrian throne. Louisburg, a large French fortification on Cape Breton Island, Canada, that had been captured by troops from Massachusetts at great cost in lives and money, was also returned to France, causing bitter friction between Massachusetts and England.

See also King George's War.

ALAMANCE, BATTLE OF (1771) Faced with mounting opposition from the North Carolina Regulators—Western frontiersmen who objected to high taxes imposed by Eastern settlers—Governor William Tryon recruited 1,500 men to put down the movement. In May of 1771, at Great Alamance Creek, near Hillsborough, 2,000 Regulators, poorly armed and undisciplined, were defeated by Tryon's militia in a battle that lasted just over two hours. Six Regulator leaders were hanged, but Tryon offered a pardon to the rest if they would give up the rebellion. During the Revolution, some of the unredeemed Regulators fought for the British.

ALARCÓN, HERNANDO DE (born 1500?) The Spanish frontiersman Alarcón commanded the supply ships assigned to rendezvous with Coronado along the coast of the Gulf of California in 1540. His party reached the mouth of the Colorado River and made the first known European contact with the Yuma Indians, then rowed in small boats past the sandbars at the mouth of the river, reaching a point not far below the beginning of the Grand Canyon. Alarcón heard from the Indians that Coronado had reached Cibola but could find no one willing to go to meet him. He made a second ascent of the Colorado and planted a cross with letters buried beneath it, which Melchior Diaz later found, and finally returned to New Spain.

See also Coronado, Francisco Vasquez de; Diaz, Melchior.

ALASKA, RUSSIA IN The name "Alaska," from an Aleut word meaning "mainland," was not applied to the far northern peninsula of North America until the American purchase in 1867, when Senator Charles Sumner suggested it to Secretary of State William Seward; it had been known to Americans and Europeans as Russian America. Until the mid-18th century the Alaskan coast was known only to the Aleuts and Inuits, but about that time the Russians began to extend their Siberian fur trapping operations across the Aleutian Islands to the mainland, following the explorations of Vitus Bering and Alexei Chirikov in the 1740s, Pyotr Bashmakov in the 1750s, and Pyotr Krenitsyn's mapping expedition of the 1760s.

The Russians employed especially brutal methods, forcing whole villages of Aleuts into slavery and furiously crushing attempts at resistance, such as the Aleut Revolt. In the 1780s Gregor Shelekhov, known as the founder of Russian America, organized a fur company that systematized the trapping on the Alaskan coast and intensified the exploitation of the native inhabitants under the guise of rules intended to protect them. In 1784 he founded Kodiak, the first permanent Russian settlement in Alaska. Although Shelekhov failed in obtaining a government monopoly for his company, it provided the nucleus of the Russian-America Company, founded in 1798.

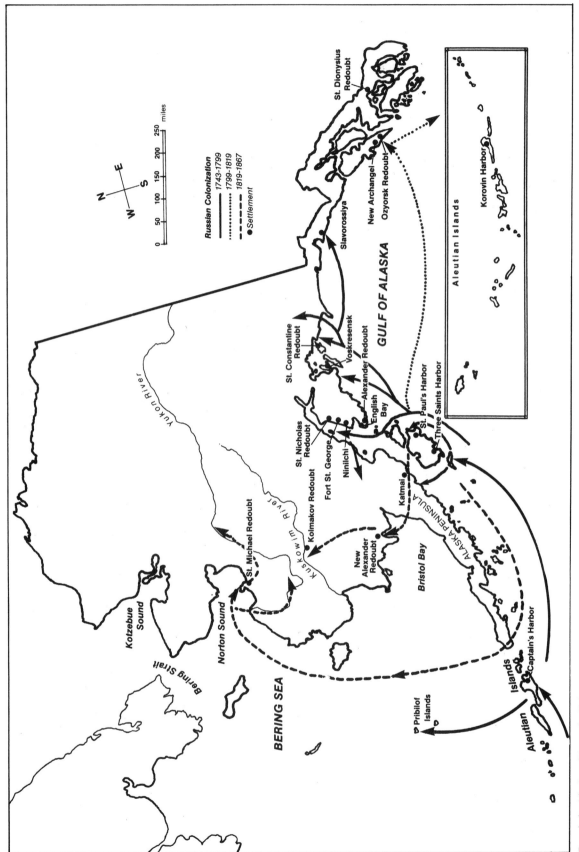

Russia in Alaska. *(Facts On File, Inc.)*

See also Aleut Revolt; Aleuts; Russian-America Company.

Bibliography: Chevigny, Hector, *Russian America: Alaskan Venture, 1741-1867* (1965; reprint, Binford 1979).

John Mack Faragher
Mount Holyoke College

ALBANY The Dutch first established Fort Orange (originally Fort Nassau) at the junction of the Hudson and Mohawk rivers in 1615, and it became the center of the successful patroonship of Rensselaerswyck as well as the center of the thriving Iroquois fur trade, from which it was given the name Beverwyck in 1652. Renamed Albany with the English conquest in 1664, Dutch merchants and landlords retained control, and it remained the most vivid remnant of Dutch America. It became the strategic center of the geopolitical alliance of English and Iroquois, and in 1754 was the site of the Albany Congress. Gradually, as the center of the New York fur trade moved west to Fort Oswego the Albany area moved to agricultural development, and the state relocated its capital there in 1797 to effect a stronger connection between metropolitan New York City and the broad upstate hinterland made available by Iroquois land cessions. With the completion of the Erie Canal in 1825, Albany became a primary transshipment point in the Great Lakes-Atlantic trade.

ALBANY CONGRESS, THE (1754) An intercolonial meeting held at Albany, New York, in July 1754, the Albany Congress was convened to strengthen relations between the British colonies and the Iroquois confederacy. French encroachments from Canada in the 1750s had coincided with growing Iroquois discontent with American trading practices and land policies. The British government, aware that war with France was imminent and con-

This contemporary illustration neatly summarized the sentiment of the plan of union developed at the Albany Congress.
(Library of Congress)

cerned about the military strength and strategic location of the Iroquois tribes, ordered the colonies to settle the Indians' complaints in one comprehensive agreement. Albany, the site of previous intercolonial meetings with the Indians, was selected as the most convenient meeting place.

The delegates—representing New York, New Hampshire, Massachusetts, Rhode Island, Connecticut, Pennsylvania, and Maryland—failed to reach agreement on matters concerning the Indians, but they did make recommendations for defensive works against the French, for a single superintendent of Indian affairs, and for Crown control of colonial acquisition of Indian lands. A committee, led by Benjamin Franklin of Pennsylvania, proposed a plan for colonial union whereby the colonies' external affairs, such as dealings with the Indians and common defense, would be governed by a grand council elected by the colonial assemblies and a president-general appointed by the Crown. The plan, known as the Albany Plan of Union, was not ratified by the colonial assemblies and was therefore never submitted to Parliament. It did, however, become important as a quasi precedent for American union. Other recommendations of the Albany Congress, such as central control of western settlement, were attempted by the British government in the years preceding the American Revolution, but with little success and to the detriment of relations between the Crown and the colonies.

Bibliography: Hamilton, Milton W., *Sir William Johnson: Colonial American, 1715-1763* (Kennikat, 1976); Labaree, Leonard W., *The Papers of Benjamin Franklin*, vol. 5:374-417 (Yale Univ. Press, 1972).

Wendell Tripp
New York State Historical Association

ALBANY CONVENTION (1689-90) A meeting of civil administrators and military officers in Albany, New York, the Albany Convention served as the government for Albany until the newly crowned British monarchs William and Mary established colonial rule, and also as a planning session for frontier defense. The convention, afraid that the French would attack the frontiers, asked for aid from Jacob Leisler, the self-proclaimed lieutenant governor of New Amsterdam to the south. Leisler refused to help unless he was named commander in chief of the area, a demand that the convention would not grant. When the French attacked Schenectady to the west, the convention acceded to Leisler's demands.

ALBEMARLE SETTLEMENTS The first permanent colonial settlements in North Carolina, they were established in the region of Albemarle Sound in 1653-54 to form a protective southern boundary for the colony of Virginia. In 1662, Samuel Stephens was placed in military command of the region, which was initially called the Southern Plantation, and later Albemarle County. In 1664, William Drummond was appointed governor, and in the following year it was formally included in the Carolina Charter. By 1689, with the arrival of large numbers of settlers in the area, Albemarle County's autonomous government was abolished, and it became a part of the Carolina colony.

ALBUQUERQUE Some attempts at settlement had been made in the area of Albuquerque before the Pueblo Revolt of 1680, but it was not until the time following Diego de Vargas's reconquest, in 1706, that several soldiers from the presidio at Bernalillo and their families founded the town. The town suffered from both Indian attacks and recurrent drought but expanded nonetheless; by 1763 there were 50 families in the town. An influx of settlers after 1780 raised the population of Albuquerque and the surrounding area to a total of 3,800 non-Indian inhabitants. The Pueblo Indians were now pacified, but the Navaho, Apache, Comanche, and Ute tribes who moved into the region ensured that Albuquerque remain a frontier outpost well into the 19th century.

ALCOHOL, CONSUMPTION OF Drinking was a commonplace of colonial culture. In an age when water sources might easily become contaminated, especially in concentrated human communities, people rejected water drinking and readily turned to hard cider, beer, or the most popular colonial beverage, rum. Brewed and distilled spirits were thought of as healthy supplements to the diet, as medications to cure colds, fevers, frostbite, even broken bones; and as relaxants. Many people consumed "daily drams" upon rising, with their meals, during work breaks, and at bedtime; workers and soldiers demanded their daily "rum ration." Public drinking to the point of drunkenness was also common at elections, court sessions, militia musters, or communal work bees. As the price of producing rum dropped in the 18th century, the consumption of alcohol increased, by the era of the Revolution reaching a per capita level approximately two to three times higher than it would be two centuries later.

With this increase in drinking, and particularly in public intoxication, came increased criticism of alcohol. Capitalists began to argue the effect of spirits on worker productivity, rationalists the effect on the mind, doctors the effect on health. In a 1784 pamphlet that became a classic of the temperance movement, Dr. Benjamin Rush condemned drinking, largely because of the consequences of abuse by patriot troops during the Revolution. Probably the most important consequence of the Revolution, however, was to cut off foreign supplies of rum, turning people

toward a greater consumption of domestic corn whiskey, distilled by the frontier descendants of the Scots and Irish.
John Mack Faragher
Mount Holyoke College

ALDEN, JOHN (c.1599-1687) Signer of the *Mayflower Compact* and colonial official, John Alden shipped on the *Mayflower* as a cooper to maintain the barrels. At Plymouth Rock, he was selected as one of the eight bondsmen responsible for the colony's debt, but he was not the first to step ashore as some legends maintain. Around 1627, he received a land grant of 169 acres in Duxbury, where, with his friend Miles Standish, he established himself as a leading citizen and arbitrer of boundary disputes. His offices included surveyor of highways, Duxbury's deputy (1641-49), member of the councils of war against the Indians, treasurer (1656-58), and governor's assistant (1632-41; 1650-86). He was deputy governor in 1664-65 and again in 1677 in recognition of his defense during King Philip's War.

Although he had an acknowledged reputation as a speaker, records do not substantiate Henry Wadsworth Longfellow's romantic poem about his winning of Priscilla Mullins, "The Courtship of Miles Standish." He did, however, marry Priscilla, and the couple had 11 children. He died in Duxbury as the last surviving signer of the *Mayflower Compact*.

See also Mayflower Compact.

ALDEN, PRISCILLA (born 1602) Perhaps the only female Pilgrim to be remembered by subsequent generations, she was born Priscilla Mullins (or Molines) in Dorking, Surrey, England. Her father William, a shoemaker, sailed with her, her mother, and younger brother on the *Mayflower*, but only Priscilla survived the first terrible winter in New England. Sometime between 1621 and 1623 she married John Alden, and therein lies her fame and place in history. An anecdote published in 1814 by one of her descendants, Timothy Alden, became the basis for a poem by Henry Wadsworth Longfellow,"The Courtship of Miles Standish." Longfellow detailed how Captain Standish, diminutive and considerably older than Priscilla, asked his good friend John Alden to convey a proposal of marriage to her. Alden also was in love with Priscilla, but still he went to her and gamely presented the desires of his rival in "simple and eloquent language." At last Priscilla interrupted "With eyes overrunning with laughter/Said, in a tremulous voice, 'Why don't you speak for yourself, John?'" The lesson of the poem was that, if you want something done properly, do it yourself. Very little is known about Priscilla Alden outside of this quite embellished episode, except that she bore John Alden 11 children.

ALEUT REVOLT (1761-66)   The Aleuts first came into contact with Russian fur traders in the 1740s. The Russians employed especially brutal methods, binding whole villages of Aleuts into slave labor, forcing the men to trap and the women to perform sexual service. Attempts at resistance were crushed, as on Kanaga Island in 1757, when an entire village was attacked, plundered, and burned to the ground. Moving east along the Aleutian chain, the Russians first encountered organized resistance in the Fox Islands, where in 1761 a native attack decimated a party of Russian traders. The following year, in a series of raids, the Aleuts destroyed a fleet of Russian ships from Kamchatka and kept up an effective resistance through 1765. The next year, however, the Russians struck back in force, crushing the rebellion and carrying out deliberate "reductions" of the Aleutian population. After the revolt, Aleutian hunters were supposedly protected by government regulations, but at best they labored under harsh contracts that robbed them of any share in the fur trade.

See also Alaska, Russia in.

ALEUTS   Inhabiting the Alaska peninsula and the Aleutian archipelago, the Aleuts speak a common language, Eskimaleut, or Eskaleut, with the Inuit (Eskimo), although the Atka Aleut of the western Aleutians and the Unalaska Aleut of the east speak somewhat different dialects. They were probably late migrants to North America, c. 5,000-3,000 B.C., and with the Inuit are of a different stock than other native Americans—shorter and broader with rounder faces, lighter skin, and a more pronounced epicanthus typical of Asian peoples. Their economy was based on the hunting of sea mammals, supplemented by fishing. Frequent contact to their south with Indians of the Northwest coast influenced much of their material culture, such as their timbered, earth-banked pit houses.

Russian explorers and fur traders made their first contact with the Aleuts in 1741 and imposed a brutal slave regime on the people, who rose up in organized resistance during the Aleut Revolt of the 1760s. As a result of warfare and disease, the precontact population of some 25,000 had been reduced by 90 percent by the end of the 18th century.

See also Alaska, Russia in; Aleut Revolt.

ALEXANDER, JAMES (1691-1756)   A lawyer and attorney general of New Jersey from 1723 to 1727, James Alexander was born in Scotland and came to America after the Scottish Rebellion of 1715. He held various positions in the governments of New Jersey and New York. After

studying law he became attorney general and worked to improve court procedures. He practiced law privately following his removal from the councils in New York (1732) and New Jersey (1735) for opposition to the Crown. Alexander volunteered to defend publisher John Peter Zenger, who was accused of libel and sedition, but was dismissed from the case in contempt of court. He died while fighting a case for colonists' rights.

ALEXANDER, MARY SPRATT PROVOOST (1677-1734)   Businesswoman in colonial New York, something of a tomboy, Mary Spratt Alexander inherited her business acumen from her mother who, in keeping with the Dutch custom, managed the affairs of her husbands after they died. Mary Spratt married Samuel Provoost (younger brother of her mother's third husband) and became his business partner, investing her inheritance in his merchant venture. The couple had three children before Samuel died. She married again in 1721, to James Alexander, descendant of the Scottish Earls of Stirling. James was a lawyer who became a leading political figure in New York and New Jersey. Mary was politically minded also, supporting her husband's ambitions and becoming deeply involved in the cause of John Peter Zenger. But Mary Alexander was first and foremost a businesswoman, importing goods and marketing them in her own store along with products made in the colonies. There was a time when, it was said, there was not a single ship anchored in New York Harbor without a consignment for her. She bore seven children by her second husband, and her estate was estimated at over 100,000 pounds sterling.

ALEXANDER, WILLIAM (1726-83)   Born in New York City, Alexander (also known as Lord Stirling) began his long career as a soldier during the French and Indian War as an aide-de-camp to Massachusetts colonial governor William Shirley. In 1756 he accompanied Shirley to England to defend the governor against a charge of neglect of duty. While there Alexander pressed a claim of his own to the earldom of Stirling. The claim was rejected, but Alexander used the title Lord Stirling even as a general for the Americans during the Revolutionary War.

When war broke out in 1775, Alexander enlisted in a New Jersey regiment as a colonel. In 1776 he was made brigadier general. His forces were badly beaten by the British in the Battle of Long Island (August 26, 1776). Alexander then participateed in the severe American defeats at Brandywine on September 11, 1777 and Germantown on October 4, 1777. Benjamin Rush, commenting on the poor quality of American military leadership, called Alexander "a proud, vain, lazy, ignorant drunkard."

The Algonquin, such as these on the Sorell River, opened the St. Lawrence to French fur traders. *(Library of Congress)*

Although his military career was not characterized by successes, Alexander, together with generals Sullivan, Greene, and Stevens, formed the core of Washington's high command in the battles in the middle colonies. He was also a founder and the first governor of King's College (now Columbia University).

ALGONQUIN INDIANS The Algonquins lived along the river drainages of the Ottawa Valley of interior Quebec and Ontario. They are often confused with the Algonquian, a widely scattered linguistic group that included most native Americans in the Northeast. During the 17th and 18th centuries these hunter-gatherers were deeply involved in the French fur trade and thus helped to shape the economic and political maps of the Great Lakes during the first half of the 17th century.

Hunter-gatherers, whose tool kit included the birchbark canoe, toboggan, and snowshoes, the Algonquins comprised several major bands: Weskarini, Matouweskarini, Keinouche, Kichesipirini, Otaguottouemin, and Onontchataronon. Sometime before 1570 they had begun to exchange their pelts for French trade goods. To protect this connection, they allied themselves with their neighbors

the Montagnai against the Iroquois, and together their successes in 1603 and 1609-10 opened the St. Lawrence to French traders. In the short run it encouraged many Algonquins about 1620 to move closer to this new route by settling at Trois-Rivières. In the long run, however, Algonquin early successes set the stage for their eventual defeat. As long as the Iroquois had threatened the St. Lawrence passage, the Algonquins enjoyed a lucrative trade between the Huron and the French via the interior Montreal-Ottawa River-Lake Nipissing-French River-Georgian Bay water route. The Kichesipirini were the most successful, but the connection put them in direct competition, first with the French who sought a direct contact with the Huron, and once again with the Iroquois, who by the 1630s sought control not only over the French-Algonquin-Huron trade but over the Algonquins' beaver-rich hunting territories as well.

Conflict with the Iroquois. With the temporary elimination of the Iroquois threat along the St. Lawrence after 1610, the French bypassed the Algonquin and established direct ties with the Huron. The Algonquin attempted to break the connection, first with diplomacy and then with threats. When these tactics failed, they attempted to establish a direct trade with the Dutch at Fort Orange (Albany). In 1634, to protect their own position, the Mohawk killed several Algonquin traders, thereby fomenting war. Since the Mohawk had access to firearms, the Algonquin, especially the Kichesipirini and Weskarini, were soundly defeated. The peace settlement of 1645 was an uneasy one because it gave the Iroquois the right to hunt in regions immediately next to the Algonquin. This proximity soon led to renewed hostilities when the Mohawk killed a number of Algonquin including their most renowned warrior, Simon Piskaret. During this war the Iroquois again defeated the Algonquin and then dispersed their major trading partners, the Huron, thus destroying the entire system. The Iroquois failed to capitalize on the situation, and the French quickly moved their trade operations into, and west of, the Great Lakes.

By 1675 most Algonquin had been dispersed from their traditional homeland, with the majority seeking refuge either in the Jesuit missions or among the French at Trois-Rivières. They remained allied to the French fighting the English and the Iroquois in the major colonial wars of the 17th century. By 1720 they were once again intermediaries in trade, this time as carriers in an illegal system of smuggling between Montreal and Albany. In the 1730s they entered the so-called Seven Nations confederacy, an alliance between mission Indians and the French, and they subsequently served in King George's War (1744-48) and the French and Indian War (1756-63).

See also French Colonies; Fur Trade; Indians of North America.

Bibliography: Hunt, George T., *Wars of the Iroquois: A Study in Intertribal Trade Relations* (Univ. of Wisconsin Press, 1940); Jennings, Francis, *The Ambiguous Iroquois Empire* (Norton, 1984); Trigger, Bruce, *The Children of Aataentsic: A History of the Huron People to 1600*, 2 vols. (McGill-Queens Univ. Press, 1972).

Richard L. Haan
Hartwick College

ALISON, FRANCIS (1705-79)   Arriving in America from Ireland in 1735, Alison made his way to New London, Pennsylvania. In 1737 he became pastor of the New London Presbyterian Church. He established a Latin grammar school there in 1743. Alison left New London in 1752 to become principal, and later rector, of the Academy and Charitable School opened in 1751 (now the University of Pennsylvania). He was a professor of moral philosophy and did much to encourage the natural rights philosophy that in many ways characterized American revolutionary thought. He founded the American Philosophical Society, of which Benjamin Franklin was the first president. Ezra Stiles, then president of Yale College, called Alison "the greatest scholar in America."

ALLEN, ETHAN (1738-89)   Revolutionary War soldier and leader of the Green Mountain Boys. Allen was born on January 21, 1738, in Litchfield, Connecticut, served in the French and Indian War, and then settled in Bennington, Vermont. He became involved in the dispute over the land that would become Vermont but was then known as the New Hampshire Grants, between New York and New Hampshire, both colonies having been given conflicting patents by the British Crown. Those who held grants from New Hampshire ejected New York's settlers and raised a defense regiment known as the Green Mountain Boys, naming Allen as colonel.

When the Revolutionary War broke out, Allen and the Green Mountain Boys joined with Benedict Arnold's Massachusetts forces to seize Fort Ticonderoga on May 10, 1775. The next day, Allen took Crown Point, thus securing control of Lake Champlain. Allen next participated in the invasion of Canada, where he was taken prisoner at Montreal on September 25, 1775, and sent to England, being exchanged in May 1778. His book *A Narrative of Col. Ethan Allen's Captivity* (1779) fails to mention Arnold's part in the capture of Ticonderoga.

Allen returned to Vermont as commander of the militia, but played no further part in the war. He and his brothers urged the British to incorporate Vermont into Canada or help it achieve separate status, but these plans collapsed with the end of the war. He settled in Burlington, Vermont, and died there on February 12, 1789, two years before his

Ethan Allen took a leading role in organizing Vermont settlers in the 1770s and was instrumental in the American victories at Fort Ticonderoga and Crown Point in 1775. *(Library of Congress)*

dream of having Vermont recognized as a state was realized.

ALLAN, JOHN (1746-1805)   Born in Edinburgh, Scotland, Allan emigrated with his parents to Nova Scotia in 1749. In the late 1760s he became a justice of the peace and a clerk of the supreme court. From 1770-76 he served in the provincial assembly. When the American Revolution broke out, Allan gave assistance to the Americas, most notably by securing a treaty with the Indians in his region, and in January 1777, Congress named him Superintendent of the Eastern Indians. Allan then became a fugitive from the British. Nova Scotia authorities burned his home, imprisoned his wife, and offered a reward for his capture. He eluded the British and, after the war, settled in Maine. In 1801, Congress gave him land in Ohio as compensation for the losses he incurred in the Revolution.

ALLEN, WILLIAM (1704-80)   A lawyer and Philadelphia businessman, he was educated in London and returned to America to take over his father's retail businesses in 1725. As a member of the Philadelphia Council from 1727, he was instrumental in securing funds to build what is now Independence Hall. He was a member of the Assembly from 1731-39, Grand Master of the Freemasons in 1732, mayor of Philadelphia in 1735, and recorder of the city in 1741. A lower court justice from 1737, he was provincial chief justice from 1750-74. Although Allen worked closely with Benjamin Franklin, he refused to support American independence and retired in England in 1776.

ALLERTON, ISAAC (?1586-1659?)   Pilgrim leader and entrepreneur, Isaac Allerton refitted the *Speedwell* for the Leyden group and sailed on the *Mayflower* to Plymouth Rock, where he served as a resourceful assistant to Governor Bradford. When the colony lost its backing in 1625, he not only convinced the backers to reinvest but borrowed enough money to resupply the desperate colony. He brought the last Leyden Pilgrims to Plymouth in 1629 and engineered the Patent of 1630, giving the colony land and property titles. His service ended in 1631 when he was censured for his expansive trading ventures. By 1644 he was a flourishing merchant in New Haven.
See also Plymouth.

ALLOUEZ, CLAUDE JEAN (1622-89)   A Jesuit missionary, Allouez was born at Saint-Didier, France, and studied to be a Jesuit at Toulouse, Billom, and Rodez. Ordained in 1655, he went to Canada as a misionary in 1658. His work among the Indians along the St. Lawrence River was so successful he was appointed vicar of all the traders and Indians in the Northwest in 1663. He traveled throughout the Northwest for 20 years, converting the Indians, founding missions, and overseeing the relations between the traders and Indians. He described his conversions and the geography of the land in his diaries. When the Northwest Territory was proclaimed for the King of France on June 4, 1671, he gave the oration at Sault Ste. Marie.

His Mission of Rapides des Pères, now an historical monument at De Pere, Wisconsin, served 2,000 Indians in 1674, and Nicholas Perrot rewarded the mission with a monstrance in 1686. During his service with the Indians, he baptized 10,000 and preached to over 100,000 Indians among the Potawatomi, Nipissirinien, Outagamie, Mascouten, Coupée, Queue, and Miami tribes. He died working among the Miami near Niles, Michigan.

AMERICA, NAMING OF   Columbus died in 1506 certain that his discovered islands lay just off the coast of Asia; the admiral had proved a fundamental point in successfully making his round trip, but his discovery never shook his faith in older geographic notions. By contrast, after his own voyage to the coast of South America in 1499, Amerigo Vespucci concluded that these lands were not islands "but a continent, because it extends along far-stretching shores that do not encompass it."

"Mundus Novus," the title assigned to Vespucci's published letter, came into the hands of the scholastic monks of St. Die near Strausburg in 1507 as they were engaged in preparing a new edition of Ptolemy's geography. The idea that these lands constituted a newly discovered "fourth part" of the globe revolutionized their thinking, and in their *Cosmographiae Introduction* of 1507, which included the world map of Waldseemuller, they christened Vespucci's New World "America" in his honor. Columbus's older notion of a small and crowded globe continued to shape popular belief and terminology for years; Cortes, in the 1520s, for example, persisted in the belief that Mexico was a part of Asia, and in Iberia the Americas continued to be known as "The Indies" for the next century. As late as 1634, when Jean Nicolet became the first European to cross Lake Michigan, he expected to land on the shores of China, and dressed appropriately for a meeting with the Great Khan. But in 1538, Mercator used "America" to refer to both North and South America, by which time this was becoming standard usage among the best educated Europeans.

See also Cartography; Columbus, Christopher; Nicolet, Jean; Vespucci, Amerigo.

Bibliography: Arciniegas, German, *Amerigo and the New World* (1955; reprint, Hippocrene).

John Mack Faragher
Mount Holyoke College

AMERICAN PHILOSOPHICAL SOCIETY   Founded at Philadelphia by Benajmin Franklin in 1743, the American Philosophical is the oldest learned society still in existence in the United States. In 1769 it merged with the American Society, the successor to Franklin's Junto of 1727, a tradesman's self-improvement club. It was established to promote "useful knowledge among the British plantations in America" and is modeled after the Royal Society of London. In 1770, the Society had 241 members (including 24 Europeans) classified into four groups: mathematical and physical sciences, social sciences, geological and biological sciences, and the humanities. The Society first published *Transactions* in 1769 and has published regularly ever since. Early contributors included Thomas Jefferson, Benjamin Rush, and Joseph Priestley. Its archives are rich with early colonial letters and manuscripts, including the papers of Franklin, Lewis and Clark, and others. Its library specializes in the beginnings of American government and the history of American science and culture. In 1787-89 the Society erected Philosophical Hall in Philadelphia where it is still headquartered.

AMHERST, JEFFREY (1717-97)   Rising quickly in the British army, Amherst was given command of an expedition going to North America in 1758. Prime Minister William Pitt placed Amherst over General Wolfe and later made him commander in chief. During the French and Indian War, he was responsible for the greatest British successes, taking forts Duquesne and Ticonderoga. He was appointed governor general of British North America after the fall of Montreal in 1760. When he failed to subdue Pontiac in the rebellion of 1763, Amherst returned to England.

Along with John Wilkes, Amherst was one of the most popular figures of his day. Acting according to his principles, he resigned the governorship of Virginia (to which he had just been named) and his other commands when he had a disagreement with George III in 1768. He was restored to favor in 1770 and given the governorship of Guernsey. As a privy councillor he advised George III during the Revolutionary War, whose prosecution he vigorously supported. He refused to serve as British commander in America, though, because he detested his previous experience there. In 1780 he succeeded in ending the Gordon Riots in London. In 1787 he became Lord Amherst, and in 1796 a field marshal.

ANDRÉ, JOHN (1751-80)   A British soldier, André joined the royal army in 1771, and rose quickly in rank. In 1778, he was appointed adjutant general (major) of the British forces in America and aide to General Clinton. Witty and artistic, he was popular with the British regulars and often organized plays to keep them entertained. In 1780, Major André acted as liaison between General Clinton and the American general Benedict Arnold. André was captured after a meeting with Arnold and taken to General Washington's headquarters. Charged with spying by an American military court, he was sentenced to death and hanged. After André's death, Washington described him as "an accomplished gentleman and gallant officer." André left behind a journal of the war years, published in 1902.

ANDROS, SIR EDMUND (1637-1714)   A British colonial governor, Andros was born in London. He was appointed the governor of New York by the Duke of York in 1674. Andros tried to force Dutch families to pledge allegiance to English rule, but he did not gain support from the English settlers and was recalled to England in 1681. After the Duke of York, who still favored Andros, became King James II, Andros was made the governor of the Dominion of New England (1686). Ignoring the traditions of local and popular politics already formed in New England, Andros enforced unpopular laws and taxes on the colonists and imposed the Anglican form of worship on Congregational Boston. The Boston militia overthrew his regime in 1689, and Andros returned to England, where he still had influence. Andros was appointed lieutenant governor of Virginia in 1692 and was a capable leader until he was recalled in 1698 after antagonizing the leading Anglican official in the colony.

See also Dominion of New England.

ANGLO-AMERICAN CULTURE   Culture in the American colonies reflected the differing regions along the Atlantic coast as well as the motives that had led various groups to come to North America. English colonization from the Chesapeake Bay south tended to be a quest for financial gain rather than an exercise in nation building. Unlike the gentlemen adventurers and ambitious commoners who arrived at Jamestown in 1607, the Massachusetts settlers of 1620 had a different, religious goal in mind.

New England Settlements.   The 35 or so Separatists who accompanied William Bradford and the other Pilgrims on the *Mayflower* were in search of a religious ideal. Their militant Calvinism would simply not allow for compromise with the Church of England. The Puritan migration of 1630, also to Massachusetts Bay, had a similar basis. But the politically more subtle group led by John Winthrop was not ready for an open breach with the established church.

The determination of both groups to build a "Zion in the Wilderness" produced a complex blend of social and cultural values altered by the realities of the New World. One of the largest sources of income for those of the Bay colony was supplying food and wood products to their countrymen in the Caribbean. The latter could then concentrate all their energies on sugar production and by the 18th century many of their slaves were paid for by their sugar converted to rum in New England. Therefore, while trade patterns in the North isolated New Englanders to some degree from the mother country, tobacco production in Virginia and Maryland drew these colonies economically and culturally closer than ever to England.

Puritan Culture.   Puritan New England was a place where passionate concern for the scriptures led to an elaborate system of public education, while Chesapeake Bay growers tended to import tutors to train their children right on the plantation. By 1647 the Massachusetts General Court declared that it was "one chief project of that old deluder Satan to keep men from knowledge of the scriptures," and therefore each township of more than 50 households was required to provide a schoolmaster for its children. Although traditional subjects like ancient languages and composition were taught, the Puritans were children of the Renaissance and also introduced students to major literary figures, including Shakespeare.

When Harvard College was founded in 1636, young men studying for the clergy were taught their Aristotelian logic as modified by the French Huguenot Peter Ramus. Later, the growing worldliness of the Harvard curriculum convinced Connecticut clergyman James Pierpont to organize a more orthodox school in 1701. Businessman Elihu Yale contributed books and trade goods for creation of a new college, eventually situated in New Haven and called Yale College.

Austere Massachusetts settlers arrived with a distrust for musical instruments and stained glass in their churches. They strongly opposed poetic translations that gave lilt and charm to the scriptures. In their opinion, since men and women were quite corrupted enough by original sin and normal desires of the flesh, "enthusiasm" was best left to the flawed teachings of other religions.

The Bible did contain poetry, however, and was filled with parables and allegories. Lecturers, as certain clergymen were called, regularly explained these to eager listeners, most of whom were plain folk like farmers and fishermen. So, rather than sophisticated literary allusions, most sermons and much popular literature tended to set ideas in the language of common people. This was one of the strengths of John Bunyan's popular work, *The Pilgrim's Progress.* Englishmen turned to the lessons of history to justify their actions and behavior. From ancient to modern history they found moral precepts to comple-

ment their theological persuasion. John Foxe's *Acts and Monuments,* better known as "The Book of Martyrs," was published in 1563 and reminded Puritans in America of why they had left England. Bradford's *History of Plymouth Plantation* was not published in book form until 1856 but was known and admired by many of his contemporaries.

New Englanders kept diaries to show how life's journey had to be meticulously observed and evaluated to provide spiritual and behavioral insights for those on the passage toward judgment. Michael Wigglesworth never printed his diary for reasons of modesty. But his epic poem, "Day of Doom," may have been the most widely read piece of theological poetry in New England. Much gentler but more sophisticated was the work of Anne Bradstreet of Andover. In 1650 her collection *The Tenth Muse Lately Sprung up in America* was well received when it was published in London. The *Bay Psalm Book,* which translates the most poetic part of the Old Testament, may have been a rigidly accurate translation, but in achieving exactness, the flow of the graceful King James version is replaced by a precise, if ill-fitting translation from the Hebrew.

Cotton Mather's epic religious history, *Magnalia Christi Americana,* was considered so important it was sent to London to be put in type in 1702. Scholars believe it was inspired by Edward Johnson's 1653 spiritual-historical survey of the Puritan mission, *The Wonder Working Providence of Sion's Saviour in New England.*

The first printing press was established in Cambridge in 1639 by Stephen Daye, and the following year the first book was published. It was the *Bay Psalm Book,* edited by Richard Mather. It was not until 1704, however, that the city's first newspaper, the *Boston News-Letter,* began its carefully censored public life.

The Middle Colonies.   Pennsylvania, to the south, was much more tolerant of diverse social and theological views. Although German immigrants came in large numbers to farm the land, English Quakers soon turned Penn's infant city of Philadelphia into a booming commercial port on the Delaware River. By 1775 it was the second largest city in the British Empire.

Benjamin Franklin was 17 when he arrived from Boston in 1723. Since the Quakers did not possess a university-trained clergy, there was no institution of higher learning in the city at that time. He worked at the printing trade his brother had taught him and in 1729 bought the newspaper he worked for, changing its name to the *Pennsylvania Gazette.* At its press, in 1757, he also published *Poor Richard's Almanac.* This collection embodies Quakerism's common sense, Puritanism's work ethic, and a Newtonian view of an ordered, rational universe. The

Junto, his self-improvement society, was organized in 1727 and matured into the American Philosophical Society. His *Proposals Relating to the Education of Youth in Pennsylvania* commenced an effort that in 1754, culminated in the founding of what became the secular University of Pennsylvania.

The Chesapeake Region and the South.   T h e squires of the Chesapeake Bay remained loyal to the precepts of the Church of England. They lived on their estates, and shipped and received goods on their own wharves. So urban development was minimal. Their British-born sense of civic responsibility was reenforced by the books and magazines they imported from London. Whether in church government or the colonial militia, they carried out their activities with a sense of *noblesse oblige*. Some of the wealthiest sent their sons to study law in London at one of the Inns of Court. The more modest had to be content with sending their sons to William and Mary College, founded in 1693. One measure of the differences between the Chesapeake Bay colonists and their northern counterparts is that in 1700, imports from Britain were eight times greater than they were for New England (and still three times larger on the eve of the Revolution). They imported Chippendale furniture and used Christopher Wren's architecture for William and Mary College. But pride in Anglo-American culture never permitted the House of Burgesses to adopt an attitude of unquestioning obedience to the royal governors.

In the deep South, the economy was driven by rice farming in the 18th century. The colonists regularly trafficked in slaves because white servants could not survive in the malarial infested fields. This drove many planters to seek the ocean breezes of Charleston, South Carolina, and Savannah, Georgia. The social season was a time to show English gowns and furniture and to listen to the music of Handel.

The Revolutionary Era.   The coming of the Revolution in 1775 brought a new and bold American culture to the forefront. Thomas Paine had been in the colonies less than two years from England when he published the pamphlet *Common Sense* in January 1776. The fact that it blamed George III for the outbreak of the rebellion is significant because only five months later Thomas Jefferson's Declaration of Independence did exactly the same thing. His demands for freedom and justice eloquently echoed John Locke's *Second Treatise on Government*, defending the Glorious Revolution of 1688.

Even the best poetry of the revolutionary era is the work of a suffering rebel, young Philip Freneau. He was locked away for two months on the British prison hulk *Scorpion*. He painted an acid sketch of the ordeal in *The British Prison Ship*. He was typical of a new generation of writers who saw culture in general, and literature in particular, as a way of justifying the revolutionary experience. In the new paintings of John Trumbull and Gilbert Stuart, and in the writings of men like Noah Webster, Anglo-American culture was to take on a nationalistic militancy.

See also Literature, Colonial; Religion, Colonial.

Bibliography: Bridenbaugh, Carl, *Myths & Realities: Societies of the Colonial South* (Atheneum, 1963); Bridenbaugh, Carl and Jessica, *Rebels and Gentlemen: Philadelphia in the Age of Franklin* (Oxford Univ. Press, 1962); Morison, Samuel Eliot, *The Intellectual Life of Colonial New England* (Cornell Univ. Press, 1960); Wertenbaker, Thomas, *The Golden Age of Colonial Culture* (Cornell University Press, 1959); Wright, Louis B., *The Atlantic Frontier: Colonial American Civilization, 1607-1763* (Cornell Univ. Press, 1964).

Allen Richman
Stephen F. Austin State University

ANGLICANS   By action of the Virginia legislature in 1619, the Church of England became the officially established ecclesiastical institution in that colony. At that early date in colonial American history, the King and his Privy Council might well have assumed that such would automatically be the case wherever England's flag flew. That this would not be the way the story turned out was only one of many surprises when it came to transplanting Old World institutions to New World shores.

In general, Anglicanism in the 17th century grew quite slowly. Clergy were few in number, competition was never far away, and in the South, towns did not develop so that anything approaching normal parish life, England-style, could evolve. To solve some of these problems, Thomas Bray, one-time commissary to Maryland, founded missionary and publication societies that would adopt the "foreign plantations" as their special interest and concern. With this aid, Anglicanism spread through all the colonies in the 18th century, although never legally favored anywhere in New England nor in Pennsylvania.

Virginia and the Chesapeake region remained the great center of Anglican strength, about one-half of all Anglican parishes in 1750 being found in just two colonies—Virginia and Maryland. Any hopes for a genuinely powerful intercolonial church were dashed, however, by the outbreak of the American Revolution. During that struggle, Anglicanism was abruptly disestablished throughout the colonies, delivering a blow from which the Church did not recover for at least a generation. Colonial Anglicanism also suffered from the unwillingness of most Americans to see a Church of England bishop take up residence in America. Never able to complete its own form of governance and never able to separate the bond between episcopacy and monarchy, the colonial Anglican estab-lishment—although heavily favored from the start—had by the 1780s, surrendered most of its advantages and much of its prestige.

See also Religion; individual colony articles.

Bibliography: Woolverton, John F., *Colonial Anglicanism in North America* (Wayne State Univ. Press, 1984).

Edwin S. Gaustad
University of California, Riverside

Anglo-Dutch Wars The first Anglo-Dutch War (1652-54), was precipitated by Britain's passage of the 1651 Navigation Act. On July 6, 1652 the Dutch govern-ment ordered its commanders to attack English shipping. In May 1653, the English began a blockade of Dutch ports. On August 4, 1653, Admiral Tromp attempted to run the blockade in an effort to link up with Admiral Witte de With. The English fleet lay in wait, and in the ensuing engage-ment Admiral Tromp was killed, and the Dutch fleet badly mauled.

Peace negotiations began in September 1653 and lasted until April 1654. The resulting Treaty of Westminster (April 5) may be described as an extraordinarily mild defeat for the Dutch, especially in light of the military situation in the English Channel. Yet during the period of the negotiations, Lord Protector Cromwell dispatched a squadron of four warships to New England, with the intent of launching an attack on the Dutch colony New Nether-land. Shortly before the expedition was to sail from New England ports, news arrived in America of the peace set-tlement. The war ended in a stalemate.

Second War. The second Anglo-Dutch War began as an undeclared maritime war in 1663. Along the West Coast of Africa, Britian's newly chartered Royal African Company clashed with the forces of the Dutch West India Company in a rivalry over the slave, ivory, and gold trade. By 1664 preparations for war were underway in both countries. On March 12, 1664, James, Duke of York and Albany, received a royal patent to a stretch of the North American coast occupied since the 1620s by the Dutch. The duke and his advisers organized and financed an expedition to attack and capture New Netherland. The English fleet under the command of Colonel Richard Nicolls, augmented with forces from New England, sailed against the poorly defended Dutch garrison of New Amsterdam on the southern tip of Manhattan Island, forc-ing its surrender without a shot in August 1664.

Meanwhile, war fever spread in both countries, and on March 4, 1665, England officially declared war on the United Provinces. For two years the war raged on with large naval engagements in the English Channel, while

England and the Netherlands sought out European allies. In January 1666 Louis XIV of France declared war on England, although French forces played little part in the war. In spring 1666 the focus shifted from diplomacy to maritime war as the British fleet under Monck and Prince Rupert was defeated by De Ruyter and the younger Tromp in the Four Days' Battle. In August, however, the forces of Monck and Rupert exacted revenge in a series of suc-cessful raids of shipping along the Dutch coast. English victories notwithstanding, the rest of the year passed without major incident. Shortages of men and supplies and the inability of either nation to win a decisive victory soon took the heart out of both commands. The English were suffering from the partial blockade as well as the plague and, in September, the Great Fire of London. By mid-February 1667, both sides were ready to negotiate.

In the Treaty of Breda (July 31, 1667) the Dutch seemed to have won many concessions, although the territory of New Netherland remained lost. On the thorny issue of the Navigation Act the Dutch won a half victory. The defini-tion of contraband as only munitions was accepted, visit and search rights were lightened, and the principle of "free ship, free goods" was acknowledged by the English. And finally, the provisions of the Navigation Act were clarified in favor of the Dutch when they were allowed to import into England, commodities of the growth, production, or manufacture of the German-speaking hinterland. In the West Indies the Dutch would never regain the dominance they once enjoyed, although they would later get back Curacao and St. Eustatius; and the retention of Surinam would permit them to establish a Dutch center for the export of South American produce. Thus the war ended.

Third War. The third Anglo-Dutch War was part of the wars of Louis XIV of France, whose aims included both the expansion of the French overseas empire and the elimination of Dutch rivalry to French trade. England was drawn into the war by the secret Treaty of Dover (1670) which established an alliance between England and France. When Louis invaded the Netherlands in 1672 and overran the southern provinces, the English and Dutch found them-selves once more in a maritime war. In this war, Dutch naval prowess proved itself once again. De Ruyter defeated the combined English and French fleets in a heroic battle in Southwold Bay, and on August 9, 1673, the combined fleets of admirals Cornelis Evertsen and Jacob Binckes forced the surrender of New York. This victory was short-lived, however, for in the negotiations that led to the second Treaty of Westminster, New York was returned to the English. When the treaty was made public on March 6, 1674, the legal niceties could not conceal the Dutch defeat, for although diplomacy had succeeded in forcing England to break with France, the two-year struggle had pressed the United Provinces hard. The peace was tantamount to an acknowledgment by the Dutch that they were no longer the dominant European naval power.

See also Navigation Acts; New Netherland.

Bibliography: Wilson, Charles, *Profit and Power: A Study of England and the Dutch Wars* (Cambridge Univ. 1957); Boxer, Charles R., *The Anglo-Dutch Wars of the 17th Century* (HMSO London, 1974).

Oliver A. Rink
California State University, Bakersfield

ANGLO-SPANISH WAR (1727-28)   Under the terms of the Treaty of Utrecht (1713), Spain was forced to give up Gibraltar to Great Britain and to sign the Asiento, an agreement giving the British the right to transport slaves to the New World. Spain accused Britain of violating its terms and began seizing British ships. A brief Anglo-Spanish war in 1718 was followed by friendlier relations, but war broke out again in February 1727 with increased English trade. A preliminary peace was established in August, and in March 1728 a convention attempted a settlement. In the Treaty of Seville (1729), Spain promised to restore normal trade, but in fact, seizures of British ships continued.

ANNAPOLIS   Capital of Maryland and seat of Anne Arundel County, Annapolis was founded in 1649 by Puritans from Virginia on the northern bank of the Severn River. First called Greensbury, and then Anne Arundel, it later became an important seaport and was named the port-of-entry to Maryland in 1668. It was renamed Annapolis in honor of the future Queen Anne in 1694, the same year it became the capital of the colony. Toward the end of the Revolution, it served as the site of the Continental Congress (1783-84). It was there that George Washington resigned his commission from the Continental Army and there that the treaty of peace with Britain was signed. The Annapolis Convention of 1786 laid the groundwork for the Constitutional Convention of the following year.

ANTINOMIANISM AND THE ANTINOMIAN CONTROVERSY   Antinomianism means "without law," and although many Christians may teach that the grace of God places them above religious legalism, the term is usually used pejoratively to denounce those who fail to conform to certain standards of conduct or belief. Charges of antinomianism usually signal quarrels over authority and power. The first designation of "antinomianism" in the New England event appeared in 1644 with the publication of John Winthrop's *A Short Story of the Rise, Reign, and Ruine of the Antinomians, Familists & Libertines, That Infected the Churches of New-England.*

The Antinomian Controversy was comprised of a series of interrogations, disagreements, and trials that took place in Boston and Cambridge between 1636 and 1638. A number of interlocking issues were at stake, including the civil authority of John Winthrop, the theology of John Cotton, the ecclesiastical power of John Wilson, and the dissenting voice of Anne Hutchinson. In the trials, conferences, and later writings, the very character of the Puritans' enterprise in New England was under debate. Theocratic assumptions were tested, and today, scholars mine the texts to understand Puritan church-state relations and the concomitant issues of sedition, Indian relations, gender roles, and the early history of dissent in America.

At the center of the Boston controversy stood Anne Hutchinson, a critic of legalistic preaching who exalted John Cotton as the exemplary teacher of grace and, in so doing, attacked the legitimacy of other ministers. Hutchinson was banished from the colony and then excommunicated from her church. Cotton defended her position until late in the church examination. Many prominent citizens, some accused of sedition, followed Hutchinson and her family into exile in Rhode Island.

See also Hutchinson, Anne.

Bibliography: Hall, David D., ed., *The Antinomian Controversy, 1636-1638: A Documentary History* (Wesleyan Univ. Press, 1968).

Jane F. Crosthwaite
Mount Holyoke College

ANTISLAVERY   Blacks had always been prominent antislavery advocates and led the challenge against bondage. Two of the earliest black abolitionists, Prince Hall and Abijah Prince, were New Englanders. Prior to the prerevolutionary period, few whites voiced any misgivings about the institution of slavery. Some had objected to the slave trade, and some religious groups, particularly the Quakers, had demonstrated opposition to the principle of human bondage. Occasionally, colonial governments imposed heavy import duties on slaves, but chiefly because they feared the presence of Africans in their midst. It was not until the revolutionary period, when egalitarian philosophies became widespread, that organized opposition to slavery appeared. But this opposition proved unable to challenge effectively the institution.

A few isolated individuals stood out as at least theoretical opponents of slavery in the prerevolutionary years. John Woolman, a Quaker, and Anthony Benezet, a Huguenot, were prominent antislavery spokesmen, as were Benjamin Franklin and Benjamin Rush. But even such well-respected philosophers as John Locke upheld the right to hold slaves; Locke wrote a constitution for the Carolina settlement that recognized slavery in those colonies.

OBSERVATIONS

On the Inflaving, importing and purchafing of

Negroes;

With fome Advice thereon, extracted from the Epiftle of the Yearly-Meeting of the People called Quakers, held at *London* in the Year 1748.

Anthony Benezet

When ye fpread forth your Hands, I will hide mine Eyes from you, yea when ye make many Prayers I will not hear; your Hands are full of Blood. Wafh ye, make you clean, put away the Evil of your Doings from before mine Eyes Ifai. 1, 15.

Is not this the Faft that I have chofen, to loofe the Bands of Wickednefs, to undo the heavy Burden, to let the Oppreffed go free, and that ye break every Toke, Chap. 58, 7.

Second Edition.

GERMANTOWN:
Printed by Christopher Sower. 1760.

Antislavery sentiment in colonial America was particularly strong among Quakers. *(Library of Congress)*

Antislavery and the Revolution. The American Revolution provoked growing numbers of people to question the inconsistencies between natural rights philosophy and slavery, by then an integral part of the colonial economy. Many times revolutionary speakers and writers described America's relationship with Britain as one resembling slavery. Many incorrectly maintained that Britain was solely responsible for slavery's existence in the colonies. As the Revolution matured, more frequent and strident calls for abolition were heard. The first formal organized antislavery society appeared in 1775; additional ones formed after the Revolution.

During the war, about 5,000 blacks continued a long tradition of Afro-American involvement in colonial wars and had a strong influence on antislavery thought. Particularly in the North, both slaves and free blacks served in the militia. Slaves and their families often won freedom for meritorious service. Black soldiers, however, were controversial. General Washington initially barred black enlistment. The governor of Virginia, Lord Dunmore, took advantage of Washington's order to declare all slaves freed and to invite them to join the king's troops. His declaration had the desired effect, and thousands escaped to British lines during the war. Alarmed by the threat that slave fugitives posed, Washington admitted free blacks into the army. Slaveholders, too, somewhat relaxed their attitudes toward blacks, and many permitted at least some noncombat black enlistment.

Policies After the Revolution. After the war, revolutionary ideals spawned several manumission and antislavery societies. The Quakers organized the first society in 1775. In 1785 they were joined by the New York Society for Promoting the Manumission of Slaves, headed by John Jay. Societies in most other colonies soon followed. They often had differing goals. Some argued for deportation and colonization, while others focused on abolition of the slave trade or gradual emancipation. Pennsylvania's legislature passed the first such plan in 1780. Many individuals manumitted their slaves, feeling it inconsistent with American ideals.

While the incongruity with bondage was apparent to many, the Revolution hardly made abolitionists of all or even most whites. Slavery was dealt with only vaguely and indeterminately in the Declaration of Independence, and then received sanction in the Constitution of 1787. In the draft of the Declaration, Jefferson blamed George III for instituting slavery, but Southern slaveholders had the passage stricken. It was the first instance of many in which slave owners would dilute or eliminate the new nation's opposition to the institution. In the Constitutional Convention, Southern planters retained recognition of slavery, based on arguments about the rights of property, the cornerstone of the new government. Each slave was reckoned as three-fifths of a person for purposes of representation, although slaves did not vote. The Convention also agreed not to end the Atlantic slave trade for another 20 years. Slavery was prohibited in the Northwest Territory, but a stringent Fugitive Slave Act faced little opposition. Through these measures, antislavery activity was overpowered effectively. As far as slavery was concerned, the Constitution represented a victory for slaveholders.

Thus the launching of the new nation ended an era in Afro-American history. By safeguarding the institution, the writers of the Constitution left a critically divisive issue untouched. The tensions it generated for 75 years culminated in civil war.

See also Slavery.

Bibliography: Davis, David Brion, *The Problem of Slavery in the Age of Revolution, 1770-1823* (Cornell Univ. Press, 1975).

Lynda J. Morgan
Mount Holyoke College

ANZA, JUAN BAPTISTA DE (1735-88)   Son of a frontiersman father of the same name, Anza in 1773 was ordered to explore the possibility of a route between Sonora and California by which food could be carried to the Pacific coast settlements.   Anza left Tubac in January 1774 and arrived at Mission San Gabriel on March 22.   He then returned to Mexico City to make his report and was ordered to lead settlers to San Francisco Bay.   The party left Tubac in October 1775 and arrived at the bay in September 1776, Anza having led them as far as Monterey.   Anza became governor of New Mexico in 1777, a post of which he was relieved in 1788 at his own request, dying soon thereafter in Sonora.

APACHE INDIANS   With the Navaho, the various Apache tribes are Athapaskan-speaking peoples who migrated into the desert region of present-day northern Mexico and Southwestern United States perhaps as late as the 16th century.   There they subsisted on small-scale gardening in the creek and river bottoms, hunting and gathering, and secondarily on plunder gathered from raids against the sedentary farming peoples of the region, such as the Pima, the Papago, and the various Pueblo.   Indeed, the name "Apache" probably comes from the Zuni word for "enemy"; the Apache call themselves N'de, or Dine, "the people."   Not all contacts between the Apache and the indigenous societies were hostile, however, for the Apache were also traders, bringing meat and hides from the plains to the Pueblo peoples.   Among Europeans, Coronado first encountered Apachean speakers in 1541, but the name was first recorded by Onate in 1598.   He made contact with the Mescalero of west Texas, one of several distinct tribes that include the Western Apache or Coyotero, of southeastern Arizona; the Chiricahua of southwestern New Mexico; the Jicarilla of northeastern New Mexico; and the Lipan of the lower Rio Grande Valley.   A sixth group, the Kiowa-Apache, became fully intermixed with the Kiowa of Oklahoma.

In the postcontact period, with the introduction of the horse, many Apache groups shifted more fully to hunting and raiding.   The Mescalero began raiding the Spanish settlements in northern Mexico and New Mexico in the early 17th century, beginning a cycle of warfare and revenge that continued for the next two centuries.   Unlike most other Indian groups, Apache numbers grew after their encounter with the Europeans, largely because of their incorporation of mestizo and Indian captives.

Bibliography: John, Elizabeth A. H., *Storms Brewed in Other Men's Worlds* (Texas A&M Univ. Press, 1975); Opler, Morris E., *Apache Odyssey* (Holt, Rinehart & Winston, 1969); Spicer, Edward H., *Cycles of Conquest* (Univ. of Arizona Press, 1962)

John Mack Faragher
Mount Holyoke College

APPALACHIAN MOUNTAINS, THE   Ranging from 50 to 200 miles in width, the Appalachian system of interlocking mountain ranges, ridges, and valleys extends from northern New England to central Alabama and presented a formidable barrier to the western expansion of the European colonies.   The Longfellow and White mountain ranges of Maine and New Hampshire are separated by the Connecticut River valley from the Green Mountains of Vermont.   Cut by the valley of the Hudson River, the system extends southward into New York where the Catskills merge into the Allegheny Plateau, which extends south through Pennsylvania into Virginia.   Here the eastern face of the system is called the Blue Ridge; the western reaches the Cumberland Plateau.

The few gaps in the Appalachians south of the Hudson are cut by the Delaware, Susquehanna, Potomac, James, and Roanoke rivers, which provided access to habitable interior valleys, particularly the great Shenandoah River valley of Virginia, west of the Blue Ridge, but did not lead over the western ridges to the interior lowlands.   That access was provided most dramatically by the Mohawk River valley in the north and the Cumberland Gap in the South—the great natural gateways through the mountains.   Other routes taken by pioneers were Braddock's Road (later the Cumberland or Old National Road) or Forbes Road across Pennsylvania and Maryland to the forks of the Ohio River.   Some pioneers followed the Watauga, Holston, or Clinch to the Tennessee.

At the end of the French and Indian War the great population increase of the seaboard colonies, supplemented by powerful waves of immigration, created enormous pressures on the Indian land of the western Appalachians and the rich interior lowlands.   The British attempted to stem this invasion by declaring, in the Proclamation of 1763, a western barrier to settlement at the divide between Atlantic and Gulf watersheds.   Even before the American Revolution, however, the Appalachians had been breeched by the pioneers.

Bibliography: Hunt, Charles B., *Natural Regions of the United States and Canada* (Freeman, 1974).

John Mack Faragher
Mount Holyoke College

ARAWAK   The Arawak who greeted Christopher Columbus in the Bahamas were members of a large group of Indians who lived from Brazil northward along the coastal regions of South America and in the Caribbean. The tribe in the Bahamas was called the Lucayo; the main group, the Taino, lived in the Greater Antilles. The Taino had an elaborate religion and a stratified society with chiefs at the top and slaves at the bottom. An aristocratic caste was under the chiefs, while the greatest number of Arawak were commoners. Wars with the fierce Carib Indians, forced labor for the Spanish, and decimation by disease all contributed to their early disappearance as an active tribe in the Caribbean.

ARCHITECTURE, COLONIAL Colonial architecture in the American colonies can be divided into two phases corresponding to the 17th and 18th centuries. By the end of the 18th century the new nation began entering a third phase.

17th Century. In the 17th century, architecture was distinguished by regional variations of late gothic vernacular types of residential design. These regional types were determined by the ethnic character of the original settlements—English in New England and Virginia, Dutch along the Hudson River, Swedish along the lower Delaware, French along the Mississippi and Great Lakes, and Spanish in Florida and the Southwest. The principal exceptions to this pervasive vernacular medieval emphasis were the late Baroque of Spanish mission churches and the few references to English Renaissance architecture in the houses of prosperous Virginia planters.

Although the English colonists along the Atlantic seaboard used the traditional heavy hewn wood frame for their houses, they quickly modified the traditional house by covering it with split planks (clapboards) and shingles, eliminating the traditional wattle-and-daub and thatch that did not weather well. The oldest surviving residence and church in New England—the Fairbanks House of Dedham, Massachusetts, c. 1637; and the "Old Ship" Meetinghouse of Hingham, Massachusetts, begun in 1681 and later modified—show well this method of heavy frame construction.

By the last decade of the 17th century, all the various settlements along the Atlantic seaboard had come under English control, and a uniform English culture had become established. About this same time, also, colonists began to emulate current architecture in England, adopting late Baroque elements in what came to be called Georgian architecture after the reigning monarchs. Georgian architecture is characterized by the use of Classical elements, particularly in window and door openings and in decoration, by a horizontal emphasis, and by restraint in form and decoration. After 1725 this late Georgian classicism was transformed in England and in the colonies by neo-Palladianism, inspired by the restrained classical designs of the mid-16th century Italian architect Andréa Palladio.

18th Century. Increasingly, too, gentlemen-amateur architects consulted proliferating architectural publications for their designs. For example, Peter Harrison of Newport, Rhode Island, based his Redwood Library in Newport (1748-50) on a plate from Edward Hoppus's *Fourth Book of Palladio* (1736).

Georgian colonial public buildings consisted largely of governmental buildings and churches. Government buildings generally derived from domestic models, as in the Old Colony House in Newport (1739-41), designed by Richard Munday, a builder-architect. More carefully studied in proportion and detail is the Pennsylvania State House (1730-41), popularly called Independence Hall, in Philadelphia, designed by gentleman-amateur architect Judge Andrew Hamilton. Except for the addition of a tower, the central block is not much different from large English brick country houses of the day.

The basic type of the 18th century church was established in such examples as Christ Church (popularly known as Old North Church), Boston, 1723-41, which in turn had been inspired by the churches designed by Sir Christopher Wren to replace those lost in the great London Fire of 1666. After James Gibbs's St. Martin-in-the-Fields, London (1721-26), was published in his *Book of Architecture* of 1728, it then became the model for church architecture in the colonies. The most thoroughly Gibbsian of these churches was the Baptist Meetinghouse (1774-75) at Providence, Rhode Island, by the gentleman-amateur architect Joseph Brown, a successful merchant.

The exact point at which Colonial architecture ends and a distinctly national American architecture appears is difficult to pinpoint. Although the colonies declared their independence in 1776, they were not able to achieve political separation from England until the signing of the Treaty of Paris in 1783; and not until 1787 was the Constitution written and self-government instituted. Economic self-sufficiency was not gained until after 1812. Yet by 1790 many builders and architects were consciously seeking a new architectural expression to symbolize the new nation and its neoclassical form of republican democracy. Some, like Samuel McIntire of Salem or Charles Bulfinch of Boston, tended to adhere to a conservative English late Baroque tradition. Others, such as Thomas Jefferson in his later work, and his protégé Benjamin Henry Latrobe, forcefully rejected the older forms and substituted a truer and more Grecian neoclassicism in the buildings of the new nation.

Bibliography: Cummings, Abbott Lowell, *The Framed Houses of Massachusetts Bay, 1625-1725* (Harvard Univ. Press,

1979); Kimball, Fiske, *Domestic Architecture of the American Colonies and of the Early Republic* (Scribner's, 1922); Morrison, Hugh, *Early American Architecture from the First Colonial Settlements to the National Period* (Oxford Univ. Press, 1952); Pierson, William H., Jr., *American Buildings and the Architects*, vol. 1: The Colonial and Neo-Classical Styles (Oxford Univ. Press, 1970); Roth, Leland M., *A Concise History of American Architecture* (Harper & Row, 1979).

Leland M. Roth
University of Oregon

ARGALL, SIR SAMUEL (flourished 1609-24) Navigator and deputy governor of Virginia, Sir Samuel Argall discovered a short route across the Atlantic to Virginia in 1609, and his resourcefulness aided the starving Virginia colony. Sent to buy hogs in Bermuda in 1610, he returned instead with a cargo of fish from Cape Cod to provide immediate food. His purchase of 1,000 bushels of corn from the Indians gave the colonists seed, and he brought grain and horses from Canada. In 1613 he sailed to Maine to oust the French missionaries from the title to the North American coast issued by Louis XIII. On his return trip, he made the Hudson River Dutch swear loyalty. He captured Pocahontas in 1612, which in turn led to a treaty with the Indians.

ARKANSAS POST In 1686, Henri de Tonti, associate of La Salle, built this trading post on the Arkansas River, near its mouth on the Mississippi. It became the first permanent European settlement in the lower Mississippi Valley and an important connecting point between French settlements in Louisiana and in the upper Mississippi. Through the 18th century Arkansas Post continued as a fur-trading station, an army garrison, and a Jesuit mission, even after the cession of Louisiana to Spain in 1762. From 1819-21 it was the first capital of Arkansas territory, until superseded by Little Rock.

ARMSTRONG, JOHN (1758-1843) Born in Pennsylvania, Armstrong served as an officer in the Continental Army in North Carolina. Major Armstrong was the reputed author of two attacks on Congress in the 1790s entitled "The Newburgh Addresses." He asserted that the officers, not the civilians, embodied the true revolutionary spirit. The Continental Army was disbanded shortly after the Newburgh crisis. Armstrong later entered politics and was elected senator from New York. From 1804-10 he served as a minister to France. In 1812 he was appointed brigadier general but in 1813 left his command to become secretary of war. He was forced to resign in September 1814 for failing to protect Washington, D.C., from the British.

ARNOLD, BENEDICT (1741-1801) An American military leader who became a renowned traitor, Arnold was born in Norwich, Connecticut. His first major military accomplishment was in May 1775, when he joined Ethan

A patriot hero early in the Revolutionary War, Benedict Arnold came to symbolize treason among Americans. *(Library of Congress)*

Allen and took Fort Ticonderoga. In September 1775, Arnold and General Montgomery made an unsuccessful attack on Quebec. Montgomery was killed, and Arnold, who suffered severe wounds, was promoted to brigadier general. During his command, he stopped a British invasion from Canada at Lake Champlain. Arnold resented Congress for promoting five brigadiers who were junior to him to major general in February 1777. After Arnold courageously attacked a British fort in Danbury, Connecticut, he was promoted to major general. Arnold was again severely wounded when he fought General Burgyone's troops at Saratoga.

In May 1779, through correspondence with Sir Henry Clinton, Arnold secretly offered to aid the British. After Arnold was given command of West Point in 1780, he arranged through Britain's Major John André to surrender the post to the British for 20,000 pounds. André was captured, exposing the plot, but Arnold escaped. He became a British brigadier general and later commanded British troops against Connecticut and Virginia. He left America for Britain in 1781.

ART, COLONIAL The intellectual, religious, social, and material life of the period—the Puritanism of many of the colonists, the growing gentility of the 18th-century colonies, the colonists' diverse national origins, the materials and opportunities available to artists and craftsmen, the interactions of the Atlantic community, and republicanism—all conditioned painting and the design of everyday artifacts. Regarding Indians and Africans as heathens, slaves, or cultivators, the European-Americans absorbed nothing artistic from them.

The Puritans brought with them a profound distrust of religious images. Their Christianity, which focused on the Bible, the orthodoxy of the community, and the inner state of each individual, forbade any representation of God. In the words of Samuel Willard, "For any to entertain or fancy any other Image of God, but those reverend impressions of His glorious Perfections that are engraven upon his heart, is highly to dishonour Him." Craftsmen who probably practiced several crafts produced for the Puritans images that were not forbidden by the Second Commandment: gravestones and portraits. Portraits such as "Mrs. Elizabeth Freake and Baby Mary" (c. 1674) and "Anne Pollard" (1721) are simple, unadorned representations, far from the European baroque with its large scale, complex forms, and emotionalism.

In the 18th century a genteel colonial class commissioned portraits, and the European courtly style influenced colonial portraiture. A provincial tradition of stock poses and surroundings, more graceful and elaborate than in Puritan portraits, began with John Smibert and Robert Feke, and continued throughout the colonial period with Joseph Blackburn and John Singleton Copley. Beginning in the 1760s, Copley transcended such provincialism with his own style, the realistic representation of a figure posed informally and close to everyday objects. Yet in 1774, Copley, like Benjamin West before him, expatriated to England in search of sophistication in technique and elevation in subject.

Charles Wilson Peale found an indigenous elevated subject in the virtue and heroism of the revolutionaries and sought to make art, through his Revolution Era portraits, a didactic force in the new nation. Yet like Puritanism, republicanism harbored distrust of the arts, which were associated with European courts and the luxuries of the aristocracy. Influential patriots such as Thomas Jefferson, John Adams, and Timothy Dwight countenanced art only when it served the public good. John Durand acknowledged this attitude in a 1768 advertisement of "cheap rates" on "historical pantings": "Men who have distinguished themselves for the good of their country and mankind may be set before our eyes as examples."

Artifacts. The design of everyday artifacts evolved from the decoration of utilitarian objects in the 17th century to the masterly craftsmanship of the silversmiths and furniture-makers who served the 18th-century elite. Women such as Anne Bradstreet decorated home-produced textiles with needlework. Blacksmiths adorned utilitarian products such as hardware, housewares, and weathervanes. The German, Dutch, and Scandinavian settlers of the middle colonies continued a folk tradition in furniture-making that retained its popularity long after the Revolution. Bostonians Robert Sanderson, John Hull, Jeremiah Drummer, and John Coney initiated a tradition of silversmithing that absorbed European style (Baroque, rococo, and ultimately neoclassical) and became intimately linked with the lives of the colonial gentry. Legendary Bostonian Paul Revere was only one of the silversmiths serving the 18th-century elite. Similarly, furniture-making using European styles and indigenous woods became more elaborate as a genteel class provided craftsmen with a market. Centered in Philadelphia, furniture-making signified the wealth of its patrons as it drew successively on the William and Mary, Queen Anne, and Chippendale styles, becoming more embellished, more curvilinear, and more imposing.

See also Puritanism; Provincialism; Republicanism; and individual artists and craftsmen.

Bibliography: Brown, Milton W., *American Art to 1900: Painting, Sculpture, Architecture* (Abrams, 1977); McCoubrey, John W., ed., *American Art, 1700-1960: Sources and Documents* (Prentice-Hall, 1965); Wright, Louis B., et al, eds., *The Arts in America: The Colonial Period* (Scribner's, 1966).

John Saillant
Brown University

ARTICLES OF CONFEDERATION The Articles of Confederation, the first national constitution of the independent United States, were drawn up in 1776-77, adopted in 1781, and replaced by the present federal Constitution in 1789. Richard Henry Lee's motion for independence in the Second Continental Congress (June 7, 1776) also included a directive that a plan of confederation be prepared. A committee, of which John Dickinson was the leading member, submitted draft articles on July 12.

Congressional debate over the draft took place in 1776 and 1777. Key issues included representation and the manner of voting, the apportionment of expenses, and the disposition of western lands. The question of allocating power between the states and the national government was also controversial, given the widespread hostility toward central authority provoked by British policy during the previous decade. Fears that the national government would take all powers not enumerated led to the adoption of an amendment (advocated by Thomas Burke of North Carolina) that reserved those powers to the states. In mid-November 1777, Congress approved the revised articles and submitted them to the states for consideration.

Richard Henry Lee proposed a plan in June 1776 that resulted in the Articles of Confederation. *(Library of Congress)*

Main Provisions. The articles as submitted provided for a single-house Congress in which each state would have one vote; delegates would be appointed annually in the manner directed by the state legislatures. (These and other arrangements preserved the operating procedures of Congress.) Delegates could serve no more than three years out of six; a president, eligible for no more than one year out of three, would chair. Decisions were by simple majority except in enumerated major policy areas, where nine votes were required. The states kept their sovereignty, freedom, independence, and every power not "expressly delegated" to Congress. Expenses were apportioned among the states by the amount of surveyed land in each and were to be met by state taxes. Congress itself had no power to tax directly. However, it was given authority over foreign affairs and the power to declare war and peace. It was the last resort in boundary and jurisdictional disputes between states. It had authority to regulate coinage and establish weights and measures, to regulate Indian trade outside the states, to establish a post office, to raise loans and emit bills of credit, and to maintain and regulate military forces. The confederation established by the articles would be "inviolably observed by every state" and could be altered only if all 13 agreed.

The issue of western lands delayed final approval of the articles. Maryland spoke for the states with no land claims and called for the cession to the national government of such claims by other states. Following Virginia's cession in early 1781, Maryland became the final state to ratify; the articles took effect in early March.

Criticism of the Articles. Despite solid success in ending the war and concluding the peace, reorganizing national finances, and drawing up fundamental ordinances for the western lands, the Confederation Congress came under severe criticism during the 1780s. This criticism gave the articles a persisting reputation for structural weakness. Specifically, the critics charged that Congress's powers under the articles were inadequate to deal with foreign affairs and commerce, that the national government required the power of direct taxation, that Congress possessed few means to enforce its measures, and that the provision for unanimous consent made amendment impossible. Discontent coalesced in 1786-87, following the failure of several attempts to give Congress limited power to raise revenue and regulate commerce. The critics then abandoned the amendment process for a federal convention, which in 1787 drew up the new constitution that replaced the articles.

See also Constitution; Continental Congress; Dickinson, John.

Bibliography: Burnett, Edmund C., *The Continental Congress* (1941; reprint, Greenwood, 1976); Jensen, Merrill, *The Articles of Confederation: An Interpretation of the Social-Constitutional History of the American Revolution, 1774-1781* (Univ. of Wisconsin Press, 1940); Rakove, Jack N., *The Beginnings of National Politics: An Interpretive History of the Continental Congress* (Knopf, 1979).

Douglas M. Arnold
The Papers of Benjamin Franklin

ASBURY, FRANCIS (1745-1816) An American Methodist bishop, Asbury was born in Birmingham, England, and by the age of 21 was a member of the Wesleyan Conference, a Methodist society. He was appointed to the colonies as a missionary and, arriving in

1771, traveled by horseback around the colonies spreading his message. Although recalled to England by the society, he chose to stay in America and become a citizen of Delaware. In 1784 he was a leader in the formation of the Methodist Episcopal Church in America and became one of its superintendents. He named himself a bishop in the church but continued to travel on horseback and to preach.

ASHE, JOHN BAPTIST (1720-81) A member of the North Carolina colonial assembly, Ashe was speaker in 1765 when Parliament passed the Stamp Act. He organized an association opposing the Stamp Act and forced the stamp-master to resign. Although he assisted Governor William Tryon in putting down the Regulator movement in 1771, he later became a zealous Whig. He served as a member of the first Continental Congress for North Carolina. He raised his own regiment during the Revolutionary War and in 1776 was appointed brigadier general. In 1779, Ashe went to Briar Creek, Georgia, where he engaged British forces under General Provost. Ashe blundered so badly that some of his men believed he had betrayed them to the British. After the defeat, Ashe returned to Wilmington, North Carolina. The town was captured by the British, and he and his family were taken prisoner. He died in prison from smallpox in 1781.

ASIENTO Initiated by Charles V in 1518, the asiento was a permit issued by the Spanish government allowing the bearer to deal in slaves in the Spanish colonies. Portugal, Genoa, the Netherlands, and France held the asiento at times in the 17th century. So great were the profits deemed possible by combining illegal trade with asiento operations that at the Peace of Utrecht in 1713, the British demanded and received the asiento as a spoil of the War of the Spanish Succession. However, the expected profits proved to be illusory, and in 1750 the asiento lapsed and was not renewed.
See also Utrecht, Treaty of.

ATKIN, EDMUND (1707-1761) Charleston merchant and Indian trader, Atkin was appointed British Superintendent of Southern Indians in 1756 after submitting a report to the Board of Trade the previous year. In his report he had argued for the protection of the tribes from the encroachments of land speculators and settlers by the creation of such an office and the construction of a series of frontier forts. His tenure during the French and Indian War was marked by controversy over his tendency to put his own business affairs over those of Indian administration and by complaints that he was slow to fortify the southern frontier. Nevertheless, his report marked the first comprehensive plan for the management of Indian affairs, removing authority from the colonies and placing it in the hands of the imperial government, thus providing a model for the later Indian policy of the United States.

ATTUCKS, CRISPUS (?1723-70) A victim of the Boston Massacre, about whom contemporaries knew little, Attucks is believed to have been a runaway slave who became a sailor. He was a leader of the mob that confronted British troops on the night of May 5, 1770. When the British opened fire, Attucks was killed instantly and became a martyr to American independence.

AUDIENCIAS Spanish colonial administrative authority. As a law court, the audiencia considered both criminal and civil matters, including the protection of the Indians. In the power vacuum of the colonies the audiencia quickly took on legislative and executive powers as well and became the chief advisory board to the viceroys. The first audiencia was established in Santo Domingo in 1511 to serve as a court that would consider lawsuits normally taken to Spain. Each large urban center in the Spanish colonies eventually received an audiencia, beginning with Mexico City (1528), Panama (1538), Lima (1542), Guatemala (1548), and Bogota (1549). Later in the colonial period, the power of the audiencia declined with that of the viceroy as the Crown began to assert its control over local affairs.

AUGUSTA, CONGRESS OF (1763) Georgia Governor James Wright, Georgia Indian Superintendent John Stuart, and the governors of Virginia, North Carolina, and South Carolina met with representatives of the Southeastern Indian tribes at Augusta in 1763. The Indians were informed that the French and Spanish had been forced to give up their lands east of the Mississippi, and were asked to sign a treaty ceding territory between the Savannah and Ogeechee rivers from Ebenezer to Little River and an area about 30 miles deep along the coast from the Altamaha to the St. Marys. An influx of settlers into the area around Augusta followed during the next decade.

AUGUSTA, FORT Fort Augusta was constructed at the head of navigation of the Savannah River by the order of James Edward Oglethorpe issued on June 14, 1736. Work was begun in 1737 and finished in 1738. Oglethorpe was convinced that his garrison there helped to eliminate abuses in the Indian trade and to preserve the friendship of the Creek nation. The fort was rebuilt in 1759 and used by refugees fleeing from the Cherokee War in 1760. About 800 Indians met with 4 colonial governors under the guns of Fort Augusta to sign a peace treaty in 1763. The garrison was removed to Boston in 1768, and the fort was abandoned.
See also Augusta, Congress of.

AUGUSTA, TREATY OF (1773)   In this treaty signed in Augusta, Georgia ceded huge tracts of land to the colony Georgia. Most of the approximately 2,000,000 acres was north of the Little River, the boundary set by the 1763 Congress of Augusta. The western limit remained at the Ogeechee River. In exchange for the cession, debts that the Indians owed to traders were canceled; the traders were to be paid out of the proceeds from the sale of the ceded lands. The Creeks bitterly resented the Treaty of 1773 and went on the warpath, preventing the occupation of the new purchase. After Georgia declared independence, the ceded lands were organized as Wilkes County.

See also Augusta, Congress of.

AYLLÓN, LUCAS VÁSQUEZ DE (c.1475-1526)   Ayllón, who had arrived on Hispaniola in 1502 and had become a justice of the supreme court, sponsored and financed two small exploring expeditions north along the Atlantic coast of North America, searching for a suitable place to colonize. In 1525, 5 ships with 500 colonists led by Ayllón set sail for the Carolina coast. Settling on the Cape Fear River in modern North Carolina, the colony was a disaster from the beginning. Malaria, problems with the Indians, and a lack of discipline all contributed to Ayllón's death on October 18, 1526. The remaining settlers sailed back to Hispaniola, with only 150 arriving safely.

B

BACKUS, ISAAC (1724-1806)   A leading writer and exponent of religious liberty, Isaac Backus was educated only in the local common school in his native Norwich, Connecticut.   Awakened by the Revivalist preacher James Davenport, Backus experienced saving grace and joined the Norwich Congregational Church in 1742.   Unable to force changes in church practices, he joined a Norwich "Separate" church in 1746.   That year he received an inner call to preach and embarked upon a number of preaching tours in Massachusetts, Rhode Island, and Connecticut.   In 1748 he was ordained pastor of the church in Titicut, Massachusetts; three years later he accepted the Baptist views of a minority of his congregation and was immersed. After several years of controversy, Backus organized a Baptist church in Middleboro, Massachusetts, where he served as pastor for the rest of his life.

Throughout his career, Backus insisted upon freedom of the church from civil control; by 1772 he was the Massachusetts Baptists' leading spokesman in matters concerning the relationship of church and state.   In his *Appeal to the Public* (1773), he denied the state's right to support churches through taxation and instead supported Baptist demands for the separation of church and state.   Backus argued similar principles in the debates over the Massachusetts constitution in 1780 and the federal Constitution in 1788.   A voluminous writer, his most notable work was *A History of New England, with Particular Reference to the Denomination of Christians Called Baptists* (3 vols., completed 1796).

Bibliography: McLoughlin, William G., *Isaac Backus and the American Pietistic Tradition* (Little, Brown, 1967).

James F. Cooper, Jr.
University of Connecticut

BACON'S REBELLION   The migration of the Susquehannah from Pennsylvania to the Virginia backcountry in the 1660s stiffened the resistance of Virginia's Indians to the further expansion of European agriculture.   Western settlers demanded a policy of armed expansion, but coastal planters advised restraint.   Led by the wealthy western planter Nathaniel Bacon, and in defiance of orders from Virginia's Governor William Berkeley, westerners marched up the Potomac into Maryland in 1675, indiscriminately murdering Indians and precipitating a frontier war.   With Bacon as leader, the westerners pushed a set of political reforms through the House of Burgesses, but impatient with the pace of change, Bacon and his followers seized control of the colony, declaring the leader "General of Virginia" and, in a "Manifesto and Declaration of the People," demanding the death or removal of all Indians and an end to the rule of wealthy "parasites."   Berkeley fled to the eastern shore of the Chesapeake.   The civil war that followed shifted in Berkeley's favor only after Bacon's sudden death from dysentery.   In the aftermath there were no drastic changes in Virginia politics or society, but the

Balboa's fame as discoverer of the Pacific led to jealousy among other Spanish colonists and his execution. (*Library of Congress*)

elite shifted to a policy of armed expansion to gain the support of western planters.

Bibliography: Washburn, Wilcomb E., *The Governor and the Rebel* (1958; reprint Norton, 1972).

BAFFIN, WILLIAM (?1584-1622)   British Arctic explorer, Baffin first served as the pilot on a 1612 expedition charting the west coast of Greenland, then as chief pilot in the service of the Muscovy Company. In 1615 and 1616 he piloted two voyages in search of a Northwest Passage, the second of which explored and named Baffin Bay. Lack of confirmation of the discovery by later explorers led to the elimination of the bay from maps, and it was not finally confirmed until 1818. His last years were spent in the service of the East India Company, and he died during a battle with the Portuguese in the Persian Gulf.

See also Northwest Passage.

BALBOA, VASCO NÚÑEZ DE (1475-1519)   A poor young adventurer, Balboa joined a pearl-hunting expedition to the Spanish Main in 1500 and settled down as a planter in Santo Domingo. Unsuccessful in his business ventures and saddled with debts, he fled to Panama, where the colony was in dire straits. Balboa usurped command and presided over the establishment of the new settlement of Darien. In 1513, hearing rumors of a rich land and an ocean over the mountains, Balboa mounted a large expedition and set out to cross the Isthmus. Struggling through swamps and fighting Indian resistance, Balboa took possession of the Southern Sea and the lands surrounding it for the Spanish Crown.

Soon afterward, the man Balboa had deposed, Martín Fernández de Enciso, succeeded in having a new governor, Pedrarias Dávila, replace Balboa in Darien. Balboa, planning to explore the Southern Sea, devoted his time to building ships on the south side of the Isthmus. In 1519, jealous of Balboa's fame and popularity, Dávila had Balboa arrested, brought back to Darien, and beheaded in the public square with four of his companions.

Thomas C. Thompson
University of California, Riverside

BALTIMORE   Port on the Patapsco River in the upper Chesapeake Bay, it was founded on August 8, 1729, and named for the second proprietor of the colony, Cecilius Calvert, Lord Baltimore. Economics played a central role in Baltimore's establishment; it was designed to serve as a convenient harbor for the export of tobacco, Maryland's most important agricultural commodity. Although the tobacco trade was eventually eclipsed by the export of

wheat to Scotland and Ireland, Baltimore's maritime traffic and the scale of its shipbuilding industry steadily increased.

The town also became well known for its openness to immigrants and religious minorities. As one of the most important centers of Roman Catholic settlement along the Eastern seaboard, Baltimore became the first Catholic archdiocese in America. In 1768 it was named the seat of Baltimore county, and in 1773 was connected by carriage road to Philadelphia. By the outbreak of the Revolution it was the third largest city in North America, with a population of approximately 6,000. Its subsequent growth was even more impressive. At the time of its incorporation as a city in 1796, its inhabitants numbered 20,000. Baltimore also briefly served as the site of the Continental Congress (December 1776-January 1777).

See also Calvert, Cecilius.

BALTIMORE, LORDS OF. *See* **Calvert.**

BANCROFT, EDWARD (1744-1821)   Later known as an American spy for the British, "Doctor" Bancroft was a native of Westfield, Massachusetts, and the author of a natural history of Guiana. A resident in England, his interests brought him into contact with Benjamin Franklin. Bancroft became an advocate for the American cause, accompanied Franklin to France, and passed information about the British to American agents. In 1776 he was approached by an American Loyalist, Paul Wentworth, and agreed to provide information about American actions to the British. From 1777 to 1783, Bancroft received a salary from the British government. He supplied information on Franklin's movements and the positions of troops and ships. The British once pretended to arrest him to protect his cover. After the Revolutionary War he lived in England, continuing to correspond with Franklin, who never suspected him. Bancroft's role as a spy was not made public until 70 years after his death.

BANISTER, JOHN (1734-88)   The grandson of a renowned botanist and naturalist of Virginia, Banister studied law at the Middle Temple in England in 1753. He returned to Virginia and was elected a delegate to the Virginia Convention in 1776. In 1777 he served in the House of Burgesses, and in 1778-79 in the Continental Congress. He signed the Articles of Confederation, which he helped write. During the war his home was occupied by British troops, and from 1778-81 he fought as a Virginia cavalryman. Banister assisted in the final expulsion of the British from Virginia. He was highly regarded by George Washington, with whom he corresponded.

BANKING AND CREDIT   The capital necessary to build colonial industry and commerce came from Great Britain.

English merchants financed colonial shipping, from 1670 to 1730 receiving a net return of from 5 to 10 percent on their investment, as well as from the fishery, shipbuilding, and iron industries. By 1700, however, in both the North and South, local merchants or planters had acquired sufficient capital to participate in local capital markets; indeed the Boston merchant class had acquired nearly half of the carrying capacity of all colonial-owned shipping. Most colonists with capital, however, rejected shipping for investments in real estate or British securities, and very few ventured into riskier industrial finance.

18th Century Expansion. The expansion of the economy in the 18th century was also financed by Great Britain. After 1740, Scottish merchant houses provided most of the funding for the expansion of tobacco production in the South; by the 1770s Glasgow merchants had established more than 100 outlets in Virginia alone, and wealthy and poor planters alike had come to rely on the availability of Scottish credit. Moreover, in the aftermath of the French and Indian War, when radical declines in British expenditure brought about a crisis in the colonial balance of payments, British merchants eagerly extended credit to importers. By the 1770s the colonial economy was deeply indebted to British capital, an important contributing factor to the coming Revolution.

After the Revolution, British merchants demanded specie in payment for the commodities and services upon which the states continued to depend, renewing a financial crisis that was deepest in New England but affected all the states. Led by Robert Morris, the first superintendent of finance under the Articles of Confederation, Congress in 1781 chartered the Bank of North America in an attempt to bring the fiscal system under American control. Other commercial corporations with lending capacity (such as the Connecticut Trading Corporation of 1723 or the Massachusetts Land Bank of 1740) had previously existed on a local basis, but this was the first private commercial bank in North America. It was followed by the chartering of the Bank of New York and the Bank of Massachusetts (both 1784), whose customers were mainly merchants and stock subscribers.

Bibliography: Bailyn, Bernard, *The New England Merchants in the Seventeenth Century* (1955; reprint Harvard Univ. Press, 1979); Davis, Andrew M., *Currency and Banking in the Province of Massachusetts Bay*, 2 vols. (1900; reprint Kelley); Redlich, Fritz, *Molding of American Banking*, 2 vols. (1947-51; reprint Johnson, 1968); Ver Steeg, Clarence L., *Robert Morris, Revolutionary Financier* (1954; reprint Hippocrene, 1970).

John Mack Faragher
Mount Holyoke College

BANK OF NORTH AMERICA The first government-sanctioned and incorporated bank in the United States, established by an act of the Continental Congress on December 31, 1781, the Bank of North America began operations in Philadelphia on January 7, 1782. The financial difficulties of the newly-established U.S. government had prompted the Continental Congress to establish a Department of Finance with Robert Morris serving as superintendent. Morris proposed the establishment of the Bank of North America as a means by which the government could maintain a stable national currency and facilitate the issuance of bonds and government loans to aid in the national war effort.

See also Morris, Robert.

BANNEKER, BENJAMIN (1731-1806) A noted astronomer and mathematician, Banneker was born in Maryland, the son of free black farmers. His grandmother's desire to hear the Bible read to her led to his attending a local school, where he first displayed an aptitude for mathematics. After the death of his father in 1759, Banneker worked the family farm but found time to dabble in mechanical endeavors. The erection of Ellicott's Mills in the vicinity stimulated further efforts on his behalf, encouraged by George Ellicott, who loaned to Banneker instruments and books.

Ellicott urged Banneker to delve into astronomy and publish an almanac, which he did from 1792 to 1806. To gain the necessary leisure time to pursue his studies Banneker gave his farm over to Ellicott in return for an annuity. Ellicott then introduced him to Pierre L'Enfant, the architect of Washington, D.C. L'Enfant so esteemed Banneker's abilities that he hired him to help survey the boundaries of the District of Columbia. Banneker died in 1806, praised for his accomplishments by Jefferson and Washington, and recognized as an equal by L'Enfant and other European scientists.

BAPTISTS Emerging from the context of English Puritanism, Baptists distinguished themselves from the latter by their opposition to infant baptism and to civil government having any authority over religious conscience. Roger Williams, exiled from Massachusetts in 1635, founded the colony of Rhode Island and Providence Plantations the very next year. Briefly a Baptist, he assisted in the organization of the country's first Baptist church in Providence in 1638. Because his colony declared itself for a "full liberty in religious concernments" (Charter of 1663), Rhode Island became a haven for all the despised and persecuted, especially Baptists and Quakers in the 17th century.

Both Newport and Providence therefore became important early centers of Baptist growth, these later to be supplemented by major settlements in Philadelphia, where Baptists gathered from Wales and elsewhere to form the first formal Association in 1707. Prior to the middle of the 18th century, however, the Baptist presence in America was limited and divided between Arminians and Calvinists, between Sunday observers and Seventh-Day observers. Following the Great Awakening, however, Baptist growth spurted sharply forward, not only in New England and the Middle Colonies but throughout the South as well. Riding the tide of Calvinist theology and of an evangelical piety, Baptists increased from fewer than 100 churches in 1740 to around 500 churches a half century later. Blacks turned to this denomination in greater numbers than to another, in the 18th century and later as well.

The activities of such clergymen as Isaac Backus in New England and John Leland in Virginia helped identify Baptists with the struggle for a full and complete religious liberty in colony after colony. Enjoying or accepting no government favor for themselves, they resisted it for all others, believing (as Roger Williams had affirmed in 1644) that no principle had done more harm to the state, the church, and all humankind than "the bloudy tenant of persecution for cause of conscience."

See also Backus, Isaac; Great Awakening.

Bibliography: McLoughlin, William G., *New England Dissent, 1630-1833: The Baptists and the Separation of Church and State*, 2 vols. (Harvard Univ. Press, 1971).

Edwin S. Gaustad
University of California, Riverside

BARD, JOHN (1716-99) One of the most outstanding physicians of early America, John Bard was born in Burlington, New Jersey, the son of a Huguenot émigré, Peter Bard, who had risen to be the judge of the state supreme court. John pioneered in the systematic dissection of human corpses for medical instruction; the development of public health measures for New York City, including the purchase of Bedloe's Island for quarantining purposes; and the careful clinical reporting of an extrauterine pregnancy in which both baby and mother survived as a result of Bard's surgical skill. In addition, he was a friend and correspondent of Benjamin Franklin.

BARRE, ISAAC (1726-1802) Born in Dublin, Ireland, Barre became one of the most eloquent spokesmen in Parliament for the American cause during the 1760s and 1770s. He had been to America during the French and Indian War, serving as a lieutenant colonel under General James Wolfe, and had fought at the siege of Quebec. In 1761 he was elected to Parliament. Barre favored Prime Minister William Pitt's efforts to prevent taxation of the American colonies, especially the Stamp Act of 1765. In a speech before Parliament, Barre called the Americans "Sons of Liberty." After the Boston Tea Party of 1773, however, Barre approved of the Boston Port Bill, the first of the five Intolerable Acts. He retired from Parliament in 1790. Several American cities were named after him, including Barre, Vermont, and Wilkes-Barre, Pennsylvania.

BARRY, JOHN (1745-1803) Born in Ireland, Barry emigrated to Philadelphia about 1760. A wealthy master of a merchant vessel, he outfitted the first Continental fleet when the Revolution broke out. In 1776 he was commissioned captain of the *Lexington*. He fought at Trenton, raided British ships in the Delaware River, and captured the first ship ever taken by an American naval officer. In 1780 he took Colonel John Laurens to France on the *Alliance*, and on the return trip he captured two British vessels. His last battle was fought in the Straits of Florida in 1783. When the navy was reorganized in 1794, he was first senior officer. Commodore Barry became known as the "Father of the Navy."

BARTLETT, JOSIAH (1729-95) Beginning the study of medicine at the age of 16, Bartlett opened his practice in Kingston, New Hampshire, in 1750. He entered politics in 1765 as a delegate to the legislature. Governor Wentworth appointed him a magistrate and, in 1770, commander of a militia regiment. Bartlett lost those offices in 1775 as a result of his opposition to royal policy. In August 1775 he was chosen to be a member of the Continental Congress. He was the first to vote for the Declaration of Independence and the second to sign it. He resigned from the Congress to provide medical help to New Hampshire regiments. In 1779 he retired to state politics, and from 1793 to 1794 served as the first governor of the state of New Hampshire.

BARTRAM, JOHN (1699-1777) Known as the father of American botany, he was born in Marple, Massachusetts. He conducted hybrid experiments in a botanical garden—the first in America—that he started at Kingsessing, Pennsylvania, in 1728. In 1765 King George III appointed him official botanist of the colonies. His *Observations* (1751), about the area around Lake Ontario, was one of many published works describing plant life in the colonies. His son William (1739-1823) followed in his footsteps and continued to care for and conduct experiments in the Kingsessing garden after the death of his father.

BASHMAKOV, PYOTR (flourished 1750s) A Russian explorer of the Aleutian Islands, Bashmakov, on a fur-hunting expedition in the Bering Sea in 1753, first sighted islands to the east; and there his vessel was wrecked. He and his men built a ship from the wreckage, returning on this ship in 1756. The next year he explored the islands further, reaching Tanaga Island, about midway in the chain, before turning back.

BATTS, THOMAS (flourished 1671) The explorer Batts was one of the first Englishmen of record to cross the Appalachian Mountains. Batts and Robert Fallam, who kept the journal of the expedition, were commissioned by Abraham Wood to cross the mountains and "make the discovery of the South Sea" in 1671. They set out from Fort Henry and with the aid of Perecute, an Indian guide, followed the Staunton (Roanoke) River through the Blue Ridge to the westward flowing New River and followed it to the falls near the present boundary between Virginia and West Virginia. Clearly they were not the first Europeans, for after crossing the divide Fallam recorded their find of initials of earlier explorers carved in trees. On their return, at the summit of the mountains, they looked back to see a "glimmering light as from water," which they supposed to be a "great bay" of the South Sea. Batts and Fallam established the English claim to the Ohio country.

See also Wood, Abraham.

BAYARD, JOHN BUBENHEIM (1738-1807) Born to a wealthy Maryland family, Bayard moved to Philadelphia in 1756 to begin his career as a merchant. By the end of the French and Indian War (1763) he had built a substantial fortune. Active in revolutionary politics, Bayard signed the Non-Importation Agreements, joined the Sons of Liberty, and served as a delegate to the Provincial Convention in 1774. He supported the choice of George Washington as commander in chief of the Continental Army and volunteered for army duty. From 1777 to 1778 he was speaker of the Pennsylvania assembly and in 1785 was elected to the Continental Congress. He moved to New Jersey in 1788, continuing to hold office there.

BAY PSALM BOOK (1640) This translation of David's psalms, properly titled *The Whole Booke of Psalms Faithfully Translated into English Metre*, was the first book printed in English in the North American colonies. The first edition of 1,700 copies was printed in Cambridge in the Massachusetts Bay Colony in 1640.

The *Bay Psalm Book* rendered the Hebrew psalms into English meter and verse so they could be sung to English tunes. One innovation brought by the Protestant Reformation was the singing of psalms by the entire congregation instead of by the choir alone. It was thought that metrical translations were better adapted to group singing. Three leading Puritan scholars of Hebrew and Greek—Richard Mather of Dorchester, and Thomas Welde and John Eliot of Roxbury—were in charge of the translation. They insisted on a threefold standard: an accurate rendering of the original Hebrew meaning, suitability for congregational singing, and a simple, comprehensible style. Some controversy ensued over the poetic merit of the translation, but despite the dispute the *Bay Psalm Book* was reprinted many times and remained in use in New England churches for more than a century and a half.

Bibliography: Miller, Perry, *The American Puritans* (Doubleday, 1956); Nye, Russel B., and Grabo, Norman S., *American Thought and Writing*, vol. I: *The Colonial Period* (Houghton Mifflin, 1965).

Suzanne Greene Chapelle
Morgan State University

BEAUFORT Agricultural settlement and town on Port Royal Island, off the coast of South Carolina, it was first visited in 1521 by Spanish explorers who gave it the name "Punta de Santa Elena." The Spanish made no attempt to establish a settlement there, but repeated attempts at colonization by the French in 1562, the English in 1670, and the Scots in 1684 proved unsuccessful. It was only in 1711, with the official establishment of a town under the jurisdiction of the colony of South Carolina, that Beaufort was finally occupied permanently. During the Revolution it served as a British garrison and observation point for the surveillance of naval traffic in the area.

BEAUMARCHAIS, PIERRE AUGUSTINE CARON DE (1732-99) Beaumarchais, a financier and writer, was born in Paris and became noted for his daring satires of royal authority in *Le Barbier de Seville* in 1775 and *Le Mariage de Figaro* in 1784. His role in helping the financially hard-pressed American colonies during the American Revolution was equally daring. Working with Arthur Lee, the colonies' agent, he engineered a French loan of 1,000,000 livres and convinced Spain to match it. His company shipped 200 guns, 25,000 muskets, and 200,000 pounds of gunpowder to the colonial forces in 1777 and sent 50 European officers, including Casimir Pulaski and Barton Steuben. Unfortunately, the Continental Congress thought the shipments were a gift, and Beaumarchais had to seek a loan of 1,000,000 francs from the French government to meet the cost. When he stopped the shipments of 1779, the Americans owed him 4,000,000 francs. His heirs finally obtained 800,000 francs in 1835.

BEAVER WARS These clashes between various Indian alliances during the 17th century grew out of the hotly contested struggle for the fur resources of the Great Lakes. As such, these conflicts reflected the new motives of expansion and acquisition in Indian warfare that came in the wake of European colonialism.

By the 1620s the Iroquois of New York had exhausted their supply of beaver in their homeland. In a series of wars between 1630 and 1697, the Iroquois aggressively wrested control of the Great Lakes region from those Indians allied to the French trading system. The Iroquois were supplied with firearms by the Dutch, and later the English, of New York. The first series of engagements, in which the Iroquois Confederacy devastated much of Canada, culminated in the dispersal of the Huron from Sault Ste. Marie in 1649. In the second series of wars, between 1650 and 1675, the Iroquois expanded into the northern Ohio region as far west as Illinois. Beginning in the 1670s, the French and their Indian allies countered the earlier Iroquois thrust. By 1697 the Iroquois had suffered such serious setbacks that they negotiated for peace, which was formally concluded in 1701.

See also Fur Trade; Iroquois Confederacy.

Bibliography: Hunt, George T., *The Wars of the Iroquois: A Study in Intertribal Trade Relations* (Univ. of Wisconsin, 1940); Jennings, Francis, *The Ambiguous Iroquois Empire* (Norton, 1984).

Richard L. Haan
Hartwick College

BEDFORD, FORT A fortified garrison designed to protect the western boundary of Pennsylvania, it was built in 1750 under the supervision of Colonel John Armstrong and initially named Fort Raystown. In 1757, soon after the outbreak of the French and Indian War, it was expanded and strengthened by Colonel Henry Bouquet. There, troops of the Virginia militia under George Washington joined the forces of General John Forbes for the campaign along "Forbes Road." The fort's name was officially changed to Fort Bedford in 1759, and its garrison withstood a siege during Pontiac's 1769 uprising. It had been abandoned, however, by the time of the American Revolution.

BELL, ROBERT (c.1732-84) A native of Glasgow, Scotland, Bell made his mark in an unusually colorful fashion—as a book auctioneer, bookseller, and, for a time, publisher. When his initial efforts in the book trade in Berwick-upon-Tweed and Dublin failed, Bell emigrated to Philadelphia. At auctions he so entertained his audiences with droll literary tales and funny and satirical comments about each author that his auctions were always crowded.

In 1776, Bell brought out the first edition of Thomas Paine's *Common Sense*. After the Revolutionary War, he fought vigorously for freedom of speech and freedom of the press by reprinting pamphlets such as John Dickinson's *Sentiments on What Is Freedom* and *What Is Slavery*.

BENAVIDES, ALONSO (died 1664) Having come to Mexico in 1598, the Catholic priest Benavides arrived in New Mexico in 1622 and spent the next few years establishing missions among the Pima and Apache. The Franciscan wrote a "Memorial" in 1630 (revised 1634) that mentioned the two kingdoms of Quivira and Aixaos to the northeast and recommended their conquest to forestall English and French expansionism. He also called for greater support for the missions. Benavides delivered his plea to Philip IV in person in 1630 and then to Pope Urban VIII before returning to New Mexico. He was then appointed assistant to the Archbishop of Goa in Portuguese India, whom he succeeded, dying in office in 1664.

BENEZET, ANTHONY (1713-84) The Quaker son of a French Huguenot immigrant, Benezet, a Philadelphia schoolteacher, worked tirelessly in the mid-18th century for social justice. Benezet believed that each man had a personal obligation to aid suffering humanity, and this belief led him to active charity work. His chief concern was that fellow Quakers would continue to recognize their duty to take care of others in society, and to this end he preached against the Quaker merchants' dangerous tendency toward acquisitiveness, believing that too much success made men callous to charity.

Benezet is best known as one of the leaders of the successful attempt to outlaw slaveholding by Quakers. With John Woolman, Benezet followed in the footsteps of other Quakers beginning in the 1690s who insisted that slaveholding was a sin. Benezet tied the practice to his condemnation of luxury, echoing non-Quakers who feared that slaveholding degraded master as well as slave. Finally, in 1776, Woolman and Benezet led the Yearly Meeting to order local meetings to disown all Quakers who owned slaves. Wealthy Quakers continued to defect to other sects during this period, however, despite Benezet's efforts.

BERING, VITUS JONASSEN (1681-1741) Danish-born pioneer Arctic explorer for Russia, Bering entered Russian service in 1703 and in 1724, by then a captain of the first rank, he led the first expedition to Kamchatka. In 1728 he sailed north in order to determine whether Asia and North America were connected but failed to answer the question conclusively. In 1733, as commander of the

Great Northern Expedition, he led some 600 men on a several-year exploration of the Siberian coast, but the search for the land bridge to America did not begin until seven years later. Bering sighted the Alaskan coast in 1741 but on his return voyage was shipwrecked on the island in the strait that later carried his name. He died there of scurvy.

BERING STRAITS HYPOTHESIS   As early as the mid-16th century, 200 years before the discoveries of Vitus Bering, Spanish chroniclers anticipated discovering a land bridge connecting northwestern America with northeastern Asia. Indeed, after Columbus's faulty notion that America was Asia had been finally disproved, Europeans persisted in assuming that the Indians were descendants of one or another wandering tribe of Eurasians—Carthaginians, Scandinavians, Moors, Welsh, or Jews. Today the conventional wisdom is that the New World was settled by Old World peoples who crossed the Bering Straits during periods when the sea level was so low that the channel served as a bridge between the continents; alternate theories of migration across the Pacific or Atlantic oceans have been largely discarded.

However reasonable, the probability of Bering Straits migration remains a hypothesis, and considerable debate continues over its parameters. Based on the archaeological evidence of various North and South American sites, scientists have proposed migrations beginning as early as

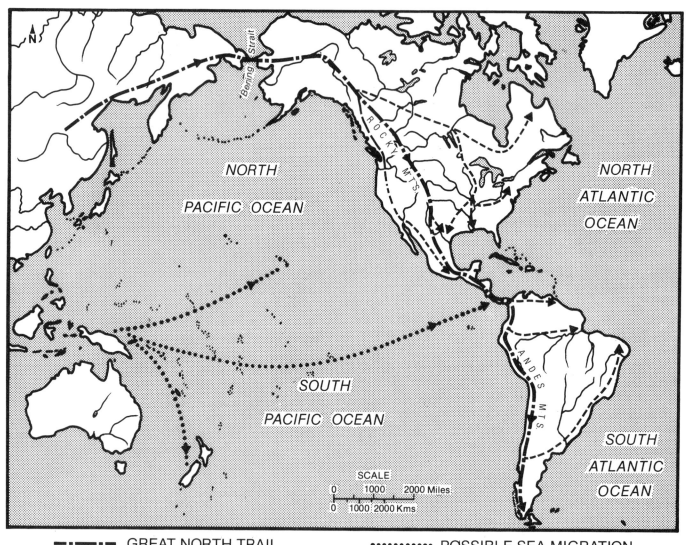

—·—·—·— GREAT NORTH TRAIL

--------- OTHER MAIN MIGRATION
ROUTES IN THE AMERICAS

············ POSSIBLE SEA MIGRATION
ROUTES

Bering Straits Hypothesis. *(Martin Greenwald Associates, Inc.)*

100,000 or as late as 12,000 years ago. Many American Indians reject the hypothesis altogether, maintaining that their ancestors evolved in the Western Hemisphere, and of late, this position has found some support among certain scientists. Recently proposed theories include the possibility that after an initial early migration, cultures that developed in the Americas may have been re- exported, via reverse migration, to Eurasia, where they may have stimulated the cultural transformations of the Upper Paleolithic or Neolithic epochs. In the absence of conclusive evidence, it is important to keep an open mind about the possibilities, distinguishing between fact and hypothesis.

Bibliography: Goodman, Jeffrey, *American Genesis* (Summit, 1981); MacNeish, Richard S., ed., *Early Man in America* (W. H. Freeman, 1973).

BERKELEY, SIR WILLIAM (1606-77) A colonial governor, he was born and educated in England and by 1639 had been knighted by King Charles I. Named royal governor of Virginia in 1642, he served until 1677 with the exception of the eight years (1652-60) of civil war in England. He was most noted for the insurrection against his administration, Bacon's Rebellion, in 1676, when Nathaniel Bacon took over the government in protest of Berkeley's Indian and expansion policies. Berkeley fled the colony and returned only upon Bacon's death from swamp fever the same year. However, because of Berkeley's harsh retaliation programs, he lost the governorship and returned to England, where he died shortly after.

See also Bacon's Rebellion.

BERKELEY, GEORGE (1685-1753) Born in Kilkenney, Ireland, of English ancestry, Berkeley was a philosopher whose theory of immaterialism was influential in colonial America. Berkeley was educated at Trinity College, Dublin, and in 1709 he published his first major work, *An Essay Towards a New Theory of Vision*. The following year he put forth his immaterialist philosophy in *A Treatise Concerning the Principles of Human Knowledge*. (In immaterialism, the world is made up of sensible, perceivable things that are essentially passive and active spirits that perceive them.)

Berkeley made plans to start a college in Bermuda to train people for the ministry and received a promise of funding from Parliament. He went to Rhode Island in 1728 to begin arrangements, and once there met and corresponded with American philosopher Samuel Johnson (who would become the first president of King's College, now Columbia University). Johnson was the first to recognize the importance of immaterialism. When the plan for the college in Bermuda fell through, Berkeley returned to England.

BERKELEY, LADY FRANCES (1634-1695?) Wife of three colonial governors, including Sir William Berkeley of Virginia, and central figure in the "Green Spring faction" of Virginia politics, she came to America in 1667 as wife of Samuel Stephens, recently named governor of the Albemarle settlements and Roanoke Island of North Carolina. Her husband died two years later, and shortly thereafter she married Sir William Berkeley and moved to the governor's residence at Green Spring. Lady Frances's hospitality was legendary and was enjoyed by, among others, her cousin Nathaniel Bacon, leader of Bacon's Rebellion. After the rebellion collapsed, Governor Berkeley was summoned to England, where he died. His wife carried on his political influence by becoming the center, at Green Spring, of opposition to the newly appointed governor, Herbert Jefferys. Her home remained a political center even after she married Philip Ludwell, who would become governor of the Carolinas.

See also Bacon's Rebellion.

BERMUDA A group of islands in the mid-Atlantic approximately 600 miles east of Cape Hatteras, North Carolina, Bermuda was settled in 1609 by English colonists bound for Virginia. The connection between Bermuda and Virginia was initially incorporated into law; from 1612 to 1615, Bermuda was included in the Virginia Company charter. With the establishment of the Bermuda Company in 1615, however, the islands were autonomously administered and were declared a crown colony in 1684. Although Bermuda's inhabitants were sympathetic to the cause of American independence, the islands were occupied by British troops in 1778 and remained under direct royal rule.

BEVERLEY, ROBERT (c.1673-1722) Born to wealth and social position, Beverley was educated both in his native Virginia and in England. He began his career as an assistant secretary, but his knowledge of law and politics caused him to rise to clerk of the General Court, clerk of the council, and clerk of the General Assembly. In the assemblies of 1699, 1700-02, and 1705-06 he sat as a burgess at the capital. On a trip to England he was asked to review a book on the British Empire in America. He found the book so inadequate that he wrote his own *History and Present State of Virginia* (1705). Written with a wry sense of humor, the history is noted for its shrewd observations and humorous sketches of Southern planters. Beverley later retired to his estate, Beverley Park, where he wrote *The Abridgement of the Public Laws of Virginia* (1722).

BEVERWYCK   The village of Beverwyck was established in New Netherland by Director General Peter Stuyvesant on April 10, 1652, when he issued a proclamation separating the main settlement of the colony of Rensselaerswyck from the jurisdiction of Fort Orange. By creating the independent village of Beverwyck, which afterward became the city of Albany, the director general denied the patroon's claim to the land that comprised the site of the West India Company's garrison at Fort Orange (erected 1624).   The proclamation established the jurisdiction of Fort Orange, a 3,000 foot arc around the fort. The Rensselaerswyck community north of the fort called The Fuyck fell within these bounds and was renamed Beverwyck with a court separate from the patroon's court of Rensselaerswyck.   The village was renamed Albany in honor of James, Duke of York and Albany, in 1664.

BIENVILLE, JEAN-BAPTISTE LE MOYNE, SIEUR DE (1680-1767)   Born in Montreal to a large and illustrious family, Jean-Baptiste Le Moyne had opportunities to distinguish himself from an early age. In 1698 he joined the expedition of his brother, the Sieur d'Iberville that founded the colony of Louisiana. In 1701, Bienville became the acting commandant of the colony, continuing in this role until 1712.

In 1717 control of Louisiana was transferred to the Compagnie d'Occident, and Bienville was appointed to the newly created position of commandant general. The following year Bienville established a company post and town at New Orleans, which shortly thereafter became the colony's capital. Bienville was removed from office by the company in 1725. In 1733 he returned to Louisiana, now a royal colony, as governor. In 1736 he led a Choctaw-French force into battle against the Chickasaw and suffered a defeat at the village of Ackia. A campaign in 1739-40 was more successful but inconclusive. These setbacks notwithstanding, Bienville was a master of Indian diplomacy. His knowledge of Indian languages and social conventions allowed him to build bridges betweeen Indian and European cultures that secured the survival of the infant colony. He retired to Paris in 1743.

BILLINGS, WILLIAM (1746-1800)   An American composer, he was born in Boston and, for the most part, was self-educated. He worked as a tanner before devoting all of his time to music, usually as a choir director and voice teacher. His works, *The New England Psalm-Singer* was published in 1770, followed by *The Singing Master's Assistant* in 1778. In 1774 he established a school of singing in Stoughton, Massachusetts. During the Revolution he wrote patriotic songs, such as "Chester." Other publications included *Music in Miniature* (1779), *The Psalm Singer's Amusement* (1781), *The Suffolk Harmony* (1786), and *The Continental Harmony* (1794).

BILOXI, FORT   A settlement in southeast Louisiana on the shore of the Gulf of Mexico, originally named Fort Maurepas, it was established in 1699 by the Sieur d'Iberville, as a part of an ambitious program of fort construction and colonization intended to secure the French possessions in the Mississippi Valley from encroachment by the British and Spanish. Initially inhabited by a core of 200 French colonists, the settlement was moved across the Mississippi to the site of the present city of Biloxi in 1719. Its name was also changed to that of the Indian nation that lived in the vicinity. Biloxi was the capital of the province of Louisiana until 1722.

BLACK LEGEND   In the mid-16th century, after the violent Spanish conquest of the Caribbean, Mexico, Central America, and Peru, a controversy erupted within Spain over the justice and morality of what had taken place. Spilling over into Europe during the decades when England, France, and other powers were considering colonizing ventures of their own, the criticism of the Spanish became part of the so-called Black Legend of Spanish cruelty to the Indians, which in turn became a prime ideological justification for competing colonial enterprises.

The single most important figure in this development was Bartolomé de Las Casas, a Dominican witness to the horrors of the conquest in the Caribbean, whose infamous 1542 text, which came to be known as *The Destruction of the Indies,* provided a detailed account of Spanish atrocities and claimed that the conquest had cost the lives of millions of Indians. Widely reissued throughout Europe, and translated into English in 1583, the Las Casas treatise (along with other histories of the conquest) added considerable fuel to the anti-Catholic and anti-Spanish passions of English nationalists and Protestants.

Although his work has been the subject of criticism for centuries, Las Casas's claims have been largely substantiated; the indigenous 8,000,000 inhabitants of Hispaniola, for example, were exterminated by 1550, perhaps the first recorded instance of genocide. But what was left out of the Black Legend was the fact that within both the New World and Spain there were moral critics like Las Casas who fervently fought against these cruelties and laid the groundwork for concepts of universal justice and international law. Moreover, the English, who argued that theirs would be an example of "moral" colonization, practiced many of the same Black Legend cruelties on the Indians of North America.

See also Las Casas, Bartolomé de.

BLACKSTONE, WILLIAM (1596-1675) New England colonist and first settler of Boston, Blackstone received his bachelor's (1617) and master's (1621) and then took orders in the Church of England. He settled in Massachusetts in 1623, but the arriving Puritans reduced his holdings by 1633. He announced that in England he did not like the herd-bishops and would not live in the colonies under the herd-brethren. In 1634 he moved near Pawtucket and aptly named his home Study Hill for his library of 186 books. He had a decided preference for solitude, except for the company of his wife and son and his friendships with the Indians. He planted the first orchard in the colony.

BLAIR, JAMES (1655-1743) Founder and president of the College of William and Mary, Blair first came to Virginia as a missionary from England to the parish of Varina. His talent for leadership was such that he was soon given supervisory authority. In 1690, Blair urged the clergy of Virginia to establish a college, but its prospects were unclear. Blair then took the unusual step of going to England, where he succeeded in getting a charter and in raising funds for the proposed college. On his return to Virginia, Blair became the first president of the College of William and Mary. As president, Blair fought bitter but successful battles with Sir Edmund Andros and Francis Nicholson in order to establish the college on a sound basis.

BLAND, EDWARD (flourished 1650-51) The explorer Bland in 1650, led by an Indian guide, undertook one of the earliest land journeys of exploration into the interior of Virginia, accompanied by several other English colonists, including Abraham Wood. Leaving Fort Henry at the site of present-day Petersburg, Virginia, they rode to the fork of the Dan and Staunton (Roanoke) rivers. Bland published their findings in *The Discovery of New Britain* (1651), which proclaimed the western land to be better than coastal Virginia, with great quantities of fish,

salt, precious metals, and wonderfully fertile soil able to sustain at least two annual crops of Indian corn.

See also Wood, Abraham.

BLAND, RICHARD (1710-76) A native of Virginia, Bland was educated at the College of William and Mary. In 1742 he entered Virginia's House of Burgesses as a representative from Prince George's County. He remained such until 1775. As a legislator, Bland was concerned about the rights of the public. Author of the Two Penny Bill curtailing ministers' salaries, he opposed the militant Anglican clergy of the 1750s and 1760s. He defended the Virginia legislature's act in an address sent to George III and both houses of Parliament. In "An Inquiry into the Rights of the British Colonies" (1766), he argued that no power outside of Virginia could impose taxes on the colony.

Bland's attitudes toward taxation were tempered by his desire to remain united with England. He opposed Patrick Henry's resolutions against the Stamp Act but did support the Non-Importation Agreements. He was a delegate to the colonial conventions of both 1775 and 1776 and to the first Continental Congress. Although he was elected to the second Congress, ill health kept him from attending and he retired from political life. After Bland's death, Thomas Jefferson, who greatly admired him, purchased his large and valuable library.

BLOCK, ADRIAEN (died 1624) A Dutch explorer, Block, following the expedition of Henry Hudson, in 1613 charted Manhattan Island, sailed up the Housatonic and Connecticut rivers, and explored Narragansett Bay, Rhode Island, and Block Island, which is named for him. His map of the southern New England coast was the first to distinguish between Long Island and Manhattan.

BLOUNT, WILLIAM (1749-1800) Frontier land speculator, Blount was born in North Carolina and entered his father's trading house. During the Revolution he was active in the Committee of Safety and served under Horatio Gates in the North Carolina Battalion. In the 1780s he entered politics, serving in the state legislature and the Confederation Congress. He was a delegate to the Constitutional Convention and later served as governor of the Southwest Territory and senator from Tennessee. Throughout his political career, his primary interest was in land speculation, and with his brothers he secured huge and sometimes fraudulent grants to lands along the Tennessee River and at Muscle Shoals. He helped to negotiate the Hopewell treaties with the Cherokee and Choctaw in 1784 and 1785. In the 1790s he was expelled from the

Senate for his role in the international intrigue over Louisiana.

See also Gates, Horatio.

BLUE LAWS   Colonial legislation regulating community standards of morality in Sabbath observance, dress, and habits came to be called "blue laws." Parliament had long enacted these laws—regulating clothing, for example, in the 14th century, Sunday closings during the Reformation—and these were generally transplanted to the colonies. Virginia required church attendance from all its citizens in 1624, Massachusetts 10 years later. Throughout the colonies there were laws forbidding work, sports, and travel on the Sabbath. Anti- tobacco laws go back to the earliest years of the colonial period. Perhaps the most extreme measures were taken in New England, where, in 1651, the Massachusetts General Court declared its "complete disapproval of men and women of mean condition who wear the clothing of gentlemen" and prohibited personal adornments of gold, silk, and fur for those with estates of less than 200 pounds. The origin of the term "blue laws" is uncertain, but it came into popular use with the publication of Rev. Samuel Peters' *General History of Connecticut* (1781), in which he ridiculed the Puritans with an imaginary code restricting mothers from kissing their children on Sundays.

BOARD OF TRADE AND PLANTATIONS (1696-1782)   A n advisory, administrative body that succeeded the Lords of Trade and Plantations in 1696, it was given authority to regulate and suggest new legislation regarding social welfare programs within England, foreign trade, and colonial affairs. The board was composed of five permanent members and a varying number of government ministers, who served in an *ex officio* capacity. From 1748 to 1761, George Dunk, Earl of Halifax, presided over the board and inaugurated an era of intensified supervision and control by the Crown over its colonies. With the outbreak of the American Revolution, however, the Board lost much of its power. It was disbanded in 1782.

See also Dunk, George Montagu, Earl of Halifax.

BODEGA Y QUADRA, JUAN FRANCISCO DE LA (1743-94)   In 1775 the Spanish naval officer Bodega commanded the schooner *Sonora* on the expedition led by Bruno Heceta to the northwest coast of North America. The Spanish were intensely concerned about growing Russian power in the region, and Heceta and Bodega were to strengthen the Spanish claim and expand Spanish knowledge. Bodega contributed by discovering Bodega and Tomales bays on the voyage and by reaching as far

north as Alaska. Bodega returned to Alaska in 1779, and in 1792, as commandant of the naval squadron stationed at San Blas, he served as the Spanish commissioner for Nootka and aided in determining the border betweeen English and Spanish territories on the northwest coast. His health broken, Bodega died in Mexico City.

See also Heceta, Bruno.

Even within his own lifetime Daniel Boone epitomized the spirit and determination of the American frontiersman. *(Library of Congress)*

BOND, THOMAS (1713-84) Bond is a seminal figure in the institutional development of American medicine. Together with his brother, Phineas, also a physician, and Benjamin Franklin, Thomas Bond helped found the American Philosophical Society, an academy that became the University of Pennsylvania. In his autobiography, Franklin credits Bond with the founding of the Pennsylvania Hospital, the first American institution solely for the care of the injured, the sick, and the mentally disturbed. His introductory lecture for medical students and his essay on pursuing health and preventing disease are still in use today.

BONNET, STEDE (died 1718) In 1717, Major Stede Bonnet abandoned his plantation on Barbados to start a new career in piracy. He captured a few ships, sold the spoils in New York, and returned to cruise the coast off the Carolinas. There he met Blackbeard, with whom he sailed for a while before striking out on his own again. He cruised from Delaware Bay to Charleston, capturing many prizes. His success aroused the citizens of Charleston, and Colonel William Rhet hired two ships and set out in pursuit of Bonnet. His force fought a five-hour battle before Bonnet surrendered. Bonnet was quickly tried, found guilty, and hanged. He was not a particularly notable pirate, but he is the only one recorded to have made some of his victims walk the plank.

BOONE, DANIEL (1734-1820) Legendary frontiersman, pioneer, and Indian-fighter, Boone was born of Quaker parents in Berks County, Pennsylvania, and as a youth moved with his family down the Valley of Virginia to settle on the Yadkin River in North Carolina in 1751. In 1767 he first traveled over the crest of the Appalachians, then in 1769, with five others including the frontiersman John Finley, crossed the Cumberland Gap and spent two years hunting and trapping the Kentucky country. In 1775, as agent for Richard Henderson's Transylvania Company, he opened a trail (the Wilderness Road) to the new country and led a party of emigrants from Virginia to a site on the Kentucky River where they constructed Fort Boonesboro, the next year guiding his own family to the settlement. He was active in the settler-Indian warfare that raged in Kentucky over the next few years, and at one point was captured by the Shawnee and held for three months, escaping in time to lead the defense of Boonesboro in 1779.

After the Revolution his title to Kentucky lands was questioned because of faulty registry, and in 1799, after being deprived of the last of his holdings, he moved his family to Spanish Missouri where he was granted land in the Osage Valley. After the Missouri country became a part of the United States he was again deprived of his claim until it was at last confirmed by Congress in 1814. He spent his last years hunting and trapping on the frontier.

Beginning with John Filson's fictionalized "autobiography" of Boone in 1784, the frontiersman began to assume a legendary status, which extended even to Europe after Byron included Boone as a figure in his epic poem *Don Juan* (1823); the title character in James Fenimore Cooper's *Leather-Stocking Tales* was patterned after Boone. Modern historians have shown much of the legend to be fiction, but in its essentials it accurately characterized the man who fought Indians, led the way for American settlement of the trans-Appalachian west, and was deprived of his lands by the very forces he served.

See also Finley, John; Transylvania Company; Wilderness Road.

Bibliography: Lofaro, Michael A., *The Life and Adventures of Daniel Boone* (Univ. Press of Kentucky 1978); Smith, Henry Nash, *Virgin Land: The American West as Symbol and Myth*, 2nd ed. (Harvard Univ. Press, 1970).

John Mack Faragher
Mount Holyoke College

BOSCH LOOPERS Independent Dutch traders in contravention of the authority of the official monopoly, the Dutch West India Company, the Bosch Loopers engaged in fur trading with the Indians. Dutch authorities at Albany complained that these men traded illegal guns and liquor with the Indians, threatening the peace and security of New Netherland; by whatever means, they succeeded in trading more pelts than did company traders. In the 18th century, after New Netherland had become New York, the Bosch Loopers carried the trade beyond the mountains and into the Ohio Valley, where they rivaled their French counterparts, the Coureurs de Bois. Similar independent Russian traders were known as the Promysheleniki.

See also Coureurs de Bois; Promysheleniki.

BOSOMWORTH, MARY MUSGROVE (flourished 1716-50) The niece of the famous chief Brims, she married John Musgrove in 1716 and the couple operated a trading post on the lower Savannah River. She was uniquely prepared to serve as a liaison between Oglethorpe and his successors in Georgia and her people, the Creek. After the death of her husband, Mary married another trader, Jacob Matthews. Following his death, she married the Reverend Thomas Bosomworth in 1744. With his help she finally obtained the rewards promised by Oglethorpe—ownership of St. Catherine's Island and the income from the sale of the Ossabaw and Sapelo islands.

BOSQUE, FERNANDO DE (flourished 1670s) Bosque, a career soldier, assisted the Franciscan Juan Larios in the establishment of the Mexican province of Coahuila in the

Boston's Faneuil Hall became a focal point of patriot agitation before the Revolutionary War. *(Library of Congress)*

1670s. As lieutenant to Antonio Balcarcel, who had been charged with Coahuila's conquest, Bosque soon became the secular leader of the expedition due to Balcarel's bad health. In 1675, Bosque and Larios crossed the Rio Grande and explored the country beyond, returning to Balcarel's newly founded capital at Guadalupe. Due to their report, missions were soon planted across the Rio Grande, and Spanish control extended well into Texas.

BOSTON   In 1621 the first English colonists settled the former Indian village of Shawmut, devastated by the plague of 1616-19. Shawmut was chosen by the Massachusetts Bay Company as the most suitable defensive and commercial site on the bay in 1630. Renamed Boston after the strongly Puritan town in England, it was the focus of the Puritan settlement of New England, becoming capital of Massachusetts Bay Colony two years later. Boston Common was set aside in 1634. With the founding of Harvard College in 1636, Boston assumed the position as a center of American intellectual life. Among other American firsts, Boston was the site of the first post office (1639), the first mint (1652), the first printing press (1674), the first bank (1686), and the first regular newspaper (1704).

With the growing prosperity of merchant shipping in the late 17th and early 18th centuries, Boston became the largest and most important town in North America, al-though it was gradually overtaken in importance by the rise of the ports of New York and Philadelphia. In 1770 its population stood at some 16,000.

Boston was one of the earliest centers of the movement for independence, the site of substantial protest over British regulations, including the Boston Massacre (1770); the Boston Tea Party (1773), which led to the closing of the port under the Boston Port Act (1774); and the Battle of Bunker Hill (1775), which became a rallying cry to unite the colonists. Under siege from mid-1775 until 1776, the British thereafter withdrew, leaving Boston undisturbed for the remainder of the Revolution.

See also Boston Massacre; Boston Tea Party; Bunker Hill, Battle of.

THE BOSTON MASSACRE (1770)   On October 1, 1768, British redcoats landed at Boston's Long Wharf and "with insolent parade" marched up King Street. They came to restore order to the town after the American customs commissioners had complained that the people controlled the reins of power in Boston and prevented them from carrying out their duties. In keeping with the traditional English fear of standing armies, Bostonians viewed the redcoats as invaders. For the next 18 months the townspeople and soldiers lived in an increasingly charged atmosphere, as taunts, name-calling, and scuffles marked the daily life of the town. Exacerbating matters, off-duty soldiers vied with unemployed workers for jobs in Boston's tight labor market.

The climax came on the night of March 5, 1770. A mêlée between workers and soldiers at Gray's ropewalk a few days earlier had prepared the way for the showdown. On the night of March 5th a crowd at the Custom House threatened the lone sentry. When his cry for help brought Captain Thomas Preston and a file of grenadiers to his rescue, the crowd enveloped them and prevented their return to the guardhouse. In the panic of the moment the troops fired. Crispus Attucks and four others died in what town leaders dubbed "the Horrid massacre." Their blood bought the removal of soldiers from the town but in the subsequent trials John Adams and Josiah Quincy, Jr., won acquittals for Preston and all but two of the soldiers. Found guilty of manslaughter, the two pleaded benefit of clergy, were branded on the thumbs, and released.

See also Attucks, Crispus.

Bibliography: Zoebel, Hiller, *The Boston Massacre* (Norton, 1970).

BOSTON PHILOSOPHICAL SOCIETY Founded in the spring of 1683 by Increase Mather, the Philosophical Society consisted of "agreeable gentlemen, who met once a fortnight for a conference upon improvements in Philosophy and additions to the stores of Natural History." The Philosophical Society, which met for almost 10 years, became a conduit for scientific and intellectual trends in Europe, passing them on to fellow colonists. It was the first scientific society in America.

BOSTON TEA PARTY To assist the East India Company, which was seriously in debt, Parliament enacted the Tea Act of May 1773. The law, by removing middlemen and eliminating all taxes on tea except the three pence Townshend tax, offered Americans tea at a price lower than colonial smugglers could charge. But Americans resisted the act, viewing it as an ill-disguised attempt to make the principle of parliamentary taxation palatable. The tea ships that arrived in New York and Philadelphia were forced to return to England with their cargo.

In Boston, however, events took a more destructive turn. When the tea ship *Dartmouth* arrived on November 28, her master was obligated by law to pay all duties on his cargo in 20 days, after which the tea could be legally seized and sold at auction. Another parliamentary statute prohibited the return of exported tea to England. Early in December two more tea ships, the *Eleanor* and the *Beaver* joined the *Dartmouth* in Boston harbor. Townspeople requested the return of the tea to England, but Governor Thomas Hutchinson, whose two sons were agents of the company, refused, determined to uphold the law. On December 16, with the *Dartmouth*'s tea subject to seizure the next day,

5,000 inhabitants of Boston and surrounding towns gathered at Old South Meeting House to make a final request to the governor, who again refused. That night 60 men disguised as Mohawk Indians rushed to Griffin's Wharf. Boarding the vessels, they emptied 342 chests of tea valued at 10,000 pounds into the harbor. Provoked at this wanton destruction of property, Parliament struck back the following year with the punitive Coercive Acts.

See also Coercive Acts; Townshend Acts.

Bibliography: Labaree, Benjamin, *The Boston Tea Party* (Oxford Univ. Press, 1964).

BOTETOURT, NORBORNE BERKELEY, BARON DE (c.1718-70) Colonial governor of Virginia, Norborne Berkeley Botetourt arrived at Williamsburg in a gilded coach drawn by white Hanoverian horses in 1768. Addressing the General Assembly in a gold-braided red coat, he offended them by his resemblance to King George at the opening of Parliament. After they protested against a requirement that Americans be taken to England for legal hearings, Botetourt disbanded the assembly. George Washington and George Mason's resolution refusing to import or buy items taxed by Parliament was adopted by the burgesses. Botetourt dropped all taxes except the sea tax, but the unsatisfied colonists still would buy no goods from English ships. Botetourt shortly died of a fever.

BOUCHER, JONATHAN (1738-1804) Arriving in Virginia from Cumberland, England, at the age of 16, Boucher became a tutor to the children of wealthy families, including the stepson of George Washington, John Custis. In 1762, Boucher went to England for ordination in the Anglican Church and then returned to Virginia, where he ministered to several parishes. He was on intimate terms with Washington until the outbreak of the Revolution in 1775. Boucher was unswerving in his loyalty to Britain, denouncing the patriots from his pulpit. He published his views on the unchallengeable power of Parliament in "A Letter from a Virginian to Members of Congress" in 1774. The idea of a worldwide British community was a more noble endeavor, in Boucher's view, than the cause of liberty, which had always attracted "knaves" and "Qua[c]ks in Politics."

Washington repudiated him, although Boucher's respect for the general seems to have transcended their differences. Boucher was forced to return to England in 1775, joining the exodus of other Loyalists. He compiled a book of his North American sermons, dedicating them to George Washington. He also wrote of his colonial experiences in *Reminiscences of an American Loyalist*. In 1785 he became vicar of Epsom and remained there until his death.

BOUDINOT, ELIAS (1740-1821) Born to a prosperous family in Philadelphia, Boudinot married the sister of his brother-in-law, Richard Stockton. A conservative New Jersey attorney who believed in gentry rule, Boudinot nevertheless opposed New Jersey's royal governor William Franklin. He became a member of the local Committee of Correspondence in 1772 and of the New Jersey Provincial Congress in 1775. He was against early attempts to declare colonial independence. In 1777 Boudinot became commissary-general of prisoners and served as president of the Continental Congress in 1782. A strong Federalist, he worked hard for ratification of the Constitution. He was the first counsellor named by the U.S. Supreme Court. From 1772 until his death he was a trustee of Princeton.

BOUQUET, HENRY (1719-65) Born to French Protestants living in Switzerland, Bouquet began his military service as a cadet for the States General of Holland in 1736 and was commissioned as a lieutenant two years later. In the War of the Austrian Succession he fought for the King of Sardinia. The Prince of Orange then recruited him for the Swiss Guards in 1755. Offered the position of lieutenant colonel in the new Royal American Regiment (also called the King's Royal Rifle Corps), Bouquet went to Pennsylvania in 1756.

America proved to be a hostile place for Bouquet, who came to detest the Quakers and who met with resistance in South Carolina when he attempted to quarter his troops. In 1758 he was promoted to colonel and accompanied John Forbes to Fort Duquesne, only to find it already abandoned by the French. His greatest success was during Pontiac's Rebellion in 1763 when he held off the Delaware and Shawnee Indians at Bushy Run (near Pittsburgh). He later went south on an expedition to obtain a peace treaty from the Indians in the trans-Ohio region. He died in Pensacola from a fever, shortly after attaining the rank of brigadier.

BOURGMONT, ÉTIENNE VENYARD (c.1680-c.1730) The French explorer Bourgmont commanded Fort Detroit in 1705 on the retirement of Alphonse de Tonty. After an Indian revolt, he deserted the fort with his mistress Madame Tichenet, "La Chenett," in 1706 and settled on an island in Lake Erie. When the French tried to arrest him, he escaped to Louisiana, where he explored the Missouri River. His article "La Déscription" (1717) earned him a captaincy and passage to France from the governor, the Sieur de Bienville. In 1723 the Company of the Indies sent him to make peace with the Comanche Indians and build Fort Orleans, which he erected on the Missouri above Grand River. In 1724 he went as far west as the Kansas border and made an alliance with the Comanche. He took several chiefs, including Chicagou, to France with him but did not return with them.

BOURNE, NEHEMIAH (c.1611-91) Shipbuilder and British rear admiral, Bourne was born in London, where his father was a shipwright. Disregarding his father's wishes for a scholarly career, he came to Massachusetts in 1638 to build ships and trade in Charlestown, Dorchester, and Boston. In 1641 he built Boston's first large vessel for Governor Winthrop, the Trial. In 1650 he left the colonies for a commission in the British navy. His fine performance in sea battles earned him a gold medal in 1650, appointment as rear admiral in 1652, and soon after, Commissioner of the Navy. He became a wealthy merchant as well.

BOWDOIN, JAMES (1726-90) A Revolutionary War leader, Bowdoin was born in Boston, graduated from Harvard (1745), and became a merchant. He was elected to the Massachusetts General Court (1753) and then to the Council (1757). An early supporter of colonial cooperation, he eventually came to support American independence. Bowdoin was a member of the executive council of Massachusetts (1775-77) until he became ill and temporarily retired from public life. He was the governor of Massachusetts (1785-87) and urged a permanent union of the states. Bowdoin was responsible for stopping Shays' Rebellion (1787) but was then defeated for reelection. In 1788 he became a member of the Massachusetts convention to ratify the federal Constitution. Bowdoin had great scientific and literary interests, and in 1780 he became the first president of the American Academy of Arts and Sciences. Massachusetts chartered Bowdoin College in Brunswick, Maine, four years after his death.

See also Shays' Rebellion.

BOYLSTON, ZABDIEL (1679-1766) Boylston grew up in Muddy River (now Brookline), Massachusetts, and received his medical training from his father, one of the first colonial physicians. Zabdiel's practice was not particularly notable until April 1721 when a ship from Tortuga brought smallpox to Boston. On June 6 the great Puritan divine, Cotton Mather, in an "Address to the Physicians of Boston," urged the city's doctors to inoculate. Mather based his argument on a paper of the Royal Society, which in turn was based upon successful inoculation in Constantinople.

Boylston's inoculation of his son and seven other citizens caused an uproar that soon threatened the personal safety of both Mather and Boylston, whose houses were attacked. A war of pamphlets failed to resolve the issue. Boylston and Mather were now called before the selectmen to explain why inoculation had been used. During the next year Boylston supplied the data for seven pamphlets supporting the efficacy of inoculation. The data were convincing. Of the 241 persons Boylston had inoculated, only six died and four of these already had smallpox at the time of inoculation. By 1726, five years after the beginning of the epidemic, Boylston took the risk of publishing under his own name, but in London, his essay, *An Account of the Small-pox Inoculated in New England*. A model of clinical discourse, it nonetheless caused the controversy to reignite. On his return to Boston, however, Boylston practiced in peace.

BRACKENRIDGE, HUGH HENRY (1748-1816)   The son of poor immigrants, Brackenridge came to York County, Pennsylvania, and ran a school to earn money to attend Princeton, where he became friends with Philip Freneau and James Madison. In collaboration with Freneau, he wrote the commencement poem, "The Rising Glory of America" (1771). During the Revolution, Brackenridge wrote two plays, *The Battle of Bunker Hill* (1776) and *The Death of General Montgomery* (1776), both praising American valor.

Because of his differences with church doctrine, Brackenridge switched from the ministry to the law, and in 1781 he moved to the frontier village of Pittsburgh, where he helped its first newspaper, the *Pittsburgh Gazette* (1786). Between 1792 and 1815 he wrote and published *Modern Chivalry*, a satire of the American West, which may be his most important work.

BRADDOCK, EDWARD (1695-1755)   Born in Scotland, Braddock entered the British military service in 1710 as an ensign in his father's regiment, the Coldstream Guards. In 1745-46 he helped suppress the Jacobite Rebellion. Braddock was a major general in the British army when he was sent to North America during the French and Indian War. He was reputed to be a strict disciplinarian. As commander in chief, he planned an expedition against Fort Duquesne in July 1755, but without the help of friendly Indians, whom he had alienated with his arrogance. One month before, Colonel George Washington, an aide to Braddock, wrote that the general had lost all patience with his men and lacked the sense and moderation necessary to a leader.

Washington's estimation seems to have been accurate, for as Braddock marched his men toward the fort at the junction of the Ohio, Allegheny, and Monongahela rivers, his confused troops were routed by a force of 900 French and Indians. There were nearly 1,000 casualties in his army of 1,400. Only 23 of 86 officers survived. Braddock himself was mortally wounded. Washington buried Braddock in the road to keep his grave a secret, as he made a hasty retreat, leading the army's remnants to safety.

BRADFORD, CORNELIA SMITH (died 1755)   Publisher of the *American Weekly Mercury* and one of a handful of female printers and journalists active before the Revolution, Bradford was a woman of great beauty and talent. She was also domineering and headstrong. Some time around 1740 she married printer Andrew Bradford and moved to Philadelphia from New York. Although he died in 1742, his wife managed to break up his partnership with his brother William in that time. Cornelia inherited Andrew's printing business, weekly newspaper, and a great deal of real estate. She decided to keep the newspaper going and, after employing an assistant for a time, became the sole editor and printer for almost two years before the *American Weekly Mercury* finally folded in 1746. Cornelia Bradford also had a head for business, successfully running a shop connected to the printing and making investments in real estate. When she died in 1755, she left a significant inheritance to five nieces and nephews.

BRADFORD, WILLIAM (1590-1657)   A colonial leader born in Yorkshire, England, Bradford joined the Separatist congregation in 1606. He went to Holland with the Separatists and lived and worked in Leiden for 11 years. Bradford sailed on the *Mayflower* in 1620 and signed the Mayflower Compact. After Governor John Carver died in 1621, Bradford was chosen governor of the colony at Plymouth and remained its leader until his death, serving 30 one-year terms as governor. He kept Plymouth together despite harsh winters, famine, disease, and Indian hostility.

Bradford, who was intensely religious, tried to govern Plymouth with strict Puritan faith. He drew up a patent in 1630 that gave the people self-government and title to the lands they settled. In 1636, he drafted new laws for the colony. Bradford's regime helped other settlements in the Pequot War (1637) and in the New England Confederation. Bradford had great literary abilities, although he had no formal education. His *History of Plymouth Plantation*, an account of the early settlement of Plymouth, is an invaluable source of the colony's history.

See also Mayflower Compact; Plymouth.

BRADFORD, WILLIAM (1663-1752)   Pioneering journalist and printer, William Bradford came to Pennsylvania in 1685 from Leicestershire in England but by 1689 had returned to England, in part because of criticism and in part because of lack of financial support for his printing projects. By 1690, however, he had returned to America where he succeeded in founding the first paper mill in the English colonies.

In 1693 the New York Council offered the position of printer to Bradford. Over the next 50 years, Bradford printed the first legislative proceedings and the first New York paper currency, as well as the first drama and first history of New York. When he was 62, Bradford began New York's first newspaper, the *New York Gazette*, on November 8, 1725. At 80, Bradford finally retired, having pioneered in colonial printing and publishing.

BRADFORD, WILLIAM (1721-91) The "patriot-printer of 1776" was born in New York City, the grandson of William Bradford, pioneer colonial printer. In 1742 he opened a bookstore in Philadelphia and published the *Weekly Advertiser*, or *Pennsylvania Journal*. Branching out, Bradford started a number of related businesses including a coffeehouse, a printshop, and a newspaper. His desire to be in the thick of things led him to enlist in the militia in 1756 during the French and Indian War, and he reached the rank of captain. The day before the Stamp Act of 1765 was to take effect Bradford issued his newspaper as being in mourning, complete with skull and crossbones. Later he signed the Non-Importation Resolutions of 1765. An advocate of the Continental Congress, he portrayed the need for unity by the device of a dissected snake and the words "Unite or Die," one of the best-known symbols of the growing American sentiment for revolution and independence.

Convinced that war with Great Britain was necessary, Bradford succeeded in playing a key role in assisting the Continental Army with the logistics of finance. Although he was then 56, Bradford did not hesitate to enlist. A major in the Pennsylvania militia, he was severely wounded at Princeton. By the end of the war Bradford's health was broken, but he never regretted his decision, telling his children, "Though I bequeath you no estate, I leave you in the enjoyment of liberty."

BRADSTREET, ANNE DUDLEY (1612-72) The first American poet to be published, Bradstreet was born in Northampton, England, and had a comfortable childhood and good education on the Earl of Lincoln's estate, where her wealthy father was steward. She married Simon Bradstreet in 1628, and they sailed to America with the first Massachusetts Bay colonists in 1630. Her father, Thomas Dudley, was deputy governor and her husband held numerous official positions in the colony throughout his life.

When she first met the American wilderness, her "heart rose" and she "was convinced it was the way of God." Mother of eight children, with numerous illustrious descendants, Bradstreet lived in Ipswich and then after 1644 in North Andover. Her poetry, rich with her intense faith in God, was published without her knowledge in 1650 in London by her brother-in-law under the title, *The Tenth Muse, Lately Sprung Up in America*. A posthumous volume included revisions and an autobiographical

memoir, plus the more personal (and perhaps best) poems from her later years.

Bibliography: Hensley, Jeannine, ed., *The Works of Anne Bradstreet* (Harvard Univ. Press, 1967).

Ruth Barnes Moynihan
University of Connecticut

BRADSTREET, JOHN (c.1711-74) An ambitious and highly capable soldier known for his ingenuity in adverse situations, Bradstreet served the British army in North America in the War of the Austrian Succession (King George's War), the French and Indian War, and Pontiac's Rebellion. Imprisoned in the French fort at Louisburg in 1744, he was later exchanged at Boston, where he met Governor Shirley. In 1745 he convinced the governor that Louisburg could be taken and was second in command of that successful expedition. In 1756, Governor Shirley gave Bradstreet charge over all transportation of supplies on the New York frontier. He became a major general in 1772.

BRANT, JOSEPH (1742-1807) An Indian leader born in 1742 in Ohio, Brant's Indian name was Thayendanegea. The son of a Mohawk chief, he received his education at Eleazar Wheelock's Indian charity school in Lebanon, Connecticut. In 1763 he aided the British against Chief Pontiac during Pontiac's Rebellion. Brant became secretary to the superintendent of Indian affairs in 1774. During the Revolution, Brant remained loyal to the British and became the leader of the Indians in the Mohawk Valley. He was particularly active on the New York-Pennsylvania frontier. In 1777 he headed the Indian forces at the Battle of Oriskany, and in 1778 Brant commanded the Indian forces during the Cherry Valley Massacre. Towards the end of the Revolution, he tried to establish peace on the Indian frontier.

After the war, he settled with the Mohawk in Canada and urged the British to compensate the Mohawk for their war losses. He failed in his attempts to form a united Indian confederacy to oppose further settlement by whites. In 1786, he received funds from Britain to purchase land in Canada (presently Ontario). Brant translated the Book of Common Prayer and St. Marks Gospel into Mohawk and built an Episcopal church in Canada.

BRATTLE, THOMAS (1658-1713) Merchant, philanthropist, and scientist, born in Boston, the son of a wealthy merchant and landowner, Brattle was educated at Harvard. After his graduation in 1676, he embarked on a lengthy period of travel and study abroad. He returned to Boston in 1689 and served as the treasurer of the Harvard Corporation from 1693 to 1713. His condemnation of the Salem witch trials made him a controversial figure. As an outspoken supporter of the Anglican church and an opponent of Cotton and Increase Mather, he was one of the founders of the Brattle Street church in 1698. As a student of the natural sciences, he published several monographs on astronomy.

BRAXTON, CARTER (1736-97)   Born in the Tidewater region of Virginia, Carter Braxton was a member of the colony's landholding elite. He graduated from the College of William and Mary and served in the House of Burgesses (1761-75). He was a conservative Whig who wholly supported the Virginia resolutions against the Stamp Act but thought republicanism an ideal never to be achieved in America. As a delegate to the Continental Congress in 1775 and 1776, he signed the Declaration of Independence. He expressed doubt, however, that all of the signers realized that they were making a permanent break from England. He continued to serve the Congress until 1785 and assisted in writing a new constitution for Virginia.

BRÉBEUF, JEAN DE (1593-1649)   The Jesuit missionary Jean de Brébeuf was born in France and came to Canada in 1625. He spent his life among the Huron Indians, learned their language, and followed their lifestyle. He was in England from 1629 to 1632 but returned to Lake Huron, where he founded St. Ignatius. When the Iroquois attacked the village, the Huron urged Brébeuf and his disciple, Gabriel Lalemant, to escape, but they would not desert their Indian congregation. The Iroquois put both missionaries to death by torture. Brébeuf's *Jesuit Relation of 1635-1636* gives a full account of the Huron, their customs, and language. His translation of Ledesma's catechism into Huron was attached to the end of Champlain's account of his voyages. Published in 1640, this translation was the first printed sample of the Huron language.
   See also Lalemant, Jérôme.

BREED'S HILL. *See* **Bunker Hill, Battle of.**

BRENT, MARGARET (1601-71)   Noted as the first American woman to demand a vote, Brent held one of the largest land grants in colonial Maryland. She arrived in 1638, shortly after the colony's founding, with her sister Mary, and they managed their holdings together. Offspring of an aristocratic Catholic family, she was so capable a businesswoman that in 1647 the dying Governor Calvert named her his executor. She then asked the Maryland Assembly for two votes, one to represent her ownership of land like all other landholders and the other to represent her power of attorney for the deceased governor. The Assembly refused because she was a woman. Brent had to sell some of the governor's cattle in order to

pay the soldiers he had hired to put down a revolt. She thus prevented mutiny and chaos in the colony. When Lord Baltimore in England found fault with her management of his brother's estate, the Maryland Assembly praised her diplomacy and unanimously insisted that it had been safer "in her hands than in any man's else in the whole Province." The Brent sisters never married. In 1651 they moved to a large plantation in Virginia for the rest of their lives.

BREWSTER, MARTHA WADSWORTH   (1710-c.1759)   Author of a small volume entitled *Poems on Divers Subjects* (1757), she was married to Oliver Brewster of Lebanon, Connecticut, and the mother of two children, Rubie (or Ruby), born in 1732 or 1733, and Wadsworth, born in 1737. Little else is known of her life. Her ingenious poem "To Rubie ..." includes wordplay about Rubie's marriage to Henry Bliss of Longmeadow, Massachusetts, and her "Acrostick for My Husband" evidences affection as well as poetic skill.

BREWSTER, WILLIAM (1567-1644)   A Pilgrim leader, he was born in England. After a brief time at Cambridge University and working for a court administrator during the reign of Queen Elizabeth, he returned to Scrooby, England, in 1589 to take over some duties of his ailing father. It was here that he joined a group of Puritans that eventually separated from the Anglican church in 1606 and emigrated in 1609 to Leyden, Holland, where he became an elder and the leader of the group. Brewster led the group through 1620 when they sailed for America on the *Mayflower* and continued as their leader during the Plymouth colony years, being the only church officer in the colony until 1629.

BRIMS (flourished 1700-30)   Brims was the acknowledged leader of the Creek nation for over three decades until his death around 1732. Usually known as "Emperor" Brims, he attached his people to the English after the establishment of Charleston. The Creek helped the English destroy the Spanish missions along the Chattahoochee River. When the English traders began to cheat their clients, Brims instigated the Yamassee to take the warpath in 1715 without risking the lives of his tribesmen. For the next 15 years Brims followed a policy of playing the English against the French and Spanish, a policy that allowed the Creek to maintain their independence.
   See also Yamasseé War.

BRITISH EMPIRE   The first British Empire reached the zenith of its power with the signing of the Treaty of Paris in 1763. The origins of this empire extended back to the early Tudors and the reign of Henry VII, who had expressed an interest in the plans of Christopher Columbus. King Henry supported the efforts of John and Sebastian Cabot in 1497-98, who explored parts of the mainland of North America, which they claimed for England. Little was done to follow up these voyages and claims, owing chiefly to the Spanish control of the high seas.

With the defeat of the Spanish Armada in 1588, English colonial interest quickened. After some abortive attempts, the first permanent settlement was made in Virginia at Jamestown in 1607 under Captain John Smith. The Pilgrims arrived at Cape Cod in November 1620, drew up the Mayflower Compact and established a settlement at Plymouth, which became the first of the New England colonies. During the 17th century, English settlements were established from Maine to Carolina, as well as in Bermuda and the West Indies, where colonists found relief from religious, political, and economic oppression at home.

The Dutch Wars.   Other European powers established colonies in the New World, and competition developed for control of American lands. The Dutch had gained their independence from Spain and shortly emerged as a leading commercial and colonial force. Rivalry between Holland and England led to three wars between 1652 and 1674, caused by friction over commercial posts in India, over slave trading in Africa and the Caribbean, and over the colony of New Netherland. The Dutch settlement in the Hudson River Valley threatened to drive a wedge between the English to the northeast in Connecticut, Massachusetts, Rhode Island, and those to the south in Virginia and Maryland.

Commercial friction led England to pass a Navigation Act in 1651, which outlawed trade with Holland and limited English trade to English ships. Various Navigation Acts were passed from time to time by Parliament in an attempt to implement the mercantile system, which was designed to preserve the profits accruing from commerce for the mother country. The system tried to encourage English trade by duties, prohibitions, and bounties. Colonies were viewed as a source of raw materials and as a potential market for finished products in a commercial arrangement that would produce a favorable balance of trade for Britain. Throughout the course of the first British Empire, the Navigation Acts remained on the books, but they were largely evaded through widespread smuggling and were never effectively enforced.

During the second Anglo-Dutch War (1664-67), London was threatened as the Dutch burned English ships in the Thames River. However, the Treaty of Breda (1667) confirmed the English possession of New Amsterdam, which had been captured in 1664 and renamed New York in honor of James, Duke of York, who was heir to the

British Empire. *(Martin Greenwald Associates, Inc.)*

throne. The third Anglo-Dutch struggle (1672-74) led to a gradual reorientation of English foreign policy, in that Parliament recognized that France posed a much greater threat to English interests than did Holland.

Competition with the French.   France under Louis XIV had become the most powerful country in the world and was thought to be seeking universal imperium, which would perpetuate its hegemony in Europe as well as gain control of America and India. England was determined to maintain a balance of power in Europe and to provide for security of its colonial empire and the expansion of its trade. Many in England believed that whoever controlled the seas controlled the trade of the world and that whoever controlled the trade possessed the wealth of the world and indeed the world itself. Colbert, minister of Louis XIV, placed a high priority on the building of a strong French navy and colonial empire. If the French navy could match the English in strength, then the danger of invasion by Louis XIV's army posed a grave threat.

The Glorious Revolution of 1688-89, which deposed Britain's King James II and brought over William of Orange from Holland was the catalyst that produced what has been termed the Second Hundred Years' War between

Britain and France. Protestant William III of Orange had been a leading adversary of Catholic Louis XIV on the continent. In coming to Britain, William injected a personal element to the deep-seated antagonism between Britain and France, which had included continental, colonial, and commercial friction. During the Second Hundred Years' War the competition for empire was a major concern, and it focused to a great degree on North America, India, and the West Indies, where conflicting claims were not resolved except by war.

The period between 1689 and 1713 was oe of almost continued warfare between England and France. After the Treaty of Utrecht in 1713, there was a generation of peace between the combatants. This was followed by a renewal of the struggle with a brief respite until 1763, when the first British Empire reached the peak of its power.

During the Second Hundred Years' War each side had certain advantages in the struggles. Britain was aided by a strong navy, the Bank of England, and a larger colonial population, while France had a strong army, a centralized government, and a larger population. With the exception of the Battle of Beachy Head (1690), the English navy held the upper hand and was the defensive shield against a French invasion of Britain as well as the offensive weapon in the overseas colonial struggle. The British navy was very effective in expanding the empire in the Caribbean and in India.

The financing of the war was a major problem for both sides. In 1694 the Bank of England was founded and became a powerful support for the war effort. It was chartered to meet the immediate need of the government for money. From the beginning, the bank was a success and freed the government from financial embarrassment. It was said that the victor in the war would be the prince who had the last coin in his treasury. Since the bank provided virtually unlimited credit, the English king would have the equivalent of the last coin in the treasury.

Hostilities in the Colonies.

The size of the English population in the overseas colonial empire was a great advantage in the war against the French. The Atlantic seaboard colonies attracted thousands of substantial, industrious, middle-class English settlers. Through natural increase and immigration the English population doubled every 20 years. The French population in Canada remained small despite effort by the government to encourage immigration. In 1689 there were about 15,000 French settlers in Canada. By the middle of the next century (1750), there were only about 54,000. Throughout this period the ratio of English to French settlers was about 20 to 1.

The first two phases of the Second Hundred Years' struggle were known in North America as King William's War (1689-97) and Queen Anne's War (1702-13). The Treaty of Ryswick (1697) called for the restoration of territory taken during hostilities. However, in 1713 the Treaty of Utrecht provided significant gains for the English as France ceded Newfoundland, Nova Scotia (Arcadia), and Hudson's Bay territory. Spain gave to England Gibraltar, Minorca, and the *asiento*, a contract for supplying the Spanish colonies with African slaves.

The renewal of hostilities between England and the Bourbon powers commenced with the War of Jenkins' Ear in 1739 and escalated into the War of the Austrian Succession (1740-48). The American phase of the conflict was called King George's War (1743-48). The outstanding event of the war for the Americans was the capture of Louisburg (1745), perhaps the strongest of the French fortresses in the New World. The Treaty of Aix-la-Chapelle (1748), which ended the war, was a disappointment for many colonists because it called for the return of Louisburg to France. This treaty was merely a truce as both sides prepared for a renewal of the conflict from the Ohio Valley to New York, New England, and Nova Scotia.

The French and Indian War (1756-63) was the American phase of the Seven Years' War. After suffering some reverses in the early part of the struggle, the English forces rallied under the inspirational guidance of William Pitt, one of Britain's greatest war leaders. The year 1759, known as the *annus mirabilis* (miraculous year) saw the capture of Quebec, which paved the way for the fall of Canada. In the West Indies the English captured Martinique, Grenada, St. Lucia, and St. Vincent. On the other side of the world, the British forces under Robert Clive dealt the French a decisive blow for the control of India. Late in the war, Manila and Havana fell to the English.

Consequences of British Victory

The Treaty of Paris (1763) reflected the complete victory of Britain over France and its allies in North America, the West Indies, Africa, and India. France withdrew from the mainland of North America with the cession of Canada and the Ohio and Mississippi Valley regions. England also received from France, Cape Breton Island and the rest of Nova Scotia. Despite the objections of William Pitt, France was allowed to keep two small islands, St. Pierre and Miquelon, near the coast of Newfoundland. In the Caribbean, France retained its rich sugar islands of Guadeloupe, Martinique, and Haiti but gave up Grenada, St. Vincent, Dominica, and Tobago. England acquired the slaving post of Senegal in Africa, but France kept Goree. In the Mediterranean the island of Minorca was returned to English control. As compensation for the return of Havana, England gained east and west Florida. Spain received from France the Louisiana territory west of the Mississippi River. The effective control of India passed to England, as France was

BRITISH EMPIRE: TOPIC GUIDE

GENERAL

Anglo-American Culture
Colonial Government (see **Topic Guide**)
Common Law
Exploration (see **Topic Guide**)
    Northwest Passage
Immigration
    English Immigrants
    Scotch-Irish Immigrants
Indians, North American (see **Topic Guide**)
Mercantilism (see **Topic Guide**)
Monarchs, English
    Divine Right of Kings
    English Civil War
    Glorious Revolution
    Regicides
Piracy
Postal Service
Privateering
Proprietary Colonies
Royal Colonies
Salutary Neglect
Slavery (see **Topic Guide**)
War (see **Topic Guide**)
Women, Legal Status of

permitted to retain only trading posts that were demilitarized.

Thus the original 13 American colonies formed the core of a vastly expanded British Empire. It was truly a worldwide enterprise, reaching unprecedented heights in commercial and colonial greatness that the world had never before witnessed.

See also Dutch Colonies; French Colonies; French and Indian War; Navigation Acts; Spanish Colonies.

Bibliography: Andrews, C. M., *The Colonial Period of American History*, 4 vols. (Yale Univ. Press, 1934-38); Gipson, Lawrence Henry, *The British Empire Before the American Revolution*, 15 vols. (Knopf, 1936-70); Osgood, Herbert L., *The American Colonies in the Eighteenth Century*, 4 vols. (Columbia Univ. Press, 1924); Rose, J. H., et al., eds., *Cambridge History of the British Empire, vol. I: The Old Empire from the Beginnings to 1783* (Cambridge Univ. Press, 1929); Williamson, James A., *A Short History of British Expansion*, 2 vols. (Macmillan, 1953-54).

Donna T. McCaffrey
Providence College

BROWNE, WILLIAM (1737-1802) Born in Salem, Massachusetts, into one of its richest and most respected families, Browne was elected to the Massachusetts Assembly in 1762. Although he initially opposed Parliament's imposition of taxes, he ultimately sided with the Crown in its disputes with Massachusetts. In 1774, Browne publicly welcomed Britain's General Gage to Boston. As governor, Gage appointed him to the superior court, giving Browne a reputation as a Tory. In 1776 he left Boston for London, joining the Loyalist refugees there. He became the governor of Bermuda in 1781. Taking an unofficial leave to return to New England, he witnessed the sale of his Salem mansion. His son's suicide in 1786 and financial difficulties compelled him to return to England in 1788.

BROWN UNIVERSITY Originally named Rhode Island College, it was founded in Warren in 1764. James Manning was the first president, and the first class graduated in 1769, the year before the college moved to Providence. It is the seventh oldest institution of higher learning in the United States. Its charter states that "all members hereof shall forever enjoy full free absolute and uninterrupted Liberty of Conscience." The college was closed during the Revolution and used as a barracks and hospital by American and French troops. It was named Brown University in 1804, after benefactor Nicholas Brown.

BRÛLÉ, ÉTIENNE (c.1592-c.1633) A French explorer, Brûlé was born in Champigny and traveled with Samuel de Champlain to New France in 1608. In 1610, Champlain sent him exploring with the Algonquin chief Iroquet. Brûlé became an expert in woodcraft and Indian dialects, and he adopted an Indian way of life. In 1615, Champlain sent him on an Indian mission, in which he also traced the Susquehanna River from its headwaters to its outlet in the Chesapeake Bay. From 1622 to 1624, as the manager of the fur trade, he was the first European to visit the Great Lakes. He lost favor with Champlain by selling his services to the English in 1629. Traditionally he was killed and eaten by the Huron, but he was probably murdered in the course of inter-tribal rivalries.

BRY, THÉODORE DE (1528-1598) An engraver and publisher, de Bry was born in Liège and settled around 1750 in Frankfurt-am-Main, where he established an engraving and publishing house. On a visit to London about 1587, he met the geographer Richard Hakluyt, for whom he made a series of illustrations for the travel books, *Collectiones peregrinationum in Indiam orientalem et Indiam occidentalem.* Many of his scenes depicted Indians greeting the Western explorers, such as Columbus and Balboa, with gifts. His imaginative renderings of the wonders of the New World have become famous, particularly the plates illustrating Thomas Hariot's *Briefe and*

True Report of the New Found Land of Virginia, published in Frankfurt in 1595.

BUELL, ABEL (1742-1822)   Printer, engraver, type founder, and silversmith, Buell was born in Connecticut. During his life he perfected machinery for cutting and polishing gems, set up and operated a cotton mill in New Haven (1795), minted copper coins for the state, and operated a line of packet boats. His most notable achievements, however, came early in his career. In 1769 he designed and cast the first font of native American type. Then in 1784, using all the available surveys, he produced the earliest large-scale map of the new nation. In his later years he became impoverished, dying in the New Haven almshouse.

BUFFALO   "Buffalo" is a misnomer for the North American species of wild bison (*Bison bison*). Unrelated to the true buffalo of Asia, this massive bovine, measuring up to 7 feet at the shoulders and 12 feet from head to tail, and weighing nearly a ton, flourished with the moderating temperatures following the last Ice Age, gradually filling the Great Plains and migrating as far east as tidewater Virginia. When the southwestern exploring expedition of Francisco Coronado first encountered the giant herds in the 1540s, the buffalo probably numbered some 40,000,000.

In pre-Columbian times, small bands of plains-dwelling Indians exploited the herds, using the hunting stick and bow and arrow to wound their prey. Their economies were transformed by their adoption of the horse in the 17th and 18th centuries, making buffalo hunting extremely efficient and allowing the development of complex high cultures among the Great Plains Indians.

Despite such hunting, the size of the buffalo population remained relatively constant until the Overland Trail of the 1840s divided them into northern and southern herds. Then disaster struck in the 1870s and 1880s as American hunters of meat and hides practically exterminated the herds. Thereafter, buffalo were replaced in the economy by farms and cattle ranches. Protected by the Canadian and U.S. governments, a few small herds exist today in national parks.

See also Great Plains Indians.

BULL, WILLIAM (1710-91)   The first native-born American to receive the degree of doctor of medicine, Bull found his interests were in politics rather than medicine. He was a member (1736-49) and speaker (1740-42, 1744-49) in the Commons House in South Carolina. In 1748 he was appointed to the Council and in 1759 became lieutenant governor. He served as governor five separate times between 1760 and 1775 and tried to quash the growing revolutionary sentiments. Bull wanted to establish a college in Charleston as well as a strong public school system, but the Revolution upset his plans. He was removed from the governorship in 1775 and left for Britain in 1782 when the British troops departed.

BUNDLING   Bundling was a courtship mode common in 18th century New England whereby unmarried couples were allowed to go to bed together, fully clothed, with a "bundling board" in the middle of the bed to keep them apart. Some authorities have held that it was practiced only by the "humbler classes," for the sake of both privacy in small crowded houses and warmth during cold New England winters, with approval and encouragement from adults. But bawdy ridicule and rising social standards generally ended the practice after the Revolution.

BUNKER HILL, BATTLE OF   Locked in Boston by American troops after the rout of British troops at Lexington and Concord (April 19, 1775), General Gage and his army of 13,000 were in a vulnerable position, exposed to bombardment from surrounding hills. American forces planned to occupy Charlestown, Massachusetts' Bunker Hill on June 16; disobeyed orders, however, resulted in the fortification of Breed's Hill, lower than Bunker but closer to Boston. An alarmed General Gage ordered a frontal assault on the hill by 2,500 men under Major General William Howe. Twice the British, weighed down by full packs on the hottest day of the year, clambered up the slope only to be cut down by withering fire. On the third attempt, relieved of their packs, the British took the hill as the Americans, out of ammunition, retreated. The bloodiest battle of the war, Breed's Hill, still remembered as the Battle of Bunker Hill, cost the British a staggering 1,054 casualties and dampened their hopes for a quick victory.

See also Revolutionary War Battles.

BURGESSES, HOUSE OF   Meeting in Jamestown, Virginia, in 1617, the House of Burgesses was the first representative legislature in America. It was convened by the governor, Sir George Yeardley, and was organized as a one-house assembly to include the governor, his council, and two citizens (or burgesses) representing each borough. In the beginning there were seven boroughs, but soon four more were added. It authorized itself to make laws and to regulate taxes. By the second half of the century the House of Burgesses was a two-house assembly, and it ruled the Virginia colony with very little interference from England.

BURGIS, WILLIAM (flourished 1718-31)   One of America's early engravers, Burgis left London and came to New York around 1718. He published by subscription "A South Prospect of Ye Flourishing City of New York," which was sent to John Harris in London to be engraved.

The patriot stand at the Battle of Bunker Hill bolstered American spirits at the outbreak of the Revolutionary War. *(Library of Congress)*

He then moved to Boston where, with his associates, he sold a view of Boston by subscription. Marriage to a well-to-do widow was followed by Burgis's disappearance. His Boston engravings include "Views of Harvard," "The Meeting-House of the Old First Church in Boston," "Plan of Boston in New England," and "Boston Light."

BURGOYNE, JOHN (1722-92) Beginning his long military career at the age of 18, Burgoyne quickly purchased a captaincy and spent several years living lavishly in London. In debt, Burgoyne moved to France until the outbreak of the Seven Years' War. He introduced the idea of light cavalry in England after reading about the Cossacks, and two successful regiments were raised. In 1761 he was elected a member of Parliament but still spent much time in military affairs.

In 1774, Burgoyne was sent to America to reinforce General Gage. After observing the Battle of Bunker Hill (1775), he returned to England, disgusted. In June 1776 he was in Canada as second in command to Sir Guy Carleton.

Again Burgoyne was dismayed by the ineptitude of his superior. He then proposed an ambitious plan to take Ticonderoga and Albany, New York. George III approved the plan, but Burgoyne found he had only half the troops promised. He was successful in capturing Ticonderoga, but his advance was blocked by colonial troops under Schuyler, who was then superseded by Gage. General Burgoyne surrendered to Gage at Saratoga on October 17, 1777. He returned to England in disgrace but enjoyed some success as a playwright. His most noted work was *The Heiress* (1786).

BURKE, AEDANUS (1743-1802) Born in Ireland, and a student of law in Virginia, Burke settled in South Carolina, serving as a lieutenant in the Second Continental Regiment until 1778. He became a judge until the British closed the courts in 1780, returning to the field as a captain. He also served in the South Carolina legislature (1781-82, 1784-89). He wrote pamphlets on amnesty for the Loyalists and on his dislike for nobility, the latter published in three languages. He opposed ratification of the Constitution, believing the presidency was a threat to liberty. He did serve in the first Congress, though, and was an advocate for slavery. He spent the remainder of his life in judicial functions, most notably in revising the South Carolina legal code.

BURNET, WILLIAM (1730-91) A graduate of the second class of the College of New Jersey (Princeton) in 1749, Burnet studied medicine and began his practice in Newark. As head of the Essex County Committee of Safety during the Revolutionary War, he was responsible for controlling the large Loyalist faction in eastern New Jersey. He became the presiding judge in the county court and sentenced Loyalists for aiding the British. In 1776, 1777, and 1780 he was a member of the Continental Congress. He was elected surgeon general of the Eastern District and had close contact with George Washington and General Lafayette. After the war he returned to his medical practice.

Prominent in New York state politics, Aaron Burr later became U.S. vice president. *(Library of Congress)*

BURR, AARON (1756-1836) Born in Newark, New Jersey, Burr graduated from the College of New Jersey (now Princeton) in 1772 and afterwards studied law. He fought in the Revolution under Colonel Benedict Arnold and General George Washington. In 1779, Burr resigned from the army and from 1782 practiced law in New York City, where he and Alexander Hamilton became rivals. Burr was elected to the New York state assembly and appointed state attorney general in 1789. He was elected to the U.S. Senate in 1790, defeating Hamilton's father-in-law, but returned to the assembly after being defeated for reelection in 1796.

In 1800, Burr was nominated for vice president. Confusion arose in the voting for vice president and president in the electoral college, which resulted in a tie between Burr and Jefferson. The decision went to the House of Representatives, where, after several days and 35 ballots, the tie still held. Using a letter-writing campaign, Hamilton, whose contempt for Burr outweighed his strong political opposition of Jefferson, was able to swing his fellow Federalists in support of Jefferson. Thus, as a result of the 36th ballot, Burr became the vice president (1801-05). He was nominated for governor of New York in 1804, but was defeated. The long rivalry between Burr and Hamilton had erupted again during the election campaign, resulting in Burr's challenge of Hamilton to a duel in 1804. Burr killed Hamilton and fled to Philadelphia. During the next few years, Burr went west and became a leader of a conspiracy, never fully understood, that either wanted to separate the western states from the Union or invade Mexico. In 1807 he was arrested and tried for treason. After his acquittal, he practiced law in New York City.

See also Hamilton, Alexander.

Bibliography: Lomask, Milton, *Aaron Burr*, 2 vols. (Farrar, Straus, 1979-82).

BURR, ESTHER EDWARDS (1732-58) Born in Northampton, Massachusetts, Burr was the third child of Jonathan and Sarah Pierpont Edwards. She grew up during the years of religious ferment known as the Great Awakening and was profoundly shaped by her parents' evangelical beliefs. In 1753 she married Aaron Burr, Presbyterian minister and president of the College of New Jersey (later Princeton). She lived in Newark and Princeton during her marriage, witnessing not only the college's formative years but the deaths of her husband and her father, who had replaced her husband as the college's president. She died at the age of twenty-six, after a brief illness, leaving two children, Sarah and Aaron, Jr. Her son later became the third vice president of the United States.

Between October 1754 and September 1757 Burr kept a careful record of her daily experience. Written as a letter-journal to her closest friend, Sarah Prince of Boston, this document speaks of her family, the college's early struggles, and the Seven Years' War then raging in the colonies. But it is most significant for the richly detailed descriptions of the work Burr did, the beliefs and values she lived by, and the sense of sisterhood she shared with Sarah Prince and several other latter-day Puritan women. The earliest surviving woman's document of its kind in the colonial period, it offers a rare glimpse into the public and private life of a spirited and articulate 18th century woman.

Bibliography: Karlsen, Carol F., and Crumpacker, Laurie, eds., *The Journal of Esther Edwards Burr, 1754-1757* (Yale Univ. Press, 1984).

Carol F. Karlsen
University of Michigan, Ann Arbor

BUSHNELL, DAVID (c.1742-1824)   Inventor of the submarine, Bushnell was born in Saybrook, Connecticut. Shy and retiring, he grew up working on the family farm. When his father and mother died, David, then in his early 20s, sold his share of the farm and, after two years of being tutored for admission, entered Yale College. He graduated four years later in 1775. At Yale, Bushnell became intrigued with the fact that gunpowder could be exploded under water.

He returned to Saybrook, where he constructed a man-propelled submarine boat. Constructed of many laminations of wood and complete with an instrument panel, the completed work was called "Bushnell's Turtle." The Revolutionary War provided him with the opportunity he had long sought. In 1776 Bushnell used the device to try and blow up British ships in Boston Harbor, off Governor's Island, New York, and above Philadelphia in the Delaware River. Although he was unsuccessful in these attempts, in 1779, General Washington appointed Bushnell a captain-lieutenant of the newly organized companies of sappers and miners.

In 1783, Bushnell was mustered out of service and went to France for the next 12 years. In 1795 he turned up in Columbia County, Georgia, where he taught school as "Dr. Bush." He soon moved to Warrenton, Georgia, where he became head of a private school and practiced medicine until his death.

BUTLER, JOHN (1728-96)   A native of New London, Connecticut, Butler was the captain of a band of pro-British Indian auxiliaries during the French and Indian War. After the outbreak of the Revolution, he fled to Canada, where he organized Butler's Rangers, a military unit of Loyalists and Indians. Butler's Rangers invaded the Wyoming Valley of Pennsylvania and massacred the inhabitants. Generals John Sullivan and James Clinton led their troops against the rangers in 1779 in New York. Although he was defeated, Butler escaped and led a raid through the Mohawk Valley in 1780. After the war Butler was appointed British commissioner of Indian affairs in Niagara, Canada.

BUTLER, RICHARD (1743-91)   Born in Ireland, Butler emigrated to America some time before 1760. He became a lieutenant colonel of a Pennsylvania regiment during the Revolutionary War. In 1777 he was in Morgan's rifle corps and by 1781 was with Lafayette in Virginia. At the close of the war, he was with the 9th Pennsylvania regiment. After the war, he was active in Indian affairs, representing the federal government. As a major general and second in command he accompanied General Arthur St. Clair on an expedition against the Indians of Ohio and

Indiana. St. Clair's men were routed by Indians near Wabash on November 4, 1791, and Butler was one of 900 casualties.

BUTTERWORTH, MARY PECK (1686-1775)   A presumed counterfeiter, Butterworth invented a method of producing currency without using a copper plate (which could have been used as evidence against her). Working with various family members, she sold counterfeits for half the face value to people in Rehoboth, Massachusetts, and Newport, Rhode Island. By all accounts, Butterworth was a domineering master craftsperson. Although a few confessions were made by her co-workers, neither Rhode Island nor Massachusetts could muster enough evidence to indict her. Butterworth managed to live the life of an obscure housewife, bearing seven children and dying of natural causes at her home in Rehoboth, Massachusetts.

BUTTON, THOMAS   In the wake of the loss of Henry Hudson, his London backers sent Button to follow up on the discovery of the great bay, thought to be the Northwest Passage. His voyage of 1612-13 checked some of this optimism by discovering the western shore and coasting it northward until he became convinced that this was a bay, not a passage.

See also Hudson, Henry; Northwest Passage.

BYRD FAMILY   The Byrd family of Virginia originated with William Byrd I (1652-1704), son of a London goldsmith, who emigrated in the mid-17th century. Byrd inherited lands at the site of modern Richmond. He repented his support of Bacon's Rebellion in time to escape punishment. As much a merchant as a planter, Byrd built his fortune in West Indian trade, the slave trade, the Indian and fur trade, and the English import trade, as well as tobacco farming. He often negotiated for Virginia in Indian affairs. He married Mary Horsmanden. He served in the House of Burgesses and the Council, of which he became president. He also held the posts of receiver general and auditor general until his death.

William I's fortune bore fruit in his son's lifetime (1674-1744). One of the best educated planters of Virginia, William II built Westover. Like his father, he served in the House of Burgesses and on the Council and as receiver general. He joined other tobacco magnates in opposing the tobacco and fur trade regulations of Governor Alexander Spotswood. Byrd's intellectual fame spread far beyond Virginia.

William III (1729-77) did not measure up to his father's record. He, too, served in the House of Burgesses and on the Council. He commanded the 2nd Virginia Regiment in the French and Indian War and succeeded George Washington to top command in 1759 but resigned after an inconclusive campaign against the Cherokee. Early in the Revolution he showed Loyalist leaning. By then he had dissipated one of the great fortunes of colonial Virginia. He committed suicide.

See also Byrd, William.

Bibliography: Tinlin, Marion, ed., *The Correspondence of the Three William Byrds of Westover, Virginia, 1684-1776* (Univ. Press of Virginia, 1977).

John E. Selby

College of William and Mary

BYRD, WILLIAM (1674-1744) In literary reputation William Byrd II was the most distinguished Virginian before the Revolutionary War generation. He studied for over a decade in England, concluding at the Middle Temple and obtaining admission to the bar. Elected to the Royal Society, he kept up his association with leading scientific and literary figures, especially his close friend, the chemist Robert Boyle. A member first of the House of Burgesses and then the Council, Byrd actively supported Governor Edmund Andros but clashed with governors Francis Nicholson and Alexander Spotswood.

Surveying the North Carolina border in 1728, Byrd drafted two accounts: "The History of the Dividing Line" and the more candid and humorous "The Secret History of the Dividing Line." He also wrote "A Journey to the Land of Eden" when he returned to his lands along the border and "A Progress to the Mines" when he visited his old rival Spotswood at Germanna. Although none were published in Byrd's lifetime, critics compare his works to the best in contemporary Britain. Byrd collected one of the largest libraries in colonial America and cultivated a garden famous for its rare specimens.

Bibliography: Marambaud, Pierre, *William Byrd of Westover, 1674-1744* (Univ. Press of Virginia, 1971).

John E. Selby

College of William and Mary

C

CABEZA DE VACA, ALVAR NÚÑEZ (c.1490-c.1557) A Spanish professional soldier who fought in Italy, Spain, and France, Cabeza de Vaca became treasurer of Panfilo Narvaez's expedition to Florida in 1527-28. Following the disintegration of the venture, he traveled west toward New Spain, reaching Culiacan with three companions in 1536. On his arrival he told stories of his travels that greatly enhanced Spanish knowledge of the southern part of North America. He also helped to spread the legend of the Seven Cities of Cibola and directly influenced De Soto's decision to mount his own expedition. In 1540 he led a party through the Rio de la Plata region of South America that mutinied against his leadership. Cabeza de Vaca returned to Spain under arrest in 1545 and remained in prison until 1551.

See also De Soto, Hernando.

CABILDO The cabildo was the town council in the Spanish colonies. Regulated by royal laws, two types of officials, regidores (aldermen) and alcaldes ordinarios (magistrates) were voting members of the cabildo. Usually between 5 and 12 of these officials sat on the cabildo and were presided over by the corregidor, a royal representative who frequently found himself in conflict with the cabildo, which spoke for the town.

The cabildo selected some municipal officers and could also call town meetings to discuss issues of general concern. It protected the poor and promoted education and charity, but the cabildo's greatest power was in the economic sphere, where it issued land grants, established wage and price controls, financed public works, and regulated trade.

Control by local interests gradually ended, for by the late 16th century the crown had begun to appoint regidores, often in exchange for money. The cabildo became increasingly ineffective until the Bourbon reforms of the early 18th century. By the early 19th century cabildos were staffed almost exclusively by creoles and served as centers of the independence movement.

Thomas C. Thompson
University of California, Riverside

CABOT, JOHN (died 1498?) Sailing for England, this Genoan-born explorer provided England with its claim to the North American continent in 1497. As a young man he moved to Venice where he engaged in the spice trade, traveling as far east as Mecca. He conceived a plan of sailing west across the Atlantic, similar to that of Columbus, and in England in 1496 Henry VII authorized him to explore for the Crown. He sailed from Bristol in the spring of 1497 on the ship *Mathew*, landing on the coast of Newfoundland or Labrador on June 24. Without making any human contact, he returned to England and reported his finding to the king. The next year he left on a second voyage, but he and his ships were lost at sea.

CABOT, SEBASTIAN (?1484-1557) Venetian-born explorer, the son of John Cabot, he claimed to have accompanied his father on his exploration of North America for the English in 1497. In 1512 he entered the service of Spain and was appointed *piloto mayor*, or chief pilot, a position previously held by Amerigo Vespucci. Although he may have made several voyages for the Spanish, the only one on record took place from 1526 to 1530, when he sailed to the Atlantic coast of Brazil and Argentina and explored the estuary of the Rio de la Plata. In the 1540s he returned to England, where he became a governor of the Company of Merchant Adventurers, or the Muscovy Company, and participated in the Russian trade.

CABRILLO, JUAN RODRÍGUEZ DE (?1495-1543) Born in Portugal, the explorer Cabrillo arrived in Mexico with Panfilo Narvaez in 1520. He accompanied Cortes at the capture of Tenochtitlan and assisted in the conquest of Guatemala. In 1542, Antonio de Mendoza, the viceroy of New Spain, named him the commander of two ships, the San Salvador and the Victoria, sent north along the Pacific coast. Cabrillo's orders were to discover the Strait of Anian, or Northwest Passage, that the European powers had long been seeking. Cabrillo discovered San Diego Bay on September 28, 1542, thus becoming the first European in California. He led the expedition up the Santa Barbara Channel, where he fell and broke his arm on San Miguel Island. He continued as far north as Point Reyes, although he did not sight Monterey or San Francisco. His arm badly infected, he turned back and died on San Miguel Island. His expedition then sailed north to the Rogue River in Oregon before returning to New Spain.

CADILLAC, ANTOINE DE LA MOTHE (1658-1730) Cadillac was born Antoine Laumet in a small village in southwestern France. Very little is known about his early years but it is evident from his letters that he was well-educated. After spending about a decade in Acadia, during which time he married and invented his now-famous name, Cadillac acquired an important patron in Frontenac, governor of New France. In 1694, Cadillac received the appointment of commandant at Michilimackinac. In three years at this position, Cadillac accumulated a sizeable estate and many enemies, chief among them the resident Jesuit missionaries.

In 1698, Cadillac returned to France and proposed a new establishment at Detroit, arguing that a strong French presence at this strategic crossroads would block English expansion into the Great Lakes region and solidify French-Indian relations in the West. Cadillac's town, founded in 1701, grew to become the important city of Detroit. By 1708 charges of deteriorating Indian relations and illegal trading with the English had undermined Cadillac's position. In 1710 he was appointed governor of Louisiana. Cadillac spent only four years (1713-17) in that colony, accomplishing little but confirming the opinion of his enemies that he was a very difficult man. Returning to France in 1717, Cadillac retired to the province of his birth.

CADWALADER, THOMAS (?1707-99) Physician and patriot, Thomas Cadwalader came from a substantial Philadelphia family. He was educated first at the Friends Public School in Philadelphia and later at the University of Rheims in France. A widely respected physician, Cadwalader was also a man of public affairs and patriotic causes. Cadwalader helped found the Trenton (New Jersey) Library and the Pennsylvania Hospital. Active in politics, he was a signer of the Non-importation Articles and protested against the Stamp Act. During the Revolutionary War he helped setup American military hospitals.

CAHOKIA On this site, across the Mississippi from present-day St. Louis, was the greatest prehistoric city north of Mexico, a part of the great Mississippian culture of North America. Laid out about 950 A.D., and covering some six square miles, Cahokia was surrounded by rich farmland, which supported a population of some 30,000 by 1100. Lesser towns along the river were linked to it by an elaborate system of roads. The great Cahokia mound, the largest man-made structure north of the pyramids of Mexico, was the center of urban life. The city fell into decline and had been abandoned by the end of the 15th century, although other Mississippian groupings, notably the Natchez, prevailed into the period of European conquest. Later the French established a mission at the site of Cahokia.

CAJUNS The familiar name given to a population of French descent living in southwestern Louisiana, Cajuns is derivative of "Cadians" or "Acadians," inhabitants of Acadia. The name Acadia was given in 1524 by Giovanni

de Verrazano to the land that he saw and claimed for France and that is now known as Nova Scotia. France lost Acadia to Britain in 1713 but the Acadians were only expelled by Britain in 1755, when they refused to take an oath of allegiance. A population of 12,000 people then began a long journey first to France, next to Haiti, and finally to Louisiana in 1762.

Bibliography: Glenn, R. Conrad, ed., *The Cajuns: Essays on Their History and Culture* (Univ. of Southwestern Louisiana, 1978).

CALEF, ROBERT (1648-1719) Author of a strong attack on Cotton Mather and the Salem witchcraft trials of 1692, Calef was born in England and settled as a cloth merchant in Boston in 1688. In 1693, Calef accused Cotton Mather of trying to stir up a Boston witchcraft frenzy following the Salem tragedy. Calef attacked Mather and his father's methods and motives. Mather responded by having Calef arrested for libel. Calef successfully explained his point of view, and the suit was dropped. Calef then sought to have printed in Boston his more extensive attack, *More Wonders of the Invisible World*, but no printer in Boston would handle it. The book was published in London and soon caused a sensation in Boston. Its devastatingly critical attack on the Salem witchcraft trials and the hysteria they caused angered the Mathers, but Calef stuck by his account.

CALIFORNIA INDIANS Speaking more than 120 distinct languages and distributed over a territory with enormous climatic and geologic diversity, the Indians of California included a great variety of peoples. They practiced hunting, fishing, and gathering, especially of acorns, and although none practiced horticulture, the population density approached the highest levels in all of North America. At the time of the first European contact an estimated 250,000 indigenous Californians lived in more than 500 small villages. In the north lived groups such as the Modoc, Shasta, and Yurok, who shared much in common with the tribes of the Pacific Northwest; in the central valleys and on the slopes of the Sierra Nevada lived the Miwok, Yokut, Salinan; and in the south were the Gabrielino, Serrano, Luiseno, and Dagueno, who brought the art of basketry to its highest expression.

These gentle peoples offered little initial resistance to the first settlements of Spanish missionaries and soldiers, planted in the 1770s in fear of an expanding Russian empire in Alaska. The coastal Indians were concentrated in mission compounds where they were forcibly converted to Catholicism. It was a brutal system, with many similarities to the concentration camps of modern history. Forced to work, to abandon their native ceremonialism, and beset with European diseases, the coastal population fell by a third within the first 50 years. There were a few attempts at organized resistance, but more typical was individual flight or a despondency that included infanticide to protect the children from the horrible mission fate. The missions were "secularized" by the Mexican government in 1834, but the succeeding rancho regime, followed by the Anglo invasion beginning in 1849, further decimated the Indians, who numbered only 15,000 by the end of the 19th century.

Bibliography: Cook, Sherburne F., *The Conflict Between the California Indian and White Civilization* (Univ. of California Press, 1967); Forbes, Jack D., *Native Americans of California and Nevada* (Naturegraph, 1969); Heizer, Robert F. and Whipple, M.A., *The California Indians* (Univ. of California Press, 1971).

John Mack Faragher
Mount Holyoke College

CALVERT, CECILIUS (1605-75)   The eldest son of Sir George Calvert, Cecilius Calvert, upon his father's death in 1632, became 2nd Lord Baltimore and inherited the proprietorship of the province of Maryland. Although he was the colony's first proprietor, Cecilius never came to Maryland. Rather, since his right to the province continually was threatened by enemies in England who challenged the validity of the colonial charter, Cecilius chose to defend his interests at home, naming his younger brother Leonard as the colony's first governor.

CALVERT, GEORGE (c.1580-1632)   Born of Catholic parents in Yorkshire, England, George Calvert became private secretary to Sir Robert Cecil, clerk of the Privy Council, in 1606. After serving as a court official in Ireland, Calvert won election in Parliament in 1609. In 1613 he was appointed clerk of the Privy Council and developed a close friendship with James I, who knighted him in 1617. Two years later he was appointed one of the government's principal secretaries of state. In 1625 the king made him the 1st Baron of Baltimore in Ireland.

Calvert had always shown an interest in the colonizing ventures of the Virginia Company. He thus applied for and received, in 1623, a charter for a colony of his own in Newfoundland which he called Avalon. He himself visited its main settlement, Ferryland, in 1627-28. Unfortunately, French attacks caused the colony to flounder, so Calvert sought another location in a better climate. King Charles I, whom he petitioned in 1632, granted him an area north of Virginia to be called Maryland in honor of the queen, Henrietta Maria. Calvert, however, died before the formal charter could be granted, so actual colonization was carried out by his son Cecilius, 2nd Lord Baltimore. Sir George Calvert's importance to America lies in the terms of the charter he had written, based on that of his Newfoundland colony, which allowed the proprietor to grant land to any religious group without being bound by England's penal laws. Under these terms both Catholics and Protestants settled Maryland, which became the first colony to grant religious freedom.

See also Maryland.

Bibliography: Hanley, Thomas, *Their Rights and Liberties: The Beginnings of Religious and Political Freedom in Maryland* (Newman Press, 1959).

Leonard R. Riforgiato
Penn State University

CALVERT, LEONARD (1606-47)   Maryland's first governor, Leonard Calvert was the second son of Sir George Calvert, 1st Lord Baltimore, and the brother of Cecilius, the colony's first proprietor. The Crown granted Maryland to Lord Baltimore in 1632, and the next year Leonard led 300 settlers aboard two ships to establish the colony. Since Sir George had died just before the charter was issued, his eldest son Cecilius inherited both the title and the proprietorship. And because the Calverts were Roman Catholics, their rights continually were threatened in England. Thus, the proprietor chose to remain at home to defend his interests and sent his younger brother Leonard to erect and govern the colony. Leonard served as Maryland's governor from the founding of the colony until his death in 1647.

As governor, Calvert enjoyed extensive power. He was military commander in chief, the chief justice, and the chief magistrate. He could call and dissolve the legislative assembly. He could grant land and choose the sites for ports, fairs, and markets. He governed with an appointed council and an elected assembly, which he first called in February 1635. He succeeded in establishing trade relations with the Indians, as well as with other English colonies. In 1644, he was driven from Maryland to Virginia by a Protestant rebellion. He returned two years later, leading an army of troops from both colonies, and recaptured control of the province, which he continued to govern until his death the following year.

THE CAMBRIDGE AGREEMENT (1629)   An agreement drafted and signed by 12 Puritan members of the Massachusetts Bay Company, in which they agreed to emigrate with their families to Massachusetts if the company's charter were transferred there. By accepting the agreement, the company shifted its interest from commerce to colonial settlement. As a result of the agreement, the Great Migration of 1630 took place, in which more than 1,000 Puritan families migrated to New England to build a colony.

See also Masssachusetts Bay Company; Puritans.

CANADA. *See* **French Colonies.**

CANARY ISLANDS A group of islands off the northwest coast of Africa that served as an important waystation and provisioning center for the Spanish fleets on their way to the New World. Although claimed by Portugal, they were ruled by Spain from the end of the 15th century. As major wine producers and traditional sugar exporters, the islands provided both the commodities and skills necessary for wide-scale colonization of the Western Hemisphere. Their wine trade, in particular, became important and was carried on with the British colonies in North America despite Parliament's Navigation Act of 1663.

CANONCHET (c.1630-76) Sachem of the Narragansett, also known as "Nanuntenoo," he was the son of Miantonomo and the nephew of Canonicus. In 1675, Canonchet signed a treaty with the British, agreeing to turn over Indian escapees from King Philip's War, but found it hard to keep this agreement. When in 1676 the British learned that fugitives were sheltered in Narragansett territory and sent a military force to capture them, the force was wiped out. Canonchet was later captured by the colonists and executed by the colonists' Indian allies. His death marked the end of Indian sovereignty in New England.
See also Canonicus; Miantonomo.

CANONICUS (c.1565-1647) Sachem of the Narragansett, his Latinized name was adapted from the Algonkuian word *Qunnoune*, meaning "high" or "tall." In 1622, Canonicus sent a war challenge to the Pilgrims at Plymouth but later established a truce with them. In 1635 he granted Roger Williams land for Providence, and he remained, on Williams's advice, neutral during the Pequot War. In 1638, Canonicus signed a treaty of peace with the British colonists, but during the Narragansett's 1643 war with the Mahican, the colonists turned over his brother Mianontomo to the Narragansett's enemies. The bad feelings that followed were later to erupt in King Philip's War.
See also Mianontomo.

CAPE COD This peninsula, jutting into the ocean from southeast Massachusetts, forms the enclosure of Massachusetts Bay. First explored for the French by Giovanni de Verrazano in 1524, it was named in 1602 by the English captain Bartholomew Gosnold. Samuel de Champlain charted its waters in 1606, Henry Hudson landed in 1609, and John Smith mapped it and its Indian villages in 1614. The first permanent European settlers were the Pilgrims, who landed first at the site of Provincetown, then entered the bay and founded Plymouth in 1620. The Cape was the site of Indian missions and cod fishing stations during the 17th century, and of whaling stations in the 18th century after the arrival of Portuguese immigrants.

CAPE FEAR SETTLEMENTS A region of North Carolina first visited by Giovanni da Verrazano for France in 1524, Cape Fear was claimed and colonized by Spain in 1526. By the terms of a royal patent awarded to Lucas Vasquez Ayllon, approximately 500 Spanish slaves were brought there from the island of Hispaniola. The experiment, however, proved unsuccessful and only 150 of the original colonists survived to return to Hispaniola.

The region was later visited by English explorers, and in 1662 a group of New England colonists, led by William Hilton, established the Cape Fear Company and attempted settlement there. Although this renewed attempt at colonization lasted only a few months, Hilton returned to Cape Fear in 1663 with a group of settlers from Barbados and established the independent county of Clarendon. Due to economic problems and hostile relations with the native populations, this colony had to be abandoned in 1667. It was only at the beginning of the 18th century, after the forcible removal of the native peoples, that European colonization finally succeeded at Cape Fear. In 1713, Landgrave Thomas Smith was granted title to the region, and it was soon settled by colonists from North and South Carolina. The establishment of Wilmington in 1733 provided the region with a major seaport.

CAPTIVITY. *See* Indian Captivity.

CARIBBEAN The Caribbean became the first part of Spain's colonial empire in the Western Hemisphere. Christopher Columbus's 1492 expedition touched land in the Caribbean, while ensuing voyages of exploration and settlement brought other Caribbean islands under Spanish domination. Until the 1519 Spanish conquest of Mexico, the Caribbean islands remained the focus of Spain's colonial activity.

Spanish colonization wreaked havoc with island Indians. Harsh Spanish treatment and European diseases for which the Indians had no natural immunity decimated their population. On some islands, such adversities virtually eliminated the pre-Spanish residents. Needing a labor force for its Caribbean commercial and agricultural economy, Spain imported African slaves, who quickly supplanted Indians as the principal non-Spanish population element. Moreover, cohabitation of Spaniards and blacks gave rise to a racially mixed group known as *mulattos*.

Spanish Administration. As Spain's colonial empire expanded throughout mainland North and South

America, the Caribbean colonies retained a critical role. They served as embarkation points for mainland exploration and as the communications center for Spain's hemispheric colonial system. Moreover, they became the fulcrum of Spanish hemispheric trade. Floats (fleets) of supply ships laden with European goods would sail from Spain to Cuba, from where smaller convoys would deliver goods to various mainland Caribbean ports. In turn, they would pick up mainland products, particularly gold and silver, and would gather again in Havana prior to leaving for Spain, guarded by heavily armed galleons. Shipments included Caribbean island products, principally sugar.

Because of its comparative closeness to the mother country, the Caribbean became the most tightly controlled area of Spain's Western Hemispheric colonies. Transformed into a military stronghold, these islands developed into the focal point of Spain's struggle against other European colonizing powers, which began contesting the area during the late 16th century. Success came first to the Dutch, who secured a number of small islands as the basis for their trading activities. With the Dutch providing the initial naval challenge to Spain, England also settled numerous islands, including Jamaica, while French expansion in the Caribbean included the capture of the western one-third of Hispaniola, which became Saint-Domingue.

The Spanish colonies erupted in revolution in the early 19th century. By 1825 the mainland colonies from Argentina and Chile in the south to Mexico in the north had won their independence.

Spain maintained its hold on Cuba and Puerto Rico throughout most of the 19th century, but the Spanish-American War (1898) ended in the defeat of Spain and the termination of its Western Hemispheric colonial era. Cuba obtained its independence, while Puerto Rico became a U.S. possession.

See also Columbus, Christopher; Las Casas, Bartolomé de; Spanish Colonies; Spanish Conquest.

Bibliography: Knight, Franklin W., *The Caribbean: The Genesis of a Fragmented Nationalism* (Oxford Univ. Press, 1978); Sauer, Carl Ortwin, *The Early Spanish Main* (Univ. of California, 1966).

Carlos E. Cortés
University of California, Riverside

CARLISLE PEACE COMMISSION (1778) An offer by Britain to repeal parliamentary legislation after the surrender to the Americans of General Burgoyne's army at Saratoga (October 1777). The British government sent a peace commission to Philadelphia headed by Lord Carlisle. The commission proposed to repeal the Tea and Coercive Acts, to impose no revenue taxes on the colonies, and to negotiate with Congress the suspension of all acts passed since 1763. The peace commission ended up being an attempt to reconcile differences with the colonies before France could make alliance with them. All hopes of negotiation disappeared after France and America signed treaties (February 1778), even though the terms of the Carlisle Peace Commission would have been satisfactory before the Revolutionary War began.

CARONDELET, FRANÇOIS LOUIS HECTOR DE (c.1748-1807) Born in Flanders, Carondelet served as governor of Salvador before becoming governor of Spanish Louisiana in 1792. His term was marked by efforts to strengthen Spanish control. In 1792, Carondelet decreed that all Spanish subjects could engage in the Missouri River trade, permitting individual enterprise in the borderlands in the hope of counteracting American expansionism. He also encouraged American separatists in the Old Southwest and formed a defensive alliance with four southern tribes in 1793. Carondelet closed his term as governor in 1797 and then became governor general of Quito. In general, although his efforts were successful, Carondelet's strengthening of Louisiana taxed the weak Spanish finances far beyond their limits.

CARROLL, CHARLES (1737-1832) Revolutionary war leader and signer of the Declaration of Independence, Carroll was born in Annapolis, Maryland, and became known as Charles Carroll of Carrollton. Although for years unable to participate in political affairs because he was a Roman Catholic, Carroll sided with the patriot cause and engaged in a newspaper debate with Daniel Dulany (1773). Carroll served in the first Maryland convention (1774-76). The Continental Congress appointed him (1776) to accompany Benjamin Franklin and Samuel Chase to seek aid in Canada for the Revolution. As a member of the Second Continental Congress (1776-78), he signed the Declaration of Independence. He was elected to the Maryland senate (1777), but declined a position in the Constitutional Convention (1787). Carroll became one of Maryland's first U.S. senators (1789-92).

CARROLL, JOHN (1735-1815) The son of a merchant who had emigrated from Ireland, Carroll was born in Maryland where he studied at Bohemia Manor, a school run by the Jesuits. In 1748 he entered the Jesuit college at St. Omer in France, joining the Jesuits in 1750. After ordination in 1769, Carroll taught in and traveled about Europe, returning to Maryland (1774) after the suppression of the Jesuit order. When the Continental Congress decided to seek French-Canadian support for the Revolution, Father Carroll and his cousin Charles Carroll of Carrollton were appointed to a diplomatic mission to Canada in 1774 along with Benjamin

Franklin and Samuel Chase. The mission failed because of French-Canadian concern over American anti-Catholicism.

In 1784, the papacy organized the newly independent United States into a mission, appointing Father Carroll as superior. Based at Baltimore, Carroll actively involved himself in community affairs, especially education, and was an effective spokesman for American Catholics. In 1789 the papacy created the first American diocese at Baltimore. By a special dispensation American priests were allowed to elect their first bishop. They chose John Carroll, who was consecrated in that year with jurisdiction over the entire country. Under his guidance the nation's first Catholic college, Georgetown, was founded in 1791. Carroll became an archbishop in 1808 when new suffragan sees were erected at New York, Philadelphia, Boston, and Bardstown, Kentucky.

Bibliography: Guilday, Peter, *The Life and Times of John Carroll: Archbishop of Baltimore, 1735-1815*, 2 vols. (Encyclopedia Press, 1922); Melville, Annabelle, *John Carroll of Baltimore: Founder of the American Catholic Hierarchy* (Scribner's, 1955).

Leonard R. Riforgiato
Penn State University

CARTAGENA EXPEDITION   During the War of Jenkins' Ear (1739-42), in which England fought with Spain over trading rights in the Caribbean and Central America, an American regiment was recruited to serve under British commanders. Known as the Cartagena Expedition, 3,500 Americans invaded the Spanish town of Cartagena on the Colombian coast in 1741. The British plan to capture the fort was ill-formed, and American troops were butchered. Military defeat was followed by an epidemic of yellow fever and a loss of supplies. Only 600 Americans survived. Many colonists saw the incident as further proof of British incompetence and disregard for American lives.

CARTERET, SIR GEORGE (1610-80)   A colonial governor and proprietor, George Carteret was born in Jersey in the Channel Islands. Appointed comptroller of the English navy in 1639, he was responsible for getting supplies to the naval forces during the English Civil War (1642-46). A Royalist, he was appointed lieutenant governor of the island of Jersey (1643), where he conducted raids against ships of the Parliamentarians, and he harbored Charles II when he took refuge (1649-50) on the island. When Parliamentarian naval forces captured Jersey (1651), he fled into exile with Charles II to France.

Upon Charles II's restoration to the throne (1660), Carteret's loyalty was rewarded by grants of land in Carolina in 1663 and in New Jersey in 1664 by Charles's brother, James, Duke of York. Although Carteret never came to America, he sent his cousin, Philip, to govern the New Jersey

colony. His term as treasurer of the navy (1661-67) was marred by suspicion of mismanagement of funds. He served as commissioner of the admiralty from 1673.

See also Carteret, Philip.

CARTERET, PHILIP (1639-82)   The first governor of New Jersey, Philip Carteret was born in Jersey in the Channel Islands. He sailed to America (1665) to assume his duties as governor of New Jersey, a position bestowed upon him by those, including his cousin Sir George Carteret, who had been granted New Jersey by James, Duke of York. He organized the first New Jersey assembly, which met in 1668.

New England settlers in New Jersey, opposed to the collection of quitrents to the proprietors, elected James Carteret, Sir George's son, to lead them in an unsuccessful rebellion against the authority of Philip Carteret. Shortly thereafter the Dutch took over New Jersey as part of New Netherland and Carteret returned to England (1672). In 1676, after the English had retaken New Netherland, he came back to America to govern East Jersey, but again he encountered opposition to the right to collect taxes—this time from New York Governor Edmund Andros who arrested and jailed him (1780). He was freed when Andros was recalled to England later that year. Philip Carteret governed East Jersey until shortly before his death.

See also Andros, Edmund; Carteret, Sir George; New Jersey.

CARTIER, JACQUES (1491-1557)   One of the most important explorers of the era of European expansion into the Americas, Cartier undertook several voyages to the New World on behalf of France and helped establish the French claim to large parts of North America. In 1533, King Francis I received an opinion from Pope Clement VII that the earlier papal bull of 1493, which had divided the New World between Spain and Portugal, applied only to lands then known to Europeans. Newly discovered territories, therefore, might be claimed, explored, occupied, and exploited by any Christian monarch. This was sufficient justification for Francis to launch an expedition to secure for France the riches of the Americas, a route to the East Indies through the Americas, or both. Cartier, an experienced Breton captain, was recommended as a likely candidate to lead such an expedition.

Cartier directed his first voyage (1534) to the Americas far to the north, hoping to discover gold or silver comparable to what the Spanish had found in Mexico or to find a sea route to China. After a 20-day voyage, Cartier's men, aboard two 60-ton vessels, encountered a few Indians eager to trade fur for metal (thereby establishing a basis for French-Indian relations that endured throughout the colonial era) but found neither the gold nor the passage to China. A year later Francis commissioned a second Cartier voyage, this one involving three ships carrying sufficient provisions for a winter in the wilderness. During this 1534 voyage Cartier sailed up the St. Lawrence River to the future site of Montreal.

Cartier's third, and last, expedition to the New World left France in the spring of 1541 with the intent of establishing a permanent settlement for a military garrison commanded by the Sieur de Roberval, the king's lieutenant. With several hundred men (some from French prisons) and five ships, Cartier reached America a year ahead of Roberval's three ships, which carried 200 settlers and included women. The French encountered some hostility from the natives and suffered terribly during the winter. By 1543 they had decided to give up their attempt to settle and return to France. For some years the French presence in the New World would be maintained by fishermen, pirates, and a few former sailors who had settled among the natives.

See also Exploration; Roberval, Sieur de.

Aaron M. Shatzman
Franklin and Marshall College

CARTOGRAPHY Many cultures developed the skills of representing graphically the earth's surface: Eskimo maps of wood and bone, Polynesian maps of stick, Chinese and Arab manuscript maps. These could be of significant local value, but with advances in printing in late 15th century Europe, published maps became the most important method of communicating the growing knowledge of the world. The first printed maps copied medieval *mappemundi,* which represented a simplified world of the continents of Europe, Asia, and Africa, centered on holy Jerusalem. But European mapmakers soon turned to the more sophisticated maps of Ptolemy, whose two-dimensional representations of a spherical earth with lines of latitude and longitude, dating from the 2nd century A.D., were rediscovered in Arab libraries by Renaissance scholars. Ptolemy's world was small, crowded with continents (including Terra Incognita in the Southern Hemisphere). It was Ptolemaic maps (such as Toscelli's map of 1472 and Martin Behaim's globe of 1492) that helped shape Columbus's thinking, allowing him to believe, until his death in 1506, that he had reached Asian shores in 1492.

Martin Waldseemuller's printed world map of 1507 was the first to incorporate Amerigo Vespucci's notion of a new continent, christening it "America" after Vespucci's first name, but he forced this "mundus novus" into a Ptolemaic-sized world. Only after Magellan's circumnavigation in 1519-22 did mapmakers begin to appreciate the size of the Pacific Ocean. Waldseemuller had used a cordiform (heart-shaped) projection for his world map. Later in the 16th century the German Gerhardus Mercator pioneered the use of a conformal projection (1569), designed for use by navigators, in which lines of constant compass direction were represented as straight lines of longitude. Used by Richard Haklyut in his published version of the world voyages of Sir Francis Drake, Mercator's projection became the standard representation of a world encompassed by the West. Placing Europe at the center of the world, like Jerusalem on the *mappemundi,* it thereby greatly exaggerated the size of the Northern Hemisphere and distorted the cartological perceptions of an epoch. Not until the mid-20th century did more objective projections challenge Mercator's *imago mundi.*

Later Developments. During the 17th and 18th centuries, cartographers focused on the development of accurate charts and maps of the coasts and interiors of a world being rapidly explored by the advance guard of European colonialism. The center of cartological activity shifted from the Spanish, whose pilot major in Seville had responsibility for keeping an up-to-date master world map, to the headquarters of the great English and Dutch trading companies, and finally to official French (1720) and English (1795) hydrographic offices.

In 1755, John Mitchell summarized the state of cartological knowledge in his printed *Map of the British and French Dominions in North America,* which was subsequently used to lay down the boundaries of the newly-formed United States in 1783, and which went through many editions. In 1784, Abel Buell, guided by Mitchell's map, produced the first map of the nation engraved by one of its citizens. A glance at these documents shows not only what was known but what remained to be discovered. Accurate and detailed topographic maps of the interior of North America awaited the work of the Army Corps of Engineers in the 19th century.

See also Exploration and Discovery, European.

Bibliography: Legear, C. E., ed., *United States Atlases* (1950; reprint Ayer, 1971); Meinig, D. W., *The Shaping of America: A Geographical Perspective on 500 Years of History* (Yale Univ. Press, 1986); Paullin, C. O., *Atlas of the Historical Geography of the United States* (1932; reprint Greenwood, 1975); Peters, Arno, *The New Cartography* (Friend Press, 1984).

John Mack Faragher
Mount Holyoke College

CARVER, JOHN (c.1576-1621) A *Mayflower* Pilgrim and governor of Plymouth, John Carver was born in Nottinghamshire or Derbyshire. From 1610 to 1611, he used the money he had made as a merchant to finance the Pilgrims in Leyden, where he was third in rank. Sent to London in 1617, he raised money for the move to America, hired the

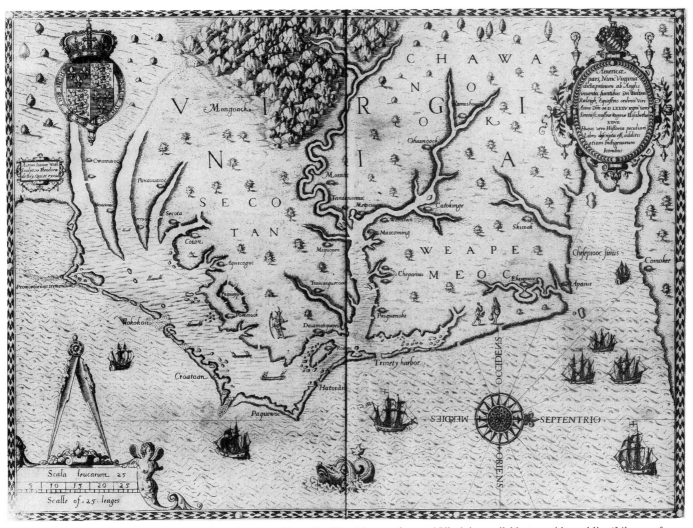

Advances in cartography and printing made early maps of America, like this one of coastal Virginia, available to a wider public. *(Library of Congress)*

Mayflower, and under the Compact of 1620 became governor. Selected to find a landing place, he may have been the first to set foot on Plymouth Rock. He helped nurse the sick during the first winter, signed a treaty with the Massasoit Indians, and died working in the fields.

CARVER, JONATHAN (1710-80)   A very early traveler of the upper Mississippi, Jonathan Carver was born in Weymouth, Massachusetts, and grew up there and in Canterbury, Connecticut. When the French and Indian War began in 1754, Carver enlisted and in 1760 attained the rank of captain. With the war over, Carver explored the upper Mississippi, including present-day Minnesota. On returning to Boston he was unable to find a publisher of his travel narrative and went to London, where he earned his living in various literary endeavors. In 1778, his *Travels in Interior Parts of America* appeared. For its second edition, Carver added sections on Indian manners and customs. He was involved closely with two other publishing projects: A *New Universal Geography* and a book on tobacco raising.

CARY, ARCHIBALD (1721-87)   Planter, industrialist, and political leader, Cary was born in Chesterfield County, Virginia, and educated at the College of William and Mary. In 1742 he founded a plantation in Henrico County and later served as a local justice and as a delegate to the House of Burgesses. After 1750, Cary's business interests turned increasingly to industry with his construction of a ropery, foundry, and flour mill. A strong supporter of American independence, he served on one of the Virginia committees of correspondence in 1773. After the destruction of his mills in 1781 by a British force, he turned to politics, being elected president of the Virginia Senate in 1787.

CASCO TREATIES (1678, 1703)   Peace agreements signed in 1678 and 1703 between the Abnaki and Pennacook confederacies of northern New England and the

Samuel de Champlain's European companions battle the Iroquois in 1609 during his exploration of Lake Champlain. *(Library of Congress)*

British colonists. The first treaty came in the wake of King Philip's War (1675-76) and was designed to restore the relative peacefulness of prewar British-Indian relations in northern New England. War captives were exchanged, and the Indians were compensated for British settlement on their lands. The second of the treaties was sponsored by Governor Joseph Dudley of Massachusetts, who feared French influence in northern New England. Although gifts were exchanged and a treaty signed, the Franco-Indian alliance continued.

CASKET GIRLS Young women sent to the colony of Louisiana by the India Company of France to become brides for the settlers, they came in 1728 with all their belongings stuffed in wooden trunks and therefore became known as "filles à la cassette," or the Casket Girls. Previous shipments of women to Louisiana had been composed of prostitutes who were taken from houses of correction. The Casket Girls were supposedly guaranteed to be virtuous and were put in the care of the Ursuline nuns until suitable husbands could be found. In Louisiana society, it would later become important to be a descendant of the Casket Girls and not of the Correction Girls.

CASTILLO, DIEGO DEL (flourished 1650) The Spanish explorer Castillo and Hernando Martín led a party of soldiers into western Texas from New Mexico in 1650, attempting to reach the Jumano Indians with whom Father Juan Salas had worked for some time in the 1620s and 1630s. Castillo and Martín not only contacted the Jumano, they also found pearls in the Nueces River. Some of the group traveled farther eastward to the country of a tribe known as the Tejas who were ruled by a king. The pearls Castillo brought back to El Paso and the tales of the Tejas stimulated further exploration in the area, notably that of Diego de Guadalajara in 1654.

See also Guadalajara, Diego de.

CATESBY, MARK (c.1679-1749) A naturalist, author, etcher, and traveler, Catesby was born in England about 1679. An early interest in botany led him first to study in London and in 1712 to go to Virginia, where he remained for the next seven years collecting and writing. Encouraged by other botanists, he undertook to write a natural history of the Southern colonies and the Bahamas. From 1722 until his return to England in 1726, he studied, collected, and drew sketches of the fauna and flora of South Carolina, Georgia, Florida, and the Bahamas. On his return to England, he became an accomplished etcher. He then wrote and illustrated *The Natural History of Carolina, Florida, and Bahama Islands,* which contained over 200 plates etched by him. In 1733 he was made a member of the Royal Society based on his observations and paintings done in America on the migratory habits of birds. Catesby died in London.

CATTLE   Domesticated cattle were first introduced by the Spanish into New Mexico in 1598, and stockraising spread through the Rio Grande Valley and into Texas by the early 18th century, then with the missionaries into California in the 1770s. These were varieties of the Andalusian longhorn, especially well-suited to arid conditions.

Meanwhile, cattle had been brought to Jamestown by the English in 1611, and several excellent dairy varieties were introduced by Swedish, Danish, and Dutch colonists. But by the late 17th century, lack of confinement had produced a hearty, free-ranging hybrid breed with low milk production. The mid-18th century saw many attempts to improve breeding and the quality of dairy products, and the middle colonies became the center of a rapidly growing dairy industry.

In the South, grazing cattle on frontier lands became an important pioneer occupation, herdsmen often forming the vanguard of European settlement. By the 1780s Atlantic stockraising culture extended across the Appalachians into the Ohio Valley and along the Gulf Coast into southern Louisiana, where Eastern breeds mingled with Spanish longhorns. There, along this Spanish-English frontier at the end of the 18th century, emerged the classic cattle culture of the West, with the mounted herdsman (or cowboy) roping and branding, and the roundup that characterized the later Western cattle industry.

Bibliography: Dobie, J. Frank, *The Longhorns* (Little, Brown, 1941).

CELORON DE BLAINVILLE, PIERRE JOSEPH (1693-1759)   The French officer and explorer Celoron de Blainville was born in Montreal and was commissioned in 1715. From 1734 to 1742 his able management of the Michilimackinac post won praise from both the French and Indians. In 1740 he led a successful expedition against the Chickasaw Indians. In 1742 he served at Detroit, in 1744 at Niagara, in 1746 at Fort St. Frederic, and in 1748 relieved Detroit during a Huron revolt. In 1749 when he was sent to the Ohio to dispel English traders and reinstate Miami loyalty, he left lead plates along the river claiming French rule. From 1750 to 1753, he commanded Detroit and then became mayor of Montreal. He died in the French and Indian War.

CERRÉ, JEAN GABRIEL (1734-1805)   A fur trader, Cerré was born in Montreal but established his network of Missouri River fur hunters in Kaskaskia, Illinois. During the Revolution, he sided with the Americans, became a

citizen, and served briefly as a magistrate of the Illinois country under Colonel John Todd in 1799. When Todd's troops left, Cerré also departed because the magistrate's authority was no longer upheld. By 1780 he was in St. Louis serving in the militia and in 1782 was one of eight syndics. He expanded his trading empire by settling his family members in the town of New Madrid and in the trading post of L'Anse-à-la-Graisse founded by him in 1780. He also sent traders to the Tennessee Indians.

CHAMPION, DEBORAH (1753-1845)   During the Revolution, Champion carried dispatches and the army payroll on horseback from her Paymaster General father Henry Champion near Norwich, Connecticut, to General Washington and his troops at Boston, accompanied by an old family slave, Aristarchus. Because she was a young woman, the British allowed her to pass through their lines without suspicion. In 1775 she became the second wife of Judge Samuel Gilbert of Gilead, Connecticut.

CHAMPLAIN, LAKE   Approximately 125 miles long and reaching a maximum width of 14 miles, Lake Champlain was named for the French explorer Samuel de Champlain, who first visited it in 1609. Providing a direct route between the Hudson and Saint Lawrence river valleys, it was the scene of conflict between English and French colonial forces during the 17th century, culminating in the English conquest of the region in the French and Indian War (1756-63).

The lake's strategic importance continued to be crucial during the American Revolution. During the operations against Fort Ticonderoga in May 1775, the American generals Samuel Herrick and Benedict Arnold tried to secure Continental control of the region. In the aftermath of the ill-fated American invasion of Canada, however, the British position there was consolidated, and a British fleet was constructed to maintain its control of the lake. In the face of this threat, Arnold mobilized a counter-effort in the summer of 1776 and supervised the construction of an American fleet. Although this American fleet was defeated and almost completely destroyed by the British in October at the Battle of Valcour Island, the resistance offered on Lake Champlain provided Continental forces farther south with desperately needed time for mobilization.

CHAMPLAIN, SAMUEL DE (1567-1563)   As an explorer, colonizer, and royal governor, Champlain, more than any other individual, contributed to the establishment of a permanent French presence in North America. A navy captain's son, Champlain joined expeditions to the West Indies in 1601 and to Canada in 1603. His long career in

A 1768 view of Charleston showed a major port, the largest American city south of Philadelphia. *(Library of Congress)*

Canada really began, however, in 1604, when he joined the Sieur de Monts in an attempt to settle a permanent colony in Acadia. The settlement lasted only three years, during which Champlain produced detailed maps and charts of the Atlantic coastal region as far south as Cape Cod.

In July 1608, Champlain established a base, which became Quebec, on the St. Lawrence River at a point where the river narrowed sufficiently to permit control of the waterway by cannon. Although Quebec's initial foundation had been dictated by the need to locate a trading base near the Indians, the site itself allowed its occupants to control access to Canada's interior. Of the 28 Frenchmen who founded Quebec, only 8 survived the first winter. That summer, Champlain joined friendly bands of Algonquin and Huron on an expedition against their rivals, the Mohawk—an Iroquois nation. One skirmish was immensely significant, for when one blast from Champlain's gun felled two Mohawk warriors, a pattern of native-European alliances was established that endured throughout the colonial era. After that minor battle the Iroquois tended to ally with the English against the French, while the Huron and Algonquin joined the French in the struggle for control of the American interior.

Although Quebec existed specifically as a base for the fur trade, Champlain acted to insure French influence, if not dominance, throughout the interior. Named commandant of New France in 1612, Champlain sent some members of his company into the wilderness each year to winter with the natives, to learn their languages and customs, and to cement their friendly ties to the French. As he had done in Acadia, Champlain ordered crops planted.

Such successes, plus the fear of competition from other European powers, led Champlain to make several trips to France in order to appeal for government support. In 1617 he requested that France establish a stable colony that could survive and grow through natural population increase by sending 400 families to Canada, to be protected by 300 soldiers. It was not until the creation of the Company of a Hundred Associates in 1627, however, that significant efforts were undertaken in France to bolster Champlain's colony. In 1632, with the French recapture of Quebec from the English (who had seized it in 1629), Champlain was made governor of the colony. That year he published his key work, *Voyages*, partly to generate interest in New France among Frenchmen. He died in Quebec three years later.

See also Exploration; French Colonies; Hundred Associates, Company of a.

Aaron Shatzman
Franklin and Marshall College

CHARLESTON, SOUTH CAROLINA Charleston, the first permanent settlement in South Carolina (1670), was settled by Governor William Sayle and 150 English and Irish colonists on the Ashley River. Until 1783 it was called Charles Town in honor of King Charles II. The settlement was moved to a more easily defended location on a peninsula between the Ashley and Cooper rivers (1680) and survived an attack by the Spanish and French fleet (1706). By 1775, it had become the largest and wealthiest American city south of Philadelphia. The provincial congress met in Charleston and adopted the first state constitution (1776). The British unsuccessfully attacked the city in 1776 and 1779, but gained control from 1780 to 1782. Legislative ordinances governed Charleston until 1783, when it received a city charter. It remained the state capital until 1790.

CHARLEVOIX, PIERRE FRANÇOIS XAVIER DE (1682-761) A French explorer and historian, Charlevoix was born at St. Quentin, graduated from the Jesuit College Louis le Grand in 1704, and sailed with the Marquis de Vaudreuil to Canada in 1705. Recalled in 1709, he taught at his former college, where one of his students was Voltaire. In 1720 he went to Canada ostensibly to review the Jesuit missions, but he was actually on a secret mission to determine the boundaries of Acadia and to find a new route to the West. He traveled by single canoe up the St. Lawrence, through the Great Lakes, and into the Illinois River, reaching New Orleans and Biloxi in 1722. His three-volume history of New France (1744) was the first complete account of France's North American colonies.

CHARTER OAK The Charter Oak was the name given to an oak tree in Hartford, Connecticut in which Connecticut settlers hid their colonial charter in 1687. The tree survived until the mid-19th century.

The original charter, given by England to John Winthrop, governor of the Connecticut colony in 1662, was almost a document of freedom from Britain. When King James II ascended the throne (1685) he tried to annul the Connecticut charter, while Connecticut petitioned the Crown to remain as it was or to be under the Massachusetts, rather than New York, government. Considering this a surrender, English officials sent Sir Edmund Andros to receive the charter for the Crown. Traditionally, when the charter was brought into a courthouse where Governor Treat was making a speech against its surrender, the charter was stolen by Joseph Wadsworth, who hid it in a hollow tree. Connecticut subsequently joined the short-lived Dominion of New England governed by

Andros. After King James was overthrown, Connecticut resumed its charter government, which continued to be the basic law of the colony and then the state until 1818.

See also Connecticut; Dominion of New England.

CHARTER OF LIBERTIES, NEW YORK (1683) Drafted by the assembly of New York and approved by James, Duke of York (the future King James II), the charter described how the government was to be organized and the functions of the governor, council, and legislative assembly. The charter guaranteed freedom of assembly and trial by jury. It protected women's property, ensured people freedom from feudal exactions, and gave exemptions from quartering soldiers. The charter also granted religious toleration to all Christians. In 1685 the assembly was abolished by James.

CHARTER OF PRIVILEGES (1701) Granted by William Penn for Pennsylvania on October 28, 1701, the Charter of Privileges was a guarantee of freedom of worship for all those who had faith in one God. The charter also stated that those who believed in Jesus Christ were eligible for office. The charter changed the form authorized by Penn's earlier Frame of Government (1682, 1683). The Council was no longer a representative body and a unicameral legislature was substituted for the Assembly.

See also Frame of Government.

CHARTES, FORT DE The administrative and commercial center of the French territory of Illinois, the fort was constructed in 1719 and named for the son of the regent of France. Because of its location on the banks of the Mississippi, it was damaged by floods in 1727 and had to be entirely reconstructed in 1732. In 1747 the settlement was relocated near the Indian village of Kashkaskia and redesigned on a massive scale by the engineer Jean Baptiste Saucier in 1751. Transferred to the British after the French and Indian War, it was renamed Fort Cavendish. It had, however, been abandoned by the time of the Revolution.

CHASE, SAMUEL (1741-1811) Signer of the Declaration of Independence and associate justice of the U.S. Supreme Court, Chase was born in Somerset County, Maryland. He began to study law in 1759 and was admitted to the bar in Annapolis two years later. Chase was elected to the Maryland legislature (1764-84) and led violent resistance to the Stamp Act with the Sons of Liberty. He sat in both the First (1774) and Second (1775-78) Continental Congresses and was appointed in 1776 to accompany Benjamin Franklin and Charles Carroll to Canada to seek a Canadian alliance in the Revolution. Chase then rejoined Congress and signed the Declaration of Independence. He voted against ratification of the Constitution by Maryland (1784). Chase became chief justice of the Baltimore criminal court (1788) and was named chief justice of the Maryland general court three years later. George Washington appointed him to the U.S. Supreme Court, where he served (1796-1811) until his death, despite an impeachment trial (1805).

CHAUNCY, CHARLES (1705-87) A religious leader born in Boston, he graduated from Harvard (1721) and soon became the minister of the First Congregational Church of Boston, where he served for 60 years (1727-87). He soon gained such an influence on religious thought that Jonathan Edwards became his only rival. Chauncy was the leader of theological liberalism in New England and was constantly in conflict with the conservative Edwards over the Great Awakening. Chauncy wrote a pamphlet (*Seasonable Thoughts on the State of Religion in New England* [1743]) in which he criticized the emotionalism in the Great Awakening. He battled the introduction of episcopacy into New England during the 1760s, and supported the patriots throughout the Revolution. Embracing Universalism in the 1780s, Chauncy began new debates with Edwards by issuing *Salvation for All Men Illustrated and Vindicated as a Scripture Doctrine* (1782), followed by *The Mystery Hid from Ages... or the Salvation of All Men* (1784).

See also Edwards, Jonathan; Great Awakening.

CHEQUAMEGON BAY This harbor on the southwest coast of Lake Superior was first explored by the Frenchman Radisson in 1659, who found it protected from lake storms by the Apostle Islands at the bay's entrance and built a trading post. Later it became the site of the mission of St. Esprit but was always known as La Pointe. Chequamegon Bay was a rallying point for the French and the western Indians in the alliance against the Iroquois and one of the most important of the lake posts. A French fort was built on Madeline Island in the bay in 1718 and a garrison kept there until 1759. Alexander Henry founded a post there for the North West Company in the late 18th century.

CHEROKEE INDIANS The Iroquoian-speaking Cherokee were centered in the Appalachian portions of what is now the Carolinas, Georgia, Alabama, and Tennessee. From Spanish expeditions in the 16th century they contracted epidemic diseases that brought heavy population losses. Late in the 17th century, the Cherokee encountered Virginia traders and Indian allies of Carolina raiding for slaves. After 1700, Carolina established a trade monopoly with the Cherokee to deter Virginia and Louisiana as well as to gain their assistance against other Indians and runaway blacks.

Initially welcome, the Carolina connection soon proved destructive. Over time, the Cherokee complained increasingly of ever-lower prices for deerskins, of cheating and unsavory debt collections by traders, and of the colony's favoring the rival Creek while providing inadequate means of defense against the Creek, Iroquois, and other enemies. Cherokee population resumed its decline, dependence on trade goods (including rum) increased, and the number of traders and other whites living among the Cherokee rose.

With the outbreak of the French and Indian War (1756-63) the Cherokee were initially divided among pro-French, pro-British, and neutralist factions. A series of violent incidents involving Virginia and Carolina settlers who had moved on to their hunting land finally provoked the Cherokee to war against the English. But with the French unable to provide support and facing an invasion of 2,500 English troops, the Cherokee were obliged to make peace and cede more hunting land. Thereafter, settlers streamed into eastern Cherokee country, fanning tensions. The Cherokee arose against the rebellious colonists in 1776, but the British failure to invade Charleston doomed their effort. In 1777 they ceded virtually all their South Carolina land. Although many continued to resist the Americans until 1792, the Cherokee were no longer a formidable people, politically, militarily, or economically.

Bibliography: Corkran, David H., *The Cherokee Frontier: Conflict and Survival, 1740-62* (University of Oklahoma Press, 1970; Crane, Verner W., *The Southern Frontier, 1670-1732* (Duke University Press, 1929).

Neal Salisbury
Smith College

CHEROKEE WARS Trading conflicts instigated the outbreak of the Stono War in 1674 between South Carolina and the Cherokee. The importance of trade to both societies increased and also mitigated this tendency toward conflict. Commercial relations were hindered by the colonial practice of enslaving Indians captured in war, but ultimately the lucrative Cherokee trade overrode all other considerations and the various colonial governments jealously protected the rights of the traders they had licensed. Although the Cherokee often allied themselves militarily with the British, the general fear of Indians precipitated further hostilities in 1759, when the Cherokee were blamed for atrocities apparently committed by another tribe. But, as before, the importance of trade asserted itself, and by 1762 the British and the Cherokee were again at least nominal allies.

See also Stono War.

CHERRY VALLEY MASSACRE (1778) During the American Revolution, attacks by the Americans on British-allied Iroquois led to reprisals by the Indians. About 100 Tory rangers under Joseph Brant and 200 Iroquois attacked the New York settlement of Cherry Valley in 1778. The rangers fired on the fort while the Indians burned and looted buildings and killed any settlers unable to reach the safety of the palisade. Thirty civilians, including women and children, were killed, and the subsequent atrocity stories spurred four American invasions of the Iroquois country during the next year.

See also Brant, Joseph.

CHESAPEAKE BAY Fed by the Susquehanna, Patuxent, Potomac, Rappahannock, York, and James rivers, this 200-mile inlet of the Atlantic was in 1607 the site of Jamestown, the first permanent English settlement in America. As a region the Chesapeake is bounded by the fall line of the rivers to the west, by the great dismal swamp to the south, and by the valleys of the Susquehanna and Delaware to the north. Its indigenous inhabitants were village dwelling Algonquian speakers, frequently allied in small confederacies, including the Powhatan Confederacy. In 1570 the Spanish founded a Jesuit mission on the lower James River, but the missionaries were soon murdered. In 1585 explorers from Raleigh's English settlement at Roanoke first recorded the name "Chesepiooc" as the name of one of these villages on the bay; in Algonquian the word seems to mean "on the big river." What became the second Roanoke expedition was supposed to settle somewhere in the Chesapeake region.

Jamestown became the nucleus of the Virginia colony; in 1634, St. Mary's City on the north bank of the Potomac became the first settlement of what was the colony of Maryland. In the 1650s both colonies began the intensive settlement of what is known as the Eastern Shore of the bay. The great port at Norfork, in Virginia, at the mouth of the bay, was founded in 1682; the other great Chesapeake port, Baltimore, Maryland, was established in 1729. For the most part, however, the lucrative tobacco plantations of both colonies established direct connections with Europe by directly trading with shippers who moved up the deep rivers to local storehouses or "factories."

CHICKASAW INDIANS A Muskohegean tribe, closely related to the Creek and the Chocktaw, they primarily occupied the area of northern Mississippi and western Tennessee, but also parts of South Carolina, Georgia, Alabama, Arkansas, and Kentucky. Called "Chicaza" when first encountered by Hernando De Soto in 1641, they lived in extensive riverside towns and were noted for their warlike character. Their Muskohegean dialect became the common language of trade throughout the entire Gulf area.

In disputes with neighboring tribes, the Chickasaw claimed territory as far north as the Ohio River.

Their military conflicts continued throughout most of the 18th century. In the first of these, in 1715, they allied with the Cherokee to drive the Shawnee from their tribal territory. Their subsequent conflicts involved the French, who were allies of the Choctaw, the Chickasaw's arch-enemies. The Chickasaw defeated a French invasion of their territory in 1739-40 and in 1769 routed the Cherokee. By the terms of the 1785 Hopewell Treaty with the U.S. government, the extent of Chickasaw territory was formally established but was subsequently whittled away in treaties of 1805, 1816, 1818, and 1832. The Chickasaw nation was later relocated in the Oklahoma Territory.

CHICKASAW-FRENCH WAR (1736-40) A conflict along the lower Mississippi River over the right of free passage, it was one of the few military encounters settled in favor of the Indians. The Chickasaw had always opposed French presence in the Gulf of Mexico area, and in 1729 they supported the Natchez in an insurrection against French rule. In 1736 the French retaliated but were driven from Chickasaw territory with heavy losses. Another French attack in 1740 failed. A treaty between the two sides later provided for the right of free travel for French traders, but sporadic attacks led to more hostility and to the eventual loss of French claims at the end (1763) of the French and Indian War.

CHICKASAW TRAIL Although sometimes referring to any of several Indian routes running through the Old Southwest, "Chickasaw" is usually reserved for the trail running 500 miles from Fort Rosalie (Natchez), in the heart of Natchez Indian country on the Mississippi, northeast to the Chickasaw towns on the headwaters of the Tombigbee, across the Tennessee River at Muscle Shoals, thence to French Lick (Nashville), the site of extensive salt deposits along the Cumberland. In 1801 the Chickasaw and the Choctaw signed treaties allowing for its improvement. The Natchez Trace, as it became known, was completed between 1806 and 1820 and became the main route of emigrant, commercial, and military traffic to the Old Southwest.

See also Natchez.

CHICKASAW TREATY (1786) An agreement between the Chickasaw nation and the United States in January 1786, the treaty determined the territorial boundaries and conditions of trade between the two peoples. This treaty and the agreement signed with the Cherokee nation two months before at Hopewell, South Carolina, were the first to recognize and codify the principle of U.S. sovereignty over the native peoples of North America. In both treaties the observance of the original terms of trade and territorial boundaries proved to be only temporary. They were revised in later treaties and eventually abrogated with the displacement of the Chickasaw to the Oklahoma Territory.

See also Hopewell, Treaty of.

Chihuahua Trail. *(Martin Greenwald Associates, Inc.)*

CHIHUAHUA TRAIL   This 1,600-mile trail connecting the northern Spanish settlements of New Mexico with Chihuahua was actually the northmost segment of the old Camino Real (Royal Road) leading out of the viceregal capital at Mexico City. Juan de Oñate pioneered this road to the colonial and Indian settlements of the upper Rio Grande in 1598, and it became the lifeline for incoming supplies and outgoing frontier products sold in the mining towns of Chihuahua. Because of the danger of Indian attack along the route, it was usually traversed in the fall by huge convoys (*conductas*) with soldier escorts totaling as many as 500 men and thousands of head of cattle and sheep.

See also Oñate, Juan de.

CHIRIKOV, ALEXEI ILYICH (1703-1748)   Chirikov, a Russian explorer of the Alaskan coast and a trained navigator, joined Vitus Bering in the late 1720s on his expeditions in the north Pacific. He sighted the Alaskan coast in 1741, but the loss of two of his ships forced him to turn back. Later that year he explored the Aleutians and made the first contact with the Aleuts. His report includes the first description of the coast of Alaska and its indigenous inhabitants. Appointed to the high post of captain commander in 1747, he spent his last years in retirement in Moscow.

See also Aleuts; Bering, Vitus.

CHOCTAW INDIANS   The largest of the southern Muskohegean peoples, closely related to the Chickasaw and the Alabama, the Choctaw occupied the area of modern Alabama and southern Mississippi. More dependent on intensive agriculture than any other of the Southern tribes, the Choctaw also possessed an elaborate system of religious beliefs and rituals, including secondary burial and the construction of funerary mounds.

Throughout the 18th century, the Choctaw were in a state of almost constant hostility with the neighboring Chickasaw and Creek. Although the Choctaw were traditionally close allies of the French, having served on the French side in the 1730 Natchez uprising, a pro-British faction was established by chief Red Shoes in 1750. After the French defeat in the French and Indian War, the Choctaw and the British maintained friendly relations, although many Choctaw migrated to French-controlled Louisiana. During the Revolution, the Choctaw rejected the appeal of Tecumseh to join the Creek in hostilities against the colonists. This was due to the intervention of chief Pushmata. Although the territory of the Choctaw was confirmed by the U.S. government in 1783, the 1830 Treaty of Dancing Rabbit mandated their relocation to the Oklahoma Territory.

CHOUTEAU, RENÉ AUGUSTE (1749-1829)   An important trader and government official, Chouteau was born in New Orleans and with his stepfather, Pierre Laclède, helped found St. Louis in 1764 as a trading post. Chouteau and his half-brother Pierre negotiated a very favorable trading agreement for furs with the Osage Indians in Missouri, an arrangement that led to the establishment of profitable trading posts by the Chouteau family. When the United States bought Louisiana in 1804, Chouteau became a justice of the first territorial court. He served as colonel in the St. Louis militia in 1808 and was selected as chairman of the board of trustees of the newly incorporated St. Louis in 1809. In 1815 he was the federal commissioner for treaties with the Sioux, Iowa, Sauk, and Fox Indians and was later the United States pension agent for the Missouri Territory (1819-20).

CHRISTINA, FORT   Located at the confluence of the Delaware and Christina rivers, Fort Christina, or Christiana, was the first permanent European colony in Delaware, established by the Dutch leader Peter Minuit and a group of Swedish colonists in 1638. Fort Christina served as the capital of New Sweden from 1638 to 1643 and again in 1654. Its control passed to the Dutch in 1655 and to the British in 1662. In the 1730s, the area became the scene of Quaker colonization, and Thomas Penn founded the city of Wilmington at the site. During the Revolution it was the scene of the Battle of Brandywine, at which the Continental Army failed to halt the British advance to Philadelphia.

CHURCH, BENJAMIN (1639-1718) Born in Plymouth, Massachusetts, and raised in various frontier towns in New England, Church in 1674 moved to Sogkonate (now Little Compton), Rhode Island, where he was the sole white settler. He got along well with the neighboring Indians, especially with Awashonks, the "squaw sachem." It was she who warned him of the onset of King Philip's War (1675-76), which she also refused to join. Church was captain of a Plymouth company during the Great Swamp Fight of December 19, 1675, and was twice wounded. He was noted for his ability to persuade other Indian tribes to fight with the British instead of with Philip's Wampanoags. With the help of his Indian assistants, Church captured Philip's wife and son, and on August 12, 1676, Alderman, an Indian in Church's company, shot Philip, himself.

Church served in King William and Queen Anne's wars as first a major and later a colonel. After one of his raids into Nova Scotia it was discovered he had "knocked" some French prisoners in the head, resulting in conflict with colonial authorities. He became embittered, though, over the meager compensation he received for his services, and he retired in 1704.

CIBOLA, SEVEN CITIES OF After the conquests of the Inca and Aztec empires, the Spanish conquistadors constantly followed tales of gold and riches. The Seven Golden Cities of Cibola was one of the subjects of these stories. As early as 1530, Nuno de Guzmán's men moved north from Mexico City seeking Cibola. Their hopes were heightened by the report of Cabeza de Vaca on his return in 1536. Marcos de Niza's 1538-39 expedition as well as Coronado's in 1540 stemmed from Cabeza de Vaca's tales. Cibola was eventually revealed as seven Zuni pueblos with very little gold or silver. Nevertheless, the hopes the Spanish had for Cibola were quickly transferred to Quivira, in what is now Kansas.

CINCINNATI, THE SOCIETY OF THE (1783) Revolutionary War army officers stationed in the Newburgh-Fishkill area of New York formed this society on May 10, 1783, before disbanding, naming it after the Roman general Lucius Quintius Cincinnati. The society was formed to promote friendship, to continue the ideals of the Revolution, and to aid members of the officers' families. The first president general of the society was George Washington, who served until 1799, when he was succeeded by Alexander Hamilton. The society was restricted to commissioned officers of the Continental forces of the United States and France who served as commissioned officers at least 30 months during the revolution. Membership was hereditary, and passed from father to the eldest son. Judge Aedanus Burke of South Carolina circulated a pamphlet criticizing the hereditary feature and restriction of membership in the society. Thomas Jefferson was also an influential critic. The society had its first general meeting (May 1784) and abolished the hereditary principle for membership, but the decision was never ratified by state societies.

CIRMENHO, SEBASTIAN RODRIGUEZ (flourished 1595-96) The Portuguese-born explorer Cirmenho was given command of the 1595 Manila galleon *San Agustín* on the understanding that he would attempt to find the legendary Strait of Anian between the Pacific and Atlantic. After a particularly rough voyage across the Pacific, Cirmenho anchored in Drake's Bay and led a small party inland. A storm beached the *San Agustín* on November 30, 1595, the ship and all its contents a total loss. Carpenters built a small launch, and the entire crew set sail in it down the coast. During the voyage Cirmenho sighted the entrance to Monterey Bay. The launch arrived in Navidad on January 7, 1596, whereupon the viceroy, Luís Velasco, criticized Cirmenho in spite of his arduous journey and successful exploration.

CITIES AND TOWNS The largest American cities were small by European standards. By the end of the 17th century, London had over 500,000 inhabitants, and several other English cities had populations in the tens of thousands. By comparison, in 1690 Boston had only 6,000 inhabitants, New York City 4,700, and Philadelphia 2,200. A century later, Boston had a population of only 18,038, while New York City had grown to 33,131 and Philadelphia to 42,444. In 1790 America was still a predominantly rural society; only 3.3 percent of the population lived in towns of 8000 or more inhabitants.

Commercial Development. Yet early American cities and towns had an impact on society that far surpassed their proportion of the total population. Especially in the North, the larger port towns quickly became the centers of economic and political life. They were the main entry points for the influx of European immigrants, ideas, and imported goods. They were also the main collection

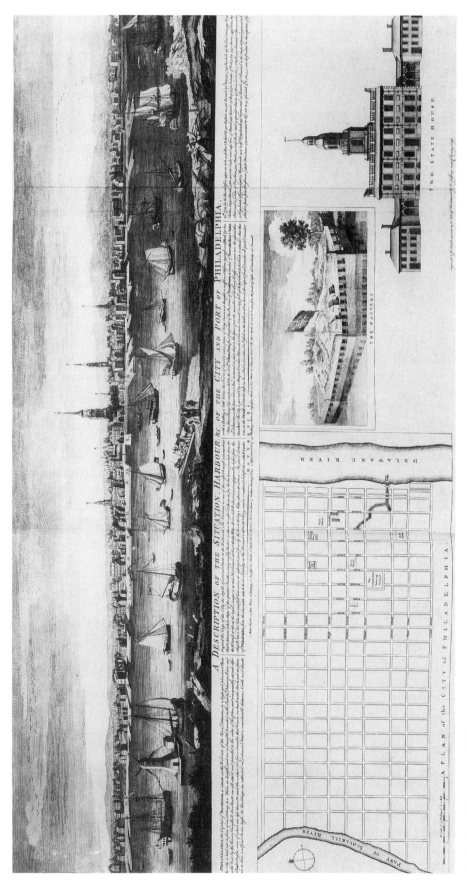

By the late 18th century, Philadelphia was the largest city in the American colonies. *(Library of Congress)*

points for American goods destined for the Atlantic trade. Thus, they represented crucial points of connection in an extensive network that linked Europe and the American interior.

The most active and important participants in this economic network were urban merchants. They supplied rural merchants with imported goods in exchange for exportable raw materials and foodstuffs. Moreover, by the end of the 17th century, merchants in the Northern seaports had developed complex commercial operations that included transportation as well as distribution. Colonial-owned ships carried goods along the coast of the American colonies, to the West Indies, and to England and Europe. The expansion of colonial shipping spurred the growth of the urban economies by creating work for local artisans and laborers, especially in the shipbuilding industry. The profits from trade did not benefit everyone in the cities, however. The Northern port towns offered remarkable prosperity to some, but recurring unemployment and poverty to others. Throughout the 18th century the urban social structure became increasingly stratified, with a growing distance between the few at the top and the majority at the bottom. Especially in Boston, this economic inequality contributed to sharp divisions in local politics; on the eve of the American Revolution, lower-class antagonism toward the ruling elite added considerably to the intensity of the protests against British policy.

Southern Cities. The main cities and towns in the South were neither as large nor as important as their Northern counterparts in the 17th century, but their size and significance increased in the 18th century. Charleston, South Carolina, grew from a population of around 4,000 in 1730 to over 16,000 in 1790. Baltimore's population growth was even more dramatic, rising from around 100 in 1750 to 13,500 in 1790. For the most part, however, these and other Southern towns did not develop the economic complexity that marked the Northern cities. In the colonial era, Southern merchants did not gain control of the shipping business, nor did the import-export trade in the ports contribute significantly to the development of local manufacturing and other sorts of enterprise. Throughout the 18th century and on into the 19th, the urban economy in the South remained subservient to the dominant slave economy in the countryside.

Bibliography: Bailyn, Bernard, *The New England Merchants in the Seventeenth Century* (Harvard Univ. Press, 1955); Bridenbaugh, Carl, *Cities in Revolt: Urban Life in America* (1955; reprinted, Oxford Univ. Press, 1971); Nash, Gary B., *The Urban Crucible: Social Change, Political Consciousness, and the Origins of the American Revolution* (Harvard Univ. Press, 1979).

Gregory H. Nobles
Georgia Institute of Technology

CLAIBORNE, WILLIAM (1587-1677) Born in England, Claiborne was appointed the surveyor of the Virginia colony (1621) and then served as secretary of state (1626-37, 1652-60). He began trading actively with Indians on the shores of the Chesapeake in 1627-28. After Claiborne received a license to trade corn, furs, and other commodities in New England and Nova Scotia, he purchased Kent Island in Chesapeake Bay from the Indians and established a trading settlement (1631). Claiborne soon came into conflict with Cecilius Calvert, the proprietor of Maryland, who charged Claiborne with inciting Indians against the Maryland colonists. Petty warfare followed, and while Claiborne was away in England, Governor Leonard Calvert of Maryland reduced Kent Island to submission (1637) and put it under the colony's jurisdiction (1638). After he was made treasurer of Virginia (1642), Claiborne joined Richard Ingle in driving Governor Calvert into Virginia, while they took control of

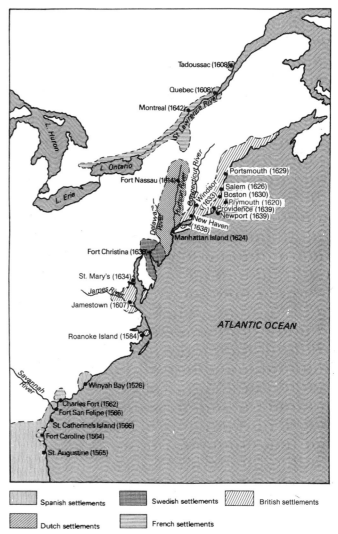

Cities and towns. *(Martin Greenwald Associates, Inc.)*

Maryland (1644-46). Claiborne was later a member of the governing commission of Maryland (1652-57).

CLARK, ABRAHAM (1726-94)   A lawyer and signer of the Declaration of Independence, he was born in Elizabethtown, New Jersey. Clark studied law informally as a means of settling land disputes. Siding with the patriot cause, he became a member of the New Jersey committee of safety (1774). Clark sat in the New Jersey provincial congress (1775) and helped draft the state's first constitution. He then served in the Second Continental Congress (1776-78; 1779-83) and signed the Declaration of Independence. After the Revolution, Clark was a delegate to the Annapolis Convention (1786), where he urged a stronger union among the states.

George Rogers Clark's Revolutionary War exploits helped to secure the Northwest Territory for the United States. *(Library of Congress)*

CLARK, GEORGE ROGERS (1752-1818)   A frontier leader and soldier born near Charlottesville, Virginia, Clark was an explorer and surveyor in the Ohio Valley and in Kentucky (then claimed by Virginia) before the Revolution. When the Revolution broke out, the Virginia legislature made him commander of frontier militia to provide protection of the western region. After he recruited 200 men in May 1778 to rid the Illinois territory of Indians and other enemy forces, he captured Kaskaskia, Cahokia, and Vincennes. The British recaptured Vincennes in October, but Clark and his men retook it in a daring attack (February

1779). As a brigadier general (1780-82), Clark successfully attacked the Shawnee and defended St. Louis against the British.

Clark's actions during the war helped to secure the Northwest Territory for the United States under the peace terms of the Treaty of Paris (1783). He used his own funds for his campaigns and never received any reimbursement. Consequently, Clark found himself in debt, a condition that continued for the rest of his life. His last military expedition was against the Wabash tribes (1786). The same year, Clark was relieved of his duties after James Wilkinson led an intrigue against him. For the next several years, Clark was active along the Mississippi River, especially for French interests. He took refuge in St. Louis (1798) to avoid surrendering his French commission as a major general. He then lived near Louisville, Kentucky, until his death.

See also Paris, Treaty of.

CLASS   In the Federalist Number 10, James Madison wrote that American society was made up of "different classes, actuated by different sentiments and views." If "class" means simply an economic and social rank order, there can be no dispute, for clearly such a social class system was in place. It extended from commercial planters and slave owners, to subsistence farmers, indentured servants, and finally to the slaves themselves, and, moving from the country to the city, from wealthy merchants to professionals, shopkeepers, artisans, laborers, and included the urban poor. The size of each category is difficult to estimate and varied between regions, but in 1760 slaves constituted 23 percent of the colonial population, servants and landless workers perhaps 15 percent, small farmers just over 30 percent, workers and artisans another 20 percent, with the wealthiest 10 percent of the colonial class structure composed of planters, merchants, and their associated crust of lawyers and other professions. This tenth controlled nearly half of the country's wealth.

These differences contributed to notably different standards of living between groups. At the lowest levels of the system, slaves, servants, and the poorest urban and rural workers might suffer seasons below the level of subsistence; at best landless workers labored from hand to mouth. But the combination of rapid expansion, a relatively limitless base of land to the west, and a tradition of geographic mobility provided for many otherwise poor people the opportunity for economic improvement. "Roast beef and apple pie" comfort was probably attainable for the majority of white Americans at any rate. Upper class standards included far more—not only fine clothing, transport, homes, and the amenities but the chance to enjoy music, art, and books. Education too, outside of New England with its tradition of free schools, was largely the province of the wealthy, especially at its higher levels.

Social Mobility and Class Consciousness.   By comparison with Europe, this class system was remarkably open, excepting of course the quarter of the population bound in slavery. There was no titled aristocracy, and although some of the terms of English class privilege found their way to the colonies—country "squire," for example—these could be rather easily acquired along with estates on one's way up the class ladder, for there was considerable social mobility in the colonies. Artisans worked their way from apprenticeship to journeyman status, and if few attained the position of master, enough did to fuel the vision of the self-made man. In the booming imperial economy of the 18th century, many men rose to wealth through trade; status was something that money could buy in America.

The issue of "class" becomes more complicated if it is broadened to include Madison's notion of "sentiments"— what another age would call "class consciousness." By the time of the Revolution wealthy merchants and planters certainly had a self-conscious view of their world, one they actively sought to protect through alliance, compromise, and rebellion when necessary. The middling groups, however, tended to view the system in more benign terms as one of pronounced equality, a kind of middle-class paradise. Class consciousness on the part of the masses, however, was a phenomenon more akin to an industrial society of manufacturers and workers. That society was already being born at the end of the Revolution; it would bring with it the growth of capitalism as well as commerce, increasing concentrations of wealth and power, an end to independent artisan labor, and a new and more rigid class system.

Bibliography: Main, Jackson Turner, *The Social Structure of Revolutionary America* (Books On Demand, 1965).

John Mack Faragher
Mount Holyoke College

CLINTON, GEORGE (1686-1761) A   colonial   administrator, he was born in England and was a captain in the Royal Navy by 1716. He served as commodore and governor of Newfoundland in 1731 and commander of a Mediterranean squadron in 1737. In 1743, heavily in debt and needing more money, he asked for and was eventually appointed governor of New York, but he lacked the ability to govern in civil matters and allowed others to speak for him and assume his duties. He was relieved of the position in 1753.   Still a naval officer, he had been promoted

through the ranks to admiral by 1747. He returned to England and served in Parliament (1754-60).

During the Revolutionary War, George Clinton pursued both military and political careers. *(Library of Congress)*

CLINTON, GEORGE (1739-1812) A   Revolutionary War soldier and political leader, Clinton was born in Little Britain, New York. After serving in the French and Indian War, he started a law practice (1762). He served in the New York assembly (1768-75) and the Second Continental Congress (1775).   The same year he was appointed brigadier general of the New York state militia and defended New York City and the Hudson River. Although he was militarily incompetent, he was given a second commission by Congress. He was elected governor of New York in 1777 and served until 1795, during which time he unsuccessfully opposed New York's ratification of the Constitution. A follower of Thomas Jefferson during the 1790s, Clinton retired from governorship (1795) but later returned (1801-04). He was elected (1804) as vice president under Jefferson but was turned down for the presidential nomination in 1808. While serving a second term as vice president, Clinton cast the deciding vote (1811) that refused to renew the charter of the 1st Bank of the United States.

CLINTON, SIR HENRY (1738-95)   A soldier from the time he was 13, Clinton came from a military family. He served in the Seven Years War as aide-de-camp to Ferdinand of Brunswick (1760-62), and in 1772 became a major general. He had a seat in Parliament, but most of his time was spent in active service in America in the Revolutionary War. After fighting in the Battle of Bunker Hill (1775) and the Battle of Long Island (1776), he was made a lieutenant general. Clinton succeeded General William Howe as commander in chief in North America in 1778, campaigned with Cornwallis in South Carolina (1779), and captured Charleston (1780). Clinton resigned in 1781 and returned to England, where he published his *Narrative of the Campaign of 1781 in North America* (1783). He later served as governor of Gibraltar (1794-95).

CLYMER, GEORGE (1739-1813)   A signer of the Declaration of Independence and the Constitution, Clymer grew up in Philadelphia and entered business with his uncle, a merchant. He sided with the patriot cause during the early stages of the Revolutionary War era and in the Philadelphia Tea Party (1773) helped force the resignation of merchants appointed by the British to sell tea. After serving as a member of the Pennsylvania Council of Safety (1775-76) he sat in the Second Continental Congress (1776-78; 1780-83) and signed the Declaration of Independence. He worked on numerous government committees during the Revolutionary War and was a Pennsylvania delegate to the Constitutional Convention.

COATS, WILLIAM (died 1752)   The explorer Coats joined Hudson's Bay Company as a sea captain in 1726 and regularly sailed annual supply ships. In the 1740s he began compiling a geography of the Bay and in 1749 was selected to renew exploration of its eastern coast. His notes and maps were not published in his lifetime, for in 1751 he was dismissed from the service for private trading and he died, perhaps by his own hand, a year later. In the 1850s these manuscripts were published, revealing one of the most thorough and complete surveys of the North American coastline.

COCKING, MATTHEW (1743-1799)   An English explorer, fur trader, and employee of the Hudson's Bay Company, Cocking was sent in 1772 to explore the interior for the Company; his journal provided the first clear account of the country and of the Saskatchewan inhabitants. The next year he further explored the country east of Lake Winnipeg, helping to open it to the exploitation of British traders. After several years in Indian country as the master of several trading posts, he returned to England where he died, leaving annuities to the children of his Indian wife.

See also Hudson's Bay Company.

CODDINGTON, WILLIAM (1601-78)   Founder of Newport, Rhode Island, William Coddington was born in England and came to the Massachusetts Bay Colony as assistant director in 1630. He served as treasurer from 1634 to 1636 and deputy from 1636 to 1637, but his support of Anne Hutchinson in the Antinomian controversy drove him from the colony in 1638. He joined Roger Williams in Rhode Island until he established himself in 1639 as governor of South Aquidneck and of its new town Newport. By 1656 he had accepted the rule of Williams' Providence Plantations. He became a Quaker, thrived in trade, and in 1674, 1675, and 1678 was magistrate of Rhode Island and Providence Plantations.

COERCIVE ACTS (1774)   The Coercive, or Intolerable, Acts were passed by Parliament in reaction to the Boston Tea Party. King George III believed the time had come to subdue the Americans and by force, if necessary. Accordingly, Parliament enacted four statutes in the spring of 1774 designed to punish Massachusetts and serve as a warning to the other colonies.

The first of these Coercive Acts, quickly dubbed the Intolerable Acts in America, closed the port of Boston until the East India Company was paid for its loss of the tea. The second act altered the charter of Massachusetts by strengthening the hand of government. Now the king would appoint the Council hitherto elected by the lower house. The third act granted magistrates accused of capital crimes the right to trial either in England or another colony. The last act allowed the governor to quarter troops in uninhabited buildings close to the scene of trouble. A fifth statute, unrelated to the Coercive Acts but passed at the same time, added to the colonists' dread: The Quebec Act recognized Roman Catholicism as that province's established religion and established a government without a lower assembly or trial by jury. Intended to isolate Massachusetts Bay from the other colonies, the Coercive Acts failed dismally. Identifying with Boston's cause, colonists from Maine to Georgia flooded the town with money, supplies, and food, while calls for a continental congress came from several towns.

See also Boston Tea Party; British Empire; Colonial Government; Quebec Act.

Bibliography: Ammerman, David, *In the Common Cause* (Norton, 1975).

COFITACHIQUE, LADY OF (flourished 1540)   In 1540, in the region where present-day Georgia and South Carolina meet, Hernando De Soto was received hospitably by the ruler of Cofitachique, whom the Spanish chroniclers called "the Lady of Cofitachique." De Soto was disappointed that she had no gold or silver. The Lady offered the Spaniards pearls instead, and De Soto took 350 pounds away with him. The Indians were said to be the most civilized the Spaniards had met and the land good for settlement. However, De Soto continued his journey, taking the Lady with him to insure the good behavior of the Indians he would meet. The Lady managed to escape, as did a black slave who belonged to a Spanish soldier. The Lady and the slave were later reported to have returned to her village.

COLBERT, JEAN-BAPTISTE, MARQUIS DE SEIGNELAY (1619-83)   A French finance minister who promoted French settlement in North America, Colbert was born in Rheims to a family of well-established bankers whose members had assumed an important political role since the 15th century. Beginning his career with his uncle, Colbert was noticed by Cardinal Mazarin, with whom he quickly advanced to the position of intendant of personal affairs. On his deathbed, Mazarin recommended Colbert to the young Louis XIV. Mazarin died in 1661 and in that same year Colbert became France's finance minister. In 1665 he assumed additional responsibilities for the navy, commerce, and forests, among others.

Colbert created and built the modern notion of the state. In the colonial domain, he rebuilt the French navy and, including the land acquired overseas in his mercantilist schemes, is credited for the development of French North America. Colbert took a personal interest in New France, overseeing the smallest details. But, as was often the case in France, demands of warfare in Europe prevented the fullest pursuit of colonial development. When Colbert died, the Iroquois were still a threat to New France, and La Salle was still struggling to establish France's effective control of the Mississippi.

Bibliography: Wolf, John B., *Louis XIV* (W. W. Norton, 1968).

COLDEN, CADWALLADER (1688-1776)   A colonial physician and scientist born in Ireland and brought up in Scotland, Colden graduated from the University of Edinburgh (1705) and went to London to study medicine. He emigrated to America in 1710 and settled in Philadelphia, where he had a medical practice. In 1718 he moved to New York, where he became a member of the governor's coun-

cil (1721). While serving in public posts, Colden published studies on cancer, small pox, and yellow fever and classified American plants. Colden also wrote the *History of the Five Indian Nations* (1727) as well as scientific treatises. Colden served as the lieutenant governor of New York (1761-76) during the critical period of colonial protest. Colden was a Loyalist who never had great popularity, especially when he refused to condemn the Stamp Act in 1765. After the Declaration of Independence, Colden retired to his Long Island estate.

See also New York.

COLDEN, JANE (1724-66)   A botanist from Newburgh, New York, Colden was the daughter of Cadwallader and Alice Colden, who had emigrated from Scotland in 1710. Her father studied medicine at the University of Edinburgh but became involved in New York City politics before moving his family to Newburgh and pursuing his interest in botany. Realizing that Jane had the mind and temperament of a scientist as well as an interest in the garden, he undertook guiding her through a rigorous educational program in botany. Although Jane never learned Latin, discipline and enthusiasm led her to compile a catalogue of over 300 local plants by 1757. Her father introduced her to other prominent botanists, some of whom visited Jane in Newburgh, others with whom she corresponded. She discovered and named the gardenia, after American naturalist Alexander Garden, and that discovery led to her only publication, in the Edinburgh Philosophical Society's *Essays and Observations*. She probably discontinued her botanical work after her marriage in 1759.

COLLEGE OF PHILADELPHIA   With its origins as a Charity School, the Academy of Philadelphia was founded in 1740 at the instigation of Benjamin Franklin. In 1755 the academy began to grant degrees and became known as the College of Philadelphia, later becoming the University of Pennsylvania. It was the first college in America not founded for the purposes of a theological education but instead had a liberal curriculum. It was also the first school in America to offer professional training in medicine. Ten signers of the Declaration of Independence and nine signers of the Constitution were associated with the college.

COLLEGES   Nine colleges, all for young men, existed in the colonies at the time of the Revolution. They were:

Name/Founded/Religious Affiliation
Harvard College (1636), Congregational
College of William and Mary (1693), Anglican
Yale College (1701), Congregational
College of New Jersey (Princeton) (1746), Presbyterian
College of Philadelphia (University of Pennsylvania)

(1754), Unaffiliated

King's College (Columbia) (1754), Anglican

College of Rhode Island (Brown) (1764), Baptist

Queen's College (Rutgers) (1766), Dutch Reformed

Dartmouth College (1769), Congregational

Harvard College, named for the minister John Harvard, who left his library and half his estate to the college, first offered instruction in Cambridge in 1638. Although approximately 70 percent of the early graduates became Puritan ministers, the college's charter referred to the goals of "the advancement of all good literature arts and sciences" and to "the education of the English and Indian youth of this Country" as well as to the training of "a learned and able ministry." William and Mary, where instruction began around 1729, stated similar purposes. Yale, whose classes predated William and Mary's, was founded by strict Congregationalists (Puritans) who believed that Harvard had grown too liberal. The other colonial colleges, founded after the Great Awakening, were less strictly denominational.

Colonial colleges modeled their curricula on the English universities at Oxford and Cambridge. Fields of study included Latin, Greek, Hebrew, classical literature, theology, logic, ethics, physics, geometry, astronomy, and rhetoric. The College of Philadelphia, influenced by the practical Benjamin Franklin, offered courses in agriculture, chemistry, mechanics, government, commerce, and modern languages. Modern mathematics and sciences were introduced by other colleges, and the study of medicine was offered at the College of Philadelphia in 1765 and at King's College in 1767.

Bibliography: Button, H. Warren, and Provenzo, Eugene F., Jr., *History of Education and Culture in America* (Prentice-Hall, 1983); Handlin, Oscar and Mary F., *The American College and American Culture* (McGraw-Hill, 1970).

Suzanne Greene Chapelle
Morgan State University

COLONIAL GOVERNMENT Colonial government progressed through several stages in the 170 years between the chartering of the Virginia Company and the Declaration of Independence. As the colonies grew, their desire to control their own affairs also developed, which put them in conflict with the authority of the English Crown and the interests of the British Empire.

1606-59. The English settlers who established themselves as freemen and the proprietors empowered by royal charters established the fundamental structures of colonial government. The first years of nearly every settlement were marked by a disparity between expectations and reality, one result of which was the growth of freemen assemblies not envisioned by the proprietors. The early governments were not democracies: Only freemen (invariably white, male property-holders) participated, and royal governors and proprietors exerted a strong, if unsteady, influence. Furthermore, although many freemen desired an assembly to represent their interests, they assumed in accordance with 18th century political thought that aristocratic authority should be represented in the figure of the governor. Other freemen, especially those far from the port towns in which authority was centered, were simply apathetic. Yet efforts by the English government to collect customs duties through the Laud Commission (1634-41) and Parliamentary Commission for Plantations (1643-59) were ineffective, and a significant number of royal governors left their offices in disgrace because of mismanagement or undue self-aggrandizement.

The 1606 charter of the Virginia Company granted its profit-seeking proprietors governance of the settlement, reflecting the notion current in the English government that proprietary charters extended its economic but not its political domain. The governing council appointed in London disintegrated in Virginia as disease, starvation, and Indians harassed the settlement, and the settlers depleted their supplies while prospecting for gold. John Smith, the forceful governor elected in 1608, organized the colony. A succession of aristocratic governors extended political and economic prerogatives to ordinary settlers in an effort to gain cooperation and revitalize the finances of the company. In 1619, Sir George Yeardley presided at the first meeting of an American elected representative assembly, the House of Burgesses. In 1624 the Crown dissolved the moribund company, declaring Virginia a royal colony, appointing a royal governor, and allowing the assembly to meet in an expedient attempt to collect customs duties. The assembly focused on the interests of freemen and their families, beginning around 1650 to define in law slave status for Africans, who worked on the tobacco plantations of wealthy freemen families.

In 1619 the Pilgrims received a charter and emigrated with a group of non-Pilgrims, landing in 1620 in Plymouth after signing the Mayflower Compact. The compact demanded settlers' obedience to law and allowed freemen to vote for a governor and an assembly, which Pilgrims dominated for several decades. The dispersion of towns from the nucleus of authority—a common impediment to the authority of the early governments—resulted in a 1636 determination to allow each town two deputies, chosen by freemen, to sit with the governor and his assistants in a General Court, which promptly prohibited the governor and his assistants from enacting legislation and granting land. The Pilgrims gradually lost governance as the settlement expanded.

A 1629 charter created the Massachusetts Bay Company, which, because of an oversight in its charter, was able to move

COLONIAL GOVERNMENT: TOPIC GUIDE

GENERAL

Blue Laws
British Empire (see **Topic Guide**)
Common Law
Deference
Democracy
Lotteries
Mercantilism (see **Topic Guide**)
Monarchs, English
    Divine Right of Kings
    English Civil War
    Glorious Revolution
    Regicides

Postal Service
Proprietary Colonies
Regulators
Religion, Freedom of
Republicanism
Royal Colonies
Salutary Neglect
Social Welfare
Suffrage
Wage and Price Controls
Whig Ideology
Women, Legal Status of

COLONIES

Connecticut
    Charter Oak
    Fundamental Orders of
        Connecticut (1639)
Delaware
Dominion of New England
French Colonies
    Coutume de Paris
Georgia
Maritime Provinces
Maryland
    Maryland Civil War (1655)
    Toleration Act
Massachusetts
    Cambridge Agreement
    Council for New England
    General Court, Massachusetts
    Massachusetts Bay Company
    Massachusetts Body of Liberties
        (1641)
    Mayflower Compact
    New England Company
    Virginia Company of Plymouth
New Hampshire
    Exeter Compact
New Jersey
    Elizabethtown Associates
    Concessions and Agreements of
        New Jersey (1665)

    Laws, Concessions, and Agreements
        (1677)
New Netherland
New York
    Albany Convention (1689-90)
    Charter of Liberties, New York
        (1683)
North Carolina
    Fundamental Constitutions of
        Carolina (1669)
Pennsylvania
    Charter of Privileges (1701)
    Frame of Government
    Great Law of Pennsylvania (1682)
Rhode Island
South Carolina
    Fundamental Constitutions of
        Carolina (1669)
Spanish Colonies
Swedish Colonies (New Sweden)
Virginia
    Fairfax Proprietary
    Virginia Company of London
    Virginia Declaration of Rights
        (1776)
    Virginia Resolves (1765) and Association
        (1774)
    Virginia Statute for Religious Freedom
        (1786)

COLONIAL GOVERNMENT: TOPIC GUIDE (continued)

INTERCOLONIAL

Albany Congress, The (1754)
Articles of Confederation
Committees of Correspondence
Continental Association (1774)
Continental Congress, First (1774)

Continental Congress, Second
  (1775-81)
New England Confederation
  (United Colonies) (1643)
Stamp Act Congress

BIOGRAPHIES

Alden, John
Allerton, Isaac
Argall, Sir Samuel
Berkeley, Lady Frances
Bowdoin, James
Bradford, William (1590-1657)
Brewster, William
Byrd, William (1674-1744)
Calvert, Cecilius
Calvert, George
Carver, John
Claiborne, William
Coddington, William
Conant, Roger
Cranston, John
Dale, Sir Thomas
De Lancey Family
De La Warr, Thomas West, 3rd Baron
Dudley, Joseph
Dudley, Thomas
Eaton, Theophilus
Endecott, John
Gates, Sir Thomas
Harrie (Harvey), John
Haynes, John

Heathcote, Caleb
Kieft, Willem
Lloyd, David
Lovelace, Francis
Ludlow, Roger
Mayhew, Thomas (1621-57)
Minuit, Peter
Moody, Lady Deborah
Morton, Thomas
Oglethorpe, James Edward
Penn Family
Penn, William
Pott, John
Printz, Johan Bjornsson
Rising, Johan Classon
Smith, John (?1580-1631)
Standish, Miles
Stuyvesant, Peter
Williams, Roger
Winslow, Edward (1595-1655)
Winthrop, John (1606-76)
Wyatt, Sir Francis
Yeardley, Sir George
Youngs, John

---

its proprietorship to the colony, establishing itself as the first American self-governing commonwealth. In 1630, Governor John Winthrop called an assembly of freemen and directed the formation of a General Court, which in violation of the charter restricted freemanship to church members. After 1634 freemen (a small minority of the population) sent deputies to the General Court, which elected the governor. In 1644 the legislature divided into a bicameral organization, not only giving the deputies a distinct voice but also marking an important division—the governor and his council representing centralized authority and the deputies representing towns often far from the center of authority. In 1646 the Court defended its legislation by asserting its independence of English law. During the 1630s settlements spread from Massachusetts into Connecticut and Rhode Island, generally approximat-

ing the Massachusetts model of government, although with complete religious freedom in Rhode Island. In 1643 the United Colonies of New England, the first intercolonial political organization, was formed by Massachusetts, Plymouth, Connecticut, and New Haven for their common defense.

In 1632, Lord Baltimore received a charter for Maryland that allowed a manorial structure of government in which the proprietor could distribute land and political prerogatives in return for proceeds from the use of the land. Royal governor Leonard Calvert called an assembly in 1634. By the 1640s this assembly had gained the right to meet separately and to introduce legislation, and by the 1650s had repudiated proprietary authority altogether and sought a government deriving authority only from the Maryland House of Burgesses. Proprietary control was re-established with force by

Philip Calvert, who handed power to the 3rd Lord Baltimore in 1661.

1660-1720. These tumultuous years were marked by the 1664 absorption of the Dutch colony of New Netherland (renamed New York) into the British Empire, the establishment of the Carolinas (1663) and New Jersey (1664) as proprietary settlements, the establishment of New Hampshire as a royal colony (1680), and the founding of Pennsylvania (1680). A series of legislative acts (1664-71) defined lifelong servitude for black slaves, and there were rebellions against governmental authority in several colonies. There was also a strong English effort to force the colonies into a mercantilist system, commencing with the Navigation Act of 1660.

The creation of governments in the years from 1606 to 1660 involved the formation of a social elite to sit in the assemblies. These men were not aristocrats as in England but entrepreneurs of recent and unsteady success who wielded power Parliament would not have allotted them in England. Although the rebellions against governmental authority in Virginia (1676), Carolina (1677), Massachusetts (1689), New York (1689), and Maryland (1689), were triggered by different events unique to each colony, they also represented a challenge against government by those who desired power and recognition of their interests but found themselves alienated from the assemblies or channels of royal power. When ambitious entrepreneurs such as Virginian Nathaniel Bacon became frustrated with the distribution and use of political power, they challenged the right of other entrepreneurs to govern.

In the early 1680s, William Penn received charters for Pennsylvania and Delaware. His Pennsylvania charter granted him total governance, stipulating only that legislation be approved by an assembly, that the Navigation Acts be observed, and that powers to review legislation, hear appeals in court, and add taxes lay with the English government. Penn faced an unruly assembly that gained from him in 1696 the power to initiate legislation and in 1701 a new Frame of Government that created representative governments for Pennsylvania and Delaware. Penn spent much of the last two decades of his life trying to resolve disputes with the assembly.

The English government sought vigorously to control the colonies through the Lords of Trade (1660-95) and the Board of Trade (after 1696), the Dominion of New England (1685-89), and the conversion of most of the settlements into royal colonies. After the 1684 annulment of the Massachusetts charter, Sir Edmund Andros, royal governor of the Dominion of New England, attempted to center authority in himself at the expense of the assemblies—a brief, doomed attempt that resulted in a compromise between colonial and imperial governmental power. Throughout the colonies, royal governors and imperial officials commissioned to enforce the Navigation Acts and Acts of Trade added a new dimension to colonial government, one that fostered a scorn for English authority and accentuated the importance of the assemblies for the furtherance of freemen's interests. The colonies resisted this imperial system not only with bribes and smuggling but also with armed insurrection in the rebellions of 1689.

1721-63. In these provincial years, Britain's policy of salutary neglect shielded the colonies from the strictures of mercantilism. The Crown established royal government in North and South Carolina (1729) and chartered Georgia (1732). After decades of social fluidity and the protests of the late 17th century, a stable class emerged as the empowered in society and politics. Southern planters, Northern land-owning descendants of the settling families, and urban merchants involved in the Atlantic trade came to dominate politics through the assemblies. Government became a field of competition not only between indigenous elites contending among themselves for sets in the government but also between royal governors and the assemblies.

Royal governors sought to consolidate their power at the expense of that of the assemblies, opposing the expansion of representation to newly-settled areas and exercising their prerogatives of convening and adjourning the assemblies. Although they never strictly enforced the Navigation Acts and the Acts of Trade, the governors entrenched royal patronage positions in the colonial government and established themselves as the sole channels of imperial authority, closing the customary channels through which the assemblies had appealed to the English government. Consequently, the colonial elite in its quest for power found itself alienated from the governors, addressing only the American freemen and lacking a say in English government when salutary neglect came to an end.

1764-76. These eventful years encompass the imperial crisis, in which the English government sought to raise revenue in the colonies and govern them more closely and in which the colonies responded by denouncing and ultimately circumventing the imperial part of colonial government. Quasi-governmental bodies evolved quickly as assemblymen, their followers, and others resisted the governors and imperial agents, often after the governor had dissolved the assembly.

In 1764 a Boston town meeting responding to the Sugar Act denounced taxation without representation and suggested a concerted protest by the colonies. Later in 1764 the Massachusetts House of Representatives instructed a Committee of Correspondence to communicate with the other colonies. In 1765 (and in 1769 with a stronger statement by George Mason), the Virginia House of Burgesses asserted its right to legislate for Virginia. Also in 1765, the Stamp Act Congress, an important advance in intercolonial cooperation, objected to another attempt to raise revenue and broached the possibility of nonimportation of English goods, a possibility realized intermittently in the next decade. After the reading of Samuel Adams's 1768 Massachusetts Circular Letter denouncing taxation without representation, Governor Bernard dissolved the assembly, which merely circumvented his authority by holding new elections that brought more patriots into the assembly. Similarly, Governor Botetourt dissolved the Virginia assembly in 1769.

Between 1772 and 1774 resistance in Massachusetts grew as Governor Hutchinson began to receive his salary from the Crown instead of the assembly, and the Massachusetts charter was dissolved and a governing council of royal appointees was installed. In 1773 the Virginia Committee of Correspondence, which included Patrick Henry and Thomas Jefferson, began to articulate the notion of complete legislative independence. In 1774 the First Continental Congress declared the Intolerable Acts unconstitutional, and in 1776 the Second Continental Congress voted for independence. The demise of colonial government was followed by the adoption of the Articles of Confederation (1777) and the composition of state constitutions.

See also specific colonies and individuals; Continental Congress, First; Continental Congress, Second; Declaration of Independence; Mercantilism; Navigation Acts; Salutary Neglect; Stamp Act.

Bibliography: Andrews, Charles M., *The Colonial Background of the American Revolution* (Yale Univ. Press, 1931); Bailyn, Bernard, *The Origins of American Politics* (Knopf, 1968); Christie, Ian R., and Labaree, Benjamin W., Empire or Independence, 1760-1776 (Norton, 1976); Kammen, Michael, Deputyes and Libertyes: *The Origins of Representative Government in Colonial America* (Knopf, 1969); Kammen, Michael, ed., *Politics and Society in Colonial America: Democracy or Deference?* (Holt, Rinehart, 1967); Maier, Pauline, *From Resistance to Revolution: Colonial Radicals and the Development of Opposition to Britain,* 1765-1776 (Knopf, 1972).

COLUMBUS, CHRISTOPHER (c.1451-1506) Columbus was born into the family of a weaver, Domenico Columbo, in Genoa, Italy, in 1451. At 19 he went to sea, eventually settling in Lisbon, where he conceived the idea of sailing west to the Indies. However, Bartholomew Dias's discovery of the Cape of Good Hope ended Columbus's chances for Portuguese support, and he solicited several other European courts for royal patronage.

In 1492, Queen Isabella of Castile decided to back Columbus and gave him three ships. The *Niña,* the *Pinta,* and the *Santa Maria* left Palos on August 3, 1492. The long voyage tested the willpower of Columbus and terrified his men, but on October 12 the lookout sighted San Salvador in the Bahamas. The fleet went on to discover Cuba and Hispaniola, where Columbus left 40 men before sailing home.

The voyages of Christopher Columbus stimulated exploration of the New World, but he failed to attain great wealth as a result. *(Library of Congress)*

Other Voyages.   Isabella commanded Columbus to sail again immediately with 17 ships and 1,000 colonists. At Hispaniola he found that the men he had left there had been killed by the Indians. He established the colony of Isabella, also on Hispaniola, and explored further, returning to Spain in June 1496.

In Spain, many returned colonists criticized Columbus, but Isabella continued to have faith in him. On his third expedition he landed on the coast of Venezuela, discovering South America. On Hispaniola, meanwhile, discontented colonists succeeded in replacing Columbus, getting Francisco de Bobadilla appointed governor in 1500. De Bobadilla arrested Columbus and sent him back to Spain in chains, where Isabella released him.

In 1502, Columbus made his last voyage, exploring the Central American coast. Marooned for a year, he returned to Spain in 1504 to find that Isabella had died. With his chief support gone, the governorship and other titles denied him, Columbus died in Valladolid.

See also Exploration; Spanish Colonies.

Bibliography: *Fernandez-Armesto, Ferdinand, Columbus and the Conquest of the Impossible (Weidenfeld and Nicolson, 1974); Morison, Samuel Eliot, Admiral of the Ocean Sea: A Life of Christopher Columbus* (Little, Brown, 1942).

Thomas C. Thompson
University of California, Riverside

COMMITTEES OF CORRESPONDENCE   Samuel Adams organized the first Committee of Correspondence in Boston in 1772, and by 1773 there were some 80 other committees in Massachusetts and more in other colonies. The Virginia House of Burgesses created a committee with legislative standing "to obtain the most early and authentic intelligence" of British actions affecting America "and to keep up and maintain a correspondence and communication with our sister colonies." This intercolonial committee system was the principal channel for directing public opinion in the years leading up to the Revolution. In 1775 the Continental Congress appointed a five-man Committee of Correspondence to organize foreign contacts.

COMMITTEES OF OBSERVATION AND SAFETY   First appointed by the Massachusetts legislature in October 1774, with John Hancock as chairman, the Massachusetts Committee of Safety was empowered to call out the militia and seize military supplies. Other colonies soon established similiar Committees of Observation and Safety. In July 1775 the Continental Congress sanctioned such committees as the best way to organize the local war effort. The committees provided the Continental Army with men and matériel and generally acted as ad hoc government during the Revolutionary War. Their operations were suspended as the states adopted their own constitutions.

COMMON LAW   That part of the English legal system based on custom and precedent, common law was distinguished from statute and from laws arising from equity, maritime, or other special branches of jurisprudence. The original Virginia "Lawes of 1612" were inspired by military example but were later replaced by the extension of common law protection to that colony. Other charters, such as that of Massachusetts, enjoined the authorities to "make no laws repugnant to the laws of England," allowing the General Court of the colony to argue in 1646 that "our government

itselfe it is framed according to our charter, and the fundamental and common lawes of England, and carried on according to the same." Common law was likewise extended to all the English colonies in America, where it became the basis of the legal systems of all the states except Louisiana, which continues to be governed by the Code Napoleon.

In 1728, Daniel Dulany, a leading Maryland lawyer and politician declared that "the Common Law takes in the Law of Nature, the Law of Reason, and the Revealed Law of God." In general, however, the practice of law in the colonies was bereft of the legal expertise and court reports necessary for a system truly based on precedent. Law books were scarce, and the few treatises published in the colonies were designed to familiarize justices of the peace with the broad outlines of jurisprudence. Yet the ideal of the common law as a repository of basic rights and liberties frequently inspired complaint and protest over British attempts to regulate colonial life and commerce—in the struggle, for example, over the vice-admiralty courts, which functioned without juries. In 1761, James Otis disputed the legality of search warrants on the grounds of the common law, and four years later John Adams similarly invoked the tradition to protest the denial of jury trial to John Hancock, arguing that such rights could not be abridged by parliamentary statute. The notion of inalienable rights found in the Declaration of Independence and the bills of rights included in the federal and state constitutions thus derive from the common law tradition. Most of the new state constitutions declared common law a continuing tradition.

Sir William Blackstone's Commentaries on the Laws of England (1765-69), which reduced the common law to a system contained in four volumes, had a great impact on Americans, who by 1775 had purchased as many sets as the English themselves. These books perhaps did more to establish the common law in American practice than anything else.

See also Declaration of Independence.

John Mack Faragher
Mount Holyoke College

COMMON SENSE   One of the most widely disseminated and influential political documents in history, Thomas Paine's *Common Sense* was published in January 1776. Refusing fees in order to allow the greatest possible circulation, Paine unequivocally called for independence: "A government of our own is our natural right." Paine is often considered a rhetorician for his incendiary statements, plain language, and biblical allusions, all of which were departures from 18th-century elite political discussion. Yet his subtle rhetoric sought not only political independence but also a renovation of humankind and society. *Common Sense* sought to instill reason and virtue in its audience, urging upon them "the simple voice of nature and reason." The notion of "common sense" was central to the revolutionary intellectuals, who believed that a healthy society must be united in a common sense, a shared set of assumptions and beliefs. *Common Sense* sought to identify reasonable belief in God and natural law, loyalty to society, and commitment to social equality as this shared set. In a healthy society, government should restrain "our vices," while allowing humankind "happiness" in "uniting our affections."

Bibliography: Foner, Philip S., ed., *The Complete Writings of Thomas Paine*, 2 vols. (Citadel, 1945).

John Saillant
Brown University

COMPAGNIE D'OCCIDENT Compagnie d'Occident, or Mississippi Company, was a business enterprise created on January 1, 1718, by John Law, a financial wizard born in Scotland who had taken the hearts and trust of France by storm. When Louis XIV died on September 1, 1715, his heir was only five years old, and the regency of the kingdom went to his great-uncle, the Duke Philippe d'Orléans. The regent was looking for a solution to the large public debt he had inherited, and Law's schemes seemed so ingenious that he was given a free hand. The timing was perfect for Law, and in 1713 financier Antoine Crozat had received a royal charter giving him monopoly of trade for Louisiana. By December 1716, Crozat had already lost an enormous sum, and in 1717 he asked for and was granted release of all his obligations.

On January 1, 1718, all Crozat's privileges were turned over to the Compagnie d'Occident. Law merged the company with his new creation, the Royal Bank, and also with the East Indian Company. In North America, the Compagnie was given a much larger territory, including Illinois as well as Louisiana. Mining in Illinois was expected to produce quick profits; however, the profits did not materialize and the shares that had been the object of speculation became worthless. Law fled France in 1720.

CONANT, ROGER (c.1592-1679) Settler and governor of Salem, Conant was born in Devonshire, England, and came to Massachusetts in 1623. As a Non-conformist, he left the Puritan colony for Nantucket in 1624, but his name remained on an island in Boston Harbor. He was briefly governor at Cape Ann but moved in 1626 to Naumkeag (now Salem), where he was governor until he was replaced by John Endicott in 1628. His courtesy in accepting Endicott's leadership earned him respect, and he represented Salem in the General Court in 1634. In 1636 he

moved to Beverly to serve as justice of the quarterly court among other public posts.

CONCESSIONS AND AGREEMENTS OF NEW JERSEY (1665) The Concessions and Agreements of New Jersey were issued by Lord John Berkeley and Sir George Carteret, joint proprietors of the colony, on February 10, 1665. The document was designed to attract settlers, hopefully from New England, to the new English colony. Its terms were almost identical to the Concessions of Carolina written six weeks earlier; Carteret and Berkeley were also proprietors there. The New Jersey Concessions outlined the form of government and explained the terms under which land would be granted. Its most important features were representative government, taxation only with consent, annual elections, and freedom of conscience "in matters of Religion."

Bibliography: Boyd, Julian, *Fundamental Laws and Constitutions of New Jersey* (Van Nostrand, 1964).

CONDÉ, FORT A settlement and trading center founded in 1711 by the Sieur de Bienville, on the banks of the lower Mississippi River, Fort Condé was constructed on the site of an earlier settlement named Fort Louis de la Mobile, which was destroyed by flood in 1702. Fort Condé served as capital of the French province of Louisiana from 1711 to 1719. Because of its political and strategic significance, the fort was continuously expanded and strengthened, its original wood stockade being replaced by brick fortifications and a sloping rampart in 1717. In 1763 it became a British possession and was renamed Fort Charlotte. In 1780 it was transferred to Spanish control.

CONFEDERATION CONGRESS (1781-89) Congress under the Articles of Confederation largely continued the politics of its predecessor, the Second Continental Congress. The Confederation Congress carried through the administrative reorganization begun by the old Congress in early 1781, entrusting affairs formerly handled by standing committees to new departments of finance, war, and foreign affairs under independent heads. Robert Morris in particular made substantial progress reorganizing finance (1781-84).

The major success of the Confederation was the conclusion of a favorable peace with Britain. Even before the military victory at Yorktown in October 1781, Congress had appointed a peace commission in Europe to replace the single negotiator. Although the commissioners violated the instruction that no action be taken without consulting France, Congress accepted the provisional peace treaty in April 1783 and made final ratification in January 1784. The treaty acknowledged American independence and established extensive western boundaries for the United

States. The year 1783 also saw the discharge of most of the Continental Army. Discontent with Congress's policies toward the army, however, had earlier led to protests at the Newburgh, New York, camp against arrangements for officers' pay and pensions. Later in the year, Pennsylvania troops mutinied, and Congress left Philadelphia as a result. It spent the rest of its years in Princeton, Annapolis, Trenton, and finally New York.

Congress's most substantial achievement following the peace was the organization of the northwest territories. After accepting Virginia's large cession of land, Congress adopted a report prepared by a committee chaired by Thomas Jefferson setting guidelines for western affairs (1784). Never fully implemented, it however served as a precedent for the Northwest Ordinance of July 13, 1787, which established U.S. policy for the development of the region and the admission of new states.

Despite these successes, the Confederation Congress came under severe criticism during the mid-1780s. These were years of poor morale in Congress: The war was over, attendance was low, and the states were often lax in meeting their financial obligations. Critics charged that Congress was ineffective in foreign policy, military affairs, trade relations, and finance. Britain held forts on American soil and discriminated against American trade. In addition, Congress had difficulties in its economic affairs, lacking authority to regulate trade and without direct power to raise revenue. After several attempts failed to amend the Articles of Confederation, the critics turned to wholesale constitutional revision in 1787. The Confederation Congress conducted its last official business on October 10, 1788 and was soon replaced by a new Congress under a new Constitution.

See also Articles of Confederation; Continental Congress, Second; Northwest Ordinance.

Bibliography: Burnett, Edmund C., *The Continental Congress* (Macmillan, 1941); Jensen, Merrill, *The New Nation: A History of the United States During the Confederation, 1781-1789* (Knopf, 1950); Rakove, Jack N., *The Beginnings of National Politics: An Interpretive History of the Continental Congress* (Knopf, 1979).

Douglas M. Arnold
The Papers of Benjamin Franklin

CONGREGATIONALISTS As a result of the migrations of Pilgrims and Puritans to Massachusetts early in the 17th century, a new denomination ultimately emerged: the Congregationalists. So designated because of their rejection of bishops or synods and their emphasis upon the authority of the local congregation, this denomination had its major and firm base in New England, specifically in Massachusetts, Connecticut, and New Hampshire. So pervasive was its influence in this region that one can speak of a "New England Way" that persisted long after the colonial period and that had impact far beyond the borders of the three colonies.

Congregationalists managed to maintain an impressive degree of homogeneity, discouraging dissent and when deemed necessary, resorting to penalties and punishments to keep the New England Way relatively unsullied. By the early 18th century, however, dissenters (particularly Anglicans, Quakers, and Baptists) had managed to gain footholds. From that time on, agitation against Congregational control continued to build. Not until the 19th century, however, did congregationalism relinquish the last vestiges of its alliance with the several state governments.

If colonial America anywhere had a truly effective establishment of religion, that place would be New England. Every town levied taxes to support the parish church, the often handsome meetinghouse serving as a center for community life as well as for religious life. By 1750, Massachusetts and Connecticut could boast of about 400 Congregational churches in those two colonies alone, a degree of ecclesiastical saturation unmatched anywhere else in North America. Revolutionary sentiment and activity did nothing to weaken or discredit Congregationalism; on the contrary, its political and religious leaders fought side by side for freedom from England's Parliament and from England's Church.

See also Pilgrims; Puritans.

Bibliography: Winslow, Ola E., *Meetinghouse Hill, 1630-1783* (Norton, 1952).

Edwin S. Gaustad
University of California, Riverside

CONNECTICUT Colonial Connecticut, excluding the western land claims, covered approximately 5,000 square miles. The state is divided by the Connecticut River, which flows through the center from north to south. The Housatonic River and its tributary, the Naugatuck, flow through western Connecticut, while eastern Connecticut has a system of small rivers that converge near the southeast corner that form the Thames River. Between upland regions in the northeast and northwest corners, the Connecticut River valley broadens into lowlands around Hartford. A narrow coastal plain includes numerous small sheltered harbors. When Hartford was settled in 1636, there were 6,000 to 7,000 Indians in Connecticut divided into 16 tribes belonging to the loose Algonquin confederation. Except for the Pequot, they generally cooperated with white settlers, sold them land, and lived peacefully close to them.

First Settlements. The first European visitor to Connecticut was the Dutch explorer Adriaen Block, who in 1614 sailed up the Connecticut River to the present site of Windsor. The Dutch built a fort at the present site of Hartford in 1633, the same year in which William Holmes from Plymouth Colony founded a trading post at Windsor. True settlement of the three mother towns of Connecticut began when a group of about 70 dissatisfied inhabitants of Dorchester, led by Roger Ludlow, moved to Windsor in 1635. They settled close to the Plymouth group and bought them out in 1637. Wethersfield was founded in 1635-36 by a group of some 30 families from Watertown. Hartford was founded when Thomas Hooker led a contingent of 100 from Newtown in June 1636 after obtaining legal clearance from the Massachusetts Bay government. Similar motives prompted all three groups of settlers: dissatisfaction with the religious and political leadership of Massachusetts Bay and the attractiveness of fertile farm lands on a navigable river.

Saybrook, at the mouth of the Connecticut River, was established in November 1635. The colony's first governor was John Winthrop, Jr., but its two real leaders were Zion Gardiner, who constructed the fort at Saybrook, and George Fenwick, who ruled over the trading post and fort until it became part of Connecticut in 1644. Puritans led by the Reverend John Davenport and Theophilus Eaton, a wealthy merchant, established their theocracy at Quinnipiac (New Haven) in 1638.

The first serious Indian threat to the colony came from the powerful Pequot, who attacked the fort at Saybrook in 1636. In 1637 Connecticut's river towns assembled a force of 90 men under Captain John Mason, who led a surprise night attack on the Pequot fort at Mystic followed by a horrible slaughter as the English set fire to the fort. Those who surrendered were given as slaves to tribes friendly to the English. The major Indian threat to Connecticut's Puritan mission and orderly expansion had been destroyed. But the Pequot War and the continuing threat of Dutch expansion led the colonies of Connecticut and New Haven to join the New England Confederation (1643-84). As a member of the confederation, Connecticut contributed several hundred men to the fighting in King Philip's War (1675-76), which occurred mainly in Massachusetts and Rhode Island.

Forms of Government. At first, Connecticut's government consisted of eight magistrates named by the Massachusetts General Court, but Connecticut had no intention of remaining part of the Bay Colony and therefore required its own formal instrument of government. Thomas Hooker's 1638 sermon provided the framework for the Fundamental Orders, a civil equivalent of a church covenant, which were adopted in 1639. The orders constituted only a brief outline of government and cannot be considered a constitution in the modern sense.

Connecticut's political integrity was further secured with its charter of 1662.

The restoration of Charles II in 1660 raised questions as to the legal foundation of the colony's government. Governor John Winthrop, Jr. sailed for England in 1661 and succeeded in securing an extraordinary document providing a clear legal basis for the colony, the absorption of New Haven, boundaries similar to the present except for the Pacific Ocean as a western border, and finally an exceedingly generous degree of self-government. The charter constituted John Winthrop, Jr. and others as a corporate body and called for a governor, deputy governor, and 12 assistants to be elected annually in May by the freemen. Twice yearly the upper house met with a lower house of two members per town to conduct the colony's business as the General Assembly. The legislature could enact laws that did not contravene those of England. New Haven, after much resistance, submitted to annexation in 1665.

The first serious threat to Connecticut's corporate integrity was an attempt by the English government to annul all colonial charters and join the New England colonies and New York into a Dominion of New England, ruled by Sir Edmund Andros. On October 27,

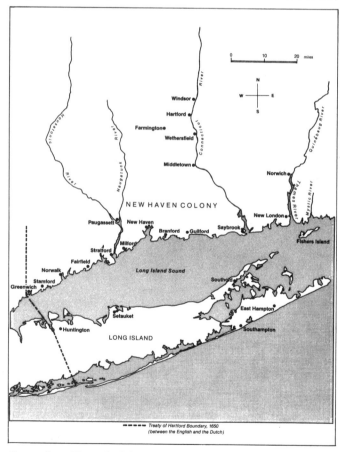

Connecticut. *(Facts On File, Inc.)*

1683, Governor Andros arrived in Hartford, where his commission as governor and the king's order to annex Connecticut to the Dominion were read. The discussion that followed lasted into the evening. When the charter was brought out and placed on the table, the lights were suddenly extinguished and the charter hidden in the Charter Oak. Despite the disappearance of the charter, the colony surrendered.

Connecticut remained under Andros's rule until the spring of 1689, when news arrived of the Glorious Revolution in England. The freemen voted to reestablish the charter government and to restore all the old magistrates to power. Fitz-John Winthrop went in 1693 to England, where he was successful in getting William and Mary to reconfirm the 1662 charter, which served Connecticut until 1818.

18th Century Development. Connecticut prospered during the 18th century. Its population, estimated in 1636 to be only 800, by the first census in 1766 had reached 130,612, including 3,019 blacks and 617 Indians. Over 90 percent of this population was engaged in agriculture, with the scarcity of capital and labor, along with inadequate transportation, keeping most farmers at the subsistence level of production. The most important early crop was Indian corn, but flax, hemp, pork, beef, grains, cattle, sheep, and swine were also produced.

By 1750 there was a shift from soil tillage to grazing as expanding markets in the West Indies and other mainland colonies encouraged farmers to expand the production of livestock and feed. Considerable geographical specialization also developed. While Connecticut's trade increased during the 18th century, the greatest volume was with Boston, New York, and the West Indies. There was some manufacturing, with clockmaking, ironmaking, and shipbuilding heading the list of industries.

Rapid growth before 1750, especially along the eastern seacoast, brought demands for currency inflation from merchants there. The New London Society for Trade and Commerce was formed in 1729 and petitioned the General Assembly to issue bills of currency, thereby supplying eastern Connecticut with an expanded supply of currency to pay off past debts and purchase goods directly from Britain. More populous western Connecticut succeeded in destroying the Society in the legislature mainly because the west feared the growing economic competition from the east. East-west resentments were also intensified by territorial claims of the Windham-based Susquehanna Company to land in Pennsylvania. Western Connecticut settlers feared that the success of the proposed settlement in Pennsylvania would result in lower prices for land in their area and attacked the company's supporters in east-ern Connecticut with bitter speeches and pamphlets. The issue was settled only in 1782 when Pennsylvania's claim to the region was recognized.

Intellectual Life. Intellectual growth in Connecticut showed in the colony's commitment to education. The Code of 1650 required a town of 50 families to employ a teacher to instruct in reading and writing and a town of 100 families to operate a grammar school to prepare students for college. Hopkins Grammar School was founded at New Haven in 1660. A 1690 law established free schools in Hartford and New Haven, and in 1700 the General Assembly established grammar schools in four county seats.

In 1712 the assembly made the society or parish the unit for schools and in 1733 employed income from the sale of western Connecticut lands to supplement other school revenues. Several private academies were established in the mid-18th century, and Yale College was incorporated by the General Assembly in 1701. It moved to New Haven from Saybrook in 1717. The colony's first newspaper was the Connecticut Gazette in New Haven in 1755, while the Connecticut Courant was launched in Hartford in 1764, making it the oldest American newspaper in continuous existence to the present.

Religious Life. Connecticut's Puritan mission was clear from the adoption of the Fundamental Orders, which charged the colony's magistrates with "preserving the disciplyne of the Churches." The law of 1644 that made the financial support of the ministers of the Puritan Congregational Church an obligation upon everyone was restated in the Code of 1650, and the provision was strengthened many times thereafter. Religious dissenters such as Quakers challenged the establishment before 1700. The Baptists and Anglicans offered even more formidable challenges during the early 18th century. Attempts to shore up the system with the Saybrook Platform of 1708, providing for "Associations" of pastors and "Consociations" of churches with considerable powers, produced only a cold formalism and growing indifference.

This decline in spirituality made Connecticut susceptible to the Great Awakening during the 1730s and 1740s. While thousands of people were converted, the Congregational Church in Connecticut became bitterly divided between the revivalist "New Lights" and the anti-revivalist "Old Lights," who were strong enough in the General Assembly to pass legislation limiting the activities of revivalist preachers. New Lights were centered in eastern Connecticut, thereby intensifying east-west divisions.

The Revolutionary Era.   By 1763, Connecticut had survived persistent efforts to bypass or seriously amend its charter and had contributed significantly in the four wars fought against the French from 1690 to 1763. In order to pay its huge war debts, the British Parliament enacted the Stamp Act. Connecticut's General Assembly approved an official protest and the Sons of Liberty arose in vigorous opposition to the Act's passage in 1765. Jared Ingersoll, the stamp distributor for Connecticut, was stopped on his way to Hartford by an angry mob that threatened him with bodily harm if he refused to resign. When Governor Thomas Fitch signed the oath to support the act, all but 4 of the 12 council members walked out in protest. Even after the Stamp Act's repeal in February 1766, the Sons of Liberty worked successfully to defeat Fitch and the four assistants who had supported him. William Pitken, Sr. was elected governor and Jonathan Trumbull elected deputy governor. Connecticut had also sent three delegates to the Stamp Act Congress. Connecticut's responses to the Townshend duties of 1767 were written protests and participation in nonimportation agreements.

The Coercive Acts, punishing Boston for the Boston Tea Party, aroused fears in Connecticut for its own charter and hurt the colony's merchants by closing the port of Boston. Committees of Correspondence were established in many Connecticut towns, which also passed resolutions denouncing British actions. The General Assembly enacted stringent anti-Tory laws, and ardent Loyalists were harassed and persecuted.

When fighting erupted at Lexington and Concord on April 19, 1775, some 3,600 Connecticut militiamen rushed to the Boston area. A special session of the General Assembly convened on April 26 to enact an embargo of food exports and ordered one-fourth of the militia to be ready for active military service. In May many Connecticut men, including Benedict Arnold, participated in the seizure of Fort Ticonderoga, and in June, Connecticut soldiers fought under Israel Putnam at the Battle of Bunker Hill. By now the assembly had authorized Connecticut's delegates to the Continental Congress to vote for independence.

During the Revolutionary War, Connecticut suffered damage from four British attacks: Danbury in April 1777, Greenwich in February 1779; New Haven, Fairfield, and Norwalk in July 1779; and New London and Groton in September 1781, when the British troops were led by Benedict Arnold. As the Provisions State, Connecticut provided large amounts of supplies as well as men and arms.

By the mid-1780s growing dissatisfaction with the Articles of Confederation resulted in Connecticut's active participation in the movement toward a new Constitution. The state's large number of state and continental bondholders would benefit from a national government with taxing powers, and there were fears of social anarchy spilling over from Shays' Rebellion in nearby Massachusetts. Connecticut's delegates to the Constitutional Convention in Philadelphia helped to engineer the Connecticut Compromise, providing for equal representation in the Senate and representation, according to population, in the House of Representatives. Connecticut ratified the Constitution by a vote of 128 to 40.

See also Hartford; New England Confederation; New Haven Colony; New London.

Bibliography: Buell, Richard, Jr., *Dear Liberty: Connecticut's Mobilization for the Revolutionary War* (Wesleyan Univ. Press, 1980); Bushman, Richard L., *From Puritan to Yankee: Character and the Social Order in Connecticut,* 1690-1765 (Harvard Univ. Press, 1967); Collier, Christopher, *Roger Sherman's Connecticut: Yankee Politics and the American Revolution* (Wesleyan Univ. Press, 1971); Main, Jackson Turner, *Society and Economy in Colonial Connecticut* (Princeton Univ. Press, 1985); Van Dusen, Albert E., *Connecticut* (Random House, 1961).

John W. Ifkovic
Westfield State College

CONNECTICUT WITS   The Connecticut Wits were a group of sophisticated, aristocratic Yale College graduates active from the 1770s until the early 19th century. They were loosely gathered around two main interests: literature and politics. The most noted members were John Trumbull (1750-1831), Timothy Dwight (1752-1817), and Joel Barlow (1754-1812). The group, also called The Hartford Wits after the literary club they formed following the Revolutionary War, had a goal of promoting a national literature. Trumbull began the campaign at Yale by satirizing the uselessness of the classical curriculum ("The Progress of Dulness," 1772) and arguing for more modern literature. He later wrote the most popular poem of the Revolution, "M'Fingal" (1776), a satire of the Tories. Dwight and Barlow similarly tried to provide their new nation with a worthy literature by writing lengthy, unreadable epics such as Dwight's "The Conquest of Canaan" (1785) and Barlow's "Columbiad" (1807). Only Barlow's mock epic "The Hasty Pudding" (1796), a celebration of American cornmeal mush, is still widely enjoyed today. In their attempt to create a national literature the Wits focused on American subjects, but they still followed British models.

The Wits also expressed their political views by collaborating on several satires that promoted their conservative Federalist beliefs and attacked the Jeffersonian democratic principles they felt threatened their nation. Barlow broke from the group by becoming a radical, a Deist, and a supporter of the French Revolution.

CONTINENTAL ARMY   The Continental Army was composed of those soldiers who served in forces authorized by the Second Continental Congress and were distinct from the forces of the state militias. In the aftermath of Lexington and

Concord, while colonial forces besieged the British in Boston in June 1775, the Congress accepted the proposal of John Adams and passed resolutions that created the Continental Army. The resolutions authorized the recruitment of several rifle companies, offered George Washington the position of commander in chief, and funded the army through bills of credit that the colonies would redeem. Charles Lee, Israel Putnam, Philip Schuyler, and Artemas Ward were appointed as major generals under Washington.

Members of the Continental Army generally served longer enlistments and were better trained than militia members but suffered from lack of supplies and irregular pay. The type of privations the Continentals endured at Valley Forge (1777-78) were frequent during the war and led to a near mutiny at Morristown, New Jersey, in 1780. During the latter part of 1783 the Continental Army's soldiers were gradually sent home. Many were furloughed in the spring and discharged in October, with most of the rest discharged in November.

See also Revolutionary War Battles; Valley Forge.

CONTINENTAL ASSOCIATION (1774) Adopted by the First Continental Congress and signed by its members in October 1774, the Continental Association was a program of economic boycott intended to pressure Parliament and the British mercantile community into supporting repeal of the Coercive Acts of 1774 and other objectionable legislation. The association, which went far beyond earlier nonimportation agreements, consisted of three major elements: (1) nonimportation of British goods beginning on December 1, 1774; (2) nonconsumption of British goods starting on March 1, 1775; and (3) nonexportation of American products to Britain, Ireland, and the British West Indies as of September 10, 1775. The association also contained pledges to discontinue the slave trade, promote frugality and economy, support agriculture and manufactures, and discourage extravagance and dissipation. The delegates were in general united behind this program, although considerations of local interest led to some disagreement and modification before adoption.

The association was enforced by local committees, which used public opinion and community pressure to win compliance by merchants and consumers. It was unsuccessful in persuading Parliament to repeal its acts but provided the Americans with an essential mechanism of unity and resistance during a crucial phase of the Revolution.

Bibliography: Ammerman, David, *In the Common Cause: American Response to the Coercive Acts of 1774* (Univ. of Virginia, 1974).

Douglas M. Arnold
The Papers of Benjamin Franklin

CONTINENTAL CONGRESS, FIRST (1774) The First Continental Congress convened in Philadelphia on Septem-

ber 5, 1774, to determine how the colonies would respond to Britain's Coercive Acts of 1774. It concluded by adopting a program of protest and resistance that led the Americans in the direction of independence. At the outset the delegates determined that each colony would have one vote, an arrangement continued in subsequent congresses. The Congress then sanctioned resistance to the Coercive Acts in Massachusetts by endorsing the militant Suffolk Resolves. The caution and conservatism of some members was nevertheless apparent in a debate over a plan of union with Britain offered by Joseph Galloway, a delegate from Pennsylvania. The Congress rejected the plan, which would have left England substantial powers over the colonies.

The Congress's main work of resistance took the form of a Declaration of Rights and Grievances (October 14) and the Continental Association (October 18). In the former, the delegates called for the repeal of the Coercive Acts, the Quebec Act, and other recent British laws and asserted that the colonial legislatures had exclusive power to tax and enact internal legislation (subject only to royal veto). They equivocated, however, about Parliament's power to regulate trade. In the latter, the Congress established a system of economic boycott against Britain. Concerned with maintaining unity both within and outside the Congress, the delegates in October adopted memorials and addresses to the King, the people of Britain, the American colonists, and the inhabitants of Quebec. Before adjourning on October 26 the Congress resolved to meet again on May 10, 1775, if American grievances were not redressed.

See also Continental Association; Continental Congress, Second; Declaration of Rights and Grievances; Suffolk Resolves.

Bibliography: Ammerman, David, *In the Common Cause: American Response to the Coercive Acts of 1774* (Univ. of Virginia, 1974).

Douglas M. Arnold
The Papers of Benjamin Franklin

CONTINENTAL CONGRESS, SECOND (1775-81) The agency that guided the thirteen colonies to rebellion and eventual military victory, the Continental Congress convened in Philadelphia on May 10, 1775. Faced with armed conflict in Massachusetts and British refusal to redress American grievances, Congress was forced to act as a national government. The delegates soon organized the Continental Army, with Washington as commander in chief. While making a conciliatory gesture to Britain in the Olive Branch Petition in July, Congress showed its resolve to resist in the Declaration of the Causes and Necessity of Taking Up Arms. During the fall and winter, Congress answered George III's August proclamation of rebellion, organized a Continental Navy, attempted to win Canada to

After the euphoria of the Declaration of Independence had dissipated, the press lampooned the politicians of the Second Continental Congress. *(Library of Congress)*

the cause, and established committees to import war supplies and explore the possibility of foreign assistance.

British intransigence and continued fighting made the possibility of American independence likely, and the publication of Thomas Paine's Common Sense in January 1776 helped crystalize thinking; however, moderate opinion remained strong. In May, Congress authorized the colonies to replace governments based on royal authority with ones grounded in the people. This was followed on June 7 by Richard Henry Lee's famous motion for independence, foreign alliance, and confederation. The debate culminated in a vote for independence (July 2) and the adoption of the Declaration of Independence (July 4).

Actions of the Congress. With independence declared, Congress took on more of the attributes of a national government, turning to the issues of union and foreign affairs. Articles of Confederation were introduced in July 1776 and were debated and amended for over a year before adoption. They were not finally ratified by all the states until 1781. In September 1776, Congress adopted a plan for treaties with foreign powers and empowered its first official European mission, a three-man commission to France.

Driven several times from Philadelphia by military emergencies, Congress was faced with persistent difficulties during the years following independence. The delegates kept their support behind Washington despite occasional discontent and dealt with other controversies involving the army's leadership. Problems of supply and finance were more vexing. Congress had to resort to large issues of paper money and widespread use of certificates promising future payment for goods and services; both money and certificates depreciated. After virtually repudiating its previous paper currency in 1780, Congress in 1781 established a Department of Finance under Robert Morris to deal with economic problems.

American foreign policy scored a major success in 1778 when the commissioners in Paris obtained treaties of alliance and commerce with France. Congress ratified them in May. The entry of France into the war provided important military and financial support, although Congress paid a price by allowing its foreign policy to become dependent on its ally. In 1779, Congress adopted peace terms and appointed John Adams negotiator; it also continued to send ministers to other European courts, hoping to attract additional foreign support.

By the time that the Confederation was finally ratified in early 1781, Congress had set most of the policies that would lead to victory and independence. Not all that it did was successful: military setbacks were common and financial problems continued. In addition, conflict within Congress, which the delegates had moderated in the early years, came fully into play in 1779 during disputes over the specifics of the peace terms and the activities of Silas Deane as agent in France. The Confederation Congress inherited the successes and problems of its predecessor.

See also Articles of Confederation; Confederation Congress; Continental Congress, First.

Bibliography: Burnett, Edmund C., *The Continental Congress* (Macmillan, 1941); Henderson, H. James, *Party Politics in the Continental Congress* (McGraw-Hill, 1974); Rakove, Jack N., *The Beginnings of National Politics: An Interpretive History of the Continental Congress* (Knopf, 1979).

Douglas M. Arnold
The Papers of Benjamin Franklin

CONTRACEPTION Methods of preventing conception require at least a rudimentary understanding of human fertility, something few regular physicians possessed during the colonial period. Although a widespread notion existed that there was a "safe" period during the ovulatory cycle, before the 20th century, expert opinion varied as to its precise timing. Folk medicine, herbal teas based largely on female superstitions, were mostly harmless and ineffective, although some of the more powerful potions were potentially poisonous. Perhaps more effective was the practice of female douching with similar potions. Condoms made from skin or gut were used as prophylactics, not contraception devices, and were only available to the wealthy and sophisticated. Certainly the most widespread contraception practice was withdrawal, or coitus interruptus; based on the frequency of its condemnation in the medical texts of the early republic it must have been

common enough. In one case from the court records of 18th-century Massachusetts, a man charged with the paternity of an illegitimate child used coitus interruptus as a defense. In general, however, contraception was ineffectively practiced in colonial America, a society with one of the highest birthrates in recorded history.

CONVICT LABOR Representing a specialized class of indentured servitude, convict labor appeared in the American colonies soon after permanent settlement. A proclamation by James I in 1615 laid the basis for convict transportation, although that form of immigration only became significant after parliamentary legislation in 1717 that provided for the transportation of certain criminal offenders. Virginia, Maryland, and the West Indies were the principal destinations of convicts in the 18th century. In the continental colonies the need for labor overshadowed protests against the practice of convict transportation.

Bibliography: Smith, Abbot Emerson, *Colonists in Bondage: White Servitude and Convict Labor in America, 1607-1776* (Univ. of North Carolina, 1947).

CONWAY CABAL (1777) Expressing dissatisfaction with General George Washington's direction of the Revolutionary War, Congress in 1777 made General Horatio Gates president of the Board of War, with Major General Thomas Conway as inspector general. In a letter to Gates, Conway criticized Washington. When the letter's contents and the movement to replace Washington became public, Gates denied complicity, and Conway was left without supporters. He resigned from the army and later in the war apologized to Washington. Although his name was attached to the incident, Conway was not the leader in this attempt by congressional opponents to take over direction of the war.

CONWAY, THOMAS (1735-1800?) A soldier born in Ireland on February 27, 1735, he was educated in France, where he joined the army (1749). He sailed to America in 1777 to help the colonists in the Revolutionary War and was appointed a brigadier general. A proposal by Congress to make Conway a major general was criticized by General George Washington, who claimed that Conway's selection was unfair to more competent American officers. After Conway threatened to resign, Congress promoted him to major general and appointed him inspector general.

Shortly after his promotion, Conway wrote a letter to General Horatio Gates criticizing Washington. When the letter and its supporters, called the Conway Cabal, became known, Conway's friends deserted him. He resigned from the army in 1778 and in the same year was severely wounded in a duel brought on by his criticisms of

Washington, to whom he subsequently apologized. After his recovery, he rejoined the French forces and was appointed governor general of French India (1787). He remained a royalist after the French Revolution and returned to England when the royalists were defeated.

See also Conway Cabal.

COOK, JAMES (1728-1779) English naval officer, explorer, and surveyor, Cook was of humble origin and entered the Royal Navy as an able seaman at the late age of 27 but quickly rose through the ranks, finally to be appointed, in 1775, First Lord of the Admiralty. He participated in the naval operations of the French and Indian War, during which he charted the St. Lawrence River and made possible the amphibious assault on Quebec of General James Wolf. From 1771 to 1779 he engaged in three historic voyages around the world in search of the great southern continent, while also charting Australia, New Zealand, and many of the islands of the Pacific. In the last of these voyages, in search of the Northwest Passage, Cook charted the northwest coast of North America, the Bering Straits, and the Sandwich Islands (Hawaii), where he was killed in a fight with the inhabitants. Among his many accomplishments, he contributed to the triumph of British power in Canada and to the opening of trade between China, Hawaii, and the Pacific coast of North America.

See also French and Indian War; Hawaii; Northwest Passage.

COOKE, ELISHA (1637-1715) A physician and politician, he was born in Boston and educated at Harvard. He served as speaker of Boston's General Court from 1682 until 1684 and then was elected to the Board of Assistants under the original Massachusetts Bay charter. When Joseph Dudley became president of New England, Cooke, strongly opposed to a new royal charter, participated in Dudley's overthrow. He continued to oppose the new charter as the colony's agent in London from 1690 until 1692. Again, he was elected to the Board of Assistants from 1694 but was prevented from serving by Governor Phips. When Dudley became governor in 1702 he stripped Cooke of all government positions.

COOTE, RICHARD (1636-1701) A colonial governor, he was born in Ireland and in 1683 inherited the title Baron Coote of Coloony. From 1688 to 1695, as Earl of Bellomont (or Bellamont) by marriage, he was a member of the English Parliament. In 1697 he was appointed colonial governor of New York, Massachusetts, and New Hampshire. During his short stay in America, he dealt with wars in Rhode Island, Connecticut, and New Jersey; illegal trade; and Indian relations. His commission of privateer

William Kidd to combat piracy against British ships was unsuccessful, for Kidd never found any pirates and, in frustration, turned to piracy himself.

COPLEY, SIR LIONEL (died 1693) Born in England, he was a member of the Royal Footguard from at least 1676 and stationed at Hull from 1681, where he was instrumental in securing the fort for King William during the 1688 English revolution. He was commissioned as the first royal governor of Maryland in 1691 and arrived to take over his duties in 1692. During his short tenure, he was responsible for establishing the Church of England in Maryland and granting an annual salary for the governor. He was also successful in regulating fees for justice and militia officers, structuring trade with the Indians, and signing peace treaties with the Indians in the area.

COPLEY, JOHN SINGLETON (1738-1815) One of the most renowned American painters, Copley was raised in Boston in the home of his stepfather, limner and engraver Peter Pelham. Beginning in the 1750s he painted commissioned portraits that together form an unparalleled view of well-to-do colonial life. Dismayed by the turmoil of incidents like the Boston Tea Party and eager for contact with European art circles, he left for England in 1774, being elected to the Royal Academy in 1779.

The European courtly tradition is reflected in his earlier portraits, which show formal balance and stock poses and surroundings. His own style, the realistic representation of a subject who is portrayed informally and close to the objects of everyday life, characterizes such mature paintings as "Boy with a Squirrel" (c. 1765) and "Portrait of Paul Revere" (c. 1768-70). His most skillful portraits, such as "Mrs. Thomas Boylston" (1766), show his capacity to represent textures, organize forms, and depict light in order to create a stunning yet intimate image. His expatriation was part of a search by many American artists for sophistication in technique and elevation in subject that they missed in America. One of Copley's most famous works, "Watson and the Shark" (1778), was produced in Europe, but art historians agree that the European painterly style and the vogue for history paintings weakened Copley's style. His paintings are displayed in many U.S. museums.

Bibliography: Prown, Jules, *John Singleton Copley*, 2 vols. (Harvard Univ. Press, 1966).

John Saillant
Brown University

CORBIN, MARGARET COCHRAN (1751-1800) A Revolutionary War heroine, Corbin was the daughter of Robert Cochran, who was killed by Indians in 1756. Her mother was also carried off at this time. Margaret married John Corbin in 1772 and accompanied him when he joined the 1st Company of the Pennsylvania Artillery at the start of the Revolution. John was killed in the battle of Fort Washington in November 1776, at which point Margaret courageously stepped in, performing his duties until she suffered incapacitating wounds. In 1779 the State of Pennsylvania granted her $30 to help pay for her necessities, and Congress later awarded her disability payments. She died in New York State.

CORN   Corn (maize) is one of the two most important New World crops developed by the indigenous peoples of the Americas (the other is potatoes). Corn was domesticated in the Mexican highlands 8,000 years ago, and thanks to its tolerance of a wide variety of climates and soils, its cultivation was diffused north and south to environments throughout North and South America, becoming the staple of all horticultural Indians. Among the many varieties in use were popcorn, flint and dent corn, sweet and flour corn, in hues from white and yellow to red, blue, and black.

Columbus carried it home from his second voyage and it quickly spread through much of Europe, Asia, and Africa, where it was grown to provision the slave ships. Corn supplied by the Indians saved the starving Jamestown colonists, and the Pilgrims survived by plundering Indian maize stores. Although European colonists preferred wheat for their bread, they found corn much less susceptible to disease, and throughout the hemisphere it quickly became the staple colonial crop.

Corn could be eaten at several of its growing stages: baby ears consumed whole, green ears eaten raw or roasted, hard ears pounded into meal. Indians and colonists alike transformed corn into hasty pudding, porridge, and hominy; ground and baked it into pone, dodger, hush puppies, johnny cake, or tortillas; rolled their game, fish, or chicken in it before cooking. Anglo colonists quickly adapted their distilling art to corn mash, and whiskey had become an important product in the early 18th century. Corn was also a forage crop for livestock. Thanks to the abundance of corn there were no famines in pioneer America.

Bibliography: Hardeman, Nicholas P., *Shucks, Shocks, and Hominy Blocks: Corn as a Way of Life in Pioneer America* (Louisiana State, 1981); Mangelsdorf, Paul C., *Corn: Its Origin, Evolution, and Improvement* (Harvard Univ. Press, 1974).

John Mack Faragher
Mount Holyoke College

CORNSTALK (c.1720-77)   A Shawnee leader also known as Wynepuechsika, Cornstalk was born in western Pennsylvania and migrated with his family to the Scioto River Valley of Ohio with his family around 1730. He served on the French side during the French and Indian War and became known in 1763, toward the end of the war, for his relentless attacks on the British settlements in western Virginia. Cornstalk and his followers remained in the area even after the formal end of the hostilities, continuing their raids against the colonists.

In 1774 he proposed territorial compromise with the settlers, but his approaches were rebuffed and answered by a militia campaign against the Indians led by Governor Dunmore of Virginia. At the Battle of Point Pleasant, the Shawnee were defeated, with heavy casualties on both sides. The hostilities were finally ended with the signing of a treaty at Chillicothe, Ohio, which was viewed by many of Cornstalk's followers as a capitulation. Uncontrolled raids followed, and in 1777, when Cornstalk attempted to negotiate with the settlers, he was held hostage and then executed in retaliation for the murder of a settler. His death sparked a war between the settlers and the Shawnee that ended only with the Treaty of Greenville in 1795.

CORNWALLIS, CHARLES (1738-1805)   A British general in the American Revolution and later governor general of India, Cornwallis was born in London, son of the 1st Earl Cornwallis. He attended the military academy at Turin and while serving in Germany during the Seven Years War became a lieutenant colonel. After his father's death (1763), Cornwallis succeeded him as earl and took various posts, including service as aide-de-camp to King George III.

During the Revolution, he took command in North America as a major general. He helped the British to victory at the Battle of Long Island (August 1776). After Washington's victory at Trenton (December 1776), Cornwallis failed to entrap Washington's men. The following year Cornwallis played a key role in the British victory at Brandywine, Pennsylvania (September 1777), which resulted in the British occupation of Philadelphia. He then became a lieutenant general, second in command to Sir Henry Clinton. Cornwallis accompanied the British army in a retreat toward New York City from Philadelphia and fought the Americans at the Battle of Monmouth (June 1778). When the main British operations shifted to the southern states, Cornwallis and Clinton besieged Charleston (1780), and after the city's fall Cornwallis took command of British forces in the South. He enjoyed a success at Camden in August 1780, but then extended his forces in pursuing the Americans, now commanded by General Nathanael Green. Severe defeats led Cornwallis to retreat to positions on the coast at Yorktown, Virginia. Hemmed in by French and American troops, Cornwallis surrendered with his forces in October 1781, effectively ending combat in the war.

After the war Cornwallis had a distinguished career, twice serving as governor general of India. He also sat in the British cabinet and held diplomatic posts. Cornwallis was promoted to general in 1793.

See also Revolutionary War Battles.

His surrender at Yorktown did not bar Charles Cornwallis from prestigious posts after the war. *(Library of Congress)*

CORONADO, FRANCISCO VÁSQUEZ DE (1510-54) The Spanish explorer Coronado came to New Spain in 1535 and was appointed governor of Nueva Galicia. In 1538 he aided Marcos de Niza in preparing for his expedition to Arizona and New Mexico and then commanded the party assigned to follow up Niza's report of great wealth there. In July 1540, Coronado, with 200 men, reached the Zuni pueblos, which made no resistance, but the rumored wealth of Cibola proved a dream. He sent exploration parties out in all directions: Melchior Diaz died attempting to rendezvous with Hernando Alarcón, although he did succeed in crossing the Colorado and going down the California peninsula; Pedro de Tovar traveled to the Hopi pueblos of northern Arizona; Garcia López de Cardenas discovered the Grand Canyon. Coronado himself reached the pueblos in the valley of the Rio Grande.

In 1541, Coronado heard rumors of a rich country to the northeast called Gran Quivira and set out to find it. The expedition descended the Pecos and marched out onto the plains. Coronado crossed the Texas panhandle and Oklahoma and reached Quivira, in eastern Kansas, only to find

that it was a settlement of Wichita Indians. Disappointed again, he returned to Mexico. Back in Nueva Galicia, his conduct toward the natives resulted in an investigation of his administration. Coronado was removed from his position and moved to Mexico City, where he worked in a minor municipal post until his death.

See also Alarcón, Hernando; Diaz, Melchior; Niza, Marcos de.

Thomas C. Thompson
University of California, Riverside

CORTES, HERNANDO (1485-1547) The conquistador Hernando Cortes attended the University of Salamanca before arriving on Hispaniola in 1504. He participated in the conquest of Cuba in 1511 and began the conquest of the Mexican mainland in 1519 under the auspices of the governor of Cuba, Diego Valasquez. When the party landed on the Mexican coast, Cortes proclaimed his independence from Velasquez and marched to the Valley of Mexico, aided by the Indian girl Malinche. Cortes conquered the Aztecs with his Indian allies doing most of the fighting. Although the Aztecs fought well, their capital city of Tenochtitlán was destroyed in the struggle and by late 1520 Cortes controlled the Valley of Mexico despite the efforts of Velasquez to stop him. By 1524 he had conquered the entire region from Guatemala to Acaponeta, which he ruled directly as captain general of New Spain.

Between 1524 and 1526, Cortes conquered Honduras, but during those years his enemies and the Crown steadily ate away at his power. Elevated to the nobility as Marquis of the Valley of Oaxaca, Cortes organized the transportation of settlers and the establishment of the Catholic Church in New Spain. From 1530 to 1540, Cortes devoted himself to the development of his own territories and sent out exploring expeditions, one of which discovered Baja California in 1536. In 1541 he returned to Spain, where he died.

Thomas C. Thompson
University of California, Riverside

COTTON, JOHN (1584-1652) The father of New England Congregationalism, Cotton was educated in Puritan doctrine, church practices, and preaching style at Trinity and Emmanuel Colleges at Cambridge University. In 1612 he was ordained vicar of St. Botolph's Church in Boston, Lincolnshire, where over the course of 20 years he earned a reputation as a great and learned preacher. In 1630, Cotton preached his famous farewell sermon, "God's Promise to His Plantation," to the passengers of the ship *Arbella*, justifying their departure for Massachusetts Bay and urging them to reform the practices of the Church of England.

Called before Church authorities for nonconformity in 1633, Cotton himself departed for the New World, where he became preacher of the First Church of Boston. The most eminent minister in the Massachusetts colony, Cotton by his evangelical preaching sparked a large number of conversions within the first two years of his arrival. Several of his students, including Anne Hutchinson, believed that Cotton's emphasis upon justification by faith alone contradicted the doctrine of other ministers, who stressed the relationship of good works to saving grace. Cotton's clarification of his positions were prerequisite to ministerial unity and Hutchinson's banishment. Church authorities frequently looked to Cotton to answer unresolved questions of Congregational church government; churches probably began to require conversion as a condition for church membership at Cotton's suggestion. Cotton spent much of his later life defining and defending New England Congregationalism in tracts such as *The Way of the Churches of Christ in New England* (1645).

See also Congregationalists.

Bibliography: Ziff, Larzer, *The Career of John Cotton* (Princeton Univ. Press, 1962).

James F. Cooper, Jr.
University of Connecticut

COUNCIL FOR NEW ENGLAND (1620-35) An English corporation that succeeded the Virginia Company of Plymouth, the Council for New England was empowered to claim and colonize all lands on the eastern coast of North America from Long Island to the Bay of Fundy. The council was composed of 40 members and was granted both commercial privileges and governmental authority over its territory. Under the presidency of Sir Ferdinando Gorges, the council intended to allot land in New England through a feudal division of fiefs and manors. However, the success of the Puritan colonies and the failure of its own attempts at colonization resulted in the return of the council's royal charter in 1635.

See also Gorges, Sir Ferdinando.

COUNCIL OF THE INDIES The Council of the Indies was established in Spain as the governing body for the Spanish colonies in the Western Hemisphere after the conquest of Mexico in 1524. Although technically subordinate to the king, the council was practically autonomous. Among its powers and duties were the right to recommend individuals for civil and ecclesiastical posts, to review administration, and to pass general colonial laws. It also functioned as the court of appeal from the various audiencias. During the 17th century its role was diminished by increased bureaucratization. This trend continued until abolition of the council in the 19th century.

See also Audiencias.

COUREURS DE BOIS AND VOYAGEURS The fur trappers, traders, and boatmen of the French Fur Trade, the so-called coureurs de bois, were unlicensed independent fur traders who began leaving the French settlements along the St. Lawrence for the interior in the second half of the 17th century in order to take up residence among the interior Indians. They not only traded with the Indians but married Indian women and raised Mixedblood or Métis children. With their knowledge of the customs, language, and geography of the country, these men played an important part in the exploration of the territory north and west of the Great Lakes. Many early French explorers of the North American interior—Duluth, Radisson, and Perrot among them—were leaders of these men. Although the title *coureur de bois* was frequently conferred on the employees of the French and English fur companies, these latter were more properly known as *voyageurs* or *engagés*; by the late 18th century there were perhaps as many as 5,000 of them in the Canadian West, divided between the *hommes du nord*, or "men of the north," those who wintered in the interior; and the *mangeurs du lard*, or "pork eaters," who made the annual supply trip from Montreal to the interior. Superb boatmen and woodsmen, they too were mostly French-Canadian or Métis.

See also Bosch Loopers; Fur Trade; Mixedbloods; Radisson, Pierre.

COUTUME DE PARIS A French legal code in colonial Canada and Louisiana, the Coutume de Paris was originally the feudal law of the area around Paris. The code was introduced in Canada in 1627 and became the only legal code in 1664. The provincial councils added edits and ordinances following the rules of the French parlement. After the British took over Canada in 1763, military and elected justices administered the coutumes. Although the English criminal code was adopted in the Quebec Act of 1774, the coutumes remained until 1792. In Louisiana use of the coutumes ended when Spanish law was imposed in 1769. In Virginia the Declaration of Rights in 1778 permitted coutumes for the French in the Illinois country. Later, Northwest Territory laws sanctioned coutumes in family relations, inheritance, and property rights involving French settlers.

COXE, DANIEL (1673-1739) Born in England, he came to America in 1702 and was appointed commander of forces of West Jersey, an area in which his father held some interests. From 1796 he was a member of the governor's council and held a seat on the provincial supreme court. He served in the assembly from 1714. Because of disagreements with Governor Hunter, he was removed from both the council and the assembly; he fled to England and wrote *A Description of the English Province of Carolina* (1722).

Returning to America in 1725, he became the first Grand Master of Masons in 1730 and served on the supreme court again from 1734 until his death.

CRAFTS Produced by workmen of varying degrees of skill and experience, craft manufactures coincided with the settlement of the colonies. Early crafts originated in the household and were generally simple, utilitarian products. Ornamentation and display were secondary considerations. Traveling artisans supplemented homemade craft production. In the 18th century the stabilization of family and society, increasing affluence, ample resources, urbanization, an expanding market, and a maturing economy generated a greater demand for crafts as well as fostering a desire for better workmanship.

As a result, commercial craft industries appeared, attaining a high level of development in urban environments. Craftsmen or artisans, sometimes with the help of apprentices or journeymen, rivaled the work of the English and French in such areas as silversmithing and cabinetmaking, and altogether produced an extraordinary variety of finished objects. Among the principal craft industries was furniture making. The colonials imported only two-fifths of their furniture in 1700, and their dependence upon overseas sources declined during the 18th century.

In addition to the dominant white, male artisans, slave craftsmen contributed significantly to craft production and women occasionally broke into the craft field. For a brief time widows might follow the occupations of deceased husbands, although usually women engaged in such occupations as millinery and dressmaking. Commercial craft production emanated from small establishments and was confined mostly to New England and the Middle Colonies. Over time some crafts were produced in standardized form for domestic sale or export, although most work remained individualized items made to order. While some American craft work was original, much reflected fashions and styles current in England and on the European continent as well as the 18th century mania for Oriental designs and techniques.

Bibliography: Bridenbaugh, Carl, *The Colonial Craftsman* (New York Univ. Press, 1950).

Alan D. Watson
University of North Carolina, Wilmington

CRANSTON, JOHN (1625-80) Physician and governor of Rhode Island, Cranston was born in London and came in 1637 to Rhode Island. He was first drummer and then captain of the Portsmouth militia band. Among his many offices, he was general attorney (1654-56) and commissioner from Newport in the General Assembly every year but three from 1655 to 1666. His studies in medicine made him the first doctor trained in the colonies. He was deputy governor from 1672 to 1676 and governor from 1678 until his death.

CREEK CONFEDERACY The Muskogean-speaking peoples of the Creek Confederacy dominated Indian-European affairs in the Southeast for most of the colonial period. Located in what is now Georgia and Alabama, they suffered massive population losses due to diseases introduced by Spanish explorers in the mid-16th century. European pressures resumed late in the 17th century as the Spanish in Florida, the English in Virginia and Carolina, and the French in Louisiana competed for influence among them.

The Creek initially allied with the Carolinians, to whom they traded deerskins and slaves, the latter captured in wars with other Indians. After repeatedly being abused by the traders, the Creek in 1715 joined the Yamasees in an unsuccessful uprising against the Carolinians. Thereafter the National Council, under the leadership of Brims, saw to it that each Creek town traded with one or another of the three powers while avoiding entanglement with any.

By so playing off the Europeans, the Creek grew wealthy and powerful—and also larger as they absorbed refugees from uprooted Indian communities throughout the Southeast. In 1733 they allowed the colony of Georgia to be established on part of their land, but settlers quickly moved beyond the boundary so that by mid-century Creek-English relations were tense. Although the Creek remained neutral during the French and Indian War (1756-63), the British victory undermined their play-off policy. Facing the land-hungry English alone, the Creek lost bargaining power as their dependence on European trade goods became painfully apparent. Over the next decade, they ceded several million acres in exchange for cancellation of their debts to English traders. At the outbreak of the American Revolution, the Creeks were bitterly divided between neutralist and pro-British factions, finally entering on the British side in 1778. When the war was over, the Creek ceded 800 square miles to the victorious new nation. Although the Creek were defeated and severely weakened, many continued to resist the Americans until 1794 and again during the War of 1812.

See also Yamasee War.

Bibliography: Corkran, David H., *The Creek Frontier, 1540-1783* (Univ. of Oklahoma Press, 1967); Crane, Verner H., *The Southern Frontier, 1670-1732* (Duke Univ. Press, 1929).

Neal Salisbury
Smith College

CREOLES The word "criollo," a colonial corruption of the Spanish verb "criado" (to breed), came into use in Spanish America in the 16th century to refer to the second and subsequent generations of colonists born in the Western Hemisphere. According to some 18th century linguistic authorities, the term was originally used by slaves to refer to their American-born children, but by the 18th century it was applied almost exclusively to whites, criollo or "creole" contrasting with "peninsulare," a person born in Spain.

Along the Gulf coast, after the English forced the relocation of several thousand French Acadians to Louisiana in 1755, the term (and later the more pejorative "Cajun") was used by original French settlers as a label of pride to refer to themselves and their dialect to the newer immigrants. Over the centuries since then, this usage has grown less distinct but no less important; by the 19th century significant numbers of blacks and mixed-race groups had appropriated the Creole label, so that today it refers to a large and diverse segment of French-dialect speakers in Louisiana, as does the term Cajun.

In English, "Creole" came to suggest, as well, a process of ethnic and racial mixture and was often applied pejoratively to suggest a resulting indolence and tropical apathy, as when Cotton Mather in the late 17th century criticized the youth of New England for falling into "Criolian Degeneracy." A less value-laden but related meaning is found in the term "creolized language," a true language of mixed elements from the tongues of both the colonizer and the colonized, which develops when mutually unintelligible speakers remain in intimate and long-lasting contact with one another.

Bibliography: Mills, Gary B., *The Forgotten People: Cane River's Creoles of Color* (Louisiana State Press, 1977).

John Mack Faragher
Mount Holyoke College

CRÈVECOEUR, FORT This trade center and military post on the Illinois River, at the site of the modern city of Peoria, Illinois, was the first French fort in the west, established by the Sieur de La Salle in 1680. The initial purpose of the small fort, constructed near the Indian village of Pimitoui, was to protect French traders from attacks by the hostile Iroquois. This military function later proved to be less important than its commercial character. Although the military structure was destroyed after only three months, the site continued to be an important fur trading center. It was transferred to British control in 1765 and renamed Fort Clark.

CRÈVECOEUR, MICHEL-GUILLAUME JEAN DE (1735-1813) A French-American writer, he was born in Normandy, France, and in 1754 went to Canada, where he fought in the French and Indian War. After exploring the area, he settled in New York and became an American citizen in 1765. He wrote essays on American life and the coming revolution, using the pen name J. Hector St. John. These essays were later collected in *Letters from an American Farmer* (1782). While he was on a visit to France (1780-83), his New York home was destroyed and his wife killed during an Indian raid. Heartbroken, he served as the French consul in New York, wrote newspaper articles signed "Agricola," and eventually retired to France in 1790.

CRIME AND PUNISHMENT Crime, its regulation, and its punishment, were perceived by the authorities as growing problems throughout the colonial period; as the Puritan leader John Winthrop put it, "as people increased, so sin abounded." The 17th century records of Winthrop's Boston, for example, reveal numerous instances of assault, arson, breaking and entering, embezzlement, fighting and brawling, manslaughter, the receipt of stolen goods, theft, and, especially, of sexual irregularity. During the 1630s, for instance, some 30 cases of fornication and adultery came before the Massachusetts Court of Assistants. As Boston developed as a market and a port, the growing numbers of seamen, runaway servants, freed blacks, wayward Indians, and widows preoccupied the authorities, who complained about the growing tendency to disorder among these "unfamilied" groups. The situation was similar in other colonial towns. Although crime was not so prevalent as in the mother country, each town was beset with its share of criminals. Similar too were the moral regulations in every colony: the rigid observance of the Sabbath, the concern with public drunkenness, the prohibitions on gambling and card playing.

The enforcement of these laws and regulations was generally handled by the local constabulary, which appeared everywhere as soon as government was organized. Seldom were constables paid, but rather they were drafted from the ranks of freemen or citizens and given the authority, in the words of one charter, "to make, signe, & put forth pursuits, or hues & cries, after murthrers, manslayrs, peace breakers, theeves, robers, burglars, where no magistrate is at hand; also to apprehend without warrant such as are over taken with drinke, swearing, breaking ye Saboth, lying, vagrant psons, night walkers, or any other yt shall break our lawes." Towns and villages organized night watches of citizens to patrol the streets.

Punishment was swift and generally consisted of fines, restitution of stolen goods two- or threefold, and public whippings; the use of pillory, stocks, and ducking stool were less common than usually supposed, and jails were commonly used merely as places of detention while awaiting punishment. An exception was imprisonment for debt, which despite frequent protests pointing to its brutality and irrationality, continued in most areas through the 18th century.

The problem of criminality grew during the extended periods of intercolonial warfare during the late 17th and 18th centuries. Highway crime and horse theft, piracy and smuggling, and increased attention to prostitution, bastardry, and infanticide characterize the judicial records of the period. With the increased issue of paper money the inevitable counterfeiters appeared. Mob violence, involving both men and women, became a problem in many cities.

The increase in crime and disorder was accompanied by an increasing frequency of public executions and punishments of mutilation, such as branding and the cropping of ears. In 1749, for example, the whole of Boston turned out to witness a double hanging; in 1769 Charlestown, Massachusetts, burned a black man and woman at the stake for the poisoning death of three whites; and in 1771 two women were hanged in New York City for being pickpockets. Prolonged jailing also became more common. Philadelphia, in 1722, became the first municipality to erect a stone prison, in which debtors were separated from common criminals; other jails were pitiful dungeons. Charles Woodmason complained that the Charlestown jail of 1767 housed 16 debtors in each 12-foot square room, with no sanitation, no cots, and no separation of the sexes; "a person would be in a better Situation," he wrote, "in the French Kings Gallies, or the Prisons of Turkey or Barbary." As bad as these facilities were, however, the jails, the punishments, and the crimes of colonial America could never really compare with the situation in England or the Continent.

Bibliography: Bridenbaugh, Carl, *Cities in the Wilderness* (Oxford Univ. Press, 1938); *Cities in Revolt* (Oxford Univ. Press, 1955).

John Mack Faragher
Mount Holyoke College

CROGHAN, GEORGE (died 1782) Irish-born Indian trader and diplomat, Croghan entered frontier commerce in the early 1740s. Over the next 15 years he conducted a growing business with the tribes of the West—to the French representing perhaps the greatest threat to their plan for control of the Ohio Valley, to the British becoming their best source of knowledge about the Indians and the aims of the French. The French and Indian War destroyed his business, and after the war he played an important role as an interpreter and messenger for the British, helping to negotiate agreements with the Western tribes. He turned thereafter to land speculation, purchasing large tracts from Indians, often fraudulently. He helped to negotiate the agreement by which the English reoccupied the Western forts after Pontiac's Rebellion, but the war severely damaged his finances. The Revolution further complicated his land business, and he died an obscure figure with an enormous debt. Croghan was a consummate diplomat to the Indians, a skilled frontiersman, and a sharp trader, as well as a gambler and a cheat.

See also Pontiac's Rebellion.

CROMWELL, OLIVER (1599-1658) A British leader and general, he represented Cambridge in the Long Parliament in 1640 and, after creating the New Model Army in 1645, distinguished himself at Naseby and Langport in 1646 at the end of the First English Civil War. After 1649, when King Charles I was executed, Cromwell ruled England, Scotland, and Ireland. In 1653, backed by his army and by an Instrument of Government, he was proclaimed lord protector of the country, presiding over a council of state and a one-house parliament. His protectorate brought order, religious freedom, prosperity, justice, and superior armed forces to England.

CULPEPER, THOMAS, LORD (1635-89) Charles II appointed Culpeper governor of Virginia for life in 1675, effective upon the death or removal of Governor William Berkeley. When Berkeley died in 1677, Culpeper appointed deputies to serve in his place, but was himself ordered to Virginia in 1680. Once there, he pardoned the participants in Bacon's Rebellion and persuaded the General Assembly to grant a tobacco export tax for the King's disposal and other monies for himself. After four months, Culpeper returned to England, leaving a deputy in charge. He was ordered back when the low price of tobacco caused planters to destroy their crops. Upon arrival he hanged some of those who had destroyed tobacco, modified proposed legislation, and dissolved the assembly. He worked to increase the power of the Crown. Culpeper left for England in May 1683. He was removed from office three months later for having again left Virginia without permission and for extortion.

Bibliography: Flippen, Percy Scott, *The Royal Government in Virginia, 1624-1775* (AMS Press, 1966).

CULPEPER'S REBELLION In 1677, farmers living in the backwoods community of Albermarle, North Carolina, were engaged in smuggling tobacco with the help of New England merchants. The proprietary group of the colony, led by acting governor Thomas Miller, then attempted to collect customs under the Plantation Duty Act of 1673, part of the Navigation Acts. Under the leadership of John Culpeper, a recent settler from South Carolina, and George Durant, a local planter, the farmers accused their opponents of treason and official misconduct. Culpeper had the proprietary group jailed and seized the government. The rebels administered the government for over a year.

Governor Miller escaped from jail in 1678, made his way to England, and presented his case to the proprietors there. The rebel assembly sent Culpeper on their behalf. Although Miller succeeded in having Culpeper tried for treason, he was acquitted of that charge. He was found guilty only of "riot," because there was no settled government in Carolina at that time (the appointed governor having died before arriving in the colony). Eventually one of the actual proprietors became governor, and the rebellion slowly quieted down.

CUMBERLAND, FORT   This trading post and storehouse, established in western Maryland in 1750 at the confluence of Wills Creek and the Potomac River, was originally named Fort Mount Pleasant and maintained by the Virginia Company. In 1755 it was enlarged and rebuilt as an open stockade to serve as a point of mobilization for the campaign of Edward Braddocks and George Washington against Fort Duquesne. At that time it was renamed in honor of the Duke of Cumberland. The British colonial forces sought shelter in the fort after their disastrous defeat at the Battle of the Wilderness. By 1765, however, Fort Cumberland had lost its importance and was abandoned.

CUMBERLAND GAP   A deep pass at the intersection of the present states of Virginia, Kentucky, and Tennessee in the Cumberland range of the Appalachian highlands, it is some 45 miles northeast of Knoxville. Offering the easiest passage across the Appalachians, the pass had been in use by Indians and herds of buffalo for centuries and was the route of the Great Trading and War Path to the Ohio River country. The pass gained public recognition after the return of Virginian Thomas Walker and his exploring company from the first recorded exploration of Kentucky, but since Walker saw crosses and other European graffiti carved on the trunks of trees at the pass it was clear that other frontiersmen had used the pass before. In 1775, Daniel Boone and others blazed the Wilderness Road over the gap, and thereafter it became the great gateway to the trans-Appalachian west for hundreds of thousands of American pioneers.

CUMBERLAND SETTLEMENTS   After the Cherokee cession at the Treaty of Sycamore Shoals in 1774-75, land speculator Richard Henderson, who had acquired the dubious land rights, encouraged settlement in Kentucky and south along the Cumberland River in what would become Tennessee. After the failure of Henderson's plans for the Transylvania Company colony in Kentucky by the preemption of authority by the Virginia legislature, he turned his attention to the Cumberland settlements. In 1780 he signed the "Articles of Agreement or Compact of Government" (known as the Cumberland Compact) with 263 settlers, setting the terms by which they could purchase land and establish a temporary elective government over the eight small communities in the area of French Lick, present-day Nashville. Like the earlier Kentucky experience, however, this compact was voided in 1783 when North Carolina incorporated the settlements as Davidson County; later they became the heart of Tennessee.

CURRENCY ACT (1764)   An attempt at monetary regulation in the American colonies by Parliament, the Currency Act prohibited the issuance of paper money after September 1, 1764. During the French and Indian War the colony of Virginia had accumulated a debt of more than 250,000 pounds, which it had indefinitely deferred by issuing bank notes. In order to control the rapid inflation of prices that resulted, Parliament passed the Currency Act, which overturned the existing fiscal legislation of the assemblies of the Southern colonies. An earlier, equally unsuccessful attempt by the New England colonies to evade debt by issuing paper money had been prohibited by Parliament in 1751.

D

DALE, SIR THOMAS (died 1619) A marshal of Virginia and naval commander, Thomas Dale was knighted in 1606 and appointed in 1611 to bring order to Virginia. When Sir Thomas Gates left in 1614, Dale's severe punishments, such as tying a food thief to a tree until he starved, caused the colonists to call his rule "cruel tyranny." His more favorable innovative measures included eliminating malaria by moving the colony away from the swamps of Jamestown to Henrico, building palisades around the cornfields, and establishing peace with the Indians. The colony in good order, he left in 1617 to defend English interests in the East Indies.

DARE, VIRGINIA (born 1587) The first English child born in America, Virginia Dare was the granddaughter of Governor John White, who settled at Roanoke Island (North Carolina) in 1587. On August 18 of the same year, the governor's daughter Ellinor gave birth to Virginia. Governor White returned to England in an effort to collect supplies for his new colony, but because of the interference caused by the war with Spain, no help came to the colony until 1591. There is no historical trace of these early colonists, and it is postulated that they either perished or were absorbed by local Indian tribes. Beyond her ninth day of life, when White sailed from Roanoke, nothing is known about Virginia.

DARRAGH, LYDIA BARRINGTON (1729-89) A Revolutionary War heroine, nurse, and midwife, Darragh earned a place in history for a single courageous act. One of the rooms in her house in Philadelphia was used by British officers as a council chamber during the British occupation. When she overheard them plotting a surprise attack on George Washington's troops at Whitemarsh in December 1777, Darragh decided to carry the news to the American army at Whitemarsh, where her son was a soldier. In order to cross British lines, she carried an empty sack, claiming that she needed to buy flour. She walked 13 miles towards the camp, eventually meeting an American officer and warning him of the impending attack. Forewarned, the Americans were able to defeat the British.

DARTMOUTH COLLEGE Funds raised in England, partly by the second Earl of Dartmouth, allowed founder Reverend Eleazar Wheelock to move his school, originally opened in 1755 as Moor's Indian Charity School in Lebanon, Connecticut, to Hanover, New Hampshire in 1770, where a college for whites was added. It was the last institution of higher learning in America to be founded by royal decree. The Indian school was eventually discontinued. A famous lawsuit, argued in front of the U.S. Supreme Court by Daniel Webster in 1819, held that the state legislature could not put the college under state control. At issue was the inviolability of private corporation charters, which the court said were contracts.

DAUGHTERS OF LIBERTY The name Daughters of Liberty was given to groups of women who in 1768-69 assembled in several communities throughout the colonies to demonstrate their support of the patriot cause by holding spinning bees. Numbering between 15 and 100 participants, the women would meet in the morning with their spinning wheels at the home of a clergyman or other sympathizer and spend the day spinning sheaves of wool or cotton yarn. Such gatherings were reported in Newport and Providence, Rhode Island; in New York City; in Boston, Beverly, Ipswich, Rowley, and Newbury, Massachusetts; and in Georgia. In most cases, the spinners gave the yarn they produced to their hosts, but in two instances it was made into clothing worn by the graduating classes of Rhode Island and Harvard colleges. The Daughters attracted considerable attention, for their activities were widely reported in the newspapers, which praised their patriotic ardor and upright characters. The spinning bees revealed the desire of colonial women to participate in the Revolutionary ferment and served as an outlet for such involvement.

Bibliography: Norton, Mary Beth, *Liberty's Daughters: The Revolutionary Experience of American Women, 1750-1800* (Little, Brown, 1980).

James K. Somerville
State University of New York at Geneseo

DAVENPORT, JOHN (1597-1669) A clergyman and author, Davenport was born in Coventry, England. He served as a minister from 1615 to 1633, when his adoption of Non-conformist views caused him to flee first to Holland and then to the Massachusetts Bay Colony (1637). By 1639 he was established in New Haven (Connecticut) Colony, as the pastor of the church and was active in church policy. He objected to the "Half Way Covenant" and petitioned in 1662 against New Haven's incorporation into

Connecticut in his pamphlet *New Haven's Case Stated*. After he lost these issues, he left New Haven for the First Church of Boston, where he died shortly after taking office.

DAVIES, SAMUEL (1723-61) An American Presbyterian minister and college president, he was born in Delaware. Ordained a minister in 1747, he was sent to Virginia to preach and gained fame as an orator. Through his early efforts, the church in Virginia was strengthened and the first presbytery in the colony was founded at Hanover in 1755. Transferred to the New York synod in 1753, he traveled to Britain to raise funds for the College of New Jersey (now Princeton University). Elected to the college presidency in 1759, he served for only two years, but raised the college's academic and admissions standards and made plans to expand the library.

DAVION, ANTHONY (died 1727) A French missionary, Father Anthony Davion was born in Issigny, Normandy, and was educated in the foreign mission seminary in Paris. Ordained in 1690, he became a church pastor in Quebec. In June 1700 he went to Biloxi in the Mississippi Valley, where he worked among the Tonica tribe. Tribal warfare forced him to leave, but in 1704 the Tonica Indians asked him to return. He destroyed their sacred temple and put out their sacred fire but made few converts except for the chief, who agreed to be

An early patriot, Silas Deane later urged Americans to reconcile with Britain. *(Library of Congress)*

baptized and wear Western dress. After several missions to the Tonica, Davion died in New Orleans.

DAVIS, JOHN (?1550-1605) English explorer, Davis devoted his career to the discovery of the Northwest Passage. With a reputation as a fine navigator, he secured royal backing for a series of voyages from 1585 to 1587 in which he explored the western coast of Greenland and the inlets and channels of Baffin Island; Davis Strait is named for him. Failing to discover a passage, in 1591 he attempted to find a western entrance; his ship was forced to turn back at the Strait of Magellan, but on his return trip he charted the Falkland Islands. He then served as pilot on the first voyages of the East India Company to the East Indies, where he was killed by Japanese pirates.
See also Northwest Passage.

DAY, STEPHEN (c.1594-1668) The American colonies' first printer, Day was born in England about 1594. A locksmith by trade, he emigrated to New England in 1638 under contract to work two years for Reverend Glover, who brought with him a printing press, font of type, and paper. Glover died on the voyage, but his wife settled in Cambridge, Massachusetts, where Day operated the press until 1649. The first imprints included annual almanacs; five Harvard commencement broadsides; the Capital Laws (1642); the *Bay Psalm Book* (1640), the first book in English printed in the colonies; and a spelling book (1643).

DEANE, SILAS (1737-89) A colonial leader, diplomat, and patriot who eventually opposed the Revolution, Deane was born in Groton, Connecticut. He graduated from Yale College (1758) and started a law practice in Wethersfield, Connecticut, in 1762. During the years before the Revolution, Deane supported the patriot cause. He led the local opposition to the Townshend Acts and sat in Connecticut's General Assembly (1772). Deane served as secretary to the Committee of Correspondence (1773) and represented Connecticut in the First and Second Continental Congresses (1774-76).

In 1776, Deane became the first colonial representative to be sent abroad as a diplomat. In France, he secured a shipment of arms (1777) that helped American victory at Saratoga, New York. He was also able to obtain for the Americans the services of many European army officers and mercenaries. He was joined in France by Arthur Lee and Benjamin Franklin to negotiate the treaties of the French alliance. Deane returned to America (1778) after charges of disloyalty and embezzlement arose because of his association with the British spy Edward Bancroft. Deane was unable to quiet the suspicions of Congress and subsequently began to denounce the war bitterly, advocating reconciliation with Britain in letters to friends. After they were published in a Tory newspaper in New York City, he then went into exile

A contemporary engraving showed the members of the Continental Congress voting to adopt the Declaration of Independence. *(Library of Congress)*

in London, where he published *An Address to the Free and Independent Citizens of the United States* (1789), a defense of his actions. Deane died while returning to North America by ship.

DEARBORN, HENRY (1751-1829)   Born in Hampton, New Hampshire, he was trained as a physician. A patriot and a captain in the militia, he participated in the Battle of Bunker Hill in June 1775. Subsequently, he joined Benedict Arnold's Quebec expedition and was taken prisoner by the British. Paroled in 1776 and exchanged in 1777, when he rejoined New Hampshire's forces he fought at Ticonderoga and Saratoga, wintered at Valley Forge (1777-78), and was commended at the Battle of Monmouth. He later served with Washington in the Yorktown campaign. After the war, he sat in the U.S. Congress (1793-97), was secretary of war (1801-09), and served as a major general in the War of 1812 but was recalled for incompetence. He died in Roxbury, Massachusetts.

DE BRAHM, WILLIAM GERHARD (1717-99)   A Dutch-born surveyor and geographer, De Brahm emigrated in 1751 with 160 Protestant Germans to Georgia, where he founded Bethany. Soon thereafter more than 1,000 relatives and acquaintances joined the original settlers. In 1754, De Brahm was appointed a surveyorship in Georgia and in 1764 he received a crown appointment as surveyor for the Southern District. He explored, surveyed, and plotted the Florida coast, marking out lands for settlement and locating town sites complete with school and church lands.

In 1770, Governor James Grant suspended De Brahm for his arrogant attitude including overcharges and obstruction of applications for land. De Brahm sailed for England, where he published a map of the Atlantic Ocean for his mariners' guide, *The Atlantic Pilot* (1772). His publications, his reports, and his own presence combined to win over the Privy Council and the Lords of the Treasury, who recommended to the Council of East Florida that he be reinstated. His work continued as did his quasi-religious efforts, such as Time an Apparition of Eternity (1791) and *Apocalyptic Gnomon Points Out Eternity's Divisability* (1795).

DECLARATION OF INDEPENDENCE   The Declaration of Independence originated in the appointment on June 11, 1776, by the Second Continental Congress of a committee to draft a formal statement declaring independence from Great Britain. The committee consisted of Thomas Jefferson, John Adams, Benjamin Franklin, Roger Sherman, and Robert Livingstone. The others delegated to Jefferson the task of composing the document, which Adams, Franklin, and later the other members of the committee modified. The Congress altered Jefferson's document during the debates of July 2–4 and adopted the Declaration on July 4, ordering handbills of the Declaration to be widely disseminated. Beginning on August 2, 56 men representing all 13 colonies signed the Declaration, which is now displayed in the National Archives in Washington, D.C. Jefferson preserved the document he presented to the Congress, presenting it to his friends and ultimately printing it with a key indicating the modifications.

Philosophical Basis.   The Declaration as adopted by the Congress reflected the ideas of the English philosopher John Locke, who argued that a divinely ordained natural law endows humankind with natural rights (to life, liberty, and property) and that government rests upon a trust with the citizens whereby the government may claim obedience of the citizens as long as it uses its power to protect their rights. If the government ceases to protect their rights, the citizens may empower a new government. The Declaration cast Americans in the role of citizens and George III in that of a ruler who had despoiled their rights. The Declaration states that "the Laws of Nature and of Nature's God" entitle the United States to political independence. The essence of the Declaration is its definition of humankind as equal, free individuals possessing the right to choose their own government.

The Declaration, along with the American Revolution that followed, was a crucial element in the creation of modern liberalism. Yet, intellectual and social ferment lay behind the ordered sentences of the Declaration. Far from a liberal individualist, Jefferson viewed individuals as tied together in society by rights and duties and as bound together in their affections by a moral sense. He sentimentally idealized the public virtue that oriented individuals away from self-interest and toward the good of society, and he did not foresee the social and political contention that would lead in the 1780s to calls for a strong federal government and even to some calls for an American king. For the growth of the economy and the population in the 1780s, combined with a greater inequality in the distribution of wealth than in 1776, led to lower-class and middle-class complaints about inequality and to a sense of crisis among the gentry, who seized upon the idea of a strong federal government to counter what the gentry perceived as an excess of liberty. Furthermore, the Congress expunged from Jefferson's document a long passage condemning George III's support of slavery. Although he owned 200 slaves in 1776, Jefferson hoped for a gradual end to slavery. He acquiesced in the deletions to gain consensus,

remarking in 1778 that "future efforts" must eradicate slavery. Without the antislavery passage the Declaration could address slavery only with the phrases about human equality and rights. Slaves, however, were considered not human beings but property. The absence of consensus over slavery was revealed in the 1784 failure by only one vote of Jefferson's ordinance to ban slavery in the western part of the United States after 1800.

Text of the Declaration.   The text of the Declaration of Independence is as follows:

WHEN in the Course of human Events, it becomes necessary for one People to dissolve the Political Bands which have connected them with another, and to assume among the Powers of the Earth, the separate and equal Station to which the Laws of Nature and of Nature's God entitle them, a decent Respect to the Opinions of Mankind requires that they should declare the causes which impel them to the Separation. We hold these Truths to be self-evident, that all Men are created equal, that they are endowed by their Creator with certain unalienable Rights, that among these are Life, Liberty, and the Pursuit of Happiness. That to secure these Rights, Governments are instituted among Men, deriving their just Powers from the Consent of the Governed. That whenever any Form of Government becomes destructive of these Ends, it is the Right of the People to alter or to abolish it, and to institute new Government, laying its Foundation on such Principles, and organizing its Powers in such Form, as to them shall seem most likely to effect their Safety and Happiness. Prudence, indeed, will dictate that Governments long established should not be changed for light and transient Causes; and accordingly all Experience hath shewn, that Mankind are more disposed to suffer, while Evils are sufferable, than to right themselves by abolishing the Forms to which they are accustomed. But when a long train of Abuses and Usurpations, pursuing invariably the same Object, evinces a Design to reduce them under absolute Despotism, it is their Right, it is their Duty, to throw off such Government, and to provide new Guards for their future Security. Such has been the patient Sufferance of these Colonies; and such is now the Necessity which constrains them to alter their former Systems of Government. The History of the present King of Great Britain is a History of repeated Injuries and Usurpations, all having in direct Object the Establishment of an absolute Tyranny over these States. To prove this, let Facts be submitted to a candid World. He has refused his Assent to Laws, the most wholesome and necessary for the public Good. He has forbidden his Governors to pass Laws of immediate and pressing Importance, unless suspended in their Operation till his Assent should be obtained; and when so suspended, he has utterly neglected to attend to them. He has refused to pass other Laws for the Accomodation of large Districts of People, unless those People would relinquish the Right of Representation in the Legislature, a Right inestimable to them, and formidable to Tyrants only. He has called together Legislative bodies at Places unusual, uncomfortable, and distant from the Depository of their public Records, for the sole Purpose of fatiguing them into Compliance with his Measures. He has dissolved Representative Houses repeatedly, for opposing with manly Firmness his Invasions on the Rights of the People. He has refused for a long Time, after such Dissolutions, to cause others to be elected; whereby the Legislative Powers, incapable of Annihilation, have returned to the People at large for their exercise; the State remaining in the meantime exposed to all the Dangers of Invasion from without, and Convulsions within. He has endeavoured to prevent the Population of these States; for that Purpose obstructing the Laws for Naturalization of Foreigners; refusing to pass others to encourage their Migrations hither, and raising the Conditions of new Appropriations of Lands. He has obstructed the Administration of Justice, by refusing his Assent to Laws for establishing Judiciary Powers. He has made Judges dependent on his Will alone, for the Tenure of their Offices, and the Amount and Payment of their Salaries. He has erected a Multitude of new Offices, and sent hither Swarms of Officers to harass our People, and eat out their Substance. He has kept among us, in Times of Peace, Standing Armies without the consent of our Legislatures. He has affected to render the Military independent of and superior to the Civil Power. He has combined with others to subject us to Jurisdiction foreign to our Constitution, and unacknowledged by our Laws; giving his Assent to their Acts of pretended Legislation: For quartering large Bodies of Armed Troops among us: For protecting them, by a mock Trial, from Punishment for any Murders which they should commit on the Inhabitants of these States: For cutting off our Trade with all Parts of the World: For imposing Taxes on us without our Consent: For depriving us in many Cases, of the Benefits of Trial by Jury: For transporting us beyond Seas to be tried for pretended Offences: For abolishing the free System of English Laws in a neighbouring Province, establishing therein an arbitrary Government, and enlarging its Boundaries, so as to render it at once an Example and fit Instrument for introducing the same absolute Rule into these Colonies: For taking away our Charters, abolishing our most valuable Laws, and altering fundamentally the Forms of our Governments: For suspending our own Legislatures, and declaring themselves invested with Power to legislate for us in all Cases whatsoever. He has abdicated Government here, by declaring us out of his Protection and waging War against us. He has plundered our Seas, ravaged our Coasts, burnt our Towns, and destroyed the Lives of our People. He is at this Time, transporting large Armies of foreign Mercenaries to compleat the Works of Death, Desolation and Tyranny, already begun with circumstances of Cruelty and Perfidy, scarcely paralleled in the most barbarous Ages, and totally unworthy the Head of a civilized Nation. He has constrained our fellow Citizens taken Captive on the high Seas to bear Arms against their Country, to become the Executioners of their Friends and Brethren, or to fall themselves by their Hands. He has excited domestic Insurrections amongst us, and has endeavoured to bring on the Inhabitants of our Frontiers, the merciless Indian Savages, whose known Rule of Warfare, is an undistinguished Destruction of all Ages, Sexes and Conditions. In every stage of these Oppressions We have Petitioned for Redress in the most humble Terms: Our repeated Petitions have been answered only by repeated injury. A Prince, whose Character is thus marked by every act which may define a Tyrant, is unfit to be the Ruler of a free People. Nor have We been wanting in Attentions to our British Brethren. We have warned them from Time to Time of Attempts by their Legislature to extend an unwarrantable Jurisdiction over us. We have reminded them of the Circumstances of our Emigration and Settlement here. We have appealed to their native Justice and Magnanimity, and we have conjured them by the Ties of our common Kindred to disavow these Usurpations, which would inevitably interrupt our Connections and Correspondence. They too have been deaf to the Voice of Justice and of Consanguinity. We must, therefore, acquiesce in the Necessity, which denounces our Separation, and hold them, as we hold the rest of Mankind, Enemies in War, in Peace, Friends.

We, Therefore, the Representatives of the UNITED STATES OF AMERICA, in GENERAL CONGRESS, Assembled, appealing to the Supreme Judge of the World for the Rectitude of our Intentions, do, in the Name, and by Authority of the good People of these Colonies, solemnly Publish and Declare, That these United Colonies are, and of Right ought to be, FREE AND INDEPENDENT STATES; that they are absolved from all Allegiance to the British Crown, and that all political Connection between them and the State of Great Britain, is and ought to be totally dissolved; and that as FREE AND INDEPENDENT STATES, they have full Power to levy War, conclude Peace, contract Alliances, establish Commerce, and to do all other Acts and Things which INDEPENDENT STATES may of right do. And for the support of this Declaration, with a firm Reliance on the Protection of divine Providence, we mutually pledge to each other our Lives, our Fortunes, and our sacred Honor.

See also Continental Congress, Second; Jefferson, Thomas.

Bibliography: Boyd, Julian P., *The Declaration of Independence: The Evolution of a Text* (Princeton Univ. Press, 1945); Malone, Dumas, *The Story of the Declaration of Independence* (Oxford Univ. Press, 1975); Wills, Garry, *Inventing America: Jefferson's Declaration of Independence* (Doubleday, 1978).

John Saillant
Brown University

DECLARATION OF RIGHTS AND GRIEVANCES (1765)   Drafted in New York City by delegates from the nine colonies at the Stamp Act Congress, the declaration denounced the Stamp Act as unconstitutional taxation levied without the consent of the colonies. Written primarily by John Dickinson, the declaration stated that the delegates had the same rights as the King's subjects in Britain and that taxation without representation in Parliament was a violation of those rights. The declaration also said that since the colonies could not be represented in Parliament, only the colonial legislatures could impose taxes. The Northhampton (Virginia) County Court declared the Stamp Act unconstitutional in February 1766.

See also Dickinson, John, Stamp Act; Stamp Act Congress.

DECLARATORY ACT (1766)   The result of a political compromise between Parliament and the American colonies in the aftermath of the 1765 Stamp Act, the Declaratory Act for the first time explicitly defined the legal relationship between the North American colonies and the British government. In agreeing to repeal the unpopular Stamp Act and the Sugar Act, Parliament officially declared that the decision-making and administrative jurisdiction of the Crown in American affairs superseded that of the colonial legislatures in all cases. This act, the wording of which closely followed that of the Irish Declaratory Act of 1719, was strongly supported by Prime Minister William Pitt.

DEERFIELD MASSACRE (1704) Incorporated in 1673, Deerfield is situated in the Connecticut River Valley in northwestern Massachusetts. As a frontier settlement, the town was exposed to Indian attacks from the beginning and in 1675 was the first town in the valley to be attacked during King Philip's War. When Queen Anne's War broke out in 1702, the Indians began their campaigns against the towns in Maine, but as the war went on, Deerfield received warnings from New York officials that the French were fitting out an expedition against it. Nevertheless, the actual attack, on February 29, 1704, was a complete surprise, and more than half of the 291 villagers were killed or carried away to Canada as captives. Following the war, Deerfield gradually became less exposed as other settlements grew up around it and never again was attacked.

DEFERENCE The world-view of 17th-century English colonists was founded on principles of hierarchy and deference to authority. Children were to be strictly governed by their parents, wives by their husbands, and the family provided the model for civil order as well. Theirs was a world of class, of slaves and servants, of the lesser- and better-born, and of ethnic hierarchies in which Indians, Africans, and other peoples were considered distinct social inferiors to English-speakers. In New England, Puritanism enjoyed the status of a state religion, as did Anglicanism in Virginia. Each of these orders of distinction demanded the deference to which it was entitled. In political terms society was dominated by the planter elite in the Southern colonies and by small groups of wealthy families in the proprietary colonies, while in New England, despite rather wide property ownership and political participation, traditions of deference returned many of the same leading families to political office year after year. In the words of John Winthrop, the people were called upon by their leaders to "quietly and cheerfully submit unto that authority which is set over you … for your own good."

The development of colonial society, however, fostered conflicts that fractured this deferential order. In Bacon's Rebellion (1676) in Virginia, backcountry planters complained bitterly about the "grandees" of the tidewater;

while issuing a challenge to the elites, however, they brutally reinforced ethnic hierarchy. By the 18th century the growing population faced increasing land shortages, with resulting conflict and violence, sometimes leading to overt revolt throughout the colonies. The Great Awakening of the 1740s introduced what became an American tradition of sectarianism in which people could follow their own religious lights.

Growing ethnic diversity and concentration created, especially in the Middle Colonies, a kind of pluralistic society, in which difference came to be expected. And the growing incidence of premarital pregnancy and geographic mobility suggested that even family governance had become less hierarchical. The Revolution, of course, might be interpreted (as it was by the conservatives) as a general revolt against deference, but the developments of the previous 50 years suggest that the crisis of authority had been a long time coming.

John Mack Faragher
Mount Holyoke College

DEKANAWIDAH (?1550-?1600) A legendary Indian prophet and lawgiver, also known as Deganawidah, meaning "two rivers flowing together," he was reported by tradition to have been born near Kingston, Ontario, one of seven brothers of a Huron family. Mythical elements are prominent in the story of his infancy: At the time of his virgin birth, his mother reportedly received an oracle that this child would someday destroy his own people, and she made several unsuccessful attempts to kill the baby.

Growing into manhood, Dekanawidah moved southward, joined the Iroquois, and met Hiawatha, another legendary figure in Iroquois history. The two men conceived the idea of a grand confederation of Iroquois peoples and set about bringing the Oneida, Cayuga, Onandaga, Seneca, and Mohawk together. Dekanawidah's greatest contribution was the formulation of the structure of that confederation, based on elected representatives from local villages and with the participation of women in the political process. This League of Five Nations later served as a model for the federal system of government of the United States. Near the end of Dekanawidah's life, the prophecy of his childhood was fulfilled with the destruction of the Hurons by the Iroquois Confederacy.

See also Hiawatha; Iroquois Confederacy.

DE LANCEY, JAMES (1703-60) Councillor, chief justice, and lieutenant governor of New York, De Lancey was the son of Stephen De Lancey and Anne Van Cortlandt. James studied law at Cambridge and was widely regarded as one of the best educated men in New York. His marriage to Anne Heathcote, cousin of Sir John Heathcote, a member of Parliament and associate of Walpole, as well as the marriages of his brothers and sisters, helped him create a powerful network of social, economic, and political allies in America and Britain.

Between 1729, when De Lancey was appointed to the provincial council, and his sudden death on July 30, 1760, he demonstrated great political savvy in manipulating the imperial system to his and his family's benefit. First appointed to the provincial supreme court in 1731, he became a close ally of Governor William Cosby and was rewarded with a promotion to chief justice in 1733. During the prosecution of Peter Zenger, De Lancey vigorously defended the royal prerogative. In 1744, Governor George Clinton, believing that De Lancey would help him defend the governor's office against the incursions of the Assembly, granted the chief justice a commission for good behavior in place of the usual tenure at pleasure. De Lancey, however, used the security of his new commission to build an independent political base from which he frequently assailed Clinton. First appointed lieutenant governor in 1747, he was, until his death, the most powerful politician in the colony.

See also De Lancey Family.

DE LANCEY FAMILY   Etienne (Stephen) De Lancey, a Huguenot immigrant who came to New York in 1686, became the sire of one of the colony's most powerful families. A wealthy New York City merchant, his marriage to Anne Van Cortlandt provided important social and political relations with New York's Dutch aristocracy. His membership in the Church of England and his commercial relations with major London merchants afforded him important connections with the colony's British community. His children, as a result of their education, political skills, and opportune marriages, increased the economic and political influence of the family not only in New York but also in Great Britain.

James (1703-60) served as chief justice (1733-60) and lieutenant governor (1753-55, 1757-60) of New York. His son James (1732-1800) promoted the family's interests until the eve of the Revolution. Oliver (1718-85) served as an assemblyman and councillor from New York until the Revolution, and during the Revolutionary War became a British general. The family's most important alliance was the marriage of Susannah to Admiral Sir Peter Warren, whose political influence in Great Britain assured the family attentive friends in Parliament and the government. The family was also allied with London merchants William and Samuel Baker, who often lobbied on their behalf before the Crown.

Although the "De Lancey interest," as the family and its adherents came to be known, frequently opposed the actions of New York's royal governors, the family's political and social influence grew from its connections within the imperial system. When the colonies broke from Britain, most of the family left New York. Their extensive estates were confis-

cated by the Revolutionary government, and family members were forced to resettle throughout the British Empire. The Crown compensated most of them for their losses, and many family members resumed their imperial political careers in their new homes.

George Miles
Yale University

DE LANGLADE, CHARLES MICHEL   (1729-c.1801)   "Father of Wisconsin" and Indian soldier, Charles Michel De Langlade was the son of a French nobleman and an Ottawa Indian. He was educated by the Jesuits, but after joining his Indian uncles in a French expedition against the Chickasaw he adopted military life and became a renowned leader of Indian troops during the French and Indian War. From 1756 to 1759 he helped defeat General Braddock and Rogers's Rangers, attacked Fort William Henry, and served in the Quebec campaign of 1759. When the French withdrew, De Langlade changed sides and gave his Mackinac fort to the English. He settled with his father in Green Bay, Wisconsin. During the Revolution he allied with the British.

DELAWARE   Delaware is located on the east side of the Delmarva Peninsula, a finger of land between the Atlantic Ocean and the Chesapeake Bay. The northwest corner of Delaware falls within the Piedmont Plateau and is the only area of elevation. The remainder is flat, a part of the Atlantic Coastal Plain. Its nearly 190 square miles of tidal wetlands provided an important resource for Native Americans and early settlers, as did its principal waterways, the Delaware River and Delaware Bay. Encompassing just 2,057 square miles, Delaware ranked by area as the second smallest colony.

By 6500 B.C., hunters and gatherers inhabited the forests and bogs that covered Delaware, but more sedentary and agriculturally oriented Indians date from about 1000 A.D. At the time of European contact, two Indian groups lived within the area that was to become Delaware. The Lenni Lenape, later known as the Delaware Indians, lived to the east along the Delaware River and Bay. The other group was known as the Nanticoke and lived to the southwest along the waterways that flowed into the Chesapeake. Both groups belonged to the Algonquian language family.

Credit for the European discovery of Delaware goes to Henry Hudson, who sailed into the bay in 1609 while looking for the Northwest Passage to Asia for the Dutch. He named the river the South River, but eventually the name given it by Samuel Argall in 1610 to honor the governor of Virginia, Lord De La Warr, prevailed. Although early explorers commented on the beauty and abundance of the area, neither the Dutch nor the English showed any early interest in establishing colonies there. Then, beginning in the 1630s, the area became of great interest to three European nations—the Netherlands, Sweden, and Great Britain—as each attempted to establish trade hegemony along the Delaware River. The early colonial history of Delaware became one of international rivalry and competive settlements.

Early Settlement. The Dutch made the first attempt at settlement in 1631. A group of investors organized a colony named Zwaanendael and sent 28 men to build a fort just inside Cape Henlopen on Lewes Creek. The colony was designed, in part, to exploit the large number of whales in the Delaware Bay and to produce whale oil in commercial quantity. A misunderstanding between the settlers and the Indians led to the massacre of the entire colony within a few months. After that unsuccessful attempt, the Dutch chose for many years to limit their activities along the Delaware to brief trading missions.

The first permanent settlement in Delaware came in 1638, when the New Sweden Company established an outpost on the Minquan Kil, later named the Christina River in honor of the child queen of Sweden. The Swedish colony on the Delaware River arose, in part, from Sweden's desire to raise itself to great power status through colonial exploitation. The New Sweden Company was originally a private company with strong government support and both Swedish and Dutch investors, many of the latter disgruntled with the Dutch West India Company.

Peter Minuit, himself previously employed by the Dutch West India Company as director general of New Netherland, served as the organizer and leader of the first Swedish expedition. He chose the site of settlement and supervised the construction of the fort, also named for the young queen. Minuit died on the return trip to Sweden, a major blow to the fledgling company and colony. New Sweden experienced many difficulties and setbacks during its year of existence. Lack of support from Sweden put the colony at a disadvantage in the fur trade and in tobacco production. The population of New Sweden never exceeded 200 Swedes and Finns, and this small number was settled over a great distance from present-day Wilmington to Philadelphia.

In 1643, the company was reorganized and a new governor sent to the colony. Johan Printz sought to revitalize New Sweden and to expand its hold on the Delaware River Valley. His aggressive administration brought the colony into increasing conflict with the Dutch, who claimed the area of right of discovery and maintained an active fur trade along the Delaware River. The Dutch built Fort Casimir on the River just below Fort Christina, but Peter Stuyvesant, the director general of New Netherland, did not conquer the much smaller Swedish colony until 1655, when Swedish colonial leadership had passed to Johan Rising.

The Dutch established the town of New Amstel around Fort Casimir and made it their center of fur trading and colonial administration on the Delaware. They established courts at present-day Lewes and New Castle, which became the foundations of two of Delaware's three counties. At its height the colony numbered about 600 settlers, including many Swedes and Finns. But Dutch control of the Delaware lasted less than a decade.

In 1664 an English fleet under the command of James, Duke of York, a younger brother of King Charles II, captured New Amsterdam. A smaller flotilla under the command of Sir Robert Carr was then sent to the Delaware River to take command of New Amstel, which was renamed New Castle. This extension of English control of the west side of the river exceeded the orders of the Duke of York and made his claim to the land tenuous, but it effectively eliminated Dutch holdings in colonial North America. Between 1664 and 1682, Delaware was governed from New York by a deputy of the Duke of York. English settlement began, and English law was introduced into the courts, but Dutch, Swedish, and Finnish landholdings were reconfirmed.

Rule by Pennsylvania. In 1682, William Penn asked for and received the area that would become Delaware from the Duke of York so that he might control the western side of the Delaware River from just below Philadelphia to Cape Henlopen. He reaffirmed the existing divisions as counties, giving the lower two their modern names of Kent and Sussex and keeping the name of the northernmost county as New Castle. The area had no proper name, being called "Government of the Counties of New Castle, Kent, and Sussex on Delaware," or, more informally, the "Lower Counties." The Duke of York's claim to much of this land was legally attenuated, and there existed a conflicting claim from the Calvert family based on a charter granted to them for Maryland in 1632 by King Charles I. The Calverts had been reluctant to challenge the Duke's claims in court, but they were not so reluctant to challenge Penn. The resultant Penn-Calvert controversy was finally settled in favor of the Penn family in 1750. Boundary questions proved difficult to settle, and finally the English surveyors Charles Mason and Jeremiah Dixon were brought in to complete the work. The boundaries of the two proprietorships had been established, but the assembly of the Lower Counties did not officially adopt the final borders of the colony until 1775.

Penn discovered that ruling the Lower Counties was difficult in other respects as well. Unlike the inhabitants of Pennsylvania, who were predominantly English Quakers, the population of the Lower Counties included a broad mixture of ethnicities, including Swedes, Finns, Dutch, and French, as well as English. Penn's attempt to consolidate the government of Pennsylvania with that of the Lower Counties through the Act of Union (1682) proved frustrating. Representatives of the two areas clashed in the assembly, especially over the issue of defense policy during King

William's War. In 1701, Penn reluctantly agreed to two separate assemblies, which began to meet in 1704, Delawareans in New Castle and Pennsylvanians in Philadelphia. Thus the Lower Counties maintained their separateness from their large neighbors to the north even though both shared the same proprietary family and governor.

The establishment of Pennsylvania and particularly the city of Philadelphia ended the pioneer phase in the socio-economic development of the Delaware River Valley. The production of wheat, predominantly for markets in the West Indies, came to dominate the valley's economy and largely replaced tobacco farming as the cash crop for Delaware's farmers. Farm incomes rose, and milling, coopering, and shipbuilding became significant activities along Delaware's tidal streams. Although Philadelphia remained the premier market center for Delaware, Wilmington and other towns arose within the Lower Counties as secondary centers of trade. The merchant gristmills built at the fall line of the Brandywine Creek adjacent to Wilmington were the largest and most productive in the Delaware River Valley.

Ethnically and religiously, Delaware remained heterogeneous. Kent and Sussex counties were populated by English settlers who subscribed to the Church of England. Many of the larger landowners had originally received their land grants from the Calverts and followed social customs characteristic of the Chesapeake region. These planters used black slaves to work their extensive lands. By contrast, New Castle County attracted more varied settlers and was socially and economically a part of the world of southeastern Pennsylvania. Quaker farmers, merchants, and millers dominated the area around Wilmington, while Scotch-Irish Presbyterians and Welsh Baptists settled in the western part of the county. The foundations of the future University of Delaware were laid by the Reverend Francis Alison, a Presbyterian clergyman who established an academy in New London, Pennsylvania, that was moved to Newark, Delaware in the early 1760s.

Revolutionary War Era. The assembly of the Lower Counties gave support to the military needs of the colonies during the French and Indian War and shared in the subsequent consternation when the British Parliament attempted to impose the Stamp Act in 1765. The assembly's speaker of the house, Caesar Rodney, an Anglican farmer from Kent County, led Delaware's delegation to the Stamp Act Congress and was one of the little colony's most outspoken patriots during the Revolutionary period. Politically, Delawareans were often divided. The Anglican planters of lower Delaware wished to remain in the British Empire, while the more radical elements in the northern part of the colony favored separation. Aside from Rodney, Delaware's leading political figures during the Revolution-

ary period were George Read and Thoms McKean, both lawyers in New Castle County.

Delaware's most noted statesman of the era was John Dickinson. Son of the largest landowner in Kent County and the son-in-law of one of Philadelphia's wealthiest Quaker merchants, Dickinson was a fine legal scholar who had trained in London. His *Letters from a Farmer in Pennsylvania to the Inhabitants of the British Colonies* (1767) helped convince colonists that the Townshend duties were as much a usurpation of parliamentary power as the Stamp Act had been.

When war broke out between Great Britain and its colonies, Delawareans made haste to establish their separate sovereignty from Pennsylvania by declaring the Lower Counties to be the Delaware State (June 15, 1776). When the question of the Declaration of Independence came before Congress, two of Delaware's three delegates were in Philadelphia and unable to agree. The third, Caesar Rodney, then at his home in Kent County, was summoned to cast the deciding ballot, which placed Delaware in the column for independence. Rodney's midnight ride from Dover to Philadelphia over the night of June 1-2 remains the single most famous event in Delaware's history.

General William Howe's army briefly invaded Delaware in 1777 as it moved from Maryland to Philadelphia. A skirmish took place at Cooch's Bridge near Newark on September 3, as the British army marched toward the Brandywine River, where the British troops won a decisive victory over General George Washington's army on September 11. British troops then occupied Wilmington for five weeks, capturing the state's chief executive, numerous documents, and money. The assembly retreated from New Castle, ultimately establishing a new state capital at Dover. The Delaware Regiment, formed by Colonel John Haslet as part of Washington's continental line, earned distinction in numerous battles from New York to North Carolina. Because of their state's small size, Delawareans were reluctant to agree to the Articles of Confederation until the question of the land claims of some of the big states were resolved in favor of the United States as a whole. By contrast, Delaware was the first state to ratify the United States Constitution, on December 7, 1787.

See also Dickinson, John; Minuit, Peter; New Netherland; Penn, William; Stuyvesant, Peter.

Bibliography: Hancock, Harold, *Liberty and Independence* (Delaware American Revolution Bicentennial Commission, 1976); Munroe, John A., Colonial Delaware (KTO Press, 1978); Weslager, C. A., *The Delaware Indians: A History* (Rutgers Univ. Press, 1972); idem, *The Dutch and Swedes at New Castle* (Mid Atlantic, 1987); idem, *The English on the Delaware* (Rutgers Univ. Press, 1967).

Barbara E. Benson
Historical Society of Delaware

DE LA WARR, THOMAS WEST, 3RD BARON   (1577-1618)   The first governor of the Virginia colony, De La Warr was born in Hampshire, England, and was knighted in 1599 by his cousin the Earl of Essex. Imprisoned and fined during the Essex conspiracy, he was restored to favor and in 1609 was appointed the Virginia Colony's first governor and captain general. In 1610 he reached the starving colony just as Sir Thomas Gates was evacuating it. De La Warr resupplied the colonists and built new fortifications, but, overcome by the summer heat, he then left for England, where he wrote a defense of the colony in 1611. On a subsequent voyage he died of food poisoning in the Azores.

DEMOCRACY   Through most of the colonial period the word "democracy," if used at all, implied rule by the lower orders, a kind of world turned upside down in which the lesser orders of society would establish the rule of the mob. It was only in the mid-18th century, with the increasing conflicts of mature colonial society and especially the conflicts with the British imperial system when colonists began to experiment with notions of popular sovereignty, that the term began to be seen in a more favorable light. Even then, it was understood not as an abstract goal but as a tendency in government to be balanced, as John Adams suggested, by aristocratic and monarchial structures.

Interpretations of colonial society that see a gradual "growth of democracy" are therefore somewhat anachronistic. One might argue that with a franchise broadened to include most adult white male property owners, the colonies were more "democratic" than the mother country, but on the other hand the colonies institutionalized slavery, generally prohibited in England. The strength of the colonial legislatures could be seen as a democratic tendency, but most legislators were representatives or agents of the colonies' leading wealthy families, not the broad mass of the people.

It was, again, the initial stages of the Revolution that first brought the people directly into the political process. During the Stamp Act riots and the nonimportation movement, urban artisans and rural farmers for the first time began to demand government based on principles of popular sovereignty and political equality. The Revolution eliminated the monarchy and a hereditary titled aristocracy and broadened the base of social, economic, and political power. It was the true beginning of democracy in America.

John Mack Faragher
Mount Holyoke College

DEMOGRAPHY, HISTORICAL. *See* **Historical Demography.**

DENONVILLE, JACQUES RENÉ DE BRISAY, MARQUIS DE (1637-1710)   The governor of Canada (1685-89), the Marquis de Denonville succeeded Le Febvre de la Barre.

Denonville attempted to end Iroquois raids by attacking their villages in 1687. The Iroquois retaliated by attacking and burning the island of Montreal and threatening the town in 1689. The Canadian settlers were in even greater danger from the enraged Indians when war was declared between France and England.

DENONVILLE, FORT   Established as a military outpost on the eastern bank of the Niagara River at its outlet to Lake Ontario in 1687 by the Marquis de Denonville, governor of New France, Fort Denonville consisted of a small stockade whose initial function was to protect the movement of French fur traders in this region. Abandoned after only one year, the fort site was again occupied and fortified in 1726 by the French at a time of increasing hostilities with the Iroquois. It was captured by the British in 1759 and renamed Fort Niagara. At the outbreak of the Revolution, it was a Loyalist stronghold and came under U.S. control only with the Jay Treaty of 1796.

DESERT INDIANS OF THE SOUTHWEST   In the years prior to the arrival of Europeans, the valleys of the desert southwest of what is now southern Arizona were populated by groups of Piman and Yuman peoples. The first, including the Pima and the closely related Papago, lived in rancherias, small communities of family homesteads strung out along the shallow watercourses of the Santa Cruz and Gila river valleys, from which they diverted water to irrigate their garden plots. Speaking a Uto-Aztecan dialect closely related to that of the Aztecs of central Mexico, they referred to themselves as "o'otam," or "the people." When Cabeza de Vaca first encountered Piman peoples (c.1540) there were perhaps as many as 30,000 of them spread over a north-south span of nearly 1,000 miles. There was little direct contact between the Piman and the Spanish, because of the lack of valuable resources in their territory, although missionary efforts to "reduce" the people into concentrated settlements contributed to hostilities that erupted into the Pima Revolt of 1751.

The Yuman, interrelated Hokum-speaking peoples, resided in the Colorado and Gila river valleys and were composed of an Upland group, including the Havasupai, who farmed the floor of the Grand Canyon, and their neighbors of the plateau, the Yavapai and Walapai, who were hunters. Downriver were the River Yumans, the Cocopa, the Quechan, the Mojave, and on the Gila, the Maricopa. Coronado's expedition in 1540 brought their first encounter with Europeans. The next extensive contact came with Father Kino's mission activity in the 1690s. It was not until 1780, however, that the Spanish established two settlements in the country of the River Yumans. The soldiers mistreated the Indians and the settlers appropriated their lands. Within a year the Yuma rose in revolt, killing 4 Franciscans, 31 soldiers, and 20 settlers. The Spanish abandoned the lower

Colorado, and the Yuman were left alone until the 19th century.

See also Pima Revolt of 1751.

Bibliography: Joseph, Alice, Spicer, Rosamond B., and Chesky, Jane, *The Desert People: A Study of the Papago Indians* (Univ. of Chicago Press, 1949); Spicer, Edward H., *Cycles of Conquest* (Univ. of Arizona Press, 1962); Weaver, Thomas, ed., *Indians of Arizona* (Univ. of Arizona Press, 1974).

John Mack Faragher
Mount Holyoke College

DE SOTO, HERNANDO (?1498-1542)   Arriving in Panama with Pedrarias Dávila in 1514, the Spanish explorer De Soto took part in Pizarro's expedition in Peru and was then named governor of Cuba in 1537. He was impressed by the stories of Cabeza de Vaca and decided to mount an expedition to explore the area beyond Florida, hoping to find the wealthy kingdom of the Seven Cities of Cibola. About 600 colonists sailed from Havana in 1539, landing near Tampa, Florida. In 1540 the party moved as far north as North Carolina, where they found their first treasure, some low-grade pearls. Needing supplies, De Soto turned back toward the Gulf of Mexico to rendezvous with his ships, but near Mobile the Spaniards were ambushed by Indians and suffered severe losses.

In 1541, De Soto moved west and crossed the Mississippi River near Memphis. Scouting parties into Oklahoma and Arkansas found no cities of gold, and in 1542, De Soto began moving south toward the Gulf, again in search of supply ships. On May 21, De Soto died from the effects of a fever, and his men weighted his body with chains and sank it in the Mississippi to prevent the Indians from finding and mutilating it. The remaining 300 men descended the Mississippi to the Gulf of Mexico, where they built boats, finally reaching the Spanish settlement at Panuco in September 1543.

See also Exploration; Cabeza de Vaca, Alvar Nunez; Spanish Colonies.

Thomas C. Thompson
University of California, Riverside

DETROIT, FORT   In 1701, Cadillac founded Fort Detroit on the strategically important Detroit River between lakes Erie and Huron, and it quickly became one of the most important commercial and military centers of the Great Lakes region. Within a few years thousands of Indians had relocated their villages about the fort, and there was considerable intermarriage and cultural mixing between the French soldiers, traders, and *coureurs de bois* (trappers) and the Indians. Surrendered to a British military force during the French and Indian War, Detroit continued to prosper under British rule, although many of

the French métis families moved south to River Raisin, nown by the British as Frenchtown. Included in United States territory by the Treaty of Paris, it was not actually transferred until 1796, after Jay's Treaty. Made capital of Michigan Territory in 1805, it was captured by British during the War of 1812.

In 1541, Hernando De Soto attacked a fortified Indian town on the Yazoo River in Mississippi. *(Library of Congress)*

DE VARGAS, DIEGO (1643-1704)   A Spanish colonial administrator who was appointed governor of New Mexico in 1690, De Vargas's task was to reconquer the province from the Indians, who had driven the Spanish out in the Pueblo Revolt of 1680. Launching his expedition from El Paso, by September 1692 he had reached Santa Fe with 50 Spaniards and the same number of Indian allies. The capital submitted to him, as did Taos and most of the other pueblos. In 1693 he led a second expedition that included colonists as well as soldiers. This expedition was forced to fight a long but successful campaign against the Pueblo.

The Indians rebelled again in 1696, but Vargas put them down with little difficulty. By the end of that year New Mexico was back under Spanish control. Vargas was killed by Apaches on a campaign in 1704.

See also El Paso.

DE VRIES, DAVID PIETERSEN (?1592-1655?) A trading captain and colonizer, De Vries was born in La Rochelle, France, but grew up in Holland. A resourceful trader, he was engaged in shipping Newfoundland cod to Spain. Commissioned to settle colonists in the New World, he sailed in 1631 to Swanendael on the Delaware River and in 1632-33 to Delaware, Virginia, and New Amsterdam. In 1634-36 he was active in Guiana, the West Indies, and New Netherland; between 1638 and 1644 he brought colonists to Staten Island and Vriessendael near Tappan. After Indians attacked his settlements in 1643, he returned to Holland, where he wrote in 1655 an account of New Netherland.

DIAZ, BARTHOLOMEW (?1450-1500) Portuguese navigator, Diaz was the first European of record to round the South African Cape of Good Hope. In the early 1480s he engaged in expeditions to the Gold Coast of Africa and in 1487 was chosen by King John II of Portugal to open a sea route to India around Africa, which he succeeded in accomplishing the next year, although his crew forced him to return to Lisbon once he had rounded the Cape. He remained in the Africa trade through the 1490s, establishing the trading post at Sofala on the east coast of Africa's Mozambique. In 1500 he was with Pedro Alvares Cabral when the African fleet blew off course and encountered the Brazilian coast; he and his ship were lost on the return voyage.

DIÁZ, MELCHIOR (died 1540) When Cabeza de Vaca and Estevanico stumbled into Culiacan in 1536 after surviving the disintegration of Narvaez's 1527 Florida expedition, the Spanish explorer Diáz welcomed them and then sent them on to Mexico City. In 1540, Diáz became one of Francisco de Coronado's chief lieutenants in his search for the Seven Cities of Cibola in Arizona and led the party sent out by Coronado to rendezvous with Hernando Alarcón's supply ships at the end of the Gulf of California. Looking for Alarcón, Diáz crossed the Colorado River and penetrated down the Baja California peninsula before giving up. On his return he found the letters left by Alarcón under a stone cross on the banks of the Colorado. Before he could report to Coronado, Diáz died in a freak accident, falling off his horse and impaling himself on his own lance.

See also Alarcón, Hernando; Coronado, Francisco Vasquez de.

John Dickinson denied Britain's taxing authority in *Letters from a Farmer* (1768). *(Library of Congress)*

DICKINSON, JOHN (1732-1808) A colonial figure and public official whose writings during the Revolution gave him the title "Penman of the Revolution," he began a law practice in Philadelphia (1757) and held many public offices in Pennsylvania and Delaware. Dickinson sided with the patriots before the Revolution, but hoped for reconciliation with Britain. The Pennsylvania legislature appointed him to the Stamp Act Congress (1765), where he drafted the Declaration of Rights and Grievances, asking for repeal of the Stamp Act. He responded to the Townshend Acts by publishing a series called *Letters from a Farmer in Pennsylvania* (1768), which challenged Britain's right to tax the colonies and which made him a popular figure.

As the Revolution approached, he drafted petitions to the King for the Pennsylvania legislature and the First and

Second Continental Congresses. He opposed separation from Britain, but supported the Second Continental Congress in its move to take up arms. Although he voted against the Declaration of Independence, he helped draft the Articles of Confederation (1776). He represented Delaware in Congress (1776-77; 1779-80) and was elected president of the Supreme Executive Council of Delaware (1781) before becoming president of Pennsylvania (1782-85). Dickinson was president of the Annapolis Convention (1786) and supported the ratification of the Constitution as a member of the Constitutional Convention (1787). Dickinson College, of which he was a founder (1783), is named for him.

See also Declaration of Rights and Grievances.

DICKINSON, JONATHAN (1688-1747)   A Presbyterian clergyman born in Hatfield, Massachusetts, Dickinson settled in Elizabethtown, New Jersey, after his graduation from Yale (1706). During the Great Awakening he was an advocate of "New Side" Presbyterianism and became the leading preacher and religious authority in the Middle Colonies. In 1746 he was a founder of the College of New Jersey (Princeton College) and became its first president.

See also Great Awakening; Princeton College.

DINWIDDIE, ROBERT (1693-1770)   An administrator of the colonies who was born in Scotland, he began his career as a customs collector in Bermuda (1727-38). He then served as surveyor general of the Southern District of America (Carolinas, Virginia, Maryland, Pennsylvania, Bahamas, Jamaica) from 1738 until 1749. Residing in Virginia, he held a seat on the Virginia Council from 1741 and was made lieutenant governor in 1751. In the absence of the governor, he defended the territory against the French. In 1753 Dinwiddie sent George Washington to warn the French about further infringement on the colony's borders and, in 1754, to defend the borders against the French.

DISEASE   Early Americans understood disease as a result of a morbid imbalance of the four bodily humors identified as blood, yellow bile, black bile, and phlegm. To restore health it was necessary to restore the balance by either depleting body liquids (bleeding, purging, salivating, sweating) or by adding drugs, food, or liquids. This theory of medical practice had come down through the centuries and was essentially unchanged from the elaboration by Galen in the 2nd century of the medical ideas of the Greek physician Hippocrates (5th century B.C.).

American Indians and Africans, on the other hand, believed that sickness was caused by spirits and was the result of violating taboos. In a similar vein, the 17th century Puritan interpreted diseases as visitations by God—a punishment for sins. But by the 18th century most European medical personnel had taken the great step of rejecting supernatural causes of disease. The cures were unchanged, but the shift to an emphasis on natural causes of disease reflected the new rational approach of the Enlightenment.

Disease was the main factor in the defeat and conquest of the Indians of North and South America. Because the Americas had been isolated from Eurasia and Africa while epidemic and pandemic diseases developed and ravaged the populations there, indigenous Americans had little or no immunities to smallpox, measles, influenza, plague, and diphtheria. Introduced to America, often at the first contact, these diseases destroyed the population, often resulting in a 90 percent decline in population during the first century of colonization. Lethal pathogens spread far beyond the face-to-face contact with Europeans, frequently seriously weakening a native society on the eve of its confrontation with the Europeans. The effect of disease on American Indians is nearly incalculable, and may rank as the greatest disaster any human population has experienced.

Classification and Diagnosis.   Diseases were classified by symptoms such as fevers, fluxes (diarrhea), dropsy (fluid retention), poxes (skin eruptions); or by the part of the body affected such as pleurisies (lung problems) or quinsies (throat disorders such as scarlet fever or diphtheria). Fevers were subdivided into various types depending on their patterns—intermittent, tertian, and quotan for the intervals between bouts. There were several poxes, including smallpox, leprosy, and syphilis. People also suffered and died from conditions vaguely laabeled as falling down, teething, old age, childbirth, fits, or the ague.

If highly contagious, a disease could be identified as a plague regardless of symptoms. Other diseases were characterized by their seasonal appearances. Autumnal fever usually meant malaria or yellow fever; summer diseases were most likely nutritional deficiencies; the winter diseases included influenza or pneumonia. During the cold months of 1749-50, for instance, 40 people died from the "winter fever" on Kent Island in Maryland.

Accurate diagnosis or a precise method of describing the symptoms of any disease was difficult because the scientific world lacked any workable notion of what distinguished one disease from another. Physicians had no way of measuring body temperature, and few autopsies were performed. Cotton Mather's theory that illness was the result of minute worms (animacular) that could be seen under a microscope was not widely believed. Instead the medical profession concentrated on questioning whether the imbalance of humors in the body resulted from a miasma ("noxious smells causing bad air") or a contagion ("communicable through personal contact"). The advocates of pesthouses and quarantine stations (the contagionists) hoped to isolate the sick and thus prevent the spread of disease. Environmentalists emphasized the need to keep the streets clean of human waste and animal decay and were indifferent to quarantine procedures.

"Seasoning" Diseases.   By far the most taxing disease in early America was known as the "seasoning," a reference to the recurrent bouts with malaria or autumnal fever feared by all newcomers south of New England. Immunity was acquired slowly with successive attacks of malaria, each of which weakened the individual and made him susceptible to other more fatal diseases. Pregnancy led to a loss of any acquired immunity, and pregnant women faced a double jeopardy with the strong possibility of miscarriage if they contracted malaria.

A second debilitating disease in the "seasoning" process was dysentery, known at the time as the bloody flux and often confused with typhoid fever because of similar symptoms. It was found in all the colonies but killed more frequently in warmer climates, often adding to the misery of malaria sufferers. During wartime, epidemics of dysentery were at their worst. Dysentery rather than typhus was the American camp fever. The disease was spread from army camps to civilians as soldiers went home to convalesce.

Smallpox and Measles.   Smallpox, the most prevalent disease in Europe, was less of a problem for European settlers in America but aroused more fear than any other disease. It was highly contagious when it did appear; the skin eruptions left permanent scars and thus it was terribly disfiguring; and it was often fatal. In Europe smallpox was a childhood disease; the survivors (no more than 60 percent of the sufferers) acquired lifelong immunity). But Americans, relatively isolated from the recurring epidemics of Europe and Africa, had fewer opportunities to acquire that immunity. The occasional smallpox epidemic could devastate a community, both adults and children suffering equally. A 1738 outbreak of smallpox in Charleston, South Carolina, killed half of the 2,100 people who contracted the disease (out of a total population of fewer than 5,000). By the middle of the 18th century, wealthy parents hesitated to send their adolescent children to school in England because of their fear of smallpox, thus indirectly encouraging the growth of colleges in America.

Inoculation with the live smallpox virus (variolation) did confer immunity and had been used in America since Cotton Mather promoted the procedure (learned from his slave Onesimus) during a 1723 epidemic in Boston, Massachusetts. Because the procedure actually gave smallpox to the person being inoculated (with less danger of dying than catching it the "natural" way), the operation could spread the infection if precautions were not taken to isolate the sick. Variolation was not a widespread practice until the Revolutionary War, when the Continental Congress ordered the inoculation of all soldiers in the Continental Army and followed approved procedures of isolation until they had recovered. At the end of the century, variolation was replaced with vaccination (using a cowpox virus), which was neither contagious nor a potential public health hazard.

Measles was another killing disease that occurred sporadically in all the colonies. In colonial America it did not follow the pattern of a mild childhood illness that conferred adult immunity. Thus a high proportion of middle-aged and elderly persons were infected by measles.

Other Common Diseases.   While the fevers and poxes took their toll on all the ethnic factions, Afro-Americans and Africans suffered to a greater degree from respiratory diseases—from colds and pneumonia to tuberculosis— than did the white population. The blacks appeared to have greater resistance to tropical diseases such as yellow fever, malaria, and dengue, but only in the case of malaria has a genetic factor been identified. However, epidemics of all kinds affected blacks, especially the American-born, with the same ferocity as they affected whites.

Although diseases of the aged—cancer, heart disease, and stroke in particular—did appear, they were not as widespread as today because few people lived long enough to suffer from them. Complaints about arthritis—called rheumatism, gout, and sciatica—received attention in the medical manuals. Benjamin Franklin, who lived to the age of 84, suffered from three ailments he described as "the gout, the stone, and old age."

Among the nutritional diseases, scurvy, resulting from a deficiency of ascorbic acid (vitamin C), was so common that physicians carried lemons or limes, when they were available, as medication. The excessive use of salt to preserve meat, the lack of fresh foods from early spring to the first summer harvests, combined with the prevalence of worms, contributed to a host of nutritional deficiencies.

Patterns of Disease.   Americans in general suffered less from diseases than did Europeans because of their relative isolation from the Old World, because of the dispersed population, and because of greater availability of food. Colonial Americans, especially in New England, lived longer and had healthier lives than did their European counterparts or Southern neighbors. The average life span in parts of 17th-century Massachusetts was about 70 years of age, due most likely to the retreat of malaria from the area. Mortality increased in the 18th century but did not reach the proportions of the Old World. Women in all places continued to die at a faster rate than men because of complications from childbirth.

Epidemics when they occurred could not travel far in America and were usually contained within narrow geographic limits. Americans, on the other hand, with fewer opportunities to acquire immunities, were more vulnerable to epidemics, a problem that created an acute crisis during the Revolution when country people were crowded into army camps.

As cities grew after the Revolution and the population became more dense, and as the sailing time across the Atlantic was reduced to within the incubation period of many diseases, American ailments began to follow the European patterns. Measles became a childhood disease; diphtheria, yellow fever, and cholera appeared more often to replace smallpox as the most dreaded scourge. Life expectancy dropped in the cities as crowded living conditions contributed to the incidence of epidemics. However, few Americans lived in cities (about five percent), and the population in general benefited from the greatest advantage of rural existence—isolation from disease centers.

As yet, medicine had few means of countering the increase in diseases. By the Revolutionary War era, educated members of the community were recommending hygienic and dietary measures—quarantine for contagious diseases, personal cleanliness that included washing all parts of the body and more frequent changing of clothes to prevent the "itch," and a reduction of salt and meat in the diet. Bathing had been frowned on for centuries in Europe because the public bathhouses had been seen as the source of venereal disease. This negative attitude toward personal cleanliness, which was not part of the ethos of either Indians or Africans, gradually changed among the Europeans in America beginning with the middle of the 18th century.

See also Medicine.

Bibliography: Crosby, Alfred W., *The Columbian Exchange: Biological and Cultural Consequences of 1492* (Greenwood Press, 1972); Duffy, John, *Epidemics in Colonial America* (Louisiana State Univ. Press, 1953); McNeill, William H., *Plagues and People* (Doubleday, 1976); Savitt, Todd L., *Medicine and Slavery: The Diseases and Health Care of Blacks in Antebellum Virginia* (Univ. of Illinois Press, 1978); Wertz, Richard and Dorothy, *Lying In: A History of Childbirth in America* (Free Press, 1977).

Elaine G. Breslaw
Morgan State University

DIVINE RIGHT OF KINGS   The political theory that rulers derive sovereignty over their people directly from God may have been articulated first in ancient Egypt, but it was asserted by the monarchs of the powerful European nation states of the 16th and 17th centuries, who argued that law was an instrument of grace, not a contrivance of human wisdom, thus making the king answerable only to God and above all promulgated law. In England, during the 17th century, opponents of the Stuart monarchy revived the Roman theory that sovereignty resides in the people and that governments were therefore responsible to those from whom their power derived. In 1651, Thomas Hobbes argued for autocracy, but one based on a social contract between the sovereign and the people to keep the peace; in 1689, John Locke stressed man's natural rights and asserted that if a government set up to protect those rights betrayed its trust it could legitimately be removed, if necessary by revolution. This theory was embodied in the Declaration of Independence, which argued that the struggle was one of popular will resisting illegitimate monarchical authority.

John Mack Faragher
Mount Holyoke College

DIVORCE   In colonial America, divorce was uncommon, but individuals who sought to break their matrimonial bonds had several options, both formal and informal. A *vinculo matrimonii*, or absolute divorce which permitted both parties to remarry, was rare; more frequent was *mena et thoro*, or legal separation from bed and board. The latter was granted through petition to one's colonial legislature, unlike in England, where divorce was the province of the ecclesiastical courts. A third remedy, available in most colonies, enabled husbands and wives to bypass agreements through an outside party. Finally, estranged couples might arrange informal separations, or the husband might simply desert.

Specific divorce provisos varied widely, with most colonies refusing to permit absolute divorce. Even in Massachusetts and Connecticut, whose comparatively liberal divorce laws reflected the Puritan belief that marriage was a civil contract rather than religious sacrament and was therefore dissoluble, divorce a *vinculo matrimonii* was expensive to obtain and infrequently granted. However, except for Connecticut, whose legislature favored absolute dissolution and refused to grant legal separations, every colony provided for separation from bed and board for such causes as desertion, bigamy, adultery, cruelty, and failure to support. Abused and abandoned wives were the most frequent petitioners, most of whom sought separate maintenance and some form of alimony.

After independence, most states revised and formalized their divorce codes, for the first time permitting absolute divorce either through judicial decree or legislative enactment. Reflecting, perhaps, higher female expectations of marriage as well as greater assertiveness in its severance, petitioners during the postwar years increasingly cited the absence of affection as evidence of marital discord and frequently sought more specific property settlements than had their pre-revolution counterparts.

Bibliography: Kerber, Linda K., *Women of the Republic: Intellect and Ideology in Revolutionary America* (Univ. of North Carolina Press, 1960); Salmon, Marylynn, *Women and the Law of Property in Early America* (Univ. of North Carolina Press, 1986).

James K. Somerville
State University of New York at Geneseo

DOLLIER DE CASSON, FRANÇOIS (1636-1701)   A Sulpician missionary, Dollier de Casson was sent to Canada in 1666, traveled with René de Brehent de Galinée in La Salle's exploring party. They voyaged up the Great River (the Mississippi) and sighted Lake Erie, of which they took possession for Louis XIV in 1668. As they preached to the Indians, they explored the Ohio River, Lake Michigan, and the upper Illinois River. In 1670, Dollier de Casson became head of the Sulpicians (1671-74, 1678-1701) and seigneur of Montreal, helping to develop the city and maintain good relations between religious and civil officials.

DOMESTIC SYSTEM   The domestic system, often called the putting-out system, emerged gradually from the traditional system of household production. Throughout the colonial era, most households, especially in rural regions, had to supply many of their own basic needs—food, clothing, and some tools and implements—but they had to obtain other items from local artisans and shopkeepers. To a large degree these purchases did not involve cash, but an exchange of goods or labor. A rural merchant, for instance, might trade imported tools, tableware, spices, or fine cloth for marketable farm produce or homespun yarn and cloth; he would then send these locally produced goods to urban merchants in exchange for more manufactured or imported goods. By the end of the 18th century, many merchants became increasingly active in promoting household production. Rather than merely accept home-produced goods in trade, they put out raw materials to be made into finished goods by men, women, and sometimes children working in the home. The early shoe and textile industries depended greatly on the putting-out system, and in many cases the profits from the system provided the capital for the introduction of the factory system. The emergence of factory production did not bring about the immediate end of the putting-out system, however.

Household production remained an important part of American industrial growth throughout the 19th century.

Bibliography: Faler, Paul, *Mechanics and Manufacturers in the Early Industrial Revolution: Lynn, Massachusetts, 1780-1860* (State Univ. of New York Press, 1981).

Gregory H. Nobles
Georgia Institute of Technology

DOMINGUEZ, FRANCISCO ATANASIO (flourished 1770s)   A Franciscan missionary and the superior of Silvestre Velez de Escalante, in that order, Dominguez accompanied Escalante on his attempt to find a route from Santa Fe to Monterey in 1776. Dominguez followed Escalante north into southwest Colorado, west into Utah, south to the Crossing of the Fathers on the Colorado River just above the Grand Canyon, and then east back to Santa Fe. Dominguez was the inspector of the Franciscan missions in the province, but his report on the deteriorating conditions in New Mexico evoked no fresh effort on the part of a government suffering from a lack of money as well as bureaucratic apathy.

See also Escalante, Silvestre Velez de.

DOMINICANS   The Order of Friars Preachers, or Dominicans as they are commonly known, labored in Spanish America during the colonial and Revolutionary War period. From the beginning of their North American missions in 1510, the Dominicans loudly and publicly denounced Spanish enslavement of the Indians. Antonio de Montesinos and especially Bartoleme de Las Casas effectively advanced the argument that Indians were not savages but rational human beings with immortal souls to be saved. Their campaign resulted in the bull *Sublimis Deus* written by Pope Paul III in 1537, which forbade enslavement of Indians.

The only Dominican activity in the pre-federal period on what was to become American soil occurred in Florida. Dominicans accompanied Spanish expeditions to conquer Florida in 1523 under Lucas Vasquez de Ayllon and, in 1528, under Panfilo de Narvaez, both of which failed. Dominicans were also with Hernando De Soto in his three-year exploration of Florida and the American Southeast (1539-42). Convinced that the reason for previous failures to settle Florida was the presence of Spanish soldiers, which caused the Indians to resist, Friar Luis Cancer de Barbastro led a purely religious, unarmed expedition to Florida in 1549. His murder by Indians on June 26, shortly after he landed alone, doomed this noble experiment. A final attempt to colonize Florida and establish Dominican missions failed in 1561. With this, Spain ceased all colonizing ventures into Florida, and Dominican activity on American soil ceased. Not until 1805 would

Dominicans establish a mission on U.S. territory, in Kentucky.

Bibliography: Ellis, John Tracy, *Catholics in Colonial America* (Helicon Press, 1965).

Leonard R. Riforgiato
Pennsylvania State University

DOMINION OF NEW ENGLAND (1686-89)   In an effort to strengthen royal rule over the colonists, the colonies of Massachusetts, Rhode Island, Connecticut, New Hampshire, and Maine were made one province, under one leader, and called the Dominion of New England. Joseph Dudley served as president until the arrival of royal-appointee Sir Edmund Andros. A council was also appointed by the Crown. No colonists were represented. Andros held a hard line regarding the Navigation Acts and taxation laws. In 1688 he added New York and New Jersey to strengthen defenses. When King James II abdicated in 1689, the colonists revolted and overthrew Andros, thus ending the dominion form of government.

See also Andros, Sir Edmund.

DORCHESTER COMPANY (1624-26)   Organized in England by the Reverend John White and the Western Merchants, the Dorchester Company's purpose was to provide an alternative for the Puritans to the Separatists in Plymouth and to end double-manning of the merchants' fishing ships by settling fishermen on Cape Ann (Gloucester, Massachusetts). To be incorporated, the colonists had to stay three years and build schools and churches. In 1625, Roger Conant became governor, but he rejected the location and took about 40 settlers to Naumkeag (now Salem). The rest left for England, but the colony was not a total loss, as the Massachusetts Bay Company was modeled on it.

DRAGGING CANOE (c.1730-92)   A Cherokee leader also known as Tsiyu-Gunsini ("he is dragging it"), he was born at Running Water Village on the Tennessee River, the son of Cherokee chief Attakullakulla. Although little is known of his early life, he came into prominence around 1775 as one of the fiercest Indian opponents of the sale of extensive territory in Kentucky and Tennessee to the American colonists. Predicting that the passive acceptance by the native peoples of the colonists' expansion would ultimately result in the Indians' exile and misery, Dragging Canoe allied himself with the British after the outbreak of the Revolution. He established a headquarters for himself and his followers at Chickamauga Creek and with arms and ammunition provided by the British began a prolonged series of attacks against the Tennessee settlers that ended in 1782 with his defeat and retreat southward.

Although he halted hostilities with the 1785 Hopewell Treaty that set the official boundaries of Indian Territory, Dragging Canoe led renewed attacks on settlers who crossed the line. Once more he accepted peace with the Treaty of Halston in 1791, but when that treaty, too, was violated by the settlers he went to war again and fell in battle at the head of his Cherokee forces.

DRAKE, SIR FRANCIS (?1543-96)   English pirate, privateer, and admiral, Drake was the most famous of the Elizabethan "sea dogs." He went to sea as a boy, and by the 1560s had taken part in voyages to the African coast and the Caribbean. In 1567 he was a member of John Hawkins's slave-trading expedition from the Guinea coast to the Gulf of Mexico, which infuriated the Spanish; thereafter he was engaged in a series of raids of towns along the Spanish Main. By the mid-1570s he had grown wealthy with the plunder of his exploits as a pirate and privateer.

From 1577 to 1580, Drake became the second man, after Magellan, to circumnavigate the globe, sailing the *Golden Hind* across the Atlantic to Brazil and the estuary of the Rio de la Plata, through the Straits of Magellan, up the coast as far north as Drake's Bay in California, where he anchored and became the first European to encounter the California natives. He crossed the Pacific, coasted the Philippines and the East Indies, crossed the Indian Ocean, rounded Africa, and returned to England with valuable spices. In 1581 he was knighted by Elizabeth I for his accomplishment.

From 1585 to 1587, Drake engaged in several plundering expeditions against the Spanish empire in America, and in 1588 led the English naval forces in defeating the Spanish Armada. He died of dysentery on his ship, off the coast of Panama, while once again raiding the Spanish Main.

Bibliography: Andrew, Kenneth R., *Drake's Voyages* (1967).

John Mack Faragher
Mount Holyoke College

DRAYTON, WILLIAM HENRY (1742-79)   A radical opponent of Britain and the Loyalists, Drayton was born near Charleston, South Carolina. He completed his education at Oxford University and returned to South Carolina, where he became a planter. He became a member of the assembly (1765). Subsequently, he wrote several articles (1769) against the nonimportation movement that made

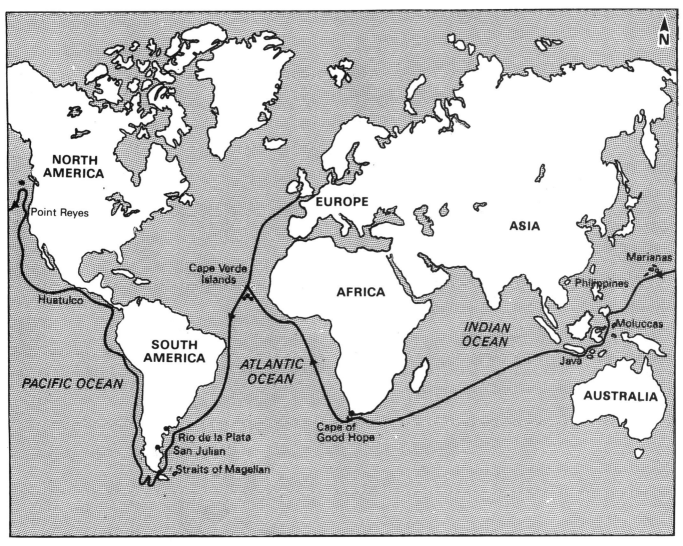

Voyage of Francis Drake, 1577-1580. (*Martin Greenwald Associates, Inc.*)

him unpopular, and he then went to Britain, where he was well received as a supporter of British rights.

Drayton soon returned to South Carolina, where he became a member of the colony's council (1772-75) and an assistant judge. Denouncing Parliament's legislation in America, Drayton published "A Letter From a 'Freeman' of South Carolina to the Deputies of North America" (1774), in which he supported a federal system. He proposed that each province should be able to regulate its own internal affairs. As war approached, Drayton actively supported the American cause and was a member of important revolutionary committees in South Carolina. He helped to prepare for armed resistance and was elected president of the provincial congress (1775). Drayton was elected chief justice under the state constitution (1776) and urged Georgians to form a union with South Carolina. He also supported the adoption of the state constitution of 1778

and was a member of the Continental Congress from 1778 until his death.

DRESS   The most notable aspect of colonial clothing was its relationship to class. Sumptuary laws throughout the colonies permitted the upper classes to adorn themselves with laces, gold and silver, ruffles, and embroidery forbidden to others. The gentleman planter attending church or county court might be seen in a broadcloth coat with silver buttons, a colored ornamented waistcoat, plush or broadcloth breeches, silk stockings, shoes with silver buckles, and a scarlet cloak; his wife might be wearing a broadcloth gown over scarlet petticoats ornamented with silver lace. Puritan and Quaker aristocrats, believing in plain adornment yet with equal conviction in the importance of signaling the differences between the classes, settled for the very best materials, although by the 18th century many of Boston and Philadelphia's men and women of quality were slavishly following the dictates of London fashion.

As for workers and farmers, they generally chose trousers over breeches; loose shirts devoid of embroidery, ruffles, or lace; and drab home-dyed colors; wives' dresses were meaner and shorter, made of rough linen or cheap cotton. A man's formal suit of clothing or a woman's gown were rare possessions, saved for marriages and funerals, passed down through generations. In 1791, Alexander Hamilton estimated that three quarters of all the country's clothing had been produced at home. Slaves were one of the few groups who wore ready-made clothes manufactured of cheap "negro-cloth." Backcountry styles were also born of poverty; in the Carolina backcountry the Reverend Charles Woodmason commented that "Females (many very pretty) come to Service in the Shifts and a short petticoat only, barefooted and bare legged—Without Caps or Handkerchiefs — dress'd only in their Hair, Quite in a State of Nature."

The most distinctive American style was the clothing of the male frontiersman. While few English pioneers went so far as the French frontiersmen who went into battle stripped of all but breechclout, their leather leggings, fringed hunting shirts, fur caps, broad sashes, and moccasins were emulations of Indian dress.

The distinctions of class became more pronounced in the late 18th century when upper-class women appeared with low cut bodices encased in stiff whalebone, surrounded by six-foot hoop petticoats, in high-heeled shoes, and elaborate coiffures. One French commentator noted he had dined with several women "dressed in great hats, plumes, &c. Two among them had their bosoms very naked. I was scandalized at this indecency among republicans." Indeed it was the French Revolution, not the American, that introduced the notion of democracy in dress.

Bibliography: Earle, Alice M., *Costume of Colonial Times* (1924; reprint Gale, 1975); McClellan, Elisabeth, *Historic Dress in 1607-1870* (1899; reprint Ayer); Wyckoff, Alexander, et al., *Early American Dress: Colonial and Revolutionary Periods* (1965; reprint, Amaryllis Press).

John Mack Faragher
Mount Holyoke College

DRINKER, ELIZABETH SANDWITH (1735-1807)   A Quaker who represented the typical upper-class Philadelphian in the late 1700s, Elizabeth Drinker's extraordinary diary is atypical in the sense that it is the longest and richest extant personal memoir written by a woman in 18th-century America. The diary covers the years 1758-1807 in great detail, presenting not only the perceptions and lifestyle of one woman but also the far more encompassing experiences and mentality of American women and men over the course of a half century. Her diary allows the reader to explore a world full of politics, literature, science, and urban development.

As the wife of an affluent merchant and mother of five children, Drinker led a busy and rewarding life. She was devoted to her family and committed to the principles of the Quakers. As the primary caregiver in a family subject to the usual and frequent 18th-century disorders, she had a broad knowledge of contemporary medicine. A sensible woman of good humor who had an extensive network of friends, Drinker read widely, enjoyed good music, and debated political issues.

DUDLEY, JOSEPH (1647-1720)   A much hated colonial governor, born in Roxbury, Massachusetts, Dudley graduated from Harvard (1665). He sat on the General Court as a representative from Roxbury (1673-76) and later became noted for his negotiations with the Indians. Philosophically, Dudley was not opposed to a system of colonial government that allowed imperial control over the colonies.

When the Charter of Massachusetts was vacated (1684), Dudley was made governor of Massachusetts, New Hampshire, and the King's Province. After Sir Edmund Andros became the governor (1686), Dudley remained an important member of Andros's council. When Andros's regime was overthrown (1689) in the aftermath of the Glorious Revolution, Dudley was arrested, and 119 charges were made against him in Britain by a committee of leading colonists. He was acquitted but remained hated in New England for his unwavering support of Crown policies. Dudley was appointed chief of the Council of New York. After taking unpopular positions during the trial of Jacob Leisler following Leisler's Rebellion, Dudley resigned his office and returned to Massachusetts (1692), where he became the governor (1702). Although there were many tensions between Dudley and the colonists, he performed valuable services for the colony, especially in military expeditions against Canada. He was replaced as governor by Governor Shute (1715) after the colonial opposition became too strong.

See also Andros, Sir Edmund; Leisler's Rebellion.

DUDLEY, THOMAS (1576-1653)   A governor of the Massachusetts Bay Colony, Dudley was born at Northampton, England. He was an able steward (1616-29) for the Earl of Lincoln, and his efficient management of the Earl's complex finances earned him both a good name and prosperity. Becoming a Dissenter, he joined John Cotton's congregation and helped plan the Massachusetts Bay Colony.

In 1630 he sailed on the *Arabella* with John Winthrop as his deputy governor. After a dispute with Winthrop, Dudley briefly moved to Ipswich but soon returned to the more centrally located town of Roxbury. He was elected governor in 1634, 1640, 1645, and 1650; he was also deputy governor 13 times. He served on the Standing Council and represented Massachusetts in the New Enlgand Confederation in 1643 as one of two commissioners. In 1630 he was a founder of the First Church of Charles Town and in 1650, as governor, signed the charter for establishing Harvard, where he served as overseer.

DUELING Prearranged contests between two persons armed with deadly weapons originated in the Middle Ages and had become associated with knighthood and chivalry in the 15th century when the purpose often was not to kill but to draw blood. It was fairly common among the aristocratic classes and by the 18th century had developed into a deadly ritual, especially in the South where, under the pseudofeudalistic conditions of slavery, a chivalric code developed. But duels were reported among all classes, even among servants and slaves, and in all areas; the first recorded colonial duel took place in Plymouth in 1621, and duels were reported in such Northern cities as Boston, New York, and Philadelphia, where in 1715 an Anglican minister challenged a parishioner to a duel for having "basely slandered a gentlewoman" but was thwarted by a Grand Jury. By the time of the Revolution the practice had been generally outlawed in the North, but the statutes against it were more lax in some states than others; both New Jersey and New York, for example, had strict laws, and after the Aaron Burr—Alexander Hamilton duel of 1804, Burr was indicted for murder in both states.

DUER, WILLIAM (1747-99) Merchant, financier, and political leader, born in Devonshire, England, Duer was educated at Eton and served briefly in the army before entering business. In 1768 he gained a contract from the British navy to provide timber for masts and spars, and in a subsequent trip to New York to acquire the timber he established his permanent residence there. A supporter of the cause of American independence, Duer served in the Continental Congress from 1777 to 1779 and as assistant secretary of the treasury under Alexander Hamilton in 1789. Unwise financial speculation, however, led to his imprisonment after the financial panic of 1792.

DUKE OF YORK'S LAWS Not required by his charter to obtain the consent of the freemen for his laws, the Duke of York ruled the colony of New York without a representative assembly for 20 years. In 1665, Governor Nicolls

drew up a code of laws and presented them to 34 New York delegates. The proceedings violated their idea of lawmaking, but the code was accepted with minor changes. Locally elected officials accountable to the governor replaced town meetings. Appointed justices of the peace adopted laws of the towns and counties. The code provided for trial by jury and for religious toleration. Each town built a church supported with tax money. Long Island Puritans objected because they were taxed without representation. The laws set up a civil and criminal code; organized local governments, courts, and militia; fixed standards of weights and measures; and provided methods of keeping records. The laws gave the impression of local control; but power remained with the Duke's deputies.

DULANY, DANIEL (1685-1753) Born in Ireland, Dulany migrated to Maryland in 1703. After apprenticeship he began the practice of law in 1709. In 1716 he continued his legal studies in London. Upon his return to Maryland he was, in 1722, elected to the provincial assembly and named attorney general. He became a leader of the antiproprietary party, which wished to extend English statute law to Maryland to replace arbitrary rule by the Calverts. His arguments for this position were expressed in *The Rights of the Inhabitants of Maryland to the Benefit of the English Laws* (1728). Gradually, Dulany moved towards the proprietor's side, accepting appointments as provincial agent (1733), judge of the admiralty (1734), and commissary general (1736). In 1742 he became a member of the Governor's Council, serving until his death. His son Daniel (1722-97) continued his father's conservative, Loyalist policies.

Bibliography: Land, Aubrey, *The Dulanys of Maryland: Daniel Dulany the Elder (1685-1753) and Daniel Dulany the Younger (1722- 1797)* (John Hopkins Univ. Press, 1968).

DULUTH, DANIEL GREYSOLON, SIEUR (1636-1710) A French explorer, Duluth was born into a noble family at St. Germain-en-Laye near Paris. He and his brother Claude, Sieur de la Tourette, emigrated to Montreal, where their cousin Henry de Tonty already lived. In 1678, Duluth left with secret instructions from the Count de Frontenac, governor of Canada, to explore Lake Superior. He succeeded in opening the lake to the French by negotiating a peace treaty between the warring Sioux and Chippewa. When the Sioux brought him to Lake Mille Lac in Minnesota, Duluth claimed the Indian lands for Louis XIV. Louis Hennepin recorded his fastening of the French arms to an oak tree in his 1683 map. In 1680 the Sioux broke their treaty and captured Hennepin, but Duluth rescued him and reinstated the treaty. In 1695 poor health forced

Duluth to leave his frontier post of Fort Frontenac and to spend his last years in Montreal.

DUMMER, JEREMIAH (1645-1718) Silversmith, engraver, portrait painter, and magistrate, Dummer was born in Newbury, Massachusetts. His father apprenticed him to John Hall, mint master. His apprenticeship over, he married in 1672. In addition to silversmithing, he painted a number of portraits. He also held a succession of offices, including constable (1675), selectman of Boston (1691-92); justice of the peace (1693-1718), treasurer of Suffolk County (1701), and overseer of the poor (1702). Perhaps his most intriguing public service followed his appointment in 1700 by the Earl of Bellomont to look for the hidden treasure of the pirate Captain William Kidd on Gardiners Island off of Long Island.

DUMMER, JEREMIAH (1679-1739) Son of silversmith Jeremiah Dummer, he was born in Boston, educated at Harvard, and took his doctorate in philosophy at Utrecht, Netherlands (1703). He then went to England, where he practiced law. In 1710 he became colonial agent for Massachusetts and, in 1712, for Connecticut. He never returned to America, but he persuaded Elihu Yale to fund a college in the colonies; thus Yale College was established in Connecticut and, in support, Dummer supplied hundreds of books for its library. He was dismissed from his Massachusetts post in 1721 when he felt that the Massachusetts Assembly was overstepping its bounds with Parliament and was relieved of his Connecticut post in 1730 for similar reasons.

DUNK, GEORGE MONTAGU, EARL OF HALIFAX (1716-71) Merchant and colonial administrator, born in Scarborough, England, Dunk was educated at Cambridge and rose to the peerage with his father's death in 1739. After brief service in 1742 as lord of the bedchamber, he was appointed president of the Board of Trade and Plantations in 1748. Dunk distinguished himself as a strong supporter of mercantile interests, for which he earned the nickname "Father of the Colonies." The city of Halifax, Nova Scotia, was named in his honor. After his resignation from the Board of Trade in 1761, Dunk served as first lord of the admiralty (1762), lord of the privy seal (1770), and secretary of state (1771).

DUNLAP, WILLIAM (1766-1839) The "father of American theater," Dunlap was born in Perth Amboy, New Jersey, where he spent his first 11 years. In 1777 his Loyalist father prudently moved to British-occupied New York, where William received instruction as a painter. At 16 he began his first career as a professional portraitist. In

1784 his father sent him to London to study under Benjamin West, but he investigated the theater instead.

Returning to New York, he tried his wings as a playwright. Dunlap's play *The Father of an Only Child* (1789) met with some success, while his father assisted his income by making him a partner in his China trade business. In 1796, Dunlap purchased a one-quarter interest in the Old American Company. Before he was forced into bankruptcy in 1805, he wrote the blank verse play *Andre* (1798), praising the military courage of both Britain's Major Andre and the Americans in the historical court martial. He also wrote *The Fatal Deception* (1794), retitled *Leicester*, and *The Italian Father* (1799). He worked at the Park Theatre in New York until 1811, when he returned to painting. In 1826 he joined a revolt against the American Academy of the Fine Arts to found the National Academy of Design and served as its vice president (1831-38). Poverty and ill health marked his declining years, but he published both his *History of the American Theatre* (1832) and the two-volume *History of the Rise and Progress of the Arts of Design* (1834).

DUNMORE, JOHN MURRAY, EARL OF (1732-1809) Born into a powerful and noble Scottish family, John Murray succeeded to his father's title as Lord Dunmore in 1756 and subsequently represented Scotland in the House of Lords. In 1770 he was appointed governor of New York and the following year received the governorship of Virginia. At first he worked harmoniously with the colony's leaders, but by 1773 he was compelled to take strong measures against open resistance to British rule. He dissolved the House of Burgesses in March 1773, when it proposed a committee of correspondence on colonial grievances, and again in May 1774, following a vote for a public fast protesting the Boston Port Act.

In September 1774, Dunmore led the Virginia militia to victory against the Indians in the Ohio territories (Lord Dunmore's War). While the Dunmore peace settlement has been called unsuccessful, it kept the western frontier quiet for the first three years of the Revolution and paved the way for the settlement of Kentucky.

Revolutionary fever in Virginia continued to grow. In June 1775, Dunmore moved the seat of government to a British warship, the *Fowey*, and refused to sign any bills unless the Burgesses moved on board. The Burgesses considered this a breach of their privileges, resolved that the governor had abdicated, and vested power in a committee of safety. Dunmore declared martial law and raised a militia to suppress the rebels. After his forces were defeated at Gwynn's Island in July 1776, Dunmore returned to England. He later served as governor of the Bahamas (1787-96).

See also Lord Dunmore's War; Virginia.

DUQUESNE, FORT In order to repel English attempts to take the Ohio country, in 1753 the governor general of New France, Ange de Menneville, Marquis de Duquesne, sent over 2,000 Canadian militia and Indians to construct a series of forts linking the Great Lakes to the headwaters of the Ohio. In the spring of 1754 his men reached the confluence of the Monongahela and the Allegheny rivers at the source of the Ohio, where they overpowered a small Virginia militia force building a fort. There the French built Fort Duquesne. From here later in 1754 they successfully defended themselves against Washington's attack and routed General Edward Braddock's expedition. Fort Duquesne remained in French hands until 1758 when they abandoned and burned it upon the approach of the army of General John Forbes. In English possession the site was renamed Fort Pitt.

DUSTON, HANNAH (1657-1736?) Lauded by Cotton Mather as a great Puritan heroine during the "Indian troubles" in the 1690s, Duston was captured in frontier Haverhill, Massachusetts, six days after the birth of her twelfth child in March 1697. With the child and another village woman, Mary Neff, she was forced to walk barefoot northward with other captives to central New Hampshire. Her captors killed the baby and threatened the women with harm and enslavement. In order to escape, Hannah killed nine Indians with a hatchet, including a man, two women, and six children (one wounded woman and one child escaped) and then scalped them to prove her story. She and two companions returned by canoe to Massachusetts, where they were voted bounties for the scalps. A monument to Duston is a landmark of present-day Haverhill.

DUTCH COLONIES. *See* **New Netherland.**

DUTCH-INDIAN WARS The Dutch-Indian Wars consisted of a series of bloody encounters between 1640 and 1664 with the Algonquian-speaking Indians of the lower Hudson River Valley and the environs of Manhattan, Staten, and Long islands. The first of these occurred in 1640 when the theft of some hogs on Staten Island was mistakenly blamed on the Raritan Indians. Governor Willem Kieft authorized a punitive expedition under the leadership of Cornelis van Tienhoven. The expedition succeeded in killing several Indians and burning their crops.

The following summer witnessed the next violent confrontation, when a band of Raritans attacked a farm on Staten Island, killing four settlers. Shortly thereafter, Governor Kieft issued a bounty of wampum for the heads of those who had murdered the farmers. When the head of the Indian who had led the raid on Staten Island was

delivered to the fort by the chief of the Haverstraw Indians, a peace was concluded.

Kieft War (1642-43). Following the brutal murder of an elderly wheelwright in late 1641, Governor Kieft called a war council of the Board of Twelve Men to advise on Indian policy. With war hysteria running high, much of it fostered by Kieft's demand for revenge, a punitive expedition was authorized in the spring of 1642 to carry the war to the Indian river villages. After a series of broken truces and a number of bloody raids on the women and children of both sides, the war was brought to a conclusion when a platoon-sized contingent of West India Company soldiers and settlers stormed two camps of Indians as they slept. Over 100 Indians, mostly women and children, were slain. In the immediate aftermath of the "Battle of Pavonia" the outlying areas of the colony were devastated as nearly every tribe in the surrounding region fell upon isolated Dutch settlements. No other significant battles took place, but the carnage continued until David Pietersz de Vries led a Dutch mission to negotiate peace in March 1643. A peace treaty was signed on April 22, 1643.

Peach Tree War (1655). New Netherland's next Indian war broke out in 1655 when a combined force of Mahican, Pachami, Esopus, and Hackensack Indians launched an assault on Manhattan Island. In the early morning hours of September 15, 1655, a force estimated at more than 500 landed in 64 canoes at New Amsterdam. With Director General Peter Stuyvesant away at the Delaware River dislodging the Swedes from their colony of New Sweden, the Indians spread through the compound, bursting into the houses on pretense of looking for Indians from the North. The real cause of the attack seems to have been revenge for the slaying of a squaw. She had supposedly been killed for stealing peaches from an orchard, thus the name Peach Tree War. After a skirmish between the Indians and a contingent of company soldiers, the Indians were forced to retreat, but the depredations soon spread to the west bank of the Hudson River, where several Dutch settlements were put to the torch.

When Stuyvesant returned from the Delaware, he quickly took charge in shoring up the colony's defenses and initiating negotiations with the Indians. After a series of prisoner exchanges, peace was concluded in October 1655. The cost had been high: 100 Europeans dead, 150 captured (eventually ransomed), 300 homeless, 28 farms destroyed, and more than 8,000 bushels of grain destroyed.

Esopus Wars (1659-64). The colony's next Indian war erupted in September 1659, when a dozen or so colonists and company soldiers attacked a handful of

Indians near the Hudson River settlement of Esopus (modern Kingston, New York). The war raged until mid-summer 1660, when hostilities were finally brought to a close when Director General Stuyvesant relieved Esopus after a 23-day siege by Indians. In the peace negotiations the Dutch agreed to return a band of Indians they had sold into slavery in Curacao and to pay gifts to the Esopus and Wappinger Indians as a gesture of perpetual friendship.

During the negotiations the sachems of the Esopus tribe had warned Stuyvesant that the location of the new settlement of Nieuwe Dorp (modern Hurley, New York) was unacceptable because it occupied land used by the tribe for farming. Failing to heed the warning, the Dutch went ahead with their new settlement, and on June 7, 1663, the new village was attacked. The so-called Second Esopus War did not end until May 1664, and then only because the Indians had been exhausted by repeated savage attacks on their farms, villages, and families. The peace treaty imposed upon the Esopus Indians ended their dominance of the region. Three months later the Dutch themselves fell to the English.

See also Kieft, Willem; New Netherland; Stuyvesant, Peter.

Bibliography: Kammen, Michael, *Colonial New York—A History* (Scribners, 1975); O'Callaghan, Edmund B., *The History of New Netherland; or, New York Under the Dutch*, 2 vols. (Appleton, 1845-48).

Oliver A. Rink
California State University, Bakersfield

DUTCH REFORMED CHURCH An active trading nation and important sea power in the 17th century, Holland established North American bases at the mouth of the Hudson River and farther north where the Mohawk River joined the Hudson. In Manhattan and Fort Orange (later Albany), Holland's national church accompanied Holland's West India Company. The Dutch Reformed (Calvinist) Church was first established in New Amsterdam in 1628, while at Fort Orange, Johannes Megapolensis served as minister through much of the 1640s. Megapolensis, like so many of the early clergy, found the religious diversity unmanageable and the Indian (in his case, Mohawk) languages impossible. By the end of the century, 25 other Dutch Reformed churches were scattered about southern New York, northern New Jersey, and much of Long Island.

Well before that time, however, the Dutch flag had yielded to a British one as Britain in 1664 sought to consolidate its North American land claims all the way from New England to Virginia. Since Holland's Church was—like Britain's—a national one, the new authorities extended specific toleration to that Church, the Articles of Surrender (the Reverend Samuel Drisius happily reported) stipulating "that our religious services and doctrines, together with the preachers shall remain and continue unchanged."

The Dutch Reformed ministers and members carried on, therefore, exercising significant influence in and around the Hudson River. Because the Great Awakening was primarily a Calvinist revival, the Dutch Reformed had no difficulty cooperating with and benefiting from that movement. Theodore Frelinghuysen in particular led in this endeavor, as well as in an effort to free the American churches from what he regarded as overly strict control by Amsterdam. His son assisted in the founding of Queen's College (later Rutgers) in 1766, this New Brunswick, New Jersey institution serving as an enduring reminder of the presence of the Dutch early in American history.

See also Great Awakening.

Bibliography: Smith, George L., *Religion and Trade in New Netherland* (Cornell Univ. Press, 1973).

Edwin S. Gaustad
University of California, Riverside

DUTCH WEST INDIA COMPANY A joint stock company established by charter of the States General of the Netherlands in 1621 as a national monopoly, the Dutch West India Company was protected for 24 years by provisions in the original charter that "no native or inhabitant of these provinces shall be permitted, to sail or trade with the coasts and countries of Africa, from the Tropic of Cancer to the Cape of Good Hope, to or with the countries of America or the West Indies ... nor to or with any islands situated on either side or between both...." The charter, which was extended in 1646 and completely rewritten in 1674, represented a victory in a long struggle by several prominent Dutch business and political leaders to establish a hemispheric monopoly of shipping and trade. Mercantile motives, however, were not the exclusive cause of the company's founding, for a secondary and in some minds perhaps a primary motivation was to continue the war against Spain in the New World. At its founding, enthusiasm among investors was not strong, but after a series of amendments to the original charter in 1623, public sentiment turned around and an initial capitalization of over 7,000,000 guilders was achieved. The administration of the company was in the hands of the College of the Nineteen, or simply the Nineteen, as it came to be called. In the day-to-day management of the company's colonies, however, the individual chambers exercised decisive control, and each was given specific responsibility for policy formulation in their areas of concern, subject to approval of the Nineteen.

The company's North American colony of New Netherland was under the administration of the Amsterdam chamber. As the chief source of furs throughout its history, the colony attracted the interest of the powerful Amsterdam merchant community, whose influence prompted the company to undertake colonization of the region in 1624. Although financial pressures forced the company to abandon its monopoly of the fur trade after 1639, New Netherland remained under company administration until its conquest by the English in 1664.

In addition to New Netherland the company administered colonies in the Caribbean and on the mainland coast of South America, where an effort to carve a Dutch colony out of Portuguese Brazil (New Holland) was abandoned in 1654. The company was also involved in the slave trade with several outposts on the west coast of Africa, many of which became targets of the Royal African Company in the 1660s.

See also New Netherland.

Bibliography: Boxer, Charles R., *The Dutch in Brazil, 1624-1654* (Oxford Univ.Press, 1957); Goslinga, Cornelis, C., *The Dutch in the Caribbean and on the Wild Coast, 1580-1680* (Univ. of Florida Press, 1971).

Oliver A. Rink
California State University, Bakersfield

DWIGHT, TIMOTHY (1752-1817) Born in Northampton, Massachusetts, Dwight was a man of remarkable educational ability whether as a Congregational minister in the pulpit, as head of the schools he founded, or as president of Yale College (1795-1817). His mother, daughter of Jonathan Edwards, provided him an early education, which included learning the entire alphabet in one lesson and reading fluently in the Bible by the age of four. When he entered Yale at 13, he had already completed most of the first two years' work. He received a master's degree in 1772 and immediately delivered A *Dissertation on the History, Eloquence, and Poetry of the Bible.*

He remained at Yale as a tutor, but after marrying Mary Woolsey in 1777 he resigned to be an army chaplain (1777-79). The death of his father required his return to Northampton, Massachusetts. There, while running two large farms, he started a coeducational school, represented Northampton in the state legislature, and was an active preacher and minister. His *The Conquest of Canaan* (1785) mirrored the triumphs of General Washington in a Biblically inspired epic poem of 11 books in rhymed pentameters. One of the Hartford Wits, he followed this work with "Greenfield Hill"

(1794), a poem celebrating his love of the American landscape and institutions, in contrast with his earlier political satire, "The Triumph of Infidelity, a Poem" (1788). Behind these efforts lay a passionate Puritanism and a belief that democracy would endanger the republic.

From 1795, when he was elected president of Yale, he lavished his abilities and talents on Yale and its students. His influence was felt everywhere. He taught seniors rhetoric, logic, metaphysics, and ethics. In addition he acted as professor of theology, spoke widely, and counseled many.

See also Hartford Wits.

A member of the Hartford Wits, Timothy Dwight was one of the most influential American educators of his era. *(Library of Congress)*

DYER, MARY (c.1610-60) Hanged in Boston for her Quaker beliefs, she was born Mary Barrett, married milliner William Dyer in London in 1633, and emigrated to Boston, joining its First Church in 1635. Called by contemporaries a "comely" woman, of "sweet and pleasant discourse ... fit for great affairs," she raised six children and was a friend and follower of Anne Hutchinson. She was said to have been the only person to walk out of church at her friend's side when Hutchinson was excommunicated in

1638. The Dyers accompanied the banished Hutchinsons to Rhode Island, where William became a colonial officer.

On a trip to England in 1652, Mary Dyer joined George Fox's new Society of Friends (Quakers), whose doctrines resembled Anne Hutchinson's belief that God's will is manifested as inner light. Drawn by this inner voice to test Massachusetts's new laws banishing Quakers on pain of death, Dyer was imprisoned in Boston in 1659 and sentenced to die by Governor John Endicott on another visit later that year. On October 27, she was led to the gallows, made to watch two co-believers die, but taken down herself and sent away. She returned the following May, desiring to "offer up her life" for "the repeal of that wicked law against God's people." Refusing to repent, and forgiving her executioners, she was hanged on June 1. The laws were repealed in 1661.

See also Hutchinson, Anne; Quakers.

E

EARLE, RALPH (1751-1801) Earle was born in Shrewsbury, Massachusetts, and in 1774 he appeared as a portrait painter in New Haven. In the same year he returned to Massachusetts and married his cousin Sara Gates. In 1775, on a visit to Concord and Lexington, he made four paintings of the battles and landscape, later engraved by Amos Doolittle. In 1777 he painted Timothy Dwight, later the president of Yale, and Dwight's wife.

Earle's whereabouts during most of the Revolutionary War are uncertain, but by 1782 he was in England, where he was a pupil of Benjamin West and painted the king and other nobility. He had left Sarah Gates in New Haven, and in England he married Anne Whitesides.

In the 1780s, Earle returned to the United States, once again deserting his wife. He painted portraits in New York, Connecticut, and Massachusetts. Although art historians have suggested that his work hurt by "habits of intemperance and procrastination," his paintings are usually interesting and lively but uneven in quality. His portrait of Mrs. Charles Jeffrey Smith shows his abilities at their best. While preferring the convention of drapes and landscapes as background or frame, on occasion he painted without these framing devices.

EAST INDIA COMPANY (ENGLISH) England's East India Company was formed in 1600 in response to commercial rivalries with the Dutch and Portuguese in Asia. The company's focus of interest was India, where it eventually took almost total control. However, the company also intruded on American colonial affairs, primarily via its trade in tea. The company's purchase of larger amounts of tea after expanding its activities into China forced it to search for larger markets. The American colonies were an obvious choice, but the introduction of a tea tax (1767) had resulted in falling American consumption: from 900,000 pounds (1769) to 237,000 pounds (1772). The East India Company surrendered some of its political power for the right, acquired under the Regulating Act (1773), to export tea directly to America because of its financial crisis. Colonial reactions to the East India Company's tea monopoly resulted in violent protests throughout the colonies, including the Boston Tea Party, and contributed significantly to the growth of anti-British feelings.

See also Boston Tea Party.

EASTON, TREATY OF (1758) During the French and Indian War the settlements of eastern Pennsylvania were under continuous attack by the French-allied Delaware Indians. Desperate for assistance, the colonial government concluded a pact with the Iroquois Confederacy, the Delaware's overlords. The Iroquois were not required by this treaty to aid the British militarily, merely to proclaim their neutrality and claim the Delaware. In return, the Iroquois regained the land west of the Susquehanna River that they had ceded at the Albany Congress in 1754. Satisfied by these provisions, the Iroquois and Delaware took no part in the fighting until the next year, when they joined the British in attacking the French. With the final defeat of the French, however, the Iroquois found themselves unable to play the two European powers off against each other.

EATON, THEOPHILUS (1590-1658) A merchant and the governor of New Haven Colony, Eaton was born at Stony Stratford, England. As a founding member of the Massachusetts Company, he was one of five English managers, but in 1637 he left his thriving London trade for New Haven with John Davenport. Eaton and Davenport ruled New Haven jointly by controlling church membership and thereby the right to hold office. Eaton was elected governor in 1639 and was reelected each year until his death. He also devised a new legal code in 1655. His personal life was less successful. During the 1640s his wife was excommunicated for lying, and he suffered losses in trading with the Dutch.

EDEN, SIR ROBERT (1741-84) A colonial governor, born in Durham, England, Eden married Caroline Calvert (1765), the sister of Lord Baltimore, proprietor of Maryland. Eden was commissioned governor of the Maryland (1768) and as governor supported the Crown, preventing the General Assembly from protesting against the Townshend revenue acts. In 1776 a letter to Eden from Lord George Germain, secretary of state for colonies, was intercepted. The letter led to suspicions that Eden was an enemy of the colonists, and the Continental Congress requested the governor's arrest. Shortly thereafter, Eden left Maryland (June 1776) and returned to England, where he was made a baronet. After the Revolution, he returned to Maryland and died in Annapolis.

EDENTON LADIES TEA PARTY   This was the satirical British label for an agreement signed by 51 women from Edenton, North Carolina, in October 1774. In the agreement the women declared their intention to give "sincere adherence" to the activities of the provincial congress and to support the "publick good" through boycotts of British imports as a matter of female duty. Similar boycott agreements, especially against British tea and textiles, were signed by many women of other colonies. Women were thus asserting a significant public role in the politics and economics of revolutionary era patriotism.

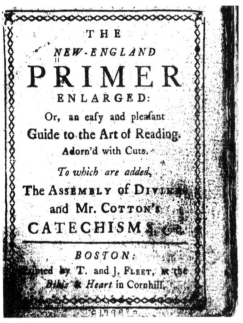

The New England Primer, like many materials used in colonial education, combined learning with religious instruction. *(Library of Congress)*

EDUCATION   Most Americans of the colonial and Revolutionary generations placed a high value on education, but not all had equal access to it. Young white men from wealthy families were most likely to be well educated. Educational facilities were more varied than they are today. Children often learned the rudiments of reading, writing, and ciphering from their parents or a local clergyman. Some towns, especially in New England, opened public schools where all resident children could learn at least to read the Bible. A Massachusetts law of 1647 required that every town with 50 families support such a school and that every town of 100 families support a "grammar" school that taught Latin, knowledge of which

was required for admission to all the colonial colleges. Similar schools were opened in other New England towns. Generally only boys attended the Latin schools and in no case did colleges admit young women.

In the Middle Colonies, education was often a sectarian affair with the local churches sponsoring schools. In religiously tolerant Pennsylvania, denominations as diverse as Anglicans, Quakers, and Moravians opened schools. The Friends Public School, founded in 1689, offered a Latin grammar school education to Philadelphia boys. One of the few good schools for girls was the Moravian Seminary, which opened in 1742 in Bethlehem, Pennsylvania.

In the Southern colonies, where the population was widely spread over rural areas, there were fewer schools. Many wealthy children were taught by private tutors. In Virginia, two Latin grammar schools opened in the 1640s and 1650s, and in Maryland at the same time there was a Catholic Latin grammar school. Churches and individual clergymen also ran schools. In all the colonies "dame schools," conducted in the homes of widows or other women needing the small tuitions they collected, provided an elementary education. In towns throughout the colonies, master craftsmen educated their apprentices. In Northern and Southern cities alike, private masters often opened schools in their own homes and charged a tuition for both elementary and higher education. Some of these teachers were graduates of Harvard, William and Mary, and other colleges. Others were barely literate.

The overall result of this widely varied education was a literacy rate considerably higher than that in Europe. By the outbreak of the Revolution, most men in the New England colonies had at least basic reading and writing skills. In the Southern colonies, over 50 percent of adult white males were literate. The women's literacy rate was lower, but more American women could read and write than could their European counterparts.

Educating Women and Minorities.   Although a few girls learned Latin, Greek, history, and geography, most were offered training in sewing, embroidery, drawing, and perhaps French beyond the basic skills. Many colonists believed that young women should spend their time at home learning domestic skills from their mothers.

Only a few blacks received any formal education in colonial America. A very small number of schools opened for black students, generally sponsored by the Anglicans or the Quakers. In New York City, the Church of England opened a school in 1704 where Elias Nean taught three nights a week for blacks, Indians, and whites. In 1743 the Anglicans in Charleston, South Carolina, purchased two slaves, had them build a schoolhouse, and then taught them to teach reading, which they did for many years. Quakers in Pennsylvania may have opened a school for black students as early as 1700, and in some Quaker schools black and white children studied together. Other blacks taught themselves to read and write. A few slave children were allowed to sit in on classes conducted by tutors for their masters' children, and a few masters instructed their own slaves even when that was illegal.

Post-Revolution Schools. The years following the Revolution witnessed major changes in education. The search for an American identity encouraged education. A new kind of school, the academy, taught "useful" subjects like modern languages, algebra, and the sciences. Women's education improved enormously as Americans decided women could be better mothers and helpmates for their husbands if their mental abilities were developed. Women's academies began closing the gap that had existed between men's and women's educations, but women were still excluded from the colleges.

The post-revolutionary period, which saw a rapid increase in the free black population, also witnessed an increase in schools for black students. New denominations like the Methodists and black congregations of several denominations opened day, evening, and Sunday schools to teach basic literacy and arithmetic and occasionally the higher subjects. Universal education for girls and boys regardless of racial background however lay a century and a half in the future.

Bibliography: Button, H. Warren, and Provenzo, Eugene F., Jr., *History of Education and Culture in America* (Prentice-Hall, 1983); Norton, Mary Beth, *Liberty's Daughters* (Little, Brown and Company, 1980); Wright, Louis B., *Life in Colonial America* (Capricorn, 1971).

Suzanne Greene Chapelle
Morgan State University

EDWARD, FORT A military base approximately 50 miles north of Albany, it was established in 1755 by General Phineas Lyman to provide support for the Crown Point expedition of Sir Wiliam Johnson. The site, on the eastern bank of the Hudson River only 14 miles south of Lake George, had long been known by the Iroquois as the "Great Carrying Place" but was renamed to honor the grandson of King George II. Even after the conclusion of the Crown Point expedition, Fort Edward remained important, especially during the French and Indian War. At the start of the Revolution, it was occupied by the Americans but abandoned at the time of General Burgoyne's 1777 advance.

EDWARDS, JONATHAN (1703-58) Edwards was one of the greatest theologians and revivalists of the colonial era. Born in East Windsor, Connecticut, he was the only son of Esther and Timothy Edwards, a minister, and the grandson of Solomon Stoddard, one of New England's most powerful and prominent Puritan ministers. After receiving his bachelor's (1720) and master's (1723) degrees from Yale College, Edwards moved to Northampton, Massachusetts, in 1726 to assist his grandfather Stoddard in ministry there. Edwards was ordained in February 1727, and two years later, when the aged Stoddard died, Edwards became pastor of the Northampton congregation. Edwards first gained widespread notice when Northampton was swept by a brief but intense religious revival, the so-called "Little Awakening" of 1734-35, which he documented in *A Faithful Narrative of the Surprising Work of God...* (1737). In the early 1740s all of New England experienced an even more dramatic revival, and Edwards played a leading role in promoting the Great Awakening. His *Sinners in the Hands of an Angry God* (1741) stands as a model "New Light" sermon, with its stress on the Calvinistic themes of human depravity and undeserved salvation through divine grace. Even after the revivalistic spirit had died down, Edwards continued to push for greater religious intensity. However, his attempt to reinstitute strict standards of church admission put him in conflict with his congregation and his fellow ministers in the neighboring towns, and he was dismissed from the Northampton pulpit in 1750. He then moved to Stockbridge, Massachusetts, where he not only served as missionary to the Indians there but also wrote some of his most celebrated works, including *A Careful and Strict Enquiry into the Modern Prevailing Notions of Freedom of the Will* (1754). In 1758 he became president of the College of New

Jonathan Edwards greatly influenced colonial religion as a leader of the Great Awakening. *(Library of Congress)*

Jersey (later Princeton University), but soon after taking office he died from the effects of a smallpox inoculation.

See also Great Awakening.

Bibliography: Miller, Perry, *Jonathan Edwards* (1949; reprint Greenwood, 1973); Tracy, Patricia Juneau, *Jonathan Edwards, Pastor: Religion and Society in Eighteenth-Century Northampton* (Hill & Wang, 1979).

Gregory H. Nobles
Georgia Institute of Technology

EDWARDS, SARAH PIERPONT (1710-58)   Evangelical Protestant and wife of theologian Jonathan Edwards, Sarah Edwards was the daughter of Reverend James Pierpont, a founder of New Haven and of Yale College, and Mary Hooker, a descendent of Connecticut settler Reverend Thomas Hooker. Intelligent, lively, and pious, she inspired her future husband to write of her "wonderful sweetness, calmness and universal benevolence of mind." In 1727 she married and moved into the parsonage at Northampton, Massachusetts, where she raised 11 children, supported her husband's ministry and writing career, and entertained a constant stream of visitors, one of whom commented that the Edwards were "the most agreeable family I was ever acquainted with."

From 1734 to 1742, during the Great Awakening, she experienced a series of conversions that culminated in a powerful mystical transport used by her husband as a model for his *Some Thoughts Concerning ... Revival of Religion ...* (1742). In 1750, following her husband's ouster from Northampton, the family moved to frontier Stockbridge. After her husband's death in 1758, while traveling to Philadelphia to care for her orphaned grandchildren, she was stricken with dysentery and died.

See also Edwards, Jonathan; Great Awakening.

Bibliography: Winslow, Ola E., *Jonathan Edwards* (Macmillan, 1941).

ELIOT, JARED (1685-1763)   Born in Guilford, Connecticut, Eliot was educated at Yale College, where he graduated in 1706. He soon settled in the southern part of Killingworth (now Clinton), Connecticut, living above the church in which he preached unfailingly every week until his death. His interest in natural science led him into a number of successful endeavors, first as a distinguished practicing physician and instructor of physicians. Eliot also pursued other scientific interests. He collected the black sand that on occasion covered the beach and transported it in his saddle bags to a nearby iron furnace. When smelted, excellent iron ore could be extracted from the sand. For his essay on this discovery, he was awarded a gold medal by the Royal Society of London. A student of agricultural practice throughout the colony, he advocated a number of agricultural improvements in an Essay on Field Husbandry in New England, published in six parts.

ELIOT, JOHN (1604-90)   A Puritan missionary, born in Widford, England, Eliot was educated at Cambridge and served as a schoolteacher in Essex, where he came under the theological influence of Thomas Hooker. Asked to minister to a group of Puritan emigrants to America, he accompanied them to Boston in 1631. Soon after his arrival however, Eliot left Boston and settled in Roxbury, where he resumed his work as a teacher. It was there that he met an Indian captive and conceived his personal mission of converting the native peoples of New England. To that end, he moved to Dorchester Mills in 1646 and began full-time preaching to the Indians, initially in English but by 1647 in various Algonquian dialects.

Eliot established the Society for the Propagation of the Gospel in New England in 1649 and, with funds raised by this organization, translated and published the Bible in Algonquian. In 1651 he founded a school for Indian converts and, with a land grant from the Massachusetts General Court, established Natick, a town of "praying Indians." By 1674, Eliot had helped found 14 other such towns throughout New England, but the ultimate impact of his life's work was severely restricted by the rise of English-Indian tensions at the time of King Philip's War (1675-76).

See also Hooker, Thomas.

ELIZABETHTOWN ASSOCIATES   On September 30, 1664, Governor Nicolls gave six English Puritans in Jamaica, Long Island, a patent to buy land west of the Arthur Kill in New Jersey. On December 1, the Indians sold them land that stretched from the mouth of the Passaic River north along the kill and 34 miles inland. Governor Philip Carteret joined with the Associates, who then numbered 80, to found Elizabethtown (Elizabeth), which was the capital of the province and of East Jersey until 1686. When the General Assembly of New Jersey met in 1668, the Associates refused to pay their taxes because of their Indian title and patent.

ELLERY, WILLIAM (1727-1820)   A signer of the Declaration of Independence, Ellery was born in Newport, Rhode Island. He graduated from Harvard (1747), became a merchant in Rhode Island, and later started a law practice. He served in the Second Continental Congress (1776-81; 1783-85) and was a member of many committees concerning commerce and the navy. Ellery was also appointed to a newly created board of admiralty (1779). After the Revolution, he was involved in the state-rights movement in Rhode Island. He was elected chief justice of the state (1785) but remained in Congress. Ellery was commissioner of the Continental Loan office for Rhode Island (1786-90). In 1790, President Washington appointed him collector of customs for Newport, a position he held until his death.

EL PASO   The major ford across the Rio Grande, El Paso stood on an important trade route from the beginning of Spanish involvement in the area, Juan de Onate's expedition crossing at that point as early as 1598. The Franciscans established a mission there in 1659, but it was not until 1681 that survivors of the Pueblo Revolt in New Mexico founded a town on the banks of the river. El Paso served as the base for Diego de Vargas's reconquest of New Mexico in the 1690s as well as for Juan Mendoza's and Nicolas Lopez's explorations eastward into Texas. In 1766 the town of about 5,000 lay at the center of an extensive complex of missions and was the key to the defense of the entire region.

EMPRESS OF CHINA   The first American merchant vessel to engage in the China trade, the *Empress of China* was commanded by Captain John Greene and arrived in Canton on August 30, 1785, after a six-month voyage from New York by way of Cape Horn. In the years following the Revolution, American overseas trade was conducted mainly with Europe, but the opening of commercial harbors in the Far East encouraged merchants in Salem, Boston, Newport, New York, and Philadelphia to expand their commercial connections. The large profits earned by the *Empress of China* in the sale of American goods and in the import of Chinese tea and silks served to sharpen American economic interest in the Far East.

ENCOMIENDA AND HACIENDA   The problem of maintaining an adequate Indian labor supply was endemic in the early Spanish colonies, and the institution of encomienda, and the hacienda system that followed it, were attempts to deal with that problem. The repartimiento system that had begun on Hispaniola during the 1490s was clearly inefficient, and the encomienda quickly evolved out of that system. Beginning in 1503 a series of crown decrees granted the labor of Indian vassals of the crown to a particular Spaniard; in return, the colonist was required to perform military service for the crown. The abuses of this system were so extreme and so widespread that it was perhaps the chief agent, after disease, in the tremendous depopulation of the Caribbean and Central American areas after the arrival of the Spanish. Dominican agitation against encomiendas, specifically that of Bartolome de las Casas, resulted in the New Laws of 1542-43. These measures aimed to decrease the abuse of the natives by the Spaniards, and after 1550 the number of encomiendas steadily decreased.

After the demise of the encomienda system, the hacienda system developed. In its basic form the hacienda was a large landed estate. Much of the land was not cultivated, and the hacienda produced only for the local market. Loans made to workers against their wages resulted in their being tied to the estate until the loans were repaid. Other payment to laborers included the use of a small plot of land and food supplies. Under the encomienda system the more laborers one controlled by crown grant, the higher one's status was in the colony; with the hacienda system, land was added to labor as a measure of social standing. Although not as brutal as the encomienda, the hacienda did perpetuate the same type of forced labor system and continued to flourish long after the wars of independence in the early 19th century.

See also Repartimiento.

Bibliography: Harris, Charles, *A Mexican Family Empire: The Latifundio of the Sanchez Navarros, 1765-1867* (Univ. of Texas, 1975); Simpson, Lesley Byrd, *The Encomienda in New Spain; the Beginning of Spanish Mexico* (Univ. of California, 1950).

Thomas C. Thompson
University of California, Riverside

ENDECOTT, JOHN (c.1589-1665)   Governor of Massachusetts and Puritan leader, John Endecott was born in Chagford, Devonshire, of wealthy parents who disinherited him when his association with the Reverends John White and Samuel Skelton led him to Puritanism. In 1628 he obtained a patent for territory on Massachusetts Bay from the Plymouth Council in England and sailed on the Abigail in 1628 to prepare the colony for the arrival of the main group.

Landing at Naumkeag (now Salem), he governed the colony for two years until John Winthrop arrived. A stern moralist, he was influenced by the Pilgrims at Plymouth and organized his own church on the Pilgrim model. His first acts were to deport John and Samuel Browne for not adopting his form of Separatism and to end Thomas Morton's licentious lifestyle by cutting down his Maypole at Merry Mount. He even cut the cross out of the English flag in 1634 because the cross was a symbol of popery. Later, he treated the Quakers very harshly. He was deputy governor in 1641-43, 1650, and 1654; and governor in 1644, 1649, 1651-53, and 1655-65. He was also an overseer of Harvard.

ENGLISH CIVIL WAR   The reign of the Stuart monarchs was marked by stormy and violent conflicts with Parliament; these so preoccupied the English during the early decades of colonization that the colonies developed a strong tradition of local autonomy. When Charles I dismissed Parliament in 1629 he appointed a commission to govern the colonies, but they were too busy in England to do anything about America. When Charles recalled Parliament in 1640, both claimed jurisdiction over the colonies, but neither was able to exercise it. The struggle led to the first Civil War (1642-46), then the second Civil War (1648), followed by the execution of Charles I and the proclamation of the Commonwealth (1649), headed by Oliver Cromwell. Cromwell articulated a general imperial scheme, but wars with the Dutch and the Irish took most of his foreign attention.

By the late 1650s, Cromwell had taken dictatorial control of the English government, and popular support quickly declined. In 1660, King Charles II restored the Stuart monarchy; under his reign, Parliament passed the Navigation Acts of 1660 and 1663 to consolidate centralized authority over the colonies. This trend toward tighter control accelerated when James II ascended the throne in 1685. He revoked the corporate charters and joined Connecticut, Rhode Island, Massachusetts, and New York in a vast new colony, the Dominion of New England. His royal governor, Sir Edmund Andros, abolished the existing legislative assemblies and ruled without representative institutions of government. Similar actions at home offended influential English political leaders, and James's Catholic sympathies aroused the mostly Protestant public. The leaders of Parliament staged a bloodless coup, forcing James into exile and placing his Protestant daughter Mary and her Dutch husband William of Orange on the throne. William and Mary agreed to respect the traditional powers of Parliament. William was busy defending England in war against France and shoring up what was left of royal prerogative. The result was another decade of neglect.

See also Andros, Sir Edmund; Dominion of New England.

Bibliography: Andrews, Charles M., *The Colonial Period of American History*, 3 vols. (1934-37, Yale Univ. Press); Lovejoy, David S., *The Glorious Revolution in America* (1972; reprint Wesleyan Univ. Press, 1986).

ENGLISH IMMIGRANTS The vast majority of 17th-century settlers in British North America were emigrants from England, Scotland, and Wales; indeed, by 1690, 90 percent of the American colonists were of English descent. The first permanent English settlers arrived at Jamestown in 1607, but the great migration of English began in the late 1620s with the establishment of the colony on Massachusetts Bay. From then until the outbreak of the English Civil War in the early 1640s, perhaps as many as 60,000 English arrived in North America, 20,000 in New England alone. New England migrants represented a cross section of the southern English society from which the majority of

them hailed, including men of all ranks, single men as well as those with wives and children, established men in their middle years, and young men seeking their fortune. Relatively few persons came to New England under terms of indenture, but by contrast the immigration to Virginia and Maryland, which averaged some 2,000 mostly English persons each year from the 1630s until the end of the century, consisted largely of indentured servants, most of whom were men, young and poor.

Migration to the colonies nearly ceased during the English Civil War, and in fact the reverse migration of Puritans back to England may have been the more population-important flow of the 1640s and 1650s. In the third quarter of the century the stream of immigrants to the newly established Middle Colonies increased, the majority of them under indenture, although there were more women and skilled craftsmen than earlier. The increasing preference of Southern planters for African slaves in the late 17th century, along with the improving conditions in England that accompanied the end of civil strife, reduced English emigration in the decades around the turn of the century.

18th Century Characteristics. Levels of immigration into the colonies increased greatly after the Treaty of Utrecht (1713) concluded over two decades of intercolonial warfare. Although statistics for the 18th century are hardly better than for the 17th, fragmentary evidence, mostly from the decade before the Revolution, suggests that 60 percent of the English were indentured servants, male, in their twenties, and from London or the urban northcountry. Although these English migrants probably constituted the single largest European immigrant group, together, the Scotch-Irish, the German, the Scotch, and the French immigrants outnumbered the English, while Africans, forced to America as slaves, were the largest single group of the century. By the first federal census in 1790 the proportion of persons of English descent had fallen to less than five in ten (six in ten among whites). Nevertheless, the overwhelming English migration of the first decades of settlement produced a society and culture that was to remain, with important ethnic and regional distinctions, predominantly English.

Bibliography: Bailyn, Bernard, *The Peopling of British North America: An Introduction* (Knopf, 1985); Bailyn, Bernard, *Voyagers to the West: A Passage in the Peopling of America on the Eve of the Revolution* (Knopf, 1986).

John Mack Faragher
Mount Holyoke College

ENUMERATED GOODS First listed in the Navigation Act of 1660, enumerated goods were products of colonial growth or manufacture that by parliamentary legislation were required to be exported only to England, Ireland, Wales, Berwick-on-Tweed, or other English provinces. From the original six in 1660, Parliament in the 18th century enlarged the list of enumerated goods to include virtually all profitable colonial exports. Reflecting mercantilist philosophy, the enumeration of goods was designed to benefit English industry and to increase customs revenue. Colonial evasion of the enumeration laws occasioned additional legislation in 1673 and 1696.

See also Acts of Trade and Navigation.

ERIC THE RED (flourished 980s) Icelandic-born Norse explorer and father of Leif Eriksson, Eric the Red was exiled from Iceland for a homicide in 982. He spent three years exploring the coast of Greenland, which he reportedly named because "men would be more ready to go there if it had a good name," but also because "green" connoted pasturage, and he found it possible to sustain the Norse pastoral economy along the narrow ice-free southern coast. With his family and others, he began the colonization of Greenland in the late 980s.

See also Eriksson, Leif.

ERIKSSON, LEIF (c.970-c.1020) Icelandic-born Norse explorer of the northern Atlantic coast of North America and son of Eric the Red, Eriksson emigrated with his father to Greenland about 985, where he may have heard of the western landfall of Bjarni Herjulfson. About 1001, with a crew of 35 men, he explored each of Herjulfson's landfalls, which he named Helluland (land of rocks and glaciers), Markland (land of forests), and Vinland, (land of meadows—not wine, as it has been misconstrued), apparently corresponding to the coasts of Baffin Island, Labrador, and Newfoundland respectively. He wintered in Vinland, where the party erected several dwellings and where Eriksson's brother Thorvald Eriksson later attempted to plant a colony.

See also Eric the Red; Eriksson, Thorvald; Herjulfson, Bjarni.

ERIKSSON, THORVALD (died 1005) Norse explorer of North America, Thorvald was the brother of Leif Eriksson. After his brother's return to Greenland, he left to explore the region further in 1003 and spent two years reconnoitering the coast of Newfoundland. There his party became the first Europeans to encounter the indigenous inhabitants of North America, the first of whom they indiscriminately slew. Not surprisingly, the Indians next attacked the party, killing Thorvald, whose men retreated and soon after returned to Greenland. In the Norse sagas the Indians are called "Skraelings," which translates as weaklings or wretches. Thorvald's importance lies in the bad omen of his contact with the Indians.

See also Eriksson, Leif.

ESCALANTE, SILVESTRE VELEZ DE (died 1792) Nothing is known of Escalante's early life, but after the Spanish missionary came to New Spain in 1769 he was active among the Franciscan missions in New Mexico. In 1775 the governor requested that he find a route to Monterey. Initially he could not get through the Hopi towns to reach the Grand Canyon. In July 1776, Escalante led (with Francisco Dominguez) another attempt to discover a trade route from Santa Fe to Monterey. The party cut across the southwest corner of Colorado, then west into Utah before dropping down to the Colorado River. Escalante and Dominguez spent 13 days searching for a ford, crossed the river, and returned to Santa Fe via Zuni on January 2, 1777.

See also Dominguez, Francisco.

ESKIMO (INUIT) Ranging over 5,000 miles from the northeastern tip of Siberia across Arctic North America to eastern Greenland, the Eskimo (or Inuit, their self-designation) are one of the most widely distributed indigenous peoples in the world. With their Alaskan neighbors the Aleut, they speak dialects of Eskaleut and are descended from rather recent migrants from Asia, circa 3000 B.C., sharing more physical traits in common with Asians than do other Native Americans. Throughout their territory they practiced an economy based on fishing and the hunting of sea mammals and the caribou, employing a particularly inventive material culture that included the harpoon with detachable shaft, the kayak, sleds and sledges pulled by their hardy dogs, and the igloo.

Among the three main divisions of the Inuit—the Alaskan, the Greenland, and the Central Eskimo—the first two were most affected by European contact in the colonial period. In the North Atlantic, the Norse first encountered the Inuit around 1000 A.D., and the extensive European search for the Northwest Passage brought them into frequent contact by the 17th century. The Russians were on the mainland of Alaska by the 1760s, and although most contact was with the Aleut, the Inuit too were drastically affected by the brutal methods of the Russian fur trade. A precontact population estimated at some 60,000 had fallen to roughly half that by the end of the 18th century.

ESOPUS WARS. *See New Netherland.*

ESPEJO, ANTONIO DE (flourished 1582-83) Espejo, a wealthy Spaniard and a well-known naturalist, financed and led (with Bernaldino Beltran) an expedition in 1582-83 to rescue three Franciscan friars who had been left unprotected in New Mexico. On arriving in the Pueblo country, Espejo found that all three were dead, but he decided to explore the territory on hearing rumors of mines farther to the west. Beltran led a small group that left the main body and returned to their Chihuahua base, but Espejo turned northeast from the Rio Grande and then traveled south along the Pecos before returning home. Espejo's journey and the stories that he brought back served to whet the appetite of the Spanish government for expansion to the north.

ESTAUGH, ELIZABETH HADDON (1680-1762) Proprietor and founder of Haddonfield, New Jersey, Estaugh was born in London to Quakers who wished to emigrate to America to escape religious persecution. To that end, her father bought two large tracts of land in Gloucester County, West Jersey, but was unable to emigrate because of business responsibilities and poor health. Elizabeth decided to go to America alone to manage the investments, an unusual decision at that time for an unmarried woman of 21, and in 1701 she arrived with a housekeeper and two male servants. In 1702 a young minister named John Estaugh, whom Elizabeth had fallen in love with in England, came to visit her at her home on the south bank of Cooper's Creek. According to Quaker tradition, Elizabeth proposed marriage to John, saying she had received a call to love him from the Lord. (This tale was retold by Longfellow in "Tales of a Wayside Inn.") Although John Estaugh became legal guardian of Elizabeth's family's holdings, he was consumed by his ministry and traveled a great deal. An intelligent and gifted woman, Elizabeth continued to manage the estate quite successfully. She had no children of her own but became the adoptive mother of her nephew. In 1713 she moved to a new site, which became the village of Haddonfield, where she died.

ESTEVANICO (flourished 1527-39) Estevanico, a black slave from Morocco, accompanied his master on Panfilo de Narvaez's expedition to Florida in 1527. After the disintegration of the Narvaez expedition on Galveston Bay, the survivors were enslaved by Indians for a year before escaping and moving southward along the coast. During the next several years the remnants of the Narvaez party alternately served as slaves and as medicine men for the natives of the Gulf Coast, but in 1535 the four survivors— Estevanico, Cabeza de Vaca, Dorantes de Carranza, and Alonso del Castillo Maldonado—escaped and headed up the Rio Grande to the Northwest. Their reputations as healers ensured welcomes from the tribes on the way. Near the site of Ciudad Juarez, they turned southwest, and as they entered Sonora they heard rumors of large cities of fixed houses to the north, which they thought were the legendary Seven Cities of Cibola. In March 1536 they met

a Spanish patrol on the Rio Sinaloa, and on April 1 they entered Spanish territory.

When Father Marcos de Niza was sent ahead of the Coronado expedition in 1539 to survey the route to Cibola, Estevanico was his guide. Estevanico stayed ahead of Niza for most of the journey and in May 1539 reached the first of the "cities," Hawikuh. There he was killed by the Pueblo Indians so that he could not communicate with the army that he claimed was following him.

See also Cabeza de Vaca, Alvar Nunez; Cibola, Seven Cities of; Narvaez, Panfilo de; Niza, Marcos de.

EXETER COMPACT (1639) Based on the Mayflower Compact, the Exeter Compact was signed by the settlers of Exeter, New Hampshire, on July 14, 1639. John Wheelwright founded Exeter in April 1638 after Massachusetts Bay exiled him for supporting Anne Hutchinson. The authorities in Massachusetts had stripped Wheelwright of his position as a clergyman, and they also claimed jurisdiction over his Exeter parish. After first Portsmouth and Dover in 1641 and then Hampton in 1642 accepted the rule of Massachusetts, Exeter also acceded that colony's authority, but Wheelwright left for Maine rather than submit.

EXPLORATION Neolithic Asian emigrants first explored and settled the Western Hemisphere; Europeans played no part in the "discovery" of America. By the time the European exploration of North America began in the 16th century, the continent was laced with an elaborate network of trails that guided colonial conquerors, missionaries, traders, and settlers alike. There was relatively little long-range exchange of goods or information before the European era. Indian cultures were essentially local, and although groups often possessed a good deal of information about adjacent areas and peoples, for the most part they lacked a continental understanding of geography. The very fact of a colonial presence in the Western Hemisphere, on the other hand, suggests the importance of long-distance exchange in European culture; it was imperial politics and commercialism that provided the incentive for the first systematic exploration of the continent and its resources. Despite the steady accretion of geographic information, however, it took nearly three centuries of colonial experience to develop an accurate overall conception of the shape, size, and character of the continent.

Spanish Exploration. Exploration began in the Caribbean by the Spanish when Ponce de Leon, the conqueror of Puerto Rico, sighted and reconnoitered the coast of Florida in 1513. This coastal knowledge was extended by Alonso de Pineda's 1519 exploration of the Gulf coast, Francisco Gordillo's 1520 voyage north as far as Cape

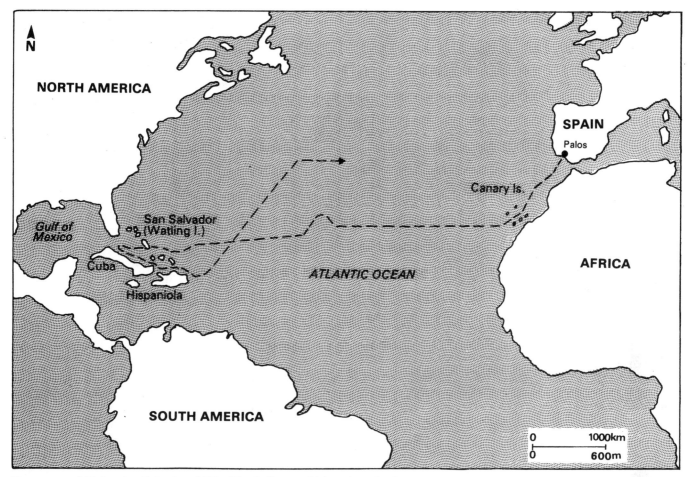

First voyage of Christopher Columbus, 1492. *(Martin Greenwald Associates, Inc.)*

Fear, and Estevan Gomez's expedition from Nova Scotia south in 1524. The exploration of the interior proved to be far more difficult. The conquistador Panfilo de Narvaez landed at Tampa Bay in 1528 hoping to duplicate the successes of Cortes in Mexico, but his expedition came to ruin along the Texas coast without finding any civilizations to plunder. One of the few survivors, Cabeza de Vaca, finally reached Mexico in 1536 after years in captivity and a long overland march, with tales of rich civilizations to plunder in the American Southwest.

Stimulated by this vision of a fabulous civilization, in 1539, Hernando de Soto inaugurated an expedition of conquest that began in Florida and moved north and west. By 1542 his troops had ravaged scores of Indian villages through much of the deep South, crossed the Mississippi River, and explored the lower reaches of the Arkansas River Valley, before returning to the great river in despair. When de Soto died, his retreating men became the first Europeans to float down the Mississippi to its mouth on the Gulf. Meanwhile in 1540, Francisco Vasquez de Coronado moved north from Mexico where he and his

lieutenants explored the Gulf of California, the Colorado River, the Grand Canyon, and the southern Great Plains in search of wealth but found only the sedentary Pueblo and other even poorer Indians. Despite their failures these expeditions were the foundations of Spanish geographic knowledge of the southern continental tier and established the approximate northern limits of Spanish control.

French Exploration. French exploration began with the voyage of Giovanni di Verrazano along the Atlantic coast in 1524 and Jacques Cartier up the St. Lawrence River in 1535; it was not until the early 17th century, however, that France began a comprehensive program of imperial exploration. Samuel de Champlain entered the estuary of the St. Lawrence in 1603 and within a dozen years had explored a water route to Georgian Bay on Lake Huron via the Ottawa River. Champlain envisioned a northern empire based on the lucrative fur trade and linked by waterways, and over the next century this goal was largely realized by his successors. In 1623, Etienne Brule was at the St. Mary's River, the strategic juncture of lakes

Huron and Superior (Sault Ste. Marie), and ten years later, Jean Nicolet was at Michilimackinac and Green Bay. After Groseilliers's exploration of lakes Michigan and Superior in 1654 and 1659 it could be truly said that the northern lakes were a French sea and the northern fur trade a French business. In the wake, and sometimes in advance, of these explorations, Catholic missionaries and fur traders invaded the country, the first proselytizing, the second marrying Indian women and raising mixed-blood children who in turn entered the trade. In the process the French contributed to the creation of a new kind of society—French and Indian at the same time.

By the 1650s the French had heard from the Indians about the great inland river system that could link the French empire of the north to the Gulf in the south. In 1673, Louis Jolliet and Father Marquette explored that connection, via Green Bay and the Wisconsin River, traveling down the Mississippi as far south as de Soto's crossing. The Sieur de La Salle reached the Gulf via the Mississippi in 1682 and claimed the entire great valley, which he named Louisiana, for France. His work was extended by the explorations of Duluth, Hennepin, and Tonty, who explored other portages to the Mississippi system. The French then pushed the fur trade farther west with the Missouri River explorations of Bourgmont in 1712-17, the expedition of St. Denis up the Red River in 1713, and, most profitably, the achievement in the 1730s and early 1740s of La Verendrye and his sons. These men opened the Grand Portage from Lake Superior to Lake of the Woods, extended the water route to Lake Winnipeg, founded a post on the site of what would become Winnipeg, reached the Mandan villages on the upper Missouri River, and penetrated the grasslands as far west as the Black Hills of South Dakota.

English Exploration. One of the persistent aims of these explorations was the discovery of the fabled Northwest Passage to the Pacific or "South Sea." To this elusive goal the English devoted the most attention. Cabot's 1497 voyage, like that of Columbus five years before, aimed to pioneer a new route to the spice islands. After Spanish and French expeditions had established the continuity of the coastline from Florida to New England, English efforts concentrated on the northern latitudes, thus gaining for them control of the route to the continent's interior provided by Hudson's Bay. Even explorers in more temperate climates, however, continued to pursue the goal of a passage through the continent; Weymouth sailed up the Penobscot River, Smith up the James in the hope that these waters led the way to the Orient. However elusive, the search provided a powerful stimulus to Atlantic coastal mapping, essentially completed by the combined efforts of the European powers by the early 17th century.

After the first English colonies were planted along the Atlantic coast, the exploration of the fertile coastal plain began immediately, stimulated less by the desire for furs or plunder than by the hope for fertile lands on which to settle. The Appalachian chain, however, prevented further exploration of the interior. Abraham Wood and Edward Blande first breeched those mountains in 1650; 20 years later John Lederer mounted the summit of the Blue Ridge, Thomas Batts with Robert Fallam became the first Europeans of record to cross the Appalachian divide, and James Needham and Gabriel Arthur conducted a successful trading mission to the interior Cherokee, whom Arthur accompanied to the Ohio River Valley. In 1698, Thomas Welch became the first Englishman to cross the Mississippi. Alexander Spotswood blazed a trail to the Shenandoah Valley in 1716 that became a much-traveled route of families who had settled the great inland valleys by midcentury. When Daniel Boone opened a road to Kentucky in the 1770s, the whole of the interior was opened to European agriculture.

The other important region of English inland exploration began on the shores of Hudson's Bay. Groseillers and Radisson, the expatriate Frenchmen who first proposed to the English the mission that resulted in the establishment of the Hudson's Bay Company, envisioned fur traders moving into the interior from posts on the bay's coast, but the English traders were mostly content to let the superiority of their trade goods draw the Indian producers to them. In 1690, Henry Kelsey explored the Canadian interior, but there was no follow-up on his efforts. Not until goaded by the western penetrations of the French in the 1730s and 1740s did the Hudson's Bay Company send Anthony Henday into the interior in 1754. He was followed by Matthew Cocking, who provided the first clear account of the Saskatchewan country, and Samuel Hearne, who in 1774 built Cumberland House, the first inland Hudson's Bay Company post. The greatest explorers of the Northwest, however, were the men of the North West Company, a Montreal fur trade combination put together in 1784 that carried on the tradition of the French trading system. Under the North West banner Peter Pond and Alexander Mackenzie opened the region north of Lake Athabasca to commercial exploitation.

Exploring the Far West. Mackenzie's trip from Athabasca to the Pacific by way of the Fraser River in 1793 finally fulfilled the old vision of crossing the continent, some 300 years after Columbus. The Pacific coast had been first explored, however, by the Spaniard Cabrillo in 1542, then again by the Englishman Drake some 35 years later; yet the coast had lain mostly undisturbed until the Russians began to extend their Siberian fur trapping operations to the Alaskan coast. Bering's expedition of 1741 was followed by explorations of the Aleutian chain by Chirikov and Bashmakov, and finally by Krenitsyn's landing on the Alaskan peninsula in 1768. In the 1780s, Gregor Shelekhov founded Kodiak.

EXPLORATION: TOPIC GUIDE

GENERAL

Alaska, Russia in
Appalachian Mountains
Bering Straits Hypothesis
Cartography
Caribbean
Cibola, Seven Cities of
Frontier (see **Topic Guide**)
Fur Trade
Geography and Culture (see **Topic Guide**)

Great Lakes
Kensington Stone
Kentucky
Mississippi River
Newport Tower
Norse Explorations and Settlements
Northwest Passage
Tordesillas, Treaty of (1494)

BIOGRAPHIES

Anza, Juan Baptista de
Baffin, William
Balboa, Vasco Nunez de
Bashmakov, Pyotr
Batts, Thomas
Bering, Vitus Jonassen
Bland, Edward
Block, Adriaen
Boone, Daniel
Buell, Abel
Cabeza de Vaca, Alvar Nunez
Cabot, Sebastian
Cabrillo, Juan
Cadillac, Antoine de la Mothe
Cartier, Jacque
Champlain, Samuel de
Chirikov, Alexei Ilyich
Coats, William
Cocking, Matthew
Columbus, Christopher
Cook, James
Coronado, Francisco Vasquez de
Cortes, Hernando
Davis, John
De Soto, Hernaando
Diaz, Bartholomew
Drake, Sir Francis
Duluth, Daniel Greysolon, Sieur
Eric the Red
Eriksson, Thorvald
Eriksson, Leif
Fox, Luke
Frobisher, Martin
Gilbert, Sir Humphry
Gorges, Sir Ferdinando
Gosnold, Bartholomew
Grenville, Sir Richard
Hakluyt, Richard
Hariot, Thomas
Hearne, Samuel
Henday, Anthony

Hennepin, Louis
Henry the Navigator
Herjulfson, Bjarni
Hudson, Henry
Jolliet, Louis
Kelsey, Henry
Knight, John
Krenitsyn, Pyotr Kuzmich
Lane, Ralph
La Salle, Robert Cavelier, Sieur de
Lederer, John
Ledyard, John
Mackenzie, Sir Alexander
Magellan, Ferdinand
Marquette, Jacques
Middleton, Christopher
Moor, William
Narvaez, Panfilo de
Nicolet, Jean
Onate, Juan de
Peralta, Pedro de
Pizarro, Francisco
Ponce de Leon, Juan
Pond, Peter
Portola, Gaspar de
Post, Christian Frederick
Pring, Martin
Radisson, Pierre Esprit
Raleigh, Sir Walter
Shelekov, Gregor Ivanovich
Spotswood, Alexander
Tonty, Henry
Varranzano, De Giovanni da
Vespucci, Amerigo
Viele, Arnouto Cornelissen
Villafane, Angel de
Walker, Thomas
Welch, Thomas
Weymouth, George
White, John
Wood, Abraham

Compelled to counter these moves in order to protect their claim to California, in 1769 the Spanish sent Junipero Serra and Portola to establish missions and presidios up the California coast while Francisco Escalante broke an overland trail connecting the new colony to New Spain. The middle regions of this coastline were explored in the 1770s by the Englishman James Cook, in the 1780s by the Frenchman Perouse, and later most effectively mapped by George Vancouver.

By the end of the colonial period, then, European exploration had fully limned the outlines of the continent and had traced the majority of its rivers and valleys. Yet the hearland of the continent—remained unknown, great blanks on the maps of John Mitchell and Abel Buel, premier American cartographers of the late 18th century. These mysteries would be gradually unveiled by the great explorations of the Americans Lewis and Clark, Zebulon Pike, Stephen Long, and John C. Fremont in the 19th century.

Bibliography: Bolton, Herbert Eugene, *The Spanish Borderlands* (Elliotts Books, 1921); Brebner, John Bartlett, *The Explorers of North America, 1492-1806* (1933; reprint AMS Press, 1983); Chevigny, Hector, *Russian America: The Great Alaskan Adventure, 1741-1867* (1965; reprint Binford- Metropolitan, 1979); De Voto, Bernard, *The Course of Empire* (1952; reprint Univ. of Nebraska Press, 1983).

John Mack Faragher
Mount Holyoke College

F

FAESCH, JOHN JACOB (1729-99) Ironmaster and businessman, born in Basle, Switzerland, Faesch immigrated to New Jersey in 1764 under a seven-year contract to a British firm to supervise the operation of its iron mills at Ringwood, Charlotteburg, and Long Pond. He succeeded Peter Hasenclever in that position. Faesch substantially expanded the New Jersey iron industry with the acquisition of more woodland for charcoal and with the establishment of a new mill at Mount Hope. He became a naturalized British subject in 1766. A supporter of American independence, Faesch produced arms for the Continental Army and served in the New Jersey Constitutional Convention of 1787.

See also Hasenclever, Peter.

FAIRFAX PROPRIETARY A grant for all the land between the Potomac and the Rappahannock rivers, the Fairfax Proprietary was based on a 1688 patent to Lord Thomas Culpeper from James II. On Culpeper's death in 1689, Lord Thomas Fairfax, the son of Culpeper's daughter Catherine, inherited the land. In 1745 the Privy Council confirmed Lord Fairfax's proprietary rights to 5,000,000 acres. Fairfax visited his land in 1735 and settled in 1747 at Greenway Court in the Shenandoah Valley. On his death in 1781, the Virginia Assembly took the Northern Neck, but the Definitive Treaty of Peace in 1783 ended seizure of Loyalist land. By 1796, Fairfax's heirs had rights to only the land he had put to use.

FAIRFAX RESOLVES In response to the Intolerable Acts, local meetings were held across Virginia in late July and early August 1774 to discuss the colony's response and to choose delegates to a Virginia convention. Many resolutions were passed at these meetings, the Fairfax Resolves being ones that are remembered. Probably written by George Mason, they called for: nonimportation of British goods, aid to Boston (whose harbor was blockaded), and united resistance by the colonies, beginning with an Inter-colonial Congress. The Fairfax Resolves also discussed the possibility of refusing to export tobacco if the colonies' demands were not met.

FALL LINE From southern Pennsylvania to Georgia, on the eastern slopes of the Appalachians, which are marked by numerous falls on the eastward-flowing rivers, the Fall Line formed the boundary between the Tidewater, or coastal section of the Atlantic coast, and the Piedmont, or upland country. The Tidewater was the region first occupied by English settlers and by the late 17th century had become a district dominated by slave plantations and a landed gentry. To guard the frontier at the Fall Line posts were established, such as Fort Henry at the falls of the Appomattox and Byrd's Fort at the falls of the James. Settlement of the upcountry in the 18th century characteristically took the form of subsistence or small commercial farms, and the two sections marked by the Fall Line experienced persistent conflict, reflected in such episodes as Bacon's Rebellion in Virginia and the movement of the Regulators in North Carolina.

See also Bacon's Rebellion; Regulators.

FEKE, ROBERT (?1705-50?) An American artist, he was born on Long Island and eventually settled in Newport, Rhode Island, where he became well known as a portrait painter. Not much is known of his life, but it is evident that he was greatly influenced in style by artist John Smibert. It is also known that Feke was in Boston in 1741 to paint a portrait of the family of Isaac Royall and also in 1748-49 when he painted, among others, the Bowdoin family. He also painted in Philadelphia during the 1740s and early 1750s. It is thought that he spent his last years, in ill health, in Bermuda. His portraits are in various museums throughout the United States.

FERGUSON, ELIZABETH GRAEME (1737-1801) A Philadelphia literary figure, she was the daughter of a physician who served on the Pennsylvania Supreme Court, and granddaughter of Sir William Keith, governor of Pennsylvania. She spent most of her life at her family's estate, Graeme Park, near Philadelphia. She was once engaged to Benjamin Franklin's son William, but the engagement was ended, at least partly because of her family's pro-British sympathies. After her disrupted engagement, Elizabeth made a translation of Fenelon's Telemague. Although it was never published, this manuscript, along with her copious correspondence, travel journals, and occasional verse, gave her a literary reputation. She was an intelligent and cultivated woman with many notable friends, and she endeavored to create a salon at Graeme Park modeled on the European salon. In 1772 she married Henry Hugh Ferguson, a Scot who spent much of his time in England. Elizabeth became involved in two incidents that led many to question where her own sympathies lay during the Revolution. In 1777 she

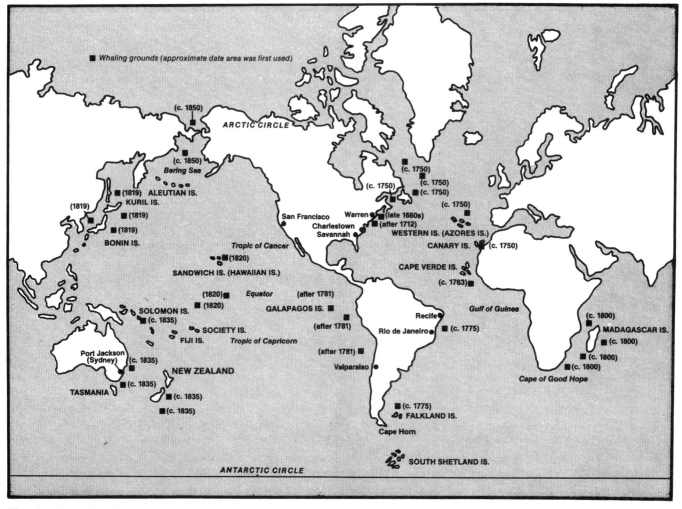

Whaling grounds (approximate date area was first used)

ARCTIC CIRCLE

(c. 1850)

(c. 1850)
Bering Sea

(1819) ALEUTIAN IS.
KURIL IS.
(1819)
(1819)
(1819)
BONIN IS.

San Francisco

Warren
Charlestown
Savannah
(late 1660s)
(after 1712)
WESTERN IS. (AZORES IS.)
CANARY IS.
(c. 1750)

(c. 1750)
(c. 1750)
(c. 1750)
(c. 1750)

Tropic of Cancer
(1820)
SANDWICH IS. (HAWAIIAN IS.)

CAPE VERDE IS.
(c. 1763)

(1820)
(1820)
SOLOMON IS.
(c. 1835)
SOCIETY IS.
FIJI IS.
Equator
GALAPAGOS IS.
(after 1781)
Tropic of Capricorn
(after 1781)

Recife
Rio de Janeiro
Gulf of Guinea
(c. 1775)

(c. 1800)
MADAGASCAR IS.
(c. 1800)
(c. 1800)
(c. 1800)

Port Jackson
(Sydney)
(c. 1835)
NEW ZEALAND
TASMANIA
(c. 1835)
(c. 1835)
(c. 1835)
(c. 1835)

(after 1781)
Valparaiso

Cape of Good Hope

(c. 1775)
FALKLAND IS.
Cape Horn

SOUTH SHETLAND IS.

ANTARCTIC CIRCLE

Fisheries. *(Facts On File, Inc.)*

carried a letter from Reverend Jacob Duche, former chaplain of the Continental Congress, to General Washington. Philadelphia had just fallen to the British, and Duche urged Washington to sue for peace. And in 1778, Elizabeth relayed a message from the British to Washington's aide Joseph Reed, offering a substantial bribe to arrange favorable peace negotiations.

FINLEY, JOHN (c.1722-69) A Scotch-Irish pioneer, Finley emigrated to Pennsylvania with his family around 1740 and by mid-decade had been licensed as an Indian trader to work the Ohio country. In 1755 he met Daniel Boone during Braddock's campaign against the French, sharing with the famous frontiersman his knowledge of the legendary Kentucky country. For the next 15 years he worked as a trapper and trader in the vicinity of Fort Pitt. Then in 1769 he accompanied, and perhaps led, Boone across the mountains

to Kentucky, where Finley died under unknown circumstances.

FISHER, MARY (1623-98) Quaker preacher and missionary, Fisher was born in Yorkshire, England, and went to Barbados after years of persecution in England for her Quaker beliefs. In the summer of 1656 she and another woman sailed to Boston Harbor and were detained by the authorities, who considered Quakers to be heretics. They were returned to Barbados. (Subsequent Quaker visitors to Boston were executed.) Some time around 1657 she set out to the Near East with six other Quakers. The party was turned back in Venice, but Fisher continued alone, going overland from Greece to Adrianople in Turkey. She presented herself as an ambassador of the Most High God and spoke with Sultan Mahomet IV at his army encampment. Because the Sultan was a most feared figure in the West, and not least because of her arduous solo trek, Fisher became a celebrated figure famous for her courage and unshakeable beliefs. She married William Bayly in 1662 and bore three children. After Bayly died, Mary remarried and emigrated to Charleston, South Carolina, where she lived for the remainder of her life.

FISHERIES The North Atlantic fisheries of the fertile continental shelf may have attracted European fishermen even before 1492. Certainly they were being exploited by the Portuguese, Spanish, and French by the time John Cabot reported, in 1497, that the northern waters were "swarming with fish." The French dominated the industry until the late 16th century, when the English successfully introduced the practice of "dry fishing," of drying the catch along the shores of Newfoundland in order to conserve salt. By the 1620s, English merchants had established a number of small fishing stations from Cape Cod north to Nova Scotia. They controlled the fisheries until the disruption of the English Civil War provided an opening for the colonists. Fishing then quickly became the single most important aspect of the New England economy. By the 18th century, fishing accounted for more than one-third of New England's exports and employed 10 percent of the region's men. This in turn contributed to the prosperity of the merchants who purchased the catch and sold it in Europe and the Caribbean.

The most productive fisheries were off the shores of Newfoundland, Nova Scotia, and Labrador, and access to those grounds was an issue during the Revolution. In the Treaty of Paris (1783) the United States won the right to continue fishing as well as the liberty to dry and cure their catch on the unsettled shores of Canada. Whaling also became a flourishing business in the 18th century with the perfection of manufacturing techniques for spermaceti candles and the development of markets for whalebone and ambergris, used in the production of drugs and perfume.

See also Whaling.

Bibliography: Stackpole, Edouard, *Sea-Hunters: New England Whalemen, 1635-1835* (Greenwood, 1973).

FLAGG, JOSIAH (1737-95?) Born in Woburn, Massachusetts, composer Josiah Flagg bridged the gap between traditional New England church music and classical secular forms. In 1764 he published as his first work, "A Collection of the best Psalm Tunes in two, three, and four parts, from the most approv'd Authors. ..." Its success led Flagg in 1766 to publish *Sixteen Anthems*, which, while religious in tone, were actually secular pieces. He became the leader of a military band, which gave its first concert June 29, 1769, at Concert Hall, Boston. At this and succeeding concerts he introduced a wide range of music from selections from Handel's *Acis and Galatea* to "vocal and instrumental musick accompanied by French horns, haut boys, etc. ..." On October 28, 1773, he gave his "final Grand Concert" in Faneuil Hall. Flagg then settled in Providence, Rhode Island, and served during the Revolu-

tion as a lieutenant colonel. Little is known about his later years.

FLETCHER, BENJAMIN (1640-1703) British soldier and colonial governor. He spent 22 years (1663-85) in the British army, and from 1692 to 1697 he served as governor of New York. To unify the defense effort during King William's War he asked the colonies to send aid to New York. When the Pennsylvania Assembly refused to provide assistance, William and Mary lifted Penn's Charter in 1692 and appointed Fletcher governor of Pennsylvania (1693-94) as well as of New York, giving him broad powers. He appointed William Markham deputy governor and ordered the election of a special assembly to pass defense bills.

The Quakers, led by Assembly Speaker David Lloyd, obstructed Fletcher's royal authority by demanding the governor's confirmation of old laws before enacting any others. After he consented and accepted affirmation in place of oaths, the Assembly granted 760 pounds for use in the war but refused to pass a militia bill. In August 1694, the King restored Penn's powers. As New York governor, he allied himself with the anti-Leislerians, enriched his political friends with favoritism and fraud in land grants, and condoned acts of piracy. In 1697, Fletcher was removed from office and sent to England under arrest for his corrupt practices. He died in Boyle, Ireland.

See also King William's War.

FLOYD, WILLIAM (1734-1821) American patriot and signer of the Declaration of Independence, Floyd was born in Brookhaven, Long Island. He became a major-general and fought for the patriotic cause in the American Revolution. Floyd was a member of the Continental Congress (1774-77; 1778-83). His support of the patriots caused his family to suffer hardships after the British invaded Long Island (1776). They took possession of Floyd's property, and his family had to seek refuge in Connecticut. Following his membership in the Continental Congress, Floyd served in the state senate and supported conservative and stable financial policies. He was a member of the first Congress (1789-91) and later ran unsuccessfully for lieutenant-governor of New York (1795).

FONTAINEBLEAU, TREATY OF (1762) A secret agreement made on November 3, 1762, between France and Spain, in which France ceded to Spain the Isle of Orleans and all territories in Louisiana west of the Mississippi River, it laid the foundation for a final resolution of the French and Indian War. Following a series of British victories in North America, King Charles III of Spain entered the war on the French side. The British then declared war on Spain and took over Spanish colonial possessions in Cuba, Florida, and the Philippines. The Treaty of Fontainebleau compensated France's Spanish allies for the loss of colonial territory and was a prelude to the final settlement of the war in the Treaty of Paris.

See also Paris, Treaty of.

FOOD Compared to the consumption standards of working people in Europe, the relative abundance of food was one of the considerable advantages of colonial life. Slaves of course were less well fed, most subsisting on hominy with a little meat two or three times a week, but for other colonists diet was probably one of the things that contributed to a generally healthier and longer life span than in Europe. The most important food in colonial America was indigenous Indian corn, or maize, the cultivation of which colonists quickly adopted. Because wheat grew poorly in most of the earliest settled regions, corn became the colonial staff of life, ground with rye to produce a loaf called "rye-an'-injun," cooked into "samp" or porridge, boiled with beans to make "succotach," soaked in lye to produce "hominy" (the Algonquian words testifying to the origins of these dishes), or served simply as roasting ears or popcorn. Other Indian crops included pumpkins, squashes, beans, and maple sugar, augmented by the colonists' cultivation of peas, turnips, carrots, domestic berries and grapes, fruit trees, and honey.

Wild game was abundant and important to the diet, whether on the frontier or in the cities; most of the meat was salted, pickled, or smoked for later use. Even more important was fish, including cod, salmon, shad, lobsters, crabs, and oysters. Colonists quickly introduced hogs, who thrived on the forest mast. Cattle and milk cows were raised in the South from the beginning of settlement, but it was not until the 18th century that milk and beef became common table items throughout the colonies. Northern farm wives became adept at cheesemaking, but the dearth of churns in colonial inventories suggests a low consumption of butter. Food was, of course, simple and plain in the kitchens of the common farmer, considerably more elaborate in the dining halls of the wealthy, but by all accounts colonists of every class loaded their tables with great quantities, in the style of the day.

Bibliography: Carson, Jane, *Colonial Virginia Cookery* (Univ. Press of Virginia, 1985); Earle, Alice M., *Home Life in Colonial Days* (Corner House, 1975).

John Mack Faragher
Mount Holyoke College

FORBES, JOHN (1710-59) A British military officer, born in Fifeshire, Scotland, Forbes joined the 2nd Royal North British Dragoons in 1735. Serving in Europe during the War of the Austrian Succession, he rose to the rank of lieutenant colonel by 1745. In 1757, as colonel of the 17th Foot Regiment, he was transferred to Halifax, Nova Scotia, and placed in command of an expedition against Fort Duquesne. Overcoming problems of supply and coordination, he led a force of 6,500 colonials westward, clearing a line of communication that was dubbed Forbes Road. On November 25, 1757, Forbes's troops took possession of the recently abandoned French fort and renamed it Fort Pitt.

FOREIGN PLANTATIONS, COUNCIL FOR (1660-65, 1670-72) An advisory committee formed to take over some of the duties of the Colonial Board, it was charged with regulating the governments of the colonies and reporting to the Privy Council. It was also empowered to enforce the Navigation Act of 1651, which allowed only trade with Britain. The board's members were from various fields and included merchants and administrators. After five years the work of the committee was incorporated into a Privy Council committee, and it was not until 1670 that the committee became separate again. By 1675 its duties had again become part of the Privy Council's Committee for Trade and Plantations.

FORTS The French and Spanish built the first forts in North America, often competing for the same sites. Charles Fort (Parris Island, South Carolina) was built and abandoned by the French in 1562; nearby the Spanish built Fort San Felipe in 1566, replaced in 1577 by Fort San Marcos, abandoned in 1586. In Florida, French Huguenots built Fort Caroline at the mouth of the St. Johns River in 1564; after the destruction of the Protestants, the Spanish conquerors built Fort San Mateo. Later, the Spanish garrisoned five different forts, including Fort San Marco, in the area of St. Augustine.

For the Spanish the mission may have been the preeminent frontier institution, but without the nearby fort, or presidio, missions would never have been so effective. The presidio soldier, with his Indian or mestizo family raising crops for their support, was the settlement policeman as well as frontier guardian against Indians and rival colonial powers. Missionaries continually complained of the loose morals, lax discipline, poor equipment, and low morale of the presidio soldiers, but knew they could not get along without them. In addition to those in Florida, important Spanish presidios included El Paso and Sante Fe in New Mexico, San Antonio in Texas, and San Diego and Monterey in California.

The Dutch also built forts to protect their settlements. They constructed Fort Nassau on the Delaware River in 1623 and Fort Orange (later Beverwyck, then Albany) on the Hudson the next year. The Swedish Fort Christina, built in 1638, was later taken by the Dutch and became Wilmington, Delaware, and in 1651 the Dutch built Fort Casimir.

English Forts.   Fortifications were one of the first preoccupations of the English settlers. What has become known as Fort Raleigh was built on Roanoke Island in the 1580s; in 1607 both Jamestown in Virginia and the Popham Colony in Maine included forts. Upon landing in Massachusetts, the Pilgrims threw up a rough barricade of logs and branches and later fortified their meeting house on a dominant position above their village. Special forts of various kinds were built all along the English frontier of settlement, stretching from Fort Pownall on the Penobscot River in Maine to Fort St. George at the mouth of the St. Johns River in northern Florida and including Fort Richmond on the Kennebec River, Forts Dummer and Bridgman on the upper Connecticut River, and Forts Shirley, Pelham, and Massachusetts in the western part of that colony. In New York, they constructed Forts Anne and Nicholson south of Lake George, Fort Johnson on the Mohawk, and Fort Oswego on the southern shore of Lake Ontario. Further south there was Fort Henry in Virginia, Fort Nohoroco in North Carolina, and a score of forts in Georgia. For the most part, however, the principal fortification was the garrison house, both dwelling and fort, found in virtually every settlement.

French Forts.   The French also used the garrison house for their early settlements in what would later be called Quebec. As they expanded into the Great Lakes country and beyond, however, they undertook the greatest program of fort-building in colonial America. They began with Fort de Baude at the Straits of Michilimackinac, constructed in the 1660s, then with the series of forts planted by La Salle in the 1680s—Fort Frontenac on the north shore of Lake Ontario, Forts Crevecoeur and St. Louis in the Illinois country, and Fort Prudhomme (later Fort Assumption) on the Mississippi at Chickasaw Bluffs. By the early 18th century French forts stretched from Fort Mobile and Fort Maurepas (Biloxi) on the Gulf of Mexico, to Fort Rosalie (Natchez), up the Mississippi to Fort de Chartes in the Illinois, Fort Massiac on the Ohio, Fort Oiatenon on the Wabash, Fort Miami (later Fort Wayne) in what would become Indiana, Fort St. Joseph in southern Michigan, Fort La Baye (Green Bay), Fort Detroit, Forts Niagara and Denonville on the Niagara River, and Fort Toronto on Lake Ontario. To the West were Forts St. Antoine and Beauharnois on the upper Mississippi, Fort D'Huillier on the Minnesota, Fort Orleans on the Missouri, and Fort La Reine on the Assiniboine. On the New York-Canadian frontier there were Forts Chambly, St. Theresa, and St. John on the Richelieu River; Fort St. Anne (later La Motte) and Fort St. Frederic on Lake Champlain; and Fort La Galette at the mouth of the Oswgatchie River on the St. Lawrence.

Later Colonial Forts.   A great deal of fort-building took place during the French and Indian War, which began over French and British competition for control of the Ohio Valley. The French first built a series of forts linking the lakes to the sources of the Ohio: Forts Le Boeuf, Presque Isle, Machault, and Fort Duquesne (later Fort Pitt and Pittsburgh). Fort Carillon (later Fort Ticonderoga) was situated between Lake Champlain and Lake George. The English countered with a string of opposing forts including Forts Necessity, Cumberland, Edward, Augusts, Bedford, Loudoun (on the Little Tennessee River), Stanwix, and William Henry.

Many of these forts were reactivated during the Revolution, although new locations came into prominence, including Fort Moultrie in Charleston harbor; Forts Clinton, Putnam, and Constitution at West Point; and Forts Montgomery, Clinton, and Independence somewhat lower on the Hudson River.

Bibliography: Peckham, Howard W., *The Colonial Wars, 1689-1762* (Univ. of Chicago Press, 1964).

John Mack Faragher
Mount Holyoke College

FORT STANWIX, TREATIES OF (1768, 1784)   Following the French and Indian War the Iroquois were no longer able to play off the French against the English. In the treaty of 1768 they gave up all claim to the Ohio Valley, hoping to deflect English settlement away from Iroquois territory. The Shawnee and some dissident Seneca joined to attack the English in Lord Dunmore's War (1774), but the Iroquois remained neutral.

During the American Revolution the Iroquois again tried to stay neutral, but constant American infringements on their territory drove most Iroquois into the British camp. After Indian victories at Wyoming and Cherry Valley, the Americans mounted four invasions of the Iroquois country in 1779. Most of the Iroquois towns were destroyed, and the weakness of the Iroquois was revealed in the Treaty of 1784. Although supposedly signing a peace treaty with the Iroquois, the American commissioners assumed that the Treaty of Paris of 1783 had transferred to the United States the sovereignty of the area east of the Mississippi River. They refused to recognize the Iroquois Confederacy and, under threat of war, coerced the Iroquois into ceding all land held west of New York and Pennsylvania in return for a reservation in New York.

See also Cherry Valley Massacre; Iroquois Confederacy; Lord Dunmore's War.

FORT WILLIAM HENRY MASSACRE (1757) This massacre, the unexpected outcome of the bitter siege of Fort William Henry on the shores of Lake George, New York, during the French and Indian War, became a rallying point for intensified hostilities by the British against the French. On August 9, the French commander, the Marquis de Montcalm, agreed to offer safe conduct to the 2,500 defenders of Fort William Henry, but on the following day when they began to leave the enclosure the defenders were set upon by the Indian allies of the French. Although only about 50 were killed, hundreds of the defenders were either captured or stripped of all their possessions. They later sought shelter at Fort Edward.

FOX, CHARLES JAMES (1749-1806) British opposition politician and the aristocratic son of the first Lord Holland, he was born in London. Fox was renowned for his dissolution and self-indulgence by the time he entered Parliament at the age of 19. Initially a political conformist loyal to his class, Fox underwent a change of heart upon the death of his parents and older brother. He withdrew his support from Lord North's government and made a brilliant speech in 1775 attacking that government's policies in America. Fox became leader of the opposition and, when North's government fell after defeat in the American Revolution, joined a Whig-led government as foreign secretary in 1782. A brilliant orator and gadfly, Fox was more effective in opposition than in government, and his political support steadily eroded.

FOX, LUKE (1586-1635) An English navigator in search of the Northwest Passage, Fox in 1631 explored Hudson's Bay, beginning where Thomas Button had left off. Carefully examining the coastline southward and eastward to the entrance of James Bay, he concluded that there was no passage to be found there. His published account of the voyage, *North-West Fox* (1635), contributed greatly to contemporary geographic knowledge.

See also Northwest Passage.

FOX-FRENCH WARS A series of conflicts between the French and the Fox tribe of the western Great Lakes region that can be traced to the first encounters of the two peoples. In 1665, soon after the appearance of the first French traders in the region, the Fox imposed a portage fee between the Fox and Wisconsin rivers, an act that angered the French authorities. Further bad feelings were created by the brusque treatment of Fox negotiators in Montreal in 1671. The Fox then attempted to prevent French contact with the Chippewa, rivals of the Fox to whom French traders were supplying arms and ammunition.

An unsuccessful 1712 attack by the Fox on Fort Detroit initiated the open warfare, and it was followed by Fox attempts to stir up anti-French feeling in Wisconsin. In 1716 the French, perceiving the extent of the threat posed by the Fox, dispatched an expedition under Louis de la Porte to break their power. Despite their crushing defeat, the Fox resumed the hostilities in 1726 with an attack on Indian allies of the French. This was answered in 1730 by a large-scale attack by the French and their Indian allies on the Fox. Fighting continued until 1738, when the Fox, now severely weakened, signed a peace treaty with the French and merged with the Sac nation.

FRAME OF GOVERNMENT Two early Pennsylvania statutes were known as the Frame of Government. William Penn wrote the first Frame of Government (April 25, 1682) to insure that "the will of one man may not hinder the good of an whole country." Penn wanted to establish a free government "where the laws rule, and the people are a party to those laws," but he reserved much power to himself or his governor. A Council of 72 men "of most note for their wisdom, virtue, and ability" had the exclusive right to initiate legislation, oversee all justice, and appoint provincial officers and committees to supervise the safety, trade, manners, and morals of the colony. The governor and the Council jointly managed finances, established courts, and chose judges. The General Assembly, a body of 200 representatives, could only approve or reject bills submitted by the Council. Freemen— those who owned land, rented improved land, or paid taxes—elected one-third of the Council and the entire Assembly annually. The second Frame of Government (April 2, 1683) preserved much of the first Frame; however, it reduced the Council to 18 members, the Assembly to 36 members, and William Penn gained greater power to appoint local officials.

Bibliography: Soderlund, Jean R., ed., *William Penn and the Founding of Pennsylvania, 1680-1684: A Documentary History* (Univ. of Pennsylvania Press, 1983).

FRANCISCANS The Order of Friars Minor, or Franciscans, focused most of its American mission work in Spanish territories. Only a few Franciscans labored in New France, erecting a short-lived monastery at Fort Niagara in 1679. Friar Louis Hennepin sailed with the Sieur de La Salle on his exploration of the Great Lakes and the Mississippi. No permanent missions resulted from this venture. The preeminence of the order in New Spain was assured by the appointment of a Franciscan, Juan de Zumarraga, as Mexico's first bishop in 1528.

Early Franciscan missions centered in what is now New Mexico, where friars had accompanied the expedition of Francisco de Coronado (1540- 42). On Coronado's return to Mexico, three friars remained to convert the Indians who, instead, murdered them. In 1598 the first permanent Spanish settlement in New Mexico was established at Real de San Juan. Nine Franciscans ministered there. In 1610, Santa Fe was established as the territorial capital. From here Franciscans directed their mission work. Missions, set up near pueblos, consisted of a church, monastery, and workshops. Indians were taught crafts and instructed in new agricultural techniques. Franciscans introduced the horse and cattle. Despite some successes, Franciscan efforts to close the pueblo kivas, the center of the kuchina cult, provoked the Indians to rebel in 1680. About 400 Spaniards died, 21 of them missionaries. Spain regained control in 1699, but the missions never recovered from Indian alienation.

Elsewhere in the Southwest, Franciscans replaced Jesuits in the Arizona missions in 1767, when the Jesuits were suppressed by King Charles III of Spain. In 1700, Jesuit Father Eusebio Francisco Kino had founded San Xavier del Bac near present Tucson along with two other missions. These Arizona missions never flourished because of Indian hostility and a lack of sufficient missionaries. Scattered Franciscan missions in Louisiana and Texas were modestly successful.

California Missions.   California was to be the scene of the greatest Franciscan success. Spain's interest in the area began in 1768, goaded by Russian settlers pushing down the west coast from Alaska. To secure the territory, Spain erected a number of presidios and mission stations. Under the leadership of Junipero Serra, missions were established at San Diego (1769), San Carlos Borromeo (1770), San Antonio (1771), San Gabriel (1772), San Francisco (1776), San Juan Capistrano (1776), Santa Clara (1777), and San Juan Buenaventura (1782). Eventually, 21 missions were created. Presidios were located at San Diego, San Francisco, Monterey, and Santa Barbara. Franciscans served these as well as the independent villages of San Jose and Los Angeles.

The missions were self-contained units with a church, monastery, Indian dwellings, workshops, and farmlands. Indian life was strictly regulated by the friars, who divided the day into periods of prayer, work, and instruction. By and large, California's missions were successful in raising Indian standards until they were secularized by the Mexican government in 1834.

See also Spanish Colonies.

Bibliography: Geiger, Maynard, *Franciscan Missionaries in Hispanic California, 1769-1848: A Biographical Dictionary* (Huntington Library, 1969); Kelly, Henry, *Franciscan Missions of New Mexico, 1740-1760* (Univ. of New Mexico Press, 1941).

Leonard R. Riforgiato
Pennsylvania State University

FRANCO-AMERICAN ALLIANCE (1778)   In February 1778, France declared war on Great Britain, bringing into the open its previously tacit support of the new United States. Although the political climate in France was favorable to the ideals represented by the American Revolution, there were other reasons for France to enter the conflict. The emotional reasons included the humiliating Treaty of Paris signed with Britain only 15 years before, at the end of the French and Indian War. Political and economic reasons included the necessity of dealing with this new power overseas whose emergence had radically changed the transatlantic trade. Vergennes, the French minister of foreign affairs, had from the start advocated support of the American colonists, in spite of France's serious financial problems. France, however, did not enter the alliance until the defeat of Britain's General Burgoyne at Saratoga, New York, gave some needed reassurance about American military capacity. During the Revolutionary War the French contributed about 12,000 soldiers in addition to their fleet. As a direct result of the Treaty of Paris signed in 1783, France recovered Senegal and two islands, St. Lucia and Tobago.

See also Paris, Treaty of.

FRANKLAND, AGNES SURRIAGE (1726-83)   Colonial tavern maid who became a titled English aristocrat, Frankland was something of an 18th-century legend. She was one of eight children born to a poor fisherman and his wife in Marblehead, Massachusetts. While working at an inn, she caught the eye of Charles (Harry) Frankland, customs collector for the port of Boston. Agnes's charming, unspoiled nature and beauty captured his heart instantly, and although ten years older he persuaded her family to allow her to go to Boston to be educated at his expense. In 1746, Harry Frankland succeeded to the baronetcy of Thirsk in Yorkshire, and Agnes became his mistress. Boston was scandalized by this public display, and the two were forced to move out of Boston to rural Hopkinton. After Agnes was rejected by Frankland's family in England, the two went on a tour of Europe. In Lisbon, Sir Harry was trapped by the earthquake of 1755 and rescued by Agnes. Legend has it that he promptly married his mistress. They returned to Boston and were finally accepted by society there. After several years as consul general in Lisbon, Sir Harry and Agnes moved to England, where Sir Harry died. Agnes remarried several years later and died in England.

FRANKLIN, ANN SMITH (1696-1765)   Printer, publisher, and businesswoman in 18th-century Newport, Rhode Island, Ann Franklin was the wife of James Franklin and sister-in-law of Benjamin Franklin. Her husband, invited from Boston to Newport in 1727, died in 1735, leaving Ann

Benjamin Franklin was perhaps the most noted colonial American, respected in the arts and business and as a patriot and diplomat. *(Library of Congress)*

with four children and a printshop. They had published *The Rhode Island Gazette* (1732-33), but James's long illness had made it impossible to continue. Ann was the colony's official printer for the rest of her life. Lucrative sidelines included printing cloth and keeping a bookshop. Her ability and integrity as editor, compositor, and printer resulted in a commission from the Rhode Island General Assembly to print an official supplement to the public laws (1736), followed by a complete revision of the *Acts and Laws of Rhode Island* (1744). She also printed numerous pamphlets and sermons by Rhode Island intellectual leaders and published *The Newport Mercury* (1763-65).

FRANKLIN, BENJAMIN (1706-90) Printer, writer, inventor, scientist, humanitarian, statesman, diplomat, and one of the most prominent Americans of his time, Franklin was born in Boston. Apprenticed in his brother James's printing shop, he ran away to Philadelphia in 1723. He gained full ownership of a printing business there in 1730, the same year he took Deborah Read as his common-law wife. Soon, he was well known as the publisher of the *Pennsylvania Gazette* and *Poor Richard's Almanack.*

Franklin also became a civic leader, developing projects for the physical improvement of Philadelphia and helping to organize a debating society, a circulating library, a hospital, the American Philosophical Society, and the Philadelphia Academy. In 1748, having made a sufficient fortune, Franklin turned the printing business over to his partner. The years that followed saw the culmination of his scientific work in experiments that made substantial contributions to electrical theory. Described in *Experiments and Observations on Electricity* (1st ed., 1751), they helped to establish Franklin's reputation in Europe.

Early Political Career. This period also saw the development of his political career. He was elected to the Pennsylvania Assembly in 1751, and in 1753 he was appointed deputy postmaster general of the colonies by the British government. At the outset of war with France in 1754 he proposed a union for defense at the intercolonial Albany Congress; the plan was rejected by both the colonies and Great Britain but nevertheless set a precedent for later American union. In Pennsylvania he led a campaign against the policies of the province's proprietors;

twice he was sent by the Assembly to London as its agent (1757-62, 1764-75).

It was during the second London mission that Franklin became involved in the politics of the American Revolution. Initially a strong imperial patriot who advocated an expanded Anglo-American empire in North America, Franklin became convinced by London's policies after the French and Indian War that Parliament should have no authority over the colonies. His role as the most prominent American spokesman in London was manifested in his 1766 testimony against the Stamp Act before the House of Commons, his appointment as agent for Massachusetts (1770), and his involvement in secret and unsuccessful negotiations to end the imperial crisis (1774-75). Despite Franklin's deep and abiding love for London, he was prepared for revolution when he sailed home in 1775.

National Leader.   On his arrival in Philadelphia, Franklin began his most strenuous years of public service. During two years as an active member of the Second Continental Congress for Pennsylvania (1775-76), he served as postmaster general, sat on key commercial and diplomatic committees, and signed the Declaration of Independence. In Pennsylvania, he was president of the state constitutional convention (1776). In 1776 he was appointed by Congress as one of three commissioners to France. As commissioner there and later as United States minister plenipotentiary (1778-85), Franklin procured supplies and raised loans, negotiated treaties of alliance and commerce (1778), and served on the commission that negotiated the Treaty of Paris (1783) with Britain that ended the war. As in London, Franklin thrived in the social, cultural, and intellectual world of Paris.

Franklin returned to Philadelphia in 1785 and was soon chosen president of the Supreme Executive Council of Pennsylvania (1785-88), president of the Pennsylvania Society for Promoting the Abolition of Slavery (1787), and a member for Pennsylvania of the Constitutional Convention (1787); in the latter he was one of the most effective advocates of conciliation and compromise. During these years he continued the intermittent work he had begun in London on his famous *Autobiography.* Left incomplete at his death, it nonetheless became the most influential model of the American success story.

See also Albany Congress; Continental Congress, Second; Franklin, Deborah; Franklin, William; Paris, Treaty of.

Bibliography: Van Doren, Carl, *Benjamin Franklin* (Viking, 1938); Wright, Esmond, *Franklin of Philadelphia* (Harvard Univ. Press, 1986).

Douglas M. Arnold
The Papers of Benjamin Franklin

FRANKLIN, DEBORAH READ (died 1774)   Wife of Benjamin Franklin, whom she met and became acquainted with while he was a lodger in her father's house, Deborah Franklin first married another man but soon left him. Since she could not get a divorce, she entered into a common-law marriage with Franklin in 1730. She often managed his affairs while he was away in England. During his two longest terms overseas, she stayed in Philadelphia, refusing to leave home, but the couple corresponded frequently. Deborah died in 1774 of a stroke while Benjamin was still in office in England. He returned to America three months later, bitterly regretting the loss of his beloved companion.

FRANKLIN, STATE OF   The State of Franklin was the name used by the government of eastern Tennessee that was organized after North Carolina ceded (1784) to the Confederation Congress its claims to lands west of the divide of the Appalachians. The cession had left the settlers there without civil authority. The next year delegates approved a constitution, named themselves the State of Franklin, and elected as governor John Sevier, frontiersman, land speculator, and leader of the Watauga Association. Franklin had a troubled history: It was never recognized by the Confederation government; it negotiated Indian treaties that were invalidated by Congress; it struggled against the reimposition of North Carolina jurisdiction in 1787; and it was divided by factionalism between groups of eastern and western settlers. The creation of the Southwest Territory by the new federal government in 1790 ended its short life.

See also Sevier, John.

FRANKLIN, WILLIAM (1731-1813)   The son of Benjamin Franklin, William was his father's protégé, assisting him in his work and scientific experiments. He served briefly as a captain on the New York frontier, returning to Philadelphia in 1750. He was comptroller of the general post office and clerk of the provincial assembly until 1756, when he accompanied his father to London. William entered the Middle Temple and was called to the bar. He was introduced to the Earl of Bute, through whom he was named governor of New Jersey in 1763.

At first, Franklin was a popular executive, but the Stamp Act crisis (1765) initiated a period of constant controversy with the patriots. He disagreed with his father's politics, and in 1774, after arguing about the Coercive Acts, the two became estranged. Benjamin called his son "a thorough Courtier," one who saw "everything with Government Eyes." The New Jersey provincial congress declared William "an enemy to the liberties of this country." After the Revolutionary War started, he was arrested and sent to

Connecticut. Exchanged in 1778, he became president of the Board of Associated Loyalists but left for England shortly thereafter. In 1784 he wrote to his father, and they were reconciled. He remained in London the rest of his life.

FREE BLACKS   Free blacks formed a small but important part of the Afro-American population of colonial and Revolutionary America. More appropriately called non-slave blacks, since they were rarely completely free, these men and women prepared the way for increasing numbers that followed them in the 1800s.

In 1790 the first federal census gave the first comprehensive count of the non-slave black population. There were approximately 60,000 free blacks (about 8 percent of all blacks). More than 27,000 were in the North, where they represented over 40 percent of all Northern blacks. Those in the South—more than 32,000—represented less than 5 percent of all blacks there. The numbers of non-slave blacks increased rapidly during the next two decades. By the census of 1810, when there were more than 185,000 free blacks (13.5 percent of the total), 78,000 were in the North (7.4 percent of all blacks there), while 108,000 were in the South (8.5 percent of the total blacks there). The majority of the Southern free blacks lived in the Upper South.

Few reliable statistics are available for the years before 1790, but it is known, for example, that in 1755, 4 percent or 1,817 of Maryland's Afro-Americans were free and that in 1769, 3.5 percent or 165 in Louisiana were free. The percentages ran somewhat higher in the North.

The sources of the non-slave black population are numerous and varied. Since the laws regulating slavery were not fully in place until the 1660s, early Africans brought to the colonies as indentured servants became free after a set number of years of service. Best known of these early free Negroes were Anthony and John Johnson, probably relatives, who owned substantial farms on the Eastern Shore of Virginia and apparently enjoyed full rights of citizenship. Descendants of early free blacks formed the basis of small groups of land-owning non-slave blacks that survived throughout the period of slavery.

Other blacks became free by running away, purchasing their freedom, or occasionally by serving in the colonial militias, where Afro-American soldiers saw action in many early conflicts including the French and Indian War. Some mulattos, or mixed-race people, were free because their mothers (black, white, or Indian) were free. Private manumissions increased the free black population. In some of these cases, slave masters manumitted their own children conceived with slave women. Several religious denominations, especially the Quakers and Methodists, encouraged their members to free their slaves, and many

complied. Around the time of the Revolution, manumissions increased as many individuals recognized the discrepancy between the Revolutionary ethic and the enslavement of fellow human beings.

Economic and Legal Status.   Non-slave blacks worked at a variety of jobs. A few became quite wealthy but most remained farmers or farm workers, craftsmen, laborers, domestic workers, and sailors or dockworkers in waterfront towns. The more successful owned some property, most commonly their own homes or small farms. Others, particularly men and women freed late in life, did not accumulate property, and some lived in real poverty.

As the free black population grew, colonies began to impose various restrictions. Before the Revolution there was no real uniformity to these. Blacks were restricted from voting and holding public office in some colonies and from mustering with the militia in others. Bringing legal suits and testifying in court were forbidden in some colonies. In all areas the restrictions grew harsher as the numbers of non-slave blacks increased. All free blacks could hold property. They could also travel freely, something they would not be permitted to do in some areas in the 1800s.

Effect of the Revolution.   The Revolution made a major impact on the free black community, primarily by increasing its size. Many individuals became free during the Revolutionary period. Some were manumitted by masters who came to believe that slavery was wrong. Others gained their freedom by service in the colonial militias, the Continental Army, the naval forces, and also by serving with the British. Many slaves took the opportunity provided by the wartime confusion to run away. Others, where allowed, brought suits and were granted freedom by court decree. By 1805 all the Northern states, where relatively few people held slaves, had passed laws providing for eventual emancipation, Pennsylvania being the first to do so in 1780.

Bibliography: Berlin, Ira, *Slaves Without Masters: The Free Negro in the Antebellum South* (Random House, 1974); Quarles, Benjamin, *The Negro in the Making of America* (Macmillan, 1964).

Suzanne Green Chapelle
Morgan State University

FREEHOLD   The English promoters of colonization in North America tempted settlers not only with promises of free land but of freeholds, a form of land tenure by which an estate is held for life. Most of those who came to America without terms of indenture had been artisans and tenants in England. In America many of these men became freeholders, although in several colonies freeholders ful-

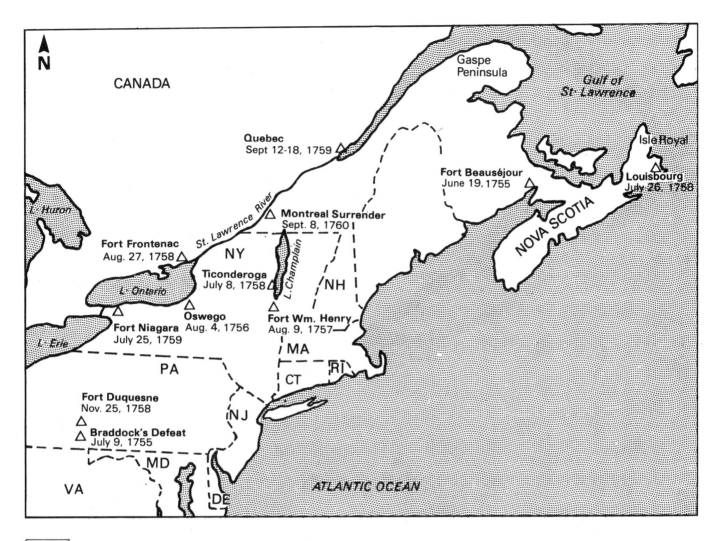

| | Major battles |

Major battles of the French & Indian War, 1755-1763. *(Martin Greenwald Associates, Inc.)*

filled their feudal obligations to the Crown with the payment of a quitrent. In most colonies the right to vote was restricted to freeholders, the landed class, alone. A separate class in many colonies, the freemen, was even more restrictive, but, at a minimum, all freemen were freeholders as well.

See also Quitrent.

FRELINGHUYSEN, THEODORUS JACOBUS (1691-1748?) A New Jersey religious leader active in the Great Awakening, he was born in Germany near the Netherlands. Trained in Dutch theology, he became a minister in 1717 and in 1720 arrived in New Jersey as minister of the Dutch Reform congregation of Raritan in the New Brunswick, New Jersey, area. Early in his ministry he came into conflict with members of his congregation and with church authorities for his departures from the traditional forms of worship. After successfully defending himself, Frelinghuysen encouraged a revivalist approach to religion that was praised by such Great Awakening leaders as Jonathan Edwards, Gilbert Tennent, and George Whitefield.

See also Great Awakening.

FRENCH AND INDIAN WAR (1754-63) The last of the great Anglo-French colonial wars, the French and Indian War eventually became part of the greater imperial struggle between Britain and France known as the Seven Year's War. Although King George's War was formally concluded in 1748, the Treaty of Aix-la-Chapelle that concluded it resembled a truce far more than a treaty of peace. It restored conditions as they had been in 1744 and failed to address the fundamental conflict between British and French interests in the interior of North America.

Thus, barely had one war ended when the preliminary skirmishes of another began. As early as the summer of 1749, French and British expeditions, the latter chiefly from Virginia, began to assert contradictory claims to the Ohio Valley. After several years of sparring, the contest came to a head in 1754 when the Canadians and Virginians each decided to build a fort at the forks of the Ohio. The French repulsed the Virginians, but their victory sounded an alarm in London that eventually led to France's expulsion from North America.

In 1755, in response to the French victory, the British sent Major General Edward Braddock to America with plans for a major offensive. In July, however, Braddock was killed and his expedition, which included George Washington, was routed by French sorties from Fort Duquesne. In September, a French expedition against English positions on Lake George was repulsed, but inflicted sufficient damage that the British canceled a planned attack against Crown Point, the French stronghold on Lake Champlain.

The colonial wars of the 17th and early 18th centuries usually developed as peripheral offshoots of European conflicts. In 1756 the importance of America reversed the process. Determined not to risk their colonies, the British formally declared war against France on May 18. France reciprocated; the numerous states of Europe chose sides, and what became known as the Seven Years War commenced. Before it ended, battles would be fought all over the world from Africa to the Philippines, and for the first time, America would emerge as a central rather than a peripheral arena.

British Successes. Britain's declaration of war had no immediate effect on France's success in America. In 1756 the French captured Oswego on Lake Ontario and menaced British settlements throughout the Mohawk Valley. The next year they captured and destroyed Fort William Henry on Lake George. The tide of battle turned in 1758, however, as Prime Minister William Pitt began to commit men and money to the American front. In July, British regulars under the command of Sir Jeffrey Amherst captured the French fort of Louisburg, at the mouth of the Saint Lawrence River. When colonial troops led by Lieutenant Colonel John Bradstreet destroyed Fort Frontenac at the head of the Saint Lawrence in August, France's ability to supply its interior posts was gravely challenged. Unable to provision a full garrison at Fort Duquesne, the French were forced to destroy it in November to prevent its capture by a joint expedition of colonial militia and English regulars led by Colonels Henry Bouquet and George Washington.

The British pressed their advantage the next year. Commanding a force of regulars and Iroquois Indians, Sir William Johnson captured Fort Niagara on July 25. By the end of August, Amherst had captured Ticonderoga and Crown Point on Lake Champlain. The stage was set for the climactic battle of the war. Convinced of the strategic importance of Quebec, Pitt determined to seize control of it. He promoted James Wolfe, a hero of the siege of Louisburg, to the rank of major general and directed him to attack by way of the Saint Lawrence. After a series of faltering attempts to land his troops, Wolfe discovered an unguarded path onto the Plains of Abraham behind the city. The British landed on September 12, routed the French forces despite Wolfe's death, and accepted their surrender on September 18. Cut off from their supplies, Montreal, Detroit and other western posts surrendered to the British the next year, bringing the war in America to a close.

In the Treaty of Paris (1763), France ceded Canada and the eastern half of Louisiana to England. New Orleans and western Louisiana were transferred to Spain. The treaty marked the end of an era and confirmed the emergence of Britain as the strongest power in Europe.

See also Abraham, Plains of; Braddock, Edward; Duquesne, Fort; Paris, Treaty of.

Bibliography: Drake, Samuel G., *A Particular History of the Five Years French & Indian War* (Heritage Books, 1984); Jennings, Francis, *Empire of Fortune: Crowns, Colonies, & Tribes in the Seven Years War in America* (Norton 1988).

George Mills
Yale University

FRENCH COLONIES   The story of New France traditionally begins with the voyages of Jacques Cartier, who first crossed the Atlantic in 1534. Although European fishermen were already quite familiar with the Grand Banks off the coast of Newfoundland, it was Cartier who discovered the Gulf of St. Lawrence. Cartier's orders from the French crown were to search for gold and other precious metals and for a route to China. Instead, a group of Micmac Indians discovered him and suggested that the French trade for furs. The fur trade would prove to be the dominant factor in the life of New France. For the remainder of the 16th century, seasonal cod-fishing expeditions and fur-trading fairs at Tadoussac, at the mouth of the Saguenay River, grew in importance without the benefit of permanent European establishments.

As the 17th century approached, French officials—and their counterparts in England—observed with covetous eyes the riches being obtained from the New World by Spain. King Louis XIV of France was determined to gain a more permanent foothold in America but was unwilling to commit royal funds to this risky undertaking. In 1588 exclusive trading rights were granted to Jacques Noel, a nephew of Cartier, in exchange for his investment in the colonization process. This action produced an immediate negative response from those merchants who favored free trade. Throughout the French regime the need and the desire of the crown to use private capital to further state-sanctioned goals was a constant source of friction. Merchants excluded from monopolistic grants argued that trade restrictions hampered economic growth. On the other hand, government officials constantly complained that merchants with such grants ignored state policy in their pursuit of profits. This dilemma was complicated by the fact that unbridled competition among Europeans engaged in the fur trade was exploited by Indians who demanded higher prices for their furs and lower prices for European goods.

Era of Champlain. Such problems threatened to delay forever the founding of permanent settlements in New France. In 1603 a monopoly was granted to the Huguenot leader Pierre du Gua, Sieur de Monts. He established a settlement at Port Royal in Acadia in 1605 but this venture lasted only two years. In 1608, de Monts sent his lieutenant, Samuel de Champlain, to build a habitation above Tadoussac at Quebec to intercept the flow of furs reaching rival traders. De Monts gave up in 1612, but Champlain remained. Champlain survived a variety of reorganizations and emerged as the true leader of New France. He secured an alliance with the Huron, who controlled the fur trade of the Great Lakes. By this alliance he also secured the Huron Iroquois enemies to the south. Champlain was responsible for persuading various native groups to bring their furs to Quebec, thus insuring that New France would have a future. His success was due in part to his policy of sending young traders as agents of the company to live in Indian villages. There they would learn native languages and customs and gather information about the country for future reference. The first such *hivernant*, or winterer, was Étienne Brulé. Brulé became, perhaps, too familiar with native ways. According to the report of one missionary, he was too familiar with too many Huron women, so his hosts put him to death and ate him.

Récollet missionaries arrived in 1615 to work with the Huron, and Jesuit missionaries followed in 1625. Finally, in 1627, Cardinal Richelieu sought to stabilize the situation in New France. Richelieu formed the Company of a Hundred Associates (Compagnie des Cent-Associés), a private corporation backed by the crown. This new joint-stock company was better capitalized and was obligated to settle 4,000 colonists by 1643 in exchange for the seigneurial rights of ownership and justice. Champlain received a boost in rank and authority. The situation

looked promising until an English expedition intercepted a fleet of French ships and forced Champlain to surrender Quebec in July 1629. Quebec was restored to France in 1632.

Champlain had secured the St. Lawrence Valley for the French, but at the time of his death in 1635, Quebec was still little more than a warehouse. New France's population of 675 permanent settlers in 1650 compared quite unfavorably to the Anglo-American colonies. Massachusetts alone contained some 15,000 settlers by that date. One bright spot was the founding of Ville-Marie in 1642 by Paul Chomedey de Maisonneuve, an agent of the Société de Notre-Dame de Montreal. This group of pious laymen and clerics wished to convert the natives and gather them in a Christian utopian settlement on Montreal Island. The Society was dissolved in 1663, but Montreal soon became the main entrepot of the fur trade.

Indian Alliances. By 1645, New France was showing signs of life. In that year a temporary truce was concluded with the Mohawk, the trading partners of the Dutch at Fort Orange (Albany). The profits from the reinvigorated fur trade of that year went to a new company, the Communauté des Habitants. The Company of a Hundred Associates, in disarray since Richelieu's death in 1642, no longer had 100 members and was beset with financial woes. In 1645 the company sold the monopoly on the marketing of all furs collected in Canada to this new Canada-based group. Two years later the company sold its rights to Acadia to Charles Menou d'Aulnay. (Acadia and Canada were separate jurisdictions. Together with the *pays d'en haut*, or western country, they comprised New France. In reality, Acadia and Louisiana, after its establishment, operated as distinct colonies.) Also in 1647 the king established a council to help govern the colony. This council evolved into the Sovereign Council (Conseil Souverain), established in 1663 and renamed the Superior Council (Conseil Supérieur) in 1703. It functioned, after 1663, much like a provincial *parlement* in France.

Several years of promise ended in 1649 when the Iroquois Confederacy launched a major campaign to destroy the Huron and their Indian allies and capture the rich fur country of the Great Lakes region. A decade of wars crippled New France and finally prompted the crown to assume ownership and control of the colony in 1663. Over the next decade Louis XIV, through his chief minister, Jean-Baptiste Colbert, undertook a number of measures designed to reorganize and strengthen New France. An administrative system similar to that of the French provinces was instituted. The system was headed by two officials, both appointed by the crown: a governor general in charge of military and Indian affairs; and an intendant responsible for justice, civil administration, and finance.

FRENCH COLONIES: TOPIC GUIDE

GENERAL

Cajuns
Chickasaw-French War
  (1736-40)
Compagnie D'Occident
Coutume de Paris
Exploration (see **Topic Guide**)
Fox-French Wars
Franco-American Alliance
  (1778)
French and Indian War
  (1754-63)
French colonies
French Immigrants
French West Indies Company
Fur Trade
  Coureurs de Bois and Voyageurs
Geography and Culture
  (see **Topic Guide**)

Huguenots
Hundred Associates,
  Company of a
Indians, North American
  (see **Topic Guide**)
King George's War
King William's War
  (1689-97)
Louisiana Revolution
  (1768)
Missions and Missionaries
  Jesuits
Mixedbloods (Mestizos, Metis)
Natchez War
Queen Anne's War
  (1702-13)
Religion (see **Topic Guide**)
Roman Catholics

BIOGRAPHIES

Allouez, Claude Jean
Beaumarchais, Pierre Augustine
  Caron De
Bienville, Jean-Baptiste Le Moyne,
  Sieur De
Botetourt, Norborne Berkeley,
  Baron de
Bourgmont, Etienne Venyard
Brebeuf, Jean de
Cadillac, Antoine de la Mothe
Cartier, Jacques
Celoron de Blainville, Pierre
  Joseph
Cerre, Jean Gabriel
Champlain, Samuel de
Charlevoix, Pierre Francois
  Xavier de
Chouteau, Rene Auguste
Colbert, Jean-Baptiste
Davion, Anthony
De Langlade, Charles Michel
Denonville, Jacques Rene De Brisay,
  Marquis De
Duluth, Daniel Greysolon,
  Sieur
Frontenac, Louis de Baude,
  Comte de
Galinee, Rene de Brehant de
Gravier, Jacques
Groseilliers, Medart Chouart,
  Sieur de
Harpe, Bernard de la
Hennepin, Louis

Iberville, Sieur de (Pierre
  Le Moyne)
Jolliet, Louis
Joutel, Henri
Laclede, Pierre
Lafayette, Marquis de
Lahontan, Louis-Armand de
  Lom d'Arce
Lalement, Jerome
La Salle, Sieur de
Laudonniere, Rene Goulaine de
Le Moyne, Jacques
Le Moyne, Simon
Mallet, Paul and Pierre
Marquette, Jacques
Montcalm, Louis-Joseph De
  Marquis
Monts, Pierre du Guast, Sieur de
Nicolet, Jean
Noue, Zacharie Robutel de la
Radisson, Pierre Esprit
Rale, Sebastien
Ribaut, Jean
Roberval, Jean Francois
  de la Rocque, Sieur de
Rochambeau, Jean Baptiste
  Donatien de Vimeur, Comte de
St. Denys, Louis Juchereau de
Tonty, Henry de
Vaudreuil-Cavagnial, Pierre
  de Rigaud, Marquis de
Verranzano, Giovanni da

The Coutume de Paris, the system and body of customary law in force in Paris, was established as the basis of all law in New France. A parochial system was initiated in 1664 by Laval, the first Bishop of Quebec. A militia system was organized in 1663 in Montreal. Two years later the crown sent an entire regiment, some 1,200 men, to bolster the colony's military strength. The Carignan-Salières regiment marched into Iroquois country in 1666. Despite two ineffective campaigns, the Iroquois, who were fighting on other fronts, sued for peace in 1667. A decade of relative calm followed.

Colbert and New France. As for domestic affairs, Colbert subsidized the immigration of some 900 *filles de roi*, female orphans raised at the king's expense. To encourage marriages the state provided dowries for poor girls. To stimulate a high birth rate the state offered monetary rewards for families with 10 or more children. Colbert also supported intermarriage between the French and Indians.

It was Colbert's hope that New France would provide staples such as furs, fish, and lumber for the mother country and become a reliable market for goods manufactured in France. He also hoped that New France would increase its agricultural production and become more self-sufficient. To encourage settlement and cultivation, Colbert offered large concessions to any entrepreneur who agreed to bring colonists and build mills. These *seigneurs*, in turn, would make land grants and receive various taxes and fees from their settlers, or *censitaires*. Grants were divided into long, narrow rectangles, or *rotures*, that ran along the river valley. This unique system reflected the dependence of all the *habitants* on the river. Such a system also discouraged the growth of nucleated villages. This seigneurial system has sometimes been mistakenly labeled a feudal system. In fact, the state regulated the entire operation to prevent the growth of private authority. Also, the *censitaires* had more rights and privileges than did their counterparts in France. The system did inhibit land speculation, but this was not likely to become an important element in the economy of New France given the abundance of cheap land, the short growing season, and the lack of markets for agricultural products.

Colbert's mercantilist dreams were only partly realized. The agricultural base developed slowly. The small, tradition-bound family farms of rural Canada stood in sharp contrast to the dynamic metropolitan world of Montreal and Quebec. Despite Colbert's efforts to limit geographical expansion and diversify the colonial economy, the fur trade, the only consistent source of profits for the crown and the colonists, overwhelmed policy. The search for new markets and fur supplies, that is, Indian consumers and producers, increased as merchants (*marchands* or *négociants*) sent out parties of *engagés* (employees: boatmen/*voyageurs*, clerks/*commis*, and traders/*traiteurs*) to the *pays d'en haut*. So many illegal traders (*coureurs de bois*) left their farms in pursuit of economic advancement and adventure that in 1681 Colbert was forced to legitimize expansion in hopes of controlling it through a system of trading permits (*congés*).

Exploration and Expansion. Exploration was encouraged by Governor Louis Buade de Frontenac (1672-82, 1689-98). Frontenac established Forts Frontenac (1673) and Niagara (1679) on either end of Lake Ontario and supported the expeditions of La Salle, who reached the mouth of the Mississippi River in 1682. (Joliet and Marquette had "discovered" the Mississippi in 1673, but they had not reached the Gulf of Mexico.) Despite the renewal of hostilities between the French and the Iroquois in the 1680s and several direct confrontations with the English during the War of the League of Augsburg (1689-97), French traders continued to expand the boundaries of New France. Expansion, however, produced a glut of furs on the market. In 1696, Louis XIV and his minister of marine, the Comte de Pontchartrain, ordered the evacuation of most of the western posts. (Vigorous protests forced a compromise. Most of the posts were retained, but the *congé* system was abandoned until 1716.) This restrictive policy was reversed two years later when the crown ordered Pierre Le Moyne d'Iberville to establish a colony at the mouth of the Mississippi. The crown, faced with the threat of an English expedition from the Carolinas, decided once and

French possessions in the New World, 1713. (*Martin Greenwald Associates, Inc.*)

for all to solidify French claims to the Mississippi Valley. (This decision was made over the protests of Montreal merchants who feared that a port on the Gulf of Mexico would loosen their control over the fur trade.) The King's ministers reasoned that Louisiana would check the expansion of the English colonies and also provide a strategic position from which to attack or defend Spanish possessions, depending on the outcome of the impending war over the Spanish succession.

Development of Louisiana.
Louisiana grew slowly at first, suffering from a well-deserved reputation for disease and mosquitoes. After several flawed attempts at private development and an attack by the Natchez Indians on a frontier post, the crown assumed full control and responsibility for the colony in 1731. Thereafter, Louisiana became more prosperous, although it remained a drain on the royal treasury throughout the French regime. New Orleans, the capital after 1722, quickly developed into the cultural, social, and economic center of a vast region. By 1763 the city had a population of around 5,000. The Illinois country to the north, officially a part of Louisiana since 1717, contained the most fertile land in all of New France. By the 1740s this region was becoming known as the granary of Louisiana, consistently producing an agricultural surplus with the help of a substantial number of black slaves. Lead and furs were also important exports. Illinois served as a crucial link between Canada and lower Louisiana and provided a jumping-off place for expeditions to the West. (The Mallet brothers traveled from Illinois to Santa Fe in 1739.) The principal villages in French Illinois were Kaskaskia on the eastern bank of the Mississippi and Ste. Genevieve across the river. French merchants continued to expand their operations in the region after the fall of New France, playing a leading role in the establishment of various cities such as St. Louis and Kansas City.

Throughout Louisiana, relations with the various Indian tribes were of critical importance. The Choctaw in the south and the Illinois, Potawatomi, and Ottawa in the north were indispensable, although occasionally unreliable allies. Certainly one feature that distinguished all the French colonies in North America from the English colonies was the dependence of the French on the Indians for military support and economic prosperity. Although the French were not above exploiting their native partners and were quite willing to destroy unfriendly groups such as the Fox and the Natchez, they also recognized the necessity of learning Indian languages and understanding Indian customs. In the Illinois country, French-Indian marriages were quite common for several decades and, in general, the French were not as racist in their attitudes as were the English.

Golden Age of New France.
With the signing of a treaty of neutrality with the Iroquois (1701) and the beginning of a 30-year respite from imperial wars in 1713, New France was ready to enter into its golden age. In 1714 construction began on a new fortress town, Louisburg (Louisbourg), on Ile-Royale (Cape Breton Island). From this port the French dominated the fishing industry in North America. Canada remained dependent on the fur trade and royal expenditures for defense; however, signs of economic diversification began to appear. By 1755 Canada's population had reached 55,000. The English colonies by that date contained over 1,000,000 inhabitants. Visitors commented on the independence and refinement of Canadians of all classes.

During this period (1713-43), French overseas commerce increased so markedly that the English began to fear for their supremacy. Unfortunately for New France, it was the French West Indies that provided the major share of this new colonial prosperity. The coffee and sugar produced on Guadeloupe, Martinique, and St. Dominque (Santo Domingo) far outweighed the value of Canadian exports. When the imperial struggle began again in earnest in 1756, the Canadians held the upper hand at first. Poor leadership and lack of support from France eventually led to defeat, and the crown abandoned New France in the Treaty of Paris (1763) in order to regain its far more lucrative possessions in the Caribbean.

See also Champlain, Samuel de; Exploration; Hundred Associates, Company of a; Indians of North America; Iroquois Confederacy.

Bibliography: Bosher, John F., *The Canadian Merchants, 1713-1763* (Oxford Univ. Press, 1987); Eccles, William J., *The Canadian Frontier, 1534-1760),* rev. ed. (Univ. of New Mexico Press, 1983); Harris, Richard Colebrook, *The Seigneurial System in Early Canada: A Geographical Study* (Univ. of Wisconsin Press, 1966); Jaenen, Cornelius J., *Friend And Foe: Aspects of French-Amerindian Cultural Contact in the Sixteenth and Seventeenth Centuries* (McClelland and Stewart, 1976); McDermott, John F., ed., *Frenchmen and French Ways in the Mississippi Valley* (Univ. of Illinois Press, 1969); Trigger, Bruce G., *Natives and Newcomers: Canada's "Heroic Age" Reconsidered* (McGill-Queen's Univ. Press, 1985).

Jay Gitlin
Yale University

FRENCH IMMIGRANTS The first French to settle on the North American continent were the companions of Samuel de Champlain, who built Quebec in 1608, taking possession of the lands claimed by the French crown. But these were not immigrants, a term defined as individuals who leave their home to find a new life in another country. As Canada was a French possession, there was, properly speaking, no French immigration to North America during the colonial period with the exception of the Huguenots whom the British Crown settled in Charleston in 1697 as part of their pressure against French establishments along the Mississippi. The famous plight of the Acadians in the mid-18th century also cannot be considered immigration, as these French, expelled by the British from Nova Scotia, merely went to another French territory, Louisiana. Huguenot immigrants, however, did continue to settle in the English colonies in the early 1700s, numbering among their descendants Paul Revere.

After the Treaty of Paris (1763) ended the French and Indian War, France renounced its possessions on the North American continent and French troops and ships left, only to return in 1778 as allies of the United States during the Revolutionary War. A few French soldiers and sailors among them remained behind, but not until 1792, during the paroxysm of the French Revolution, was there a noticeable immigration from France to the United States. These were a few Girondins (the moderate faction), soon to be followed by their enemies, the partisans of the Terror. They came to Boston, Baltimore, and Philadelphia, where they earned a meager living. Simultaneously, some clerics and nuns fleeing the French Revolution found their way to Canada via England. Further, a slave revolt in Santo Domingo brought thousands of French planters and their household slaves to New Orleans, then a Spanish possession, reinforcing its Creole character. The next significant immigration occurred when the collapse of the Napoleonic empire brought another wave of a select group of French exiles to the United States.

See also Cajuns; French Colonies.

Bibliography: Eccles, William J., *France in America* (Harper and Row, 1972).

Charles J. Balesi
The French Colonial Historical Society

FRENCH WEST INDIES COMPANY   Known in French as Compagnie des Indes Occidentales, this company was created on May 28, 1664, as an attempt by Colbert to unite France's commerce with the West Indies, South America, West Africa, and Canada into one organization with a trade monopoly. The 42 articles of its charter were very similar to those of the East Indies Company, stipulating among others that the minimum subscription had to be 3,000 livres, that a 20,000 livre investment entitled one to a director's seat, and that the company owned forts and lands but that the King appointed the governor. Investments were slow in coming. In 1667 the King's direct financing represented 54 percent of the total capital. Although all sorts of fiscal advantages were extended to the company, it had great difficulty maintaining essential operations. The company was expected to supply

the French West Indies with cattle and slaves, yet the islands were never able to make due without Dutch contraband. The company was able nevertheless to build a large commercial fleet: There were 70 ships in service in 1670 and 89 in 1672, but continuous warfare inflicted heavy losses. In 1674 the company was liquidated and a serious effort was made to reimburse the volunteer contributors.

Bibliography: Cole, Charles W., *Colbert and a Century of French Mercantilism* (Columbia Univ. Press, 1939).

FRENEAU, PHILIP (1752-1832)   Later known as "the poet of the Revolution," Freneau was born in New York City. He showed an early interest in politics when as a student at the College of New Jersey (later Princeton) he adopted the liberal Whig viewpoint of his friend James Madison. Freneau also wrote with Hugh Henry Brackenridge the 1771 commencement poem "The Rising Glory of America." Freneau joined the New Jersey militia in 1778 and later served on a privateer. Captured in 1780, Freneau described the atrocities and injustices he experienced in his poem "The British Prison Ship" and in many other harsh political satires. He continued to express his liberal democratic views after the war as a newspaper editor and journalist, and he pursued his interests right up until the end, when at age 80 he froze to death walking home from a political discussion.

His literary contributions were not always of a political nature. From about 1783 to 1790, while working as a ship captain, Freneau wrote light verse, mostly character sketches of simple American types that delighted his countrymen. Freneau also wrote more serious philosophic verse on such themes as the transience of life and the presence of God in nature. Perhaps his best poem of this type is "The Indian Burying Ground." Because Freneau's work includes both satires written in the neoclassical style of the 18th century and philosophical nature poems that anticipate the romanticism of the 19th century, he is often considered a transitional literary figure.

James F. Cooper, Jr.
University of Connecticut

FRIENDLY ASSOCIATION FOR REGAINING AND PRESERVING PEACE WITH THE INDIANS BY PACIFIC MEASURES   A private organization for fostering peaceful coexistence between Pennsylvania colonists and Indians, it was founded during the French and Indian War. In 1756 the colony of Pennsylvania officially declared war on the Indians, who in turn gained French support for retaliatory attacks. Since most of the Indians' grievances were territorial, a group of Pennsylvania Quakers established the association, holding peace conferences at Easton in 1757 and 1758 and spending more than 7,000 pounds to settle the Indians' claims. This activity was violently opposed by the colony's settlers, who claimed that the association had no authority to negotiate on their behalf.

FROBISHER, MARTIN (?1535-94)   An English adventurer and explorer, born to a family of country gentry, Frobisher joined the Africa trade as a young man, explored Guinea, was captured by Africans, turned over to the Portuguese, and shipped back to England, where he engaged in smuggling. Beginning in 1576 he made three voyages in search of the Northwest Passage, during which he charted Frobisher Bay (which he thought to be the passage entrance), traded with and kidnapped Eskimos, and mined several hundred tons of what turned out to be worthless ore. He spent the rest of his life as an admiral and adventurer in the service of Queen Elizabeth I. He died as a consequence of a wound incurred during an attack on a Spanish fort.

See also Northwest Passage.

FRONTENAC, LOUIS DE BUADE, COMTE DE (1622-98)   Twice governor of Canada (1672-82, 1689-98), Frontenac, originally an army officer, was known for his fiery temper. He angered Louis XIV by installing a free feudal government, quarreled with the Jesuits, quarreled with the governor of Montreal, Nicholas Perrot, over illegal fur trading, and finally lost the governorship in 1682 by fighting with his military director, Duchesneau. In 1689, after the Marquis de Denonville had provoked the disastrous Iroquois war, Frontenac was made governor of Canada again and brought order by sending war parties to burn and raid the Iroquois lands. A retaliatory English attack on Quebec failed. He greatly expanded French influence in the Great Lakes region and in Canada by revitalizing the fur trade.

See also French Colonies.

FRONTIER   In the 20th century the term "frontier" has generally meant the sparsely settled region of European civilization bordering on the wilderness. Many now reject this definition because it ignores the frontier's social essence: the interpenetration of two distinct societies, European and Indian. Indeed, in its original usage, the term referred to the boundary, often military, between two conflicting societies, from which was also derived the concept of the military "front." In this sense, the colonial frontier was characterized not so much by a confrontation with the wilderness as by a confrontation between cultures. Moreover, rather than the triumph of "civilization" over "savagery," the frontier is now generally understood as a process of acculturation affecting both Europeans and Indians, marked by interchange or diffusion of cultural traits and by the eventual emergence of European social and cultural dominance.

Impact of European Conquest.   There was, from the first invasions of Europeans on the Atlantic coast in the early 16th century, to the first European settlements in trans-Appalachia in the 1770s, to the far Western penetrations of Americans in the 19th century, a discernible pattern to the frontier process. Of foremost importance was the impact of disease. Isolated from the virulent diseases that had devastated Europe during the late Middle Ages, Indians were exceptionally vulnerable to contagion from European contact. Indeed, disease often preceded direct contact, arriving with the first trade goods or in the blood or on the breath of Indian intermediaries. Death rates from the first outbreaks of measles, influenza, bubonic plague, and especially smallpox commonly reduced the size of Indian communities by half. Historical demographers have estimated that as a consequence of disease the native population of greater Florida, the first area to be invaded in the early 16th century, fell from some 900,000 in 1500 to a little over 100,000 in 1596, and a 90 percent decline in population within the first century of contact was common throughout the hemisphere. The subsequent history of the frontier was dramatically shaped by native population collapse.

Also characteristic was the universal European demand for the expropriation, for their own use, of the indigenous resources of land and people. The Spanish sought to bind the Indians of Mexico and the Southwest to a form of peonage; the French to incorporate the labor of the Indian hunters and trappers of the Northern lakes into the international fur trade; the English, mostly ignoring Indian labor, instead concentrated on acquiring Indian lands, and ultimately all the colonial powers were implicated in various stratagems of expropriation. It was sometimes the opening scene—the Pilgrims settling on the forlorn site of a coastal village devastated by the plague that struck the northern Atlantic coast in 1615-19. Sometimes it came late in the final act—the Cherokee being concentrated and removed from their southeastern homelands on the Trail of Tears in the 1830s after three centuries of encounter; but dispossession was inevitably part of the frontier tragedy.

The persistent violence of the Indian-European frontier was the direct result of this struggle over land and resources. The first European visitors, from Columbus in the Caribbean of the 1490s to Cook in the Pacific of the 1780s, were invariably greeted with great hospitality; but the efforts of these two agents of colonization to dictate terms quickly led to violent encounters. Jamestown had been established only 14 years before its aggressions resulted in

FRONTIER: TOPIC GUIDE

GENERAL

Agriculture (see **Topic Guide)**
Alaska, Russia in
African-Indian Contact
Appalachian Mountains
Buffalo
Captivity x-ref
Cumberland Gap
Cumberland Settlements
Exploration (see **Topic Guide)**
Fall Line
Franklin, State of
Fur Trade
   Bosch Loopers
   Coureurs de Bois and Voyageurs
   Promyshleniki
Great Lakes
Land Companies

Land Ordinance of 1785
Land Policy
Log Cabin
Missions and Missionaries
   Franciscans
   Jesuits
   Moravians
Mississippi River
Mixedbloods (Mestizos, Metis)
Northwest Ordinance (1787)
Paxton Boys
Population
Proclamation of 1763
Roads and Trails
Surveying
Transportation
Watauga Association
War (see **Topic Guide)**

BIOGRAPHIES

Adair, James
Atkin, Edmund
Blount, William
Boone, Daniel
Chouteau, Rene Auguste
Clark, George Rogers
Croghan, George
Eliot, John
Finley, John
Girty, Simon
Gist, Christopher
Gookin, Daniel
Henderson, Richard
Heckwelder, John Gottlieb
Johnson, Guy

Johnson, Sir William (1715-74)
Kirkland, Samuel
Lawson, John
Moore, James
Nairne, Thomas
Needham, James
Priber, Christian
Pynchon, William
Robertson, James
Rowlandson, Mary
Sevier, John
Weiser, Johann Conrad
Woodmason, Charles
Woodward, Henry
Zane, Elizabeth

a concerted Powhatan attack that nearly wiped out the colony in 1622; Plymouth was but a year or two older when it went to war against the neighboring Pequot in 1637. Indians and Europeans were frequent and deadly adversaries throughout the colonial period, although Indians were as likely as not fighting one European nation as the mercenaries of a competing European colonial power.

Acculturation. Although violence may have been its most notable feature, the frontier was more broadly a process of mutual acculturation. Additions to Indian life included metal goods, firearms, and domesticated animals (notably the horse) that dramatically affected methods of production, and textiles that significantly improved clothing and housing; but other less positive additions accompanied these, including alcohol, a drug to which Indians seem to have developed a powerful addiction. Moreover, to obtain these commodities, Indians were required to become members of an international exchange network, most notably as producers in the fur trade. Market dependency became as pervasive as disease, dispossession, and violence.

The debt of the European colonists to the Indians may be less obvious, but much of what was familiar about colonial life was directly the result of acculturation. Maize (corn) was the staff of life, and indeed, without the whole panoply of New World crops, we would have to imagine colonial folkways without baked beans, pumpkin pie, maple sugar, even roast turkey. Settlement and survival techniques including forest gardening; herbal medicine; the fashioning of canoes, moccasins, and snowshoes; and styles of woodland warfare were adopted wholesale by the colonists. Indian trails directed settlers to resource and settlement sites; the majority of colonial towns were located on the ruins of former Indian villages. It is true, as one historian had commented, that colonists utilized Indian means to pursue European ends, but that was equally true about the Indian use of European goods.

Indeed, from the perspective of colonial officials, European acculturation to Indian ways often appeared deeply subversive. New France struggled for decades with the tendency of its sons to run away to the woods where they lived with the Indians, trading furs and perhaps marrying Indian women, and English officials had similar worries. By the 18th century a large class of settlers along the frontier from New England to Georgia was described by denigrating officials as "white Indians," or "savages"; of course these backwoodsmen were also implacable Indian haters and fighters. Throughout the colonial period, however, Indian life and culture had a powerful appeal and draw for many Europeans, as the common phenomenon of captives refusing to return home after the wars suggested. It is no accident that rebels opposed to officials of a royal government often dressed themselves as Indians.

It is clear nonetheless that acculturation had many more debilitating effects upon traditional Indian life than upon European life, including the deterioration of traditional norms and standards with the corresponding disintegration of authority, the rise of factionalism, and the introduction of profound cultural demoralization. These negative effects, however, were more the result of the unequal configurations of power implicit in the confrontation between a people organized along lines of locality and kinship, on the one hand, and central states with the ability to mobilize incomparably greater resources of men and matériel on the other. Acculturation itself did not lead to destruction. At the end of the colonial period, despite their defeats, Indian people remained culturally distinct if politically encapsulated and militarily subordinated.

One of the most significant outcomes of the frontier process of colonial America was its polarizing effect. "Indian," it should be remembered, was a European term without any contingent meaning in North America until Europeans came to think of the indigenous, as a group, as the "other." Every group tends to develop a self-identity in opposition to some other, and because of the primary place of the frontier and its violence in colonial life, the "other" of colonial America was the Indian. The particular identity of "American" that had been at least partially developed by the time of the Revolution had much

to do with the historic contrast and competition with the Indian on the frontier.

See also Fur Trade; Indians, North American.

Bibliography: Axtell, James, *The European and the Indian* (Oxford Univ. Press, 1918); Jennings, Francis, *The Invasion of America* (Univ. of North Carolina Press, 1981); Lamar, Howard R., and Leonard Thompson, eds., *The Frontier in History* (Yale Univ. Press, 1975).

John Mack Faragher
Mount Holyoke College

FUCA, JUAN DE (flourished 1590s?) In 1625 a work called *Purchas, His Pilgrims* contained the claim of one Juan de Fuca to have discovered in 1592 a passage leading from the Pacific Ocean to the polar sea. Fuca's claim exercised a powerful attraction on the Spanish, who were concerned that the English or French might find the strait and use it to attack the Spanish colonies in the Pacific. In the years following 1592 both Cirmenho and Vizcaino attempted to find the strait, but their voyages proved fruitless. Neverthelesss, when the broad passage between Vancouver Island and the mainland was discovered in 1787 it was immediately named after Fuca.

See also Cirmenho, Sebastian Rodriguez; Vizcaino, Sebastian.

FUNDAMENTAL CONSTITUTIONS OF CAROLINA The Fundamental Constitutions represented the notion of the Carolina colony's proprietors of how an ideal society ought to be ordered. Probably drafted by John Locke, secretary to Lord Ashley, one of the proprietors, the document draws heavily on ideas of the English political philosopher James Harrington, who suggested that social order and harmony depended on a balance between the popular or democratic elements and the aristocracy.

The Fundamental Constitutions, sent to Carolina in 1669, proposed to make use of the proprietary control over land distribution to insure that a landed, titled aristocracy would control two-fifths of the land in each of Carolina's counties, while common settlers would hold three-fifths. Those who invested in the colony, by providing capital or settlers, would receive elevation to the colonial peerage, which included lords designated as landgraves and caciques. The commoners (or their representatives) would sit with the lords together in an assembly to draft the colony's laws, every freeholder who controlled at least 50 acres might vote, and those who held more than 500 acres could be elected to the parliament. The document even included provisions extending freedom of worship to any person who acknowledged a god. In spite of repeated requests from the proprietors that the colonists enact the

Fundamental Constitutions, they never were adopted by Carolina's settlers.

orders were incorporated in a charter in 1662 and again in the state charter of 1776.

FUNDAMENTAL ORDERS OF CONNECTICUT (1639) The orders were established to bring a form of government to the Connecticut colony river towns of Windsor, Hartford, Wethersfield, and, for a time, Springfield. Eleven orders provided for a general assembly, an elected governor and elected judges, voter qualifications, the election of court deputies, the requirements for calling an election and organizing the courts, and dividing taxes. It also gave freemen the right to establish a court if the governor or judges refused to do so. These

FUR TRADE The fur trade directly stimulated the European exploration and colonization of North America more than any other single activity. For the French of the St. Lawrence and Great Lakes, the English of the Hudson's Bay Company, the Russians of the Alaska coast, as well as the Dutch and English traders of upstate New York, fur trading remained a major economic force throughout the colonial period, and competition for access to furs was one of the contributing causes of the great colonial wars. The fur trade was also unique as one of the only economic enterprises that employed Indian producers in an interna-

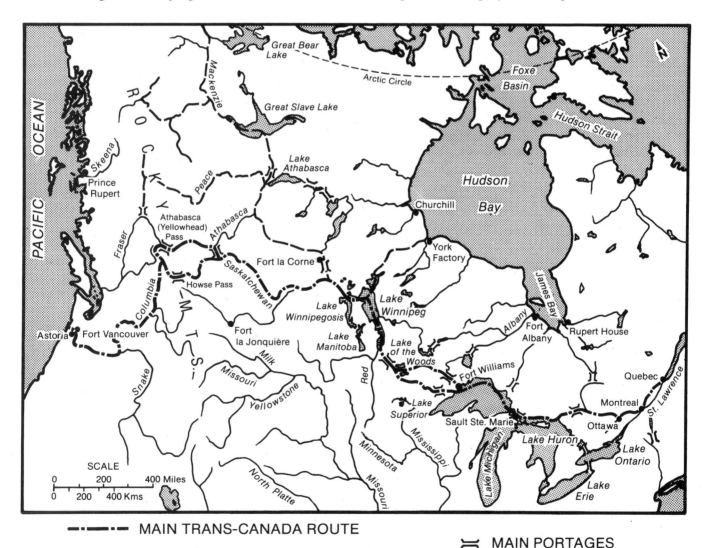

— ·· — ·· — **MAIN TRANS-CANADA ROUTE**

— — — — **OTHER MAIN FUR TRADE ROUTES**

⋈ **MAIN PORTAGES**

Fur Trade. *(Martin Greenwald Associates, Inc.)*

tional economic system, profoundly altering their way of life.

Europeans as well as Indians had traditionally depended upon furs for their winter clothing, but the radical depletion of European small game during the population expansion of the late Middle Ages resulted in a sharp decline in supply. Throughout Europe the price of furs rose and sumptuary laws restricted their use to the upper classes, thus making the trade far more profitable. Russian merchants with access to fur-rich Siberia supplied much of the demand, but the abundant mammal resources of North America came to assume the greatest importance.

Early Fur Trade.   In the early 16th century European fishermen drying their catch on sandy Atlantic shores began sporadic trading with Indian hunters attracted by iron and steel utensils; by the latter part of the century Norman merchants were systematically collecting furs from Indians along the Newfoundland and New England coasts. In 1603 the French monarch Henry IV granted the first North American fur monopoly. With the founding of Quebec, the French established themselves in the St. Lawrence Valley and over the next decade established an alliance with the powerful Huron Indians who, because of their control of access to the rich fur-bearing regions north of the Great Lakes, became middlemen in the trade. By the early 17th century merchants of the French monopoly, as well as independent, illegal traders known as *coureurs de bois*, were supplying the European demand, and French-Americans remained a major force in the trade through the colonial period.

Early Dutch exploration of the Atlantic coast was also motivated, in part, by the search for furs. In 1614 they founded a post on the Hudson River that became Fort Orange (later Albany), where they eventually established an important trade relationship with the Iroquois Confederacy, consequently the great rival of the Huron for the Great Lakes trade. New Amsterdam's greatest profits came from the fur trade, much channeled through their official monopoly, but the Dutch, too, had a problem with independent traders, known as Bosch Loopers.

English Colonies.   The trade was also the economic mainstay of the Pilgrims of Plymouth, the first successful English colony in the North. The Pilgrims traded with Narragansett and Massachusetts Indians, operated trading posts on Cape Cod and on the Kennebec River in Maine, and succeeded in eliminating the competition of independent traders such as Thomas Morton. The Puritans traded along the Merrimack River and in 1636 founded the inland town of Springfield to exploit the resources of the Connecticut River Valley, in which the Dutch had also established a post near present-day Hartford. By the late 17th century, however, the wild game of New England had been largely depleted. In Virginia the fur trade was negligible, but in the Carolinas and Georgia the trade with interior Indians for deerskins was extremely profitable, leading to the founding of the ports of Charleston and Savannah.

Canadian Trade.   Much more important to the English, however, was the trade of northern Canada, which they secured with forts and "factories" (trading posts) along the coast of Hudson Bay. The official English monopoly, Hudson's Bay Company, founded in 1670, engaged in active and frequently violent competition with French traders. By the early 18th century the rival English and French companies were pressing into the North American interior, exploring as far west as the Rockies by 1750.

Influence of the Fur Trade.   In the fur trade each party had a distinctive and interdependent role to play. Europeans traded; some Indian men also traded, while others trapped, guided parties, or worked as boatmen, all in exchange for European goods that transformed the technology and culture of their societies; Indian women dressed skins, supplied the essential foodstuffs for the trading parties, and manufactured the snowshoes, canoes, and functional clothing of both Indians and Europeans. On the frontier European traders, both company men and independents, lived with Indians, often marrying and raising mixed-race children and entering into a new and distinctive fur-trade society.

But the fur trade was much more destructive than constructive. Commercial lust directed a war on the animals that radically and forever altered the ecology of North America. Commercial warfare between rival European-Indian combinations inaugurated centuries of brutal warfare that included the Beaver Wars, marked by the destruction of the Huron in the 1640s, and led finally to the great colonial wars for empire. By the 1730s Pennsylvania traders were entering the Ohio Valley; blocked there by the French, the confrontation led directly to the French and Indian War.

See also Albany; Beaver Wars; Coureurs de Bois; Exploration; French and Indian War; Hudson's Bay Company; Huron Indians; Pilgrims; Plymouth; Puritans.

Bibliograpy: Axtell, James, *The European and the Indian* (Oxford Univ. Press, 1981); Phillips, Paul C. and Smurr, J. W., *The Fur Trade*, 2 vols. (Univ. of Oklahoma Press, 1961); Van Kirk, Sylvia, *Many Tender Ties: Women in Fur Trade Society, 1670- 1870* (Univ. of Oklahoma Press, 1980).

John Mack Faragher
Mount Holyoke College

G

GAGE, THOMAS (1721-87) A British military commander and the last royal governor of Massachusetts, Gage was born in Firle, England. He became the lieutenant colonel of the 44th Foot regiment (1751) and at the outbreak of the French and Indian War went to America with his regiment under General Braddock (1754). He took part and was wounded in Braddock's disastrous Pennsylvania campaign in 1755. As a brigadier general Gage succeeded Sir William Johnson (1759) and helped to complete the conquest of Canada. He was made governor of Montreal and promoted to major general (1761). In 1763, Gage was appointed the commander-in-chief of North America and was in charge of all American military affairs until 1773.

He returned to the colonies as a vice admiral and governor of Massachusetts (1774). Gage took office at a time when the colonies were at their greatest unrest and had to put the Port Act into effect. Gage's attempt to seize stores of colonial arms led to the conflict at Lexington and Concord and was soon followed by the imposition of martial law. A few months after the battle at Bunker Hill (1775), Gage returned to England.

See also Massachusetts.

GALINÉE, RENÉ DE BREHANT DE (died 1678) A French Sulpician missionary, Galinée was sent to Canada in 1668. He traveled with François Dollier de Cassan in La Salle's 1669 exploring party, but the two missionaries parted from La Salle early in their journey. After traveling along the shores of lakes Erie and Huron, the two Sulpicians took possession of the region for Louis XIV. During their mission to preach to the Indians, they also explored the Ohio River, Lake Michigan, and the upper Illinois River. Galinée returned to France in 1671.

GALLOWAY, JOSEPH (1731-1803) Born to a family of prominent merchants, Galloway studied law in Philadelphia and became one of the city's most popular advocates. In addition to his legal practice, he took an interest in commercial land speculation and politics. He was elected an assemblyman in 1756. In 1764 he lost his seat, along with Benjamin Franklin, for their joint petition for a royal instead of proprietary governorship. He returned, however, in 1765 and from 1766 to 1775 was speaker of the assembly. At the same time he served as vice president of Franklin's American Philosophical Society.

Galloway was a delegate to the First Continental Congress in 1774. His major contribution was a plan for an imperial legislature and written constitution. The idea was rejected, and Galloway did not return to the Congress. He adamantly opposed independence from England. Afraid for himself, Galloway sought the protection of General Howe, providing him with information for the Philadelphia campaign. In 1778, Galloway fled to England, becoming a spokesman for the Loyalists. His estates in America were seized, and he was forbidden to return. He died in England.

See also Continental Congress, First; Galloway's Plan of Union.

GALLOWAY'S PLAN OF UNION When the First Continental Congress met in September 1774, the colonial delegates were concerned with the problem of preserving the British Empire while still maintaining colonial freedoms. A plan, closely resembling that of the Albany Congress of 1754, was proposed by Joseph Galloway, a conservative delegate from Pennsylvania. Galloway called for a federation of the colonies under a president-general appointed by the king. A grand council elected by colonial legislatures would, with the president, regulate intercolonial affairs as an American section of Parliament. The plan was defeated by the vote of one colony, setting the tone for a radical rather than a moderate Congress.

See also Continental Congress, First; Galloway, Joseph.

GÁLVEZ, BERNARDO DE (1746-86) Bernardo de Gálvez's family had long been concerned with governing the Spanish colonies in the Western Hemisphere, his father having been viceroy of New Spain and his uncle the minister-general of the Indies. Bernardo himself had served with the Spanish army in Portugal, Algiers, and New Spain before being appointed governor of Spanish Louisiana in 1777. He immediately allied himself with the French Creoles by marrying a native Louisianian. During the Revolutionary War, Gálvez played the decisive role in driving the British from the lower Mississippi and the eastern Gulf Coast. Even before Spain declared war on Great Britain, Gálvez allowed Oliver Pollock to set up a supply base for the American rebels in New Orleans. After the formal declaration of war, Gálvez conquered West Florida from the British in three campaigns (1779-81). His success was the main reason Britain ceded Spain both East and West Florida in the Treaty of Paris in 1783.

As a reward for his actions, Gálvez was made viceroy of New Spain in 1785. He immediately began to transform Spanish policy toward the Indians. In his "Instrucciones" to the frontier commander Jacobo Ugarte y Loyola, written in 1786, Gálvez discarded the old solutions to the Indian problem, the mission and presidio, in favor of a policy designed to tie the Indians to the Spanish through economic and technological dependence. He died of fever before he could bring his ideas to fruition.

GAMA, VASCO DA (?1469-1524) A Portuguese explorer and navigator, da Gama stimulated European intent in transoceanic exploration. Following up Bartolomé Dias's voyage around the Cape of Good Hope in 1487-88, da Gama left Lisbon on July 8, 1497, and was piloted as far as West Africa by Dias. Swinging out into the Atlantic to take advantage of the westerly winds, da Gama reached Calicut, India, on May 22, 1498, thus opening up a new, Portuguese-controlled trade route to the riches of the East. Like Dias, da Gama also searched for the kingdom of Prester John, but in this he was disappointed. In 1502, da Gama voyaged again to India. He conquered Calicut and made it a Portuguese colony, killing or expelling the large Muslim trading community. He then retired, but returned in 1524 as viceroy, dying soon after his arrival.

See also Exploration.

GARCES, FRANCISCO (1738-81) Garces, a Franciscan missionary in Sonora, Mexico, from 1768 onward, was based at San Xavier del Bac but traveled extensively, making four long journeys through northern and western Arizona before 1774. In that year, convinced of the feasibility of an overland route to Monterey, he joined Juan Bautista de Anza and went with him as far as San Gabriel before returning to Arizona. Accompanying Anza again on his second expedition (1775) Garces penetrated the San Joaquin Valley. Garces was killed in the Yuma revolt of 1781.

See also Anza, Juan Bautista de.

GARDINER, JOHN (1737-93) Massachusetts lawyer and legislator, born in Boston, Gardiner was educated at the University of Glasgow and practiced law in England, where he became an ardent Whig. After a stint as attorney general of the Carribean island of St. Christopher, Gardiner returned to Boston in 1783 and built a successful law practice. He was elected to the Massachusetts General Court in 1789 as representative from Pownalboro and became known as a zealous reformer willing to take full advantage of the latest political issue. He was best known for reforming probate laws and as an advocate for repeal of laws restricting theaters. Gardiner drowned off of Cape Ann, Massachusetts, as he seemed on the verge of achieving high office.

GARONKONTHIE, DANIEL (c.1600-76) An Iroquois chief whose name means "moving sun," he was born in Onandaga (New York) and became an important French ally among the Iroquois. He settled near Montreal around 1654 and was deeply impressed with the culture of the French colonists there. In 1657 he led French Catholic missionaries in a short-lived attempt to settle near Onandaga, and in 1661 he served as a guide for the Jesuit missionary Jacques LeMoyne. He later prevented LeMoyne's assassination and served as a French-Iroquois intermediary. In 1669 he was baptized in Quebec and took the Christian name Daniel. He spent the rest of his life as a Catholic missionary to the Iroquois.

GASPÉE INCIDENT (1772) In the spring of 1772 the British navy's Lieutenant William Dudingston, commander of the schooner *Gaspée* had made himself resented through his overzealous enforcement of the Navigation Acts in Rhode Island waters. When the *Gaspée*, pursuing a suspected smuggler, ran aground on June 9, several boatloads of Providence citizens boarded the vessel at night, wounded Dudingston, removed him and his crew, and burned the vessel to the water's edge. A royal commission of inquiry could learn nothing of the identity of the criminals and so the government allowed the matter to drop. Disturbed by the powers of the commission, the Virginia House of Burgesses set up a committee of correspondence and urged the other colonies to do the same, that they might keep one another informed of their constitutional concerns.

GATES, HORATIO (1728-1806) A prominent American general in the Revolutionary War, Gates was born in England. He served in North America during the French and Indian War, accompanying General Braddock during his unsuccessful attempt to capture Fort Duquesne (1755). He retired from the British army in 1765 and took up residence in Virginia in 1772. Gates supported the patriot cause during the Revolution and was commissioned adjutant general in the Continental Army in 1775. In 1776 he was promoted to major general and was appointed commander, over General

The burning of the British ship *Gaspée* heightened colonial tensions with Britain. *(Library of Congress)*

Sullivan, of the Northern Army. In 1777 he was appointed commander of the army at Ticonderoga over General Schuyler. Most historians credit Gates' rapid promotions to the influence of several New England delegates to the Continental Congress.

His victory against Burgoyne at Saratoga in 1777 encouraged an attempt, known as the Conway Cabal, to replace Washington as commander in chief with Gates. In November 1778, Gates was appointed president of the Board of War. Gates did not object publicly to the ultimately unsuccessful Congressional schemes to replace the commander in chief although he and Washington eventually reestablished a working relationship. Between 1778 and 1780, Gates commanded the Northern and Eastern departments of the army. He was appointed commander of the Southern Army in June 1780. After his defeat at Camden in August 1780, Gates was replaced by General Nathanael Greene. Gates freed his slaves in 1790 and moved to New York City, where he died.

See also Conway Cabal; Revolutionary War Battles.

GATES, SIR THOMAS (died 1621) Governor of Virginia, Thomas Gates was born in Colyford, Devonshire. He sailed with Sir Francis Drake in 1585 to attack St. Augustine, Florida, and rescue the Roanoke colonists. In 1606 he left his military post in The Hague to be a grantee of the Virginia and Plymouth companies. As the lieutenant general, he set out in 1609 for Virginia with a pinnace and eight ships filled with 500 men and women. He was shipwrecked on Bermuda, and his experience, recorded by William Strachey, provided the background for William Shakespeare's *The Tempest*. Shocked by the colonists' state when he reached Virginia the next May, he was loading them on his ship when Lord De La Warr's arrival stopped the exodus. Gates, who was sent to England for supplies, returned in 1611 with three ships and three caravels holding 100 cows, 200 pigs, and 280 men and women, including his wife and daughters. After his wife died en route, he sent his daughters back, but he stayed to take the governorship from Thomas Dale. Although Virginia suffered hardships, the efficiency of the Gates administration improved colonial life. In 1614 he went to England to help the Virginia

Company but sold his stock in 1620 to return to The Hague, where he died.

GENERAL COURT, MASSACHUSETTS The governing body in New England colonies, a general court was first provided for and established in the charter of the Massachusetts Bay Colony. The court was empowered to govern, correct, punish, and make rules. It consisted of a governor, 18 assistants (or, in the case of the courts in the Connecticut and New Haven colonies, magistrates), and all the freemen in the colony. Meetings were conducted four times a year. At these meetings whatever was necessary for the running of the colony was brought up and acted upon. It was a time for new freemen to be admitted, for taxes to be established, for justice to be administered, and for fines to be assessed.

GEOGRAPHY AND CULTURE North America was characterized by a profoundly diverse human geography both before and after the beginning of European colonization. Thousands of indigenous Indian communities supported themselves with a wide variety of subsistence strategies, combined themselves into various political alliances, and spoke over 200 languages that were further divided into scores of distinct dialects. To this continent of villages European expansion added Spanish, French, Dutch, and English colonizers as well as African slaves. By the mid-18th century these had been joined by immigrant Germans, Irish, Scots, Welsh, Swedes, Finns, and Jews. A regional approach to colonial North America helps to bring some spatial order to this complexity.

Indian Cultures. Anthropologists group North American Indians, for example, into several major regions broadly defined by subsistence practice. This "culture area" concept is based on the premises that a regional ecology requires a good deal of similarity in the procurement of food and shelter and that a group is likely to share cultural features in common with its nearby neighbors. This concept is essentially static and says nothing about the process of historical change, but it supplies a convenient device for ordering Indian diversity.

The Indians of Mesoamerica and the Southwest based their societies on intensive irrigation farming, while those of the Great Basin and California depended upon gathering, primarily of seed resources. The Indians of the Northwest coast relied on the abundant fisheries of the rivers, those of the prairie plains on bison hunting. East of the Mississippi River, societies depended upon corn (maize) cultivation, but increasingly supplemented it with hunting as one moved from the Southeast to the Northeast. The peoples of the Subarctic and Arctic relied on the exploitation of land and sea mammal populations. Although overgeneralizations

should be avoided about different groups from the same area that had their own distinctive histories, groups from the same culture area as different as the Aleut and the Eskimo of the Arctic, the Iroquoian and Algonquian speaking peoples of the Northeast, or the Hopi and Pueblo of the Southwest shared many cultural similarities.

Europeans and Indians. European conquest and settlement introduced a dynamism into North American history that cannot be contained by the concept of subsistence culture areas. By 1750 colonialism had created an Atlantic coastal zone in which Indians remained as remnant populations only. Further west was a zone that included Indian groups as yet unconquered but, nevertheless, connected to the colonial system. The most important of these were the Iroquois Confederacy and the Creek Confederacy, which controlled much of the fur trade in the North and South,

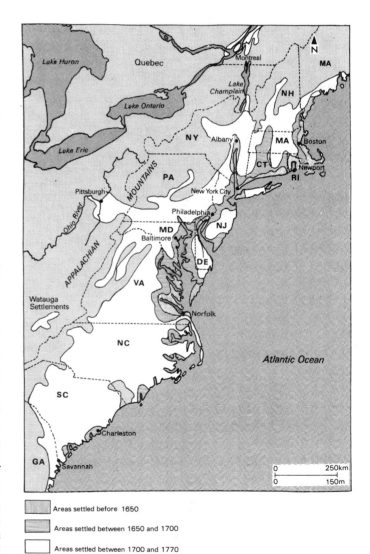

Geography and Culture. *(Martin Greenwald Associates, Inc.)*

GEOGRAPHY AND CULTURE: TOPIC GUIDE
GENERAL

Alaska, Russia in
Appalachian Mountains
Bermuda
Canary Islands
Connecticut
  Hartford
  New Haven Colony
  New London
Delaware
Forts
French Colonies (see **Topic Guide**)
  Arkansas Post
  Cahokia
  Chequamegon Bay
  Green Bay
  Kaskaskia
  Montreal
  Natchez
  Natchitoches
  New Orleans
  Prairie du Chien
  Quebec City
  Sault Saint Marie
  Saint Louis
  Vincennes
Georgia
  Savannah
Great Lakes
Hawaii
Kentucky
  Cumberland Gap
  Cumberland Settlements
Maine
  Kennebec River Settlements
  Saint Croix Settlement
Maritime Provinces
  Louisburg
  Newfoundland
Maryland
  Annapolis
  Baltimore
  Saint Mary's City
Massachusetts
  Boston
  Cape Cod
  Plymouth
  Plymouth Rock
  Salem
Mississippi River
New Hampshire
  Portsmouth

New Netherland
New Jersey
New York
  Albany
  Beverwyck
  Champlain, Lake
  New York City
  Hudson River
  Long Island
  Mohawk River
North Carolina
  Albemarle Settlements
  Cape Fear Settlements
Ohio River, The
Pennsylvania
  Philadelphia
Rhode Island
  Newport
  Providence Plantation
Rupert's Land
Saint Lawrence River
Spanish Colonies
  Albuquerque
  Caribbean
  El Paso
  Los Angeles
  Monterey
  Pensacola
  Rio Grande
  San Antonio
  San Diego
  Santa Fe
  Saint Augustine
  Tenochtitlan
  Tucson
  Yuma
South Carolina
  Beaufort
  Charleston
Swedish Colonies
Vermont
Vinland
Virginia
  Chesapeake Bay
  Jamestown
  Norfolk
  Williamsburg

respectively. However, the zone included many smaller Indian groupings as well as many mixed-blood peoples who played important intermediary roles in the trade. Finally, there was a third zone into which few Europeans had yet penetrated but within which the reverberating effects of colonialism had been felt. The effects included for example, the importation of European tools, weapons, and domestic animals (like the horse), as well as the imperatives of the trading system, which the Indians used in order to obtain more of these valuable things.

New England. Within the zone of European dominance, several distinct regional societies had emerged by 1750. These societies were larger and more culturally important than the geopolitical units of colonies or provinces, although they sometimes adhered to general political boundaries. With over 400,000 Euro-Americans, New England was the largest region; settled almost entirely by English dissenting Protestants, it was also the most homogeneous in North America. The pattern of contiguous settlement of compact villages and towns provided

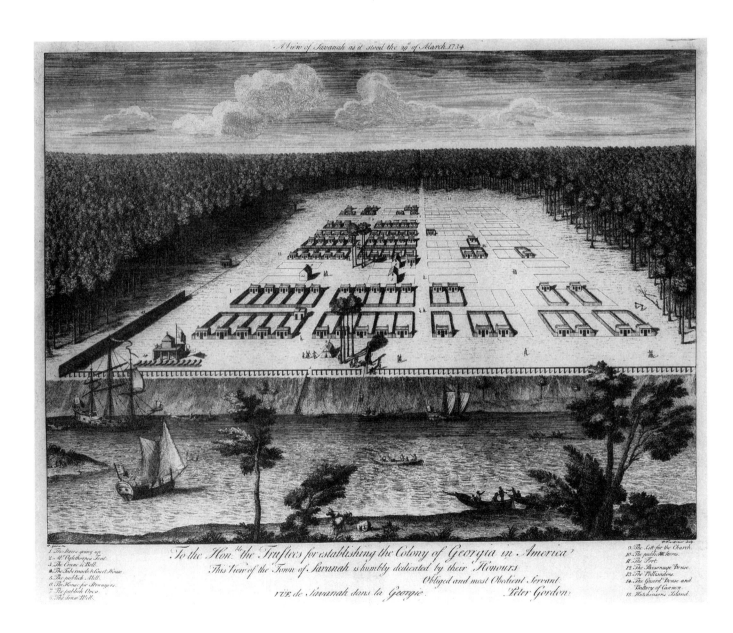

In 1734, a year after Georgia was settled, Savannah had begun to emerge from the wilderness. *(Library of Congress)*

the society with an ordered and uniform culture. It was also a society with enormous potential for demographic growth, which was manifested in its expansion north and west. Acadia and Newfoundland were spheres of strong New England influence, as were areas bordering on Long Island, the Hudson, and the St. Lawrence.

Canada.   Like its southern neighbor, the society along the St. Lawrence was essentially homogeneous; controlled immigration produced a population of some 55,000, the vast majority of whom were Roman Catholic and French. With its centralized authority located at the anchoring cities of Quebec and Montreal, it was also the most urbanized of all North American colonial societies, although its urbanism was more administrative than commercial. This region extended south via the Richelieu River to the shores of Lake Champlain.

The Hudson Valley.   In contrast to both these, the Hudson Valley's 100,000 settlers were ethnically heterogeneous. Especially along the lower Hudson, in the area of New York City, diversity was accompanied by a tendency for populations to mix and mingle, producing a new ethnic identity, the "Yorker." It was also a society dominated by merchant or land-owning patrician families; much of the farming was performed by tenants, continuing a tradition that began with the Dutch. This region stretched from East Jersey up the Hudson to Albany and included a growing number of settlements along the Mohawk River.

The Middle and Southern Colonies.   Nearly as populous as New England was Virginia with some 390,000 inhabitants. But Virginia was a biracial society composed almost entirely of English Anglicans and African slaves in the ratio of 2 to 1 and as a result was a strongly hierarchical society with a powerful gentry. Virginia was also unique for the absence of towns and cities, since most plantations dealt directly with shipping agents from their own wharves along the rivers. The county was the primary unit of local society. Virginia was also expansionist, its influence extending from eastern Maryland south to the Albemarle district of North Carolina, its frontier moving through the gaps in the Blue Ridge chain into the long Shenandoah Valley.

In the Shenandoah, Virginians met streams of settlers moving down Pennsylvania, which with 230,000 was the third most populous region at the time. There a history of Quaker tolerance and extensive recruitment of immigrants introduced a cultural variety unparalleled elsewhere in North America. The rich countryside was a veritable patchwork of ethnic and religious identities within a relatively open social structure. Less compactly settled than

New England, all Pennsylvania roads led to the great urban center of Philadelphia, which by the time of the Revolution had become the second greatest English-speaking city in the world, fed by the grain trade to Europe. This society also experienced great growth, its Scotch-Irish and German immigrants streaming into the great corridor of the Shenandoah, carrying Pennsylvania culture as far south as backcountry Carolina.

Greater Carolina extended from Cape Fear to Florida, including much of North Carolina and Georgia, and its population numbered some 90,000. Like Virginia, this was a biracial society but with the important difference that here blacks outnumbered whites 2 to 1. This was the most slave-dependent society in North America but also the one in which Africans had the most direct influence upon culture. It was dominated by a central metropolis, Charleston, with the consequent enfeeblement of local society. Planters regularly abandoned the countryside to their slaves and drivers, fleeing to the urban life of Charleston, a pattern they inherited from their Caribbean forebears. The backcountry of Carolina, by contrast, shared much in common with that of Virginia.

Spanish Settlement.   The final important region was New Mexico, with perhaps some 20,000 Spanish-speaking residents and many more Indians. This was a racially stratified society of Spaniards (mostly Creoles), mestizos, and Indians, each occupying its own caste position. Like all of the Spanish empire in the New World, this was a society based on the clustered town and village, although here isolation reduced the marketplace to a mere ghost of what it was in more economically vital regions. Florida and Texas shared some of these characteristics with New Mexico.

Bibliography: Hofstadter, Richard, *America at 1750: A Social History* (Random, 1971); Kehoe, Alice B., *North American Indians: A Comprehensive Account* (Prentice-Hall, 1981); Kroeber, Alfred L., *The Cultural and Natural Areas of Native North America* (1939; reprint Kraus); Meinig, D. W., *The Shaping of America*, vol. 1, *Atlantic America, 1492-1800* (Yale Univ. Press, 1986)

John Mack Faragher
Mount Holyoke College

GEORGIA   Geography shaped Georgia's history. The Appalachian Mountains in the northern part of the state blend into the rolling hills of the piedmont. At the fall line of the rivers the coastal plain begins. The Savannah River forms Georgia's eastern boundary, while the Chattahoochee River, which rises in the same northeast sector of the state, runs across Georgia to form the western boundary. The Ogeechee, Oconee, and Ocmulgee rivers parallel the Savannah as they slice through the interior, while the Flint River joins the Chattahoochee and empties into the Gulf of Mexico.

The first people to enter Georgia were nomadic hunters who followed buffalo and deer. Later, prehistoric Indians settled along rivers and streams and lived by fishing and farming as well as by hunting. Huge burial mounds may still be seen at Ocmulgee, near Macon; at Etowah, north of Atlanta; and at Kolomoki, in southwest Georgia. Less impressive artifacts may be found on almost every waterway.

Hernando De Soto was the first European to traverse the region in his search for the riches of Cufitachiqui in 1540. After a brief occupation of the coastal region by Jean Ribault's French Huguenots (1562-65), Menendez de Aviles restored the area to Spain in 1565. A chain of missions flourished along the sea islands and into the interior as far as the Chattahoochee.

England challenged Spain's claim by founding Carolina in 1664. Military expeditions from Charleston destroyed the mission settlements and forced the Spanish out of Georgia. An uprising of Yamassee Indians in 1715 alarmed the Carolinians and caused them to welcome the new "buffer" colony of Georgia between the Savannah and Altamaha rivers.

Oglethorpe and Early Colonization.

General James Edward Oglethorpe and his friends had originally intended for Georgia to be a debtors colony, but Parliament was not interested in helping prisoners. Parliament granted a 21-year charter to the Trustees of Georgia in order to protect Carolina and to produce silk and wine. Hardworking poor people and foreign Protestants were sent to the new colony, where each head of family received 50 acres of land to cultivate. Oglethorpe arrived at Yamacraw Bluff on the Savannah River with 114 settlers on February 12, 1733, and supervised the surveying of the town of Savannah with its unique pattern of alternating squares. Tomochichi, chief of the Yamacraw, offered his help as did Mary Musgrove, the Indian wife of a Carolina trader.

After settling a group of German Lutherans at Ebenezer, 45 miles up the Savannah River, Oglethorpe returned to England, where he and the trustees secured the passage of three acts of Parliament. The Indian Act gave Oglethorpe control of the Indian trade west of the Savannah River; the Rum Act forbade the use of strong drink; the third act prohibited slavery in Georgia. During that year, 1735, a group of Highland Scots founded the town of Darien on the Altamaha River.

Oglethorpe returned to Georgia in 1736 and honored Frederick, Prince of Wales, and his new bride, Augusta of Saxe-Gotha, by naming two new towns after them. Frederica was his garrison town on St. Simon's Island. Augusta, 130 miles up the Savannah River, was his outpost for controlling the Indian trade. Anticipating a war with Spain, Oglethorpe returned again to England to persuade Prime Minister Robert Walpole to send a regiment to Georgia.

The expected war began in 1739. With his regiment of 500, an equal number of Carolinians, and 1,000 Indians, Oglethorpe besieged but failed to capture St. Augustine in 1740. A Spanish expedition retaliated in 1742. Oglethorpe's men defeated the invaders in the Battle of Bloody Marsh on St. Simon's Island. After another unsuccessful invasion of Florida in 1743, Oglethorpe left Georgia for good. By that time, the Georgia experiment seemed a failure. The population dwindled, and those who stayed complained about restrictions on landholding and slavery. The trustees reluctantly abandoned their plan, and in 1752, a year before their charter was due to expire, they handed Georgia over to Parliament.

The Royal Colony.

Georgia began to prosper as a royal colony. In 1752 a Puritan settlement was established at Midway, between Savannah and Darien. The influx of planters with their slaves caused the lowcountry to resemble South Carolina's plantation society.

The administration (1754-57) of Georgia's first royal governor, John Reynolds coincided with the beginning of the French and Indian War (Seven Year's War). Reynolds proved to be as clumsy in his treatment of Indians as he was unskillful in dealing with the members of his own council. Georgians complained about Reynolds's arbitrary conduct and succeeded in having him replaced in 1757 by Henry Ellis, a more gifted and tactful governor. Ellis maintained friendly relations with the Creek during the war. When the Cherokee overran the Carolina and Georgia backcountry in the winter of 1759-60, the Creek came to the rescue. After the Cherokee were driven back to their mountains, Governor Ellis asked to be recalled.

Georgia's third colonial governor, James Wright, enjoyed the longest tenure, 1760-82. The first important achievement of his administration was hosting a congress of Indians at Augusta in 1763. The governors of Virginia, North Carolina, and South Carolina joined Wright in signing a treaty by which the English were permitted to settle as far as the Ogeechee River, 40 miles west of the Savannah, and as far north as Little River, 20 miles above Augusta. Georgia's new southern border was the St. Marys River.

During the decade that followed the population increased rapidly. By 1773 there were about 35,000 people living in Georgia; in the next three years 20,000 more entered the state. The Georgia Assembly encouraged immigration by establishing townships in the backcountry. Prosperous Indian traders John Rae and George Galphin brought settlers from northern Ireland to Queensborough on the Ogeechee. A group of North Carolina Quakers petitioned for and received a township that they named Wrightsborough in honor of the governor. In addition to these organized efforts at colonization, thousands of drifters crowded into the backcountry, spilling over the Indian boundary. This led Governor Wright to call the Indians to Augusta again in 1773 and extract more land from them. Most of the ceded territory lay above the Little River between the Ogeechee and Savannah rivers. The Cherokee, whose debts to the Georgia traders were canceled as part of the bargain, were satisfied with the Treaty of 1773. However, the Creek who claimed the same region and who were not so heavily in debt were furious at the surrender of land. Their young warriors took up the war hatchet in the winter of 1773-74 and spread terror along the frontier.

The Revolutionary War Era.   The Indian uprising explains the protestations of loyalty by backcountry Georgians in August 1774. When a group of Savannah merchants gathered at Tondee's Tavern and signed petitions denouncing the British Intolerable Acts, the inhabitants of the backcountry drew up counterpetitions saying that the Savannah residents had different interests from theirs. However, when Governor Wright failed to obtain more land as a condition of peace, many backcountrymen joined the lowcountry Whigs in opposition to Lord North's policies. The Midway settlement was the hotbed of revolutionary sentiment. That community sent Lyman Hall to the Second Continental Congress in 1775 before other Georgia parishes were ready to act.

The news of the clash at Lexington and Concord in April 1775, combined with the rumor of a British-inspired Indian offensive on the frontier, inflamed Revolutionary sentiment. Georgia adopted the Continental Association, and local committees of "Liberty Boys" began to make examples of those who refused to take the pledge to boycott British trade. By the end of 1775, Governor Wright was only a figurehead. The real power was exercised by a Committee of Safety.

Governor Wright left Georgia on a British naval vessel in March 1776, and Georgia drew up a short and simple constitution called Rules and Regulations. George Walton and Button Gwinnett were sent to Philadelphia to join Lyman Hall, and the three signed the Declaration of Independence. Gwinnett returned to Georgia and was elected to a constitutional convention. He headed the committee that drafted Georgia's first state constitution, a democratic document which entrusted power to a one-house legislature.

During each of the first three years of the war, Georgia attempted to invade Florida, but failed each time. In 1778 the British high command turned its attention to Georgia.

An invasion force from New York under Lieutenant Colonel Archibald Campbell captured Savannah on December 28, 1778. Campbell occupied Augusta on February 1, 1779, but was forced to retreat two weeks later in the face of a reinforced American army. The British turned on General John Ashe's pursuers and routed them in the Battle of Briar Creek on March 3, 1779.

A large French army under Count Henri D'Estaing, combined with an American force under General Benjamin Lincoln, conducted a three-week siege of Savannah climaxed by a gallant but futile assault on October 9, 1779. The British lines held, and the French sailed away. With Savannah secured and royal government restored in Georgia, General Henry Clinton used Georgia as a base for another expedition, which captured Charleston. Whig resistance in the two states collapsed for a time.

However, Elijah Clarke conducted a bold raid on British-held Augusta in September 1780. A British detachment tried to intercept Clarke but was itself defeated in the Battle of Kings Mountain, the turning point of the war in the South. Lieutenant Colonel Henry (Lighthorse Harry) Lee of General Nathanael Greene's army forced the British surrender of Augusta in June 1781, and General Anthony Wayne compelled the British to evacuate Savannah in July 1782.

The peace treaty of 1783 placed Georgia's western boundary on the Mississippi River. By the same treaty, Spain regained Florida and contested Georgia's southern border. The Creek Indians under the skillful leadership of Alexander McGillivray opposed Georgia's efforts to cross the Ogeechee River. Georgia currency, based on the unobtainable Indian land, declined drastically in value. Under the Articles of Confederation, Congress was too weak to help against the Creek and the Spanish. In the expectation of receiving help from a stronger union, Georgia promptly ratified the new constitution on January 2, 1788, the fourth state to do so.

See also Augusta, Congress of; Augusta, Treaty of; Cherokee Wars; Oglethrope, James Edward; Revolutionary War Battles.

Bibliography: Cashin, Edward J., ed., *Colonial Augusta: "Key of the Indian Country"* (Mercer Univ. Press, 1986); Coleman, Kenneth, *The American Revolution in Georgia* (Univ. of Georgia Press, 1958); Coleman, Kenneth, *Colonial Georgia: A History* (Scribner's, 1976); Jackson, Harvey H., and Spalding, Phinizy, eds., *Forty Years of Diversity: Essays on Colonial Georgia* (Univ. of Georgia Press, 1984); Reese, Trevor, *Colonial Georgia: A Study in British Imperial Policy in the Eighteenth Century* (Univ. of Georgia Press, 1963); Wood, Betty, *Slavery in Colonial Georgia, 1730-1775* (Univ. of Georgia Press, 1984).

Edward J. Cashin
Augusta College

GERMAINE, LORD GEORGE (1717-85) Born in England, a son of the first Duke of Dorset, who was lord-lieutenant of Ireland, Germaine served in the British army in Germany but was condemned for disobeying orders at Minden in 1759. Family influence and public opinion, nevertheless, enabled Germaine to enter Parliament in 1761. He supported Lord North and replaced Lord Dartmouth as secretary of state for colonies in 1775. In this position he had control of the British army in America, although the court-martial that had tried him for his conduct at Minden had found him unfit to serve in the military. Germaine supported the use of military force, including mercenaries, against the colonists. He quarreled with generals Carleton, Clinton, and Howe, and the British defeat in America has been partially blamed on Germaine's interference. He resigned as colonial secretary in 1782.

GERMAN IMMIGRANTS Although a few Germans undoubtedly came to the North American colonies during the early 17th century, the first group of identifiable German immigrants, under the leadership of Francis Daniel Pastorius, arrived in Pennsylvania in 1683, where they founded Germantown. Large-scale immigration, however, did not begin for another quarter century, after the harsh European winter of 1708-09, the wars of Louis XIV, and overpopulation in the region of the Rhine River forced migration. Although the first Germans landed in New York, they soon moved to Pennsylvania, where lands were not encumbered with feudal dues.

From 1710 until the outbreak of the Revolution, perhaps as many as 100,000 Germans immigrated to the colonies. According to the first federal census of 1790, the centers of German population included New York (where they constituted 8 percent of the inhabitants), New Jersey (9 percent), Maryland (12 percent), and especially Pennsylvania (33 percent). Not surprisingly, therefore, Philadelphia had been their principal port of entry and, since most of the German immigrants were farmers, they spread out across the rich agricultural plain of the Middle Colonies.

Most German immigrants came as "redemptioners," that is, they were allowed passage to America on credit and were then given a short time after arrival to arrange payment or otherwise be sold into servitude for a period of four to seven years. Historians estimate that from one-half to two-thirds of those Germans who arrived in the colonies in the 18th century came as redemptioners. As the century wore on, however, most German redemptioners were purchased by other Germans, who had arrived earlier and had worked their way into independence. Indeed, emigrating in groups, sharing language and (often) pietistic Protestantism, the Germans tended to cluster in their own distinct communities. By the time of the Revolution they had established a reputation as frugal and industrious farmers, with good barns and snug houses. The so-called "Pennsylvania Dutch" are descended from those German communities.

This large-scale German immigration ended with the Revolution; it did not resume until the second quarter of the 19th century. By that time the 18th-century Germans had largely assimilated to American life, adopting English, intermarrying with persons of other ethnic backgrounds, and even Anglicizing their names.

See also Pennsylvania.

Bibliography: Diffenderfer, Frank R., *German Immigration into Pennsylvania* (1900, reprint Genealog. Pub., 1979); Rippley, LaVern J., *The German-Americans* (Univ. Press of Amer., 1976).

John Mack Faragher
Mount Holyoke College

GERMAN REFORMED CHURCH Major emigrations from Germany to North America, especially to the Middle Colonies, occurred early in the 18th century. The first wave came in 1708 to 1710 as refugees from the Palatinate (with Britain's assistance and encouragement) found their way to New York and to settlements along both sides of the Hudson River. Far greater numbers entered Pennsylvania from the 1730s, this migration helping to give Penn's colony its immmportant Germanic stamp. By 1740, 50 German Reformed churches had been founded, the vast majority of these being in Pennsylvania and, by 1780, the numbers had risen to over 200.

Since British Quakers had already occupied the Pennsylvania lands closest to the Delaware River, the German Reformed, arriving approximately a half century later, took up residence in Montgomery, Lehigh, Northampton, Lancaster, Berks, and York counties. Close cooperation existed between the Dutch Reformed and these German Calvinists, the latter even being ruled by the Classis (synod) of Amsterdam. One of Pennsylvania's best known clergymen, John Philip Boehm, appealed to that Classis when his own ministerial credentials were challenged. In fact, Boehm, a schoolmaster and farmer, had entered upon a ministry to the German Reformed at the entreaties of friends and neighbors who had no other ecclesiastical leadership to assist them. Boehm filled the vacuum impressively from around 1720 to his death in 1749. Recognizing the great merit of his contribution, the Classis supported Boehm and arranged for his regular ordination in New York in 1729.

In 1793 the German Reformed organized their own synod at Lancaster, Pennsylvania, their membership of some 15,000 extending from New York to backcountry Virginia. Language prevented any merger with the Dutch, while theology precluded alliance with the Lutherans. Continuing to minister, therefore, to their own immigrant group, the German Reformed later entered into a series of mergers, losing their separate ecclesiastical identity in the 20th century.

See also Dutch Reformed Church.

Bibliography: Dubbs, Joseph H., *A History of the Reformed Church, German* (Scribners, 1895).

Edwin S. Gaustad
University of California, Riverside

GERMANTOWN   A settlement near Philadelphia, also known as German Towne and Germanopolis, it was founded in 1683 by a group of German Quakers and Mennonites led by Francis Daniel Pastorius, agent for the Frankfort Land Company.   The purchase of its 25,000 acres from the Pennsylvania territory chartered to William Penn marked the beginning of large-scale German colonization in the region.   During the Revolution and the British occupation of Philadelphia, Germantown was the scene of Washington's last battle before wintering the Continental Army at Valley Forge.

A signer of the Declaration of Independence, Elbridge Gerry was long influential in both Massachusetts and national politics. *(Library of Congress)*

GERRY, ELBRIDGE (1744-1814)   An active patriot in the Revolution and a signer of the Declaration of Independence, Gerry later became U.S. vice president (1813-14).   Born in Marblehead, Massachusetts, he graduated from Harvard (1762) and joined his father's business. Gerry, a friend of Samuel Adams, was a member of the Massachusetts General Court (1772-74) and served on the Committee of Correspondence. He supported a separation from Britain in the Continental Congress (1776-81) and signed both the Declaration of Independence and the Articles of Confederation. After devoting some time to business interests, he returned to the Continental Congress (1783-85).

As a delegate to thee Constitutional Convention (1787), he opposed the final document but afterwards announced that he would support it. He then served in Congress (1789-93), where he supported both anti-Federalist and Federalist (particularly financial) measures. As a diplomat Gerry joined John Marshall and Charles C. Pinckney in France during the XYZ Affair (1797-98). He was elected the governor of Massachusetts (1810-11), and during his second term he isolated Federalist strongholds to insure Republican domination in elections, leading to the term "gerrymander." Gerry was vice president (1813- 14) under James Madison, serving until his death.

GILBERT, SIR HUMPHREY(?1539-83)   An English soldier and adventurer, half-brother of Sir Walter Raleigh, Gilbert is more important for his ideas than for his single expedition to North America. As a young soldier he entered the service of Princess Elizabeth, remaining a member of her household after her accession. In 1576 he published *A Discourse of a Discoverie for a New Passage to Cataia* [Cathay], which argued for the existence of a Northwest Passage and did much to advance the cause of English exploration.   In 1578, Queen Elizabeth I authorized him to colonize western lands not claimed by another Christian prince, and along with Raleigh he set out on a western voyage that failed completely.   In 1583, Gilbert sailed from Plymouth on a second attempt, landing at St. John's Bay, Newfoundland, which he claimed for his queen, and encountered fishermen of several European nationalities. He was lost on the return voyage.

See also Northwest Passage.

GIRTY, SIMON (1741-1818)   A British agent among the Indians, Girty was born near Harrisburg, Pennsylvania, where at 15 he was captured by Senecas and adopted into their tribe, learning Indian language and customs. Released near Pittsburgh, he worked as an interpreter at Fort Pitt and as a military scout during Lord Dunmore's War. Joining the rebels at the outbreak of the Revolution, he later deserted at Detroit to the British, for whom he worked as an interpreter and agent among the Indians of the Old Northwest. Several times he led warrior raids on settlements in western Pennsylvania, joining in the torture of captives and thereby becoming one of the rebels' most despised enemies. After the Revolution he continued his anti-American agitation among the Indians, participating in the conflict of the 1790s. Afterward settling in Canada, he was nearly captured by the Americans at the Battle of the Thames in 1813. Known as the "White Savage" and the "Great Renegade," Girty became perhaps the most hated man on the Northwestern frontier.

See also Lord Dunmore's War.

GIST, CHRISTOPHER (c.1705-59) The first to explore the Ohio River country, Gist was a native of Maryland but in 1745 moved his family to the Yadkin River in North Carolina, where he became a trader, surveyor, and scout. In 1751 he traversed trans-Appalachia for the Ohio Company, writing journals that provide an illuminating portrait of the mid-18th century frontier. An associate of George Washington, twice saving his life during the French and Indian War, Gist was an active participant in those campaigns.

See also Ohio Company.

GLORIOUS REVOLUTION The Glorious Revolution—the assumption of the English throne late in 1688 by the Protestant William of Orange (William III) and his wife Mary in place of the deposed Catholic James II—had a counterpart in the American colonies, where a series of "rebellions" occurred in direct response to events in England. In Massachusetts the government established to administer the Dominion of New England was overthrown, and in New York, officials were also replaced. In Maryland, the Catholic Calvert regime succumbed to Protestant rebels. Although these political revolts resulted in part from discontent generated by circumstances unique to each colony, the fundamental cause was shared: Officials whose authority derived from James II could not maintain it once he had been removed from the throne. Additionally, in each of the American rebellions, the insurgents based their case at least partly on fears that Protestants were in jeopardy from Catholics (either English or French) or those allied to Catholics (Indians).

New England.   Initiated by Charles II, the Dominion of New England was an attempt by the English Crown to unite the Northeastern colonies under one government led by a single royal governor. This alone proved threatening to the individual colonies, whose charters, guaranteeing their liberties, were revoked. Resentment was especially bitter in Puritan Massachusetts, for the Dominion's governor, Sir Edmund Andros, not only flaunted his Anglicanism, but while governor of New York, had refused to help the colony during King Philip's War (1675-76). Once news of the revolution in England reached Massachusetts, rumors spread that Andros was secretly a

papist and that he would hand control of the Dominion to the French. On April 18, 1689, a mob of Bostonians captured Andros and a number of other officials, who were jailed. Although William and Mary were proclaimed as the colony's monarchs, Massachusetts lacked a legally constituted government.

New York and Maryland.   It took a week for New Yorkers to learn of the mob action in Boston. Francis Nicholson, Andros's lieutenant in New York, had suppressed news of William and Mary's accession. With Andros in prison, Nicholson chose to do nothing, increasing uncertainty in the colony. When Nicholson left for England in June, the militia, led by Captain Jacob Leisler, assumed control (Leisler's Rebellion). Leisler proclaimed William and Mary as king and queen, and, having received the new king's instructions addressed to Nicholson or whomever "in his absence" was administering the colony's affairs, took the title of lieutenant governor and proceeded to govern.

The Calvert family's government in Maryland was also overthrown in 1689, even though the proprietor, away from the colony since 1684, had ordered the new sovereigns proclaimed. But the messenger carrying Lord Baltimore's instructions died before reaching the colony, and local officials failed to act on their own. Amid rumors of a French-Indian-Catholic plot to seize Maryland and massacre all the Protestants, a newly-formed Protestant Association directed the seizure of power. The Association called for a special assembly, which proclaimed the new king and queen, and asked the Crown to assume control of Maryland.

Results.   The Maryland rebels did succeed in removing the Catholic Calverts from heading the colony's government. In 1692, Maryland became a royal colony, a status it retained until 1715. In 1691, Massachusetts received a new charter, and New York received a new governor, who promptly ended Leisler's Rebellion.

See also Andros, Sir Edmund; Dominion of New England; Leisler's Rebellion.

Aaron Shatzman
Franklin and Marshall College

GLOVER, JOHN (1732-97) Born in Salem, Massachusetts, Glover became a member of the Marblehead committee of correspondence in 1772 and in May 1775 was commissioned a colonel in the 21st Massachusetts Regiment, for which he raised 1,000 men. He joined the Continental Army at Cambridge, Massachusetts, in June and was ordered by General Washington to equip armed ships for the colonies. After the British left Boston, Glover's regiment was ordered to New York, where it evacuated

American troops from Long Island. He later transported Washington's troops across the Delaware and led an attack on the British at Trenton. He then ferried Hessian prisoners back across the Delaware in a subzero storm. In 1777, Glover fought with General Gates against Burgoyne at Saratoga, New York. After escorting the Convention Army to Cambridge, he fought with generals Greene and Sullivan. He resigned from active military service in 1782.

GNADENHEUTTEN MASSACRE (1782) This attack by the Pennsylvania militia ended a Moravian attempt to establish a Christian-Indian village. In 1772, Moravian missionaries from Pennsylvania led a group of their Indian converts to establish a village on the frontier of the Ohio territory. During the Revolution, the pacifism of this community aroused suspicions, and its members were forcibly expelled to the village of Gnadenheutten in the Sandusky Valley in 1781. In 1782 some members of this community retaliated against settlers in Washington County, Pennsylvania. The result was an attack on March 7, 1782, by the Pennsylvania militia against the village of Gnadenheutten in which 100 men, women, and children were killed.

GODDARD, MARY KATHERINE (1738-1816) Designated by the Continental Congress as official printer of America's Declaration of Independence, Goddard was an influential newspaper editor and publisher in Baltimore, Maryland, throughout the Revolution as well as its highly respected postmistress for 14 years. She had learned her trade by working with her mother, Sarah Goddard, on the *Providence Gazette* in the 1760s and then by managing her brother William's *Pennsylvania Chronicle* in Philadelphia. When he established the *Maryland Journal*, she moved to Baltimore to run it until their collaboration was disrupted by a bitter quarrel over his attempt to take the business without compensating her. When the government also ousted her from the post office in 1789, on grounds that a woman could not properly travel enough for the position, 200 admiring Baltimore businessmen unsuccessfully supported her petition for reinstatement. She continued to operate her bookshop until her impoverished death at 78.
See also Goddard, Sarah Updike.

GODDARD, SARAH UPDIKE(c.1700-70) Influential Rhode Island printer of the *Providence Gazette* and *Country Journal* (1763-68), Goddard was born into the prominent Rhode Island family of Lodowick and Abigail (Newton) Updike. She was tutored in Greek, Latin, and French, as well as in math, literature, and history. Married in 1735 to Dr. Giles Goddard, she lived in New London, Connecticut, until his death in 1757. Then she used her inheritance to get training for her son William so they could set up in 1762 the publishing business.

The newspaper's colonial rights articles circulated widely in pre-revolutionary America, and a special August 1765 issue helped organize colonists against the Stamp Act. After her son left the business, she reorganized as Sarah Goddard and Company, publishing books and the newspaper with her daughter Mary Katherine and other apprentices. Times were so hard that she told subscribers that "Provisions ... will be received in Lieu of Cash." Her son forced her to leave Providence in November 1768 by selling the business despite her objections. She died in Philadelphia.
See also Goddard, Mary Katherine.

GODFREY, THOMAS (1704-49) Glazier, mathematician, and inventor of a mariner's quadrant, Godfrey was known as a self-educated, brilliant, but argumentative person. Godfrey was an original member of Benjamin Franklin's Junto society, where Franklin objected to his precise, mathematical style "forever denying or distinguishing upon trifles, to the disturbance of conversation."

Born in Bristol Township, Philadelphia, he was apprenticed to a glazier. The windows of Independence Hall are his work. Governor James Logan, a skilled mathematician himself, noted Godfrey's natural abilities in mathematics, astronomy, and optics while Godfrey was glazing the windows of the governor's home, "Stenton." Aided by Logan, Godfrey developed his talents, and in 1730 he began work on improving Davis's quadrant, which demanded such dexterity in calculating a ship's latitude that ships were often off course. Godfrey sent his improved quadrant to London, where the inventor James Hadley saw it and may have based his own quadrant on Godfrey's design. In the ensuing debate, Logan defended his protégé to the Royal Society, which eventually recognized Godfrey's contribution with a gift of furniture valued at 200 pounds.

GODFREY, THOMAS (1736-63) A poet and playwright, Godfrey was the son of Thomas Godfrey, inventor of the improved quadrant. He grew up and studied in Philadelphia, while he practiced his father's trade of a glazier. At the College of Philadelphia, he became friends of painter Benjamin West and poet-composer Francis Hopkinson. During the French and Indian War, Godfrey took part in the successful campaign to take Fort Duquesne.

Godfrey benefited from the teaching and friendship of William Smith, the first provost of the Academy and Charitable School of Philadelphia and editor of the *American Magazine*, in which virtually all of Godfrey's lyrics and verse were published. "The Court of Fancy" (1762) showed imaginative power although, as he knew, the work was imitative of Chaucer and Pope. Nonetheless, it marks the emergence of poetry that was becoming distinctly American. *The Prince of Parthia* bears the distinction of being the first drama by a native American produced professionally by the American Company (c.1760). While Godfrey drew on Shakespeare and other playwrights, *Parthia* was not fundamentally derivative. It continues to be revived periodically. Critics have called it both "powerful in diction and in action" and remarkable only for its "measured dullness."

GOLDEN HILL, BATTLE OF (1770) The incident known as the Battle of Golden Hill, indicative of the escalating tension between colonists and British officials, was actually a street riot between British soldiers and colonial patriots in New York City. A dispute over the Quartering Act had been revived when the New York assembly refused to vote supplies for the British troops (1768) and then did so (1769). A leader of the Sons of Liberty, Alexander McDougall, criticized the assembly in a broadside; the British cut down the city's liberty pole; and the Sons of Liberty made countermoves to prevent soldiers from posting broadsides. After a patriot leader seized three soldiers who were posting insulting placards, other soldiers came to the rescue, and a street fight took place between 30-40 soldiers with bayonets against citizens armed with knives and clubs. Several were wounded in each group, but there were no deaths. McDougall was arrested for writing the broadside. After pleading not guilty, he was released on bail. The case never went to trial, but McDougall was imprisoned for several months for contempt.

GOMEZ, ESTEVAN(flourished 1519-25) Gomez, a Portuguese mariner, emigrated to Spain where he was considered for the post later given to Ferdinand Magellan. He commanded a ship on Magellan's global circumnavigation voyage, but resentful of Magellan's preferment, Gomez mutinied at the entrance to the Straits of Magellan. He took his ship back to Spain, where he offered to find a more practical passage to the Indies through North America. He left in September 1524 and landed at Cape Breton (Nova Scotia). Discarding the Gulf of St. Lawrence as too icebound to be a good passage to the Pacific, he sailed south as far as Rhode Island. Returning empty-handed to Spain, Gomez disappeared into obscurity.
See also Exploration; Magellan, Ferdinand.

GOOKIN, DANIEL (1612-87) Gookin, a Massachusetts soldier and Indian agent, was born in England, emigrated to Virginia with his family, and then moved to New England in 1644 because of his deep Puritan convictions. There he was elected to the General Court and continuously

returned for 35 years. Interested in the Indians, he wrote *Historical Collections of the Indians in New England* (1674; published 1792), a valuable early work of ethnography, and assumed the position of protector of the Praying Towns of Christianized Indians during King Philip's War (1675-76). His *An Historical Account of the Doings and Sufferings of the Christian Indians* (1677; published 1836) sought to exonerate the mission Indians from charges that they had collaborated with their pagan kinsmen during the war. In 1681 he was appointed major general of the Massachusetts militia.
See also King Philip's War; Praying Towns.

GORGES, SIR FERDINANDO (c.1568-1647) An English promoter and organizer of early colonizing efforts, Gorges, the youngest son of an aristocratic family, entered the army and was knighted for action at the siege of Rouen (1591). As the military governor of Plymouth, he became an organizer of the Virginia Company of Plymouth (1606) along with Sir John Popham. In 1607 he fitted out a colonizing expedition to the New England coast led by George Popham (cousin of Sir John) and Raleigh Gilbert (son of Sir Humphrey Gilbert); they established a post (the Sagadahoc colony) at the mouth of the Kennebec River, but ineffectual leadership, factionalism, and poor relations with the Indians led to its abandonment within a year.

In 1614 he and John Smith planned a New England colonizing expedition; Smith reconnoitered the coast, returning with a valuable cargo of fish and furs, but he was captured by the French and the plans collapsed. In 1620, Gorges led in organizing the Council for New England, from whose grants developed the colonies of Plymouth and Massachusetts, both of which were able to circumvent the authority of the council. Gorges finally succeeded in securing title to the province of Maine in 1639, which his grandson sold to Massachusetts in 1677.
See also Council for New England; Gilbert, Sir Humphrey; Smith, John.

GORTON, SAMUEL (c.1592-1677) A heterodox religious leader, Gorton was born near Gorton, England, and settled in London around 1615, making his living in the textile trade. Due to his strong religious opinions, he was eventually drawn into the camp of the Dissenters and, believing that he could find true religious toleration in America, emigrated to Boston in 1637. Gorton found, however, that he had overestimated the extent of freedom available to newcomers in the Massachusetts Bay Colony. His personal views on the nature of the Trinity, the professional clergy, and heaven and hell had little relation to orthodox Puritan doctrine, and within two months of his arrival he was accused of heresy, tried, and banished, with a similar legal process occurring in the Plymouth Colony in the following year.

Leaving with a few followers for Rhode Island, Gorton was eventually involved in land disputes with the local Indians and was arrested again in 1644 by the Massachusetts authorities and shipped in chains to England on a charge of blasphemy. In 1648, after serving a sentence at hard labor, Gorton received a letter of safe conduct back to America from the Earl of Warwick. Settling again in Rhode Island, he established the town of Warwick and became one of its leading citizens.

GOSNOLD, BARTHOLOMEW (?1572-1607)   An English captain, Gosnold in 1602 commanded an exploring expedition along the coast of New England for the Earl of Southampton. Striking the mainland near Cape Neddick, Maine, he was met by a group of Indians hailing him in English, wearing French clothing, and rowing out to meet him in a Basque shallop, all tokens of many years of contact with European fishermen who had stopped along the coast to dry their catch. Sailing south, he anchored on a sandy shore where the crew fished the abundant waters; Gosnold christened the spot Cape Cod, perhaps the first English place name in New England. Rounding the Cape, he landed at Cuttyhunk Island, where he successfully traded knives and implements for tobacco, food, and furs with the Indians. Tensions with the Indians later caused his men to refuse to maintain the fortification planned as a permanent settlement. The successful fishing and trading, however, encouraged further English exploration. Commanding the *God Speed*, he subsequently carried some of the first settlers to Jamestown, Virginia, where he died of malaria.

GRAFFENRIED, CHRISTOPHER, BARON DE   (1661-1743)   Swiss colonizer Christopher Graffenried was born in Bern of titled parents. His exploits depleted his fortune, and in 1708 he entered into a venture with Franz Ludwig Michel and Georg Ritter to bring Swiss settlers to North Carolina for mining. In 1709 he received a grant of 5,000 acres and the appointment as landgrave from the Lords Proprietors of North Carolina. By 1710 he had an option on 100,000 acres between the Neuse and Trent rivers, where he planned to establish Swiss emigrants and Palatine exiles. Half the group died on the voyage, and Graffenried had to replenish his supplies by mortgaging his land to Thomas Pollock.

Further troubles came with the revolt of the Tuscarora Indians in 1711. Graffenried was captured but succeeded in negotiating a short-lived truce. He then turned to Governor Spotswood of Virginia for aid and received a patent for land on the upper Potomac near present-day Washington.

He hoped the land would provide silver mines and a safe refuge for the settlers, but his associate Michel would not agree to uprooting the settlers for this scheme. Graffenried had no more resources, and he returned to Switzerland in 1713 to live in Bern.

GRAND PORTAGE   This nine-mile trail bypassing the falls and rapids of the Pigeon River was established in 1732 by the Sieur de La Verendrye. The Pigeon River flows into Lake Superior just south of the present Canadian boundary, so the development of the Grand Portage opened a water route to the chain of lakes extending to Lake Winnipeg and thus opened the rich fur-bearing lands of the Assiniboine and Saskatchewan to the French. The portage became a rendezvous point for Montreal traders in the late 1760s, and in 1779 the North West Company built its inland headquarters on the south bank of the Pigeon River. Claimed by the United States under the Treaty of Paris (1783), the position continued to be held by the British until 1803 when they moved the post to Kaministiquia.

GRAVIER, JACQUES (1651-1708)   A Jesuit missionary to the Illinois Indians, Jacques Gravier was born at Moulina, France, educated in Paris, and came to Canada in 1685. He worked as a missionary and aided Father Allouez in his ministry to the Miami Indians. After Allouez's death, Gravier became the vicar general of the Illinois Indians in 1689. In 1693 he baptized over 200 Indians. When the Illinois Indians moved south, Gravier followed them and recorded the tribes and plants of the river's course. He also wrote an Illinois grammar. When he returned to his mission on Lake Peoria, the Indians attacked him, and he eventually died of his wounds.

GREAT AWAKENING   A massive religious revival that swept across English America in the early 1740s, the Great Awakening dramatically altered the lives of many colonists. It also tended to break down the distinctions people perceived between various sects, thereby lessening the competition, mutual resentment, and even conflict that had marred relationships among the various Protestant denominations. The thrust of the message proclaimed by revival preachers focused on an individual's personal relationship with God; their words commonly were directed more to a listener's emotions than to her or his intellect. Their appeal thus depended little on fine points of doctrine, nor did they devote much attention to specific observational practices that defined the several Protestant groups. Indeed, the ministers most closely identified with the great revival (that is, those who attracted the largest audiences) were itinerants—preachers who carried their message from church to church and sometimes preached outdoors, unrestricted by walls that could be identified with a particular sect.

Origins of the Revival.　It is hardly surprising, then, that the Great Awakening began with the arrival of a visiting minister, George Whitefield, who came to America from England in late 1739 to raise money for an orphanage he was building in Georgia. In the decades prior to Whitefield's appearance the religious life of the colonies—overwhelmingly Protestant—seemed settled, stable, peaceful, and comfortable. New England, reflecting its Puritan roots, was largely Congregationalist, while Anglicanism was the most prevalent denomination in the South. Yet the religious fervor that had marked at least the New England colonies through the 17th century had passed by the third decade of the 18th century. Americans had overcome the uncertainties and resolved the anxieties associated with building new societies in the wilderness (which might have caused them to turn to religion) and were now more secure, more "enlightened." If in the 17th century bright and ambitious young men went to college to become ministers, increasingly in the 18th century they turned to other, secular professions.

During the decades prior to the Awakening the various Protestant sects had established formal institutional structures to coordinate their activities. The Church of England, in threatening to send a bishop to the colonies, stimulated other denominations to organize, for Congregationalists, Baptists, and Presbyterians feared that if an Anglican bishop were placed in America to unify and direct his churches, their own influence and membership might decline. While such associations did provide a setting for doctrinal disputes, organization tended to lead to formalization. For many, religion was more an intellectual exercise than an emotional experience.

As early as the 1720s, a few ministers broke out of that pattern and stirred their congregations into revivals of religious fervor. In New Jersey, Theodore Frelinghuysen's evangelical style and passionate calls for his flock to focus on faith rather than on good outward behavior "awakened" his congregation. His remarkable success led a neighboring Presbyterian minister, Gilbert Tennent, to preach in an emotional, extemporaneous, virtually spontaneous style that ignored fine points of theological doctrine and directed its message at his listeners' hearts. In the 1730s, Jonathan Edwards, preaching in Northampton, Massachusetts, aroused his congregation with sermons that made salvation and damnation visible, graphic realities.

Whitefield's Impact.　Thus, when Whitefield reached Philadelphia in November 1739 and accepted an invitation from the minister William Tennent Sr. (Gilbert's father) to undertake a tour of the Middle Colonies, the seeds for a revival had already been planted. The earlier success of Tennent, Frelinghuysen, and Edwards in awakening their congregations suggests that many colonists were "ready" to have their religious lives changed, that they were anxious to receive and respond to the emotional message Awakening preachers offered.

Prior to Whitefield's arrival, colonial newspapers had reported his evangelical accomplishments in England, where his fiery, impassioned preaching had both alienated conservative ministers and attracted thousands to hear him. During his nine days in Philadelphia, Whitefield seized the emotions of the city's residents. Benjamin Franklin remarked that "all the world [seemed to be] growing religious." Men and women were "struck pale as Death"

George Whitefield's evangelical preaching sparked the religious revival known as the Great Awakening. *(Library of Congress)*

as Whitefield described the horrors of damnation. Some fell to the ground, others screamed in anguish for God to help them.

Although an Anglican minister, Whitefield chose not to base his message on the theology or doctrine of any specific sect. His appeal, thus, was aimed at all Protestants. For a month, Whitefield toured from Philadelphia to New Jersey to New York to New England. He then headed to the South before returning to the Middle Colonies and New England. During three days in Boston more than 19,000 people came to hear him. Everywhere he went, Whitefield's words threw men and women into a religious frenzy. And reports of his accomplishments in one location only heightened the hysterical anticipation of those awaiting his arrival.

Heritage of the Awakening.

Before returning to England, Whitefield persuaded Gilbert Tennent to carry on the work by undertaking a tour of his own. Others, such as James Davenport, whose emotional excesses on the pulpit proved too outrageous even for many fellow evangelicals, followed. All over the colonies revivals were ignited, and congregations everywhere demanded that their ministers adopt the emotional preaching style that caused men and women to experience the kind of religious fervor that signified regeneration. Some who could not or would not give up the practice of delivering carefully prepared, sober, somber, theologically "correct" sermons (which had caused Whitefield to refer to them as "dead men") lost their pulpits.

Ironically, while the Awakening had a kind of unifying, homogenizing impact through its tendency to minimize doctrinal distinctions between the various Protestant sects, it simultaneously precipitated serious conflicts as not only many individual congregations but also entire denominations split into pro- and anti-revival factions. Among Congregationalists, "New Lights" opposed "Old Lights"; Presbyterians broke into "New Side" and "Old Side" groups. Antirevivalists argued that the emotionalism displayed under the impact of evangelical preaching was but a manifestation of insanity and could not be trusted as a sign of genuine salvation. Moreover, they feared that the movement undercut the authority of traditional church leaders, as it undermined the historical foundations upon which their denominations had been built.

One sect that benefited from the Awakening was the Baptists, whose observational practices had always had an emotional "flavor." The division between Presbyterians became so severe that for a time two separate synods existed, with the New Side faction founding its own college (later to emerge as Princeton University) to train pro-revival ministers. By the end of the century most such conflict had been resolved. In fact, the broad toleration of a variety of religious groups, each offering a slightly dif-

ferent approach to the same end, which has become a natural aspect of religious life in America, was encouraged by, if it did not originate in, the Great Awakening. For during the revival itinerant preachers were welcomed to conduct their ministries in churches identified with sects other than their own, members of all denominations gathering together in one place to hear and respond to the same message. Specific points of doctrine that divided the various Protestant sects were glossed over, or ignored, as preachers focused not on observational practices but rather on their listeners' feelings, emotions, and faith.

See also Edwards, Jonathan; Religion; Tennent, Gilbert; Whitefield, George.

Bibliography: Ahlstrom, Sidney E., *A Religious History of the American People* (Yale Univ. Press, 1972); Bushman, Richard, ed., *The Great Awakening* (Univ. of North Carolina Press, 1970); Gaustad, Edwin S., *The Great Awakening in New England* (1957; reprint Quadrangle, 1968); Hofstadter, Richard, *America at 1750* (Knopf, 1971).

Aaron Shatzman
Franklin and Marshall College

GREAT BASIN AND ROCKY MOUNTAIN INDIANS Because of their isolated and rugged environment, the Indians of the Great Basin and the Rocky Mountains had almost no contact with Europeans before the 19th century. In the area that is now Nevada and Utah the Paiute and Ute— peoples later derogatorily described as "Diggers"— practiced variations of a Desert Culture that had remained largely unchanged for thousands of years. They hunted small game but, more important, gathered roots and nuts, a subsistence strategy that demanded a mobile and flexible social structure and low population density. This way of life would continue until overland transport brought thousands of Americans through their country in the mid-19th century with white settlement not far behind.

To the north, the Bannock and the Shoshoni (often designated "Snake" by Americans) were able to exploit the larger fauna of the mountains. By the end of the 17th century the differences between the southern and northern groups were greatly exaggerated by the arrival of the horse in the northern regions. These animals effected a remarkable cultural transformation in the region, for with them came the rapidly developing Plains horsehunter complex with its new ritual styles, the tepee, and social organization based in mounted bands. The Nez Percé became noted breeders of the Appaloosa breed and traded horses throughout the region. Over a century before the first Europeans came to the region — with the expedition of Lewis and Clark — European contact and articles had substantially transformed the way of life of an isolated area.

See also Indians, North American.

Bibliography: Euler, Robert C., *The Paiute People* (Indian Tribal Series, 1972); Josephy, Alvin M., Jr., *The Nez Percé Indians and the Opening of the Northwest* (Yale Univ. Press, 1965); Steward, Julian H., *Basin-Plateau Aboriginal Sociopolitical Groups* (Smithsonian Institution, Bureau of American Ethnology, 1938); Wheat, Margaret M., *Survival Arts of the Primitive Paiutes* (Univ. of Nevada Press, 1967).

GREAT LAKES The Great Lakes—Ontario, Erie, Huron, Michigan, and Superior—form the largest group of lakes in the world and together form a collective body of inland water second only to the Caspian Sea. The lakes offered abundant fishing, access to the rich fur resources of the northern woods, and, at the south, access to the rich alluvial and glaciated soil of the central lowlands.

Drained by the St. Lawrence River, this system allowed the French to penetrate to the very center of the North American continent by waterway. Long blocked at Lake Ontario by the Iroquois, the French forged a canoe route via the Ottawa River to Georgian Bay and from there struck out to found posts at the strategic lake linkages of Sault Ste. Marie (1668), and Michilimackinac (1689). Later, by placing posts at Detroit (1701) and Niagara (1726), the French dominated lake transport. Low divides between the lakes and the tributaries of the Mississippi made for relatively easy transport to waters draining into the Gulf of Mexico at carrying places such as Chicago, the Fox-Wisconsin connection out of Green Bay, the St. Joseph-Maumee link from Lake Michigan to the Wabash, and the St. Mary's-Miami portage from Detroit to the Ohio. By 1730 the French had built a water transport system that formed a continuous arc about the English colonies to the east.

The British assumed control of this great waterway at the conclusion of the French and Indian War. They supplemented the French system by building shipyards and operating a great inland navy. In the Treaty of Paris (1783) the British agreed to joint control of the lakes with the United States, a mutual system tested during the naval engagements on the lakes during the War of 1812, then confirmed in the Great Lakes Disarmament Agreement of 1817.

GREAT LAW OF PENNSYLVANIA (1682) An assembly of representatives of the Delaware counties of Kent, Sussex, and New Castle and delegates of the Pennsylvania counties of Chester, Bucks, and Philadelphia convened at Chester and enacted the Great Law on December 4-7, 1682. The Chester Assembly passed an Act of Union, joining the Pennsylvania and Delaware governments, and an Act of Naturalization, extending rights of Englishmen to all Swedes, Finns, and Dutch who promised allegiance to the King and obedience to William Penn. The Great Law, an embodiment of the "Laws Agreed Upon in England," contained many principles of the Quaker religion. It defined freedom of conscience, provided for religious liberty, and afforded protection of the law and equal rights of the ballot for all religions. It also abolished oaths, limited brutal punishment, lifted the death penalty except for the crimes of murder and treason, provided for trial by jury, defined weights and measures, and outlined election procedures.

Bibliography: Soderlund, Jean R., ed., *William Penn and the Founding of Pennsylvania, 1680-1684: A Documentary History* (Univ. of Pennsylvania Press, 1983).

GREAT PLAINS INDIANS The Great Plains was the largest culture area of indigenous North America. Extending from central Canada through Texas, from the eastern slope of the Rocky Mountains to the forests of the Mississippi Valley, this huge semiarid grassland was the habitat of the American bison, or buffalo, which congregated in great summer herds that totaled some 60,000,000 at the end of the 18th century. Indigenous populations on the Great Plains established a symbiotic relationship with the bison, hunting the herds for the lean meat, the sweet fat, the pliable hides, the workable bone, horn, and hair, and in turn firing the plains to encourage the tender grasses favored by the herds.

Early Cultures. The Great Plains were generally inhospitable to all but the most simple human exploitation until a combination of environmental and technological change during the 1st millennium A.D. A moist climatic phase encouraged the extension of horticultural settlement up the valleys of the Arkansas and Missouri river systems and into the parklands along the borders of the plains. Descendants of these horticultural people in the historic era included the Mandan, Hidatsa, Arikara, Omaha, Kansa, and Missouri village peoples. Simultaneously the diffusion of the use of bow and arrow stimulated a more efficient exploitation of the buffalo, although the lack of effective transport other than the dog kept down the numbers of truly nomadic peoples. Typically, hunters moved onto the plains for summer and fall hunts, returning to horticultural base camps at the fringe of the plains for the winter.

A severe drought in the 14th century contracted the areas of horticulture and encouraged more peoples to experiment with a more nomadic way of life. The historic era of plains settlement, however, which saw scores

GREEN BAY 177

of peoples moving onto the grasslands, arrived with the coming of the horse to North America. Indians were adopting the use of horses in the Southwest as early as 1630. By the late 17th century the horse had spread from the Arkansas Valley north into present-day Kansas and Nebraska, and by 1730 horses were being traded in the north along the Saskatchewan. Horses allowed for greatly improved exploitation of the bison and for the accumulation and transportation of possessions. Horses were, in short, the key to a higher standard of living on the plains and made nomadism an attractive subsistence strategy.

18th Century Developments. Beginning in the 18th century, then, there occurred vast and historic movements of people on to the plains from all directions. From the Mississippi Valley the Assiniboine and the Sioux moved west across the Missouri River to occupy the northern plains, while the Cheyenne and Arapaho moved south and west to the western slope of the Rockies, and the Crow left the Missouri Valley to settle eastern Montana. From the south, Caddoan peoples such as the Wichita, Pawnee, and Arikara moved north to the central plains. From the Great Basin, Uto-Aztecan-speaking Comanche moved west into Texas and the Kiowa into Oklahoma. From the north, Atabascan-speaking Sarsi established themselves on the far-northern plains in Alberta. These migrations were in response to both the pull of attractive options and the push of increasing European disruptions and movements of populations to the south and east.

The Great Plains thus became home to peoples of different backgrounds, speaking several distinct languages. Yet, a common plains culture developed. Plains nomadism was predicated upon the existence of the bison herds and depended upon the use of the horse. Because mobility was essential, the most significant social unit was the band of 50 to 100 persons. Because of the need for horses, and the length of time spent breeding them, raiding and warfare became an endemic practice. On the other hand, there was a premium placed upon flexible and open social structures, and there was widespread incorporation of captives into societies with little evidence of ethnic prejudice, although there seems to have been persistent conflict between certain groups contesting for the same resources. The summer rendezvous brought hundreds, even thousands of people together, often from different ethnic groups, for the largest social occasion of the year. At these meetings trading, gambling, athletics, visiting, courting, council meetings, and ritual participation in events such as the Sun Dance took place. By the end of the colonial period plains culture had achieved a florescence that would in the 19th century present a most difficult obstacle to continued Euro-American expansion.

See also Indians, North America.

Bibliography: Ewers, John C., *The Horse in Blackfoot Indian Culture* (Smithsonian Institution, 1958); Hoebel, E. Adamson, *The Cheyennes* (Holt, Rinehart and Winston, 1978); Hundley, Norris, Jr., ed., *The American Indian* (CLIO Press, 1974); Meyer, Roy W., *The Village Indians of the Upper Missouri* (Univ. of Nebraska Press, 1977); Wedel, Waldo R., *Prehistoric Man on the Great Plains* (Univ. of Oklahoma Press, 1961).

Richard L. Haan
Hartwick College

GREAT TRADING AND WAR PATH Perhaps the best known trail in colonial America, this ancient Indian route ran down the Valley of Virginia along the western slope of the Blue Ridge. Among the colonists it became known as the Great Road of the Valley. At its northern end, on the Potomac River at Wadkin's Ferry, it connected to the rich farming country of southeastern Pennsylvania via the Philadelphia Road, in use by traders as early as 1700. At its southern end, on the Holston River (Tennessee), it forked in several directions. To the southeast, it went down the Watauga and Yadkin rivers to the Catawba Indian villages, later the backcountry Carolina settlements. To the southwest, it followed the Holston down to the Cherokee towns, later to the eastern settlements of Tennessee. In the west, it went over the Cumberland Gap into Kentucky, where it connected with the Scioto Path, running farther north to Fort Sandusky on Lake Erie. The section over the Cumberland Gap and a fork northwest into Kentucky became known as the Wilderness Road.

See also Cumberland Gap; Roads and Trails; Wilderness Road.

GREEN, ANNE CATHERINE HOOF (c.1720-75) The official printer to the Province of Maryland from 1767 to 1775, she was probably born in Holland and brought to Pennsylvania as a child. In 1738 she married Jonas Green, a printer from Boston. They moved to Annapolis, Maryland, where Jonas was named printer to the province and was responsible for publishing the laws of the colony and the votes and proceedings of the assembly. In 1745 he began publishing the *Maryland Gazette*, the only newspaper in Maryland until 1773. When Jonas died in 1767, Anne took over both jobs. She published the newspaper during the crucial years preceding the Revolution, carrying stores of colonial protests despite her official appointment. Following her death in 1775, her son Frederick took over the printing business.

GREEN BAY When the French built Fort St. François Xavier in 1684 at the place they called "La Baye" it was the first European settlement west of Lake Michigan. By the early 18th century, Green Bay had become a mercantile center for the upper Mississippi fur trade, and like other French trading towns was characterized by a great deal of mixing among traders, trappers, and Indians. When the English arrived in 1761, most of the residents were métis, or mixedbloods, and the process of mixing continued into the 19th century. Green Bay flourished and remained in British hands until 1816.

Nathanael Greene's greatest triumphs came in the South, where he outmaneuvered General Cornwallis. *(Library of Congress)*

GREENE, NATHANAEL (1742-86) One of the most brilliant American generals in the Revolutionary War, Greene was born in Warwick, Rhode Island. He became the youngest brigadier general in the Continental army when he was named Commander of the Rhode Island brigade sent to the siege of Boston (1775). At Boston, Greene for the first time served with George Washington, who sent him to defend New York (1776) against the British. Greene did not fight in the Battle of Long Island (August 1776) because of a fever, but he commanded American troops in New Jersey. Although he urged the takeover of Fort Washington on Manhattan Island, the British captured the fort (November 1776). Greene then commanded one of the two columns in an attack against Trenton (December 1776). Congress next sent Greene to Philadelphia to help stop the British at Brandywine (1777). Greene was made quarter-master general (1778), and his successful efforts ensured that Americans would not go through another experience similar to the winter at Valley Forge.

He was then appointed by Washington to command American operations in the South (1780), succeeding Horatio Gates. Greene exercised remarkable leadership, inflicting heavy losses on General Cornwallis at Guilford Courthouse (March 1781) and restricting British control in South Carolina to the Charleston area. He returned to Rhode Island a hero (1783) and then retired near Savannah, Georgia (1785).

See also Revolutionary War Battles.

GREEN MOUNTAIN BOYS The Green Mountain Boys, a band of Vermont settlers who achieved fame in the early stages of the Revolutionary War, were members of an informal group organized to defend land claims. After Governor Benning Wentworth of New Hampshire began (1749) to grant lands west of the Connecticut River in what is now Vermont to settlers, New York asserted its claim to the area. After the Crown gave New York jurisdiction (1764) and after the New York supreme court said that the early grants were invalid (1770), irate Vermonters organized military companies to defend their claims. Ethan Allen was elected the commander of the Green Mountain Boys, who terrorized New York settlers in Vermont and ignored New York officials. The British government refused to intervene and directed New York to suspend land grants until the dispute ended.

As the Revolutionary War neared, the Green Mountain Boys sided with the patriot cause and helped in the capture of Fort Ticonderoga in May 1775. They raised a separate regiment and were influential in the British defeat in the Battle of Bennington (1777). Led by Ethan's brother Ira Allen, Thomas Chittenden, and others, Vermont declared itself an independent republic (1777). By 1791, New York had dropped its claim to Vermont, which was admitted to the union.

See also Allen, Ethan.

GRENVILLE, GEORGE (1712-70) A British government official, Grenville introduced tax policies that caused anger and unrest among the colonists. Born into a prominent family, he first entered Parliament in 1741 and often held ministerial posts. As prime minister, first lord of the treasury and chancellor of the exchequer (1763-65), Grenville wanted to relieve the burdens of British taxpayers by imposing colonial tax programs. He proposed that Americans should pay the costs of maintaining British troops that defended the colonies in North America. He introduced the Sugar Act (1764) and the Stamp Act (1765). After leaving office in 1765, he strongly defended his policies, voting against the repeal of the Stamp Act.

GRENVILLE, SIR RICHARD (?1541-91) A naval commander and leader of the first English colony in North

Later views romanticized the capture of Fort Ticonderoga by Ethan Allen's Green Mountain Boys in 1775. *(National Portrait Gallery)*

America, Grenville was the son of a distinguished Cornish family. As a young man he fought against the Turks, was knighted, sat in Parliament, and served briefly as sheriff of Cornwall. In association with Sir Humphrey Gilbert, and representing the interests of his cousin Sir Walter Raleigh, he commanded a fleet of seven ships that sailed for Virginia in 1585, remaining in America only long enough to settle the colony before returning. He sailed again with supplies in 1586, only to find that the colony had already been abandoned. He was active in the naval campaigns against the Spanish, dying during a battle off the Azores.

GROSEILLIERS, MÉDART CHOUART, SIEUR DE (?1625-97?) This great explorer of the western Great Lakes first came to French Canada in the late 1630s as an assistant to the Jesuit mission among the Huron. After the destruction of the mission by the Iroquois in the late 1640s, he formed a fur-trading partnership with his brother-in-law Pierre Radisson, and they explored lakes Michigan and Superior in 1654 and 1659. Groseilliers was one of the first to suspect that the lakes could be connected, by short portages, to the great Mississippi River system, thus connecting the French empire of the north to the Gulf of Mexico in the south. After a successful fur-trading expedition, the furs of the two men were confiscated by the French authorities in 1660, and in anger Groseilliers and Radisson entered the service of the English, for whom they opened the trade into Hudson Bay that became the basis of the Hudson's Bay Company. In 1670, however, unhappy with the English reluctance to explore the interior, Groseilliers returned to French allegiance and settled in Canada.

GUADALAJARA, DIEGO DE (flourished 1654) In 1654, Guadalajara was sent into western Texas to follow up the explorations of Hernando Martín and Diego del Castillo. In 1650, Martín and Castillo brought back pearls from the Nueces River and tales of a tribe of Indians called the Tejas who were ruled by a king. Guadalajara reached the Jumano

Indians, with whom the Spanish maintained friendly relations, then continued 30 leagues farther. At that point the Spanish were met by the Cuitao Indians, whom they defeated, taking 200 prisoners and many furs. Guadalajara then returned to El Paso in triumph.

GWINNETT, BUTTON (?1735-77) A public official and signer of the Declaration of Independence, Gwinnett was born in Gloucestershire, England. He immigrated to a large plantation on St. Catherine's Island, Georgia (1765) and became involved in local politics. He served a term in the Assembly (1769) and was a delegate to the Second Continental Congress (1776), where he signed the Declaration of Independence. The same year he was a speaker at the Georgia assembly, supporting the drafting of a state constitution. In 1777 he was named president of Georgia and put in command of the civil militia. A dispute between Gwinnett and a military commander over who was responsible for the failure of an expedition against British posts in Florida led to a duel in which Gwinnett was mortally wounded.

H

HABERSHAM, JAMES (1712-75) A businessman and colonial administrator, he was born in England and came to Georgia in 1738. With his friend George Whitefield he established the Bethesda Orphanage and was in complete charge of it by 1741. In 1744 he turned to business, organizing a large trading firm. He also invested in land and, eventually, after fighting for laws to allow slavery in Georgia (passed in 1749), he planted extensive rice fields. In 1754 he was councillor and secretary of the province. He presided over the upper house of the General Assembly in 1767, and from 1771 to 1773 he was acting governor.

HAKLUYT, RICHARD (?1552-1616) An English historian of exploration, Hakluyt developed his interests in geography under the tutelage of his guardian-cousin, Richard Hakluyt the Elder. Trained and ordained a minister in the Church of England, Hakluyt served in the 1580s as chaplain to the English ambassador in Paris, where he learned about the explorations of the European powers. In 1584 he wrote the unpublished state paper, "A Discourse of Western Planting," in which he made a powerful argument for English exploration and colonization in the Western Hemisphere as a part of the search for a Northwest Passage. In order to further stimulate his countrymen to undertake a systematic program of colonization he then turned to the collection and publication of accounts of exploration and travel. *The Principall Navigations, Voiages and Discoveries of the English Nation,* which included not only English accounts but those of foreign explorers as well, was published in three volumes in 1598-1600 and has continued to be the most important collection of exploration documents extant.

HALE, NATHAN (1755-76) Revolutionary War soldier and a martyr to American Independence, Hale was born in Coventry, Connecticut. He graduated from Yale (1773) and taught school until the Revolution broke out and he was commissioned in the Connecticut militia (1775). Soon after, he joined the Continental Army and helped in the siege of Boston. In 1776 he was promoted to captain and served in the defense of New York City. Tradition claims that he was one of a small, daring band who captured a provision sloop underneath the guns of a British man-of-war. In September 1776 he volunteered to undertake a mission behind British lines on Long Island to obtain military information. He was captured by the British while disguised as a Dutch school teacher, and brought before General Sir William Howe, who ordered him to be hanged the next day. Standing on the gallows before his execution, he reportedly made a short speech that he concluded by saying, "I only regret that I have but one life to lose for my country."

HALLAM, LEWIS, JR. (c.1740-1808) An actor and theatrical manager, Hallam made his American debut in 1752 with his parents in *The Merchant of Venice* at Williamsburg, Virginia. This performance at the age of 12 as a servant to his mother's Portia ended in tears, but as he matured he became the company's leading actor, played the first American Hamlet, the hero in the first American play (1767), *The Prince of Parthia* by Thomas Godfrey, and was a virtuoso in tragedy, comedy, and pantomine. Hallam left the North American colonies during the Revolutionary War, but by 1785 he had reestablished the company, only to clash with a succession of partners, including William Dunlap in 1796. In 1806 he lost his contract but continued his "final" performances until his death in Philadelphia.

HALLAM, MRS. LEWIS (died c.1774) A Shakespearean actress, Mrs. Hallam came to America in 1752 to form with her actor husband Lewis and their son Lewis Jr. a new company under the auspice of Lewis's brother, William Hallam. Their opening in *The Merchant of Venice* at Williamsburg, Virginia, established their reputation. In 1754 the company went to Jamaica, where the elder Lewis died. Mrs. Lewis married the actor David Douglass, who brought the reorganized American company back to the Northern colonies in 1758. Her most famous roles were Desdemona, Cordelia, Portia, Jane Shore, and even Juliet to her son's Romeo.

HALL, LYMAN (1724-90) A signer of the Declaration of Independence, Hall was born in Wallingford, Connecticut. He was ordained by Fairfield West Consociation (1749) but was dismissed after he was charged with immoral conduct (1751). He subsequently studied medicine and practiced in Wallingford. Hall joined a group of New England Congregationalists, and they migrated to Georgia and founded Sunbury (1758), where Hall became the leader of St. John's Parish. It became the largest Puritan organization for the Revolutionary cause. The parish elected Hall a delegate to the Second Continental Congress (1775-80), and he signed the Declaration of Independence. After the Revolution, Hall lived in Savannah, whence he continued to practice medicine. He later served as governor of Georgia (1783).

A trusted aide of George Washington, Alexander Hamilton rose to great prominence after the war, particularly as a supporter of the Constitution. *(Library of Congress)*

HAMILTON, ALEXANDER (?1755-1804)   The statesman Hamilton, born in the British West Indies, went to the mainland in 1772 and soon entered King's College (Columbia). He became involved in Revolutionary politics, precociously writing pamphlets in support of the American cause. In the army by 1776, he then became George Washington's aide-de-camp (1777). Hamilton quickly demonstrated a grasp of military and political affairs, developing a characteristic preference for a strong, vigorous, and "high-toned" central government. In 1781, Hamilton left Washington's service but took part in the Yorktown campaign before leaving the army. Soon afterward, he started a legal practice and went to the Continental Congress as a New York delegate (1782-83); later in the decade he sat in the state legislature and once again in Congress.

During the mid-1780s, Hamilton continued to show a distaste for what he saw as defects in the Confederation's government and finances. In 1786 he took part in the decision of the Annapolis Convention to recommend a constitutional convention. New York appointed him one of its delegates to the convention in Philadelphia, where he took a strongly nationalist stand (1787). Later he played a key role in the struggle for the ratification of the new Constitution as one of the three authors of The Federalist (1787-88), a series of 85 essays of which Hamilton wrote 50, and as a leader of the pro-ratification forces in the New York convention (1788). Hamilton had an outstanding later career as first U.S. Secretary of the Treasury (1789-95). He died in a duel with long-time political enemy Aaron Burr on July 12, 1804.

See also Annapolis Convention; Burr, Aaron.

Bibliography: Cooke, Jacob E., *Alexander Hamilton* (Scribner's, 1982).

Douglas M. Arnold
The Papers of Benjamin Franklin

HAMILTON, ANDREW (1676-1741)   Public official and lawyer, who defended John Peter Zenger. Having come to Accomac County, Virginia, late in the 17th century, Hamilton married Anne (Brown) Preeson in 1706, established valuable connections in Maryland, built his law practice, and served in the Maryland Assembly. Later he moved to Philadelphia and was appointed attorney general of Pennsylvania in 1717. For his work, the Penns granted him a 153-acre estate in Philadelphia, where he became recorder of the city of Philadelphia and prothonotary of the supreme court. From 1727, he represented Bucks County in the Pennsylvania Assembly for 12 years, 9 of them as speaker. In 1737 he was appointed judge of the vice admiralty court.

Hamilton is best known for his successful defense of John Peter Zenger, printer of the New York *Weekly Journal*, against a charge of seditious libel. In April 1735, after Zenger's counsel was disbarred, Hamilton argued to the jury and public opinion the need for liberty of the press to expose arbitrary government. He convinced the jury to rule on the truth of the articles printed: if accurate, then acquit Zenger. Zenger was freed, and Hamilton was presented the key to New York City in a gold box. He died in 1741, a champion of "the rights of mankind and the liberty of the press."

HAMMON, JUPITER (1711-c.1806)   Preacher, essayist, poet, lifelong clerk on his owner's Long Island estate, Hammon was the first black American to appear in print. His *An Evening Thought: Salvation by Christ was Penetential Cries* (1760), a broadside for Christmas Day, arranges the "common measure" of the hymns in call-and-response couplets. The verse "Address to Miss Phillis Wheatley" (1778), the essay *A Winter Piece* (1782), published with three poems, and the sermon *An Evening's Improvement* (c.1783), published with a dialogue between master and slave, all deal with issues of slavery and Christianity. His *Address to the Negroes of the State of New York* (1787) was reprinted in 1806 by local Quakers as a memorial to the poet.

Bibliography: Ramsom, Stanley Austin Jr., ed., *America's First Negro Poet: The Complete Work of Jupiter Hammon of Long Island* (Kennikat, 1970).

A leader of the Massachusetts patriots, John Hancock was the first to sign the Declaration of Independence. *(Library of Congress)*

HANCOCK, JOHN (1737-93)   A merchant, public official, and first signer of the Declaration of Independence, Hancock was born in Braintree (now Quincy), Massachusetts. He graduated from Harvard (1754) and inherited his uncle's mercantile business and a large estate 10 years later. He sided with the patriot cause and protested and evaded the Stamp Act of 1765 by smuggling. He was elected to the Massachusetts General Court after the British seized one of his ships, the *Liberty*, in 1769 and remained a member until 1774. As a result of the Boston Massacre, the Boston town committee was formed, and Hancock was made the chairman. Hancock became the president of the first and second Provincial Congresses (1774-75). He was one of the rebels expected to be captured by General Thomas Gage, and fled with Samuel

Adams for Lexington, and then to Philadelphia (1775). He became a delegate to the Continental Congress, serving as president for the first two years. As president he was the first person to sign the Declaration of Independence. Hancock had limited military abilities but was very disappointed when he was denied command of the Continental Army, a position he greatly desired. He served in the convention to draft the Massachusetts constitution, and was elected the state's first governor (1780). He was the governor until he was elected to Congress (1785), and returned to the governorship two years later. Hancock played a key role in Massachusetts' ratification of the U.S. Constitution (1788) and died in his ninth term as governor.

HARD LABOR CREEK, TREATY OF (1768)   This was an agreement made on October 14, 1768, between the colony of Virginia and the Cherokee nation marking the boundaries of permitted British colonization. By the mid-1760s, many Virginia colonists had settled within the territory of the Cherokee, and the governor of Virginia, Lord Shelburne, convened a conference at Hard Labor, South Carolina, to ratify this new status quo. Under the supervision of the Virginia negotiator, Commissioner of Indian Affairs John Stuart, a new line was drawn, but this agreement proved to be only temporary. Continuing colonization pressure on this territory forced the repeated redrawing of the line and eventual relocation of the Cherokee.

HARIOT, THOMAS (1560-1621)   The first Englishman to embark upon a critical examination of the flora and fauna of North America, Hariot was an accomplished mathematician and astronomer and professor at Oxford. He was persuaded by Sir Walter Raleigh to join Richard Grenville's ill-fated attempt to plant a colony on Roanoke Island in 1585. He published the results of his observations in *A Briefe and True Report of the New Found Land of Virginia* (1588), the first English book on the first English colony in North America. His companion in this venture, John White, produced the original watercolors of the accompanying illustrations.

HARPE, BERNARD DE LA (flourished 1717-22)   Mapper of the Arkansas River, Harpe explored the Red River in 1717 and the Arkansas River in 1721. In 1717 the governor of Louisiana, Jean Baptiste Le Moyne, sent him on an exploring trip from Natchitoches up the Red River. He reached the Wichita Mountains and followed the Arkansas River back to the Mississippi. In 1722 he made his camp on a small rock formation visible from the river. He is credited with naming his campsite Little Rock, a name also adopted by the town that sprang up around the rock.

HARRIS, BENJAMIN (c.1673-1716) Bookseller, author, and first American printer, Benjamin Harris spent eight years in the colonies (1686-95). Harris left England because his outspoken Protestant tracts had brought public censure and imprisonment. His first and last publications in Boston were editions of John Tulley's *Almanach*. Because of his publications, such as the influential *New England Primer*, his London Coffee House bookshop became the meeting place of Puritan scholars, including Cotton Mather. In 1690, Harris published the first newspaper printed in America, *Publick Occurrences Both Forreign and Domestick*. The newspaper, notable for concentration on American news, was suppressed by the royal governor for creating "much distaste because not Licensed." In spite of his strong Protestant bias, Harris became the governor's official printer for a year in 1692. During his Boston period, he outsold his rivals, formed a partnership with John Allen, and published 10 books. His later quarrels in London with fellow writers inspired Jonathan Swift's *Bickerstaff Papers*.

HARRISON, PETER (1716-75) An American architect, he was born in England and came to Newport, Rhode Island, in 1740. He worked at farming and was in the trading business with his brother Joseph. He also drew maps of the area in 1745 and helped to strengthen Newport against attack in 1746. He designed the Redwood Library in Newport (1748-50), King's Chapel in Boston (1749-54), the Brick Market in Newport (1761), Christ Church in Cambridge, Massachusetts (1761), and the Synagogue in Newport (1762-63). In 1761 he moved to New Haven with his family and served as customs collector from 1768.

HART, NANCY (?1735-1830) A Revolutionary heroine, Nancy Hart was said to wield a rifle with an aim as true as any man's in all of Georgia. She and her husband Benjamin moved to Georgia in 1771, where they were embroiled in the civil strife between Whigs and Tories. Her hatred of Tories is exemplified by the celebrated anecdote of the time that five of them appeared at her home demanding supper. She filled them with whiskey, grabbed one of their rifles and shot one, holding the others hostage. The mother of eight children, Nancy Hart was reputed to have been illiterate and of generally crude manners.

HARTFORD A city on the Connecticut River, it was established in 1635-36 by a group from the Massachusetts Bay Colony led by Thomas Hooker. Hartford was first named "New Towne," after the hometown of the migrants (the modern Cambridge, Massachusetts). The founding of Hartford and the towns of Windsor and Wethersfield began a westward colonial movement. In 1639, Hartford was incorporated into the Colony of Connecticut and was granted a royal charter in 1662. In 1687, during the rule of Governor Edmund Andros, that charter was hidden in the city's legendary Charter Oak. From 1701, Hartford served as the capital of Connecticut, at first jointly with New Haven.

HART, JOHN (?1711-79) A legislator and a signer of the Declaration of Independence, Hart was born in Stonington, Connecticut, and later moved to New Jersey. A farmer and mill owner, Hart was appointed justice of peace of Hunterdon County (1775 and 1761) and was elected to the state assembly (1761-71). He opposed the Stamp Act (1765) and giving provisions to royal troops in New Jersey. While judge of the court of common pleas (1774), he served in the provincial congress of New Jersey (1774-76). In 1776, he was sent to the Second Continental Congress and became its vice president and signed the Declaration of Independence.

HARTFORD, TREATY OF (1650) An agreement between New Netherland and the United Colonies of New England, the Treaty of Hartford addressed the question of trade conflicts and determined the territorial boundaries between the two colonial entities. In order to resolve lingering disputes, Peter Stuyvesant, Governor of New Netherland, traveled to Hartford and met with commissioners of the United Colonies of New England. Although the main commercial issues remained unresolved, the Dutch and the English agreed to establish a formal boundary between them on Long Island at Oyster Bay and on the mainland at Greenwich. This treaty remained in effect until the conquest of New Netherland in 1664.

HARVARD UNIVERSITY The oldest college in America, Harvard was founded in 1636 at Cambridge, Massachusetts with a grant of 400 pounds from the Massachusetts General Court to foster the rigorous Puritan scholasticism. Its name is from John Harvard's gift of half his property and all of his library. Nathaniel Eaton gave up the presidency to Henry Dunster, who established the charter in 1650 of two governing bodies, a corporation of the president and five fellows and a board of overseers. This charter was suspended from 1686 during Increase Mather's presidency (1685-1701) to 1707. By 1780, Harvard was a university and added a medical school in 1782 and a law school in 1815.

HARVIE (HARVEY), JOHN (1742-1807) Patriot and member of the Continental Congress, John Harvie was born in Albemarle, Virginia, son of the Scotch immigrant, John Harvie (1706-67), who was the guardian of Thomas Jefferson. Trained as a lawyer, the son was appointed to the Virginia conventions of 1775 and 1776 and to the

Continental Congress in 1776 to represent Indian affairs. He signed the Articles of Confederation and, as a militia officer, helped organize the Continental Army's supplies in 1778. He resigned from the Congress in 1778 and turned his talents to serving Richmond in the land office and as its mayor (1785-86).

HASENCLEVER, PETER (1716-93)   Ironmaster, born in Remscheid, Prussia, son of a merchant and iron manufacturer, Hasenclever began his apprenticeship in a local steel mill in 1730. In 1732 he completed his training in Liege, Belgium. After establishing a trading partnership in Lisbon he immigrated to England, where he became a naturalized subject in 1764. Backed by a British firm he established several iron mills in Morris County, New Jersey, in 1764. Unexpected financial problems, however, resulted in his dismissal and replacement by John Faesch. In 1773, Hasenclever returned to Prussia and supervised the iron works at Landshut until his death.

See also Faesch, John Jacob.

HAT ACT (1732)   The Hat Act was one of a series of measures passed by Parliament and designed to protect the industrial economy of Britain through mercantilist trade sanctions. Already feeling the adverse effects of French competition in the hat industry, and fearing even more competition from the American colonies, Parliament decreed that hats produced in America could not be exported from one colony to another and that all American hatmakers must serve a seven-year apprenticeship before being licensed to practice their trade. In addition, no hatmaker would be permitted to train more than two apprentices at any one time, and blacks were barred from the industry.

HAWAII   The Sandwich Islands, as this group of eight large and dozens of small islands in the central Pacific was christened by the first European visitor of record, English Captain James Cook, in 1778, lie some 2,400 miles west of the California coast. They were first populated by voyagers from Polynesia as early as 800 A.D. By the time of Cook's landing, Polynesians had inhabited seven of the largest islands and had developed a horticultural society as well as a system of native kingship. On a return visit in 1779, Cook was killed in a battle with the Hawaiians, but his voyage opened the way to the further use of the islands by English ships, as well as visits by scientists and collectors. They remained largely isolated, however, until the coming of American merchants, missionaries, and whalers in the early 19th century.

See also Cook, James.

HAYNES, JOHN (?1594-1654)   Governor of Massachusetts and of Connecticut, Haynes was born in Essex. In 1633 he sailed with John Cotton and Thomas Hooker on the *Griffin* to Massachusetts, where he was an officer for Newtown (Cambridge). Governor of Massachusetts in 1635, he refused a salary but approved Roger Williams's exile. After he moved to Hartford in 1637 he improved Indian relations and signed a treaty with the Narragansett and Mohican in 1638. In 1639 he became the first governor of Connecticut, an office he held for every alternate year until his death. He worked to unite New England and represented Connecticut in the New England Confederation in 1646 and 1650.

HAZARD, EBENEZER (1744-1817)   Editor, scholar, and first postmaster general of the United States (1782-89), Hazard was born in Philadelphia and graduated from the College of New Jersey (Princeton) in 1762. Appointed surveyor-general of the Post Office in 1776, he traveled extensively and assisted in the extension and improvement of mail delivery. As postmaster general during the difficult Confederation period he withstood the pressures of competing states, and under his guidance the system was self-supporting. In the 1790s he published one of the first, and still valuable, collections of American historical documents.

HEADRIGHT   A grant of land, usually 50 acres, by a colonial government to any man who paid his own or another's transportation costs to the colony, the headright was awarded by many of the colonies in the 17th century. It was most common, however, in Virginia (where the system was instituted in 1618), Maryland, the Carolinas, and Georgia, where headrights were granted in conjunction with the importation of indentured servants or slaves and thus played a key role in the development of a large-scale plantation economy. By the late 17th century the system had become notably corrupt, with planters claiming headrights each time they reentered the colony from abroad and ships' captains claiming grants for each member of their crews. In the 18th century headrights were replaced by the direct sale of land.

HEARNE, SAMUEL (1745-92)   The first European to reach the Arctic by land across Canada, Hearne as a young man joined the Hudson's Bay Company and was stationed at Fort Churchill, at the mouth of the Churchill River on Hudson Bay. From there, in the early 1770s, he explored the frozen lands to the north, traveling with Indian guides. In his journals, he provided the first extensive account of the Arctic landscape and the lives of the Eskimos. In 1774 he supervised the construction of Cumberland House, the Company's first interior post, designed to compete with the expansion of the aggressive North West Company. In 1782 he was captured by a French naval officer and taken to France, where he was released, then returned to Canada. He died after ill health forced his retirement.

See also Hudson's Bay Company.

HEATHCOTE, CALEB (1666-1721)   New York merchant, landed proprietor and bureaucrat, Heathcote was from a politically accomplished English family and immigrated to New York in 1692. Appointed the same year to the royal council, he served in a variety of military, legislative, and judicial offices in the course of his career. After establishing himself as a successful New York City merchant, he moved to Westchester County (1696). There he helped found the borough of Westchester, which he served as mayor throughout the rest of his life. He acquired extensive tracts of land in Westchester, Ulster, and Richmond counties as well as in New York City itself, and in 1701 received a patent for the Manor of Scarsdale, the last manorial grant in the British Empire. A devoted member of the Anglican Church, Heathcote promoted its establishment throughout the province.

Heathcote's most important imperial service was as collector and receiver general, in which capacity he oversaw the customs service for New York. In 1715 the Crown appointed him surveyor-general for the Northern Department, comprising all of Britain's colonies north of the Delaware River. Frustrated by Rhode Island and Connecticut's defiance of customs regulations, he recommended a variety of policies to curb their independence and improve the efficiency of imperial administration. Although his proposals were not implemented, they reflect the emergence in the early 18th century of an increasingly complex colonial bureaucracy with important connections in America and Britain.

HECETA, BRUNO (1751-1807)   As commander of the schooner Santiago, Heceta was sent out in 1775 by the viceroy of New Spain to explore the Pacific coast of North America. Heceta's expedition was part of the effort by the Spanish to strengthen their claims to the area in the face of growing Russian power. With his subordinate, Juan de la Bodega y Quadra, Heceta sailed north. Bodega and Heceta separated at Bodega Bay, and Heceta went on to discover Trinidad Bay and the mouth of the Columbia River, which he at first thought was the western entrance of the Northwest Passage. Heceta reached as far north as Nootka,

on Vancouver Island, before returning south. He was then transferred to the Philippines.

HECK, BARBARA RUCKLE (1734-1804)   Born in Ireland, Heck is known as the "Mother of Methodism in America." After coming to New York in 1760 with other Irish Methodists, she was distressed at their loss of religious fervor. During a card game in 1766 she is said to have swept the cards from the table, denouncing all the players. This event caused her to go to the home of Philip Embury, a preacher originally from Ireland, to declare, "Philip, you must preach to us, or we shall all go to Hell, and God will require our blood at your hands!" This incident marked the inception of the Wesleyan movement, and Heck planned the building of the first Wesleyan chapel in America.

HECKWELDER, JOHN GOTTLIEB   (1743-1823)   Heckwelder, a Moravian missionary to the Indians of Ohio, emigrated from his native England in 1754 and by the close of the French and Indian War was serving as a Moravian messenger to the frontier Indians. From 1771 to 1786 he worked as an assistant to David Zeisberger, living among the Christian Delawares and helping in their removal to Ohio and Canada. In 1792-93 he helped arrange treaties concluding hostilities in the Northwest. His two books, summarizing his experiences, strongly influenced many Americans, including James Fenimore Cooper, who drew on them in constructing his *Leatherstocking Tales.*

See also Zeisberger, David.

HENDAY, ANTHONY (flourished 1750-62)   The first European explorer of western Canada, a native of the Isle of Wight, Henday joined the Hudson's Bay Company and came to America in 1750. When, goaded by French explorations, the Company decided to explore the potential of the western country in 1754, Henday volunteered. Accompanied by a large party of Cree Indians, he traveled by canoe southwest to the Saskatchewan River, where he was met and threatened by a group of French traders. Striking out over the prairies, he traded with Plains Indians (perhaps Assiniboine or Blackfoot), providing one of the first written descriptions of the horse and buffalo culture of the Great Plains. Moving within sight of the Rockies, the party wintered and returned the next year. Henday had been farther west than any other European and provided valuable information about the Indians and the French posts of the interior, thus making possible the opening of the western British fur trade. He made another western trip in

1759 but, failing promotion, left the Company's service two years later.

HENDERSON, RICHARD (1735-85) A North Carolina lawyer, jurist, and land speculator, Henderson organized a company for the exploitation of western lands in 1769 and hired Daniel Boone as its agent. In 1774, Henderson organized the Transylvania Company, negotiating an illegal cession from the Cherokee of what would become most of Kentucky, and then established the first settlement of his projected colony at Boonesborough. The objections of Virginia and North Carolina to this infringement of their colonial grants ended his scheme. In 1780 he founded the settlement at French Lick, later Nashville, Tennessee.

See also Transylvania Company.

HENDRICK (c.1680-1755) The Iroquois chief Hendrick, also known as Tiyanoga, was an important British ally among the Iroquois. Always a friend of British traders and colonists, Hendrick was taken to England in 1710, where he was formally presented to Queen Anne. Returning to America as "King Hendrick," he attempted to limit French influence among his people. In 1751 he met with Jonathan Edwards to discuss a large-scale settlement of Iroquois at Stockbridge, Massachusetts, and in 1754, at the Albany Congress, he urged the British to wage open war on the French. Hendrick was killed in battle during William Johnson's expedition, soon after the victory over the French at Lake George.

HENNEPIN, LOUIS (1640-c.1701) A Recollect friar and author, Louis Hennepin was born in Ath in the Flemish province of Hainaut. Baptized as Johannes, he changed his name when he joined the order. He traveled widely before he journeyed to Canada in 1675 with La Salle, who requested his services at Fort Frontenac on Lake Ontario. In 1679 he accompanied La Salle on the *Griffon* through the Great Lakes and Illinois country, where Hennepin named Lake St. Claire. When the party was captured by the Sioux Indians, Duluth rescued Hennepin and took him to Canada. In 1682, Hennepin returned to France and wrote the first description of Niagara Falls and his explorations with La Salle in *Description de la Louisiane* (1683). In later books, he gave himself the credit for discovering the Mississippi. He was eventually exiled from France and lived the rest of his life abroad.

HENRY, PATRICK (1736-99) An outstanding orator and a leader of the American Revolution, Henry was born in Hanover County, Virginia. After failing as a store owner, he became a lawyer (1760) and achieved a good

reputation. In the Parson's Cause case, Henry was the defense attorney and argued that since the king had disallowed a Virginia law, he had violated the compact between ruler and ruled, and therefore, he had forfeited his claims to obedience.

Patrick Henry's initial opposition to complete independence from Britain tarnished the status he had achieved through early speeches calling for liberty. *(Library of Congress)*

Henry entered the House of Burgesses (1765), where he vividly protested against British tyranny while introducing radical resolutions against the Stamp Act that led to great personal popularity. He was a delegate to the First and Second Continental Congresses (1774-76) and a member of Virginia's first Committee of Correspondence. When Governor Dunmore dissolved the House of Burgesses (1775) Henry led a Virginia Convention in its place and resolved to arm and train a militia, declaring "Give me liberty or give me death." Although Henry felt that war with Britain might be necessary, he opposed (1776) complete independence. This stance cost him a national leadership role. In Virginia he helped draft the state's constitution and was elected governor (1776-79, 1784-86). He opposed the Constitutional Convention (1787) and led the opposition against ratification of the Constitution in Virginia. Henry began a campaign that helped adopt the

10 amendments comprising the Bill of Rights. Subsequently, Henry gradually withdrew from politics. George Washington asked him to run for the state legislature as a Federalist in order to oppose the Kentucky and Virginia resolves (1799), and he was elected, but died at his estate in Charlotte County before taking office.

HENRY, WILLIAM (1729-86) Gunsmith and scientist, born in Chester County, Pennsylvania, Henry received no formal schooling but was apprenticed to the gunsmith Matthew Roesser in Lancaster in 1744. In 1750 he formed a partnership with Joseph Simon and produced rifles of exceptional accuracy. During the French and Indian War, Henry served as a government armorer. Deeply interested in the natural sciences, he carried out important experiments with steam power and provided assistance to Robert Fulton. He was elected to the American Philosophical Society in 1768. He supplied arms to the Continental Army and served in the Continental Congress from 1784 to 1786.

HENRY THE NAVIGATOR (1394-1460) This Portuguese promoter of navigation and exploration was the third son of King John I of Portugal. After winning a victory over the Muslims in northern Morocco in 1415, he was appointed governor of the southernmost province of Portugal by his father and used revenues of the province to establish a school of oceanography at Sagres. There scientists, shipbuilders, and mapmakers, many of them Jewish, made great advances in knowledge, including the development of the caravel. There Henry also forged a comprehensive program of exploration in order to capture the African gold trade and locate the mythical Christian kingdom of Prester John.

His program first took ships westward into the Atlantic, where the Madeiras were rediscovered (1419) and then colonized (1425). In 1427 the Azores, a group of islands yet farther west, were explored and settled. Meanwhile, other ships under his sponsorship were coasting southward along Africa. In 1434 they rounded Cape Bojador, the traditional southern limit of the Atlantic, and in 1441 reached Cape Blanco, from where his captains began to bring home African slaves, marking the beginning of the modern slave trade. The exploration of Cape Verde, the Guinea coast, the Cape Verde Islands, and Sierra Leone from the mid-1440s to the early 1460s was marked by the frantic search for gold and slaves that from that time forward characterized European exploration. Although Henry himself never went to sea, he is generally acknowledged to be the founder of the modern age of exploration.

See also Exploration.

John Mack Faragher
Mount Holyoke College

HERJULFSON, BJARNI (flourished 980s) The Norse discoverer of North America, Herjulfson was blown off course while sailing from Iceland to Greenland in 985 with the colonizing party of Eric the Red. Driven far to the southwest, Herjulfson made landfall at three distinct coastal landscapes—two heavily wooded, the northernmost mountainous and glaciated. He did not land, nor did he name these coasts, but continued back toGreenland, where the tale of his discovery may have inspired Leif Eriksson.

See also Eriksson, Leif.

HERRMAN, AUGUSTINE (c.1605-86) Cartographer, merchant, and landholder, Herrman was born in Prague, Bohemia, and came to the colonies as a trader for the Dutch West India Company. From 1643 to 1651, he represented the prestigious firm Peter Gabry & Sons, in New Amsterdam. He also formed a lucrative beaver skin trade, grew and exported indigo from Manhattan Island, and was the largest exporter of tobacco in America. His prosperity ended when Governor Peter Stuyvesant, who had appointed him one of his "Nine Men" in 1647, ruined him for signing the *Vertoogh* complaint in 1649 to the States General of the Netherlands. In 1653 he was restored to Stuyvesant's favor.

When Stuyvesant sent him to Maryland to settle a boundary dispute, Herrman prepared such a fine draft of a map that he was granted Maryland residency in 1660 and citizenship in 1666. The map, *Virginia and Maryland as it is Planted and Inhabited This Present Year 1670 Surveyed and Exactly Drawne by the Only Labour & Endeavour of Augustin Herrmann*, required 10 years to execute and was engraved in London in 1673. Lord Baltimore, the colony's proprietor, rewarded Herrman with an 13,000-acre land grant in Cecil County, where he built Bohemia Manor.

HESSELIUS, JOHN (1728-78) A portrait painter, Hesselius was born in Prince Georges County, Maryland, the son of the portrait painter Gustavus Hesselius and his wife Lydia. Young Hesselius was trained by his father and the English painter, John Wollaston, whose "almond-eyed" portraits of Maryland landowners are similar in style to Hesselius's mature work. His marriage to a wealthy plantation owner's daughter, Mary Woodward, brought him financial comfort and secured him commissions with the local society. He completed nearly 100 paintings, but his later work is regarded as wooden and stereotyped. His best earlier work is represented by his portraits of Samuel Chew and his wife and the children of Benedict Calvert. The portraits of Governor Johnson, Mrs. John Moale, and Colonel Edward Fell and his wife illustrate his later, more rigid style. He made his home at Bellefield plantation on the Severn River near Annapolis, but he painted portraits for wealthy families in Philadelphia and Virginia as well as most for of the Maryland families living near him.

HESSIANS   A general term for all German mercenaries who fought for Britain during the Revolutionary War. Faced with a shortage of its own soldiers, Britain asked the landgrave of Hesse-Cassel, whose first wife was a daughter of King George II, to supply trained mercenaries. About 17,000 men were sent by Hesse-Cassel, along with about 12,000 other German troops who were trained on the Prussian system (1776). The Hessians represented about one third of the soldiers fighting for Britain. They took part in almost every campaign, including victories at Long Island and Brandywine, yet they were defeated at Trenton, which raised the morale of Washington's men. After the war, a substantial number of them settled in the United States and Canada.

HEWES, JOSEPH (1750-79)   A signer of the Declaration of Independence, Hewes was born in Kingston, New Jersey. After running a successful mercantile business in New Jersey, he moved to Edenton, North Carolina, where he established a mercantile and shipping business. He was a member of the colonial assembly (1766-75) and all five provincial congresses. Hewes was elected to the Continental Congress (1774-77). After failing to gain reelection, he became a member of the North Carolina legislature (1778-79) and died in Philadelphia during the session.

HEYWARD, THOMAS (1746-1809)   A South Carolina patriot and signer of the Declaration of Independence, Heyward was born in St. Luke's Parish, South Carolina. He was admitted to the bar (1771) and was elected to the colonial legislature the following year. Heyward was a delegate to the provincial congress (1774) and became a member of the Council of Safety (1775, 1776), which had much power over the government. After serving in the second provincial congress, he helped adopt a state constitution (1776). As a delegate to the Second Continental Congress (1776-78), he signed the Declaration of Independence. During the Revolution he joined the state militia and helped defend Charleston. He represented Charleston in the legislature (1782-84) and became a founder and first president of the Agricultural Society of South Carolina (1785).

HIGGINSON, FRANCIS (1586-1630)   Clergyman and writer, Francis Higginson was born in Claybrooke, Leicestershire, England. In 1613 he received his degree from Jesus College, Cambridge, and was ordained as deacon in 1614. He was his father's curate and a popular speaker at St. Nicholas until Thomas Hooker turned him

into a Nonconformist. In 1629 he sailed with his wife, Anna Herbert, and eight children on the *Talbot* to Massachusetts. Three editions of *New England Plantation*, his journal on the voyage and on life in Naumkeag (Salem), were sold in 1630. He also wrote a confession of faith and church covenant.

The defeat and capture of the Hessians at the Battle of Trenton improved American morale. *(Library of Congress)*

HILLEGAS, MICHAEL (1729-1804)   A merchant and political leader, born in Philadelphia, Hillegas took over the family business with his father's death in 1750 and amassed a considerable fortune in the iron and sugar trade. Active in promoting the cause of American independence, he served in the provincial assembly (1765-75) and was appointed one of the two "Continental Treasurers" by the

Continental Congress in 1775. From 1777 to 1789 he served as Treasurer of the United States. Hillegas was one of the founders of the Bank of North America, and in 1792 he established the Lehigh Coal Mining Company. He served as a Philadelphia alderman from 1793 until his death.

See also Bank of North America.

HILLSBOROUGH, WILL HILLS, 1ST EARL OF (1718-93)   The Earl of Hillsborough was appointed the first secretary of state for the colonies in January 1768. President of the Board of Trade in 1763-65 and again in 1766, he was well qualified for the new post. But Hillsborough, a "King's Friend" and defender of Parliament's authority, was a hardliner on American affairs who believed in the efficacy of force. One of his first official actions was to respond tactlessly to the Massachusetts Circular Letter of February 1768, thereby promoting the colonial unity he sought to forestall. A minor incident in March provoked his order to send troops to Boston; by June he thought that two more regiments were necessary to maintain order. Poor judgment and overreaction marred his performance as secretary, and Lord Dartmouth replaced him in 1772. Hillsborough later returned to government service (1779-82).

See also Massachusetts Circular Letter.

HISTORICAL DEMOGRAPHY   Historical demography is the social science concerned with the study of population in the past. The demographer's primary objectives are to determine the total population of an area; identify trends in growth, stability, or decline of that population; describe its age structure, sex ratio, ethnic composition, and density; and explain how the interaction of births, marriages, deaths, and migration produced the detected population patterns and trends. Analysis of fertility, mortality, and migration rates reveals the factors that produced, for example, an increase in population—an excess of births over deaths, an excess of in-migration over out-migration, or a combination of the two variables. Other objectives are to interpret the influences of demographics on social and economic trends and to identify social, economic, and political conditions that had demographic consequences.

Formal historical demographic questions include: What was the population of this area? What were the levels and trends in fertility and mortality rates and how did these influence population growth, stability, or decline? Who were the migrants into the American colonies, and who were those who moved out of settled areas to frontier regions? How did migration affect the age, sex, and ethnic composition of the population? What differences existed in the birth, death, and migration rates and trends in New

England, the Middle Colonies, and the South? To what extent did differences in fertility, mortality, and migration bring a spatial redistribution of population?

Historical demography is interdisciplinary. The demographer explores other variables for causes of the population trends and their consequences and employs the concepts, questions, and discoveries of medical science, geography, economics, biology, political science, sociology, and anthropology, among other fields, to interpret the significance of population structure and trends. The historian's skills and imagination in using traditional sources are essential in interpreting demographic data. And women's, Afro-American, family, and Native American Indian historical studies have made valuable contributions to knowledge of the demographic history of early America.

Demography Techniques.   American scholars, using techniques similar to those developed by the French demographer Louis Henry and the English scholar E. A. Wrigley, analyze the populations of American colonies. Because of the state of the sources, colonial demographers have made adjustments to European methods of analyzing parish registers. They employ census data analysis where such sources exist; use aggregative analysis of church records, vital records of towns, and genealogies; engage in family reconstitution relying on church records, town records, and genealogies; and make prosopographical studies to create "collective biographies" of a community.

Aggregative analysis of a series of birth, death, and marriage records has the advantage of quickly providing gross population trends. Demographers record the monthly total of all births, deaths, and marriages on a preliminary extraction form and plot the annual totals on graphs. The scholar analyzes the relationships of births to deaths and marriages by the month and the year; establishes an independent estimate of total population at the beginning and end of the series of data; and calculates crude birth, death, and marriage rates.

Family reconstitution provides a more detailed view of the interaction of the population's vital events and solves the problem of establishing rates because once the vital data for the families have been compiled on family reconstitution forms, age-specific marriage, fertility, and death rates may be calculated from them. Family reconstitution, employing methods similar to genealogy, assists in developing sets of vital data useful in observing the details of family structure and demographic trends. Crucial measurements drawn from reconstitution exercises include marriage ages, family sizes, infant mortality, and life expectancy for the population examined. Changes in these conditions assist in assessing the standard of living, evaluating expressions of satisfaction or dissatisfaction in the community, and understanding the way people perceived themselves in society.

In prosopographical studies the scholar creates a collective biography of a town, village, county, or city using "record stripping" procedures. All people mentioned in a record series are culled and reassembled by name. The people included in other series of documents are added through "record linkage," and all are organized on a name and subject basis. From these biographical files it is then possible to investigate the collective characteristics of the people's lives. Typically, such studies have other than demographic content and seek to discover people's deeper beliefs and interests that influenced political behavior, or seek answers to questions about social structure and social mobility, or analyze networks of relationships to comprehend the nature of community.

American Records.   Prior to the first federal census of 1790, there are only limited census data for the area that became the United States. The 40 extant censuses taken before 1776 are unevenly distributed in time and among the colonies. For example, there are 10 known censuses for New York but none for Pennsylvania. Given these circumstances, historians have had to resort to other sources to reconstruct the population history of communities in early America.

Demographers employ a variety of sources, including a town's vital records, church records, tax assessment lists, and property records— including wills, deeds, and inventories of estate. They use "bills of mortality" because they are especially helpful for establishing causes of death and understanding the disease environment. Journals, diaries, wills, correspondence, account books, and orphans' court records, supplemented with knowledge of laws concerning migration, marriage, medical practice, and inheritance, enhance the answers to questions about the causes of population trends and explain how vital events shaped the adjustments that people made in their lives in response to demographic patterns.

Bibliography: Vinovskis, Maris, ed., *Studies in American Historical Demography* (Academic Press, 1979); Wells, Robert V., *Revolutions in Americans' Lives: A Demographic Perspective on the History of Americans, Their Families, and Their Society* (Greenwood, 1982); Wrigley, E. A., ed., *An Introduction to English Historical Demography from the Sixteenth to the Nineteenth Century* (Basic Books, 1966).

Rodger C. Henderson
Pennsylvania State University

HOBBY, SIR CHARLES (c.1665-1715) Merchant and colonial administrator, born in Boston, the son of a prominent merchant, Hobby spent his early adult years in Jamaica. There he distinguished himself in defending the British control of the island, an act that earned him a knighthood. Hobby returned to Boston in 1700 and entered private business, also serving as selectman and justice of the peace. In 1710 he joined the British expedition against Port Royal, Nova Scotia, and in 1711 was appointed lieutenant of Annapolis Royal, as the city was called after its capture. Although Hobby returned to Boston in 1712, he maintained financial and political ties to Nova Scotia.

HOLT, JOHN (1721-84) A printer, journalist, and postmaster, Holt was born in Williamsburg, Virginia, and married into a printing family, the Hunters. After an initial business career, Holt went to New York City with a letter to the influential printer James Parker, who set him up in the printing business, first in New Haven, Connecticut, and then in New York City. In 1766, Holt issued his own newspaper under the title of the *New York Journal*, or *General Advertisor* and then as the Gazette, or *Post-Boy*, a title formerly used by Parker. During the Revolutionary War, English troops burned his printing shop in New York City, then those subsequently set up in New Haven; Kingston, New York; Poughkeepsie, New York; and finally in New York City again. In spite of the property loss and the constant flights, Holt continued issuing the paper during the war. A second printing press in Norfolk, Virginia, was run by his son, John Hunter Holt. This paper, *The Virginia Gazette*, or the *Norfolk Intelligencer*, also angered the British, and on September 20, 1775, English soldiers dismantled the shop.   Appointed deputy postmaster in New Haven in 1775, Holt applied his experience to the postal improvements he had recommended to Samuel Adams in 1776.

HOOKER, THOMAS (1586-1647) A colonial religious leader born in Marfield, England, Hooker was educated at Emmanuel College, Cambridge. He served as a minister in Essex parishes (1620-30), where he became an important Puritan leader gaining the attention of Archbishop William Laud. After Hooker was ordered to appear before the ecclesiastical Court of High commissions, Hooker fled to Holland (1630) and then sailed for the Massachusetts Bay Colony three years later.

He settled in New Towne (now Cambridge, Massachusetts), where he became popular. He disagreed with colonial leaders over the extent of magisterial authority and limited suffrage. Hooker led a group of his parishioners to Connecticut, where he helped settle Hartford (1636), and he supported the general Puritan thought of the Fundamental Orders (1639) that became Connecticut's constitution. Hooker helped Massachusetts defend Congregationalism against Presbyterianism and assisted in forming the New England Confederation, which was the first union of the colonies. His most important work, *A Survey of the Summe of Church Discipline*, appeared a year after his death.

See also Fundamental Orders of Connecticut; New England Confederation.

HOOPER, WILLIAM (1742-90) A signer of the Declaration of Independence, Hooper was born in Boston. He graduated from Harvard (1760) and began to study law under James Otis. After being admitted to the bar, he went to Wilmington, North Carolina (1764). He was a member of the military expedition against the Regulators as a deputy attorney general (1771). Hooper became a member of the colonial assembly from Campbellton (1773). He was placed on the Committee of Correspondence and was elected to all five provincial Congresses. He served in the First and Second Continental Congresses (1774-77), signed the Declaration of Independence, and became a member of the state legislature (1777-82).

HOPEWELL, TREATY OF (1785) An agreement between the Cherokee nation and the United States, signed at Hopewell, South Carolina, on November 28, 1785, the treaty determined the territorial boundaries and conditions of trade between the two peoples. This treaty and those soon afterward signed with the Choctaw and Chickasaw nations were the first to recognize and codify the principle of U.S. sovereignty over the native peoples of North America. The observance of the original terms of trade and territorial boundaries proved, however, to be short-lived and were superseded by later treaties and the eventual removal of the Cherokee to the Oklahoma Territory.

HOPKINS, SAMUEL (1721-1803) A Congregationalist theologian, Hopkins was born in Waterbury, Connecticut, and graduated from Yale College in 1741. After ordination as a Congregationalist minister in 1742, he spent several months in the household of Jonathan Edwards in Northampton, Massachusetts, where he was deeply influenced by Edwards's theology. In 1743, Hopkins was appointed minister to the congregation in Great Barrington, Massachusetts, where he served until differences with the local community resulted in his dismissal in 1769. Still a close associate of Jonathan Edwards, he became minister in Newport, Rhode Island, in 1770. Hopkins was an early opponent of slavery and, with Ezra Stiles, promoted an African colonization program for free blacks.

With the outbreak of the Revolution and the British occupation of Newport, Hopkins fled with his family, briefly preaching in Newburyport, Massachusetts, and in Canterbury and Stamford, Connecticut. He returned to Newport in 1780 to rebuild the badly damaged church and remained its minister until his death. Hopkins's greatest achievements were in the field of religious philosophy and

his most famous work, *System of Doctrines Contained in Divine Revelation, Explained and Defended* (1793), presented his doctrine of disinterested benevolence.

See also Edwards, Jonathan; Stiles, Ezra.

HOPKINSON, FRANCIS (1737-91) Author, judge, and signer of the Declaration of Independence, Hopkinson was born in Philadelphia. He graduated from the College of Philadelphia (later the University of Pennsylvania) in 1757, was awarded his M.A. (1761), and was admitted to the bar. Hopkinson then moved to Bordentown, New Jersey, to set up a law practice. He became prominent enough to be elected to the Second Continental Congress (1776) and signed the Declaration of Independence. Throughout the Revolution, he was a popular political satirist and pamphleteer. He helped design the first national flag (1777) and was judge of the Pennsylvania admiralty court (1779-89). He urged the adoption of the Constitution and became the federal district judge for eastern Pennsylvania (1789-91).

HORSE The wild horse (*Equus caballus*) originated in North America, spreading into Asia, Europe, and Africa before becoming extinct in its homeland about 7,000 years ago. Domesticated horses were reintroduced into the Caribbean by Columbus in 1493 and into Mexico by Cortes in 1519. By the time of Coronado's exploration of the Southwest in 1540, these horses had multiplied sufficiently to outfit the expedition.

Spanish stockmen, using horses to tend their pasturing cattle and sheep, colonized the Rio Grande Valley in the early 17th century, and from there horse culture spread onto the plains, reaching all the buffalo hunting tribes by the mid-18th century. The development of complex Great Plains Indian cultures depended upon the horse. By 1800 there were millions of wild horses, or mustangs, in the West.

Along the Atlantic coast, horse populations developed from Spanish stock introduced from the West Indies into Florida, then northward to the Southern colonies, as well as from English and Flemish stock introduced by the French and English colonists. After 1650, New England exported horses to other colonies and especially to the West Indies, where horses often powered sugar refining mills. In the colonies horses were used mostly for transport and rarely for draft until the development of the heavy Conestoga breed in Pennsylvania in the mid-18th century.

See also Great Plains Indians.

Bibliography: Roe, Frank Gilbert, *The Indian and the Horse* (1955; reprint Univ. of Oklahoma Press, 1979).

HOUSEHOLD INDUSTRIES Farmers in colonial America, from Southern planters to Northern yeomen, strove to achieve a high degree of self-sufficiency, an important part of which involved not only the provision of food, but the production of nearly all that the family required. In addition to family farms, the local agricultural complex typically included blacksmiths to work metal, millers to grind corn and saw lumber, and perhaps a variety of other craftsmen, depending upon the state of development and the location of the community. But the basic needs of most households were supplied by the work of people at home, and it was the work of farm wives that often made the difference between success or failure. Besides bearing and caring for large numbers of children, preparing at least three meals every day, cleaning, washing, ironing, and mending, women produced an abundance of goods. They raised vegetables, herbs, and flax; set hens, plucked geese, milked cows, churned butter, made cheese; and carded, spun, wove, cut, and tailored the family wardrobe.

The expansion of the colonial export economy had a contradictory effect on household industries. On the one hand, there was a great increase in the amount of manufactured goods in circulation in the 18th century; clearly, some households had become far less independent in the provision of their subsistence. On the other hand, some Southern planters took advantage of increasing wealth to divert the labor of slaves from commodity production to work in gardens or at crafts, designed to increase the self-sufficiency of the operation. In the North, the growth of the domestic or putting out system, in which merchants contracted with farm women or whole families to complete cloth- or shoe-making operations at home, suggested that old economic strategies were being used to advance new ones. The nonimportation movement of the early Revolutionary period played an important role in strengthening the tradition of household manufactures at the beginning of the nation's history.

See also Domestic or Putting Out System; Self-sufficient and Market Farming.

Bibliography: Ulrich, Laurel T., *Good Wives: Image and Reality in the Lives of Women in Northern New England, 1650-1750* (Knopf, 1982).

John Mack Faragher
Mount Holyoke College

HOWARD OF EFFINGHAM, FRANCIS, LORD (1643-95)

Appointed governor of Virginia in 1683, Howard of Effingham quickly set about accruing power to his office by increasing fees and persecuting all opponents. Besides feeling threatened politically, the main Protestant colonists also feared religious persecution at the hands of Howard and King James II, both Catholics.

In 1688 the House of Burgesses sent a petition to England protesting Howard's policies. By the time it arrived, the Glorious Revolution had removed James II, and the petition was well received by the new Protestant king, William. In October 1690 a lieutenant governor was appointed. Howard kept his commission, stayed in England, and drew half-pay for the next two years. Under his administration the Assembly had lost many of its privileges, including the right to appoint its own clerk, to receive judicial appeals, and to control all revenues.

Bibliography: Flippen, Percy Scott, *The Royal Government in Virginia, 1624-1775* (AMS Press, 1966).

HOWE, GEORGE AUGUSTUS, VISCOUNT (c.1724-58)

British military leader and commander in chief of the British forces in North America, Howe was born in Nottingham, England, son of Viscount Emmanuel Scrope Howe (governor of Barbados, 1732-35) and Maria Sophia Charlotte, Countess of Darlington, who was related to King George I. Succeeding to his father's title in 1735, Howe entered the Grenadier Guards in 1745 and was named aide-de-camp to the Duke of Cumberland. He also served in Parliament (1747-58).

In 1757, in the French and Indian War, Howe became a battalion commander in northern New York. His expedition to relieve German Flats was successful, but his mission to Fort Ticonderoga proved to be a failure. Appointed brigadier general in late 1757, Howe retrained the British soldiers for frontier warfare, utilizing the tactics of the Rangers of Robert Rogers. In July 1758 he was second in command of a renewed attack on Fort Ticonderoga but was killed in a preliminary skirmish with the French near Lake George. Howe was buried at St. Peter's Church in Albany. He was the elder brother of William Howe, British commander in chief during the Revolution.

HOWE, RICHARD (1726-99)

A British admiral who led British naval forces during the Revolutionary War, Howe was born in London. The brother of Sir William Howe, Richard went to North America at the outset of the French and Indian War as captain of the Dunkirk, and seized the French Alcide on the St. Lawrence. Howe was a member of the Admiralty board (1765-70) and treasurer of the navy. Howe was sympathetic to the colonists as commander of North America (from 1775), but was unable to prevent war. Early in the conflict Howe defended Sandy Hook and Newport, Rhode Island, from the French. Differences with the British government led him to resign his command in 1778. He later became first lord of the admiralty (1783-88) and won important victories against the French.

See also Howe, Sir William; Revolutionary War Battles.

Engraved for Murray's History of the American War.

LORD HOWE.

Printed for T. Robson, Newcastle upon Tyne.

As commander of North America from 1775, Admiral Richard Howe tried to prevent war with the colonists. *(Library of Congress)*

HOWE, ROBERT (1732-86) A Revolutionary War soldier, Howe was born in Bladen (now Brunswick) County, North Carolina. Before the outbreak of the Revolution, he was a rice planter, sat in the colonial assembly, and served in the militia, commanding Fort Johnston (1766-67; 1769-73). He was a colonel of artillery in Tryon's expedition against the Regulators. As the Revolution approached, Howe served in the first three provincial congresses and was a member of the provincial Committee of Correspondence.

During the Revolutionary War he helped drive Lord Dunmore out of Virginia as colonel of the 2nd North Carolina regiment and commanded the forces that captured Norfolk. He was promoted to brigadier general (1776) and led an unsuccessful mission against St. Augustine, Florida, as a major general (1777). Howe then commanded (1778)

at Savannah, but was forced to evacuate the city (1778) after the British landed, which led to a court martial in which he was exonerated. Transferred to the North, he commanded the West Point garrison, suppressed mutinies among Pennsylvania and New Jersey troops (1781), and dispersed a mob that had driven Congress out in Philadelphia (1783). He was later elected to the state legislature but died before taking his seat.

HOWE, SIR WILLIAM (1729-1814) A British general during the Revolutionary War and brother of Richard Howe, William Howe entered the army in 1746. During the French and Indian War (Seven Years War), he helped in the battle for Quebec at the Plains of Abraham (1759). He then defended Quebec with his own regiment (1759-60), led a brigade to Montreal, and fought in the European theater of the war. He became a major general in 1772. Although he did not agree with Britain's policies towards the colonists, he led the British troops in the battle of Bunker Hill (1775) and succeeded General Thomas Gage as the British commander in North America.

Besieged in Boston by colonial troops, he evacuated his forces to New York early in 1776. During the 1776 and 1777 campaigns, Howe faced George Washington's forces several times, defeating the Americans at Long Island (1776) and Brandywine (1777) but having less success at White Plains (1776) and Germantown (1777). Feeling unsupported by the government, Howe asked to be relieved and was succeeded by Sir Henry Clinton in 1778. He then returned to England, where he was promoted to full general (1793).

See also Howe, Richard; Revolutionary War Battles.

HUDSON'S BAY COMPANY In 1670 the "Governor and Company of Adventurers of England tradeing into Hudsons Bay" was granted a royal charter by Charles II. The charter conferred upon the company a trade monopoly, mineral rights, and proprietary rights to the land itself in a vast region of the Canadian West known as Rupert's Land. From its posts on Hudson Bay at Churchill and York Factory, and on James Bay at Fort Albany and Moose Fort, the company had access to some of the richest fur country on the continent and to some of the best trappers, notably the Cree Indians. However, the isolation of the company's coastal facilities made them vulnerable to attack by the French until the Treaty of Utrecht (1713) confirmed British possession of the Bay.

Starting in the 1740s, traders moving inland from the Great Lakes to the Saskatchewan region began to compete with the company. Serious opposition emerged in 1783 from the North West Company and convinced the

Hudson's Bay Company that it must maintain posts in the interior. After a long period of struggle and occasional violence, made worse by the Napoleonic Wars and their adverse effect on the fur market, the two companies merged in 1821. The dominant figure in the postmerger period was George Simpson, who eliminated surplus posts and tried to make the remaining ones more self-sufficient. For the Indians, the days of competition had been a blessing. Now the company reaped the profits.

A number of factors, including an increasing interest in the agricultural potential of company land, led to the end of the company's trade monopoly in 1859. Finally, in 1870 the company sold Rupert's Land to the new Dominion of Canada for 300,000 pounds. The company continues to operate a chain of department stores in Canada.

See also Fur Trade.

Bibliography: Brown, Jennifer S. H., *Strangers in Blood: Fur Trade Families in Indian Country* (Univ. of British Columbia Press, 1980); Rich, E. E., *History of the Hudson's Bay Company, 1670-1870*, 3 vols. (Macmillan, 1961).

Jay Gitlin
Yale University

HUDSON, HENRY (died 1611)   An English explorer in service for the English and the Dutch, Hudson made several enormously important explorations of North America. In 1607, in search of the Northwest Passage, he explored the islands of Svalbard northeast of Greenland, opening the way for the beginnings of the English whaling there. The next year he explored the icy waters off Novaya Zemlya, but his failure to find passage from the east lost him the backing of the Muscovy Company. In 1609 he sailed for the Dutch East India Company with a mixed Dutch-English crew on the famous *Half Moon*. Headed again for northeastern waters, he was forced by a mutiny among his crew to turn instead to the waters off North America, where he explored the Hudson River, opening the way for Dutch occupation and settlement, which began the next year. After this success the English state refused him permission to sail again for their cross-channel rivals, and in 1610, in the employ of a group of London merchants, he sailed for the northwest Atlantic, where he explored the strait and great bay that now carry his name. He spent a hard winter at James Bay, where discontentment among the crew finally broke out in mutiny. Hudson, his son, and seven loyal crew members were set adrift on the bay and were never heard of again.

See also Hudson River; Northwest Passage.

HUDSON RIVER   At the time of the first European exploration of the lower Hudson Valley by Giovanni da Verrazano in 1524, the area was a rich homeland for a dense concentration of Algonquian and Iroquoian speaking peoples. French traders, moving east from Lake Ontario via the Mohawk River, reached the Hudson in 1540, but the Dutch established the first European settlement in 1614, following the exploration by Henry Hudson in 1609. With its mild climate and rich soil, the valley was perfect for European agriculture; and with its ice-free harbor and deep channel, the river was the perfect corridor for the rich Indian trade of the interior.

When the English took over New Netherland in 1664 some 10,000 Dutch settlers lived along the river, most concentrated near Manhattan, but others living as tenants on large upriver estates. Under British rule, English, German, Scotch, and Afro-Americans colonized the lower valley, producing one of the most ethnically diverse and secular communities in colonial America, distinguishing New York from more homogeneous and religious New England. By 1750 the population of the Hudson Valley had increased to more than 100,000.

The Hudson was witness to much conflict during the 18th century. During the Indian wars, settlers along the upper river and its tributaries were frequent targets of raids. Somewhat later, land-hungry New Englanders encroached on the estates of Hudson Valley landlords, resulting in persistent and often violent conflict. During the Revolution tenants were among the most active of the rebels, with the struggles along the Hudson having much to do with the quasi-feudal conditions of land tenure.

See also Hudson, Henry; New Netherland.

HUGUENOTS   During the colonial era Huguenots, or French Protestants, intermittently played important roles in their country's overseas colonial ventures. King Henry II's Huguenot first minister, Gaspard de Coligny, attempted to establish a French foothold in Portuguese Brazil that would be both a base for further exploits as well as a sanctuary for his fellow Protestants. In 1535, Coligny sent an expedition to Rio de Janeiro, but this threat to Portuguese control ended in 1550, when the French garrison was overwhelmed.

Coligny next moved against the Spanish in Florida, by attempting to erect a Huguenot colony there in 1562 and again in 1564. Both efforts failed, partly because of internal strife among the settlers. Such disorder mirrored the disunity of France itself, where the presence of Huguenots seemed an intolerable abomination to many in the Catholic majority, resulting in the Saint Bartholomew's Day Massacre of Huguenots in 1572. Although many of their leaders perished, Protestants endured in France and eventually received full civil rights.

West Point, a defensive key to American control of the Hudson River, was painted by Pierre L'Enfant about 1778. *(Library of Congress)*

Although Huguenots were active in early Canada as fur traders and fishermen, they made no attempt to erect a permanent Protestant settlement in the colony. Some prominent French Catholics saw Canada as fertile ground on which to build a pure, Catholic society. Thus Cardinal Richelieu, the king's first minister, in 1625 permitted Canada's Catholic viceroy to bar Huguenots from New France. Two years later, Richelieu organized the wholly Catholic Company of a Hundred Associates, gave its shareholders feudal title to the land and a monopoly on the fur trade, and supported its goals of establishing French Catholic settlers in the colony and converting the Indians to Catholicism.

Periodically groups of refugee Huguenots settled in the Americas, but never in Canada. Indeed, some scholars have suggested that the severe population shortages which plagued New France, and which weakened it, might have been overcome had French leaders been less determined to insure that Canada remain religiously pure and permitted Huguenots to emigrate to the colony. English America did provide a haven for French Protestants throughout the colonial era, and their contribution to the emerging American society was great. A few Huguenots settled in Canada after the mid-17th century, and one 18th century official even claimed that much of the colony's trade was controlled by Protestants. Nevertheless, unity of religion marked French Canadian society, in dramatic contrast to the situation in the English colonies to the south or in France itself.

See also French Immigrants.

Aaron Shatzman
Franklin and Marshall College

HUME, SOPHIA WIGINGTON (1702-74)   Quaker minister and writer, granddaughter of Mary Fisher, Sophia was raised as an Anglican by her prosperous land-owning family in Charleston, South Carolina. Well educated and of aristocratic bearing, she married Robert Hume in 1721 and bore a son and a daughter. Her husband died in 1737, and Sophia suffered through two illnesses that left her convinced that she must forsake luxury for a simpler Quaker lifestyle. She moved to England and finally joined the Society of Friends. In 1747 she answered a divine call to return to Charleston and spread the Quaker message. She wrote *An Exhortation to the Inhabitants of the Province of South Carolin*a to spread the word about the evils of vanity. In an attempt to get it published she went to Philadelphia in 1748. Her considerable gifts as a writer were further explored in *A Caution to Such as Observe Days and Times* (1763). Hume's talent and erudition were somewhat in conflict with her belief in Quaker principles about the role of women in society. But she never wavered in her belief, and she returned to England after her ultimately unsuccessful attempt to strengthen Qukerism in Charleston.

See also Fisher, Mary.

HUMPHREYS, JOSHUA (1751-1838)   One of America's most noted shipbuilders, Humphreys was born in Delaware County, Pennsylvania. He opened his own shipyard, and by the age of 25 he became the foremost marine architect in America. Congress asked him (1776) to refit eight small merchant vessels for a naval fleet for the Revolutionary War. He thought much about America's problem of naval inferiority during the war. Congress appointed him naval constructor (1794), and he prepared models for six frigates that carried more cannons and more sails than was common at the time. These ships became the main force of the U.S. navy and later took part in some of its most celebrated battles. He was commissioned to build a naval yard in Philadelphia (1806), and his design ideas became widely adopted by other nations.

HUNDRED ASSOCIATES, COMPANY OF A   Formed by Cardinal Richelieu in 1627, the Company of a Hundred Associates, also known as the Company of New France, united more than a hundred investors in an effort to secure a French presence in Canada through sponsorship of carefully supervised colonization. Allied to that goal was an aim to create an ideal society in the empty space of the New World by barring from the colony groups that had disrupted French society. Thus the company permitted only Catholics to settle in New France, thereby eliminating the "threat" posed by Huguenots, or French Protestants. Through the creation of seigneuries, or feudal estates, land was distributed to nobles. Although the desire to create a perfect Catholic feudal society may have provided the primary motivation for many investors, the company's monopoly on all trade (except for fishing) in the colony, which promised great profits, doubtless proved attractive also.

Composed of government officials, merchants, nobles, and churchmen, each of whom invested 3,000 livres, the company sent an expedition of 400 settlers to Canada in the spring of 1628. But an English force, with help from Huguenots, captured the convoy, and Quebec itself fell to English invaders in 1629. When the French returned to Canada in 1632, the company looked to individuals, and to the Church, to carry out its goals. Since fur trade profits were insufficient to pay for colonization costs, the company granted seigneuries and titles to persons able to transport settlers to the colony and sustain them. Begun in 1634, this policy succeeded in achieving the creation of 70 such estates by the 1660s. Although feudal rents were nominal in Canada, few Frenchmen proved willing to give up their lives as peasants in France merely to maintain that status in Canada's harsh climate and frontier environment. And many who did come as habitants deserted the estates to which they "belonged" to take up life as couriers des bois—fur trappers who lived outside the control of organized society.

Although profits from the fur trade could be great, they proved erratic given the uncertainties imposed by fluctuating Indian relations, the distance from the colony to France, and competition from the English. Unable to sustain its efforts to keep the colony supplied, and heavily in debt, the company in 1645 ceded the fur trade monopoly, and much administrative control, to the colonists in return for an annual payment. After Louis XIV assumed personal power, Canada was made a royal colony (1663) and the king assumed responsibility for its survival.

See also French Colonies; Fur Trade.

Aaron Shatzman
Franklin and Marshall College

HUNTER, ROBERT (died 1734)   A popular colonial governor, he was born in Scotland and served in the English army. From 1709, as governor of New York and New Jersey, Hunter healed many rifts between the two settlements, particularly those of a financial nature. He brought German refugees with him to set up manufacturing facilities to supply naval stores to Britain. When the project failed, the Germans went on to settle Schoharie, New York, and parts of Pennsylvania. He was partly responsible for setting up the first postal system—between Boston and Albany—in America. In 1719 he served as comptroller of customs in England, and he was governor of Jamaica from 1727.

HUNTINGTON, SAMUEL (1731-96)   A signer of the Declaration of Independence, Huntington was born in Windham, Connecticut. He began a law practice in Norwich (1758), and represented Norwich in the Connecticut legislature (1765-84). He served on many committees in Connecticut during the Revolution, and the General Assembly appointed him a member of a committee for the defense of the colony (1775). Representing Connecticut in the Continental Congress (1775-84) he signed the Declaration of Independence, and became president of the Congress (1779-81; 1783). After the war he became chief justice of the superior court of Connecticut (1784-85). He was elected governor of Connecticut (1786) and served until his death. During this time he vigorously supported the ratification of the Constitution.

HURON INDIANS A confederacy of Iroquoian speaking nations, the Huron, when they first encountered Europeans, lived near the shores of Georgian Bay east of Lake Huron. Estimates of their precontact population range from 18,000 to 22,000. They practiced a mixed economy of farming, hunting, and gathering. They had already developed an extensive trading network with their Algonquian speaking neighbors in which they exchanged their agricultural surplus for meat and skins. The Huron quickly broadened their trading network when European goods became available.

In 1615, Samuel de Champlain made France's first official contact with the Huron. From then on French missionaries and traders were permanent fixtures in Huron villages. Between 1634 and 1640 a series of epidemics swept the Huron villages, reducing their population to some 9,000. In the 1640s the confederacy came under increasing pressure from members of the Iroquois Confederacy who began to mount large, well-organized war parties against the Huron. In 1647, 1648, and 1649 a series of Iroquois attacks drove the Huron from Georgian Bay. Some moved to Lorette near Quebec. Others resettled among Iroquoian speakers further west or moved in among the Ottawa.

See also Fur Trade; Indians, North American; Iroquois Confederacy.

HUTCHINSON, THOMAS (1711-80) The last civilian governor of Massachusetts Bay, Hutchinson was born to an old Boston merchant family. At 26 he began his political career by winning a seat in the Massachusetts assembly, which he held (except for 1739) until 1749. Competent and of unquestioned integrity, Hutchinson inevitably made political enemies over the years. The hard-money plan he backed in 1748 benefited the colony but made him unpopular with debtors. Already holding a string of offices (lieutenant governor, councillor, judge of probate), Hutchinson in 1760 became chief justice of the supreme court. His role in the Writs of Assistance case (1761) angered smugglers, numerous among Boston's merchants. He unfairly fell victim (his house was sacked) to the Stamp Act riot of August 26, 1765, for Hutchinson had written London opposing the act. Patriots, however, perceived him as an enemy to American liberty, and that perception would subsequently only deepen.

He became acting governor (1769) and was then confirmed (1771) in that office. While acting governor, he ordered the removal of British troops from the city in the aftermath of the Boston Massacre. Hutchinson's announcement in June 1772 that the Crown would pay his salary as governor appeared to threaten the colony's charter. In 1773 an angry house petitioned for his removal from office when the incriminating Hutchinson Letters fell into its hands. Finally, his adherence to principle caused the tea to be dumped into Boston harbor in December 1773, for he refused to allow the return of the cargo to England. Replaced as governor by General Thomas Gage, Hutchinson sailed for England on June 1, 1774, never to return. He died in exile, despised by his countrymen.

See also Boston Massacre; Boston Tea Party; Hutchinson Letters.

Bibliography: Bailyn, Bernard, *The Ordeal of Thomas Hutchinson* (Harvard Univ. Press, 1974).

Henry J. Halko
Simmons College

HUTCHINSON, ANNE MARBURY (1591-1643) Born in England to a dissenting Puritan family, Hutchinson became a leader of Dissenters in the early New England Puritan theocracy. Barely two years after her arrival in Boston in 1634, Hutchinson was involved in the so-called Antinomian Controversy. She was associated with Henry Vane, political opponent of John Winthrop; with her brother-in-law John Wheelwright, preacher of a controversial Fast Day sermon who was subsequently charged with sedition; and with John Cotton, whose religious influence had initially led her to New England. This swirl of civil and religious issues led to a civil trial where she was banished and to a church examination in which she was excommunicated. Hutchinson was accused of holding banned religious meetings in her home, of insulting the clergy by charging that they preached a Covenant of Works rather than a Covenant of Grace, and of various other issues that arose during the course of the trials. Hutchinson was supported in her theological position by John Cotton until near the end of her church trial.

Hutchinson and a large number of associates then moved to Rhode Island in 1638. Following the death of her husband, William, in 1642, she and some of her younger children moved to the Pelham region of the Hutchinson River in New York where all but the youngest daughter were massacred by Indians in 1643.

See also Antinomianism and the Antinomian Controversy; Wheelwright, John.

Jane F. Crosthwaite
Mount Holyoke College

HUTCHINSON LETTERS In December 1772, Benjamin Franklin, agent in England for the Massachusetts Bay Colony, sent to patriot leader Thomas Cushing 13 letters written to a British official by Massachusetts Governor Thomas Hutchinson, Lieutenant Governor Andrew Oliver, and two others. The letters corroborated for Franklin what he had long suspected, that America's problems originated not with the ministry but in the plots of renegade Americans such as Hutchinson and Oliver. How Franklin came by the letters remains a mystery, but he forwarded them on condition that they be neither printed nor copied and that they be returned to him. The six Hutchinson letters, written 1768-69, contained nothing that Hutchinson had not publicly stated or written previously, but one contained the statement that if the connection with Great Britain were to continue there would have to be "an abridgement of what are called English liberties." Boston's leaders, themselves long convinced that Crown officials were sending false, slanderous reports to the ministry, could not resist the temptation to use the evidence now in hand. The letters were read to the Massachusetts House on June 2, 1773, and shortly after printed in newspapers and in pamphlet form. Further, the House petitioned the King to remove Hutchinson and Oliver from office. The request was refused, but the letters nonetheless destroyed whatever remained of Hutchinson's effectiveness as governor and made his recall a mere matter of time.

See also Hutchinson, Thomas.

Bibliography: Bailyn, Bernard, *The Ordeal of Thomas Hutchinson* (Harvard Univ. Press, 1974).

HUTCHINS, THOMAS (1730-89) A geographer, military engineer, and journalist, Hutchins was born in Monmouth County, New Jersey, became an orphan at 16, and later served with the British troops (1759-80). He fought in the French and Indian War, laid out military designs for Fort Pitt and Pensacola, Florida, and illustrated his journals with maps. Refusing to serve against the Americans in the Revolutionary War, he was imprisoned in London but escaped to France, where Benjamin Franklin gave him a letter to Congress that resulted in his appointment as geographer to the Southern army on May 4, 1781, and as "geographer to the United States" on July 11.

After the war, Hutchins mapped land for the United States and individual states. He prepared map work for Pennsylvania and Virginia when Congress recalled him to survey the western territory of the Land Ordinance of 1785. In spite of threats from the Indians, he made three expeditions to plot four of the seven ranges of public lands, mapped the boundary line between New York and Massachusetts, and was leaving Pittsburgh to finish the survey when he died.

See also Land Ordinance of 1785.

HYDE, EDWARD, VISCOUNT CORNBURY (1661-1723) A colonial governor, he was educated in Switzerland and served in the British Parliament. Due to heavy debts he asked to be appointed to the colonies and arrived in 1702 to be governor of New York and New Jersey. His rule of each was disastrous. He embezzled monies intended for defense, prosecuted those not of the Church of England, and accepted bribes. He was recalled to England in 1708 but, facing arrest due to his unpaid debts, he was only able to go after inheriting his father's title and becoming Earl of Clarendon. In 1711 he served on the British Privy Council, but his administrative career was, for the most part, over.

I

IBERVILLE, PIERRE LE MOYNE, SIEUR D'
(1661-1706) Known as the "Canadian Cid," Iberville was the third son of Charles Le Moyne de Longueuil et de Chateauguay and of Catherine Thierry. He first distinguished himself during Pierre de Troyes's campaign to drive the English from Hudson Bay in 1686. He took part in the savage attack on Corlaer (Schenectady, New York) in 1690 and led the expedition that captured York Fort on Hudson Bay in 1694. In 1697, Iberville secured his reputation as a brilliant naval commander when his flagship, the Pelican, defeated three English warships in Hudson Bay. His victories in Newfoundland and Hudson Bay were reversed at the conference tables of Europe, but in 1698, Iberville set sail for the first of three voyages (1698-99, 1699-1700, 1701-02) to Louisiana and the Gulf of Mexico, voyages that brought Iberville fame as the founder of French Louisiana. Throughout his career Iberville carefully exploited any opportunity to increase his personal fortune. He invested his profits from the fur trade and other enterprises in several estates in western France and a cocoa plantation in Santo Domingo. Iberville represented a new, energetic generation of native-born French Canadians and became a legendary hero after his death.

IMMIGRATION The growth of the colonial population was first, and perhaps foremost, due to the great movement of European and African peoples across the Atlantic. This movement began slowly; 25 years after the founding of Jamestown, the population of the British colonies of North America (excluding Indians) totaled fewer than 5,000 people.

Characteristics of Mobility. Beginning in the late 1620s and extending to at least 1650, however, thousands of immigrants came to America, a movement known at the time as "The Great Migration." To New England this movement was one of families and congregations, to the Chesapeake colonies one of indentured men; in both cases these immigrants were largely English. Small but important groups of Dutch, Swedes, and French also settled in New York, New Jersey, and Maryland. By the end of the 17th century, mainly as a result of this immigration, British colonial population stood at 250,000. This steady flow of immigrants became a great flood early in the next century, as Scots, Scotch-Irish, Germans, French, and Africans joined the English in the trans-Atlantic crossing. Over the next 75 years the population of the colonies grew tenfold, reaching more than 2,700,000 by 1780. By that same date perhaps as many as 75,000 French-speakers lived in Quebec, 30,000 Spanish and another 40,000 Spanish-speaking (mestizos) in the provinces of Florida, Texas, and New Mexico.

The peopling of North America was an expansion in scale and an extension outward of previously established patterns of mobility in the lands of the immigrants' origins. In England, Scotland, Ireland, the Palatinate region of Germany, and elsewhere, the movement of men, women, and families was a confirmed fact of social life before the cross-Atlantic traffic began; the North American immigration was a spill-over of these patterns. During the 1630s, while 21,000 Puritans emigrated to New England, another 120,000 Englishmen relocated in Ireland. European domestic patterns, therefore, shaped the development of the American population. The large numbers of indentured servants moving to the colonies along Chesapeake Bay, for example, fell off in the 1650s when English population growth slackened and as fire and plague reduced the population of London and created a greater local demand for labor. The consequently reduced emigration of English servants stimulated the forced emigration of African slaves and forever changed the character of America's population. Likewise, the African slave trade had begun much earlier, in the 15th century. Over the centuries, approximately 10,000,000 African slaves landed in the Western Hemisphere, but fewer than 1 of every 20 of them went to British and French North America.

The Pilgrims, here leaving Holland to begin their journey to North America, were an example of typical 17th century New England immigration. *(Library of Congress)*

Ethnic Diversity. The immigration to colonial America was characterized by great ethnic diversity. It is clear that the two largest immigrant groups during the colonial period were the English and the Africans, each totaling, according to good historical estimates, perhaps 400,000 to 500,000 persons. The Scotch-Irish, Protestants from Ulster or northern Ireland, numbered at least 250,000, and the Germans 100,000 more. Other important groups included the Scots, Irish, Dutch, and French.

Carefully kept immigration registers compiled during the years between the end of the Seven Years' War (1763) and the signing of the Declaration of Independence (1776) suggest something of the same outline: Into the colonies poured some 55,000 Protestant Irish; 40,000 Scots; 30,000 Englishmen; 12,000 Germans and Swiss; and 85,000 Africans — a total of 222,000 immigrants, an average of nearly 15,000 persons each year. An analysis of the first federal census (1790) provides another method for arriving at the proportional contribution of these various nationalities to the colonial population. According to the census, 49 percent of the American population in 1790 was English; 18 percent African; 15 percent Scotch-Irish, Scottish, or Irish; 7 percent German; 3 percent Dutch; and 2 percent French.

Immigration and Labor Needs. The difference between the proportions of English and Africans in the population of 1790, despite the rough equivalence of the size of the emigration from the two areas, testifies to the extreme exploitation of the slave condition. Africans were involuntary migrants, and during the colonial period it was cheaper to import new slaves than it was to rear new ones. It should be noted, however, that while European immigrants were sooner or later free to marry and reproduce at some of the highest rates in recorded history, from half to two-thirds of them came to British North America as indentured servants or "redemptioners"; many packed into ships' holds duplicating at least some of the horrors of the African "middle passage." This marks another important characteristic of colonial immigration: that the majority of migrants came in a state of bondage. In addition to the slaves, the indentured servants, and the redemptioners, among the ranks of bound immigrants were 20,000 English convicts who reached the shores of Virginia and Maryland, the survivors of some 30,000 who were transported from England in the 18th century to labor on tobacco plantations.

The African slave trade and the transportation of convicts were the most extreme expressions of the deliberate engineering of overseas migration. But in Europe as well, immigration agents combed the Rhineland and the British Isles for recruits. In the 17th century English indentured servants filled this demand. These servants were mostly unskilled and became field workers in the Chesapeake colonies. Later the need for this kind of labor was largely filled by African slaves. With the growing complexity of the colonial economy the demand for European labor grew more sophisticated, and skilled workers in manufacturing, trade, and crafts were recruited. On the eve of the Revolution 6 of 10 arriving indentured servants from England and Scotland claimed to be trained artisans.

Although historians have often stressed the role of religion in the settlement of the colonies, in fact it was of secondary importance when compared to the demand for labor. It can be argued that labor shortages were one of the prime motivating factors in the establishment of relatively tolerant policies toward religious differences in Pennsylvania and Maryland, one of a number of recruitment incentives that included guarantees of rights and liberties and grants of land. Indeed, New England probably had the most restrictive religious tests for immigrants, which was not unrelated to the fact that the largely subsistence farm economy created a relatively low demand for labor.

Driven to populate their colonies, officials established de facto and de jure naturalization procedures for immigrants. Again, New England's was most restrictive; to become a "freeman" one had to demonstrate a Puritan faith. In other colonies, however, naturalization was easily granted, giving immigrants the opportunity to own land and enjoy the full protection of the laws. These local statutes, however, did not include the coverage of British law; a general naturalization law was not passed by Parliament until 1740, and even this liberal provision excluded Catholics. Most immigrants continued to be naturalized by local or colonial ordinance until 1773, when Parliament invalidated all such statutes. This became another contributing factor to the growth of the movement for independence.

See also Puritans; Slavery; articles on individual colonies.

Bibliography: Bailyn, Bernard, *The Peopling of British North America: An Introduction* (Knopf, 1986); Proper, Emberson E., *Colonial Immigration Laws* (1900; reprint AMS Press).

John Mack Faragher
Mount Holyoke College

INDENTURED SERVITUDE   An institution of bound labor, indentured servitude originated early in the 17th century as a means of defraying the transportation cost of English immigrants unable or unwilling to pay their passage to America. To meet the expense of the ocean voyage, the prospective immigrants sold their labor services, in effect borrowing against future returns from their labor. The term derived from the contract between the immigrants and the purchasers of their labor services, which was written in duplicate on a large piece of paper and divided along a jagged or indented edge.

The origin of indentured servitude is somewhat clouded. It may have been a novel creation to solve at least partially the problem of peopling a new world, an adaptation of English apprenticeship, or, more probably, an outgrowth of the English system of service in husbandry. In any event, the institution had appeared in Virginia by 1620, instigated by the Virginia Company to transport workers to its colony.

Initially servants came from England, but increasingly during the 18th century the English were joined by Germans, Scots, and Irish. Although all the English colonies utilized indentured labor, Virginia and Maryland were the only ones to continue to import significant numbers of servants throughout the colonial period. Beyond the Chesapeake, Pennsylvania was the most popular entrepot for servants.

Quantitatively, indentured servants were a major presence in English America, comprising perhaps three-quarters of Virginia's 17th century settlers and half to two-thirds of the whites coming to the colonies after the 1630s. Although servant immigration peaked in the mid-17th century, roughly 350,000 servants were imported into the colonies before 1775.

Terms of Indenture.   As the institution developed, two contractual options were open to prospective servants. Indentures might be consummated in England or in America. In the first instance emigrants negotiated the best contract possible in terms of length of service, destination, and compensation. The length of time of the indenture varied roughly according to the amount of indebtedness entailed by their transportation but inversely with age, skill, and education. Those going to the West Indies might secure shorter terms due to the undesirable conditions of their destination.

Some emigrants went to America without contracts. Upon arrival they were sold according to the "custom of the country," or legislation devised by each colony to deal with such persons and to provide them with some legal protection. Their indentures, made in the local courts, indicate that such servants were younger, less skilled, and served longer terms. In the 18th century another broad class of servants called redemptioners, mainly Germans, swelled the ranks of those going to the colonies without contracts.

Supplementing those who voluntarily went to America were the servants sent without consultation or against their will, mainly convicts. Added to the convicts as involuntary servants were the rogues and vagabonds sent to America by order of English judicial authority, political and military prisoners, and the kidnapped. The last were subject to the

This contract for indentured servitude described in detail the conditions of labor and personal conduct. (Library of Congress)

shadowy business of "spiriting," an illicit but highly profitable trade in servants in the 17th century. Parliamentary directives and municipal ordinances were required to curb the practice, which, while prevalent, has probably been overstated.

Although opinion differs widely about the social origins of the servants, they apppear to have represented a broad segment of English society, ranging from the gentry to paupers. Usually 15 to 25 years of age, these servants were predominantly male. Approximately three-fourths of the migrants in the 17th century were males, and the proportion rose to nine-tenths in the 18th century. From an equal division between skilled and unskilled in the beginning, a trend develoepd toward the importation of unskilled in the latter years of the 17th century, only to reverse in subsequent years as perhaps 80 percent of the servants were skilled by the time of the Revolution.

According to their indentures, servants contracted for two to seven years' labor, usually three or four. The length of time varied roughly according to the amount of indebtedness entailed by their transportation. Children served until their legal majority; convicts 7 or 14 years depending upon the severity of their offenses. In return for promised faithful service by the indentured, masters agreed to furnish sufficient food, clothing, and lodging. Variations included the possibility of skilled workers securing wages or children obtaining the rudiments of an education. At the end of the indenture, masters paid "freedom dues," generally clothes, tools, guns, spinning wheels, or corn, so the servants could make a start in life. Some colonies offered a headright grant of land to freed servants.

The terminability of labor service and possession of contractual rights distinguished servants from slaves. Yet during the period of indenture servants possessed little personal freedom. They could not travel, marry, or own property without the consent of their masters. The harshness of the institution was manifested in many ways. Local courts entertained servant complaints of immoderate correction, lack of appropriate food and clothing, failure to receive freedom dues, and refusal of masters to release servants from their contracts at the expiration of their indentures. Runaway servants were common, although if apprehended their period of indenture was often lengthened by twice the time of their absence plus additional time for charges incurred in their capture. Women bearing children during their servitude often served a year or two years beyond their original indenture to compensate for time lost to childbirth and infant care. Indeed, households with servant women raised troublesome questions of morality for local authorities.

Servants and Slaves. Indentured servitude antedated slavery in the English colonies and constituted the principal source of bound labor in America until overshadowed by slavery after 1700. Initially, slaves replaced servants as unskilled laborers; then, as slaves were trained to skilled jobs, they replaced servants altogether. Although there is no necessary connection between the two labor systems, servitude was quantitatively important in two regions of English America in which slavery took its firmest roots: the Chesapeake and the West Indies. The early purchase and sale of servant indentures or contracts prepared whites psychologically to accept the institution of slavery.

The American Revolution disrupted indentured servitude by curtailing immigration but did not end the institution. State legislation in the 1780s revived servitude with only minor changes. However, more reliance was placed upon the importation of Germans and Irish as Parliamentary enactments apparently restricted English emigration. The demise of indentured servitude is obscure. The system persisted into the 19th century, although quantitatively it was insignificant after the close of the 18th century.

Indentured servitude met several needs. First, as an immigration agency for the American colonies it helped to relieve the critical labor shortage. However, it also relieved England of a supposed surplus population and allowed the English government to send some of its less desirable citizens to America. Indentured servitude also enabled poor but ambitious Europeans to gain a new lease on life by taking advantage of opportunities in America.

Bibliography: Galenson, David, *White Servitude in Colonial America: An Economic Analysis* (Cambridge Univ. Press, 1982); Jernegan, Marcus, Laboring and Dependent Classes in Colonial America: 1607-1783 (1960; reprint Greenwood, 1980); Morris, Richard B., *Government and Labor in Early America* (1946; reprint Northeastern Univ. Press, 1981).

Alan D. Watson
University of North Carolina at Wilmington

INDEPENDENCE HALL A brick building on Chestnut Street, Philadelphia, where the Declaration of Independence, Articles of Confederation, and United States Constitution were signed. Governor Andrew Hamilton drew the plans for the hall, and it was erected between 1732 and 1741. The Second Continental Congress, and later the state supreme court, met there. Independence Hall now has a museum of furniture, documents, and articles of the Revolutionary period and a set of portraits of the signers of the Declaration of Independence by Charles Willson Peale. The Liberty Bell stands in the central rotunda.

INDIAN CAPTIVITY One important aspect of the numerous wars between colonists and the indigenous inhabitants of North America was the taking of captives by the Indians. From 1689 to 1713, during the intercolonial wars known in America as King William's and Queen Anne's Wars, for example, over 600 men, women, and children were taken captive by the Indian allies of the French. Over the whole colonial period the number surely ran into the thousands. The "captivity narrative," a literature spawned by this phenomenon, became the most popular literary genre in the colonies and was perhaps the first truly American literature.

Ransom was always a prominent motive for the taking of captives; payments, often from the public treasury, secured the release of many. But an even more important motive was the Indian search for replacements for the men, women, and children who had died in the conflicts. Nearly all Indian tribes practiced adoption, and it was not unusual for a captive to find that he or she was intended as a surrogate for a deceased Indian relative. Through such a process, hundreds of colonists were incorporated into tribal life. Out of the 600 captives of the late 17th-century New England wars, for example, only about 30 percent returned to their settler families; the rest remained either with the Indians or with the French in Quebec.

Contemporaries were greatly disturbed by the reluctance of many captives to return. As one wrote, "all men naturally wish for ease, and to avoid the shackles of restraint." Certainly by contrast with English civilization, Indian culture offered social equality, adventure, and, for women, perhaps a less subordinate status. As one former captive wrote, Indian life offered "the most perfect freedom, ease of living, and absence of those cares and corroding solicitudes which so often prevail with us."

Perhaps the first well-known captivity narrative was John Smith's probably fictitious account of his confinement by Powhatan and salvation by Pocahontas. The first to be published in the colonies, however, was Mary Rowlandson's Sovereignty and Goodness of God (1682), which went through 15 editions before 1800. Rowlandson's was a kind of "pilgrim's progress," but by the 18th century, the heyday of the captivity narrative, the genre had been secularized and sensationalized, with a great deal of blood and gore, and even more anti-Indian propaganda. Perhaps the captivity narrative had to take this form, to mask the true and disturbing nature of the captivity phenomena.

Bibliography: Axtell, James, *The European and the Indian* (Oxford Univ. Press, 1981).

John Mack Faragher
Mount Holyoke College

INDIANS AND THE AMERICAN REVOLUTION The American Revolution was a disaster for native Americans, in contrast to its liberating effects on whites. With their commitment to a political and economic order that gave full rein to market forces and the prerogatives of property, the rebellious colonists posed a direct threat to the land and other resources basic to native Americans and their way of life.

After the expulsion of France from North America in 1763, Britain attempted to establish its authority over territory west of the Appalachians so as to control Indian-white trade and colonial expansion. but these efforts, including the Proclamation of 1763 and a strengthened Indian affairs bureaucracy, had little effect. British supplies of trade goods were insufficient, and from Maine to Georgia the Proclamation Line went unenforced in the face of colonial land hunger. The result was native-settler tensions, punctuated by outbreaks of violence and by cessions of land, especially in Kentucky (1768) and Georgia (1773), that were widely resented among the natives affected.

Allegiances and the War. With the outbreak of war between Britain and its colonies, some Indians, such as the Mingoe, Shawnee, and Delaware on the Ohio River, and the Cherokee in Carolina, used the occasion to strike against encroaching settlers. The Creek and Six Nations Iroquois, whose factionalism had formerly enabled them to play the British off against the French, were internally divided. While the Creek remained neutral at the outset, the Six Nations were split between the Oneida and a few others who joined the Americans and the rest who sided with the British. In 1777 the council fire symbolically uniting the Six Nations went out, and Iroquois fought one another alongside British and American troops in several battles. Among relatively autonomous Indians, the Abenaki of northern New England—where the British presence was minimal and where the natives had longstanding ties with the French—were the most significant group to align with the rebels. The colonists also drew on the aid of Indians completely subjugated to their governments, such as the Catawba in South Carolina and the small bands of southern New England.

The Americans quickly recognized the Indian contribution to the British cause and took drastic measures to counter it. The failure of the British to seize Charleston in 1776 enabled rebel troops to organize an expedition against the Cherokee that destroyed the Lower Towns. The effect was to force the cession in 1777 of virtually all Cherokee land in South Carolina and much of that in North Carolina and eastern Tennessee. Some Cherokee and pro-British Creek continued the struggle after the British captured Savannah in 1778 but to little avail. To the north, the Americans launched a scorched earth expedition through Iroquois country, beginning in 1778, driving most Iroquois to Canada. In 1780, American troops undertook a similar march through Delaware and Shawnee villages on the Ohio. Along much of the western frontier, fighting continued even after the British surrendered at Yorktown in October 1781.

Effects of the War. The British-American Treaty of Paris (1783), ending the war, made no mention of the Indians. By implication, the British had agreed that their former allies were subjects of the new republic and, in the treaty conferences that followed, the Indians were obliged to cede vast tracts of land. The cumulative effect of the war and the British abandonment was to break the power of most of the Indian nations to the west of the colonies, especially the Iroquois and Cherokee. While thousands of natives fled north or west to avoid further depredations by the self-proclaimed "empire of liberty," resistance to the Americans continued until 1795 and resurged a decade later under the inspiration of the Shawnee Prophet Tenskwatawa and his brother Tecumseh. Only in 1814 were the last Indian opponents of the American Revolution suppressed militarily.

See also Creek Confederacy; Iroquois Confederacy.

Bibliography: Downes, Randolph, *Council Fires on the Upper Ohio: A Narrative of Indian Affairs in the Upper Ohio Valley until 1795* (Univ. of Pittsburgh Press, 1940); Graymont, Barbara, *The Iroquois in the American Revolution* (Syracuse Univ. Press, 1972); O'Donnell, James H., III, *Southern Indians in the American Revolution* (Univ. of Tennessee Press, 1973).

Neal Salisbury
Smith College

INDIANS, LATIN AMERICAN The enormous ethnographic variation of the indigenous peoples of Latin America is perhaps best ordered by classification into several broad culture areas based on patterns of subsistence strategy, material culture, and social structure. The major areas are the Caribbean, the Andes, the grasslands, and the forests.

Caribbean Region. Columbus first made contact with people of the Circum-Caribbean, an area including the islands, the isthmus of Central America, and the northern coastal areas of Colombia and Venezuela. These farming peoples raised maize, beans, sweet potatoes, bitter and sweet manioc, fruit trees, and cotton. They were skilled artisans, producing loom-woven textiles, ceramics, and gold jewelry. Vulnerable to virulent European diseases such as smallpox and plague, which spread quickly in their dense settlements, and ravaged by Spanish warfare and economic exploitation, the peoples of the Caribbean were decimated in the 16th century and largely replaced by African slaves. The few Indians who remained were hunting and warrior tribes, such as the Caribs, saved by their isolation and lower population density.

Caribbean horticultural techniques had diffused from the great central corridor of the Americas. Maize was first developed in central Mexico from where it spread north to the St. Lawrence Valley of Canada and south to central Chile. Mesoamerican maize farming supported a dense and expanding population and, eventually, grand states and civilizations. The Mayans of Yucatan were unique in their construction of great religious centers while remaining dispersed practitioners of slash-and-burn horticulture.

The peoples of central Mexico, including the Aztecs who flourished somewhat later than the Mayans, practiced more efficient irrigation agriculture, centralized their populations in great cities like Tenochititlan, and organized their social and political system around warfare. Indeed, the rise of endemic warfare to supply tribute may account for the decline of the Mayans. When the Aztec empire was conquered by Cortes in 1519, the population of central Mexico numbered some 25,000,000; a century later it had fallen to no more than 1,000,000. Even then, the Spanish remained in the midst of a vast Indian sea. Since women accounted for only 1 in 10 colonists, there was much miscegenation with the Indians, producing a large mixed-blood, or mestizo, population. In 1810, 60 percent of the population of Mesoamerica was Indian, and another 20 to 30 percent was mestizo.

Andes Region.   The people of the Andean culture area were responsible for the domestication of the potato, varieties of which spread throughout South America and into the Caribbean. With 50 different cultivated crops, including potatoes, maize, beans, squash, manioc, peanuts, peppers, fruit trees, and cotton in their terraced, irrigated, and fertilized fields; with their domesticated llamas, alpacas, dogs, and ducks; with loom-weaving, ceramics, and metallurgy in gold, silver, copper, and tin, the Andeans enjoyed the most efficient and productive system in the Americas. Great population centers grew up in the narrow, fertile valleys of the Andes, linked together by a complex system of roads, canals, and public works, requiring centralized control. Out of this context grew the great Inca empire, with its highly developed class structure, its state religion, and its pattern of territorial conquest, eventually subjecting the peoples from central Colombia to central Chile and western Argentina to Inca authority. Disease spread to Peru in advance of the Spanish, weakening the empire and preparing it, as it were, for conquest. The Indian population continued to fall well

into the 18th century; yet in 1810 Indians constituted two-thirds of the population of Peru.

Grasslands and Forest Regions.   In the grasslands of the south, now Argentina, lived hunting peoples who practiced little or no horticulture. In the 17th century they began to acquire horses and developed an equestrian way of life that paralleled in many respects the culture of the Plains Indians of North America. Nomadic, in politically autonomous bands, they presented an effective barrier to European expansion onto the pampas until systematically extirpated by the Argentinians in the 19th century.

Most of the remainder of the South American continent, including the great Amazonian Valley, may be defined generally as tropical forest. In these regions lived an enormous number of peoples who in spite of their diversity of language and custom shared certain common traits. They farmed, fished from dugout canoes, wove baskets and cotton textiles, and practiced a war complex that included captive-taking and ritual cannibalism. They were generally without domestic animals or the arts of metallurgy and lived in relatively isolated, politically autonomous villages without classes.

For most of the colonial period, these Indians remained outside the perimeter of European control, escaping both the exploitation and disease that destroyed their more densely settled and wealthier cousins. Beginning in the 19th century with the expansion of Brazilian coffee growing, and particularly in the 20th century with the development of rubber, timber, and other forest resource exploitation, these forest peoples have become the most recent victims of a familiar historic pattern.

Bibliography: Lyon, Patricia J., *Native South Americans* (1974; reprint Waveland Press, 1985); Sanchez-Albornoz, Nicolas, *The Population of Latin America: A History* (Univ. of California Press, 1974).

Richard L. Haan
Hartwick College

INDIANS, NORTH AMERICAN   More than 10,000 years of human history had elapsed in North America when the first Europeans arrived. Before the Christian era, small, kin-based bands had moved into virtually every ecological niche on the continent, exchanging resources, goods, and ideas with neighbors near and far. Such exchanges later facilitated the spread of the bow and arrow and (where climate permitted) of agriculture, the development of religiously based exchange networks in the Midwest and Southeast, and the consolidation of pueblos struggling to overcome the effects of the Southwest's aridity. Despite the diversity of their environments, lifeways, and histories, most native Americans lived in autonomous, self-sufficient communities linked by wide-ranging exchanges.

First European Contacts.   During the 16th century, natives from Frobisher Bay to the Gila River met countless European fishermen, sailors, explorers, missionaries, and would-be colonizers. Wherever the visitors attempted to exercise coercive authority, inflict gratuitous violence, or kidnap natives, they met with passive or active resistance. While few Europeans ventured far inland and none (except some Spanish missionaries in Florida) established themselves permanently, they profoundly affected many natives. Their epidemics so drastically depopulated the Southeast as to undermine the centralized Mississippian chiefdoms there. And their glass, copper, and iron wares spread throughout the East as natives came to appreciate their utilitarian value or spiritual power. By the last quarter of the century, a commercial fur trade was fostering new alliances and deadly rivalries among Indians in the Northeast. On returning to the St. Lawrence Valley in the 1580s, the French found a war-torn no man's land from which their Iroquoian-speaking hosts of 40 years earlier had been driven.

The earliest colonies were shaped by this prior history of Indian- European relations. The Powhatan confederacy that confronted Jamestown in 1607 had arisen over three generations in response to rivalries generated by trade, to Spanish and English colonizing efforts, and to depopulation by disease. The disappearance of the St. Lawrence Iroquoians enabled the French to establish themselves in the Canadian interior without intruding on Indian land. In 1609 and again in 1610, they used guns to aid the Huron and Canadian Algonquin in excluding the feared Mohawk from the St. Lawrence trade. The Mohawk then turned to the newly-arrived Dutch on the Hudson for guns and other goods for themselves and their fellow Iroquois. English efforts to penetrate Dutch and French trade networks in the future "New England" succeeded only after two epidemics, in the late 1610s and early 1630s, depopulated portions of the region by as much as 90 percent.

Early Conflicts.   All the early colonies relied heavily on Indians for food, trade, legitimacy in European eyes, and support against hostile natives. Where epidemics, native cooperation, and mere pronouncements failed to stifle resistance against European domination or expansion, the newcomers resorted to coercion, violence, and, frequently, total war. Such was the case in the Pequot War (1637) and several lesser conflicts in New England, Governor Kieft's War (1642-45) and the Peach War

(1655-57) in New Netherland, the various Powhatan wars in Virginia, and the earliest Pueblo revolts in New Mexico.

Behind the settlement frontier in the Northeast, the Iroquois Confederacy became the linchpin of New Netherland's economy and a perennial threat to New France's. With their own hunting territories largely depleted of beaver, the Iroquois used Dutch-supplied guns to raid Indians trading with the French in Canada. Above all they sought trade goods, furs (which could themselves be traded), and captives for adoption to replace those lost to disease and warfare. These raids escalated into the Beaver Wars of the 1640s and 1650s during which the confederacy dispersed the Huron, Erie, and Neutrals of the eastern Great Lakes and established itself as the most formidable military and political power on the continent.

In the Southwest, the normally autonomous and peaceful Pueblo, along with some Apache and Navaho, also united in revolt. The Pueblo Revolt (1680) was directed against the abuses of *encomenderos*, civil officials, and, above all, the Franciscan missionaries who were systematically uprooting native religion. Although the Spanish reconquered New Mexico in 1692, they wisely refrained from trying to reimpose total control of Pueblo life. Indians attended Catholic services if they chose but were simultaneously permitted to continue their traditional religious practices undisturbed.

Role in International Politics.   After the English conquest of New Netherland in 1664, both England and France sought to make the Iroquois instruments of their imperial policies. In 1675-76, settler pressures on Indian land led to armed conflicts in the New England and Chesapeake colonies. With New York's backing, the Iroquois helped defeat the New England Indians in King Philip's War and then joined Albany in establishing and overseeing the "Covenant Chain" system of alliances linking Indians and colonies from Virginia to Massachusetts. In the meantime, Jesuit missionaries made inroads among the Iroquois, creating religious and political divisions that widened during the 1680s as Iroquois warriors fought Indian allies of the French along a front extending from Maine to Minnesota. The Iroquois turned their factionalism to diplomatic advantage by signing a treaty of neutrality with France in 1701 to augment their special relationship with England.

Imperial competition and English settlement likewise affected native life in the southeast, where South Carolina (settled 1670) and Louisiana (settled 1699) quickly surpassed the influence of Virginia and Florida. Shawnee, Yamasee, Creek, Chickasaw, Cherokee, and Catawba obtained guns from Carolina traders in exchange for deerskins and for Tuscarora, Westo, Timucua, Apalachee, Guale, and Choctaw captives, who were then resold as

INDIANS, NORTH AMERICAN: TOPIC GUIDE

GROUPS

Aleuts
Algonquin Indians
Apache Indians
Arawak
California Indians
Cherokee Indians
Chickasaw Indians
Choctaw Indians
Creek Confederacy
Desert Indians of the Southwest
Eskimo (Inuit)
Great Basin and Rocky Mountain Indians

Great Plains Indians
Huron Indians
Indians, Latin American
Iroquois Confederacy
Lumbee Indians
Navaho Indians
Northwest Coast Indians
Powhatan Confederacy
Pueblo Indians
Seminole Indians
Subarctic Indians
Wappinger Confederacy

THEMES

African-Indian Contact
Bering Straits Hypothesis
Black Legend
Buffalo
Disease
Encomienda and Hacienda
French Colonies (see **Topic Guide**)
Friendly Association for Regaining and
    Preserving Peace with the Indians by Pacific
    Measures
Frontier (see **Topic Guide**)
Fur Trade
Horse
Indian Captivity

Indians and the American Revolution
Mesa Verde
Missions and Missionaries
New World Crops
Norumbega
Praying Towns
Proclamation of 1763
Requerimiento
Revitalization Movements
Sachems
Scalping
Spanish Colonies (see **Topic Guide**)
Wampum

BIOGRAPHIES

Bosomworth, Mary Musgrove
Brant, Joseph
Brims
Canonchet
Canonicus
Cofitachique, Lady of
Cornstalk
Dekanawidah
Dragging Canoe (Tsiyu-Gunsini)
Duston, Hannah
Eliot, John
Garankonthie, Daniel
Hendrick
Jemison, Mary
Kino, Eusebio Francisco
La Demoiselle ("Old Briton")
Las Casas, Bartolome de
Logan, James
McGillivray, Alexander
Malinche
Massassoit
Metacomet (King Philip)
Miantonomo
Montezuma
Montour, Madame
Neolin (the Delaware Prophet)

Oacpicagigua, Luis
Occom, Samson
Oconostota
Opechancanough
Outacity
Pocahontas
Pontiac
Pope
Powhatan
Red Jacket
Red Shoes
Rowlandson, Mary
Sassacus
Serra, Junipero
Shikellamy
Skaniandariio
Skenandoa
Squanto
Tammany
Teedyuskung
Tekawitha, Catherine
Tomochichi
Uncas
Ward, Nancy
Wheelock, Eleazar
Zeisberger, David

slaves in the West Indies. From the turn of the century, the Creek also traded with the French, playing off the two powers as a means of maintaining their autonomy. And the Choctaw found in French guns an effective defense against Chickasaw and Creek slave raiders. Trader abuses and settler encroachments eventually contributed to resentment among South Carolina's allies. In 1715 the Yamasee led the Shawnee and Creek in the largest Indian rebellion yet in the British colonies. Only the assistance of the Cherokee enabled the English to suppress the uprising.

Expansion of the Colonies. Through the first half of the 18th century, most native groups located east of the Mississippi River but west of the English settlements exchanged furs for trade goods with any and all Europeans in their vicinity. In so doing, they reinforced older practices of exchanging gifts as a means of cementing ties within and between autonomous communities. As the century wore on, however, the impact of a growing, land-hungry colonial population became more apparent, especially in the Southeast, where the Creek ceded land for the new colony of Georgia in 1733, and in eastern Pennsylvania, where the Delaware lost all their land after a series of fraudulent seizures by the colony culminating in 1741. Although most colonial expansion was English, the spread of tobacco plantations in Louisiana led the French to attack and disperse the Natchez between 1729 and 1731. Meanwhile, beaver and deer populations dwindled as Indian indebtedness and dependence on the fur trade increased, along with the prominence of alcohol as a commodity. At many places Indians came under pressure to cede land as a means of settling their debts. Increasingly, Britain and France used the trade to distribute gifts and thereby secure native allies, underscoring the fact that the Indians' value to Europeans was no longer in their productivity but in their ability to aid one power in making territorial gains at the other's expense.

During the French and Indian War (Seven Years' War, 1756-63), the Delaware, Shawnee, and Cherokee retaliated against settler encroachments by siding with the French and their allies in the Northwest. But for the Creek and Iroquois, accustomed to playing the two powers off against one another, a decision was more difficult. The presence within each of pro-British, pro-French, and neutralist factions—formerly a source of strength—now weakened these two nations. While the Creek remained neutral, Iroquois fought on both sides until 1759 when, sensing the outcome, the confederacy joined the English. After France's defeat in 1763, its Indian allies attempted unsuccessfully to expel the British from their newly-seized Northwestern forts in the uprising known as Pontiac's Rebellion. Thereafter, native-settler tensions along the frontier intensified despite Britain's efforts to assert control over its colonies and their Indian affairs.

The Revolution and Its Effects. With the outbreak of the American Revolution, the Indians formerly allied with France readily joined the British against the expansionist rebels. The Creek and Iroquois were again weakened by divisions within their own ranks, although large numbers of each eventually contributed significantly to the British cause. Rebel retaliation against pro-British Indians inflicted particular damage on the Iroquois, Cherokee, Shawnee, and Delaware. After the war all the inland groups were obliged to recognize the sovereignty of the new republic and to cede vast tracts of additional land.

By the end of the colonial period, nearly all Indians in North America had been affected by the European invasion

---

INDIAN WARS: TOPIC GUIDE

Aleut Revolt (1761-66)
Augusta, Congress of (1763)
Augusta, Treaty of (1773)
Beaver Wars
Casco Treaties (1678, 1703)
Cherokee Wars (1760-81)
Cherry Valley Massacre (1778)
Chickasaw-French War (1736-40)
Chickasaw Treaty (1786)
Deerfield Massacre (1704)
Dutch-Indian Wars
Easton, Treaty of (1758)
Fort Stanwix, Treaties of, 1768 and 1784
Fox-French Wars
French and Indian War (1754-63)
Gnadenheutten Massacre
Hard Labor Creek, Treaty of
Hopewell, Treaty of
Indians and the American Revolution
Iroquois Treaties (1684, 1791)
King Philip's War (1675-76)
Lochaber, Treaty of
Lord Dunmore's War (1774)
Natchez Revolt (1729-31)
Niagara, Great Indian Council at (1741)
Pavonia Massacre
Pequot War (1637)
Pima Revolt (1751)
Pittsburg, Treaty of (1775)
Pontiac's Rebellion
Pueblo Revolt (1680)
Shackamaxon, Treaty of (1682-83)
Susquehannock War (1676)
Sycamore Shoals, Treaty of (1775)
Tuscarora War (1711-13)
Walking Purchase
War (see **Topic Guide**)
Westo Wars (1680)
Yamassee War (1715-16)

that began nearly three centuries earlier. Along the Eastern seaboard, native communities struggled to retain their distinctive identities and traditions in the face of depopulation from disease, the ravages of alcohol, the loss of resources and skills, and pressures to sell additional land and convert to Christianity. After 1783 these same factors confronted the recently powerful Iroquois, Cherokee, Creek, and other inland groups. While many of these Indians avoided confronting the United States, others—particularly France's former allies in the Northwest plus the pro-British Creek—continued to resist militarily until 1794, and some rallied once again during the War of 1812.

In the upper Great Lakes and Illinois areas, the fur trade and attendant conflicts had uprooted many native communities, driving them southward and westward. Some of these joined other groups on the Great Plains where, adopting Spanish horses and French guns, they developed a nomadic way of life based on the pursuit of buffalo. On the Pacific coast, Spanish missionaries in California and Russian and British traders on the Northwest coast were transforming the lives of Indians they met and indirectly affecting many others. Only a few remote bands in the western mountains remained oblivious to Europeans as the 18th century drew to a close.

Bibliography: Axtell, James, *The Invasion Within: The Contest of Cultures in Colonial North America* (Oxford Univ. Press, 1985); Jennings, Francis, *The Invasion of America: Indians, Colonialism, and the Cant of Conquest* (Univ. of North Carolina Press, 1975); Salisbury, Neal, *Manitou and Providence: Indians, Europeans, and the Making of New England, 1500-1643* (Oxford Univ. Press, 1982); Spicer, Edward, *Cycles of Conquest: The Impact of Spain, Mexico, and the United States on the Indians of the Southwest, 1533-1960* (Tucson: Univ. of Arizona Press, 1962); Wright, J. Leitch, Jr., *The Only Land They Knew: The Tragic Story of the American Indians in the Old South* (The Free Press, 1981).

Neal Salisbury
Smith College

INDIGO This most important natural blue dye, native to India, was introduced into Europe in the 16th century. In the late 17th century New World colonists adapted indigo culture to the West Indies, where the French monopolized production on the island of Montserrat. But despite attempts the English had great difficulty in transplanting indigo to their colonies. In the 1740s, Eliza Lucas (Pinckney), a young Antigua woman managing her father's South Carolina plantations, spent several years experimenting with indigo and, with the help of a West Indian overseer and slaves experienced in indigo culture, developed techniques that turned indigo into Carolina's second largest export crop. Rice, the most important crop, was grown in the lowlands, while indigo required high

ground, and the two commodities had different growing seasons, placing them in perfect harmony. Carolina indigo was inferior to West and East Indian varieties, but Parliamentary bounties helped the industry to flourish until the Revolution.

INGLIS, CHARLES (1734-1816) An Anglican clergyman, Loyalist, and first colonial bishop, Inglis was the son of an Irish minister and took a preaching post in 1755 at the Free School in Lancaster, Pennsylvania. In 1758 he was ordained deacon and priest of Dover, Delaware, and Kent County. In 1766 he became assistant to the Reverend Samuel Auchmuty at Trinity Church in New York City and fostered the Anglican church with Reverend Thomas Bradbury Chandler of Elizabethtown, New Jersey. His letters to English leaders document his efforts to convert the Mohawk Valley Indians.

A firm Loyalist, Inglis deplored the American Revolution and responded to Thomas Paine's *Common Sense* in a pamphlet, *The True Interest of America Impartially Stated*, in 1776. He fled New York when General Washington arrived but returned with the British and saved St. Paul's Church from burning. In 1777, Auchmuty died, and Inglis succeeded him. He defended the Loyalists' position in his numerous writings, such as his letters published under the pen name of "Papinian." These letters tried to persuade the rebels to abandon the war and appeared as a pamphlet (1779). He left the United States in 1783, and in 1787 he was appointed Anglican bishop in Nova Scotia.

INQUISITION, SPANISH The Holy Office of the Inquisition arrived in the Spanish colonies as early as 1517, its task to preserve religious orthodoxy and thus contribute to the stable union of church and state. Not until 1570 was the first tribunal established in Lima, Peru; previous to that date its authority was exercised by regular and secular clergy. Most inquisitorial procedures were carried out against Europeans, but Indians could be prosecuted until 1570, when jurisdiction over native orthodoxy was transferred to the episcopal courts. Arguments over jurisdiction and the clear misuse of power for personal gain by Inquisitors constantly created conflict between the Holy Office and other religious and secular authorities, but the Inquisition continued to function in the Spanish colonies until the 19th century wars for independence.

INSURANCE Since most investment in the colonial economy was placed by British merchants and capitalists, most insurance for indemnifying them against risk of loss was English as well. With the growth of colonial-owned shipping in the 18th century came the establishment of the first American marine insurance companies—at Philadelphia in 1721, and at Boston in 1724. The first mutual fire insurance society was established in Charleston in 1735; the first life insurance group in Philadelphia in 1759. The construction of precise mortality tables, upon which modern insurance depends, began in America with the work of Harvard professor Edward Wigglesworth, who compiled the first American table in 1789. By the end of the 18th century, some 30 American companies were issuing policies against a number of risks.

IRON ACTS (1750, 1757)

The Iron Acts passed by Parliament in 1750 and 1757 were part of a series of measures designed to protect Britain's industrial economy of Britain by means of mercantilist trade sanctions. In order to maintain a high level of supply of raw material for the British iron industry in the aftermath of a drop in iron imports from Sweden, Parliament decreed that no new iron forges or mills could be established in the American colonies. Unfinished pig and bar iron from America would, however, be granted a preferential lowering of import duties, which was dropped altogether in the Iron Act of 1757. This act did not, however, substantially increase iron imports to Britain.

IRON MANUFACTURING

Many of the earliest European explorers, John Smith among them, noted an abundance of both iron ore and wood fuel in America. Bog ores, found in eastern Massachusetts and along the Jersey shore, supplied the first colonial furnaces, such as the Lynn Iron Works, founded in 1643 by John Winthrop, Jr. He brought over from Europe a number of skilled iron workers, men who became the founders of the industry throughout the Northeast. The Lynn Works, at its peak producing eight tons a week, ranked with the best European furnaces, turning out pots, kettles, and hollow ware, as well as pigs and wrought bars. Most early iron works, however, were little more than large blacksmiths' forges (known as bloomeries). In 1700 colonial production amounted to little more than one percent of world production.

In the 18th century rock ores were discovered in outcroppings along the Connecticut and Hudson rivers and in northern New Jersey and eastern Pennsylvania. These were the ores used in the furnaces of the Principio Company of Maryland (1715); of Henry William Stiegel, who built a large iron and glass works in Pennsylvania; and of Peter Hasenclever, who in the 1760s operated a works in northern New Jersey with six blast furnaces and seven forges—the largest industrial enterprise in colonial America prior to the Revolution. These large works benefited from the passage of the Iron Acts (1750, 1757). By 1775 the colonial proportion of world production had risen to nearly 15 percent.

Production was sufficient to supply the military needs of the Revolution, but with the loss of the English market for pig and bar iron and English capital for maintenance and expansion, the industry fell into decline thereafter, not to revive until the late 19th century.

See also Iron Acts.

IROQUOIS CONFEDERACY

Based in what is now upstate New York, the Iroquois Confederacy, or League, was the most powerful and influential Indian group in colonial North America. While most scholars date its founding to shortly before the arrival of Europeans, many Iroquois claim it has far greater antiquity. Either way, it arose through the efforts of Deganawida and Hiawatha to end war among the Five Nations by establishing laws and customs for preserving unity and rituals for exchanging wampum "words" of peace and condolence. The result was a confederacy modeled on the multifamily Iroquois longhouse, with the Seneca as keepers of the western door, the Mohawk as keepers of the eastern door, the Onondaga as keepers of the council fire, and the Cayuga and Oneida as younger brothers.

As European trade goods generated rivalries among native Americans, the confederacy made its presence felt. After being expelled by the French and their Indian allies from the St. Lawrence Valley in 1609-10, the Mohawk turned to the Dutch in the Hudson Valley. Here they obtained guns and other goods plus New England wampum for circulation among the Five Nations. Heavily armed Iroquois then attacked Indians trading with the French and carried the furs they captured to the Dutch. During the Beaver Wars of the 1640s and 1650s, the Five Nations dispersed the Huron, Neutrals, and Erie as political entities so as to control the Great Lakes fur trade and gain captives to replace the many Iroquois lost through disease and warfare.

Iroquois strategy shifted after 1660 as Anglo-French imperial expansion brought the fall of New Netherland to England, a militarily stronger New France, and the arming of the confederacy's Indian rivals. Seeking to accommodate both powers, the Iroquois accepted French Jesuit missionaries while joining New York in establishing and overseeing a "Covenant Chain" of alliances linking subject Indians to the English colonies from Virginia northward. But their ties to the British remained stronger, and they were drawn into further struggles with the French and their allies until 1701, when, in simultaneous agreements at Montreal and Albany, they agreed to remain neutral in future Anglo-French conflicts.

The 18th Century. During the next half century, the Iroquois traded peacefully on all sides while expanding their Covenant Chain role in the English colonies. They adopted the Tuscarora as the sixth nation of the confederacy after the latter fled from North Carolina, oversaw the relocation of Shawnee, Delaware, and other groups in western Pennsylvania and Ohio, and waged incessant warfare with the Catawba and Cherokee. Meanwhile, French and English traders were moving inland, and the English colonies were growing at an explosive rate. The result was a heightened Anglo-French competition, centered after mid-century on the Ohio Valley, that threatened the delicate balance of forces underlying Iroquois peace and prosperity. At the outbreak of war between England and France in 1755, the confederacy remained neutral while members fought on both sides. As the final outcome of the French and Indian War became apparent, the confederacy joined the English cause in 1759 in return for guarantees of trade goods and the security of its lands. With France's exodus from North America as a result of the English victory, the commercial and military roles of the confederacy ended just as settler land-hunger became irrepressible.

During the American Revolution, the Oneida and a few others joined the Americans but most fought with the British. In retaliation the rebels conducted scorched earth raids in Iroquois country, driving many inhabitants to Canada. The Treaty of Paris (1783), settling the war, left confederacy members to deal with the victorious Americans on their own. The result was extensive cessions of land to New York and Pennsylvania, leaving only scattered settlements in upstate New York. Although the confederacy continued to serve as a focal point for Iroquois identity, its decisive political role was ended.

See also French and Indian War.

Bibliography: Jennings, Francis, *The Ambiguous Iroquois Empire: The Covenant Chain of Indian Tribes with English Colonies from Its Beginnings to the Lancaster Treaty of 1744* (W. W. Norton, 1984); Merrell, James H., and Richter, Daniel K., eds., *Beyond the Covenant Chain: The Iroquois and Their Neighbors in Indian North America, 1600-1800* (Syracuse Univ. Press, 1987); Wallace, Anthony F. C., *The Death and Rebirth of the Seneca* (Knopf, 1970).

Neal Salisbury
Smith College

IROQUOIS TREATIES (1684, 1701) In 1684 the Iroquois sought to extend their control over both the Illinois country and northern Virginia. They hoped to make the Indians of those regions tributary to the Iroquois Confederacy without the mediation of European colonists. The English reaction to the ensuing raids was muted by the need to uphold the Iroquois against the French, for if the French defeated the Indians there would be no further English expansion westward. The treaty concluded in 1684 between Virginia and the confederacy did not punish the Iroquois in any way and encouraged the Seneca especially to continue to push west.

By 1701 the escalating warfare between the Iroquois and the French had resulted in the invasion of confederacy territory by French-allied Indians and the subsequent suing for peace in Montreal by Iroquois representatives. The French desired only to detach the Iroquois from the British while retaining the confederacy as a buffer between the two colonial empires and were therefore content to force the Iroquois to declare neutrality. As the new century began the confederacy found itself in the unenviable position of being officially neutral between two powers almost continuously at war.

IZARD, RALPH (1741-1804) A wealthy Revolutionary patriot, diplomat, and senator, born near Charleston, South Carolina, Izard inherited his father's estate and was sent to school in England. He returned to Carolina (1764) and took charge of the family's plantations. He returned to England to use his influence in mending the conflict with the colonists (1775). Becoming sympathetic with the patriot cause, he moved with his family to Paris (1776). He bitterly resented Benjamin Franklin for not recognizing his right in France as an American diplomat. In Philadelphia, Izard helped General Greene to take command of the southern army (1780) and was chosen a delegate from South Carolina to Congress. He served in the legislature and sat in the U.S. Senate (1789-95).

J

JAMES, THOMAS (c.1593-1635) An English navigator who sailed to Hudson's Bay in search of a Northwest Passage in 1631, James explored the southern extension of the bay, which thereafter took his name. His narrative, *Strange and Dangerous Voyage* (1633), remained popular for many years.

See also Northwest Passage.

Later illustrations of the founding of Jamestown ignored the harsh environment of the first years. *(Library of Congress)*

JAMESTOWN Jamestown (Virginia) was England's first successful colony in America and followed several abortive attempts. Captain Christopher Newport landed 104 men and boys on the shore of the James River in April 1607. The unhealthy environment caused a horrifying death rate and the earliest settlers seldom had the needed skills for frontier living. The colony survived only through the aggressive leadership of Captain John Smith. After the "Starving Time" of 1609-10, the survivors abandoned the colony but returned upon meeting supply ships in Chesapeake Bay. Governors Thomas Dale and Thomas Gates imposed martial law and stabilized the colony. With tobacco promising economic salvation, an improved land policy after 1616, along with establishment of a representative assembly, built the population to about 2,000 and spread settlement beyond the confines of the town. The Indian attack of 1622 reversed the trend. The town of Jamestown served as the colony's capital until 1699 when the burning of the capital occasioned a new start in Williamsburg. During the next century, Jamestown dwindled to virtually a ghost town.

Bibliography: Morton, Richard L., Colonial Virginia, vol. 1 (Univ. of North Carolina Press, 1960).

Primarily a diplomat during the Revolutionary War, John Jay later served as chief justice of the United States and as governor of New York. *(Library of Congress)*

JARRATT, DEVEREUX (1733-1801) An Episcopal religious leader, born in New Kent County, Virginia, Jarratt was raised on a plantation and spent much of his youth training racehorses. Largely self-taught, he served briefly as a schoolmaster before beginning serious religious studies with Alexander Martin in 1758. Jarratt was ordained by the Church of England in 1762 and in the following year was appointed rector of Bath parish in Dinwiddie County, Vir-

After writing the Declaration of Independence, Thomas Jefferson reformed Virginia's laws while governor and then returned to national politics. (*Library of Congress*)

ginia. From 1764 to 1772 he preached along the Virginia frontier, sparking a wave of religious enthusiasm. Jarratt's ministry, although Episcopal, was seen as a forerunner of the Methodist movement.

JAY, JOHN (1745-1829) A statesman, diplomat, and jurist, Jay was born to a prominent New York family and educated at King's College (now Columbia). Subsequently admitted to the New York bar, he practiced law until becoming immersed in political activity during the 1770s. Jay served as a delegate to the First and Second Continental Congresses; he was also a principal architect of the New York constitution and chief justice of the state. He was president of Congress

from December 1778 until September 1779, when he went to Spain on an unsuccessful mission as U.S. minister.

In 1782 he joined the American peace commission in Paris and played a key role in the decision to negotiate a peace treaty with Britain without consulting America's ally France. When Jay returned to the United States, he became secretary of foreign affairs (1784-89). Among many activities as secretary, he was involved in inconclusive negotiations with Spain over U.S. rights to navigate the Mississippi River. Convinced by experience of the nation's weakness in foreign affairs, Jay supported the new and strengthened U.S. Constitution as one of the three authors of The Federalist (1787-88). In later years Jay was the first chief justice of the United

States (1789-95), negotiator of a major treaty with Britain in 1794, and governor of New York (1795-1801). He died after a long retirement.

See also Paris, Treaty of (1783).

Bibliography: Morris, Richard B., *Witnesses at the Creation: Hamilton, Madison, Jay, and the Constitution* (Holt, Rinehart & Winston, 1985).

Douglas M. Arnold
The Papers of Benjamin Franklin

JEFFERSON, THOMAS (1743-1826)   Leader of the American Enlightenment, republican political philosopher, and deist, Jefferson was born in Albemarle County, Virginia, and died there in his home, Monticello. As a young lawyer, he joined the Virginia House of Burgesses in 1769, soon promoting an unsuccessful bill to allow manumission of slaves and joining Patrick Henry in advocating resistance to British colonial policies.

National Leader.   In 1775 he joined the Second Continental Congress, composing the Declaration of Independence in 1776. In the late 1770s, and as a governor of Virginia (1779-81), he guided the historic reform of the laws of Virginia, abolishing the laws of primogeniture and entail and of the establishment of religion. In 1783 he returned to the Continental Congress, introducing in 1784 an unsuccessful ordinance to ban slavery in the western part of the United States after 1800 and traveling to France to negotiate treaties with European governments. He was U.S. minister to France (1785-89) during the composition and ratification of the Constitution.

After 1789, Jefferson's distinguished political career included the positions of George Washington's secretary of state (1790-93), John Adams's vice president (1797-1801), and third president of the United States (1801-09). He headed the new Democratic-Republican party (opposed to the Federalist party headed by Alexander Hamilton) through which he sought to preserve citizens' individual liberties. The Louisiana Purchase of 1803, which almost doubled the size of the United States, was his most important act as president.

Intellectual Achievements.   "A Summary View of the Rights of British America" (1774), the Declaration of Independence (1776), "An Act for Establishing Religious Freedom" (1779), and *Notes on the State of Virginia* (1781-83) define his republicanism and secure his position in the Enlightenment. He believed that humankind possesses natural rights, which included liberty and self-government; reason, which allowed discovery of the laws of nature; and a moral sense, which united individuals through affection. He thought that society should be a union of individuals who have both duties and rights, a union ruled by a natural aristocracy and representative government. Believing education necessary for citizens living under a representative government, he devoted his last years to the establishment and management of the University of Virginia.

Jefferson mingled the classical ideal of a unified society of virtuous citizens with the modern ideal of free citizens protected in the pursuit of their interests. Fearing miscegenation and future discord between whites and blacks, he envisioned no place in his republic for blacks, whom he advocated shipping to Africa after they had been sufficiently educated to found their own society.

See also Declaration of Independence; Republicanism; Virginia.

Bibliography: Boyd, Julian P. et al., eds., *The Papers of Thomas Jefferson* (Princeton Univ. Press, 1950); Koch, Adrienne, *The Philosophy of Thomas Jefferson* (Columbia Univ. Press, 1943); Malone, Dumas, *Jefferson and His Time*, 6 vols. (Little, Brown, 1948-81); Peterson, Merrill D., ed., *Thomas Jefferson: A Reference Biography* (Scribners, 1986).

John Saillant
Brown University

JEMISON, MARY (1743-1833)   Adopted member of the Genesee nation, Jemison was born at sea to Irish immigrant parents and spent her early childhood in western Pennsylvania. In 1758, during the French and Indian War, she was captured by Indian allies of the French and was adopted by two Seneca women. She later married a Delaware warrior who settled in the Genesee Valley of western New York. Refusing an offer of return after the conclusion of the war and having become accepted among the Genesee, she married Chief Hiokatoo after the death of her first husband. A supporter of the cause of American independence, she spent her last years on the Buffalo Creek Reservation.

JENCKES, JOSEPH (1632-1717)   An iron manufacturer and colonial leader born in Hammersmith, England, Jenckes was the son of an ironmaster who immigrated to the Massachusetts Bay Colony. In 1650, Jenckes followed his father to America and settled in Rhode Island, where iron ore had been discovered. Purchasing a tract of land on the Pawtuxet River in 1669, he built a sawmill and a forge and founded an independent community. Although Pawtuxet was attacked and burned during King Philip's War (1675-76) Jenckes directed the reconstruction and encouraged further settlement. In 1679 he served as deputy in the General Assembly and from 1680 to 1698 was assistant to the colonial governor.

JENKIN'S EAR, WAR OF (1739-43)   This colonial conflict between Great Britain and Spain was the American counterpart of the War of Austrian Succession in Europe. In the early 18th century, tensions between British and Spanish colonial authorities had steadily intensified. The name of this conflict arose from a violent naval incident off Florida in which Robert Jenkins, a British seaman, lost an ear in a skirmish with the Spanish fleet. The incident served as the justification for Great Britain's declaration of war against Spanish colonial possessions in June 1739, which was followed by naval operations in the Caribbean and land engagements along the Georgia-Florida border. At sea, British Admiral Edward Vernon captured Puerto Bello in Panama in 1739 but suffered a serious defeat off Cartagena, Colombia, in the following year. On land, Georgia Governor James Oglethorpe gained the alliance of the Creek nation for an invasion of Florida in 1740, initially capturing the Spanish forts of San Francisco de Pupo and Picolata on the St. Johns River but failing to take St. Augustine in 1742. The Spanish mounted a counterinvasion of Georgia in 1743, but by that time the focus of the conflict, now known as King George's War, had shifted to Canada and Europe.

See also King George's War.

JESUITS   Jesuits, members of the Society of Jesus, comprise the Roman Catholic religious order most closely associated with missionary work in Britain's North American colonies. In 1642, Iroquois Indians, raiding in what was to become Michigan, captured French Jesuit Father Isaac Jogues and two lay brothers. They were brought to Ossernenon, a Mohawk village near present-day Auriesville, New York, where they were tortured for a year. Rene Goupil was murdered. Father Jogues escaped, only to return to New York, where he was captured and killed in October 1646 along with a lay helper, Jean de LaLande. With the English conquest of New York, Jesuit activity there ceased until the arrival of Father Ferdinand Farmer (Steinmeyer), who established the first Catholic church in New York during the Revolution.

Steinmeyer's main missionary work was in southeastern Pennsylvania where, in 1741, German Jesuits had established two missions, at Conewago and Goshenhoppen. Jesuits also founded St. Joseph's, Philadelphia's first Catholic church, in 1733. From 1655 to 1658 there was a temporary Jesuit presence in Virginia, composed primarily of exiles from the Puritan revolution in Maryland. The bulk of Jesuit activity in the colonies, however, occurred in Maryland.

Maryland Jesuits.   English Jesuits led by Father Andrew White sailed with the first settlers to Maryland in 1634. Centered in the south of Maryland, around St. Mary's, Jesuits supported themselves by farming while pursuing mission work. Expelled during the English Civil War, they returned to Maryland in 1648. Because the Calvert family, the proprietors of the colony, wished to keep tight control over the clergy and avoid affronting Protestant settlers or the British Crown, Maryland Jesuits were technically Gentlemen Adventurers, holding land on the same terms as other settlers and subject to taxation. This deviation from canonical procedures caused constant friction between the proprietors and the Society. When Pope Clement XIV suppressed the Society of Jesus in 1773, Maryland Jesuits retained their lands and organization, functioning as secular priests until their restoration in 1814. An American Jesuit, Father John Carroll, became bishop of Baltimore, the first American see, after the Revolution.

Bibliography: Hughes, Thomas J., *History of the Society of Jesus in North America: Colonial and Federal*, 4 vols. (Longmans, Green, 1907-17); Parkman, Francis, *The Jesuits in North America in the Seventeenth Century*, 2 vols. (1895; reprint Corner House, 1970).

Leonard R. Riforgiato
Pennsylvania State University

JEWS   In 1654, 23 Dutch Jews disembarked from the small French frigate *Sainte Catherine* at the trading colony of New Amsterdam. These refugees, fleeing north from the Portuguese, who had recaptured Brazil from Holland, constituted the beginning of North American Jewish life. A small but steady trickle of Jewish immigrants followed these first pioneers. Some emigrated from Spain, Portugal, Holland, and Italy (Sephardic Jews), others from Poland, Hungary, Germany, and Lithuania (Ashkenazic Jews). Although the vast majority of Jewish immigrants settled in large urban centers—Newport, New York, Philadelphia, Charleston, and Savannah—an enterprising few were inevitably drawn to smaller communities that offered them the hope of economic advancement. By the time of the American Revolution, there were between 1,500 and 2,500 Jews in the colonies (or .05 to .10 percent of America's total population).

Jews came to the New World for many reasons, but the most compelling factor was probably economic ambition. They sought to escape the political oppression and economic disabilities that dominated their European existence. Religious persecution motivated some, but for the most part early settlers—if loyal to their faith—were hardly punctilious about observing it. The absence of a Jewish communal infrastructure in the colonies meant that Jewish settlers would necessarily forgo the customary ritual and religious amenities that characterize an established community.

The Jew of 18th-century America was most likely to be a shopkeeper or merchant, but colonial Jews were also found in a variety of trades that included watchmaking, soapmaking, baking, shoemaking, wigmaking, engraving, snuffmaking, distilling, indigo sorting, and candlestick-making. Some Jews participated in the African slave trade and even in the hazardous enterprise of privateering. The army and navy supply business attracted several Jewish merchants, as did trading and land speculation. The most successful were those engaged in the triangular trade with Europe and the West Indies. Even though Jews could have conceivably become farmers in the New World (a vocation from which they were barred in Europe), most avoided that type of life with which they had little experience. Some Southern Jews, however, were plantation owners combining farming, ranching, and commerce. There were practically no Jews in the profession of law, which in some colonies was restricted to Christians, but a few individuals did practice medicine, then still considered a craft.

Religious Observance. Participation and membership in the Jewish community was essentially voluntaristic. Unlike the European governments, colonial governments did not empower local Jewish communities to coerce membership. Social pressure did urge affiliation, however, and the fear of not receiving a proper Jewish burial was a particularly compelling reason to become a paying member. Worship services were held in most communities just as soon as a *minyan* (the requisite quorum of ten males 13 years of age or older) could be assembled. Yet, the acquisition of cemetery grounds usually preceded the erection of a synagogue structure.

From its inception, the synagogue has been the central organ of Jewish life in the New World. Large communities employed a cantor (who chanted the worship service), a sexton, and also a ritual slaughterer. Prior to 1840, no synagogue was led by an ordained rabbi. Synagogues also provided education for children of the poor, relief for the needy, medical care for the sick, and burial for the indigent dead.

The first colonial congregations convened in rented houses or rooms. It was not until the mid-18th century that some colonial Jewish communities could afford to erect their own synagogue buildings: New York in 1730, Newport in 1763, Philadelphia in 1782, and Charleston in 1794.

Up to the Revolution, colonial Jewry remained fundamentally an immigrant group. Notable Jews during this period, with few exceptions, were foreign-born. Yet, these early settlers forged patterns of existence that influenced and directed the character of American Jewry during subsequent years. During their first century on the North American continent, Jews adapted themselves to the realities of colonial and frontier life. They established a cohesive community based on voluntarism; they struggled to legitimate the rights of Jews to differ from the Christian majority within which they existed; and they sought to maintain their Jewish identity in an open society, an environment in which Jews mixed freely with non-Jews.

Era of the Revolution. Jews participated politically, economically, and militarily in the American Revolution. Like their fellow colonists, their loyalties were often divided: Some remained staunch Loyalists; others were devoted patriots; many vacillated according to prevailing conditions. In the wake of the Revolution, Jews received full and equal citizenship. Article VI, section 3, of the Constitution insured that no religious test would ever be required for any office of the federal government—a provision that guaranteed political equality, at least on the federal level. This assurance imbued American Jews with the confidence to sustain a protracted struggle to safeguard and broaden American principles of religious freedom in the years ahead.

See also Religion.

Bibliography: Borden, Morton, *Jews, Turks, and Infidels* (Univ. of North Carolina Press, 1984); Goodman, Abraham V., *American Overture: Jewish Rights in Colonial Times* (Jewish Pub. Society of America, 1947); Marcus, Jacob Rader, *The Colonial American Jew*, 3 vols. (Wayne State Univ. Press, 1970); Marcus, Jacob Rader, *Early American Jewry*, 2 vols. (Jewish Pub. Society of America, 1951, 1953); Marcus, Jacob Rader, ed., *The Jew and the American Revolution: A Bicentennial Documentary Revolution* (Greenwood Press, 1975); Sarna, Jonathan D., Kraut, Benny, and Joseph, Samuel K., eds., *Jews and the Founding of the Republic* (Markus Wiener, 1985).

Gary P. Zola
Hebrew Union College-Jewish Institute of Religion

JOHNSON, EDWARD (1598-1672) A writer and town official in Massachusetts, Johnson was born in Canterbury, England. He received training as a joiner and came to Boston in 1630, where he was licensed to trade with the Indians and was acknowledged a freeman in May 1631. He returned to England to bring back his family and settled in Charlestown, Massachusetts, in 1636. In 1640, Johnson was a founding member of the town of Woburn, Massachusetts, and served for 32 years in various town offices, such as proprietor, clerk, selectman, militia captain, surveyor, inspector of arms, and "perfector of lawes." He was a deputy to the Massachusetts General Court from 1634 to 1672 except 1647-48.

In May 1650 he started his detailed chronicle of life in New England, *The Wonder-Working Providence of Sion's Saviour in New England*, which was first published anonymously in London in 1653. The stories and verse were written to prove how God favored New England with miraculous acts, but Johnson's precise accounts are also an excellent source for early colonial activities.

JOHNSON, GUY (1740-88) Loyalist and Northern superintendent of Indian affairs (1774-82), Johnson was born in Ireland but immigrated to New York to join his relative Sir William Johnson, whose son-in-law he became. After Sir William's death, he assumed the leadership of the Johnson family and the position of superintendent of the Northern colonies. Building on the years of goodwill built by his father-in-law, he organized the Iroquois to fight on the side of the British during the Revolution, afterward returning to England.

See also Johnson, Sir William.

JOHNSON, SIR JOHN (1742-1830) A Loyalist leader and superintendent of Indian affairs in Canada, Johnson was born in New York's Mohawk Valley, the son of Sir William Johnson. As captain of a company of the New York militia, Johnson served in the campaign to suppress Pontiac's Rebellion (1763). He was commissioned colonel of a New York militia regiment and then went to England, where he was knighted (1765). After his father's death (1774), Johnson was heir to much of his estate, succeeded to his title of baronet, and took his father's post as major general of militia.

Johnson sympathized with Britain in the Revolution, and corresponded with Governor Tryon about organizing the settlers and Indians in the Mohawk region. Johnson fled to Montreal with some followers after he learned that General Schuyler wanted to arrest him. In Montreal, he was made a lieutenant colonel and commanded a force called the Royal Greens. He assisted General Barry St. Leger on an expedition against Fort Stanwix (1777) and led a successful attack in the Mohawk Valley (1778). He aided Indians in Niagara and Oswego (1779) and conducted devastating raids in the lower Mohawk Valley and the Schoharie Valley (1780). England commissioned him superintendent general and inspector general of the Six Nations and Quebec Indians (1781), an assignment renewed in 1791. Compensated by the British for his losses in New York with large land grants in Canada, Johnson stayed active in Indian and Loyalist affairs for many years.

See also Johnson, Sir William.

JOHNSON, SAMUEL (1696-1772) Born in Guilford, Connecticut, Samuel Johnson graduated from Yale College in 1714 and was appointed a tutor two years later. With junior tutor Daniel Browne he coordinated the activities of the college until the arrival of Rector Timothy Cutler in 1719. Prolonged access to the books donated to the college by Jeremy Dummer led Johnson to question the ecclesiastical foundations of Congregationalism in favor of Episcopalism. Suppressing his convictions, he was ordained as pastor of the West Haven (Connecticut) Con-

gregational Church in 1720. By September 1722 he could no longer conceal his sentiments and, along with Rector Cutler, Tutor Browne, and several area ministers, declared his allegiance to the Church of England. The ensuing scandal rocked the colony.

Although some of his fellow dissenters eventually recanted, Johnson went on to become a leader of the Episcopalian Church in America. Following his declaration, he abandoned his pulpit and sailed to England, where he was ordained as a priest in the Anglican Church. He was appointed by the Society for Propagating the Gospel as the minister of the first Episcopalian church in New England (Stratford, Connecticut) and published several tracts defending the Church of England's liturgy and missionary efforts. In 1753 he became the president of King's College (later Columbia) in New York. Following his resignation in 1763, he reassumed his ministry at Stratford, where he served until his death.

Kenneth P. Minkema
University of Connecticut

JOHNSON, SIR WILLIAM (1715-74) Land baron and superintendent of Indian affairs, Johnson was born in Ireland and in 1738 immigrated to New York to take charge of the Mohawk Valley estate of an uncle. There he entered the Iroquois trade and became a close associate of the Mohawks, speaking their language, wearing their clothes, and enjoying their trust. He entered into relationships with at least two tribal women, including Mary (Molly) Brant (sister of Chief Joseph Brant), with whom he had several children. Given huge grants of land by the tribe, and made fabulously wealthy by his Indian business, Johnson turned his mansion, Johnson Hall, into the center of the relationship between the Iroquois and the British. During King George's War (1744-48) he was appointed superintendent of Indian affairs and worked successfully to keep the Iroquois from siding with the French. He repeated this role during the French and Indian War (1755-63) and, commissioned as major general, led attacks against the French, including the capture of Montreal. After the war he was rewarded with a baronetcy by the King. He advocated a boundary line separating American settlers from the Indians and opposed the colonists' movement for independence.

See also Brant, Joseph; Brant, Mary (Molly); King George's War.

JOHNSTON, HENRIETTA (c.1670-c.1728) Possibly the first woman artist in America, Johnston was married in 1705 to Reverend Gideon Johnston in Dublin, Ireland, where she was born. Financial difficulties led them in 1707 to emigrate to Charleston, South Carolina, where the reverend was to become rector of St. Paul's Church. By the time he assumed his ministry his health was broken and the family's financial status was very marginal. Henrietta helped support her family by utilizing her talent as a portraitist. She did more than 40 portraits on paper, using dry colored chalk and finishing them with a fixative. The materials were undoubtedly difficult to obtain, and it was a most unusual choice of media, because the use of pastels was only being explored at that time in Europe. The portraits show the influence of Edward Lutterell, an English painter, but their directness and optimism are distinctly American. Whatever their artistic merits, they served their purpose of putting food on the family's table. Reverend Johnston drowned in Charleston Harbor in 1716, and little is known about Henrietta after that point, except that she continued to do portraits.

JOLLIET, LOUIS (1645-1700)   Born at Quebec, the explorer Louis Jolliet (also Joliet) had received an excellent education from the then newly founded Jesuit College in Quebec when he turned toward a life of Indian trade, at first as assistant to his older brother, Adrien Jolliet. Well-liked by Jean Talon, the intendant of New France, Jolliet, by then conversant in several Indian languages and familiar with the West through several trips, received a *conge*, a special license, to lead a mission at his own expense to the mysterious large waterway many hoped connected with the Pacific Ocean.

On October 1, 1672, in Quebec, Jolliet entered into a partnership with seven associates to finance the expedition, joining with Father Jacques Marquette at his Mission of St. Ignace (Wisconsin). Jolliet, Marquette, and five other Frenchmen pushed west through rivers and portages, reaching the Mississippi River on June 15, 1672. They continued south down the Mississippi to an Indian village in present-day Arkansas and established that the river flowed to the Gulf of Mexico. Returning north, they traveled on the Illinois River to Lake Michigan via the Chicago portage. Jolliet's canoe capsized near Montreal on July 21, 1673, obliging him to report on his journey from memory. Later, refused permission to colonize Illinois, he married and ran a successful business. Three years before his death he was appointed royal hydrographer for New France.

See also French Colonies; Mississippi River.

Bibliography: Delanglez, Jean, *Life and Voyages of Louis Jolliet, 1645-1700* (Institute of Jesuit History, 1948).

JONATHAN   First applied as a derisive term by the English for the American colonists, the term "Jonathan" or "Brother Jonathan" was adopted by the Americans themselves as a friendly term for an unsophisticated country boy venturing into town. An English satirist used the term as early as 1643 to describe a dedication to Queen Elizabeth:

"... her *Epitaph* was one of my Brother *Jonathan's* best *Poems*, before he abjured the *University*, or had a thought of *New-England*." During the Revolutionary War, the British taunted the American patriots with this label in cartoons referring to "plaguy Cold Jonathan," and English soldiers marked bundles of hay "Welcome, Brother Jonathan" before they left Bunker Hill. After the new nation was established, New Englanders used the expression for country boys, and Royall Tyler presented a Yankee "Jonathan" in his play *The Contrast*, the first comedy written in America (1787). By 1812 the nickname had a firm place in American slang. Earlier efforts by scholars to trace the term to George Washington's devotion to Jonathan Trumbull are without foundation.

JONES, JOHN PAUL (1747-92)   A famous Revolutionary War sea captain and naval officer, he was born in Kirkcudbrightshire, Scotland, as John Paul. He had his first command on the merchant ship *John* (1769), and a year later he was arrested in Scotland for murder after he flogged the ship's carpenter to death. Cleared of these

IOHN PAUL IONES,
Commander of a Squadron in the Service of
THE THIRTEEN UNITED STATES OF NORTH AMERICA. 1779.

The victory of John Paul Jones over Britain's *Serapis* in 1779 boosted America's naval reputation. *(Library of Congress)*

charges, he later commanded a ship in the West Indian trade. After killing the leader of a mutiny, he fled to Fredericksburg, Virginia, where he added "Jones" to his name.

After the Revolutionary War started, Jones was commissioned senior lieutenant of the Continental Navy (1775), sailed to the Bahamas with a small fleet commanded by Esek Hopkins (1776), and was there given the command of the sloop *Providence*, capturing numerous prizes. Sailing from French ports in command of the *Ranger* (1777-78), Jones made two shore raids in Britain and captured the first British naval sloop to surrender to America. Given command of the *Bonhomme Richard* in 1779, he had a squadron of five ships and encountered a Baltic trading fleet and its British naval escorts. There followed a fierce naval battle in which the *Bonhomme Richard* was so badly damaged that it soon sank, but Jones captured and boarded the British flagship, the *Serapis*. Asked to surrender during the battle, Jones is supposed to have replied, "I have not yet begun to fight." He was subsequently lionized in France, and Louis XVI made him a chevalier of France. During the last years of the war he commanded the *America*. Congress honored Jones's service in the Revolution with the only gold medal presented to a Continental naval officer (1787). He subsequently served as a rear admiral in the Russian navy (1788-89) and retired to Paris.

JOSSELYN, JOHN (flourished 1638-75) Personal details about the scientific and travel writer John Josselyn are obscure. He was the second son of Sir Thomas Josselyn of Essex, England; may have received training as a physician; and never married. He visited New England on two occasions, from the summer of 1638 to October 1639 and then from July 1663 to August 1671, to see his brother, Henry Josselyn, in Black Point, Maine. On the first trip he also stayed with John Cotton and John Winthrop. On his return to England, he chronicled his careful observations in *New-Englands Rarities Discovered* (1672). This book gave the first published description of the plants and animals in New England and received a favorable review in the Royal Society's July 15, 1672, issue of *Philosophical Transactions*. Josselyn followed his first success with *An Account of Two Voyages to New England* (1674), which combined scientific observation with stories of the settlers and general comments on life in New England.

JOUTEL, HENRI (c. 1645-1723) The French explorer Henri Joutel was born in Rouen and accompanied La Salle's expedition to America in 1684. The expedition did not land at the mouth of the Mississippi River as planned, and Joutel was left in charge of a mutinous force while La Salle searched for the Mississippi. Unlike La Salle, Joutel escaped death from his own men and eventually made his way to Henry de Tonty's fort on the Illinois River. Joutel traveled from the fort along the Great Lakes and Ottawa River to Canada, where he set sail for France in 1688. In 1713 he published his journal recording La Salle's unsuccessful attempt to explore the Mississippi.

See also La Salle, Sieur de.

JUNIUS, LETTERS OF Published in the London *Political Advertiser* (1769-72), the Junius Letters slandered and criticized Tory-minded English ministers, especially the Duke of Grafton, the prime minister. The letters were signed with the pseudonym "Junius." The unidentified writer was possibly Sir Phillip Francis. The letters criticized the ministers for inconsistent measures that caused the colonies to come close to rebellion. Frequently reprinted, the letters of Junius are considered polemic masterpieces that reflected colonial opinion and gave moral support to the early Revolutionary cause. Junius forecasted that the colonies would strive for independence.

K

KALB, JOHANN (1721-80) A Revolutionary War general, he was born in Germany and served in the French army in European conflicts from the 1740s to the 1760s, reaching the rank of major. Kalb traveled to America on a secret mission for the French government (1768), but had to return to France after his reports were intercepted. Wishing to fight in the colonies, Kalb went to America with a promise from Silas Deane that he would be made a major general.

When Kalb arrived in America in 1777, the young friend he traveled with, the Marquis de Lafayette, was made a major general, and Kalb was left without a command. Later in the year, he spent the winter with General George Washington at Valley Forge (1777-78) and was a member of the Continental Army until 1780. In April 1780, Kalb served in South Carolina under General Horatio Gates. Against Kalb's advice, Gates advanced against the British at Camden, where the Americans met the forces of Lord Cornwallis. After failing in three advances, Kalb led his remaining men forward in a desperate attack in which he was mortally wounded.

KAMINISTIQUIA The mouth of the Kaministiquia River, on Thunder Bay, northwest coast of Lake Superior, was the site of a supply and trading post built by Duluth in 1679. The river was an important route to the interior until La Verendrye opened the more southern Grand Portage on Lake Superior in the 1730s. After the settlement of the boundary between the United States and British Canada in the early 19th century, the North West Company relocated its major post of Fort William at Kaministiquia. Today it is the site of Thunder Bay, an important industrial and transshipment lake port.
See also Grand Portage.

KASKASKIA Founded in 1703 by French Jesuits on a site above the mouth of the Kaskaskia River, the town of Kaskaskia was the largest of the six French villages along the Mississippi bottomland in the Illinois country. The others were Cahokia (1698), Fort de Chartres (1721), St. Philippe (1735), and Prairie du Rocher (1735) on the east bank, and Ste. Genevieve (1735) on the west. Because of their isolation, these villages enjoyed considerable autonomy and developed their own traditions, including a unique architectural style with both Canadian and Caribbean influences.

After the French and Indian War, many of the inhabitants fled to the west bank of the Mississippi where St. Louis was founded in 1764, and when the British arrived they found the communities largely evacuated. In 1778, Kaskaskia was captured by George Rogers Clark as the first step in his conquest of Illinois. It became the first Illinois territorial capital in 1809 and was the first state capital from 1818 to 1820, after which it was succeeded by Vandalia. The changing course of the rivers eventually obliterated the original site of the village.

KELLER, IGNACIO JAVIER (1702-59) Born in Moravia, Keller entered the Jesuit order in 1718. In 1729 he was sent to New Spain and ordered to the northern frontier. Until his death he was stationed at the mission of Suamca in Sonora, where the tradition established by his fellow Jesuit Eusebio Kino exerted a great influence on him. For most of his time at Suamca, Keller, like Kino, worked among the Pima Indians, but in 1742 he received orders to go north and establish relations with the Moquis (northern Hopi), with whom there had been no contact since the Pueblo Revolt of 1680. On his way north his party was attacked by Apaches, who stole all their livestock. When his escort refused to go any farther, Keller was forced to return to Suamca.
See also Kino, Eusebio Francisco.

KELSEY, HENRY (c.1667-1724) An explorer for the Hudson's Bay Company of western Canada, Kelsey came to North America as an apprentice in 1684. During 1690-92, traveling into the interior to encourage the Indians to come to the Hudson Bay to trade, he became the first European to visit the Saskatchewan country, the first to make contact with the Indians there, and the first to describe grizzly and buffalo hunting. He stayed with the Company, later serving as an overseas governor, and was twice a prisoner of the French. His journals constitute a major source for the early history of the West.

KENNEBEC RIVER SETTLEMENTS These colonial settlements along the coast of Maine were established in the wake of the explorations of Bartholomew Gosnold (1602), Martin Pring (1603), and George Weymouth (1605). The first of the settlements was founded by George

Weymouth at the mouth of the Kennebec River in 1607 but abandoned in the following year. Later settlements established by European fishermen on Monhegan Island and at Pemaquid Point proved more durable, and their inhabitants provided supplies to the Plymouth colonists in 1622. In 1625, John Brown purchased the lands of New Harbor from the Abenaki; in 1626, Abraham Shurt established a new settlement on Monhegan Island; and in 1630, Thomas Purchase founded the settlement of Brunswick at Pejebscot Falls.

In the following decades, European colonization spread up the Kennebec River and along the coast with the foundation of such settlements as Georgetown Island (1648) and Bath (1661). This movement continued until the outbreak of hostilities with the Abenaki toward the end of the 17th century. The Kennebec settlers were also in constant competition over the fur trade of the region with the Massachusetts Bay colonists, whose governor, William Bradford, obtained a royal patent for the upriver region of Cushenoc.

KENSINGTON STONE   A slab of rock found in 1898 near Kensington, Minnesota, with runic inscriptions describing a Norse exploration of North America in the 14th century, the Kensington Stone was subsequently declared a fraud. Investigators found that its inscriptions were replete with anachronistic runes and grammar and that its carving had been accomplished with modern chisels. Other bogus artifacts of Norse settlement include the Newport Tower.

See also Newport Tower.

KENTUCKY   First publicly explored during the 1750s, Kentucky, with its rich hunting, soon became a favorite spot for the "long hunters," including Daniel Boone, who in 1775 helped to cut the Wilderness Road across the Cumberland Gap and founded Boonesboro, thus opening the country for immigration. As Boone noted, this was a "war of incursion," and the Indians fought the settlers on the "dark and bloody ground" with a fury unmatched in the colonial period. Yet immigration hardly slackened, and by 1790, Kentucky's population stood at 70,000. Boone's employer, land speculator Richard Henderson, hoped to organize the country as the separate state of Transylvania, but in 1776, Virginia organized it as Kentucky County. Without a land system, conflicting settlement claims ruined many of the early immigrants, including Boone himself, and resulted in a rapid accumulation of land in the hands of the wealthy. During the 1780s there was much sentiment for separation from Virginia, even from the United States, but finally a convention in

1792 drafted a state constitution and Kentucky was admitted as the 15th state.

See also Boone, Daniel; Cumberland Gap; Wilderness Road.

KIEFT, WILLEM (1597-1647)   Director general of New Netherland (1637-45), Kieft is chiefly remembered for his rash Indian policy, which embroiled the colony in a series of disastrous wars. A merchant who later worked for the Dutch West India Company, he was sworn in as director general in 1637 and arrived in New Amsterdam in March 1638. During his tenure of office, New Netherland established the first form of consultative government with the appointment of the Board of Twelve Men in August 1641. This board was called into session to assist the governor in his prosecution of a punitive war against the Raritan Indians. The Twelve Men, who had been chosen by the leading citizens of New Amsterdam, advised caution, but Kieft was determined to punish the Indians guilty of depredations on Staten Island. Some months later, after having agreed to assist in the governor's Indian war, the Twelve Men petitioned Kieft for a larger role in the governance of the colony. In a fit of pique he dismissed them in February 1642.

However, with the Indian war going badly for the Dutch following Indian attacks in the wake of the murder of 80 Indians in February 1643, Kieft was forced once again to consult the citizens of the colony. Consequently, in September 1643 a Board of Eight Men was selected by the governor's counsel from a list of acceptable candidates approved by the leading citizens of New Amsterdam. This board eventually came to oppose most of Kieft's policies, and in response to the public clamor for the governor's removal they addressed a long memorial to the States General and the directors of the West India Company, calling for Kieft's dismissal and a public investigation of his conduct in office. Officially succeeded in office by Peter Stuyvesant in 1645, Kieft perished in a shipwreck on his voyage home to the Netherlands in 1647.

See also Dutch-Indian Wars; New Netherland; Stuyvesant, Peter.

Bibliography: Rink, Oliver A., *Holland on the Hudson: An Economic and Social History of Dutch New York* (Cornell Univ. Press, 1986).

Oliver A. Rink
California State University, Bakersfield

KING GEORGE'S WAR (1744-48)   Known in Europe as the War of the Austrian Succession, King George's War ended three decades of peace between Britain and France and opened the final round of colonial wars in North America. The war began in Europe in March 1744 but quickly spread to America. News of the war reached Cape

An engraving of an Indian encounter with the colonists in King Philip's War showed the superior weapons of the colonists. *(Library of Congress)*

Breton before it arrived in Boston, and the French seized the English village of Canseau and attacked the English post at Annapolis Royal, Nova Scotia.

Aware of the threat that the French post at Louisburg posed, but also aware from former prisoners that the fort was in disrepair, Governor William Shirley and the Massachusetts Bay legislature decided to attack. Supported by colonies south to Pennsylvania, an expedition was placed under the command of William Pepperell. Commodore Peter Warren, stationed in New York, joined the party with three British naval vessels. On June 17, after a siege of seven weeks, the garrison at Louisburg capitulated. Meanwhile, however, the French and their Indian allies began to raid the border towns of New England and New York. Over the next four years, hundreds of British subjects were killed or captured. Attempts to organize an intercolonial invasion of Canada failed repeatedly, and border communities were at the mercy of the French until the Treaty of Aix-la-Chapelle ended hostilities in 1748. The treaty, which returned Louisburg to France in exchange for French concessions in Madras, India, temporarily ended the fighting but did nothing to resolve the fundamental conflicts between the British and French empires. The peace it brought proved fragile.

See also British Empire.

George Mills
Yale University

KING PHILIP'S WAR (1675-76)   King Philip's War represented the final effort by some southern New England Indians to retain autonomy in the face of English expansion. By 1670 the native population was declining precipitously in the face of new diseases and altered subsistence patterns, while a second generation of healthy settlers began reaching adulthood and desiring land. As fur-bearing animals were depleted and as commercial prosperity ended the colonists' use for wampum as a currency substitute, many Indians no longer interacted freely with both colonists and other natives. Instead they faced heightened pressures to sell land and to submit to the political, legal, and religious authority of the English.

Tensions were most acute in Plymouth, where the war actually began in June 1675 after three Wampanoag were hanged for murdering a Christian Indian. The latter had alleged to the English that the Wampanoag planned an uprising. Under the leadership of Metacom (known to the English as "King Philip"), most Narragansett, Nipmuc, and Connecticut Valley Indians north of Springfield joined the Wampanoag against Plymouth, Massachusetts, Connecticut, and Rhode Island. Initially, the war went against the English as they repeatedly exposed their troops to enemy attacks while persecuting nonhostile Indians at home. The tide only turned during winter as disease weakened the fighting Indians, as the colonists began using Indian troops, and—most importantly—as the Mohawk entered the conflict on the English side.

Effects of the War. By August 1676 the Wampanoag and their allies were defeated. Friendly or hostile, those Indians who had not left the colonies as refugees or as slaves were confined to reservations. While the uprising actually reversed English expansion for a time, the long-range effect was to open most remaining Indian land for settlement. And the Mohawk's decisive role enabled British authorities to draw New England into the English-Iroquois Covenant Chain, a major force in shaping English policy and expansion in the Northeast for the next century.

Bibliography: Jennings, Francis, *The Invasion of America: Indians, Colonialism, and the Cant of Conquest* (Univ. of North Carolina Press, 1975); Leach, Douglas Edward, *Flintlock and Tomahawk: New England in King Philip's War* (Macmillan, 1958).

Neal Salisbury
Smith College

KING'S COLLEGE (COLUMBIA UNIVERSITY) King's College received its royal charter on October 31, 1754, as the College of the Province of New York. Its first eight students studied in the English charity schoolhouse with the president, Reverend Samuel Johnson, and graduated in 1758. Its next president, Reverend Myles Cooper, modeled the college after the English system, moved it to Park Place in 1760, and started a medical school in 1767. The American Revolutionary army turned the college into a hospital. After the war the college was reestablished as Columbia College (1784) under the Regents of the State of New York and in 1787 returned to its original city charter.

KING WILLIAM'S WAR (1689-97) A part of the larger war in Europe at the time, it was the first phase of the British wars with the French and Indians in America. British-allied Iroquois Indians raided an area near Montreal. In retaliation, the French and their allied Indians ravaged settlements in New York, New Hampshire, and Maine. Colonists marched by land toward Montreal. A fleet under William Phips sailed from Boston and captured Port Royal, Nova Scotia, but was unable to penetrate heavily fortified Montreal. The land forces never arrived. The remainder of the war consisted of small border fights. It ended with the inconclusive Peace of Ryswick (1697).

KINO, EUSEBIO FRANCISCO (?1645-1711) An Italian Jesuit, Kino came to New Spain in 1681 and was involved in the 1683-86 attempt by Isidor de Atondo to colonize Lower (Baja) California. He arrived on the northwest frontier in 1687 and for the next 25 years traveled incessantly, building missions as he went. The Pima Indians were his special charge; he protected them against proposals to turn the missions over to secular clergy and against the encroachment of Spanish settlers. Kino also mapped northern Sonora and southern Arizona and explored the valleys of the Gila and Colorado rivers. As a result of his discoveries, Kino claimed that California was a peninsula, not an island as the Spanish had previously thought.

KIRKLAND, SAMUEL (1741-1808) A Congregationalist missionary to the Iroquois, Kirkland was born in Connecticut. He first preached among the Seneca in the mid-1760s and then among the Oneida until his death. During the Revolution he worked successfully to align the Oneida and the Tuscarora with the patriot cause; they were the only important Indian groups to do so. During the Indian conflicts in the Northwest Territory in the 1790s, he was again successful in keeping the Six Nations neutral. In 1793 he was a founder of Hamilton College, established as an institution for the education of both white and Indian youth.

KNIGHT, JOHN (died 1606) An English explorer, Knight sailed for the Danes, then for the East India and Muscovy companies to search for the Northwest Passage. In 1606 he explored the coast of Labrador, following it southward, but the ship was badly damaged in a storm. With three others, including his brother, Knight went ashore to scout the terrain; the party never returned and was probably killed by Eskimos.

KNIGHT, SARAH KEMBLE (1666-1727) An early chronicler of colonial society, Knight was the daughter of Boston merchant Thomas Kemble and apparently had a literary education. She kept a shop on Boston's Moon Street and also ran a boarding house after husband Richard Knight's death. She is most notable for her salty and observant description of a horseback journey that she made alone from Boston to New York in 1704 to settle some family business. The journal is a valuable source of information about colonial life and speech. When her only daughter married New London, Connecticut's John Livingston, Knight herself moved to Connecticut in 1714, buying property and maintaining several inns and shops in the Norwich, Connecticut area until her death.

KNOWLTON, THOMAS (1740-76) A Revolutionary War officer, Knowlton was born in West Boxford, Massachusetts, and grew up in Ashford, Connecticut. He saw military service during the French and Indian War (1755) and was promoted to lieutenant. Accompanying General Lyman to Cuba, he took part in the siege of Havana (1762). After the clash at Lexington and Concord, he became captain of an Ashford company and marched to Massachusetts. At the Battle of Bunker Hill, Knowlton's defense of entrenchments at the base of the hill protected the colonial withdrawal. Promoted to major, he made a successful attack on Charlestown (January 1776) and was promoted to lieutenant colonel in August. A month later Knowlton prematurely attacked the British in the Battle of Harlem Heights and was killed.

The greatest successes of Henry Knox came with artillery, including the siege of Yorktown. *(Library of Congress)*

KNOX, HENRY (1750-1806) A Revolutionary War leader, he established a bookshop in his native city of Boston at the age of 21. He became a student of artillery tactics as a member of the Boston Grenadier Corps (1772) and sided with the patriots as soon as war broke out. Knox was commissioned a colonel and commanded the Continental army artillery (1775). After great difficulties, he was able to bring the artillery pieces captured at Fort Ticonderoga to Boston, where their emplacement forced the British to evacuate the city (1776).

Knox was a good friend of General George Washington and was his adviser throughout the war. Knox served in the campaigns around New York City and in New Jersey and organized the movements of troops to Trenton after Washington crossed the Delaware River. After the Battle of Trenton, Knox was promoted to brigadier general and was with Washington in the winter at Valley Forge (1777-78). After directing the artillery in the siege of Yorktown (1781), he was promoted to major general. He was the chief organizer of the Society of the Cincinnati (1783) and commanded the fort at West Point (1782-84). After resigning from the military (1784), Knox served as secretary of war (1785-94).

See also Cincinnati, Society of the; Revolutionary War Battles.

KOSCIUSZKO, TADEUSZ ANDRZEJ BONAVENTURA (1746-1817) A Revolutionary War soldier and Polish patriot, he graduated from the Royal College of Warsaw with the rank of captain (1769). Hearing of the revolution in America, he went to Philadelphia, where he became a colonel of engineers in the Continental Army (October 1776). He joined the Northern army under General Gates at Ticonderoga (1777) and contributed to the American victory over General Burgoyne at Saratoga. Kosciuszko was placed in charge of building fortifications at West Point (1778-80). Stationed in the south, he became one of the first Continentals to enter Charleston after the British evacuated and was later promoted to brigadier general (1783). After the Revolutionary War ended, he became major general of the Polish army (1792) and led resistance against the Russians.

KRENITSYN, PYOTR KUZMICH (died 1770) A Russian naval officer and explorer of the North Pacific, Krenitsyn in 1768 commanded an expedition that left from Kamchatka and explored the Aleutian Islands and the western coast of the Alaska Peninsula. Although he died upon his return in 1770, his notes were the basis of the first map of the Aleutians, published in St. Petersburg in 1777.

L

LABOR COMBINATIONS Colonial authorities were not friendly to combinations and collective actions of workers. The earliest laws of Virginia defined strikes as mutiny and riot, punishing the offense with whippings, commitment to the galleys, and years of forced labor. These codes were particularly draconian, but in general the colonies closely followed the precedents of English statute and common law, which defined worker combinations to raise wages as criminal conspiracies. In 1680 striking New York City coopers were the first of a rather long list of colonial worker associations to be convicted on charges of conspiracy. In many cases the authorities used the argument of "public interest" to prohibit work stoppages, as in New York in 1741 when striking bakers were tried and convicted during the panic attending the so-called Negro Plot.

Both the 1680 and 1741 cases involved master and journeymen craftsmen. Combinations by journeymen or unskilled workers to secure better working conditions from employing masters were rarer. In 1741 journeymen caulkers of Boston refused to work in protest to the payment of wages in depreciated paper currency. In 1768, New York journeymen tailors ceased working because of a wage cut by masters, being careful to argue that theirs was not a strike but a refusal to accept remuneration upon which their families could not survive.

Workers frequently formed benevolent societies to protect the widows and orphan children of deceased members, but trade unions themselves did not begin to be organized until the close of the Revolutionary War, when the decline of custom work, an increase in factory production, and a decline in the apprentice system sharpened class lines. In the 1780s and 1790s unions of New York and Philadelphia shoemakers, typographers, carpenters, masons, and coopers were organized. In response, employers organized trade associations, arguing that they would not employ journeymen "as society men, but as individuals." Workers' unions were subject to the same criminal conspiracy provisions of common law.

Bibliography: Morris, Richard B., *Government and Labor in Early America* (1946; reprint Northeastern Univ. Press, 1981).

John Mack Faragher
Mount Holyoke College

LACLÈDE, PIERRE (LIGUEST) (c.1724-78) Founder of New Orleans, Pierre Laclède was born in Bedous in the French Pyrenees. Although his legal name was Liguest, he called himself Laclède. He jointly formed a trading company, Maxent, Laclède & Company, and received an eight-year franchise to trade with the Indians on the Missouri River. In 1764 he traveled with his stepson Pierre Auguste Chouteau to the French western side of the Mississippi, where he ordered Chouteau to build a trading post. He named the post St. Louis in honor of King Louis IX. Although the trading post grew and prospered, Laclède fell into financial difficulty and died on his way back from New Orleans, where he had gone to seek additional funds.

LA DEMOISELLE ("OLD BRITON") (died 1752) Chief of the Piankashaw band of the Miami, La Demoiselle was born in the lower Wabash Valley of Indiana and became an important British ally in the region. His nickname, "Old Briton," arose from his constant support of an alliance between his people and the British. In 1747 he participated in an insurrection of the Huron against the French and subsequently moved with his followers to Pickawillany in western Ohio, then under nominal British control. His signing of a trade treaty with Pennsylvania angered the French authorities, and he was killed during the French capture of Pickawillany in 1752.

LAFAYETTE, MARIE-JOSEPH, MARQUIS DE (1757-1834) The French soldier and statesman Lafayette was orphaned at an early age. After inheriting considerable wealth he married at 16, purchased a captain's commission, and seemed destined for an indolent courtier life when in 1776 he convinced the American agent in Paris to give him a commission as a major general in the Continental Army. While serving first as a volunteer in the staff of General Washington, he rapidly proved his valor and intelligence on the battlefield and received important commands. Temporarily returning to France in 1779, where he had become a popular figure, he had a major role in getting France to lend full support to the

United States. Once more in America, his action at the Battle of Yorktown (1781) was critical.

Returning to France, Lafayette quickly became involved in the charged atmosphere preceding the French Revolution. As commander of the National Guard in 1789, he introduced the three colors as a national emblem. While commanding one of the armies on the northern border in 1792, he was accused of treason by the radical faction in Paris and had no choice but to cross over to the Austrian lines, remaining a war prisoner until 1797. He did not participate in public life during the Napoleonic Empire, but returned to politics under the Bourbons and remained until his death a staunch supporter of Republican principles.

Bibliography: Ballantine, Orpha, *Lafayette: A Historical Perspective* (Moran, 1980).

Charles J. Balesi
The French Colonial Historical Society

LE GÉNÉRAL   LA FAYETTE

The popularity of the Marquis de Lafayette in both France and the United States helped promote the Franco-Ame rican alliance. *(Library of Congress)*

LAFORA, NICHOLAS DE (?1730-89?) A captain in Spain's Royal Engineers, Lafora accompanied the Marques de Rubi on his inspection tour of the northern frontier of New Spain in 1766 and 1767. Lafora had much experience, having already served in Italy, Africa, and Portugal before arriving in New Spain in 1764. With Rubi, Lafora traveled from the Texas coast to the head of the Gulf of California. An accomplished military engineer, Lafora not only contributed to Rubi's report, commenting on the construction and defense capabilities of the presidios and missions, but drew a map of the territory that was perhaps the most comprehensive map of northern New Spain in the colonial period.

See also Rubi, Marques de.

LAHONTAN, LOUIS-ARMAND DE LOM D'ARCE, BARON (1666-c.1716) Soldier and author, Baron Lahontan was born in Lahontan in the south of France. In 1683 he was sent to New France as a military officer to fight the Iroquois. He joined the unsuccessful 1684 search for the Iroquois on Lake Ontario. He went with Duluth and Tonty on their western expedition as interpreter to the Indians. He was a commander for a year at Fort St. Joseph on the St. Clair River above Detroit and then explored westward. By 1689 he had returned to Quebec and was sent to France to report the news of French victories. In 1691 he returned to Quebec to serve the governor, Count de Frontenac, and left in 1692 after a disastrous love affair. His memoirs describing his various travels, *Nouveaux Voyages dans l' Amérique Septentrionale*, was published in 1703 and enjoyed great popularity.

LAKE GEORGE, BATTLE OF (1755) French and Indian War engagement at the head of Lake George, in northern New York. On September 8, 1755, a British force composed of Indians and troops from New York and New England defeated a French and Indian force and captured its commander, General Baron de Dieskau. The American commander, William Johnson, was criticized for abandoning his original objective, the occupation of Crown Point on Lake Champlain, but his victory and the capture of Dieskau were in such sharp contrast to British failures elsewhere that he was awarded a baronetcy and 5,000 pounds. The great Iroquois leader King Hendrick was killed in the battle. Earlier historians credited the victory to Johnson's second in command, Phineas Lyman of Connecticut, but more recent scholars cite Johnson's organizational ability and inspiring presence in the battle.

LALEMANT, JÉRÔME (1593-1673) A French Jesuit missionary, Jérôme Lalemant was born in Paris. He was sent to Canada in 1638 to convert the Huron and founded a model town. He was superior of missions (1645-50), and in 1647, as vicar-general of all French possessions, he went to France to seek help from the Canada Company for the Huron who had fled from the Iroquois to Quebec. He returned to France on the same fruitless mission in 1656. In 1659, Bishop Laval asked him to return to Canada as supervisor-general of the missions, where he worked among the Huron until 1665. His nephew Gabriel (1610-49) joined the Jesuits in 1630 and followed his uncle to Canada in 1646. He and Jean de Brébeuf were killed at their Huron mission by the Iroquois on March 16, 1649.

See also Brébeuf, Jean de.

LANCASTER, TREATY OF (1744)   An agreement between representatives of the Iroquois Six Nations and of Maryland and Virginia, the Treaty of Lancaster resulted in territorial adjustments favorable to the colonists. Because of intensive colonial settlement in lands previously regarded as belonging to the Iroquois Confederacy, the colonial commissioners, in their meeting with representatives of all the confederated tribes except the Mohawk, agreed to offer monetary compensation in return for title to the disputed lands. Between June 22 and July 4, 1744, a comprehensive settlement was negotiated. These negotiations also led to the alliance of the Iroquois Confederacy with the British during King George's War.

See also Iroquois Confederacy; King George's War.

LAND COMPANIES   The 17th century settlement of English and Dutch peoples in North America was promoted by state-chartered companies that planned to profit from trade but were much more financially successful in the sale and grant of lands. As the press of population growth and economic development turned the attention of investors to trans-Appalachia in the mid-18th century, both English and American speculators formed western land companies with either royal or colonial charters. With few exceptions these companies produced conflict rather than profit.

The first and perhaps most famous was the Ohio Company, organized in 1747, whose efforts at exploration and settlement of land north of the Ohio River were a factor in the beginning of the French and Indian War. The Susquehanna Land Company, chartered in 1753 under the provisions of Connecticut's original sea-to-sea grant, began the settlement of the Wyoming Valley in northeastern Pennsylvania over protests from that colony, and with years of resulting turmoil. Among others, the Mississippi Company (headed by George Washington), the Illinois and Indiana companies, and the Transylvania Company tried to secure grants from the British Board of Trade to sanction their illegal purchases from the Indians. Like the settlement ventures, these attempts at land speculation failed due to intercompany and intercolonial rivalries.

See also Ohio Company; Transylvania Company.

Bibliography: Livermore, Shaw, *Early American Land Companies* (1939; reprint Hippocrene Bks., 1968).

LAND ORDINANCE OF 1785   This land law passed by the Confederation Congress established the basic features of the federal land system. At the conclusion of the American Revolution in 1783, the relationship between the victorious states and the settlements in the lands west of the Appalachians was undefined, and the Congress under the Articles of Confederation quickly moved to clarify this relationship. The Land Ordinance of 1784, drafted by Thomas Jefferson, provided that as sufficient population developed, territories would be created northwest of the Ohio River and that eventually they would be admitted as states. This ordinance, however, would go into effect only when all the states had ceded their western lands, but as this was something that North Carolina and Georgia did after 1787 the ordinance never became operative and was superseded by the Northwest Ordinance (1787).

In the 1785 ordinance, Congress, again led by Jefferson, reflected on the lessons from the colonial past and decided that prior to sale all lands would undergo a rectilinear survey into townships composed of 36-square-mile sections, that those lands would undergo compact and orderly settlement, that sale would take place at public auctions with a minimum price of one dollar per acre, that one section in each township would be reserved for the support of common schools, and that there would be military tracts set aside for the provision of lands to veterans of the Revolution. Unlike the ordinance of the year before, in the Land Ordinance of 1785, Congress established a basic system of land distribution that would prevail for the next 200 years and that provided the fundamental shape of the American landscape.

See also Land Policy; Northwest Ordinance.

Bibliography: Stilgoe, John R., *The Common Landscape of America: 1580-1845* (Yale Univ. Press, 1982).

John Mack Faragher
Mount Holyoke College

LAND POLICY   Although the earliest European interest in North America focused on the possibility of plunder or commerce, settling the land with colonists soon became more important. Land policy thus was a major influence in the organization of the social and economic life of the colonies. Promoters of colonization tempted settlers with promises of free land. Most colonial charters established the right of freehold tenure under obligations of "free and common socage" that were filled by the payment of a fixed rent or quitrent and the taking of an oath of fealty to the king. Several colonies attempted to institute manorial systems of land ownership, but with the exception of the patroonship system established along the Hudson River, the tenant system along the St. Lawrence in New France, and the Spanish grants of huge estates in New Mexico, Texas, and California, these attempts at recreating feudalism in America were doomed to failure in an environment of abundant land and open frontiers.

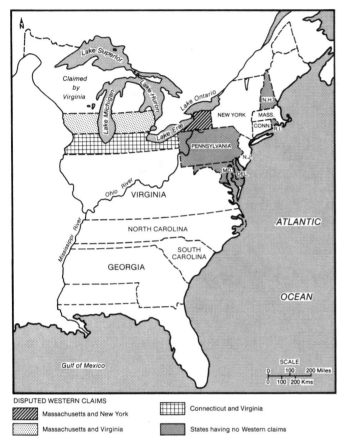

DISPUTED WESTERN CLAIMS

- ▨ Massachusetts and New York
- ▨ Massachusetts and Virginia
- ▦ Connecticut and Virginia
- ▨ States having no Western claims

© Martin Greenwald Associates, Inc.

Land Ordinance of 1785, based on surrender by states of western land claims. (*Martin Greenwald Associates, Inc.*)

Early Policies.   In 1618 the Virginia Company introduced the system of headrights, grants of land to any man who paid for passage, a program subsequently adopted by many other colonies in the 17th century. This system facilitated the accumulation of large tracts of land by men with capital and linked the establishment of large plantations directly to the importation of the forced labor necessary to work them. Servants who worked out the time of their indenture often found land priced too high for them and so either worked as wage laborers, took up some form of tenancy, or migrated to the frontier where they squatted on Indian lands. Moreover, since the claimants of headrights were generally allowed to site their own plan-

tations, in the Southern colonies there was little overall planning regarding the shape or direction of settlement. Plantations tended to be scattered over the landscape, and there were relatively few towns or villages.

In New England, by contrast, Puritan authorities developed a highly disciplined land distribution system in which contiguous tracts of some 36 square miles were granted to groups of proprietors, who distributed lots to individual settlers not only on the basis of status and wealth but on need as well. Clusters of house lots formed the centers of the towns, with outlying individual and common fields, pastures, and woodlots. The result was more broadly based ownership, compact settlement, and an orderly landscape.

18th Century Policies.   In the 18th century sale largely replaced the grant of land. Township proprietors were transformed into land speculators in New England, and by mid-century the nucleated village had given way to more dispersed patterns of settlement. Virginia and Carolina planters, often incorporated into Land Companies, intrigued with colony and crown governments and negotiated illegal treaties with Indians for the release of massive tracts of western lands. George Washington, for one, made his fortune speculating in western lands. Nevertheless, the price of colonial land was usually low enough to permit free men of moderate means to find farms, especially if they were willing to move west.

After the Revolution the members of the Confederation Congress seriously thought through the implications of colonial land policy in designing the land policy of the new nation, which became embodied in the Land Ordinance of 1785 and the Northwest Ordinance (1787).

See also Freehold; Headright; Land Companies; Land Ordinance of 1785; Northwest Ordinance; Patroonships; Quitrent.

Bibliography: Bidwell, Percy W. and Falconer, John I., *History of Agriculture in the Northern United States, 1620-1860* (1925; reprint Kelley); Gray, Lewis Cecil, *History of Agriculture in the Southern United States to 1860*, 2 vols. (1933; reprint Kelley).

John Mack Faragher
Mount Holyoke College

LANE, RALPH (c.1530-1603)   An enterprising English colonist, Lane was as a young man a courtier of Elizabeth I and a privateer in the wars against Spain and Ireland. In April 1585 he accompanied Richard Grenville and over a hundred colonists to Virginia and after Grenville's August departure commanded the settlement at Roanoke Island. When relations with the Indians deteriorated, due to the insatiable demand of the colonists for supplies, Lane led an attack on a nearby village, the first open hostilities between English colonists and natives. By June 1586 the colony was on its last legs and the settlers were saved only by the fortuitous arrival of Sir Francis Drake, who transported the survivors back to England. In later years Lane served in Ireland, where he was knighted and where he died.

La Salle's descent of the Mississippi River extended France's claims in North America. (*Library of Congress*)

LANGDON, JOHN (1741-1819)   A colonial and early national military and political leader, Langdon was born in Portsmouth, New Hampshire. Originally a seaman and then a merchant, he became active in New Hampshire patriot activities in 1774, capturing British military supplies in Portsmouth. He then entered the state legislature and sat in the Second Continental Congress (1775-76; 1783). After the Revolutionary War erupted, he was instrumental in organizing and financing the opposition to General Burgoyne's advance from the North against the Americans and led New Hampshire militia at the battles of Bennington, Vermont (1777) and Saratoga, New York (1777). He later fought in Rhode Island.

After the war he was govenor of New Hampshire (1785-86; 1788-89) and was a delegate to the Constitutional Convention (1787). He urged the Constitution's ratification and then entered the U.S. Senate (1789-1801) before returning to New Hampshire to serve again as governor (1805-09; 1810-12).

LARIOS, JUAN (1636-75?)   A Franciscan missionary in New Spain, Larios was in Guadalajara, the capital of the province of Jalisco since 1651, when he responded in 1670 to the entreaties for missionaries by emissaries from the Indians of Coahuila and the area beyond the Rio Grande. For three years Larios preached on the Coahuila frontier, returning to Guadalajara in 1673 to enlist help from his brother Franciscans. In 1675 he was the spiritual leader of the Balcarcel-Bosque expedition that was charged with conquering Coahuila. With Fernando de Bosque, Larios penetrated not only into Coahuila but well across the Rio Grande into Texas. Larios and Bosque's recommendations led directly to the establishment of four missions across the Rio Grande and the first Spanish colonizing effort in southern Texas.

LA SALLE, ROBERT CAVELIER, SIEUR DE (1643-87)   Born in Rouen, France, to wealthy parents, La Salle received the best possible education from the Jesuits. Entering their seminary in 1658, he took some of the vows and taught until 1667, when he left the order. At 23, La Salle arrived in New France, where he quickly adopted a life of action. By 1673 he had become an experienced explorer and obtained the support of Governor Frontenac, whose name he gave to the first fort he built, Fort Frontenac (Kingston, Ontario). La Salle returned to France in 1678 to raise funds to further his explorations. During his stay, he received patent letters from the king authorizing him "to work at discovering the western parts of our country of New France."

That same year, with his assistant, Henri de Tonty, and a small group of soldiers and craftsmen, he launched the first vessel to navigate the Great Lakes, the *Griffon*. His objective was to reach the Mississippi River and sail to the end of its course. He failed on his first try but was successful the second time. After an uneventful descent, he reached the Gulf of Mexico where, on April 9, 1682, he claimed all the land east and west for the king of France. His third exploration, by sea, ended disastrously, as he confused the Texas coast with the delta of the Mississippi. La Salle was assassinated by a group of mutineers.

Bibliography: Parkman, Francis, *La Salle and the Discovery of the Great West* (1889; reprint Corner House, 1968); Terrell, John Upton, *La Salle, Robert Cavelier, Sieur de, 1643-1687*, Weybridge and Talley, 1968).

Charles J. Balesi
The French Colonial Historical Society

LAS CASAS, BARTOLOMÉ DE (1474-1566)   The Dominican Las Casas became the champion of the Indians in the Spanish colonies and their spokesman at the court in Madrid. Arriving on Hispaniola in 1502, he became the first priest ordained in the Western Hemisphere in 1510. During this time he, like most of his fellow Spaniards, exploited the Indians for their labor. Around 1516, Las Casas became convinced of the unchristian character of the Spanish treatment of the Indians, and from that time forward he fought for the abolition of the encomienda system.

In the early 1540s, Las Casas wrote his *Very Brief Account of the Destruction of the Indies*, the basis for the Black Legend of the Spanish genocide of the Indians. So powerful was this account that it is credited with influencing Charles I's promulgation in 1542 of the New Laws, which were intended to phase out the encomienda. But the New Laws were ignored by Spanish colonists, and as Bishop of Chiapas, in New Spain, Las Casas met with so much resistance from his congregation when he urged them to restore their stolen wealth to the Indians that he resigned in 1550. After 1550, Las Casas continued to debate the morality of Spanish treatment of the Indians and succeeded in blocking an attempt by the Peruvian conquistadors to have their encomiendas declared perpetual.

See also Black Legend; Encomienda and Hacienda; Repartimiento.

LAUD COMMISSION   The Laud Commission, formally known as the Commission on Foreign Plantations, was established April 28, 1634, as a standing committee of the Privy Council. It took its name from its chairman, Archbishop Laud. Unlike previous commissions, its authority extended over the entire British Empire. Subject to the approval of the Crown and Privy Council, it was authorized to govern the colonies, erect courts, appoint and remove governors and other officials, and, especially, to examine charters and patents. The commission was largely established in response to increasing Puritan immigration to Massachusetts and the growing independence of that colony. In general, the commission accomplished little. There is no record of it after 1641.

See also Massachusetts.

Bibliography: Beer, George Louis, *The Origins of the British Colonial System* (Peter Smith, 1959).

LAUDONNIÈRE, RENÉ GOULAINE DE   (flourished 1562-82)   A French Huguenot and colonist, Laudonnière accompanied Jean Ribaut's Huguenot colonists sent by Admiral Coligny in 1562. As Ribaut's lieutenant, Laudonnière helped to establish the colony at Charlesfort (now Port Royal, South Carolina) and then returned to France. In 1564, Laudonnière, arriving with supplies for the colony, found it abandoned. He built a new colony, Fort Caroline, on St. John's River in Florida. Laudonnière barely kept the mutinous colony under control, and when Sir John Hawkins came Laudonnière paid Hawkins four cannon to ship his starving colonists home. Ribaut's sudden arrival prevented the departure, but instead of helping the colonists Ribaut left to fight the Spanish, who attacked Fort Caroline from the land and killed most of the inhabitants, except Laudonnière and the artist Le Moyne. Laudonnière returned to France in 1566; his account, *L'Histoire notable de la Floride*, was published posthumously in 1586.

LAURENS, HENRY (1724-92)   A merchant and political leader, Laurens was born in Charleston, South Carolina, and became an active importer-exporter. The wealthiest man in Charleston, Laurens's business interests gave way to political involvement. He served in the state assembly (1757-64; 1765-74), and he sided with the colonists. After attempting diplomatic reconciliation with Britain, he served on the Council of Safety in South Carolina (1775), helped draft a state constitution, and became vice president of the state (1776). He served in the Second Continental Congress and became its president (1777-78). On a mission to gain financial support from the Netherlands (1780), he was captured by the British. His papers outlining a treaty between the United States and the Netherlands led Britain to declare war against the Dutch. Exchanged for Lord Cornwallis, Laurens joined John Adams, Benjamin Franklin, and John Jay in negotiating the Treaty of Paris (1783).

See also Paris, Treaty of.

LAWS, CONCESSIONS, AND AGREEMENTS (1677)   Written by William Penn, they were the framework and regulations for colonizing West Jersey. The land was to be divided into 10 sections and then each of those into 10 parts again. One of these parts was called a proprietorship. A bill of rights was included that guaranteed religious freedom, trial by jury, right of petition, freedom from imprisonment for debt, and a say in taxation. They provided for an annually elected assembly (whose first meeting was in 1681) that was charged with lawmaking, dispensing justice through courts, and enforcing the law. They provided government for the colony until 1702.

LAWSON, JOHN (died 1711)   An English colonist, explorer, and colonial official, Lawson came to the Carolinas in 1700 as a colonial official. Later in the decade he traveled throughout the backcountry of South Carolina and Georgia. His notes of these travels, published in England under the title *A New Voyage to Carolina* (1709), provide a valuable record of Southern Indian and frontier life in the early 18th century. He returned in 1710 as surveyor-general of North Carolina and assisted Christopher Baron de Graffenried in the founding of New Bern, a colony of German Palatines, but was killed by Indians the next year.

LEAGUE OF ARMED NEUTRALITY (1780) Catherine II, Empress of Russia, declared in 1780 that the Russian navy would be used to free neutral trade from belligerent interference. This was a blow to British blockade efforts against France and Spain. Catherine invited European countries and the United States to a conference, and the United States accepted (1780). Francis Dana was appointed the minister to Russia to gain recognition of the United States as an independent nation and to maintain freedom of the seas. The mission was a failure, for Catherine refused to receive Dana because American independence was not recognized by Britain. James Madison pointed out that it would have been unwise for America to be in the league anyway, for America's interests would have become complicated with the politics of Europe.

LEDERER, JOHN (flourished 1668-71) A German explorer, Lederer came to Virginia in 1668. Authorized by Governor Berkeley to explore the western country, the next year he led three expeditions through the foothills of Virginia to the Blue Ridge, twice reaching the summit of the first range. His explorations were publicized in his book *The Discoveries of John Lederer* (1672).

LEDYARD, JOHN (1751-89) An American explorer, born in Groton, Connecticut, he left Dartmouth to go to sea in 1773. In 1776, Ledyard joined the expedition of James Cook to the Sandwich Islands (Hawaii) and, with Cook on the Oregon coast, realized the great possibilities in the Pacific fur trade. On his return he was imprisoned in London for two years for refusing to fight against his countrymen. In America after the Revolution he published a narrative of his adventures with Cook and made several attempts to secure backing for a trading voyage to the Pacific but failed despite encouragement from Thomas Jefferson. In 1787 he traversed Europe with a plan to walk across Asia in order to reach the Pacific but was arrested by the Russians as a spy; later an account of this adventure was published. In England the following year he organized an expedition to explore the sources of the Niger River in Africa; this strange explorer committed suicide while delayed in Cairo.

LEE, ARTHUR (1740-92) A Revolutionary War diplomat, Lee was born in Westmoreland County, Virginia, and was the brother of Francis Lightfoot, Richard Henry, and William Lee. He received a medical degree from the University of Edinburgh (1764), established a medical practice in Virginia (1766), and then returned to England to study law (1768). Soon, he became involved in the political controversy over the colonies and wrote a series of ten "Monitor Letters" in the *Virginia Gazette* and in London the "Junius Americanus Letters" (1769), defending the stance of the colonies.

His reputation as a writer helped him to the appointment as colonial agent of Massachusetts in London (1770). After he was admitted to the British bar, Lee became a diplomat (1775), and the Continental Congress asked him to be the London agent (1776). He joined Benjamin Franklin and Silas Deane in Paris to negotiate an alliance with France. Lee also sought aid in Spain with some success (1777), and then in Berlin, where he had no success at all. Lee, Franklin, and Deane signed important treaties of commerce and alliance with France (1778). Lee unsuccessfully tried to charge Deane with disloyalty and embezzlement, and Deane made counter charges against Lee that caused Lee's recall (1779). He was elected to the Virginia House of Delegates (1781), served in the Continental Congress (1781-84), and argued against ratification of the Constitution.

See also Deane, Silas.

LEE, FRANCIS LIGHTFOOT (1734-97) A signer of the Declaration of Independence, Lee was born at Westmoreland County, Virginia, and was the brother of Arthur, Richard Henry, and William Lee. Lee served in the House of Burgesses from Loudoun County (1758-68). Settling a plantation in Richmond County, Lee became a burgess of the county during the crucial years preceding the Revolution (1769-76). Taking part in defiance of the British government, Lee signed the Westmoreland Association against the Stamp Act (1766), helped form the Virginia Committee of Correspondence, and called for a Virginia convention (1774). A member of the Continental Congress (1775-79), Lee signed the Declaration of Independence. While in Congress, he urged free navigation of the Mississippi River for American citizens.

LEE, HENRY (1756-1818) A soldier and public official, known as Light Horse Harry for his daring cavalry tactics, Lee was born in Prince William County, Virginia. Lee graduated from the College of New Jersey (now Princeton) in 1773, and with the outbreak of the Revolution, he was made a calvary captain (1776). As a major, he commanded three troops of calvary and three companies of infantry known as Lee's Legion (1778). The legion captured the fort at Paulus Hook, New Jersey, one of the most daring actions in the war (1779). He was sent to aid Nathanael Greene in the Carolina campaign and distinguished himself in the battles at Guilford Courthouse, Eutaw Springs, and

Augusta. As a lieutenant colonel, he helped in the siege of Yorktown (1781).

A war hero and a close friend of George Washington, Lee became prominent in Virginia politics after the war. He sat in the state legislature and the Continental Congress (1785-88) and voted to ratify the Constitution (1788). He also served as the governor of Virginia (1792-95) and helped Washington suppress the Whiskey Rebellion (1794). Lee retired from politics after serving in the House of Representatives (1799-1801). While involved in western land speculation, Lee became financially ruined and was confined to debtor's prison, where he wrote his memoirs (1808-09). Confederate leader Robert E. Lee was his son.

A cavalry leader known as Light Horse Harry, Henry Lee earned his nickname during Revolutionary War campaigns in New Jersey and North Carolina. *(Library of Congress)*

LEE, MOTHER ANN (1736-84)   Mother Ann Lee was the charismatic leader of the religious community called the Shakers (officially organized as the United Society of Believers in Christ's Second Appearing). In 1774 she led a band of eight followers to America from England. Six years later in Albany, New York, they were joined by New Light Baptists and began to attract followers throughout New England. Following a brief imprisonment in Albany and Poughkeepsie in 1780 under suspicion for her pacifism, Mother Ann was released by order of Governor George Clinton. She led a missionary venture through Massachusetts for the next four years, calling on people to confess their sins, take up the cross of celibacy, and live a new and perfect life in the presence of the Christ Spirit. Although the interpretations varied over time, most Shakers believed Mother Ann was the occasion of Christ's second apppearance—the first was in the male Jesus, the second now in the female. Over the next 200 years, Mother Ann's teachings inspired the development of some 19 communities, only 2 of which continue today.

See also Shakers.

LEE, RICHARD HENRY (1732-94)   A Revolutionary War era public official and signer of the Declaration of Independence, Lee was born in Westmoreland County, Virginia, and was the brother of Arthur, Francis Lightfoot, and William Lee. He became a justice of the peace in Virginia (1757) and then entered the House of Burgesses (1758-71). An advocate of liberal policies, Lee was an early opponent of Britain's colonial administration. In the House of Burgesses he drafted many petitions and protests and became friends with Patrick Henry and Thomas Jefferson. To coordinate the efforts of the colonies, he proposed (1773) a system of intercolonial committees of correspondence.

From 1774 to 1779 he was a delegate to the First and Second Continental Congresses. He introduced a resolution that led directly to the drafting of the Declaration of Independence (1776), and he advocated a confederation among the colonies. Lee was elected to the Virginia legislature (1780) and then returned to Congress (1784-89). He refused to be a delegate to the Constitutional Convention because of his membership in Congress. Arguing against ratifying the Constitution, he wrote a series of articles, "Letters of the Federal Farmer," in which he argued against the Constitution because of its provision for a strong central government and because of its lack of a bill of rights. As a U.S. senator (1789-92), he proposed several resolutions to correct omissions he saw in the Constitution, and many of these were adopted in the Bill of Rights (1791).

LEE, WILLIAM (1739-95)   A diplomat in the Revolution, Lee was born in Westmoreland County, Virginia, and was the brother of Arthur, Francis Lightfoot, and Richard Henry Lee. He and his brother Arthur engaged in mercantile pursuits in London (1768). They became involved in London politics as members of John Wilke's movement, and Lee was elected a sheriff and alderman in London (1775). A secret committee of Congress appointed Lee and Thomas Morris commercial agents in Nantes, France (1777). While in France, William Lee became involved in his brother's notorious Lee-Deane controversy. Lee was chosen by Congress in May 1777 as commissioner to the courts of Berlin and Vienna. These missions failed, but he did negotiate a treaty of commerce between the United

States and Holland. His government service ended in 1779.

See also Lee, Arthur.

LEISLER'S REBELLION (1689-91)   The Glorious Revolution (1688) in Britain that brought William and Mary to the throne and forced James II to abdicate caused a revolt in the colonies by Protestant colonists alarmed at the prospect of a Catholic-French plot. Captain Jacob Leisler (1640-91) took control of southern New York after Fort James on Manhattan Island was seized by a mob (May 1689). Leisler, taking the title of lieutenant governor, influenced representatives of Massachusetts, Plymouth, Connecticut, and New York to meet in New York City to unite in an offensive against Canada. Leisler took charge of the campaign (1690) but his efforts were spoiled when the colonies refused to cooperate. After Colonel Henry Sloughter was commissioned governor of New York by William and Mary, Major Robert Ingoldesby arrived in New York City with a force of English soldiers in early 1691. Leisler and his allies resisted Ingoldesby but surrendered to Sloughter upon his arrival in March. Leisler was tried for treason and executed in May 1691.

LELAND, JOHN (1754-1841)   A Baptist minister, he was born in Massachusetts. In 1774 he went to Virginia, where he established a Baptist congregation at Orange. In 1788 his congregation sent him to the Virginia convention to speak against the Constitution, but he was convinced by advocates such as James Madison that religious freedom would not be curtailed. He was against slavery and proposed its abolition at the Baptist General Committee meeting in 1789. In 1791, Leland moved back to Massachusetts, where he led both the Massachusetts and Connecticut Baptists and continued to fight for religious freedom and separation of church and state. He wrote *Virginia Chronicle* in 1790.

LE MOYNE, JACQUES (died 1588)   Watercolorist Jacques Le Moyne was the first European artist known to have visited the Americas. He was a member of the Laudonnière expedition to Florida, Georgia, and the Carolinas in 1564. He survived the Spanish attack on the Huguenot settlement on St. John's River in 1565. His watercolors of American animals and Indians were engraved and published with his narrative of the expedition in 1591 (translated into English as *Narrative of Le Moyne*, 1875). After he left America, he settled in London and executed watercolors of animals and portraits of the nobility.

LENNOX, CHARLOTTE RAMSEY (1720-1804)   A novelist, dramatist, and translator, Lennox was born in New York City, where she spent most of her unhappy childhood. She was sent to England at 15 to be educated and in 1747 married Alexander Lennox, the same year that her first book, *Poems on Several Occasions*, was published. The most important friendship of her life was with Samuel Johnson, who advised her and promoted her writing career. Her novels have been described as a mixture of the novel of manners and sentimental romance. Some of her major works include *The Life of Harriet Stuart* (1750) and *The Female Quixote, or the Adventures of Arabella* (1752).

LEONARD, DANIEL (1740-1829)   Born to the most socially and politically dominant family in southern Massachusetts, Leonard graduated from Harvard in 1760 and took up the study of law. He became the Crown attorney for Bristol County in 1769 and proceeded to the General Court in 1770. Initially opposed to George III, Leonard was persuaded by Thomas Hutchinson to adopt a Loyalist position. He authored 17 articles as "Massachusettensis" against John Adams's "Novanglus." After the Revolutionary War broke out, Leonard took refuge with the British in Boston, and after independence was declared and his property confiscated, he left for England. From 1782 to 1806 he was chief justice of Bermuda. He died in England from a pistol wound, possibly a suicide.

LEVERETT, JOHN (1662-1724)   President of Harvard College (1707-24), Leverett instituted a liberal curriculum that roused the ire of former president Cotton Mather. Descended from an early governor of Massachusetts, Leverett studied at Boston Latin School, graduated from Harvard College (1683), and was appointed fellow and tutor at Harvard (1685). He also trained as a lawyer and was made judge of the superior court and judge of probate for Massachusetts' Middlesex County in 1702 and was elected to the Provincial Council in 1706. Governor Dudley sent him on missions to New York, to the Iroquois, and to the Port Royal Company.

LEWIS, FRANCIS (1713-1802)   A merchant and political leader, born in Glamorganshire, Wales, Lewis was orphaned at an early age, educated at the Westminster School, and apprenticed to a London mercantile house. In 1738 he immigrated to America and settled in New York, engaging in the international trade. In 1756, as a private provisions contractor during the French and Indian War, he was captured at the fall of Fort Oswego and spent several years as a prisoner of war in France. Lewis later became a strong supporter of American independence and served as a member of the Continental Congress (1775-79) and as commissioner of the Board of the Admiralty (1779-81).

LEXINGTON AND CONCORD, BATTLE OF
(1775) The opening engagement of the Revolutionary War, the Battle of Lexington and Concord followed a period of increasing hostility between Crown officers and the citizens of Massachusetts. Warned by Paul Revere and William Dawes that the British were on their way to Concord to seize colonial military supplies, 70 militiamen stood on Lexington Green the morning of April 19, 1775. Captain John Parker and his men, realizing they were no match for the 700 British regulars under Lieutenant Colonel Francis Smith, intended only to stand in symbolic protest. But someone fired a shot, and the resulting skirmish left eight American dead. Moving on to Concord, the Redcoats lost three men at North Bridge. Then began their agony, the bloody 20-mile retreat to Boston. Bedeviled by the fire of minutemen from 40 towns, British troops suffered 273 casualties while inflicting 93 on the Americans.

Following the battle, colonial forces began the siege of Boston.

See also Revere, Paul; Revolutionary War, Battles of the.

LIBERTY BELL Following a reading of the Declaration of Independence at the state house (later called Independence Hall) in Philadelphia, the Liberty Bell first proclaimed American independence on July 8, 1776. Not until the 19th century did it come to symbolize American independence. The Liberty Bell was originally planned by the provincial council for the golden jubilee (1751) of William Penn's 1701 Charter of Privileges. The bell was cracked in testing upon arrival and recast in Philadelphia. It was hidden in Allentown (1777-78) during the Revolution. The Liberty Bell rang frequently, but became fatally cracked while being rung on George Washington's birthday (1846). It was first called the Liberty Bell during the anti-slavery movement (1839). On the bell is inscribed: "Proclaim Liberty throughout all the land unto all the inhabitants thereof."

See also Independence Hall.

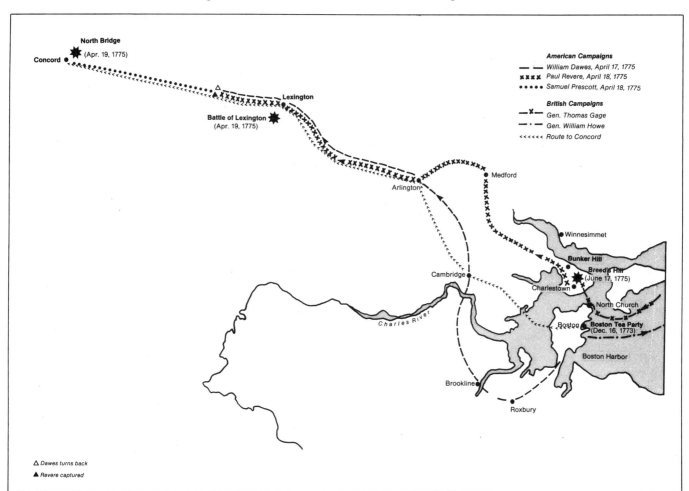

Battle of Lexington and Concord. *(Facts On File, Inc.)*

LIBERTY INCIDENT (1768) The Liberty Incident typified the growing tension between Massachusetts citizens and Crown officials. On June 10, 1768, customs officials in Boston seized John Hancock's sloop *Liberty* for unloading cargo without paying customs duties. The customs officers, fearing that a gathering crowd might rescue the *Liberty*, had her towed under the guns of the man-of-war *Romney*, whose captain had antagonized the town by impressing seamen. The crowd rioted, throwing stones at *Romney*'s crew and beating the customs men. When Governor Bernard could offer them no protection, the customs commissioners fled to the safety of Castle William in the harbor and again asked England to send troops for their protection. News of the incident reached London in July; two regiments reached Boston in October.

LINCOLN, BENJAMIN (1733-1810) A soldier and public official, Lincoln was born in Hingham, Massachusetts. Lincoln served in the legislature (1772-73) and the provincial congress (1774-75). He became a brigadier general when the Revolutionary War broke out. Promoted to major general, Lincoln commanded troops in New York (1776) and Vermont (1777), where he took command of the milita. In the Battle of Saratoga (1777), he played an important role in defeating General John Burgoyne. After recovering from wounds he received at Saratoga, Lincoln commanded the Continental Army in the southern department. Unfamiliar with southern terrain, Lincoln blundered and had to surrender his army to General Henry Clinton in the siege of Charleston (1779). Later freed, he rejoined General Washington at Yorktown, where he accepted the sword of Lord Cornwallis. The Continental Congress made him secretary of war (1781-83), after which he returned to Massachusetts, where he commanded the troops that suppressed Shays' Rebellion (1787).

See also Shays' Rebellion.

LINCOLN, LEVI (1749-1820) A lawyer and politician, born in Hingham, Massachusetts, Lincoln graduated from Harvard (1772). He began a law practice in Worcester and was elected to the convention that drew up the first state constitution (1779). In landmark court battles in 1781, Lincoln argued successfully against the legality of slavery in Massachusetts in view of the state's bill of rights. After the war Lincoln became an anti-Federalist and Republican leader, serving in numerous state offices and as U.S. attorney general (1801-04).

LINING, JOHN (1708-60) A physician, Lining typified the curiosity and scientific interest of the American Enlightenment. At the age of 22 he began his medical practice in Charleston, South Carolina. He soon became fascinated by yellow fever and wrote the first American analysis of its pathology. Using himself as a subject, Lining sought to study tropical conditions as they are experienced daily. To do this he kept a careful record of his daily intake of food and water and the weight of his excretions. Although these efforts did not result in conclusive data, they proved helpful to later researchers. Lining was also fascinated by electricity and replicated Franklin's famous kite experiment.

LITERATURE Because of the conditions of life and the Puritan scorn for entertainment, very little of what we now regard as "literature" was written between 1607 and 1787 during the colonial period and the era of the Revolution. The colonists had to tame the new world, and they concentrated on their task. Their communications, therefore, were usually either descriptions of their colonies to England or definitions of the colonies to themselves. A good example of the first type is *A True Relation of Such Occurrences and Accidents as Hath Happened in Virginia Since the First Planting of That Colony* (1608), written by Captain John Smith to show the material benefits of colonization. The second type was mostly produced by New England colonists, because the Puritans came with a vision of a New Zion. This millennialistic vision led to their sense of the importance of the moment, recorded in their many histories, biographies, and sermons. William Bradford's book *Of Plymouth Plantation* (1650), for example, is both a history and a chart of God's sacred plan for the new world. Similar millennialistic works were *Magnalia Christi Americana* (1702) by Cotton Mather and *The Wonder-Working Providence of Scion's Saviour* (1653) by Edward Johnson. In addition, many works of piety and doctrine were produced in the 17th century by John Cotton, Thomas Shepard, and Nathaniel Ward.

For Puritans, literature always had a didactic or religious purpose. For example, Calvinist doctrines were conveyed in the popular poem "The Day of Doom" (1662) by Michael Wigglesworth. Acclaimed as the two best Puritan poets were Anne Bradstreet, who wrote *The Tenth Muse Lately Sprung Up in America* (1650), and minister Edward Taylor, whose works remained unpublished until 1939.

The 18th century. In the 18th century the literature of the colonies became more diverse and secularized. Nevertheless, there was Jonathan Edwards, the last of the great Puritan preachers, who wrote many famous religious essays. The *Journal* (1774) of John Woolman, a modest Quaker preacher, was also important. The Deism of the Enlightenment dispensed with all forms of orthodox religion, however, favoring instead individual reasoning, as shown in Thomas Paine's *The Age of Reason* (1794). Another deist, famous statesman and inventor Benjamin Franklin, espoused common sense and pragmatism in his

Poor Richard's Almanack (1733-1758), an immensely popular amalgamation of folk humor and philosophy.

Much of the literature was concerned with the pressing political issues of the day. Paine's pamphlet *Common Sense* (1776) argued boldly for separation from England. The eloquence of Thomas Jefferson was evident in The Declaration of Independence (1776) and Philip Freneau championed the Revolution in verse, satirizing the British as did John Trumbull in *M'Fingal* (1776), a satire on Tories. Alexander Hamilton, James Madison, and John Jay published *The Federalist Papers* (1787-1788), while the Federalist poets known as the Connecticut Wits defended their beliefs by collaborating on political satires. They also tried individually to create a national literature, but while they focused on American subjects, they still used Old World forms and models. Royall Tyler had the same intentions and results in his play *The Contrast*, although he did introduce some authentic American types. The American people and their land were also described in *Letters from an American Farmer* (1782) by Michel Guillaume St. John de Crevecoeur, but the real American Renaissance in literature did not come until the middle of the 19th century.

See also Bradstreet, Anne; Connecticut Wits; Freneau, Philip; Mather, Cotton.

Bibliography: Boynton, Percy H., *A History of American Literature* (Ginn, 1919); Parrington, Vernon Louis, *The Colonial Mind, 1620-1800* (Harcourt, Brace, 1927); Stern, Milton R. and Gross, Seymour L., eds., *American Literature Survey: Colonial and Federal to 1800* (Viking, 1962).

James F. Cooper, Jr.
University of Connecticut

LIVINGSTON, PETER VAN BRUGH (1710-92)   A New York merchant and politician, grandson of Robert Livingston (born 1654) and son of Philip Livingston (born 1686), Peter graduated from Yale College in 1731. During the French and Indian War he made a fortune fulfilling government supply contracts and joined his brothers and cousins in opposing the DeLancey interest. Never elected to the provincial assembly, he was nonetheless active in opposition to the sugar and stamp acts. Unlike the rest of his family, he seems to have been comfortable with the aggressive tactics of New York City's merchants and mechanics. In 1775 he was elected presiding officer of New York's first provincial congress, but he fell ill later that year and retired from public life.

LIVINGSTON, PHILIP (1716-78)   A New York merchant, philanthropist, and signer of the Declaration of Independence, Philip was the grandson of Robert Livingston (born 1654) and son of Philip Livingston (born 1686). Philip reaped large profits trading during the French and Indian War, but unlike his grandfather, who was notorious for his parsimonious ways, Philip devoted considerable attention to civic projects. Among the institutions to which he contributed were King's College (now Columbia), New York Hospital, the St. Andrews Benevolent Society, and the New York Society Library.

Livingston began his political career in 1754 with his election as a New York City alderman. He entered the Assembly in 1758 and represented New York at the Stamp Act Congress. Although he was chosen speaker of the Assembly in 1768, he was swept from office the next year. He represented New York at the First and Second Continental Congresses where he counseled caution but signed the Declaration of Independence. He served in both the Continental Congress and the Senate of New York until his death in 1778.

LIVINGSTON, ROBERT (1654-1728)   A New York merchant, landed proprietor and politician, he was the son of John Livingston, a Scottish Presbyterian minister who took his family to Rotterdam, Holland at the time of the Stuart Restoration (1660). Robert became fluent in Dutch and by the age of 16 was engaged in commercial shipping under his own name. In 1674 he moved to Albany, where his bilingualism and economic savvy assured his mercantile success. He quickly entered the community's political life and the next year became town clerk and secretary to the board of Indian commissioners. He soon transformed the latter office into one of the most important in New York. Livingston's marriage in 1679 to Alida Schuyler Van Rensselaer, sister of soon-to-be mayor Peter Schuyler and widow of wealthy patroon Nicholas Van Rensselaer, established his connections with two major dynasties of the Upper Hudson Valley and confirmed his entrance into the provincial elite.

Throughout his life Livingston made good use of his social and political connections. In 1686, with the help of his friend Governor Thomas Dongan, he received a patent for the manor and lordship of Livingston, comprising some 160,000 acres in present day Dutchess and Columbia counties. He enjoyed close relationships with Governors Bellmont, Cornbury, and Hunter, from whom he often received political favors and valuable contracts for supplying governmental stores. A member of the provincial assembly (1709-25), Livingston served as speaker from 1718 until his retirement. He died one of New York's wealthiest men.

George Mills
Yale University

LIVINGSTON, ROBERT R. (1718-75)   A New York jurist and landed proprietor, he was the grandson of Robert Livingston (born 1654) and son of Robert Livingston of

Clermont (born 1688). Robert married Margaret Beekman, sole heir of Colonel Henry Beekman, in 1742. Taken together, the Livingston and Beekman land holdings represented one of New York's largest estates. Elected to the provincial assembly in 1758, Livingston was appointed judge of the Admiralty Court in 1759 and associate judge of the provincial Supreme Court in 1763. As chairman of New York's Committee of Correspondence he supported convening an intercolonial conference to resist the Stamp Act. Although Livingston was prepared to pursue aggressive measures to protect colonial rights, his association with New York's landlords made him a primary target of the "popular party." Defeated in the election of 1768, he never regained a seat in the Assembly.

Robert Livingston helped to frame the Declaration of Independence and later directed foreign affairs. *(Library of Congress)*

LIVINGSTON, ROBERT R. (1746-1813) A jurist, diplomat and gentleman farmer, Robert was often referred to as "Chancellor" to distinguish him from his father, Judge Robert R. Livingston (born 1718), and was commonly regarded as the most important member of the family in his generation. A 1765 graduate of King's College (later Columbia), he was admitted to the bar in 1770. As a member of the Second Continental Congress he served on the committee to draft a declaration of independence, but was called back to New York before the resulting document was signed. During the Revolution he served on numerous congressional committees, in particular those concerning judicial, financial, and foreign affairs. In 1781 he was named secretary of the Department of Foreign Affairs in which capacity he corresponded regularly with the American commissioners negotiating peace with Great Britain.

Livingston was also a member of the committee that drafted the first constitution of the state of New York in 1777 and served as Chancellor from 1777 to 1801. He supported the U.S. Constitution but disagreed with Hamilton's economic policies, and by the early 1790s he emerged as a member of the Republican party. Jefferson appointed him minister to France in 1801, and Livingston capped his political career by negotiating the acquisition of Louisiana in the spring of 1803. He resigned his post in 1804 and returned to the family estate, Clermont. During the last decade of his life he pursued a variety of agricultural experiments and worked closely with Robert Fulton to develop a commercially feasible steamship.

George Mills
Yale University

LIVINGSTON, WILLIAM (1723-90) A lawyer and first governor of the state of New Jersey, William was the grandson of Robert Livingston (born 1654) and son of Philip Livingston (born 1686). He graduated from Yale College in 1741. Admitted to the bar in 1748, he was a close associate of John Morin Scott, William Peachtree Smith, and William Smith, Jr. An aggressive opponent of New York's commercial gentry, he was generally credited with orchestrating the Livingstons' defeat of the DeLancey faction in the provincial assembly elections of 1758. A proponent of colonial home rule, he clearly favored patrician leadership within New York, and, like most of his family, was defeated in the election of 1769.

Livingston's loss so disappointed him that he left New York, taking up residence on his estate near Elizabethtown, New Jersey. He did not, however, retire from politics. He joined the Essex County Committee of Correspondence and represented New Jersey at both the First and Second Continental Congresses. Elected the first governor of the state of New Jersey, he served for 14 years (1776-90). In 1787 he attended the Constitutional Convention and was credited with arranging New Jersey's ratification early the next year.

LLOYD, DAVID (1656-1731) Born in Wales, this lawyer and jurist left his imprint on the legal, political, and constitutional development of Pennsylvania. His legal skills caught the attention of William Penn, who appointed him attorney general on April 24, 1686. Lloyd held many public positions and shaped the law of early Pennsylvania while serving in the county and provincial courts and the Philadelphia city court. He also sat for many terms as a delegate in the Pennsylvania Assembly between 1693 and 1729. Lloyd was also a member of the provincial council in 1695-96 and 1698-1700. He served as chief justice, interpreting laws he had written, from 1717 until his death.

Lloyd protested the subordinate status of the Assembly under the 1683 Frame and supported its stronger legislative role in Markham's Frame (1696) and in the Charter of Privileges (1701). In 1689 he was removed as clerk of the provincial court for refusing to produce court records demanded by the provincial council. In the period 1692-94 Lloyd battled the royal governor, Benjamin Fletcher, and fought for the rights of the Assembly. In 1698 vice-admiralty court judge Robert Quarry accused Lloyd of resisting enforcement of the Navigation Acts. Quarry complained about Lloyd's antiauthoritarianism and the Board of Trade demanded that Penn remove him as attorney general and suspend him from the provincial council. Lloyd adopted a strong antiproprietary position and led the Popular party, composed of the poorer backcountry Quakers, against the Proprietary party, composed of Penn's wealthy counselors, headed by James Logan.

Lloyd advocated the right of affirmation for jurors and witnesses, opposed the appropriation of military funds, insisted upon constitutional reform, and demanded the right of the Assembly to meet and adjourn at its own decision. Lloyd authored a list of grievances sent to Penn in 1704 and attempted to impeach Logan in 1707. Lloyd had great technical skill in drafting the laws passed by the Assembly. He spent his life weakening the power of the proprietor and strengthening the power of the popular Assembly.

Bibliography: Lokken, Roy Norman, *David Lloyd: Colonial Lawmaker* (Univ. of Washington Press, 1959).

Roger Henderson
Pennsylvania State University

LOCHABER, TREATY OF (1770) This agreement, signed on October 18, 1770, between Virginia and the Cherokee nation superseded the Treaty of Hard Labor Creek in delineating the boundaries of permitted British colonization. Since the signing of the earlier treaty, Virginia colonists had continued to settle within the territory of the Cherokee, and the government of Virginia sought to lend legal status to the new status quo. Under the supervision of Colonel John Donelson, a new line was agreed upon and surveyed. Its actual course, however, added even more area to the colony of Virginia than that agreed to in the treaty, and the Cherokee nation lost more than 9,000 square miles of their tribal territory.

See also Hard Labor Creek, Treaty of.

LOCKE, JOHN (1632-1702) An English philosopher, inspirer of the age of Enlightenment and Reason in England and France, he was born at Wrington, Somershire. His political philosophies directly influenced the American Revolution, especially the Declaration of Independence. Locke held that the government should protect man's property and possessions and that man has the right to think, worship, and speak as he wishes. Man must subject himself to civil law and find freedom in voluntary obedience. Locke advocated a constitution under which the legislative body is elected. The executive branch has one ruler and is separate from the legislative. The people are ultimately sovereign. Locke also believed that a ruler's authority is conditional rather than absolute and that the people have the right to withdraw their support and overthrow the government if it does not fulfill its trust. Locke's political philosophy had a great influence on Thomas Jefferson, the drafting of the Declaration of Independence, and the Constitution of the new government.

LOGAN, JAMES (1674-1751) A colonial administrator and political leader, he was born in County Armaugh, Ireland, the son of a prominent Quaker churchman and teacher. Raised and educated in Bristol, England, he briefly began a business career before making the acquaintance of William Penn, who asked him to become his personal secretary in 1699. Sailing with Penn to Pennsylvania, Logan served as secretary of the province and clerk of the provincial council (1701-17).

After Penn's return to England, Logan was appointed commissioner of property and receiver general of lands, a position that required him to protect Penn's private interests and forced him to negotiate with the native peoples of the province for trade rights and territory. He established close relations with many of the tribes of western Pennsylvania and gained considerable personal wealth from business transactions with them. Logan also served as mayor of Philadelphia (1722), justice of Philadelphia County (1726), chief justice of the Pennsylvania supreme court (1731-39), and acting governor of Pennsylvania (1736-38). He retired from public life in 1747, devoting himself to the study of natural science. The plant family *Loganiaceae* was named by Linnaeus to honor him.

LOGAN, JAMES (?1725-80) An Indian leader, born in the Delaware Indian village of Shamokin, his Indian name was Tah-gah-jute. Prominent among the Mingo bands,

Logan was a friend of the whites in Pennsylvania and Ohio. Logan's friendship with the whites ended after his Shawnee wife and relatives were killed at the Yellow Creek massacre, an event that helped to precipitate Lord Dunmore's War (1774). He scalped 30 white men during the war and spent the rest of his life seeking revenge for the massacre. His eloquent refusal to discuss peace was reprinted in many colonial newspapers, and Thomas Jefferson used the oration to show the degrading effects of living in the New World in *Notes on the State of Virginia*. Until his death, Logan continued to brutalize white settlements. While aiding the British at Detroit during the Revolutionary War he was killed by a relative.

LOGAN, MARTHA DANIELL (1704-79)   A colonial teacher and horticulturist, Logan ran a boarding school in Wando River, South Carolina, where students were taught reading, arithmetic, drawing, and needlework. She is best known for her gardening and is the assumed author of the "Gardener's Kalendar," which was published in John Tobler's *South Carolina Almanack* for 1752. Different versions of this calendar appeared in South Carolina and Georgia almanacs into the 1780s. Her writings did not bear her name until they appeared in the *Palladium of Knowledge* (1796). According to Pennsylvania botanist John Bartram, with whom she corresponded eagerly, "Her garden is a delight."

LOG CABIN   The earliest European settlers in North America frequently utilized log construction in structures of all types and styles. However, the first cabins utilizing the horizontal construction of flattened logs, mortised together at the corners, filled or "chinked" with chips and clay, were probably introduced by German or Scandinavian colonists in the lower Delaware River Valley during the 1630s. English and Scotch-Irish immigrants fused these ideas with the traditional spatial concepts of the British Isles, where single-room, gable-end cottages of mud or stone housed most rural people. Pioneers might spend their first winter in a simple hut made of poles, with an open side facing away from prevailing winds and toward a large log fire, but soon they would construct a full enclosure, with a fireplace along one wall and a floor of log puncheons, and later might add a lean-to in the back or even a second story.

Such cabins came to typify the housing of backwoods people in western Pennsylvania, the Valley of Virginia, and the Piedmont of the Carolinas and Georgia, from where it was carried into trans-Appalachia. Although New Englanders generally used frame-construction techniques, the log cabin could even be found in the late colonial period in the northern settlements of Vermont, New Hampshire, and Maine.

Bibliography: Glassie, Henry, *Pattern in the Material Folk Culture of the Eastern United States*, rev. ed. (Univ. of Pennsylvania Press, 1971); Shurtleff, Harold, *The Log Cabin Myth: A Study of the Early Dwellings of the English Colonists in North America* (1939; reprint Peter Smith, 1967).

LOG COLLEGE   From 1726 to 1742, William Tennent, an Irish Presbyterian minister in Noshaminy, Pennsylvania, conducted classes in the log schoolhouse that he had constructed. The schoolhouse was about 20 feet square and served as the first training school for American Presbyterian ministerial candidates. In 1746 the Presbyterian Synod recognized the importance of Tennent's work and established an official school, the College of New Jersey (later Princeton) to prepare young men as Presbyterian ministers. Tennent helped to raise money for the new college.

LONDON, TREATY OF (1604)   The agreement known as the Treaty of London marked the end of a period of hostilities between England and Spain that had existed since 1585. The fighting had interrupted the colonial activities of both powers in the New World. By the terms of the treaty all captured territories were to be returned and free trade was to be allowed. Spain, however, maintained that English merchants had never been permitted to trade with its colonies and that the treaty merely restored prewar conditions. English objections to this interpretation led to intensive privateering in the Caribbean that went on until the issue was resolved in the Treaty of Madrid (1670).

See also Madrid, Treaty of.

LONG ISLAND   Long Island was granted in 1620 by King James I to the Virginia Company of Plymouth. With the replacement of the Plymouth Company in 1635 by the Council for New England, Long Island was granted to William Alexander, Earl of Stirling. In 1636 competition for control of Long Island arose when the Dutch rulers of New Amsterdam began to grant patents for lands opposite Manhattan Island. By the mid-17th century, the western end of Long Island was occupied by both Dutch and English settlements. The eastern end of the island was, however, colonized only by English settlers, and the 1650 Treaty of Hartford incorporated all of Long Island east of Oyster Bay into the Connecticut colony.

With the English conquest of New Amsterdam in 1664, the entire island technically came under English control, but it was not until the Treaty of Westminster (1674) that the title to Long Island was legally given to the Duke of York, brother of Charles II. During the Revolution, control of Long Island was crucial to the defense of New York City, and the defeat of the Continental Army at the Battle of Long Island in August 1776 marked one of the early turning points in the war.

LOPEZ, ANDRES (flourished 1750-1812) Lopez is remembered as the greatest Mexican painter of the late colonial period. A disciple of Miguel Cabrera, Lopez, who was active for more than 50 years, was known for his decorative murals. In addition, he painted several portraits of government officials in New Spain, including the viceroy Bernardo de Gálvez. His acknowledged masterpiece, "Via Crucis," is in Aguascalientes and was painted with the help of his brother Cristobal between 1798 and 1800.

LÓPEZ, NICOLAS (flourished 1683-84) In 1683 the Jumano Indian chief Juan Sabeata arrived in El Paso and requested that missionaries be sent to proselytize in his tribe. López, a Franciscan missionary, and Captain Juan Dominguez de Mendoza traveled east to the Colorado River, surveying the general situation in the region. On their return the Franciscan and the soldier went to Mexico City to ask for support in extending the mission and presidio system into Texas. While they were in Mexico, the viceroy received a report that a French fleet led by La Salle had sailed for the Gulf coast. The need to meet this threat overshadowed their requests, and they returned disappointed to the northern frontier.

See also Mendoza, Juan Dominguez de.

LORD DUNMORE'S WAR (1774) This conflict between the government of Virginia and the Shawnee nation over territory in western Pennsylvania and eastern Ohio can be traced to the hostility of the Indian peoples of Ohio against Virginia settlers and to the competition between the colonies of Virginia and Pennsylvania for control of the strategic Fort Pitt, on the site of modern Pittsburgh. In 1774, Colonel John Connelly, on orders from Virginia governor Lord Dunmore, began the war by capturing Fort Pitt, renaming it Fort Dunmore, and using it as the headquarters of a campaign of retaliation against the Indians for attacks against Virginia settlers.

While General Andrew Lewis and the Virginia militia embarked on a campaign against the Shawnee towns in nearby Ohio, Dunmore himself arrived at Fort Dunmore to encourage further Virginia settlement in the vicinity. The Shawnee, under the leadership of Cornstalk, were defeated

The Battle of Long Island, shown in a 1776 illustration, was a major setback for the Continental Army. *(Library of Congress)*

at the Battle of Point Pleasant by the Virginia forces, and they agreed to negotiate for peace. Lord Dunmore subsequently established a camp near the site of Chillicothe, Ohio, and supervised the signing of a peace treaty and an exchange of prisoners that established, at least temporarily, peace on the Pennsylvania-Ohio frontier.

See also Cornstalk; Dunmore, John Murray.

LOS ANGELES　In 1542, Juan Rodríguez de Cabrillo sighted the Bay of San Pedro, which he called the Bay of Smokes because of the Indian fires on the plain surrounding it. It was not until after Gaspar de Portolá and Junipero Serra penetrated California by land in the 1770s that the region was explored, however. The mission of San Gabriel was established in 1771, and in 1781, Felipe de Neve founded the Pueblo de Nuestra Senora la Reina de Los Angeles de Porciuncula. Forty-four settlers from Sinaloa were its first inhabitants.

Within 20 years Los Angeles had over 300 residents and a new mission at San Fernando. The town, although by far the largest in California, was of only minor importance in a society that revolved around huge, self-sufficient landed estates. Through the rest of the colonial period Los Angeles and its port at San Pedro were occasionally visited by foreign ships, which were quickly ordered away by the Spanish authorities. The town's chief function was to be the center of governmental authority, such as it was, in the south, and it served as a social center for the vast hinterland surrounding it. The main export of California, hides taken from the hundreds of thousands of cattle, were shipped out through San Pedro. Throughout the colonial and Mexican periods, however, Los Angeles remained a small town catering to the needs of the ranchos around it.

See also Serra, Junipero; Portolá, Gaspar de.

LOTTERIES　Reflecting the popularity of gambling, private and public lotteries were common in the 17th-century English colonies. City lots and houses were frequently sold through lotteries, which were often conducted at taverns, as for example in Boston in 1719 when 100 tickets were sold for five pounds each. Similiar sales occurred throughout colonial cities, although they were frequently condemned by auctioneers and merchants as prejudicial to legitimate trade. Reflecting these criticisms several colonies, beginning with Massachusetts in 1732, outlawed private lotteries, while at the same time they increasingly turned to them as a convenient and painless method of raising money for public purposes. Benjamin Franklin convinced the city of Philadelphia to hold a lottery in 1747 in order to construct a battery on the river, and in 1752 Newport held one to finance the first paving of the town streets. The endowment for King's College (later Columbia), established in New York City in 1754, was provided by an assembly-approved lottery, and in 1763 the first lighthouse at Sandy Hook outside New York harbor, was constructed after a public lottery raised 6,000 pounds. Lotteries continued as an important method of public finance until the second quarter of the 19th century when they began to be attacked as weakening the morals of the community. Most states had outlawed them by 1850.

LOUDON, JOHN CAMPBELL, FOURTH EARL OF　(1705-82)　A British military officer and commander in chief of the British forces in North America, Loudon was born in Ayrshire, Scotland, and joined the 2nd Royal North British Dragoons in 1717. Elected a Scottish representative peer in 1734, he served as governor of Stirling Castle in 1741. During active service in Flanders in 1743, he was named aide-de-camp to King George II and was promoted to the rank of colonel of the 30th Foot Regiment in 1749. As a hard-line disciplinarian, Loudon was appointed commander in chief of the British forces in North America by the Duke of Cumberland in 1756. Serving also as governor general of Virginia, he gained the admiration of many prominent Americans in his attempts to reorganize the regular army and galvanize the support of the various colonies. Loudon was credited with playing a crucial role in the British conquest of Canada but failed to overcome the opposition of some colonies to full financial participation in the war. While admired as an administrator, he was viewed as a poor tactician. The French general Montcalm easily overran Loudon's defense of Forts Oswego and William Henry. He was recalled by William Pitt in 1757 and later served as governor of Edinburgh Castle.

See also Fort William Henry Massacre; Oswego, Fort.

LOUISBURG　The French began the construction of a major fortress and naval station on Cape Breton Island in 1720, after their loss of mainland Acadia to the British in 1713. Called Louisbourg by the French and Louisburg by the English, it overlooked the rich offshore fisheries and guarded the entrance to the Gulf of the St. Lawrence. It quickly became a major military center as well as an entrepôt used illegally by the Acadians. During King George's War, in 1745, Governor William Shirley of Massachusetts mounted a large naval expedition against the fortress. Land forces laid siege and captured the town, then captured the French fleet upon its arrival. By the Treaty of Aix-la-Chapelle (1748), however, Louisburg was returned to the French in exchange for Madras in India, an agreement greeted with disgust in British North America. Captured by the British in 1758, Louisburg became General Wolfe's base for operations against Quebec and a major staging area for the deportations of the Acadians to other

Louisburg's strategic importance at the entrance to the St. Lawrence River made it a frequent target during struggles between the French and English. *(Library of Congress)*

parts of North America and Europe. It was finally razed by the British in 1760.

LOUISBURG, BATTLES OF (1748, 1757, 1758) The conflicts between British and French forces over the control of a fortress on Cape Breton Island known as the Battles of Louisburg were a prelude to the British conquest of Canada. The French citadel and town of Louisburg, built soon after the Treaty of Utrecht (1713), was always viewed as a direct military threat by the British colonies in New England. In 1745, during King George's War, the New Englanders moved to remove this perceived threat. Massachusetts Governor William Shirley organized a military expedition against Louisburg, in which troops from Pennsylvania, New Jersey, New York, Connecticut, and Rhode Island also participated. Under the command of William Pepperell, the town and fortress were taken, but in 1748, under the terms of the Treaty of Aix-la-Chapelle, they were returned to France.

In 1757, during the French and Indian War, a large-scale attack on Louisburg was made by the Earl of Loudon but it failed, owing to unexpected French reinforcement of the garrison. In the following year, Generals Amherst and Wolfe achieved the final conquest of Louisburg. With a large force of colonials, they overran and destroyed both the citadel and the town, ending forever the French presence in the Gulf of St. Lawrence.

See also French and Indian War.

LOUISIANA *See* **French Colonies.**

LOUISIANA REVOLUTION (1768) In November 1762, France ceded Louisiana to Spain. Delays in the actual transfer exacerbated the economic chaos that already existed in the colony at the end of the French and Indian War (Seven Years' War). Antonio de Ulloa was named the first Spanish governor of Louisiana in May 1765. After his arrival Ulloa, bothered by a lack of troops and funds, requested that Charles Philippe Aubry, the French commandment and acting governor, continue to govern the colony, but in the name of the king of Spain.

It was in this climate of political uncertainty that the revolution took shape. Led by Attorney General Nicolas Chauvin de Lafrénière and another official, Denis-Nicolas Foucault, and fueled by an unpopular Spanish mercantile decree, the movement gathered momentum in October 1768. A petition was circulated demanding the removal of Ulloa, and an armed group of Creole, German, and Acadian militiamen persuaded the Spanish governor to withdraw to his ship on October 28. After this successful and bloodless coup, the Superior Council at New Orleans considered the idea of establishing a republic. The period of uncertainty came to an end when Spain's General Alexander O'Reilly entered New Orleans in August 1769, established Spanish rule once and for all, and brought the leaders of the insurrection to trial. Six of the rebels received the death penalty; the execution earned the Spanish general the nickname "Bloody O'Reilly."

Jay Gitlin
Yale University

LOVELACE, FRANCIS (c.1621-75) Governor of New York, Francis Lovelace's famous family included his brother Richard, the Cavalier poet. In 1667, Francis was appointed governor of New York as a loyal royalist. For five years he adminstrated his office well, dealing with epidemics, Indian attacks, revolts in New Jersey and Delaware, and a population of Dutch, English, and Swedes. He started regular sessions of the New York Council, bought Staten Island from the Indians, began the merchants' exchange, and improved land and water transportation. While he was in Connecticut to promote the first post road between New York and Boston, the Dutch took New York in August 1673. He returned to England a ruined man.

LOYALISTS The Americans who remained loyal to Great Britain during the Revolutionary War came from a variety of backgrounds, pursued a variety of objectives, and met a variety of fates. Some were Crown officials and appointees who were attached to the imperial regime through personal interest. Some were Anglican clergy and

Loyalists evacuated Boston in March 1776 as colonial forces gained control of the city. *(Library of Congress)*

lay people who wished to maintain and extend the position of the church in America. Other Loyalists belonged to social, ethnic, or cultural minorities that had historically been separate from or in opposition to the dominant groups in the colonies—and who looked to England for support. They included many backcountry settlers and members of religious minorities as well as some tenant farmers, slaves, and Indians. Many Loyalists, including royal officers, were sincere believers in the superiority of traditional British rule. Others were primarily afraid of political and social upheaval and temperamentally opposed to any form of resistance to established authority; many such feared that the patriots were mere conspirators who promoted disobedience to gain selfish ends. Never truly united, the Loyalists were ineffective politically and militarily during the Revolutionary War.

Few became active Loyalists until forced to by the course of events. Many who remained loyal began as critics of specific British policies in the 1760s and 1770s. However, they were unable or unwilling to follow their patriot neighbors into military resistance and outright rebellion. The final imperial crisis of 1773-76, when Britain faced colonial resistance with force rather than concession, was the turning point. Many who, like the Massachusetts governor Thomas Hutchinson, had long considered themselves loyal to both their colony and the Empire now chose to follow the lines of constitutional obedience to Britain that Hutchinson had outlined earlier. Those who, like Pennsylvania's Joseph Galloway, had worked during the months before independence to maintain imperial ties saw their proposals swept aside.

Loyalists in the Revolution. The outbreak of war placed Loyalists in jeopardy. Vilified as traitors by the patriots, they were subject to a variety of punitive measures. Suspected Loyalists were investigated by local committees of safety and harassed by crowds. Known partisans of Britain and others who refused to take oaths of allegiance and support the new revolutionary regimes found themselves deprived of the vote, barred from office, doubly taxed, exiled, and stripped of their property by the state legislatures and the courts; some even were executed.

The British government overestimated Loyalist strength in the colonies. This led Britain, particularly during the later years of the war, to follow the unrealistic hope that the Loyalists would provide decisive military and political support. At the same time, Britain failed to give the consistent leadership necessary to rally such support. Loyalists did serve in a number of special corps and did at times provide useful help to the imperial forces. But more Loyalists were inactive or ineffective; they never formed a solid base on which to rebuild British authority.

The Treaty of Paris (1783) committed Congress to recommending that the states restore rights and property to the Loyalists. Despite much patriot opposition, most states did restore political rights to those who had remained in America. It was those who left who suffered the most. It is estimated that between 60,000 and 80,000 Loyalists departed the United States for Great Britain and Canada during the war and at its end. Some were compensated by Britain for their losses. As a percentage of the population, this figure is higher than that for the émigrés who left France during the French Revolution. When viewed from this angle, the American Revolution showed the mark of a real social upheaval.

See also British Empire; Galloway, Joseph; Hutchinson, Thomas.

Bibliography: Bailyn, Bernard, *The Ordeal of Thomas Hutchinson* (Harvard Univ. Press, 1974); Calhoon, Robert M., *The Loyalists in Revolutionary America, 1760-1781* (Harcourt Brace Jovanovich, 1973); Nelson, William H, *The American Tory* (Oxford Univ. Press, 1961); Palmer, R.R., *The Age of the Democratic Revolution: A Political History of Europe and America, 1760-1800*, vol. 1: *The Challenge* (Princeton Univ. Press, 1959); Smith, Paul H., *Loyalists and Redcoats: A Study in British Revolutionary Policy* (Univ. of North Carolina, 1964).

Douglas M. Arnold
The Papers of Benjamin Franklin

LUDLOW, ROGER (flourished 1659-1664) A codifier of laws, Ludlow was born in Wiltshire, England, entered Balliol College, Oxford, in 1610, and studied law at the Inner Temple in 1612. On February 10, 1630 he was elected an assistant of the Massachusetts Bay Company and sailed on the *Mary and John* in March. He helped found the town of Dorchester and was chosen deputy governor in 1634. He joined the settlers along the Connecticut River and in 1636 presided at Windsor over the first court held in Connecticut. He drafted the Fundamental Orders that, except for some changes in the Charter of 1662, formed the basis for Connecticut government from 1639 to 1818. At the request of the General Court in 1646, he collected and codified all laws enacted in Connecticut into what became known as "Ludlow's Code" or "The Code of 1650."

In 1639 he founded Fairfield as an outpost against attacks from the Pequot and the Dutch. For the next 15 years the town elected him as magistrate or deputy governor. From 1651 to 1653 he was the commissioner of the United Colonies of New England. In 1654 he returned to England to decide cases of land forfeiture for Cromwell in Dublin until 1660 and then retired there.

LUMBEE INDIANS   A mixed Indian-white people, also known as the Croatan Indians, whose traditional territory is in Robeson County, North Carolina, they claim to be the direct descendants of the local Indians and the English colonists of Sir Walter Raleigh's "Lost Colony" on Croatan Island in 1585. Their name is derived from the Lumbee or Lumber River that flows through Robeson County. The origin of this people has long been a matter of controversy among scholars. Some suggest that they are the descendants of the offspring of intermarriage between the Hatteras tribe and the early English colonists. Other suggested origins include descent from the Cherokee, Tuscarora, and eastern Sioux, or from a heterogeneous population of English settlers, Indians, escaped slaves, and shipwrecked sailors along the North Carolina coast.

From colonial times, the legal status of the Lumbee Indians has been problematic. During most of the 19th century, they were classed as free blacks, receiving a separate classification only in the 1880s. In 1953 the North Carolina legislature recognized their status as a tribe, and in 1956 the U.S. Congress followed suit, although it declined to make the Lumbee Indians eligible for federal Indian benefits.

LUMBERING   In the scramble for what Richard Hakluyt, the Elizabethan propagandist for colonization, called "merchantable commodities" in the colonies, timber resources ranked high. The forests of New England, in particular, contained valuable woods, notably white oak for the timbers and planking and black oak for protecting the underwater portions of ships; pine for pitch, turpentine, and rosin; and, most important, white pine for ship masts. In the Northern forests white pine 4 to 6 feet in diameter towered 120 to 200 feet, a size unknown in Europe and perfect for ship masts. Colonial forests were an important resource for maintaining the English navy.

Having experienced a shortage in its domestic wood supply since the 15th century, Parliament enacted measures designed to conserve the forest resources of the colonies, including a restriction on lumbering in the Massachusetts charter of 1692 and the Naval Stores Act of 1729. Colonists largely ignored these measures. Backcountry sawmills, often utilizing water power, became the center of many emerging communities, and commercial lumbering in Maine and New Hampshire was fully underway by the mid-17th century. Softwoods were floated downriver to port markets, establishing a system of logging that would move to the Mississippi Valley and the Pacific Northwest in the 19th century.

By 1750 much of coastal North America had been cleared, but responsibility rested not with the lumberer but with the farmer. Colonists saw the forests as inexhaustible; small, half-timbered, thatch-roofed English cottages gave way to large, full-timbered, clapboarded, shingle-roofed American houses. Much forest land was burned to clear the ground for agriculture. By the 19th century shortages of the most valuable trees had begun to occur in the Northeast.

LUNA Y ARELLANO, TRISTAN DE (1510-73)   A Spanish colonial official who arrived in New Spain in 1530, Luna went on Francisco de Coronado's expedition and led the main body of men into Cibola after Coronado and Marcos de Niza had explored ahead. In 1559, Luna was chosen to command an expedition to forestall French occupation of Florida. He was assigned 13 ships, 500 soldiers, and about 1,000 colonists to found two settlements in Florida, one in Alabama country and one near the site of Ayllón's unsuccessful colony on the Carolina coast. A hurricane destroyed most of his fleet, and bickering among his subordinates put an end to the venture. Luna was relieved of his command in 1561 and died in poverty.

See also Coronado, Francisco Vásquez de; Ayllón, Lucas Vásquez de.

LUTHERANS   Lutheranism first penetrated the North American continent when Swedish colonists arrived at Fort Christina (Wilmington), Delaware, in 1638. Sweden's King Gustavus Adolphus had envisioned an expansion not only of his kingdom but of his country's Protestantism as well. Along with economic and political instructions, the governors of New Sweden were directed to see that true honor and worship be paid to God and that divine service "be zealously performed according to the unaltered Augsburg Confession, the Council of Uppsala, and the ceremonies of the Swedish Church." New Sweden, however, quickly fell before the Dutch in 1654, they in turn surrendering to the British a decade later.

The far more significant Lutheran migration came in the next century, and it was German rather than Swedish. In the 1730s and 1740s, more than 60,000 Lutherans poured into Pennsylvania alone, with Philadelphia becoming the logical base of operation for Henry Muhlenberg, leading Lutheran cleric and organizer, who arrived in 1742. By 1748, Muhlenberg had established America's first Lutheran synod, while he toured widely up and down the Atlantic coast to preserve and encourage all isolated Lutheran groups. At the middle of the 18th century, Lutheran churches could be found all the way from Maine to Georgia, with the greatest concentration by far in the Middle Colonies.

While Muhlenberg himself could preach in three languages (German, Dutch, and English), most Lutheran worshippers in the colonial period were interested in hearing only one: namely, German. This linguistic limitation kept Lutheranism from swift expansion but helped it to be a haven and cultural center for Germans arriving daily at the busy port of Philadelphia. Even as late as mid-19th century, well over a third of all the nation's Lutheran churches were located in Pennsylvania.

Bibliography: Wentz, Abdel R., *A Basic History of Lutheranism in America* (Fortress Press, 1964).

Edwin S. Gaustad
University of California, Riverside

LYNCH, THOMAS (1749-79)   A signer of the Declaration of Independence, Lynch was born in Winyaw, South Carolina, where he held many civil offices. Lynch was a member of the first and second provincial congresses (1774-75), the constitutional committee for South Carolina (1776), the first state General Assembly (1776), and the Second Continental Congress (1776-77). The provincial Congress made him captain in the South Carolina Regiment (1775). As a member of the Continental Congress, he voted for and signed the Declaration of Independence.

M

McCAULEY, MARY. *See* **Pitcher, Molly.**

McCREA, JANE (1752-77) McCrea became a celebrated martyr of the Revolutionary War after her death at the hands of General Burgoyne's Indian allies sparked the support of patriots, contributing to the American victory at Saratoga. Legend says that she was waiting to meet her fiancé, David Jones, a member of the British army, when she was shot and scalped by Indians in July 1777. Jones had written that he would see her at Fort Edwards, New York, where the British troops would march. News of the killing caused Edmund Burke in a speech in Parliament to denounce the British policy of using Indian allies. The event was used as propaganda, persuading many neutral Americans to choose the patriot cause.

MacDOUGALL, ALEXANDER (1732-86) Emigrating from Scotland with his parents, MacDougall arrived in New York City in 1738. During the French and Indian War he was a privateer and afterwards settled in New York as a merchant. Arrested for libel for attacking the General Assembly, he refused to answer questions and was jailed for over a year. He held radical mass meetings against British rule in 1774 and in 1775 became colonel of a New York regiment. Rising to major general by 1777, he was present at the battles of Germantown and the Highlands of the Hudson. A quarrel with General Heath in 1782 led to his court-martial for insubordination, but he later served in the Continental Congress (1781-82; 1784-85) and the New York state senate (1783-86).

McGILLIVRAY, ALEXANDER (?1759-93) The son of Lachlan McIntosh, a Scottish Indian trader in Georgia, and of a Creek princess, McGillivray was reared in the Creek town of Little Tallassie until he was 14, then taken to Charleston to be educated. For a time he worked in a mercantile house in Savannah. When the American Revolution began, he returned to his nation. He was commissioned to serve as a deputy to John Stuart and later to Thomas Brown, British superintendents of the Creek and Cherokee.

When the British were defeated in 1783, McGillivray assumed the leadership of the Creek and sought help from the Spanish in Florida to oppose the land-hungry Georgians. He refused to recognize a series of treaties that Georgia extracted from a few chiefs and sent his warriors on the warpath in 1786. Georgia was unable to cope with the Creek threat and willingly entered into the federal union in 1787. President George Washington invited McGillivray to New York in 1790 and concluded a treaty that secured a portion of the territory Georgia wanted but guaranteed the lands west of the Oconee River to the Creek. Thus, by his diplomatic skill, McGillivray managed to preserve the independence of the Creek nation for a decade until his death.

McKEAN, THOMAS (1734-1817) A lawyer, political leader, and judge, McKean was born and educated in Chester County, Pennsylvania; later he trained for law in Delaware. A lawyer, assemblyman, and justice there, McKean became a patriot, serving in the Stamp Act Congress (1765), the First and Second Continental Congresses (1774-76, 1778-83), and other Revolutionary bodies. While in the Second Continental Congress he signed the Declaration of Independence and served as president (1781). McKean was active in Pennsylvania affairs as well, accepting appointment as chief justice (1777) while continuing to hold office in Delaware. McKean was an opponent of Pennsylvania's state constitution of 1776 and a supporter of the new federal constitution (1787). He left the chief justiceship to become governor of Pennsylvania (1799-1808).

MACKENZIE, SIR ALEXANDER (1764-1820) A Scottish-born fur trader and explorer in far northwestern North America, Mackenzie emigrated to New York with his father in 1774 but was sent to school in Montreal (1778) after the outbreak of the Revolutionary War. He entered

Later president, James Madison was active in Virginia affairs during the Revolution and also sat in the Continental Congress. (*Library of Congress*)

the Canadian fur trade in 1779 and joined the North West Company as a partner in 1787. In 1789 he explored the river running from Great Slave Lake to the Arctic Ocean, a river now named for him. In 1793, in the company of Indians, he became the first European to reach the Pacific from the interior by way of the northern river system, preceding the expedition of Meriwether Lewis and William Clark by more than a decade. His journals were published in England in 1801. He was knighted the next year, returned to Canada, and later retired to Scotland.

MADISON, JAMES (1751-1836) The fourth president of the United States, Madison was born in Port Conway, Virginia, and graduated from the College of New Jersey (Princeton) in 1771. Returning to Virginia, he was active

in Revolutionary politics; by 1776 he was a member of the Virginia convention, where he established his reputation as an advocate of religious freedom. After serving in various state offices, Madison was an active Virginia delegate to the Continental Congress from 1780 to 1783 and again in 1787-88. In the middle years of the decade he served in the state assembly. During this period he demonstrated a wide-ranging grasp of public issues and emerged as an advocate of a stronger central government.

In 1786 he attended the Annapolis Convention and soon thereafter was chosen a delegate to the Constitutional Convention in Philadelphia. A leader there (1787), he was a principal architect of the centralized Virginia Plan, which served as the basis for the federal constitution. In addition, he took the notes that are the primary source of knowledge about the meeting. In his speeches to the convention and as one of the three authors of *The Federalist Papers* (1787-88), he presented a powerful analysis and defense of balanced popular government in a geographically extended republic. In 1788 he led the fight to ratify the Constitution in the Virginia convention. During his outstanding later career Madison was a U.S. Congressman (1789-97), secretary of state (1801-09) under Jefferson, and fourth U.S. president (1809-17).

Bibliography: Brant, Irving, *James Madison*, 6 vols. (Bobbs-Merrill, 1941-61).

Douglas M. Arnold
The Papers of Benjamin Franklin

MADRID, TREATY OF (1670) An agreement between Great Britain and Spain, the treaty established a legal relationship between the colonies of the respective powers. At issue was the right of free trade between the British and Spanish colonies, which Spain had opposed since the 1604 Treaty of London. At Madrid, Great Britain formally agreed not to allow trade between its colonies and Spanish possessions, but with Spain's acknowledgment of that agreement Great Britain gained legal recognition of its right to claim territory in the Americas. Although border disputes soon arose between British Georgia and Spanish Florida, semiofficial British piracy in the Caribbean ended.

See also London, Treaty of.

MAGELLAN, FERDINAND (?1480-1521) Born in Portugal, Magellan served in the Portuguese possessions in India and Asia and returned in 1512 a decorated captain. Accused of trading with the Moors, he renounced his allegiance to the Portuguese crown and went to Spain. He became obsessed with finding a southwestern passage to the Orient that would counter the Portuguese trade monopoly and lobbied Charles V until the monarch gave him his support.

Magellan's fleet of five ships left for Brazil on September 20, 1519. He decided to winter on the coast of Patagonia, and three of his crews mutinied at the prospect. Magellan managed to put down the mutiny and in October 1520 entered the straits that would bear his name. One ship had been lost on the Patagonian coast and another, captained by Estevan Gomez, now mutinied and returned to Spain. After 38 days in the straits, Magellan reached the Pacific. His three remaining ships sailed for 12,000 miles through open sea and clear weather, arriving at Guam on March 6, 1521. They then went on to the Philippines, where Magellan was killed in a dispute with natives on April 27. On September 8, 1522, one ship with 18 men aboard sailed into Seville harbor, nearly three years after they had left.

See also Gomez, Estevan.

MAINE   Visited by French, English, and Portuguese explorers and fishermen during the 16th century, the first settlement in Maine was planted by the French in 1604 on an island in the mouth of the St. Croix River, but it failed after the first winter. In 1607, Sir Ferdinando Gorges attempted to establish an English colony on the Kennebec River, but it too failed. Referred to as the "country of the Main Land" in an English document of 1620, it was called "the Province of Maine" in the 1622 grant of all the lands between the Merrimack and Kennebec rivers issued to Gorges and John Mason. Permanent settlements were first made along the coast in the 1630s. By mid-century commercial lumbering operations had begun, establishing a system of logging that would be the center of Maine's economy through the 20th century.

The Massachusetts Bay Company purchased the proprietary rights to Maine in 1677, and the absorption of the colony was confirmed by the Massachusetts charter of 1691. Maine did not separate from Massachusetts until 1820, when it was admitted to the union as a state as part of the Missouri Compromise.

MAKEMIE, FRANCIS (c.1658-1708)   The Presbyterian minister Makemie was born in Donegal County, Ireland, at a time of persecution against Presbyterians. After graduation from the University of Glasgow in 1682, he was sent to Maryland as a missionary, subsequently preaching in North Carolina, Virginia, along the east shore of Maryland and Virginia, in Philadelphia, and in Barbados. Although strongly opposed by the Anglicans and Quakers, Makemie was the first Dissenter licensed under the Virginia Toleration Act (1699). He is best remembered as

successfully challenging New York's religious establishment laws in 1707 and as one of the founders of the Presbyterian Church in America.

MALINCHE (flourished 1519-28)   One of 20 girls given to Cortes in 1519 by the Tabasco Indians, Malinche came from an interior tribe and spoke Nahuatl, the language of the Aztecs, as well as Tabascan and Mayan. She quickly became a trusted adviser of Cortes as well as his mistress and accompanied the Spanish on their campaign in the Valley of Mexico. On converting to Roman Catholicism she took the name of Marina and, although she had a son by Cortes, she married the conquistador Juan Jamarillo around 1523 and settled on land given to her by Cortes. Information about Malinche passes from view after 1528.

MANUFACTURING AND INDUSTRY   Although overshadowed by a predominantly agrarian economy, manufacturing and industry gained prominence throughout the colonies, and they achieved greater significance during the Revolutionary War, which diverted resources into the indigenous production of goods that previously were obtained from abroad.

Extractive industries such as fishing, fur trapping, and lumbering preceded agriculture and remained consequential throughout the colonial era. Whaling supplemented fishing in New England. Naval stores, particularly tar, pitch, and turpentine, gained prominence in the South as did potash in the North. Mining, mostly iron ore along with a little copper, established the basis of an important colonial export and manufacturing industry.

Manufacturing centered in individual households, which produced food, drink, clothing, and furniture among a host of goods. Closely related to agriculture was the ubiquitous enterprise of grist milling (flour and meal). The forests were the basis for the manufacture of various wood products, including boards, shingles, and staves. Clothing (textiles, hats, shoes), finished iron products, and shipbuilding, all confined mostly but not exclusively to New England, comprised the remaining principal manufactures. Of lesser importance were the glass, paper, brick and tile, distilled beverage, machinery, and carriage and wagon industries. The variety of manufacturing is demonstrated by the fact that in 1697 as many as 50 manufacturing handicrafts besides the building trades were followed in Philadelphia.

Although widespread, manufacturing industry was concentrated in New England and to a lesser degree in the Middle Colonies, which shipped finished products to the Southern colonies and to the West Indies in competition with England. Parliament met that threat in part by attempting to curb the colonial manufacture of woolens, hats, and iron products. Other deterrents to manufacturing included the scarcity of labor and capital, a poor transportation network, high freight rates, a scattered population, a lack of ready money, the lure of agriculture independence, and the general reliance upon household industry.

Bibliography: Clark, Victor S., *History of Manufactures in the United States*, 3 vols. (McGraw-Hill, 1929); McCusker, John J. and Menard, Russel R., *The Economy of British America, 1607-1789* (Univ. of North Carolina Press, 1985).

Alan D. Watson
University of North Carolina at Wilmington

MAPLE SUGAR   Maple sugar, the rendered sap of the sugar maple tree (*Acer saccharum*) was a common sweetener and a good substitute for expensive West Indian sugar during the colonial era. Everywhere within the growing range of the maple, from Nova Scotia to North Carolina, west to the Mississippi Valley, and north to the Great Lakes, Indians harvested maple sap in February and March, long before the coming of the colonists. Women tapped the trees, collected the sap in wooden troughs, boiled it by dropping in hot stones, and stirred until granulation occurred. They used the sugar with vegetables, fish, and meat. In late winter, when food stores were nearly depleted, maple sugar mixed with the remaining parched corn, might serve as the principal food until the first crops of the spring.

Indians first taught tapping the sugar maples to the French. Brass or copper kettles allowed for more efficient rendering, and by enclosing the kettles in a "sugar house," straining the syrup through linen, and clarifying it with eggs, colonists learned to remove the impurities from the sap. As early as the 1720s, farmers from northern New England to Virginia manufactured a refined variety of maple sugar. The Sugar Act of 1764, imposing high duties on imported sugar, stimulated domestic production, and abolitionists later urged Americans to boycott slave-produced cane in favor of maple. Maple remained the principal form of sweetener well into the 19th century.

See also Sugar Act.

Bibliography: Nearing, Helen and Scott, *The Maple Sugar Book* (Schocken, 1971).

MARION, FRANCIS (?1732-95)   Born in South Carolina, Marion was a planter and a "natural born soldier," known as the Swamp Fox. His earliest military campaigns were against the Indians. In 1775 he was elected to the provincial congress, simultaneously serving as captain of a parish regiment that attacked the British at Savannah. After the British had almost completely overrun the colony, he effectively harassed them by cutting off their communications and freeing American prisoners. Two attacks on

Georgetown, South Carolina, however, were failures. He gained a reputation for his ability to keep order among his men and even gave his troops permission to court-martial or kill the bandits who roamed South Carolina's back-country.

In January 1781, General Nathanael Greene's forces, the core of popular resistance in the South, attempted to push Britain's General Cornwallis northward and out of South Carolina. Marion and Henry Lee attacked Fort Watson, brilliantly executing their part of the plan. Greene himself was unsuccessful. Marion's heroism, demonstrated by his use of guerilla tactics, led to Marion's appointment as brigadier general and his place in American history and legend as the Swamp Fox. After the war he commanded a fort in Charleston and worked a plantation.

MARITIME PROVINCES   The Canadian provinces of Nova Scotia, Prince Edward Island, and New Brunswick, known collectively as the Maritime Provinces, are composed of the islands and mainland on the south side of the Gulf of the St. Lawrence. They were first claimed by John Cabot for the English in 1497 but were first effectively settled by the

Called the Swamp Fox, Francis Marion used guerrilla tactics to harass British forces in the South. *(Library of Congress)*

MARQUETTE DESCENDING THE MISSISSIPPI.   79

Jacques Marquette explored the Mississippi River as part of his missionary activities in the upper Midwest. *(Library of Congress)*

French. The French dominated the 16th-century coastal fisheries and in 1605 founded Port Royal on the Bay of Fundy and established the colony of Acadia, extending from Prince Edward Island south into what would become Maine. French colonists, who began arriving in the 1630s and soon became known as Acadians, settled on the eastern shore of the Bay of Fundy, on Ile Royale (Cape Breton Island) and Ile St. Jean (Prince Edward Island), where they diked and reclaimed the tidal flats, practiced subsistence agriculture, and traded with the Micmac Indians.

In 1710 the British captured Port Royal (which they renamed Annapolis Royal), then by the terms of the Peace of Utrecht (1713) gained possession of Acadia (which they renamed Nova Scotia). Only Ile Royale and Ile St. Jean remained in French possession. In 1720 the French built the fortress of Louisburg on Ile Royale, to which many mainland Acadians removed. As a counter-

weight, the British founded the port of Halifax on the Atlantic coast of Nova Scotia in 1749, settling it with a mixture of Germans and New England emigrants. Halifax became a center for the deportation of thousands of Acadians who refused to swear allegiance to British rule. The British gained possession of the Gulf of St. Lawrence islands in 1763 after their victory in the French and Indian War, renaming them Prince Edward Island and Cape Breton Island and attaching them to Nova Scotia, although both later had identities as separate colonies. Thousands of French were expelled, while English and Scotch immigrants replaced them.

During the Revolutionary War, Halifax became a major staging area for British naval forces after the evacuation of Boston in 1775. After the war, the city became the primary refuge for Loyalists, 32,000 of whom arrived in 1783 alone. Many settlements, including Sydney, the capital of Cape Breton Island, were founded as a result of this emigration. The western shore of the Bay of Fundy became so settled with Loyalists that it was separated from Nova Scotia in 1784.

When the French entered the Revolutionary War in support of the Americans, they seized the small outer Gulf of St. Lawrence islands of Miquelon and St. Pierre south of Newfoundland, and these were ceded by Britain in the Treaty of Paris (1783). Although England retook them during the Napoleonic Wars, they were later returned to France and remain overseas territories.

MARQUETTE, JACQUES (1637-75) Born in Laon, France, to a prominent family, the missionary Jacques Marquette showed a precocious interest in religion, entering the College of Jesuits of Reims at the age of nine. Fully ordained in 1666, he left for New France, where he soon was sent to the Mission of St. Ignace, by the Straits of Mackinac on Lake Michigan. It was there that Louis Jolliet arrived with five companions on May 15, 1673, with the letter from the Jesuit superior directing that he join their expedition to the Mississippi River. While on their return north, Father Marquette established the first parish in Illinois, of the *Mission de l'Immaculé Conception*, promising the Illinios Indians in attendance that he would soon return. In 1674, Father Marquette traveled back to Illinois with two veterans of the previous journey. They wintered in very difficult conditions at the Chicago Portage, where Father Marquette fell sick with a pulmonary infection. He still managed to celebrate Easter Mass to a large gathering of Illinois at their main village (Uticca, Illinois) but died after returning home to his Mission of St. Ignace on the eastern shore of Lake Michigan, near the present town of Ludington. His evangelization laid the foundation for the conversion to Catholicism of the Illinois Indian Confederation.

See also Jolliet, Louis.
Bibliography: Donnelley, Joseph P., *Jacques Marquette* (Loyola Univ. Press, 1968).

Charles J. Balesi
The French Colonial Historical Society

MARTIN, HERNANDO (flourished 1650) In 1650, Martin and Diego del Castillo left El Paso and headed east into Texas. Their assigned task was to reestablish contact with the Jumano Indians, who had welcomed Father Salas among them two decades earlier. The Jumano again welcomed the Spaniards and encouraged them to explore farther to the east, where they said a tribe of Indians known as the Tejas were ruled by a king. Intrigued, Martin and

Castillo went on, never reaching the Tejas but finding fresh-water pearls in the Nueces River. Their report to the governor at El Paso stimulated the assembling of another expedition, this time led by Diego de Guadalajara, into the region in 1654.

See also Castillo, Diego del; Guadalajara, Diego de.

MARTIN, JOSIAH (1737-86) Born in the West Indies, Martin entered the British army in 1757 and attained the rank of lieutenant colonel. In 1771 he was appointed royal governor of North Carolina. Immediately he became enmeshed in battles with the colonial assembly. The judicial system collapsed in 1773, and criminal courts were opened by royal prerogative. The legislature then met in an extralegal provincial congress in August 1774. Martin fled and, devising a plan for taking the Southern colonies, formed his own regiment. Defeated in 1776, he joined General Clinton and later General Cornwallis in their Southern expeditions. He returned to England in 1781, continuing to support Loyalists in their claims for restitution.

MARTIN, LUTHER (1748-1826) A graduate of the College of New Jersey (Princeton) in 1766, Martin began practicing law in Maryland in 1771 and continued until the eve of the Revolution. He attended Maryland patriot conventions in 1774 and in 1777 wrote a reply to General Howe's letter ordering Maryland citizens to cooperate with the British. Appointed Maryland's attorney general in 1778, he enthusiastically prosecuted Loyalists throughout the war. He was a delegate to both the Continental Congress and the Constitutional Convention in Philadelphia. He opposed ratification of the Constitution, but his dislike for Thomas Jefferson allied him with the Federalists. He assisted Salmon Chase in the justice's impeachment trial in 1804 and defended Aaron Burr against charges of treason in 1807. His last important court appearance was against Daniel Webster and William Pinkney in *McCulloch v. Maryland* in 1819.

MARYLAND During the 17th century the English Crown used great proprietary grants in America both as a reward to prominent gentlemen for loyal service and as a way to secure England's foothold in the New World without having to deplete royal resources. Proprietary grants conveyed vast territories and extensive governmental privileges to private men who planned to use their own fortunes to settle and to sustain colonies. The Stuart monarchs were willing to surrender a degree of control in

English America to accomplish those goals, especially since the proprietaries thus created promised to strengthen those men who had served as the Crown's allies during its long struggle with Parliament before the English Civil War and after the Restoration. And, if one of the consequences of proprietary grants was the creation of a new American nobility, reasoned royal advisors, so much the better for the Crown's interests in the New World and the Old.

Among those benefiting from royal generosity in the form of a proprietary grant was George Calvert, an Oxford graduate who had served as secretary to Sir Robert Cecil (who advanced Calvert's career), as clerk of the Privy Council, as a secretary of state under James I, and as a member of the Council for New England. Calvert's service in the English government ended with his public announcement that he had converted to Roman Catholicism. Charles I, married to a Catholic, was hardly disposed to see a royal ally of Calvert's status diminish and rewarded him for his loyalty by elevating Calvert to the peerage as 1st Lord Baltimore.

The Calvert Grant. Calvert already held a grant to the Avalon Peninsula in Newfoundland. In 1628 he took his family and 40 colonists to this American estate, but both the climate and the French proved hostile. Calvert soon departed for Virginia, then for England to seek a royal grant for territory to the south. Charles I responded to Calvert's request by granting him, in 1632, about 10,000,000 acres between Virginia to the south and the 40th parallel to the north. Charles named the place after his wife, Henrietta Maria. The New England colony of "Mary Land," carrying the name of a Catholic Queen and owned by a Catholic lord, surely struck observers as a likely home for persecuted religious dissenters, or at least for English Catholics.

Lord Baltimore's charter certainly gave him the authority to follow his personal inclinations in erecting his colony. As absolute lord and proprietor of Maryland he owned every acre in the province. Grants he chose to make would be in his, not the King's, name. Equally awesome were his governmental powers, which were virtually unlimited since he could appoint all magistrates and judges, or exercise executive or judicial powers himself. Only Calvert enjoyed the right to initiate legislation. The proprietor could establish his own colonial nobility, composed of lords loyal to him and, since all the rights and privileges conveyed to Baltimore by the Maryland charter would be passed on to succeeding generations of Calverts, to his heirs. The only limits on the proprietor's powers imposed by the charter were stipulations that the colonists might provide advice about, and give their formal assent to, Maryland's laws before they were enacted; that the colony's laws not contradict those of England; and that the

Crown be allowed to determine the province's external affairs (war and trade) and receive one-fifth of any metals previously discovered there. In essence, Calvert's powers in Maryland were as extensive as the Crown's were in England.

Since Lord Baltimore died before the King's seal had been affixed to the Maryland charter, his 26-year-old eldest son and heir, Cecilius Calvert, received Maryland from the crown, thus becoming the colony's first official proprietor. Given significant English anti-Catholic sentiment, including rumors suggesting that Maryland would become a base for Catholic-Spanish expansion in the Americas, Cecilius chose to remain in England in order to defend his rights in America and to protect his family's interests in England. He selected his younger brother Leonard Calvert to serve as Maryland's first governor and to lead the first group of colonists to his province. In November 1634 two ships, the *Ark* and the *Dove*, left England carrying more than 200 settlers—a majority of whom were Protestants—to the colony, along with 2 Jesuits and 17 gentlemen. The first English Marylanders purchased land from Indians at St. Mary's, where they built their settlement. In spite of the Catholic "nature" of the Maryland enterprise, never in the colony's history did Catholics outnumber Protestants.

Early Settlement. To entice settlers, the Calverts offered a degree of religious toleration and land on generous terms. The first governor received instructions to be scrupulous in insuring that the colony's Catholic leaders give "no scandal or offense" to the Protestants. Perhaps more important in peopling the colony was the use of a headright system to dispense Maryland's acres. The Calverts granted 100 acres for every adult (free or servant) a settler transported to the colony and 50 acres for every child under 16 years of age. Those bringing five adult inhabitants to Maryland not only were to receive 2,000 acres, but also might identify their plantations as "manors" and enjoy all the "royalties and privileges" that status connoted in England. In return, those receiving land were to pay a yearly quitrent to Lord Baltimore of 2 shillings for every 100 acres they owned.

After resolving conflicts generated by the settlers' unwillingness to accept the proprietor's right to initiate all the colony's laws (the settlers rejected a code of laws Lord Baltimore sent from England; the proprietor agreed to give the assembly limited rights to formulate laws), the colonists proceeded to establish a flourishing society. Indeed, Maryland prospered virtually from the outset of settlement, ample testimony to the care with which the Calverts planned their colonization enterprise and to the value of prior English experience in settling Virginia. Maryland's economy resembled Virginia's, with tobacco rapidly coming to assume a preeminent place among the crops planted in the colony. Since Maryland's topography, like Virginia's, was marked by the prevalence of navigable waterways, settlers soon discovered that not only could they raise tobacco, but that they could also transport it to the coast, from where it could be shipped abroad to ready markets. So dominant did tobacco become in the Virginia-Maryland economy that both colonies enacted legislation requiring settlers who planted tobacco simultaneously to plant a number of acres of corn.

The small family farm on which essentially self-sufficient settlers produced everything they needed in order to survive, typified Maryland society. Tobacco substituted for rare specie, serving as the means by which colonists paid taxes or purchased manufactured goods. Labor was nearly as scarce as coin since at the outset of settlement slaves were an insignificant part of the population, so few colonists were able to clear and then cultivate vast tracts of land, no matter how extensive their actual holdings. Cattle, hogs, sheep, wild game, fruits, vegetables—all from the small farm itself—fed Maryland's inhabitants.

Religious Dissension. In spite of proprietary efforts to insure harmony among Maryland's Protestant and Catholic settlers, religious differences destroyed social tranquility. After a decade of living together, open strife between the groups erupted in 1644 when Governor Leonard Calvert arrested a Protestant, Richard Ingle, for making treasonable statements. During a minor civil war, the Protestants drove Calvert from the colony. In 1648, Lord Baltimore acted to restore peace by naming a Protestant, William Stone, as Maryland's new governor. The next year the colonial assembly passed the Act Concerning Religion, initiated and partly written by the proprietor, which guaranteed toleration for every settler who professed faith in Jesus Christ. With these actions Lord Baltimore sought both to resolve the religion-inspired disorder that plagued his colony and at the same time to disarm his Protestant critics in England. These critics argued that the Maryland charter ought to be prorogued since it authorized a Catholic-dominated colonial government that suppressed or persecuted Protestants.

Such efforts did not prevent Baltimore from losing his colony when the Puritans gained control in England. In 1651, Parliament sent a group of Commonwealth Commissioners to the Chesapeake to insure acceptance of England's Puritan government. Among them was William Claiborne, who had served during the 1620s as Virginia's secretary of state, had explored what was later to become part of Maryland, had acted as Virginia's agent to oppose the original Maryland grant to Lord Baltimore (since it seemed to infringe on Virginia's

claims), and had in 1631 established his own colony on Kent Island (included in the Maryland grant to Lord Baltimore). Claiborne was intensely anti-Catholic and anti-Maryland, especially since Leonard Calvert in 1637 had invaded Kent Island, seized control, and with the cooperation of Maryland's assembly, deprived Claiborne of all his property in the colony. Claiborne had retaken Kent Island during the civil war in 1644 and now, in 1652, he replaced the proprietor's Protestant governor Stone, and Stone's council, with his own government.

Although Parliament refused to sanction Claiborne's actions, Baltimore's government failed to survive, for a group of Puritans initiated a rebellion against the proprietary, sparked when Lord Baltimore insisted that all settlers take an oath of loyalty to him (which the English government would not tolerate). The antiproprietary forces defeated Governor Stone's troops at the Severn River in 1655. Stone became a prisoner, and a Puritan, William Fuller, became Maryland's new governor. The Act Concerning Religion was repealed by a Puritan assembly (thus depriving Catholics of protection), and Baltimore lost his colony for three years, until 1658.

Late 17th Century. The restoration of the Stuart monarchy in 1660 returned Lord Baltimore to control of Maryland. And control was profitable: As the colony's population and prosperity rose during the second half of the 17th century, so did proprietary revenues. Maryland rents and duties yielded at least 10,000 pounds a year to Lord Baltimore.

Although Maryland provided the proprietor with substantial revenues, the colony proved difficult to govern. In both 1660 (with Governor Josias Fendall's cooperation) and 1669 (when it submitted a list of complaints) the assembly sought to assert its power at the expense of the proprietor's. In spite of the colony's general economic well-being, religious differences among its inhabitants generated turmoil. Just when Virginia was enduring the strife of Bacon's Rebellion, the leaders of a protest in Maryland, William Davyes and John Pate, were hanged by the government. Several years later, in 1681, rumors of a papist-Indian plot to destroy Maryland's Protestant citizens stimulated a major uprising against the proprietary led by former governor Fendall and a former Anglican minister named John Coode, who were banished for their behavior. These were preliminary acts for the climactic events of 1688-89, when, as part of the Glorious Revolution in America, Protestant forces overthrew Maryland's Catholic government.

During 1688 rumors spread in the colony that members of the government, with the help of the colony's Catholics,

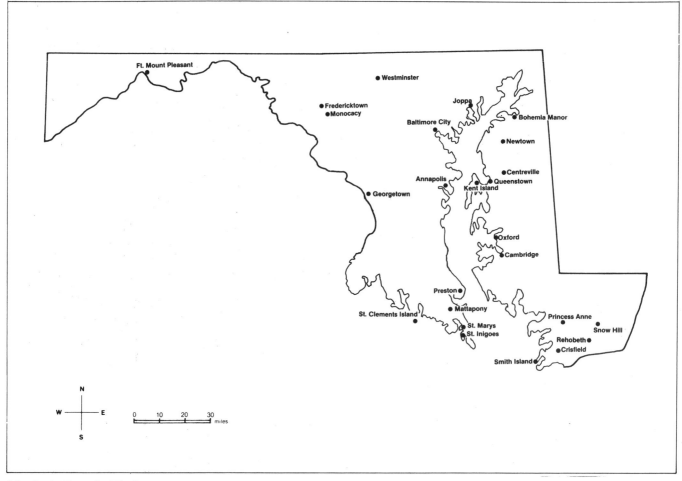

Maryland. *(Facts On File, Inc.)*

French, and Indians, were planning to slaughter Maryland's Protestants. When news of William and Mary's ascension to the English throne reached Maryland in 1689 ahead of Lord Baltimore's instructions that the new monarchs be proclaimed in the colony, his opponents suggested that Baltimore planned to reject allegiance to the English Crown and to hold Maryland as his own Catholic province. In response, a Protestant Association emerged, headed by Coode; Coode's brother-in-law Nehemiah Blakiston, the customs collector; Kenelm Cheseldyne, a former assembly speaker; and Henry Jowles.

In July 1689, Coode led 250 men to St. Mary's, seized the government on behalf of the association, and held power until the assembly gathered, proclaimed its loyalty to William and Mary, and asked the new monarchs to govern Maryland as a royal colony. Coode and the association controlled Maryland's government until 1692, when Sir Lionel Copley arrived as the colony's first royal governor. But the Crown allowed the Calverts to retain title to Maryland's land and to continue to collect revenues in the colony. Indeed, their charter never was revoked formally, and in 1715, after the 4th Lord Baltimore converted to Protestantism, the family again received control of Maryland's government, which they retained until the colonies declared their independence from England.

Population and Economic Characteristics. Although the community of Baltimore was the most important port on the Chesapeake, and second only to Charleston in the South, Maryland remained essentially a rural province throughout the colonial era. Most residents lived on farms worked by the owner, his family, and perhaps a few servants or slaves. On most farms tobacco was the most important crop. As the 18th century progressed, however, increasingly the large plantation of more than 1,000 acres and with a labor force of 50 or more black slaves, came to dominate the image of life in the colony. While Maryland's population grew steadily throughout the colonial era, the slave population grew dramatically and came to comprise an ever larger percentage of the total. In 1633, "200 English" lived in Maryland. By 1660 the number had grown to 8,000. In 1688, 25,000 persons, slave and free, lived there. In 1707, of the nearly 34,000 residents, 3,003 were white servants, while 4,657 were slaves. By 1715, of 50,200 Marylanders, 40,700 were white, while 9,500 were black. In 1748, of 130,000 inhabitants, 94,000 were white and 36,000 were black. The 1755 census counted 107,208 whites (6,870 of whom were servants) and 42,764 blacks (plus another 3,592 mulattoes).

Tobacco and slavery marked both Maryland and Virginia, creating a kind of Chesapeake society. In spite of declining tobacco prices, a continual reduction in profits, and escalating debts to English merchants during the 18th century, Chesapeake planters resisted altering their traditional dependence on tobacco, which they shipped abroad each autumn on the annual "great fleet." Although a few planters had begun to substitute wheat or other grains for tobacco by the middle of the century, tobacco ruled Maryland's economy. While many realized that if freed from English trade regulations they might increase their profit per hogshead of tobacco (commonly as little as 15 shillings) by a full three pounds, internal antagonisms between Protestants and Catholics, or between those who supported or opposed the proprietary, worked to divide Maryland's citizens and to divert their attention from the consequences of imperial policies that provoked unified opposition in other colonies.

Early Statehood.   During the debates in 1776-77 over the Articles of Confederation, Maryland led the six states with established western boundaries in their insistence that the seven states with claims to unsettled lands west of the Appalachian Mountains cede such territory to Congress, both because the Revolutionary War had been a common effort in which all the states had shared and because conflicts between states with competing claims surely would disrupt the new government. When Congress declared that any such land given up by states would be "disposed for the common benefit," and when New York and Virginia finally gave up their claims to western territory, Maryland ratified the articles in 1781, the last state to do so. Marylanders displayed little opposition to the Constitution, since that document promised to protect the institution of black slavery, important both as a source of labor on their plantations and farms, and as a form of social control over the 64,445 blacks (nearly a third of the population) living as slaves in the state. Maryland ratified the Constitution on April 28, 1788.

See also Articles of Confederation; Calvert, Cecilius; Calvert, Leonard.

Bibliography: Clemens, Paul G., *The Atlantic Economy and Maryland's Eastern Shore From Tobacco To Grain* (Cornell Univ. Press, 1980); Kulikoff, Allan, *Tobacco and Slaves* (Univ. of North Carolina Press, 1986); Land, Aubrey C., *Colonial Maryland* (Kraus International, 1981); Main, G. L., *Tobacco Colony: Life in Early Maryland* (Princeton Univ. Press, 1982).

Aaron M. Shatzman
Franklin and Marshall College

MARYLAND CIVIL WAR (1655)   The causes for the Maryland Civil War can be traced back to 1649. In that year Puritans executed King Charles I and proclaimed the Commonwealth, and Cecilius Calvert wrote Maryland's Act Concerning Religion, which granted religious liberty to all in the colony who professed Jesus Christ and the Trinity. This was intended by Calvert to protect his Roman Catholic co-religionists, now a hopeless minority in Maryland. In an effort to hold onto the colony, Calvert in 1653 instructed the governor, the Puritan William Stone, to administer an oath of allegiance to the proprietor. Maryland's Puritan-dominated assembly responded by repudiating Calvert's authority, repealing the Act Concerning Religion, and proscribing Roman Catholicism. Civil War resulted in March 1655 between southern Maryland, which backed Calvert and Stone, and the northern part, which supported the assembly. A Puritan victory led to expulsion of Jesuit missionaries, who fled to Virginia. The British Parliament restored the colony to Calvert in 1657.

See also Maryland.

Bibliography: Steiner, Bernard, *Maryland Under the Commonwealth: A Chronicle of the Years 1649-1658* (Johns Hopkins Press, 1911).

MASON, GEORGE (1725-92)   An influential Virginia leader during the Revolution, Mason was the son of a wealthy Virginia planter. He studied law but never practiced. His knowledge of public law proved useful, though, in both the management of his plantation and his activities as a member of the Ohio Company. In 1759 he served in the House of Burgesses, but between 1760 and the Revolution he held no political office. He actively opposed the Stamp Act, and in response to the Boston Port Bill of 1774 he authored the Fairfax Resolves (1774), accepted by the First Continental Congress. He was a close associate of George Washington, and when the latter became commander in chief of the Continental Army, Mason took his place at the July 1775 Virginia convention.

In 1776, Mason wrote the Declaration of Rights, accepted by the Virginia convention on June 12, 1776. The document influenced Thomas Jefferson in composing the Declaration of Independence and was the foundation of the

Bill of Rights of 1789. Mason also drafted the greater part of the Virginia Constitution and revised its penal code. As a delegate to the Constitutional Convention, he was extremely active, eventually opposing its adoption. Besides lacking the protections later included in the Bill of Rights, the Constitution, Mason believed, perpetuated slavery and did not afford adequate protection to the states. He did not sign the Constitution.

See also Fairfax Resolves.

MASON, JOHN (c.1600-72)   Soldier and magistrate, John Mason was born in England, served as a soldier in the Low Countries, and came to Massachusetts about 1633. He was captain of the Dorchester militia and in 1635 helped found Windsor, Connecticut. During the Pequot War, he took 8 settlers and 100 Indian allies led by Uncas deep into Pequot leader Sassacus's territory. He and Captain John Underhill's Massachusetts militia surprised Sassacus's camp along the Mystic River and killed all 700 Indians, including women and children. He described his victory in *A Relation of the Troubles That Have Happened in New England* (1677).

After the Pequot War, he held many offices in Connecticut. He was deputy (1637-42), magistrate (1642-60), deputy governor (1660-69), and assistant (1669-72). He was also chief military officer and managed Indian relations for Connecticut and for the New England Confederation. He founded Norwich, Connecticut, in 1660 and lived there until his death. His first wife died in Windsor in 1638, and he had seven children by his second wife, Anne Peck.

MASON-DIXON LINE   The present boundary between the states of Pennsylvania, Maryland, and West Virginia is also known as the Mason-Dixon line. In the 1680s a dispute arose between Cecilius Calvert, 2nd Lord Baltimore and first proprietor of Maryland, and William Penn, proprietor of Pennsylvania, over the boundary between their grants. Despite numerous surveys and conferences between the disputants, the conflict continued between the two families and colonies for the next 80 years, becoming so tangled that the British Privy Council in 1763 demanded its settlement by royal survey. Conducted from 1763 to 1768 by English astronomer Charles Mason and Jeremiah Dixon, with the assistance of the colonial surveyor David Rittenhouse, the survey began at an agreed point east of the Delaware River and extended 233 miles to a point west of the Monongahela River. It was confirmed by the Crown in 1769. In 1784 it was extended farther west as the boundary between Pennsylvania and Virginia. Although at the time the boundary implied nothing about slavery, in the early 19th century it became known in popular parlance as the dividing line between the slave and free states and continues to connote the boundary between North and South.

MASONS (FREE AND ACCEPTED MASONS, FREEMASONS)   A secret society of men that claims a long history, the masons hold as their central tenet a belief in the "Grand Architect of the Universe and the Bible," with its symbolism and ceremony apparently derived from the medieval guilds. Roman Catholics do not join and consider Masons to be antipapal. Many colonists were initiated into Masonic lodges in Europe and continued on in America, but the first lodge assembled in America was probably in Philadelphia around 1730. Benjamin Franklin was instrumental in the society, and George Washington was initiated in 1752. Although in modern times Masons shun politics, it was not always so. Washington took the oath of office on a Masonic Bible and laid the cornerstone for the Capitol with a Masonic trowel. This ignited a great controversy and led to opposition to the participation of Masons in other cornerstone layings. The site of the Bunker Hill Monument was donated by the Masons. In 1775, 14 blacks were initiated into the order in Boston, forming a separate branch that has remained so ever since. Many presidents were Masons, including Jefferson, Madison, Monroe, and Jackson.

MASSACHUSETTS   Massachusetts was the first of the New England colonies to be settled permanently by the English, and throughout the colonial era it remained the largest and most prominent. In 1620 the so-called Pilgrims, a group of Puritan separatists fleeing religious persecution in England, landed at Cape Cod and established Plymouth Colony. Ten years later, a larger group of Puritans under the leadership of John Winthrop settled Massachusetts Bay. Unlike the Pilgrims of Plymouth, the Massachusetts Bay Puritans did not intend to turn their backs on England. Rather, they sought to create a model society—what Winthrop referred to as a "city upon a hill"—that would encourage social and religious reform in England. Ultimately, they failed to have much influence on English society, but they had a profound effect on the development of American society.

Puritan Settlement.   The arrival of hundreds of English Puritans in the 1630s caused a rapid expansion of the number of Massachusetts settlements. By 1650 the population had climbed to over 15,000, and there were 11 towns in Plymouth Colony and 29 in Massachusetts Bay, some as far west as the Connecticut River Valley. The growth of the Puritan population provided the impetus for the founding of the first American college, Harvard (1636),

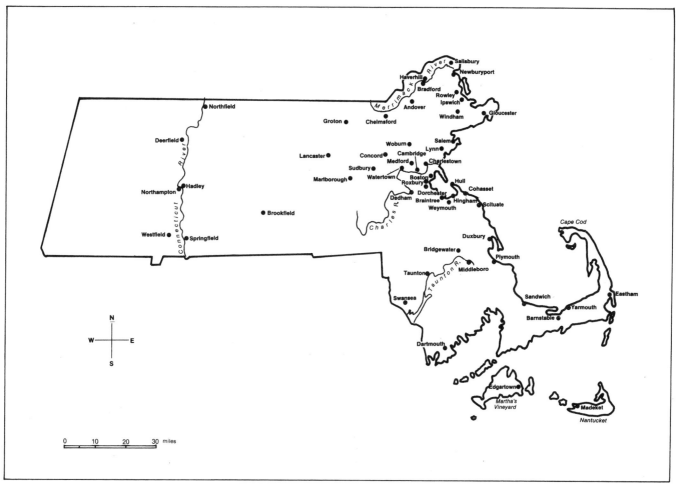

Massachusetts. *(Facts On File, Inc.)*

as a training school for Puritan ministers. As was the case in most North American colonies, the expansion of English settlement led to the domination, even the destruction, of the native Indian tribes. Indeed, years before the English Puritans established permanent settlements, the natives' initial contact with European fishermen had exposed them to devastating diseases. By the time of the Puritan migration, the Indian population of the region had already declined by as much as 90 percent. The Puritan settlers completed the conquest of the native tribes in two 17th-century wars, the Pequot War (1636-37) and King Philip's War (1675-76). Although there were occasional Indian attacks in resistance to further English encroachment on the western frontier, the native population of Massachusetts had been effectively subdued or removed by the beginning of the 18th century.

Control of the interior enabled English settlers to spread rapidly across the landscape. In 1700 there were more than 80 towns in Massachusetts, and by the time of the American Revolution the number would increase to over 300. The vast majority of 18th-century Massachusetts towns were small agrarian villages, with an average population of under 1,000 inhabitants. The economy of these towns was centered on the production of food and other homemade goods primarily for local consumption. But in many cases, especially in the older and somewhat larger communities, people also produced a substantial surplus for trade—usually grain or cattle. Several towns in the countryside became important market centers where rural merchants collected locally produced goods for shipment to urban seaports.

These farm products comprised only a small part of Massachusetts's exports. Fish and timber products were much more significant commodities; indeed, the Massachusetts fishing industry provided the major source of foreign trade throughout the colonial era. Massachusetts merchants also made an important contribution to the colony's economic development by establishing their own shipping fleet. Yet for all its economic activity and development, colonial Massachusetts generally suffered a negative balance of trade. By the middle of the 18th century, Massachusetts was dependent both on England and on other American colonies not only for manufactured goods but for some basic foodstuffs as well.

Early Political Development.   Massachusetts always struggled to maintain its political independence, however.   The original 1629 charter of the Massachusetts Bay Company did not specify that control of the corporation had to remain in England, and when Winthrop and the other settlers came to the New World, they brought the charter with them.   By doing so, they established Massachusetts as a self-governing religious commonwealth.   All officials—from the governor and his assistants to the representatives in the General Court to the selectmen and lesser officers in the individual town meetings—were subject to election by the freemen, the adult male church members.   Thus by 17th-century standards, Puritan Massachusetts had a comparatively wide degree of suffrage.

The first serious challenge to Massachusetts's traditions of self-government came in the 1680s.   In 1684, in response to unfavorable reports by a royal customs official about the lax enforcement of the Navigation Acts and the lack of religious toleration in Massachusetts, the English government annulled the colony's original charter.   In the following year King James II attempted to reorganize the Northern colonies into a single administrative unit, the Dominion of New England.   The new governor of the Dominion, Sir Edmund Andros, almost immediately generated intense hostility in Massachusetts, because his policies seemed to threaten the main foundations of independence in the local communities—land ownership, the town meeting, and the Puritan church.

When word reached Massachusetts that the English Parliament had deposed James II in the so-called Glorious Revolution in 1688, the inhabitants of Boston overthrew Andros and forced him to return to England in 1689.   Despite the hopes of most Massachusetts political leaders that the new monarchs, William and Mary, would restore the old charter, the English government issued a new charter.   In 1691, Massachusetts and Plymouth were incorporated into one royal colony with a governor appointed by the king.   The new charter did restore the representative assembly (the General Court) and gave the representatives the power to choose the governor's council.

Throughout the first half of the 18th century, political life in Massachusetts was comparatively peaceful.   Representatives in the General Court occasionally challenged the prerogative and authority of the royal governors, but the governors also played on factional divisions among members of the General Court.   The balance of power, although delicate, remained stable.

Era of Protest.   In the 1760s, however, with the imposition of new Parliamentary regulations and taxes in the wake of the Seven Years' War (1756-63), the tone of Massachusetts politics changed dramatically.   Radical political leaders in Boston allied themselves with urban artisans, mariners, and other members of the lower classes to protest both the new British policies and the power of the local governing elite.   In August 1765, Boston's "Sons of Liberty" made violent attacks against the houses of Andrew Oliver, the local stamp tax collector, and Thomas Hutchinson, the lieutenant governor of Massachusetts.   Boston merchants engaged in a less violent but no less important form of protest by agreeing not to import British goods.   Throughout the late 1760s and into the early 1770s, Boston remained a center of radical action.   The Boston Committee of Correspondence sent out repeated alarms and appeals to Massachusetts towns and thus established an important network of communication with the countryside.

In 1774, after Parliament imposed the Coercive Acts to punish Boston for the destruction of imported tea at the so-called Boston Tea Party, the people of Massachusetts began to reject the authority of the British government.   Above all, the Massachusetts Government Act, which limited the right of Massachusetts towns to hold town meetings, led inhabitants of the countryside as well as the city to fear the prospect of British oppression.   Local militia units organized themselves into companies of "minutemen" and began to make preparations for armed resistance.   On April 19, 1775, Massachusetts farmers faced British regulars who were coming to seize munitions at Concord, and the first shots of the American Revolution were fired.

The Revolutionary War.   After the first battles at Lexington and Concord and the protracted siege of Boston in 1775-76, Massachusetts did not experience the immediate impact of warfare.   The British evacuated Boston in March 1776, and the main theater of war moved outside New England.   During the war, however, Massachusetts contributed greatly both to the Revolutionary army and to the Revolutionary government.   John Adams, for instance, served as one of the leading members of the Continental Congress, and he also played a major role in drafting a new constitution for Massachusetts.

The Massachusetts constitution stands as one of the major political achievements of the Revolutionary era.   It was the first written constitution to be drafted by a special convention and approved by the voters at large. An initial draft of the constitution was rejected by the people in 1778, in fact, and it was not until 1780 that a second version was finally ratified. With its division of powers among an executive, a senate, and a house of representatives, the Massachusetts constitution provided one of the main Revolutionary-era models of republican government for the U. S. Constitution.

Achieving independence from England and framing a state constitution did not mean the end of political strife in Massachusetts, however. In 1786 farmers in the central and western parts of the state rose up in arms to protest what they saw as economic oppression at the hands of private creditors and indifference on the part of state officials. Shays' Rebellion, as this agrarian insurrection came to be called, threatened the political stability of Massachusetts in the post- revolutionary era. Even though the authorities eventually suppressed the rebellion, they still had to make concessions to the disaffected farmers in order to regain their allegiance to the new republican state. Clearly, the spirit of political independence and resistance to authority still survived in Massachusetts, a condition that was reflected in the fairly close vote in 1788 to ratify the federal constitution.

See also Adams, John; Andros, Sir Edmund; Coercive Acts; Puritans; Revolutionary War, Causes of; Shays' Rebellion; Winthrop, John.

Bibliography: Morgan, Edmund S., *The Puritan Dilemma: The Life of John Winthrop* (Little, Brown, 1958); Nash, Gary B., *The Urban Crucible: Social Change, Political Consciousness, and the Origins of the American Revolution* (Harvard Univ. Press, 1979); Zemsky, Robert M., *Merchants, Farmers, and River Gods: An Essay on Eighteenth-Century American Politics* (Gambit Press, 1971); Zuckerman, Michael, *Peaceable Kingdoms: New England Towns in the Eighteenth Century* (Knopf, 1970).

Gregory H. Nobles
Georgia Institute of Technology

MASSACHUSETTS BAY COMPANY In 1628 a number of prominent English Puritans bought their way into the defunct Dorchester Company, which had tried to plant a farming and fishing settlement at Cape Ann. The new company obtained a charter authorizing settlement of the area known as Massachusetts Bay, north of Plymouth colony, and in 1629 was reorganized as the Massachusetts Bay Company with a royal charter giving the company full authority to govern its own territory. The Puritans voted to transfer the company to Massachusetts, which meant that when company members emigrated they would have full control of the government under which they would live.

The Puritan migration began in 1630 when John Winthrop and a dozen other company members led more than 1,000 settlers to Massachusetts Bay. Over the next ten years they were followed by over 15,000 others who planted towns throughout eastern Massachusetts.

In 1631, Winthrop and his associates transformed the trading company into a colonial commonwealth in which male members of the Puritan congregations would become voting freemen. In 1634 the freemen insisted that the lawmaking powers assigned to them by the charter be delegated to "executives" elected from each settlement. By 1644 the executives and advisors had separated into two houses, together forming the General Court and introducing the concept of bicameral legislatures to America. The company/commonwealth continued as the constitutional basis of government until 1684, when the Crown rescinded the charter.

Bibliography: Bailyn, Bernard, *The New England Merchants in the Seventeenth Century* (1955; reprint Harvard Univ. Press, 1979); Haskins, G. L., *Law and Authority in Early Massachusetts* (1960; reprint Univ. Press of America, 1980); Morgan, Edmund S., *The Puritan Dilemma: The Story of John Winthrop* (1958; reprint Little, Brown, 1962); Morison, Samuel E., *Builders of the Bay Colony* (1930; reprint New England Univ. Press, 1982).

MASSACHUSETTS BODY OF LIBERTIES (1641) A code of laws that established the power of the representatives in the General Court in Massachusetts, the Massachusetts Body of Liberties was written by Nathaniel Ward and adopted in 1641. Attempts had been made by committees in 1635, 1636, and 1638 to draw up a code, but none had been successful. In 1636, John Cotton presented a code to the General Court, but it was not accepted. Finally, in 1639, Ward and Cotton were charged with the job; each came up with a code, and Ward's was accepted in 1641 with changes made by the towns and reductions made by the court. It was not renewed after its three-year probation period because it was felt that it still gave too much power to the General Court.

MASSACHUSETTS CIRCULAR LETTER (1768) Samuel Adams persuaded the Massachusetts house of representatives on February 11, 1768, to adopt a circular letter to the other assemblies, encouraging a united colonial response to the Townshend Acts. A moderate statement that recognized Parliament's legislative authority over the colonies but denied its power to tax them, the letter only repeated the constitutional position of the Stamp Act Congress of 1765. However, Lord Hillsborough, first secretary of state for America and a champion of parliamentary supremacy, found the letter seditious and informed Governor Bernard that the house must either rescind the letter or be dissolved. When the Massachusetts house on June 28 voted down a motion to rescind by an overwhelming 92 to 17, Bernard, following orders, ended the session.

See also Townshend Acts.

MASSACHUSETTS LAND BANK A financial institution founded in 1740 to aid the economic growth of Massachusetts, which was plagued by a constant shortage of capital, the land bank issued paper money backed by promissory notes secured by land. The notes issued by the Massachusetts Land Bank gave a sudden boost to the local economy, and similar land banks were established in Connecticut, Rhode Island, New York, New Jersey, Pennsylvania, and North Carolina. The resultant inflation and political opposition led Parliament to outlaw the Massachusetts bank in 1741 and to prohibit New England land banks in the Currency Act of 1751.

MASSACHUSETTS SCHOOL ACT (1647) Called the "Old Deluder Act," this 1647 Massachusetts law began public education in America. The act decreed that every town of 50 families must employ a schoolmaster to teach reading and writing and that every town of 100 families had to found a grammar school because "one chief project of that old deluder, Satan, was to keep men from the knowledge of the Scriptures." Education was important to the Puritans because translations of the Bible into the vernacular made it accessible to everyone who could read English and not just to Latin scholars. The 1647 act grew from a 1642 act requiring parents to teach their "children to read and understand the principles of religion and the capitall laws" and left to the individual towns whether the schools were to be funded by taxes or use fees.

MASSASOIT (c.1580-c.1662) Chief of the Wampanoag, also known as Ousamequin, or "Yellow Feather," he was an important ally of the Puritans of Plymouth colony. Massasoit became chief in 1607 and established his center near Pawkunnakut in Rhode Island, from which he eventually extended his control over the peoples of Rhode Island and eastern Massachusetts. His rule was severely weakened by the disastrous plague among his people in 1617 and the rising power of the Narragansett. He therefore recognized that the arriving English colonists could be potentially important allies and offered them land, a treaty of mutual protection, and the practical agricultural knowledge they needed to survive. His recovery from serious illness, due to the efforts of an English physician,

strengthened his bond with the colonists, and he warned them of an impending Narragansett attack in 1632.

Subsequently branded as a collaborator, Massasoit fled for protection to the Plymouth colony until peace was restored through the intervention of Roger Williams. In 1649 he sold land to the colonists for the establishment of Duxbury. His children were educated in the English style. One of them, Metacomet, also known as Philip, headed the anti-English confederation in King Philip's War.

See also King Philip's War.

MASTERS, SYBILLA (died 1720) An inventor, probably born in Bermuda, she lived with her Quaker family in West New Jersey and was married to Thomas Masters sometime between 1693 and 1696. Her husband was a prosperous merchant who was alderman of Philadelphia, then mayor and provincial councillor. Sybilla raised four children and tinkered with her mechanical inventions. In 1716 she was awarded her first patent, in England, for a device that pounded corn into meal, using either water power or horses to drive it. The meal was marketed as "Tuscarora Rice," a cure for consumption, and is considered the first American patent medicine. Sales were disappointing, possibly because it was of little medicinal value. She secured another patent for a new way of working and staining palmetto leaf and straw for use in making hats. After receiving a monopoly for importation of palmetto leaf from the West Indies, she opened a shop in London that sold hats and furniture. Sybilla returned to Philadelphia in 1716, published her patents in America in 1717, and died three years later, after making her mark as an inventor and marketer of great ingenuity.

MATHER, COTTON (1663-1728) A clergyman, author, and scholar, Mather was born in Boston, Massachusetts, the son of Increase Mather. He graduated from Harvard (1678), studied medicine for a time, and received his master's degree (1681). Turning to the ministry, he was ordained (1685) and became associated with his father at Boston's Second Church. Through his writings, Mather promoted the revolt against the royal appointment of Sir Edmund Andros as governor. His writings became studies of spiritualism and possession. "Memorable Providences Relating to Witchcraft and Possession" (1689) contributed to the hysteria of the Salem witchcraft trials (1692). Some of the trials were narrated in Mather's "Wonders of the Invisible World," (1693).

His fame grew as he worked hard for the cause of orthodox Congregationalism. He wrote 450 works on natural history, church music, church polity, and moral essays. *Magnalia Christi Americana* (1702) was the most complete history of New England for many years. Mather fought against heterodoxy, and when Harvard became less Congregationalist he resigned his fellowship (1703), promoting Yale as the new bastion of the faith. He was elected to Britain's Royal Society (1713) and joined his father in an unpopular campaign to urge Zabdiel Boylston to administer inoculations against smallpox. After his father's death, Mather succeeded as pastor of the Second Church (1723).

See also Congregationalists; Mather, Increase; Witchcraft. One of the most influential colonial clergymen, Cotton Mather opposed departures from orthodox Congregationalism.

MATHER, INCREASE (1639-1723) A religious and political leader, Mather was born in Dorchester, Massachusetts. He graduated from Harvard (1656), and received a master's degree from Trinity College, Dublin (1658). Returning to America, he became a teacher at Boston's Second Church (1664), where he was at the pulpit for the rest of his life. His son Cotton joined him there in 1685. Increase was appointed licenser of the press (1674) and a fellow of Harvard (1675), where he later became president (1685-1701).

The dispute over the Massachusetts Charter during the 1680's drew him into political affairs, and he led a protest against revocation of the charter. He went to England to have the charter restored (1688) but his negotiations were unsuccessful. He was appointed the official agent of the colony (1690), and the new charter joined the Massachusetts Bay and Plymouth colonies (1691). Mather returned to Boston in 1692 with the new royal governor, Sir William Phips, and discovered that the new charter and the new governor were unpopular. Thus, Mather found himself in the middle of a controversy that cost him the presidency of Harvard (1701). During the Salem witchcraft trials, Mather wrote *Cases of Conscience Concerning Evil Spirits* (1693), a work that was greatly responsible for ending the hysteria. Mather, who wrote more than 150 works on theology, history, science, and politics, remained a leader of New England Congregationalism until his death.

See also Congregationalists; Mather, Cotton; Witchcraft.

MAURY, JAMES (died 1770) A descendant of French Huguenots who settled in Virginia, Maury attended William and Mary College. After graduating, he went to England in 1741 for ordination as an Anglican priest, returning to Virginia in 1742. In 1762, when he was the rector of a church in Louisa County, he brought suit in a Hanover County court (as part of the Parsons' Cause case) to recover the unpaid portion of his salary. Maury argued that his jury was illegal because the members were religious dissenters and not gentlemen. The defense attorney, Patrick Henry, eloquently insisted that plain farmers made an honest jury. Maury was awarded one penny.

See also Henry, Patrick; Parson's Cause.

MAVERICK, SAMUEL (c.1602-c.1676) Colonist and commissioner, Maverick was born in Devonshire, England, and came to Massachusetts in 1624. He welcomed John Winthrop in 1630 and took the oath of freeman in 1632. Winthrop wrote of Maverick's concern for the Indians and settlers. He was a successful merchant and respected by the Puritans, but in 1647 they fined him for joining Dr. Robert Child's plea to allow worship for non-Puritans. He left for England in 1650, discussed Puritan intolerance in *A Briefe Discription of New England and the Several Townes Therein* (1660), and received a commission in 1664 to hear complaints in Massachusetts and New York.

MAYFLOWER COMPACT A legal and political agreement signed on November 11, 1620, by the 41 male passengers on the *Mayflower* before disembarking at Plymouth, this document established the principles of self-government and majority rule among the Pilgrims. Since, during their voyage, the Pilgrims, led by William Bradford, had unexpectedly decided to change their destination and settle in New England rather than in Virginia, the land patent granted to them in London by the Virginia Company was no longer valid.

In the face of angry threats by some of the settlers that they would not be bound by the group's leaders, Bradford drafted the Mayflower Compact, patterning it after common Puritan church covenants. By signing this document, the members of the community committed themselves to become an autonomous "Body Politick" and to observe all rules issued by a vote of the majority. Although this document still had to be approved in London before becoming legally binding, and was subordinate to the subsequent religious rulings of the Pilgrim leadership, the signing of the Mayflower Compact marked the beginning of democratic ideas in the New England colonies. It remained in force as the basic political document in Plymouth until the annexation of Plymouth by Massachusetts Bay Colony in 1691.

MAYHEW, JONATHAN (1720-66) A religious leader who helped to pave the way towards American independence, Mayhew was born in Chilmark, Martha's Vineyard, Massachusetts. He graduated from Harvard (1744) and became pastor of West Church, Boston, three years later. He moved quickly away from older Puritanism to a less rigid religious position. In 1649, on the centennial of the execution of England's Charles I, Mayhew delivered

"Discourse Concerning Unlimited Submission and Non-Resistance to the Higher Powers," a sermon in which he attacked the divine right of kings and ecclesiastical absolutism and showed discontent with the laws imposed on the colonies by Britain. His sermons were considered the first to abandon traditional Trinitarian doctrine (1755) and moved towards Unitarian congregationalism. Mayhew's sermons had profound effect in Boston, and his political sentiments were considered ahead of his time. He attacked the Calvinist view of predestination, defended free will, and opposed religious and political arbitrary rule. At Harvard, he preached against popish idolatry (1765). The next year he gave a sermon on the Stamp Act, justifying the possibility of citizens taking the government administration into their own hands.

MAYHEW, THOMAS (c.1621-57) Clergyman and Indian missionary, Mayhew was born in England and came to America in 1631 with his father, also named Thomas. In 1642 father and son were awarded Martha's Vineyard, Nantucket, and the Elizabeth Islands. The younger Thomas became pastor at Edgartown, but his interest was in converting the Indians. He learned their language and soon his first convert, Hiacoomes, could give sermons. Mayhew and John Eliot described their conversions in *The Glorious Progress of the Gospel* (1649) and *Tears of Repentance* (1653). In 1657 his ship was lost as he sailed to England with an Indian convert to seek financial aid.

MECKLENBURG COUNTY RESOLUTIONS (1775) Meeting in Charlotte in May 1775, the South Carolina Committee of Safety drew up 20 resolves demonstrating the commitment to the Revolution. They declared on May 31 that all laws and commissions confirmed by King George III and Parliament were "annulled and vacated" and suspended the colony's constitution. Forming a provincial congress, which they placed under the direction of the Continental Congress, the delegates assumed all legislative and executive powers. They reorganized local government, elected county officials, and formed nine militia companies. The resolutions were to remain in force until the British government put a stop to its injustices and corruption.

MECOM, JANE FRANKLIN (1712-94) The favorite sister of Benjamin Franklin, Mecom in her letters left an enduring record of the difficulties of her life and the affectionate nature of her relationship with her brother. Youngest of her father's 17 children and her mother's 10, she married Edward Mecom when she was 15 and had 12 children between 1729 and 1751. She ran a boarding house and later a shop to alleviate their poverty, and several of her children apparently inherited serious mental illness from their father.

MEDICINE The medical profession in Europe and America had few tools with which to treat illnesses during the colonial era. Based on the current theories of disease, medicine depended on the depletion of blood through venesection or leeches, or the reduction of other bodily fluids through purging, vomiting, salivation, sweating, or blistering. The tools of the trade consisted of lancet (scalpel), clyster (enema syringe), calomel to purge the bowels, ipecac or rhubarb as emetics, and wine as a diuretic. A poultice was used to blister the skin to infect it and, in accordance with the prevailing theory, to draw out the disease with the resultant pus.

Colonial doctors, lacking academic interests and far too busy to be concerned with theories of diseases, were not embroiled in the controversies over nosologies, the classification of diseases, that preoccupied European physicians. Nor did they go to extremes in their treatments, preferring less heroic measures of diet, rest, and mild purgatives. Induced excessive bleeding, associated with Benjamin Rush's theories of nervous spasms in the blood vessels, came at the end of the 18th century after the Revolution; the practice, however, never became a popular remedy in America.

In spite of theories and systems, the doctor's role was to provide moral support, set broken bones, and dispense medication from his herb garden. Much like the witch doctor of the Indians or the herb doctor among the Afro-Americans, his air of authority was one of the most potent medicines available.

Medications. Medicine had only a few effective remedies. It was possible to alleviate pain with opiates and cure some cases of syphilis or gonorrhea with mercury, or scurvy with citrus fruits. The physician could inoculate to prevent smallpox but care had to be taken to stop the spread of the disease. In Norfolk, Virginia, in 1774 a mob rioted against the practice of inoculation without safeguards and marched a recently inoculated group and their doctors to the pesthouse, forcing a quarantine of the infected persons.

One of the few specific medications available until the 19th century was cinchona bark (quinine). Malaria could be treated successfully with quinine, but ignorance of the exact quantity needed often meant that the patient did not receive an adequate dose. On the other hand some physicians prescribed quinine for any fever, assuming that if it was good for one fever it was good for all. If "the bark" did not work to cure a nonmalarial fever, physicians were known to reject it altogether as a useless remedy.

MERCANTILISM: TOPIC GUIDE

GENERAL

Acts of Trade and Navigation
   (1650-1767)
Currency Act (1764)
Hat Act (1732)
Iron Acts (1750, 1757)
Molasses Act (1733)
Naval Stores Act
Proclamation of 1763
Stamp Act (1765)
Sugar Act (1764)
Townshend Acts (1767)
Wool Act (1699)
British Empire (see **Topic Guide**)
Banking and Credit
Colonial Government (see **Topic Guide**)
Enumerated Goods
Fisheries
Salutary Neglect
Smuggling
Wage and Price Controls

COMPANIES

Compagnie D'Occident
Dorchester Company
Dutch West India Company
East India Company (English)
French West Indies Company
Hudson's Bay Company
Hundred Associates, Company of a
Massachusetts Bay Company
New England Company
Royal Africa Company
South Sea Company
Virginia Company of London
Virginia Company of Plymouth

BOARDS AND COMMISSIONS

Board of Trade and Plantations
Council for Foreign Plantations
Council of the Indies
Laud Commission
Warwick Commission

BIOGRAPHIES

Cromwell, Oliver
Pitt, William (The Elder)
Townshend, Charles

The Profession of Medicine. The medical profession in the colonies did not follow the distinctions used in Europe—physicians, surgeons, and apothecaries (pharmacists). There were no guilds to enforce requirements nor effective legal regulation of the profession to preserve the differences. Doctors acted as pharmacists and surgeons. Midwifery, however, maintained its separate identity as a female occupation until shortly before the Revolution, when the male midwife made his appearance. With the advent of licensing and academic qualifications in the 19th century, midwifery gave way to the male-dominated medical profession.

Most doctors in colonial America received their training through apprenticeship and not all had the benefit of a college degree. An elite few went to Europe—usually to Edinburgh—for graduate medical education. The first medical school in this country was not established until 1765 in Philadelphia and only a handful of doctors were able to attend classes. New York followed suit in 1768 with King's College (now Columbia) Medical School. Plans in Massachusetts for a medical school were halted by the Revolution, and Harvard College did not set up such a training institution until 1780. No graduate medical education was available in America until Johns Hopkins University opened its doors after the Civil War.

See also Disease; Rush, Benjamin.

Bibliography: Duffy, John, *The Healers: A History of American Medicine* (Univ. of Illinois Press, 1976); Marti-Ibanez, Felix, ed., *History of American Medicine: A Symposium* (MD Publications, 1959); Shryock, Richard Harrison, *Medicine and Society in America: 1660-1860* (Cornell Univ. Press, 1960).

Elaine G. Breslaw
Morgan State University

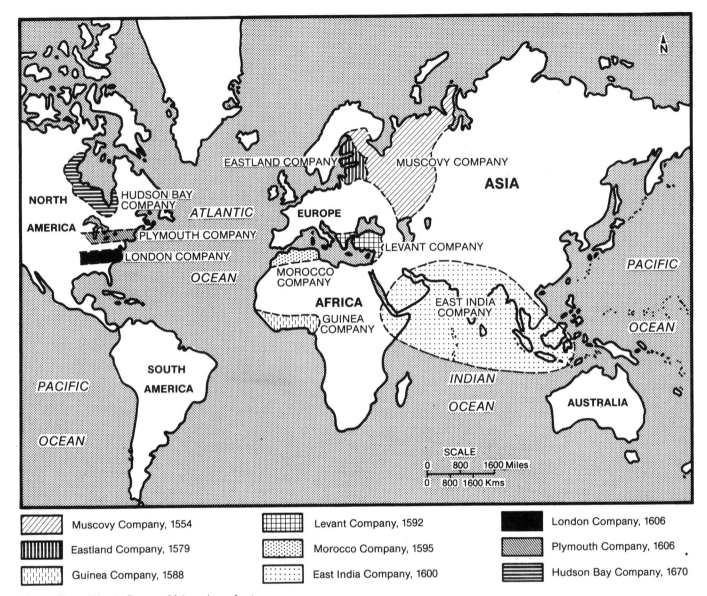

NORTH AMERICA

ATLANTIC

EASTLAND COMPANY

MUSCOVY COMPANY

ASIA

HUDSON BAY COMPANY

EUROPE

PLYMOUTH COMPANY

LEVANT COMPANY

PACIFIC

LONDON COMPANY

OCEAN

MOROCCO COMPANY

AFRICA

GUINEA COMPANY

EAST INDIA COMPANY

OCEAN

SOUTH AMERICA

PACIFIC

INDIAN

OCEAN

AUSTRALIA

OCEAN

SCALE

0 800 1600 Miles

0 800 1600 Kms

Muscovy Company, 1554	Levant Company, 1592	London Company, 1606
Eastland Company, 1579	Morocco Company, 1595	Plymouth Company, 1606
Guinea Company, 1588	East India Company, 1600	Hudson Bay Company, 1670

Mercantilism. *(Martin Greenwald Associates, Inc.)*

MENDOZA, JUAN DOMINGUEZ DE (flourished 1656-86) Mendoza had entered the Franciscan Order in 1656 and was assigned to the presidio in El Paso in 1683 when Juan Sabeata, chief of the Jumano tribe, arrived in the town requesting that the Franciscans send some of their brothers to his tribe to preach to them. Governor Cruzate instructed Mendoza to explore the Nueces River, bring back samples of commodities, and discover what he could about the Indians. Mendoza and the Franciscan Nicolas López penetrated deep into Texas. They became convinced that Spain should extend its power into the region. After returning to El Paso, the two went to Mexico City, where they sought the viceroy's support for their efforts. While they were in Mexico a French fleet sailed for the Gulf coast, and the attention of the government shifted to this threat. Mendoza and López were forced to return to the northern frontier without promise of support.

See also López, Nicolas.

MENÉNDEZ DE AVILÉS, PEDRO (1519-74) Recognized by his contemporaries as Spain's most capable sea captain, and captain-general of the Indies fleet from 1555 to 1563, Menéndez in 1565 received a royal order to sweep Florida's Atlantic coast clean of the French and found a Spanish settlement there. In Florida, Menéndez first slaughtered the French colonists at Fort Caroline and then destroyed the survivors of Ribaut's shipwrecked fleet. Founding St. Augustine in 1565,

Menéndez crossed to Spain seven times between 1565 and 1571 to get supplies and colonists for his new settlements. Philip II recalled Menéndez to Spain in 1572 to protect home waters, which he did until his death.

See also Saint Augustine.

MENNONITES   An Anabaptist church, the Mennonites were founded by Menno Simons (1496-1561), a Dutch priest who joined the Reformation in 1536. At first a Dutch phenomenon, the church soon spread to the German Palatinate and Switzerland. It is strongly pietistic, emphasizing the need for rebirth through a conversion experience that results in personal commitment to Christ and the leading of a godly life. From this it follows that baptism should only be adminstered to adults who can testify to their rebirth. Mennonites also believe in separation of church and state, freedom of conscience, pacifism, and the idea of visible saints, meaning that only the converted be admitted to church membership. In addition to baptism, Mennonites accept as a sacrament the Lord's Supper. They observe the rituals of foot washing and the kiss of peace derived from primitive Christianity and refuse to swear oaths.

American Mennonites are descended from two waves of immigration: One from Holland settled in New York in 1650 and, in 1683, at Germantown, Pennsylvania, now a part of Philadelphia. In 1688 the second wave of Palatinate German Mennonites entered Pennsylvania, settling in the southeast. The Amish who migrated to Pennsylvania during the 18th century were led by Jakob Amman, a Swiss Mennonite who broke from the church in 1693. A religious conservative, he insisted on simple dress and lifestyle and on separation from non-Amish society. Eventually the entire church emigrated to America, where they became known as the Pennsylvania Dutch, a corruption of the word Deutsch, meaning German.

See also Religion.

Bibliography: Wenger, John, *The Mennonite Church in America* (The Herald Press, 1966).

Leonard R. Riforgiato
Pennsylvania State University

MERCANTILISM   A highly nationalistic economic theory, mercantilism originated in governmental practices of Western European countries from 1500 to roughly 1800. Known as mercantilism in England after Adam Smith used the term in his Inquiry into the Nature and Causes of the Wealth of Nations (1776), the theory has been called Colbertism in France after Jean Baptiste Colbert, finance minister of Louis XIV, and cameralism in the Germanic states. Whatever the terminology, mercantilism buttressed and rationalized the state-making process of modern Western Europe.

By means of sustained governmental intervention in the economy, mercantilism sought to achieve a powerful, prosperous, independent state. As such, the theory exhibits elements of nationalism and paternalism. Early mercantilists were bullionists, emphasizing the need to accumulate the precious metals of gold and silver. Gradually their strictures relaxed to an appreciation of a favorable balance of trade, which in turn emphasized the importance of national self-sufficiency.

Mercantilist ends were secured by means of legislation designed to regulate every facet of economic life. Commerce required close attention. A large merchant marine ensured commercial independence. An efficient navy protected shipping. Government sought to promote agriculture, to protect manufactures, and to control wages, prices, and product quality, all in an effort to realize national self-sufficiency.

At that point mercantilism revealed another characteristic—imperialism. According to Thomas Mun, in *England's Treasury by Forraign Trade* (1664), the state must pursue an active role of colonization, for colonies could nourish the mother country. If not sources of gold and silver, overseas possessions served the mother country as producers of raw materials and markets for manufactures. In all cases, the interest of the mother country was paramount; actions of a dependent provincial government must redound to the advantage of the mother state to which it owed its existence and protection.

Mercantilism and the Colonies.   The application of mercantilism to the English colonies derived most immediately from parliamentary legislation and from Crown directives to executive officials. The Navigation Acts, a series of parliamentary enactments beginning in 1651 and extending through the colonial period, regulated colonial trade. By law Parliament also sought to discourage colonial manufacturing, particularly woolen goods, hats, and iron products. Restrictions on currency emission and the refusal to curb the slave trade also reflected mercantilist policy. Conversely, by means of bounties Parliament encouraged the colonial production of naval stores and indigo.

While English mercantilism apparently operated to the overall detriment of the colonies, a century and a half elapsed before the provincials mounted an effective protest. The cost imposed by the Navigation Acts upon the colonies was no more than three percent of colonial income, and perhaps far less. Moreover, with cheap land and scarce labor, the colonies generally complemented the economy of the mother country. The provinces also enjoyed the advantage of English naval protection, restricted foreign competition, guaranteed markets, cheap English manufactures, and easy credit. Overall, the English laxly enforced the mercantilist legislation; when threatened, the colonials resorted to an evasion of the laws.

Patterned after the mother country, the English colonies exhibited mercantilist tendencies of their own in the promotion and regulation of their provincial economies. The heritage of mercantilism carried over to the United States in state and national policies of the early republic. By then, however, mercantilistic thought already clashed with the visions of republicans who sought a more pluralistic, democratic marketplace of equally competing individuals.

Bibliography: Andrews, Charles M., *The Colonial Period of American History*, 3 vols. (Yale Univ. Press, 1934-38); Heckscher, Eli F., *Mercantilism*, 2 vols., rev. ed. (1955: reprint Garland Pub., 1983); Schmoller, Gustav F. von, *The Mercantile System and Its Historical Significance* (1897; reprint A. M. Kelley Pub., 1965).

Alan D. Watson
University of North Carolina at Wilmington

MERCER, HUGH (?1725-77)   Born in Scotland and trained as a doctor, Mercer emigrated to Pennsylvania about 1746. He practiced medicine on the Pennsylvania frontier and during the French and Indian War served as an officer in a Pennsylvania regiment. He became acquainted with George Washington during this campaign and subsequently moved to Virginia. In 1775, Mercer was elected a colonel of minutemen and then of a regiment. He was a delegate to the Virginia convention, and Congress elevated him to brigadier general. He helped carry out the surprise attack at Trenton on December 26, 1776. On January 3, 1777, in the battle of Princeton, he was beaten and stabbed by British soldiers, dying from the wounds.

MESA VERDE   Mesa Verde is a high plateau in southwestern Colorado that is cut by deep canyons. The term has come to refer to the series of cliff dwellings, adobe buildings inside caves, that dot the region. From 1500 B.C. to 1300 A.D. there were four occupation periods of the villages: the Basket Makers, Modified Basket Makers, Developmental Pueblo, and the Great Pueblo. The Indian inhabitants of Mesa Verde were agricultural, building their settlements in the cliffs for greater security. They apparently left the area around 1300 A.D. due to a prolonged drought that made agriculture impractical in the area. The region was first visited by Father Escalante in 1776.

METACOMET (KING PHILIP) (c.1642-76)   Metacomet, a Wampanoag Indian leader better known to the colonists by his English name of King Philip, is commonly identified as the instigator of the wide-ranging conspiracy that was the last serious Indian resistance to European settlement in New England. The image of King Philip's War, however, is as distorted as his English title, given as a derisive comment on his purported "ambitious and Haughty spirit."

The war grew out of Plymouth Colony's expansion, especially with the settlement of Swansea in 1667 on Wampanoag land, and the competing land claims of Massachusetts, Plymouth, and Connecticut. Under these circumstances, Metacomet was pressured by the English to surrender his people's sovereignty. In 1675 three of his men were executed for the murder of John Sassamon, a "Praying Indian" and

Metacomet, known as King Philip by the English, led Indians in the last serious opposition in New England to colonial settlement. *(Library of Congress)*

English spy, and Metacomet found it increasingly difficult to control his warriors. The war erupted when the English killed an Indian rifling an abandoned house.

Metacomet's warriors were successful until December when the Mohawk defeated Metacomet's forces and, in the Great Swamp Fight, the Narragansett suffered a devastating defeat. Although remnants joined Metacomet as did some Nipmuck from the north, it was not enough. Short of supplies and constantly harassed by the English, Metacomet was killed in August 1676.

See also King Philip's War.

Bibliography: Leach, Douglas E., *Flintlock and Tomahawk: New England in King Philip's War* (Macmillan Co., 1958); Alden Vaughan, *The New England Frontier: Puritans and Indians* (Little, Brown and Co., 1965).

Richard L. Haan
Hartwick College

METHODISTS   Although a late arrival in colonial America, Methodism quickly made up for lost time. Originating as a pietistic movement within the Church of

England, Methodism found in America its most fertile soil. With the assistance of dedicated lay people, Methodism entered Maryland and New York in 1766 and had managed to build or buy churches there as well as in Philadelphia before the decade was out. Other lay evangelists, dispatched by John Wesley in England, arrived in the early 1770s to strengthen the advance elements; of these, Francis Asbury was the most important.

Asbury, arriving in 1771, proceeded to organize and stimulate the youthful movement with such effectiveness that Wesley bestowed upon him the title of "Superintendent of the American Colonies." With his headquarters established in Baltimore in 1773, Asbury set both the example and the policy of an itinerant ministry, the famous Methodist "circuit rider." By 1776 some 26 itinerants carried the Methodist message from New York to Virginia, and a decade later the number had grown to about 100.

The American Revolution, by severing all ties with England, might have threatened a movement still so young, still so dependent upon Wesley's direction. The opposite turned out to be the case, as Methodism declared its independence along with that of the nation, organizing in 1784 as a wholly indigenous church. At that point, Asbury and others accepted ordination, Methodism in America up to then having been almost wholly a lay rather than a clerical movement.

Growth through the remainder of the century was phenomenal, with Methodists increasing from around 8,000 in 1780 to more than 80,000 two decades later. By that time Methodism had already moved to the western frontiers, into Ohio, Indiana, and Kentucky. Also by that time Methodism had attracted a large following among blacks, notably in New York and Philadelphia, this leading early in the 19th century to separate "African Methodist" denominations.

Bibliography: Bucke, Emory S., ed., *History of American Methodism*, 3 vols. (Abingdon Press, 1964).

Edwin S. Gaustad
University of California, Riverside

MIAMI, FORT Located on the site of present-day Fort Wayne, Indiana, the French built Fort Miami (or Miamis) in 1749 to control the important portage between the Maumee and Wabash rivers, which linked the military and commercial center at Detroit with the waters of the Mississippi River system. Taken over by the British in 1763, Fort Miami was abandoned during Pontiac's Rebellion.

MIANTONOMO (c.1600-43) A Narragansett chief, whose name was derived from the word *miantonimi*, "he who wages war," he was a leader of Indian opposition to English colonial expansion in New England. Although he agreed to the granting of land to Roger Williams for his

Providence colony, Miantonomo feared the effect of continued colonization on his people and in 1642 conferred with leaders of the Wyandanch and Montauk tribes on Long Island about the possibility of unified military action against the English.

Although this plan was never implemented, word of it reached the leaders of the Massachusetts Bay Colony, and Miantonomo was summoned to Boston to face charges of plotting against the English. He was subsequently released but forced to sign a peace treaty with the English colonists. In 1643 the Narragansett were attacked by the neighboring Pequot, who had gained the support of the English. Miantonomo was captured in one of the early battles and handed over by the Pequot to face a show trial in Boston by the commissioners of the United Colonies of New England. His unrelenting nationalism and longstanding friendship with Roger Williams angered the judges, and he was executed. One of his sons, Canonchet, was chief of the Narragansett at the time of King Philip's War.

See also Canonchet.

MICHILIMACKINAC, FORT Michilimackinac includes the strategic passage between lakes Huron and Michigan, the land on both sides, and the island now called Mackinac. A historic meeting place for Great Lakes Indians, its first European settlement came in 1671, when French Jesuits founded St. Ignace as a mission for emigrant Huron. In 1689 a French garrison was established at Fort de Buade. Meanwhile, a great commerce in furs began between the French *coureurs de bois* and the Indians. By the 1710s there were over 600 Frenchmen living at the straits, many of them with Indian women, rearing mixedblood or métis children. A stable community existed from at least 1720.

In the summer thousands of Indians and traders turned the straits into a bustling commercial center for the Great Lakes trade, while military men and merchants used the strategic site as a distribution point for the northern and western lakes. The British took over in 1761, causing many of the Francophone residents to flee to more isolated posts. During the Revolutionary War, the garrison was moved to the island. The United States gained possession in 1783, but England captured the straits during the War of 1812 and held them until 1816.

MIDDLETON, ARTHUR (1742-87) Born into the South Carolina gentry at his father Henry's estate, Middleton Place, and trained in England as a lawyer, Arthur Middleton became a prominent political and social figure in Charleston. He disliked the new wave of Scottish and Irish immigrants that flowed into South Carolina seaports in the early 1770s and held himself above the settlers of the backcountry. In spite of his haughty attitude, Middleton believed in the cause of liberty. He served as a delegate to the Second Continental Congress (1776-78; 1781-83) and signed the Declaration of Independence. He also served on the state legislature and was the author of the first draft of the South Carolina state constitution.

See also Middleton, Henry.

MIDDLETON, CHRISTOPHER (died 1770) An explorer and master navigator, Middleton began his long naval career on board privateers during Queen Anne's War (1701-13), joined the Hudson's Bay Company in 1721, and made 16 annual voyages to Hudson Bay before 1740. In 1737 he was elected a fellow of the Royal Society in recognition of his contributions to the theory and practice of navigation. Based on this reputation, in 1741 he was commissioned in the navy and appointed commander of an expedition to discover the Northwest Passage leading westward out of Hudson Bay. After wintering at Churchill, the northernmost post on the bay, he explored Wagner and Repulse bays and observed the entrance to Frozen Strait. On his return his career was wrecked by a campaign of denigration by believers in the passage because of his conclusion that there was no passage in those waters. His map of the western Hudson Bay has proved to be one of the best of the 18th century.

See also Northwest Passage.

MIDDLETON, HENRY (1717-84) A member of the Charleston, South Carolina, gentry, who became one of South Carolina's largest landowners, Middleton held various official positions from 1747 to 1754 before becoming speaker of the colonial assembly. He later became a member of His Majesty's Council. He was conservative in his politics and opposed a popular legislative appropriation of money to the John Wilkes Fund. A delegate to the Continental Congress and its second president, he resigned in February 1776 when more liberal delegates began to dominate. He was succeeded by his son Arthur. After the defeat of Charleston in 1780 he put himself under British protection, but his loyalty to the American cause was never questioned.

See also Middleton, Arthur.

MIFFLIN, THOMAS (1744-1800) Born to a Quaker family in Philadelphia and educated at the College of Philadelphia (later the University of Pennsylvania), Mifflin entered mercantile business in 1765. A patriot leader, Mifflin was a Pennsylvania assemblyman and delegate to the First and Second Continental Congresses (1774-76; 1782-84). From 1775 to 1778 he was quartermaster general of the Continental Army but he eventually resigned under criticism. Out of the army, Mifflin again sat in Congress, serving as president in 1783-84. In 1787 he was

a Pennsylvania delegate to the Constitutional Convention and a supporter of the new Constitution. Later he was president of the supreme executive council of Pennsylvania and governor of the state (1790-99).

MILITIA In the 17th century most colonies required all able-bodied male citizens of the towns, usually excepting ministers, to own weapons and to assemble for periodic training and inspections. These militia, perhaps related to the Anglo-Saxon institution of the "fyrd," or the "posse comitatus," were more likely simply immediate, practical responses to the continuing danger of Indian attack. Colonial militia were also used by colonial governments to suppress internal disorders, such as Bacon's Rebellion or the Regulator movement, and were the main forces in the intercolonial wars until the entrance of British regular troops during the 1760s. In these irregular bodies, discipline was haphazard; enlistments were short-term; desertions were common; and coordination between colonial militias was difficult to achieve. The combination of these factors created nearly insurmountable obstacles during the Revolutionary War, which was fought, on the patriot side, largely by militia forces.

Nevertheless, the notion of a citizen soldiery, called out to defend the homeland but disbanded at the conclusion of the crisis, came to be the republican ideal, while standing armies were seen as the potential instrument of tyranny. This belief was embodied in the Second Amendment to the Constitution: "A well regulated Militia, being necessary to the security of a free State, the right of the people to keep and bear Arms, shall not be infringed." The 1792 Militia Act authorized the organization of state militia.

Bibliography: Dupuy, Richard E. and Dupuy, Trevor, *Military Heritage of Americans* (1968, reprint Hero Books, 1984); Ekirch, Arthur A., Jr., *The Civilian and the Military* (1956, reprint Myles, 1972).

MILLS The first recorded mill in North America was built at Plymouth in 1631, but Spanish colonists in Florida or New Mexico may have constructed primitive horizontal wheels before then. Although windmills were common on Cape Cod, Long Island, and other coastal locations, in English and French North America mills typically utilized large vertical waterwheels to capture the kinetic energy of the many rushing streams and rivers. Waterwheels turned slowly and gearing was necessary in order to secure the speed necessary to turn the massive millstones, which were quarried in several locations from Massachusetts to North Carolina. By the end of the 17th century, mill-building had become an important part of an emerging American tradition of common engineering.

Grain Mills.   Grist mills were a component part of the local agricultural economies of Europeans at least as early as the 12th century, and in America the grinding of grain was the first of the household industries to be socialized. Gristmills were rather widely scattered in the South, where indentured servants or slaves were often employed to grind grain by hand, but in New England and the mid-Atlantic colonies nearly every village had one or more examples of these little processing plants. The typical mill could grind about four bushels of corn an hour, and most settlers brought only enough for a week's use, so the mill was usually a busy social center. On the frontier, a millsite often became the center of settlement. Throughout the colonial period, gristmills were so essential to local economies that they were considered public utilities. Millers were granted tax exemptions or monopolies, and their fees were subject to scrutiny and regulation.

Sawmills.   Sawmills were uncommon in England but took on great importance along the Atlantic coast of North America, where labor was scarce and timber abundant. The first was built in Virginia in 1632, and by 1700 there were sawmills serving nearly every established community in the English colonies. As early as the beginning of the 18th century, large mills at the mouths of Maine and New Hampshire rivers were producing great quantities of board for export to coastal towns and overseas. The construction of dams and millponds blocked both the drainage of silt and the passage of spawning fish, which were also driven away or destroyed by sawdust indiscriminately dumped into the stream, a process first noted with dismay by the Indians. And the mills provided the means for the great deforestation of the eastern half of the continent, well under way by 1750. The sawmill was a powerful agent in the transformation of the North American ecology.

Other Mills.   Fulling mills, which shrank and sized homespun cloth, also became common features of the Northern colonial landscape in the 18th century. Over the years many fullers gradually added wool carding and fabric dyeing to their repertoire of services, socializing these important domestic industries. When the fuller also took up power spinning, as some did late in the century, the fulling mill became a "woolen mill." Gradually other kinds of mills appeared—paper mills, powder mills, spice mills, and oil mills—all first steps in the industrialization process. Unlike grist and saw mills, however, these were not a part of the self-sufficient economy.

See also Household Industries.

Bibliography: Stilgoe, John R., *Common Landscape of America, 1580-1845* (Yale Univ. Press, 1982).

John Mack Faragher,
Mount Holyoke College

MINUIT, PETER (1580-1638)   As director general of New Netherland and governor of New Sweden, Minuit left his mark on Dutch colonial history, but little is known of his early life. It is probable that he was born at Wesel in the German Duchy of Cleves. His presence among those accompanying Willem Verhulst in the 1625 expedition to New Netherland suggests that he had become an employee of the Dutch West India Company, serving perhaps as a factor. In various documents he is mentioned as a member of the governing council of the colony. It is presumed that he shortly thereafter sailed back to the Netherlands and returned to the Netherland colony in May 1626.

Upon his return, he discovered that Verhulst had had a falling out with the council and had been placed under house arrest. Appointed director general by the council, Minuit immediately set to work bringing the colony to order. During his administration of New Netherland (1626-31), he consolidated settlement on Manhattan Island (leaving a force of company soldiers at Fort Orange), purchased Manhattan Island from the Indians for trade goods valued at 60 guilders, and opened diplomatic channels with Governor Bradford of New Plymouth. He was recalled by the company to the Netherlands in 1631 and eventually dismissed.

He was later recommended by Samuel Blommaert (former director of the Amsterdam chamber of the West India Company) as the man to command an expedition to plant a Swedish colony on the Delaware Bay. In 1637, as a co-founder with Blommaert and others of the Swedish West India Company, he led an expedition to the Delaware and in March 1638 erected Fort Christina. Later that year he was lost at sea in a hurricane off the coast of the island of St. Christopher in the Caribbean.

See also New Netherland.

Bibliography: Rink, Oliver A., *Holland on the Hudson: An Economic and Social History of Dutch New York* (Cornell University Press 1986).

Oliver A. Rink
California State University at Bakersfield

MINUTEMEN   Minutemen was a term given during the Revolutionary War era to those soldiers who would be ready for an emergency at a minute's warning. The Worcester, Massachusetts convention and the provincial congress met to reorganize the Massachusetts militia (1774).

Tories were forced out and new officers were elected who formed new regiments in which one third of the troops were designated as minutemen. They turned out together to resist the British at Lexington and Concord. The British killed minutemen on Lexington green, and minutemen marched on Concord bridge. A subsequent reorganization of the Massachusetts military eliminated the minutemen there, but by the recommendation of the Continental Congress, Connecticut, Maryland, and New Hampshire united.

MISCEGENATION

MISCEGENATION   The term "miscegenation" was not coined until 1865, but the intimate, sexual contact between European colonists, Indians, and African slaves, resulting in the creation of large numbers of people with varied and mixed ancestry, has been an important theme of American history from the beginning of European colonization.

Sexual relations were surely one of the very first forms of contact between Europeans and Indians, probably dating from the time the first sailors dropped anchor in American harbors. Well known is the story of Pocahontas, the daughter of Chesapeake chief Powhatan, who not only saved the life of John Smith but married English tobacco trader John Rolfe. Less well known is the fact that quite a number of Jamestown colonists were drawn to Powhatan's village, where they married Indian women and raised families and where many remained. In the backcountry, where during the colonial period Indians and English participated in a trading economy, and where traders were generally without European women English men and Indian women commonly married.

Sexual relations between Europeans and Africans were suffused with the coercive reality of slavery. Sex and even marriage apparently took place with some regularity between English indentured servants and African slaves of the 17th-century Chesapeake region. Fearful of the consequences of a unified servile class, and as part of their general strategy of "divide-and-rule," the colonial elite enacted a series of laws, beginning with statutes in Maryland (1661) and Virginia (1662) that prohibited and severely punished interracial sex and marriage, which clearly marked Africans as a socially inferior group and which, in effect, legislated a racial caste system into existence.

Over the following decades sexual exploitation by masters made life a hell for thousands of slave women, as well as for their brothers, husbands, and sons, but the real intent of the law, after all, was to shape the attitudes and behavior of the masses. The relationships between Indian women and Europeans may have been generally conducted on mutually agreeable terms, but slavery determined that miscegenation between Europeans and Africans would be dominanted by violence, guilt, and shame.

See also Mixedbloods (Mestizos, Métis); Mulattoes.

Bibliography: Nash, Gary, *Red, White, and Black: The Peoples of Early America*, 2d ed., (Prentice-Hall, 1982).

John Mack Faragher
Mount Holyoke College

MISSIONS AND MISSIONARIES

MISSIONS AND MISSIONARIES   Propagation of the Christian religion was a goal of all the major European colonial powers, although there were important variations in their commitment. The Spanish missions in the Southwest and West were the best known, but there was also a substantial French effort and some English missionary activities.

Spanish Missions.   For the Spanish the mission was arguably one of the most important agencies of colonialism. In theory the Spanish mission was to be temporary, preparing the Indians to be loyal subjects of Crown and church; in practice, however, it became a fixed colonial institution. The Franciscan order began work in Florida in 1528. In the 1570s the Franciscans were among the Pueblo in the Southwest, where by 1630 there were 25 missions. Most were destroyed during the Pueblo Revolt of 1680, but 70 years later, after the reconquest, they had reestablished 20 of them. The Franciscans founded missions in east Texas in the early 18th century, most notably the chapel of the Alamo at San Antonio, and in California beginning in the late 1760s under the leadership of Junipero Serra. In southern Arizona the Jesuits, led by Eusebio Francisco Kino, founded more that 20 missions, including San Xavier del Bac near Tucson. In addition to evangelizing and converting the native population, the Spanish missions played an important role in introducing economic institutions such as peonage and pastoralism and assisted in spreading epidemic European diseases that decimated the Indians.

French Missions.   Missions were far less institutionally important among the French, and yet no history of New France can ignore the missionaries for their impact on French-Indian relations. The first missionaries in Canada, in the early 17th century, were Recollects, who the Crown hoped would cement commercial ties to the natives. Never numbering more than a handful, theirs was a pitiful record of conversion. They were succeeded by the Jesuits, who first came in 1625. Although their numbers were also few, they were notably more successful, largely because they lived among the Indians, learning their languages and customs. Some, including Jean de Brebeuf (the patron saint of Canada), died bravely as martyrs.

In general European missionaries linked conversion with acculturation, holding that Indians could not accept Christianity without accepting, as well, European cultural norms. To this rule, the Jesuits offered an important exception, working to introduce Christianity within the con-

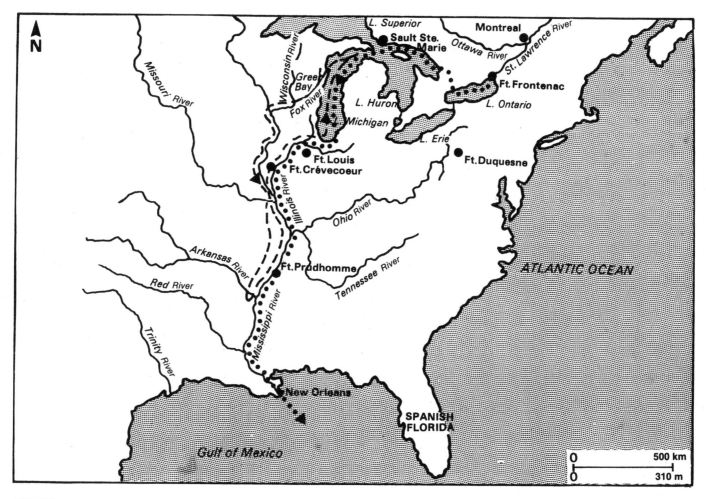

Route of Pierre Marquette and Louis Jollet, 1673

Route of Robert Cavelier de La Salle, 1682

Mississippi River Explorations, 1673-82. *(Martin Greenwald Associates, Inc.)*

text of native culture. "Blackrobes" such as Claude Jean Allouez and Jacques Marquette helped to open up the Great Lakes and the Mississippi Valley to French trade and settlement in the 17th century, and as a result the West long retained a French Catholic influence. The Jesuits of New France also produced a long series of "Relations," which were reports on their activities and which form one of the most valuable records of European-Indian contact in existence.

English Missions. By contrast with the Spanish and French Catholics, the Protestant missionaries of the English colonies achieved little of note. Anglican Alexander Whitaker at Jamestown in 1612 succeeded in converting Pocahontas, among a few others, and the first charter of the Massachusetts Bay Colony declared its prime objective to be the conversion of the Indians, but neither effort amounted to much more than public relations. For the English the equation of conversion with acculturation was never seriously challenged and formed the basis of the program of the Society for the Propagation of the Gospel in New England. The society supported the efforts of John Eliot and Thomas Mayhew, who founded the "praying towns" that, in 1670, included some 20 percent of the surviving Indians of the region.

Efforts in the other colonies produced even more disappointing results, although William Penn and the Quakers enjoyed some success in Pennsylvania. In the South the Society for the Propagation of the Gospel in Foreign Parts, organized by the Anglicans in 1701, spent most of its energies among white colonists and made little headway among Indians. Missionaries paid some attention to slaves, but conversion was generally opposed by masters as potentially subversive. The most successful Protestant missionaries were the Moravians, including John Gottlieb Ernestus Heckwilder, Johann Conrad Weiser, and David Zeisberger, who in the 18th century worked among the Iroquois and Delaware. Like the Jesuits, the Moravians attempted to introduce Christianity while respecting Indian cultural values, and for this they were often opposed by colonial authorities and settlers.

See also Franciscans; Spanish Colonies.

Bibliography: Axtell, James, *The Invasion Within: The Contest of Cultures in Colonial North America* (Oxford Univ. Press, 1985); Gray, Elma E. and Leslie R., *Wilderness Christians: The Moravian Mission to the Delaware Indians* (1956; reprint Russell, 1973); Shea, John D. G., *History of the Catholic Missions Among the Indian Tribes of the United States, 1529-1854* (1857; reprint Ayer, 1969).

John Mack Faragher
Mount Holyoke College

MISSISSIPPI BUBBLE   The spectacular failure in 1720 of the Mississippi Company, a French trading monopoly organized as a privately-owned royal stock company in 1718 by the Scottish financier John Law, was popularly referred to as the bursting of the "Mississippi Bubble." The Mississippi Company, or Company of the Indies, controlled the French foreign trade monopolies, the mint, the royal revenues, and the management of the royal bank, all of which were tied to the promotion of colonization and land speculation in Louisiana. A period of frantic speculation began when the state allowed stock to be purchased with depreciated royal bonds. The stock quickly soared to highly inflated values that could not be backed by real assets. The inevitable failure came in 1720, and many investors lost everything. The failure of the South Sea Company in England also occurred in 1720, the year both "bubbles" burst.

MISSISSIPPI RIVER   The Mississippi, the greatest of all North American rivers and the world's third longest (after the Nile and the Amazon), is fed by runoff from 31 states and 2 Canadian provinces. From its source in north-central Minnesota it runs south for more than 2,300 miles, passing first from lake to lake in a narrow passage marked by many falls and rapids, then descending into a broad valley where it is fed by the Minnesota, Chippewa, and Wisconsin rivers. By its juncture with the Missouri it has grown to monumental proportions that are expanded by the waters of the Ohio, the Arkansas, and the Red, where the delta begins, the river branching into thousands of bayous and draining into the Gulf of Mexico.

Before the European era, the lower and middle reaches of the river were the sites of the flowering of the great Mississippian Indian cultures, complex societies based on the horticultural production of corn, beans, and squash, with centralized political organization, social stratification, and a highly developed religious system. At Cahokia, one of the great urban centers of Mississippian culture and the largest city north of Mexico, some 30,000 persons lived at its peak phase about 1100 A.D. In the first decades of European colonization the Natchez of the lower river were a powerful remnant of that era.

Among the Europeans, Hernando De Soto first reached the Mississippi in 1541, but it was first explored by Marquette, Jolliet, and La Salle for the French in the 1670s and 1680s, and French influence extended well beyond the colonial period. The first French settlement on the river was New Orleans, founded in 1718. Navigating the river in their flat-bottomed bateaus and barges, the French founded other important posts on or near the Mississippi at Natchez, Arkansas Post, Kaskaskia, St. Louis, and Prairie du Chien. From these centers they explored and traded west up the Red River and into Texas, up the Arkansas (finally reaching Sante Fe), and up the Missouri and Osage.

At the end of the French and Indian War the Mississippi River became the international boundary between English and Spanish America. In 1783 it was made the western boundary of the new nation, with navigation of the river guaranteed. The Spanish continued to block passage at New Orleans, a continuing source of tension, until the Louisiana Purchase of 1803 finally guaranteed the great river system to the United States.

See also Exploration, French Colonies.

John Mack Faragher
Mount Holyoke College

MITCHELL, JOHN (died 1768)   John Mitchell was a man of many talents and accomplishments. As a physician practicing in Urbana, Virginia, he pioneered in the successful treatment of yellow fever. As a botanist he wrote learned essays on the principles of botany and zoology as well as "An Essay upon the Causes of the Different Colours of People in Different Climates." These accomplishments are overshadowed by the achievement of Mitchell's great *Map of the British and French Dominions in North America with Roads, Distances, and Limits and Extent of the Settlements*. Done on a scale of 1:2,000,000, Mitchell's map has been used for a century and a half in the resolution of boundary disputes both between states and between the United States and England.

MIXEDBLOODS (MESTIZOS, MÉTIS)

Social and demographic factors were the most important determinants of patterns of Indian-European miscegenation. Intermarriage with Indians in the English colonies was not as extensive as in Spanish Mexico, where by the end of the colonial period the mestizo, or mixed Indian-European population, had become as large as the Indian, and considerably larger than the white, population. But that difference had less to do with different "national characters" of the colonizers than with the distinction between an economy like Mexico's which directly incorporated Indian communities into the colonial labor system, and one like Virginia's, based on the labor of indentured servants and African slaves.

Along the Atlantic coast, from New England to Florida, the character of Indian-European relations was shaped by wars over control of the arable land; and by the rapid immigration of large numbers of colonists of both sexes; there were relatively few intimate contacts between the Europeans and the Indians. But in the backcountry, wherever the fur trade placed a premium on more cooperative relations, English traders intermarried with Indians with a frequency at least as great as that among the *coureurs de bois* and Indians of New France. By the end of the colonial period, nearly all surviving tribes with a history of trade relations included large mixedblood components among their populations.

But mixed ancestry did not necessarily lead to a distinctively ethnic identity. Indeed, the majority of Indian-European offspring remained with their Indian mothers and identified themselves as Indians. It was only late in the colonial period, when groups of mixed ancestry came to play special mediating economic or social roles, as did the western Canadian people who became known as the métis, that mixedbloods assumed a unique identity. At the same time, influenced by the increasing importance of racial categories in late colonial culture, Americans came to think of these persons no longer as Indians but as "half-breeds" or "half-castes."

See also Miscegenation.

Bibliography: Crane, Verner W., *The Southern Frontier, 1670-1732* (1928; reprint Norton, 1982); Giraud, Marcel, *The Metis in the Canadian West* (English translation, Univ. of Nebraska Press, 1986); Van Kirk, Sylvia, *Many Tender Ties: Women in Fur-Trade Society in Western Canada, 1670-1870* (Univ. of Oklahoma Press, 1980).

John Mack Faragher
Mount Holyoke College

MOBILE, FORT

The Lemoyne brothers, sieurs d'Iberville and de Bienville, established a fort on Mobile Bay on the Gulf of Mexico in 1702 in order to counter the Spanish settlement of Pensacola, itself intended to consolidate their possession of Florida. Over the first decade of their founding, both towns were captured and recaptured during the War of the Spanish Succession between France and Spain. Both a garrison and a mission, the fort at Mobile drew about it several hundred Muskhogean-speaking Indians who, by mid-century, had blended with the colonist population. Along with Biloxi and New Orleans it was one of the most important towns of lower Louisiana. Transferred to the British in 1763, it was taken by Spain during the Revolutionary War.

See also French Colonies.

MOHAWK INDIANS   *See* **Iroquois Confederacy.**

MOHAWK RIVER

The Mohawk is the only major river that breaches the Appalachian highlands and thus was the most strategically important east-west route of the northeast during the colonial and early national eras. Long under the control of the powerful Iroquois, the Mohawk River was the route of the lucrative New York fur trade, drawing pelts from the deep interior to the market at Albany. Farmers moving west along the corridor had settled 80 miles of the valley with their riverine lots by 1750 and became prime targets during the French and Indian War. The improvement of the river route to Lake Ontario, connecting the Mohawk River to the sources of Lake Oneida and the Oswego River, became an important objective in the early national period, a project finally completed with the opening of the Erie Canal in 1825.

MOLASSES ACT (1733)

British legislation that put duty of six pence a gallon on molasses, nine pence on every gallon of rum, and five shillings per 100 pounds on sugar that was imported from non-British colonies to the American colonies. These duties were to be paid before landing, but colonial smuggling alleviated the impact of the Molasses Act. The act was, in effect, a protective tariff in favor of the British planters in the West Indies and was repealed by the Sugar Act (1764).

See also Acts of Trade and Navigation.

MONARCHS, ENGLISH

From the beginning of colonization to the Revolution, the English monarchy was deeply involved in the course of American history. Henry VII (reigned 1485-1509) sponsored John Cabot's exploration of the northern coastline of North America in 1497 and began the consolidation of monarchial power that was a prerequisite to serious overseas expansion. Henry VIII (1509-47) further strengthed that power, began a century of conflict with Spain that included seaborne privateering, and broke with the Roman Catholic Church, giving impetus to the Protestant movement in England that would become a main force in planting colonies.

After the reigns of Edward VI (1547-53) and Mary I (1553-58), both inconsequential for the Americas, came that of Elizabeth I (1558-1601), not only one of the most important English monarchs but crucial to early colonization. Elizabeth finished the task of building a powerful monarchy, brought the privateering war against Spain to its peak (which drew increasing English attention to America's riches), and granted Sir Humphrey Gilbert the first royal charter to settle an American colony (1578). After the death of Gilbert, who had been attempting to plant a colony in Newfoundland, she continued the project with a royal charter to her favorite courtier, Sir Walter Raleigh, in 1584. This resulted in the founding of Virginia at the unsuccessful settlement of Roanoke. Under her aegis Sir Francis Drake sailed around the world (1577-80), bringing great publicity to overseas expansion.

The 17th and 18th Centuries. James I (1601-25) chartered the Virginia Companies to begin the colonization of North America and saw the founding of Jamestown in 1607. In 1624, as a result of mismanagement, the King dissolved the company and assumed control of the colony. During the reign of Charles I (1625-49) the great Puritan migration to Massachusetts began, dropping off when the King recalled Parliament in 1640, beginning the struggle with the Puritans that resulted in his execution in 1649. The restoration of the monarchy, with the ascension of Charles II (1660-85), brought about efforts to strengthen the inefficient imperial system through the Navigation Acts of 1660 and 1663; but Charles further dispersed central power in the empire by granting charters allowing self-government to Rhode Island and Connecticut. In the last year of his reign, Massachusetts's charter was revoked for nonenforcement of the Navigation Acts.

James II (1685-88) attempted to extend royal power by consolidating the Northern colonies into the Dominion of New England in 1685, which abolished the local assemblies. Charles was removed and replaced by William II (1689-1702) in the "Glorious Revolution" of 1689. William allowed the colonies to return to their old governments, although after the imperial reorganization of 1696 most of the colonies reverted to direct royal control. A war with France (1689-97), known in Europe as the War of the League of Augsburg, was called King William's War in America. During the reign of Anne (1702-14), there was another war with France, known in Europe as the War of the Spanish Succession and dubbed Queen Anne's War (1702-13) in America.

During the reigns of George I (1714-27) and George II (1727-60), English government was dominated by Parliament and the powerful group of families known as the Whigs. George III (1760-1820) resolved to enhance royal power once more, and his resulting conflict with Parliament during the 1760s resulted in an inconsistent and incoherent colonial policy. As an active participant in efforts to enforce imperial prerogatives in the colonies, George became identified as a threat to American liberties. First declared a tyrant in Thomas Paine's *Common Sense*, the King became the focus in the Declaration of Independence of nearly all the colonies' grievances. The American Revolution thus became a struggle to throw off monarchy altogether.

See also British Empire; Dominion of New England; King William's War; Queen Anne's War; Revolutionary War, Causes of.

Bibliography: Andrews, Charles M., *The Colonial Period of American History*, 4 vols. (Yale Univ. Press, 1934-38); Lovejoy, David S., *The Glorious Revolution in America* (1972; reprint Wesleyan Univ. Press, 1986).

John Mack Faragher
Mount Holyoke College

MONCKTON, ROBERT (1726-82) A British military officer and son of John Monckton, Viscount Galway, Robert Monckton began his military career in the 3rd Foot Guards in 1741. Serving on the Continent during the War of Austrian Succession, he rose to the rank of major by 1747. In 1751 he was promoted to the rank of lieutenant colonel in the 47th Regiment and served as a member of Parliament. In the following year he was transferred to Nova Scotia and appointed provincial councillor and commander of Fort Lawrence. In those positions Monckton restored order to the province by quelling an uprising of German immigrants.

During the French and Indian War he won acclaim by capturing Fort Beauséjour and clearing French forces from the isthmus of Nova Scotia. He was later appointed lieutenant governor of the province and oversaw the forced deportation of more than 1,100 French Acadians. Monckton was acting governor at the time of Lord Amherst's 1758 Louisburg expedition and led British forces up the St. John's River in the following year. In 1760 he was transferred to the southern district of Pennsylvania and New York and served as New York governor in 1761. After commanding a successful 1762 expedition against Martinique, Monckton returned to England where he held various civil and military posts.

See also Louisburg, Battles of.

MONEY   Because the export of coin from Britain was forbidden, 17th-century colonists depended upon wampum, commodity money (furs, skins, and hogsheads of tobacco among others), or illegal local coinage (such as the Massachusetts-minted "pine-tree shillings" of 1652-84). As foreign trade became more important the specie-scarce Americans heavily discounted their produce in order to obtain foreign coinage. By the early 18th century the most common circulating medium had become the Spanish silver peso or "piece of eight," usually called a "dollar" from the English transliteration of the German "thaler" (another large silver coin of the time). In 1785, in deference to the wide acquaintance with this medium, Congress adopted "dollar" as the name of its new decimal-based currency; other monetary terms — "quarter" from the practice of dividing the large Spanish coin into four pieces, "two bits" from the two "reales" in a quarter — also continued.

Colonial paper money was first issued by Massachusetts in 1690, but because of the colony's failure to back the issue with adequate taxes, the bills were enormously devalued. The Massachusetts Land Bank of 1740, declared illegal by Parliament the next year, was an attempt to capitalize the bills. In 1751, Massachusetts was prohibited from printing any more money, but during the French and Indian War the other colonies turned to the practice. The resulting inflation caused Parliament to pass the Currency Act of 1764, which until the Revolution, prohibited any further printing.

The currency issued by the Continental Congress was backed by promises alone. Continental dollars traded against Spanish dollars at the rate of 3 to 1 in 1777, 40 to 1 in 1779; in 1781, by which time Congress had issued over $190 million in continentals, the ratio was 146 to 1: thus the phrase "not worth a continental." State governments reacted to the economic crisis of the Revolutionary War and its aftermath by printing currency of their own. It was not until the new federal government established the federal mint (1792) and began issuing currency (1794) that the monetary situation began to stabilize.

Bibliography: Billias, George A., *The Massachusetts Land Bankers of 1740* (Univ. of Maine, 1959); Harrod, Roy F., *The Dollar* (Norton, 1963); Nettels, Curtis P., *Money Supply of the American Colonies Before 1720* (1934; reprint, Gordon Press); Newman, Eric P. and Doty, Richard G., eds., *Studies on Money in Early America* (American Numismatic, 1967); Ver Steeg, Clarence L., *Robert Morris, Revolutionary Financier* (1954; reprint Hippocrene, 1970).

John Mack Faragher
Mount Holyoke College

MONTCALM, LOUIS-JOSEPH DE, MARQUIS (1712-59)   Born into a military family, the Marquis de Montcalm had received a solid education from a tutor, an education continued even after he joined the Regiment of Hainaut as an ensign at the age of 12. A captain in 1729 and colonel in 1743, he had been wounded several times before he became a major general in 1756 and was given command of the troops in Canada during the French and Indian War. Forgotten by the French government, his army greatly outnumbered by the adversary, and lacking supplies, he had nevertheless managed to frustrate British efforts, winning several early encounters (Fort Carillon, Fort George) during the British campaign against New France and in 1758 became a lieutenant general.

In September 1759, while defending the seemingly impregnable Quebec from the British, he was confronted with the appearance of British forces under General James Wolfe on the Plains of Abraham outside the city. In the ensuing battle both Montcalm and Wolfe received mortal wounds, with Montcalm dying the next day. His death brought to an end what had been a gallant defense facing insurmountable odds. On September 18, the French army surrendered Canada to the British, a surrender which became final with the Treaty of Paris in 1763.

See also Abraham, Plains of; French and Indian War; Wolfe, James.

MONTEREY   The Spanish explorer Sebastián Vizcaíno first sighted the curve of Monterey Bay in 1602; he described in glowing terms its capacity and the sheltered nature of its harbor. However, not until 1769 did the viceroy order Gaspar de Portola to go north from Baja California and found settlements at San Diego and Monterey. The Portola party reached Monterey in October but did not recognize the site from Vizcaíno's description and went on to San Francisco Bay. The following year, Portola returned and succeeded in establishing a presidio on Monterey Bay. In 1774, Juan Bautista de Anza first opened a land route between Monterey and the Spanish towns in Arizona, and in 1777 the capital of California was moved from Baja to Monterey, where it remained for the rest of the Spanish period.

See also Anza, Juan Bautista de; Portola, Gaspar de; Vizcaíno, Sebastián.

MONTEZUMA (1466-1520)   An Aztec emperor of Mexico (1503-20), Montezuma was born in Tenochtitlan (Mexico City). Montezuma ordered that the shores be guarded when word was brought to him of the landing of the white man (1518). Hernando Cortes and his men arrived a year later and were met by embassies from Montezuma bearing gifts. Soon, Cortes marched to the capital, and used Montezuma in designing his conquests.

As shown in 1768, Montreal was the most important French city in North America. *(Library of Congress)*

The Spaniards were attacked by natives of Mexico City (1520), and Montezuma stood on a palace roof to order his people to stop fighting. Angered by Montezuma's action the Indians attacked and mortally wounded him.

MONTGOMERY, RICHARD (1738-75) A native of Ireland, Montgomery served with the British colonial army from 1756 to 1772. He then settled in King's Bridge, New York, unable to purchase a commission as a major. The Coercive Acts of 1774 convinced him to join the patriot cause, and he was one of the first appointed to the rank of brigadier general when the Continental Army was formed. With General Philip Schuyler, Montgomery led an expedition against Canada in 1775. He captured Montreal but was killed while attempting to take Quebec, an unsuccessful mission for the Continentals. "The Death of General Montgomery," painted by John Trumbull and modeled after Benjamin West's tribute to Britain's General James Wolfe, depicted him as a tragic hero.

MONTICELLO The residence in which Thomas Jefferson lived throughout his political career, Monticello ("little mountain") was an estate that developed in character with its owner. Jefferson began constructing the house in Albemarle County, Virginia, in 1769. He turned to classical architecture for his inspiration, informed by his reading of the Italian architect Andrea Palladio. He then added his own distinctive touches: Side terraces in the slope of the hill conceal stables, laundries, and servants' quarters. The plans for the house were constantly altered over the years. The dwelling was completed in 12 years, but work on the estate lasted until 1809.

MONTOUR, MADAME (c.1684-c.1752) Interpreter and Indian agent in New York and Pennsylvania. Although she spent most of her life among the Indians, her origins are somewhat mysterious. She was thought to be of mixed French and Indian blood, and she is variously described as being the daughter of Count Frontenac (Canadian governor), or the daughter of a fur trapper and his Indian wife, or possibly a captive of Iroquois from Canada. Madame Montour first was used as an interpreter by the English in the summer of 1711, at a conference between the chiefs of the Iroquois and New York governor Robert Hunter. In 1712 she aided Colonel Robert Schuyler in dissuading the Iroquois from joining the Tuscaroras in their war in the

Carolinas. She was so skilled at promoting good relations between the English and the Iroquois that the French sought to buy her services. She moved to Pennsylvania in 1717 and continued her interpretership between that colony and the Iroquois in conferences in 1727, 1728, and 1734. She eventually settled in Western Pennsylvania. There is a county, a town, and a mountain in Pennsylvania named in honor of Madame Montour and her son Andrew, who served the English in the French and Indian War.

MONTREAL   The Iroquoian village of Hochelaga was the farthest penetration of the St. Lawrence River by the French explorer Cartier in 1535. When next explored, by Samuel de Champlain in 1603, the site had been abandoned. Named "Mount Royal," it became the location of a missionary colony in 1642 and grew to become the base of the French fur trade, with the largest western tributary area of any North American colony as well as the western anchor for French riverine settlement.

Montreal prospered after falling to the British in 1760. The Montreal fur trade system continued to grow, with Scotch as well as with French traders. The Montreal-based North West Company became a major competitor of the Hudson's Bay Company until the two firms were united in 1821. The Quebec Act of 1774 guaranteed the "ancient laws, privileges, and customs" of the French citizens. Later that year American Revolutionary forces occupied the city without resistance, but they found no significant support among the Canadians, and the British retook the city in 1776. By the boundary provisions of the Treaty of Paris in 1783, Montreal traders lost the productive districts south and west of the Great Lakes, but they continued to operate in the American sector until the late 1790s, by which time their attention had been redirected to the rich northwest territories of Athabasca. The city was a major center of Loyalist relocations during and after the Revolution.

MONTS, PIERRE DU GUAST, SIEUR DE   (?1560-1628)   A French explorer and colonist in Canada, the Sieur de Monts was born a Roman Catholic but joined Henry IV as a Protestant. He traveled to the St. Lawrence River in 1603, and King Henry gave him the directorship of the Canada Company and land grant in Acadia. Joined by Samuel de Champlain, de Monts sailed in March 1604. He explored the Bay of Fundy, discovered Annapolis harbor and St. John River, which he named. After settling a colony on the St. Croix River, he founded a second colony in 1605 at Port Royal (now Annapolis), Nova Scotia. When he returned to France, he had lost favor with the King and received no money for his work. In 1606 he managed to relieve the colony in Canada and send Champlain to

explore the St. Lawrence River. In 1608, de Monts helped the endangered colony at Quebec.

MOODY, LADY DEBORAH (died 1659)   Lady Moody, born Deborah Dunch in Avedon, England, came from an ancient family of Berkshire known for its Non-conformist leanings. She married Sir Henry Moody of Garesden in Wiltshire around 1605. Her husband, a member of Parliament like her father, died in 1632. She left England for Massachusetts in 1639 with her son Henry and several families from her estate in England. She settled in Lynn but joined the church at Salem in 1640.

In 1642 she was brought before the Quarterly Court of the colony for refusing to accept the doctrine of infant baptism. With a group of friends and sympathizers, she left Lynn to settle in New Netherland where the Dutch authorities, eager to attract colonists disaffected with the orthodox regime in Massachusetts, promised "free liberty of conscience." In 1645, Governor Kieft granted a patent to the new town of Gravesend on Long Island. The patent recognized Lady Moody as the prime mover for the group. An educated, cosmopolitan widow with friends in high places, she had the power and the determination to make a home in America where small-minded people could not decide her beliefs for her.

MOORE, SIR HENRY (1713-69)   A colonial administrator, born in Jamaica, Moore studied in England and at the University of Leyden. Returning to Jamaica, he served successively as assemblyman, councillor, secretary, and lieutenant governor. From 1756 until 1762 he served as acting governor, in which capacity he quelled a major slave rebellion. The Crown named him a baronet in 1764 and appointed him governor of New York in July 1765.

Moore arrived in New York in the midst of the Stamp Act crisis. Discovering that he was at odds not only with the colony's assembly but also the council, he chose to avoid confronting them and devoted considerable attention to Indian affairs, which he could conduct without the legislature's involvement. He worked closely with Sir William Johnson and twice visited the Six Nations before his death.

MOORE, JAMES (died 1706)   A trader and colonial official, born in Ireland, Moore emigrated to Charleston, South Carolina, in 1675, where he entered the Indian trade. He soon became involved in protests against the rule of the proprietors. In 1700 he was elected governor by the council and served until 1703. During Queen Anne's War (1702-13), he led the English expedition against St. Augustine, during which he engaged in slave raids against both Indians and free blacks.

See also Queen Anne's War.

MOORE, JOHN (1659-1732) A colonial administrator, he was born in England and came to South Carolina in 1680. After serving at several administrative jobs in the colony, he moved to Philadelphia, where by 1700 he was the attorney general and register-general of Pennsylvania. Moore's membership in the Anglican church and his intense loyalty to the king caused many disagreements between him and Governor William Penn, and in 1704 he was removed from both offices. From 1704 until 1728, he was collector of the port of Philadelphia and after that, until 1732, served as deputy collector of the port. He was also deputy register- general of the city from 1724 until 1726.

MORAVIANS The Moravians or *Unitas Fratrum* were the heirs of the Slavic reformer John Hus, who was burned at the stake in 1415 for heresy. In 1457 they founded their church, which accepted only two sacraments and repudiated the doctrines of the Mass, purgatory, confession, image and relic worship, and the efficacy of good works. Steadily diminished by constant persecution, the few surviving members fled Bohemia in 1722 to settle at Herrnhut, the German estate of the Count von Zinzendorf, a Saxon court official. Strongly pietistic, Zinzendorf decided in 1727 to reconstitute the church on the basis of a novel and radical ecumenical scheme that he called *ecclesiolae in ecclesia*. The universal church, or *ecclesia*, was composed of separate components called *ecclesiolae*, or denominations. Moravians, posing as ministers of other sects, would infiltrate and unite them into a whole. In 1732 the Saxon government ordered the church at Herrnhut dissolved because Lutheranism was the established religion.

Zinzendorf sent his followers to the West Indies, Georgia, and Pennsylvania while he received Lutheran ordination, followed by consecration as a Moravian bishop. In 1742 he arrived in Philadelphia, where he tried unsuccessfully to unite the German sectarians. His efforts to infiltrate the Lutheran church were likewise frustrated by the arrival of the Lutheran leader Henry Melchior Muhlenberg. Frustrated, Zinzendorf returned to Europe, while his followers were granted (1749) a charter as a church by Great Britain. Operating from their centers at Bethlehem and Nazareth in Pennsylvania, Moravians sent missionaries to Ohio and set up missions for Pennsylvania Indians. As pacifists they played no part in the Revolution.

See also Muhlenberg, Henry Melchior; Religion.

Bibliography: Hamilton, John T. and Hamilton, Kenneth G., *History of the Moravian Church: The Renewed Unitas Fratrum, 1722-1957* (Moravian Church in America, 1967).

Leonard R. Riforgiato
Pennsylvania State University

A conservative who supported a strong national government, Gouverneur Morris helped to write the Constitution. *(Library of Congress)*

MORGAN, DANIEL (1736-1802) A general in the Revolutionary War, Morgan was born in New Jersey. He accompanied General Braddock's disastrous Pennsylvania expedition in 1755 and later served in other frontier military campaigns. With the coming of the Revolution, he was commissioned as a captain. By late 1776 he commanded a regiment as a colonel, serving in major campaigns under Generals Gates and Washington. Although George Washington later characterized Morgan as "intemperate" and "illiterate" and commented that "there are different opinions with respect to his abilities," Morgan, then a brigadier general, received a gold medal for his skill and bravery at the battle of Cowpens, South Carolina, in 1781. After the war he commanded troops (1794) in Pennsylvania charged with suppressing the Whisky Rebellion. He served as a Federalist representative in Congress from 1797 to 1799.

MORRIS, GOUVERNEUR (1752-1816)   A lawyer, statesman and diplomat, Morris was born to a wealthy landed family in Morrisania, New York, and educated at King's College (now Columbia). He studied law with William Smith and started a legal practice in New York City. Although conservative by temperament, Morris joined the patriot cause, helping to write New York's first constitution in 1776; serving on the state council of safety; and sitting in the Continental Congress (1778-79), where he drafted several important state papers.

In 1781, Morris, by then a resident of Philadelphia, began over three years as assistant to Robert Morris, the superintendent of finance. In 1787, Gouverneur was an active member of the Pennsylvania delegation to the Constitutional Convention, where he called for a strong national government sensitive to the interests of property. He favored a vigorous executive department and opposed the convention's concessions to slavery. As the leading member of the Committee on Style he was responsible for the final wording of the Constitution. In later years, Morris returned to New York, pursued various business interests, and served as U.S. minister to France during the French Revolution.

MORRIS, LEWIS (1726-98)   A signer of the Declaration of Independence and a half brother of Gouverneur Morris, Lewis Morris was born into a prominent family in Westchester County, New York. He served one term in the provincial assembly (1769) and became a member of the Second Continental Congress (1775). The Provincial Congress of New York made Morris a brigadier general. He took his post, but was able to return to Congress to sign the Declaration of Independence. He took part in the New York campaign (1776), but his military ventures were continuously interrupted by his civil duties. He was a member of the state legislature (1777-90) and retired as a major general of militia. He urged the ratification of the Constitution.

MORRIS, ROBERT (1734-1806)   Morris, the Philadelphia merchant who was known as the "Financier of the American Revolution," was born in England. He came to America as a youth and joined the Philadelphia mercantile house of the Willings, where he later prospered as a partner. An active patriot, Morris was elected in 1775 to the Continental Congress, taking a leading role in the key commercial and diplomatic committees, while also borrowing money and procuring supplies for the military. Morris brought his business resources to the service of the cause,

often advancing his own fortunes in the process. He opposed independence in July 1776 over the question of timing but later signed the Declaration of Independence.

Morris left Congress in 1778 but continued his commercial and political activities in Pennsylvania. In 1781, Congress asked him to head the newly created Department of Finance. As superintendent (1781-84), Morris devised an ambitious plan to reform the country's finances and strengthen the central government. Included in the program were a revenue system, a national bank, and a plan to fund the national debt. Despite success in making economies, improving administration, and raising loans, Morris only partially achieved his goals. However, his plans set a precedent for the Federalist financial program in the 1790s. Morris was a member of the Constitutional Convention of 1787 and strongly supported the new constitution. His later years were marred by unsuccessful land speculations.

Bibliography: Ver Steeg, Clarence L., *Robert Morris, Revolutionary Financier* (Univ. of Pennsylvania Press, 1954).

Douglas M. Arnold
The Papers of Benjamin Franklin

MORTON (MOURT), GEORGE (1585-1624)   A Pilgrim father, Morton was born into a Roman Catholic family not far from the Pilgrim community in Scrooby, Nottinghamshire. William Brewster converted him, and he soon joined the Scrooby group in Holland, where as a wealthy merchant he could help support the Pilgrims. When he negotiated with the London merchants in 1619, he changed his name to Mourt, perhaps to protect himself from his Catholic family.

In 1622, Mourt's name was on the preface of the account, *A Relation or Journall of the beginning and proceedings of the English Plantation setled at Plimoth in New England, by Certain English Adventurers both Merchants and Others.* The account may have been sent by William Bradford and seized by a French privateer, but it has come to be known as *Mourt's Relation.* It contains the Mayflower Compact and details on settling the colony. Morton himself arrived with his wife and four children and his sister-in-law, Alice Southworth, at Plymouth in 1623. Morton died in 1624, the same year that Alice married Bradford, who cared for his family's interests.

MORTON, JOHN (c.1724-77)   A signer of the Declaration of Independence, Morton was born in Ridley, Pennsylvania, of Swedish ancestry. He was elected to the provincial assembly in 1756 and served until 1767. In 1765 he was a member of the Stamp Act Congress in New York. He returned to the colonial legislature in 1769 but in 1770 was appointed as judge for cases involving blacks. In 1774 he became an associate justice of the Pennsylvania

George Washington's beloved home of Mount Vernon was built along the Potomac River about 1743. *(Library of Congress)*

supreme court. He was a delegate to the First and Second Continental Congresses (1774-77) and signed the Declaration of Independence. The chairman of the committee on the Articles of Confederation, Morton died before they were implemented.

MORTON, THOMAS (?1590-1647?)   Adventurer and rake, Morton may have been a lawyer and identified himself as "of Clifford's Inn, Gent." He visited America in 1622 and returned to settle at Quincy, Massachusetts, where he built his house called Merry Mount. His home was the center of riotous living, and in 1627 the Pilgrims cut down his Maypole, deeming it a symbol of sin. Moreover, he monopolized the fur trade and even sold guns to the Indians to obtain choice furs. In 1628 Captain Miles Standish seized him and sent him to England, but by 1630, Isaac Allerton had brought him back. John Endecott cut the Maypole down a second time. Morton

was arrested again and his property burned. He was sent to jail in England but was soon released.

In 1637 he published a diatribe against the Puritans called *New England Canaan*, but he would not keep away from the colony, and by 1643 he was in Plymouth. Ordered to leave, he went to Maine, Rhode Island, and Massachusetts, where he was promptly imprisoned for speaking against the colony in the Privy Council. After a year in the Boston jail his health was broken, and he died about two years later. His disregard for social mores inspired Nathaniel Hawthorne's short story "The Maypole of Merry-Mount."

MOULTRIE, WILLIAM (1730-1805)   A general during the Revolutionary War, Moultrie was born in Charleston, South Carolina, and was active in the military from his youth. George Washington recalled years later that Moultrie had been engaged in "considerable actions" against the Cherokee. An officer in the

French and Indian War, he was appointed colonel immediately upon the outbreak of the Revolution. In 1775 he raised the first flag on Fort Johnson. Later he commanded a palmetto fort on Sullivan's Island in Charleston Harbor, holding off the attack of Britain's Admiral Parker (1776). Also in 1776 he attained the rank of brigadier general. He was captured in 1780 at the fall of Charleston, exchanged in 1782, and promoted to major general later in the year. While a prisoner, he completed his memoirs. He was governor of South Carolina in 1786-88 and 1792-94.

MOUNT VERNON Located on the Potomac River in Fairfax County, Virginia, Mount Vernon was the home of George and Martha Washington from 1752. Built by George's half brother Lawrence about 1743 and named after Admiral Edward Vernon, the mansion was made of wood in the style common to Virginia planters. Shaped as a rectangle, a central hall divided the house into two rooms on each side, the second floor exactly as the first. Later a third story was added. Washington spent much of his youth at Mount Vernon before he finally inherited it from Lawrence, to whom he had always been particularly close. He and Martha are buried near the house.

MOUNT VERNON CONFERENCE (1785) Under the Articles of Confederation, Congress had little central authority. One of the most crucial problems was the inability of Congress to regulate commerce. It was up to the states individually to work out agreements. In March 1785, commissioners from Maryland and Virginia met at George Washington's home, Mount Vernon, to discuss navigation of the Potomac River. In a successful meeting, Maryland gained access to certain commercial activities in the Chesapeake, while Virginia received rights in the Potomac. James Madison was so impressed with the outcome of the conference that he initiated a movement to call delegates to Philadelphia to increase Congressional power.

MUHLENBERG, HENRY MELCHIOR (1711-87) Born in the duchy of Hanover in Germany, Muhlenberg studied theology at the pietistic University of Halle and was ordained to the Lutheran ministry in 1739. In 1741 he accepted a call to the United Congregations of Philadelphia, New Hanover, and Providence in Pennsylvania, arriving in Philadelphia on November 25, 1742. To combat voluntarism, a practice in which laymen dominated congregational affairs, Muhlenberg created the first Lutheran synod in America, the ministerium of Pennsylvania, in 1748. This body not only placed all participating ministers under its control but forbade lay interference in congregational matters. Gradually Muhlenberg extended his authority throughout Pennsylvania, New Jersey, and New York, replacing more conservative ministers in the latter two areas with his own recruits from Halle.

Theologically, Muhlenberg pursued a middle ground between the arid legalism of Lutheran orthodoxy and the excessive emotionalism of pietism. He insisted the revival practices be expressed within the liturgy and opposed George Whitefield and the Great Awakening as well as the pietistic Moravians. From the beginning Muhlenberg urged his fellow Germans to acculturate themselves to the American environment. For this reason he set up charity schools, supported by the Anglican Church, whose purpose was to teach German youngsters English language and culture, to the dismay of German sectarians. Muhlenberg supported the American Revolution, viewing it as God's punishment on England for misrule. Two of his sons were actively involved, Peter as a general with George Washington, Frederick as a member of the Continental Congress. Muhlenberg died in Providence in 1787 universally recognized as the patriarch of American Lutheranism.

Bibliography: Riforgiato, Leonard, *Missionary of Moderation: Henry Melchior Muhlenberg and the Lutheran Church in English America* (Bucknell Univ. Press, 1980).

Leonard R. Riforgiato
Pennsylvania State University

MULATTOES Throughout the Western Hemisphere, miscegenation between European colonists and African slaves produced thousands of children of mixed white and black ancestry. The Spanish term for these persons, "mulatto," obscurely drawn from the word for mule, and thus implying mixed parentage, entered the English language in the 17th century, at about the same time that England energetically entered the slave trade and embarked on its own history with blacks.

By the time of the Revolution, mulattoes constituted some 10 percent of the nonwhite population of the English colonies. Certainly the best known source for these persons of mixed race was the coercive sexual relations between masters and their female slaves, but while these relations were certainly responsible for shaping the troubled sexual dynamics between white and black in America, they were probably not the main source for the American mulatto population. That came, rather, from the sexual mixing of European servants and African slaves in the 17th century Chesapeake area, before the creation of racial castes had fully proscribed this form of intimacy.

Two distinctive patterns in regard to mulattoes emerged in the colonies. In the upper South, the ruling elite opposed miscegenation among the lower classes as a potential threat to their supremacy, and the mulattoes descended from those 17th-century unions were generally treated precisely as if they were blacks and nothing more. But in areas of the lower South, such as South Carolina and

Louisiana, where slavery was imported from the Caribbean with the very first settlers, where there was no large white servant class, and where masters found themselves in the racial minority, the mulatto population, slowly emerging out of the relations between masters and slave women, was useful as an intermediate element between white and black, free and slave. As a result both of their kinship ties to the master class, and their social usefulness, many more mulattoes became freemen in the lower than in the upper South. And while the degree of blackness counted for little in Virginia, in New Orleans and Charleston the many possible shades of distinction among mulattoes (half black), quadroons (quarter black), and octoroons (eighth black) became important determinants of social status.

See also Miscegenation; Mixedbloods (Mestizos, Métis). Bibliography: Reuter, Edward Byron, *The Mulatto in the United States; Including a Study of the Role of Mixed-Blood Races Throughout the World* (1918; reprint Johnson, 1970); Williamson, Joel, *New People: Miscegenation and Mulattoes in the United States* (Free Press, 1980).

John Mack Faragher
Mount Holyoke College

MURRAY, JOHN (1741-1815) A Universalist religious leader born in Alton, England, Murray was raised in a strict Calvinist home and settled with his family in Cork, Ireland, in 1751. After meeting John Wesley, he became deeply involved in religious work and later, while living in London, became an adherent of James Relly's doctrine of Universalism. In 1770, after the death of his wife and serious financial reverses, Murray emigrated to America and began to preach the ecumenical message of Universalism in New Jersey and New England, much to the displeasure of the various local religious authorities. In 1774, under the patronage of shipmaster Winthrop Sargent, he founded the first Universalist Society in America, in Gloucester, Massachusetts.

With the outbreak of the Revolution, he was appointed chaplain of the Rhode Island regiments by the troops. Opposition to his appointment by other chaplains in the Continental Army was personally overruled by George Washington. In 1779, Murray established the Independent Church of Christ in Gloucester, Massachusetts, and became its first minister. Continuing controversy forced him to defend his religious rights under the Massachusetts constitution. He was vindicated in 1788 and from 1793 served as pastor of the Universalist Society in Boston.

MURRAY, JOSEPH (1694-1757) A lawyer, he was born in Ireland and came to New York, where he practiced law from 1718. He specialized in real estate law and worked on

the city's boundary dispute with Harlem and on the long-term battle with Brooklyn over ferry rights. In 1754, when he became a commissioner, he worked on boundary disputes with Massachusetts and New Jersey. In 1754 he was a delegate to the Albany Congress, on the board of trustees of the New York Society Library, and a governor of King's College (now Columbia), to which he willed his extensive library. He was the author of *Opinion Relating to the Courts of Justice in the Colony of New York* (1734).

MURRAY, JUDITH SARGENT (1751-1820) One of the first American feminists, Murray was a Gloucester, Massachusetts, writer who publicly advocated women's equal education and equal opportunity for self-sufficiency. Her articles, published under the pseudonym "Constantia," first appeared in 1784 and during the 1790s, claiming that women were capable of much more than just "contemplating...the mechanism of a pudding, or the sewing of the seams of a garment." Young women, she said, should have enough self-respect not to rush into marriage too young or out of fear of spinsterhood. These essays were widely read by others interested in improving the condition of women and appeared in the three-volume *The Gleaner* in 1798.

Sargent made an unhappy marriage at 18 to sea captain John Stevens, who finally left her in 1786 to escape imprisonment for debt. After his death in the West Indies, she married John Murray, who had come to Gloucester in 1774 as pastor of the first Universalist Church in America. Land for the church had been donated by Winthrop Sargent, Judith's wealthy shipowner father.

MUSIC The most important musical tradition of early America was hymnody. The Puritans restricted church music to the singing of traditional psalms, such as those that appeared in the *Bay Psalm Book* (1640), the first book published in the English colonies. Texts without music, these psalms were "lined-out" by the minister and sung back by the congregation employing traditional folk melodies, with various singers ornamenting the tune, producing what many contemporaries likened to the braying of a collection of jackasses. Others have noted that this heterophony creates great musical tension and evokes powerful emotions. This tradition was part of the tendency toward congregational participation that characterized the Reformation and continued as a major component in the making of American folk music.

From the early 18th century critics of this style of singing sought to reform it, beginning with John Tufts's publication of the first singing book in America, *An Introduction to the Singing of Psalm Tunes* (1712) and with Cotton Mather's *Psalterium Americanum* (1718). About this time the English compilations of Isaac Watts became popular and continued to be very influential. Thomas Walker introduced the modern system of musical notation to America in *The Grounds and Rules of Music Explained* (1721). The first hymn book with musical notation, *A Collection of Psalms and Hymns* (1737) was edited by John Wesley during his missionary residence in the Southern colonies.

Nonchurch Music. Outside of the church, music as an art developed very slowly. German immigrants to Pennsylvania were responsible for the first musical organizations. In 1730, Johann Conrad Beissel founded Ephrata Cloister at Lancaster, Pennsylvania, the first center for musical education and publication. Moravians at Bethlehem, Pennsylvania, organized singing groups and a Collegium Musicum (1744-1820) that performed chamber music and symphonies of Haydn, Mozart, and others. In Charleston, South Carolina, the St. Cecilia Society (1769-1912) was the first musical society in America. In 1763 a music school opened in Philadelphia. By the time of the Revolution, musical societies and schools were present in nearly all the important cities and towns.

Influence of Billings. William Billings of Boston became the first American to make a profession of musical composition. Along with other 18th-century American composers, Billings was determined to reform and enliven American religious music, turning to early Bach for his models, and developing a counterpoint style, the "fuguing" tune that employed a kind of harmonic round. His publication of *The New England Psalm Singer* (1770) demonstrated the continuing importance of the religious tradition. During the Revolution he wrote patriotic hymns and anthems.

See also Bay Psalm Book.

Bibliography: Kingman, Daniel, *American Music: A Panorama* (Schirmer Books, 1979); Lomax, Alan, *The Folk Songs of North America* (Doubleday, 1960); McKay, David P. and Crawford, Richard, *William Billings of Boston* (Princeton Univ. Press, 1975).

N

NAIRNE, THOMAS (died 1715) An Indian agent, planter, and colonial legislator, Nairne was born in Scotland but emigrated to South Carolina at the end of the 17th century, becoming a plantation owner on St. Helena Island. Active in Indian affairs as early as 1702, he became the colony's first Indian agent in 1707 and sought to regulate the trade to and establish missions among the Yamassee. He was burned at the stake by that tribe.

NARVÁEZ, PÁNFILO DE (c.1478-1528) A Spanish soldier in the New World, Narváez helped Diego Velasquez pacify Cuba from 1515 to 1518 and was then sent by him to Mexico to arrest Hernando Cortes in 1520. Narváez lost an eye in the attempt and was imprisoned for two years by Cortes. In 1527, Narváez led a colonizing expedition into Florida in search of the mythical kingdom of Appalachee. While Narváez was exploring inland, the ships in his fleet sailed back, taking with them the women of the colonists. The stranded soldiers traveled west, trying to reach the Spanish settlement on the Rio Panuco in New Spain. Narváez drowned in Matagorda Bay, and only four survivors, among them Estevanico and Cabeza de Vaca, reached Mexico (1536).
See also Cabeza de Vaca, Alvar Nunez; Estevanico.

NASSAU, FORT(CASTLE ISLAND) A trading post established by Dutch sailors on Castle Island near Albany, Fort Nassau first appeared on a Dutch map of 1614, the legend of which describes it as being 36 feet long and 26 feet wide. It is probable that the post was established to provide a wintering place for Dutch fur traders. It is mentioned in several Dutch notarial documents from the city of Amsterdam and in the work of Johannes de Laet, a Dutch chronicler of the 17th century. Sketchy evidence suggests that it was abandoned in 1618 because river waters had washed it out.

NASSAU, FORT (DELAWARE RIVER) Established by the Dutch West India Company in 1623 in an expedition headed by Captain Cornelis Jacobsen May, Fort Nassau was shortly thereafter abandoned but was reoccupied in the summer of 1633 when a house was built and other improvements made. Deserted again in the winter of 1633-34, it was occupied by the English under the command of George Holmes in 1635. A Dutch vessel soon recaptured the fort and brought the English prisoners to New Amsterdam.

This last experience convinced the Dutch that they must either occupy the fort or lose it to others, and it is probable that a small garrison and a commissary were sent there in the spring of 1636. In June 1645, Governor Johan Printz of New Sweden challenged the Dutch presence at Fort Nassau, which at this time contained a garrison of about 20 West India Company soldiers. The Dutch were to remain at Fort Nassau, however, until Peter Stuyvesant ordered it abandoned in 1651 and the freemen and soldiers living there removed to Fort Casimir. In 1655 an expedition headed by Stuyvesant drove out the Swedes and annexed New Sweden to New Netherland.
See also New Netherland.

NATCHEZ In 1716, the Sieur de Bienville established Fort Rosalie on the site of present-day Natchez, in the heart of the country of the Natchez, the strongest Indian confederacy in the lower Mississippi River region. By the 1720s bad relations between the colonists and the Indians had turned violent; in the resulting Natchez Revolt the natives attacked and destroyed the fort, killing more than 200 colonists. Rebuilt, the fort continued as an important way station along the Mississippi between upper and lower Louisiana. Taken by the English in 1763, it was renamed Fort Panmure. It was captured by Spain in 1779 and surrendered to the United States in 1798. In the early 19th century Natchez became a commercial center as the southern end of the Natchez Trace, running from Nashville.
See also Natchez Revolt.

NATCHEZ REVOLT (1729-31) The conflict between the Natchez people of the southern Mississippi Valley and the French over control of territory and trade routes can be traced to the establishment of Fort Rosalie on the Mississippi by the French in 1714. The subsequent arrival of French settlers in the traditional area of Natchez and its annexation to the colony of Louisiana provoked sporadic hostilities in 1716 and again from 1722 to 1724.

Relations between the Natchez and the French further deteriorated with the appointment of a new commandant at Fort Rosalie. In 1729, with the support of the neighboring Chickasaw, the Natchez attacked and destroyed Fort Rosalie, killing more than 200 French settlers. In the following year the French and their Choctaw allies carried out retaliatory raids against Natchez villages, inflicting heavy losses and forcing the surviving Natchez to abandon their traditional territory and flee across the Mississippi. The French forces pursued them and resumed their attacks, decimating the remnants of the Natchez tribe and selling many into slavery in Santo Domingo. A few Natchez escaped the French to find shelter in Chickasaw territory farther up the Mississippi, but the power of the Natchez was destroyed forever.

NATCHEZ WAR (1729-31) The French settled in the Natchez (Mississippi) district early in the 18th century. The Natchez tribe of about 1,000 warriors at first had friendly relations with the French. Jean Baptiste Le Moyne, Sieur de Bienville, the governor of Louisiana, built Fort Rosalie at the site of what is now the city of Natchez. As French-Indian tensions increased, the French nearly conquered the Natchez (1723). The Natchez retaliated unsuccessfully (1728), but the next year they succeeded in killing over 200 Frenchmen and destroying Fort Rosalie. A war followed, and the French enlisted the Choctaw tribe and drove the Natchez from their villages. Most of them took refuge with the Chickasaw, Creek, and Cherokee tribes. In 1731, the last group of Natchez were defeated and more than 400 of them were sold into slavery in the West Indian trade.

NATCHITOCHES As part of a French offensive against Spanish influence in eastern Texas, Louis Juchereao de St. Denis founded in 1713 the French frontier post of Natchitoches on the Red River, from which point he opened a Red River route to Texas and eventually to Sante Fe. From Natchitoches the French expanded their influence into Texas, trading with the Indians. In response, the Spanish in 1721 founded Los Adaes, near the Sabine River, 45 miles from Natchitoches. This area, near the present-day boundary of Texas and Louisiana, became the frontier between French Louisiana and New Spain.

NAVAHO INDIANS Like their Athapaskan-speaking Apache cousins, the Navaho migrated to the Southwest from western Canada via the Great Plains from the 10th to the 16th centuries, establishing themselves in the high plateau of what is now called Four Corners country. They were not a unified tribe but rather a series of matrilineally connected kinship bands, each with its own leadership. They practiced small-scale farming, hunting and gathering, and, in the postcontact period, much raiding of neighboring sedentary Indians and Spanish communities for goods, especially horses and sheep.

The Franciscans failed in their attempts to acculturate the Navaho through their missions in the 18th century, but the Navaho proved to be great imitators of the culture of their neighbors. From the Pueblo they took agrarian tech-

niques, as well as practices such as sand painting and blanket weaving; from the Spanish they adopted the care of livestock. By the 18th century many Navahos were living as pastoralists, and Navaho rugs had already begun to make the people's artistic reputation.

NAVAL STORES ACT (1705) Passed by Parliament during the era of the Navigation Acts, the Naval Stores Act was designed to protect raw materials obtained from the North American colonies for marine industries. Under the act, which expired in 1713, naval stores could only be sent to Britain or its colonies. Britain started to pay bounties on pitch, turpentine, hemp, ship spars, and similar articles. Britain's maritime interests were later safeguarded by legislation (1727) to limit severely the cutting of white pines, which were extensively used in ship building.

See also Navigation Acts.

NAVAL STORES INDUSTRY Broadly encompassing tar, pitch, turpentine, resin, hemp, and lumber (masts, yardarms, and bowsprits), the naval stores industry emerged as a profitable enterprise in the New England and Southern colonies. Needing such commodities for its extensive navy and merchant marine corps and then dependent upon expensive Scandinavian and Russian products, Parliament in 1705 placed a bounty on the manufacture of colonial naval stores to encourage their production. As a result of this bounty, naval stores production soared in South Carolina but then succumbed to the ascendancy of rice, leaving North Carolina to become England's leading supplier of naval stores by the eve of the Revolution.

Naval stores production not only profited the wealthy but also offered the small farmer a marketable product that might be pursued when crops did not demand attention. Using slave labor and crude techniques, colonials generally sacrificed quality to quantity. Despite provincial inspection systems to improve the quality of exports, English merchants constantly complained that American tar and pitch were inferior to European products.

See also Manufacturing and Industry.

Bibliography: Gray, Lewis Cecil, *History of Agriculture in the Southern United States to 1860*, 2 vols. (Carnegie Foundation, 1933).

NECESSITY, FORT As a part of the English attempt to drive the French from the Ohio River Valley, in the spring of 1754 George Washington, leading a company of Virginia militia, was sent by Governor Robert Dinwiddie to attack Fort Duquesne. At Great Meadows, on the Monongahela River, some 50 miles from Duquesne, Washington met and defeated a small advance party of French on May 28, then with his men forted up in a crude log breastwork they called Fort Necessity. Here they were attacked by a large number of French and Indians, who defeated the Virginians on July 3. Washington was forced to sign a capitulation and retreated back to Virginia. These battles were the first of the French and Indian War.

See also Dinwiddie, Robert; French and Indian War; Washington, George.

NEEDHAM, JAMES (died 1673)   An English explorer, Needham came to South Carolina from Barbados in 1670 and became a planter. In 1673, outfitted by Abraham Wood, and accompanied by Gabriel Arthur, he headed the expedition that first opened direct trade with the interior Cherokee, who welcomed the English because the Spanish, their former trading partners, had attacked a band of their kinsmen and enslaved some of them the year before. Leaving Arthur behind, Needham went back to Ft. Henry, Virginia. On his subsequent return to the interior he was murdered by a party of Occaneechi Indians.

NEGRO PLOT OF 1741   In 1740 a wave of arson began in New Jersey and then swept into New York. A white servant girl implicated in some of the crimes told tales of a slave conspiracy to burn the city to the ground and kill all its white inhabitants. Paranoia seized the citizenry, and many slaves were arbitrarily arrested and threatened with torture unless they disclosed the details of the conspiracy. By the time the scare abated a year later, over 100 slaves had been thrown into jail; 30 had been tortured, hanged, or burned at the stake; and 70 had been transported to the West Indies. Many of the fears of slave uprisings usually associated with the plantation societies of the South flourished in urban settings as well.

NELSON, THOMAS, JR. (1738-89)   A Revolutionary War general, Nelson was a Virginian to his core although he was educated at Cambridge University. He began his career in the House of Burgesses in 1761. In 1775 he served in the Second Continental Congress and signed the Declaration of Independence. He left the Congress in 1777 to return to Virginia and lead the state's troops throughout the remainder of the Revolutionary War. During that time he was appointed general and fought with the Marquis de Lafayette. In 1779, Nelson was elected once again to the Continental Congress, soon resigned because of poor health, and returned to Virginia where he served in the state legislature, and as governor (1781). He became impoverished by paying public debts with his own money.

NEOCLASSICISM   A style of art and architecture based on a return to antiquity, neoclassicism became popular after the discovery and excavation of the ancient cities of Herculaneum and Pompeii in the mid-18th century. The style swept north, finding fertile ground in Napoleon's France, and eventually crossed the Atlantic to America. Benjamin West was its most famous American proponent in the art world, and his painting "Agrippina with the Ashes of Germanicus" is a fine example of the style.

It was in architecture, however, that the influence of neoclassicism was most strongly felt in America for over 100 years. Many American architects identified with the straightforward, sturdy qualities of the ancient Roman republic of Cato and Cincinnatus. Specific design features include columned porches, found especially in the South. Among the prominent examples of neoclassical architecture are the capitol buildings of Virginia (designed by Thomas Jefferson, who used a neoclassical design for Monticello) and Massachusetts (designed by Charles Bulfinch). The most famous neoclassical structure is the Capitol in Washington (designed by Bulfinch, Thornton, Hallet, and Latrobe).

NEOLIN (THE DELAWARE PROPHET)   (?1725-75?)   A religious leader and visionary of the Delaware nation, whose name means "the enlightened one," Neolin was born in the eastern Great Lakes region and came to prominence at the time of Pontiac's attempted unification of the Indians of that area during the French and Indian War. Few details of his life are known with certainty, but its central event was apparently a mystical journey to heaven and a meeting with the "Master of Life." In that encounter, Neolin received a code of divinely inspired laws and returned to the world of the living to preach them among the Delaware.

The core of his teaching was that the white settlers had brought evil influences to the country and had destroyed the Indian's traditional, moral way of life. Neolin therefore urged his people to avoid all contact with the settlers, return to their traditional ways, and prepare for an eventual holy war against the European colonists. This teaching gained many enthusiastic converts, among them Pontiac, who utilized Neolin's doctrine to organize a coordinated attack on British forts in 1763. After the defeat of Pontiac, however, Neolin faded into obscurity.

See also Pontiac's Rebellion.

NEWBURGH ADDRESSES (1783)   With the fighting of the Revolution coming to an end, and their pay months in arrears, a group of army officers in Newburgh, New York, were on the verge of staging a coup. Two unsigned addresses written in March 1783 by Major John Armstrong, Jr., who was then serving under General Gates, extolled the patriotism of the officers and deplored their treatment by Congress. George Washington, who sympathized with the financial hardships of the officers, was nevertheless determined to prevent any action against Congress. Washington appealed to the officers' honor, but what most convinced them to disavow the addresses was the example of Washington himself.

NEW CAESAREA   The original name of the colony of New Jersey as it appeared on the 1664 charter granted to John Berkeley and Sir George Carteret, "New Caesarea" was chosen to commemorate Carteret's heroic defense of the island of Jersey in the English Channel in 1649. It was believed at the time that the name "Jersey" was itself a corruption of the name "Czar's Eye" or "Caesar's Isle." Much of the territory of the new colony had been controlled by the Dutch West India Company until the British conquest of New Amsterdam in 1664. Toward the end of the 17th century, Berkeley and Carteret sold much of their lands to the Quakers, but in 1701 control of the New Jersey colony reverted to the Crown.

NEW CASTLE   A settlement in Delaware first named Fort Casimir, New Castle was founded by the Dutch in 1651 to counteract the influence of Swedish Fort Christina. Dutch presence in the area sparked hostilities, and in 1654 the garrison at Fort Casimir surrendered to Johan Rising, governor of New Sweden. Under the Swedish, it was renamed Fort Trefaldighet but was recaptured and renamed New Anstel by the Dutch in the 1655 military expedition of Peter Stuyvesant to the Delaware Valley. In 1664 it was taken over by the English and renamed yet again, this time New Castle. Purchased by William Penn from the Duke of York in 1683, it became the capital of Delaware (1775-77) until a British invasion forced the patriots to move the capital to Dover.

NEW ENGLAND COMPANY   A commercial corporation, legal successor to the Dorchester Company, the New England Company was granted the right to colonize the area around Massachusetts Bay. In 1628, following an unsuccessful attempt to establish a plantation at Dorchester, a group of English Puritans received a patent from the Council for New England for the land between the Merrimack and Charles rivers. Led by John White of Dorsetshire, the first settlers established themselves at Naumkeag, later known as Salem. In 1629, with the issuance of a royal patent to the Massachusetts Bay Company and the appointment of John Endecott as governor, the New England Company was formally dissolved.
See also Massachusetts.

NEW ENGLAND CONFEDERATION (UNITED COLONIES) (1643)   With the growing need for unification of the colonies, the New England Confederation was formed by Massachusetts, Plymouth, Connecticut, and New Haven to provide defense (in the wake of the Pequot War) as well as to assist the spread of a common religion and the handling of common problems. Its governing board consisted of eight commissioners, two from each colony. Six votes were needed to pass legislation. It met annually, sometimes more often, and acted as a court when there were conflicts between colonies. Each colony, in proportion to size of male population, bore the expense of war, which seemed unfair to the largest colony, Massachusetts. Nonetheless, the confederation formally existed until 1684.

NEW ENGLAND PRIMER   This fundamental textbook for teaching young New England colonists to read and write was first published in 1690 by Benjamin Harris. Harris had also published the first (and quickly suppressed) newspaper in the colonies, *Public Occurences Both Forreign and Domestick*. For 50 years, the New England Primer was the only grammar school textbook used in the region, and it was still in use in the mid-19th century. It sold well over 5,000,000 copies in that time. A combination of alphabet rhymes and a syllabary, the primer extolled a Calvinistic piety with religious and moral injunctions. Every edition contained the Lord's Prayer, the Shorter Catechism, and the Apostles' Creed. The book was illustrated with crude yet eloquent woodcut prints. The child's prayer "Now I lay me down to sleep ..." first appeared in this seminal American text.

NEW ENGLAND RESTRAINING ACT (1775)   Enacted by Parliament in response to the First Continental Congress (and in particular to the economic boycott it established in the Continental Association), the Restraining Act of March 30 prohibited New Englanders from trading anywhere except with Britain, its West Indies, and Ireland and excluded them from the North Atlantic fisheries. In April, Parliament extended the trade provisions of the act to five other American colonies. The prohibitions were to remain in effect until "peace and obedience" were restored in the colonies and commerce with Britain was resumed. Instead, the Americans moved to further acts of resistance and rebellion.

NEWFOUNDLAND   Claimed by both France and England, this large island guarding the northern approach to the Gulf of the St. Lawrence was ceded to Britain in 1713 and became a separate colony. In the 18th century it was settled by English Anglicans and Irish Catholics who practiced a fishing economy. In 1763 the colony assumed jurisdiction over Labrador, although that territory remained under the effective administration of the Hudson's Bay Company until the 1870s.

NEW FRANCE   *See* **French Colonies.**

NEW FRANCE, COMPANY OF *See* **Hundred Associates, Company of a.**

NEWGATE PRISON Connecticut's first state prison, located in Simsbury (now East Granby), Newgate Prison was a failed copper mine taken over by the state in 1773 to house criminals and to employ them in the operation of the mine. The mine failed for the state, but the Revolutionary War had increased the need for prison quarters in the colonies. In 1775, a contingent of British Loyalists was delivered to Newgate on the orders of General George Washington, thus making Newgate the first national prison. Tories and other political dissidents were kept, along with petty and hardened criminals, in the mine's caverns, 50-70 feet below ground. In spite of the subterranean location of the cells, attempts at escape were numerous and often successful.

Bibliography: Phelps, Richard H., *A History of Newgate of Connecticut* (Arno, 1969).

NEW HAMPSHIRE In both area and population, New Hampshire was one of the smallest English colonies along the Atlantic coast. Its land area of 9,304 square miles lacks a coastal plain; its small rivers and streams are generally unnavigable, although numerous rapids and falls provided freshwater fishing opportunities and power sufficient for colonial sawmills and gristmills. New Hampshire's uneven terrain was covered by a mixture of hardwood and softwood trees in the 17th century, insuring that timber products would be a staple of the colonial economy. Of particular interest to English authorities were stands of white pine throughout the region. The tallest of these were ideally suited for ship masts, which in turn helped to reduce English dependence on the Baltic states for naval stores.

Indian Culture. The land that would become New Hampshire has been inhabited for approximately 10,000 years. At the time of European contact and settlement, small tribes of the Algonquian language group maintained regular seasonal villages in the coastal region and along the valleys of the Merrimack, Connecticut, and Saco rivers. New Hampshire's tribal groups spent much of each year at central villages, planting and harvesting crops. They raised no domestic livestock. Instead, they sent out hunting parties and migrated seasonally to the best fishing spots. Following, and probably as a result of contact with Europeans in the first decade of the 17th century, Indians in New Hampshire's coastal region either died of disease or migrated inland. Thereafter, the largest tribal group living in the colony was known as the Penacook, whose central village of the same name was located along the Merrimack River at present-day Concord. Until the 1680s, the Penacook chose to remain at peace with English authorities in New Hampshire and Massachusetts.

Early Settlement. Throughout the 16th century, French and English expeditions skirted the coastline of New England and its rich offshore fishing grounds. Fishermen based on Newfoundland at the turn of the 17th century may have been the first Europeans to set foot on New Hampshire soil. In 1604, English merchants financed an expedition led by Martin Pring that sailed up the Piscataqua River. The failure of the Sagadahoc colony in Maine in 1607, however, dampened the spirits of English investors until 1620, when a group of merchants from England's western ports was chartered as the Council for New England.

In theory, the council had the right to settle and exploit resources along America's Atlantic coast from the 40th to the 48th parallel, between present Philadelphia and central Newfoundland. The council's most active members, Sir Ferdinando Gorges and Captain John Mason, were primarily interested in lands north of the mouth of the Merrimack River and over the next 15 years gave themselves and other council members much of this land in a series of vague and conflicting grants. In 1622, for instance, they awarded themselves all of the land between the Merrimack and Kennebec rivers, extending inland to the "furthest heads of the rivers," although no one at the time knew where the "furthest heads" were located.

In spite of geographic uncertainty, council members followed up the 1622 grant by sending a small party, led by David Thomson, to the mouth of the Piscataqua River in 1623. Thomson's people built a substantial stone building at Odiorne's Point, in present Rye. Thomson called his "plantation" Pannaway, and although regarded as the first English settlement in New Hampshire, it was a disappointment to Thomson, who left after four years.

In 1629, Captain John Mason was awarded all of the lands between the Merrimack and Piscataqua Rivers, which he named New Hampshire. In the remaining six years of his life, he sponsored a number of ventures in this rather poorly-defined grant. Under the terms of a council charter to Mason, authorizing him to establish the "Laconia Company," employees were sent to New Hampshire to initiate fur trade with the Indians and set up a sawmill. Laconia Company employees not only mixed with remnants of Thomson's group, but they joined with refugees and settlers from Massachusetts Bay to found four towns in the New Hampshire seacoast area.

By 1640, the four towns of Strawbery Banke (later Portsmouth), Dover, Exeter, and Hampton existed as independent units; there was no provincial authority. Whereas Strawbery Banke, which included Thomson's Pannaway, originated directly from the efforts of Mason and Gorges, the town of Dover was a confusing blend of Laconia Company employees and Puritan settlers from Massachusetts. Exeter was founded in 1638 by minister John Wheelwright and his Antinomian followers in the wake of their expulsion from Massachusetts. Finally, that same year, authorities in Boston extended their northern boundary, located three miles north of the Merrimack River, by authorizing Stephen Batchellor and his followers to settle the town of Hampton.

During the 1640s, New Hampshire's four towns not only lacked central authority, but civil war in England virtually assured that they would receive no direction from London. In order to protect land titles and maintain civil order, majorities within all four towns eventually agreed to become a part of Norfolk County, Massachusetts. The political stability brought about by this arrangement resulted in economic growth for the four towns. The small rivers leading into the Great Bay powered dozens of sawmills. Portsmouth, Dover, and Exeter exported timber products, sometimes in locally-made ships, and in time, farm families began to derive income from trade, shipbuilding, logging, and a host of specialized urban trades.

Proprietary Colony. New Hampshire might have remained a part of Massachusetts had not political and legal affairs in London intervened. Events were precipitated by Robert Tufton Mason, grandson of Captain John Mason, who claimed his grandfather's proprietary rights to New Hampshire. Officials in London, angered by the Bay Colony's apparent disregard for their authority, accepted Mason's claims and declared New Hampshire a proprietorship in 1679. While New Hampshire leaders grudgingly accepted their independence from Massachusetts, they denied Mason's proprietary claim.

For the next 20 years, New Hampshire suffered social and political turmoil. Provincial leadership was divided between proprietary interests, who sought to capitalize on John Mason's original claim, and local landowners, who feared losing title to their farms. The chaotic political situation was compounded by the outbreak of Indian hostilities during King William's and Queen Anne's wars. Although New Hampshire's Penacook had remained neutral throughout King Philip's War, the loss of fishing rights and other grievances led them to ally with the Abenaki in Maine in the mid-1680s. In the summer of 1689, Indians from "the eastern parts" attacked frontier settlements. New Hampshire villages, particularly the mill villages in Dover, were unprepared and vulnerable. By the end of King William's War in 1696, approximately 300 settlers—roughly one-tenth of New Hampshire's population—had been killed in raids, with another 100 taken captive.

Unable to govern or defend itself, New Hampshire turned to Boston and London for relief. Some in New Hampshire sought re-annexation, and their arguments were bolstered when Massachusetts sent militia units to defend New Hampshire settlements. Authorities in London, however, sought a compromise. New Hampshire would remain a separate province, but would share a governor with Massachusetts. The first joint governor, the Earl of Bellmont, visited New Hampshire briefly in the summer of 1699, and immediately took a dim view of the Masonian claims. In 1708, during the joint governorship of Joseph Dudley, British courts upheld a provincial court ruling in favor of local residents, effectively ending proprietary claims to New Hampshire.

18th Century Growth. Having attained distinct political identity, New Hampshire entered the 18th century facing two new problems: the question of provincial boundaries and the more troubling dilemma of political, social, and economic cohesion. The boundary question emerged following the Peace of Utrecht in 1713. Investors in Boston, and to a lesser degree Portsmouth, sought to control the rich timberlands of Maine and central New Hampshire. Boston interests interpreted their boundaries in a manner that would have virtually confined New Hampshire to coastal regions. New Hampshire authorities, on the other hand, assumed their southern boundary with Massachusetts ran in an east-west direction until encountering New York—an interpretation that would have included most of present Vermont. As settlers from Massachusetts, coastal New Hampshire, and Ulster began moving into the Merrimack Valley, the boundary question came to a head. Between 1720 and 1740, both sides used legal and illegal tactics to support their claims to the valley and lands to the west. In 1740, authorities in London finally ruled in favor of New Hampshire and supplemented their decision by appointing a separate royal governor to sit in Portsmouth.

New Hampshire's victory in 1740 was due in large part to the efforts of the Wentworth family. Lieutenant Governor John Wentworth had championed New Hampshire's cause in the 1720s; his son Benning became governor in 1741. During the boundary controversy, New Hampshire settlement had pushed beyond its original four towns, extending westward almost to the Merrimack River. By 1741, New Hampshire boasted close to 25,000 residents—better than double the numbers of a decade earlier. In spite of the growth of central farm towns, the older seacoast towns dominated the colony's social, economic, and political life during Benning Wentworth's long reign. He used a combination of local patronage, imperial diplomacy and flattery, and economic manipulation to survive in office longer than any other colonial governor in America. By the time he was finally forced to resign in 1767, the Wentworth "clan" had become a virtual hereditary dynasty, and no one was surprised when his nephew succeeded him as governor.

Benning Wentworth not only led New Hampshire through two major Indian wars, but following the Treaty of Paris in 1763, he encouraged provincial expansion on a grand scale. He granted approximately 200 townships in western and northern New Hampshire, as well as the "New Hampshire Grants" in Vermont. In the 1760s alone, New Hampshire's population jumped from approximately 39,000 to 62,000. Despite the growth of Merrimack and Connecticut valley towns, Wentworth resisted pressure to create counties and give adequate representation to farm towns in the interior.

Benning Wentworth's legacy fell to his talented nephew John Wentworth. Realizing that the coastal towns were becoming increasingly unrepresentative and removed from the rest of the province, the young governor encouraged the creation of counties in 1771, promoted road construction, and granted a charter to Dartmouth College in the Connecticut Valley town of Hanover in 1769. Yet, John Wentworth never had his uncle's political contacts in London, nor did he ever gain effective political control over newer interior farm towns. This left him vulnerable when Revolutionary events swept into New Hampshire.

Revolutionary War Period. New Hampshire's relative political stability in the 1760s resulted in a reluctance to become associated with Revolutionary leaders in Virginia and Massachusetts. Resistance to the Stamp Act and Townshend duties had been mild in New Hampshire, partially because local leaders realized that the Wentworths were personally opposed to British policy. Events in Massachusetts, however, forced John Wentworth to take sides. New Hampshire communities were already sympathetic to Boston in the wake of the Coercive Acts. When John Wentworth agreed in 1774 to help General Gage build barracks for British troops stationed in Boston, New Hampshire leaders were incensed. In December 1774, mobs assaulted Fort William and Mary at Newcastle, carrying away powder and guns. Through all of this, John Wentworth tried repeatedly in vain to secure the election of a sympathetic assembly. In March 1775, he went so far as to add three seats to the assembly, but the assembly refused to seat the new members, one of whom was later dragged from Wentworth's house at gunpoint and thrown into the Exeter jail. Following this incident, Wentworth and his family fled to Fort William and Mary. In the summer of 1775, Wentworth sailed for Boston in a British warship, and royal government was ended.

Ironically, New Hampshire, a province that had been slow to enter Revolutionary politics, became one of the first American colonies to take up arms against British troops, and the very first to organize a formal state government. Upon hearing about the Battle of Lexington and Concord in April 1775, New Hampshire militia rushed to Boston.

There, under the leadership of John Stark, they fought at Bunker Hill. Meanwhile, the sudden collapse of royal government forced New Hampshire leaders into drastic political action. A provincial congress, meeting in Exeter, wrote to the Continental Congress in Philadelphia, asking for guidance. John Adams urged New Hampshire to do what no other province had yet done—draft a state constitution. Out of necessity, New Hampshire adopted a "Form of Government" on January 5, 1776. Although seen as a temporary measure, the "Form" served as New Hampshire's state constitution until the adoption of the present state constitution in 1784. This version was adopted after Vermont had agreed to dissolve its union with 34 New Hampshire towns along the Connecticut River.

During the Revolutionary War, New Hampshire raised three regiments for the Continental Army, and New Hampshire troops played a key role at the Battle of Bennington (1777) in Vermont. Its many privateers, sailing from Portsmouth to raid British shipping, were the state's most significant contribution to the war effort. After the war, opposition in New Hampshire to the federal Constitution delayed ratification until June 21, 1788, when New Hampshire became the ninth state to ratify.

See also Council for New England; Gorges, Sir Ferdinando; Massachusetts; Privateering; Wentworth, John.

Bibliography: Daniell, Jere R., *Colonial New Hampshire: A History* (KTO Press, 1981); Clark, Charles E., *The Eastern Frontier: The Settlement of Northern New England, 1610-1763* (Knopf, 1970); Upton, Richard F., *Revolutionary New Hampshire* (Dartmouth College Press, 1936); Daniell, Jere R., *Experiment in Republicanism: New Hampshire Politics and the American Revolution, 1741-1794* (Harvard Univ. Press, 1970); Van Deventer, David E., *The Emergence of Provincial New Hampshire, 1623-1741* (Johns Hopkins Univ. Press, 1976).

R. Stuart Wallace
Director, New Hampshire Division of
Historical Resources

NEW HAVEN COLONY A group of Londoners, along with recruits from Massachusetts and Connecticut, under the leadership of John Davenport and Theophilus Eaton, planted the New Haven Colony in 1637 on the site of the Indian village of Quinnipiac on Long Island Sound. Lacking a royal charter, the land was purchased from the Indians, and the colony gradually expanded to include the towns of Stamford, Branford, Guilford, and Milford on the north shore, along with Southhold across Long Island Sound on Long Island.

The official government established in 1643 was based on a theocratic model stricter than that of Massachusetts or Connecticut; not only were political privileges limited to members of the Congregational church but because the

Bible did not mention trial by jury, for example, the magistrates ruled without this English institution. In 1662 the royal charter of Connecticut included New Haven. Its proprietors resisted this absorption, but after the conquest of New Amsterdam by the Duke of York they concluded that their future would be better secured under Connecticut rule, and the colony voluntarily joined Connecticut, dissolving its separate identity, in 1664.

NEW JERSEY New Jersey was a small colony with a complex history. It covered 7,500 square miles from the Hudson River and Atlantic Ocean on the east to the Delaware River on the west. Geographically this region is divided into three diagonal bands that include a sandy coastal plain in the east with pine barrens in the southern section, then a piedmont, and finally highlands in the northwest. The land was occupied by the Lenni-Lenape (Delaware) Indians. There were 2,000- 3,000 members of this Algonquin tribe engaged in hunting and fishing when whites arrived. Conflict with the natives was acute in the 1640s and 1650s, but in the years that followed few Indians remained in the colony and relations between them and the later English settlers were more harmonious.

The first white settlers came from Holland and Sweden. In the north the Dutch moved across the Hudson from New Netherland, while in the south the Swedes crossed the Delaware from New Sweden. In 1655 the Dutch forced the Swedes to submit to their authority. Neither ethnic group arrived in large numbers; in 1664 there were an estimated 200 Dutch and 100 Swedes in the area, as well as an undetermined number of other white settlers, mostly Englishmen who came from New England.

In 1664, because of commercial rivalry with the Dutch, the English government sent a royal commission backed by troops to conquer New Netherland. Charles II then issued a grant, which included parts of present New York, New Jersey, Nantucket, and Maine, to his brother James, Duke of York. James quickly deeded the lower portion, the "most improveable" part, to Lord John Berkeley and Sir George Carteret, two loyal supporters and friends.

Berkeley and Carteret, also proprietors of Carolina, hoped to make a profit from their venture. With this in mind, they issued Concessions and Agreement in January 1665 to attract settlers from New England, offering representative government and liberty of conscience. But neither profits nor peace followed, and the history of proprietary New Jersey was marred by conflict, confusion, and turmoil. In 1672 the Dutch reconquered the region; it was returned to England in 1674. In the meantime Berkeley, who never exerted himself to settle the region, sold his half to two Quakers, John Fenwick and George Billing. In 1676 the colony was divided into an East and a

West, a step that had an important impact on its subsequent history.

West Jersey. Fenwick and Billing wanted to establish a haven for English Quakers persecuted under the laws for religious conformity. In this they were successful; West Jersey acquired a substantial Quaker population that dominated the section in the early period. The proprietors' fortunes were another matter, and relations between the two were bitter. A dispute over how much each had purchased was submitted to a group of Quaker arbitrators, including William Penn, who divided the province into 100 shares and decided that Fenwick was entitled to 10, Billing to 90. Billing sold most of his shares, often in fractional amounts, so there soon were more than 100 shareholders. In 1688 the Council of Proprietors of West Jersey was formed by resident proprietors to deal with land matters. This corporation has survived to the present.

In the meantime Fenwick proceeded to the colony, where he established the town of Salem and tried to exercise the powers of governor. His political pretensions were disputed by both Billing and the governor of New York. In 1683 title to the government of West Jersey, divorced from the land rights that remained with the shareholders, was assigned to Billing by the Duke of York. In 1687 the title was purchased by Dr. Daniel Coxe, an English physician and speculator, who sold it in 1693 to the West Jersey Society, a corporation formed to speculate in shares of West Jersey and East Jersey as well as Pennsylvania lands. In 1702 the West Jersey Society surrendered its political rights to the Crown.

East Jersey. Unlike Berkeley, George Carteret in East Jersey tried to settle the lands. In 1665 he sent his nephew Philip Carteret and a group of colonists to the province. Already present were Dutch and New England settlers, some of whom had obtained land titles from Richard Nicolls, the governor of New York. These residents, particularly in Elizabethtown, disputed proprietary claims to the land and quitrents through the colonial period and beyond. This, plus disagreements about the governor's political powers, resulted in brief revolts in 1672 and 1681. Challenges to Carteret's authority were also raised by the governor of New York.

In 1682, George Carteret's widow sold East Jersey to a consortium consisting mostly of Quakers from England, Ireland, and Scotland. The 12 original investors divided their portions in half, resulting in 24 shares that, as in West Jersey, were sold in fractional amounts. In 1685 the Board of Proprietors of East Jersey was formed to distribute land due on the shares. It also still exists today. In settling the land, the Scottish proprietors took the lead. As a result, several hundred Scots moved to the colony where they

Small farms were the most common land division in colonial New Jersey. *(Library of Congress)*

were significantly present in politics and on the proprietary board. These East Jersey proprietors assumed that they had purchased the right of government along with the land, but questions about this persisted through the colonial period. In 1702 they, too, surrendered their governmental claims to the Crown.

Development of the Royal Colony. In New Jersey, proprietors' political pretensions fell victim to efforts to centralize the empire. In 1688 both East and West Jersey had been incorporated into the Dominion of New England. After the Glorious Revolution both sections were returned to their respective proprietors, but questions about their rights to exercise the powers of government continued. There also remained questions about land titles, quitrents, and the right to establish ports. This resulted in a great deal of disorder by the end of the 1690s, including rioting and jail breaks. In 1702 the two sections were united and placed under the authority of the governor of New York, although with a separate legislature. It was hoped peace and order would follow.

By the time the Crown took over East and West Jersey the colony had taken on distinctive characteristics. The province had a diverse population, mixed in terms of ethnicity and religion. There were Dutch, Swedes, English, Scotch, Irish, and German settlers. Quakers predominated in the west, Anglicans in the east, and Presbyterians in the central section. Although there were more instances of large landholdings in the east than in the west, the colony as a whole was primarily middle-class and overwhelmingly rural. In 1748, Governor Belcher described it as "the best country I have seen for middling fortunes, and for people who have to live by the sweat of their brows." One of the "bread colonies," New Jersey farmers produced livestock and grains. In the 18th century iron became the only industry of significance.

East-West Struggles. Government under the Crown was not much more peaceful than it had been under the proprietors. During the period up to 1738, most royal governors were more interested in New York than in New Jersey. Moreover, the governors—particularly the first, the notorious Lord Cornbury—were concerned with lining their own pockets. Political divisions in the colony were complicated by the persistence of an east-west division (the legislature alternated its meetings between Perth Amboy and Burlington), by religious differences, and by conflicts between resident proprietors and those who remained in

England. In addition, as in other colonies, the legislature continually tried to wrest additional powers, particularly over financial affairs, from the governors. In 1738, in an attempt to smooth affairs, the Crown appointed the first separate governor of the colony. The choice, Lewis Morris, a New York and New Jersey landowner and politician, did not help, for by then he was an irascible old man who fought with the colonists even more than had previous governors.

Important issues in the 18th century were the amount of paper money issued by the colonial government to help finance its share of colonial wars (and used to avoid taxes), land titles, and boundaries. The old question of proprietary titles raised its head again in East Jersey, leading to riots in the 1740s and 1750s. Also important were two particular boundary disputes because both brought land titles into question. The first was the location of the boundary between the eastern and western divisions of the colony. Several attempts were made to run a line and one, by the East Jersey proprietors in 1743, eventually became the de facto division line. The second involved the northern boundary with New York. This was resolved in 1774, after much bitterness, by resorting to a royal commission. The protracted disputes made land titles uncertain, served to discourage immigration, and kept down the population of the colony.

Statehood and War. In 1763, William Franklin, son of Benjamin Franklin, was appointed governor. He was a politically astute man who served the Crown well in trying times. New Jersey dragged its heels on the Revolution because it was a rural, provincial colony, where the robbery of the treasury assumed greater significance than did imperial regulations. But Franklin was also an important factor; he succeeded in keeping the lid on revolutionary sentiment longer than any other royal appointee (only to end up imprisoned in Connecticut). In the end the colony followed the lead of its neighbors, New York and Pennsylvania, and joined in the "common cause." It sent representatives to the Stamp Act Congress and both Continental Congresses, elected members of a provincial congress that gradually superseded the royal government, and voted for independence. In July 1776 the state hastily wrote a constitution that was conservative and even included a statement making it "void" if the dispute with the Crown were resolved.

New Jersey has been called the "cockpit" of the Revolution. For much of the war, armies marched back and forth through its territory. Washington fought several important battles in the state (Trenton, Princeton, and Monmouth) and camped the Continental Army within its borders during three cold winters. By the time the war was over the state had suffered economic disruption, extensive destruction of both public and private property, and the effects in several areas of bitter civil war. William Livingston, governor from 1776 until his death in 1790, was an able leader handicapped by a constitution that provided for a weak governor.

Postwar Politics. During the Confederation period the most important issue facing New Jersey politicians was the question of returning to paper money, a measure pushed by debtors and opposed by conservative property owners. In 1786 the legislature passed a law providing for a new issue of paper money. Also important were the boundary line between East and West and relations with the central government under the Articles of Confederation.

From the outset, New Jersey favored a stronger central government that could control western lands and tax all states uniformly. Because under the Articles of Confederation the government could do neither, New Jersey residents felt they were under a disadvantage. The legislature pushed the issue when it refused to meet its requisitions from the national government in 1785. It was quick to appoint delegates to the Annapolis Convention (1786) and then to the Constitutional Convention in Philadelphia (1787). The state's delegates, led by William Paterson, were concerned that small states be protected under the Constitution and proposed the New Jersey Plan to do so. Once this issue was resolved by the Connecticut Compromise they supported the new document. The state was third to ratify the Constitution and did so unanimously in December 1787, putting aside the divisions that usually characterized its politics. Livingston, Paterson, and other politicians looked forward to the new government with a great deal of hope and optimism.

See also Concessions and Agreement; Franklin, William; New Netherland; Revolutionary War Battles.

Bibliography: Craven, Wesley Frank, *New Jersey and the English Colonization of North America* (Van Nostrand, 1964); Gerlach, Larry R., *Prologue to Independence: New Jersey and the Coming of the American Revolution* (Rutgers Univ. Press, 1976); McCormick, Richard P., *New Jersey From Colony to State, 1609-1789* (1964; reprint New Jersey Historical Society, 1981); Pomfret, John, *Colonial New Jersey: A History* (Scribner's, 1973); Pomfret, John, *The Province of East New Jersey, 1609-1702: The Rebellious Proprietary* (Princeton Univ. Press, 1962); Pomfret, John, *The Province of West New Jersey, 1609-1702: A History of the Origins of an American Colony* (Princeton Univ. Press, 1956).

Maxine N. Lurie
Rutgers University

NEW LONDON In 1644, John Winthrop, Jr., procured a grant from Massachusetts to plant a settlement, called Pequod, at the mouth of the Thames River; when the New

England Confederation ruled that the area was within the jurisdiction of Connecticut, the grant was reconfirmed by that colony. By 1658 the town had been renamed New London. In the 18th century New London became an important ship-building and shipping center, and in the two decades before the Revolution it was the fastest-growing town in the colony. It was also a center of rebel activity, and during the Revolutionary War its harbor sheltered one of the largest concentrations of privateers along the coast. In 1781 the British, under the command of General Benedict Arnold, invaded the port, destroying most of the warehouses and many of the residences in the town.

Peter Stuyvesant's long governorship of New Netherland ended in 1664 when he surrendered the colony to a British fleet. *(Library of Congress)*

NEW NETHERLAND The colony of New Netherland may be said to have its beginnings in 1609 when the English explorer, Henry Hudson, sailing for the Dutch East India Company in search of a northeast passage to Asia decided, after failing to find a navigable passage above Norway, to sail west across the Atlantic in search of a northwest passage. After skirting the coast above Cape Cod, he and his crew aboard the ship *De Halve Maen (Half Moon)* sailed as far south as the Delaware Bay before coming north into the mouth of the river that would bear his name.

Hudson's voyage established the Dutch claim to the area, but the East India Company failed to follow up on the discovery after English authorities confiscated Hudson's ship and protested the Dutch incursion. Private merchants in Amsterdam, however, were quick to cash in on the discovery, and it is probable that a privately financed voyage was made to the area as early as 1610 or 1611. The period from 1611 to 1614 witnessed increased competition among merchants of Amsterdam and Hoorn to control the fur trade of the region, and as the competition increased so too did the political maneuvering. In 1614 matters were settled when a resolution of the States-General (Dutch parliament) established a "grant of exclusive trade" to a company of merchants calling themselves the New Netherland Company. Since the charter of the company is the first known document to refer to the region of Hudson's discovery as "New Netherland" it is reasonable to date the colony's history from that year.

The New Netherland Company continued to exploit the area after 1614 through the organizing of annual voyages and the establishment of Fort Nassau on Castle Island (near Albany). When the company's charter expired in 1618, some effort was made to renew it, but plans were already afoot for the establishment of a national joint-stock company to oversee trade and colonization in the western hemisphere. That company would become a reality in 1621 with the chartering of the West India Company. Under the provisions of its charter, New Netherland became an administrative responsibility of the Amsterdam chamber of the company.

Early Colonization. The first colonization attempt occurred in 1624 when the West India Company sponsored an expedition to settle 30 families of Walloons (French Belgians) in New Netherland. In the following year a relief expedition arrived with building materials, tools, and the first commander, Willem Verhulst. Settlement did not go smoothly for the colonists or the company in the first two years. The settlers turned out to have more interest in the fur trade than in farming, and since the fur trade remained a company monopoly much friction developed between the company administration and the settlers. Matters had reached a head in 1626, when Peter Minuit arrived and took over the colony's administration. Minuit's regime (1626-31) accomplished much. In an effort to improve the colony's defenses, he consolidated settlement on Manhattan Island by evacuating all but a handful of soldiers from Fort Orange, which had been established in 1624 near present-day Albany, and bringing back the colonists from the Connecticut and Delaware rivers. He also opened diplomatic relations with Plymouth and purchased Manhattan Island from the Indians for trade goods valued at 60 guilders. He was recalled to the Netherlands in 1631.

In the late 1620s the company experimented with the so-called Patroonship Plan. June 7, 1629, proposal, "Freedoms and Exemptions for the Patroons and Masters who would plant a colony and cattle in New Netherland," invited citizens of the Netherlands to apply for a patroonship by sending surveyors to the colony to lay out their claims, purchasing the claims from the Indians, and registering the purchase with the company at Fort New Amsterdam on Manhattan Island. Several patroonships were granted, but only one, Rensselaerswyck, founded by Kiliaen van Rensselaer, an influential Amsterdam merchant and former director of the Amsterdam chamber, succeeded. All the others were eventually abandoned and sold back to the company.

By the mid-1630s the patroonship system was abandoned, and the West India Company sought other ways to make the colony attractive to colonists. In 1639, after repeated calls for a loosening of the company's grip on the fur trade, the directors approved the so-called Articles and Conditions, which expanded the colonists' trade privileges to encompass a virtual free trade in all commodities including furs. In subsequent years revised Freedoms and Exemptions were issued that included expanded privileges and free land for all who would emigrate to the colony.

Expansion and Conflict. The 1630s also witnessed increased tension between New Netherland and New England. In an effort to establish a Dutch presence in the Connecticut River Valley, Director General Wouter van Twiller sent an expedition from New Amsterdam to the Connecticut River that succeeded in erecting a small trading post wistfully named House of Good Hope. The presence of the Dutch in the valley excited the fears of the English and soon a scramble was on to establish control there. After a number of angry encounters in the valley, the Dutch were forced to back down, and although they would remain as traders for some time, the inability of the company to push its claim through diplomatic channels in Europe and the unwillingness of the authorities at New Amsterdam to risk an armed conflict with the more numerous New Englanders resulted in the loss of the Connecticut Valley in the Treaty of Hartford (1650).

Despite this setback the decade of the 1640s saw increased emigration to New Netherland as settlers responded to the generous land and trade policies of the Articles and Conditions. As the number of Europeans increased, however, relations with the Indians deteriorated. Dutch Indian policy underwent changes in the decades after 1640. In the upper reaches of the Hudson Valley, where the needs of the fur trade dictated a careful policy of appeasement with the Iroquois Confederacy, the Dutch authorities maintained peace. In the lower Hudson Valley, however, the Algonquian-speaking Indians came to be viewed as an obstacle to European settlement. Under the leadership of Director General Willem Kieft a series of disastrous Indian wars were undertaken to bring the Indians to heel. For the most part the so-called Kieft Wars succeeded in crushing the power of the river Indians, but Indian wars would continue to plague the administration of Kieft's successor.

Stuyvesant's Administration. In 1647, New Netherland welcomed Director General Peter Stuyvesant. Stuyvesant's administration would be the longest in the colony's history and in many aspects the most successful. During the 17 years of the Stuyvesant era, the colony of New Netherland grew as the tide of emigration brought thousands of new settlers.

The European population of New Netherland differed significantly from other European colonies in terms of national origin, age distribution, racial mix, and religion. Recent research has revealed a colony of amazing ethnic and linguistic diversity, containing perhaps as many as 50 percent non-Dutch, a majority of people under 25 years of age, and large numbers of blacks, the last imported by the company as slaves. Moreover, the New Netherland of the 1650s and 1660s contained a wide range of religious sects, including Lutherans, English Congregationalists, Quakers, and Jews. At the time of the English conquest in 1664, New Netherland was the most heterogeneous colony in North America. The last years of the colony's existence were marked by several Indian wars (1655, 1659-64) as well as by the conquest of New Sweden (1655), increased tension and finally outright war between the Dutch and the English, and the expansion of local government in the form of town charters. The Stuyvesant years were difficult ones for the Dutch, because the very success of New Netherland made it a prize to be taken in the Anglo-Dutch Wars. The Dutch era ended in September 1664 when an English war fleet under the command of Colonel Richard Nicolls forced the surrender of the colony. Stuyvesant's surrender would be harshly criticized by his superiors in the Netherlands, but the evidence speaks overwhelmingly to the wisdom of the Dutch decision to abandon their possession without a fight. Indeed, the impossibility of defending the colony against a sea-launched attack was proven in 1673, when a Dutch fleet forced the capitulation of English New York in the Third Anglo-Dutch War. New Netherland was not to have a second chance, however, for in the Second Treaty of Westminster (November 1674), New York was restored to the English, and the Dutch abandoned their claim to North America.

See also Anglo-Dutch Wars; Dutch East India Company; Dutch-Indian Wars; Dutch West India Company; Kieft, Willem; Minuit, Peter; Stuyvesant, Peter.

Bibliography: Gehring, Charles T., *A Guide to Dutch Manuscripts Relating to New Netherland in United States Repositories* (State Univ. of New York, 1978); Gehring, Charles T., ed. and trans., New York *Historical Manuscripts: Dutch Land Papers* (Genealogical Pub. Co., 1980); Rink, Oliver A., *Holland on the Hudson: An Economic and Social History of Dutch New York* (Cornell Univ. Press, 1986).

Oliver A. Rink
California State University, Bakersfield

NEW ORLEANS   Established in 1718 by the Sieur de Bienville, governor of Louisiana, New Orleans lies between the Mississippi River and Lake Ponchartrain, approximately 100 miles from the Gulf of Mexico. The foundation of New Orleans was part of an ambitious program of territorial expansion pursued by the French throughout the Mississippi Valley at the beginning of the 18th century. Its specific purpose was to protect the inland water route to Fort Biloxi and to maintain the French commercial and military presence on the lower Mississippi. The city was named in honor of the regent of France, the Duc d'Orleans, and served as the capital of Louisiana from 1722.

New Orleans's population was composed of many distinct immigrant groups, among whom the French and the Spanish, locally known as Creoles, dominated the aristocratic, land-owning class. In 1755 groups of exiles from Acadia, later known as Cajuns, settled in the region. In the territorial adjustments that followed the French and Indian War, New Orleans was placed under Spanish control but was returned to France by the Treaty of San Ildefonso (1800). It came under U.S. jurisdiction only with the Louisiana Purchase of 1803.

NEWPORT   Newport, Rhode Island, was founded in May 1639, by William Coddington, John Clarke, and others seeking more religious freedom than Massachusetts Bay Colony offered. The city practiced religious freedom similar to Roger Williams' settlement at Providence, and Newport became a haven for the persecuted. The second Baptist church in America was founded in Newport. The Quakers settled in Newport (1657), and one year later the first Jews arrived. Shipbuilding began early on, and Newport became an important colonial seaport, a rival of Boston and New York. James Franklin Jr. established Rhode Island's first permanent newspaper in Newport, the *Mercury*, in 1758. The city was occupied by the British (1776-79) during the Revolution, and in 1780 it became the headquarters for America's French allies commanded by General Rochambeau. During this period, war damage

and changing trade and economic patterns dealt Newport blows from which it never fully recovered.

NEWPORT, CHRISTOPHER (died 1617)   A sea captain, Newport served with Sir Francis Drake's Cadiz expedition in 1587 and also raided the West Indies. As the authorized carrier of the Virginia Company, he brought colonists to Jamestown in 1607, explored the James River, and claimed he found gold. He returned in 1608 with new settlers to find the leaders in prison and Captain John Smith on the gallows. In 1609 he carried Sir Thomas Gates, skilled craftsmen, and a crown for Powhatan to Virginia. On his last trip, in 1611, Sir Thomas Dale pulled Newport's beard because the colony was in such desperate condition. Newport later joined the East India Company and died at Bantam after historic voyages.

NEWPORT TOWER   In the 19th century the Newport Tower, a two-story circular structure of native stone in Newport, Rhode Island, was widely believed to have been built by the Norse during their stay in Vinland. It was one of a number of such relics that included the Kensington Stone and later the Vinland Map. The tower was subsequently shown to have been built as a mill by English settlers of the 17th century.

See also Kensington Stone; Vinland Map.

NEW SMYRNA COLONY   In 1768, some 1,400 colonists from Greece, Italy, and Minorca were brought to East Florida by Dr. Andrew Turnbull, an English promoter, and settled on a site near the present city of Daytona Beach. This mass migration was second in size only to the migration of German Palatines to New York in 1710. Laboring under harsh contracts of indenture, under which colonists were to receive land grants after seven years, the colonists quickly became disillusioned, and the first year a number of them engaged in a revolt, which was suppressed. New Smyrna was a dismal failure, and in 1776 the 600 survivors straggled into St. Augustine, some 75 miles north, petitioning the British there for relief from their indentures and settling in the vicinity.

NEWSPAPERS   The first newspaper to appear in the colonies was *Public Occurences*, published in Boston, which was suppressed by colonial authorities after one issue which criticized the conduct of King William's War (1689-97). The first two continuously published papers, the *Boston News-Letter* (1704-76) and the *Boston Gazette* (1719-41), were both conservative organs of those authorities, the former holding the distinction of publishing the first newspaper illustration in America. A later *Gazette* (1755-98) became the leading advocate of independence, publishing contributions from John and Samuel Adams.

The *New England Courant* (1721-26), founded by James Franklin, provided lively and critical journalism that landed its publisher in jail in 1723.

Franklin's brother Benjamin soon moved to Philadelphia where he worked for the *American Mercury* (1719-41) before purchasing the *Philadelphia Gazette* (1728-1815), which he edited from 1729 to 1766. Here Benjamin Franklin printed much of his writing, including the first ruminations of Poor Richard, weather reports, and the first political cartoon in the colonies (1754). The *Pennsylvania Journal and Weekly Advertiser* (1743-97), published by William Bradford, later the printer of the Continental Congress, became the leading competitor of Franklin's *Philadelphia Gazette*.

The first newspaper in New York City, the *New York Gazette* (1725-44), was founded by Bradford's grandfather. It was followed by John Peter Zenger's *New York Weekly Journal* (1733-52), which opposed the official political line of the *New York Gazette*. Zenger's criticisms resulted in an indictment of seditious libel in 1735. His acquittal established the principle that truth is a defense against libel and is considered the foundation of American freedom of the press.

Other important colonial papers included Baltimore's *Maryland Gazette* (1727-34, 1745-1839), Charleston's *South Carolina Gazette* (1732-1802), and Williamsburg's *Virginia Gazette* (1736-80). Several papers founded in the 18th century have continued in publication to the present: Portsmouth's *New Hampshire Gazette* (founded 1756), the *Newport Mercury* (1758), and Hartford's *Connecticut Courant* (1764). On the eve of the Revolution there were 37 papers published in the colonies. By 1790 the number had grown to 92, including 8 dailies, the first of which was the *Pennsylvania Evening Post*, founded in 1783.

See also Zenger, John Peter.

Bibliography: Brigham, C. S., *History and Bibliography of American Newspapers, 1690-1820*, 2 vols. (1947; reprint Greenwood Press, 1976).

John Mack Faragher
Mount Holyoke College

NEWTON, THOMAS (1660-1721) A lawyer and colonial administrator, he was born in England. He practiced law in Boston beginning in 1688. In the 1691 Jacob Leisler high treason trial in New York, he was attorney for the Crown. He also served in that capacity for a brief time at the beginning of the witch trials in Salem, Massachusetts, during the next year. Newton was secretary of New Hampshire from 1692; deputy judge of the Court of Admiralty for Massachusetts, Rhode Island, and New Hampshire from 1702; customs comptroller in Massachusetts from 1707; and attorney general of Massachusetts from 1720. He was the first to use the term "barrister" for "lawyer" in Massachusetts, and he was known for his extensive law library.

NEW WORLD CROPS In addition to the many wild plants gathered for food, botanists have identified 154 aboriginal crops domesticated and cultivated by pre-Columbian Indians. The most important of these were corn (maize) and potatoes, the first developed in Mexico and diffused widely throughout both continents, the second domesticated in the Andean highlands and in use throughout South America, although varieties of sweet potatoes were also grown in the Northern Hemisphere. These complex carbohydrates, the staff of life for the majority of Indians, formed the material base for the growth of the Indian population and for the development of complex Indian cultures. Both cultigens were introduced into Europe, Asia, and Africa soon after contact and gradually came to assume an importance in the Old World nearly equal to that in the New. Today corn and potatoes rank second and fourth, respectively, in the order of the world's seven staple foods, and they constitute the only important additions to the world's supply of staples since ancient times.

Mesoamerica was birthplace to most of the supplementary crops that made up the complex of cultigens in aboriginal North America. Corn, beans, and squash (including pumpkins) were known by many Indian peoples as "the three sisters," so closely were they associated. Nutritionists now know that in combination these three provide a correct balance of protein and amino acids. Other important vegetable crops included cassava, melons, chilis, sunflowers, tomatoes, peanuts, cashews, Jerusalem artichokes, and avocados, all unknown to the Old World before the 16th century.

Indians developed fiber plants such as agave, sisal, henequen, and New World cotton, which was superior to Asian varieties and became the commercial fiber that clothed the world as a result of the industrial revolution in the production of textiles. Cotton was but one of the New World tropical cultigens that became key commodities of colonial plantation agriculture; tobacco was the most important, but others include cacao (chocolate), vanilla, pineapples, and papayas.

Tobacco was grown for ritual and medicinal uses by the Indians, and early European promoters proclaimed its pharmacological properties. Other New World medicinal plants included coca and cinocha trees (from which are derived cocaine and quinine, respectively), cascara, ipecac, witch hazel, wintergreen, and arnica. In the four centuries that Europeans have been examining and analyzing the flora of America, they have yet to discover a medicinal herb not known to the Indians.

See also Corn; Potato; Tobacco.

Bibliography: Axtell, James, *The European and the Indian* (Oxford Univ. Press, 1981); Driver, Harold, *Indians of North America*, 2nd rev. ed. (Univ. of Chicago Press, 1969).

John Mack Faragher
Mount Holyoke College

NEW YORK   New York State's topography determined both its precontact and European settlement patterns. Extensively mountainous, the state is scored by two river systems that form a historic corridor to the interior of the continent. The Hudson River, a tidal estuary navigable for 150 miles north from Manhattan Island, combines with Lakes George and Champlain to form a contiguous water route to Canada. The Mohawk River extends from the Hudson, near Albany, 150 miles westward to the lakes and plains of western New York. Paleo- Indian groups entered the region about 10,000 B.C. By the time Europeans arrived, Algonquian-speaking tribes occupied the Hudson Valley and Long Island; Iroquoians in five tribal groups occupied the Mohawk corridor and much of the western lake plains. During the colonial period, European settlement was confined to the Hudson Valley and the eastern 100 miles of the Mohawk. In addition, Long Island extends 118 miles from the mouth of the Hudson River northwesterly along the New England coast. It was settled early in the colonial period and influenced New Netherland's and New York's contact with New England.

First European explorations.   Giovanni da Verrazano, a Florentine navigator seeking a route to the Pacific for King Francis I of France, briefly entered New York Bay in 1524. This gives him the honor of discovery, but the first significant European contact came in September 1609 when Henry Hudson, also seeking a westerly route to the Orient, sailed 90 miles up the Hudson to a site below present-day Albany. Hudson's employers, the Dutch East India Company, did not exploit his discovery, but other Dutch merchant groups began to explore the coastal areas and the river (which they named the Mauritius) and to make contact with the natives. By 1614 they had begun a profitable trade in furs and established a trading post near the site of Albany. In 1621 the Dutch government chartered the West India Company, a national joint-stock company with a commercial monopoly of the entire Western Hemisphere. The company always regarded its venture on the Hudson as an expensive distraction from its activities in the Caribbean and in South America, but it did support the settlement of the region, which it ruled through an appointed governor.

Dutch Settlement.   In 1624 the West India Company sent 30 families to New Netherland. Some settled at the mouth of the Hudson, while others moved upriver to settle Fort Orange (later Albany). Because Manhattan Island could be easily defended and because it was centrally located among several Dutch settlements, the Dutch purchased it from the Indians in 1626 and established New Amsterdam at its southern tip. To encourage settlement and to make the colony a source of supply for other American ventures, the company granted vast tracts of land—fronting 16 miles on navigable rivers but extending indefinitely inland—to any man who would settle 60 colonists upon the tract. The grantee, called the patroon, would have complete feudal lordship of the tract and its settlers. Only one of these succeeded, that of Kiliaen van Rensselaer.

In the first two decades of company rule, the colony grew slowly. The fur trade flourished, but the company monopoly prevented investment in the colony by other Dutch merchants. English competition in commerce and in colonization, with New Englanders settling in numbers in Long Island and in the Connecticut Valley, created a debilitating unease. The population was heterogeneous—perhaps only 50 percent Dutch, the rest comprising several European nationalities and African slaves and freemen. This diversity compelled a certain spirit of tolerance, but its practical effect was in contrast to the single-minded effort of the homogeneous English settlements. In addition, the colony was affected externally by the Anglo-Dutch maritime wars and internally by several wars with the Algonquian-speaking tribes of the Hudson Valley. The first of these, 1641-45, left barns and homes destroyed and fields abandoned, some for several years. Shorter conflicts in the 1650s and 1660s had similar effects, although in all the wars the Indians suffered more serious and permanent losses than did the Dutch.

The turning point in the colony's fortunes came in 1640 when the West India Company gave up its trade monopoly. This enabled other Amsterdam merchants to invest in New Netherland, which they did for selfish reasons. Profits, to the colony's detriment, flowed to Amsterdam not to New Netherland, but they did encourage new economic activity in the production of foodstuffs, timber, and tobacco, in addition to trade in furs and slaves. At the same time, the Freedoms and Exemptions of 1640 offered 200 acres of free land to each colonist who brought with him five other people. This recognized, at least implicitly, that to the average settler the New World's greatest attraction was free land. And in 1647, Peter Stuyvesant, the most capable of all New Netherland's directors, was appointed to a term that would last until 1664. In 1650 he negotiated a treaty at Hartford, Connecticut, that gave up some Dutch lands but compelled the New Englanders to recognize the existence of definite boundaries to their expansion.

British Conquest and Early Rule. The candle of New Netherland flickered most brightly just before it went out forever. The colony enjoyed its greatest growth in its last decade when the population increased from about 2,000 in 1655 to about 9,000 in 1664. By then the Algonquin tribes were subjugated and their lands under Dutch control. The population now comprised increasing numbers of stable families instead of single adventurers. The frontiers were quiet. The 60 years of control by distant merchants did not, however, instill a spirit of unified independence in New Netherland. When the British decided to take the Dutch colony, it fell without a struggle.

New Netherland was a geographical and commercial nuisance to the British and a pawn in the broader conflict between Britain and the United Provinces. In 1664, Charles II gave his brother James, Duke of York, a vast American territory that included all of the Dutch colony. James immediately sent a small fleet that forced the surrender of Manhattan, and New Netherland became New York, at least in name. The process of anglicizing the colony lasted for a full generation, and throughout the colonial period the colony's most distinguishing characteristic was its ethnic and religious heterogeneity.

James, as Duke of York and later as King James II, had complete control of the government and administration of New York. His charter, however, stipulated that New York's laws must conform to those of England, and he was more concerned about making money than in the empty exercise of authority. From the beginning his governors sought the advice and assistance of local citizens. In 1683, James granted, via Governor Thomas Dongan, a guarantee of representative legislature and personal freedoms. Dongan also granted liberal charters to New York City and Albany.

When James became king in 1685, he disallowed the charter and annexed New York to the multicolony Dominion of New England, but when William and Mary succeeded James, the Dominion was dissolved and New York's elected assembly was restored. In the meantime, Jacob Leisler, who had come to New Netherland as a soldier and then married a wealthy widow, led a local revolt (Leisler's Rebellion) against James's policies and established an arbitrary government of his own. Leisler was executed for treason, but his actions polarized internal differences—part ethnic, part economic, part geographical—that remained for years.

William and Mary recast New York as a royal colony in 1691. Thereafter the colony grew slowly but steadily, while certain tendencies became enduring characteristics: great influence in the hands of a few powerful families; land granted in great tracts, including manorial estates; a conflict of interests between New York City and inland settlements. These were equaled in their influence upon New York's development by an external factor: the protracted conflict between Britain and France. New York played an active role in the North American theater of this conflict because of its strategic location. It was the most vulnerable of England's colonies and the colony most oppressed by expenditures for defense. New York was the only colony that hosted a body of British regulars throughout this entire period.

Anglo-French Conflicts. The Hudson-Lake George-Lake Champlain waterway created an invasion route between New York and Canada, while the St. Lawrence River and Great Lakes gave access to the western region. The Iroquois Confederacy controlled all of the western area and much of the Mohawk Valley and was a constant but unpredictable factor in the defense of New York as Britain and France attempted to gain Iroquois support and were in turn played upon by Iroquois diplomats for their own purposes. International conflict was heightened by competition in the fur trade, New York's most important commerce. With local peltries used up, furs came from the west, and the commerce was therefore controlled by the Iroquois—a matter of deep concern to the French and their Indian allies.

In the first three of the colonial wars—King William's War (1689-97), Queen Anne's War (1702-13), King George's War (1744-48)—French and Indian parties attacked frontier settlements, unsettled the fur trade, and led New York to take part in expeditions against Canada. In the French and Indian War (1754-63), New York played an even more critical role. The lake area north of Albany was a battleground for five years, and Albany itself was the center of British operations in North America. Frontier communities again endured French and Indian raids, and New York was forced to garrison a large force of British troops. In the end the British were victorious. Sir William Johnson secured the active participation of the Iroquois in behalf of Britain; the seizure of strongpoints at Oswego and Niagara paved the way for the conquest of Montreal and Quebec. The French menace was finally removed.

Development and Growth. New York had become politically mature during these decades of conflict. Its general assembly gained power as the royal governors made political concessions in return for increased revenues and in the process became entangled in local party politics. By the 1730s two major factions, the generally cosmopolitan Court party and the generally provincial Country party, and several smaller groups had developed—all influenced by ethnic and social matters, economic and constitutional differences, family alliances, religious differences, geographic interests, and the force of individual personalities. The common features were that each faction had an elite leader-

British troops landed in New York City in 1776; the state was a primary objective of both the British and Americans during the Revolutionary War. (*Library of Congress*)

ship and that all tried to manipulate the general population. The best known incident of this factionalism was the 1735 case in which a New York jury acquitted the printer John Peter Zenger of the charge of libeling Governor William Cosby. The press was thereby recognized as a political weapon. In the following years the Assembly began to appeal more directly to a growing number of voters, while the governor's authority declined.

Although the Iroquois presence, the French menace, and restrictive land policies slowed New York's growth in comparison to other colonies, the population did increase, while remaining an ethnic mixture. Palatine Germans, encouraged by the British Crown, settled on the Hudson and in the Schoharie Valley; French Huguenots, Germans from the Rhineland, Scots, and Scotch-Irish founded several inland settlements. Of greatest long-range importance, land-hungry New Englanders began to move into the Hudson Valley in increasing numbers. In the 1760s they confronted owners of Hudson Valley manors in disputes that led to violence and a call for British troops. The presence of large numbers of free blacks and slaves (15 percent of the population in mid-18th century New York City) resulted in periodic hysterical episodes—the most infamous in 1741 when the discovery of a "Negroe conspiracy" led to the torture and execution of 31 slaves and 4 whites.

Era of the Revolution. New Yorkers expected that after the conquest of New France that they would be able to gain complete control of the fur trade and also expand into western lands. They were disappointed. Although the Treaty of Fort Stanwix (1768) did open some Iroquois lands to settlement, Britain's Proclamation of 1763 placed a limit on expansion while the fur trade shifted to Montreal. Widespread anger at various revenue-raising measures by the British government, notably the Stamp Act (1765), built upon this disappointment and New York, although perhaps the most conservative of the colonies, was the first to suggest an intercolonial congress, known as the Albany Congress, to resist British measures. As always, the elite attempted to guide and control the populace. New York did not approve the Declaration of Independence until July 9, 1776, and a large, though indeterminate, number of New Yorkers remained loyal to the Crown.

New York's colonial status came to a formal end in 1777 when the provincial congress created and approved a state constitution. By then New York had become a major battlefield.   Nearly one-third of all Revolutionary War engagements were fought in New York. The British captured New York City in 1776 and held it throughout the war, and the area north of Manhattan was wracked by several years of vicious partisan warfare. In 1777 a three-pronged British invasion of the Hudson and Mohawk valleys ended with General John Burgoyne's surrender at Saratoga—the turning point, many historians think, of the Revolution. Thereafter, the major battles were fought in Southern states, but Loyalist and Indian raids laid waste the agriculture of the Mohawk Valley for four successive years, 1778-81. In response, a force under General John Sullivan invaded the Iroquois domain in 1779 and so severely ravaged villages and crops that the Iroquois, though still a military threat, never recovered economically.

In 1780 the enduring strategic importance of the Hudson Valley was dramatized when Benedict Arnold's effort to betray West Point to the British was foiled by the capture of his accomplice, Major John André. The British evacuation of New York City on November 25, 1783, was the final military event of the Revolution. After the Constitutional Convention (1787), the debate over ratification was especially bitter in New York. The Constitution's supporters, led by Federalist authors Alexander Hamilton and John Jay, plus Robert R. Livingston, finally carried the day; and the Constitution was ratified on July 26, 1788.

See also Albany Congress; Anglo-Dutch Wars; Dominion of New England; Dutch-Indian Wars; French and Indian War; New Netherland; Revolutionary War Battles.

Bibliography: Bonomi, Patricia U., *A Factious People: Politics and Society in Colonial New York* (Columbia Univ. Press, 1971); Kammen, Michael, *Colonial New York: A History* (Scribner's, 1975); Lustig, Mary Lou, *Robert Hunter, 1666-1734: New York's Augustan Statesman* (Syracuse Univ. Press, 1983); Richter, Daniel K., and Merrell, James H., eds., *Beyond the Covenant Chain: The Iroquois and Their Neighbors in Indian North America* (Syracuse Univ. Press, 1987); Rink, Oliver A., *Holland on the Hudson: An Economic and Social History of Dutch New York* (Cornell Univ. Press, 1986); Ritchie, Robert C., *The Duke's Province: A Study of New York Politics and Society* (Univ. of North Carolina Press, 1977).

Wendell Tripp
New York State Historical Association

NEW YORK CITY   Founded in 1626 by the Dutch West India Company and named New Amsterdam, what is now called New York City was confined throughout the colonial period to the southern tip of Manhattan Island at the mouth of the Hudson River. The company's director, Peter Minuit, bought the island in 1626 from the Indians for 60 florins' worth of goods. By year's end, New Amsterdam comprised 30 houses, a blockhouse, a mill, and cultivated land. A center of commerce and government, it had grown to about 1,500 inhabitants by 1664, when it was seized by Great Britain. The Dutch recaptured the city in 1673 and named it New Orange, but with its return to Britain in 1674 it permanently became New York City.

The Dutch West India Company in 1653 granted the city its first municipal charter. This was succeeded by charters from royal governors Thomas Dongan in 1686 and John Montgomerie in 1731, the latter charter confirmed by the state constitution of 1777. It was thus governed by an appointed mayor and aldermen elected by city districts. Repressed by wars and depression until about 1715, it thereafter became a commercial center with shipyards, refineries, mills, a slave market, and a thriving Caribbean trade. By 1776 its population was about 22,000, including some 3,000 slaves, and it could claim a college (King's, later renamed Columbia, founded 1754), a city hall, a hospital, a poorhouse, a jail, a library, 400 taverns, and 22 churches. Despite a conservative ruling class, the city was the scene of vigorous, sometimes violent, opposition to the Stamp Act, tea tax, and Quartering Act and in 1774 formed the first committee of correspondence.

Captured by the British in September 1776, the city was occupied throughout the Revolutionary War and attracted a large Loyalist refugee population. It suffered the physical damages of an occupied city, including major fires in 1776 and 1778. Following British evacuation in November 1783, Whig lawyers and merchants flocked to the city, which gradually regained its commercial and financial prominence. It became a center of advocacy for the Constitution and was the first capital of the United States under the Constitution.

See also Minuit, Peter; New Netherland; New York.

Bibliography: Archdeacon, Thomas J., *New York City, 1664-1710: Conquest and Change* (Cornell Univ. Press, 1976); Klein, Milton M, ed., *New York: The Centennial Years 1676-1976* (Kennikat Press, 1977); Rink, Oliver A., *Holland on the Hudson: An Economic and Social History of Dutch New York* (Cornell Univ. Press, 1986).

Wendell Tripp
New York State Historical Association

NIAGARA, FORT   This Lake Ontario fort, built by the French in 1726 at the mouth of the Niagara River, which runs from Lake Erie over one of the world's most spectacular falls, was the principal defense of this narrow gateway to the rich Ohio country. Captured by the English in 1759 during the French and Indian War, it became a key fortress in the control of the Great Lakes. Despite the Treaty of Paris (1783), the British refused to evacuate the fort until after Jay's Treaty in 1796. The British recaptured it during the War of 1812, after which it was returned to the United States.

NIAGARA, GREAT INDIAN COUNCIL AT (1741)   The largest peace conference ever held between representatives of the British colonial government and the native peoples of North America, it was convened by William Johnson, the superintendent of Indian affairs. In response to continued attacks on settlers in western New York, Johnson notified the leaders of the tribes in that area that he was about to embark on a retaliatory campaign but that any tribes preferring to avoid war should immediately send representatives to sign a peace treaty at Niagara. Among the more than 2,000 leaders that attended this meeting (July 9-18) were representatives of the Ottawa, Huron, Seneca, Menomini, Chippewa, and Iroquois.

NICHOLAS, ROBERT CARTER (1728-80)   The grandson of Robert "King" Carter, a powerful Virginia planter, Nicholas was educated at the College of William and Mary. He took up law and became head of the provincial bar. He represented York County in the Virginia House of Burgesses from 1756. He opposed Patrick Henry's Stamp Act Resolves (1765) and later, independence. He was a conservative patriot who condemned Parliament's policies of taxation and the Boston Port Bill of 1774. He exposed corruption in the Virginia treasury and then became treasurer himself. He defended the established religion against Thomas Jefferson's 1776 bill for religious freedom but helped draft a declaration of rights for the new Virginia government.

NICHOLSON, FRANCIS (1655-1728)   Born in Yorkshire, England, he first came to America as a soldier under the command of Sir Edmund Andros. By 1688 he was commissioned as lieutenant governor of the Dominion of New England but returned to England when Jacob Leisler gained control of New York. From then on he made several crossings to America to serve as lieutenant governor of Virginia until 1692 and as governor of Maryland from 1694 until 1698; to lead Massachusetts's troops in the capture of Port Royal in Canada in 1710 and 1711, and to serve as governor of Nova Scotia in 1713 and as governor of South Carolina from 1720 until 1725.

NICOLET, JEAN (1598-1642)   French explorer Jean Nicolet was born in Cherbourg, France. Nicolet was one of the young men Samuel de Champlain chose to live among the Canadian Indians as an interpreter and explorer. In 1618, Nicolet was sent to the Indians on Allumette Island on the Ottawa River to learn their language and woodcraft. In 1624 he became the much respected interpreter of the Nipissing. When the English took the territory, he returned to Canada to become the interpreter for the colony.

In 1639 he traveled west in a canoe paddled by seven Huron to search out a tribe called the Winnebago, or "Men of the Sea." He had hoped to find Orientals but instead discovered that the "Men of the Sea" lived beside a great lake. He was the first known European explorer to see Lake Michigan and the countryside of Wisconsin. The Indians thought he had come from the gods and called him "manitouiriniou" or "wandering man." He returned to his post at Three Rivers, Quebec, and drowned two years later in a boating accident on the St. Lawrence River.

NIXON, JOHN (1733-1808)   A prominent Philadelphia merchant and patriot leader, Nixon supported nonimportation during the Stamp Act crisis (1765-66) and served on many Revolutionary bodies, including the Committee of Correspondence, during the years before independence. Nixon took part in the New Jersey campaign of 1776-77 as a militia officer and served in various civilian posts throughout the war. Later he was involved in public finance; in 1784 he became a director of the Bank of North America and was thereafter president (1792-1808). Throughout his life Nixon was involved in civic affairs; he became a Philadelphia alderman in 1789.

NIZA, MARCOS DE (c.1500-58)   A Franciscan missionary and New World explorer from Nice, Marcos de Niza had accompanied Pedro de Alvarado to Peru and had witnessed the execution of the Inca leader Atahualpa (1533). In 1538 the viceroy commissioned him to explore the territory beyond Culiacan. Taking his lead from Cabeza de Vaca's stories, Niza left in 1539 with Estevanico as guide and reached the neighborhood of Cibola, although he did not actually enter the city. On his return he spread stories of the vast size and wealth of Cibola. In 1540, Niza led Coronado back to Cibola but was discredited when the great city he had described turned out to be made of mud.

See also Cibola, Seven Cities of; Coronado, Francisco Vásquez de; Estevanico.

NONIMPORTATION   A tactic of resistance employed on several occasions before independence by the American colonists, nonimportation—the suspension of imports from Britain—was intended to pressure the English government into changing American policy. It was first used with effect in opposition to the Stamp Act (1765-66) and was revived in protest of the Townshend legislation in 1767; during the latter crisis nonimportation had some influence in obtaining partial redress (1770), despite hesitation among some American merchants. In the final imperial crisis of 1773-76 nonimportation was part of a system of American economic resistance established by

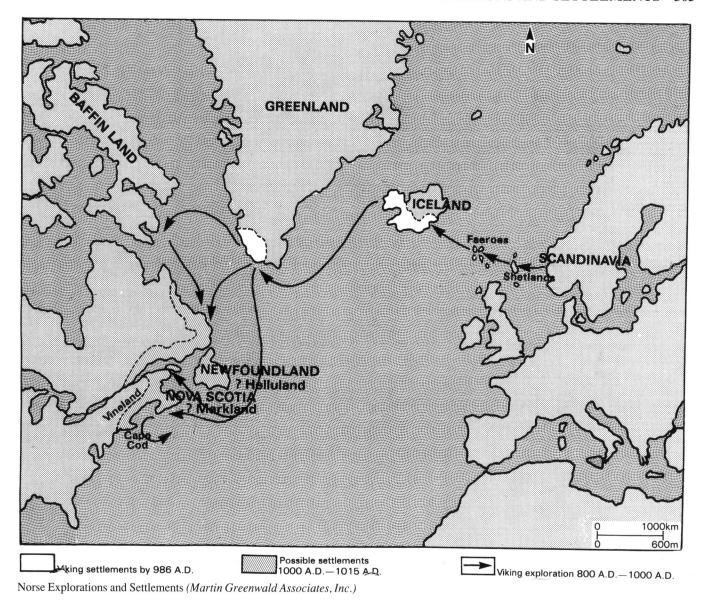

Viking settlements by 986 A.D.

Possible settlements
1000 A.D. — 1015 A.D.

Viking exploration 800 A.D. — 1000 A.D.

Norse Explorations and Settlements *(Martin Greenwald Associates, Inc.)*

the Continental Association of the First Continental Congress (1774). This time Britain did not repeal the objectionable measures, and the eventual result was independence.

NORFOLK Originally a settlement in southeastern Virginia established in 1682 as a port for the export of the tobacco of neighboring North Carolina, Norfolk eventually served the planters of the Cheasapeake Bay region as well. Throughout the 18th century, Norfolk was an active commercial center on the North American leg of the triangular trade. At the outbreak of the Revolution, the majority of its population remained Loyalist, and it was occupied by the governor of the colony, Lord Dunmore. Dunmore was, however, driven out by Revolutionary forces who burned

down Norfolk's commercial district. It was rebuilt and prospered again after the war.

NORSE EXPLORATIONS AND SETTLEMENTS At the end of the 1st millennium A.D., the Norse were the greatest sailors, navigators, and colonists in Europe. In the last years of the 8th century, Danes and Norwegians settled the northern Atlantic Shetland and Orkney islands, and from this base they raided and colonized the Hebrides, the Irish and English coast, Normandy, and even southern France on the Mediterranean. This intense expansionist drive was also evidenced in Norse island-hopping across the Atlantic, which by the year 1000 had taken them to the shores of North America. Norse expansion in the north

Atlantic, unlike 16th-century trans-Atlantic European expansion, was not directed by royal or merchant design but was a folk movement. Modern knowledge of this expansion likewise comes from oral sagas, written down generations later, which provide a broad outline of their achievements but are unreliable for precise details.

North American Discoveries. The Norse discovery of Iceland, about 850, was a result of their sail-driven ships being blown off course in the fierce and unpredictable north Atlantic. By the end of the century the Icelandic coast was dotted with permanent settlements based upon a pastoral economy. Greenland was similarily discovered in the 980s by Eric the Red, then colonized. The encounter with the coast of North America was a logical extension of this process of accidental discovery.

About 985 the ships of Bjarni Herjulfson, sailing from Iceland to Greenland, were blown off course and, struggling to return, encountered three distinct coastlines, thought now to be those of Newfoundland, Labrador, and Baffin Island. Leif Eriksson followed this discovery with a voyage of exploration in 1001. At the southernmost of Herjulfson's landfalls he built dwellings and wintered before returning to Greenland, where he named his encampment Vinland (from the Norse *vin*, meaning "meadow"). Thorvald Eriksson and Thorfinn Karlsefni made several later attempts to colonize the site, but because of the uncertainty of the supply lines to Greenland, and conflicts with the aboriginal inhabitants, these were unsuccessful, and by 1014 the site was abandoned.

Historians have proposed a multitude of locations for the site of Vinland. Artifacts from an archeological site at the fishing village of L'Anse aux Meadows in Newfoundland are similiar to those found in the Shetlands, Iceland, and Greenland, and clearly document a Norse presence in North America. But carbon-14 tests indicate an occupation as early as the 9th century, a hundred years or more before the dating provided for Eriksson's Vinland in the oral sagas, suggesting that there may have been several Norse landfalls, of which only Herjulfson's and Eriksson's were long-remembered. Other possible sites of Norse settlements exist at Pamiok Island and Ungava Bay in northern Quebec.

Norse Influence. Common knowledge of these Norse discoveries was evident in the literature of medieval Europe. English fishermen were in Iceland as early as 1410, and what they learned there may have helped inform John Cabot in Bristol. One tradition relates a trip made by Christopher Columbus to Iceland before his famous voyage, but even in mainland western Europe he could have learned of the Norse demonstration of the feasibility of trans-Atlantic navigation and of the possibility of western lands.

See also Eric the Red; Eriksson, Leif; Eriksson, Thorvald; Exploration; Herjulfson, Bjarni; Thorfinn Karlsefni; Vinland.

Bibliography: Magnusson, Magnus and Palsson, Herman, eds., *The Vineland Sagas: The Norse Discovery of America* (Penguin, 1965); Morison, Samuel Eliot, *The European Discovery of America: The Northern Voyages, A.D. 500-1600* (Oxford Univ. Press, 1971).

John Mack Faragher
Mount Holyoke College

NORTH CAROLINA North Carolina covers over 52,000 square miles—about the size of England—and stretches across three clear physiographic zones: the mountain region of the west, the rolling Piedmont plateau, and the flat Coastal Plain bounded by the Outer Banks, these distinctive barrier islands that give North Carolina a tidal shoreline as long as California's. The first inhabitants entered this area more than 10,000 years ago as hunters, and by 1200 A.D. their successors had become agriculturists, raising corn, beans, and squash. Algonquian-speaking groups populated the northeastern coastal plain, and Siouan language tribes inhabited much of the Piedmont, while the Tuscaroras in the east and the Cherokees in the west were descended from Iroquoian speakers.

In 1524, Giovanni da Verrazano sought to do for the French in the North Atlantic what Magellan had just done for the Spanish in the South Atlantic—locate a western route to China. Approaching the Outer Banks in search of a "strait to penetrate to the Eastern Ocean," Verrazano glimpsed Pamlico Sound beyond the sandy isthmus and reasoned it must be the Pacific. Soon many European maps showed a Sea of Verrazano, longer than the Mediterranean, stretching east from the west coast of the Outer Banks almost to Cape Hatteras. Hopes of controlling such an access route, as the Spanish controlled the Isthmus of Panama, may have reinforced Sir Walter Raleigh's desire for an English colony at Roanoke (Virginia) in the 1580s.

First European Settlements. Between the activities of Verrazano and Raleigh, occasional Spanish explorers probed the region by sea and land. In 1526, Lucas Vásquez de Ayllón brought 500 people to the Carolina coast from Hispaniola. Whether his short-lived colony reached Cape Fear or remained farther south is uncertain, but the few blacks who stayed behind probably joined local Indian groups. Hernando de Soto saw evidence of Ayllón's visit when his large expedition approached the Piedmont from the south in 1540. His army also brought new races and animals, new trade goods and diseases, as it marched west through southern Appalachia. In 1566-67, other Spanish explorers penetrated the western mountains again, and Dominicans visiting the Outer Banks proclaimed Spain's title to the land. But the Roman Catholics established no permanent presence to defend the claim against Protestant rivals.

In the 1580s, England's "Virgin Queen," Elizabeth I, granted courtiers the right to settle the American coast and name it Virginia in her honor. In 1584, Raleigh sent Philip Amadas and Arthur Barlow to explore the coast and claim it for England. The next spring he sent a contingent of men (including scientist Thomas Harriot and artist John White) to Roanoke Island, but their outpost failed. In 1587, White delivered more than 100 colonists to the same location. When he finally returned to Roanoke in 1590, after Spain's threatened invasion of England, he found the settlement deserted. A carved word—without the agreed sign for distress—showed that at least some had moved to "Croatoan" (Okracoke) Island south of Cape Hatteras, joining Indians who eventually moved inland and whose descendants continue in the state today.

English Development. Although the English gained a successful foothold at Jamestown in 1607, colonization farther south proved slow. Englishmen were gathering pine pitch near the Chowan River by the 1630s, and a few Virginians took up permanent residence near Albemarle Sound after 1650. The 1629 patent from Charles I, bestowing "Carolana" on Sir Robert Heath, was vacated after the English Restoration, and Charles II granted eight of his loyal supporters a sweeping proprietary charter in 1663. He defined Carolina two years later as including all the land from sea to sea between 36 degrees 30 minutes and 29 degrees north latitude. Two settlement efforts on the Cape Fear River after 1662 failed within five years, and by 1670 the proprietors had turned to developing the more southerly and accessible portion of their grant.

Migration from Virginia continued, especially after Bacon's Rebellion of 1676. Newcomers opposed to proprietary rule seized political ascendancy over Albemarle in Culpeper's Rebellion of 1677, but the proprietors soon regained control. In 1689 they named a separate governor for the portion of Carolina "That Lies north and east of Cape Feare." English passage of the Naval Stores Act in 1705, promoting colonial production of tar, turpentine, pitch, and hemp, spurred further migration. Bath Town on the Pamlico River was incorporated in 1706, and New Bern was founded by Swiss and German colonists beside the Neuse River in 1710. The next year, Governor Thomas Cary aligned himself with these new dissenters against the Anglican elite (located around the town that became Edenton) and refused to relinquish the governorship to his successor until routed by troops in July. Cary's Rebellion hinted the start of a longstanding north-

south rivalry—economic, political, and religious—between coastal counties.

In September 1711 a deeper rivalry erupted into open war. The powerful Tuscarora Indians, hurt by smallpox, slave raids, and the encroachment of white settlers on their hunting grounds along the Neuse, launched a war of retribution behind their militant leader, Hancock. Hundreds of colonists took refuge at Bath, but authorities in Albemarle remained cool to their plight. The Tuscarora were also split, with one faction, led by Tom Blunt, seeking a negotiated peace. A foray of South Carolina Indians under John Barnwell, intended largely to capture natives for sale in Charleston as slaves, nearly unified the divided tribe. But a second expedition, under James Moore, destroyed Hancock's forces in 1713. Surviving Tuscarora migrated north to join the Iroquois Confederacy, and ambitious Carolinians eyed the depopulated Cape Fear region.

Growth of the Colony. By 1712 the term "North Carolina" was in official use, although the dividing line with Virginia was not surveyed until 1728. Boundary commissioners who joined William Byrd in that endeavor received "blank patents" for valuable new estates in the Cape Fear area, where Brunswick Town was laid out in 1726 and Newton (Wilmington) in 1733. Pine forests yielded timber and naval stores; the climate invited lucrative rice production by enslaved blacks brought from South Carolina; and the Cape Fear River provided the colony's only deep-water port, giving direct access to the hinterland. New immigrants spread up the river valley—Welsh colonists from Pennsylvania in 1730, thousands of Highlanders from Scotland after 1732—founding Cross Creek and Campbellton after 1760 (which merged as Fayetteville by 1783). As they grew more numerous, tension between Albemarle and Cape Fear increased.

These newcomers obtained land patents from the British Crown, which had bought out seven of the eight Carolina proprietors in 1729. But English politician John Carteret refused to sell his share, and in 1744 (as Earl Granville) he received rights to the vast Granville Tract, constituting roughly the northern half of North Carolina, just as immigration from the north began to increase. Settlers in the Middle Colonies were facing scarce land, depleted soil, and hostile Indians, so thousands began pressing south down the Great Wagon Road. Pennsylvania Quakers, German Lutherans, and Scotch-Irish Presbyterians poured into the fertile Piedmont, making North Carolina the fastest growing American colony. Fraud by tract surveyors and quitrent collectors, plus rivalry between Granville's agents and other speculators, led to the Enfield Riot of 1759.

In the west the Cherokee, reduced by smallpox, waged an unsuccessful war during 1760-61 against the encroaching Carolinians, whose white and black population now

The Battle of King's Mountain in 1780 slowed the advance of General Cornwallis in North Carolina. *(Library of Congress)*

exceeded 110,000 and was doubling every 15 years. (To prevent further conflicts, George III in the Proclamation of 1763 prohibited American colonists from settling beyond the Appalachian divide, but negotiations with the weakened Cherokee soon pushed the boundary farther west.) To the east, over 28,000 Afro-Americans made up a quarter of the colonial population by 1760; most were forced to live as slaves on plantations near the coast, where they made up a majority in many coastal counties.

In the Piedmont new arrivals from the north, with family farms and few slaves, felt increasingly at odds with the colony's eastern establishment and the small local elite. With hard currency scarce and corruption among officials common, indebted farmers found themselves paying exorbitant fees and regressive taxes, such as those imposed to build a mansion for Governor Tryon in New Bern. Drastically underrepresented in the general assembly, they organized (around prosperous yeomen like Herman

Husband) to "regulate" their own affairs more honestly. When these Regulators closed the court in Hillsborough and intimidated local creditors and placemen, Tryon brought troops to the region. He crushed the popular movement at the Battle of Alamance in May 1771, hanging seven of its leaders, but many defiant farmers migrated rather than swear allegiance.

The Revolutionary War Era. Eastern merchants and lawyers, while hostile to the Regulators, had mounting political and economic grievances of their own against the Crown. Spurred by England's arbitrary acts, plus local events such as the Mecklenburg County Resolutions (May 1775) and the defeat of Scottish Loyalists at Moore's Creek Bridge (February 1776), provincial delegates in April 1776 drafted the Halifax Resolves. These empowered their representatives in Philadelphia to concur "in declaring Independency"—the first such formal sanction adopted by any colony. A new congress, convening again at Halifax in November, drew up a state constitution that endured, despite perpetual controversy, until its revision in 1835.

The war to secure political independence entered the region in 1780. Western militiamen destroyed a British force at King's Mountain in October, slowing the northern advance of Cornwallis, and in December Nathanael Greene led a retreat across North Carolina that weakened the enemy considerably. Engaging the British at Guilford Courthouse in March 1781, Greene's American forces relinquished the field but inflicted heavy losses. With the surrender of Lord Cornwallis at Yorktown, Virginia, in October, the rights of the state's minority of white male property holders became more secure.

Postwar Development. Familiar differences of rank and region continued to divide the state's electorate during the postwar depression. Influential merchants, lawyers, and planters in the northeast, involved in commerce, land speculation, and agriculture-for-export, favored stronger government that would protect the financial and trading concerns of creditors. So they supported the Annapolis Convention of 1786 and the subsequent meeting in Philadelphia to revise the Articles of Confederation. But subsistence farmers in the west, plus many indebted planters in the southeast, opposed policies and supported protection for debtors and issuance of paper money.

The subsistence farmers and their allies far outnumbered the prosperous northeasterners, so their delegates dominated the convention that met in Hillsboro in July 1788 to consider the proposed new federal constitution. It was rejected, and the convention voted to adjourn. But 11 states had already voted to ratify, economic conditions were improving, and word spread of James Madison's willingness to draft amendments incorporating a bill of rights. Moreover, James Iredell and William R. Davies led an intensive campaign for ratification, and Federalists in Edenton and the northeast even hinted at that region's secession if North Carolina as a whole, along with Rhode Island, continued to reject the new structure. A second convention, assembled in Fayetteville in November 1789, voted 195 to 77 to approve the Constitution.

See also Albemarle Settlements; Cape Fear River Settlements; Cherokee Wars; Regulators.

Bibliography: Crow, Jeffrey J., *The Black Experience in Revolutionary North Carolina* (North Carolina Division of Archives and History, 1977); Ekirch, A. Roger, *"Poor Carolina": Politics and Society in Colonial North Carolina, 1729-1776* (Univ. of North Carolina Press, 1981); Fenn, Elizabeth A. and Wood, Peter H., *Natives and Newcomers* (Univ. of North Carolina Press, 1983); Lawson, John, *A New Voyage to Carolina*, Hugh T. Lefler, ed. (Univ. of North Carolina Press, 1967); Lefler, Hugh T. and Powell, William S., *Colonial North Carolina: A History* (Scribner's, 1973); Merrens, Harry Roy, *Colonial North Carolina in the Eighteenth Century* (Univ. of North Carolina Press, 1964); Milling, Chapman, *Red Carolinians*, 2nd ed. (Univ. of South Carolina Press, 1969).

Peter H. Wood
Duke University

NORTH, FREDERICK, LORD (1732-92) British prime minister during the Revolutionary War, North was born in London and educated at Eton and Oxford. In 1754 he was elected to the House of Commons, where he remained for nearly 40 years. In 1767 be became chancellor of the exchequer and in 1770 prime minister. Aligning himself with King George III and opposing George Grenville, William Pitt, and the Marquis of Rockingham, North carried out measures for taxing the colonies, although he had personal doubts about the policy. A plan for the colonies to tax themselves was proposed too late to stop the Battles of Lexington and Concord in Massachusetts (April 1775), but North always hoped for an early peace. After Lord Cornwallis surrendered at Yorktown in Virginia in 1781, North resigned. He continued to serve in Parliament and was named Earl of Guilford in 1790.

NORTHWEST COAST INDIANS Along the narrow coastal strip from the Alaskan panhandle to the northern border of California, there developed what some have described as the most elaborate nonagricultural societies in the world, and certainly one of the most original cultures of North America. Despite some 30 or more tribal and linguistic distinctions — including the Tlingit, Haida, Kwakiutl, Nootka, Chinook, and Tillamook — the Indians of the Northwest coast shared a basic common culture based on local fisheries, especially of the salmon, along with supplemental hunting and gathering. Permanent villages developed to exploit the various local sites, and the great abundance they produced contributed to societies with the greatest precontact population densities in North America, north of Mexico.

The seasonal nature of this subsistence strategy provided ample leisure to develop a complex social structure based largely on the accumulation of wealth, and the time to produce the goods that measured that wealth, including wooden plank houses, dugout canoes, watertight containers, carved masks, and totem poles. Northwest coast sculpture and painting rivaled the best indigenous art in the world. Among these Indians the potlatch ("giveaway" in Chinook trade jargon) was a social occasion to display that wealth by giving it away; potlatches were held at times of ceremony, of mourning, of achievement, or of transition, and the preparation for a major occasion might take several years.

The protection afforded by the coastal mountains kept contacts with Europeans to a minimum until the very end of the colonial period. By the 1780s the Russians were forcing their way south from Alaska, impressing the Tlingit into their service with great resulting violence on both sides. In the 1790s the French and the English began the exploration of Juan de Fuca Strait and the mouth of the Columbia River. But the great disruptive effects of alcohol, disease, and dispossession awaited the 19th century.

Bibliography: Gunther, Erna, *Indian Life on the Northwest Coast of North America* (Univ. of Chicago Press, 1972); Holm, Bill, *Northwest Coast Indian Art* (Univ. of Washington Press, 1965); Stewart, Hilary, *Indian Fishing* (Univ. of Washington Press, 1977).

John Mack Faragher
Mount Holyoke College

NORTHWEST ORDINANCE (1787) Passed by the Confederation Congress, then in 1789 reenacted by the Congress elected under the newly ratified federal constitution, the Northwest Ordinance provided for the structure of territorial government and created a procedure for the admission of territories as states. Congress had previously outlined such a process in the Land Ordinance of 1784, but the law had never taken effect since enactment of its provisions awaited the final cession of Western lands by the states. Meanwhile, Congress had negotiated the sale of great tracts of land to the Ohio Company, and American settlement had begun in Ohio as well as at Detroit, Vincennes, and American Bottom on the Mississippi; immediate provision had to be made for government there.

The ordinance first laid out a structure for territorial government. A governor, secretary, and three judges of the territory were to be appointed by the president, each required to live within the territory. The governor was given wide powers to command the territorial militia, to appoint magistrates and civil officers, to lay out counties and other civil divisions, to convene and dissolve the territorial assembly, and to veto its acts. The first assembly, consisting of these federal officers sitting together, was to adopt a code of criminal and civil laws. A second territorial stage would be reached when the resident population rose above 5,000 free adult males; they would then elect representatives to a lower house; with the governor, these representatives would nominate candidates which the president would select for an upper house. The two houses together would select a nonvoting representative to Congress. There were property qualifications for voting and for holding office, and in general this structure restricted democratic rights. Out of the territory northwest of the Ohio River no less than three, and not more than five, states would be admitted to the Union.

These states were guaranteed republican government and admission with status equal to the original states.

Secondly, the ordinance guaranteed the residents of the territory religious freedom, the writ of habeas corpus, trial by jury, and the protections of common law. Indians were to be protected in their rights and lands. Slavery was prohibited, but provisions were enacted for the extradition of fugitives from slavery. In 1790, Congress enacted these exact same provisions, with the exception of the anti-slavery clause, for territory south of the Ohio.

With the Land Ordinance of 1785, the Northwest Ordinance was the greatest achievement of the Confederation government. It provided for the constitutional governance of the territories, for an orderly procedure for attaining statehood, and for the guarantee of basic civil rights of all residents. Under its basic provisions 32 new states would be admitted to the Union.

See also Land Ordinance of 1785; Ohio Company.

Bibliography: Jensen, Merrill, *The New Nation: A History of the United States During the Confederation* (1950; reprint Northeastern Univ. Press, 1981).

John Mack Faragher
Mount Holyoke College

NORTHWEST PASSAGE A sea route from the Atlantic Ocean to the Pacific, cutting through or around northern North America, was the object of an intensive European search for over 300 years before its existence was verified in the mid-19th century. The search began as soon as navigators and geographers agreed that Christopher Columbus's landfall was, as Amerigo Vespucci declared, a new continent. After the earliest explorers for the passage—Giovanni da Verrazano and Estevan Gomez in the 1520s; Jacques Cartier in the 1530s—established the continuity of the North American coast to the latitudes of Labrador and eliminated the possibility of a passage at the St. Lawrence River, attention shifted to the far north. The Spanish and Portuguese, who had developed southern empires and trade routes, left the field to the northern Europeans.

The English, who first attempted to locate a northeast passage through the Arctic waters north of Asia in the 1550s but could get no farther than Novaya Zemlya, inaugurated a long series of explorations of the northwest Atlantic with the voyages of Martin Frobisher in the 1570s and John Davis in the 1580s. Their failures delayed further progress until Henry Hudson, in 1610, passed through the strait and into the great bay that thereafter took his name. He took Hudson Bay to be the Pacific and died before Thomas Button in 1613 and William Baffin in 1615 proved otherwise. The continuing explorations of Hudson Bay—by Luke Fox and Thomas James in the 1630s and Christopher Middleton and William Moor in the 1740s—finally demonstrated conclusively the lack of an outlet to the Pacific from the bay. Vitus Bering pointed toward the possibility of a western approach to the passage with his discovery of the strait between Asia and North America in 1741. James Cook was on such a search in the 1770s, as was Jean-François de Galaup, Comte de La Perouse, in the 1780s. George Vancouver surveyed the area of the Strait of Juan de Fuca for the inlet to a passage in the 1790s. These various explorations established the continuity of the Pacific coast of North America from Oregon to northern Alaska and ruled out any but the most northerly passage.

This northernmost passage, through the straits and channels of the Arctic Ocean, was shown to exist in the 1850s, but the first European to pilot through them was Roald Amundsen in 1906. Even today the Northwest Passage is impractical as a commercial seaway because of the severe ice and weather.

See also Exploration; individual biographies.

Bibliography: Morison, Samuel Eliot, *The European Discovery of America: Northern Voyages, A.D. 500-1600* (Univ. of Oxford Press, 1971).

John Mack Faragher
Mount Holyoke College

NORUMBEGA Norumbega was the name used to describe a mythical city, province, or kingdom on the northern Atlantic coast of North America. It appeared for the first time, as "Aranbega," on the Verrazano map of 1529. Later in the 16th century it was used as a general geographical term for the North American coast north of Florida, but its original Algonquian form *Nolumbeka*, meaning "falls and still water," probably referred only to the lower Penobscot Valley in Maine. More fanciful and unverified interpretations suggest that the name was evidence of early Viking colonization in America and that it was derived from the Scandinavian *Norroenbygda*, or "Norway Land."

NOUE, ZACHARIE ROBUTEL DE LA (1624-91)   A French explorer in South America, Noue trained as a priest but spent his life as a scientist. In 1665 he explored Tierra del Fuego and the west coast of Patagonia. Taken prisoner by the Indians, he adopted their customs and learned their language. They finally permitted him to leave on a French ship, but his two-volume journal of his experiences with the Indians, published in 1675, was so vivid that the French abandoned further attempts to settle the region.

NURSE, REBECCA (1621-92)   A victim of the Salem witch trials, Rebecca Nurse lived in Salem, Massachusetts, with her prosperous farmer husband. Her family, having been involved in a number of local squabbles, had enemies who capitalized on the witchcraft frenzy of 1691. Nurse, although 71 years old, ill, and feeble, was denounced, arrested for witchcraft, and examined in 1692. She denied any such guilt, but certain town women threw contrived fits because of her presence, which led to her indictment and trial. The verdict, although at first "not guilty," was reversed after the judges pressured the jury to reconsider her testimony. The governor granted her a reprieve, but public outcry led to her execution in 1692. Public outcry of another kind was to follow: Those outraged by the events leading up to and resulting in Nurse's execution initiated what is thought to be the first significant counteraction to the Salem witch trials.

O

OACPICAGIGUA, LUÍS (flourished c.1750) A rebel leader of the Pima people of southern Arizona and northern Mexico, Oacpicagigua was born in Saric, Mexico, and urged his people to expel the Spanish from their territory. The most obvious foreign presence among the Pima were the nine Catholic missions founded by the Jesuit Eusebio Francisco Kino in the late 17th century. In 1751, Oacpicagigua openly accused the mission priests of the oppression of the local population and personally killed 18 priests in his hometown. This revolt did not gain the general support of the Pima, but before it was suppressed and Oacpicagigua was captured more than 100 Jesuit missionaries had been killed.

OCCOM, SAMSON (1723-92) A Presbyterian missionary to the Indians, Occom was a Mohegan, born in New London, Connecticut. He was educated by Dr. Eleazar Wheelock, who baptized him in 1741 under the Christian name "Samson." In 1749 he settled on eastern Long Island and in 1759 was ordained by the Presbyterian Church as a missionary to the Montauk tribe. Maintaining his ties to Wheelock, he traveled to England in 1765 to raise funds for Wheelock's proposed Indian college. He later bitterly opposed the decision to restrict that college, which Wheelock had named Dartmouth, to whites. In 1786, Occom founded the Brotherton Community of Christian Indians in western New York.
See also Wheelock, Eleazar.

OCONOSTOTA (c.1710-83) Cherokee war chief, whose name was derived from the Cherokee word *aganu-stata*, "groundhog sausage," he was a leader of Indian resistance to colonial expansion. In 1760 he gained the support of the Creek for an attack on Fort Prince George, South Carolina, an act that initiated an escalation of hostilities between the Cherokee and the colonists. His subsequent attack on Fort Loudon in Tennessee provoked a retaliatory raid against the Lower Towns of the Cherokee. In 1768, Oconostota made peace with the Iroquois, but in 1783, after a series of disastrous defeats at the hands of the Continental Army, he gave up the military command of the Cherokee to his son Tuksi.

OGLETHORPE, JAMES EDWARD (1696-1785) The founder of the colony of Georgia, Oglethorpe was born in

James Oglethorpe wanted Georgia to serve as a haven for hardworking poor people. *(Library of Congress)*

London, and received a typical gentleman's education. In 1722 he was elected to Parliament and he devoted himself to a number of good causes, including the establishment of a foundling hospital in London. He conceived the idea of sending debtors to America and joined with others in petitioning Parliament for permission. However, Parliament was reluctant to help prisoners of any sort. Oglethorpe and his friends broadened their objectives. They would send hard-working poor people who would produce silk and wine for the mother country while protecting the valuable colony of South Carolina against the Spanish in Florida and their Indian allies. Thus, few if any debtors accompanied Oglethorpe to the colony of Georgia. The ship *Ann* landed her passengers on Yamacraw Bluff in February 1733.

Oglethorpe proved to be a good friend to the Indians. Tomochichi, the elderly chief of the Yamacraw, and Mary Musgrove, niece of the Emperor Brims, served as intermediaries with the Creek nation. Oglethorpe won the trust of the Creek by reforming the Indian trade. He conducted an unsuccessful siege of St. Augustine, Florida, in 1740 and two years later defeated a Spanish counterattack near his military town of Frederica on St. Simon's Island. After another attempt to capture St. Augustine in 1743, he returned to England. Oglethorpe was venerated as a hero by the time of his death on June 30, 1785.

See also Creek Indians; Georgia.

Edward J. Cashin
Augusta College

OHIO COMPANY This most famous of the colonial land companies was organized in 1747 by a group of Virginia planters interested in speculation in western lands. Two years later Britain's Privy Council, on the condition that a fort be built and the lands be settled, granted the company 200,000 acres bounded by the Ohio and Great Kanawha rivers and the Allegheny Mountains. Alarmed by the explorations and settlement projects of such company agents as Christopher Gist, the French in 1753 built a series of forts to defend their claim to the Ohio country. This imperial rivalry inaugurated the last intercolonial war for the control of North America—the French and Indian War. A later company, the Ohio Company of Associates, organized in 1786 by New Englanders, founded Marietta (1788) and settled the Western Reserve in the area of present-day Cleveland.

See also French and Indian War.

OHIO RIVER From its source at the "Forks of the Ohio," the junction of the Allegheny and Monongahela rivers at the site of present-day Pittsburgh, the Ohio ("great river" in Iroquoian) flows 981 miles to its mouth on the Mississippi, forming a natural link between the Appalachian highlands and the central valley of the North American continent. The Sieur de La Salle was supposedly the first European to navigate its waters (1669-70) as far as the rapids opposite present-day Louisville, Kentucky, although the English claimed that a fur trader, Abraham Wood, had discovered and claimed the river for Britain in the 1650s. It was completely mapped by the 1680s but little used by either French or English until the early 18th century when they entered an intense competition for the trade of the valley and the heart of the continent. The French and Indian War began over the issue of control of the Ohio country.

OLD NORTH CHURCH It was in the belfry of the Old North Church that sexton Robert Newman, following his arrangement with Paul Revere, hung two lanterns on the night of April 18, 1775, to warn Charlestown's patriots that

British troops were crossing the Charles River on the eve of their fateful march to Lexington and Concord.

The Old North Church (officially Christ Church) on Salem Street in the North End is modern Boston's oldest church. When King's Chapel could no longer contain Boston's growing Anglican community, Old North was erected in 1723 with the Reverend Timothy Cutler as its first rector. The architect is believed to have been William Price, who patterned the structure after a Christopher Wren church in England. Built of Medford brick, Old North boasts walls 2 1/2 feet thick, a chime of eight bells (1774), a graceful spire, and one of the nation's earliest monuments erected to the memory of George Washington (1815).

Boston's Old North Church became a symbol of the American Revolution after Paul Revere's famous ride.(Library of Congress)

OLD SPANISH TRAIL This overland route between Santa Fe (New Mexico) and Los Angeles (California) was pioneered in 1776 when two Franciscan missionaries first blazed a path into Utah but were turned back by snowstorms. The route was used for trade with the Indians of the Utah country, but the connection to California awaited the early 19th century. The Old Spanish Trail led up the Rio Chama Valley, passed through present-day

Durango, Colorado, crossed the Grand and Green rivers, then went southwest across the desert to the Mojave River, and over the Cajon Pass to Los Angeles. In the 1830s it became a regular trading route and later, in the 1850s, an important emigrant route to southern California.

OLIVE BRANCH PETITION (1775) With the battles of Lexington, Concord, and Bunker Hill behind them, the Congress assembled at Philadelphia in the summer of 1775 faced a crucial decision: Should a continental army be raised to fight against the British? Before Bunker Hill in June, Americans had favored a reconciliation, but opinions were beginning to shift. Congress decided to make a final overture of peace by drafting in July the Olive Branch Petition to King George III. The letter requested the King to find a resolution to the conflict. Congress, though, proceeded with plans for war, the numbers growing of those who no longer believed in the King as America's advocate. The petition went unanswered.

OÑATE, JUAN DE (?1549-1624?) A Spanish soldier and explorer in the New World, Oñate served for 20 years on the northern frontier of New Spain before contracting with the viceroy of New Spain in 1595 to outfit and lead a party at his own expense in search of the mines rumored to exist in New Mexico. Beginning in 1598, Oñate conquered much of New Mexico in a fruitless search for treasure. Scouting parties sent out by Oñate reached Kansas (1601) and the Gulf of California (1605) but the Spanish government became increasingly frustrated despite Oñate's assurance that mines did exist. A sudden upswing in native conversions convinced the government to declare New Mexico a crown colony, but in 1608 Oñate was replaced as governor by Pedro de Peralta.

OPECHANCANOUGH (c.1545-1644) A Powhatan chief, also known as Mangopeomen, he was the brother of Powhatan and a committed enemy of the English colonists in Virginia. He first came to prominence with his capture of Captain John Smith in 1608, an incident that ended with Smith's dramatic rescue by Pocahontas. Smith later appealed to Opechancanough for food for the hungry Jamestown colonists, but when Smith's request was angrily refused, Opechancanough was taken prisoner by the English and ransomed in return for a treaty of friendship.

In 1618, after the death of Powhatan, Opechancanough gained power, even though the tribe was nominally ruled by his elder brother Opitchipan. Having been humiliated by the English, he planned their destruction, and on March 22, 1622, he led coordinated attacks on the English settlements along the James River in which almost 350 colonists were killed. Opechancanough's hostility continued and even intensified in his later years. In 1644, although con-

fined by old age to a litter, he again led an attack on the English colonies, during which he was captured and brought to Jamestown. His long career as an enemy of the English had aroused the intense hatred of the colonists, and he was executed by his guards.

See also Powhatan.

OSBORN, SARAH HAGGAR (1714-96) A religious teacher and schoolmistress; born in London, she immigrated with her parents to Newport, Rhode Island, in 1729. At the age of 17, she defied her parents and married a seaman, Samuel Wheaton, with whom she had one child before Wheaton was lost at sea three years later. Thrown on her own resources, she took over a girls' school, advertising "Reading, Writing, Plain Work, Embroidery, Tent Stitch, Samplers, etc. . . . on reasonable Terms." She probably originated one of the Newport sampler designs, recognized as the liveliest and most colorful of schoolgirl art.

In 1741, she organized the first Female Prayer Society in the Congregational Church, and the same year she married merchant Henry Osborn, an older widower with three children. In 1744, Sarah's son died, Henry's business and health failed, and Sarah resolved "to enter again into the calling of keeping school." By the early 1760s her school had grown to nearly 70 students; during Newport's religious revivals she also taught large numbers (300-500) of black and white children and adults during the evenings. Some saw her religious leadership as inappropriate, but Osborn defended her work as inspired by God and regenerative to herself. Her diary and some letters were published after her death by her minister, Samuel Hopkins.

OSWALD, RICHARD (c.1705-84) A peace negotiator for the British government during the Revolutionary War, Oswald was a native of Scotland. He made his way to London as a young man, becoming a contractor for supplying troops during the Seven Year's War. Afterwards he went to Germany as a commissary-general and then to North America. Returning to London as a merchant before the American Revolution, he became acquainted with Adam Smith and Lord Shelburne. He met Benjamin Franklin in Paris in 1777. Business connections with Americans, such as Henry Laurens, made him a valuable consultant to Shelburne. In 1782, Shelburne, as prime minister, sent Oswald to Paris to meet with Franklin and discuss a peace treaty to end the Revolutionary War, which they concluded. But because Shelburne was out of office, Oswald was recalled before he could sign the final agreement. The Treaty of Paris was signed on Britain's behalf by others on September 3, 1783.

See also Paris, Treaty of.

James Otis led the opposition in Massachusetts to the Stamp Act. *(Library of Congress)*

OSWEGO, FORT   Fort Oswego was established after a trading post was founded in 1722 by English and Dutch traders at the mouth of the Oswego River on Lake Ontario. The fort, built five years later to anchor the western end of the Mohawk corridor, became the most important English position on the Great Lakes. Burned by the French (1756) during the French and Indian War, it was rebuilt by the British and renamed Fort Ontario three years later, and it was the staging area for Lord Jeffrey Amherst's final attack on Montreal in 1760. By this time Oswego had become the mercantile center of the New York fur trade. After the Revolutionary War, the British continued to occupy the area in defiance of the Treaty of Paris (1783). They finally evacuated it after Jay's Treaty in 1796, but recaptured it during the War of 1812, after which it reverted to the United States.

OTIS, JAMES (1725-1783)   An American lawyer and politician, he was born in West Barnstable, Massachusetts, educated at Harvard College, and studied law. Advocate general of the British admiralty court in Boston until 1760, he resigned his position to serve in the Massachusetts legislature. During this time he protested, sometimes with passionate speeches and pamphlets, the British writs of assistance that allowed British customs agents to search private property for illegal goods. In 1765, at the Stamp Act Congress, he opposed the Stamp Act on the grounds that it represented taxation without representation in Parliament. A head injury received in a political dispute in 1769 curtailed his career, and from 1771 he lived quietly. He was killed by lightning in 1783.

OUTACITY (flourished c.1720)   A Cherokee chief also known as Otassite, Outassatah, and Wootasite, he was one of the predecessors of Attakullakulla and Oconostota. He was influential during a time of relative tranquility between the Cherokee nation and the British colonists; the Cherokee's main concerns in this period were the territorial incursions of neighboring Indian tribes. In 1713 the Cherokee joined with the British in a victorious campaign against the Tuscarora, but this alliance was not to last. After the embassy of Sir Alexander Cumming in 1730 and the arrival of a new wave of settlers, Outacity's successors adopted a far more militant policy.

P

PACA, WILLIAM (1740-99) Born in Maryland, Paca was 31 when he became a member of the colony's legislature. He was a staunch opponent of royal government and in 1774 was sent as a delegate to the Continental Congress. He remained until 1779 and was a signer of the Declaration of Independence. From 1777 to 1779 he also served as a Maryland state senator and in 1778 was appointed the state's chief justice. He rapidly changed public offices, becoming chief judge of the court of appeals in 1780 and governor in 1782. In 1788 he was a member of the state convention to ratify the U.S. Constitution and in 1789

Thomas Paine's American writings emphasized the potential for a new and pure nation state in North America. *(Library of Congress)*

became a U.S. district judge, serving until his death in 1799.

PADILLA, JUAN DE (c.1500-42) Padilla, a Franciscan missionary, accompanied Francisco Coronado in 1540 during his exploration of Arizona and New Mexico and belonged to the Tovar expedition that Coronado sent out after he had reached Cibola. With Trevor, Padilla was one of the first white men to see the Hopi towns of northeastern Arizona. It was in these towns that the Spanish first heard rumors of the great river to the west. When Coronado's army turned south in 1542 to return home, Padilla remained in Quivira (Kansas), where he was killed by Indians, becoming the first missionary killed by Indians on future U.S. soil.

See also Coronado, Francisco Vásquez de.

PAINE, ROBERT TREAT (1731-1814) A native of Boston and a Harvard graduate, Paine entered the ministry in 1755. He served as a chaplain in the French and Indian War but afterwards decided to study law. He acted as prosecutor, with Samuel Quincy, in the trial of the British soldiers involved in the Boston Massacre. Paine was a member of both the General Court and the Provincial Congress of Massachusetts. He attended the Continental Congress and signed the Declaration of Independence. From 1777 to 1790 he was the state attorney general and was responsible for disposing of Loyalist property. He also helped draft the state constitution in 1780 and was a state supreme court judge.

PAINE, THOMAS (1737-1809) Born in Thetford, Norfolk, England, Paine devoted his life to American affairs between his arrival in Philadelphia in 1774 and his departure for Europe in 1787. He put his substantial eloquence and rhetorical skills in the service of the cause of political liberty, publishing "African Slavery in America" (1775), "A Dialogue between General Wolfe and General Gage" (1775), *Common Sense* (1776), *The American Crisis* (1776-83), and *Public Good* (1780), which argues for "a continental constitution, defining and describing the powers and authority of congress." After 1787 he lived an eventful life that included indictment for treason in England, a seat in the French National Convention, imprisonment under Robespierre, and two major works, *The Rights of Man* (1791-92) and *The Age of Reason* (1794-96), the former banned in England and the latter an influential statement of Enlightenment deism and natural science.

Paine's rhetoric joined nature, common sense, virtue and an American republic against custom, superstition, vice, and European monarchy. He nourished a sense of American exceptionalism by invoking the notion of a new, pure republic in America, independent of European corruption. He wrote, "We have it in our power to begin the world over again. A situation, similar to the present, hath not happened since the days of Noah until now. The birthday of a new world is at hand, and a race of men, perhaps as numerous as all Europe contains, are to receive their portion of freedom from the events of a few months." Although reviled as an atheist, he believed that through nature God spoke the lessons of "science and the arts" to allow humankind to pursue its "own comfort, and Learn from My Munificence to All, to Be Kind to Each Other." He died in poverty in New York City in 1809, his anticlerical deism and his belief in the possibility of a pure social union without conflict rendered irrelevant by historical change.

See also Common Sense.

Bibliography: Aldridge, Alfred Owen, *Thomas Paine's American Ideology* (Univ. of Delaware Press, 1984); Foner, Eric, *Tom Paine and Revolutionary America* (Oxford Univ. Press, 1976); Foner, Philip S., ed., *The Complete Writings of Thomas Paine*, 2 vols. (Citadel, 1945).

John Saillant
Brown University

PARIS, TREATY OF (1763)   A treaty between Great Britain on the one hand and France and its ally Spain on the other, the 1763 Treaty of Paris concluded the French and Indian War (Seven Years War). It effectively recognized the end of French power in North America. Britain received from France all of Canada and all territory west of the Mississippi River except New Orleans. Spain ceded Florida to Britain and in return had Cuba restored to it. France claimed the islands of St. Pierre and Miquelon in the Gulf of St. Lawrence and received fishing privileges along the northern and western coasts of Newfoundland. Britain retained the islands of St. Vincent, Tobago, and Dominica in the West Indies, while St. Lucia was given to France. In the earlier, secret Treaty of Fontainebleau (1762), France had given Spain all of Louisiana west of the Mississippi, plus New Orleans. As a result of the Treaty of Paris, the British and Spanish were the greatest colonial empires in the Western Hemisphere.

PARIS, TREATY OF (1783)   To end the Revolutionary War, diplomats had to negotiate separate treaties between Great Britain and four separate nations: the United States, the Netherlands, and the Bourbon monarchies of France

and Spain. This process was complicated by the fact that each combatant pursued its own objectives and by the fact that the four powers were not a true alliance, but rather cobelligerents who might or might not be obligated by existing relationships. For example, in June 1781 when the Continental Congress empowered a team to handle any peace talks, its five members (Benjamin Franklin, John Adams, John Jay, Henry Laurens, and Thomas Jefferson) were instructed to consult only with France.

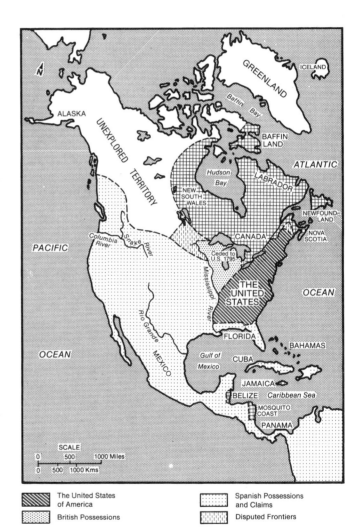

Treaty of Paris. *(Martin Greenwald Associates, Inc.)*

Opening Negotiations.   Movement towards peace in the aftermath of Lord Cornwallis's defeat at Yorktown began when a new British government took office on

March 27, 1782, under the Marquis of Rockingham (until his death on July 1) and then under the Earl of Shelburne. The ministry wanted to end the conflict, but hoped to win favorable conditions by playing their opponents against each other. As a first step they sent Richard Oswald to Paris to open informal talks with Franklin, and later with Jay and Adams. Neither Jefferson (detained in Virginia by family problems) nor Laurens (captured at sea and imprisoned in the Tower of London until exchanged for Cornwallis) played a substantive role. Other British overtures were made to the French and Spanish.

Final Conditions. The original Franklin-Oswald meeting produced on July 12, 1782, a specific set of American demands for London to consider. During a second round of talks in late September, Jay used the British to forestall a Spanish plan to gain control of the entire Mississippi River watershed. By dropping claims in Canada, the Americans persuaded Oswald to agree to setting the nation's western boundary at the river itself. On October 5, Jay, Franklin, and Oswald signed a draft agreement to that effect, contingent upon the French and British coming to terms. Shelburne insisted on some modifications, primarily trade clauses and protection for Loyalist property, and once these were added, a preliminary Anglo-American treaty was signed in Paris on November 30.

Parallel negotiations resulted in similar agreements between Great Britain and the two Bourbon nations on January 20, 1783, and with the Dutch on September 2, 1783. Once the individual governments ratified the initial treaties (Congress's approval came on April 15), work began on the final or definitive versions. Ironically, Parliament turned Shelburne out of office for being too generous, but the Fox-North coalition that came to power next could not win any additional concessions, and on September 3 its agents signed three definitive treaties. Late in the morning, in Paris, Britain's David Hartley, who had replaced Oswald, and Jay, Adams, Franklin, and Laurens for the United States concluded their agreement. Several hours later in the palace at nearby Versailles, the French and Spanish treaties were also completed, basically restoring prewar conditions. France and the Netherlands (whose definitive treaty followed in early 1784) each received minor concessions in the Caribbean, with the former also picking up Senegal. Spain fared somewhat better, receiving title to both Minorca and Florida.

The Anglo-American accord (ratified by Congress on January 14, 1784) recognized the United States as an independent nation with Mississippi as its western boundary and with important fishing rights off Canada. Both parties agreed not to impede the collection of prewar debts. Congress promised to "earnestly recommend" to the states that Loyalist property seized during the war be returned;

and the British pledged to evacuate remaining forces "with all convenient speed." Actually, each party evaded full compliance for about a decade, but the membership of the United States in the family of nations never was seriously questioned again.

See also Revolutionary War, Battles of; individual biographies.

Bibliography: Hoffman, Ronald and Albert, Peter J., eds., *Peace and the Peacemakers: The Treaty of 1783* (Univ. Press of Virginia, 1986).

Robert K. Wright, Jr.
U.S. Army Center of Military History

PARKER, JOHN (1729-75) A farmer and a mechanic, Parker held various town offices in his native Lexington, Massachusetts, throughout his life. During the French and Indian War he fought at Louisburg and Quebec and may have been a member of Roger's Rangers. As the Revolution neared, Parker became a captain of the Minutemen. On April 19, 1775, he placed a guard around the house in Lexington in which John Hancock and Samuel Adams were staying. He assembled his Minutemen, who were then ordered by British Major Pitcairn to disperse and disarm. The colonists refused, and shots were fired. Parker was among the 10 wounded; 8 others died. Parker himself was dead by autumn.

See also Lexington and Concord, Battle of.

PARRIS, SAMUEL (1653-1720) An American minister, he was born in England and by 1689 had been contracted to serve as minister for the church in Salem Village, now Danvers, Massachusetts. Three years later his daughter and his niece came down with illnesses that local physicians could not explain and so blamed them on the Devil. Parris accepted hysterical evidence against his West Indian slave and others and ordered the execution of some 20 "witches." Although he was later vindicated of any crime, he was asked to leave. He refused and, in lieu of salary, took over some church land. A court order to relinquish the land caused his return to Boston in 1697.

PARSONS' CAUSE In 1748 a Virginia statute required that Anglican clergymen be paid 17,280 pounds of tobacco per year. As the price of tobacco climbed, planters sought help from the legislature, which in 1758 declared that debts could be paid in currency at two pennies per pound of tobacco. Religious tensions between Anglican ministers and their parishioners added to the problem. Anticlerical sentiment had risen, especially in counties such as Hanover and New Kent, as the number of religious dissenters increased. Through a petition by the clergy, the Privy Council in England disallowed the Two Penny Act in 1759. Several clergymen then sued to recover the full value of their salaries. Reverend James Maury won his case but failed to recover damages when Patrick Henry made a stirring speech to the jury, declaring the clergy disloyal to the community. Henry added that King George himself had degenerated into a tyrant by interfering in colonial matters of that nature.

The Parsons' Cause represents one of the challenges to law and authority that began in the 1740s and that culminated in the Revolution. The most direct connection between the two events was Patrick Henry, who saw in both the Parsons' Cause and the Stamp Act crisis an encroachment of colonial liberties.

See also Henry, Patrick.

PASTORIUS, FRANCIS DANIEL (1651-c.1720) A German-born lawyer, author, educator, Pastorius acted as an agent for German Pietists and Mennonites in Frankfurt-am-Main. He organized the first group of German immigrants to come to the colonies (1683) and settled with them on land he purchased in Quaker William Penn's colony of Pennsylvania, near Philadelphia, a place soon known as Germantown. He served as mayor, teacher, and land agent and wrote several books about his adopted land. In 1688 he authored the first protest against slavery in the colonies.

PATROONSHIPS In 1629 the Dutch West India Company attempted to promote settlement of its colony of New Netherland by offering large estates to those transporting 50 settler families. The grantees, or patroons, were given feudal rights of perpetual ownership as well as control of local offices and civil and criminal courts. They could also exact payment from their tenants in money, goods, or services. Three patroonships were established: Pavonia, which included Staten Island; Swaanendael, on the west side of Delaware Bay; and Rensselaerswyck, near Fort Orange (later Albany) on the Hudson River. Only the last of these was successful, ruled first by the absentee landlord Kiliaen van Rensselaer, Amsterdam diamond and gold merchant, and later by his descendants, who lived upon the estate. The perpetual leases of the patroons were not abolished until the Anti-Rent War (1839-46).

See also New Netherland; Van Rensselaer, Kiliaen.

PAVONIA MASSACRE (1643) The opening attack of the Dutch-Indian War (1643-45), it came as the result of the decision of New Amsterdam's Governor Willem Kieft to attack a band of Wecquaesgeeks who had encamped near the village of Pavonia on the western bank of the Hudson, opposite Manhattan. This band had sought shelter among the Dutch colonists from their Iroquois enemies, but the brutality of February 25, 1643, by the Dutch soldiers killed more than 80 defenseless Wecquaesgeek men, women, and children, united all the Indian peoples of the area in recognizing the threat posed by the Dutch. Attacks against Dutch settlements on Long Island and Manhattan and in Westchester lasted until 1645.

PAXTON BOYS The mob of Pennsylvania frontiersmen known as the Paxton Boys massacred a group of peaceful Indians in 1763 and, joined by hundreds more frontiersmen, marched on Philadelphia the next year. After the violence of the French and Indian War, and immediately following the bloody summer battles of Pontiac's Rebellion in 1763, this frontier lynch mob, seeking revenge, had attacked the small remnant of the once powerful Susquehannock Indians at their village of Conestoga, killing seven men, five women, and eight children, including one old man who had witnessed their treaty signing with William Penn in 1701.

The Pennsylvania assembly ordered that these Paxton Boys be brought to Philadelphia for trial. Instead, some 600 frontiersmen marched to the capital to demand military protection. The city was thrown into panic and mustered its militia in defense but, in part through the efforts of Benjamin Franklin, the frontiersmen were persuaded to issue a formal protest, which later resulted in their obtaining greater representation in the legislature. This incident was illustrative of the tensions that existed between frontier and coastal sections, evident in other conflicts such as Bacon's Rebellion and the Regulator Movement; and instructive of the fate of Christian and pacified Indians during frontier conflicts, such as King Philip's War.

See also Bacon's Rebellion; Regulators.

PEALE, CHARLES WILLSON (1741-1827) The most famous portraitist of the Revolutionaries, Peale was born in Queen Annes County, Maryland. He traveled incessantly from 1765 to 1776, including two years of study in London, until he settled in Philadelphia, where he participated actively in public affairs, including two years in the militia and three in politics. He painted commissioned portraits and in 1782 opened his "Gallery of Great Men," an exhibition of portraits of leading Revolutionaries. He painted George Washington from life seven times, first in 1772, leaving a record of Washington's development as a public icon and bringing himself fame and several public commissions to paint Washington. After 1786 he expanded his interests to include mezzotints, *trompe l'oeil* painting, inventions, and natural science, opening in 1786 a museum (the first major one in the United States) of portraits, mounted animals, fossils, and curios. His most enduring paintings date from the years after 1786: "Thomas Jefferson" (1791), "The Staircase Group" (1795), "The Exhumation of the Mastadon" (1806-08), and "The Artist in his Museum" (1822).

He was an ardent republican who sought government support for art and a didactic role for art in the promotion of public virtue. Using the Revolutionaries, he sought public edification through the depiction of virtuous, heroic individuals in the service of the republic. His Revolutionary portraits depict the serene, dignified individuals he believed should be social models, even though he himself had recorded the horror of war in his wartime diary.

See also Republicanism; Art.

Bibliography: Ellis, Joseph J., *After the Revolution: Profiles of Early American Culture* (Norton, 1979); Richardson, Edgar P., *Charles Willson Peale and His World* (Abrams, 1982); Sellers, Charles Coleman, *Charles Willson Peale* (Scribner's, 1969).

John Saillant
Brown University

Following his religious convictions, William Penn made Pennsylvania a center of religious tolerance from its founding. *(Library of Congress)*

PELHAM, PETER (c.1695-1751) A mezzotint engraver and painter, Peter Pelham was born a "gentleman" in England, established a very profitable mezzotint engraving practice, and emigrated to Boston at an unknown date for obscure reasons. The London artist who engraved portraits of Queen Anne, George I, the Earl of Derby, and other English aristocrats seems to be the same one who came to America. Scholars believe that he may have abandoned his thriving London trade because of private troubles.

He brought a portrait he had begun in 1724 for Massachusetts Governor Samuel Shute as an entrée into Boston society, and he did do a portrait and engraving of Cotton Mather and of the painter John Smibert, who came to Boston in 1730. Pelham was unable to earn enough to support his family through his artistry and started a school where he taught arithmetic and dancing. Twice a widower, he then married Mary Copley in 1748, who brought her late husband's tobacco shop as another source of income. Both Mary son, John Singleton Copley, and Mary and Peter's son, Henry Pelham, grew up to be artists in their own rights.

PENDLETON, EDMUND (1721-1803) Active in Virginia politics from his youth, Pendleton was elected to the House of Burgesses in 1752 and later became its speaker. He was trained in law and served on various courts in his lifetime. In 1774 and 1775 he acted as a delegate to the Continental Congress but returned to Virginia to preside over the state convention held in 1776. Pendleton drew up the resolutions upon which Jefferson based the Declaration of Independence. Thomas Pendleton's abilities as a moderator made him a natural leader of the Virginia convention ratifying the U.S. Constitution in 1788. A strong Federalist, he believed the opposition to the Constitution was based on fears "improperly implied to this government."

PENN, JOHN (1729-95) The grandson of William Penn and one of the proprietors of Pennsylvania, John Penn was schooled in Switzerland at the University of Geneva. He was a Pennsylvania councillor in the 1750s and served as a delegate to the intercolonial Albany Congress (1754). After a stay in England he returned to Pennsylvania in 1763 as lieutenant governor, holding that office with one interruption until the end of the proprietorship (1776). Penn defended the proprietary interests while attempting to hold a middle course during the controversy between Britain and the colonies. After independence the new regime confirmed his share of family property in Pennsylvania where he lived the rest of his life.

See also Penn Family.

PENN, JOHN (1740-88) A signer of the Declaration of Independence, Penn was born in Caroline County, Virginia. He practiced law in Virginia for 12 years before moving in 1774 to North Carolina, where he was sent to the provincial congress (1775). After serving on several committees, he was elected to the Second Continental Congress. He urged independence from Britain and signed the Declaration of Independence (1776). Penn served as a member of the Continental Congress (1775- 77, 1778-80) and became a member of the North Carolina board of war (1780), but Governor Thomas Burke abolished the board (1781). Penn then practiced law for the rest of his life.

PENN, WILLIAM (1644-1718)   An English Quaker and the founder and proprietor of Pennsylvania, Penn was born in London, the son of Admiral Sir William Penn. He received his education at Christ Church College, Oxford, from which he was expelled in 1661 for religious nonconformity. He also took instruction from the French Protestant theologian Moses Aymrault at Saumur while on a two-year visit to the continent (1662-64), and he studied law at Lincoln's Inn, London, upon his return.

Association with Dissenters and absorption of Quaker beliefs in his youth decisively influenced the course of Penn's adult life. He was deeply moved in 1657 when he heard the dynamic speaker Thomas Loe, a follower of George Fox, founder of the Society of Friends (Quakers), preach with conviction on the "Inner Light." Loe's spirited sermons were instrumental in pulling Penn away from the Anglican faith and converting him to the Society of Friends in 1666.

Penn developed an intense belief in the right of the individual to worship as he pleased. Between 1666 when he converted to the Society of Friends and 1681, Penn traveled, preached, and wrote extensively defending his ideas, explaining Quaker beliefs and practices, and advocating liberty of conscience. Among the many works in which he argued these views, the most significant written in this period included *The Sandy Foundation Shaken* (1668), *Truth Exalted* (1668), *No Cross, No Crown* (1669), *The Great Case of Liberty of Conscience* (1670), *The Christian Quaker* (1674), *A Treatise of Oaths* (1675), and *An Address to Protestants of all Persuasions* (1679). Authorities imprisoned him four times for writing his thoughts, attending Quaker meetings, and preaching the word.

Despite religious persecution and the fact that the monarchy moved to tighten royal control over the colonies in this period, Charles II made William Penn proprietor of Pennsylvania through charter rights granted on March 4, 1681. This transaction settled a debt of 16,000 pounds the King owed Penn's father. In 1682 the Duke of York, later King James II, added to Penn's holdings by deeding to him his claims to Delaware. The proprietor envisioned the colony as "the seed of a nation," and he planned it as a "holy experiment."

Colonial Proprietor.   Penn's success in obtaining the charter culminated several years of Quaker interest in establishing a New World colony. His hand in the Concessions and Agreement (1676) of West Jersey provided

experience in founding a "holy experiment" based on liberty of conscience, Whig republicanism, and the traditional rights of Englishmen. Penn was not unaware of the financial benefits to be derived from land sales, quitrents, and flourishing trade. Penn wrote four frames of government for his colony: 1682, 1683, 1696, and 1701. He visited the settlement twice: 1682-84 and 1699-1701. During the first stay he planned the city of Philadelphia, established peaceable relations with the Delaware Indians, and developed the Great Law of 1682. Conflict with Lord Baltimore over the Pennsylvania boundary with Maryland required his return to England. During the second visit he implemented the Charter of Privileges (1701) that established unicameral legislative predominance in Pennsylvania government to 1776.

In 1712 a paralytic stroke cut short his planned return of Pennsylvania's government to the Crown. Hannah, his second wife, assumed the administrative duties of the province. Penn lingered on and died July 30, 1718. Three sons, John, Thomas, and Richard, participated in the proprietorship after their mother died in 1717.

See also Concessions and Agreement; Delaware; Frame of Government; New Jersey; Pennsylvania; Quakers.

Bibliography: Bronner, Edwin B., *William Penn's "Holy Experiment": The Founding of Pennsylvania, 1681-1701* (Temple Univ. Publications, 1963); Dunn, Mary Maples, *William Penn: Politics and Conscience* (Princeton Univ. Press, 1967); Illick, Joseph, *William Penn the Politician: His Relations with the English Government* (Cornell Univ. Press, 1965); Peare, Catherine Owens, *William Penn: A Biography* (Lippincott, 1957); Soderlund, Jean R., ed., *William Penn and the Founding of Pennsylvania, 1680-1684: A Documentary History* (Univ. of Pennsylvania Press, 1983).

Rodger C. Henderson
Pennsylvania State University, Fayette

PENN FAMILY   Four generations of the Penn family aided in the founding and development of colonial and Revolutionary America. Admiral Sir William Penn (1621-70), born in Bristol, England, was promoted to the position of vice admiral of the English fleet by 1652. He remained active under the Cromwellian regime to 1655 but sympathized with the monarchy and supported the Restoration of Charles II. The Crown knighted Penn in 1660, and he was later appointed a commissioner of the navy. The admiral was honored after his death when Pennsylvania, given to his son William as a proprietary holding, was named for him.

William Penn (1644-1718), a founder of New Jersey, Delaware, and Pennsylvania was born in London, the son of Admiral Sir William and Margaret Jasper Penn. His heirs included William, born to Penn and his first wife Gulielma Springett; and John, Thomas, and Richard, sons of Penn and his second wife, Hannah Callowhill. William Penn was part owner in East Jersey; as a trustee of West Jersey, he formulated the Laws, Concessions, and Agreements for Government, of 1677. Penn became proprietor of Pennsylvania through charter rights granted by Charles II in payment of a 16,000-pound debt the Crown owed Admiral Penn. The Duke of York gave Delaware charter rights to Penn. Penn served as proprietor of Pennsylvania from 1682 to 1692 and from 1694 to his death in 1718.

Thomas Penn (1703-75), the son of William and Hannah Callowhill Penn, shared proprietary power with his brothers, John and Richard. Thomas inherited one-fourth of the Pennsylvania proprietorship from his mother in 1727 and another half from his brother John in 1746. Thomas Penn went to Pennsylvania in 1732 after the Court of Exchequer supported his claim to the colony and after William Penn Jr.'s son William gave up his claim to the province. John Penn, joined by his sister Margaret and her husband, also went to Pennsylvania in 1734. Thomas, who remained in the colony until 1741, viewed Pennsylvania as a source of income, discounted his father's idealism, and made a large fortune through land sales.

John Penn (1729-1811) was born in London, a grandson of William Penn and the son of Richard and Hannah Lardner Penn; he served the colony to the end of proprietary rule. John was a member of the provincial council from 1752 to 1755 and served as lieutenant governor of Pennsylvania from 1763 to 1777, except for the period of 1771-73, when his brother Richard held office. John was in office when proprietary rule was abolished in 1776. He faced boundary disputes, frontier problems, and Indian troubles throughout his tenure. He died in Philadelphia. John's brother Richard (1735-1811) was given authority by the Continental Congress to make the last conciliatory offer to King George III in 1775. He died in England.

The Revolution brought independence from British authority and ended proprietary rule with the creation of the commonwealth of Pennsylvania under the constitution of 1776. By the Divesting Act of November 27, 1779, the commonwealth took over ownership of all the unsurveyed lands of the proprietors, paid the proprietors 130,000 pounds as compensation, and allowed the Penns to retain their private estates.

See also Delaware; New Jersey; Penn, John; Penn, William; Pennsylvania.

Bibliography: Dunn, Mary Maples, *William Penn: Politics and Conscience* (Princeton Univ. Press, 1967); Peare, Catherine Owens, *William Penn: A Biography* (Lippincott, 1957); Pound, Arthur, *The Penns of Pennsylvania and England* (Macmillan, 1932); Soderlund, Jean R., ed., *William Penn and the Founding of Pennsylvania, 1680-1684: A Documentary History* (Univ. of Pennsylvania Press, 1983); Trussell, John B., Jr., *William Penn: Architect of a Nation* (Pennsylvania Historical and Museum Commission, 1980).

Rodger C. Henderson
Pennsylvania State University, Fayette

PENNSYLVANIA Several European nations contended for possession of the Delaware Valley during the 17th century, but settlement remained sparse until the 1680s. Henry Hudson established a Dutch claim to the area in 1609. The Swedes made the first permanent settlement in 1643 on Tinicum Island in the Delaware River. Governor Johan Printz established the government and courts of the colony. In 1655 Dutch forces led by Peter Stuyvesant conquered the Swedish colony, but in 1664 the English captured, in the name of the Duke of York, Dutch possessions in America including those in the Delaware Valley. On March 4, 1681, King Charles II of England granted the area to William Penn, who in 1682 founded the colony of Pennsylvania. Thereafter, religious, governmental, and economic conditions attracted settlers, and the colony thrived under English jurisdiction.

Early Development. Proprietor William Penn commented that "the country itself, its soil, air, water, seasons and produce, both natural and artificial, is not to be despised." Indeed, the colony had the blessings of a rich diversity of natural resources and geographic features. Philadelphia, with a population of 42,000 by 1790, was the most populous city in British North America and it was the political, commercial, and cultural capital of the colony.

New York, New Jersey, Delaware, Maryland, West Virginia, Ohio, and Lake Erie and the Delaware River form the border of Pennsylvania. The Appalachian Mountains cut diagonally across the state from northeast to southwest. The average length of Pennsylvania from east to west is about 285 miles; the breadth from south to north is 150 miles. Major rivers include the Delaware, providing access to Atlantic commerce; the Susquehanna, emptying into the Chesapeake; and the Ohio, providing an outlet to the west. Pennsylvania's border with Lake Erie gives access to the Great Lakes and the Gulf of St. Lawrence. The moderate continental climate provides cold winters and warm summers, with a growing season of about 120 days per year in the north but approaching 170 to 200 days in the southeast. The colonists came into a region covered by dense forests. Farmers cleared the land and tilled the rich soil of the gently rolling hills and broad valleys of southeastern Pennsylvania.

William Penn's charter was publicly proclaimed on April 2, 1681. Penn promoted settlement of the colony he envisioned as a "Holy Experiment." His First Frame of Government (1682) provided for civil liberties, elected

William Penn concluded a treaty with the Delaware Indians shortly after receiving his charter for Pennsylvania. *(Library of Congress)*

representatives, and a governor representing the proprietor. The Council had power to enact bills into laws, and the elected Assembly had the power to approve or reject, but not initiate, legislation. The Second Frame of Government (1683) altered the distribution of power but the Assembly, still lacking authority to initiate legislation, began to take such powers to itself. In Markham's Frame of Government (1696), the Assembly gained the right to initiate laws. The Constitution of 1701 curtailed the legislative power of the Council, which became an advisory body; gave the Assembly control over legislation and taxation; and made the legislature independent of the executive branch.

By the conclusion in 1701 of his second visit, Penn had established religious liberty, agreed to popular government in the province, provided for the sale of relatively cheap land, and promoted peaceable relationships with the Indians. Provincial politics pitted the proprietor and his supporters against the popular interests of the people represented in the Assembly. In the early years James Logan led the proprietary forces and David Lloyd spoke for the popular cause.

Establishing Boundaries. Disputes with Maryland, Virginia, and Connecticut, deriving from overlapping charter rights, provoked political and military conflict during the 18th century. The dispute with Maryland was eventually resolved in 1767 when both colonies agreed to the Mason-Dixon line. Penn's grant also conflicted with Virginia's charter rights. Between 1770 and 1776 tensions erupted in Lord Dunmore's War as Virginia and Pennsylvania settlers engaged in sporadic fighting. In 1779 a joint commission agreed upon by both states extended the Mason-Dixon line to five degrees west of the Delaware River and drew a straight line boundary due north to form Pennsylvania's western border. Penn's grant conflicted with Connecticut's charter of 1662. In 1753 the Susquehanna Company, an enterprise financed by Connecticut business people, purchased land in the Wyoming

Valley (along the Susquehanna) from the Iroquois and promoted settlement in the area. The Penns protested and obtained a British court order to prevent further occupation of the disputed territory, but a series of disputes known as the Yankee-Pennamite Wars ensued, extending to the end of the 18th century.

Negotiations and purchase eased conflicts with New York, Massachusetts, and later the U.S. government. Penn's charter granted him land north to 43 degrees north latitude, but in 1774 the proprietors asked British authorities to approve the northern extent of the colony at 42 degrees. New York's western limits conflicted with Massachusetts's charter rights, and both claimed the Erie Triangle. New York ceded its claims to the U.S. government in 1781. Massachusetts did the same in 1786. In 1792, Pennsylvania purchased the Erie Triangle from the United States for $151,000.

Indian Relations. Before European settlers arrived, nearly 15,000 native Americans made their homes in the region that became Pennsylvania. Most belonged to the Algonquian language group but some Iroquoian peoples resided in Pennsylvania. Among the Algonquian peoples were the Lenni-Lenape or Delaware, who lived along the Delaware River; the Nanticoke and Conoy who lived south of the Potomac; the Shawnee along the Ohio and Susquehanna rivers and near Easton; and the Mohican along the Hudson. Conquered by the Iroquois by 1680, the Susquehannock also lost many people to European diseases and attacks by white settlers. The remnants of this group, the Conestoga, were massacred in 1763 by the Paxton Boys.

William Penn initiated fair dealings with the Indians. Granted sole proprietary rights to the land, he did not sell or permit settlement on it until purchased from the Indians. Peaceable dealings gave way to bitter bloody struggles by Indians to retain possession of their land. All Indian groups were pushed aside by encroaching European settlers who had the major advantage of a superior material culture. In Penn's lifetime, Indians shared their knowledge of farming and sold pelts to merchants. In the 1730s heavy Scotch-Irish immigration and the 1737 Walking Purchase that cheated the Indians departed from Penn's early plans. When the Penns turned to the Iroquois for assistance in pushing the Delaware off the land, the Delaware turned to the French for support of their claims. Pennsylvania, shielded by the Iroquois, maintained peaceful frontiers into the 1750s. Pioneers moved into western Pennsylvania in search of land and furs. The French built a chain of forts from Lake Erie to the forks of the Ohio River and pressured the Indians to break with the British. The French and Indian War (1754-63), ultimately won by the British, en-

sued. British General John Forbes won a major victory at Fort Duquesne and built Fort Pitt (1759-61).

Immigration and Growth. Immigration contributed most to Pennsylvania's population growth in the early years before 1720 but natural increase played a greater part in promoting rapid settlement of the interior by the 1730s. Philadelphia's population increased from 10,360 in 1740 to 22,814 by 1767. According to the first federal census (1790), about 42,520 inhabitants lived in the city. Lancaster, the largest inland town, grew from 1,800 residents in 1751 to nearly 3,800 by 1790. At mid-century (1750) the colony's population was nearly 120,000; by 1790 it was about 434,000. Pennsylvania's population doubled about every 25 years. The major factors contributing to this growth rate were a low age at first marriage for women and a low infant mortality rate.

Pennsylvania attracted immigrants from several countries. Welsh, English, and Irish Quakers came to the colony in large numbers during its early years. Anglicans, German Lutherans, and Reformed Church members came to the province for religious liberty, economic opportunity, and enjoyment of political rights. Pennsylvania's early immigration also included many lowly members of society. Slaves, indentured servants, redemptioners, and convicts found a home in Penn's province. English predominated among the flood of new arrivals from the 1680s to 1710. Another wave of migrants, arriving between 1710 and the 1750s, mostly of German origins, settled on rich productive farmland in Lancaster, Berks, and Northampton counties. The Amish, Mennonites, Moravians, Dunkers, and the Schwenkfelders came to Pennsylvania during this period. By the 1770s one-third of some counties' populations were of German origins. Scotch-Irish Presbyterians moved to Pennsylvania in large numbers from about 1720 to the Revolution and by 1776 accounted for one-fourth of the state's population.

A population profile shows the rich ethnic, religious, and linguistic diversity of the colony's inhabitants. Before 1700 Swedes, Dutch, and English settled the land inhabited by the Delaware Indians. They were joined in the 18th century by more English, German, Swiss, and Welsh migrants as well as French Huguenots. The mix of peoples created a society characterized by ethnic and religious diversity and cultural pluralism. Despite an antislavery tradition, Pennsylvania imported black slaves. Slavery continued in Pennsylvania to 1780, when the Assembly enacted a gradual emancipation law that virtually ended racial bondage in the commonwealth by the early 19th century. Blacks as a percentage of total population remained steady at about two percent from 1700 to 1790 due to the small importations of slaves in the colonial period.

Economic, Cultural, and Social Development. Pennsylvania became one of the wealthiest of the colonies through commerce with New England, the South, the Caribbean, and English and European markets. A combination of rich natural resources and an industrious population created a thriving agricultural and commercial economy. By 1700 the productive economy contributed to the colony's reputation as "the breadbasket of America," while the fur trade added to the economic development of the province. Merchants exported crops and foodstuffs to the Caribbean.

In 1700 Pennsylvanians exported goods to England worth 4,608 pounds. By 1760 Pennsylvania's exports to England had risen to a value of 22,754 pounds. The province became a leading producer of cereals, hay, and livestock; housed thriving shipbuilding and extensive iron manufacturing industries; produced textiles and glass; and engaged in lumbering and papermaking. In 1770, Pennsylvanians built 2,354 tons of vessels, including 18 topsails and 8 sloops and schooners. Iron deposits and timber for charcoal fueled a thriving iron industry. By 1730 the colony sold to England 189 tons of pig iron. This figure increased to 1,381 tons by 1770. Wealth increased the inhabitants' consumption of valuable goods from England. In 1700 Pennsylvanians imported goods from England worth 18,529 pounds; by 1770 this figure rose to 134,881 pounds.

Pennsylvanians made major contributions to artistic and scientific achievements and promoted educational and cultural advancements by creating institutions for the dissemination of knowledge. The University of Pennsylvania was originally established as a charity school in 1740; Benjamin Franklin and others transformed it into an academy. In 1765 it opened the first medical school in North America and in 1779 became the first university. Philadelphia became the center of provincial intellectual, cultural, and political life. With Franklin's leadership and contributions by others, many newspapers, magazines, and libraries emerged. Pennsylvania had its first newspaper, the *American Weekly Mercury*, in 1719 and continued to lead the colonies in the world of journalism. Franklin published the *Pennsylvania Gazette* from 1730 onward and printed *Poor Richard's Almanack* from 1732. Christopher Saur published German-language newspapers and almanacs. In 1786 the *Pittsburgh Gazette* began publication. The Pennsylvania Hospital of Philadelphia, founded by Franklin and Thomas Bond and chartered in 1751, had on its staff several prominent doctors, including John Morgan, William Shippen, Jr., Benjamin Rush, and Philip Syng Physick.

A number of prominent individuals contributed to the social, cultural, and intellectual climate of the province. Charles Willson Peale painted portraits, and Benjamin West became a noted artist. John Bartram was recognized as the foremost American botanist. Benjamin Franklin was a printer, author, diplomat, scientist, and inventor, and he participated in drafting the Declaration of Independence. Francis Hopkinson, the financier Robert Morris, the physician Benjamin Rush, and James Wilson all signed the Declaration of Independence. Wilson participated in the Constitutional Convention of 1787 and later became a U.S. Supreme Court justice. David Rittenhouse, an astronomer and mathematician, made major contributions to surveying the boundaries of the province.

18th Century Conflicts. During the French and Indian War (1754-63) much fighting occurred in Pennsylvania. In 1753, George Washington went on an expedition from Virginia to the Ohio Valley to warn the French against further claims to the region. In 1754, at Fort Necessity, the French defeated Washington. On July 9, 1755, the French and their Indian allies defeated General Edward Braddock near Fort Duquesne. In the meantime, Indians and the French attacked Pennsylvania settlers. The Albany Congress (1754) convened to consider means of organizing an intercolonial plan of unified resistance. The Pennsylvania Assembly considered a militia bill on November 26, 1756, but, dominated by pacifist Quaker members, forced the British authorities to provide the bulk of troops, weapons, and ammunition for frontier defense. Britain's eventual triumph in the war ended barriers to western development, but British imperial policies initiated after the war generated tensions between Pennsylvania and England.

After England's triumph in 1763 the Crown developed plans to reorganize colonial administration. New trade regulations and taxes prompted colonial resistance to British authority and generated a revolutionary movement against British policies and proprietary government. Philadelphia merchants organized protests against the Stamp Act (1765), the Townshend Act (1767), and the Tea Act (1773). Westerners who resented the eastern political domination of the Assembly participated in protests that evolved into a revolution. The Proclamation of 1763 limited further migration, but settlers continued to flood into the west. Pennsylvanians reacted to the Stamp Act by forming the Association. John Dickinson protested against the Townshend Act that imposed taxes on lead, glass, paint, paper, and tea with his *Letters from a Farmer in Pennsylvania*. In reaction to the Tea Act about 8,000 Philadelphians gathered and resolved that a British ship should sail out of Delaware Bay.

Protests defending colonial rights shifted to a movement for independence. Pennsylvanians responded enthusiastically to news of Bostonians' resistance to the Intolerable Acts. In July 1774, a provincial congress convened in Philadelphia and elected delegates to the First Continental Congress, which met at Carpenter's Hall in Philadelphia.

The Provincial Conference on January 23, 1775, called for the collection of military supplies and promoted vigorous enforcement of the Association. Later conferences called for removal of the proprietors from power, sought enlistments in regiments of the Continental Army, and created a navy. The Second Continental Congress convened in Philadelphia on May 10, 1775, and in 1776 adopted the Declaration of Independence. Benjamin Rush, Thomas Paine, Timothy Matlack, James Cannon, and Thomas Young, among other radicals, led the revolutionary movement. The revolutionaries instituted a new social and political system; they overturned proprietary government, extended greater representation to the western counties, wrote the state constitution of 1776, disfranchised Loyalists and confiscated their property, and enacted a gradual emancipation law (1780).

Pennsylvania played a major part in the Revolutionary War. The state sent 13 regiments to the Continental Army. As many more served in militia units. The state also furnished hospital facilities and supply depots; constructed prisoner-of-war camps; and, because of its numerous forges and furnaces, furnished vast quantities of war matériel. Citizens manufactured weapons, supplied horses and wagons, and produced quantities of food for the cause. Franklin helped to negotiate the military alliance with France in 1778, and Robert Morris, among others, organized the finances of the war. Nevertheless, the war sharply divided Pennsylvanians on the question of independence.

Many Pennsylvanians voiced opposition to the war, and others opposed the radicals who gained the upper hand in 1776. Religious pacifists wanted to remain neutral during the struggle. Many were fined, imprisoned, or banished for acting on their religious beliefs. When the British evacuated Philadelphia in 1778, an estimated 3,000 Loyalists left with them. Radical supporters of the Constitution of 1776 opposed anticonstitutionalists, or moderate elements who called themselves "Republicans"; the two factions disagreed on the Pennsylvania constitution (1776). The Divesting Act of November 27, 1779, the gradual emancipation law of 1780, and the Test Act of June 1777, requiring oaths of allegiance, promoted strong opposition among groups of Pennsylvanians.

Structure of State Government. The Revolutionary Pennsylvania constitution of 1776 was the most democratic of any of the 13 original states. It transformed the British proprietary colony into an independent commonwealth. The preamble and Declaration of Rights reiterated most of the rights pronounced by the various Revolutionary bodies and proclaimed in the Declaration of Independence. The plan replaced the proprietary governor with a Supreme Executive Council, provided for an ap-

pointed judiciary, and established a Council of Censors elected every seven years with authority to conduct a census and direct the reapportionment of the legislature. Its major constitutional responsibility was to discover any violations of the constitution and recommend amendments. The most important branch of government created by the 1776 constitution was a unicameral legislature. The assembly, composed of members elected annually, remained the center of power in the government. Representation was based on the taxable population of the state; the right to vote belonged to all free men.

Pennsylvania sent eight representatives to the Constitutional Convention in Philadelphia in May 1787: Benjamin Franklin, Thomas Mifflin, Robert Morris, George Clymer, Thomas FitzSimons, Jared Ingersoll, James Wilson, and Gouverneur Morris. Franklin moderated contending forces in the convention and on several occasions paved the way for compromise on major issues that divided the delegates. Gouverneur Morris argued at length for the nationalist cause and composed the final form of the Constitution, while James Wilson suggested many ideas that structured the Constitution. The Pennsylvania representatives supported a stronger national government, signed the Constitution on September 17, 1787, and promoted quick ratification of the new plan. On December 12, 1787, the delegates voted 46 to 23 to ratify; Pennsylvania became the second state to adopt the new plan.

The politics of the 1780s in Pennsylvania found Republicans in bitter controversy with the Constitutionalists. Radicals, or Constitutionalists, fought for independence from Britain, defended the Articles of Confederation and the Pennsylvania constitution of 1776, and many later became "antifederalists." They resisted Republican efforts to revise the 1776 constitution. Republicans opposed the 1776 constitution, sought to change it during the 1780s, strongly supported the U.S. Constitution in 1787, and in 1790 successfully brought a new plan forward for Pennsylvania's government. The Pennsylvania constitution of 1790 replaced the unicameral Assembly and Supreme Executive Council of the Revolutionary era with a bicameral legislature and a fairly strong governor. The 1790 constitution had many features similar to the newly adopted U.S. Constitution. Federalism had triumphed in Pennsylvania by 1790.

See also Declaration of Independence; Frame of Government; Penn, John; Penn, William; Penn Family; Philadelphia; Yankee-Pennamite Wars.

Bibliography: Bronner, Edwin B., *William Penn's "Holy Experiment"* (Temple Univ. Publications, 1963); Hawke, David, *In the Midst of a Revolution* (Univ. of Pennsylvania Press, 1961); Illick, Joseph E., *Colonial Pennsylvania* (Scribner's, 1976); Lemon, James T., *The Best Poor Man's*

Country (Johns Hopkins Univ. Press, 1972); Nash, Gary B., *Quakers and Politics* (Princeton Univ. Press, 1968); Ryerson, Richard, *The Revolution is Now Begun* (Univ. of Pennsylvania Press, 1978); Tully, Alan, *William Penn's Legacy* (Johns Hopkins Univ. Press, 1977).

Rodger C. Henderson
Pennsylvania State University, Fayette

PENSACOLA   First settled in 1559 and later abandoned, Pensacola was resettled in 1696, when Martin Zavala and Juan de Reina were sent out from Havana, Cuba, to the Gulf Coast of western Florida. The new town of Pensacola became Spain's chief outpost in West Florida. The outbreak of war with France in 1719 enabled the Sieur de Bienville, governor of Louisiana, to surprise and capture Pensacola on May 14, 1719, but Spain regained the port after the war. The British occupied West Florida from 1763 to 1783 after seizing Pensacola during the Seven Years War, and although Spain recovered the territory again, most of the Spanish inhabitants had left in the interim. Pensacola and West Florida were seized by the United States in 1810.

PEPPERELL, SIR WILLIAM (1696-1759)   An American businessman and soldier, he was born in Kittery, Maine, in the Massachusetts colony. He ran lumber, fish, and shipbuilding businesses and invested some of his profits in real estate. By 1730 he was chief justice of the General Court of Massachusetts and the leader of a Maine militia company. In 1745 he commanded the expedition that captured French-held Fort Louisburg on Cape Breton Island. For this heroic deed he became the first native-born American to be given the English title of baron. Pepperell gathered and commanded troops during the French and Indian War and in 1759 was made a lieutenant general by the British.

PEQUOT WAR (1637)   The Pequot War was rooted in trade rivalries among Indians and Europeans and in English expansionism. During the 1620s, New England's south coast was transformed when the Dutch discovered that Indians throughout the Northeast paid dearly in furs for the purple and white shell beads called wampum, found in greatest abundance along the shores of Long Island Sound and Narragansett Bay. To the Iroquois and other native groups, wampum strings represented sacred "words" that they presented during rituals associated with warfare, diplomacy, death, and adoption. By the end of the decade, the Pequot and their coastal neighbors devoted the better part of each winter to gathering, drilling, and stringing wampum.

During the early 1630s, the Pequot incurred the hostility of the Mohegan, Narragansett, and other Indians, as well as the Dutch, with their efforts to monopolize Indian-Dutch trade. Diplomatically isolated, they sought an alliance with the rapidly growing Massachusetts Bay Colony, for whom the Connecticut Valley had become attractive after a smallpox epidemic devastated the native population there in 1633-34. But the English made demands, including the turning over to themselves of the alleged killers of two English trading parties, that the Pequot found unduly humiliating.

Warfare.   After a year of skirmishing during which the colony of Connecticut was established, English troops along with some Narragansett and Mohegan staged a surprise predawn attack on the Pequot's Mystic River village, shooting or burning most of the sleeping residents. The Pequot sachem, Sassacus, and a few followers fled to the Mohawk with a large gift of wampum in order to gain support for a counterattack. But the Narragansett had gotten to the Mohawk first, and the latter repudiated and murdered Sassacus. With the elimination of Pequot power, Connecticut was open to English settlement, and wampum flowed unimpeded to the English, Dutch, and Iroquois.

Bibliography: Jennings, Francis, *The Invasion of America: Indians, Colonists, and the Cant of Conquest* (Univ. of North Carolina Press, 1975); Salisbury, Neal, *Manitou and Providence: Indians, Europeans, and the Making of New England, 1500-1643* (Oxford Univ. Press, 1982).

Neal Salisbury
Smith College

PERALTA, PEDRO DE (c.1584-1666)   A Spanish official in the New World, Peralta was appointed as Juan Oñate's replacement as governor of New Mexico in 1609. Peralta's first act was to build a new capital at Santa Fe, and under his rule New Mexico began to grow. His term as governor was marked by violent conflict with the Franciscans, whom he angered by asserting the rights of the Spanish crown over theirs. He was even held under house arrest by them for a year, finally escaping to Mexico City and returning with reinforcements. After 1612 he moved first to Acapulco, then to Caracas. He held various colonial and mercantile positions in South America before arriving as an invalid in Madrid in 1652, when he retired.

See also Franciscans.

PEREZ, JUAN (died 1775)   A Spanish explorer along the Pacific coast of North America, Perez was chosen in 1774 to lead an expedition north along the California coast to chart the shoreline and search for Russian settlements. Monterey was his last port of call before he set off. The first land he sighted after swinging out into the Pacific was near the present border of Alaska and Canada. Turning south, he came upon Vancouver Island and was the first

European to discover Nootka Sound, which for the next two decades would be the source of much friction between Spain and England. Coasting south, Perez surveyed the shore of latter-day Washington and Oregon, arriving back in San Blas on November 3. The next year he went on the Heceta expedition, dying soon after that squadron arrived back in port.

See also Heceta, Bruno.

PÉROUSE, JEAN-FRANÇOIS DE GALAUP, COMTE DE LA (1741-88?)   A French navigator and explorer of the Pacific, Pérouse entered the French navy at age 15, fought off the coast of North America during the Seven Years War, and served in the Indian Ocean in the 1760s. During the Revolutionary War he led a naval attack on the British trading posts along Hudson Bay, capturing Samuel Hearne. In 1785, Pérouse began a Pacific expedition designed to open the fur trade for the French and to search for a Northwest Passage. After stops at Cape Horn, Easter Island, and the Hawaiian Islands, the next year he reached Yakutat Bay, Alaska, where he finally laid to rest the claims of a passage. On his return trip he was lost in the South Pacific, but fortunately he had already sent his journal home from Australia.

See also Hearne, Samuel; Northwest Passage.

PERROT, NICOLAS (1644-1718)   An explorer and fur trader, Perrot was trained by Jesuit missionaries in New France. During his travels as a fur trader in the Green Bay region of Wisconsin, he helped spread French authority into the Northwest. He also became fluent in several Indian languages and visited many Indian tribes, including the Fox Indians, whose village at Questatinong he described as "destitute of everything." Father Allouez later established his mission of St. Marc there. In 1683, Perrot followed the Fox portage route from the Upper Great Lakes in Wisconsin to the Mississippi, where he helped build forts. Although he was accused of corrupting the Indians, he left a valuable record of their activities in his *Mémoire*, and his explorations also extended French knowledge of the continent.

PETER, HUGH (1598-1660)   A clergyman, Peter was the son of Thomas Dirkwood in Cornwall, who later changed his name to Peter or Peters. Hugh Peter graduated from Trinity College, Cambridge, in 1617 and received his master's in 1622. He became a deacon in 1621 and a priest in 1623. He became a Puritan and in 1629 left England. Settling in Rotterdam, he wrote a church convenant for William Ames, but eventually gave his church to John Davenport and sailed for New England in 1635.

He took over Roger Williams's pastorship of the church at Salem, Massachusetts, in 1636, drafted laws for the colony (1637-38), participated in the examination and trial of Anne Hutchinson (1637-38), became an overseer of Harvard College (1642), and encouraged trade in New England. He was a strong believer in the "New England Way," the restriction of church membership and government office. In 1641 he represented Massachusetts Bay in England, where he obtained a credit extension and support for Harvard, but was unable to resolve the border dispute between New England and New Netherland. He became embroiled in the English Civil War and never returned to the colony.

PHILADELPHIA, COLLEGE OF   Fostered by Benjamin Franklin, what later became the College of Philadelphia opened on January 7, 1751, as the Academy. Franklin served as president from 1749 to 1756 and hoped to start an English school to teach "everything … useful and … ornamental." The Academy was associated with a Philadelphia charity school (founded 1740) during its early years and in 1755 was renamed the College and Academy of Philadelphia. Ten years later it established the first school of medicine in the colonies. After the Revolution the school was rechartered (1779) as the University of the State of Pennsylvania. In 1791 it was renamed and organized as the University of Pennsylvania.

PHILADELPHIA   Philadelphia became the urban center of Pennsylvania, a focal point of continental affairs, and a link connecting the colony with the Atlantic world. From its origins in 1682, Philadelphia developed into the largest and wealthiest city in America by 1790. In the 1680s about 75 families lived in William Penn's "greene countrie towne." Its population grew to more than 42,000 inhabitants in 1790. The city was the entrepôt, social and cultural center, and political capital of Pennsylvania to 1799 and of the United States from 1790 to 1800.

Penn instructed his agents to create Philadelphia on land between the Delaware and the Schuylkill rivers as the seat of proprietary government and as a market town for the surrounding counties of Philadelphia, Bucks, and Chester. The plan reflected his religious idealism and practical business sense. The Society of Friends (Quakers) found in Philadelphia a refuge from persecution in England. English, Irish, and Welsh Quakers joined earlier European settlers— Swedes, Finns, and Dutch—on land inhabited by the Delaware Indians. A later influx of German, Swiss, Scots, and Scotch-Irish immigrants added to the diversity.

Philadelphia's geographic location boosted development of the hinterland and spurred the expansion of trade, industry, and finance. Increasing numbers of laborers, craftsmen, and merchants contributed to economic growth. Businessmen tapped the rich resources of the interior, buying furs, timber, grain, and iron to exchange in intercoastal trade, West Indian markets, and direct commerce with England. One contemporary observed in 1756 that "everybody . . . deals more or less in trade."

Philadelphia became a cosmopolitan community and enjoyed numerous cultural achievements and civic improvements. The city introduced paved and lighted streets and a "city watch"; established numerous schools, including the University of Pennsylvania; founded the Pennsylvania Hospital and the Library Company; organized fire

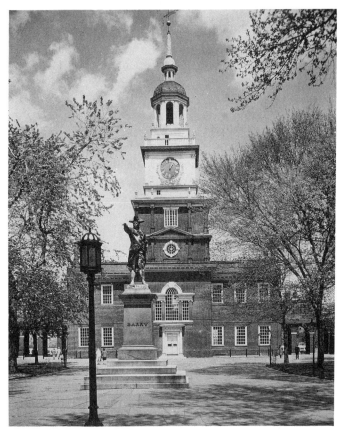

Philadelphia's State House, or Independence Hall, where the Declaration of Independence was adopted, houses the Liberty Bell. *(Courtesy State of Pennsylvania)*

insurance companies; and created the American Philosophical Society. Printers published the *American Magazine*, the *Pennsylvania Gazette*, and *Poor Richard's Almanack*. By the mid-1770s citizens had access to two dozen newspapers. In addition to Benjamin Franklin, one of the best known figures in the colonies, the city boasted many prominent men: David Rittenhouse in mathematics and astronomy, Benjamin Rush and John Morgan in medicine, Gilbert Stuart and Charles Willson Peale in art, and John Bartram in botany.

Philadelphia played a major part in the creation of the American republic. Residents protested British tax policies from 1765 to 1774. In 1774, 56 delegates from 12

colonies convened in the First Continental Congress at Carpenter's Hall. In May 1775 the Second Continental Congress met at the State House and, in July 1776, issued the Declaration of Independence. Philadelphians wrote the most democratic state constitution of the revolutionary era. During the Revolutionary War, Americans suffered defeats near Philadelphia at Brandywine Creek, Paoli, and Germantown, and the British occupied the city from September 26, 1777, to June 18, 1778. Congress reconvened there from July 1778 to June 1783. Philadelphia remained the center of the new nation's political activities as 55 men met at the State House from May to September 17, 1787, to revise the Articles of Confederation, ultimately producing the Constitution. The state's ratification convention met in the capital and voted 46 to 23 on December 12, 1787, to adopt the Constitution.

See also Pennsylvania.

Bibliography: Bridenbaugh, Carl and Jessica, *Rebels and Gentlemen: Philadelphia in the Age of Franklin* (Reynal and Hitchcock, 1942); Illick, Joseph E., *Colonial Pennsylvania* (Scribner's, 1976); Weigley, Russell F., ed., *Philadelphia: A 300- Year History* (Norton, 1982).

Rodger C. Henderson
Pennsylvania State University, Fayette

PHILIP, KING. *See* **Metacomet.**

PHILIPSE, MARGARET HARDENBROOK (flourished 1659-90) The daughter of Adolph Hardenbrook, a Dutchman who emigrated to Bergen in the early 17th century, Margaret Hardenbrook married Peter Rudolphus de Vries, a New Amsterdam merchant in 1659. When Rudolphus died in 1661 Hardenbrook inherited a considerable estate. Although she married Frederick Philipse in October 1662, she retained the management of her former husband's business. In that capacity she made frequent trips between New York and the Netherlands and traded in her own name. In time, Margaret and Frederick emerged as one of New York's wealthiest couples. She died sometime before 1693.

PHIPS, SIR WILLIAM (1650-95) A colonial governor, he was born in Maine and worked with ships in Boston. He was knighted in 1687 for recovering a sunken Spanish ship off the coast of Haiti for the British. Commissioned provost marshal of the Dominion of New England, he was an unpopular administrator. By 1690 he was an accepted member of Puritan Increase Mather's church and commanded Massachusetts's forces in the capture of Port Royal in Nova Scotia. Appointed the first native-born governor general of the colony in 1692, he brought the witchcraft trials to an end and supported a free-trade policy, but he did not defend the Massachusetts frontiers nor help other colonies defend theirs.

PICKENS, ANDREW (1739-1817)   Born in Paxton, Pennsylvania, Pickens was a farmer and local justice of the peace. He was also a captain in the militia when the Revolutionary War broke out in 1775. He participated in the battle at Ninety-Six, an important British interior post that housed over 500 Tories. As a result he was promoted to colonel. His most significant victory was the Battle of Kettle Creek in Georgia in 1779. In 1780 he joined General Nathanael Greene for the battle at Briar Creek, where a number of Americans were taken prisoner. From 1781 to 1793 Pickens served in the Pennsylvania assembly and then (1793-95) as a representative in the U.S. Congress. He moved to South Carolina in 1795.

PICKERING, TIMOTHY (1745-1829) A   native   of Salem, Massachusetts, Pickering graduated from Harvard in 1763 and began teaching sacred music. He then read law under William Pynchon but participated little in the profession. In 1772 he became a selectman and by 1774 was a member of the Massachusetts committee of correspondence. He petitioned General Gage to reopen Boston's port and was arrested. Although his father was a Tory, which could have made the son's sympathies suspect, Pickering replaced the Loyalist William Browne as colonel of the First Essex Regiment. He wrote a drill book for the militia and recruited men for the Continental Army. During the war he was an adjutant general (1777-78) of the army, sat on the Board of War (1777-80), and served as quartermaster general (1780-83).

After the war he was a delegate to the Constitutional Convention (1787) and held numerous posts in George Washington's cabinet (1791- 97), continuing as Secretary of State (1797-1800) under John Adams. He later served in both the Senate (1803-11) and the House (1813-17).

PILGRIMS   In the later years of the reign of Queen Elizabeth I (1558-1603), a wing or faction within the Church of England pushed for a more clearly, more forthrightly Protestant national church, that is, one that would remove all remaining elements of Roman Catholic liturgy or tradition. While many were willing to work slowly from within to try and reform the whole Church, others grew impatient and decided to become schismatics, or Separatists. Since to live in England and not conform to the Church of England was to risk discovery and imprisonment or worse, some of these Separatists (known to American history as the Pilgrims) moved first to Holland in 1609.

After several years in Holland, these English Separatists grew restless and dissatisfied in a foreign land where their own children grew up learning Dutch rather than English and becoming strangers within their own families. A hard dilemma presented itself to these Pilgrims: to remain in Holland and cease to be English or to return to England and cease to be faithful to their own consciences. The existence of the New World presented a third, possibly more palatable, alternative: By going 3,000 miles away from the king and his officers, perhaps they could remain English and at the same time remain true Christians according to their own understanding. With "great hope and inward zeal," they resolved to advance and propagate "the gospel of the kingdom of Christ in those remote parts."

After much delicate negotiation and difficult trials, the *Mayflower* set out alone from Plymouth, England, on September 6, 1620. Sixty-six days and four deaths later, the Pilgrims, now diminished to fewer than 100, made landfall not in northern Virginia as planned but off Cape Cod in New England. This Plymouth Colony, soon to be outpaced by the Massachusetts Bay Company to the north, never grew to great size. Slowly though steadily increasing from around 1,500 at mid-century, Plymouth numbered over 7,000 in 1691, when the colony was absorbed into Massachusetts.

Bibliography: Langdon, G. D., Jr., *Pilgrim Colony: A History of New Plymouth* (Yale Univ. Press, 1966).

Edwin S. Gaustad
University of California, Riverside

PIMA REVOLT (1751)   An insurrection by a militant faction of the agricultural Pima Indians in the Spanish province of Pimería Alta (the area of the modern Mexican state of Sonora and the southern portion of Arizona), its goals were to overthrow the Spanish colonial government and eradicate all traces of Spanish culture among the local peoples. The dispute had its origins in the late 17th century, with the establishment of missions in this area by the Jesuit Eusebio Kino. These early missions were eventually augmented with additional priests and supported by a military garrison. By 1731 there were nine Spanish missions in Pimería Alta.

The central figure in the planning and execution of the revolt was Luís Oacpicagigua, who lived in the town of Saric in northern Sonora. Accusing the Spanish of economic and religious oppression, he sparked the revolt by killing 18 Spaniards in Saric and by leading his followers in an attack on the mission at Tubutama. Although the majority of the Pima did not participate in the violence, Oacpicagigua's message caught on briefly among disaffected elements of the population, and more than 100 Spanish missionaries and administrators were killed. The revolt was suppressed with Oacpicagigua's capture by the Spanish forces.

PINCKNEY, ELIZABETH LUCAS (1722-93)   A plantation manager, celebrated for her role in the adaptation of indigo culture to South Carolina, and the mother of two patriot leaders of the Revolution, Eliza, as she was best known, was born in Antigua, British West Indies, and educated in England, where she cultivated a literate and lively intelligence.   In 1738 her father moved his family to South Carolina; recalled to active military service, he left Eliza in charge of her ailing mother and several plantations.   A decline in the demand for rice left Carolinian planters desperate for another valuable tropical commodity. Despite several earlier failures, Eliza began experimenting with indigo culture in 1741 and was able to ship her first crop in 1744.   By 1750 indigo had become an important export crop.

In 1744, Eliza married Charles Pinckney and raised three children to adulthood: Charles Cotesworth (born 1746), Harriott (1748), and Thomas (1750). Upon her husband's appointment as commissioner for South Carolina in 1753, the family moved to London, but she returned to America after her husband's death in 1758 and directed the family's plantations. Her sons distinguished themselves in the Continental Army during the Revolution and in public service thereafter. Her later years were spent with her widowed daughter and her grandchildren at her plantation on the Santee River. She became a good friend of George Washington, who served as a pallbearer at her funeral in 1793.

See also Indigo; Pinckney, Charles Cotesworth; Pinckney, Thomas.

PINCKNEY, CHARLES (1757-1824)   A native of Charleston, South Carolina, Pinckney was 19 years old when he assumed his first political role as a delegate to the Second Continental Congress. He was a lawyer, a lieutenant in the militia, and a member of the provincial legislature in 1779. H e was captured by the British in 1780 at Charleston and held until 1781. After the Revolution he served in Congress (1784-87) and was one of the committee who drew up the rules for the Constitutional Convention in 1787. He continued to serve in government positions as governor of South Carolina (1789-92; 1804-06), a U.S. senator (1798-1801), and ambassador to Spain (1801-04). He ended his career as it had begun—as a member of Congress (1819-21).

PINCKNEY, CHARLES COTESWORTH   (1746-1825)   Born in Charleston, South Carolina, Pinckney was hailed by George Washington as a man of "unquestionable bravery ... strict honor, erudition, and good sense." The brother of Thomas Pinckney, Charles served as a member of the provincial congress in 1775 and in the same year joined the first South Carolina regiment, and then was an aide to Washington. He became a colonel in 1776 and fought in several Southern campaigns. The capture of Charleston in 1780 by Britain's General Provost put an end to his military career, but he continued to serve in the state government.

He was a member of the Constitutional Convention in Philadelphia in 1787; in 1796 he became the U.S. minister to France, where he became embroiled in the XYZ Affair. In 1800 he was an unsuccessful candidate for vice president and in 1804 and 1808 for president.

See also Pinckney, Thomas.

PINCKNEY, THOMAS (1750-1828)   The brother of Charles Cotesworth Pinckney, Thomas studied at Oxford and the Middle Temple. In 1774 he was admitted to the bar. He was stationed at Fort Moultrie from 1776 to 1778 and participated in an ill-fated campaign in Florida. In 1780 he fought vigorously to keep Charleston from the British. He was wounded at the Battle of Camden and captured; after his exchange he fought with the Marquis de Lafayette at Yorktown, Virginia. Pinckney became governor of South Carolina (1787-89), but was criticized for his leniency toward Loyalists. While minister of Great Britain (1792-96), he was appointed a special envoy to Spain, and in 1795 he negotiated a treaty with Spain establishing the Florida boundary and U.S. navigation rights on the Mississippi River. He subsequently sat in the House of Representatives (1797-1801).

See also Pinckney, Charles Cotesworth.

PIRACY   Piracy is merely robbery at sea, but the legends that surround buccaneers have made piracy more than mere robbery. The English were known as a nation of pirates, and that tradition came to the colonies at an early date. Voyages of exploration commonly turned into raids on the Spanish Caribbean colonies as a means of paying for the cost of the voyage. Pirates became endemic in the Caribbean in the 17th century, and their raids became even greater in size and frequency. Henry Morgan's raid on Panama in 1671 with nearly 2,000 men represented the height of buccaneering power.

Piracy was familiar among the port towns of the North American colonies. They were not so much victims as active participants. The infant economies of the colonies welcomed pirate ships because they brought cheap but valuable commodities. The pirates also needed supplies, and the money they spent for them enriched merchants in Boston, Newport, New York City, Philadelphia, and Charleston. New York City was particularly involved in the piracy business and was associated with such notorious pirates as William Kidd.

By the 1680s the buccaneers began expanding out of the Caribbean to Africa, the Indian Ocean, and into and across the Pacific. Their increased activity would eventually raise the anger of states and merchants who were growing accustomed to the profits of regular trade. Ultimately governments, particularly the English government, refused to tolerate their activities and at the end of Queen Anne's War in 1713 the Royal Navy was unleashed against the pirates.

Decline of Piracy.   In the struggle against the navy, the long-term odds were against the pirates. They were also cut off from their old suppliers in the colonial ports. As their economies grew stronger, the colonial merchants did not need pirate goods and refused them access to their facilities. The pirates, however, were not easily defeated. They continued to recruit men who were willing to abandon their homes to go with the sea raiders. And they could terrify whole communities as Robert Teach (Blackbeard) and Stede Bonnet did to Charleston in 1717 and 1718. By 1730 large-scale piracy, so prevalent in the 17th century, was at an end. Piracy would continue with such men as Jean Lafitte, but it was never on the scale of importance that was true earlier.

See also Bonnet, Stede; Privateering; Teach, Robert.

Bibliography: Rediker, Marcus, *Between the Devil and the Deep Blue Sea: Merchant Seamen, Pirates and the Anglo-American Maritime World, 1700-1750* (Cambridge Univ. Press, 1987); Ritchie, Robert C., *Captain Kidd and the War Against the Pirates* (Harvard Univ. Press, 1986).

Robert C. Ritchie
University of California, San Diego

PITCHER, MOLLY (1754-1832)   Molly Pitcher, whose real name was Mary McCauley, was a Revolutionary War heroine, born in Trenton, New Jersey. In 1769 she married John Caspar Hays, who later joined the Pennsylvania Regiment of Artillery. On June 28, 1778, a brutally hot day, John was involved in the Battle of Monmouth. Molly was on the battlefield, carrying water from a nearby well to the weak and wounded. This earned her the epithet "Molly Pitcher." When John, overcome by the heat, could no longer fight, Molly took his place, filling a cannon for the remainder of the battle. In what they called "An act of relief for Molly M'Kolly," the General Assembly of Pennsylvania rewarded her with an annuity until her death.

PITT, WILLIAM (THE ELDER) (1708-88)   A British government minister and first Earl of Chatham, William Pitt was born in London and educated at Eton and Oxford. Entering Parliament in 1735, he supported the defense of imperial interests at sea. In 1746, King George II appointed him vice treasurer of Ireland and paymaster-general of the army. In 1756 he was asked to form a ministry to direct the ongoing wars against the French on the Continent and in North America. Opposing the peace policies of King George III, Pitt resigned from the government in 1761 and opposed the 1763 Treaty of Paris as a private citizen. Illness forced his retirement from public life in 1768.

PITT, FORT   This settlement and fort at the confluence of the Allegheny and Monongahela rivers, established in 1758 by General John Forbes after the rout of the French at Fort Duquesne, was named in honor of the British statesman William Pitt the Elder. In 1759, General John Stanwix expanded the commercial functions of the fort and the adjoining settlement of Pittsburgh. In 1764 the fort was redesigned by Colonel Henry Bouquet. It was occupied and briefly renamed Fort Dunmore in 1774. With the outbreak of the Revolution, Fort Pitt was taken over by the Continental Army and became the base for its western campaigns. It was rebuilt for the last time in 1782.

PITTSBURGH, TREATY OF (1775)   Also known as the Treaty of Fort Pitt, this agreement established a temporary peace in western Pennsylvania on the eve of the Revolution. In the aftermath of Lord Dunmore's War, tensions ran high between settlers and Indians, and representatives of the Virginia Assembly and the Continental Congress sought to avert a possible Anglo-Indian alliance by negotiating with the Delaware, Shawnee, Mingo, Seneca, Wyandot, and Ottawa nations at Fort Pitt. With Chief White Eyes of the Delaware as spokesman, the Indians agreed to remain neutral in the coming conflict in return for recognition of their territorial claims west of the Ohio River.

See also Lord Dunmore's War.

PIZARRO, FRANCISCO (c.1470-1541)   A Spanish conquistador in South America, Pizarro arrived in the Caribbean in 1502 with the fleet of Governor Ovando of Hispaniola. In 1513 he accompanied Balboa across the Isthmus of Panama and later arrested him on the orders of Pedrarias de Avila. Pedrarias showed his gratitude in 1524 when he granted Pizarro the rights to explore in Colombia. By 1528, Pizarro was certain that an Indian empire comparable to that of the Aztecs existed to the south, and in 1531 he led some 200 men into the Inca Empire. Outnumbered by the Indians, Pizarro ambushed the Inca Atahualpa's bodyguards and captured Atahualpa, holding him for ransom and then executing him. Following the conquest of Peru, civil war broke out among the Spanish, and Pizarro was assassinated in the governor's palace in Lima in 1541.

See also Balboa, Vasco Núñez de.

PLANTATION SYSTEM   The Plantation System, also called the South Atlantic System, refers to the use of African slaves on agricultural plantations in the Americas from the 17th through the 19th centuries. It first appeared in the Caribbean, where it was used to grow tobacco, some cotton and indigo, and especially sugar, an enormously profitable crop there. From the West Indies, the Plantation System spread southward into Brazil and Latin America and northward into the British colonies. There, it adapted readily to the profitable growth of tobacco, indigo, and rice. Plantations were located on the best lands available, usually near rivers for transportation and soil quality.

The successful transformation from tobacco to sugar in Barbados in the 1640s was followed by an acceleration in the Atlantic slave trade, which increased the black population from 6,000 to 80,000 by the end of the century. Many West Indian islands followed similar patterns of growth. Extraordinarily high mortality rates and harsh working conditions kept slave imports high. Masters considered it cheaper to import more slaves than to provide for those present. Consequently, food, clothing, shelter, and medical care were scarce and of poor quality. Because blacks outnumbered whites dramatically, slave codes were harsh and discipline often brutal.

When the Caribbean economies declined in the late 17th century, planters sold many slaves to the British mainland. Previously, European immigrants to the British colonies had been slow to adopt plantation slavery, in part because they could not find a profitable use for it. When they discovered how lucrative slave labor could be in the production of tobacco, rice, and indigo, they adopted the system. By the early 18th century, plantation economies had become integral components of colonial society.

North American Systems.   Plantation agriculture on the British mainland engendered two chief systems, one on the Tobacco Coast in the Chesapeake region, and another in the Carolina and Georgia lowcountry, where rice and indigo were grown. Tobacco plantations were typically small, holding 20 slaves or fewer, because tobacco did not require huge tracts of land in order to be grown, as did sugar and rice. As tobacco depleted the soil, its cultivation spread westward into the Piedmont, carrying the Plantation System with it. Large tobacco estates did exist, however, and were often described as small towns, since many became self-sufficient enclaves holding numerous highly skilled artisans as well as field laborers. By the 1780s, several areas had as many as 78 percent of all householders owning slaves.

Most of the rice estates for which the 18th-century Carolina lowcountry was known were among the largest on the mainland. Because rice required large tracts of land in order to be grown, a few grandees carved out sections of the coast and then took refuge in Charleston from the malarial swamps. They supervised their holdings through the use of overseers and were known for their cosmopolitan and leisurely lifestyles. The lowcountry plantation system featured a black majority, an urban seasonally-absentee slaveholding class, and a skilled and often urban Creole society that had little contact with the vast numbers of Africans placed on the plantations.

Although they hardly came to dominate the economy as they did in the South, plantations were not unknown in the colonial North. Large plantations could be found in the Hudson and Connecticut Valleys as well as in parts of New Jersey, Rhode Island, and Delaware. But the Plantation System was never successful in this increasingly commercial economy where soils and climates could, for the most part, support only subsistence agriculture.

See also Afro-Americans; Slavery.

Lynda J. Morgan
Mount Holyoke College

PLYMOUTH   First located as the Indian village of Patuxet by John Smith in 1614, then renamed Plymouth by Prince Charles on the published version of Smith's map, this became the site of the planting of the first permanent English colony in New England when the Pilgrims landed in 1620. They built their settlement on the ruins of that former village, which had been devastated by the plague of 1616-19 that struck the inhabitants of the southern New England coast. During the first winter more than half of the original settlers died, and food shortages continued to imperil the colony during its first years. Originally financed by the London merchants of the Plymouth Company, the settlers bought them out in 1627, established other villages in the environs, and became the colony of New Plymouth, organized under the auspices of the Mayflower Compact. First governor John Carver was succeeded in 1621 by William Bradford, who governed more than 30 years. In the 1630s Plymouth was overshadowed by Massachusetts Bay Colony and was absorbed by its larger neighbor by the terms of the royal charter of 1691.

See also Bradford, William; Mayflower Compact.

PLYMOUTH ROCK   The traditional site for the landing of the Pilgrims, Plymouth Rock is located near Provincetown Harbor, Massachusetts, which the *Mayflower* reached on November 11, 1620. In 1741, Elder John Faunce, at the age of 95, identified the large rock as "the place where the forefathers landed," but William Bradford's 1646 account, Of *Plymouth Plantation*, described several landings by exploring parties before the passengers disembarked. The Pilgrims first sent out a small boatload of 16 men under the command of Captain Miles Standish on November 15. After investigating the coastline for several days and being attacked by Indians, they discovered an abandoned Indian camp near a large pond. They took corn back to the ship as a sign of God's favor, and this location near Truro became known as Corn Hill. On December 20, a landing party of men successfully rode the breakers into a harbor during a sleet storm. The next morning on a "fair sunshining day" they saw that they were on an island and after celebrating the Sabbath they landed on Monday on the mainland covered with "divers cornfields and little running brooks." Bradford's account does not give a rock as a landmark.

POCAHONTAS (c.1595-1617) Daughter of the chief Powhatan of the Virginia confederacy, Pocahontas, whose name was derived from the Algonquian *pocahántesu*, "she is playful," first gained a reputation among the English settlers at Jamestown, Virginia, by the dramatic story of her rescue of Captain John Smith from execution in 1608. The historical authenticity of that story, however, has long been the subject of scholarly debate. In 1613, Pocahontas and a number of other Indian notables were taken prisoner by the Jamestown colonists in their effort to secure a treaty of peace with her father. During her stay at Jamestown, Pocahontas was impressed with the way of life of the English and under the spiritual guidance of Alexander Whitaker was converted to Christianity and baptized as "Rebecca." Her subsequent marriage to John Rolfe, one of the Jamestown colonists, was sanctioned by Governor Thomas Dale in his hope of improving relations with the Powhatan Confederacy. In 1616, Pocahontas accompanied Rolfe and Dale on an official visit to England, where she was received as royalty and greeted personally by King James and Queen Anne. As she was returning to America in 1617, however, she fell ill and died of smallpox. She was buried in the church cemetery of St. George's Parish in Gravesend, England.

POLLOCK, OLIVER (c.1737-1823) A merchant and financier, born in Coleraine, Northern Ireland, Pollock immigrated to Carlisle, Pennsylvania, in 1760. Later moving to Philadelphia, he entered the merchant marine and became a shipmaster in the Caribbean trade. In 1768 he settled in New Orleans and acquired extensive landholdings. As a supporter of American independence, he arranged for the secret importation of arms and ammunition from Cuba for the Continental Army after the outbreak of the Revolution. Pollock was appointed commercial agent for the United States in 1778 and lost a substantial part of his fortune by providing credit to the financially strapped government.

PONCE DE LEÓN, JUAN (c.1460-1521) Ponce de León may have arrived in the New World as early as 1493, on Christopher Columbus's second voyage. In 1502-04 he aided in the further conquest of Hispaniola and was rewarded by being named governor of Higuey province. In 1508 an Indian from Puerto Rico appeared in the province bearing gold, and Ponce de León fitted out a small party to find its source. In 1509 he undertook the conquest of Puerto Rico and became its first governor.

Stories of the Carib Indians fascinated Ponce de León, especially tales of a rich island called Bimini that contained a fountain with the magical property of restoring youth. In 1512 he received a royal commission to find Bimini, and he set out with three ships early in 1513. Sailing up the Antillean chain of islands, he struck the eastern coast of the mainland on April 2, although he thought that the coast was that of an island. Sailing west, he passed along the Florida Keys and then returned to Puerto Rico. In 1514 he received a royal commission to settle Bimini and Florida, but it was 1521 when he set out with about 200 men. He landed on the mainland again, this time on Florida's west coast, and immediately received a mortal wound in a fight with the Indians. He died in Cuba a few days later.

POND, PETER (1740-1807) An explorer and trader, born in Connecticut, Pond moved west, entering the fur trade at Detroit in 1765. Working for the North West Company, he explored north of the Saskatchewan River in the 1780s, blazing the Methye Portage, which linked the Churchill River with the Athabasca-Mackenzie system. His maps of these explorations (1784) were the first of the western Canadian interior. In 1788 he supervised the construction of Fort Chipewyan on Lake Athabasca, the starting point for the journey of Alexander Mackenzie the next year.

See also Mackenzie, Alexander.

PONTIAC (?1720-69) An Indian leader in the Old Northwest, Pontiac became the chief of the Ottawa (1755). He headed a confederation of tribes that resented the British after the French and Indian War. He enlisted several tribes in a confederacy, hoping to attack and destroy British frontier forts and settlements. The Indian conspiracy became known as Pontiac's Rebellion. Pontiac's tribes succeeded in ransacking and burning western forts and settlements from Niagara to Virginia. After British forces became too strong for Pontiac's confederation, he signed a treaty (1766). Pontiac became a symbol and legend of Indian resistance.

See also Pontiac's Rebellion.

PONTIAC'S REBELLION   Pontiac's Rebellion (1763-65) was a loosely coordinated effort by Indians of the Ohio Valley and Great Lakes to drive the British out of the land between the Allegheny Mountains and the Mississippi River. The defeat of France in the French and Indian War (Seven Years War) marked the end of competition between the empires to win Indian favor through presents and trade concessions. Britain now demanded that the western Indians bring all furs to the former French forts while offering fewer goods in return, especially rum and ammunition. In addition, the English general Sir Jeffrey Amherst had seized some Seneca land in violation of a Six Nations New York treaty. As early as 1761 the Seneca urged Indians gathered at Detroit to begin an uprising there. Although that appeal failed, anti-British sentiment grew over the next two years, fanned by the nativist message of the Delaware prophet Neolin. Neolin reported a vision in which the Master of Life made clear that the Indians' close ties to Europeans had brought them to the verge of extinction. Salvation was possible only by foreswearing European goods (except guns, for self-defense) and returning to the old ways.

The Rebellion and the Peace.   In May 1763 an Ottawa named Pontiac led an attack on Detroit while Potowatamie, Miami, Huron, Ojibwa, Shawnee, and Delaware joined in assaults on 11 other western forts. Although the Indians captured most of the forts, low supplies of food and ammunition plus disease (including an English-induced smallpox epidemic) handicapped them in the face of British reinforcements. In 1766, Pontiac and some of his followers accepted a peace in which Britain retained its posts, promising ample supplies of trade goods. But many Indians remained resentful as settlers poured into Ohio in violation of Britain's Proclamation Line, hastily established during the rebellion. As a partisan of the English, Pontiac lost much of his influence and was assassinated by some Illinois Indians in 1769. Although the rebellion failed, it nourished a tradition of pan-Indian resistance that manifested itself most forcefully through the Shawnee Prophet, Tenskwatawa, and his brother Tecumseh during the War of 1812.

See also French and Indian War; Proclamation of 1763.

Bibliography: Peckham, Howard H., *Pontiac and the Indian Uprising* (Princeton Univ. Press, 1947); Wallace, Anthony F. C., *The Death and Rebirth of the Seneca* (Knopf, 1970).

Neal Salisbury
Smith College

POOR RICHARD'S ALMANACK   Published annually between 1732 and 1796, *Poor Richard's Almanack* was the creation of Benjamin Franklin. Despite the competition of seven Philadelphia almanacs, Franklin decided to bring out a new one because he wanted a forum for his philosophy of frugal living and because the market for almanacs was excellent. An almanac containing weather forecasts, tide calculations, and sundry information was the staple book in colonial households. The first edition of Franklin's almanac appeared late in December instead of the customary October or November printing, but within three weeks, three printings had been made. The almanac's main character, Richard Saunders, caught the public imagination, as he and his fictional wife Bridget engaged in a running public battle. Although *Poor Richard's Almanack* was printed until 1796, Franklin probably did not contribute to it after 1748. In 1757 he separated from the almanac and in 1758 collected what he regarded as the best from his editions into a long speech by Father Abraham, which Richard said he had heard at an auction. *Father Abraham's Speech* is now known as *The Way to Wealth*.

POPÉ (died 1690)   A famous San Juan Pueblo medicine man and leader, Popé got his name from the *Tew po'pñ*, "pumpkin mountain." Against the background of harsh Spanish colonial rule, Popé began to preach among his people, condemning the loss of territory and cultural integrity that had come as a result of the Spanish colonial administration. He believed that the gods of the Pueblo disapproved of the Spanish and would help exterminate them. Arrrested several times for preaching this subversive doctrine, Popé was eventually flogged in the main square of Santa Fe and imprisoned with 47 other Pueblo medicine men. The pressure of public appeals, however, eventually persuaded Governor Antonio de Otermin to release Popé and his colleagues.

Following his release from prison, Popé went into hiding at the Taos Pueblo, where he gained the alliance of the Catiti of Santo Domingo, the Tupatu of Picuris, and the Jaca of Taos for an armed insurrection to begin in August 1680. Having the benefit of surprise, the rebels killed 500 Spaniards and laid siege to Santa Fe, ultimately forcing the governor to flee to Texas. This success was short-lived. Popé's autocratic manner in office led to his deposition by his own people and the eventual return of the Spanish in 1692.

POPHAM, GEORGE (died 1608)   A Maine settler, Popham was born in Huntsworth, Somerset, England. His uncle was Sir John Popham, who recommended with Sir Ferdinando Gorges that England settle a colony in Virginia. George was in the Virginia Company Patent of April 10, 1606, as one of the seven ruling council members. In 1607 he and Raleigh Gilbert filled two ships, the *Gift of God* and the *Mary and John*, with colonists and reached the Maine coast in July. They held church services on

Monhegan Island and then settled on the western Kennebec. Popham was elected governor, but he died the next winter, and the colonists returned to England.

ESTIMATED TOTAL POPULATION OF AMERICA (1630-1790)

1630	4,646
1640	26,634
1650	50,368
1660	75,058
1670	111,935
1680	151,507
1690	210,372
1700	250,888
1710	331,711
1720	466,185
1730	629,445
1740	905,563
1750	1,170,760
1760	1,593,625
1770	2,148,076
1775	2,204,500
1780	2,780,369
1790	3,929,214

POPULATION OF THE ORIGINAL THIRTEEN STATES (1790)

New England	
Massachusetts	475,199
Connecticut	237,655
New Hampshire	141,885
Rhode Island	68,825

Middle States	
Pennsylvania	434,473
New York	340,120
New Jersey	184,139
Delaware	59,096

South	
Virginia	747,610
North Carolina	393,751
Maryland	319,728
South Carolina	249,073
Georgia	82,548

POPULATION Population growth rates at the outset of settlement in early 17th-century America fluctuated wildly because the entry of large numbers of immigrants rapidly increased the total white population. From 1660 until the first federal census in 1790 the population grew at a rate of nearly 35 percent per decade. Most of the growth may be attributed to an excess of births over deaths but immigra-

tion was also an important factor. By the 1800-10 period, however, natural increase accounted for 96 percent of the total population growth, while immigration contributed only 4 percent. In 1800 the crude birth rate still approached the physiological maximum of between 50 and 60 births per 1,000 population. The estimated white birth rate per 1,000 population in 1800 is estimated at 55 and the rate per 1,000 women between ages 15 and 44 is about 278. These rates began to decline early in the 19th century.

In early 18th century America rapid population growth began. From 1700 to the end of the century the American population nearly doubled every 25 years. Most of this accumulation came from natural increase, an excess of births over deaths, but immigration, especially from the British Isles and Germany, and slave importations also promoted rapid population growth rates. Immigrants streamed into the British North American colonies from England, Scotland, Ireland, Germany, and the Swiss cantons. In this way American population grew rapidly and became increasingly diverse. Pennsylvania, more than any other colony or state, showed the results, first, of rapid growth, and second, of increasing diversity of migrants. By 1790 only 35.3 percent of the state's population was of English origin, 8.6 percent Scotch, 14.5 percent Ulster and Free State Irish and 33.3 percent of German origins. The black population increased dramatically in Virginia, the Carolinas, and Maryland to 1780. In 1780, 220,582 blacks lived in Virginia, which had a total population of 538,004 people. Rapid population growth and increasing proportions of non-English settlers changed the nature of early American communities in the 18th century. The total colonial population, white and black, grew from 250,888 in 1700 to 466,185 in 1720. At mid-century British North America had 1,170,760 inhabitants. By the end of the Revolution more than 2,780,369 people lived in the United States.

Factors of Population Growth. Several factors help explain the rapid growth of population in colonial America. First, couples married when younger than their counterparts in England or Europe. Fairly universal marriage and an average age at first marriage for American women generally lower than that of European women promoted a higher birth rate in the colonies. Moreover, lower infant and child mortality rates than those for Europeans ensured that greater proportions of Americans survived to adulthood, married, and raised families. Colonials, then, lived healthier lives than did Europeans. New immigrants in America suffered higher death rates than long-term residents. Colder winters in the Northern colonies caused higher mortality to some extent. But the mortality rate in America registered only about 25 deaths per 1,000 population, whereas, in Europe it approached an average of 40 deaths per 1,000. Better supplies of nutritious food, ample fuel supplies, and higher real wages contributed to better living conditions and a higher standard of living. There is little evidence of malnutrition contributing much to the death rate in the colonial population.

Better living conditions and a scattered, rural, agricultural population (protected to some extent from raging epidemics) meant that Americans lived better and longer than Europeans. Epidemic diseases, however, strongly influenced infant mortality rates of 180-200 deaths per 1,000 in the Northern colonies and even higher figures than these in the Southern colonies. Lower infant mortality rates than in Europe indicate that American males and females, at birth, could anticipate life expectancies in the range of 36 to 40 years. Those who survived to adulthood, about age 20, had life expectancies of an additional 35 to 40 years. Finally, American women apparently experienced lower rates of death in childbirth, in part, because of healthier living conditions and ready supplies of nutritional food.

A combination of lower age at first marriage, high birth rates, low mortality, and immigration patterns increased colonial population. From 1640 to 1700 colonial population grew from approximately 26,000 to just over 250,000. From 1700 to the end of the 18th century, it more than doubled every 25 years at an annual rate of 2.5 percent. There were more than 1,000,000 Americans by 1750 and about 2,500,000 in the Revolutionary period. Immigration added an important increment to colonial population growth, but the most important reason for rapid growth was natural increase, which for white colonists amounted to at least 26-30 percent per decade. The lower age at marriage, high birth rates, and relatively lower death rates accelerated the rate of colonial population growth.

Importation of large numbers of slaves into the Southern colonies produced a dramatic increase in population in that region. From 1700 to the Revolution, slave traders brought approximately 250,000 blacks into the British North American colonies. During the 1760s alone, slave traders imported about 75,000 blacks. Probably 90 percent of these went to work in the Southern colonies. By the Revolution, black slaves composed nearly 40 percent of the population of the five Southern colonies. Because of these heavy importations the Southern colonies' share of total population increased from 42 to 46 percent from 1700 to 1770.

1790 Census Characteristics. By 1790, when the first federal census was taken, the regional distribution of population varied considerably from North to South. From the beginning of the 18th century to the Revolutionary era (1770), the Middle Colonies' share of total population

increased from 19 to 26 percent and the South's proportion rose from 42 to 46 percent, while New England's share declined from 39 percent in 1700 to 28 percent by 1770. In 1790 the regional population distribution had shifted as follows: New England, 25.7 percent; Middle States, 25.9 percent; South, 48.5 percent. During the 18th century the Middle Colonies' population grew at the highest rate. The region had the highest birth rates in North America and attracted some 300,000 to 350,000 white immigrants, mostly Scotch-Irish and Palatine Germans who settled in Pennsylvania, New Jersey, and New York. The South's population grew at the next fastest rate because the region imported some 200,000 black slaves from 1700 to the Revolution. New England experienced a relative decline in the proportionate share of population because fewer immigrants settled in the area and birth rates declined in the region as marriage ages rose in response to land shortages and relative economic decline.

Bibliography: Curtin, Philip D., *The Atlantic Slave Trade: A Census* (Univ. of Wisconsin Press, 1969); Sutherland, Stella H., *Population Distribution in Colonial America* (1936; reprint AMS Press); Thompson, W. S. and Whelpton, P. K., *Population Trends in the United States* (1933; reprint Gordon & Breach, 1969); Vinovskis, Maris A., ed., *Studies in American Historical Demography* (Academic Press, 1979); Wells, Robert V., *The Population of the British Colonies in America Before 1776* (Princeton Univ. Press, 1975); Yasuba, Y., *Birth Rates of the White Population in the United States, 1800- 1860* (1962; reprint AMS Press).

Rodger C. Henderson
Pennsylvania State University, Fayette

PORTOLÁ, GASPAR DE (c.1723-86)   A Spanish official in California, Portolá had just been appointed governor of Baja California (1767) when he was ordered to undertake the settlement of Alta California. Sending an advance party under Rivera y Moncada ahead, Portolá and the Dominican Junipero Serra set out for San Diego. On July 16, 1769, the mission of San Diego was founded, the first of 21 on the California coast. Portolá then went on to found another settlement at Monterey, but he did not at first recognize the bay from the explorer Sebastían Vizcaíno's 1603 description and stumbled onto San Francisco Bay instead. In March 1770 he finally reached Monterey and established a mission and presidio before returning to Mexico. In 1784, Portolá returned to Spain, where he died.

See also Rivera y Moncada, Fernando; San Diego; Serra, Junipero; Monterey.

PORT ROYAL   One of the first permanent European settlements in North America, Port Royal, Nova Scotia, became the most important city of French Acadia and the scene of bitter Anglo-French conflict. Established in 1605 by Samuel Champlain and Pierre du Guast, Sieur de Monts, Port Royal was destroyed in 1613 by an English force under Samuel Argall of Virginia. The possession of Port Royal was contested again by the English in 1654, 1670, and 1690 but was temporarily ceded to France by the Treaty of Ryswick (1697). During Queen Anne's War, it was again invaded by the English and was ceded to England by the Treaty of Utrecht (1713). However, its importance declined after the founding of Halifax in 1749.

PORT ROYAL COLONY   A settlement on Port Royal Island off the southern coast of South Carolina was established in 1562 by Huguenot leader Jean Ribault and 30 French colonists. Although Spanish explorers had already visited the island and named it Santa Elena, Ribault's was the first permanent settlement. After Ribault's return to France in the following year, however, the colonists revolted and abandoned the island, which was occupied and fortified by the Spanish in 1566. In 1577 the Spanish constructed Fort San Marcos on the site of the earlier settlement but abandoned it in 1586. A Scottish colony, founded in 1684, was similarly short-lived.

PORTSMOUTH   This city and harbor at the outlet of the Piscataqua River was established in 1623 by David Thomas and four other English colonists who had been dispatched there by Captain John Mason, a London merchant and holder of a territorial grant from the Council of New England. The settlement was originally named "Strawberry Banke." Incorporated as the town of Portsmouth in 1653, it remained under the jurisdiction of the Massachusetts Bay Colony until 1679, when the separate colony of New Hampshire was established. A center of Revolutionary agitation, Portsmouth served as a shipbuilding center for the Continental navy. It was capital of New Hampshire until 1808.

POST, CHRISTIAN FREDERICK (1710-85)   A Moravian missionary, Post was born in East Prussia and emigrated to Pennsylvania in 1742. His missionary work with Indians in New York and in the Wyoming and Ohio valleys helped to ally a number of important tribes with the British during the French and Indian War.

POSTAL SERVICE   Massachusetts in 1639 became the first colony to attempt to regulate the delivery of mail, and over the next four decades several other colonies made similiar attempts. But it was not until 1691, when the British created a private postal monopoly, that an intercolonial system was first organized. Although never effective in the South, in the North the service pioneered a primitive network of postal roads extending from Portsmouth, New Hampshire, to New Castle, Delaware,

with way stations for keeping fresh horses and riders, including the famous Boston Post Road (New York-Boston) and Old Post Road (New York-Albany). Although never profitable, the service was taken over by the British government in 1707 and continued to provide fair mail delivery in the Northern colonies. By 1720 mail between New York and Philadelphia was carried once a week in summer, twice a month in winter. Regular service was extended to Virginia in 1732, but it remained spotty in the rest of the South.

Great improvements took place after 1753, when the post of deputy colonial postmaster was filled by Benjamin Franklin, who later admitted that the improved service, with reduced rates for newspapers, significantly increased the profitability of his publishing business. He extended service to Canada and South Carolina and cut the time of delivery between Northern cities. Meanwhile the British established regular trans-Atlantic mail packet service to New York and Charleston. This new efficiency was both a sign and a cause of the growing unity among the English colonies in America. Newspapers, in particular, became an important medium of intercolonial communication.

The revolt against the imperial administration that began in the 1760s included the postal system. Boycotted by the colonists, the royal post system was closed and Franklin dismissed in 1774, but the next year the Second Continental Congress appointed him continental postmaster and extended regular service south to Georgia. Ebenezer Hazard, appointed postmaster general by Congress after the Revolution, successfully guided the system through the crisis of the Confederation period. By 1789 the mails were being carried to 75 post offices on over 2,400 miles of post roads.

See also Hazard, Ebenezer.

Bibliography: Fuller, Wayne E., *The American Mail* (1972; reprint Univ. of Chicago Press, 1980).

John Mack Faragher
Mount Holyoke College

POTATO   Reckoned by the proportion of the world diet supplied by this tuber, the potato is the most important of the New World crops. It was first cultivated by Andean Indians, who called it "papa," or, in the Taino language of the Arawaks encountered by Christopher Columbus, "batata," from which the Spanish took the name. Yellow "sweet potatoes" (*Ipomoea batatas*) were brought back by Columbus, "white potatoes" (*Solanum tuberosum*) by soldiers returning from Pizarro's conquest of Peru. By the middle of the 16th century both forms were grown in Europe. Walter Raleigh introduced potatoes to Ireland during the English wars of conquest, and they became the staple of the exploited Irish peasantry. Likewise, potatoes were destined to provide the margin between famine and subsistence for peasant peoples throughout eastern Europe and became known as the food of the poor.

Although several varieties of sweet potatoes were being cultivated in North America, white potatoes were unknown until introduced by Irish immigrants in the 18th century. By the Revolution the white potato was a common field crop throughout New England and the Middle Colonies but still considered fit only for livestock and the lower classes. Only in the 19th century did the potato become a staple in the American diet.

See also Food.

Bibliography: Salaman, Redcliffe N., *The History and Social Influence of the Potato* (Cambridge Univ. Press, 1985).

POTT, JOHN (died c.1642) Physician and governor of Virginia, Pott was born in Cheshire, England. The Virginia Company gave Pott and his family free passage and shipment of a "chest of phisique" and "Books of phisique." He was a respected colonial doctor, and as deputy governor from 1629 to 1630 he improved Virginia's defenses. His rivals brought him to court in 1624 for poisoning the Indians, and in 1630 Governor Sir John Harvey fined him for cattle theft to discredit Pott's effort to keep Lord Baltimore out of Virginia. In 1635, Pott and his brother Francis were accused of treason for deposing Harvey, but John was never tried before he died near Williamsburg.

POWHATAN (c.1550-1618) The founder and leader of the Powhatan Confederacy of the eastern Virginia Algonquin was named Wahunsonacock but was called Powhatan (the name of his village) by the English. Born into a matrilineage of paramount chiefs with authority over a handful of tribes, Powhatan in the years before permanent European settlement (1607) exploited the unstable conditions produced by the disruption of European contact, including pandemic diseases sweeping through the tidewater, to extend his rule over another 25 tribes, creating a powerful chiefdom.

During the first years of contact, Powhatan established tentative relations with the English and on the basis of trade increased the power of his chiefdom. Conflict and warfare were continually threatening, however, as when John Smith became his captive in 1607 or when the English kidnapped his daughter Pocahontas in 1613. The marriage of Pocahontas to colonist John Rolfe finally sealed peaceful relations with the English until Powhatan's death in 1618. He was succeeded by his brother Opechancanough, who was less sanguine about the Europeans and led the confederacy through 28 years of almost continual conflict with the English.

See also Pocahontas; Powhatan Confederacy; Opechancanough; Smith, John; Virginia.

POWHATAN CONFEDERACY When the English settled the Chesapeake in 1607 they confronted a powerful alliance of Algonquian-speaking tribes, including such tribes as the Appamatuck, Chesapeake, and Mattaponi, headed by a paramount chief from the village of Powhatan, on what would later become the site of Richmond, Virginia, near the falls of the James River. The English applied this village name to both the chief and his chiefdom of some 30 tribes of perhaps 10,000 Indians living between the south bank of the Rappahannock River on the north, the Dismal Swamp on the south, and the falls of the rivers on the west.

Powhatan had been born into a matrilineage of paramount chiefs, but he added greatly to his chiefdom during the last quarter of the 16th century, probably encouraged by the general disruptions of war and epidemic disease that attended the first European contacts, including the establishment and destruction of a Spanish Jesuit mission on the York River in 1570-71 and an English colony on Roanoke Island in Abermarle Sound in the 1580s.

Other Virginia Algonquins, including the Rappahannock, Pamunkey, and Chickahominy, together numbering perhaps another 10,000 persons, lived in much the same way. All were primarily horticulturists, producing plentiful stores of maize (corn), beans, pumpkins, and tubers; but they also fished for the abundant seafood of the rivers and bay and hunted in the backcountry for food and hides. They lived in densely populated palisaded villages composed of several large wooden houses, with outlying fields, each with its own chief. Chiefs exacted tribute, which sustained their more opulent style of life, and in return organized and protected the communal storehouse. Powhatan sat at the apex of this system of chiefdoms.

The Powhatan met the English with mixed feelings. Contact had already brought conflict and disease, but the entrance of these powerful strangers, hungry for corn, promised lucrative trade and potential allies in the struggles between chiefs. Indian vacillation between friendship and hostility gave the English room to survive the first hard years. Small-scale warfare depopulated large parts of the peninsula between the York and James rivers, where the English had gained a foothold. When Powhatan died in 1618, he was succeeded by his brother Opechancanough, who decided to expel the English. The uprising that began in 1622 nearly wiped out the English settlements, but holding on at Jamestown the colonists were gradually able to take the struggle to the Indian homelands. The war continued intermittently until 1636. In 1644, Opechancanough tried once again, but the English crushed the rebellion and killed the chief in 1646, breaking up the confederacy.

In the early 18th century the former Powhatan were living on several small reservations where they were inter-mixing with whites and runaway slaves. By the time of the Revolution, there were perhaps 1,000 Virginia Algon-quins, most notably in the continuing tribal remnants of the Pamunkey and Mattaponi.

See also Jamestown; Opechancanough; Powhatan; Virginia.

Bibliography: Barbour, Philip L., *Pocahontas and Her World* (Houghton Mifflin, 1969); Jennings, Francis, *The Invasion of America: Indians, Colonialism, and the Cant of Conquest* (Univ. of North Carolina Press, 1975); Lurie, Nancy O., "Indian Cultural Adjustment to European Civilization," in: Smith, James H., ed., *Seventeenth-Century America: Essays in Colonial History* (W. W. Norton, 1972).

John Mack Faragher
Mount Holyoke College

POWNALL, THOMAS (1722-1805) A British colonial official, Pownall graduated from England's Cambridge University in 1743 and entered the office of the Board of Trade. In 1753 he arrived in New York as secretary to the governor and subsequently became friends with Benjamin Franklin and William Shirley, the governor of Mas-sachusetts. In 1755, Pownall was appointed lieutenant governor of New Jersey; in 1757 he succeeded Shirley in Massachusetts, where he was very popular. The Board of Trade recalled him, however, and he remained in England until 1761, when he was commissioned to an army post in Germany. In 1764-65 he published *The Administration of the Colonies*, in which he argued for centralization. In 1780 he retired from public life.

PRAIRIE DU CHIEN At the mouth of the Wisconsin River on the Mississippi, in present-day southern Wiscon-sin, Prairie du Chien was first noted when Father Marquette and Louis Jolliet traveled west from Green Bay in 1673 and encountered a large body of Indians there. The site had long been a thoroughfare and market center for the Sioux, Sauk, Fox, and French *coureurs de bois*, and French explorer Nicholas Perrot established Fort Nicolas there in the 1680s. After the French and Indian War, the post was taken over by the British, but the population remained French and Indian, with a majority of métis or mixedbloods. Retained by the British after the Treaty of Paris (1783), Prairie du Chien was finally transferred to the United States in 1816.

PRATT, MATTHEW (1734-1805) A portrait painter, Pratt was born in Philadelphia. His father was a goldsmith and friend of Benjamin Franklin and his uncle, James Claypoole, a painter. Pratt was apprenticed to Claypoole from the ages of 15 to 22. After practicing as a painter for several years, he made a trip to London and spent four years studying with painter Benjamin West, whom he represented in his 1765 painting, "The American School," working with his pupils. In 1768 he returned to Philadelphia, reopened his shop, and received good commissions, such as the full-length portrait of Cadwallader Colden (1772). He also painted Benjamin Franklin. A trip to Ireland in 1770 to look after his wife's inheritance gave him the opportunity to paint battle scenes of Oliver Cromwell's campaign and a noteworthy portrait of Archdeacon Mann.

During the Revolution, he was driven to sign painting to support his family. Although none of his signs has survived, they were very popular, particularly his sign depicting the 38 members of the Constitutional Congress. He was an ac-complished man and sometimes wrote poems to accompany his signs.

PRAYING TOWNS These small communities of Chris-tianized Indians included villages of the Iroquois founded by Jesuit missionaries, Delaware and Shawnee settlements founded by the Moravians in Ohio, and the villages of various eastern New England peoples, organized and su-pervised by Puritan missionary John Eliot. Eliot first devised the concept of praying towns, beginning with his attempts at religious education and persuasion at Nonan-tum near Boston in 1646.

In 1650, after organizing the Society for the Propagation of the Gospel in New England, he founded the first of the Christianized Indian villages at Natick. Other towns were established on Martha's Vineyard and Nantucket and along the eastern New England coast, despite the intense hostility to this missionary work expressed by the Narragansett and Mohegan. By 1674 there were 14 praying towns in New England: Chabanakong-Komun, Hassanamesit, Manchaug, Magunkaquoag, Manexit, Nashobah, Natick, Okommakamesit, Pakachoog, Punkapog, Quantisset, Wabaquassit, Wacuntug, and Wamesit. The anti-Indian sentiment and violence of King Philip's War (1675-76) resulted in the destruction of many of these towns and the virtual end of the missionary work.

See also Eliot, John.

PRESBYTERIANS As a consequence of the Protestant Reformation of the 16th century, Scotland under the guidance and prodding of John Knox turned to Pres-byterianism. Some English Protestants, rejecting a church governance by bishops in favor of one by presbyters and synods, also embraced Presbyterianism, conspicuously so during the period of the Long Parliament (1640-53, 1659-

60). Presbyterians came to America from England, Scotland, and that portion of northern Ireland called Ulster.

Although some Presbyterians emigrated in the 17th century, major growth came only in the 18th. By 1706 the first presbytery had been formed in America and, a decade later, the Synod of Philadelphia was established. In much of this organizational activity, Francis Makemie served as a powerful catalyst. Coming to the colonies in 1683, Makemie worked with particular effect in Maryland and Virginia, although he pressed on into Pennsylvania and New York. In the latter colony, a famous encounter took place in 1707 between Makemie and the royal governor, Lord Cornbury, who had held the Presbyterian preacher a prisoner for six weeks. Makemie claimed the protection of England's Declaration of Religious Toleration (1689), while Cornbury contended that the law did not apply in New York. Makemie won that battle as another Presbyterian itinerant, Samuel Davies, won a series of battles in Virginia against the Anglican establishment there.

In the Great Awakening of the 1740s, Middle Colony Presbyterians proved to be powerful itinerants, especially Gilbert Tennent, who traveled far beyond his home base in New Jersey to bring evangelical piety into much of New England. New Side (or prorevivalist) Presbyterian clergy brought the College of New Jersey (later Princeton) into being in 1746. Aided by education, evangelism, and patriotic fervor, Presbyterians had more churches in America by 1780 than any other denomination except the Congregationalists. Close cooperation between these two groups further enhanced the power of each.

See also Great Awakening; Tennent, Gilbert.

Bibliography: Trinterud, L. J., *The Forming of an American Tradition: A Re-examination of Colonial Presbyterianism* (Westminster Press, 1949).

Edwin S. Gaustad
University of California, Riverside

PRESCOTT, SAMUEL (1751-77) Born in Concord, Massachusetts, Prescott became a physician like his father and grandfather before him. On April 18,1775, Prescott was leaving the home of a friend when he encountered Paul Revere and William Dawes riding to warn patriots of the approaching British troops. He rode with them toward Concord, but they were stopped by British soldiers. Dawes escaped; Prescott tried to push through but, finding that unsuccessful, jumped his horse over a wall and got away. He was the only one to complete the "midnight ride." In 1776, Prescott fought at the Battle of Ticonderoga and was captured and taken aboard a privateer. He died in prison at Halifax, Nova Scotia.

See also Revere, Paul.

PRESCOTT, WILLIAM (1726-95) A soldier in King George's War and in the French and Indian War, Prescott was a farmer in Pepperell, Massachusetts, when Boston's port was closed in 1774. He was colonel of a company of Minutemen, and on April 19, 1775, he led his men to Concord but arrived too late to engage in fighting. He became a member of the council of war at Cambridge, Massachusetts. Prescott was then ordered to fortify Bunker Hill, but he decided that Breed's Hill was a better location. In charge of the redoubt, he was one of the chief commanders. He participated in later battles, most notably the surrender of Britain's General Burgoyne at Saratoga, New York. Prescott retired to his farm after the war but once again was called to arms to suppress Shays' Rebellion in 1787.

PRIBER, CHRISTIAN (died c.1744) A mystic missionary among the Cherokee, Priber was born in Saxony and emigrated to South Carolina in 1734 after being expelled from his homeland for his radical views on the corruption of European society. In 1736 he took up residence among the Cherokee, adopted Indian language and dress, and found them sympathetic to his notions of communal ownership of property and the equality of the sexes. The Cherokee were most interested, however, in Priber's counsel that the Southern Indians unite to form a confederation against European encroachment and in his lessons on the use of weights and measures so the Indians could guard against notoriously unscrupulous British traders. Carolinians made several attempts to capture him but were prevented by Indians who considered him a "great beloved man." He was eventually captured, however, and taken to Georgia, where he died in confinement.

PRIMOGENITURE AND ENTAIL English legal customs governing the inheritance of property, primogeniture and entail were designed to protect the integrity of family estates from generation to generation. In the instance of intestacy, primogeniture required the devolution of property upon the eldest son. The law of entail vested title to property in a future heir, thereby preventing its sale or alienation for debt or other purposes.

As vestiges of English feudalism in colonial America, primogeniture and entail existed in several colonies with varying degrees of success. In Rhode Island alone of the New England provinces, property descended to the eldest son, but in New York and in the Southern colonies entail was the rule of inheritance. Land might be entailed by will in New York, Pennsylvania, and the southern colonies. Both primogeniture and entail appeared more frequently in the 18th century with the advent of large landed estates that proprietors wished to secure and retain within their families.

The Revolution brought an eventual end to primogeniture and entail. Within a decade and a half of independence, every state but Rhode Island, which acted in 1798, had abolished primogeniture, first for real property, then for personal property. South Carolina moved against entail in 1775, followed by Virginia, Georgia, and Pennsylvania in 1776-77, and the remaining states by 1786. Neither primogeniture nor entail enjoyed widespread favor in America, where bountiful land and a more fluid society militated against those relics of European aristocracy and feudalism.

Alan D. Watson
University of North Carolina, Wilmington

PRINCE, THOMAS (1687-1758) A theologian, scholar, and historian, Prince was born at Sandwich, Massachusetts, graduated from Harvard in 1709, and served as a minister in Suffolk. In 1718 he joined Joseph Sewell as minister at Old South Church in Boston and stayed there until his death. Prince's publications include his funeral sermons, papers on Indian conversions, scientific observations, and, most important, his historical work, *A Chronological History of New England in the Form of Annals,* begun in 1730 and published in 1736. He also collected the works of the Mather family and kept a large library. His *The Christian History* (1744-45) is an admiring account of the appearances in America during the Great Awakening of the controversial evangelist George Whitefield.

PRINCETON COLLEGE Established in 1746 as the College of New Jersey, Princeton was the fourth colonial college and had three New Jersey locations: at the home of its first president, Reverend Jonathan Dickinson, in New Brunswick; in Newark with the second president, Reverend Aaron Burr; and in 1756 in Robert Smith's newly-built Nassau Hall in Princeton. The Presbyterian founders were members of the New Light movement who wanted to follow John Tennent's work at Log College to train ministers for the Great Awakening. John Witherspoon, president from 1768 to 1794, signed the Declaration of Independence, and James Madison, class of 1771, was the fourth president of the United States. It took its present name in 1896.

See also Log College; Witherspoon, John.

PRINCIPIO COMPANY An iron forge established in 1715 in Maryland by the Principio Iron Works, the Principio Company was one of the most important industrial installations in the American colonies. Soon after its first export of bar iron to England in 1718, the Principio forge was purchased by a group of British and American stockholders, among them, Augustus Washington, father of George. In 1724 the forge was enlarged and supplied from iron mines in Virginia that had come under the control of the Principio Company. By 1750 the company operated five forges in Maryland and Virginia. Its British-controlled assets were confiscated by the state of Maryland during the Revolution.

PRING, MARTIN (1580-1626) An English sea captain commissioned by Bristol merchants to trade along the New England coast in 1603, following the voyage of Bartholomew Gosnold, Pring sailed along the coast from Penobscot Bay south into Massachusetts Bay. Exploring in turn the mouths of the Saco, Kennebunk, York, and Piscataqua rivers, he concluded that none was the eagerly sought-after Northwest Passage. He landed at the northern end of Cape Cod and there encouraged the local Indians to engage in trading and to help his men gather sassafras (thought to be a miracle cure for syphilis). But when he tired of the natives' company, Captain Pring turned the ship's two large mastiff dogs on them. The Indians then grew hostile, finally driving the English from the site of what would become Provincetown, Massachusetts.

See also Exploration.

PRINTING AND PUBLISHING The first printing press in North America was set up in Mexico City by Spanish missionaries in 1535; it was more than a century later that Stephen Day established the first press in the English colonies in Cambridge, Massachusetts (1639). Day issued the first book published in America, *The Bay Psalm Book* (1640). In 1685 print shops were opened in Maryland by William Nuthead and in Philadelphia by William Bradford, who also established the earliest commercial paper mill in America. In 1693, Bradford moved his operations to New York City, where he was the first and sole printer for 30 years. In the early 18th century presses were set up in Connecticut (1709), Rhode Island (1727), and South Carolina (1731) to print public documents; like these, most presses in the colonies were under government control.

In the 18th century the proliferation of newspapers accounted for the growth in the number of printing presses. Newspaper offices often issued many other kinds of publications, including books. Benjamin Franklin opened one of the most important colonial presses in Philadelphia in 1728. Bradford's grandson, also named William Bradford, established a Philadelphia printing office in 1741 that continued in service for 80 years; he became the printer for the Continental Congress. These two Philadelphia competitors published the first American magazines in 1741, Bradford's *American Magazine* and Franklin's *General Magazine,* both of which soon disappeared. Other American magazines were issued irregularly, usually reprinting English material.

During the colonial period, printers charged authors for the publication of books and pamphlets. Authors then arranged with merchants to sell their writings on commission. The royalty system of payment did not develop until the 19th century.

See also Bay Psalm Book; Bradford, William (1663-1752); Bradford, William (1722-91); Day, Stephen; Freedom of the Press; New England Primer; Newspapers; Poor Richard's Almanack.

Bibliography: Wroth, Lawrence C., *An American Bookshelf, 1755* (1934; reprint Ayer, 1969).

PRINTZ, JOHAN BJORNSSON (1592-1663)   A Swedish colonial governor, Printz was born in Bottnaryd, Sweden. After a military career, he succeeded Peter Hollender Ridder as governor of New Sweden in 1642. For ten years he was the unquestioned ruler of New Sweden, which stretched from Cape Henlopen to Sankikan (Trenton, New Jersey). He ruled by his physical power but made peace with the Indians (who called him "Big Guts"), gave land to farmers, and built forts, a grist mill, a brewery, and a yacht. After a protest in 1653, when he hanged its leader for trying to make an official complaint, he returned to Sweden to hold other posts.

PRIVATEERING   Until the end of the 16th century it was difficult to tell where piracy began and privateering ended. By then privateering was understood to be the legal seizure of enemy ships in wartime while operating under the license of a letter of marque. Frequently those involved in English exploration and settlement funded their enterprises from the profits of privateering. Men such as the Earl of Warwick invested in the Virginia Company to get a base camp from which to raid Spanish shipping. Thus at a very early date privateering was introduced to the American colonies, where it would find a welcome home.

The great struggle between France and Britain for dominance in the race for empire produced four wars between 1688 and 1763. There were other conflicts against the Dutch and the Spanish, but the Anglo-French wars provided the main opportunities for privateers. In port cities, especially New York City and Newport, individual investors and syndicates took fast-sailing merchant ships, outfitted them with cannon, and attracted a large number of sailors with a no-prey—no-pay contract. Once outfitted, American privateers scoured the seas from the Grand Banks, where fishing ships provided easy targets, to the waters of the Caribbean, where the prizes were more numerous and richer. During the wars of 1739-48 it is estimated that American privateers captured prizes worth 17,000,000 pounds sterling. Their success also seriously hindered the trade of France and Spain, helping to weaken the hold they had on their colonies.

During the Revolution, American privateers such as John Paul Jones once again put to sea; but this war brought them not only the pleasures of prize but also those of striking a blow for liberty. The Revolution, however, marked the last great era of American privateering.

See also Piracy.

Bibliography: Morison, Samuel E., *John Paul Jones: A Sailor's Biography* (Little, Brown, 1959).

Robert C. Ritchie
University of California, San Diego

PROCLAMATION OF 1763   The royal proclamation issued by King George III on October 7, 1763, sought to bring order to the chaos in Indian-white relations that ensued with Britain's victory in the French and Indian War (Seven Years War). France's departure deeply concerned Indians between the Appalachian Mountains and the Mississippi River, most of whom had either been allied with the French or accustomed to playing them off against the British. In the absence of French competition, British trade goods became scarce while soldiers and settlers encroached on Indian land. In May 1763, France's erstwhile Indian allies in the northwest attacked 11 British-held forts in the uprising known as Pontiac's Rebellion. It was in this atmosphere that the king issued his proclamation.

Terms and Effects.   The proclamation as a whole dealt with several issues arising from the outcome of the recent war, including the disposition of lands and establishment of governments in Quebec, the Floridas, and other newly-acquired British territory. But above all it dealt with Indian policy. Land lying west of the Appalachian watershed was reserved for Indian use and could not be obtained by non-Indians without specific license from the Crown. Land sales to the east were to be regulated carefully by the colony governments. The trade monopolies about which Indians had long complained were replaced with competitive, licensed traders. British military and Indian affairs officials were to keep criminals and fugitives out of the Indian reserves. Through these measures the British government sought to allay the anxieties of Indians who, many feared, would otherwise keep the frontier in constant turmoil.

In the end, the proclamation was a complete failure. Britain failed to maintain garrisons in the west to enforce its authority there; conditions in the fur trade failed to improve; speculators obtained numerous exceptions to the ban on western land purchases; and ordinary settlers simply crossed the line and squatted. Although the line was subsequently readjusted at several points, native-settler tensions remained acute and continued directly into the American Revolution.

See also French and Indian War; Pontiac's Rebellion.
Bibliography: Alden, John Richard, *John Stuart and the Southern Colonial Frontier* (Univ. of Michigan Press, 1944); Sosin, Jack M., *Whitehall and the Wilderness: The Middle West in British Colonial Policy, 1760-1775* (Univ. of Nebraska Press, 1961).

Neal Salisbury
Smith College

PROMYSHLENIKI   The Promyshleniki were members of a group of private Russian trappers engaged in the fur trade along the Alaskan coast. In the mid-18th century, before they were suppressed by the monopolistic Russian-America Company, established in the 1780s, the Promyshleniki made numerous voyages, mostly unrecorded, across the Bering Sea from Siberia to the Aleutian Islands and the Alaskan mainland in search of the sea otter, which they practically hunted out of existence. Their relations with the Eskimos, Aleuts, and Indians were generally hostile, for they did not rely on the Indians as hunters or trading partners. Among the indigenous peoples they left death, disease, and alcoholism in their wake. But like the fur trappers of other nations—the *coureurs de bois* and the Bosch Loopers for example—they frequently intermarried with the local population, producing an interracial group, known as the Russian Creoles, that played an important role in the later sociey of Russian Alaska.

See also Alaska; Bosch Loopers; Coureurs de Bois; Fur Trade.

PROPRIETARY COLONIES   The English Crown created two quite different types of colonies in the New World. In royal colonies the king retained ownership of the land, which he alone (or his agents) could grant, and appointed both the governor and the council. In charter colonies the king gave such powers to groups or individuals who agreed to undertake the establishment of an English presence in the territories they received from the Crown. This agreement involved substantial risks since the costs involved were great and the promise of future profits no more than a hope. In such colonies as Virginia or Massachusetts Bay, for example, the king gave the charter to a corporation or company. These were referred to as corporate colonies. In other charter colonies, called proprietary colonies, the king gave a charter, which was a license to rule, to an individual or to a small private group of individuals who enjoyed, at least in theory, greater power in their colony than did the king in England.

A proprietor was the absolute lord over the territory he held, as were his heirs. The land he distributed to settlers would be titled in his (not the king's) name. He could erect virtually any type of government he chose, and all colonial officials received their appointments and derived their authority from him. He could create a colonial nobility by granting titles to those who served him. These awesome powers mirrored those which had been granted in the 14th century to the Lord Bishop of Durham in order to allow him to govern his county when it was being threatened by Scot invaders. The "Bishop of Durham clause" came to distinguish proprietary charters, appearing in Lord Baltimore's charters for Maryland and Newfoundland, as well as in that issued to the eight proprietors of Carolina. Its provisions defined the powers typically granted to others who received such charters from the Crown.

Growth and Decline of Proprietary Colonies.   The erection of proprietary colonies was a phenomenon limited to the 17th century, when the Crown, anxious to secure an English foothold in the Americas, proved willing to surrender control over the actual settlement—and to give away anticipated profits from taxation, trade, and land sales—in order to speed colonization. Those who received proprietaries were highly placed persons whose private resources enabled them to send colonists out from England and to support them during the years during which building settlements in the wilderness would require all their energies. Bestowing a proprietary charter was also a useful way for the Crown to repay a debt or return a favor. The proprietary, or great feudal estate, defined the status of the Carolinas, Maine, Maryland, New Jersey, New Hampshire, New York, Nova Scotia, and Pennsylvania.

During the 18th century, as the Crown asserted its power and its prerogatives in America, proprietary colonies were gradually turned into royal colonies, frequently with the happy consent of the settlers who anticipated that the king and Parliament would prove more liberal and protective governors than their proprietors had been. By 1720 only Maryland and Pennsylvania (attached to Delaware) remained as proprietary estates in English America.

Aaron Shatzman
Franklin and Marshall College

PROVIDENCE PLANTATION   In 1636, when Roger Williams left Massachusetts for Seekonk on Narragansett Bay, he thanked "God's merciful providence" for his deliverance and named his settlement Providence Plantation. He bought a large tract from the Narragansett and drew up a covenant for majority rule, permitting religious toleration. In 1644 his settlement joined with Newport, Portsmouth, and (in 1647) Warwick to form the Providence Plantations, later the colony of Rhode Island, which still officially retains the earlier name as its own.

PUEBLO INDIANS   Sharing a common culture based on intensive agriculture and religious ceremonialism, but speaking a variety of languages and divided into autonomous villages, the Pueblo peoples of present-day Arizona and New Mexico reside in the oldest continuously occupied sites within the limits of the United States. Given a general name from the Spanish word for village—evocative of their large, multistoried apartments of adobe—today's Pueblo people include Hopi and Zuni villagers to the west, in addition to 20 villages in New Mexico, of which the largest are Laguna, Acoma, Isleta, Santo Domingo, Jemez, San Felipe, and Taos.

When Francisco Coronado arrived in 1540, some 35,000 Indians lived in over 70 pueblos. The Spanish, especially after the conquering expedition of Juan de Oñate in 1598, demanded submission to their imperium, imposed tribute systems that extracted labor and goods, and introduced Franciscan missionaries who set about rooting out native religious practice. Although ultimately unsuccessful in eliminating the Europeans, the Pueblo Revolt of 1680 resulted in the Spanish lessening the burden of their regime, and on this basis of accommodation the Pueblo became a permanent part of the Spanish colonial system in New Mexico. Nevertheless, largely as a result of European diseases, the Pueblo population had fallen to 12,000 in 40 villages by 1750 and to merely 9,000 by 1821. The population began to rebound in the late 19th century and today totals about 35,000.

See also Pueblo Revolt.

PUEBLO REVOLT (1680)   Founded in 1598, the isolated colony of New Mexico still numbered less than 3,000 Spanish inhabitants by 1680. The Europeans lived off the labor of the Indians and maintained a tenuous hold over the region. Five years of prolonged drought and famine from 1667 to 1672 made a bad situation worse. The brutal suppression of a native religious revival in 1675 led to a direct confrontation between the Spanish and the Tewa Pueblo Indians, who forced the release of a number of captive Indian leaders. Among those released was Popé, one of the chief organizers of the intertribal revolt in 1680. That revolt began in August 1680 and by August 21, the Indians could claim a decisive victory: All the missions had been destroyed; 21 of 33 Franciscan missionaries had been killed; and the surviving Spaniards, led by Governor Otermin, were retreating to the south, arriving eventually at El Paso.

Although Spanish control was reestablished from 1692 to 1698, the revolt, one of the most successful in the history of European-Indian relations, did have a number of long-term effects: The *encomienda* system was abandoned in New Mexico; missionary attacks on the Pueblo religion decreased, especially as native practices went underground; royal land grants were made to Pueblo villages; and a public defender was appointed by Spain to protect Indian rights.

Puritan dress and religion were simple and severe. (*Library of Congress*)

PULASKI, CASIMIR (?1748-79)   A Polish officer with the patriot forces during the Revolutionary War, Pulaski was the eldest son of a Polish count. His first military service was in the guard of Duke Charles of Courland. Pulaski joined in a rebellion against the Polish monarch in 1768 and was impoverished after rebels were defeated. In 1772 he fled to Turkey, hoping to convince the Turks to attack Russia. His plot failing, he went to Paris in 1775. A French agent introduced him to Benjamin Franklin, and shortly thereafter Pulaski arrived in Boston.

In August 1775, Pulaski met George Washington and in 1777 accompanied the general at the Battle of Brandywine.

Given command of a small patrol, he met with defeat at Germantown, Pennsylvania, on October 4, 1777. That winter he was in charge of the cavalry at Trenton, New Jersey, and with General Anthony Wayne was sent to obtain supplies for Valley Forge, Pennsylvania. Pulaski refused to serve with Wayne and resigned his commission. He was soon back in command of his own cavalry, though. At Egg Harbor, New Jersey, in October 1778, he was ambushed by the British. He was then ordered to serve under General Lincoln in South Carolina. Always full of bravado, Pulaski was prone to make hasty decisions. One year after the Egg Harbor fiasco, he was fatally shot at the siege of Savannah while making a charge.

PURITANS Puritans, so named from their desire to "purify" the Church of England, resolved to remove from it all lingering evidences of Roman Catholicism. The national church that had separated from Rome during the reign of Henry VIII had followed a zigzag course that left many uncertain whether England was Protestant or Catholic. During the reigns of Elizabeth (1558-1603) and James I (1603-1625), Puritans tried hard to make their case for moving the entire Church in a more Calvinist direction theologically and toward simpler forms liturgically. When Charles I came to the throne in 1625, many Puritans grew discouraged about the prospects of ever reforming the whole Church of England.

Yet Puritans were reluctant to take that dreaded step of schism, reluctant to leave the church in which they had been nurtured. Perhaps in New England they could create a new Church of England, one fully reformed and fully faithful to the New Testament as well as the spirit of the Reformation. And, fondest dream of all, if they managed to create such a true church, perhaps Old England would behold and so admire what they had done that it would then zealously execute its own reforms. Such a grand vision, such an errand into the wilderness, led these Puritans to leave their homes, farms, and churches to settle in and around Boston, bringing with them their own charter for the Massachusetts Bay Company.

Growth in the Colonies. The decade of the 1630s, the "Great Migration," brought thousands of settlers inspired by this vision and zealous for their cause. In the words of the many-time governor of Massachusetts Bay, John Winthrop, "God hath provided this place to be a refuge for many whom He means to save out of the general calamity." A true church, he continued, has "no place left to flee into but the wilderness." Yet that wilderness could, by divine assistance, turn out to be a place where "some great work" might come to pass.

In that very first decade of settlement, the Puritans founded Harvard College (in 1636) in order to assure a learned ministry and a literate laity. With many of the Puritan ministers being themselves graduates of England's Cambridge University, the town in which Harvard was located understandably changed its name from Newtown to Cambridge, another measure of the ambitious vision embraced. Two generations or so later, Connecticut Puritans created their college, Yale, to guide and propagate "the blessed reformed Protestant religion, in the purity of its order and worship."

Theologically, Puritans stood in the Calvinist tradition, expressing their doctrines in terms of covenants or agreements between God and his creatures, or among those pledged to follow him. By the terms of the covenant of grace, God made clear his free gift of salvation; men and women could do nothing to earn it, for God had done all when he granted it. If foreordained to be one of God's elect, individuals could accept that gift of grace and could never fall away from it. Only those who were visible saints constituted the proper membership of a church; a church was not defined by geographical boundaries or by a building's dimensions, but only by the fellowship of believers. And those believers would come together in another covenant that pledged each one to "walk together in all [God's] ways, according as he is pleased to reveal himself unto us in his blessed word of truth."

Puritanism's most brilliant theologian, Jonathan Edwards, in the middle of the 18th century assisted the descendants of the original Puritans to recapture their theological vision and their ecclesiastical purity. Affirming the absolute sovereignty of God, Edwards emphasized the weakness and sinfulness of humankind without transcendent help. He also saw God as lord of all history, no less than of all life, as he looked toward a millennial fulfillment of the Kingdom of God on earth and the New Jerusalem being established— perhaps in America itself.

See also Edwards, Jonathan; Pilgrims.

Bibliography: Morgan, Edmund S., *The Puritan Dilemma* (Little, Brown, 1958); Stout, Harry S., *The New England Soul* (Oxford Univ. Press, 1985).

Edwin S. Gaustad
University of California, Riverside

PUTNAM, ISRAEL (1718-90) Born in Danvers, Massachusetts, Putnam was a farmer and a soldier. During the French and Indian War he was appointed a captain of Roger's Rangers (1755) and by 1759 had advanced to the rank of lieutenant colonel. He was once taken prisoner by the Indians. According to Putnam, just as they were about to burn him, he was rescued. He went on to fight with Jeffrey Amherst at the capture of Montreal in 1760. He was also part of the expedition to Detroit to put down Pontiac's Rebellion (1763).

Rash but daring, Putnam loved adventure. He was an eager member of the Sons of Liberty in 1765. In 1773 he traveled to the West Indies and up the Mississippi River to survey lands. Almost immediately after returning home, he abandoned his plow to fight at the Battle of Lexington. He commanded troops in New York until George Washington's arrival. Washington was unimpressed with Putnam, and the disastrous Battle of Long Island confirmed his low opinion. Putnam was given command of the Highlands on the Hudson, losing both Fort Montgomery and Fort Clinton to the British. He was accused of being unfit to command but was exonerated of the charge. In 1778 he led troops in Connecticut. He suffered a stroke in 1779, which forced him to retire from military life.

PUTTING-OUT SYSTEM. *See* **Domestic System.**

PYNCHON, WILLIAM (?1590-1662) An Englishman who became a frontier trader, colonist, and land speculator, Pynchon arrived in Massachusetts in 1630 with consider-able capital, opening a fur-trading establishment at Roxbury and subsequently serving as treasurer of the colony. In 1636 he was appointed one of the commissioners to govern the new settlements on the Connecticut River and supervised the foundation of Springfield, Massachusetts. He established a post in Springfield that became the center of the western New England fur trade and pioneered the use of the Connecticut River as a commercial route to Long Island Sound and the Atlantic, thus opening the region to commercial development. Through his agents, Pynchon negotiated a set of arrangements with the Indians in which they gave up nearly all the arable land of the upper Connecticut Valley, in the process becoming one of the biggest landowners in New England.

In 1638 he severed connections with Thomas Hooker, the leader of the Hartford settlement and linked Springfield with the administration of Massachusetts Bay. In the early 1650s he published a tract questioning certain tenets of Puritan doctrine and fell from establishment favor. Soon after, he deeded his holdings to his son John Pynchon and returned to England, where he died.

See also Hooker, Thomas.

Q

QUAKERS (SOCIETY OF FRIENDS)   One sect among the many born during the turbulent Protectorate of Oliver Cromwell, the Quakers survived the Restoration in 1660 and far beyond. Widely persecuted in England, they found a refuge exceeding all expectations when King Charles II granted to William Penn an enormous expanse west of the Delaware River. The colony of Pennsylvania, coming a half century later than settlements in Virginia or New England, profited from the mistakes and miscalculations of others. Penn, himself a Quaker and outspoken defender of his people in England, planned his colony in the early 1680s with great care, also taking pains not to alienate or offend the Indians.

Quakers were particularly welcome in Pennsylvania, of course, and that welcome was gladly received because, apart from their acceptance in Rhode Island, Quakers had known little but persecution and rejection throughout North America. But Pennsylvania, despite its "Quaker State" nickname, was never intended to be a haven for Quakers alone. As the 1682 Frame of Government indicated, "All persons living in this province who confess and acknowledge the one almighty and eternal God" would find themselves under no civil penalty or disability whatsoever. Quakers not only proclaimed a broad toleration, they made it attractive by seeing that their colony prospered.

As pacifists, Quakers found their governance of the colony increasingly problematic, just as other non-Quaker settlers did. When they lost authority by the middle of the 18th century, they could concentrate even more intently on the cultivation of the inner life and the careful supervision of their monthly, quarterly, and annual meetings far beyond the confines of Pennsylvania. Eschewing a formal ministry as well as fixed sacraments, the Quakers encouraged both men and women to take active roles within the religious community, and from there to the larger world outside. Sensitive to the cruelties practiced upon both Indians and slaves, Quakers helped sensitize many around them. New Jersey Quaker John Woolman, for example, called upon the Philadelphia Yearly Meeting in 1758 to abolish all slaveholding by Quakers and to do so promptly; otherwise, he said, "God may by terrible things in righteousness answer us in this matter."

See also Frame of Government; Penn, William.
Bibliography: James, Sydney V, *A People among Peoples* (Harvard Univ. Press, 1963). Soderlund, Jean R., ed., *William Penn and the Founding of Pennsylvania* (Univ. of Pennsylvania Press, 1983).

Edwin S. Gaustad
University of California, Riverside

QUARTERING ACTS   Quartering Acts were parliamentary acts providing for the housing and supply of British troops in America; these acts became grievances during the Revolutionary era. A 1765 act authorized government officials to hire public houses and vacant buildings to house the troops if the barracks provided by the colonies were not sufficient and directed officials to procure supplies at the expense of the colonies; this law provoked a crisis in New York. An act passed in 1774 at the time of the "coercive" Massachusetts legislation permitted royal officers to procure additional buildings for quarters if those provided were too far from where the troops were needed. Quartering in occupied private residences was never authorized.

QUEBEC CITY   Originally the Iroquoian village of Stadacona visited by Jacques Cartier in 1535, the site was abandoned when Samuel de Champlain founded the settlement of Quebec City in 1608. Made the capital of New France in 1663, it became the civil, military, and ecclesiastical center of French North America. The object of English attacks in 1629, 1690, and 1711, the city was captured from the Marquis de Montcalm by Britain's General James Wolfe in 1759, marking the French defeat in the French and Indian War and France's expulsion from North America. Although a few leading families departed, most of the French, at all levels of society, remained. The Quebec Act of 1774 guaranteed the protection of the rights of these French citizens of Canada but antagonized the English colonists to the south. After taking Montreal in 1775, the American revolutionaries led a violent but unsuccessful assault on Quebec the next year, finally retreating south.

See also Champlain, Samuel de; French and Indian War; French Colonies.

QUEBEC ACT (1774)   An act of the British Parliament, the Quebec Act alarmed the Americans by extending the boundaries of Quebec to the Ohio and Mississippi rivers, an area in which the colonies had claims. The Americans also opposed its provision for a nonrepresentative government in Quebec subordinate to home authority, the estab-

QUAAKERS VERGADERING.

Wech quaakfter deeje Post is uniet aenhevoolen:
De Woordeit-Godts die fyn u nummer toeyertrouwt:
Aarons-Borftlap is van alte fynen Gouvt.
Dat gy hem draagen fouwt met uw bemorfte Soolen.
— Paulus heeft uw mont gegrendelt in Godis-kerk:
— loerd uw Preekftoel om en weeft uw mutjen wek.

Wat Tuymel-geeft heeft u befeeten in dees Cowen:
Ruk af de Mom, en fwygh de Katten kyken uyt,
Wil v segrim verfpuedt uw weefen en geluyt:
En komt u met uw Volk voor fyn Geflagt wt fchreewen:
Waarom Vrouw Iennes-Hondt van fyrt her, y ftok haylt
Daar, uns een andre Dogh ivs Iurteis rok hevudt.

FRONTI NULLA FIDES.   THE QUAKERS MEETING.

Woman in Publi: Speaks not, St. Paul fayd,
Veelding refpector filence to her Head;
Shee on th Barrels head rai'd yet Valls this Right;
Raves darkly, &Cries, Ah Freinds Mind the Light;
They Mind it fure; for fee as faft afleep,
Theyr eyes quite clos'd; others as it Bo-peep

In the mean while look where a Female ftands
As Modeftic her felf with un-feen hands.
Silently confenting to all as true;
Goves th next hee faint a Fellow-feeling too.

Frontis — Ous non meus, Vintu

The Quakers avoided formal sacraments in their meetings and encouraged both men and women to participate. (Library of Congress)

lishment there of rights and privileges for the Roman Catholic Church, and the absence of trial by jury under restored French civil law.

The American patriots listed the Quebec Act among their major grievances with Britain, although the British government did not identify the measure as belonging to its current package of "coercive" American acts. English leaders had long been planning to reorganize the government of the province (acquired from France in 1763), and the law was largely an attempt to solve specifically Canadian problems and to accommodate French Canadian opinion.

QUEEN ANNE'S WAR (1702-1713)   A conflict between British and French colonial forces in North America and the Caribbean, contemporary with the War of the Spanish Succession in Europe (1701-14), Queen Anne's War was fueled by the territorial rivalries of the two powers not settled in the 1697 Treaty of Ryswick. The immediate cause of the hostilities in Europe was the coronation in 1700 of a grandson of France's Louis XIV as king of Spain. This family connection aroused fears in Britain that the French would gain control of the vast Spanish possessions in America, and on May 4, 1702, Queen Anne of England officially declared war on France.

Soon afterwards, British colonists from the Carolinas attacked St. Augustine, and in 1704 they destroyed other Spanish missions in Florida. In the Caribbean, after an unsuccessful attempt in 1703 to take Guadeloupe, the

British navy began widespread privateering against the French and Spanish fleets, which in 1706 attacked Charleston, South Carolina. Farther north, in response to French and Indian raids on New England settlements, three British expeditions were mounted against Port Royal, the last of which in 1710, led to the conquest of the city and peace negotiations in 1711. The hostilities were concluded in 1713 by the Treaty of Utrecht.

See also Ryswick, Treaty of; Utrecht, Treaty of.

QUINCY, JOSIAH (1744-75)   Raised in Braintree, Massachusetts, and educated at Harvard, Quincy studied law and took over his master's practice before he was 21. He was an ardent patriot and believed Thomas Hutchinson, then chief justice of Massachusetts, prevented him from becoming a barrister solely because of his politics. Quincy loathed Hutchinson and attacked him through the newspapers. Quincy was, however, a leader in defense of the British soldiers accused in the Boston Massacre (1770). In 1773 he went south to help organize the colonial cause. He spoke in Boston just before the Tea Party. In 1774 he sailed to England and met with Lord North to present colonial grievances. He died on the ship home.

QUITRENT   In England quitrents were fees collected by a lord in abeyance of obligations of service tied to land tenure. In the colonies quitrents took the form of nominal levies established in most cases by charter and collected in the royal colonies by the Crown and in the proprietary colonies by the proprietor. Generally absent in New England, quitrents in the other colonies were abolished after the Revolution on the ground that they were not levied as taxes but as a source of private income.

QUO WARRANTO   In English law, quo warranto is a proceeding that determines the right to use or exercise an office and to remove the holder if his claim is not well founded or if he has abused the privilege. In colonial America quo warranto was used to initiate proceedings to annul the charter of the Massachusetts Bay Colony (1684).

R

RACE AND RACISM Definitions of race and their symptomatic expressions in 17th- and 18th-century British North America varied considerably with region, class, and time. (As historical entities, race and racism are products of discrete circumstances and resist examination as timeless, observable physical facts.) Prior to the 17th-century conversion to slave labor in the Chesapeake, racial contempt was nearly indistinguishable from familiar English forms of class discrimination. When Chesapeake rulers lost control over poor white freemen on the frontier, they regained it by shifting to racially defined slavery and by permitting the economic status of poor whites to rise. By legally defining all whites regardless of class as superior to all blacks, Chesapeake rulers thus instituted a commonplace strain of American racism and labor control.

In contrast, some mid-18th century European and Euro-American philosophers and religious bodies, such as the Quakers, repudiated the principle of slavery as incompatible with the egalitarian ideals of the Age of Revolution. They conceived of race within the context of Enlightenment environmentalism and usually explained racism in terms of existing economic and political conditions. They regarded blacks as humans and argued that blacks' "degraded condition" was essentially the result of their entanglement in slavery. Thus inequality did not result from any genetically defined traits nor did it reflect evolutionary patterns. The potential to improve human conditions by altering the physical world was always considered a possibility. The more familiar and rigid psuedoscientific rationale that emphasized genetic inferiority developed alongside accelerated industrialization and 19th-century Social Darwinism.

Basis for Colonial Racism. The philosophers' generally abstract interpretations of race did not prevail, however, in white colonial society. Racism abounded throughout the colonies. Hobbled by certain cultural predispositions to racism embodied in their languages and religions, Englishmen employed a variety of justifications for their attitudes and behavior toward Africans. Their obvious physical differences, their "heathen" religions, their political, social, and economic organizations, and their presumed sexual behavior were all cited as evidence of inferiority. In short, many English felt that Africans were uncivilized. Slaveholders increasingly employed arguments about inherent black inferiority to justify slavery, although they would not produce a coherent proslavery ideology until the 19th century. During the 18th century most whites believed that blacks were alien beings who could never be equally incorporated into American society.

Much debate among historians has centered on the relationship between racism and slavery. Did racism precede slavery or did slavery foster racism? Without question, Elizabethan Englishmen were disposed to look contemptuously on many peoples who differed from them. But once slavery became firmly established in British America, racism assumed a new stridency needed to justify human bondage and establish control over an increasingly important labor force. Afterward, slavery and racism interacted in such ways as to perpetuate one another.

See also Slavery.

Bibliography: Frederickson, George M., *The Black Image in the White Mind: The Debate on Afro-American Character and Destiny, 1817-1914* (Wesleyan Univ. Press, 1987); Jordan, Winthrop D., *White Over Black: American Attitudes Toward the Negro, 1550-1812* (Univ. of North Carolina Press, 1968); Van Deburg, William L., *Slavery and Race in American Popular Culture* (Univ. of Wisconsin Press, 1984).

Lynda J. Morgan
Mount Holyoke College

RADISSON, PIERRE ESPRIT (1636-1710) A French explorer in Canada, Radisson was born near Lyons, France, and came to Canada in 1651. On a hunting trip near Three Rivers, he was captured by the Iroquois. During his captivity (1652-53), he learned their language and realized their usefulness in expanding fur trading. In 1657 and 1659 he traveled with the Sieur des Groseilliers deep into the western territory. Both men recognized the importance of controlling the ports of New York and Hudson Bay, but the uncooperative governor of Canada confiscated their furs on their return.

The pair joined the English, and their explorations of Hudson Bay in 1670 and 1672 inspired the founding of the Hudson's Bay Company. Radisson rejoined the service of France in 1674, but by 1684 he had settled in England, where he again joined the Hudson's Bay Company. After returning to Canada (1685-87) and helping the company to take some French outposts, Radisson settled permanently in England. His colorful accounts of his expeditions were published in 1652, 1654, 1657, and 1659.

RALEIGH, SIR WALTER (?1552-1618) An English courtier, promoter of colonization, and explorer, Raleigh was the son of a country gentleman and half-brother of Sir Humphrey Gilbert, with whom he outfitted a fleet of privateering ships and sailed into the West Indies in 1578. At court Raleigh became a favorite of Queen Elizabeth I, who granted him lucrative trading monopolies; for her he fought in Ireland and built up a great estate there. He had a large interest in the ill-fated 1583 Newfoundland voyage of Gilbert. The next year he sent out a preliminary expedition to the North American coast under Philip Amadas and Arthur Barlow, who claimed the inlets, islands, and mainland south of Chesapeake Bay for the queen; upon their return, she christened these lands "Virginia." It was with Raleigh's financial backing, and under his plan, that the colonization of Virginia at Roanoke Island, led by Sir Richard Grenville and Ralph Lane, began the next year. The failure of this settlement cost Raleigh a fortune.

Active for the rest of his life as a courtier, entrepreneur, and investor in imperial schemes, Raleigh also wrote several accounts of his adventures that had direct bearing on the history of the New World. In 1595 he led a fleet to the Caribbean where he sailed up the Orinoco River in a futile search for the gold mines of El Dorado. In the early 1600s he was directly responsible for setting up the trade in fish between Jersey and Newfoundland. In 1617, after falling from favor at court with the death of Elizabeth and spending several years with his family in the Tower of London under sentence of death, he was allowed to try once again to capture the Spanish mines of Venezuela, but failing once again he was arrested and executed. Although he never reached the shores of North America, his efforts at Roanoke have led to his reputation as the "father of Virginia."

See also Gilbert, Sir Humphrey; Grenville, Sir Richard; Lane, Ralph; Virginia.

Bibliography: Armitage, Christopher M., ed., *Sir Walter Raleigh: An Annotated Bibliography* (Univ. of North Carolina, 1987); Lacey, Robert, *Sir Walter Raleigh* (Atheneum, 1979); Whitehead, Charles, *The Life and Times of Sir Walter Raleigh* (1854; reprint Arden Library, 1980).

RALE, SEBASTIEN (?1654-1724) A Jesuit missionary, Rale was born in Pontarlier, France, and completed his Jesuit studies in 1675. In 1689 he sailed with Comte de Frontenac to Canada, where he first worked among the Abnaki and Huron Indians. In 1691, as a fluent speaker of Indian dialects, he succeeded Father Allouez at the Illinois mission and sent letters to his brother reporting the customs of the Ottawa Indians. In 1693 he went to the Abnaki mission in Maine. There he became embroiled in the warfare between the English settlers and the French. His church was twice burned (1705, 1721) by English troops.

In 1724 the British shot him in front of his house and carried his scalp to Boston. He was loved by the Maine Indians, who still use his prayers.

RAMAGE, JOHN (1748-1802) A painter of miniatures, Ramage was born in Dublin, Ireland, and attended the Dublin Society of Art in 1763. He moved to Halifax, Nova Scotia, and by 1772 was noted as a goldsmith, miniaturist, and designer of hair patterns in Boston by 1775. As a Tory, he joined the Loyal Irish Volunteers and fled briefly to Halifax, but his skill was so great that he secured commissions from both the occupying British forces and the American patriots. George Washington had him paint his miniature as a present for Martha Washington. From 1777 to 1794, Ramage executed his delicate miniatures encased in elaborate gold frames for prominent New Yorkers, including the Van Cortlandt, Rutgers, and Van Rensselaer families. In 1794 debts forced him to leave New York; he died poor in Montreal.

RAMSEY, MARTHA LAURENS (1759-1811) A renowned intellectual, Ramsey was a member of South Carolina society. Her father approved of her assiduous study habits but stressed that the first requisite in female education should be a knowledge of housewifery. She spent many years abroad, nursing her uncle and then her father, returning to South Carolina in 1785. Two years later she married David Ramsey, a former member of the Continental Congress. Martha Ramsey taught herself Latin and Greek so that she could educate her sons. Modern speculation is that a tension existed between her questioning mind and her deference to a woman's traditional role in society.

RANDOLPH, EDMUND JENNINGS (1753-1813) Born to a prominent Virginia family with a tradition of service to the Crown, Randolph seemed destined for the same. He graduated from William and Mary College and studied law under his uncle Peyton Randolph and his father John, both attorney generals for the Crown. In 1775, though, Edmund joined George Washington as an aide-de-camp (1775-76), aligning himself against his father. He became the youngest member of Virginia's state constitutional convention and served as the first attorney general. From 1779 to 1782 he sat as a delegate to the Continental Congress.

A staunch Republican, Randolph served as governor of Virginia (1786-88) and was sent to the federal Constitutional Convention (1787), at which he proposed the Virginia Plan, favoring the large states. He disapproved of a one-man executive and in the state's ratifying convention voted against the adoption of the Constitution. He served as attorney general for the new government (1789-94) and as secretary of state (1794-95). His actions in the Jay Treaty negotiations were called into question by

Washington, who accused him of making improper revelations to the French minister to the United States. Randolph resigned, ending his national public career and returned to a law practice. He later acted as counsel to Aaron Burr.

See also Randolph, John; Randolph, Peyton.

RANDOLPH, EDWARD (c.1632-1703)   A colonial agent responsible for the revocation of the Massachusetts Charter, he was born in England and was sent to Massachusetts in 1675 to report on conditions there, especially regarding the enforcement of the Navigation Acts. Upon his return to England in 1676, he was critical in his report of colonial enforcement of laws. After a term as customs collector in New England, he complained that the colonists had no regard for the law and, upon his recommendation, the Massachusetts Charter was revoked in 1684. From 1691 he served as surveyor general of customs for North America, but he was unsuccessful in his quest for customs compliance.

RANDOLPH, JOHN (?1727-84)   A native of Virginia and member of a prominent family, Randolph trained for his career in London, returning to Williamsburg to practice. In 1751 he was elected to the Common Council of Williamsburg and then served as clerk in the House of Burgesses (1752-56). He succeeded his brother Peyton as attorney general for the Crown (1756-75). He began to side with the royal governor against the revolutionaries. His son Edmund remained behind as a patriot, while John, his wife, and his daughters fled to England in 1775. Randolph drew up a plan of conciliation with America that he sent to Thomas Jefferson in 1779. At the same time he led a group of Loyalists who offered military services to the king.

See also Randolph, Edmund.

RANDOLPH, PEYTON (1721-75)   President of the First and Second Continental Congresses and a grandson of William Randolph, Peyton Randolph was born in Virginia. Educated at the college of William and Mary and in England, he was admitted to the bar (1744) and then became the king's attorney for Virginia (1748-66). Also a member of the House of Burgesses from 1748, he became its speaker (1766-75). He was a conservative and came into conflict with the royal governor, Robert Dinwiddie, who had Randolph replaced as the speaker. He served on the Virginia committees of correspondence (1759-67) and wrote a moderate protest to the king against the Stamp Act (1765) for the House of Burgesses. Between 1765 and 1774 he moved towards the patriot cause and in 1773 was named chairman of the Virginia committee of correspondence. Appointed by Virginia to both Continental Congresses, he was elected president of each (1774-75). He died suddenly from a stroke.

See also Randolph, William.

RANDOLPH, WILLIAM (1651-1711)   A planter and colonial official, Randolph came to Virginia from England (1673). He soon amassed large landholdings, including 10,000 acres in Henrico County by 1705. His wealth and extensive social connections made him a leading member of the colony's conservative political group. Importing a large number of slaves, Randolph became a leading planter in the colony. A distinguished figure in Virginia, Randolph held numerous official appointments. He succeeded his uncle as clerk of Henrico County (1673-83) and subsequently held several other positions. Randolph was named attorney general for the crown in Virginia (1694). After holding various military appointments, he became lieutenant-colonel of militia (1699). He was speaker of the House of Burgesses (1696, 1698) and served as clerk of the Burgesses (1699-1702).

READ, GEORGE (1733-98)   A Revolutionary War patriot and signer of the Declaration of Independence, Read was born in Cecil County, Maryland, and moved to New Castle, Delaware, as a child. He began a law practice in New Castle (1754), and was appointed attorney general of the Lower Counties of Delaware (1763-74). He spoke out against the Stamp Act (1765) and was elected to the provincial assembly and the First Continental Congress (1774). As a member of the Second Continental Congress (1775-77), he did not vote for the Declaration of Independence, but signed it after its adoption (1776). He became the first speaker of the legislative council as officer of the state constitutional convention (1776) and was extremely active in rallying Delaware to the patriot cause during the Revolutionary War. Active as both a judge and lawyer after the war, he supported a new federal constitution and was a member of the Annapolis Convention (1786). He headed the Delaware delegation to the federal Constitutional Convention (1787). He then served as one of the state's U.S. senators (1789-93), resigning to become chief justice of Delaware (1793-98).

REDEMPTIONERS   Representing a specialized class of indentured servants, redemptioners emigrated to America without contract but with the understanding that upon arrival they would be given a limited amount of time to raise their passage fare through friends or family or by contract. Otherwise, the shipmaster would sell the immigrants. Redemption apparently originated in the 18th century to accommodate German immigrants who tended to leave their homeland in families, sometimes in neighborhood or community groups, and to gravitate to Pennsylvania. The Germans seemed to have left the Palatinate and Rhineland more because of attractive advertising by recruiting agents than because of famine and vicious landlords. By the 1760s and 1770s, the practice decreased as the family migration pattern had declined; most German immigrants were single males, representative of indentured servants in general.

See also Indentured Servitude.

Bibliography: Smith, Abbot Emerson, *Colonists in Bondage: White Servitude and Convict Labor in America, 1607-1776* (Univ. of North Carolina Press, 1947).

RED JACKET (c.1756-1830)   A Seneca chief also known as Sagoyewátha, "He Who Causes Them To Be Awake," Red Jacket was born near Canoga in western New York under the name Otetiani, "Always Ready." As a noted and persuasive orator, he was a strong supporter of the British. His English nickname was given to him because of his fondness for the red military jacket he wore during his service with the British in the Revolutionary War. His military career was, however, controversial. He was accused of cowardice by the Iroquois chief Cornplanter in the battles against General John Sullivan during the invasion of Iroquois territory.

After the Revolution, Red Jacket became increasingly influential as a political leader. At the great Indian council at Detroit in 1786, he spoke passionately against any accommodation with the government of the United States, and although accepting the necessity of a treaty of peace with the new government, he opposed territorial compromise. In 1792, Red Jacket was one of 50 Iroquois chiefs who met with George Washington in Philadelphia and was presented with a silver medal as a token of Washington's friendship. He later sided with the Americans during the War of 1812 and died on the Seneca reservation near Buffalo, New York.

RED SHOES (c.1700-48)   A Choctaw chief, also known as Shulush Homa, Red Shoes was born in the area of Jasper County, Mississippi. Throughout his early life, the Choctaw maintained a close alliance with the French colonial authorities in the lower Mississippi Valley, and as a young warrior he served in the French-Choctaw campaigns against the neighboring Natchez and Chickasaw. The British were, however, attempting to make inroads into this region and in 1734, after the rape of his wife by a French soldier, Red Shoes severed his longstanding allegiance to the French.

Since the British traders arriving in the lower Mississippi Valley offered high quality goods at lower prices than their French competitors, Red Shoes was able to persuade many Choctaw that an alliance with the British would be desirable. His efforts led to the formation of a Choctaw

"peace party" that sought to unite the nation and negotiate with their traditional enemies the Chickasaw, who were already British allies. In 1748 the French governor of Louisiana, Marquis de Vaudreil, succeeded in undermining Red Shoes's plan by fomenting a bloody civil war within the Choctaw nation. At its conclusion, the French-Choctaw alliance remained intact, and Red Shoes was killed by his political rivals.

REED, ESTHER DE BERDT (1746-80)   A notable patriot, Reed organized a major fundraising campaign for George Washington's army during 1780 when the revolutionaries desperately needed morale building in order to survive. "Sentiments of an American Woman" was her carefully reasoned argument, citing numerous historical precedents, about why women should participate in the public affairs of the new republic. It was distributed as women went door to door soliciting a total of $7,500, which she wanted to distribute among the men as cash. General Washington insisted that the ladies make 2,000 shirts instead.

Reed's enthusiastic patriotism was nourished by family upbringing in London; her merchant father had helped secure repeal of the Stamp Act as a colonial agent. She married Philadelphia lawyer Joseph Reed in 1770, and his presidency of Pennsylvania during the Revolution added to her responsibilities. She had six children, the youngest born a year after she had endured smallpox and lost one child, and in the midst of her fundraising and shirt making. She died suddenly of dysentery that summer before the work was completed, but her work provided a model for all future American women's organizations.

REED, JOSEPH (1741-85)   Lawyer, patriot, soldier, and statesman, Reed was educated at the College of New Jersey (Princeton) and at the Inns of Court in London. Following activity as a patriot in Philadelphia, Reed served in the Continental Army (1775-77), first as George Washington's military secretary and then as adjutant general. Later he sat as a Pennsylvania delegate to the Continental Congress (1777-78), and in 1778, he was elected president of the Supreme Executive Council of Pennsylvania. Although he failed to harmonize the state's clashing political parties, his three years as chief executive saw an invigoration of the war effort.

REGICIDES   Those judges and court officers responsible for the trial and execution of Charles I were condemned as "regicides," Latin for "king killers," upon the restoration of Charles II to the English throne in 1660. Of these officials, 10 were condemned to death, 25 to life imprisonment. Some escaped, including Edward Whalley and his son-in-law William Goffe, who fled from England to Boston, then to New Haven, where for a month they were hidden in a cave on a promontory overlooking the harbor. They remained in Connecticut until 1664 when attempts were again made to arrest them. They then fled to Hadley, Massachusetts, where they were joined by a confederate, John Dixwell, who had previously hidden in Germany. Successfully evading capture, Whalley died in Hadley in 1675, Goffe settled under an assumed name in Hartford, where he died in 1679, and Dixwell moved to New Haven, where he married and lived under a pseudonym until his death in 1689.

REGULATORS The Regulators were members of vigilante movements of both backcountry South Carolina and North Carolina. In South Carolina backcountry settlers organized in the late 1760s to suppress roaming bands of outlaws who challenged local order in the aftermath of the French and Indian War. The Regulators also attempted to impose their own variety of moral discipline on the hunters, squatters, and propertyless laborers who made up the "irregular" people of the frontier, even including forced labor for idle persons without a visible way of making an honest living. Tidewater officials, fearing an uprising that might create the opportunity for a slave revolt, tolerated the movement and created locally controlled courts in the backcountry in 1769 but refused to accede to the Regulators' demands for legislative reapportionment.

In neighboring North Carolina another Regulator movement formed in 1768, protesting the use of the legal system by merchants to collect debts, thus violating their tradition of accepting commodities in lieu of cash and of scheduling repayment flexibility. These Regulators intimidated judges, closed the courts by force, and broke into jails to free debtors and their arrested leaders. In 1771, Governor William Tryon led a force of 1,200 militia into the backcountry and defeated some 2,000 Regulators at the Battle of Alamance near Hillsboro, executing 7 leaders and compelling over 6,000 farmers to swear allegiance to the established government.

The Regulator revolts were the largest uprisings since Bacon's and Leisler's rebellions in the 1670s. Although somewhat different in their targets and their outcomes, both of the Carolina Regulator movements reflected the deep hostility westerners held toward eastern officials and planters, sentiments soon thereafter seen in Pennsylvania in the rebellion of the Paxton Boys and later in Shays' Rebellion and the Whiskey Rebellion.

See also Paxton Boys; Shays' Rebellion.

John Mack Faragher
Mount Holyoke College

RELIGION In early America religion wore many different faces. Notorious for their individuality and

The 18th Century church of St. James in Santee, South Carolina, showed colonial America's religious diversity. The church was used by both Hugenots and Anglicans, with a separate pulpit for each faith. *(State of South Carolina)*

parochialism, the several colonies right down to the Revolutionary era rarely presented a united front on any issue. This was also true with respect to religion, that fact helping to account for the reluctance of delegates to the Constitutional Convention in 1787 to take up the subject of religion in any substantial way. Each colony had its own history and to some degree its own agenda with respect to religion. And each colony had its own suspicions of what the nearest neighbors might be up to in the realm of ecclesiastical affairs.

When Jamestown, Virginia, was settled in 1607 or St. Augustine, Florida, a generation before, the religious wars of continental Europe and the religious strife of England were fresh and lively memories. Religion was no parlor game, no idle option; rather it was more often than not a matter of life or death, an issue that divided nations and families, that determined how or where one might live. This does not imply that all who came to America in the 17th or 18th centuries made religion their highest priority; it does imply that religion could never quite be safely ignored or put aside as a purely private affair not to be discussed in polite society. Legislatures wrestled with it, governors addressed it, charters and frames of government endeavored to shape it.

The early probes of Spain and France into North America represented the respective interests of each nation, but they also represented the interests of the Roman Catholic Church. The papal line of demarcation, drawn by Alexander VI in 1493 to diminish potential conflict between Spain and Portugal, serves as a useful symbol of religion's involvement in New World discovery, exploration, and colonization. And when Richard Hakluyt the Younger urged England in 1584 not to let all Europe beat England to bounties beyond the seas, he put the matter in religious terms: "It remains to be thoroughly weighed and considered by what means and by whom this most godly and Christian work may be performed of enlarging the glorious gospel of Christ, and leading of infinite multitudes of these simple people that are in error into the right and perfect way of their salvation." For Hakluyt as for most of his countrymen, "the right and perfect way" meant that Protestantism, not Catholicism, must be planted in America.

Anglicanism. Virginia became a test case not only for English colonial policy in general but for the spread of "right" religion in particular. Virginia was expected to manifest the same conformity to the Book of Common Prayer and the Thirty-nine Articles of Faith that the mother country demonstrated in the early 17th century. Political authorities would establish and protect the Church of England in Virginia just as their counterparts did at home. The people would be taxed to support and obliged by law to attend that Church, just as at home. Nonconformists would be excluded or exiled or worse, just as at home. Religion was an affair of the state, not of the heart.

The path that Virginia would take could then be followed by all other English colonies coming into existence in the decades ahead. That, of course, did not happen since colonies came about in so wide a variety of ways: some proprietary, some royal, some the ventures of joint-stock companies. In addition, however, Virginia never achieved that model of success that invited widespread emulation. With its population widely scattered along the broad rivers, with a shortage of clergy and a total absence of bishops, with competition between economic and spiritual interests, with concerns about sheer survival overriding every other consideration in the earliest years, the Anglican Church in Virginia had first to save its own soul before turning its thoughts to other colonies and grand plans.

By the middle of the 17th century, Anglicanism was limited to lands around the Chesapeake Bay. A century later, however, England's national church had been planted—although not always firmly—in all 13 colonies. Its status in those colonies varied widely, ranging from effective establishment (as in Virginia and Maryland) to indifferent penetration (as in North Carolina) to resentful

acceptance (as in much of New England). Much of Anglicanism's 18th- century progress resulted from missionaries employed and supervised by the Society for the Propagation of the Gospel, a London-based, privately financed philanthropic organization. Society missionaries extended the Church's influence but simultaneously reduced its native-born leadership. When Revolutionary passions began to mount in the 1760s and 1770s, these missionaries whose strongest ties were to England remained Loyalist almost without exception. Their sentiments as well as their wholesale departures damaged the status of Anglicanism and thwarted any chance of a national "Americanized" Episcopal Church.

Also in the years just prior to the Revolution, the intense campaign to bring Church of England bishops to America aroused equally strong suspicions and resentments. Many Americans, recalling that England's bishops were political forces more often than they were spiritual ones, resolved to keep such overlords forever out of America. In 1767, Anglican clergyman Thomas Bradbury Chandler published *An Appeal to the Public* in which he argued for the absolute necessity of having a bishop sent to America: necessary for the Church, necessary for the Crown, and necessary for the continued close ties between the colonies and the empire. Presbyterian lawyer William Livingston objected strongly that this was as great a threat to American liberties, civil and ecclesiastic, as the Stamp Act itself had been. Every part of Chandler's *Appeal*, Livingston wrote in 1768, intends "to introduce an evil more terrible to every man who sets a proper value either on his liberty, property, or conscience: than even "the deservedly obnoxious Stamp Act." Americans united in their opposition to the Stamp Act; so also they united in their opposition to England's bishops. None ever came to America, but the fear that they might come further damaged the prospects of England's Church in England's colonies.

New England and the Middle Colonies. The church establishment of Congregationalism, being a product of native leadership and in no way tied to England's monarchy or Parliament, might seem to be a better candidate for an intercolonial church of universal appeal. Yet the Congregationalists remained a regional church, with virtually no force outside of New England itself. This establishment, like the Anglican one, also succeeded in arousing resentments and fears since the colonies of Massachusetts and Connecticut had so often resorted to fines and whips and gallows to maintain their religious purity. To be sure, Congregationalism was strong in those areas, in comparative terms far more concentrated and controlling than Anglicanism was anywhere. That strength came at a price, however—alienating Quakers, Baptists, Anglicans, and others who resisted or dissented from the New England Way. So truly national churches never emerged in the colonial period. Rather, individual colonies maintained their special loyalties or even encouraged a broad and shocking diversity.

Rhode Island launched its "livelie experiment" of full religious freedom in the 1630s, with the consequence that Baptists and Quakers flourished there within a generation. Pennsylvania, founded in the 1680s, invited all who were peaceable and God-fearing to settle there. Quakers came early but were soon joined by Roman Catholics, Anglicans, Baptists, Lutherans, and other sects. In fact, Pennsylvania became a byword for a diversity that apparently knew no limit. Anglican missionary Thomas Barton reported in 1764 that Lancaster County, with a population of around 40,000, had perhaps only a mere 500 Anglicans in the neighborhood: "the rest are German Lutherans, Calvinists, Mennonists, Moravians, New Born, Dunkers, Presbyterians, Seceders, New Lights, Covenanters, Mountain Men, Brownists, Independents, Papists, Quakers, Jews &c." Barton held very little hope for a society awash with "a swarm of Sectaries all indulged and favored by the Government." Pennsylvania's pluralism was typical of the Middle Colonies generally where, even from the early years of Dutch rule, variety more than conformity reigned.

The South. Nor was the South, even with its early Anglican bias, able to fend off other religious options. Maryland began as a Roman Catholic colony in 1634, although Lord Baltimore kept the immigration policies broadly hospitable with the toleration of all Christians made explicit in 1649. By the end of the 18th century, Baltimore had lost his proprietary authority, and Maryland had become another Anglican colony; nonetheless, Roman Catholics remained in greater strength there than in any other American colony. Maryland, although strongly Anglican by 1750, was also manifestly heterogeneous in religion.

North Carolina, late to be settled and looked upon as inferior territory by Virginia to the north and South Carolina below, proved ripe for settlement by Quakers, New Light (that is, evangelical) Baptists, Lutherans, Scotch Presbyterians, German Reformed, and others. An Anglican missionary, Charles Woodmason, traveling there in 1766 found religion from his point of view in a totally disgraceful and disorderly state: what passes as worship, led by "Ignorant Wretches," can only give offense "to all Intelligent and rational Minds." And Georgia, although not founded until 1732, in its earliest years saw Moravians, Jews, Lutherans, Presbyterians, and others in what was officially another Anglican colony. In 1758 the Georgia legislature created eight Anglican parishes, stipulated the salaries to be paid to ministers, and gave its proper but not particularly effective blessing to the established church.

St. Luke's Parish Church in Smithfield, Virginia, is the oldest standing church in English America. *(Library of Congress)*

But here, too, diversity proved stronger than calls for or traditions of uniformity.

To Georgia the powerful revivalist George Whitefield came, first in 1738 and repeatedly thereafter. An effective and energetic orator, Whitefield journeyed up and down the Atlantic seaboard, preaching a message of salvation and repentance. The catalyst for that wave of religious passion known as the Great Awakening, Whitefield (himself an Anglican) played down all denominational differences and drew many persons and churches into his following. Congregationalists, Presbyterians, German and Dutch Reformed, later Baptists, and still later Methodists either participated in or shared in the benefits of this Awakening. A movement both intercolonial and interdenominational had major potential for welding the discrete colonies and discrete churches into a popular unity. No uniformity resulted, but enough common ground was found to assist those who a generation later made common cause against England.

Membership. In 1780, Congregationalists had the largest number of churches in the country (around 750), with

RELIGION: TOPIC GUIDE

GENERAL

Antinomianism and the Antinomian Controversy
Blue Laws
Great Awakening
Inquisition, Spanish
Mayflower Compact
Missions and Missionaries
Music
    Bay Psalm Book (1640)

Praying Towns
Religion, Freedom of
    Toleration Act
    Virginia Statute for Religious Freedom (1786)
Revitalization Movements
Society for Promoting Christian Knowledge
Society for the Propagation of the Gospel
Witchcraft

GROUPS

Anglicans
Baptists
Congregationalists
Dominicans
Dutch Reformed Church
Franciscans
German Reformed Church
Huguenots
Jesuits
Jews

Lutherans
Mennonites
Methodists
Moravians
Pilgrims
Presbyterians
Puritans
Quakers (Society of Friends)
Roman Catholics
Shakers

BIOGRAPHIES

Asbury, Francis
Backus, Isaac
Brebeuf, Jean de
Carroll, John
Charlevoix, Pierre Francois Xavier de
Chauncy, Charles (1705-87)
Cotton, John
Davenport, John
Davies, Samuel
Dyer, Mary
Edwards, Jonathan
Edwards, Sarah Pierpont
Eliot, John
Fisher, Mary
Frelinghuysen, Theodore Jacobus
Gorton, Samuel
Heck, Barbara Ruckle
Heckwelder, John Gottlieb
Higginson, Francis
Hooker, Thomas
Hopkins, Samuel (1721-1803)
Hume, Sophia Wigington
Hutchinson, Anne Marbury
Jarratt, Devereux
Johnson, Samuel (1696-1772)
Kino, Eusebio Francisco
Las Casas, Bartolome de
Lee, Mother Ann

Leland, John
Makemie, Francis
Marquette, Jacques
Mather, Cotton
Mather, Increase
Mayhew, Jonathan
Morton (Mourt), George
Muhlenberg, Henry Melchior
Murray, John
Neolin (the Delaware Prophet)
Nurse, Rebecca
Occom, Samson
Peter, Hugh
Serra, Junipero
Starbuck, Mary Coffyn
Tennent, Gilbert
Tennent, William (1673-1746)
Weiser, Johann Conrad
Wheelock, Eleazar
Wheelwright, John
Whitaker, Alexander
White, Andrew
Wilkinson, Jemima
Williams, John (1664-1729)
Wise, John
Woodmason, Charles
Zeisberger, David

Boston's Old South Meeting House was used as both a church and a town meeting hall, demonstrating the close relationship of government and religion in colonial Massachusetts. *(Massachusetts Department of Commerce and Development)*

Presbyterians the next largest number at nearly 500. These two denominations, sharing a common theology, often worked together informally as later in the 19th century they would formally cooperate; thus the "Presbygational" combination was by far the strongest link in what came to be called the Evangelical Empire. Baptists had over 400 churches in 1780, with Methodists just getting started but already enjoying a membership of around 10,000. Anglicans had about 400 churches but, at this point was in retreat rather than advance. Lutherans, next in strength, had about 240 churches, with Quakers and German Reformed each with about 200 meetings or churches. Dutch Reformed churches numbered around 125, with Roman Catholics having a few over 50, almost wholly in Maryland and Pennsylvania. With only five synagogues, Judaism awaited the major immigrations of the 19th century.

Church membership figures for the colonial period are not particularly revealing. First, there is a scarcity of reliable data; second, church membership was restrictive and often privileged, with the result that the size of congregations frequently exceeded the lists of members. The church was regularly the locus of community life, the information center, the leading dispenser of charity, advocate of causes, and

promoter of education. The colonial churches gathered an entire society within their outstretched arms.

See also Great Awakening; Penn, William; Pilgrims; Puritans; Society for the Propagation of the Gospel; Whitefield, George; articles on individual religions.

Bibliography: Ahlstrom, Sydney E., *A Religious History of the American People* (Yale Univ. Press, 1972); Bowden, Henry W., *Dictionary of American Religious Biography* (Greenwood Press, 1977); Gaustad, Edwin S., *Historical Atlas of Religion in America* (Harper & Row, 1976); Hudson, Winthrop S., *Religion in America* (Scribner's 4th ed., 1986); Ruether, R. R. and Keller, R. S., eds., *Women & Religion in America*, 3 vols. (Harper & Row, 1981-86).

Edwin S. Gaustad
University of California, Riverside

RELIGION, FREEDOM OF   There were at least three different approaches to religious freedom in colonial America: (1) those who sought freedom chiefly for themselves; (2) those who on theological grounds endeavored to extend freedom to all; and (3) those who on rationalistic or Enlightenment presuppositions sought to restrict or eliminate the power of institutional religion over free and open inquiry. Beyond these groups, of course, early America also heard from many who found the very notion of freedom in religion to be wholly unsettling and unwelcome.

Many came to America to escape persecution, hoping therefore to find a haven for their own religious freedom but not necessarily for the freedom of all others. Pilgrims and Puritans most conspicuously represent this position, that is, they left England not to create a society where all religious options (or none) would be equally acceptable but to practice without interference or penalty their own particular manner of worship and way of life. But many others also fled the fires of persecution, not having developed any major theory regarding religious liberty, only knowing that their own liberty and lives were endangered. Lutherans from Salzburg, Austria, thus came to Georgia in the 1730s; Jews from the Iberian Peninsula fled to Holland or Brazil and then to North America; Moravians who found temporary refuge in Bohemia hoped in Georgia or Pennsylvania or North Carolina to know even greater security and safety. All of these and more saw religious freedom chiefly in terms of their own ability to worship and to believe as they felt God had commanded them to do.

Broad Interpretations.   Others argued more broadly for a community or a colony in which not only they would be free but all others as well. To these persons, a religion that was coerced was a religion not worth embracing. In Rhode Island, Roger Williams would allow no persecution for cause of conscience, for such persecution had caused enormous amounts of needless bloodshed even as it had blasphemed God. In Pennsylvania, William Penn opened doors not only to his fellow Quakers but to all other peaceable worshippers of God. While still in England, Penn had written a major treatise entitled *The Great Case of Liberty of Conscience* (1670), arguing there for the rights of Quakers and all other dissenters simply to be left alone so far as their religion was concerned. In choosing a different path from the majority, "I know no treason," Penn wrote, "nor any principle that would urge me to a thought injurious to civil peace." And in Maryland an Act of Toleration was passed in 1649 that, while limited to Christians, moved far beyond what most 17th-century ecclesiastics were prepared to accept.

In the second half of the 18th century, several important political leaders concluded (along with their Enlightenment counterparts in Europe) that institutional religion should never carry with it the force of political power and potential oppression. Thomas Jefferson and James Madison in Virginia led in the struggle against disestablishment of the Anglican Church there, but also against the notion of any intimate bond between the state and the church. Government, Jefferson observed, should have no more to do with religious opinions than it does with opinions in physics or geometry. The civil magistrate, Madison pointed out, was not a competent judge of religious truth nor was religion ever properly "an engine of Civil policy." Madison's famous Memorial and Remonstrance of 1785 led to the passage in Virginia of Jefferson's Statute for Religious Freedom in 1786. If in Virginia, where establishment had been oldest and strongest, the case for religious liberty could be made and carried, then what of the nation as a whole?

No single steady development led to the adoption of the Constitution's 1st Amendment in 1791, and no single motive characterized all those who voted for it. The three strains noted all contributed: those weary of all religious persecution, those concerned about the inviolability of the soul, and those convinced that a separation of church and state was an essential step in moving from the medieval to the modern world.

Bibliography: Gaustad, Edwin S., *Faith of Our Fathers* (Harper & Row, 1987); Miller, William Lee, *The First Liberty* (Knopf, 1986).

Edwin S. Gaustad
University of California, Riverside

RENSSELAERSWYCK A patroonship, or semifeudal estate, founded by Kiliaen van Rensselaer on August 13, 1630, near present-day Albany, New York, the estate was one of several authorized by the June 7, 1629, "Freedoms and Exemptions" issued by the Dutch West India Company to promote settlement in its colony of New Netherland.

Rensselaerswyck was the only patroonship to succeed; all the others were eventually abandoned and sold back to the company.

As late as 1660, Rensselaerswyck consisted of about 40 houses and some 200 inhabitants. The size of the estate was determined by its river frontage, which extended from the Mohawk River south along the Hudson to near present-day Coeymans, New York, and east and west of the Hudson encompassing all of modern Rensselaer and Albany counties, comprising in all about 1,000,000 acres. After the fall of New Netherland to Britain in 1664, the heirs of Kiliaen van Rensselaer were to petition the English governors of New York for years in an attempt to have their rights recognized. Finally, on November 4, 1685, Governor Thomas Dongan granted to Kiliaen, son of the late Jeremias van Rensselaer, a patent whereby the colony of Rensselaerswyck was designated an English manor in exchange for the family's abandoning all rights to the city of Albany.

See also New Netherland; Patroonships.

Bibliography: Nissenson, S. G., *The Patroon's Domain* (Columbia Univ. Press, 1937); Rink, Oliver. A., *Holland on the Hudson: An Economic and Social History of Dutch New York* (Cornell Univ. Press, 1986).

REPARTIMIENTO A term meaning "share," the repartimiento was a basic economic institution for the government assignment of Indian labor in the early Spanish colonies. It initially evolved on Hispaniola before 1500, as discontented colonists divided up the Indians and lived off of their labor. Christopher Columbus officially established the practice in 1499 as a grant to a local Spaniard, held at the governor's pleasure, of the labor of the subjects of a particular chief. The bestowal of a repartimiento included no land or mining rights. The practice tended to disappear quickly where many Spanish were bidding for labor, as for example in central Mexico, where it had disappeared by the early 17th century. At Potosi, Bolivia, it survived into the 19th century.

See also Encomienda and Hacienda.

REPUBLICANISM Ideas about republicanism—government based on popular consent and representation—came from a variety of classical and European sources and affected the way Americans thought during the Revolutionary War era about a wide range of political, economic, and social issues. Englishmen and Americans detected underlying republican elements in Britain's system of constitutional monarchy; the elimination of the Crown and the imperial structure in 1776 offered what many Americans saw as an opportunity to perfect and expand political liberty.

According to an influential strain of republican thought, popular governments were uniquely dependent upon the "virtue"—the unselfishness, self-reliance, and civic spirit—of the people, and in the first years after independence the Americans wrote state constitutions entrusting predominant power to the legislature, the traditional representative branch of the people. But it also followed that since republican governments were uniquely dependent on public virtue they were also uniquely exposed to the dangers of political and economic corruption. Corruption and tyranny were always poised to undermine hard-won liberty.

By the 1780s many prominent Americans were convinced that not only were their state legislatures becoming corrupt and tyrannical but that the people themselves were selfishly falling away from the virtue and unity of the early years of the Revolution into the pursuit of individual and group interest. In a new wave of constitution-making, which culminated in the U.S. Constitution of 1787, American Federalist leaders devised and justified republican systems that placed more emphasis on structural checks and balances than on public virtue as safeguards of liberty. However, not all agreed with the Federalist analysis of popular politics. The republican debate over liberty and tyranny, virtue and corruption, governmental structure, and the good of society continued to influence the affairs of the nation in the years after the adoption of the Constitution.

Bibliography: Wood, Gordon S., *The Creation of the American Republic, 1776-1787* (Univ. of North Carolina Press, 1969).

Douglas M. Arnold
The Papers of Benjamin Franklin

Paul Revere's fame rests on his ride in 1775 to warn the colonists of approaching British troops, but he was also prominent in politics and commerce in Massachusetts. *(Library of Congress)*

REQUERIMIENTO   The requerimiento was a document read to Indians that required them to acknowledge the power of the pope and the Spanish crown and to accept missionaries in their midst. It explained the provisions of the Treaty of Tordesillas and ended with a notarized confirmation of its reading. If the Indians refused to submit, or if they made no response, the Spanish might conquer and enslave them. The document was usually read in Spanish to Indians who understood no Spanish, and Bartolomé de Las Casas, the champion of the Indians, agitated against it for decades. The requerimiento was finally superseded by the general law on exploration and conquest of 1573.

The requerimiento was composed in 1513 after a debate at the court of King Ferdinand II over the nature of the Spanish conquests in the New World. It was to be read to all unconquered Indians and was based on the Old Testament justification for the conquest of Jericho. Its supporters argued that, just as Joshua had the right to demand the surrender of Jericho because God had given the city to the Jews, so did the Spanish have the right to demand the surrender of Indians in the New World.

See also Las Casas, Bartolomé de.

REVERE, PAUL (1735-1818)   A revolutionary patriot and noted American silversmith, Revere was born in Boston, the son of a Huguenot silversmith. Paul owned a silversmith shop in which he also made copper engravings of sheet music, portraits, surgical instruments, political cartoons for patriot causes, and dental plates. At the same time he was becoming active in Boston politics. After the Tea Act (1773), Revere became a leader of the Sons of Liberty and participated in the Boston Tea Party. He became a celebrated figure in the colonies as a messenger for the Massachusetts provincial assembly. He carried news of the Boston Tea Party to New York City (1773) and of the Suffolk Resolves to Philadelphia (1774).

Revere was famous for his ride from Charlestown to Lexington to warn John Hancock and Samuel Adams that the British were seeking them and military supplies and to alert the entire Middlesex countryside that British troops were approaching. Poet Henry Wadsworth Longfellow immortalized the event in his poem "Paul Revere's Ride." During the Revolutionary War, Revere served as an officer and engraved the first Continental money and the official seal of the colonies. As a member of the Massachusetts Committee of Correspondence, he commanded Castle William in the Boston Harbor for a time and participated in failed expeditions to Rhode Island (1778) and Penobscot Bay (1779). He continued his silversmithing while also manufacturing gunpowder, copper balls, and cannons, and helped make the hardware for frigates, including the *Constitution*.

REVITALIZATION MOVEMENTS   In the early 1760s, as the British completed their victory over the French in the French and Indian War, a Delaware spiritual leader named Neolin moved through the Ohio River Valley, claiming to have received a visitation from the Master of Life. He preached that the Indian's only hope lay not in further acculturation but in the abandonment of alcohol and European material culture, in the revival of the ancient ways, and in fierce armed resistance to further encroachment on Indian lands. Neolin's most famous convert was Pontiac, who adopted the message of the Delaware Prophet, as Neolin came to be known, as the spiritual foundation of his Northern Indian uprising of 1763.

Neolin and Pontiac were leaders of a nativistic revival, but in subtle ways their doctrines were a blend of native and European elements. Neolin argued against many old war rituals, proposed the general restructuring of sex roles along European lines, and incorporated the notion of written prayers and the "Great Book" or Bible into his doctrine. He was not the last Indian prophet to preach a syncretic message. Handsome Lake, a Seneca religious leader of the early 19th century, and his contemporary Tenskwatawa (known as the Shawnee Prophet) advocated similar nativistic reforms that incorporated European elements into a renaissance of native culture. Later in the 19th century the Paiute Wovoka preached a similar message that sparked the great pan-Indian movement known as the Ghost Dance.

Revitalization movements such as these took place worldwide during the penultimate stage of native resistance to colonial rule. They were religious movements, usually led by prophets claiming revelation, preaching millennialism and a reversal of the existing order, if the colonized returned to the old ways. Yet in nearly every case, those old ways included subtle reforms that made it more possible for the colonized to deal with colonial culture while at the same time striking a nativist stance.

See also Neolin; Pontiac; Pontiac's Rebellion.

Bibliography: Wallace, Anthony F. C., *The Death and Rebirth of the Seneca* (Knopf, 1969).

John Mack Faragher
Mount Holyoke College

REVOLUTIONARY WAR, BATTLES OF   The Revolutionary War, or more properly the War of American Independence, has two phases. After three years as a localized rebellion by North American colonies, Great Britain's struggles expanded to include operations against France (1778), Spain (1779), and the Netherlands (1780). From that point until the signing of the Treaty of Paris (September 1783), fighting spread to the Mediterranean and Caribbean seas, Africa, India, and European waters, as part of the "Second Hundred Years' War."

Hostilities began on April 19, 1775, when General Thomas Gage's troops imposing martial law on Massachusetts collided with colonial militia. After skirmishes at Lexington (probably inadvertently triggered by a shot fired by a junior British officer) and Concord, the British retreated, narrowly avoiding destruction in the running battle that followed. Within days all four New England colonies raised armies to besiege Boston.

On June 14, 1775, the Continental Congress created a national force, the Continental Army, and one day later gave command of it to General George Washington. The army consisted of the New England and New York troops plus companies of riflemen from Virginia, Maryland, and Pennsylvania, but in time would expand to contain regiments from all 13 colonies plus Canada. These regulars provided the war's primary field armies, leaving local defense to the militia.

The new organization's first combat came in the Battle of Bunker Hill (June 17, 1775), before the troops involved even knew that their status had changed. Gage sent General William Howe to gain control of the Charlestown peninsula, hoping that overwhelming force might bring the war to a swift end. Three frontal assaults eventually captured the hasty fortifications (actually located on Breed's Hill), but high British losses weakened the garrison, and London eventually replaced Gage with Howe.

Americans hoped for reconciliation during the first full year of the war and limited military efforts to defensive measures. Washington blockaded Boston until Howe evacuated the city on March 17, 1776. Other troops consolidated control elsewhere by overawing Loyalists and ousting Royal governors. Even the invasion of Canada was defensive in nature, being prompted by fears that Governor Guy Carleton's British regiments would move south. On May 10, 1775, locals seized Fort Ticonderoga; in September Generals Philip Schuyler and Richard Montgomery led a Continental force across Lake Champlain, hoping that Canada would join the rebellion. Carleton's outer defenses at Chambly (September 18) and St. John's (November 2) fell, allowing Montgomery to push on to Quebec City where he linked up with Benedict Arnold, who had led a second element across Maine. Their New Year's Eve assault ended in defeat and Montgomery's death.

During the winter of 1775-76, Britain decided to crush the rebellion in North America rather than negotiate. Throughout the war strategists in London overestimated Loyalist strength, and they initially reasoned that resistance was centered in New England. Therefore, large forces, including regiments of German mercenaries, were dispatched in three contingents to restore control in the other areas of the continent. Until those objectives were met, the recalcitrant Yankees would be harassed by naval raids.

General Henry Clinton led the smallest of the three forces against the south, but was repulsed at Charleston (June 28, 1776) by General Horatio Gates. The second expedition under General John Burgoyne reached Quebec

REVOLUTIONARY WAR:TOPIC GUIDE

GENERAL

Afro-Americans and the American
  Revolution
Antislavery
Articles of Confederation
Boston Massacre, The (1770)
Boston Tea Party (1773)
British Empire (see **Topic Guide**)
Carlisle Peace Commission
Cincinnati, Society of the
Coercive Acts (1774)
Colonial Government (see **Topic Guide**)
Committees of Correspondence
Committees of Observation and Safety
Common Sense
Continental Army
Continental Association (1774)
Continental Congress, First (1774)
Continental Congress, Second (1775-81)
Conway Cabal
Daughters of Liberty
Declaration of Rights and Grievances
  (1774)
Declaration of Independence
Democracy
Divine Right of Kings
Edenton Ladies Tea Party
Fairfax Resolves
Franco-American Alliance (1778)
Galloway's Plan of Union
Gaspee Incident
Green Mountain Boys
Hessians
Hutchinson Letters (1773)
Independence Hall
Indians and the American Revolution
Land Ordinance of 1785
League of Armed Neutrality
Liberty Bell

Liberty Incident (Riot)
Loyalists
Massachusetts Circular Letter (1768)
Mecklenburg County Resolutions (1775)
Mercantilism (see **Topic Guide**)
Monticello
Monarchs, English
Mount Vernon
Mount Vernon Conference (1785)
New England Restraining Act
Newburgh Addresses
Nonimportation
Northwest Ordinance (1787)
Old North Church
Olive Branch Petition
Paris, Treaty of (1783)
Parsons' Cause
Quartering Acts
Quebec Act (1774)
Republicanism
Revolutionary War, Battles of
Revolutionary War, Causes of
Religion, Freedom of
Shays' Rebellion (1786-87)
Sons of Liberty
Stamp Act Congress
Stars and Stripes
Staten Island Peace Conference (1776)
Suffolk Resolves
Suffrage
"Taxation Without Representation"
Valley Forge
Virginia Declaration of Rights (1776)
Virginia Resolves (1765) and Association (1774)
Virginia Statute for Religious Freedom (1786)
Whig Ideology
Wyoming Valley Violence
Yankee Doodle

BIOGRAPHIES

Adams, Abigail
Adams, John
Adams, Samuel
Alexander, William
Arnold, Benedict
Attucks, Crispus
Bland, Richard
Boucher, Jonathan
Boudinot, Elias
Burgoyne, John
Burr, Aaron
Burr, Esther Edwards
Clark, George Rogers
Clinton, George (1739-1812)
Clinton, Sir Henry
Colden, Cadwallader
Conway, Thomas

Corbin, Margaret Cochran
Cornwallis, Charles
Crevecoeur, Michel-Guillaume Jean de
Darragh, Lydia Barrington
Deane, Silas
Dearborn, Henry
Dickinson, John
Drayton, William Henry
Franklin, William
Freneau, Philip
Gage, Thomas
Galloway, Joseph
Gates, Horatio
Gerry, Elbridge
Greene, Nathanael
Grenville, George
Hale, Nathan

---

on May 6, 1776. By July 1, including a critical victory at Three Rivers (June 8), Carleton had driven American forces weakened by disease, poor logistics, and a lack of popular support from Canada. Carleton wrested control of Lake Champlain from Arnold at Valcour Island (October 11), but was forced to fall back by the onset of winter.

British strategy in 1776 focused on New York City, whose superb harbor was essential for the Royal Navy. Howe, with the largest reinforcements, arrived there on June 25 and embarked on a campaign to achieve victory with minimal losses. Washington did win a handful of skirmishes including Harlem Heights (September 16) and Pell's Point (October 18), but Howe outmaneuvered him in the important battles of Long Island (August 27), Kip's Bay (September 15) and Fort Washington (November 16).

The latter blow, a major American disaster, opened the way for a British invasion of New Jersey that drove Washington all the way across the state by December 7.

At this point Howe halted for the winter, allowing Washington to strike back at Trenton (December 26) and Princeton (January 3). These two small victories allowed the Americans time to rebuild the Continental Army on an expanded basis to serve for the duration of the war.

Britain resumed its basic strategy in 1777. On June 18, Burgoyne started south from Canada, quickly taking Ticonderoga (July 6), before slowing in bad terrain. Flanking operations met defeat at Fort Stanwix (August 3-23) and Bennington (August 16). The main column then ran into Gates and Arnold outside Saratoga. American victories at Freeman's Farm (September 19 and October 7) plus the mobilization of huge militia forces cut Burgoyne off and led to his surrender on October 17.

The second major offensive, under Howe, left New York on July 23 and sailed up the Chesapeake Bay to capture Philadelphia. Once again he outmaneuvered Washington in battles at Brandywine (September 11) and

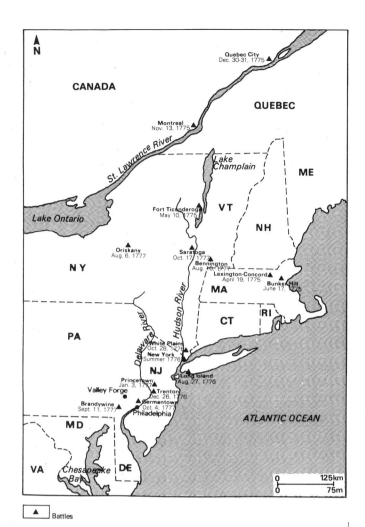

Major Battles of the Revolutionary War, 1775-1777. *(Martin Greenwald Associates, Inc.)*

by capturing Charleston and General Benjamin Lincoln's army after a siege (April 1-May 12, 1780). He then turned over Southern operations to General Charles Cornwallis.

Although troubled by irregulars under leaders like Francis Marion and Thomas Sumter, Cornwallis easily repulsed the first counterattack by defeating Gates at Camden (August 16) and then advanced into North Carolina, hoping to hold the Continentals at bay so Loyalists could organize and deal with backcountry unrest. General Nathanael Greene, the final American commander in the theater, neutralized this plan by exploiting Cornwallis's shortage of reliable troops, especially after the latter lost most of his light forces at King's Mountain (October 7) and Cowpens (January 17, 1781).

Greene regrouped behind the safety of the Dan River and then launched his offensive campaign. Cornwallis was badly mauled at Guilford Court House (March 15) and forced to move to the coast to refit. Greene then bypassed him and proceeded further into the Carolinas. Without ever "winning" a single battle, he coordinated his operations with irregulars and militia. Punished at Hobkirk Hill (April 25), 96 (May 22-June 19) and Eutaw Spring (September 8), the British soon found themselves restricted to toeholds at Charleston and Savannah.

In the meantime, Clinton and Cornwallis, acting on orders from London, moved into the Chesapeake Bay in an attempt to sever Greene's lines of communications and to halt the tobacco trade, the only form of American revenue

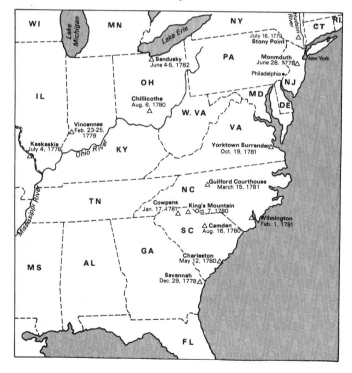

Major Battles of the Revolutionary War, 1778-1782. *(Martin Greenwald Associates, Inc.)*

Germantown (October 4). The victory proved to be a hollow one, for Washington's army remained intact, retiring to Valley Forge to improve its training.

French entry into the war dramatically changed the strategic picture in 1778. London planners ordered Clinton, who replaced Howe, to shift his attention to the south. After evacuating Philadelphia, holding off Washington's pursuit at Monmouth (June 28) and a Franco-American attack on Newport (August), fighting in the North stagnated. Washington occupied a defensive zone centered on West Point (which Arnold tried to betray to the British on September 25, 1780), neutralizing New York. Both sides restricted themselves to minor actions such as General Anthony Wayne's capture of Stony Point on July 16, 1779.

The new British Southern strategy initially produced success. Relatively small forces captured Savannah (December 29, 1778) and held it against a Franco-American attack (September 11-October 9, 1779). Clinton next inflicted the worst defeat on any American contingent export left. After inconclusive skirmishing, Cornwallis occupied Yorktown on August 1, 1781. Washington, taking advantage of the arrival from the Caribbean of a huge French fleet under Admiral Comte de Grasse, abandoned plans to strike at New York and moved south with part of his main army and a French expeditionary force under General Comte de Rochambeau.

De Grasse's victory of the mouth of the Chesapeake (September 5) trapped Cornwallis and cut him off from relief by Clinton. On September 28, Washington and Rochambeau moved forward from Williamsburg to begin a formal European-style siege. Operations proceeded flawlessly. Trenches were dug according to precise plans by head engineer General Louis Duportail; artillery commanded by General Henry Knox went into action on October 9; and the last outworks (Redoubts 9 and 10) fell to allied bayonet attacks on the evening of October 14. Relentless pressure and bad weather that frustrated a desperate plan to flee finally forced Cornwallis to lay down his arms (October 19, 1781). Although unknown at the time, Yorktown turned out to be the final major action of the war in North America.

Bibliography: Higgenbotham, Don, *The War of American Independence* (Northern Univ. Press, 1983); Royster, Charles, *A Revolutionary People at War: The Continental Army and American Character, 1775-1783* (Univ. of North Carolina Press, 1980).

Robert K. Wright, Jr.
U.S. Army Center of Military History

REVOLUTIONARY WAR, CAUSES OF The British Empire reached the zenith of its power as a truly worldwide enterprise of unprecedented commercial and colonial greatness with the signing in 1763 of the Treaty of Paris, ending the French and Indian War (Seven Years War). The English seaboard colonies cooperated significantly in the elimination of the French peril from North America. At that point, the British position in the New World seemed secure, yet in 20 short years 13 American colonies declared their independence, fought a seven-year war, and eventually brought forth the United States of America. Among the many and complex causes that created the atmosphere for the coming of the American Revolution were several significant factors: the distance between Europe and the New World, British mercantilist policies, and attempts by Britain to reorganize imperial administration.

Effects of Distance. The physical separation of America from Great Britain nurtured a spirit of self-reliance. Many settlers left their homes to flee from oppression in one form or another and to build new lives for themselves and their children. After surviving a perilous crossing of 3,000 miles of ocean, they faced a unique environment with challenges that were unknown at home. They learned to adapt to trying circumstances in order to survive. Imperial authority was hampered by long and slow channels of communication, which resulted in little protection or correction for the expanding settlements. The lack of effective imperial authority contributed to the development of the spirit of local autonomy and promoted the seeds of independent thinking and action.

Impact of Mercantilism. Another general cause for the American Revolution lay in the difficulties arising from British adherence to mercantilism. The object of this system was to subordinate the entire economic life of the colonies to the welfare of the mother country. Dominating 18th-century economic thought, mercantilism held that a country's wealth was measured by the amount of precious metal in its treasury. In the absence of gold and silver, this wealth was acquired through a favorable balance of trade, with an excess of exports over imports. England regarded the colonies both as sources of raw materials and as markets for manufactured articles. This economic theory was perceived by many colonists as contrary to their vital interests since it conflicted with their political ideals of self-government and freedom of trade. Colonial opposition was largely dormant during the first half of the 18th century by reason of the British policy of salutary neglect, which did not effectively enforce the theory of mercantilism. An example of this neglect was Robert Walpole's passage of the Molasses Tax on the import of foreign molasses by the American colonies. The measure was adopted to please the West Indian lobby; however it was largely unenforced so as not to upset the Americans. Although the Americans objected to the theory of mercantilism, they were complacent with the British practice of nonenforcement.

Regulating the Empire. A third general cause of the Revolution was the new attitude prevalent in England, as a consequence of the accession of George III in 1760 on the death of his grandfather. The King and his advisers were determined to implement a new program for regulating the empire with its vastly enlarged boundaries of Canada, Florida, and the West Indies. Their plans called for a military force of 10,000 soldiers for security in America and an increased naval presence to put an end to smuggling. To meet the increased expenditure, a revenue had to be found in the form of new taxes in America. As these recommendations were under consideration, the Americans were enjoying a new-found freedom from the threat of French invasion, as well as a sense of accomplishment for their part in the defeat of the French in the North American phase of the Seven Years War. The Americans looked to the future for greater freedom and less regulation from the mother country. The conflicting points of view clearly placed the American colonies and the mother country on a collision course.

The Stamp Act Crisis.   After the conclusion of the peace in 1763, the British Treasury took up the question of the debt which had escalated from 73,000,000 pounds to 137,000,000 pounds during the war. The income of the British Treasury was 8,000,000 pounds and it paid out approximately 5,000,000 pounds for interest on the national debt. A main source of income for the Treasury was the English land tax, which had been raised to four shillings per pound as a temporary war measure. This tax fell heavily on the landed aristocracy, whose members sought a reduction. The Treasury was also faced with an increase in the budget items for the imperial administration of the enlarged frontiers in North America. The expenses of the new army of 10,000 troops for America would be paid by Britain for the first year and thereafter the charges would be borne by the colonies. In order to provide a fund to defray these imperial expenses, Parliament passed the Stamp Act (1765), which was sponsored by George Grenville. All legal documents in the colonies, along with other items, would require a stamp which had to be purchased from British agents. It was estimated that the stamp duties would raise the sum of 100,000 pounds a year. In 1765, Benjamin Franklin was a colonial agent in England and offered no objection to the measure. During the course of the debates, Isaac Barre opposed the bill and referred to the Americans as the "Sons of Liberty," a phrase that captured the imagination of the patriots.

In the colonies, protests against the Stamp Act were immediate, with the first mob action taking place in Boston on August 14, 1765. The Massachusetts stamp master, Andrew Oliver, was hanged in effigy from a tree in the center of town as a destructive crowd shouted protests against tyranny. The shop and home of Oliver were partially destroyed, and he resigned his post. The cry of "Liberty and No Stamps" enflamed political emotions. As the protest spread throughout the colonies, it became evident that the Stamp Act could not take effect on the appointed date of November 1. "No taxation without representation" was chanted as the Stamp Act Congress met in New York and solemnly proclaimed its intention to import nothing from Britain until the objectionable law was repealed.

Lord Rockingham replaced Grenville in July as the head of the British government and faced a major crisis in the fall of 1765. Reports reached London of protests, violence, and nonimportation agreements drawn up by the colonists. Trade figures declined drastically and English merchants demanded action by the government. After discussing various options, the government decided to repeal the Stamp Act on the grounds that it was causing undue hardship for the British merchants and not for the reasons presented by the Americans. Parliament took the occasion to affirm that it had the full authority to make laws binding the American colonies "in all cases whatsoever."

It is doubtful if Rockingham would have had the votes to repeal the Stamp Act if he had not supported the Declaratory Act. During the repeal sessions, Benjamin Franklin made the distinction between internal and external taxes, assuring Parliament that the colonies did not object to external taxes that were imposed in order to regulate trade but only to internal taxes whose sole purpose was the raising of a revenue. The expert on American affairs, Charles Townshend, listened as Franklin explained this distinction. The Rockingham government had solved the imperial crisis, and there was rejoicing by the Americans, who took little notice of the Declaratory Act or the other irritants. New York voted to erect statues in honor of King George III and William Pitt, who spoke eloquently in favor of the repeal.

Townshend's Government.   In the summer of 1766, William Pitt, Earl of Chatham, formed a new government with Charles Townshend as chancellor of the Exchequer. At this critical point in British history, illness removed Pitt from the scene, and Townshend seized control of the Cabinet. He adopted a new program of taxation that steered Britain back on a collision course with the colonies. Convinced that British authority had been eroded by colonial encroachments on the powers of the Crown, Townshend sought to reorganize the empire by rendering governors, judges, and other officials independent of the provincial assemblies. Parliament would tax the colonies in order to provide a fund to pay the salaries of the officials and thus limit the influence of the assemblies. In presenting his plan to Parliament, Townshend observed the distinction between internal and external taxes by levying duties on various imports, such as glass, lead, tea, painter's colors, and paper. Townshend also sponsored the law to suspend the New York Assembly because of its refusal to comply with the unpopular Quartering Act. (New York had not voted the funds required for the support of the British troops.)

The Townshend taxation program (1767) reopened the entire controversy and led eventually to the clash of arms between America and Britain. Colonial opposition took the form of nonimportation, and lists were drawn up of British goods that were not to be purchased. Constitutional arguments against the taxes were drafted by John Dickinson, entitled "Letters from a Farmer in Pennsylvania." Dickinson rejected the Townshend duties as unconstitutional and assailed the suspension of the New York Assembly as an attack on the liberties of all the colonies. The distinction between internal and external taxes was repudiated. Massachusetts led the way in drawing up a circular letter (1768) to keep all informed of the protest activities against actions of Parliament in violation of the principle of no taxation without representation. In 1770, Lord North introduced the repeal of the Townshend duties on all the imports with the exception of tea. The duty on tea was retained in order to maintain Parliament's right to taxation.

Colonial Protests.   Protests and friction continued in the colonies. Civilians and the military clashed in the Boston Massacre of 1770 in which five died as a result of soldiers firing into a mob. The first to die was a black man and former slave, Crispus Attucks. The withdrawal of the troops from the town prevented a general uprising.

In 1773, Parliament passed the Tea Act, which was designed to alleviate a crisis in the East India Company resulting from a vast tea surplus. The company received a drawback of the taxes paid on tea imported into Britain if and when it was shipped to America. At the colonial port, the regular tax of three pence per pound would be collected. Although tea could be purchased more cheaply in Boston than in London, the Americans opposed the act for it gave a monopoly to the company and was taxation without representation.

The destruction of a large quantity of tea during the Boston Tea Party (December 1773) led to severe punitive action by Parliament. The Coercive Acts included the closing of the port of Boston, the withdrawal of some chartered rights, the increase in the governor's powers, as well as the Justice and Quartering Acts. The Quebec Act was not part of the penal legislation but it was resented, for it extended the boundaries of Canada down to the Ohio River and gave the Roman Catholic Church a privileged position.

War and Independence.   The collision course had come full circle as a result of the harsh penalties. The First Continental Congress met (1774) in Philadelphia and drew up a declaration of rights and grievances and supported the nonimportation of English goods. Failure of compromise plans and the Battle of Lexington and Concord preceded the convening of the Second Continental Congress in May 1775. The troops around Boston were designated as the Continental Army, and George Washington was appointed commander in chief of the forces. Thomas Jefferson drafted in July 1776 the Declaration of Independence, providing for the birth of the new nation, the United States of America.

Bibliography: Andrews, Charles M., *The Colonial Background of the American Revolution* (1942; reprint Yale Univ. Press, 1961); Bailyn, Bernard, *The Ideological Origins of the American Revolution* (Harvard Univ. Press, 1967); Countryman, Edward F., *A People in Revolution* (Johns Hopkins Univ. Press, 1983); Forster, Cornelius P., *The Uncontrolled Chancellor Charles Townshend and His American Policy* (Rhode Island Publications Society, 1978); Maier, Pauline, *From Resistance to Revolution* (Random House, 1973); Morgan, Edmund S. and Morgan, Helen M., *The Stamp Act Crisis*, rev. ed. (Macmillan, 1983); Namier, Lewis B., *England in the Age of the American Revolution*, 2nd ed. (St. Martin's Press, 1974); Thomas, P. D. G., *British Politics and the Stamp Act Crisis* (Oxford Univ. Press, 1975); Thomas, P. D. G., *The Townshend Duties Crisis* (Oxford Univ. Press, 1987).

Donna Therese McCaffrey
Providence College

REYNOSO, ALONSO DE (flourished 1570)   A Spanish official in the New World, Reynoso helped to establish the Spanish presence in Florida. Following the founding of St. Augustine in 1565, the Spanish government sought to solidify its hold on the Florida peninsula. Other towns were founded, but their lifespan was short. The Franciscans sought to do their part by creating a mission system reaching into the interior as well as northward along the coast. Beginning in 1573 the chief architect of the chain of missions that extended along the Georgia coast was Alonso de Reynoso. Reynoso was aware of growing English interest in the continent to the north, and he sought to forestall them, even building missions on the many islands in the Atlantic east of Georgia. Due to Reynoso's efforts, the Spanish hold on Florida, once very tenuous, was firm for the time being.

RHODE ISLAND   Before the arrival of the first European settlers, the Narragansett Indians inhabited the area of Rhode Island from Providence south along Narragansett Bay to the present towns of South Kingstown and Exeter. Their principal rivals, the Wampanoag, dominated the eastern shore region, while the Nipmuck, a weak tribe by comparison, maintained a tenuous foothold in the inland regions north and west of Providence. To the south the Niantic populated much of the coastal area of what is now the towns of Charlestown and Westerly. These tribes subsisted on farming, fishing, and to a lesser extent, hunting.

Anthropologists have estimated that approximately 10,000 Indians lived within the present boundaries of Rhode Island by 1650, with the Narragansett accounting for 6,000 of that number. In 1675 the Narragansett joined forces with the Wampanoag in King Philip's War, a futile struggle to rid New England of the white man. Decimated by battle and famine, remnants of Narragansett, Wampanoag, and other tribes sought refuge with the Niantic, who had maintained a neutral stance in the war. This aggregate of remnant groups, which also included the Pequot, became the foundation of a new Indian community in Rhode Island that ultimately assumed the name Narragansett.

Settlement and Colonial Period.

In 1524, Florentine navigator Giovanni da Verrazano, sailing in the employ of France, became the first European to explore Rhode Island and record his activities and impressions. By comparing Block Island with the Mediterranean island of Rhodes, he unwittingly gave the state its name.

The first permanent settlement was established at Providence in 1636 by English clergyman Roger Williams and a small band of followers who had left the repressive atmosphere of the Massachusetts Bay Colony to seek freedom of worship. Williams was granted a sizeable tract for his village by Canonicus and Miantonomi, friendly sachems of the Narragansett. Other Nonconformists followed him to the Narragansett Bay region, including Anne and William Hutchinson and William Coddington, who founded Portsmouth in 1638 as a haven for Antinomians. A short-lived dispute sent Coddington to the southern tip of Aquidneck Island (also purchased from the Narragansett), where he founded Newport in 1639.

The fourth original town, Warwick, was settled in 1642 by Samuel Gorton, another dissident from Portsmouth. During this initial decade two other outposts were established—Wickford (1637) by Richard Smith and Pawtuxet (1638) by William Harris and the Arnold family.

Because title to these lands rested only on Indian deeds, neighboring colonies began to covet them, and so Roger Williams journeyed to England and secured a parliamentary patent in 1644 uniting the towns into a single colony and confirming his settlers' claims to their land. This legislative document served as the basic law until the Stuart Restoration in 1660 made it wise to seek a royal charter.

At that time Dr. John Clarke was commissioned to secure a document consistent with the religious principles upon which Rhode Island was founded and one that would safeguard Rhode Island lands from the encroachment of speculators and neighboring colonies. He succeeded admirably. The royal charter of 1663 guaranteed complete religious liberty, established a self-governing colony with great local autonomy, and strengthened Rhode Island's territorial claims. It was the most liberal charter to be issued by the mother country during the entire colonial era, a fact that enabled it to serve as the basic law until May 1843.

The religious freedom that prevailed in early Rhode Island made it a refuge for several persecuted sects. America's first Baptist church was formed in Providence in 1639; Quakers established a meeting on Aquidneck in

1657 and soon became a powerful force in the colony's political and economic life; a Jewish congregation came to Newport in 1658; and French Huguenots settled in East Greenwich in 1686.

Among the more important events of the 17th century were King Philip's War (1675-76); the interruption in government caused by the abortive Dominion for New England (1686-89); and the beginning of the intermittent colonial wars between England and France (1689-1763), a long struggle for empire that frequently involved Rhode Island men, money, and ships. By the end of the century Newport had emerged as a prosperous port and the dominant community, nine towns had been incorporated, and the population exceeded 6,000 inhabitants.

The first quarter of the 18th century was marked by the long and able governorship (1698-1727) of Samuel Cranston, who established internal unity and brought his colony into a better working relation with the imperial government in London. The middle decades of this century were characterized by significant growth. Newport continued to prosper commercially, but Providence began to challenge for supremacy. This rivalry assumed political dimensions, and a system of two-party politics developed by the 1740s. Opposing groups, one headed by Samuel Ward and the other by Stephen Hopkins, were organized with sectional overtones. Generally speaking (although there were notable exceptions), the merchants and farmers of Newport and South County (Ward's faction) battled with their counterparts from Providence and its environs (led by Hopkins) to secure control of the powerful legislature for the vast patronage at the disposal of that body.

A major boundary dispute with Connecticut was resolved in 1726-27, and a very favorable boundary settlement with Massachusetts in 1746-47 resulted in Rhode Island's annexation of Cumberland and several East Bay towns, including the port of Bristol. During this midcentury period the plantations of South County reached their greatest prominence. The spread of agriculture on the mainland resulted in the subdivision of Providence and other early towns. By 1774 the colony had 59,707 residents, who lived in 29 municipalities.

The Revolutionary Era.

Rhode Island was in the vanguard of the Revolutionary movement. Having the greatest degree of self-rule, it had the most to lose from the efforts of England after 1763 to increase its supervision and control over the colonies. In addition, Rhode Island had a long tradition of evading the poorly enforced Navigation Acts, and smuggling was commonplace.

Beginning with strong opposition to the Sugar Act (1764) with its restrictions on the molasses trade, the colony engaged in repeated measures of open defiance, such as the burning of the British revenue schooner Gaspée in 1772. Gradually, Ward and Hopkins put aside their local differences and united against alleged British injustices. Finally, on May 4, 1776, Rhode Island became the first colony to renounce allegiance to King George III.

During the war itself, Rhode Island furnished its share of men, ships, and money to the cause of independence. Volunteers included a significant number of black and Indian slaves, who gained distinction as the "Black Regiment," a detachment of the first Rhode Island Regiment. Esek Hopkins, brother of Stephen, the signer of the Declaration of Independence, became the first commander in chief of the Continental navy—a force that Rhode Island helped create. The able Nathanael Greene of the Kentish Guards became George Washington's second-in-command and chief of the Continental Army in the South.

The British occupied Newport in December 1776, and a long siege to evict them culminated in August 1778 in the large but inconclusive Battle of Rhode Island, a contest that was the first combined effort of the Americans and their French allies. The British voluntarily evacuated Newport in October 1779, and in July 1780 the French forces under the Comte de Rochambeau landed there and made the port town its base of operations. It was from Newport, Providence, and other Rhode Island encampments that the French march to Yorktown began in 1781.

Postwar Developments. The revolution did not alter Rhode Island's governmental structure (even the royal charter remained intact), but it had some important effects, including the decline of Newport, the passage of an act providing for the gradual abolition of slavery (1784), and a law prohibiting Rhode Islanders from engaging in the slave trade (1787).

In 1778 the state had quickly ratified the Articles of Confederation, with its weak central government, but when the movement to strengthen that government developed in the mid-1780s, Rhode Island balked. The state's individualism, its democratic localism, and its tradition of autonomy caused it to resist the centralizing tendencies of the federal Constitution. This opposition was intensified when an agrarian-debtor revolt in support of the issuance of paper money placed the parochial Country party in power from 1786 through 1790. This political faction, led by Charlestown's Jonathan Hazard, was suspicious of the power and the cost of a government too far removed from the grass-roots level, and so it declined to dispatch delegates to the Philadelphia convention of 1787, which drafted the U.S. Constitution. Then, when that document was presented to the states for ratification, Hazard's faction delayed, and nearly prevented, Rhode Island's approval.

In the period between September 1787 and January 1790, the rural-dominated general assembly rejected no fewer than 11 attempts by the representatives from the mercantile communities to convene a state ratifying convention. Instead, the assembly defied the instructions of the Founding Fathers and conducted a popular referendum on the Constitution. That election, which was boycotted by the supporters of a stronger union (the Federalists), rejected the Constitution by a vote of 2,711 to 239.

Finally, in mid-January 1790, more than eight months after George Washington's inauguration as the first president of the United States, the Country party reluctantly called the required convention, but it took two separate sessions—one in South Kingstown (March 1-6) and the second in Newport (May 24-29)—before approval was obtained. The ratification tally, 34 in favor and 32 opposed, was the narrowest of any state.

In the end, a nearly immovable object yielded to an irresistible force; Rhode Island joined the union that had left it behind and embarked upon a new era of economic and political development.

See also Dominion of New England; Hutchinson, Anne; King Philip's War; Newport; Revolutionary War, Battles of; Williams, Roger.

Bibliography: Bridenbaugh, Carl, *Fat Mutton and Liberty of Conscience: Society in Rhode Island, 1636-1690* (Brown Univ. Press, 1974); Conley, Patrick T., *Democracy in Decline: Rhode Island's Constitutional Development, 1776-1841* (Rhode Island Historical Society, 1977); James, Sydney V., *Colonial Rhode Island* (Scribner's, 1975); Lovejoy, David S., *Rhode Island Politics and the American Revolution, 1760-1776* (Brown Univ. Press, 1958); Polishook, Irwin H., *Rhode Island and the Union, 1774-1795* (Northeastern Univ. Press, 1969).

Patrick T. Conley
Providence College

RIBAUT, JEAN (?1520-65) A French mariner and colonizer, Ribaut was born at Dieppe and came to New France in 1562 to establish a colony of Huguenots. He explored the St. Johns River in Florida but settled his group of 150 colonists farther north at what is now Port Royal, South Carolina. Ribaut returned to France and promised to resupply the colony the following year, but civil war had broken out, and Ribaut fled to England, where he was imprisoned for refusing to join an English colonizing venture. The Port Royal colony was soon abandoned.

When Ribaut was finally released in 1565, he set out to resupply a second colony, which his companion René de Laudonnière had founded at the St. Johns River. Ribaut's rescue attempt was a failure. He reached the colony but instead of staying to help the settlers threatened by Spanish force, he sailed off to fight the Spanish fleet. The colony was destroyed in September 1565 by the Spanish, and only a few, including Laudonnière, escaped. Ribaut himself was shipwrecked in a storm and killed by the Spanish.

RICE One of the world's most important crops, rice (*Oryza sativa*) was introduced into the colonies from the Mediterranean by the English in the 1620s, but it was not until the late 17th century, in the colony of South Carolina, that it became an important crop. The success of the crop depended upon the skill of slaves transported from Africa's "rice coast" (Ghana and Sierra Leone), where rice cultivation had been introduced a century earlier. The extension of rice production and the growth of slavery developed apace. By the first quarter of the 18th century, rice had become one of the Southern colonies' most successful exports.

After the British captured Charleston during the Revolution (1780), they shipped home the entire rice crop, leaving no seed. Only after Thomas Jefferson smuggled rice seed out of Europe in 1787 did the rice industry revive, eventually spreading in the early 19th century throughout the South. Rice became a staple in Southern, Creole, and Mexican cuisine, combined with seafood and meat, baked into rice cakes, bread, or pudding, or simply served boiled and buttered.

Bibliography: Kahn, E. J., Jr., *The Staffs of Life* (Little Brown, 1985).

RIO GRANDE The Rio Grande rises in the San Juan Mountains in Colorado and then flows south through New Mexico to El Paso, where it turns to the southeast on its way to the Gulf of Mexico. The full length of the river is about 1,800 miles. Its major tributaries in New Mexico are the Rio Taos, Rio Chama, Rio Puerco, and Rio Salado. Along the Texas-Mexico border it receives the flow of the Rio Conchos, Rio Alamo, and the Pecos and Devils rivers. In northern New Mexico the river falls into the Rio Grande Gorge for 75 miles before debouching onto a wide floodplain suitable for agriculture. In west Texas the terrain is mountainous and broken up by numerous dry washes. Nearing the delta, the river swells and provides the water for massive irrigation projects on both sides of the border. Among the major settlements on its banks are Albuquerque, El Paso, Laredo and Nuevo Laredo, Ciudad Juarez, Brownsville, and Matamoros.

The Rio Grande was first discovered by Europeans in the 1530s, when Cabeza de Vaca, Estevanico, and their companions worked their way west from Florida. At that time the river was known as the Rio Bravo del Norte. Their tales of the Seven Cities of Cibola stimulated further Spanish exploration, chiefly along the upper Rio Grande. Settlement began in 1598 when Juan de Onate gave the river its present name on his campaign to conquer New Mexico.

For the rest of the colonial period the Rio Grande served as the chief line of defense for the northeastern frontier of New Spain. Although settlers pushed well beyond its

course, it was to the presidios and towns along the Rio Grande that colonists retreated when in trouble. After the Pueblo Revolt in New Mexico in 1680, refugees poured into El Paso, which in the next decade was the base for Diego de Vargas's reconquest of the province. To the east, priests and soldiers penetrated west Texas from bases on the river and thrust north from Coahuila, founding the presidio and mission at San Antonio.

The Indian population along the river was greatest in central and northern New Mexico, where the Pueblo Indians were well established when the Spanish arrived. Along the eastern section of the Rio Grande the tribes were nomadic, but their penetration and pacification through the mission system was fairly successful. The arrival of the Comanches came too late in the colonial period to threaten seriously the Spanish hold on the river.

See also El Paso; Onate, Juan de.

Bibliography: Horgan, Paul, *Great River: The Rio Grande in American History*, 2 vols., (Holt, Rinehart and Winston, 1954).

RÍOS, DOMINGO TERAN DE LOS (flourished 1661-91) Through the late 17th century the Spanish government in New Spain was in constant fear of French expansionism along the coast of the Gulf of Mexico. In 1691 the viceroy, alarmed by reports of French settlement in Texas, ordered Ríos to explore deeper into the interior of the far north. Ríos had served in Peru (1661-81), and as governor of the combined provinces of Sonora and Sinaloa he commanded respect among all elements of the frontier population. His expedition traveled along the coast and then up the Red River Valley, but he never found the French. By 1693, Texas was deemed too costly to man, the missions were abandoned, and Spain pulled the frontier back to Coahuila and Nuevo Leon.

RISING, JOHAN CLASSON (1617-72) A Swedish colonial governor, Rising was born in Ostergotland, Sweden. In 1651 he was made secretary to the Commercial College, which controlled New Sweden, and in 1652 he was appointed to succeed Johan Printz as governor. During his tenure in the colony (1654-55), Rising had good relations with the Indians and the colonists and fostered commerce and agriculture, but he lost the colony for Sweden by seizing the Dutch Fort Casimir at New Castle. In 1655, Peter Stuyvesant, on behalf of the Dutch, retaliated by capturing the Swedish supply ship and then took Fort Christina on the Delaware River in a two-week battle that cost the Dutch no men and the Swedes only one.

RITTENHOUSE, DAVID (1732-96) Few early Americans were so proficient in such a variety of scientific and

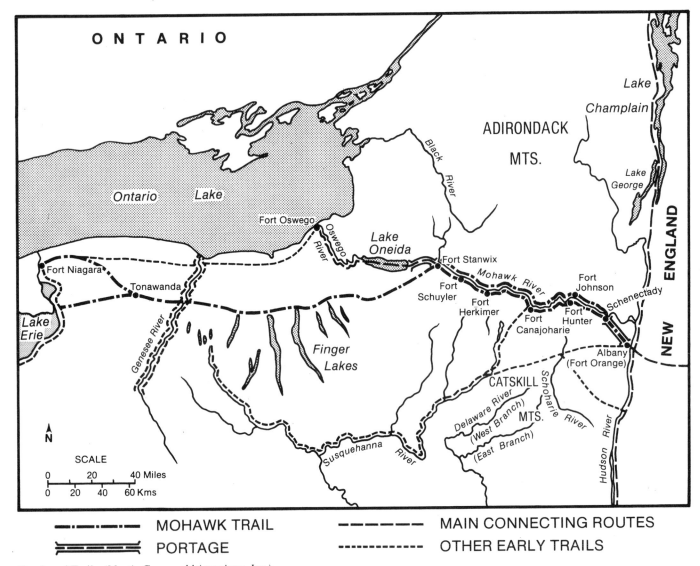

ONTARIO

Ontario Lake

Fort Oswego

Oswego River

Lake Oneida

Fort Stanwix

Black River

ADIRONDACK MTS.

Lake Champlain

Lake George

Fort Niagara

Tonawanda

Lake Erie

Genesee River

Finger Lakes

Fort Schuyler

Fort Herkimer

Mohawk River

Fort Canajoharie

Fort Johnson

Fort Hunter

Schenectady

Albany (Fort Orange)

NEW ENGLAND

CATSKILL MTS.

Delaware River (West Branch)

(East Branch)

Schoharie River

Hudson River

Susquehanna River

N

SCALE

0   20   40 Miles

0   20   40   60 Kms

—··—··—··— MOHAWK TRAIL

⬭⬭⬭⬭⬭⬭ PORTAGE

— — — — — — MAIN CONNECTING ROUTES

-- -- -- -- -- OTHER EARLY TRAILS

Roads and Trails. *(Martin Greenwald Associates, Inc.)*

technical fields as Philadelphian David Rittenhouse. Born at Paper Mill Run, near Germantown, Pennsylvania, Rittenhouse mastered skills as an instrument maker, astronomer, mathematician, and surveyor. He exhibited extraordinary ability by teaching himself to make finely-crafted clocks and mathematical instruments, using the library and tools of a relative. He designed a pendulum that allowed more accurate timekeeping. By expanding clockmaking skills, he produced compasses, levels, barometers, thermometers, and surveying instruments, each with a precision and workmanship unequaled at the time. His surveying was so accurate that it was accepted by Mason and Dixon for the Pennsylvania-Maryland border. Rittenhouse's interest in astronomy led him to develop what is believed to be the first American-made telescope. In 1767 he designed his famous orrery, a precise

model of the solar system, which is considered the forerunner of the present-day planetarium. In 1785 he introduced the use of spider threads as cross hairs in the eyepieces of his instruments.

During the Revolutionary era, Rittenhouse served as engineer, vice president, and president of the Committee of Safety. He gathered lead for bullets, oversaw the casting of cannon and the manufacture of saltpeter, and devised chain protection for the harbor. He was an active member of the general assembly and the state constitutional convention in 1776. He served on the board of war and as state treasurer (1777-89). His work on the commission to organize the United States Bank led George Washington to appoint him as the first director of the mint (1792-95). At the death of long-time friend Benjamin Franklin, Rittenhouse was elected president of the American Philosophical

Society in 1791 and by reelection held this office until his death.

Bibliography: Ford, J. Edward, *David Rittenhouse, Astronomer-Patriot* (Univ. of Pennsylvania Press, 1946); Hindle, Brooke, *David Rittenhouse* (Princeton Univ. Press, 1964).

Rodger C. Henderson
Pennsylvania State University

RIVERA Y MONCADA, FERNANDO DE (1725-81) A Spanish colonizer in the West, Rivera served in Baja California in the 1760s and explored the California coastline with the Jesuit Wenceslaus Linck. After the 1768 expulsion of the Jesuits he was chosen to lead the advance party of the Portolá-Serra expedition of 1769. His small group of scouts reached San Diego on May 14. Rivera then accompanied Portolá on the subsequent abortive attempt to found Monterey. In 1775 he explored the San Francisco peninsula, looking for a suitable site to colonize. As a reward for his services he was named lieutenant governor of California in 1777. Rivera was killed by Yuma Indians in 1781 while escorting settlers to found Los Angeles.

See also Portolá, Gaspar de; Serra, Junípero; San Diego.

RIVINGTON, JAMES (1724-1802) Bookseller, printer, and journalist, Rivington, born in Chesterfield, England, published with other printers the first daily newspaper in America and was a business entrepreneur whose schemes brought him first success and then bankruptcy in both England and America. Rivington's London issue of Samuel Smollett's *History of England* made 10,000 pounds, but poor business practices ruined him. He made a fresh start in 1760 in Philadelphia by becoming the chief distributor of English books in America. He soon added merchandise and a picture gallery and operated stores in Boston in 1762 and a Maryland land lottery in 1766. Reestablished in New York after bankruptcy again, he formed J. Rivington & Company, received 2,200 advance subscriptions for Charles Churchill's poems, and began publication in 1773 of his bipartisan paper, Rivington's *New-York Gazetteer*. After the Sons of Liberty destroyed his printing press in 1775, he resumed his paper as Rivington's *New-York Loyal Gazette* (1777-83), with a decidedly Tory slant. Troubled by public disapproval, he was sent to debtor's prison and died a poor bookseller and stationer.

ROADS AND TRAILS Early Spanish, French, and English maps document the extensive and complicated trail networks within regional Indian societies, as well as more fragile "traces" linking these regions. Indian trails either wound through major river valleys, such as the

Connecticut, Mohawk, Susquehanna, and Shenandoah, or, more typically, clung to ridges where hard ground and thin forest cover facilitated travel. During the nearly two centuries of colonial development these narrow footpaths were widened by the movement of horse and ox, cart and wagon, as well as by the action of the men of local communities, who worked out their tax obligations by performing primitive road improvements. For the most part, overland transport followed the ancient pathways blazed during millennia of Indian occupancy prior to European colonization.

The most notable of these Indian and colonial trails surmounted the mountains. Massachusetts was linked to the Hudson Valley by the Old Bay Path, which began at Boston and led west, crossing the Berkshire hills, or by the Mohawk Trail which began at Turner's Falls, and in New York sent offshoots to Lake Champlain and the St. Lawrence, to the east-flowing Susquehanna and the westering Allegheny. Westward travelers from the greater Philadelphia area followed the Kittanning Trail over the Appalachians from the Susquehanna to the Allegheny. A bit farther south Nemacolin's Path offered another trans-Appalachian route from the head of navigation on the Potomac to Fort Pitt at the junction of the Allegheny and Monongahela rivers. Later this was renamed Braddock's Road after British General Edward Braddock, who used this route to move his troops over the mountains during the French and Indian War. Later still it was incorporated as a section of the Cumberland or Old National Road and carried thousands of settlers to the Ohio Valley in the late 18th and early 19th centuries. A western extension leading from Fort Pitt to Detroit was known as the Great Trail.

The most famous of all colonial trails, known by the Indians as the Great Trading and War Path and by the colonists as the Great Road of the Valley, carried traffic over the Appalachian chain at Cumberland Gap. The approaches to the Gap and the routes to the first Kentucky settlements were marked by Daniel Boone in 1775 as the Wilderness Road, the great pioneer highway to the trans-Appalachian West. Important trails in the West included the Chickasaw Trail, known after 1806 as the Natchez Trace, running southwest from French Lick (Nashville) on the Cumberland River to Natchez on the Mississippi; the Chihuahua Trail, connecting the northernmost Spanish settlements clustered around Santa Fe with the administrative and commercial centers 1,500 miles south; and the Old Spanish Trail, connecting Santa Fe with Spanish California.

Atlantic Coast. Along the Atlantic coast the slow growth of a colonial postal service in the 18th century facilitated the gradual improvement of intercolonial roads. Two of the first were the Boston Post Road (New York-

Boston) and the Old Post Road (New York-Albany), both in service by the 1710s. By 1789 a continuous system of some 2,000 miles of post roads extended from Portland, Maine, to Savannah, Georgia. None of these, however, were hard-surfaced; the first macadamized road in America was Pennsylvania's Lancaster Turnpike, opened in 1795. Moreover, only a small percentage of the roads, those linking major cities north of Richmond, Virginia, were fit for stagecoach service. Indeed, the condition of the road network at the end of the Revolution was deplorable; 10 miles a day was very good progress for a wagon on the roads. According to George Washington, in 1784, one of the most serious problems facing the new nation was the fragility of the links between regions and sections, especially between the coastal cities and the interior; this problem was taken up during the era of transportation revolution that began late in that decade, beginning with the rage for turnpikes and canals.

See also Chickasaw Trail; Chihuahua Trail; Cumberland Gap; Great Trading and War Path; Old Spanish Trail; Transportation; Wilderness Road.

Bibliography: Dunbar, Seymore, *History of Travel in America* (1915; reprint Greenwood Press, 1968); Hulbert, Archer B., *The Paths of Inland Commerce* (Elliots Books, 1920).

John Mack Faragher
Mount Holyoke College

ROBERTSON, JAMES (1742-1814) Frontiersman and early leader of Tennessee, Robertson was born in Virginia but removed to settlements on the Holston River, west of the Appalachians, before 1770. He became a leader in the Watauga Association, was a founder of Nashville in 1779, and played an important role among the western leadership of the Revolution. In the 1780s he engaged in land speculation and participated in the struggles over the founding and organizing of the State of Franklin. In later years he worked as an Indian and land agent, and he took the side of Andrew Jackson in his feud with John Sevier.

See also Franklin, State of; Watauga Association.

ROBERVAL, JEAN FRANÇOIS DE LA ROCQUE, SIEUR DE (?1500-60) A French colonial official in Canada, Roberval received his commission as lieutenant general of Canada from Francis I in 1541. He occupied Jacques Cartier's settlement in Quebec in 1542 after Cartier left. A disastrous winter for his party of 200 was followed in the summer of 1543 by exploration in the Montreal region and a return to France by Roberval and the other colonists who had survived. The failure of Roberval's colonizing expedition dampened French enthusiasm for settlement and ruined him financially.

ROBINSON, BEVERLEY (1722-92) A Loyalist and military leader, Robinson was a member of a well-connected Virginia colonial family. His first military service came in 1746, when he was appointed to raise a company for a British expedition against Canada. He subsequently settled in New York and became active in the affairs of that colony. He later provided important logistical support for the colonial troops during the French and Indian War. Although a friend of George Washington, Robinson opposed the idea of American independence and in 1777 fled from his home in the Hudson Valley to the safety of British-occupied New York City. During the Revolution, he served the British side as colonel of the Loyal American Regiment; four of his sons also served in the British forces. Robinson's most important military contribution came in espionage and intelligence, with his service as colonel of the Loyal Guides and Pioneers. In 1779, his property in the Hudson Valley was confiscated by the American authorities, and he and his family were banished from New York State. Fleeing to England, he was compensated for his wartime services by an act of Parliament. Robinson spent the rest of his life in Great Britain.

ROCHAMBEAU, JEAN BAPTISTE DONATIEN DE VIMEUR, COMTE DE (1725-1807) Commander of the French army in North America during the Revolutionary War, Rochambeau was born into a noble family of Vendome, France, and was a distinguished officer before he received the command of the forces to go to America in 1780. His command was complicated by a lack of ships for his 7,600 soldiers and a lack of money from the crown. He sailed in May 1780 with part of his army and quartered his men in Newport, Rhode Island. He refused to attack New York until the French controlled the sea. In July 1781, after the Comte de Grasse arrived with a large fleet, Rochambeau brought his men to join George Washington's forces at White Plains, New York. The combined force of 10,000 men slipped past the English and defeated Lord Cornwallis at Yorktown with the help of de Grasse's blockade. Although the Marquis de Lafayette received the greatest public praise for the victory, Rochambeau was given an important appointment at Calais. During the French Revolution he barely survived the Terror but was later honored by Napoleon.

RODNEY, CAESAR (1728-84) A Delaware political and military leader, Rodney was born in Dover and served in the colonial legislature from 1758 to 1776, rising to the position of speaker. He was named a Delaware representative to the Stamp Act Congress (1765) and served in the First and Second Continental Congresses (1774-76, 1777-78). In July 1776 he voted on behalf of the Delaware delegation in favor of American independence and signed the Declaration of Independence. During the Revolution, Rodney served as brigadier general of the Delaware militia. His later civilian posts included provisional president of Delaware (1778-81), Delaware war executive (1781), and speaker of the upper house of the Delaware legislature (1783).

ROGERS, ROBERT (1731-95)   A colonial soldier of fortune, Rogers was born in Methuen, Massachusetts, and raised on the New Hampshire frontier. In 1755, he joined the New Hampshire regiment and participated in William Johnson's Crown Point expedition. In 1756, he was appointed captain of a company of rangers and, two years later, promoted to the rank of major in command of nine ranger companies. The daring raid of Roger's Rangers during the French and Indian War gained him fame in both America and England. After leading colonial troops against the Cherokee in South Carolina and against the forces of Pontiac near Detroit (1763), Rogers resigned his commission and traveled to London, where he published his memoirs and produced a play about his own exploits. Returning to America, Rogers was placed in command of Fort Michilimackinac in the Northwest, but was dismissed from that post after accusations of treason for dealing with the French. His later career was unsuccessful. In London in 1769, he was held in debtors' prison, and he later served as a mercenary for the Bey of Algiers. After his return to America in 1775, he was imprisoned as a British spy. During the Revolutionary War, he served the Loyalist cause as commander of the Queen's American Rangers. In 1780 he fled to England, where he spent the rest of his life in poverty.

See also Fort Michilimackinac.

ROLFE, JOHN (1585-1622)   A colonial settler, he sailed from England for Virginia in 1609. Shipwrecked on Bermuda, he and his crew sailed in homemade boats to Jamestown, Virginia. There he conducted experiments with tobacco to produce stronger, sweeter leaves. It is because of these experiments that tobacco became the staple crop of Virginia. In 1614 he married Pocahontas, a captive Indian, thereby achieving peace with the Indians for a time. In 1616 he returned to England, where his wife died, but he came back the next year, continued as secretary and recorder of the colony until 1619, and served on the Council of State from 1621. He was killed by Indians.

See also Pocahontas; Tobacco.

ROMAN CATHOLICS   Early in the 16th century, long before Jamestown or Plymouth, Roman Catholicism made

forays into Florida and later into Texas and New Mexico. Under the flag of Spain, Jesuit, Dominican, and Franciscan missionaries labored on behalf of the Church, sometimes with enduring effect, sometimes with tragic results for both the Indian and the Spanish missionary. Florida proved especially inhospitable, and ventures north of that peninsula were so costly in human lives that the Jesuits in 1571 determined to pull back. Santa Fe, New Mexico, became both an ecclesiastical and political center as early as 1610; in 1680 a widespread Indian revolt brought Spanish rule temporarily to an end. That revolt, like many others, came in direct response to practiced cruelties and enslavement that often made a mockery out of any effort to Christianize the native Americans. The gospel, one Franciscan reported from New Mexico in 1601, "is despised by these people on account of our great offences and the harm we have done them." Two generations earlier, the Dominican Bartholemew de Las Casas had intervened on behalf of the Indian, persuading Pope Paul III to issue an official statement requiring that Indians be treated as human beings and not deprived of their life, liberty, or property "even though they may be outside the faith of Jesus Christ." The papal document (*Sublimus Deus*, 1537) helped for a time, but the Spanish Conquest remained primarily just that.

Spanish Catholicism, especially in the American Southwest and far West, survived as a major religious force in the North American continent. Weathering wars and rapid changes in national ownership, the region even in the late 20th century continued to reveal Spain's colonial dominance centuries before. And Hispanic Catholics, quite significant numerically, gradually became significant in influence and power within the American Church.

France's penetration, much farther to the north initially, came by way of the St. Lawrence River and the Great Lakes. From there, due to the labors of Jesuit Jacques Marquette and others, French trade and French Catholicism moved down the Mississippi River, ultimately all the way to the Gulf of Mexico. With the Society of Jesus taking greatest responsibility, the national Church of France colored much of eastern Canada and interior America. Because the Jesuits had been so central in this development, the banishment of that order from all North America by 1770 sharply altered the fortunes of Roman Catholicism among both Indians and Europeans. At the close of the colonial period, French Catholics could still be found at both the headwaters and the mouth of the Mississippi River, but no ecclesiastical authority supplanted the Jesuits so suddenly ordered back home. As a consequence, the Church's early advantages in much of the interior of the continent were largely nullified.

English Catholics.   English Roman Catholics participated in the settlement of Maryland, a proprietary colony granted to the Calverts, prominent members of the Catholic nobility. While Catholicism never enjoyed much domestic tranquillity, even in its own colony, Maryland nonetheless remained the center for English Catholics in a British America generally antipopish in its sentiments. From Maryland, Catholicism also moved timidly into the southeastern corner of Pennsylvania. During the American Revolution, "no popery" became part of the popular cries for liberty. But anti-Catholicism in that period was mitigated by the visible and important patriotism of such Maryland Catholics as Charles and John Carroll, as well as by the indispensable assistance that Catholic France rendered to the colonial cause. When the new nation's first Catholic bishop, John Carroll, reported on the state of his Church in 1785, he could count only about 24,000 communicants in the entire country. Of this number, about 90 percent lived in Maryland and Pennsylvania. Modest in size throughout the colonial period and during the first years of U.S. independence, Roman Catholicism would soon leave all other denominations far behind.

Bibliography: Ellis, John Tracy, *Documents of American Catholic History* (Bruce, 1956); Hennesey, James, *American Catholics* (Oxford Univ. Press, 1981).

Edwin S. Gaustad
University of California, Riverside

ROSS, BETSY (1752-1836) Legendary maker of the first stars-and-stripes, Ross was raised in Philadelphia. Her husband, John, was killed in 1776, leaving her to carry on their upholstery business. The story of George Washington, Robert Morris, and George Ross commissioning her to make the first flag is based on a family tradition that came to light in a paper written by her grandson in 1820. Other than this, no historical evidence connects Betsy Ross with the flag. The stars-and-stripes was adopted as the national flag in 1777, and her role in its development was less romantic than her descendants supposed.

ROSS, GEORGE (1730-79) Born in Delaware, Ross studied law in Philadelphia and established a practice in Lancaster, Pennsylvania; he was a provincial assemblyman before American independence. Ross became a patriot in the 1770s, serving on Revolutionary committees in Pennsylvania and in the First and Second Continental Congresses; he was a signer of the Declaration of Independence. Vice president of the Pennsylvania convention in 1776, Ross eventually joined the opposition to the constitution it established. Later he was a judge of admiralty in Pennsylvania; he was involved in controversy

over the prize case of the sloop *Active* at the time of his death.

ROWLANDSON, MARY WHITE (?1635-82?) An Indian captive and author, Rowlandson was born in England and emigrated first to Salem, Massachusetts about 1640, then in 1653 to the frontier village of Lancaster, where she married (1656) the minister, Joseph Rowlandson. In February 1676, during King Philip's War, she and three of her children were taken captive during a bloody Indian attack on the town. Driven westward with the retreating Indians, Rowlandson lost one of her children and experienced grueling hardship; after three months of captivity she was ransomed and released. Rowlandson's fame rests on the account of her sufferings she wrote for her children. Published in 1682, *The Soveraignty and Goodness of God ... Being a Narrative of the Captivity and Restauration of Mrs. Mary Rowlandson* went through numerous editions, becoming one of the bestselling American books of the colonial period as well the prototype of a literary genre, the narrative of Indian Captivity.

See also Indian captivity; King Philip's War.

ROYAL AFRICAN COMPANY Organized in 1672, the Royal African Company inherited the monopoly on West African trade originally held by the Company of Royal Adventurers Trading into Africa. The shareholders were dominated by mercantile interests rather than the aristocracy, as had been the case in earlier joint stock companies. Although the company's monopoly was lost after the Glorious Revolution in 1688, it enjoyed a profit for several years, importing ivory and gold and exporting cloth. By far the most lucrative activity of the company was the transportation and sale of black slaves. Approximately 100,000 slaves were taken from West Africa to the Western Hemisphere by company ships. Continual war from 1689 to 1713 severely hurt business, and after 1713 the company steadily declined until its eventual dissolution in 1752.

ROYAL COLONIES All of the 13 original colonies, excluding Connecticut and Rhode Island, began as chartered or proprietary colonies. Most proprietary colonies surrendered their charters to the Crown because of governmental problems and subsequently became royal colonies. This new form of government, in which the colony's legal existence was authorized directly by the king, first began in Virginia (1624). A royal governor assisted by a council of 12 represented the king in each colony. The people were represented by an elected assembly, which directed law making, taxes, and revenue collections. By 1767 royal governors and judges had become financially independent of the assemblies and were paid directly by American revenue. The Crown also appointed judges, who after 1760, could be removed by the Crown just as governors were. From the mid-18th century, as Britain's government departments became more active in colonial affairs, colonial-mother country tensions mounted in the royal colonies and were a major factor in the outbreak of hostilities in 1775.

See also Revolutionary War, Causes of.

ROYAL DISALLOWANCE   An essential principle of the British imperial administration of its American colonies, the Royal Disallowance provided the Privy Council with the right to overturn any acts or decisions of the colonial legislatures that it deemed to be violations of English law, colonial charters, or governor's instructions. Royal Disallowance was used mainly as a tool by the Board of Trade and Plantations, as advisers to the Privy Council, to enforce British mercantilist policy by hindering colonial economic development.   The exercise of Royal Disallowance created resentment in the colonies and was frequently evaded by the passage of temporary legislation.

RUBI, MARQUES DE (flourished 1765-67)   A Spanish official in the New World, the Marques de Rubi was commissioned by Charles III of Spain in 1765 to inspect the military organization and the state of defense on the northern frontier of New Spain. Rubi spent 1766 and 1767 on the frontier, traveling about 7,500 miles through the provinces of Nuevo León, Coahuila, Texas, Nayarit, Nueva Vizcaya, and Nuevo Mexico. In his report he proposed establishing a line of presidios from the Rio Concepcion in Sonora to the Rio Guadalupe in Texas. This plan entailed closing, building, and moving presidios to more advantageous positions. The map of the expedition by Rubi's aide, Nicolas de Lafora of the royal engineers, is probably the best map of the Spanish borderlands.

See also Lafora, Nicolas de.

RUGGLES, TIMOTHY (1711-95)   A jurist and military leader, Ruggles was born in Rochester, Massachusetts, and graduated from Harvard in 1732. In 1753 he represented Worcester County in the Massachusetts General Court. He joined William Johnson's 1755 expedition against Crown Point and then served as a brigadier general under Lord Jeffrey Amherst in the French and Indian War. In 1762 he was appointed chief justice of Worcester County and served as president of the Stamp Act Congress (1765). His sympathies, however, were Loyalist, and at the outbreak of the Revolution he fled with his family to Boston, where he commanded three Loyalist companies. He was banished from Massachusetts in 1778 and spent the remainder of his life in Nova Scotia.

RUM TRADE   The rum trade began in the New England colonies in the 17th century and was an essential part of the income for an area unable to produce profitable staple crops such as tobacco. Initially, New England traded lumber and fish with the West Indies for molasses, from which rum was manufactured. Rum became New England's earliest industry, and by the 1730s more than 1,000,000 gallons of rum were made annually in Boston. Capitalizing on the need for slaves in the West Indies, New England merchants soon became involved in the triangular trade: molasses from the West Indies was shipped to New England to become rum, which was traded in Africa for slaves who were sold in the West Indies for more molasses. The rum trade brought colonial merchants into conflict with England, however, because colonial traders found it more profitable to deal with the French, Dutch, or Spanish sugar interests, rather than with more expensive English sources. Britain initiated the Molasses (1733) and Sugar (1764) acts to impose high duties on non-British molasses imported into New England. To evade customs duties, smuggling molasses and rum became an acceptable, even patriotic, practice by the time of the Revolution.

See also Molasses Act; Sugar Act; Triangular Trade.

RUPERT'S LAND   According to the royal charter of the Hudson's Bay Company (1670), the company was granted title to an area of nearly 1,500,000 square miles. The owners of this domain named it Rupert's Land in honor of King Charles's cousin, Prince Rupert, the first governor of the company. These boundaries included all the lands draining into Hudson Bay. This meant that west of the Great Lakes, where the valley of the north-flowing Red River of the North begins some 200 miles into present-day North Dakota and Minnesota, Rupert's Land extended considerably south of the 49th parallel.

RUSH, BENJAMIN (1746-1813)   Physician, humanitarian, writer, and statesman, Rush was born in Pennsylvania and educated at the College of New Jersey (Princeton) and the University of Edinburgh. In 1769, Rush began his influential medical practice in Philadelphia, where he was one of America's leading doctors, theorists, and teachers. His patriot activities led to election to the Second Continental Congress (1776-77), and he was a signer of the Declaration of Independence.

Rush was appointed surgeon general of the Middle Department of the Continental Army in 1777 but soon resigned as a result of controversy. In Pennsylvania he was a critic of the unicameral state constitution of 1776 and later a supporter of the new Constitution of the United States, serving in the state convention that approved it (1787). Rush's hopes for America and its revolution found characteristic expression in humanitarian and social programs aimed at developing a virtuous republican society: antislavery, education, penal reform, and temperance. He collected many of his writings on humanitarian topics in *Essays, Literary, Moral and Philosophical* (1798). Rush devoted his later years to medicine and died in Philadelphia.

A signer of the Declaration of Independence, Benjamin Rush was one of the most influential doctors in 18th century America. *(Library of Congress)*

RUTGERS UNIVERSITY First called Queen's College, Rutgers received its charter in 1766. The leaders of the Dutch Reformed Church founded the college to educate "youth in the learned languages, liberal and useful arts and sciences, and especially in divinity, preparing them for the ministry and other good offices." Like Princeton, Brown, and Dartmouth, the establishment of Rutgers was inspired by the Great Awakening, the religious revival movement that swept the country in the mid-1700s and led to a greater emphasis on training church leaders. Rutgers is located in New Brunswick, New Jersey. Its name was changed to

Rutgers in 1825 in honor of its benefactor, Col. Henry Rutgers.

RUTLEDGE, EDWARD (1749-1800) A South Carolina lawyer and political leader, brother of John Rutledge, Edward was born in Charleston and educated in the law in England. After his admission to the London bar in 1772, he returned to South Carolina and served in the First and Second Continental Congresses (1774-77), signing the Declaration of Independence. Rutledge was a strong supporter of American independence and helped in the defense of South Carolina at the outbreak of the Revolution. He was taken prisoner at the fall of Charleston (1780) and released in 1781. Following the war, he resumed his public career, serving in the South Carolina state senate (1782-96) and as governor of South Carolina from 1798 until his death.

See also Rutledge, John.

RUTLEDGE, JOHN (1739-1800) A political leader and jurist, brother of Edward Rutledge, he was born in Charleston, South Carolina, and was educated in the law. In 1762 he served as a representative to the provincial assembly and in 1765 as a delegate to the Stamp Act Congress. Rutledge was a member of the First Continental Congress and one of the main authors of the South Carolina constitution in 1776. He was later elected president of the general assembly (1776-78). As governor (1779-82) during the British invasion of South Carolina in 1779, he organized local resistance and encouraged the guerilla campaigns of Thomas Sumter and Francis Marion. Rutledge later served in the U.S. House of Representatives (1782-83, 1784-90) and attended the Constitutional Convention of 1787. He was one of the first associate justices of the U.S. Supreme Court (1789-91) but never attended any sessions, resigning to serve as chief justice of South Carolina (1791-95). In 1795, with the retirement of John Jay, Rutledge accepted a presidential appointment to become chief justice of the United States. Strong political opposition, however, led the Senate to reject Rutledge's nomination after he had already served as chief justice for one term. Increasing mental instability toward the end of Rutledge's life finally ended his public career.

See also Marion, Francis; Rutledge, Edward; Sumter, Thomas.

RYSWICK, TREATY OF (1697) An agreement between England and France, the Treaty of Ryswick ended King William's War, which was contemporary with the European War of the League of Augsburg. At stake in the hostilities were persistent colonial conflicts in North America in which the English opposed the French and the French opposed the Iroquois Confederacy. The fighting was mainly restricted to the frontiers of New England, Hudson's Bay, James' Bay, and Port Royal. By the terms of the treaty, all territorial conquests were to be returned and a joint commission was to be appointed to determine the conflicting claims to Hudson's Bay. That commission met once, in 1699, but reached no acceptable solution.

See also King William's War.

S

SACHEMS Sachem is an Algonquian word (*sakima, sagomo, sagamore*) which came to refer to the leader of either Algonquian or Iroquoian peoples of northeastern North America. These men were commonly the visible leaders during family and clan gatherings, village ceremonies, and diplomatic councils with outside groups. Among some groups, the position was hereditary; for others, merit was the sole criterion; among the Iroquois, women made the appointments. Although "sachems" usually referred to civil leaders, such men could also be war captains. Given the variety of possibilities, colonists tended to shade this term with European meaning and thus engendered much misunderstanding over the nature of authority in Indian societies.

While European settlers often referred to Indian leaders as "kings" or "emperors," sachems actually exercised very limited authority. Sachems relied heavily on their social prestige to persuade others to follow. A good hunter or brave fighter might command respect, but sachems were also expected to put concerns for family, clan, and village first and to show wisdom in council. This emphasis on generosity was also expressed through gift-giving. This practice not only redistributed wealth and reduced social tensions, it provided sachems with a powerful political tool. Gifts were more than an act of positive morality; they placed the recipient in a position of social and political indebtedness. It was through such mechanisms of persuasion, rather than coercion, that sachems built a consensus around the issue at hand. Therefore, sachems rarely provided the instant obedience from their people that settlers expected.

Bibliography: Jennings, Francis, *Invasion of American Indians, Colonialism, and the Cant of Conquest* (Univ. of North Carolina Press, 1975); Trigger, Bruce G., ed. *Handbook of North American Indians: Volume 15: The Northeast* (Smithsonian Institution, 1978).

Richard L. Haan
Hartwick College

ST. AUGUSTINE The struggle between the French and Spanish over control of Florida came to a head when the Spanish sea captain Pedro Menéndez de Avilés arrived in 1565. Philip II had ordered him to destroy any French he found in Florida and to establish a Spanish settlement there. Menéndez de Avilés slaughtered the French forces under Jean Ribaut in two battles and founded what would become the oldest permanent settlement in the United States, St. Augustine, on September 8, 1565.

Menéndez de Avilés established several other towns in Florida, but St. Augustine alone survived, thanks to his indefatigable efforts to obtain supplies and colonists. In 1586, Sir Francis Drake swept down on the town and destroyed it, but it was soon rebuilt. In the 17th century the Franciscan system of missions in Florida was further strengthened and expanded, and this helped shield St. Augustine from Indian attacks. In 1708, however, English attacks from their new base at Charleston reduced the Spanish- controlled territory in Florida to the area surrounding St. Augustine. In the 1740s the English besieged the town twice but were unsuccessful.

Following the Treaty of Paris in 1763, Florida became English and most of the Spanish inhabitants of St. Augustine, around 3,000 in all, evacuated the city. Although St. Augustine passed to the Spanish again in 1783, the chief influence in the area continued to be British until the United States seized the territory from the weak Spanish government in 1819.

See also Menéndez de Avilés, Pedro.

Thomas C. Thompson
University of California, Riverside

ST. CLAIR, ARTHUR (1736-1818) A Revolutionary War soldier and statesman, St. Clair was born in Scotland. He joined the British army in 1757 and served in Canada. After resigning in 1762 he purchased a large tract of land in western Pennsylvania, where he became involved in frontier affairs. An active patriot, St. Clair entered the army, eventually becoming a major general. He served in Canada and then with George Washington in the New Jersey campaign. In 1778 he was court-martialed for evacuating Fort Ticonderoga in 1777 and exonerated, but he held only minor military posts thereafter. St. Clair sat in Congress from 1785 to 1787, serving as Congress president in the latter year. In Pennsylvania, he was a critic of the state constitution of 1776. In 1787 he was appointed governor and later military commander of the newly organized Northwest Territory; troubles with the Indians led to a military defeat in 1791. St. Clair was governor until 1802.

ST. CROIX SETTLEMENT This Canadian settlement was founded by the French in 1604. It occupied an island in the mouth of the St. Croix River, which had been so named by Jacques Cartier in 1535 because he landed there on Holy Cross Day (September 14). After the first winter, when scurvy killed 35 of the original 100 settlers, the colony was moved across the Bay of Fundy to Port Royal (Nova Scotia), later renamed Annapolis Royal by the English. In 1613 the few remaining structures on the original site were destroyed by an English expedition from Virginia.

ST. DENYS, LOUIS JUCHEREAU DE (1676-1744) A French explorer, born in Canada, St. Denys made several trips to Louisiana with other explorers from 1698. In 1713, Cadillac sent St. Denys to east Texas to buy livestock and to find Francisco Hidalgo, a Spanish priest who wanted help in establishing missions among the Tejas Indians. St. Denys traveled along the Mississippi and the mouth of the Red River, where he founded Natchitoches, the oldest settlement in Louisiana, in 1714. He then crossed into the Indian Tejas country, traded goods for livestock and hides, went as far north as Colorado, and finally with one remaining companion was captured in an Indian village near San Antonio. He was taken to Mexico City, where he found Hidalgo and became a guide for his Spanish party of 80. From 1716 to 1717 he helped establish six missions in Louisiana. In 1719 he returned to Natchitoches and commanded the French post there for the rest of his life.

See also Cadillac, Antoine de la Mothe; French Colonies.

ST. JOSEPH, FORT Fort St. Joseph was built by the French before 1689 to protect the strategic portage between Lake Michigan and the Kankakee River leading to the Illinois settlements, The fort became a center for trade with the Potawatomi, the French traders mixing with the Indians and, over several generations, producing a métis or mixed-blood community. Taken over by the British in 1760, it was briefly held by Spanish forces in 1781 during the Revolution.

ST. LAWRENCE RIVER One of the principal rivers of North America, the St. Lawrence flows 744 miles from the outlet of Lake Ontario to its gulf and, with the Great Lakes, forms a 2,350-mile waterway into the heart of the continent that was followed by several centuries of explorers, fur traders, and missionaries. Entering from the Atlantic, the river forms a deep and broad channel for its first 550 miles, providing easy access to ocean-going vessels, like those of Jacques Cartier, who in 1535 sailed to the site of present-day Montreal. Indeed, the river offered such a superb highway that until the 19th century the most common forms of Canadian transport were the canoe and the ice sled, and roads were considerably underdeveloped.

Beyond Montreal, both the St. Lawrence and its tributary the Ottawa break into dangerous rapids, blocking the passage to ships and requiring transportation by canoe and portage.

After Cartier, the next European to explore the river was Samuel de Champlain, who laid out the village of Quebec and selected the site of Montreal. Between them lay nearly the whole of what would become New France. On the north bank at Quebec, the river meets the Laurentian Shield, where retreating glaciers had scraped bare the topsoil, and between Quebec and Montreal the alluvial bottomlands are not more than a few miles wide. The band of fertile land is wider on the bank south of Montreal but again narrows as the river flows to the gulf. Consequently, French settlement huddled along those banks in long lots, each with river frontage for access to the riverine highway. A visitor sailing to Montreal could almost literally watch the entire population of the colony as he glided along the river.

See also French Colonies.

Bibliography: Eccles, W. J., *The Canadian Frontier, 1534-1760*, rev. ed. (Univ. of New Mexico Press, 1983).

John Mack Faragher
Mount Holyoke College

ST. LEGER, BARRY (1737-89) A British military officer and member of a family of Huguenot descent, St. Leger was educated at Cambridge in England and joined the Royal 28th Foot Regiment in 1756. Distinguishing himself during the French and Indian War for his service at the siege of Louisburg (1758) and the fall of Quebec (1759), St. Leger was promoted to the rank of colonel in 1762. He is best remembered for his participation in General John Burgoyne's invasion from Canada during the Revolutionary War (1777). Laying siege to American-held Fort Stanwix, he was forced to retreat by forces under Benedict Arnold. St. Leger spent the rest of the war in Montreal in command of rangers. He resigned his army commission in 1785.

ST. LOUIS After the cession of New France to England in 1763, many of the French settlers in Kaskaskia and the other villages of Illinois retired west across the Mississippi River to Spanish Louisiana, where, south of the mouth of the Missouri, Pierre Laclede and René Auguste Chouteau founded St. Louis in 1764 to take advantage of the commerce between the settlements of the upper and lower river. Under Spanish administration, its French merchants quickly captured the growing fur trade of the west, and it soon outpaced its competitors, Natchitoches and Arkansas Post, and came to rival the position of New Orleans as the crown jewel of Louisiana. It was transferred to the United States with the Louisiana Purchase in 1804.

See also Chouteau, René Auguste.

ST. MARY'S CITY   In 1634 the first 200 colonists of Maryland, including many Catholics, settled on the north bank of the Potomac River near its mouth on the Chesapeake Bay. Established at the site of an Indian village named Yacomaco, which they renamed St. Mary's City, it became the capital of the colony. After the Protestant uprising of 1689 and the establishment of the Church of England in 1692, the capital was moved from Catholic St. Mary's to Protestant Annapolis in 1694. Thereafter the city declined to only minor importance.

SALEM   Founded by the English in 1626 on the site of the former Indian village of Naumkeag, the original Massachusetts settlement was abandoned after the devastating plague of 1616-19. The colonists kept the name of Naumkeag, however, until 1629 when Puritan emigrants renamed it "Salem," possibly a foreshortening of Jerusalem. That year Salem became the location for the first Puritan church built in New England and was briefly the capital of Massachusetts before the founding of Boston in 1630. It developed as an important fishing and shipping center and by the end of the colonial period was a leading American seaport and home of many prosperous merchants. Salem is most famous as the site of the witchcraft scare and trials of 1692.

See also Witchcraft.

SALTONSTALL, DUDLEY (1738-96)   A Revolutionary War naval officer, born in New London, Connecticut, the son of General Gurdon Saltonstall, he established his reputation as a privateer during the French and Indian War. In 1775, Saltonstall was placed in command of the harbor fort at New London and later commanded the flagship Alfred of the Continental fleet, participating in the capture of New Providence Island in the Bahamas in 1776. In 1779, as captain of the Warren, he joined in the disastrous Penobscot Expedition, for which he was dismissed from the Continental navy. After the war, Saltonstall became active in commercial shipping. He died of yellow fever in Haiti.

SALUTARY NEGLECT   "Salutary neglect" describes the circumspect American colonial policy of Robert Walpole, first English prime minister (1721-42). It survived until the end of the French and Indian War, when the English government initiated a reorganization of its empire.

Beginning in 1660 Parliament passed laws, the Navigation Acts and Acts of Trade, to organize colonial trade according to mercantilist principles, whereby the colonies would supply raw materials to England, trade only with English merchants, and avoid competing with English enterprises. These laws, with their long list of enumerated articles, which could be shipped only within the British empire, were never enforced. Walpole was persistently concerned with continental affairs and the stability of English politics, and he believed that more gold (the mercantilist definition of wealth) would flow to England through unrestricted trade than through taxation. Colonial producers and custom officials often found it convenient and profitable to circumvent the laws. Some enterprises, such as rum production in New England, could survive only by breaking such laws as the 1733 Molasses Act, which sought to protect British West Indian sugar production by setting prohibitively high duties on French and Dutch West Indian sugar.

Several factors led to the end of salutary neglect. Both English exports to the American colonies and the portion of English subjects residing in the colonies quadrupled between 1700 and the 1760s. A huge national debt, a decision to maintain a standing army in America to secure territory gained from France, and a perception that the colonies were not contributing to the maintenance of the empire resulted from the French and Indian War. English attention turned to the prospect of gaining revenue from the colonies. The 1764 Sugar Act, the first law designed to gain revenue from the colonies and the first of the Grenville Acts, enacted under Lord of the Treasury George Grenville, marked the end of salutary neglect and the beginning of the imperial crisis.

See also Acts of Trade; French and Indian War; Grenville Acts; Mercantilism; Navigation Acts.

Bibliography: Barrow, Thomas C., *Trade and Empire: The British Custom Service in Colonial America, 1660-1775* (Harvard, 1967); Kammen, Michael, *A Rope of Sand: The Colonial Agents, British Policies, and the American Revolution* (Cornell Univ. Press, 1968).

John Saillant
Brown University

SAMPSON, DEBORAH (1760-1827)   During her service as a soldier in the 4th Massachusetts Regiment during the Revolutionary War, Sampson dressed as a man and called herself Robert Shurtleff. For this behavior she was excommunicated by the First Baptist Church of Middleborough, the town in Massachusetts where she had lived as an indentured servant after her father abandoned their family when she was a child. In 1785 she married farmer Benjamin Gannett, with whom she had three children. In 1802 she lectured publicly about her army experience, and the government eventually granted her a pension for her service.

SAN ANTONIO   In 1716 the viceroy of New Spain ordered Martin de Alarcón and a Franciscan, Antonio Olivares, to establish a settlement on the San Antonio River as part of the attempt to strengthen Texas against French encroachment. After some delay, Alarcón and Olivares laid out a presidio and mission at the site in 1718. In 1721, San Antonio served as the base for the Marquis de Aguayo's successful campaign to secure Texas for the Spanish crown. Through the mid-18th century, San Antonio continued to grow, due in part to an influx of settlers from the Canary Islands and to success in missionary efforts. San Antonio was also the key to defending the northern frontier against the Apache, as was noted during an inspection tour in 1767.

As Spain's control of its American colonies loosened, San Antonio became the target of Mexican nationalists, who captured it in 1813. Loyalist forces soon retook the town, which remained Spanish until Mexican independence.

See also Aguayo, Marquis de.

SAN DIEGO   The Spanish explorer Juan Rodríguez de Cabrillo first sighted San Diego Bay in 1542, and when the Spanish decided to expand north into California, San Diego was their first objective. In 1769, Gaspar de Portolá joined with the Franciscan Junípero Serra to lead the successful colonizing effort in Alta California. Portolá sent off Fernando de Rivera y Moncada with an advance party. Rivera y Moncada reached the bay on May 14; Portolá and Serra arrived on July 1, 1769. Serra laid out the first Alta California mission on a hill above the harbor, and Portolá founded the first Spanish town. The population grew slowly, but the port remained a vital link in land communications with the northern settlements through the Spanish and Mexican periods.

See also Portolá, Gaspar de; Serra, Junípero; Rivera y Moncada, Fernando de; Cabrillo, Juan Rodríguez de.

SANDYS, GEORGE (1578-1644)   A Virginia colonist and poet, George Sandys was the seventh son of Edwin Sandys, Archbishop of York. He was associated with colonial enterprises from 1611, when he became an investor in the Virginia Company. From 1621 to 1628, he served as treasurer of Virginia, during which time he built the first American water mill; increased shipbuilding; encouraged iron, glass, and silk production; and grew grapes on his 1,500 acres. He also fought the Tappahannock Indians. After he failed to receive a colonial secretaryship in 1631 he lived in England, where he subsequently succeeded in having Virginia's charter renewed (1640) by Parliament.

This action led King Charles I to appoint a royalist governor for the colony. Sandys is noted for his translations of Ovid's *Metamorphosis Englished by G. S.* in 1626 and his *A Paraphrase upon the Psalmes of David* in 1638 and *The Song of Solomon* in 1641.

SANTA FE   The settlement of Santa Fe was founded in 1609 by Pedro de Peralta, governor of the province of New Mexico, and the town grew to more than 1,000 inhabitants by 1630. During the Pueblo Revolt (1680), Santa Fe suffered severely and was abandoned by the Spanish until 1692. It remained vulnerable to raids by the Navaho and Comanche during the early 18th century. Santa Fe became a major trading city for French traders from the Mississippi Valley during the late 18th century. Their activities were continued by Americans over what became known in the 19th century as the Santa Fe Trail. Santa Fe became part of the United States after the Mexican War (1846-48).

SASSACUS (c.1560-1637)   Pequot chief Sassacus, whose name was derived from the Massachusett *sassakusu*, "Wild Man," ruled from Narrangansett Bay to the Hudson River. Born near Groton, Connecticut, son of the Pequot chief Wopwigwoot, he greatly expanded the tribal lands after his father's death in 1632. In 1634, however, Sassacus offered to exchange his newly won territories for a peace treaty with the English colonists, an act that enraged his son-in-law Uncas, leader of the Mohegans. The peace was short-lived. In the Pequot War (1637) more than 700 of his people were killed by the English, and Sassacus himself was captured and killed by Mohawks in an attempted flight to the west.

SAULT SAINTE MARIE   By the time Jacques Marquette founded the mission of Sault Ste. Marie in 1668 on the St. Mary's River, the strategic linkage between lakes Superior and Huron, it had already been traversed by Etienne Brule, Jean Nicolet, and Pierre Radisson. The French hoped not only to convert the northern Indians but, more importantly, to use the "Soo" as an outpost to compete with the Hudson's Bay Company. It was not until 1751, however, that the French built a fort, which was taken over by the British 10 years later. In 1783 the fur-trading Canadian North West Company built a post on the south side, which they moved across the river when the boundary was run through the middle of the lakes, marking the beginning of the Canadian city. With the construction of canals and locks in the 19th century, both cities became important commercial centers.

SAVANNAH   Savannah, Georgia, was established by the colony's founder, James Oglethorpe, on February 12, 1733. Oglethorpe supervised the survey of the town lots and was responsible for the unique design of alternating squares. The town languished under the restrictions of the Georgia Trustees but revived when Georgia became a royal colony in 1752. Savannah was the metropolis of colonial Georgia. During the Revolution, Savannah was overrun by British forces on December 28, 1778. A combined army of French and Americans failed to recapture the town in October 1779. The British were forced to evacuate Savannah in July 1782 by an American army under General Anthony Wayne.

SAYRE, STEPHEN (1736-1818) A merchant and diplomat, Sayre was born in Southampton, Long Island, and educated at the College of New Jersey (later Princeton). Much of his early adult life was spent as an agent of the De Berdt banking house of London. Always a strong supporter of American independence, he offered his diplomatic services to the new nation in 1777. Appointed first as secretary to the American embassy in Berlin, Sayre later on his own initiative established diplomatic contacts in Amsterdam and Stockholm. These initiatives were largely unsuccessful, and Sayre was unable to convince Congress that he deserved back payment for his services. In 1793 he retired to his New Jersey estate.

SCALPING Although the practice varied from region to region among Indian tribes, the basic goal of scalping was to cut a circular pattern through the skin of the head and lift off the hair and skin of the skull in one motion. The "scalp" was then stretched on a hoop, attached to the end of a pole, and paraded into the village as a sign of meeting the responsibility to family and clan for avenging either a loss of a relative or a perceived insult.

In spite of a widespread popular belief to the contrary, scalping was an indigenous practice unique to North America. Archeological and linguistic evidence suggests a date of at least the 1st century A.D. in the southeastern United States. It then spread into the Northeast before the 16th century. Among the Iroquois and Huron it was an alternative to beheading, a scalp being equal to a head as a war trophy.

For colonists the practice was proof of the "savage" nature of native Americans. Few recognized its restricted use to war and the preference among Indians to take captives for adoption or torture. Nor did many colonists note the Indians' encouragement of scalping over beheading among their own people through the payment of scalp bounties.

Bibliography: Axtell, *The European and the Indian: Essays in the Ethnohistory of Colonial America* (Oxford Univ. Press, 1981).

SCHUYLER, PHILIP JOHN (1733-1804) A military and political leader, born in Albany and educated in New Rochelle, New York, Schuyler gained prominence in New York society early in life. His first military experience came with his participation in William Johnson's 1755 expedition against Crown Point; for the rest of his life he maintained an interest in military logistics and provisioning. In 1768 he was elected to the New York colonial assembly and was a delegate to the Second Continental Congress in 1775.

With the outbreak of the Revolution, Schuyler was appointed a major general by George Washington and placed in command of the Northern Department. In that position he organized the defense of New York's northern boundaries and participated in the American invasion of Canada in 1775-76. After the fall of Fort Ticonderoga in 1777, Schuyler was replaced in the Northern Department by General Horatio Gates. He nevertheless remained a valued adviser to Washington on economic and organizational affairs. In 1781 he was elected to the New York state senate and was a strong supporter of the position of his son-in-law Alexander Hamilton at the 1787 Constitutional Convention. Along with Rufus King, Schuyler was elected to the U.S. Senate from New York in 1788, serving 1789-91 and, again elected, 1797-98.

SCIENCE Although the English colonies produced relatively few contributions to theoretical science, many leading figures, men of education and training, worked within the tradition of enlightenment science, offering particularly important observational data. During the 1650s and 1660s, Bostonian John Winthrop, a member of the Royal Society of London, made the first systematic astronomical observations in the colonies. Another Bostonian, Thomas Brattle, published his advanced astronomical observations in his *Almanack* (1678), a contribution later praised by Sir Isaac Newton. In natural history, John Banister published the first systematic observations in his *Catalogus Plantarum in Virginia Observatarum* (1693) and Puritan scholar and minister Cotton Mather contributed 13 letters on natural history to the Royal Society of London's *Philosophical Transactions* (1712). Mather possessed one of the most accomplished scientific minds in the colonies; he was one of the first to accept inoculation against smallpox, wrote the first account of the hybridization of corn and squash, and in his *Christian Philosopher* (1721) offered the first lengthy American explanation of Newtonian physics. James Logan of Philadelphia had first introduced Newton's *Principia* into the colonies in 1708.

Franklin and His Contemporaries. Philadelphia in the 18th century was the center of scientific curiosity and boasted some of America's most notable men of science. Logan's friend and associate, John Bartram, in 1728 established the first botanical garden at Philadelphia and traveled widely through the colonies collecting specimens of rare plants, often with his son, William. William Bartram's 1751 list of American species of birds was the most complete up to that time. David Rittenhouse, clock- and instrument-maker, built the first orrery (planetarium) and the first telescope in the colonies and made notable astronomical observations during the 1760s and 1770s. It was Benjamin Franklin, though, who was perhaps the most remarkable product of this environment. He began his experiments in electricity in 1747, and his *Experiments and Observations on Electricity* (1751) was published in 11 foreign editions before 1776. His contributions represented the highwater mark of American science in the colonial period.

But notable work was being done elsewhere as well. In New York, Cadwallader Colden studied and wrote about the local flora in the 1740s and published his *Principles of Action in Matter* (1745-51), propounding an original theory of gravitation. In Boston, John Winthrop IV, as professor of mathematics and natural philosophy at Harvard, was the first in the colonies to lecture on electricity and to teach a course in Newtonian calculus. In the 1740s and 1750s he published papers on sunspots, lunar eclipses, comets, and earthquakes. In Connecticut, Yale-trained Jared Eliot published in 1760 the first colonial work on scientific agriculture. His associate, Yale president Ezra Stiles, himself a noted scientific observer, expressed the scientific mood when he advocated in 1761, "the classing and generalizing of experiments or facts, and pursuing their obvious inductions to certain general Laws; with which we may be prepared for useful and interesting applications."

Franklin helped to organize the first scientific society, the American Philosophical Society, in 1743 and served as its president from 1769 to 1790. In 1780, John Adams was a principal organizer of the Boston-based American Academy of Arts and Sciences. Societies for the development of scientific agriculture were organized in 1781 in New Jersey and in 1785 in Philadelphia and South Carolina.

See also American Philosophical Society; Banister, John; Bartram, John and William; Colden, Cadwallader; Franklin, Benjamin; Logan, James; Rittenhouse, David.

Bibliography: Hornberger, Theodore, *Scientific Thought in the American College, 1638-1800* (1945; reprint Hippocrene, 1968).

John Mack Faragher
Mount Holyoke College

SCOTCH-IRISH IMMIGRANTS "Scotch-Irish" is an Americanism that by 1700 was used to refer to the immigrant descendants of the Scottish Presbyterians who had settled the British colony of Ulster, in northern Ireland, during the 17th century. There they were burdened by excessive tithes, high rents, short leases, and insecure tenure under the rule of English landlords. Attracted by the promise of abundant land and indenture contracts that paid their passage, large-scale Scotch-Irish emigration to North America began in 1717 and continued for the next 60 years, averaging 3,000 to 4,000

persons per year, but rising to as many as 10,000 annually in the early 1770s. During the colonial period as a whole, an estimated 250,000 Scotch-Irish settled in the colonies.

Although the precise proportion of Scotch-Irish who came to America as indentured servants is unknown, one authority suggested in 1728 that 9 of 10 emigrants were unable to pay their fares and were thus compelled into servitude. Few servants were needed in New England, with its small freehold farms, or in the South, where African slaves were replacing white field hands, but there was considerable demand for their labor in the Middle Colonies. In addition, established commercial networks from Ulster led to Philadelphia, New Castle, and Wilmington, where most of the Scotch-Irish disembarked.

Clustering in distinctive settlements, unified by their Presbyterianism, the Scotch-Irish were soon pushing westward up the Delaware and Susquehanna rivers into the rich lands of the Cumberland Valley. After 1730 others moved south into western Maryland and down the Shenandoah Valley of Virginia. Significant numbers also settled the backcountry of the Carolinas. Many colonial officials believed that because of their legacy of frontier fighting in Ireland, these settlers were uniquely qualified as a barrier to French and Indian attack, and the Scotch-Irish played a large and active part in frontier violence, especially during the French and Indian War.

Most historical attention has focused on the colonial phase of Scotch-Irish immigration, so much so that the history of their continuing settlement in the United States after 1783 has been largely neglected. It should be noted, however, that from 1814 to 1845 about 500,000 Irish Protestant immigrants entered the country. But the historical concentration on the Scotch-Irish experience during the colonial period is understandable since, after the English and the Africans, the Scotch-Irish were the largest immigrant group before the Revolution.

See also Immigration.

Bibliography: Dunaway, Wayland F., *The Scotch-Irish of Colonial Pennsylvania* (1944; reprint Genealogical Pub., 1985); Leyburn, James G., *The Scotch-Irish: A Social History* (Univ. of North Carolina Press, 1962).

John Mack Faragher
Mount Holyoke College

SEABURY, SAMUEL (1729-96) A religious leader and first bishop of the Episcopal Church in America, Seabury was born in Groton, Connecticut, and educated at Yale College. After his graduation in 1748, he studied medicine at the University of Edinburgh (1752-53) and was ordained a minister in the Anglican Church in 1754. Seabury was subsequently dispatched by the Society for the Propagation of the Gospel to take up a religious post in the colony of New Jersey. In that position he became an eloquent spokesman for the Anglican Church in America. He later led congregations on Long Island and Westchester County, New York, where he combined his pastoral duties with a medical practice. In 1767 he organized a convention of the New York Anglican clergy to campaign for the appointment of an American bishop.

With the outbreak of the Revolution, his Loyalist political sympathies resulted in a brief imprisonment in New Haven in 1775, after which he fled with his family to British-held New York during the war. Seabury joined the British forces as a chaplain to the king's American Regiment. In 1783 he received the long-sought ordination as the first Episcopal bishop in America, ministering from New London over the bishopric of Connecticut and Rhode Island until his death in office at age 68.

SEARLE, JAMES (1733-97) A merchant and political leader, Searle was born in New York City and began his career in Madeira as an agent of John Searle & Co. In 1762 he became the company's agent in Philadelphia, and despite his commercial interests, he became active in the American resistance to British taxation and supported the idea of an American trade boycott. In 1775 he was appointed a lieutenant colonel in the Pennsylvania militia and in 1778 served in the Second Continental Congress. Accepting a diplomatic assignment for Pennsylvania in 1780, Searle visited Paris and Amsterdam in an unsuccessful attempt to raise funds. He devoted his later years to private business activity.

SEARS, ISAAC (1730-86) A Revolutionary War leader, born in West Brewster, Massachusetts, Sears first gained fame as a privateer during the French and Indian War. During the agitation against the Stamp Act (1765), he was a leader of the Sons of Liberty and chairman of the New York committee of correspondence. In 1775 he directed the seizure of British arms and the banishment of Loyalists from New York City; his radicalism was condemned officially but hailed publicly. From 1777 to 1783, Sears, operating from Boston, coordinated the activity of coastal privateers. After the war he served in the New York state assembly. Engaged in overseas trade, he died of fever in Canton, China, while on a private business venture.

SEGRESSER, FELIPE (1698-1762) Born in Switzerland, Segresser entered the Jesuit order in 1708. He arrived in Mexico in 1730 and was sent to the northern frontier. At the mission of San Javier del Bac outside Tucson he followed in the tradition of Father Eusebio Kino and like him made several exploring journeys through southern Arizona and northern Sonora, corresponding with fellow Jesuits such as Ignacio Keller at Suamca in Sonora until his death in 1762.

See also Keller, Ignacio; Kino, Eusebio.

SELF-SUFFICIENT AND MARKET FARMING "W e live here very plentifully without money," one Virginian wrote blissfully toward the end of the 17th century; yet William Fitzhugh was a capitalist farmer and merchant, deeply involved in the international market economy. Some historians have sketched the colonial farmer as an entrepreneurial type, competitive, profit-conscious, driven by the lust for accumulation. Others have described him as community-oriented rather than individualistic, motivated primarily by the goal of family security.

The English colonies developed as a part of the general expansion of the Atlantic economy, and it is clear that the production of exportable commodities was, from the beginning, a primary goal of British colonial policy. Americans operated in an environment where prices were attached to their labor and goods, and usually these prices had been affected by regional, continental, and international markets. In this context, few colonial farmers could be unaware of the fluctuating prices for essential farm commodities, for land, and for labor. Moreover, every farmer had to introduce a portion of his annual produce into the market in order to purchase essential goods such as salt, gunpowder, and lead as well as cash for the payment of taxes. In the backcountry of the South, small farmers usually worked a tobacco patch in order to raise a little cash; by the end of the colonial period, it had become common for such small farmers to purchase a slave or two to maximize their labor resources. Even in their most primitive stage of development, it is estimated that Shenandoah Valley farmers sent 10 percent of their goods to market as "surplus."

On the other hand, compared to fully commercialized farmers who commit the whole of their produce to market, this is a miniscule proportion; even in the highly commercialized Middle Colonies during the mid-18th century, the surplus exported to foreign markets constituted only 15 to 20 percent of total production. In itself the word "surplus," that which remained after the provision of household subsistence, suggests that market sales were a secondary rather than a primary consideration of farmers. Moreover, as Fitzhugh suggested, rural communities were commonly bereft of hard currency, and local economies operated mostly on principles of barter and face-to-face exchange. Colonial farmers' account books, the record of such exchanges, routinely listed current market prices after the entrance of credits or debits, but farmers made little attempt to balance their books at regular intervals and charged no interest, behavior apparently governed very little by commercial calculation.

Subsistence Requirements. The provision of subsistence demanded a bewildering array of skills from family members, especially from women, as well as a complete ensemble of productive means. Studies of Massachusetts in the 1770s suggest that over half the farms of the commonwealth were lacking in the tools and resources necessary for self-sufficiency; only half owned spinning wheels, for example, and less than one in ten owned looms. Another study of Virginia showed that in the mid-17th century, only one percent of estate inventories listed spinning wheels. By the 1770s, however, when the colony was generally much wealthier, the percentage had risen to 71 percent, and indeed, throughout the colonies, the ownership of such implements of self-sufficiency was highly correlated with wealth. The point would seem to be that contrary to popular images, it was the richest planters and farmers who were the most self-sufficient.

Most poor farmers, then, simply could not have been self-sufficient. In practice, it was the interdependence of farmers in the local community that permitted the viability of poor households, who sent their members to work for more well-to-do neighbors in exchange for the use of tools, land, or goods. This local exchange system did not constitute a market economy in the full sense, for price was not sovereign, and the maximization of profit was less important than the meeting of household needs and the maintenance of established social relationships. Sharp distinctions between self-sufficient and commercial agriculture can not be sustained in an agrarian economy in which production for home consumption and production for sale or exchange were complementary, not mutually exclusive, objectives.

See also Agriculture; Household Industries.

John Mack Faragher
Mount Holyoke College

SEMINOLE INDIANS In the late 17th century the Timucua and Apalachee Indians of northern Florida, who had been thoroughly missionized by the Spanish, came under the sustained attack of the Lower Creek Indians, who were encouraged by the English in Carolina who wanted to destroy their Spanish competitors. By 1705 the area had become so depopulated that it began to be resettled by the Creek, their numbers gradually augmented by remnants of indigenous Floridians, of the Hitchiti, and by refugees from the Yamasee War, in addition to large numbers of fugitive slaves from the expanding English rice and indigo plantations. The Spanish authorities encouraged such emigration in order to repopulate their frontier as a buffer against the English.

Over the next 50 years this new grouping expanded and overran the entire Florida peninsula, by the end of the 18th century numbering some 20 towns totalling perhaps 5,000 persons. The first references to them as the Seminole dated from the 1760s, the name probably deriving from the Spanish *cimarron* transformed into the Creek *simanoli*. From the 1810s until the 1840s the Seminole furiously resisted American expansion into Florida. By this time the people were so thoroughly intermixed with Afro-Americans that President Jackson argued it was not an Indian war but a "servile insurrection." Most were removed to Oklahoma in the 1840s, but a large remnant remained in central and south Florida.

Bibliography: Wright, J. Leitch, Jr., *Creeks and Seminoles: Destruction and Regeneration of the Muscogulge People* (Univ. of Nebraska, 1986).

SERRA, JUNÍPERO (1713-84) Serra, a Majorcan, entered the Franciscan order in 1730. In 1750, already established as a brilliant scholar and orator, he arrived in New Spain and was assigned to the missions of Sierra Gorda, northeast of Queretaro. Recalled in 1759, he was due to be sent to the San Saba missions in Texas, but the plan was never implemented. From 1759 to 1766, Serra stayed in Mexico City as a preacher and confessor, but in 1767 the Jesuits were banished from the Spanish empire, and Serra was assigned as *presidente* of the missions in Baja California.

In 1769, Serra and five other Franciscans accompanied the Portolá expedition north into Alta California, the Dominicans having been given responsibility for the Baja California missions. On July 16, 1769, the mission of San Diego was founded, the first of 21 on the California coast. For the next 15 years Serra worked indefatigably to found and support the Franciscan establishments, leaving California only for a short trip to Mexico in 1773. By the time of his death more than 6,000 baptisms had been recorded, 9 more missions had been founded, and the missions owned more than 30,000 head of stock. He died at San Carlos Mission, near Monterey.

See also Portolá, Gaspar de.

SEVIER, JOHN (1745-1815) Frontiersman, land speculator, and early leader of Tennessee, Sevier was born in Virginia and moved west in 1773. He was chosen as one of the commissioners of the Watauga Association and was a leader in the western battles of the American Revolution. At first opposed to the movement to organize the State of Franklin, he soon joined and was elected governor in 1785. Over the next few years he engaged in furious and often violent battle with other factions, finally moving farther west in disgrace. As a supporter of the federal Constitution in 1787, he was rehabilitated and elected to the North Carolina senate and to the U.S. Congress (1789-91). By that time he had become a wealthy landowner and planter. He became the first governor of the state of Tennessee

(1796-1801, 1803-09), served in the state senate, and once again in the U.S. Congress (1811-15), where he was a bitter enemy of Andrew Jackson.

See also Franklin, State of; Watauga Association.

SHACKAMAXON, TREATY OF (1682-83)   Also known as the "Great Treaty," this agreement was the first between the local Indians and the Pennsylvania colonists. In 1682, William Penn met a delegation of Delaware Indians at their chief village, Shackamaxon, to establish their legal and territorial relationship. The Delaware were represented by their chief, Tammany. Few details of the treaty's specific provisions have been preserved, but it is clear that on June 23, 1683, several agreements were signed which transferred lands in southeastern Pennsylvania to the colonists. This peace conference was immortalized by Benjamin West's 1772 painting "Penn's Treaty with the Indians."

See also Tammany.

SHAKERS   Acknowledged today for their furniture, architecture, and music, the Shakers began in the 1750s in England as a charismatic religious community and achieved their greatest success in the 19th century. Following a period of visions and of persecution, Ann Lee led a small group to the Albany, New York, area in 1774. The group began to flourish in 1780 with the addition of New Light Baptists who chose to follow Ann Lee's teachings of celibacy, pacifism, and continuing revelation.

After Mother Ann's death in 1784, the group organized as the Millennial Church, or the United Society of Believers in Christ's Second Appearing. Believing Mother Ann Lee to be the occasion of God's revelation in the female, the community that developed was notable in its beliefs and practices. It was celibate, communal, egalitarian, millennial, perfectionist, separatist, and spiritualist. The Shakers were industrious and inventive, displaying an orderly and productive communal life while practicing ecstatic dancing in its ritual life. In 1820 there were about 19 communities in New England and in Kentucky and Ohio with between 100 and 500 members each. Following a dynamic revival period between 1830 and 1860, communities began to combine and close. Today, at the end of a long decline, two communities with active members remain.

See also: Lee, Mother Ann.

Bibliography: Andrews, Edward Deming, *The People Called Shakers: A Search for the Perfect Society* (Dover, 1953).

Jane F. Crosthwaite
Mount Holyoke College

SHAYS' REBELLION (1786-87)   Shays' Rebellion engulfed much of rural Massachusetts, especially the central and western counties, and posed a brief but serious threat to the stability and legitimacy of the Massachusetts government. Many farmers resented the growing pressure from merchants and state officials to pay their debts and taxes in hard currency, which was extremely scarce in the aftermath of the Revolutionary War. They especially feared the prospect of imprisonment for debt or the confiscation and sale of their property. In the summer of 1786 representatives from dozens of agrarian villages met in county conventions and petitioned the state government for relief. When the government failed to make an adequate response to their appeals, the farmers resorted to armed protest. In the first stages of the insurrection, mobs of so-called Regulators closed the local courts and prevented creditors and county officials from carrying out further legal proceedings. Under the alleged leadership of Captain Daniel Shays, a Revolutionary War veteran who disclaimed sole responsibility for the rebellion, the Regulators continued to petition the government for relief even as they organized themselves militarily. The government refused to yield to their appeals but offered pardon to all rebels who would take an oath of allegiance. The government also organized a large militia force—financed largely by contributions from merchants and other members of the Massachusetts elite—to crush the rebellion. The critical conflict took place in January 1787, when over a thousand Shaysites attempted to capture the federal arsenal at Springfield, Massachusetts. Militia troops guarding the arsenal fired cannon and dispersed the rebels. Several weeks later, the militia routed the remnants of the insurgent force at Petersham, Massachusetts, and effectively ended the insurrection. Shays and some of the other leaders fled into Vermont or New York, but most of the rebels eventually signed the oath of allegiance and returned to their farms. Although short-lived and unsuccessful, Shays' Rebellion did have a significant political effect. In the spring of 1787 the state's voters elected a governor, John Hancock, and legislators who were more sympathetic to the plight of the western farmers, and the new government enacted laws that offered a measure of economic and legal relief. On the national level, Shays' Rebellion provided a vivid example of the internal unrest that still plagued the individual states and thus added to the growing sentiment for establishing a stronger national government under the U.S. Constitution. Still, in 1788, when Massachusetts held its ratifying convention, representatives from many of the former rebel communities contributed greatly to the state's sizeable (and almost successful) Antifederalist opposition.

Bibliography: Szatmary, David P., *Shays' Rebellion: The Making of an Agrarian Insurrection* (Univ. of Massachusetts Press, 1980); Taylor, Robert J., *Western Massachusetts in the Revolution* (Brown Univ. Press, 1954).

Gregory H. Nobles
Georgia Institute of Technology

SHELBURNE, WILLIAM PETTY, LORD   (1737-1805)   A British statesman and prime minister, born in Dublin, Petty was educated at Oxford University and served as an officer in Germany during the Seven Years War. In 1760 he succeeded his father as a member of the House of Commons. In 1761, after the death of his father, he rose to the peerage and became a member of the House of Lords. He subsequently filled various cabinet posts concerned with colonial affairs, among them privy councillor and first lord of trade. In 1782-83, he served as prime minister and supported the hardline war policy toward the American colonies of King George III. In 1784 he became the Marquis of Landsdowne and retired from public life.

SHELBY, ISAAC (1750-1826)   A military leader and politician, Shelby was born in Washington County, Maryland, and raised on the Virginia frontier. In 1773 he moved with his family to southwestern Virginia (an area later to become Tennessee) and gained distinction as a militia lieutenant in the Battle of Point Pleasant against the Shawnee (1774). In 1775-76 he directed the survey of lands in Kentucky and Tennessee and led a company of Virginia Minutemen. After serving as commissary for military supplies in Virginia in 1777, he led forces in the Carolinas (1780-81), especially at King's Mountain (1780). After the war he settled in Kentucky, was a leader in the movement for statehood, served as the state's first governor (1792-96), and returned as governor (1812-16) in the War of 1812, during which he also held a military command.

SHELEKHOV, GREGOR IVANOVICH   (1747-95)   Founder of Russian America, Shelekhov in 1775 helped organize a fur company that would exploit the Asian and American coasts of the northern Pacific. Leaving Okhotsk, Siberia, in 1783, he sailed to Bering Island in the Aleutians and in 1784 founded a settlement at Kodiak. During the next two years he explored the coast of the Gulf of Alaska, establishing other Russian settlements before leaving for Siberia in 1786. Shelekhov was ruthless in dealing with his men as well as with the indigenous inhabitants of the coast. Although his company failed to gain the government monopoly he sought, after his death it became the nucleus of the Russian-America Company, founded in 1798.

See also Alaska, Russia in.

SHERMAN, ROGER (1721-93)   A legislator and jurist, born in Newton, Massachusetts, Sherman settled in New Milford, Connecticut, in 1743 and served as the official surveyor of New Haven County from 1745 to 1758. During that time he acquired considerable property and held various public offices. After years of private study he

was admitted to the Connecticut bar in 1754 and from 1755 to 1761 served in the provincial assembly. In 1760, Sherman moved to New Haven, where he became a patron of Yale College and the city's representative in the Connecticut assembly. He also served as judge of the Connecticut Superior Court (1766-67. 1773-88).

A strong supporter of American independence, Sherman was chairman of the Connecticut Committee of Correspondence, a member of the First and Second Continental Congresses (1774-81, 1783, 1784), and one of the drafters and signers of the Declaration of Independence. He subsequently helped to write the Articles of Confederation, which he signed. In 1783 he supervised a revision of the Connecticut statutes. His most important legislative achievement came during the Constitutional Convention of 1787, when he introduced the Connecticut Compromise, providing for a dual system of representation in the federal legislative branch. He also signed the Constitution. Sherman was a member of the U.S. House of Representatives (1789-91) and served in the Senate from 1791 until his death.

Roger Sherman signed the Declaration of Independence, the Articles of Confederation, and the Constitution. *(Library of Congress)*

SHIKELLAMY (died 1748)   An Oneida chief, Shikellamy, also known as Ongwateronhiathe, "He Who Lightens the Sky for Us," was born to Cayuga parents but adopted by the Oneida at an early age, spending his early adult years in the upper Schuylkill River Valley. In 1727 he was dispatched by the Oneida nation to the Susquehanna Valley to serve as an intermediary with the Pennsylvania colonists and in that position concluded several treaties, among them a 1736 agreement for compensation for expropriated land. Shikellamy also maintained close connections with the Moravian missionaries in the Susquehanna Valley and encouraged their establishment of a forge at the Oneida village of Shamokin.

SHIPBUILDING Establishing a shipbuilding industry was an early concern in the colonies. Massachusetts and Connecticut both appointed special inspectors to guarantee the quality of vessels built in their yards and encouraged the immigration of master shipwrights who established the trade. The requirement in the Navigation Act of 1660 that trade be confined to British- or colonial-built vessels encouraged the growth of the industry, as did the bounties offered by colonies from South Carolina to Massachusetts. Domestic demand for fishing and coastal vessels was supplemented by European buyers, attracted by the low cost of materials and the favorable rates of exchange. With the proceeds from their cargoes, English merchants contracted to build ships in America, loaded them with lumber, and sailed them to southern Europe or England, where they and their cargoes were sold. Boston quickly became the center of the industry, although Philadelphia came to rival it in the 18th century. In the decade before the Revolution, Britain's North American colonies produced a capacity of over 25,000 tons annually, and by 1760 a third of the total British tonnage was colonial-built.

During the Revolution the decline in foreign trade crippled the industry and its subsidiary trades of carpentry, ropemaking, coopering, and dock work. The revival of trade during the 1790s, however, inaugurated the golden age of American shipbuilding.

See also Navigation Acts.

SHIPPEN, WILLIAM (1736-1808) A physician, academician, and patriot, Shippen came by his broad array of talents in large part as the result of his father's careful parenting. His father was not only a prominent and much respected physician in Philadelphia but also a member of the Continental Congress. In 1754 William graduated from the College of New Jersey (later Princeton) and then studied medicine with his father in Philadelphia and abroad. In 1761 he received his medical degree from the University of Edinburgh in Scotland.

On returning to Philadelphia the next year, he pioneered new approaches to the teaching of what today would be called obstetrics and gynecology. His techniques included not only the use of paintings and sculpted castings but, even more important, the dissection of human bodies. Dissection then was still taboo, and Shippen's dissecting rooms were mobbed by angry protesters. Nonetheless, his classes were immensely popular and led to his giving courses on midwifery both to male medical students and to women who planned to be midwives.

During the Revolutionary War, Shippen plunged into the emerging field of military medicine. He rapidly progressed from the substantial position of chief physician and director of the hospital in the Continental Army in New Jersey to chief physician and director general of all the Continental Army hospitals. Shippen also had the satisfaction of having Congress adopt his plan for the reorganization of the army medical department. Not all was instant success. At one point Shippen had to endure a court martial on charges of financial irregularity. Acquitted, he remained chief physician until his voluntary reesignation in 1781.

Shippen also played a prominent role as a founder and then president of the College of Physicians of Philadelphia. In 1791 he was appointed professor of anatomy, surgery, and midwifery at the University of Pennsylvania.

SHIPPING In the 17th century English merchant traders handled most of the export of agricultural produce from the colonies; from 1670 to 1730 the net return on British capital invested in colonial shipping provided a lucrative annual net return of between 5 and 10 percent. In the Southern colonies British control over exports continued into the 18th century. In the north, however, the development of coastal trading as well as the Atlantic fisheries gradually brought colonial merchants into the industry. By 1700, Boston merchants controlled some 40 percent of the carrying capacity of all colonial-owned shipping.

At that time, by contrast, New York and Philadelphia were relatively small ports. In the 1710s the total tonnage of ships clearing Boston was twice that of the other two ports combined. But with the great expansion of their agrarian hinterlands in the second quarter of the 18th century, these ports gradually overtook Boston; in the 1770s Boston's population stood at 16,000, about what it had been for the previous 30 years, while New York had grown to 22,000 and Philadelphia to 25,000, making Philadelphia the largest port in the colonies. These cities also developed a local merchant class that began to participate in the Atlantic trade as well. Whether in Boston or Philadelphia, these merchant traders owned both the ships and the cargo and conducted most of their business on barter or through the medium of bills of exchange. The Revolutionary War seriously disrupted American shipping, which did not recover until the revival of Atlantic trade in the 1790s.

SKANIANDARIIO (c.1735-1815) An important Seneca religious leader, whose name means "Handsome Lake," Skaniandariio was born in New York's Genesse Valley, half-brother of Chief Cornplanter. Under the influence of European traders, he spent his early adult years plagued by drunkenness and rebelliousness but later in life began to preach the traditional values of sobriety, chastity, and thrift among his people. In 1796, during a sudden illness, he was reportedly visited by supernatural messengers from the Artificer of Life who provided him with a divinely-inspired code of conduct. This code formed the basis of a new religion that spread quickly throughout the Iroquois confederacy.

SKENANDOA (c.1706-1816) An Oneida chief whose name was derived from the Iroquois *skennon'do*, "deer," he suffered from a drinking problem in his early adult years but in 1755 was rehabilitated and converted to Christianity by the Reverend Samuel Kirkland. Although Skenandoa was an ally of the British during the French and Indian War, he favored the colonials during the Revolution and, on the urging of Kirkland, prevented the Oneida and Tuscarora from forming an alliance with the British. He was one of the authors of the Oneida Declaration of Neutrality in May 1775 and personally ensured the safety of the settlers at German Flats, New York, throughout the war.

SLAVE CODES Slavery in British North America had been in existence, informally and on a small scale, several decades before it became defined by law. Slave codes developed gradually over the latter part of the 17th century, the result of the growing significance of slavery and the increase in the black population.

The first 20 Africans—or perhaps West Indians—arrived at Jamestown in 1619. Blacks slowly trickled into the Chesapeake region over the next half century, and their status varied. After 1640, some clearly were being held in hereditary slavery. But before midcentury, blacks could also be found laboring as indentured servants. Others lived as free men and women, having been either emancipated by their masters or born of unions between white women and black men. Some had managed to purchase themselves.

Growth of Slave Codes. The development of the slave codes in the Chesapeake reflected three general stages. Prior to 1640, slavery was not well-defined. Between 1640 and 1660, as the Plantation System developed and increasing numbers of blacks and their offspring became enslaved, a legal framework emerged. Laws closed off several loopholes to freedom. Children followed the status of the mother, which prevented claiming freedom by dint of white paternity. Conversion to Christianity was no

longer a lawful rationale for manumission, and slaves could not carry guns, possess liquor, or legally own property. The first clear indication of slavery occurred in 1640, when the Virginia General Court sentenced two runaway white indentured servants to a year's extra service, while remanding their black companion to lifetime slavery. Similar incidents, along with the increasing price of black laborers, testified to the growing importance of slavery and slave control.

After 1660 slavery and the slave code developed rapidly. Miscegenation and interracial marriage were outlawed, and in 1669 it was ruled that a master who killed a rebellious slave could not be held guilty of a felony. In 1705 Virginia legislators gathered together the laws enacted over the past six decades into a harsh slave code, on which many others were later modeled.

Bibliography: Jordan, Winthrop D., *White Over Black: American Attitudes Toward the Negro, 1550-1812* (Univ. of North Carolina Press, 1968).

Lynda J. Morgan
Mount Holyoke College

SLAVE RESISTANCE Historically, bondsmen everywhere, whether serfs in Russia or black slaves in North America, resisted their debasement in various ways, ranging from large-scale armed rebellion to what has been called silent sabotage. Resistance included such individual acts as running away, killing an overseer with an axe or poisoning a master, and feigning illness or being maddeningly literal-minded. Individuals or small groups of slaves committed arson. One of the earliest acts of slave arson in North America occurred late in 1526 at the ill-fated settlement established by Lucas Vásquez de Ayllón near the Peedee River in what is now South Carolina. Outright conspiracies and revolts usually involved both greater numbers of slaves and higher risks of discovery. There is also some evidence, particularly from South Carolina, that slaves recently arrived from Africa were among those most likely to rebel and that conspicuous unrest frequently coincided with upsurges in the importation of Africans. African-born slaves dominated both the New York revolt of 1712 and the Stono Rebellion of 1739 (where slaves from Congo and Angola were preponderant).

Despite Herbert Aptheker's pioneering research on American slave revolts, only during the last two decades have American historians intensified their interest in localized outbreaks of slave resistance during the 18th century. Two of the most substantial colonial slave conspiracies occurred in New York City in 1712 and 1741. In 1712 a group of 25 to 30 slaves set fire to a building and killed close to a dozen white people before being captured by local soldiers. In the 1741 conspiracy, known as the Negro Plot, slaves were believed to be conspiring to torch the city and massacre the whites. The upshot was mass arrests, a trial, the deportation of 70 blacks to the West Indies, and the execution of some 30 blacks. Some historians are still uncertain whether the 1741 plot was more substantial in the panic-stricken minds of whites than in the minds of the slave conspirators.

South Carolina and Georgia.   In 1739, when South Carolina whites were grappling with both hostile Indians and resourceful black maroons, the Stono Rebellion involved nearly 100 slaves who killed 30 whites before being overtaken and routed (with more than 40 deaths) by a crew of armed planters. Georgia's slaves, on the other hand, never engaged in organized resistance on the scale of Stono but ran away in substantial numbers between 1763 and 1775. One of the most serious outbreaks of slave violence in the Georgia lowcountry happened in St. Andrew Parish in 1774 when 12 slaves, 11 of whom were "New Negroes" (recently shipped directly from Africa), killed 4 whites before being captured and having their 2 "ringleaders" burned alive.

General Characteristics.   Organized rebellion, while less common than other forms of resistance, was the type most feared by whites. Running away was probably the most common. Although male slaves were preponderant among advertised runaways (as they were among incoming slave cargoes), slaves of both sexes, including some pregnant and nursing mothers, ran away to join family members and friends, to augment bands of maroons, to seek refuge among the Indians, or to head to some city like Baltimore or Savannah where they might blend into substantial free black populations. During the Revolutionary War, the number of fugitive slaves expanded even more, occasionally reaching the proportions of mass flight.

See also Negro Plot of 1741; Slavery; Stono Rebellion.

Bibliography: Aptheker, Herbert, *American Negro Slave Revolts* (Columbia Univ. Press, 1943); Davis, Thomas J., *A Rumor of Revolt: The "Great Negro Plot" in Colonial New York* (Free Press, 1985); Genovese, Eugene D., *From Rebellion to Revolution: Afro-American Slave Revolts in the Making of the New World* (Louisiana State Univ. Press, 1979); Mullin, Gerald, *Flight and Rebellion: Slave Resistance in Eighteenth-Century Virginia* (Oxford Univ. Press, 1972); and Wood, Peter H., *Black Majority: Negroes in South Carolina from 1670 through the Stono Rebellion* (Knopf, 1974).

Robert L. Hall
Northeastern University

SLAVERY   Slavery has appeared in a multiplicity of social, political, and economic contexts since antiquity, and consequently it has varied enormously in character.

Slavery in 17th-century British North America evolved haltingly within the wider hemispheric context of the Plantation System, also called the South Atlantic System. Despite great diversity, slavery generally provided a plantation labor force for the production of tobacco, naval stores, indigo, and rice. Slavery knew no regional boundaries prior to the American Revolution, but it was always more prevalent in the South, where by 1789 the two most developed systems were located. Although seriously challenged by antislavery advocates during the Revolutionary period, slavery had solidified into an established class relationship manipulated by race that proved impossible to uproot. Significantly, Africans and Afro-Americans produced distinct autonomous cultures by 1789 that represented important techniques of survival and resistance against the repressions of slavery.

The vast majority of blacks in colonial America were slaves living in the Southern colonies. Most lived in Virginia, oldest and largest of the colonies, where they numbered 300,000 in 1790. Virginia and Maryland together made up the rich Tobacco Coast and were the most economically important of all the colonies to the British Crown. Most Virginia slaves worked on tobacco plantations, most of them small but some quite large. In South Carolina, the total number of slaves was smaller than in Virginia, but because blacks constituted a majority after 1708 they had a heavier impact on society. Most of them worked on large rice plantations along the coast and lived together in much larger numbers.

Chesapeake Region.   Slavery first developed in the Chesapeake region over the course of the 17th century. In this tobacco-growing area, the abundance of land, a shortage of labor, and high mortality rates were key factors influencing slavery's adoption. The first European settlers, adventurous and greedy, patented large tracts of the best land along the rivers and experimented with a variety of labor systems. Attempts to enslave Indians failed, and although some black slaves were present, the use of indentured servitude, predominantly white, prevailed. Indentured servants contracted with wealthy landowners to work on tobacco plantations from four to seven years in return for their contracts or died soon after. Thus, temporary servants who labored for short periods of time were cheaper than hereditary bondsmen bought at higher prices but who also died quickly. High mortality also limited the numbers of freemen in search of land, thus promoting concentrations of land and power among a few great men.

After 1640 mortality declined, and indentured servitude posed problems for large landowners. As life expectancy increased, slaves became cheaper than servants, since they and their increase were owned for their lifetimes. Moreover, servant immigration subsided even while growing numbers of freemen swelled Chesapeake society, seeking land on which to make their own tobacco fortunes. Forced to settle on the poorer frontiers, heavily taxed, involved in frequent Indian conflicts, and dependent upon great planters for a market, their resentments festered. In 1676 such disputes erupted in Bacon's Rebellion, a reflection of escalating class and racial antipathies, demographic changes, and settlement patterns. The shift to black slave labor around this time helped satisfy planters' needs for social control and a dependent labor force.

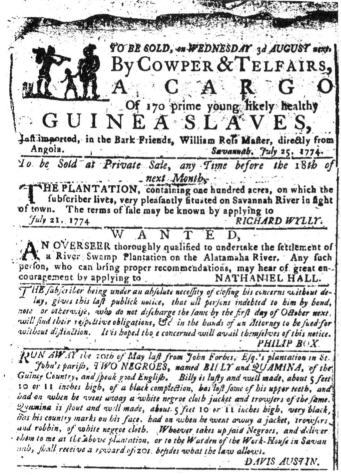

The importation and sale of blacks captured in Africa spurred the growth of slavery in the American colonies. (Library of Congress)

Lowcountry Slavery. In the Carolina and Georgia lowcountry, conversion to slavery occurred at the close of the 17th century, upon discovery of the exportable staples of naval stores, rice, and indigo. Although present earlier, slavery's character changed dramatically at that juncture. Prior to the transformation, most slaves arrived from the West Indies with masters who had been squeezed out in the sugar revolution. Afterward, African slave importations accelerated rapidly. By 1708 a black majority inhabited the region; by the 1720s blacks outnumbered whites two to one. Their presence reshaped lowcountry society by greatly altering demographic patterns, permeating the region with African cultural traits, and introducing a population that had become skilled in West Africa in the complexities of rice cultivation. As plantations swelled in size, more and more planters lived as seasonal absentees in urban centers such as Charleston. Under these conditions, lowcountry slaves retained more of their African cultural heritage than any other group of colonial slaves.

Status of Free Blacks. Although all slaves in colonial America were black, not all blacks were slaves. The free black caste, found in all the colonies, came into existence in a variety of ways. Some descended from early black indentured servants, like Anthony Johnson of Maryland's Eastern Shore, who lived there as a free man in 1622. Many were runaways. Some enterprising slaves persuaded their masters to let them hire out, earning money and then freedom through self-purchase. Some masters manumitted their mulatto children; some mulattoes were children of white women and therefore exempt from slavery. Emancipation for meritorious service, especially in the colonial wars, charted another road to freedom. A sizeable number were old or crippled, abandoned by their masters after lifetimes of service.

Revolutionary philosophy, in conjunction with a faltering tobacco economy, led to a spate of private manumissions. In the Revolution's aftermath, most Northern states enacted gradual emancipation laws. Natural increase among free blacks increased their numbers further. In 1790, more than 32,000 free blacks resided in the South Atlantic states. Over 27,000 lived in the Middle Atlantic and New England states. They represented about 8 percent of the total black population.

Compared to the restrictions levied against them in the 19th century, free blacks in the colonial and particularly in the Revolutionary periods enjoyed a relatively high status. They were few in numbers, and the law dealt with them ambiguously. Their right to hold property and in most cases firearms remained unobstructed. In many instances they voted and testified in court.

Restrictions gradually appeared, however, in colonies increasingly dependent upon slavery, where free blacks jeopardized slaveholder claims that slavery was a natural condition for blacks. After the 1660s in Virginia, for example, when slavery became an inextricable component of the economy, increasing strictures on free blacks likewise appeared. They were barred from officeholding, voting, testifying, militia service, and sexual relations with whites. Frequently they were heavily taxed and subjected to more severe punishments than whites. Occasionally, Northern free blacks petitioned for their freedom during the pre-Revolutionary period, and they also formed self-help and improvement societies. Generally, the status of all free blacks in 1789 was unsettled.

African Culture and Slavery.

Methods of slave control were predicated in part upon the erasure of African heritage. Slaveholders rightly feared the power of cultural unity and its potential to breed rebellion and resistance. Despite the slaveholders' efforts to subdue these processes, slaves successfully transmitted many elements of African and Afro-American culture across generations. They employed two chief institutions for this purpose: the family and religion. Additionally, through elaborate patterns of day-to-day resistance as well as outright rebellion, they indicated their desire for freedom.

Slavery disrupted families through sale or estate divisions, the acquisition of a preponderance of men, or isolation on small remote farms. African women, shocked by the rigors of Middle Passage and enslavement, typically had low fertility. Nevertheless, slaves gradually entered into families and began to reproduce successfully around the turn of the 18th century. Some masters encouraged family formation in order to enhance reproduction, and sometimes control, of the labor force. Slaves typically lived monogamously, although polygamous unions reminiscent of Africa were not unknown. In rearing their children they taught skills necessary for survival, such as how to avoid the whip, and the power of silence or deception when dealing with the master. They transmitted and reinforced awareness of family ties and the African past through distinct naming practices, songs, and folklore. If the family were broken apart, reliance either upon extended kin—aunts, uncles, and grandparents—or fictive kin, unrelated members of the slave community who assumed kinship responsibilities, was widespread. Where small farms predominated, slaves often entered "broad marriages," visiting spouses on nearby plantations at night or on weekends. On larger units, families more often lived on the same plantation.

Role of Religion.

Religious beliefs also helped sustain Afro-Americans in their struggles against slavery. Afro-Christianity embraced themes of freedom, rejected those of slavery, and fostered a sense of self-worth and self-esteem. Many slaves embraced this interpretation of Protestant Christianity despite slaveholders' opposition. Afro-Christianity also contained transmuted elements of African religions. Harvest festivals, commonplace in West Africa, occurred also in the colonies. Ring shouts, singing and dancing, and call-and-response behaviors were similar to rituals found in some areas of Africa, and analogous as well to many Protestant evangelical rites. Nevertheless, African religious practices were far less in evidence in the colonies than they were in the Caribbean and Brazil. Native-born populations and the presence of Protestantism, rather than the more malleable Catholicism, rendered the African past more distant on the British mainland.

Slave Resistance.

A spectrum of resistant behavior also characterized slave culture. Several instances of outright rebellion occurred; two of the more important included a 1712 uprising in New York City and the Stono Rebellion in South Carolina in 1739. Running away was a widespread form of resistance, and sometimes runaways founded maroon communities in remote areas. In the 18th century many runaways lived with the Seminole Indians in Spanish Florida. Huge numbers of runaways escaped to the British army during the Revolution, particularly after Virginia Governor Lord Dunmore's proclamation of freedom for all slaves who left the service of their masters in favor of serving with the British forces. Resistance could also involve poisoning, arson, shirking at work, and feigning illness. Although far less common, infanticide and self-mutilation, particularly among newly-arrived Africans, have been documented.

Slaves and Work.

All slaveholders faced the problem of labor management, since they could not expect cooperation from enslaved workers. Consequently, most plantation slaves worked either as gang laborers or as task laborers. Gang labor, the more common system, divided slaves into gangs under the supervision of drivers who kept them at a steady pace. The task system prevailed in the rice districts, in many ways an adaptation to the peculiar needs of that crop. Task slaves had specific work assignments to complete at their own pace and could quit when the task was completed. Generally, gang labor is considered more rigorous and disciplined, whereas task labor had the advantage of providing slaves with time of their own that could be spent, for example, working their own gardens and spending time with family and friends. Because the task system prevailed in a region where there was a large black majority heavily composed of Africans and their children, it is often considered to have facilitated a stronger African heritage than was true elsewhere in the colonies.

Not all slaves worked as rural plantation laborers. Skilled artisans lived both in urban areas, where often they were hired out, and on plantations. Their occupations were extremely diverse. Slave craftsmen could be found laboring as engineers, carpenters, blacksmiths, coopers, stone masons, shoemakers, mechanics, brickmakers, weavers, and caulkers. Many such workers were literate and had two or more languages at their command. Domestic servants, especially on large plantations, worked as coachmen, laundresses, cooks, butlers, housemaids, nurses, and personal servants. On smaller plantations, such skilled workers were often put to work in the fields when needed.

Historians have studied 19th-century slavery far more extensively than slavery in the colonial period. As study proceeds, it is clear that the colonial institution was multifaceted and complex and that it bequeathed an important legacy to post-Revolutionary generations. As it developed over the 17th and 18th centuries, it became an entrenched institution that resisted attempts to destroy it.

Bibliography: Boles, John B., *Black Southerners, 1619-1869* (Univ. Press of Kentucky, 1983); Hoffman, Ronald, and Berlin, Ira, eds., *Slavery and Freedom in the Age of the American Revolution* (Univ. Press of Virginia, 1983); Jordan, Winthrop D., *White Over Black: American Attitudes Toward the Negro, 1550-1812* (Univ. of North Carolina Press, 1968); Kulikoff, Allan, *Tobacco and Slaves: The Development of Southern Cultures in the Chesapeake, 1680-1800* (Univ. of North Carolina Press, 1986); Morgan, Edmund S., *American Slavery, American Freedom: The Ordeal of Colonial Virginia* (W. W. Norton & Company, 1975); Wood, Peter H., *Black Majority: Negroes in Colonial South Carolina from 1670 through the Stono Rebellion* (W. W. Norton & Company, 1974).

Lynda J. Morgan
Mount Holyoke College

SLAVE TRADE   Over 500,000 Africans were imported into what later became the United States between 1565 and 1807, when Congress finally outlawed overseas slave trade. Although most were shipped into South Carolina, Virginia, and Maryland, colonial New York, Massachusetts, Rhode Island, Pennsylvania, New Jersey, and Georgia all received black newcomers from Africa and the West Indies. By the time of the Constitutional Convention in 1787, only Georgia and South Carolina had not prohibited the transatlantic slave trade. Georgia did so in 1798.

South Carolina and Virginia.   South Carolina and Virginia were the two main receiving areas. Although dates and records do not correspond neatly, the data available makes it clear that these two colonies were well ahead of the others in slave imports. Between 1735 and 1775 some 70,435 to 74,098 slaves were imported into South Carolina in 401 cargoes (a yearly average of between 1,520 and 1,568 slaves). Over 84 percent of them were shipped directly from Africa with no seasoning (acclimation) in the West Indian Islands. About 40 percent of all African slaves reaching the British mainland colonies arrived in South Carolina, especially at Charleston's Sullivan's Island, which has been called the "Ellis Island of black Americans." According to recent estimates, 58,445 slaves were landed in Virginia between 1710 and 1769, a figure about 11 percent higher than previous totals. More than 90 percent of the 69,260 blacks imported into colonial Virginia (1670-1769) were brought directly from Africa. In 1778, after repeated efforts to control the flow of Africans, Virginia ended the legal slave trade.

Maryland.   Although persons of African descent, like the Portuguese mulatto Matthias de Sousa, arrived with Maryland's earliest European settlers in the 1630s, the expansion of its slave population began in the 1650s, and there was a sharp increase in importations during the middle 1670s. Before the 1680s, most of these slaves were purchased from Dutch merchants and had some experience in the West Indies. Like the other Southern colonies, Maryland did not develop a robust direct trade in slaves with Africa until its economy could absorb cargoes larger than 150 slaves. For Maryland that point came about 1695, and thereafter, until the trade was outlawed by the state legislature in 1783, over 90 percent of the black immigrants were imported directly from Africa. In fact, as in South Carolina and Virginia, "New Negroes" (blacks shipped

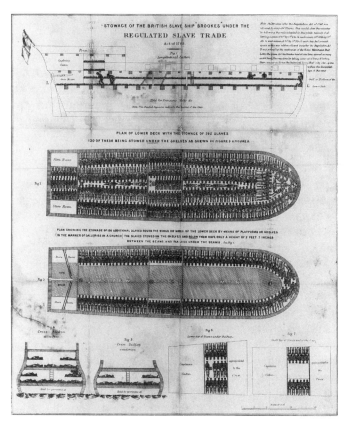

Merchants active in the slave trade tightly packed their ships with human cargo. *(Library of Congress)*

directly from Africa) were preferred over slaves seasoned in the islands, partly because of the suspicion that wily West Indian planters were palming off "rogues" and incorrigible rebels on unsuspecting mainland buyers. This clear aversion for West Indian blacks was reflected in differentially high import duties on slaves from the islands.

Personal and Cultural Aspects. Despite the numerical emphasis of most recent scholarship, occasional personalized glimpses of the trade emerge. Both the father and maternal grandfather of Benjamin Banneker, America's first black man of science, were imported into Maryland from Africa as slaves during the late 1600s and early 1700s. After being captured by hostile Africans, Olaudah Equiano (also known as Gustavus Vassa), the author of the best-known 18th-century slave narrative, was shipped from West Africa by a European trader about 1775. Equiano, a Niger Ibo, sailed from the Guinea coast to Barbados and then to Virginia within two weeks of his arrival in the Caribbean, a stay hardly long enough to qualify as seasoning. In August 1761, George Washington advertised for Jack, Neptune, and Cupid, three African-born slaves who had run for freedom. After describing their height, "country marks" (ritual scarification), and speech, Washington stated that both Neptune and Cupid "were bought from an African ship in August 1759." Runaway slave advertisements in the 18th century, as well as other observations recorded by whites with sound business reasons to attend to such details, contain numerous references to African cultural carryovers among the new arrivals: a thick African "country dialect," or a filed tooth, or a "country mark." Scholars are only beginning to explore these and other traces of Africa in colonial America, and their impact on the genesis of North American speech, agriculture, religion, music, food habits, and other folkways has not yet been fully delineated. There can be little doubt, however, that the imported Africans in 18th-century North America were cut off from the heritage of their African roots. After all, they were no longer in Africa. But by the same token it does not appear that they experienced an immediate or absolute cultural amnesia upon reaching the colonies.

See also Slavery.

Bibliography: Curtin, Philip D., *The Atlantic Slave Trade: A Census* (Univ. of Wisconsin Press, 1969); Du Bois, William Edward Burghardt, *The Suppression of the African Slave Trade* (Harvard Univ. Press, 1896); Kilson, Martin L. and Rotberg, Robert I., eds., *The African Diaspora* (Harvard Univ. Press, 1976); Wood, Peter H., *Black Majority: Negroes in South Carolina from 1670 Through the Stono Rebellion* (Knopf, 1974).

Robert L. Hall
Northeastern University

SMIBERT, JOHN (1688-1751) An American artist, he was born in Scotland, studied in England and Italy, and came to America in 1729 with George Berkeley to establish a college of science and arts in the Bermudas. They landed at Newport, Rhode Island, where Smibert painted a group portrait of the ship's passengers. In 1730, Berkeley's college not having materialized, Smibert settled in Boston and by 1731 had begun to establish a reputation as a portrait painter. In order to supplement his income, he opened an art supply, print, and sculpture shop. He continued to paint portraits and some landscapes until his eyesight failed in 1748.

SMITH, JAMES (?1719-1806) A signer of the Declaration of Independence, Smith was born in Northern Ireland and immigrated with his family to York County, Pennsylvania, in 1729. After his admission to the Pennsylvania bar in 1745, he moved to Cumberland County. An early supporter of American independence, Smith served in the provincial assembly (1774- 79), and as a member of the Pennsylvania delegation to the Second Continental Congress in 1776, he signed the Declaration of Independence. He later served as judge of the Pennsylvania high court of appeals (1780-81). He was named brigadier general of the state militia in 1782 and after the war returned to the practice of law.

SMITH, JOHN (?1580-1631) Explorer and colonizer, Smith was born in Willoughby, Lincolnshire, England. From the age of 16 he traveled in Europe, fighting in several wars. While serving with the Austrians, he was taken prisoner by the Turks and made a slave. He escaped and eventually made his way back to England (1604). Smith actively promoted a plan by the London Company to found a colony in America and sailed (1606) with the first Virginia colonists to found Jamestown, Virginia (1607). As a member of the governing council, he began to explore the region. In an episode later embroidered by legend, he was captured and sentenced to death by the Indian chief Powhatan. He escaped death when Powhatan's daughter Pocahantas supposedly intervened.

After being returned to Jamestown by the Indians (1608), Smith found that the governing council had been taken over by personal enemies, and he was sentenced to death for losing the men of his exploring party. When new settlers arrived, Smith was released and rejoined the council. In England that year he published *True Relation of such Occurances and Accidents of Noate as Hath Hapned in Virginia Since the First Planting of That Colony.* He was elected president of the colony and through strong leadership brought it through many hardships (1608-09), but after being injured in a gunpowder explosion, he returned to England (1609). He sailed to America to explore the coast of New England for the Plymouth Company in 1614 and, upon his return, wrote *A Description of New England* (1616), which included an accurate map of the region. For the rest of his life he remained in England and promoted colonization.

John Smith's vigorous leadership was a key factor in the survival of the Virginia colony in 1608-09. *(Library of Congress)*

SMITH, ROBERT (?1722-77) An architect, Smith was apparently born in Glasgow, Scotland, and settled in Philadelphia while a child. His first recorded construction was Nassau Hall for the College of New Jersey (Princeton) in 1754. He also built the president's house for the college. His masterpiece was St. Peter's Church in Philadelphia (1758). By the end of the 1750s, he was a noted Philadel-phia builder and received commissions for churches and municipal buildings, such as Zion Lutheran Church (1766), Carpenters' Hall (1768), and Walnut Hill Prison (1773). In 1768 he also became a member of the American Philosophical Society. His simple, graceful Georgian buildings are excellent examples of the period's style.

He supported American independence and was active in Philadelphia patriot organizations before the Revolutionary War. His last efforts were the design of river barriers on the Delaware River to prevent the British from reaching Philadelphia from the sea. Smith did not live to see the success of his barricades.

SMITH, WILLIAM (1727-1803) An influential educator and clergyman, Smith was born in Aberdeen, Scotland, and graduated from its university in 1747. He came to New York City in 1751, and his 1753 pamphlet on education, *A General Idea of the College of Mirania*, interested Benjamin Franklin. He joined Franklin's Academy (later the College of Philadelphia), expanded the charter in 1754, made himself provost, and wrote a new curriculum in 1756. He soon became a bitter enemy of Franklin because of his allegiance to the Penn interests and because of his 1755 pamphlet, A *Brief State of the Province of Pennsylvania*, which advocated a loyalty oath to the king, loss of voting rights to non-English-speaking Germans, and the banning of foreign-language periodicals.

Smith was a member of the Anglican Church, as a priest and deacon (1753), doctor of divinity (1763), and rector of Trinity Church in Oxford, Pennsylvania (1766-77). He wrote theological articles for a magazine he started in 1757, *The American Magazine and Monthly Chronicle of the British Colonie*s. He became a member of the American Philosophical Society in 1768. His writings include *An Historical Account of the Expedition Against the Ohio Indians* (1765); *Sermon on the Present Situation of American Affairs* (1775), opposing the Stamp Act; and a pro-British paper, written under the name of Candidus, *Plain Truth; Addressed to the Inhabitants of America* (1776). Criticized for his Loyalist sympathies, he left Pennsylvania for Maryland, where he established a school, later chartered as Washington College (1782). He subsequently returned to Pennsylvania and became active in his old school's affairs.

See also Philadelphia, College of.

SMUGGLING Smuggling was a prevalent feature of colonial trade. Parliament's attempts to control colonial commerce by constantly expanding the Navigation Acts system failed to achieve its goals. Unfortunately, it was easier to write legislation than to provide a police force to ensure compliance. Great Britain had an equally difficult problem in controlling the endemic smuggling along its own coasts.

In the 17th century the colonists discovered the necessity of smuggling, and it was more pervasive then than it would be during the 18th century. There were two main areas that attracted smugglers: the importation of European manufactured goods and the trade in sugar and its products, molasses and rum, from foreign plantations. Ready markets existed for these goods, and merchants simply wanted to meet demand as cheaply as possible and found it easy and profitable to avoid the minimal customs bureaucracy. Often they simply undermined the whole apparatus by bribing the customs agents.

The pattern of smuggling changed during the 18th century. As the industrial revolution gathered speed in England, the colonists found it cheaper to import directly from England than to continue to smuggle European goods, thus one cause of smuggling declined. The Caribbean remained a smuggler's paradise. The English sugar islands could not absorb all of the foodstuffs produced in the colonies so the Spanish, French, and Dutch colonies became important centers of the illicit trade for sugar products. The 1733 Molasses Act unsuccessfully tried to stop this trade. The colonists were unwilling to abandon these markets even during wartime when the English discovered that trading with the enemy was a way of life for the colonists. As the colonial economy matured, however, the volume of smuggled goods diminished.

During the American Revolution, when the British sought to punish Americans for their opposition to royal policy, well-known smugglers such as John Hancock were singled out for harassment. The publicity surrounding their persecution made smuggling a heroic act of resistance. It was probably never as important to the colonial economy as such legend made it out to be.

See also Navigation Acts.

Bibliography: Pares, Richard, *Yankees and Creoles: The Trade Between North America and the West Indies before the American Revolution* (Harvard Univ. Press, 1956); Tyler, John W., *Smugglers and Patriots: Boston Merchants and the Advent of the American Revolution* (Northeastern Univ. Press, 1986).

Robert C. Ritchie
University of California, San Diego

SOCIAL WELFARE   The Elizabethan poor laws, a version of which each colony adopted, supplied the framework for care of the dependent: they were the responsibility of the home community, the able-bodied had to work, and those who needed shelter would be segregated in almshouses or workhouses. Local officials scrutinized all newly arrived persons, "warning out" potential paupers and returning them to their native villages. In 1636, Boston authorities forbade residents from boarding out-of-towners without official permission and through the 18th century warned hundreds out of town each year. New York City constables sought out strangers and presented their names to the mayor; Newport, Rhode Island, officials compiled a warning-out list of "What Strangers Comes into ye Town," after 1727 subjecting any who returned to 39 lashes. Early in the 18th century, Philadelphia required strangers to post bond and printed daily warnings to them in the press.

Yet by the 18th century, from various sources—the Indian wars, foreign immigration, and, most important, the process of local economic growth itself—all the major towns had developed substantial homegrown populations of the poor and dependent. Many private charities were organized in response. In Philadelphia, for example, private Quaker associations were housing and boarding the poor from the town's beginning, and in 1767 the Friends (Quakers) opened Bettering House, widely touted as a model for the urban care of the poor. Local self-help associations such as the St. Andrews Society (founded 1749) for Scots; the Deutschen Gesellschaft von Pennsylvanien (1764) for Germans; the Friendly Sons of St. Patrick (1771) for Irish; and the Sea Captain's Club (1765), which attended to the "Relief of Poor & Distressed Masters of Ships, Their Widows & Children," all had their counterparts in other cities.

Private charity hardly relieved the problem, however. Mid-century Boston, for example, expended over 5,000 pounds annually to provide a measure of support to the poorest tenth of its population: 1,200 widows with out-relief (public relief for those not residing in poorhouses), hundreds of orphans in apprenticeship contracts, and nearly 300 men, women, and children in its almshouses and workhouses. In large measure such programs were motivated less by philanthropy than by concerns about the ill social effects of unemployment and idleness. Workhouses, common features of the colonial urban landscape, were dumping grounds not only for the poor without families to care for them but for the homeless insane, for "idle, drunken, and disorderlie persons," and frequently for criminals as well. Laboring on public projects, or bound out to private employers, workhouse inmates throughout the colonies were required to wear distinguishing patches—a large red "P" in New England and Pennsylvania, a blue "NY" in New York. Such work, argued Boston officials, prevented street orphans graduating from the "picking of Sticks to picking of Pockets" and "modest Maidens" from having to earn "their Bread at the Expense of their Innocence."

Bibliography: Bridenbaugh, Carl, *Cities in Revolt* (1955; reprint Oxford Univ. Press, 1971); Kelso, R. W., *History of Public Poor Relief in Massachusetts 1620-1920* (1922; reprint Patterson Smith, 1969); Schneider, David M., *History of*

Public Welfare in New York State, 1609-1866 (1938; reprint Patterson Smith, 1969).

John Mack Faragher
Mount Holyoke College

SOCIETY FOR THE PROPAGATION OF THE GOSPEL

Thomas Bray, one-time emissary to Maryland, upon his return to England in the 1690s diagnosed the problems of the Anglican Church in America to be chiefly an inadequate supply of, and insufficient merit in, its colonial clergy. Founded in 1701, the Society for the Propagation of the Gospel (SPG) therefore took as its chief purpose the sending of worthy clergy to England's "foreign plantations." Screening the candidates, hiring those found acceptable, paying the salaries (always criticized by the missionaries themselves as being far too low), and maintaining a steady direction of the activity in America, the SPG rescued Anglicanism from neglect and near defeat.

Although taking Christianity to the Indian and enslaved black as one of its major missions and challenges, the SPG had in the long run more impact among the English in America. With over 70 missionaries in the colonies by 1760, the way to Anglican dominance seemed assured—if only a bishop might be sent to America to give the whole operation direct and immediate guidance. Not only did the colonial Church receive no bishop, it in addition suffered a revolution that forever dashed the possibility in America of a politically powerful Anglican Church.

SOCIETY FOR PROMOTING CHRISTIAN KNOWLEDGE

Founded in London by Thomas Bray in 1699, the Society proposed to raise the education level of the colonists in general and to provide good Anglican literature to raise the religious level as well. As a publishing arm of missionary Anglicanism, the privately-supported society concerned itself with distribution and accessibility as well. Bray even envisioned a parish library in every colonial Anglican church, a vision realized only in a limited way. Where schools and colleges did not exist or could not be easily reached, the society hoped to fill what it regarded as a most dangerous void.

SONS OF LIBERTY

The Sons of Liberty were secret societies that sprang up in numerous colonial communities in reaction to Parliament's passage of the Stamp Act of 1765. They took their name from a speech against the act in the House of Commons. These colonists were outraged by what they saw as Britain's continued interference in colonial affairs and "taxation without representation."

The Sons of Liberty circulated petitions, published inflammatory anti-British tracts, tarred and feathered Loyalists, and attacked the homes and offices of British officials, including the home of the royal governor, Thomas Hutchinson. As a result of these acts of aggression, every British stamp agent in the colonies resigned his post before the Stamp Act became law. Merchants were persuaded to cancel and discontinue orders for British goods intended for sale in the colonies. These agitations continued, even after the nullification of the Stamp Act. In 1773, The Boston Sons of Liberty held their famous tea party in Boston Harbor.

Many prominent colonial citizens were active members of these societies, including Samuel Adams and Paul Revere of Massachusetts. Gathering at "Liberty Trees" or "Liberty Poles," the Sons of Liberty called for colonial self-government and an "end to British tyranny."

See also Stamp Act.

SOSA, GASPAR CASTANO DE (flourished 1590)

A Spanish official in colonial New Spain, Sosa, the lieutenant governor of Nuevo Leon, assumed control of the province after the governor was arrested by the Inquisition in 1590. Later that year Sosa was captivated by the glowing reports about New Mexico and decided to move north without official permission. He organized the population of the mining camp of Nuevo Almaden into a colonizing party and started north with almost 200 people. Ascending the Pecos River, he captured the chief pueblo on the river and then continued north, eventually reaching Taos. However, the viceroy, having heard of Sosa's insubordination, had despatched a force to arrest him. Sosa was captured and returned to Mexico City for trial. His colonists were unsuccessful without Sosa to guide them, and most made their way back to Nuevo Almaden.

SOUTH CAROLINA

The English were not the first Europeans to attempt to colonize the part of North America they would name Carolina. During the 16th century both the Spanish and the French organized expeditions aimed at erecting permanent settlements there. These efforts, by agents of Spain in 1520-21, 1525, 1526, 1561, 1564, 1566, and 1577, and by their counterparts from France in 1562, 1564, and 1577 all failed under the impact of inadequate supplies, malcontent or mutinous colonist/adventurers, or military attack by either hostile Indians or the forces of a European rival. The legacy of early European experience in the area between Virginia and Florida offered little basis for hope that a thriving colony might be established there.

Planning the English Colony. In spite of a history of failed attempts by Europeans to settle Carolina, just after the Stuart Restoration of 1660 a group of prominent Englishmen expressed interest in the area as a site for a new

English colony. These men—Virginia's Governor Sir William Berkeley; his brother John Berkeley; Sir Anthony Ashley Cooper (the future Earl of Shaftesbury); George Monck, Duke of Albemarle; Sir George Carteret; William, Earl of Craven; Edward Hyde, Earl of Clarendon; and Sir John Colleton—were sufficiently powerful that Charles II in 1663 granted them his first colonial charter, naming them Lords Proprietors over their colony of Carolina.

The idea for a Carolina colony probably originated with Colleton, a royalist who had taken refuge in Barbados and who, after the Restoration, received a knighthood and a position on the Council for Trade and Plantations, whose members included his fellow Carolina proprietors Cooper, Hyde, Carteret, and William Berkeley. The charter these men received conveyed the part of America between Virginia's southern boundary at 36°34' and the northern part of Spanish Florida at 31° from sea to sea—an area that the British Crown previously had granted in 1629 to Sir Robert Heath, who later assigned the patent to the Duke of Norfolk. Like Heath, the Duke of Norfolk had done nothing with the grant. The new proprietors, whose charter included a "Bishop of Durham" clause identical to that in Maryland's, guaranteeing them virtually unlimited authority in the province, intended to succeed where others had failed.

Almost at once the proprietors issued "A Declaration and Proposals to All That Will Plant in Carolina," promising extensive religious and political freedom, as well as land, to any who chose to settle in Carolina. At the same time, a group of Barbadians sponsored an exploratory voyage to the area and received a highly favorable report. Soon groups of colonists from both Virginia and Barbados erected settlements in the province—the Virginians around Albemarle Sound, the Barbadians at Cape Fear. But while the settlement at Albemarle Sound survived, serving as the basis for the colony of North Carolina, the Barbadian expedition failed. The proprietors had invested little in their colony, relying instead on the lure of land and liberty to attract settlers and induce them to invest their own resources. The failed Barbadian attempt demonstrated that future success would require both leadership and capital from England.

Ashley, who like Colleton had owned a plantation in Barbados, acted to meet these needs. Seeking to control the manner in which the colony's society and government developed, Ashley determined to provide the colonists with a master plan they might follow in building a new community in the open space of America. With his secretary, the philosopher John Locke, Ashley drafted the Fundamental Constitutions of Carolina (1669), a document that described an ideal society in which the interests of a landed hereditary aristocracy were neatly balanced with those of independent land-owning common planters.

Based on ideas formulated by James Harrington, Ashley and Locke's constitutions aimed at guaranteeing the independence of competing factions by strictly allocating three-fifths of the land in each county to ordinary settlers, while giving the remaining two-fifths to a hereditary nobility composed of landgraves and caciques, who might enjoy traditional feudal privileges in their "baronies." The proprietors, the nobles, and the freeholders' representatives would, according to the constitutions, sit together in an assembly, which was to respond to bills initiated by the "Grand Council," in which only the nobility was represented. This grand design never took effect in the colony, for the settlers consistently refused to adopt the Fundamental Constitutions.

While his master plan for Carolina failed to achieve realization, Ashley's efforts to energize his fellow proprietors and to create a viable settlement in America succeeded. Initially the proprietors had sought to use America to make a profit. They wanted to invest little and to rely on those already in America to migrate to their colony where, in return for land and freedom, settlers would pay rents, fees, and duties. Ashley recognized that success would require not only that colonists be recruited and transported to Carolina by the proprietors, but also those sponsoring the settlement must be prepared to support the community during its formative years. He convinced each of his fellow proprietors to invest 500 pounds to support a new colonizing expedition to Carolina and to provide an additional 200 pounds a year for the next four years to insure the colony's survival. Next, Ashley purchased three ships, the *Carolina*, the *Port Royal*, and the *Albemarle*, filled them with colonists, and in August 1669 sent them to America.

Proprietary Rule.   The expedition first headed for Barbados, where the *Albemarle* was lost in a storm. After replacing the wrecked vessel with a sloop, *The Three Brothers*, the colonists finally reached Carolina in May 1670. Perhaps influenced by the advice of friendly natives, the settlers established their community—Charles Town—not at their intended location of Port Royal but rather several miles up the Ashley River on a site they named Albemarle Point. In 1680, Charles Town, soon shortened to Charleston, was relocated to the junction of the Ashley and Cooper rivers, a place the colonists referred to as Oyster Point.

Although the settlers carried out some planting, food was scarce at the outset, and they remained for some time dependent on supplies sent out from England at the proprietors' expense and on foodstuffs provided by the natives. Nevertheless, the colony attracted settlers. In 1670 and 1671 two groups of Barbadians migrated to Carolina, and before 1672 nearly 100 New Yorkers ar-

Slave quarters at Boon Hall Plantation, North of Charleston, South Carolina. *(State of South Carolina)*

rived. These immigrants sought land on generous terms, which they received. By the end of the century nearly 5,000 persons lived in the colony.

Charleston served as the focus of the colony's political, social, and, especially, economic existence. Settlement inevitably followed the course of major waterways on which goods could be transported. Carolina planters raised cattle and hogs, grew corn, and converted felled trees into lumber—all of which they sent downriver to Charleston. Since many of the colony's early inhabitants came from Barbados, it was only natural that most ships carrying Carolina goods headed there and that slave labor, common on Barbados's sugar plantations, soon emerged as the norm in Carolina. By the first decade of the 18th century, the governor and council reported that of the 9,580 persons living in the colony, 5,500 were slaves (4,100 black, 1,400 Indian), while only 3,960 were free whites. White indentured servants, a group that had dominated Carolina society during the colony's first years, numbered only 120. By the

18th century, then, Carolinians were prosperous enough to be able to afford the costs involved in purchasing slaves (indentured servants cost a master only the amount needed to cover transportation to the colony) and also sufficiently optimistic about the future that such a long-term investment of capital seemed both safe and wise.

Simultaneous with the ascendancy of black slavery as the dominant form of labor in Carolina was the emergence of rice as the colony's principal crop. Indeed, some have speculated that African slaves should be credited with the introduction of rice into the Carolina economy, for rice cultivation was common in areas from which slaves came—East Africa and Madagascar, as well as in Spanish America and Portuguese Brazil. Introduced to Carolina as late as 1685, rice was the colony's second most important export commodity by 1690 and dominated the economy by 1705. Combined with an ever-increasing commerce in furs, deerskins, and naval stores—products that appeared as Carolinians moved into the colonial interior—rice production served as the basis for an expanding economy and stimulated the growth of Charleston as a center of American trade.

Success in peopling the wilderness and creating a flourishing economy did not mean, however, that the proprietors realized profits from their colony. By 1679 they estimated that between 17,000 and 18,000 pounds had been invested, with no return. Not until 1694 did the assembly pass a rent collection statute, which yielded only 73 pounds for the proprietors. Proprietary control deteriorated dramatically after 1715, when natives on the colony's southern border attacked the province. During the Yamasee War more than 400 settlers were killed, the Indian trade was ruined, and perhaps as much as half the cultivated land in the province was abandoned. The Indian war combined with increasing pirate activity off the Carolina coast to provoke an economic crisis. Discontent in the colony only increased when the proprietors, frustrated by their failure to collect rents on land already granted, both refused to grant additional acres and retained for themselves all the land seized from the Yamasee. In November 1719 a bloodless rebellion occurred, and the English government assumed control of Carolina's government. In 1729 the original proprietors' heirs sold their rights to the Crown for 2,500 pounds each, plus a lump sum of 5,000 pounds to cover uncollected quitrents. Over the 66 years the Carolina proprietary endured—from 1663 until 1729—the proprietors had spent about 25,000 pounds on their colony.

Royal Colony.   From 1729 to 1776 the Crown sent seven royal governors to South Carolina. To the extent the rebellion of 1719 expressed concern that the proprietors could not protect their colony from hostile forces (Indians, pirates, and Spanish), royal control proved reassuring and successful. Ironically, it was precisely the increased royal presence in the colony, or the consequences of that presence in the form of powerful colonial officials, royal troops, and the taxes required to pay for them, that led South Carolinians to participate in the destruction of royal government in America.

Westward and northward expansion into the frontier during the 18th century promoted tensions between Carolinians and the natives as well as among the colonists themselves. The Cherokee Indians attacked the Carolina backcountry in 1760. Although troops sent from Charleston helped to end the war within two years, frontier settlers complained that their protectors had inflicted greater damage through requisition or outright plunder than had the Cherokee. Indeed, the Carolina frontier seemed to attract groups of men whose lawless activities threatened the existence of ordered life. In response, in 1767 extralegal groups of settlers—Regulators—acted to purge the backcountry of such men. Decent frontier settlers not only resented the Charleston-based government's failure to insure social order by providing protection from outlaws but also its maintenance of a tax system that treated them unfairly, its failure to provide adequate schools, its refusal to establish local courts, and the inequitable distribution of legislative seats, which favored long-settled areas. The division between the coastal area and the Carolina backcountry endured throughout the colonial era.

The Revolution and Its Aftermath.   As the only major urban center south of Philadelphia, Charleston was a focus of activity during the American Revolution. Britain's General Clinton, with 8,000 troops, captured the city in the spring of 1780. Four years earlier an English attack by sea had failed to subdue the American fortress at the mouth of Charleston's harbor, as had a land assault during the Carolina campaign of 1779. But in 1780 a massive bombardment subdued the city, and the English took 5,000 prisoners. When English troops soon defeated American forces at Waxhaws and Camden, South Carolina fell, remaining under English control until the 1781 campaigns forced the British northward, ultimately to Yorktown, Virginia.

Since Carolina's economy depended on slavery, South Carolina failed to legislate against the slave trade during the Revolution. Moreover, the sheer numbers of slaves in South Carolina meant that, when the Articles of Confederation were being drafted, Carolinians objected to including slaves as part of the official population when computing the amount they would be assessed to support the central government. Conversely, during the debates over the Constitution, South Carolinians wished to include slaves when a state's inhabitants were counted in order to determine the number of representatives to which it would be entitled in Congress. South Carolinians readily accepted the Constitution, for compromises on the question of the continued existence of slavery and over how slaves ought to be counted, protected the state's economic interests.

See also Charleston; Fundamental Constitutions of Carolina; Regulators; Revolutionary War, Battles; Yamasee War.

Bibliography: Crane, Verner, *The Southern Frontier 1670-1732* (1929, reprint Norton, 1982); Sirmans, M. Eugene, *Colonial South Carolina: A Political History, 1663-1763* (Univ. of North Carolina Press, 1966); Ver Steeg, Clarence L., *Origins of a Southern Mosaic: Studies of South Carolina and Georgia* (Univ. of Georgia Press, 1975); Wood, Peter, *Black Majority: Negroes in Colonial South Carolina from 1670 Through the Stono Rebellion* (Knopf, 1974).

Aaron M. Shatzman
Franklin and Marshall College

SOUTH SEA COMPANY A British commercial corporation, the South Sea Company was established in 1711 to facilitate the sale of slaves to the Spanish colonies in America. By the terms of the Treaty of Utrecht in 1713, Spain granted Britain the right to import annually up to 4,800 slaves into its American colonies for the following 30 years. This trade proved less lucrative than expected, however, and the South Sea Company was granted the right to engage in domestic financial transactions. With its commission to underwrite the British national debt in 1720, the value of shares in the South Sea Company soared and then quickly crashed, in a financial panic known as the "South Sea Bubble."

SPANISH COLONIES Beginning in 1492, Spain built a western hemispheric colonial empire that stretched from the southern tip of South America to what is today the U.S. Southwest. It maintained its grip on these colonies for more than 300 years. To govern this immense territory, Spain divided the colonies into four administrative units known as viceroyalties—the Viceroyalty of New Spain, the Viceroyalty of Peru, the Viceroyalty of New Granada, and the Viceroyalty of the Rio de la Plata.

New Spain, the northernmost of these units, encompassed Central America, Mexico, the Philippines, Spain's Caribbean islands, Florida, and the present-day U.S. Southwest, particularly California, Arizona, New Mexico, and Texas. Huge distances isolated the latter four colonized areas, which had little communication with each other and only limited contact with Mexico City, capital of the viceroyalty. By the time of Mexican independence, some 80,000 settlers and their descendants lived in New Spain's northern borderlands.

Both commonalities and diversity characterized the Spanish colonies. Spanish culture and institutions—like government, the military, the Roman Catholic Church, large landholdings (*ranchos* and *haciendas*), cities, and towns—formed a basic pattern throughout the colonies. At the same time, intracolonial diversity developed as a result of a variety of factors, including differences in location, natural resources, the era in which each colony was settled, and the hemisphere's myriad Indian civilizations.

Spanish Governmental Structure. Foremost among colonial institutions was Spanish government. Under the Hapsburg regime during the 16th and 17th centuries, Spain constructed a highly centralized colonial system headed by the Council of the Indies. All laws and procedures emanated from Spain, which also demanded extensive reporting from colonial officials so that it could monitor and direct matters even in the farthest outposts of its empire. The ascension of the Bourbons to the Spanish throne at the beginning of the 18th century led to the establishment of a more flexible colonial system, including less restrictive trade regulations. In addition, the Bourbons emphasized improved efficiency and the generating of greater economic benefits for Spain.

However, the immensity of the Spanish empire, the rigidity of officially sanctioned transportation patterns, and the agonizing slowness of pre-electronic communications caused centralized governance to break down in practice. The more distant the colony, the more de facto its autonomy. Unable to wait for long-delayed instructions from the top, colonial officials had to act with greater initiative than envisioned in the official governmental system, particularly under the Hapsburgs. *Cabildos* (municipal councils), composed of local elites, became more activist, while private citizens often displayed disdain for the niceties of official Spanish policy. In the northern borderlands of New Spain, for example, the great distance from Mexico City and the resulting limitations of contact with the central government engendered a spirit of separateness and uniqueness.

Role of the Military. Within the Spanish system, the military played a special role, maintaining internal security, spearheading territorial expansion, and resisting foreign challenges. A principal military institution, particularly on the frontier, was the *presidio* (fort), sometimes situated in close proximity to a municipality or Catholic mission. In response to the French movement down to the mouth of the Mississippi River, Spain erected a string of presidios in eastern Texas in the early 18th century, while four presidios were established along the coast of California from San Diego to San Francisco in the late 18th century.

The extensiveness of Spain's global empire restricted its ability to commit large numbers of professional soldiers to these distant outposts. Therefore the burden of frontier defense, particularly on the fringes of the empire, fell greatly upon local residents, further strengthening their sense of self-reliance and autonomy. Career soldiers were few. In New Spain's northern borderlands, many soldiers were merely fixed-term recruits, poor men who joined the army and took their families north in search of new opportunities. Upon leaving the army, they usually settled in local towns and sometimes even became landowners through government grants that they had obtained while in the service.

The Catholic Church. The main nongovernmental colonial institution was the Catholic Church. Priests accompanied virtually every Spanish expedition. While the Spanish military and soldiers of fortune conquered and sometimes physically destroyed Indian civilizations, priests converted Indians and sometimes effected radical

SPANISH COLONIES: TOPIC GUIDE

GENERAL

Adobe
Anglo-Spanish War (1727-28)
Asiento
Audiencias
Black Legend
Cabildo
Chihuahua Trail
Cibola, Seven Cities of
Council of the Indies
Creoles
Encomienda and Hacienda
Exploration (see **Topic Guide**)
Geography and Culture (see **Topic Guide**)
Indians, Latin American

Indians, North American (see **Topic Guide**)
Inquisition, Spanish
Madrid, Treaty of (1670)
Missions and Missionaries
   Dominicans
   Franciscans
Mixedbloods (Mestizos, Metis)
Old Spanish Trail
Religion (see **Topic Guide**)
Repartimiento
Requerimiento
Roman Catholics
Spanish Colonies
Spanish Immigrants

BIOGRAPHIES

Aguayo, Josef de Azlor Y Virto de Vera,
   Marquis de
Alarcon, Hernando de
Anza, Juan Baptista de
Ayllon, Lucas Vasquez de
Balboa, Vasco Nunez de
Benavides, Alonso
Bodega y Cuadra, Juan Francisco De La
Bosque, Fernando de
Cabeza de Vaca, Alvar Nunez
Cabrillo, Juan Rodriguez
Carondelet, Francisco Luis Hector De
Castillo, Diego del
Cirmenho, Sebastian Rodriguez
Columbus, Christopher
Coronado, Francisco Vasquez de
Cortes, Hernando
De Soto, Hernando
Diaz, Melchior
Dominguez, Francisco Atanasio
Escalante, Silvestre Velez de
Espejo, Antonio De
Estevanico
Fuca, Juan de
Galvez, Bernardo de
Garces, Francisco
Gomez, Estevan
Guadalajara, Diego de
Keller, Ignacio Javier
Kino, Eusebio Francisco
Lafora, Nicolas de
Larios, Juan

Las Casas, Bartolome de
Lopez, Andres
Lopez, Nicolas
Luna y Arellano, Don Tristan de
Magellan, Ferdinand
Martin, Hernando
Menendez de Aviles, Pedro
Mendoza, Juan Dominguez De
Montezuma
Narvaez, Panfilo de
Niza, Marcos de
Onate, Juan de
Padilla, Juan de
Peralta, Pedro de
Perez, Juan
Pizarro, Francisco
Ponce de Leon, Juan
Portola, Gaspar de
Reynoso, Alonso de
Rios, Domingo Teran de los
Rivera y Moncada, Fernando de
Rubi, Marques de
Segresser, Felipe
Serra, Junipero
Sosa, Gaspar Castano de
Ulloa, Antonio de
Unamuno, Pedro de
Vargas, Francisco
Vigo, Joseph Maria Francisco
Villasur, Pedro
Vizcaino, Sebastian

changes in their cultures. In addition, Catholic missionaries, operating alone or in small groups, brought the gospel to Indians as yet untouched by Spanish government or by private exploration. In these forays, missionaries carried out their traditional dual functions of Catholicizing and Hispanicizing the Indians.

The major Catholic frontier institution was the mission, which proselytized Indians and provided for the religious needs of Spanish settlers. Some Indians peacefully accepted Catholicism and resettled around missions. Others became victims of Spanish violence, as priests meted out corporal punishment and the military conducted sweeps, uprooting Indian villages and bringing their inhabitants to the missions. More than religious institutions, missions often became major landowners and developed highly profitable economic enterprises. For example, the California missions developed a lucrative cattle business and, after Mexican independence in 1821, engaged in an active hides-and-tallow trade via U.S. ships.

The growing wealth and power of the missions inevitably created concern on the part of the Crown and later national governments, as well as envy by private citizens. The Spanish government periodically moved against the Church, such as expelling Jesuit missionaries and expropriating their considerable property in 1767 for what was deemed to be subversive activities. Following independence, Mexico secularized the powerful California missions, taking away their economic prerogatives, restricting them to religious functions, and distributing their land to private entrepreneurs.

Social and Economic Institutions. Cities, towns, *ranchos*, and *haciendas* developed throughout the colonies. Northern New Spain saw the rise of communities like San Antonio (Texas), Albuquerque and Santa Fe (New Mexico), Tucson (Arizona), and Los Angeles, San Diego, Santa Barbara, Monterey, San Francisco, and San Jose (California). These towns and cities provided a focus for political activity, economic exchange, fine artisanry, cultural creativity, and social life. On ranchos and haciendas, agriculture and livestock-raising relied on Indians, often mission-trained Indians. Highly skilled *vaqueros* (cowboys) initiated many of the practices and traditions that later would be passed on to American cowboys. Often isolated from urban communities, ranchos and haciendas also created their own social and cultural life, with activities ranging from rodeos to fiestas, and from musical presentations to poetry readings.

New Mexico developed a special institution, the communal landholding. To obtain communal land grants from the government, groups of settlers would agree to establish their towns according to Crown specifications, to carry out frontier defense, and to share governance and natural resources. These grants generated a particularly intense cooperation and sense of community.

Throughout the Spanish colonies a combination class-caste social system developed. Upward mobility was limited, but in northern New Spain that system attained greater-than-usual flexibility, with some poor settlers achieving wealth and social status. However, most residents of northern New Spain remained in the lower and lower-middle classes.

Racially the Spanish colonies were a mixture. They included *peninsulares* (born in Spain), *criollos* (born in the colonies of pure Spanish ancestry), Indians, blacks, *mestizos* (mixed Spanish and Indian ancestry), *mulattos* (mixed Spanish and black ancestry), and *zambos* (mixed Indian and black ancestry), as well as varying combinations of these major classifications. But race mixture did not eliminate racial prejudice or discrimination. Racial identity influenced socioeconomic mobility, with those of pure (or presumably pure) Spanish background having a great advantage. In general, whites obtained the major government positions, Catholic Church offices, and large landholdings. Indians, blacks, and mixedbloods remained concentrated at the lower levels of the socioeconomic structure. Faced with this restrictive system, mestizos strove, sometimes successfully, to become identified as pureblooded Spaniards. Occasionally they managed to

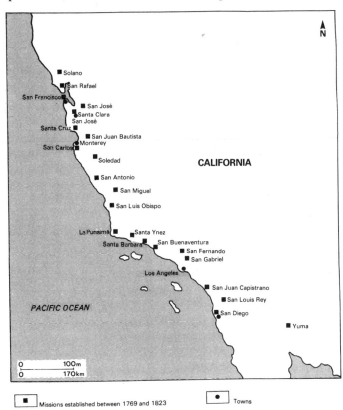

Spanish Colonies. *(Martin Greenwald Associates, Inc.)*

rise socially and economically, a process that was often accompanied by a change of ethnic identity.

A rich and varied culture developed throughout the colonies. The northern frontier witnessed a boom in creativity. Music, both religious and secular, played a central role, as did the composition and reading of poetry and the creation and presentation of religious dramas. New Mexico, in particular, became a center for popular art. Residents demonstrated skills in gold and silver filigree, weaving, and tin and iron crafting. Of special significance were New Mexico's striking, affecting *retablos* (religious scenes) and *santos* (saints), carved by artists known as *santeros* (saint makers), who continue this artistic tradition to the present.

End of the Colonial Era.   During the first three decades of the 19th century, revolution rocked Spain's western hemispheric empire, bringing its colonial period to a virtual end by 1825. Among those areas gaining independence was Mexico in 1821. In 1819, Spain sold Florida to the United States via the Adams-Onís Treaty. Only Cuba and Puerto Rico remained under Spain's control. The end of Spain's American colonial empire came in 1898, when the United States defeated Spain in the Spanish-American War. Cuba became independent, and Puerto Rico became a United States possession.

For northern Mexico, independence brought only a brief interlude between the end of the Spanish colonial period and absorption into the westwardly expanding United States. American settlers in Texas rapidly outnumbered local Mexicans, rebelled, won their independence from Mexico in 1836, and joined the United States in 1845. The following year, the Mexican War broke out between the United States and Mexico. Defeated militarily, Mexico ceded much of northern Mexico, including most of the current states of California, Arizona, and New Mexico, to the United States. In 1851, the United States purchased from Mexico the southern sliver of today's New Mexico and Arizona via the Gadsden Purchase. Through these events, one-half of Mexico's territory and some 80,000 Mexican citizens joined the United States.

See also Audiencias; Cabildos; Council of the Indies; Encomienda and Hacienda; Repartimiento; Spanish Conquest; Spanish Immigrants.

Bibliography: Bannon, John Francis, *The Spanish Borderlands Frontier, 1513-1821* (Holt, Rinehart and Winston, 1970); Knight, Franklin W., *The Caribbean: The Genesis of a Fragmented Nationalism* (Oxford Univ. Press, 1978); Liss, Peggy K., *Mexico Under Spain, 1521-1556: Society and the Origins of Nationality* (Univ. of Chicago Press, 1975); Lockhart, James and Schwartz, Stuart B., *Early Latin America: A History of Colonial Spanish America* (Cambridge Univ. Press, 1983); Morner, Magnus, *Race Mixture in the History of Latin America* (Little, Brown, 1967).

Carlos E. Cortés
University of California, Riverside

SPANISH CONQUEST   The Spanish Conquest of the Western Hemisphere has been popularly characterized by the words, "God, Gold, and Glory." In other words, the Spanish came to convert heathens to Catholicism, to reap economic gains, and to achieve some sort of renown through feats of daring. However, the Conquest was far more complex and should be viewed from at least five perspectives: Spanish institutions; Spanish individuals, Indian institutions; Indian individuals; and other European nations.

Spanish Institutions and Individuals.   Two powerful Spanish institutions—the crown and the Roman Catholic Church—had sometimes consonant, sometimes conflicting goals. The crown saw the Conquest as a process for extending its global empire, for bringing economic benefits to Spain, and for spreading Catholicism. The Church considered the spreading of Catholicism to be paramount, but it also sought to Hispanicize Indian converts and to enrich itself through the acquisition of land and the development of economically viable enterprises. While these two institutions generally provided mutual support, the crown periodically placed restrictions on Church activities in order to ensure the maintenance of royal authority.

Individual Spaniards involved in the Conquest usually shared the goals of these two institutions, at least nominally. However, they also sought personal power, economic rewards, and upward social mobility. At times they came into conflict with both crown and Church, such as when the crown attempted to restrict the prerogatives and practices of landowners (*hacendados*) or when the Church attempted to limit their use of Indian labor.

Indians and Other Europeans.   The Conquest destroyed or enfeebled Indian institutions. Some managed to survive, although usually in severely modified form and particularly when Spaniards could absorb and use them in their colonial system. For example, the Spanish sometimes manipulated Indian social structures to maintain community control or adopted Indian labor systems for the benefit of Spanish enterprises.

Individual Indians felt the full brunt of the Spanish Conquest. Huge numbers died in battle, from harsh working conditions, and from European diseases for which they had no immunity. Others became subject to Spanish colonial government, the converting pressures of the

Catholic Church, and the oppressive treatment of Spanish entrepreneurs.

Finally, the Spanish Conquest posed a challenge to those other European nations that had designs on the Western Hemisphere. As they attempted to extend their own empires, these nations had to contend with Spanish (and Portuguese) territorial claims and military opposition. On the other hand, early Iberian colonial experiences provided a type of education in Western Hemispheric conquest and colonization for other European nations.

The Spanish Conquest extended well into what is today the mainland United States. The first thrust came from the Caribbean islands, as Spanish explorers penetrated the Gulf Coast, culminating in the founding of St. Augustine, Florida, in 1565. A second series of thrusts emanated from the Viceroyalty of New Spain, whose capital was Mexico City. In 1598, Juan de Oñate led an expedition that settled what is today New Mexico. This was followed by the formation of a late 17th-century mission frontier in Arizona, the establishment of a series of *presidios* (forts), missions, towns, and ranches in eastern Texas in the early 18th century, and the creation of a string of missions, presidios, and towns along the coast of California in the late 18th century.

Spain's northern colonies remained modest in size. The Conquest managed to subdue some Indian societies, but others successfully resisted Spanish efforts to dominate them, while Indian revolts also occurred. Most dramatic was the 1680 Pueblo revolt in New Mexico, which forced the Spanish to abandon their northern New Mexican settlements. This set in motion what has become known as the New Mexico Reconquest, which recaptured the territory for Spain by 1694. As a result of the Spanish Conquest, the northwestern tier of New Spain stretched from California to Texas by the end of the 18th century, while Florida remained Spain's northeastern foothold.

See also Columbus, Christopher; Coronado, Francisco Vazquez de; Cortes, Hernando; DeSoto, Hernando; Onate, Juan de; Requerimiento; Spanish Colonies.

Bibliography: Bannon, John Francis, *The Spanish Borderlands Frontier, 1513-1821* (Holt, Rinehart and Winston 1970); Liss, Peggy K., *Mexico Under Spain, 1521-1556: Society and the Origins of Nationality* (Univ. of Chicago Press 1975).

Carlos E. Cortés
University of California, Riverside

SPANISH IMMIGRANTS   Spanish immigrants into the Western Hemisphere represented a broad spectrum of Iberian society. They ran the gamut from lower class peasants and urban workers to nobility, from soldiers to clergy, and from adventurers to settlers seeking new economic opportunities. In the early years, men comprised

most of Spanish immigration, with women and families coming later in the colonization process. A social distinction on the basis of birthplace ultimately arose. Persons born in Spain became known as *peninsulares* (Spain being the larger component of the Iberian peninsula). Those born in the Western Hemisphere of pure Spanish ancestry received the less prestigious designation of criollo (Creole).

However, Spaniards did not monopolize immigration into the Spanish colonies. Black Africans, some already residents of Spain, but most victims of the transatlantic slave trade, became a second major immigrant component. For example, in the Viceroyalty of New Spain, which included what is today Mexico and the U.S. Southwest, blacks worked in coastal agriculture and sometimes even became overseers of Indian work crews on *haciendas* (plantations) and in *obrajes* (textile mills).

Particularly as a result of the paucity of Spanish immigrant women, *peninsulares* and *criollos* had considerable sexual contact with Indians and blacks. Their racially-mixed offspring consisted of *mestizos* (Spanish-Indian) and *mulattos* (Spanish-black), while the children of Indian-black unions were called *zambos*. However, with continued racial mixture, it often became impossible to determine a person's precise racial heritage.

This extensive and complex racial mixture was reflected in Spain's northward expansion. For example, Indians outnumbered whites in Juan de Onate's 1598 expedition, which initiated Spanish colonization of New Mexico, while only 2 of Los Angeles's 46 residents claimed to be Spanish in its census of 1781, the year the city was founded. In short, while Spanish immigrants and their pure-Spanish, American-born descendants comprised most of the powerful colonial elite, Indians, blacks, and racially-mixed people played a substantial role in the Spanish colonial empire.

See also Asiento; Council of the Indies; Spanish Colonies; Spanish Conquest.

Bibliography: Mörner, Magnus, *Race Mixture in the History of Latin America* (Little, Brown, 1967); MacLachlan, Colin M. and Rodríguez, O. Jaime, *The Forging of the Cosmic Race: A Reinterpretation of Colonial Mexico* (Univ. of California Press, 1980).

Carlos E. Cortés
University of California, Riverside

SPOTSWOOD, ALEXANDER (1676-1740)   A British colonial official and explorer, born in Tangier, Spotswood entered the British army and fought in the War of the Spanish Succession. In 1710 he became lieutenant governor of Virginia, where he fought for the regulation of the Indian trade and for the prerogatives of the Crown against the interests of the planters, involving him in violent disputes with the House of Burgesses. He pursued an active program of exploration, himself conducting a series of expeditions. In 1716, with rangers, servants, and Indian guides, he crossed the mountains at the pass now called Swift Run Gap, descended west, and crossed the Shenandoah River into the great Valley of Virginia at a point near modern-day Elkton, an expedition which called much attention to lands in the west. After he left office in 1722, he devoted his time to iron mining and smelting.

SQUANTO (c.1580-1622) A member of the Pawtuxet tribe of eastern New England, Squanto, whose name was derived from the Algonquian *tisquantum*, "door," was kidnapped in 1605 by the British navigator George Weymouth and reportedly sold into slavery in Spain by Captain Thomas Hunt. The details of his escape from slavery are uncertain, and some historians reject the authenticity of the story, suggesting that Squanto was brought directly to England by Weymouth to provide Sir Ferdinando Gorges with firsthand information on the native populations of New England. In 1619, after an absence of 14 years, Squanto returned to New England aboard a ship commanded by John Slaine. There Squanto learned to his horror that his tribe had been almost entirely wiped out by a recent catastrophic epidemic, and he settled among the Wampanoag. In 1620 he served as interpreter for the Wampanoag chief Massasoit in his dealings with the Pilgrim settlers at Plymouth and later instructed the Pilgrims in the techniques of local agriculture. After Squanto's increasingly close relationship with the English eventually aroused suspicions among the Wampanoag and Narragansett, he was protected by the members of the Plymouth colony until his death.

See also Massasoit.

STAMP ACT (1765) One of the most controversial acts of Parliament in the aftermath of the French and Indian War, the Stamp Act imposed a tax on the citizens of the

After the Stamp Act Congress, Benjamin Franklin presented the colonies' grievances to Parliament. *(Library of Congress)*

American colonies to be used for the maintenance of the standing army in America. The British government, having resolved to raise part of its colonial defense budget through the sale of legally required stamps for legal documents, periodicals, almanacs, pamphlets, and playing cards in America, faced unprecedented opposition to what was considered in the colonies "taxation without representation." In 1766, following unrest, organized protest, and the appeals of prominent Americans, the Stamp Act was repealed.

STAMP ACT CONGRESS (1765) Great Britain emerged in 1763 from the era of the French and Indian War (Seven Years War) with a victory and a doubled national debt that weighed heavily on the British taxpayer. When George Grenville's ministry sought to burden lightly taxed Americans with part of the cost of the empire through the Sugar Act (1764) and the Stamp Act (1765), it triggered colonial protests. Alarmed by the preambles of the two acts, which stated that their purpose was to raise a revenue, and therefore to tax, colonial legislatures, not hitherto noted for intercolonial cooperation, recognized the wisdom of collective action and responded to the call from Massachusetts to meet in New York City in the Stamp Act Congress. New Hampshire declined to attend but later approved of the work of the congress, as did Georgia, which, like Virginia and North Carolina, was prevented from attending by its governor.

The 27 delegates from the remaining 9 colonies, sitting from October 7 to 24, 1765, drew up a list of 14 declarations and 3 petitions to King, Lords, and Commons that showed how far any notion of independence was from American minds at that time. The delegates did, however, draw limits to Parliament's authority over Americans, denying Parliament's right to tax them, since taxation rested on representation and Americans sent no representatives to Parliament. The colonial representatives agreed that Parliament's role as the empire's supreme legislature allowed it to pass laws for them, regulating their trade. While in no way contributing to the Stamp Act's ultimate repeal (1766), the congress did initiate the colonial cooperation that would later prove vital to the fight for independence.

See also Grenville, George; Stamp Act.

Bibliography: Morgan, Edmund S. and Helen M., *The Stamp Act Crisis* (Univ. of North Carolina Press, 1953).

STANDISH, MILES (c. 1584-1656) A member of the group that arrived in America on the *Mayflower* in 1620, Standish was born in England and sought his fortune in the Netherlands, where he was hired as a military adviser to sail the Pilgrims to the New World. He helped the Pilgrims explore Cap Cod and land at Plymouth and stayed with them. Elected as the colonists' military leader in 1621, his

expertise in handling the Indians and building and defending the fort enabled the Pilgrims to survive. In 1625 he returned to England to negotiate a colony charter and, the next year, helped to underwrite the debt of the colony. It was Standish who was attorney for the Council of New England under the new land grant. In 1631 he founded Duxbury, Massachusetts, with Pilgrim John Alden, and in popular legend he is associated with John's wife Priscilla.

See also Alden, John.

STARBUCK, MARY COFFYN (1644-1717) Quaker minister on Nantucket Island. Her father initiated the plan to colonize the island, and he moved his family to Nantucket about 1660. Mary married Nathaniel Starbuck shortly after the move, and they had 10 children. Although raised in the church of Massachusetts orthodoxy, she joined her husband's church, called the Electarians, around 1665. It was the belief of the Electarians that, once you believed in Christ, you could not fall from grace. Mary Starbuck felt that it was improper for a minister to be a paid professional, and it was this, along with Electarian belief, that attracted her to Quakerism. When she and her eldest son Nathaniel were converted to the Society of Friends (Quakers), it began a wave of conversions that made Quakerism the dominant religion on Nantucket. In 1708 the members on the island applied for permission from the New England Yearly Meeting to form a meeting of their own. Articulate and self-possessed, Mary Starbuck became the first recognized Quaker minister on Nantucket. She was also active in public affairs, with her home earning the nickname "Parliament House" because of all the public business that took place there.

STARK, JOHN (1728-1822) A Revolutionary War military leader, born near Londonderry, New Hampshire, the son of Scotch-Irish immigrants, Stark first distinguished himself as a frontiersman and guide with Roger's Rangers during the French and Indian War. At the outbreak of the Revolution he was appointed colonel of the New Hampshire regiment and saw action at the Battle of Bunker Hill, in the invasion of Canada, and at the battles of Trenton and Princeton. In 1777 he was named a brigadier general and directed the American defense against General John Burgoyne's invasion from Canada. Stark's greatest triumph was the Battle of Bennington in that campaign. Later named commander of the Northern Department and promoted to major general, Stark retired in 1783.

STARS AND STRIPES The official flag of the United States, the Stars and Stripes was adopted by the Continental Congress in its Flag Resolution of June 14, 1777, which determined that "the flag of the 13 United States be 13 stripes, alternate red and white; that the union be 13 stars, white in a blue field, representing a new constellation...." This vague description originally resulted in a wide variety of U.S. flags, among them the famous Bennington Flag, with an arch of stars over the numeral "76," but the now-standard form soon predominated. The popular story of Betsy Ross's role in the design of the American flag seems to lack a historical basis. The U.S. flag remained unaltered until the admission of Vermont and Kentucky to the union on May 1, 1795.

STATEN ISLAND PEACE CONFERENCE (1776)   The Staten Island Peace Conference was an unsuccessful attempt to bring a negotiated end to the American Revolution, initiated by the American general John Sullivan, who was taken prisoner by the British at the Battle of Long Island. Believing that the British commander, Admiral Richard Howe, had the power to conclude a treaty with the Americans, Sullivan suggested that he be released to arrange a meeting with members of the Continental Congress. A committee, consisting of Benjamin Franklin, John Adams, and Edward Rutledge, met with Howe on Staten Island on September 11, 1776, but learned that Howe had no power to negotiate without prior approval from London, and the talks were immediately broken off.

STEUBEN, FRIEDRICH WILHELM, BARON VON (1730-94)   Born in Magdeburg, Germany, the son of a Prussian military officer, von Steuben spent his childhood in Russia and joined the Prussian army in 1747. After service in the Seven Years War, he was appointed aide-de-camp to King Frederick II but left the Prussian service under mysterious circumstances in 1763. In 1777 he was hired by the Continental Congress as a logistical advisor and supervisor of military instruction. He made an indelible impression upon George Washington and the Continental forces at Valley Forge during the winter of 1778. His success in training those troops led to his appointment as inspector general of the Continental Army. While serving in this important post until the end of the war, von Steuben played a key role in transforming independent American militias into an effective fighting force. Following the war he helped to found the Society of the Cincinnati and became an American citizen.

STIEGEL, HENRY WILLIAM (1729-85)   An ironmaster and glass manufacturer, born in Cologne, Germany, Stiegel immigrated to Philadelphia in 1750 and was apprenticed to the ironmaster Jacob Huber in Lancaster County. In 1758 he purchased Huber's forge and property and began large-scale production of iron stoves and kettles for the West Indian sugar refining industry. Stiegel expanded his commercial interests to glassmaking in 1764, and "Stiegel glassware" gained great popularity throughout the American colonies. Financial reverses and bankruptcy in 1774, however, resulted in Stiegel's sentencing to debtors' prison. He ended his life in obscurity, as a laborer in the forges he once owned.

STILES, EZRA (1727-95)   A Congregational minister, lawyer, and college president, he was born in Connecticut and educated at Yale College. By 1749 he was preaching and by 1753 practicing law. In 1755 he was ordained a minister and held a position in Newport, Rhode Island, until 1776. While there he continued his interest in science, conducting experiments in chemistry and promoting the manufacture of silk. He also prepared the charter for Rhode Island College (now Brown University) in 1763 and was elected to the American Philosophical Society in 1768. From 1778 he was president, as well as professor of ecclesiastical history, at Yale.

STOCKTON, RICHARD (1730-81)   An attorney and political leader, Stockton was born in Princeton, New Jersey, and graduated from the College of New Jersey (Princeton) in 1748. He subsequently studied law at Newark, where he was admitted to the bar in 1754, and gained a reputation as one of the most brilliant lawyers in the Middle Colonies. He also remained an active supporter of the College of New Jersey. From 1768 to 1776 he sat on the provincial council and served as an associate justice of the New Jersey supreme court (1774-76). Always a moderate regarding relations with Great Britain, he was nevertheless elected to the Continental Congress in 1776 and was one of the signers of the Declaration of Independence. His capture and imprisonment (1776-77) by the British ruined his health.

STONE, THOMAS (1743-87)   An attorney and political leader, born in Charles County, Maryland, Stone studied law in Annapolis and was admitted to the bar in 1754. As a member of the Second Continental Congress (1775-78), he participated in the framing of the Articles of Confederation and was one of the signers of the Declaration of Independence. In the fall of 1776 he was one of the most outspoken supporters of American negotiations with General Howe at the Staten Island Peace Conference. In 1783 he served as chairman of the Congress of Confederation, and in 1787 he was elected to the Constitutional Convention but did not attend because of poor health.

See also Staten Island Peace Conference.

STONO REBELLION (1739)   This slave rebellion, also known as the Cato Conspiracy, occurred at the beginning of the war between England and Spain, which had offered runaway slaves refuge in Florida. In 1739 some 75 slaves rose up in the country near the Stono River, some 20 miles southwest of Charleston, South Carolina, killed a number of whites, and marched south toward Florida. The white militia prevented a general rebellion by attacking the runaways. A total of 30 whites and 44 blacks were killed. The resulting fear of slave uprisings led to the discovery of another plot in Charleston in 1740, when 50 blacks were hanged, and to the bloody repression in New York in 1741.

See also Negro Plot of 1741; New York; Slave Resistance; Slavery.

STUYVESANT, PETER (?1610-72) Director general of New Netherland from 1647 until 1664, Stuyvesant was born sometime between 1610 and 1612 in Weststellingwerf, in Friesland, son of the Reverend Balthazar Johannes Stuyvesant and Margaretta Hardenstein. He attended but did not graduate from the University of Franeker and signed on with the West India Company before 1635, serving in various capacities including a stint as commissary of stores for Curacao (1639-42). He became governor early in 1642 when Jan Claeszoon van Campen suddenly died. While governor of Curacao, he undertook an aggressive policy toward the Spanish that included an attack on Puerto Cabello on the coast of Venezuela and an assault on the island of St. Martin. In the latter operation he suffered a wound to his right leg, which had to be amputated. Upon the recommendation of his doctors, who feared the tropical climate was not permitting his leg to heal properly, Stuyvesant returned home to the Netherlands at the end of August 1644. While in the Netherlands in 1645, he married Judith Bayard, with whom he had two sons. In 1646 he received his commission as director general of New Netherland, Curacao, Bonaire, Aruba, and their dependencies.

Governor of New Netherland. He arrived in New Amsterdam on May 11, 1647, and set to work bringing the colony to order. In the wake of the recent Indian wars and incessant controversies that had plagued the administration of his predecessor, Willem Kieft, Stuyvesant became a whirlwind of activity, issuing edicts, regulating taverns, clamping down on smuggling, and trying to bring to bear the authority of his office on a populace inured to a long line of incompetent directors general. His would be the longest reign of any Dutch governor, and his accomplishments would not be without controversy. As the son of a minister and son-in-law of another, he was a strict follower of the Reformed Church, and many of the controversies involved attempts to enforce religious conformity on the polyglot population of the colony. Although he was required by the provisions of the West India Company charter to maintain the orthodoxy of the Dutch Reform Church, in his efforts to root out nonconformity Stuyvesant

was chastised by his superiors in the company who felt his zeal in persecuting Quakers, forcing conformity on Lutherans, and restricting the activities of Jews was hindering the company's efforts to attract colonists.

In other matters, Stuyvesant's administration was clearly a resounding success. In 1650 he concluded the so-called Treaty of Hartford with the English colonies to the north, which established tentative boundaries between New Netherland and New England; and, in a series of Indian wars, he succeeded in removing the threat to the colony's existence posed by the Algonquian-speaking Indians. In these same years he directed the construction of a wall to the north of Fort New Amsterdam to serve as defense against the English. The small street that ran along this wall became known as Wahl Straat, or in English, Wall Street. As part of the same effort to defend the colony from the English in the first Anglo-Dutch War (1652-54), he established militia posts on Long Island. In 1655 he led an expedition against the Swedish settlements on the Delaware River and finally brought this long-disputed region under Dutch jurisdiction. In 1664, however, he was to suffer his most humiliating defeat when, upon the urgent pleas of his subjects and against his own inclination to fight it out, he gave over the colony to an English war fleet commanded by Colonel Richard Nicolls.

Stuyvesant was recalled to the Netherlands in 1665 to explain his actions in surrendering New Netherland. After spending months in a spirited defense of his actions, he returned to New York, where he was to live out the remainder of his life.

See also Anglo-Dutch Wars; New Netherland.

Bibliography: Gehring, Charles T. and Schiltkamp, J.A. trans. and eds., *New Netherland Documents*, Vol. 17: *Curacao Papers*, 1640-1665 (Heart of the Lakes Publishing, 1987); Kessler, Henry H., and Rachlis, Eugene, *Pieter Stuyvesant and His New York* (Random House, 1959); Rink, Oliver A., *Holland On the Hudson: An Economic and Social History of Dutch New York* (Cornell Univ. Press, 1986).

Oliver A. Rink
California State University, Bakersfield

SUBARCTIC INDIANS The hunting peoples of the subarctic can be divided into two regional language groups. East are the Algonquian-speaking tribes of the Canadian Shield, including the Cree, Montagnais, Naskapi, and Ojibwa. West and north of the drainage of the Churchill and North Saskatchewan rivers are more than 25 separate Athabascan groups of the western boreal forest, known collectively as the Dene but including the Chipewyan west of Hudson Bay, the Yoyukon of the Yukon drainage in Alaska, and the Carrier of the Rockies in British Columbia. Within these two broad language spheres, dialects grade into one another without clear-cut boundaries, and Indians organize themselves into small hunting groups and somewhat larger bands; larger ethnic identifications were imposed by Europeans and in the 20th century became the basis for native cultural revival.

Within North America the homeland for the Dene was in east-central Alaska, from where, perhaps a millennium ago, they dispersed east and south, the Apache and Navaho pushing as far as the Southwest. Algonquian-speakers, on the other hand, probably entered the eastern boreal forests from the south. Both groups practiced the hunting of large game—caribou to the west, moose to the east—supplemented by fishing and some gathering. This subsistence strategy was the most persistent and longest-lasting on the continent because it was so well suited to a harsh environment that allows few alternatives.

European fishermen first made contact with Algonquians along the Labradoran coast in the early 16th century, spreading the fur trade and disease into the interior long before the arrival of traders and causing great disruptions of traditional patterns. As fur-bearing animals were hunted out, the French pressed further inland, reaching the Great Lakes by the mid-17th century. About the same time, the Hudson's Bay Company established its first posts and by the early 18th century was in direct contact with the Chipewyan. European rifles and traps altered the strategies of these hunters, increasing their productivity but hastening the extermination of many animals. Violence between European traders and companies drew Indians into conflict among themselves, particularly between Algonquians and Denes, Denes and Eskimos. Finally, smallpox pandemics, like the great one of 1781, left populations at only 10 percent of their precontact levels. European colonization of the great interior north did not begin until the late 19th and 20th centuries, stimulated by gold rushes and oil booms. These final threats to the Dene and the Algonquian have produced the circumstances for a powerful nativist revival in recent years.

See also Indians, North American.

Bibliography: Nelson, Richard K., *Hunters of the Northern Forest* (Univ. of Chicago Press, 1973).

John Mack Faragher
Mount Holyoke College

SUFFOLK RESOLVES On September 9, 1775, delegates from towns in Suffolk County, in which Boston was located, met in Milton and adopted the Suffolk Resolves, a bold and radical statement drawn up by Dr. Joseph Warren. Essentially, the statement said that the Coercive Acts should not be obeyed; royal courts should close; taxes should be paid to the provincial congress rather than the royal government; and militias should prepare to defend the towns. Carried by Paul Revere to Philadelphia, where the First Continental Congress was meeting in Carpenters'

Hall, the resolves won approval for their wisdom and fortitude on September 18, but the Congress made no commitment to Massachusetts Bay. On October 8, however, the Congress unanimously approved the resolves and encouraged the support of the other colonies, should Britain implement the Coercive Acts by force.

See also Coercive Acts; Continental Congress, First; Warren, Joseph.

SUFFRAGE The privilege of voting in the English colonies was hedged by significant qualifications, although they operated differently in the various colonies. In early 17th-century Virginia with its high poll tax, for example, the electorate was composed exclusively of the very wealthy. After the protest and rebellion of the 1670s, these rates were lowered, and by the 1690s some 60 percent of the adult white males owned enough property to vote. However, this apparently broad franchise had little political significance, for the planter elite so dominated politics that poorer planters did little more than assent to their rule. In New England, Puritans originally enfranchised all the adult male property-owning members of their congregations, thus adding a religious test. Roger Williams was expelled, in part, for questioning this Massachusetts test, and Rhode Island was the first colony in the region to broaden the suffrage to all male property holders. The property qualifications were frequently ignored in town-meeting government, and after 1692 the religious test was abolished by royal order, thus making the suffrage wider in New England than in the South or in the mother country.

The state constitutions of the Revolutionary War era generally broadened the suffrage, but only Pennsylvania and Georgia allowed all taxpayers to vote, while others retained property qualifications or poll taxes, although generally somewhat more leniently applied. On the other hand, free blacks were disfranchised, either by raising their property qualifications, or removing them from the voting rolls by statute. Women, of course, remained without the vote, in theory represented by their fathers and husbands, although in an interesting anomaly, in New Jersey a loophole in the constitution of 1776 permitted widows and spinsters who met the residency and property requirements to vote in its elections until disfranchised by statute in 1807.

John Mack Faragher
Mount Holyoke College

SUGAR Many sweeteners have gone by the name "sugar" (a word derived from Sanskrit), including maple sugar and honey but, unless otherwise specified, in the colonies the word sugar referred to refined sugar cane (*Saccharum officinarum*), imported from the West Indies.

European sugar production began in the Atlantic islands of Cape Verde, Madeira, and the Canaries in the late 15th century, and was intimately associated with the spread of European colonization and the growth of African slavery. The Portuguese introduced sugar and slaves into Brazil in the 16th century, and from there sugar production spread into the Caribbean, where Dutch, Spanish, French, and English colonists established profitable plantation colonies and a market for slaves. The greatest number of Africans forcibly transported to the Western Hemisphere were sent to work on the sugar plantations. Sugar cane was introduced in Louisiana by the French, in Florida by the Spanish, and elsewhere in the southern colonies by the English, but with the competition from the slave islands of the Caribbean it failed to became an important crop.

By the mid-17th century extensive reciprocal trading networks based on the production of sugar had developed. Often described as the Triangular Trade, in reality these were a complicated series of links. In one classic connection, New England merchants shipped fish, livestock, flour, and lumber to the islands in exchange for molasses; then shipped rum (distilled from the molasses) to Africa in exchange for fresh slaves, transported to the Caribbean. Together, slave and sugar formed the most profitable trades of the colonial era.

See also Maple Sugar; Triangular Trade.

Bibliography: Mintz, Sidney W., *Sweetness and Power: The Place of Sugar in Modern History* (Viking, 1985).

SUGAR ACT (1764)   An act passed by Parliament to discourage smuggling between the French West Indies and the British colonies in America, the Sugar Act lowered the high duty on foreign-produced molasses but added hides, iron, lumber, whale fins, and silk to the commodities covered by the Enumerated Articles Act. Ever since the passage of the 1733 Molasses Act, New England merchants had preferred to acquire smuggled molasses rather than pay the high duties. The Sugar Act, sponsored by Sir George Grenville, Chancellor of the Exchequer, reduced this underground trade by declaring that all ships in violation of the act would be subject to immediate seizure and confiscation.

See also Enumerated Goods.

SULLIVAN, JOHN (1740-95)   A military and political leader, born in Somersworth, New Hampshire, Sullivan was the son of indentured Irish immigrants. He gained an education in the law and practiced at Portsmouth, New Hampshire. In 1772 he was appointed a major in the New Hampshire militia and was elected to the First and Second Continental Congresses (1774-75). At the outbreak of the Revolution, he led the seizure of British positions and supplies in Portsmouth harbor and served as a brigadier

general in the siege of Boston and the retreat from Canada. In 1776 he was promoted to major general and taken prisoner at the Battle of Long Island. Exchanged for the captured British general Richard Prescott, Sullivan initiated the contacts between General Howe and the Continental Congress that led to the unsuccessful Staten Island Peace Conference in 1776. He later saw active service in New Jersey at Trenton and Princeton and in the attempt to retake Newport, Rhode Island. He then won an important victory in western New York against a combined Loyalist-Indian force in 1779. After the war he served in various political posts in New Hampshire: member of the New Hampshire constitutional convention (1782), attorney general (1782-86), and provisional president (1787-89). His last post was as a U.S. district judge (1789-95).

See also Staten Island Peace Conference.

SUMTER, THOMAS (1734-1832)   A guerilla leader and politician, born near Charlottesville, Virginia, Sumter moved in 1765 to Eutaw Springs, South Carolina, where he served as justice of the peace and as delegate to the first and second provincial congresses. With the outbreak of the Revolution, he saw service against the British and the Cherokee in Georgia and Florida. He is best remembered for his effective guerilla tactics during the British invasion of South Carolina in 1780. After the war, he was elected to the South Carolina legislature. Although he initially opposed ratification of the U.S. Constitution, Sumter subsequently served in both the U.S. House (1789-93, 1797-1801) and Senate (1801-1810). Fort Sumter at Charleston Harbor was named in his honor.

SURVEYING   Accurate surveys of land were rare in the colonies but in the South there was no organized survey whatsoever. Headright claimants, for example, were permitted to make their own selections and to run their own boundaries, provided they did not encroach upon the lands of others, reckoning "metes and bounds" by the features of the landscape. Despite frequent disputes over boundaries, this approach worked well enough along the Atlantic coast, but as expansion into the interior gained momentum it resulted in a chaos of competing titles. In New England, while surveying was still rough, the township system of land distribution resulted in a somewhat more systematic approach.

By the 18th century surveying techniques had been greatly improved by the innovations of English mathematician Edmund Gunter, especially by his portable quadrant and standardized surveyor's chain, which allowed the incorporation of measures by rod, statute mile, and acre. Also increasing the accuracy of surveys were the astronomical contributions of David Rittenhouse, who helped survey the Mason and Dixon Line and drew the boundaries of more than half of the 13 colonies. Such techniques were essential to the surveyors of the trans-Appalachian west, including young George Washington, appointed surveyor of Culpepper County, Virginia, in the 1740s, and George Rogers Clark, who surveyed for the Ohio Company along the Kentucky River in the early 1770s.

Reflecting upon the multiple conflicts over title in trans-Appalachia, Congress laid out the fundamental principles of a national land distribution in the Land Ordinance of 1785, which provided for the systematic survey of public lands before settlement.

See also Land Ordinance of 1785; Mason-Dixon Line; Rittenhouse, David.

Bibliography: Stilgoe, John R., *Common Landscape of America* (Yale Univ. Press, 1982).

SUSQUEHANNOCK WAR (1676)   The immediate cause of Bacon's Rebellion, this struggle between the Susquehannock Indians and the Virginia colonists resulted in a bloody campaign of extermination against the native peoples of southwestern Virginia. The sequence of events began in the autumn of 1675 with a series of violent engagements between the Susquehannock, fleeing southward from the more powerful Iroquois, and settlers from Virginia and Maryland. In the following spring, Nathaniel Bacon, a planter from Henrico County, urged that the Virginia militia immediately undertake retaliation against all Indians in the colony, but his request was rejected by the governor, Sir William Berkeley, who sought to avert a full-scale war.

Bacon nevertheless initiated unauthorized, punitive raids against the formerly friendly Occaneechee and Pamukey tribes on the colony's southern border, and when Berkeley still refused to sanction his actions he and his supporters laid siege to Jamestown and forced the governor to flee. Berkeley eventually succeeded, with the help of reinforcements from England, in restoring order, but not before many of the surrounding Indian tribes, with whom the colony of Virginia had maintained peaceful relations, were almost entirely wiped out.

See also Bacon's Rebellion.

SWANENDAEL COLONY   Swanendael was a Dutch colony on the Delaware River, established under a patent issued to Samuel Godijn under the West India Company's Freedoms and Exemptions of June 7, 1629. The colony was called a patroonship, and its patent carried with it semifeudal rights of jurisdiction. Joining Godijn in this endeavor were Samuel Blommaert and David Pietersz de Vries. The tract of land was described in the accompanying documents that served to justify the 1630 patent on the South River (Delaware) on a tract of land "extending

northwards about thirty miles from Cape Henlopen to the mouth of the said river and inland about two miles."

An expedition containing two vessels departed the Netherlands in December 1630. One vessel, the *Salm*, was captured by Dunkirk pirates, but the other, the *Walvis*, arrived in the Delaware in the spring of 1631 with its cargo of indentured servants, tools, firearms, and trade goods. The little colony was destroyed by Indians within the year, and although the investors continued their efforts to re-establish the colony, it was eventually sold back to the West India Company for 15,600 guilders in 1635. Since this early Dutch settlement nullified the Lord Baltimore patent claim to the region, it led to the settlement of the boundary dispute between Pennsylvania and Maryland. The compromise reached created the province of Delaware.

SWEDISH COLONIES   In 1633 the New South Company was organized with infusions of capital in equal parts from Dutch and Swedish investors. Granted a Swedish royal charter to settle on the Delaware River, in 1638 a small group of Swedes and Finns arrived under the leadership of Peter Minuit (who had left the Dutch and entered the service of the Swedes), purchased a tract of land on the west shore from the Indians, and established Fort Christina (near present-day Wilmington) as the center of the sole Swedish colony in the Americas. Over the next 20 years small outlying forts were added on the Jersey side and near the present locations of Philadelphia and Chester, Pennsylvania. These settlers probably introduced log-cabin construction to America.

In 1642 the Swedish crown bought out the Dutch investors. It extended its control of the organization, now called the New Sweden Company, and entered into a period of intense conflict with neighboring New Netherland. In 1654 the colony captured the Dutch fort at New Castle, built by Peter Stuyvesant, establishing control of the entire valley. But the Dutch retaliated the next year with a large force that wiped out Fort Christina, established a Dutch fort in its place, and thus put an end to New Sweden.

See also Minuit, Peter; New Netherland.

Bibliography: Johnson, Amandus K., *Swedish Settlements on the Delaware: Their History and Relations to the Indians, Dutch and English, 1638-1644*, 2 vols. (1911; reprint B. Franklin, 1970).

SYCAMORE SHOALS, TREATY OF (1775)   An agreement transferring approximately 17,000,000 acres of land in Kentucky from the Cherokee nation to the colony of North Carolina, the Treaty of Sycamore Shoals was signed on March 14, 1775. It took its name from the village of Sycamore Shoals on the Watauga River, where it was signed by Judge Richard Henderson on behalf of North Carolina and Chief Attakullakulla for the Cherokee. Following a 1769 reconnaisance of the Kentucky territory by Daniel Boone, the Louisa Land Company and the Transylvania Company were founded to encourage colonial settlement in that region. After extended negotiations, the Cherokee agreed to cede the lands between the Kentucky River and the Cumberland Gap for a payment of 10,000 pounds.

T

TAMMANY (?1625-?1701) Chief of the Delaware nation, whose name was derived from *támanend*, "the affable," Tammany lived along the Delaware River and became the subject of many popular stories and myths among both the Indian and non-Indian populations of the Middle Atlantic region. It is not, however, always possible to separate fact from fiction in the surviving accounts of Tammany's life. He reportedly welcomed and pledged friendship to William Penn in 1682 at Shackamaxon, and a signature identified as his appears on the Shackamaxon treaties of 1682 and 1683. In 1694 he officially pledged his friendship to the provincial council of Pennsylvania.

His most famous exploits were, however, more supernatural: Delaware myths told of his Herculean battle with an evil spirit who attempted to take over the lands of his tribe, a contest in which huge expanses of land were desolated and whole forests were turned into prairies. During the American Revolution, "Saint Tammany" became a popular symbol of American independence, and his legendary exploits were recounted during May-Day celebrations. In 1789, William Mooney, former member of the Sons of Liberty, founded the Society of St. Tammany, an organization that later dominated Democratic party politics in New York from its headquarters in "Tammany Hall."

See also Shackamaxon, Treaty of.

TARLETON, BANASTRE (1754-1833) A British army officer, the son of a prominent merchant and public figure, Tarleton was born in Liverpool and educated at Oxford. He joined the King's Dragoon Guards in 1775. Arriving in America in 1776, he served in the Charleston expedition and the New York campaign. He was promoted to the rank of lieutenant colonel in the British Legion in 1778. His most noted engagements took place during the British invasion of the Carolinas in 1780. Defeated at Cowpens, South Carolina (1781), he later served under Lord Cornwallis in Virginia. Tarleton returned to England in 1782, later serving as a member of Parliament and as a military governor of southern Ireland.

TAVERNS In the colonies taverns and inns (or "ordinaries," as they were usually called) could be found open from dusk to dawn, and sometimes longer, from Maine to Georgia, in both town and country, at crossroads and ferry crossings. The official function of a tavern was to furnish room and board for travelers, but in an age when most of life was lived within the confines of the household, taverns also offered a place where local men could leisurely drink, gossip, and gamble with their neighbors. Because few farmers could afford newspapers, the keepers of country ordinaries commonly subscribed to several, making the tavern a sort of reading room where patrons read and discussed the topics of the day. During the Revolution, taverns were the site of many of the political meetings that mobilized the populace. But men also bowled, played at dice and cards, gambled on horse races and cockfights; especially in the South, billiard tables were expected at every inn.

The consumption of wine, ale, and rum enjoyed general acceptance throughout the colonies; in 1737 there were 177 ordinaries dispensing alcohol in Boston, one for every 25 adult males, and similiar establishments were almost as common in the countryside. The tavern was a social center well suited to the farmers and tradesmen of a traditional society.

See also Alcohol, Consumption of.

TAXATION WITHOUT REPRESENTATION A quote from the British orator John Hampden, used against King Charles I in 1637, this slogan, often extended to "taxation without representation is tyranny," became the watchword of American resistance to a series of tax measures initiated by the British government beginning in 1761. The legal question at issue was whether the king and his ministers had legitimate power to tax; a 1724 decision indicated that only Parliament or the representative bodies within the colonies could raise taxes. Many Americans believed that they were not represented even in Parliament and that all taxes initiated by the government in London were therefore unjust and illegal.

The first use of this slogan in the colonies was credited to James Otis of Massachusetts in his 1761 attack on the Writs of Assistance to British customs collectors at the port of Boston. Agitation against British taxation became especially strong with the passage of the Sugar Act (1764) and the Stamp Act (1765). Public pressure soon brought about the repeal of the Stamp Act, but the Townshend Acts of 1767 and a continuing tax on imported tea provoked boycotts and demonstrations throughout the colonies, the most famous of which was the 1773 Boston Tea Party. The issues of taxation and governmental authority were central motivations for the American Revolution.

TAXES Taxes in early America proceeded from several sources. Royal taxation assumed the form of tariffs or duties incidental to commercial regulation (Plantation Duty Act, 1673) and tariffs (American Revenue Act, 1764; Townshend Acts, 1767) and excise taxes (Stamp Act, 1765) designed to raise revenue. Additional royal as well as proprietary taxation included the imposition of quitrents.

Colonial governments—provincial, county, parish, and town—relied upon a variety of taxes that varied in kind and importance from section to section and colony to colony. The New England provinces utilized a combination of property, poll, and means (faculty) taxes (listed in descending order of their importance in generating revenue). The Middle Colonies depended mainly upon property taxes, supplemented by means (faculty) taxes (most extensive in Pennsylvania) and excises (most significant in New York). Poll taxes, unpopular at the provincial level of government, were used by counties and towns.

The Southern colonies imposed a combination of poll, property, and commercial taxes. Maryland, Virginia, and particularly North Carolina relied on poll taxes at all levels of government to raise public revenue. Those provincial governments also enacted various tariffs on exports (tobacco) and imports (slaves among others). South Carolina and Georgia utilized tariffs, a capitation tax on free blacks, a means (faculty) tax, an acreage land tax, and assessments on money at interest and annuities.

Overall, taxation policies varied according to the relative strength of contending political factions and interest groups. Tax systems were fraught with loopholes, subject to fraud in collection procedures, and usually designed for the benefit of the wealthy, landed elite. As such, taxation was regressive, particularly in the Southern colonies. Town residents complained of undue, discriminatory assessments on urban property by provincial lawmakers. Adding to the tax burden everywhere were fees and public work obligations. Despite such exceptions as North Carolina, the tax burden in most colonies apparently was light compared to that of England. In all cases, however, the colonials were extremely jealous of the taxation power of their provincial legislatures.

Bibliography: Becker, Robert A., *Revolution, Reform, and the Politics of American Taxation, 1763-1783* (Louisiana State Univ. Press, 1980).

Alan D. Watson
University of North Carolina at Wilmington

TAYLOR, GEORGE (1716-81) A metallurgist and political leader, Taylor was born in Northern Ireland and arrived in America in 1736. After working at forges in Chester County, Pennsylvania, he established his own ironworks in Bucks County in 1754. A supporter of American independence, Taylor served in the provincial assembly (1764-70) and on a committee of correspondence in 1775. With the outbreak of the Revolution, he was appointed a colonel in the Bucks County militia. In 1776 he was elected to the Second Continental Congress and signed the Declaration of Independence. He last held public office in 1777, when he served on the Supreme Executive Council of Pennsylvania.

TAYLOR, JOHN (1753-1824) A political leader and commentator, popularly known as "John Taylor of Caroline," he was born in Caroline County, Virginia, and educated at the College of William and Mary. After graduation he studied law and was admitted to the bar in 1774. With the outbreak of the Revolution, Taylor joined the Continental Army, seeing active service in Pennsylvania and New York. He resigned his commission in 1779, having reached the rank of major. In 1781 he briefly resumed his military career as a lieutenant colonel in the Virginia militia, serving under the Marquis de Lafayette. Taylor was a member of the Virginia House of Delegates (1779-85), and he later served three terms in the U.S. Senate (1792-94, 1803, 1822-24). He was best known as a political philosopher and writer whose pamphlets and books were widely circulated.

Among the causes that he supported throughout his career were the strict separation of church and state and the direct representation of all citizens in the machinery of government. At the time of the Constitutional Convention in 1787, Taylor joined Patrick Henry and George Mason in opposing the draft document, fearing that it did not sufficiently protect the rights of individuals and the states. Taylor was also known as an agrarian reformer.

TEACH, ROBERT (BLACKBEARD) (died 1718) Piracy produced a number of improbable figures, but none more so than Robert Teach, better known as Blackbeard. A large, fearsome man, he grew a thick beard that he twisted into braids that danced around his head. In battle he added to his terrifying presence by shoving a slow fuse, burning at both ends, under his hat, thereby producing a wreath of smoke around his head.

A privateer in the West Indies during Queen Anne's War, he drifted into piracy after the war ended in 1713. In 1717 he appeared off Charleston, South Carolina, in his ship *Queen Anne's Revenge* and quickly set to capturing every ship entering or leaving the port and kidnapping a number of citizens for ransom. The townspeople were helpless, and he left only after he received a chest of medicine in return for his prisoners. He then sailed to North Carolina, where he grounded his ship near Cape

Fear. After transferring to an accompanying sloop, he sailed to a nearby sandbank and forced off half the men, keeping only his cronies and, of course, the treasure.

He then accepted a general pardon from Governor Charles Eden, whom he had probably bribed. After a brief rest Blackbeard returned to piracy, causing a reign of terror on the Carolina coast. The government of Virginia sent a fleet after him and in a tough fight on November 22, 1718, Lieutenant Robert Maynard killed Teach, but only after the pirate had received 25 wounds, 5 of them from bullets.

TEEDYUSKUNG (c.1705-63) A Delaware chief, whose name was derived from *kekeuskung,* "the healer," Teedyuskung was born near Trenton, New Jersey, and settled in the Upper Delaware Valley of eastern Pennsylvania around 1730. In 1750 he was converted to Christianity by the Moravian missionaries and baptized under the name Gideon. As a lifelong opponent of Iroquois domination over his people, Teedyuskung became war chief in 1753 and independently negotiated with the colonial authorities, gaining recognition of the territorial inde-

Gilbert Tennent, a Presbyterian minister, was one of the leaders of the Great Awakening. *(Library of Congress)*

pendence of the Delaware in 1756. During the French and Indian War he served as an ally of the British and spent his last years in the Wyoming Valley of Pennsylvania.

TEKAKWITHA, CATHERINE (1656-80) A Roman Catholic nun, also known as "The Lily of the Mohawks," Tekakwitha was born near Fonda, New York, to a Mohawk father and a Christian Algonquin mother, both of whom died in a smallpox epidemic while she was a small child. She was attracted to the teaching of the Jesuit Father Lamberville and in 1675 was baptized as Catherine. In 1677 she entered a convent at Sault St. Louis near Montreal and gained fame throughout Canada for the supernatural visions and miraculous cures attributed to her faith. She was also known for her practice of physical penance, insisting at one point on being whipped in public every Sunday for a year.

TENNENT, GILBERT (1703-64) A Presbyterian minister and leader of the Great Awakening, Tennent was born in Ireland, the eldest of four sons of William Tennent and Catherine Kennedy, who emigrated to Pennsylvania in 1718. From his father, the founder of the Log College in Pennsylvania, Gilbert learned the classics, Hebrew, and theology and was granted an honorary degree from Yale in 1725, the same year that he was licensed by the Philadelphia Presbyterian Synod.

In 1726 he was called to New Brunswick, New Jersey, where, under the influence of Dutch Reform evangelist and Great Awakening leader Theodore Frelinghuysen, he intensified his emotional preaching style and his emphasis on saving conversions. In 1738 the "Old Side" Philadelphia Synod sought to control the evangelism of the "New Side" Tennents by emphasizing formal education over personal piety in ministerial candidates. Tennent answered with his 1739 sermon *The Danger of an Unconverted Ministry,* which was experienced as accusatory by the Old Side and became a precipitating cause of the 1741 schism in the Philadelphia Synod. Following George Whitefield in 1741, Tennent toured the Middle Colonies and New England "harvesting" large numbers of souls. In 1743 he moved to Philadelphia's Second Church and moderated both his preaching style and the extremity of his views, calling for a reunion of his divided church in his 1749 sermon *A Humble, Impartial Essay on the Peace of Jerusalem.* This reunion finally took place in 1758 in Tennent's church. In 1753, Tennent traveled to England and raised 1,200 pounds for the College of New Jersey (later Princeton). His first wife died in 1740, after which he married Cornelia De Peyster, who died in 1753. His third wife was Sarah Spofford, with whom he had three children.

See also Great Awakening; Presbyterians; Tennent, William; Whitefield, George.

Laurie T. Crumpacker
Simmons College

TENNENT, WILLIAM (1673-1746) Founder of the "Log College" Presbyterian Seminary, Tennent was born in Scotland and received a master's degree from the University of Edinburgh in 1695. He was licensed by the Scottish Presbytery in 1701 and, perhaps because of Ireland's severe 1703 laws against Presbyterians, took Anglican orders in 1704. In 1702 he married Catherine Kennedy, with whom he had one daughter, Eleanor, and four sons, Gilbert, John, William, and Charles. In 1718 they emigrated to the American colonies, where Tennent was admitted to the Philadelphia Presbyterian Synod and became a pastor in East Chester and Bedford, New York. In 1726 he founded the church in Neshaminy, Pennsylvania, and the next year began to build an 18-by-20-foot log house as a seminary for the training of Presbyterian ministers. A leader of the "New Side" or evangelicals, he was criticized for requiring evidence of personal piety in ministerial candidates. Log College candidates were denied ordination without special examination by the "Old Side" Philadelphia Synod in 1738, and Tennent himself, after being censured, moved to the "New Side" New York Synod. Upon his death in 1746, the Log College closed, but there Tennent had trained his own sons and 17 other influential Presbyterian ministers, including founders in 1746 of the College of New Jersey (later Princeton).

See also Log College; Presbyterians; Tennent, Gilbert.

TENOCHTITLÁN The capital of the Aztecs, Tenochtitlán was founded in 1369 on a mud flat in Lake Tezcoco and was the forerunner of Mexico City. The temples of Huitzilopochtli and Tlaloc dominated the center of the city, which was divided into four quarters, each of which was further divided into wards. Tenochtitlán was connected to the shore by causeways that doubled as aqueducts. Its population may have reached 150,000. Tenochtitlán began its rise to power by conquering its twin city of Tlatilulco, also on Lake Tezcoco, in 1473, but Hernando Cortes besieged and destroyed the city in 1521, shortly thereafter reconstructing it as a Spanish colonial city.

See also Cortes, Hernando.

THEATER Colonial America had an ambivalent attitude toward the theater: fascination with the excitement of the stage, fear of the impact on morals. In many of the colonies and towns, theater was outlawed as a breeding ground for immorality and vice. In Virginia in 1665 three men were prosecuted (but acquitted) for producing the English play *Ye Bare and Ye Cub*, but this may suggest that amateur theatricals were being performed clandestinely throughout the colonies in the 17th century. By the early 18th century strolling players were circulating throughout the Southern and Middle colonies, performing in coffeehouses, barns, or fields on the outskirts of towns where they might avoid persecution. The first legitimate theater was built at Williamsburg, Virginia, in 1716 but was closed seven years later and afterward became the town hall.

The first acting company in the colonies was organized in 1749 in Philadelphia, where it performed Addison's *Cato,* moving to New York the next year where it opened with Shakespeare's *Richard III,* the first known performance of the bard's work in the colonies. This company's repertoire included 24 plays by Shakespeare, Addison, Dryden, Fielding, and others, and its members performed as well in Williamsburg, Fredericksburg, and Annapolis. In 1752 a company of English actors headed by Lewis Hallam opened in Williamsburg with *The Merchant of Venice.* This company, with a repertoire of 40 plays, also performed in New York and Philadelphia. In 1758, English actor David Douglass organized the "American Company," which opened in New York. During the next two decades this touring troupe stimulated a new interest in drama. The colonies' first permanent theater, the Southwark, was built in Philadelphia in 1766; others were built in New York City (1767), Annapolis (1770), and Charleston (1773).

During the Revolution the Continental Congress banned all "exhibitions of shews, plays, and other expensive diversions and entertainments," but performances by British actors were given for British troops and citizens in the occupied cities and towns, further awakening interest in drama. After the Revolution the Douglass troupe returned and competed with numerous others touring the major cities. Now the theater was finally accorded social approval by the attendance of such public figures as George Washington, who loved the drama.

The first indigenous playwrights belonged to the Revolutionary generation. Thomas Godfrey, perhaps America's first playwright, wrote *The Prince of Parthia* (1763), which was first performed at the Southwark in Philadelphia in 1767. Patriot playwrights included: Mercy Otis Warren, who published *The Adulateur* (1773) and *The Group* (1775); Hugh Henry Brackenridge, who wrote *The Rising Glory of America* (1771), *The Battle of Bunker's Hill* (1776), and *The Death of General Montgomery* (1777). Royall Tyler's *The Contrast* (1787) was the first American comedy.

See also Brackenridge, Hugh Henry; Dunlap, William; Godfrey, Thomas; Hallam, Lewis; Tyler, Royall; Warren, Mercy Otis.

Bibliography: Quinn, Arthur H., *A History of the American Drama: From the Beginning to the Civil War*, 2nd ed. (1943; reprint Irving, 1982); Seilhamer, George O., *History of the American Theatre before the Revolution* (1891; reprint Greenwood Press, 1969).

John Mack Faragher
Mount Holyoke College

THEUS, JEREMIAH (?1719-74) A portrait painter, Theus was probably born in Switzerland and arrived with his parents and two brothers at a Swiss-German settlement in Orangeburg County, South Carolina, around 1739. By 1740 he had established himself as a painter in Charleston and in 1744 opened an evening school to teach painting. He was connected with the prominent planters of the region and painted them at their plantations if a trip to Charleston was inconvenient. Forty portraits by Theus are catalogued, including several of Huguenot planters, but there are probably more unidentified paintings by him in private collections. His figures are stiff but exact and the features of his subjects are well drawn. His work has been mistaken for that of John Singleton Copley because of similarities in style.

THOMSON, CHARLES (1729-1824) A scholar, merchant, and statesman, Thomson was born in Ireland. He came to America as a youth and was educated at an academy in Chester County, Pennsylvania; subsequently he taught school in Philadelphia. Later a successful merchant and an active patriot, he earned the title of "the Sam Adams of Philadelphia" while helping to lead resistance to Britain. In 1774 he was chosen as the first and only secretary of the Continental Congress, serving until it was replaced by the new federal government in 1789. Thomson devoted his later years to Biblical scholarship.

THORFINN, KARLSEFNI (flourished 1010) The first European to attempt the colonization of North America, Thorfinn landed at Leif Eriksson's Vinland, circa 1010, with a party of 60 men and 5 women, the first European women in America. At the settlement, which apparently included livestock, the Norse colonists engaged in trading with the Indians, whom they called "Skraelings," or "wretches." In one such encounter, the Indians proposed trading for Norse weapons, and when the Norse refused a fight ensued in which there were deaths on both sides. Thorfinn sailed home in 1013, carrying two captive In-

dians, the first of many to be kidnapped and taken to Europe.

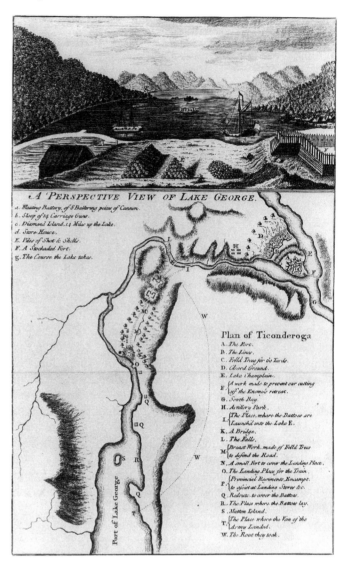

Both the British and the French wanted Fort Ticonderoga for its command of the route between Lake Champlain and Lake George. *(Library of Congress)*

THORNTON, MATTHEW (1714-1803) A physician, jurist, and political leader, Thornton was born in Ireland and immigrated with his family to Worcester County, Massachusetts. After completing medical studies in 1740, he moved to Londonderry, New Hampshire. In 1745 he served in the Louisburg expedition and was later appointed a lieutenant colonel in the New Hampshire militia. He was elected to the New Hampshire assembly in 1758. Active in patriot affairs, including the agitation against the Stamp Act (1765), Thornton was named president of the provincial congress in 1775. He was a member of the Second Continental Congress in 1776 and signed the Declaration of Independence. He then served as judge of the New Hampshire superior court (1776-82) and in the state senate (1784-86).

TICONDEROGA, FORT   A fortified point on the New York side of Lake Champlain that commanded the short land route between the southern extremity of that lake and the northern tip of Lake St. Sacrament (later Lake George), Fort Ticonderoga was the key to the historic invasion route between Canada and the Hudson River. Begun by the French in 1755 and named Fort Carillon, it was unsuccessfully assaulted by the British under General Abercrombie in 1758 but was taken the following year by a force led by Sir Jeffrey Amherst and renamed Fort Ticonderoga. It was seized by Ethan Allen in May 1775, and its cannon were transported to George Washington's army in the siege of Boston. The Americans, under General Arthur St. Clair, abandoned the fort to General John Burgoyne's invading army in 1777 but reoccupied it following Burgoyne's defeat at Saratoga. Never used after the American Revolution, it is maintained as a museum and historic site.

TOBACCO   Tobacco, or *Nicotiana tabacum*, is one of the most powerful stimulant plants known—and one of the most toxic and addictive of all drugs. Indians throughout the Americas used it in religious and medical rituals, and nearly every native language had a word for the plant. "Taboca" was the word Christopher Columbus heard the Arawak use for the plant he found them smoking "to become benumbed and almost drunk," for consuming the potent tobacco varieties they cultivated had a hallucinatory effect. Bartolomé de Las Casas reported that desperate African slaves of early 16th-century Hispaniola soon learned that tobacco smoking helped them "to lose their reason [and] fall down as if they were dead." Spanish colonists complained that newly-arrived slaves quickly became addicted to the habit. Before long tobacco had entered Europe, where doctors prescribed it as an antidote against the plague and other diseases, but others, following the slaves' example, used tobacco as an intoxicant, inhaling deeply and holding the smoke in their lungs to maximize the effect. In 1604, King James I of England declared tobacco smoking to be "loathsome to the eye, hatefull to the Nose, harmfull to the brain, dangerous to the Lungs." But despite royal disapproval the practice persisted.

In the early 1610s, John Rolfe of the Virginia Company experimented with a South American tobacco variety, and in 1613 he shipped his first crop to England. This milder tobacco found quick acceptance, for rather than inducing hallucinations, it provided pleasant and addictive smoking. By 1620 tobacco was the leading export crop of the Chesapeake colonies, and it built the foundation of Virginia's prosperity. Along with Maryland and the Al-

bemarle section of North Carolina, Virginia became the center of New World tobacco production. Tobacco was the most valued North American export.

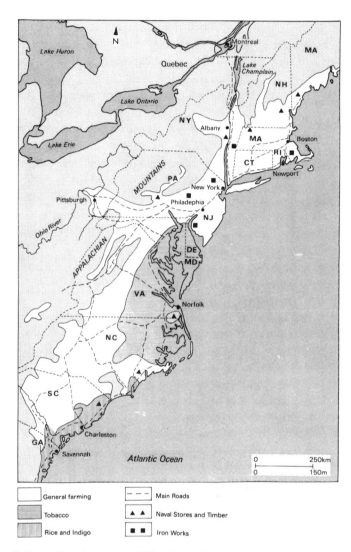

Tobacco Growing Areas, 1770. *(Martin Greenwald Associates, Inc.)*

Because growing tobacco quickly exhausted the soil, the growing tobacco trade demanded the expansion of available land, thus driving the Chesapeake colonists ever deeper into the interior, sweeping aside the Indians. Tobacco culture, moreover, was particularly demanding, requiring a heavy commitment of labor, thus stimulating the rapid growth of indentured labor and slavery.

See also Slavery.

Bibliography: Main, Gloria L., *Tobacco Colony: Life in Early Maryland, 1650-1720* (Princeton Univ. Press, 1982).

TOLERATION ACT   Perhaps the most famous, and frequently misunderstood, of Maryland's colonial statutes, the Act Concerning Religion, commonly known as the Toleration Act, was drafted by Cecilius Calvert, Lord Baltimore, in 1649. Calvert was a Roman Catholic, and Puritan rule in England meant that his financial and political interests there and in his American colony, and his faith as well, were threatened. Calvert wanted to assure English officials that, in fact, Protestants, especially Puritans, not only were safe, and secure in their faith in his colony, but also welcome. Additionally, he wished to insure that his own religion would be preserved there, not merely for those Catholics already residing in the colony but also for any potential refugees who might need a safe haven. His Toleration Act, therefore, ensured freedom of conscience in matters of religion for any who professed faith in Jesus. It did not offer protection for, or toleration of, non-Christians. The act declared that anyone who disturbed a colonist because of his or her Christian religious beliefs would suffer severe punishment.

The Maryland assembly, dominated by Protestants, modified the draft of the act to exclude any Christian who denied the Trinity. Thus, as passed in April 1649 and accepted by Calvert the following August, the act was even narrower in its application than he desired. In fact, the law merely placed in Maryland's code a practice that already had legal status, for the instructions issued in 1633 to Leonard Calvert, the proprietor's younger brother and the colony's first governor, included the provision that different religious groups tolerate one another. Also, Maryland's first Protestant governor, William Stone, had been required in 1648 to swear that under his leadership no Christian, and particularly no Roman Catholic, would be harassed because of his or her religious views.

See also Maryland; Religion; Roman Catholics.

TOMOCHICHI (died 1739) Tomochichi was chief of a small band of Yamacraw Indians who gave James Edward Oglethorpe permission to establish Savannah, Georgia. Through him Oglethorpe invited the larger Creek nation to send representatives to meet with him. About 55 Creek signed a treaty on May 21, 1733, ceding land between the Savannah and Altamaha rivers as far as the tidewater line. In 1734, Tomochichi, his wife Senauki, his nephew Tooanahowi, and five other Indians accompanied Oglethorpe to England. Tomochichi's party visited King George II, the Archbishop of Canterbury, and the Georgia Trustees, winning favorable publicity for Oglethorpe's work in Georgia. After the Indians returned to Georgia, Oglethorpe continued to deal with the Creek through Tomochichi. When the chief died at an advanced age on October 5, 1739, Oglethorpe honored him with a military

funeral. A large boulder marks Tomochichi's grave in Wright's Square, Savannah.

TONTY, HENRI DE (?1649-1704) A French explorer in the Great Lakes and Mississippi Valley regions, de Tonty was probably born in Paris and lost his right hand during his service in the French army. He accompanied La Salle in 1678 to New France, where he managed the building of La Salle's boat, the *Griffon*, for exploring the Great Lakes. While he was in charge of Fort Crèvecoeur on Lake Peoria, his men mutinied. He was wounded during a visit to the Iroquois to bring peace but escaped to Green Bay (Wisconsin) by avoiding the Iroquois encampments and living on roots.

He and La Salle built another fort on the Illinois River, Fort St. Louis, and in 1682 explored the Mississippi to its mouth, claiming the river valley for France. La Salle returned to France, leaving Tonty to control the Illinois fort. He searched twice for La Salle, who was supposedly bringing colonists from the mouth of the Mississippi. On one of these vain trips in 1686, he established Arkansas Post in the lower Arkansas Valley. After a decade of managing the fort and caring for missionaries and traders, he left Illinois and settled in Louisiana.

TORDESILLAS, TREATY OF (1494) The Treaty of Tordesillas, between Portugal and Spain, set a line of demarcation between their respective colonial domains. After Christopher Columbus's successful return from his first voyage, the Spanish monarchy applied to the pope for a monopoly of the trade and conquest of the western Atlantic. The request was inspired by a similar Portuguese petition to the pope that resulted in a series of papal bulls (notably *Aeterni regis*, 1481) granting King John exclusive Catholic rights to the booty from his African voyages, south of a line extending west across the Atlantic from the Canary Islands.

In a series of bulls (*Inter Caetera I* and *II*) issued in 1493, Pope Alexander VI (a Spaniard) confirmed Spanish rights to all discoveries west of a meridian beginning 100 leagues west of the Canaries and running south from the *Aeterni regis* line. The Treaty of Tordesillas, negotiated the next year, shifted that meridian 270 leagues westward, providing the basis for the later Portuguese colony of Brazil. The treaty helped to control competition between the Iberian nations, although other European states likely agreed with the judgment of the king of France, who remarked: "I should very much like to see the passage in Adam's will that divides the New World between my brothers, the Emperor Charles V and the King of Portugal."

TOWNSHEND, CHARLES (1725-67) The son of a viscount and known for his wit, charm, and speaking ability,

Townshend spent his career as an English public servant. As chancellor of the exchequer he sponsored legislation (Townshend Acts) that contributed to the widening rift between the American colonies and England. Educated at Leyden, and perhaps at Oxford, Townshend was elected to Parliament in 1747. When his parliamentary ally the Earl of Halifax was named head of the Board of Trade in 1748, Townshend received a position on the board. Subsequently he served not only in Parliament but in the admiralty, on the privy council, as secretary-at-war, as president of the Board of Trade, and as paymaster-general. Townshend rejected offered positions as first lord of the admiralty and secretary of state. In 1766 he became chancellor of the exchequer.

Since Prime Minister William Pitt was ill, Townshend assumed virtual leadership of the government. When Parliament reduced his proposed land tax, thereby creating a revenue deficit in his budget, Townshend declared that he would "find a revenue in America nearly sufficient" to compensate. Thus he instituted port duties on glass, red and white lead, paint, paper, and tea. The Americans were outraged that trade regulations were being employed not to regulate trade but rather to raise money, that they were being taxed by persons they had not elected to office. Townshend died "of a neglected fever" before the colonists enacted nonimportation, nonconsumption agreements to oppose the measures.

See also Townshend Acts.

Bibliography: Forster, Cornelius P., *The Uncontrolled Chancellor, Charles Townshend and His American Policy* (The Rhode Island Bicentennial Foundation, 1978).

TOWNSHEND ACTS (1767)

Although by 1767 the crisis caused by Parliament's passage of the Stamp Act (1765) had, with the act's repeal (1766), passed, the English government still was determined to establish its right to govern the American colonies. Simultaneously, many in England believed the colonials were receiving substantial benefits, such as defense, from their membership in the empire but were not contributing to their costs. Since the colonists, in resisting the Stamp Act because it seemed to represent an internal tax imposed by a body in which they were not represented, had acknowledged Parliament's right to regulate trade, Chancellor of the Exchequer Charles Townshend proposed that a set of duties confined "to regulations of trade" be enacted as a way to satisfy both sides in the conflict. His Townshend Revenue Act was meant to be seen by the Americans as a compromise—indeed, as a conciliatory gesture. Passed on July 2, 1767, the act set import duties on all glass, paint, paper, and tea.

At the same time, to help enforce this act as well as the other trade regulations, Parliament created an American Board of Customs Commissioners in Boston, to which all American customs officials would report. Parliament also established four American vice admiralty districts, where the appointed judges would hear not only cases on appeal from colonial vice admiralty courts but would also have original jurisdiction. Since such courts were juryless, their establishment promised to make enforcement of English trade laws highly effective.

Americans responded to these measures by arguing that though Parliament surely had the right to regulate the empire's trade, the purpose of any such levies must be limited exclusively to that specific end. The use of trade duties primarily to raise revenue violated their rights as Englishmen to be taxed only by representatives they had elected. Early in 1768 the Massachusetts House sent a "Circular Letter" to other colonial assemblies, denouncing the acts as illegitimate since the colonists were being taxed by persons they did not elect. The letter was warmly supported in many of the assemblies. At the same time a massive nonconsumption, nonimportation movement began, in which Americans chose not to use the imported goods that were taxed. English leaders, alarmed by such activities, concluded that troops were required to help local officials maintain order and to enforce the laws. The Townshend Acts, then, crafted to serve as a moderate compromise, failed to accomplish any of the goals that dictated their enactment.

See also Nonimportation; Revolutionary War, Causes of.

Aaron Shatzman
Franklin and Marshall College

TRANSPORTATION

The rivers of North America provided the first and foremost highways of inland commerce. For the French, the St. Lawrence River and the Great Lakes, extending 2,000 miles into the heart of the continent, provided unrivaled access to the treasures of the fur trade. From Montreal they traveled west in large birchbark canoes up to 30 feet long on La Grande Rivière (the Ottawa) with its many laborious portages, entering Georgian Bay, paddling across Lake Huron to the passages to Lake Michigan at the Straits of Michilimackinac, or Lake Superior by way of St. Marys River. The Sieur de La Salle pioneered a southern lake route to these passages. Later the canoe was supplemented with bateaux and the Mackinaw boat, both powered by mast and sail, and these vessels also connected the French settlements along the Mississippi River with the administrative center at New Orleans.

Along the Atlantic, colonists were blessed by a series of deep rivers that provided miles of access for ocean-going vessels. In New England the Penobscot, Kennebec, Androscoggin, Saco, Piscataqua, Merrimack, and Connecticut rivers were important conduits for the fur and

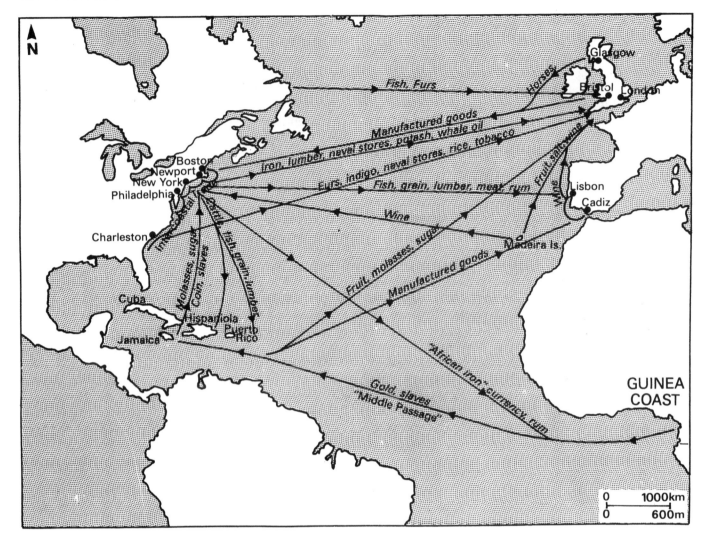

Triangular Trade. *(Martin Greenwald Associates, Inc.)*

timber industries, but only the last two drained farming land and became important routes of agricultural commerce. The Hudson (with the connecting Mohawk), the Delaware, and the Susquehanna all offered deep penetration of the backcountry of the Middle Colonies and from earliest settlement were commercial highways. On the southern coast, where the Atlantic plain widens considerably, below the falls of the Potomac, Rappahannock, York, James, Roanoke, Santee, and Savannah rivers, the valuable commodities of the growing plantation system were carried to port by shallop and pinnace.

Road Transportation. But the same rivers, streams, and creeks that facilitated boat transport were a serious barrier to overland travel, and road transport developed slowly. While Southerners rolled their hogsheads of tobacco to market over "rolling roads," in the North people at first used pack animals almost exclusively, later turning to primitive carts in summer, sleds in winter. The underdeveloped state of overland transport is suggested by the fact that in 1697 Philadelphia's tax rolls showed only 30 wheeled vehicles in the city. By the second decade of the 18th century, however, German craftsmen of southeastern Pennsylvania had developed the Conestoga wagon with its long, deep, bowed bed, its huge wheels, its distinctive tricolor of red bed, blue running gear, and white canvas cover. Pulled by large teams of native-bred Conestoga horses, these wagons supplied the British during the French and Indian War, then transported settlers to the trans-Appalachian west after victory in 1763.

The colonial upper classes along the coast traveled in sedan chairs, horse litters, or on horseback, women perched on cushions behind the saddled men. Coaches began to appear in the mid-18th century, the first on the stage line from Philadelphia to New York, a trip taking three days, opening in 1756. But lines developed very slowly, largely because the cumbersome English coach required well-graded roads, few and far between in the colonies. After the Revolution craftsmen began to design and market American coaches, part of a general revolution in transportation over the next 50 years that included macadamized turnpikes, bridges, dredged rivers, canals, locks, keelboats, then steamboats and railroads.

See also Fur Trade; La Salle, Sieur de; Mississippi River; New Orleans; Plantation System; Roads and Trails; Shipping.

Bibliography: Dunbar, Seymour, *History of Travel in America* (1915; reprint Greenwood Press, 1968); Meyer, B. H., et al., *History of Transportation in the United States Before 1860* (1917; reprint Peter Smith).

John Mack Faragher
Mount Holyoke College

TRANSYLVANIA COMPANY Organized in 1774 by Richard Henderson and other influential North Carolina investors to speculate in western lands, the Transylvania Company illegally negotiated with the Cherokee Indians for land between the Ohio and Cumberland rivers, most of what would later become Kentucky. The company's organizers encouraged pioneer settlement, framed a preliminary government, and in 1778 petitioned the Continental Congress for recognition. Its petition was rejected because of the opposition of Virginia and North Carolina, which complained of encroachment on their western grants. The company was nevertheless granted 200,000 acres on the Ohio by the state of Virginia.

TRIANGULAR TRADE Signifying routes of colonial commerce, triangular trade denoted patterns of shipping that involved a round trip of three destinations. One such route encompassed the shipment of fish, grain, lumber, and provisions from New England, New York, and Philadelphia to the West Indies; the acquisition there of sugar, molasses, fruit, and bills of exchange to take to England; and the exchange in England for manufactured products to take to the port of origin. Another route saw fish, lumber, and wheat taken to Spain, Portugal, the Azores, and the Madeira Islands; an exchange made at that point for salt, fruit, and wines; and the shipment of those goods to England where manufactures were obtained and returned to America. The African slave trade formed the best known of the triangular trades: Rum and trade goods were sent to Africa and exchanged for slaves who were taken (on the "Middle Passage") to the West Indies or to America's Southern colonies, at which point they were sold for indigenous products or bills of exchange.

Despite a longstanding emphasis on triangular trade, that shipping pattern was relatively unimportant in relation to the totality of colonial commerce. New England historians in the late 19th century, primarily through their investigation of the slave trade, erroneously originated the concept of "triangular trade." However, less than one percent of the annual average tonnage that cleared New England between 1768 and 1772 was destined for Africa. Moreover, relatively few vessels from the New England or Middle Colonies departed for the West Indies and then continued to England. Evidence to support the triangle involving southern Europe and returning to the provinces is so similar that it indicates the prevalence of a direct, two-way trade. Although some commerce followed multilateral patterns or involved route switching, route specialization and bilateral trade were predominant.

See also Rum Trade; Slavery.

Bibliography: Shepherd, James F. and Walton, Gary M., *Shipping, Maritime Trade, and the Economic Development of North America* (Cambridge Univ. Press, 1972).

Alan D. Watson
University of North Carolina at Wilmington

TROWBRIDGE, EDMUND (1709-93) A colonial jurist, born in Cambridge, Massachusetts, Trowbridge graduated from Harvard in 1728 and soon gained a name for himself as one of the most respected jurists in the American colonies. He served as Massachusetts attorney general (1749-67), becoming recognized as an authority on real property and mortgage notes. In 1767 he was appointed judge of the Massachusetts superior court, a position he held until the outbreak of the Revolution in 1775. Trowbridge was a Loyalist, but his impartiality in such cases as those of the Berkshire rioters, the Writs of Assistance, and the Boston Massacre won him the respect of all political factions.

TRUMBULL, JOHN (1750-1831) A poet and jurist, Trumbull was born at Westbury, Connecticut. His father, John, was a fellow at Yale College and a cousin of Governor John Trumbull. When only 13, young John matriculated at Yale, where he wrote neoclassical verse and bawdy, comic poetry. He graduated with a master's degree in 1770. Before graduating, he wrote a well-received long poem, "The Progress of Dullness," satirizing collegiate instruction. In 1773, Trumbull moved to Boston to study law with John Adams. It was here he acquired the political background that was to figure in his most famous poem, "M'Fingal," a work of 1,500 Hudibrastic couplets. First published in 1775, the poem was a satire of both the hapless Tory M'Fingal and the fervid Patriots. The original version was mild enough to be published in England without much comment, but in 1782 Trumbull sharpened the work, including a climax that saw M'Fingal being tarred and feathered. The poem is essentially a burlesque of the bombast and rhetoric of the early Revolution and as such is a plea for moderation. It was enormously popular. Trumbull never again published a major work, preferring to devote his energy to his law practice and becoming the leader of the "Hartford Wits." He became active in Connecticut politics and served on the state supreme court (1808-19).

TRUMBULL, JOHN (1756-1843) An American artist, Trumbull was born in Connecticut, graduated from Harvard College in 1773, and served in the colonial army until 1777. He studied painting in Boston and under Benjamin West in London from 1780. There he painted *Battle of Bunker's Hill* (1786), as well as portraits of historical figures, earning him the title "Painter of the Revolution." He returned in 1789 to America, where he painted portraits and gathered more material for his painting *Declaration of Independence*. He served John Jay as his personal secretary from 1793. In 1817 he was commissioned to paint four pictures for the rotunda of the Capitol building in Washington, D.C.

TRUMBULL, JONATHAN (1710-85) Connecticut's Revolutionary War governor graduated from Harvard College (1727) and spent his whole adult life in his native Lebanon, Connecticut. While licensed as a Congregational minister, Trumbull joined his brother Joseph in 1731 in a mercantile partnership. After Joseph was lost at sea, Jonathan became a full-time merchant on his own. From 1731 to 1749 he operated as an inland merchant, selling to customers in Lebanon and nearby towns goods that he purchased in Boston. In late 1749, with Elisha Williams and Joseph Pitkin, he formed a partnership that soon acquired large debts attempting a direct trade with England. A later firm, founded in 1764 and composed of Jonathan, son Joseph, and Eleazer Fitch, also tried but failed to realize a profitable English trade. In 1735 he married Faith Robinson of Duxbury, Massachusetts, with whom he had six children. All four sons played active roles during the Revolutionary War.

Trumbull first entered public service in 1733 with election to the General Assembly where he served as speaker in 1739. He was also a justice of the peace and judge of the county, probate, and superior courts, as well as a colonel of the Twelfth Regiment. A strong opponent of the Stamp Act, Trumbull and others walked out in 1765 when Governor Thomas Fitch took the required oath of support. In 1766 Trumbull was elected deputy governor and in 1769 governor. The only incumbent colonial governor to serve throughout the war, he established a close relationship with General George Washington, providing large amounts of food and arms for the Continental Army. While he frequently convened the Council of Safety, much of the burden of running the state fell on him. In 1784, Trumbull

retired from public service, acutely aware of the disunity that had plagued the American cause. He therefore urged the establishment of a much stronger central government.

See also Connecticut; Trumbull, Jonathan, Jr.

John W. Ifkovic
Westfield State College

TRUMBULL, JONATHAN, JR. (1740-1809) An ardent nationalist and Federalist, he was the son of Jonathan Trumbull, Connecticut's Revolutionary War governor. Educated at Tisdale's school in his native Lebanon, Connecticut, and at Harvard College, Trumbull began his long career of public service in several town offices, including selectman (1770-75). In 1774 he served the first of seven terms representing Lebanon in the General Assembly, where he actively resisted British infringements on colonial rights while also serving on Lebanon's committees of correspondence and safety. In 1775, Congress appointed him paymaster for the New York Department with the rank of colonel. After he resigned in 1778, he served as the first comptroller of the treasury for six months. From June 1781 to August 1783 he served as military secretary for George Washington, who became a steadfast and intimate friend.

Trumbull's strong nationalistic views resulting from his wartime experience, his active membership in the "exclusive" Connecticut Society of the Cincinnati, and his support for commutation put him in disfavor with his fellow townsmen, who denied him election to public office. Connecticut's ratification of the Constitution meant the triumph of nationalism, and Trumbull was rewarded with election to the first three Congresses (1789-95) and to the U.S. Senate (1795- 96), where he ardently supported all the Federalist programs. Elected Connecticut's lieutenant governor in 1796, he was also elected governor repeatedly from 1798 to 1809. His defiance of the Enforcement Act of 1809 demonstrated the depths of his commitment to Federalism.

See also Trumbull, Jonathan.

John W. Ifkovic
Westfield State College

TRUMBULL, JOSEPH (1737-78) The commissary-general of the Continental Army, Trumbull was born in Lebanon, Connecticut, the son of Governor Jonathan Trumbull and brother of painter John Trumbull. He graduated from Harvard in 1756. He served in the Connecticut General Assembly (1767-73) and was elected as an alternate to Roger Sherman at the Continental Congress of 1774. Trumbull's initial experience in supplying troops came in April 1775 when the General Assembly appointed him commissary-general to Connecticut's forces. He came to the attention of General George Washington, who influenced Congress to give Trumbull the rank of colonel and the job of supplying the Continental Army on July 19, 1775.

The problems associated with feeding the army of colonies in revolt were enormous. Funds were marginal, and currency was depreciating. Transportation was arduous. Worst of all were conflicts within Congress and the states, which appointed numerous commissaries, creating senseless competition. Despite the difficulties, Trumbull did an admirable job and was warmly praised by Washington for his efforts. In early 1777, Congress reorganized the commissary's office into two branches, one for purchases and one for issues, and offered one to Trumbull. He refused but was elected to the board of war. Ill health led to his return to Lebanon, and he died shortly thereafter.

TRYON, WILLIAM (1729-88)   A British colonial governor, born in Surrey, England, Tryon was commissioned as a lieutenant in the Foot Guards in 1751 and reached the rank of lieutenant colonel in 1758. In 1764 he received an appointment from Lord Hillsborough to become lieutenant governor of North Carolina, and in 1765, the year following his arrival, he became acting governor with the sudden death of Arthur Dobbs. As an uncompromising administrator during the Stamp Act agitation, Tryon brought the colony's coastal trade to a near standstill. In 1768 he led government troops against tax rioters in Hillsboro County, completely crushing their protest.

Tryon was transferred to New York in 1771 to replace Lord Dunmore as governor, and he continued to display a hardline attitude toward civil unrest. With the outbreak of the Revolution and the collapse of civil government in New York, Tryon commanded a Loyalist force, rising to the rank of major general in 1778. His personal animosity toward the American rebels and his brutal retaliatory raids along the Connecticut coast brought protests even from the British authorities. In 1780 illness forced him to return to England. Soon after his promotion to lieutenant general in 1782, he retired from public life.

TUCSON   When Jesuit missionaries, among them Father Eusebio Kino, visited in the 1690s what would later be known as Arizona, they found Papago Indians living in villages along the watercourses. The most important early Spanish settlement in the area was the presidio of Tubac, on the Santa Cruz River, which was established after a rebellion of the Pima Indians. The building of the mission of San Xavier del Bac and the northward extension of the frontier influenced the shifting of the Tubac garrison to the new presidio of San Agustin del Tucson, also on the Santa Cruz River, in 1775. Silver mines in the area contributed to Tucson's prosperity, and efforts to pacify and settle the nearby Apache were sporadically successful, but Tucson remained a frontier town through the colonial period.

TUFTS, JOHN (1689-1752)   An innovative composer of church music, Tufts was born in Medford, Massachusetts, to Mercy and Peter Tufts. Graduating from Harvard College in 1708, he became minister of the Second Church of Christ in West Newbury, Massachusetts, in 1714. He soon astounded his congregation by setting the psalms to music with letters instead of notes on the staff. This music, *A Very Plain and Easy Introduction to the Art of Singing Psalm Tunes*, was called "Quakerish and Popish," but the music sold 11 editions and was printed in the last issue of the *Bay Psalm Book* in 1774. Tufts also wrote the religious tracts *Anti-Ministerial Objections Considered* (1725) and *A Humble Call to Archippus, Or the Pastor Exhorted, To Take Heed That He Fulfill His Ministry* (1729). In 1738 he left his church after parish complaints and moved to nearby Amesbury.

TURELL, JANE COLMAN (1708-35)   A poet and religious mystic in Massachusetts, Turell was the daughter of Benjamin Colman, pastor of the Cambridge Brattle Street Church, and Jane Clark, daughter of a wealthy pewterer. Trained by her father, Jane could read and recite Scripture by age two and by her teens had devoured most of her father's library, concentrating on the prescribed spiritual writings, poetry, and other "polite literature" of the day. Her poetry was didactic, religious, and emotional, often occasioned by personal trauma and sometimes by homely details of daily life. She married Ebenezer Turell, a pastor in Medford, when she was 18 and continued to keep a diary that recorded household events and spiritual struggles.

Like those of any latter-day evangelical Puritan, her writings are filled with an overwhelming sense of sinfulness and anxiety about salvation. Sickly from childhood, during the last nine years of her life she endured four pregnancies, with one surviving child. A typical poem, written after three infants' deaths, concludes, "Farewell sweet Babes I hope to meet above/ and there with you to sing the Redeemer's Love." She is perhaps best known for the manner of her dying, which, because of its resignation and model piety, was recorded in detail by her husband and published with excerpts from her diary and poetry.

TUSCARORA WAR (1711-13)   This conflict in North Carolina between the Lower Tuscarora and British colonists over the continuing enslavement of the native population and territorial expropriation began with the murder of John Lawson, the surveyor general of North Carolina, by the Tuscarora in September 1711. That action was just a prelude, for Chief Hencock of the Lower Tuscarora was soon joined by the Coree, Pamlico, Machapunga, and Bear River Indians in attacks on settlements along the Trent and Pamlico rivers during which 130 colonists were killed.

The North Carolina authorities quickly appealed for help from the other colonies. New York convinced the Seneca not to assist their kinsmen the Lower Tuscarora; Virginia prevented the involvement of the Upper Tuscarora; South Carolina dispatched Colonel John Barnwell and later Colonel James Moore to mount a retaliatory campaign against Lower Tuscarora villages. The decisive battle took place in March 1713 at Fort Nohoroco, a fortified enclosure to which the surviving Lower Tuscarora had fled near Snow Hill, North Carolina. After a three-day battle, the colonists were victorious, and with the migration of the last of the Lower Tuscarora to join other tribes in Virginia and New York, large-scale colonial expansion in the Carolinas finally began.

TYLER, ROYALL (1757-1862) A satiric playwright, novelist, and jurist, Tyler was born to Royall and Mary Steele Tyler in Boston. Receiving degrees from both Harvard and Yale in 1776, Tyler in his early career practiced law and saw service against Shays' Rebellion. His reputation as a delightful wit apparently did not win the approval of John Adams, who ended his daughter Abigail's engagement with Tyler, who then married Mary Palmer. His comedy of manners, *The Contrast*, the second play and first comedy written by an American, introduced in 1787 the naive Yankee "Jonathan" and was an instant success. His other plays, except for four unpublished manuscripts, are lost, but his 1797 novel, *The Algerine Captive*, satirizing social conditions north and south, survived. His verse under the name "Spondee" lampooned the Federalist period and was collected in *The Spirit of the Farmers' Museum* (1801).

After practicing law in the Boston area until 1791, he moved to Vermont. His legal career included positions in Vermont as state's attorney for Windham County (1794-1801), assistant judge (1801-07), chief justice of the supreme court of Vermont (1807-13), and professor at the University of Vermont (1811-14).

U

ULLOA, ANTONIO DE (1716-95) As the first governor of Spanish Louisiana after the French cession of the territory to Spain in 1762, Ulloa was a complete failure. He arrived in the colony in 1766 and worked with the last French governor in ruling Louisiana. The French inhabitants eventually broke into open revolt and drove Ulloa from the colony. In 1767 he sent Francisco Riu upriver from New Orleans to report on the situation in the middle Mississippi Valley as part of an attempt to establish Spanish control, but his efforts were in vain. Ulloa was replaced in 1769 by Alejandro O'Reilly, who established Spanish authority in the next six months by executing those who had rebelled against Ulloa. Ulloa was also a noted natural scientist, known throughout Europe for his account (1748) of an expedition (1735-44) in South America.

UNAMUNO, PEDRO DE (flourished 1587) In 1587 the trade winds brought a small frigate to the coast of Alta California. The commander of the ship, Pedro de Unamuno, had been ordered to find two large islands thought to be in the ocean to the east of Japan. Although unsuccessful in this effort, Unamuno made landfall in the vicinity of Morro Bay. The harbor invited further exploration, and Unamuno led a small expedition that not only examined the shoreline but also penetrated into the interior to the vicinity of the later mission of San Luis Obispo. After a fight with the natives, Unamuno decided to continue down the coast to New Spain, arriving in Acapulco on November 22. His report was largely ignored by the administration.

UNCAS (c.1606-c.1682) A Mohegan leader, whose name was derived from the Algonquian *wonkas*, "the fox," Uncas was the son of Owenoco, a Pequot sachem and son-in-law of Sassacus, supreme Pequot chief. After condemning Sassacus's 1634 peace treaty with the English colonists, Uncas was banished from Pequot territory and became the leader of the dissident Mohegan in northern Connecticut. A bitter rival of the Narragansett, Uncas himself concluded a treaty with the English in 1643, for which they handed over to him his arch-rival Miantonomo for execution. In 1656, English colonial forces again came to Uncas's aid during his conflict with the Narragansett chief Pessacus.

During King Philip's War (1675-76), Uncas and his Mohegan followers fought on the side of the English in their campaign of extermination against the Narragansett. With the conclusion of that conflict, the Mohegan were the only Indians in New England to maintain sovereignty over even a portion of their original territory. However, they later sold off their remaining territory to the colonists and were eventually restricted to a reservation. Uncas served as the model for the main character in James Fenimore Cooper's *The Last of the Mohicans*. The town of Uncasville, Connecticut, is named after him.

See also King Philip's War; Sassacus.

UTRECHT, TREATY OF (1713) A set of agreements between Britain, France, and Spain, the treaty briefly resolved the colonial rivalry that had caused Queen Anne's War (1702-13). On April 11, 1713, France ceded to Britain St. Christopher Island in the Caribbean and Acadia and Newfoundland in Canada and also restored to Britain the Hudson Strait and Bay. While reserving fishing rights in those areas and being assured of the safety of French residents, France also acknowledged the sovereignty of the English over the Iroquois. On July 13, Spain promised never to transfer its American colonies to another power and offered British merchants the right to sell slaves in its American domains.

See also Queen Anne's War.

V

VALLEY FORGE Famed as the winter quarters of the Continental Army (December 1777- June 1778), Valley Forge was the scene of both suffering and reorganization after the British occupation of Philadelphia. Situated on the Schuylkill River, about 25 miles from Philadelphia, Valley Forge was an easily defensible position, yet logistical misplanning resulted in a critical lack of food, clothing, and shelter. Of the 10,000 troops quartered there, approximately 2,500 died during the winter. The arrival of spring, news of the alliance with France, and the organizing efforts of Baron von Steuben and Nathanael Greene dramatically altered the dire condition of the Continental Army.

See also Greene, Nathanael; Steuben, Baron von.

VAN CORTLANDT FAMILY The American branch of this prominent New Netherland and New York family was founded by Oloff Van Cortlandt (1600-84). Oloff was born in Wijkbij Duurstede in Utrecht Province (Netherlands) and emigrated to New Netherland aboard the ship *Haering* in 1638 as a West India Company soldier. In 1640 he was appointed commissary of stores and soon thereafter began to acquire real estate. In 1645 he was elected one of the Eight Men chosen to assist Director General Willem Kieft in the Indian Wars and continued to hold important offices in the government of New Netherland until the end of the Dutch era. After the English conquest of the colony he served several terms as an alderman of New York City. During the last 10 years of his life he was rated the fourth richest person in the colony. He had married Anneken Loockermans in 1642 and with her had seven children, including some of singular importance. Stephanus Van Cortlandt (1643-1700) was born in his father's house on Brouwer Street in New Amsterdam. Trained as a merchant, he served as a factor for Jan Baptist Van Rensselaer of Amsterdam and continued to import Dutch goods into New York after the English conquest. Stephanus married Gertrude Schuyler, daughter of Philip Schuyler of Albany. He served Governor Sir Edmund Andros in various capacities and was appointed the first native-born mayor of the city of New York in 1677. During the period of Leisler's Rebellion he was forced to flee, but upon Leisler's overthrow he was one of the principal prosecutors of the rebel and pushed vigorously for his execution. In 1683 he purchased a tract of land on the east bank of the Hudson that eventually became the site of the Van Cortlandt estate at Croton-on-Hudson. The manor lands included 87,713 acres according to a survey of 1732. Divided among his heirs in 1753, it became the source of the family's wealth.

See also Van Cortlandt, Philip; Van Cortlandt, Pierre; Van Rensselaer, Maria Van Cortlandt.

Bibliography: Judd, Jacob, ed., *Correspondence of the Van Cortlandt Family*, 4 vols. (Sleepy Hollow Press 1977-81).

Oliver Rink
California State University, Bakersfield

VAN CORTLANDT, PIERRE (1721-1814) The first lieutenant governor of New York state, Van Cortlandt was born in New York City, the youngest son of Philip and Catharine (De Peyster) Van Cortlandt and the grandson of Stephanus. He grew up on the family manor at Croton-on-Hudson and in 1748 married Joanna Livingston, his second cousin. Soon thereafter he inherited a portion of his father's estate and became involved with the management of the farms and mills. Although a moderate Whig with Loyalist tendencies, he declared for the patriots in the American Revolution and served in many provincial offices during the war. He presided over the New York state constitutional convention in 1776 and was elected the state's first lieutenant governor, a post to which he was periodically reelected for 18 years. He withdrew from politics in 1795 to manage the estate and died at his manor house.

See also Van Cortlandt, Philip; Van Cortlandt Family.

VAN CORTLANDT, PHILIP (1749-1831) A Revolutionary War officer and member of Congress, Van Cortlandt was the eldest son of Pierre and Joanna (Livingston) Van Cortlandt. Although born in New York City, he grew up on the family's estate at Croton-on-Hudson where as a young man he gained experience as a surveyor, overseer of his father's estate, and supervisor of gristmills. In 1775 he declared for the patriot cause in the American Revolution and was chosen one of Westchester County's delegates to the first provincial congress.

Commissioned a lieutenant colonel in the 4th New York regiment in June 1775, he was to serve with distinction on George Washington's staff and in various

The harsh winter at Valley Forge, Pennsylvania, severely weakened the Continental Army. *(Library of Congress)*

other capacities. Van Cortlandt saw action at Saratoga, Valley Forge, and Yorktown and retired as a brigadier general. In the years following the Revolution he was prominent in New York politics. In 1788 he supported the ratification of the Constitution, but his subsequent political career was as an Antifederalist. He held many offices in later life: New York assembly twice (1788 and 1790); New York state senate (1791-93; and U.S. House of Representatives (1793-1809). In 1809 he retired from politics to his family estate, where he died.

See also Van Cortlandt, Pierre; Van Cortlandt Family.

VAN RENSSELAER, KILIAEN (1580-1643)   First patroon of Rensselaerswyck, Van Rensselaer was born in 1580 in Hasselt, the Netherlands, son of Hendrick Van Rensselaer and Maria Pasraat. Trained as a jewel merchant by his uncle, he eventually formed his own merchant enterprise, which in 1614 he merged with another

jewelry firm. In 1616 he married Hillegond Van Bijler, niece of his uncle. In 1623 he appears as a principal shareholder in the Amsterdam chamber of the West India Company. He was to serve in various capacities in the company, including a stint as director of the chamber and a member of the New Netherland Commission, which was charged with the responsibility of developing policy for the company's North American colony of New Netherland.

In 1628 he was instrumental in the development of the patroonship system for New Netherland whereby private investors would, in exchange for grants of land, establish semifeudal estates in the colony. The first plan of 1628 was never implemented, but an even more generous plan was developed in 1629 and under the provisions of this plan, entitled the "Freedoms and Exemptions," Van Rensselaer acquired title to a tract of land encompassing nearly 1,000,000 acres in and around present-day Albany, New York. His heirs were to continue his efforts to make this patroonship, Rensselaerswyck, succeed, and in 1685 the family's rights were recognized by the English governor of New York, Thomas Dongan, after which the estate passed into the English manorial system. It was the only patroonship to succeed in the Dutch period and the only one to survive into the English era.

See also New Netherland; Patroonships; Rensselaerswyck.

Bibliography: Nissenson, S. G., *The Patroon's Domain* (Columbia Univ. Press, 1937); Rink, Oliver A., *Holland on the Hudson: An Economic and Social History of Dutch New York* (Cornell Univ. Press, 1986); Van Laer, A. J. F., ed. and trans., *The Van Rensselaer-Bowier Manuscripts* (Univ. of the State of New York Press, 1908).

Oliver A. Rink
California State University, Bakersfield

VAN RENSSELAER, MARIA VAN CORTLANDT (1645-89) Wife of the patroon of Rensselaerswyck (Jeremias Van Rensselaer), she was born in New Amsterdam, the third child of Oloff Van Cortlandt and Anna Loockermans. On July 12, 1662, Maria married Jeremias, who had succeeded his brother, Jan Baptist Van Rensselaer, as patroon of Rensselaerswyck in 1658. By him she had four sons and two daughters; her youngest son, Jeremias, was born shortly after her husband's death in 1674.

At the time there was no one available who could succeed Jeremias as director of the patroonship, and consequently the burden of its administration fell temporarily upon her. She was aided by her brother Stephanus Van Cortlandt. Her efforts were made more difficult by disputes with her late husband's family in the Netherlands. For two years (1676-78) she had to be content to serve as treasurer for the estate at an annual salary of 150 bushels of grain, which she was forced to share with Stephanus, who served as the estate's book-keeper. Upon the death of Nicolaes Van Rensselaer in November 1678, she took over charge of the estate, although her brother was named director. Since Stephanus continued to reside in New York City, the actual management of the estate fell to her. From that time until her death, Maria ran the estate. She maintained a voluminous correspondence with the English authorities, much of which was devoted to efforts to have the family's right to the estate of Rensselaerswyck recognized by the English government. By the time she died, the title had been recognized, and her eldest son, Kiliaen, had succeeded to the title of lord of the manor that had been founded by his grandfather.

See also Rensselaerswyck.

Bibliography: Van Laer, A. J. F., ed. and trans., *The Correspondence of Maria van Rensselaer, 1669-1689* (Univ. of the State of New York, 1935).

Oliver A. Rink
California State University, Bakersfield

VARDILL, JOHN (1749-1811) A clergyman and British espionage agent, Vardill was born in New York City and graduated from King's (later Columbia) College in 1766. As one of the college's most promising theology students, he received a master's degree in 1769 and soon afterwards joined the faculty. Vardill was also an avid political debater and pamphleteer; he was one of the most eloquent spokesmen in New York for the Loyalist cause. In 1773 he was appointed professor at King's College and subsequently left for England, where he was ordained a deacon in 1774.

Although he received an additional appointment to become assistant minister of Trinity Church in New York, Vardill chose to remain in London after the outbreak of the Revolution in an attempt to influence the opinion of Americans there against an outright break with England. Failing that, Vardill served as a British spy from 1775 to 1781. Occupying an office in London at 17 Downing Street, he and his staff kept a close watch on American sympathizers in London and succeeded in intercepting highly sensitive diplomatic mail. His greatest intelligence coup was his interception of the secret Franco-American correspondence relating to their proposed alliance. Vardill never returned to America after the war and spent his later life in Ireland.

VARGAS, FRANCISCO (flourished 1584) After the return of the expedition of Antonio de Espejo, Vargas, the regidor of Puebla, petitioned the Spanish crown for authority for the northern frontier in 1584. He claimed that the region explored by Francisco de Coronado and Espejo contained no minerals and no provisions but that a great salt river lay beyond, as well as lakes around which the Indians mined gold and silver. Vargas assumed that the river was the Strait of Anian, or Northwest Passage, and he volunteered to equip and provision 70 men at his own expense and travel beyond New Mexico to explore and settle the country. His offer was turned down.

See also Espejo, Antonio de.

VAUDREUIL-CAVAGNIAL, PIERRE DE RIGAUD, MARQUIS DE (1698-1778) The last French governor of Canada, Vaudreuil-Cavagnial was born in Canada as the third son of Governor de Vaudreuil. He fought against the Fox Indians in Wisconsin in 1728, received the cross of the Order of St. Louis in 1730, and became governor (1733-42) of Three Rivers, the third largest settlement in New France. He then succeeded Jean Baptiste Le Moyne, Sieur de Bienville, as governor of New Orleans (1742-53). Vaudreuil-Cavagnial was a respected governor during his term. Although he led one expedition against the Chickasaw Indians, he saw little military action. In 1755 he was appointed governor of Canada to conduct the defense against the English. His refusal to agree to the Marquis de Montcalm's request for a guard led to the French defeat on the Plains of Abraham in 1759. In 1760 he was besieged in Montreal and in September accepted defeat from the English. He was tried in France for his conduct but was exonerated.

VERMONT   The first European to explore this region, in 1609, was Samuel de Champlain, who named the Green Mountains ("Les Monts Verts") and provided the origin of the fanciful name "Vermont," which came into use only in the 1770s. The French first built a fort at Isle la Motte at the north end of Lake Champlain in 1665, and in 1690 English colonists from Albany planted a settlement at Chimney Point at the south end of the lake, but the first permanent villages were established along the Connecticut River after the construction of an English fort near Brattleboro in 1724. Most settlements moved north up the Connecticut Valley or east from New York.

In 1749, New Hampshire claimed its jurisdiction extended to Lake Champlain, calling the territory the "New Hampshire Grants." In 1764 the New York claim to the same area, under its charter of 1664, was confirmed by the Crown. Then in 1771, Ethan Allen and his Green Mountain Boys took up arms in defense of their indigenous claims. In 1775, with help from Connecticut forces, they captured Fort Ticonderoga and took part in the expedition against Canada. In 1777 local representatives met at Westminister and adopted a declaration of independence; after encouragement from the Continental Congress, they adopted their own state constitution, becoming the first jurisdiction to abolish slavery and to provide for universal manhood suffrage. The claims of the Green Mountain Boys were confirmed on the battlefields of Bennington and Saratoga. Agreement on the boundary was reached with New Hampshire in 1782 and with New York in 1790 after cash payments. Vermont was admitted to the union in 1791.

See also Green Mountain Boys; New Hampshire.

VERRAZANO, GIOVANNI DA (?1485-1528?)   One of the most important early explorers of both Americas, Verrazano was probably born either in Tuscany or in France, of parents who belonged to the flourishing community of Italian bankers and merchants of Lyons. His name also appears in its French form, Jean de Verrazane. At that time there were many Italians at the French court since the kings of France had begun to intervene in Italy in an attempt to establish indirect sovereignty if not outright domination.

Verrazano's first voyage across the Atlantic in 1524 is well-documented in a detailed report to France's King Francis I and was written upon Verrazano's return to Dieppe, France, his home port on the English Channel. Having left France on January 7, he reached present-day North Carolina and then, turning north, surveyed the American coast as far as Nova Scotia, a land he named "Arcadie." He made several landfalls along the way, the most famous at present-day New York City. During this voyage Verrazano first saw the expanse of water we now know as Chesapeake Bay and thought he had discovered a direct link with the Pacific Ocean. In 1526 he led a new expedition, again from Normandy, this time to Brazil. Although the circumstances and date of his death are uncertain, it may have occurred in January 1528, as he was returning to France. He was supposedly surprised and killed on a Jamaican beach by Carib Indians along with the landing party he had led on a supply search.

VESPUCCI, AMERIGO (1454-1512)   The Florentine navigator for whom the Americas were named, Vespucci spent 40 years as a commercial representative of the Medici, the powerful Italian trading family that sent him to Seville, Spain, in 1492. There, in 1498, he met Christopher Columbus, who was preparing for his third voyage. The next year Vespucci accompanied the Spanish conquistador Alonso de Ojeda on an expedition to the Pearl Coast (Venezuela), and from there he voyaged south to Brazil and may have explored the mouth of the Amazon River. *The Soderini Letter*, an account of this exploration supposedly written by Vespucci in 1504, precipitated a controversy (that has continued to this day) by antedating the voyage to 1497, thus giving Vespucci credit for having reached the mainland of "Las Indias" before Columbus.

Vespucci sailed across the Atlantic a second time in 1501, this time on a Portuguese vessel. Although some have questioned his authorship, he published an account of this expedition in *Mundus Novus (New World)*, a work translated into several languages and reprinted in scores of editions over the next five years. "These regions we may rightly call *Mundus Novus*," the author wrote, "because our ancestors had no knowledge of them." Vespucci, in other words, was probably the first to recognize Las Indias as a new continent, although he continued to believe that it was very near to Asia. In 1508 the Spanish crown named him the first pilot major of Spain, with responsibility for the licensing of mariners and the updating of maps of the world.

See also America, Naming of.

VIELE, ARNOUT CORNELISSEN (1640-c.1704)   An interpreter and negotiator with the Indians in New Netherland and New York, Viele was born in New Amsterdam, the son of Dutch emigrants, and by 1659 was living in Albany. He entered the Indian trade and by 1675 had become a valued interpreter with the Iroquois, developing a special skill in the art of Indian oratory. He was the agent of Governor Thomas Dongan and in the 1680s led a large party of New York traders north of the Great Lakes, where they were captured by the French; he escaped after being held prisoner in Quebec for four months. He played an important and active role in the implementation of the Indian policy of the colony for the rest of the century, acquiring extensive property from Indians along the Hudson River.

VIGO, JOSEPH MARIA FRANCISCO (1747-1836) A soldier and trader in the Mississippi Valley, Vigo was born in Italy and joined the Spanish army. He was stationed in New Orleans, where he became interested in the fur trade. After his discharge, Vigo built a trading network that reached as far north as St. Louis. During the American Revolution, Vigo aided the Americans with information and money and was invaluable in financing George Rogers Clark's campaign to gain control of the western frontier. By 1783, Vigo was living in Vincennes (Indiana) and soon became a citizen of the United States. Most of his later years were spent in straitened circumstances, but his friendship with William Henry Harrison was advantageous.

VILLAFANE, ANGEL DE (flourished 1651) A Spanish naval commander and explorer, de Villafane succeeded to the command of Don Tristán de Luna y Arellano, charged with colonizing the Florida coast. In 1651 he tried to move Luna y Arellano's colonists from Pensacola Bay to Santa Elena (Port Royal), but, buffeted by storms, he was finally driven back to Hispaniola after possibly traveling as far north as Cape Hatteras, North Carolina. The Spanish colonizing project was abandoned later that year when King Philip IV barred further efforts to settle Florida.

VILLASUR, PEDRO (died 1720) The chief lieutenant of Governor Valverde of New Mexico, Villasur was ordered in 1720 to reconnoiter on the Great Plains to the northeast to determine if rumors of Indian unrest were true. The Spanish government feared that the Pawnee had obtained guns from the French and would push other Indians, notably the Comanche, into the Spanish settlements. Reaching the North Platte River in August, Villasur sought to communicate with a nearby Pawnee village. The attempt was in vain, and the Pawnee ran off most of their horses and killed all but 13 of the Spaniards, including Villasur. The remnant of the group reached Santa Fe on September 6.

VINCENNES The French had established a Wabash River trading post, in present-day Indiana, on the site of an Indian village as early as 1700. Vincennes, named in 1736 after the Sieur de Vincennes, who had fortified the site in 1732, became the southernmost of the Great Lakes fur-trade centers, supplied from Detroit. By 1750 the surrounding countryside was being farmed by French-speaking families, many of them métis or mixedbloods. In 1763, after the French and Indian War, control of the post was transferred to the British. American Revolutionary War leader George Rogers Clark captured it as a part of his Illinois campaign in 1779, and from 1800 to 1813 it served as the first capital of Indiana Territory.

VINLAND In the medieval Scandinavian epics, "Vinland" from the Norse *vin* meaning "meadow") was the name for a land visited by Norse mariners about 1000 A.D. Artifacts from an archeological site at the fishing village of L'Anse aux Meadows in Newfoundland document the Norse presence in North America, and this may be the location of Vinland, although other possibilities are Pamiok Island and Ungava Bay in northern Quebec.

See also Norse Exploration and Settlement; Vinland Map.

VINLAND MAP This parchment map of the known world, supposedly drawn in the early 15th century, showed an insular land mass in the North Atlantic labeled "Vinland." In 1965, Yale University Press published the map, claiming that it was the earliest depiction of the New World, and a confirmation of the voyages of Norse exploration and settlement. In 1974 a test of the ink suggested that it was a forgery. Although a more comprehensive test of both ink and parchment in 1987 seemed to contradict the 1974 findings, much doubt has remained about the map's authenticity.

See also Norse Exploration and Settlement.

VIRGINIA Founded at Jamestown in April 1607, Virginia became the first permanent English colony in the Western Hemisphere. The Virginia Company of London established the colony to trade with natives, serve as a base against the Spanish in the Caribbean, and promote Protestantism. The colony almost failed before John Rolfe introduced tobacco cultivation in 1612. In 1616 the company increased settlement by offering land (headrights) to whomever paid for a passage and large tracts (particular plantations) to wealthy settlers. Similar motives inspired the company to call the first representative assembly in the New World in 1619. An Indian attack (whites called it a "massacre") in 1622 halted expansion, and in 1624 the Crown revoked the charter, converting Virginia into a royal colony.

Tropical diseases for which immigrants lacked immunity resulted in a terrifying death rate that prevented the population from becoming self-sustaining until the

An 18th-century map of Virginia was illustrated with a busy port scene. *(Library of Congress)*

1690s. Only the continued influx of settlers, lured by tobacco, allowed growth. Most arrived as bonded (indentured) laborers, and few survived the contract period. Those who did and could obtain land and more "unfree" labor to work it prospered. After mid-century few achieved wealth who did not have the resources to come originally as freemen. Suppressive policies, especially after a second major Indian attack in 1644, drove natives out of the middle and lower peninsulas by mid-century.

Parliament's victory over the king in the English Civil War forced the royal governor William Berkeley into internal exile until the restoration of the monarchy in 1660. Berkeley championed the planters' opposition to the Navigation Acts (1660, 1663, 1673) by which the English monopolized the tobacco trade. The laws initially brought higher costs and lower prices and a 20-year depression. Berkeley became the spokesman for the Virginia establishment (the Green Spring faction), but those outside resented him. Nathaniel Bacon seized upon anti-Indian feeling on the frontier to raise a general rebellion against the governor in 1676. On the verge of victory, Bacon died. Berkeley vindictively executed many of his followers. The Crown recalled Berkeley and took the opportunity to impose tighter imperial controls.

As planters relentlessly acquired tobacco lands, large commercial farms (plantations) developed. Economies of scale helped offset the lower prices and higher costs of the English monopoly. In time, the access to larger markets that the English provided turned their control to Virginia's advantage. Yet, as the need for labor intensified, economic

improvements and easing of political and religious tensions in England lessened the desire of whites to come as indentured servants.

Although a few blacks had been in the colony since 1619, significant migration did not occur until the great planters turned to slavery as a principal source of labor after 1680. The largest number came after the end of the royal monopoly over the slave trade in 1698. By 1740, blacks comprised 30 to 40 percent of all Virginians, and their population had become self-sustaining.

Expansion of the Colony. During the 18th century, tobacco production continued to increase, reaching 70,000,000 pounds annually by the third quarter. Glasgow merchants, whom the English monopoly excluded before the Union of England and Scotland in 1707, dominated the trade by mid-century. The Scots' business skills opened a vast new European market to Virginians.

Prosperity fostered a golden age in Virginia in the 18th century's second quarter when the wealthiest planters strove to emulate the British gentry. Construction of the College of William and Mary, for which James Blair obtained a charter in 1693, and of buildings for the new capital established in Williamsburg in 1699 introduced the architectural ideas of Sir Christopher Wren and inspired the magnificent mansions of the Tidewater.

Governor Alexander Spotswood led a promotional expedition (the Knights of the Golden Horseshoe) to the Shenandoah Valley in 1716 to dramatize the opening of the West. Land grants escalated from initially a few thousand acres apiece to several million after mid-century. From 1690 on, settlement also moved westward through the proprietary grant that the Crown bestowed on Lord Fairfax along Virginia's northern border. The new areas followed the model of the Tidewater in creating a plantation society.

Although about 55 to 60 percent of the white adult males held enough land (25 acres and a house) to qualify for the suffrage, the larger planters dominated in the Council, the House of Burgesses, the county courts, and the church vestries. Election contests seldom materialized among the ethnically, religiously, and economically homogeneous white majority. Elections were social rather than political events in which candidates "treated" participants to a good time more to win their confidence than to promote an issue.

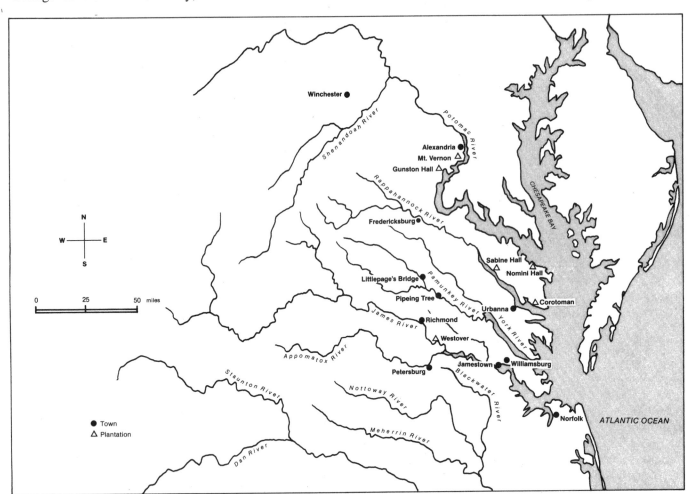

Virginia. (*Facts On File, Inc.*)

By mid-century the House of Burgesses moved ahead of the Council to become the voice of the planter class as the size of the gentry exceeded the number a 12-member board could effectively represent.

Westward bound Virginians met the French in the Ohio Valley, where the young George Washington surrendered Fort Necessity in 1754, precipitating the Seven Years War in Europe (1756-63). General Edward Braddock, whom Washington served as aide, suffered a greater defeat in 1755. Washington's First Virginia Regiment helped stabilize the southern frontier as the main theater shifted northward. The Treaty of Paris (1763) transferred Canada and the lands east of the Mississippi River to Britain and its colonies. To avoid Indian wars, the British Proclamation of 1763 confined white settlement east of the Appalachian Mountains. Virginia negotiators persuaded the Indians to set the actual border on the Kentucky River to the west of the mountains. Daniel Boone led the first settlers through the Cumberland Gap into Kentucky in 1774.

War debts and the expense of the expanded empire pushed Parliament to enact the Stamp Act in 1765. The American colonies unanimously protested that only their representatives in their legislatures could tax them. Although Virginia leaders hoped for a more cautious statement, Patrick Henry set the pace with his defiant "Caesar- Brutus" speech in support of his May 30 resolution for resistance. Virginia joined the colonies' boycott of British imports even though Governor Francis Fauquier (1758-68) kept the burgesses from sending delegates to the Stamp Act Congress in New York. The economic sanctions resulted in the Stamp Act's repeal in 1766. When Governor Botetourt (1768-70) dissolved the House of Burgesses in 1769 before they could protest the Townshend Acts duties (1767), the members met in extralegal session at a tavern in Williamsburg. Most colonists complied with a boycott long enough to compel repeal of all but the tea duty in 1770. Again, when Governor Dunmore (1771-76) dissolved the burgesses in 1774 before they could resolve against the Coercive Acts punishing Boston for its Tea Party, the house moved to the tavern. In August the first Virginia Convention convened to adopt a boycott (the Association), to begin arming the colony, and to send delegates to the First Continental Congress in Philadelphia in September.

War and Statehood. Simultaneously, a border dispute with Pennsylvania over the region around modern Pittsburgh lured the governor to the west. From June to December 1774 he led a successful expedition (Lord Dunmore's War) to expel Indians from the area and to establish Virginia's claim. He won considerable

popularity but for eight crucial months sent only scanty intelligence about Virginia opposition to British authorities. A raid on the Williamsburg public magazine two days after the Battle of Lexington and Concord bred rumors of a conspiracy to suppress American liberty. Fleeing to Norfolk in June, Dunmore conducted a successful military campaign until his defeat at the Battle of Great Bridge on December 9. He evacuated Norfolk. A proclamation of emancipation for slaves who joined his forces confirmed his iniquity in many Virginian eyes.

Although the British fired first at Norfolk on New Year's Day 1776, American troops ran amuck and burned the town. Its place as the center of the Scottish tobacco trade condemned it as a Loyalist stronghold in rebel minds. Popular opinion blamed Dunmore for the fire, and the episode fanned support for independence. On May 15, 1776, the convention directed its delegates in Congress to propose independence, and on June 7, Richard Henry Lee entered the resolution that produced the Declaration of Independence.

On June 12, Virginia became the first state to adopt a declaration of rights and, on June 29, the first republican constitution. The convention elected Patrick Henry governor (1776-79). Once Dunmore abandoned the Chesapeake Bay in August, the British conducted only privateering raids in the bay. The first major invasion occurred in May 1779, followed by Alexander Leslie's in October 1780, Benedict Arnold's in January 1781, and William Phillips's in March 1781. Lord Cornwallis arrived with the main British army in May 1781 for a campaign climaxing in his defeat by George Washington at Yorktown in October 1781. North of the Ohio River, George Rogers Clark in 1779 won spectacular victories though the gains proved difficult to sustain as the war wore on. The British conceded the territory east of the Mississippi River and south of the Great Lakes to the United States in the peace of 1783.

Postwar Virginia. The issue of whether the states or Congress should have title to the western lands blocked adoption of the Articles of Confederation. Not until 1781 did Virginia, which had the most extensive claims, agree to cede the bulk of its lands north of the Ohio River to "the Continent," permitting ratification. The question of how powerful the central government should be sharply divided Virginians. George Washington and James Madison supported the movement that eventually resulted in the Philadelphia Constitutional Convention of 1787; George Mason, Patrick Henry, and Richard Henry Lee opposed ratification of the proposed new federal constitution. The Antifederalists probably represented the majority opinion in the state, but Madison's skillful leadership and Washington's enormous prestige narrowly prevailed in the state's ratifying convention. In June 1788, Virginia became the 10th state to accept the federal constitution.

See also Henry, Patrick; Jamestown; Jefferson, Thomas; Lee, Richard Henry; Lord Dunmore's War; Virginia Company of London; Virginia Declaration of Rights; Washington, George.

Bibliography: Billings, Warren M., Selby, John E, and Tate, Thad W., *Colonial Virginia: A History* (Kraus International, 1986); Isaac, Rhys, *The Transformation of Virginia, 1740-1790* (Univ. of North Carolina Press, 1982); Morgan, Edmund S., *American Slavery-American Freedom: The Ordeal of Colonial Virginia* (Norton, 1976); Tate, Thad W. and Ammerman, David L., eds., *The Chesapeake in the Seventeenth Century: Essays on Anglo-American Society* (Univ. of North Carolina Press, 1979).

John E. Selby
College of William and Mary

VIRGINIA COMPANY OF LONDON   The royal charter of 1606 authorizing the founding of a colony named Virginia in America provided for two joint stock companies distinguished by the principal location of their stockholders: London and the West Country, especially Plymouth. The latter's grant included present New England, where a colony failed in 1607; the former's grant extended from modern North Carolina to Long Island Sound. Its colony at Jamestown succeeded in 1607. A second charter in 1609 reduced royal supervision of the London Company and permitted public sale of stock. The reformed company postponed dividends for seven years during which settlers worked as employees. A third charter in 1612 gave the company jurisdiction over newly discovered Bermuda, which promised to be more profitable, and authorized the company to hold a public lottery.

The introduction of tobacco in Virginia helped the colony but came too late to save the company. Dissatisfied stockholders ousted the treasurer, Thomas Smith, in 1619. The company instituted private landholdings to encourage settlement and, also in 1619, offered settlers a voice in policy through a representative assembly. A major Indian attack in 1622 defeated the effort at growth. Continued internal rancor led the Crown to dissolve the company in 1624.

See also Virginia.

Bibliography: Morton, Richard L., *Colonial Virginia*, vol. 1 (Univ. of North Carolina Press, 1960).

VIRGINIA COMPANY OF PLYMOUTH (1606-20)   One of two private corporations granted territory in the Virginia charter of 1606, the Virginia Company of Plymouth was owned by English mer-

chants from the ports of Plymouth, Bristol, and Exeter. While the rival Virginia Company of London was granted the right to establish plantations in southern Virginia, from 34° to 41° north latitude, the Virginia Company of Plymouth was granted the lands to the north, from 38° to 45° north latitude. In the overlapping area between the two patents (38°-41°), settlements were to be established no closer than 100 miles from each other.

Technically under the jurisdiction of the Royal Council for Virginia, the Plymouth Company was directed by a self-governing council of 13 members, led by Sir John Popham and after his death in 1607 by Sir Ferdinando Gorges. The company's first expedition lost its way and was captured by the Spanish off Puerto Rico in 1606. In the following year, a settlement was established at the mouth of the Kennebec River, but with the death of its resident governor, George Popham, and with discontent among the colonists it was abandoned in 1608. No further attempt at permanent settlement was made until 1620, when the Virginia Company of Plymouth was reorganized as the Council for New England.

See also Council for New England; Gorges, Sir Ferdinando; Virginia; Virginia Company of London.

VIRGINIA DECLARATION OF RIGHTS (1776)   A forthright declaration of individual liberty adopted as tensions with Britain were rapidly building, the Virginia Declaration of Rights influenced other state constitutions and later the federal Constitution's Bill of Rights. George Mason submitted a draft to the Virginia Convention shortly after it passed its resolution for independence. Mason drew the principles from English tradition, especially the 1689 Bill of Rights. Of the final version, he proposed 13 of the 16 clauses. James Madison amended the clause on religion to grant "freedom" instead of "toleration." The convention adopted the declaration on June 12, 1776.

See also Mason, George.

VIRGINIA RESOLVES (1765) AND ASSOCIATION (1774)   Patrick Henry's Virginia Resolves in the House of Burgesses on May 30, 1765, and his defiant "Caesar-Brutus" speech in their defense, set the tone of colonial resistance to the Stamp Act (1765). More cautious leaders expunged one resolve, but newspapers printed the five Henry introduced plus two that he did not. In 1774 Virginians again took the lead. The convention proposed expanding the boycott of British imports used against the Stamp Act and the Townshend Act's duties to include an "Association" against exports to oppose the Coercive Acts. The Continental Congress concurred.

See also Henry, Patrick; Stamp Act; Townshend Acts.

Bibliography: Morgan, Edmund S. and Morgan, Helen M., *The Stamp Act Crisis: Prologue to Revolution* (Univ. of North Carolina Press, 1953).

VIRGINIA STATUTE FOR RELIGIOUS FREEDOM (1786) Ranked by Thomas Jefferson among his achievements second only to the Declaration of Independence, the Virginia Statute for Religious Freedom is one of the earliest American statements of absolute religious liberty. It barred discrimination based on religious belief and outlawed compulsory church attendance and support.

The Virginia Declaration of Rights (1776) inspired Virginia dissenters, who had multiplied over the previous generation, to demand disestablishment of the Anglican Church as soon as the new legislature met. Although authorities seldom strictly enforced the rule, colonial law mandated church attendance. Anglican vestries could tax (tithe) citizens to run the church and pay for the care of the poor, with which the law charged the church. Jefferson, returning from Congress in 1776 to broaden Virginia's guarantees of freedom, opened the debate in the first assembly. Only a temporary suspension of the tithe resulted. Jefferson opposed the alternative of a general assessment benefiting all Christian sects. Although he drafted his bill earlier, he found no time appropriate to submit it until 1779.

The legislature did not enact it until 1786 when James Madison reintroduced it.

See also Jefferson, Thomas; Virginia Declaration of Rights.

Bibliography: Buckley, Thomas E., *Church and State in Revolutionary Virginia, 1776-1787* (Univ. Press of Virginia, 1977).

VIZCAÍNO, SEBASTIAN (c.1550-c.1628) A Spanish explorer, Vizcaíno was assigned to explore the Pacific coast in 1602, following the failure of the expedition led by Sebastian Cirmenho in 1595. Vizcaíno was not new to the west coast: In 1596-97 he had been involved in an attempt to plant a colony at La Paz in Baja California and had also worked with pearl fisheries in the Gulf of California. Vizcaíno sailed in May 1602 from Acapulco, but bad weather kept him from reaching San Diego Bay until November. He discovered Monterey Bay later that month and pushed on to the north to Cape Mendocino before returning to Acapulco in March 1603of Monterey Bay notwithstanding, for the next century there was no concerted attempt to follow up on his discoveries. He later commanded an expedition (1611-14) across the Pacific to Japan.

See also Cirmenho, Sebastian.

W

WAGE AND PRICE CONTROLS During the colonial period both official and popular attitudes favored wage and price regulation. Low wages, mercantilists argued, would assure a favorable balance of trade and also keep workers in their place. Following the precedent set in the Tudor Statute of Artificers (1562), 17th-century colonial officials, especially in the North, placed maximum limits on wages. Such statutes were soon found impractical and were replaced by the more traditional practice of wage regulation by justices of the peace, usually local men of wealth who hardly represented the interests of workers. While wages in the labor-scarce colonies were generally higher than those for comparable work in England and while regulations in practice thus tended to set minimums rather than maximums on wages, colonial courts convicted many individuals for accepting "excessive" wages.

Popular attention, meanwhile, focused on "fair prices." Colonial officials regulated the "assize" of bread — its price, quality, and quantity — and sometimes the assize of meat, leather, and bricks as well. They legislated against market manipulations such as engrossing (creating and holding a monopoly), forestalling (buying up the entire stock of a particular commodity), and regrating (reselling forestalled stock for a profit). Local authorities set the fees of quasi-public functionaries such as chimney sweeps, gravediggers, millers, pilots, porters, and smiths, as well as the prices charged at public accommodations such as taverns and ferries.

The regulation of wages and prices was on the decline by the mid-18th century. During the inflation and economic disruption of the Revolutionary War, however, significant popular demand developed for a return to regulation. In 1774 the Continental Congress encouraged the states to control the prices of imported goods, labeling price gougers "enemies of the American cause." Many attempts were made on the state level to enact such controls, most of them unsuccessful, but the debate demonstrated that deep support continued to exist for what some have called a "moral economy."

See also Mercantilism.

John Mack Faragher
Mount Holyoke College

WALKER, THOMAS (1715-94) An explorer, physician, and Revolutionary patriot, born in Virginia, Walker studied medicine at Williamsburg. In 1748 he joined a company of land speculators exploring the southern stretches of the Shenandoah Valley. Two years later he became the first American of record to explore the Kentucky country. During the Revolutionary War he was a member of the executive council of Virginia and a member of the House of Delegates.

WALKING PURCHASE In 1737, Thomas Penn arranged with the Delaware Indians to consummate a treaty supposedly made with his father, William Penn, in 1700. Under the terms of this treaty the elder Penn had bought a tract of land extending along the Delaware River as far as a man could walk in a day and a half. Thomas Penn wanted to sell land to settlers along the Delaware and on Tohickon Creek, but without clear title no one would buy. An altered map was shown to the Delaware as illustrating the area covered by the purchase, and the walk took place, a distance of 64 miles in the stipulated time. Although the Indians protested, the proprietary government backed up the swindle, and settlers quickly occupied the land.

WALTER, THOMAS (1696-1725) A clergyman and composer, Walter was born in Roxbury, Massachusetts, to Sarah Mather and Reverend Nehemiah Walter and graduated from Harvard (1713). His grandfather Increase Mather preached his ordination sermon when Walter became his father's assistant pastor in 1718. Walter wrote *A Choice Dialogue Between John Faustus, a Conjurer, and Jack Tory His Friend* in 1720 in response to his friend John Checkley's unorthodox proposals to change church government. Walter's 1721 publication, *The Grounds and Rules of Musick Explained; or, an Introduction to the Art of Singing by Note*, was influenced by John Tufts's music. Walter also wrote *The Sweet Psalmist of Israel* in 1722. His uncle Cotton Mather recorded both Walter's participation in a controversial smallpox inoculation experiment and his early death from consumption.

WALTON, GEORGE (1750-1804) Walton was a dominant figure in Georgia politics for over a decade. Born in Virginia, he was orphaned at an early age. He moved to Savannah in 1769, studied law, and had started a successful practice when the American Revolution began. In December 1775, Walton was elected president of the Council of Safety. In 1776 he was named to Congress where, with Button Gwinnett and Lyman Hall, he

WAR: TOPIC GUIDE

GENERAL

Abraham, Plains of
Aix-La-Chapelle, Treaty of (1748)
Alamance, Battle of (1771)
Anglo-Dutch Wars
Anglo-Spanish War (1727-28)
Bacon's Rebellion
Cartagena Expedition
Culpeper's Rebellion (1677-80)
English Civil War
Fontainebleau, Treaty of (1762)
Forts
Fort William Henry Massacre (1757)
French and Indian War (1754-63)
Hartford, Treaty of (1650)
Indian Wars (see **Topic Guide at Indians, North American**)
Jenkin's Ear, War of (1739-43)
King George's War

King William's War (1689-97)
Lake George, Battle of (1755)
Lancaster, Treaty of (1744)
Leisler's Rebellion (1689-91)
London, Treaty of (1604)
Louisburg, Battle of
Madrid, Treaty of (1670)
Militia
Paris, Treaty of (1763)
Paris, Treaty of (1783)
Queen Anne's War (1701-13)
Revolutionary War, Battles of (see **Topic Guide**)
Ryswick, Treaty of
Utrecht, Treaty of (1713)
Wilderness, Battle of the (1755)
Yankee-Pennamite Wars (1769-72, 1775, 1784)

BIOGRAPHIES

Amherst, Jeffery
Bouquet, Henry
Braddock, Edward
Bradstreet, John
Church, Benjamin (1639-1718)
Forbes, John (1710-59)
Hobby, Sir Charles
Howe, George Augustus, Viscount

Loudoun, John Campbell, Fourth Earl of
Mason, John (1600-72)
Monckton, Robert
Pitt, William (The Elder)
Winslow, John
Winslow, Josiah
Winthrop, Fitz-John
Wolfe, James

signed the Declaration of Independence. At the age of 26, he was the youngest signer. He served in Congress until 1778 and again in 1780-81 and 1787-88.

He returned to Georgia in 1778 and participated in an abortive invasion of Florida. When the British captured Savannah in December 1778, he was severely wounded. Following his recovery and exchange, he helped organize a government in Augusta and was elected governor (1779). When the British surrendered Georgia in 1783, Walton was elected chief justice (1783-86). A few years later he disposed of his holdings near Savannah and moved to Augusta. He was elected governor a second time in 1789 and after that served as superior court judge. In 1795-96 he filled an unexpired term in the U.S. Senate.

WAMPUM   Wampum, or wampompeage, are tubular beads, created from the shells of whelks and quahog clams found along the coasts of Long Island Sound and Cape Cod, Massachusetts, which were strung on sinew or woven into belts and used as a unit of exchange in Indian-white trade and diplomacy. Their use was indicative of the complex interplay of cultures in colonial North America. For Indians, wampum held artistic and symbolic meanings. Among the Northeast tribes wampum beads were made into bracelets, necklaces, and adornment on clothing. Among the Iroquois, however, wampum, when exchanged between negotiators as a gift also assured the truth of what was spoken at treaties or special rituals.

When Euro-Americans recognized that Indians valued wampum, they quickly moved to monopolize its source and production. Wampum soon became a medium of exchange in the fur trade as well as a unit of currency among whites during the early years of New England's colonization. This mutually useful misunderstanding had two significant consequences: First, it connected New England and New York, through the Iroquois, with the tribes of the Great Lakes. Second, by the 1630s wampum was a necessary requisite to all Indian-white negotiations until Euro-Americans contacted the calumet complex farther west.

Richard L. Haan
Hartwick College

WAPPINGER CONFEDERACY   A coalition of nine Algonquian-speaking tribes inhabiting the eastern shore of the Hudson River, from Poughkeepsie to Manhattan, as well as a section of the Connecticut coast, the Wappinger Confederacy suffered heavy losses and was eventually disbanded after a war with the Dutch of New Amsterdam in 1640-45. The members of the confederacy were the Wappinger, Manhattan, Wecquaesgeek, Sintsink, Kitchanwack, Tankiteke, Nochpeem, Siwanoy, and Mattabesec. Several of the tribes were further subdivided.

The members on the Connecticut coast and on eastern Long Island never came into conflict with the English or Dutch colonists, since they agreed to sell their traditional lands and migrate out of the area, eventually merging with the Scaticook, Stockbridge, and various groups in Canada. The western members of the Wappinger Confederacy, however, were drawn into conflict with the Dutch beginning with the 1640 Pavonia Massacre. After suffering heavy losses, the Wappinger tribe being particularly hard hit, the confederacy sold off its lands to the Dutch colonists and initially merged with the Mahican and Nanticoke, later to join the Delaware nation. A few members remained in the lower Hudson Valley, where isolated Wappinger communities existed as late as 1756.

See also Dutch-Indian Wars.

WAR   War affected the colonists in North America in two ways: local wars, such as conflicts with the Indians, had immediate, direct impact; others, such as the French and Indian War, were the colonial part of large-scale wars between European powers. King William's War (1689-97) was part of Europe's War of the League of Augsburg, while Queen Anne's War (1702-13) played out in North America the European struggles in the War of the Spanish Succession. Similarly, King George's War (1744-48) also concerned royal succession, in this case the War of the Austrian Succession. Finally, the French and Indian War, which secured British domination in North America, was fought in conjunction with the Seven Years War (1756-63), in which Britain established colonial superiority over the French around the globe.

WARD, ARTEMAS (1727-1800)   A Revolutionary War general, born in Shrewsbury, Massachusetts, Ward graduated from Harvard in 1748 and, after a brief period as a teacher, opened a general store in his hometown in 1750. He participated in the attack on Fort Ticonderoga

(1758) during the French and Indian War and was promoted to the rank of colonel in the local militia. He entered public life in 1762 with his appointment as justice of the Worcester County court of common pleas, becoming chief justice in 1775. A staunch opponent of Britain's authority, Ward served in the General Court but in the late 1760s was kept from office by Massachusetts's hardline Governor Bernard.

In 1775, soon after the Battle of Lexington and Concord, Ward took command of the provincial militia and, as general and commander in chief of the Massachusetts troops, directed the operations at Bunker Hill and in the siege of Boston. The Continental Congress appointed him second in command to George Washington in June 1776, and in that position he helped force the evacuation of the British from Boston. Ward resigned his commission in 1777, owing to declining health. He later served as a member of the Continental Congress (1780-81) and the U.S. House of Representatives (1791-95).

WARD, NANCY (c.1738-c.1824)   A Cherokee notable, whose name was adapted from *nanvehi*, "one who goes about," Ward was born at Chota, near Fort Loudon, Tennessee. She was the daughter of the famous warrior Fivekiller and half-sister to Attakullakulla, who was later to become chief of the Cherokee. Also known as *Tsistunagiska*, "Wild Rose," she fought alongside her husband, Kingfisher, at the battle of Taliwa during the 1755 Cherokee-Creek War. For her heroism she earned the title *Agigau*, "Beloved Woman," of her nation. After the death of her husband, she married Bryant Ward, a white trader, and later served as intermediary between the colonists and the Cherokee.

WARREN, JAMES (1726-1808)   A political leader, born in Plymouth, Massachusetts, Warren graduated from Harvard in 1745 and engaged in commerce. He married the author Mercy Otis Warren in 1754. Appointed sheriff of Plymouth in 1757, he later served in the Massachusetts provincial congress (1766-78). Warren was a radical supporter of American independence and, after the death of Joseph Warren at Bunker Hill in 1775, he was named president of the provincial congress. He also served as paymaster general of the Continental Army but resigned his commission in 1777, and in 1777-78 he was speaker of the Massachusetts House of Representatives. After the war he was less influential in politics, although he did return to the state House of Representatives in 1787 and was elected speaker again.

See also Warren, Mercy Otis.

WARREN, JOHN (1753-1815)   A noted surgeon, born in Roxbury, Massachusetts, and the brother of patriot and physician Joseph Warren, John Warren entered Harvard College at the age of 14 and graduated (1771) with distinction. At Harvard, Warren became fascinated with anatomy and formed a club to promote the study of anatomy through dissection and other techniques. On graduating, Warren set up a medical practice in Boston in which he specialized in surgery.

In 1773, Warren joined the patriots and is thought to have participated in the Boston Tea Party. General George Washington appointed Warren, only 22, surgeon of the army hospital in Cambridge, Massachusetts, after the Battle of Bunker Hill (1775). Later, Warren accompanied the Continental Army to Long Island and New Jersey. On his return to Boston in 1777, he became the city's preeminent surgeon, and in October 1783 he was appointed the first professor of anatomy and surgery at Harvard's newly-founded medical school. He remained a key figure in Boston's medical and civic affairs until his death.

WARREN, JOSEPH (1741-75) A physician and political leader, Warren was born in Roxbury, Massachusetts, and graduated from Harvard in 1759. After a brief period of teaching, he studied medicine under Dr. James Lloyd. Warren was an early and active supporter of American independence; he was one of the leaders of the protest against the Stamp Act (1765) and headed a committee to protest the Boston Massacre in 1770. In 1775 he dispatched Paul Revere and William Dawes to warn the American troops at Lexington and Concord, and succeeded John Hancock as president *pro tempore* of the Massachusetts provincial congress. As a major general in the militia, he was killed at the Battle of Bunker Hill.

WARREN, MERCY OTIS (1728-1814) A historian of the American Revolution and a patriotic poet and playwright, Warren was the third of 13 children born to the prominent family of James and Mary Otis of Barnstable, Massachusetts. Warren obtained an unusually good education by listening to her brothers' lessons and by extensive reading in her minister uncle's library, although she always wished that she and other women had been allowed opportunities for further study. She married James Warren of Plymouth in 1754, and they had five sons.

As the Revolution approached, her home became a center of opposition to British policy, and she wrote numerous satirical plays for publication in Boston. Angering her previously close friends John and Abigail Adams, she and her husband later opposed the ratification of the federal Constitution and then defended the French Revolution, arguing against the New England Federalists and in favor of greater local and state self-

government. Warren's three-volume *History of the Rise, Progress and Termination of the American Revolution*, which she began writing in the 1770s, was published in 1805 and remains useful for its firsthand reports and strong personal opinions about events and people of the time.

WARWICK COMMISSION (1643-49) A committee appointed by the British Parliament, the Warwick Commission was charged with overseeing colonial affairs during the Puritan Revolution in England. It was empowered to make appointments and to administer and was headed by colonial governor in chief, the Earl of Warwick. During its short life it contained the expansion of the Massachusetts colony by granting a charter to Rhode Island. It did not generally become intimately involved in the everyday affairs of the colonies, leaving the colonists to settle smaller problems. The commission ceased to exist when the British Commonwealth was established in 1649.

WASHINGTON, GEORGE (1732-99) Born at Wakefield in Westmoreland County, Virginia, Washington appeared destined to the modest career typical of the younger sons of Virginia's colonial gentry. The premature death in 1752 of his half-brother Lawrence, which made George the family heir, abruptly changed that situation, leading to ownership of Mount Vernon, a large plantation on the Potomac River, and a lifetime of public service.

Early Military Career. The military consumed over a quarter of his adult years, beginning with appointment at the age of 21 as one of Virginia's four militia adjutants. Between 1754 and 1758 he participated in the British Empire's struggle to control the Ohio Valley as commander of Virginia's provincial forces deployed on the colony's frontier. His first combat experience in a minor skirmish at Fort Necessity in Pennsylvania in 1754 turned out to be the opening action of the French and Indian War. During these years, as a lieutenant colonel, Washington exhibited courage, especially in General Edward Braddock's disastrous defeat in 1755 at the Battle of the Wilderness, and a capacity for leadership that resulted in command of a brigade when General John Forbes captured Fort Duquesne in Pennsylvania (1758). Washington was the only native-born American to reach this rank during the war.

At the conclusion of the 1758 campaign, Washington retired to his plantation, married (1759) the wealthy widow Martha Custis, and entered politics as a member of the Virginia House of Burgesses. By 1774, when he was elected to the First Continental Congress, he had also emerged one of the better-known moderate opponents of Great Britain's colonial policies.

Revolutionary War Leadership.   After the Battle of Lexington and Concord, the Second Continental Congress quickly took advantage of Washington's experience, appointing him to committees handling military matters. On June 15, 1775, his fellow delegates unanimously elected him "General and Commander in Chief" of Continental forces. Washington accepted the assignment only out of a profound sense of duty, refusing any salary. For eight years, the longest American war before Vietnam, he led the main elements of the army in combat while also carrying out the broader responsibilities of the Revolution's senior officer.

He first took the field (July 1775) as commander of the patriot forces besieging Boston and, after the British withdrew from the city (March 1776), then directed the forces in New York. He was soon outflanked by British forces and suffered defeats at Long Island and White Plains. After withdrawing to New Jersey in late 1776, his troops surprised the British at Trenton (December 1776) and Princeton (January 1777), victories that greatly improved American morale. Defeats in 1777 led to the privations at Valley Forge during the winter of 1777-78. The American alliance with France (February 1778) was followed in the spring by Washington's pursuit of the British across New Jersey. He then concentrated his forces on the Hudson River above New York City. During the next two years, Washington's troops engaged the British inconclusively, and he weathered a near mutiny of his unpaid and poorly supplied soldiers at Morristown, New Jersey, in May 1780. In 1781, Washington dramatically moved his forces south to force Lord Cornwallis to surrender at Yorktown, Virginia.

Washington correctly realized that he had to keep the Revolution alive by preserving his army and avoiding activities that undermined the political goals of the movement. A superb organizer, he molded a competent professional force during the conflict. Although his combat record lists more defeats than victories, the successful engagements at Trenton, Princeton, and Yorktown mark him as a gifted general. His greatest contribution to the cause, however, came from the way he dismantled the army after victory was achieved, establishing an American tradition of military subordination to civilian authority.

Postwar Career.   After the Revolution, Washington wanted to resume his agricultural pursuits, but returned to public service as a leader of the movement for a stronger union. His stature resulted in unanimous elections as presiding officer of the 1787 Constitutional Convention

and, in 1789, as the country's first president. Once in office, he tried to make the promises of the Revolution and of the Constitution realities. Applying experiences gained in commanding the Continental Army, he set about organizing the new government. With quiet authority he balanced emerging political factions, pursued a neutral foreign policy, and concentrated on economic expansion and the settlement of the west. He also defended federal authority, quickly employing militia forces to suppress the Whiskey Rebellion of 1794. Always a precedent-setter, he refused to accept a third term and returned to Mount Vernon, where he died two weeks before the close of the century. At that time he was serving as commanding general of the army raised during the "Quasi-war."

Among the Founding Fathers, Washington most clearly embodied the classic concept of the soldier-statesman. As the architect of Revolutionary War victory, in the Constitutional Convention, and as president, he personified nationhood and established the essential precedents for the new republic.

George Washington's heroic reputation among Americans was captured in many portraits. *(Library of Congress)*

See also French and Indian War; Revolutionary War Battles; Virginia; Wilderness, Battle of the; Yorktown, Surrender at.

Bibliography: Flexner, James T., *George Washington: A Biography*, 4 vols. (Little, Brown, 1972); Freeman, Douglas S., *George Washington*, 7 vols. (1948-57; reprint Kelley).

Robert K. Wright, Jr.
U.S. Army Center of Military History

WASHINGTON, MARTHA CUSTIS   (1731-1804) Wife of George Washington. Born to moderate circumstances, the oldest of eight children of the Dandridge family, she married Daniel Custis in 1749 and moved to his family's opulent plantation on the Pamunkey River in Virginia. With Custis she had four children, two of whom survived, and in 1757 her husband died. Martha Custis was left with a sizeable fortune and was soon being courted by another Virginia plantation owner, George Washington. They were married on January 6, 1759, and Martha and the children moved to Mount Vernon. Although the couple was childless, George was devoted to his wife and her children. In 1773 her daughter Martha ("Patsy") died of epilepsy. When her husband was named commander of the Continental Army, Martha did her best to support him, venturing outside of Virginia for the first time in her life. She visited him in Cambridge, Massachusetts; Valley Forge, Pennsylvania; and Newburgh, New York, doing her best to keep him in good spirits and becoming a reassuring presence to the troops. Her surviving son John ("Jackie") died in 1781, and George and Martha raised his two youngest children. After the war, the couple spent five tranquil years at Mount Vernon before George was elected president. During his two terms in office, Martha was criticized for adopting an excessively formal and opulent style for social gatherings. But she was a kind, warm, and gracious person whose style reflected her background. She died at Mount Vernon.

WASHINGTON, WILLIAM (1752-1810)   A military leader and distant relative of George Washington, William Washington was born in Stafford County, Virginia, and briefly studied theology. With the outbreak of the Revolution, he was appointed captain in the Virginia militia and was wounded in action during the battles of Long Island and Trenton. He was promoted to the rank of major in 1777 and to lieutenant colonel in 1778. In 1779 he took part in the defense of South Carolina and in the following year won an impressive victory against the British colonel Banastre Tarleton at Rantowles,

South Carolina. He was taken prisoner briefly in 1781 and was later promoted to the rank of brigadier general.

WATAUGA ASSOCIATION   The first local governmental compact in Tennessee, the Watauga Association was formed in 1772 by Virginia and North Carolina settlers who had emigrated over the divide of the Appalachians into the river valleys of the upper Tennessee, including the Watauga, Holston, and Clinch valleys. This emigration increased after the negotiation of the Treaty of Hard Labor Creek with the Cherokee in 1768 opened these valleys for settlement. The association, governed by a written code and administered by commissioners (including John Sevier and James Robertson) chosen by the majority vote of the settlers, formed an important western barrier to Indian and British attacks during the Revolutionary War and insured a minimum of civil order west of the mountains until the organization of the State of Franklin in 1785.

See also Franklin, State of; Hard Labor Creek, Treaty of; Robertson, James; Sevier, John.

WAYNE, ANTHONY (1745-96)   A soldier and statesman, Wayne was born in Waynesboro, Pennsylvania, was educated at a private academy in Philadelphia, and, after a career as a surveyor, inherited his father's estate. Active as a patriot before independence, he served on local committees and in the Pennsylvania assembly. In early 1776 he was appointed a colonel in the Continental Army and joined Pennsylvania troops in Canada shortly thereafter. In 1777, Wayne was made a brigadier general and fought in the Philadelphia campaign; he then served at Valley Forge. In 1779 he led a successful and celebrated attack on Stony Point, New York, and in 1781 participated in the operations in Virginia. During the war he became known as "Mad Anthony" for his daring leadership. He retired from the army as a major general in 1783. During the 1780s, Wayne served in the Pennsylvania assembly and then moved to Georgia, where he supported the federal Constitution of 1787. In the 1790s he was first a U.S. congressman (1791-92) and then an army commander (1792-96). He conducted a successful campaign against Indians in the Northwest Territory and died in 1796 while on active duty.

WEBSTER, NOAH (1758-1843)   A successful American lexicographer, publicist, and self-promoter, Webster was born in West Hartford, Connecticut, graduated from Yale College (1778), and died a staunch Federalist. His *Grammatical Institute of the English Language* (first part, 1783) eventually provided him with an income for life. His most enduring legacy dates from 1828, *An American Dictionary of the English Language*, progenitor of later dictionaries.

Webster's life parallels the late-18th-century birth of a modern liberal, capitalist society. He absorbed and publicized some of the republican ideology that had fueled the Revolution, including in his writings the notions that America was free of the corrupt social conditions of Europe and that America was a pure, natural society. Yet he altered the republican notion of public virtue by merging it with the notion of self-interest that was to be typical of laissez-faire capitalism: "... *patriotism* or *public spirit* is nothing but self-interest, acting in conjunction with other interests for its own sake." He promoted a strong federal government that would protect the pursuit of self-interest. In the 1780s he lobbied for uniform state copyright laws, to protect himself and others who published for profit.

Bibliography: Babbidge, Homer D., Jr., ed., *Noah Webster: On Being American* (Praeger, 1967); Ellis, Joseph J., *After the Revolution: Profiles of Early American Culture* (Norton, 1979).

John Saillant
Brown University

WEISER, JOHANN CONRAD (1696-1760)   An Indian agent and interpreter, Weiser was born in Germany and emigrated to New York with his family in 1710. A few years later he left home and took up residence among the Iroquois, with whom he maintained close lifetime ties, marrying a Mohawk woman in 1720. Beginning in the 1730s, he served both Indians and Europeans as an interpreter and negotiator. One important contribution was his negotiation of Philadelphia agreements with the Iroquois in 1731 and 1736, although perhaps his greatest was helping to maintain the alliance between the Six Nations and the British. He was also instrumental in the notorious Walking Purchase with the Delaware (1737) and the Treaty of Lancaster (1744). He served as Indian agent for Pennsylvania, worked with the missionary David Zeisberger, and conducted many Christian and state missions among the tribes of the Western frontier. During the French and Indian War Weiser served as a militia colonel but was too ill to participate actively in these culminating events of his career.

See also Walking Purchase; Lancaster, Treaty of; Zeisberger, David.

WELCH, THOMAS (flourished 1690-1705)   A Carolina trader with the Indians and a slave raider, Welch became the foremost English trader to the Chickasaw. He performed one of the most notable exploits in the early history of the Southern Indian trade when, in 1698,

he journeyed from Charleston to the Quapaw village at the mouth of the Arkansas River, becoming the first English colonist to cross the Mississippi. He returned with important intelligence on the French control of the lower Mississippi.

WENTWORTH, JOHN (1737-1820)   A colonial governor, born in Portsmouth, New Hampshire, Wentworth was educated at Harvard and entered private business soon after graduation in 1755. Dispatched to London as an agent of the family firm in 1763, he helped influence the repeal of the Stamp Act. In 1766, Wentworth succeeded his uncle as governor of New Hampshire. Committed to the development of the interior of the colony, he established a division of five counties, sponsored mapping and road building, and helped found Dartmouth College in 1769. With the outbreak of the Revolution in 1775, the Loyalist Wentworth fled New Hampshire,

Later noted for his dictionary, Noah Webster supported the belief that a new and pure type of government could emerge in America. *(Library of Congress)*

finally settling in 1783 in Nova Scotia, where he later served as lieutenant governor (1792-1808).

WENTWORTH, PAUL (died 1793)   A British espionage agent and mysterious relative of New Hampshire Governor John Wentworth, he was apparently born in New Hampshire and spent his early adult years engaged in the plantation trade in London, Paris, and the West Indies. Refusing an appointment in 1770 to the New Hampshire provincial council, he later became that colony's London agent. With the outbreak of the Revolution, Wentworth became a British spy, coordinating agents and informers in Europe. In the winter of 1777-78, he unsuccessfully attempted to stop the Franco-American alliance talks. He was elected to Parliament in 1780 and retired to his Suriname plantation in 1790.
See also Wentworth, John.

WEST, BENJAMIN (1738-1820)   An American artist, West was born in Pennsylvania. In 1760 he traveled in Europe and settled until 1763 in Rome, where he studied classical art. West visited London in 1763, was received enthusiastically, and became historical painter to King George III in 1772. A founder of the Royal Academy in 1768, he served as its president from 1792, except 1806, until his death. He served as a mentor for, taught, and influenced numerous American artists who came to London for training. West's works include *Agrippina with the Ashes of Germanicus* (1768), *The Departure of Regulus from Rome* (1769), *Penn's Treaty with the Indians* (1772), *The Death of General Wolfe* (1771), and *Death on the Pale Horse* (1802). *The Death of General Wolfe*, which created a controversy when it was exhibited because historical figures were shown in contemporary dress, greatly influenced subsequent historical paintings.

WEST, SAMUEL (1730-1807)   A religious and political leader, West was born in Yarmouth, Massachusetts, graduated from Harvard in 1754, and was ordained a minister in Dartmouth, Massachusetts, in 1761. He was a strong supporter of American independence and after the outbreak of the Revolution served as a chaplain in the Continental Army. His most important military contribution was his deciphering of a treasonous letter from Benjamin Church to a British admiral. After the war, West served on a committee to draft the Massachusetts constitution and was delegate-at-large to the Constitutional Convention in Philadelphia in 1787. He later returned to the pulpit, retiring in 1803.

WESTON, THOMAS (c.1575-c.1664)   An English merchant and colonist, Weston was a successful ironmonger in London when his censure for unlicensed trading in textiles led to a search for new opportunities. Patented under the name John Peirce and Associates, he financed the Pilgrims, who rejected his terms after he had hired the *Mayflower*. Weston soon reconciled with them and arrived at Plymouth in 1622 with a group of settlers seeking commercial gain. In 1623, Governor Robert Gorges, named as governor by the Council for New England, planned to arrest Weston for illegal trading and inciting the Indians, but Plymouth's William Bradford sent Weston to Virginia. He was a member there of the House of Burgesses in 1628 and obtained a 1,200-acre land grant in Maryland in 1642, but returned to England in 1644.
See also Council for New England; Plymouth.

WESTO WARS (1680-83)   The result of economic competition between South Carolina planters and colonial proprietors, this conflict led to the extermination of the Westo tribe. In order to monopolize the lucrative trade in deerskins, the proprietors of South Carolina established exclusive agreements with the inland Westo who handled the trade. Many of the independent planters in the colony, however, saw these commercial agreements as a threat to their own interests, and in 1680 they hired groups of migrating Shawnee to attack and wipe out the main Westo settlements. By 1683, with no more than 50 Westo surviving the genocide, the proprietors' monopoly was broken.

WETHERILL, SAMUEL (1736-1816)   An industrialist and religious leader, born in Burlington, New Jersey, Wetherill was a carpenter by trade, having served as an apprentice in Philadelphia in 1751. As a supporter of the political and economic independence of the American colonies, he established the "United Company of Pennsylvania for the Establishment of American Manufactures" in 1775. He was successful in the spinning-and-weaving industry and later supplied clothing to the troops at Valley Forge. Although a Quaker, Wetherill approved of armed resistance to the British. Expelled from the sect for that opinion, he founded the "Free Quakers" in 1777, remaining their leader until his death.

WEYMOUTH, GEORGE (died c.1612)   An English sea captain, Weymouth, following the voyage of Martin Pring, explored the New England coast in 1605 for the Earl of Southampton, who had earlier sent out the expedition of Bartholomew Gosnold. Striking landfall at Nantucket Island off of Massachusetts, he was driven north by storms until he landed on one of the islands in Penobscot Bay. He became the first Englishman to explore the Maine interior, navigating some 40 miles up St. George's River. Before returning, Weymouth kidnapped five Abenaki tribesmen for use as translators, guides, and political intermediaries on later voyages. He authored several books on navigation and shipbuilding.

WHALING Whales provided the raw materials for a number of important colonial commodities. Lamp oil, candles, fishing rods, umbrellas, corsets, and perfume were all made from whale by-products. Whaling's presence in the New World dates to the 1650s when early settlers, primarily in the Cape Cod and Long Island areas, engaged in small-scale shore whaling. The sperm whale was first caught by New England whalers in 1712, and this species of whale became the prime target of the whaling boom of 18th- and 19th-century America.

New Bedford and Nantucket Island, both in Massachusetts, became the largest whaling centers in the world. When whaling expanded into the Pacific after the War of 1812, a majority of the ships there were registered out of New Bedford. These ships would sail from New England around Africa or South America to the Pacific, where they would stay for four to five years before returning home. The decline of whaling began in the mid-1800's. The California Gold Rush and the Civil War, followed by the discovery of petroleum and the innovative uses of electricity, had devastating effects on the industry.

WHARTON, RICHARD (died 1689) A businessman and entrepreneur, Wharton was born in England and came to America to seek his fortune, partly achieved by marrying in succession three women from wealthy families. He supported the Navigation Acts and was a force behind driving the Dutch from New York, hoping to eliminate the Dutch as competitors. He obtained exclusive rights to salt production and was briefly granted a commission as sole producer of naval stores. His investment in 500,000 acres in Maine failed because such large-scale projects were against the Puritan ethic. The Dominion of New England (1686) was based in part on his ideas.

WHEAT This most important of the cereal grains was introduced to the New World by Christopher Columbus, then in Mexico by Hernando Cortes. From Mexico it spread northward with the Spanish colonists, reaching California by the late 18th century. Along the Atlantic, the English at Jamestown in 1607 and the Dutch at New Amsterdam in 1626 typically attempted to make their beloved wheat the first transplanted European crop. Their first sowings, however, were failures, as were those of the Pilgrims who, in order to conceal from the Indians the deadly toll of that first winter, broadcast their wheat seed atop the graves of their kin. Many Northern areas, it turned out, were ill-adapted to wheat cultivation. Additionally, wheat was always difficult to grow during the early stages

of farm-making, unlike corn which could be grown amid the stumps. Moreover, corn could be ground into meal by hand; wheat required a nearby grist mill.

Wheat, unlike corn, enjoyed the great advantage of bringing a high price in relation to its shipping weight, and as farming matured, especially in the river bottoms of New York, the plains of southeastern Pennsylvania, and the Virginia Piedmont, wheat became a successful cash crop. By 1770 wheat and wheat products constituted one fifth of the total exports of the colonies. The size of the wheat surplus was kept down by persistent problems with disease. Black stem rust appeared in New England as early as 1660 and by the Revolutionary War was common wherever wheat had long been cultivated. The Hessian fly appeared in the aftermath of the war and by the early 19th century had drastically reduced the wheat crop throughout the Northeast, by which time the center of wheat production had shifted to the Ohio Valley.

Bibliography: Kahn, E. J., Jr., *The Staffs of Life* (Little, Brown, 1985).

WHEATLEY, PHILLIS (c.1754-84) One of the best-known American poets of her time, Wheatley was the African-born domestic slave of a Boston tailor, John Wheatley, and his wife Susanna. The Wheatley family bought her as a child and educated her. *An Elegaic Poem* (1770) on the evangelist George Whitefield made her famous. It was published in Boston, Newport, and Philadelphia and printed with the funeral sermon for Whitefield in London. She visited her admirers in that city in 1771, accompanied by her owner's son, and it was in London that *Poems on Various Subjects, Religious and Moral* (1773) later appeared. A newspaper appeal for subscribers for a Boston edition had failed. *Poems* was her only book. She published widely in newspapers, but readers ignored appeals for contributions to finance a second volume. Susanna Wheatley freed Phillis soon before dying in 1774. In 1778, Phillis married John Peters, an enterprising free black whose schemes all failed. Their three children died as youngsters. After Phillis died in Boston and was buried with her last child in 1784, her husband went to jail for debt. Phillis Wheatley's poems are mostly elegies, in couplets, using classical imagery to discuss contemporary issues of Christianity, nationalism, and slavery.

WHEELOCK, ELEAZAR (1711-79) A Congregational missionary and educator, Wheelock was born in Windham, Connecticut, and graduated from Yale in 1733. After his ordination in 1734, he was appointed pastor in Lebanon, Connecticut, and established a reputation as a charismatic speaker during the era of the Great Awakening. After his conversion and tutoring of the Indian Samson Occom,

Wheelock became deeply involved in missionary work among the Indians of New England, and in 1754 he established a religious college in Lebanon for the education of Indian youths.

By 1765 the school had grown dramatically, and Wheelock dispatched Occom and Alexander Whitaker to England to raise funds for an expansion of the work. Wheelock's plan of establishing a new school in Iroquois territory, however, was bitterly opposed by New York's governor, William Johnson, who feared that the presence of missionaries would endanger the peace established by the Treaty of Fort Stanwix. As a result, Wheelock shifted the location. In 1769 he received a charter and land grant from Governor John Wentworth of New Hampshire and founded Dartmouth College, naming it for the Earl of Dartmouth, a prominent philanthropist. Wheelock served as the president of Dartmouth from its opening in 1770 until his death.

See also Dartmouth College.

WHEELWRIGHT, JOHN (c.1592-1679) A clergyman, Wheelwright was born at Saleby, Lincolnshire, England. He received his master's degree from Sidney College, Cambridge, in 1618 and was ordained in the Anglican church in 1619. Silenced as a Nonconformist, he went in 1636 to New England, where he was the pastor at Mount Wollaston (now Quincy), Massachusetts. He was banished from Massachusetts in 1637 for speaking out to support his sister-in-law, Anne Hutchinson, in the Antinomian controversy. In 1638 he founded Exeter, New Hampshire. Despite Massachusetts' claim over the area, he was the pastor until Exeter accepted the Massachusetts Bay Colony's rule. He then moved to Wells, Maine, before he resolved his differences with Massachusetts (1644). For most of the rest of his life he was a minister in Hampton and Salisbury, New Hampshire.

WHIG IDEOLOGY Whig Ideology comprised a cluster of values, beliefs, and anxieties that emphasized the blessings of liberty, the evils of tyranny, and the dangers that the inherent human desire to dominate others posed to liberty. Whig Ideology stressed the importance of the citizenry remaining morally upright and ever vigilant to check the growth of executive power in the state. Developed by an assortment of political radicals, pamphleteers, and journalists in 18th-century England, Whig Ideology interpreted the Glorious Revolution of 1688 that overthrew the Stuart monarchy as the creation of a delicate constitutional balance between power and liberty, and its proponents warned ceaselessly of the expansion of ministerial power.

Transmitted to the New World through the writings of a variety of groups and individuals, Whig Ideology took root in America because of (1) the perceived similarities of the English and colonial political structures, (2) the pervasive factionalism of American politics, and (3) the instability of colonial political leadership and the colonial economy. American champions of Whig Ideology deplored the evils of party and faction, found evidence of conspiracies against liberty, and stressed the importance of public and private virtue.

Such perspectives became the dominant elements of American political culture, particularly after 1763 with Britain's triumph in the Seven Years War. When Britain sought to strengthen royal authority in the colonies and curb the power of the legislatures, American Whigs responded by invoking the specter of ruthless, power-hungry men in England—supported by their dissolute lackeys in the colonies— plotting to institute despotism in the colonies. These alarms gradually transformed moderate opposition to British policy into an uncompromising defense of traditional American rights and prerogatives.

See also Colonial Government; Revolutionary War, Causes of.

Bibliography: Bailyn, Bernard, *Ideological Origins of the American Revolution* (Harvard Univ. Press, 1967); Bailyn, Bernard, *The Origins of American Politics* (Knopf, 1968).

James K. Somerville
State University of New York at Geneseo

WHIPPLE, WILLIAM (1730-85) A political leader, born in Kittery, Maine, Whipple went to sea at an early age. In 1750, as the master of a merchant vessel, he engaged in the slave trade. Wentworth entered private business in Portsmouth, New Hampshire, in 1759, but as a strong supporter of American independence he retired in 1775 to devote himself to public life. In 1776 he was a member of the Continental Congress and a signer of the Declaration of Independence. As general of the New Hampshire brigade of the Continental Army, Whipple saw action in the Rhode Island and Saratoga, New York, campaigns. After the war he served in the New Hampshire legislature and was associate justice of the superior court (1782-85).

WHITAKER, ALEXANDER (1585-1617) An Anglican missionary born in Cambridge, England, Whitaker was the son of a divinity professor at Cambridge University. After receiving a bachelor's degree from the university in 1605 and a master's degree in 1608, he was ordained as a minister in the Church of England and assigned to the American colonies. Arriving at Jamestown in 1611, he began to preach among the settlements along the James River and was also active among the local Indians. His most famous convert was Pocahontas, whom he baptized in 1613 before her marriage to John Rolfe. Whitaker's sermon, *Good Newes from Virginia* (1613), was among the first describing conditions in the colony.

WHITE, ANDREW (1579-1656) A Jesuit missionary born in London, White was educated at various Catholic institutions in Europe and was ordained at Douai, France, in 1605. He subsequently served as a missionary of the Catholic Church in England, at the time a highly illegal activity, for which he was arrested and banished. Settling in the Low Countries, White entered the Jesuit College in Louvain in 1609 and was appointed one of its professors in 1619. Risking arrest, he returned to England in 1629 and became acquainted with George Calvert, Baron Baltimore, who was then planning a colonization project in America. White gained the approval of the Jesuit order to accompany the colonists, and he established a Catholic school in Maryland in 1634. For the next 10 years he worked among both the English colonists and the local Indian population. Arrested during the 1644 Puritan insurrection of William Claiborne, White was sent to England, where he was convicted of treason and banished once again. He was refused permission to return to Maryland and spent the next few years in the Low Countries. In his later years he risked execution by returning to England and resuming his missionary work.

WHITE, JOHN (flourished 1577-93) An artist and colonist, White in 1585, along with Thomas Hariot, accompanied the colonizing expedition organized by Sir Walter Raleigh that landed on Roanoke Island off the Virginia coast. Hariot was to provide the written description of their findings, White the visual record. White's watercolors of the flora and fauna and the native life he observed provided the basis for a series of engravings by Theodore de Bry, used to illustrate the second edition of Hariot's book (1590), then reissued as a portion of de Bry's massive illustrated history of America. Not until the 20th century were the original watercolors published (in *The American Drawings of John White*, 1964), revealing what were perhaps the most accurate and sensitive images of North American Indians made at the moment of their contact with Europeans.

After this initial experiment in colonization ended in conflict between the settlers and the natives, White returned to England. He came to Roanoke Island again in 1587 as governor of a colony of English families—the first attempt at a self-sustaining and reproducing settlement. The next year he left his followers, including his daughter and granddaughter (Virginia Dare, the first English child born in North America) to go to England for supplies. His return was delayed by the war with Spain, and by the time he again stepped ashore at Roanoke in 1591 the colony had disappeared. Nothing is known of his later years.

See also Bry, Theodore de; Dare, Virginia; Hariot, Thomas.

WHITEFIELD, GEORGE (1714-70) A clergyman and evangelist, Whitefield was born in Gloucester, England, and was educated at Oxford, where he befriended Methodist John Wesley. Becoming a deacon in the Church of England in 1736, he quickly gained a reputation as a preacher. He came to America in 1738 as a missionary. In Georgia he made plans to establish Bethesda orphanage and then returned to England to raise money to build it. Ordained a priest in 1739, he believed that all people—not just Church of England members—should hear the word of God and evangelized to large groups in places other than churches. Whitefield soon found that he had to defend himself against criticism by his fellow clergymen.

He returned to America in late 1739 and became a prominent leader in the Great Awakening movement. Because of his views on the clergy and slavery, he was censured by the Church of England and eventually (1740) was suspended from office. He returned to England in 1741, came back to America in 1744 as a Calvinist Methodist, and continued to preach, from Maine to Georgia, until his return to England in 1748. He visited America four more times (1751, 1754-55, 1763-64, 1769-70). During the last visit, Whitefield died in Newburyport, Massachusetts.

See also Great Awakening.

WICKES, LAMBERT (1735-77) A naval officer, born in Kent County, Maryland, Wickes was trained as a merchant seaman and commanded commercial vessels in the Chesapeake Bay. Becoming part-owner of a vessel in 1774, Wickes, a radical supporter of American independence, refused to comply with British customs regulations. In 1776 he was named captain of the Continental navy ship *Reprisal*, which carried William Bingham to Martinique and Benjamin Franklin to France. In 1777, while privateering in the English Channel and off the Irish coast, he was detained briefly by the French authorities. Returning to America, Wickes's ship foundered off Newfoundland, and he was lost at sea.

WIGGLESWORTH, EDWARD (c.1693-1765) The son of Michael Wigglesworth and a graduate of Harvard College (1710), Edward Wigglesworth stayed on at Harvard to pursue his theological studies. In 1722 he became the first holder of Harvard's Hollis divinity chair. During the Great Awakening he fought the evangelism of George Whitefield whom he called "an uncharitable, censorious, and slanderous man." His leadership of the anti- evangelical cause led to his being offered (1761) the Yale College rectorship, which he declined. Theologically he is important for accenting the freedom of will, which he characterized by saying that no man is "under irresistable motions either to do good or evil." His son Edward followed him in the Hollis chair.

See also Wigglesworth, Edward (1732-94); Wigglesworth, Michael.

WIGGLESWORTH, EDWARD (1732-94) Educator, theologian, and early demographer, Edward Wigglesworth was much advantaged by his father Edward's eminence at Harvard. Like his father a Harvard graduate (1749) and a clergyman, Wigglesworth succeeded to his father's chair of divinity in 1765 and remained connected with the college until his death. He was also very much interested in public affairs. His *Calculations on American Population* (1775) predicted that the British-American population would double every 25 years. This calculation led him to predict that America's population would reach 1,500,000,000 by the end of the 20th century. Devout and an admirer of the Crown, Wigglesworth sought reconciliation with Great Britain before the Revolutionary War.

WIGGLESWORTH, MICHAEL (1631-1705) A theologian and poet, Wigglesworth was born in Yorkshire, England, and came to the Massachusetts Bay Colony with his Puritan parents in 1638. He graduated from Harvard (1651) and then taught there (1652-54). He served as minister at Malden, Massachusetts, from 1657 until his death. Afflicted throughout his life by poor health, he worried about his performance of religious duties, but he was so respected that he was often chosen to preach prestigious public sermons. His ill health prevented him from becoming president of Harvard, but he served as a fellow of the college from 1697. Married three times, he had eight children.

He used his poetic talents to exhort the Puritans to more godly thoughts. "God's Controversy with New England" was a response in 1662 to the drought that Puritans regarded as a sign of God's displeasure. His most famous work, the poem "The Day of Doom," pictured the day of judgment in a ballad of 224 stanzas. It was extremely popular from its publication in 1662 and had numerous editions. "Meat out of the Eater or Meditations Concerning the Necessity, End, and Usefulness of Afflictions Unto Gods Children" (1669) was also reprinted several times.

WILDERNESS, BATTLE OF THE (1755) This engagement between British colonial and combined French and Indian forces during the French and Indian War was a setback for the British in their plan to conquer Fort Du-quesne in Pennsylvania. On July 9, 1755, on the banks of the Monongahela River, about 8 miles from Fort Duquesne, 1,400 regular troops under General Edward Braddock and 450 colonials under Colonel George Washington were surprised and badly defeated in a guerilla engagement by about 900 French and Indian troops. With Braddock mortally wounded, Washington led the retreat to Fort Cumberland. In this battle, the British losses were more than 1,000, with the French forces losing only 43.

See also Braddock, Edward; French and Indian War.

WILDERNESS ROAD This trail leading from Virginia through the Cumberland Gap into Kentucky, an extension of the Great Trading and War Path, was marked and named by Daniel Boone for the Transylvania Company in 1775 when it became apparent that a treaty of cession would be negotiated with the Cherokee. Boone led a party that blazed the trail from the junction of north and south trails at the Holston River and into Kentucky. In what is now Laurel County it forked, a west branch going to Harrodsburg, then to the Falls of the Ohio (Louisville), while an east fork continued north to Boonesborough on the Kentucky River, and later extended to Maysville on the Ohio River. Wagons first passed over the road in 1795, and when it was improved as a turnpike in the early 19th century it became the main connecting link between the Virginia, Tennessee, and Ohio valleys, carrying thousands of emigrants to the trans-Appalachian West.

See also Boone, Daniel; Cumberland Gap; Great Trading and War Path; Roads and Trails; Transylvania Company.

WILKES, JOHN (1727-97) A British political leader and social critic, Wilkes was educated at the University of Utrecht in the Netherlands and was elected a Fellow of the Royal Society in 1749. He entered public life as high sheriff of Buckinghamshire, in England, in 1754 and as a member of the House of Commons in 1757. Initially a close political ally of English statesman William Pitt, Wilkes soon aroused controversy as editor of the satiric *North Briton* and *New Briton*, some of whose articles resulted in his conviction on libel charges and his expulsion from Parliament in 1764. To avoid the charges, Wilkes spent several years in France and Italy, renewing scholarly friendships and devoting himself to writing.

Returning to England in 1768, he was elected to Parliament from Middlesex, but was arrested and imprisoned for the outstanding libel charges. Elected yet again while in prison, Wilkes was seen as a victim of the government and as a defender of liberty. Released, he was elected sheriff of London and was finally readmitted to the House of Commons in 1774. Together with Isaac Barre, he opposed the British attempts to prevent American independence and

Banished from Massachusetts in 1635, Roger Williams was sheltered by Rhode Island Indians. *(Library of Congress)*

argued for equal representation within Great Britain itself. He retired from public life in 1790. The city of Wilkes-Barre, Pennsylvania, preserves his name.

WILKINSON, JEMIMA (1752-1819) Known as the Publick Universal Friend, Wilkinson was a traveling preacher during the Revolutionary War era, with a large following of disciples in southern New England and the Philadelphia area. A voracious reader and eccentric mystic, Wilkinson was brought up in a strict Quaker family in Cumberland, Rhode Island. Dismissed from the Friends (Quakers) for attending a Baptist meeting in 1776, she had a vision, during a severe illness, that she had returned from the dead to preach. Dressed like a clergyman in flowing black robe with masculine hairstyle, Wilkinson advocated pacifism, antislavery, and celibacy. Although opponents accused her of charlatanism and sexual immorality to discredit her in-

fluence, many freed their slaves because of her teaching, and Judge William Potter of South Kingston, Rhode Island, built a mansion for her New England headquarters. After the Revolution she pioneered one of the first settlements in western New York State and established Jerusalem Township. Her religious movement disintegrated after her death.

WILLARD, SAMUEL (1640-1707) A clergyman and writer, Willard was also vice president of Harvard (1700-07). He was born at Concord, Massachusetts, graduated from Harvard in 1659, and became minister at Groton, Massachusetts, in 1633. As a prominent theologian, he was active in the colony's controversies. A "diabolical seizure" in a member of his parish inspired his psychological study of witchcraft, and during the witchcraft trials he sided with the Mather family for more humane treatment of the accused. In 1678 he became pastor at the Old South Church in Boston, where he was criticized for his liberal policies for admitting new members, which included waiving public confession and opening baptism to more applicants. He initially supported the Crown's revocation of the colony's charter but later wrote a pamphlet against the action, *The Character of a Good Ruler* (1694). His many lectures were published as the *Compleat Body of Divinity* (1726).

WILLIAM AND MARY, COLLEGE OF   Founded in 1693 at Williamsburg, Virginia, the College of William and Mary received its charter and its name from King William and Queen Mary who gave the Reverend James Blair its educational grant. Christopher Wren built the first building, which was destroyed and rebuilt in 1705. The college had an Indian school through funding from the physicist Robert Boyle and by 1729 grammar, philosophy, and divinity schools. These schools were replaced in 1779 with modern languages, medicine, and law. Several prominent Revolutionary War leaders, including Thomas Jefferson, James Monroe, and Edmund Randolph, graduated from the college, which was attacked during the war.

WILLIAMS, JOHN (1664-1729)   A clergyman and religious writer, Williams was born in Roxbury, Massachusetts, and graduated from Harvard in 1683. After serving briefly as a teacher, he became in 1688 the first pastor in the frontier settlement of Deerfield, Massachusetts. His family was killed during an Indian raid, and Williams taken prisoner after which he spent three years in Indian and French captivity before Governor Dudley of Massachusetts negotiated his release. His pious memoir, *The Redeemed Captive Returning to Zion* (1707), was written in collaboration with clergyman Cotton Mather. Williams later served as chaplain on the 1711 Massachusetts expedition to Canada against Port Royal.

WILLIAMS, ROGER (1603-83)   The founder of the Rhode Island colony, and its governor from 1654 to 1657, Williams came to America in 1630 as a Puritan minister. Born in London, he graduated from Cambridge University (1627) and became an Anglican minister. A Separatist, or one who had left the Anglican Church because he believed that it was corrupt and had Catholic practices, Williams, along with thousands of other Puritans, migrated to Massachusetts Bay Colony, where his own views were widely shared.

Almost at once settlers in the Bay Colony became aware of Williams's adherence to a strict set of beliefs,

for he rejected a position in Boston's church because its members had not fully renounced the Anglican Church. In Plymouth, founded by Separatists, Williams found a more acceptable environment in which to live. There he established ties with the Indians, and as he became increasingly familiar with them, he concluded that since America really belonged to them the English Crown had no right to give pieces of it away. Nor, he continued, did the English king enjoy the authority to rule, or his agents to govern, colonies that he had no right to charter. Such ideas were dangerous, not only for Williams personally, but also for the Puritan leaders of Massachusetts if word reached England that the Puritan authorities tolerated their expression.

If Williams's political views were disturbing, his assertions that church and state must be totally separated (to insure the purity of the church) and that a variety of religious sects ought to be tolerated, challenged the fundamental principles upon which Massachusetts Bay had been founded. Since he was immensely likeable, logical, and dedicated, no one wished to punish him for expressing such dangerous notions. But since Williams refused either to alter his opinions (which few expected he would) or simply to keep them to himself, the magistrates finally banished him from the colony in 1635.

Because he believed the Indians owned America, Williams purchased land in Rhode Island from them and in 1636 founded a settlement he named Providence. In Rhode Island colonists enjoyed the freedom to worship according to their own views. In 1643, Williams traveled to England to secure a charter (1644) for the colony he founded. He returned to Rhode Island in 1644 and remained active in the colony's affairs until his death, supporting his ideas for religious liberty and democracy in *The Bloody Tenent Yet More Bloody* (1652) during another visit to England and while he was governor. His efforts to maintain good relations with the Indians were ultimately unsuccessful, and he commanded troops during King Philip's War (1675-76).

See also Rhode Island.

Aaron Shatzman
Franklin and Marshall College

WILLIAMS, WILLIAM (1731-1811)   A political leader, born in Lebanon, Connecticut, Williams graduated from Harvard in 1751. After service in the French and Indian War, he engaged in business and held several local offices in his hometown. From 1757 to 1776, he was a member of the provincial assembly, later serving in the Continental Congress (1775-78, 1781-84) and signing the Declaration of Independence. During the Revolution, Williams raised funds and provisions for the Continental Army. His later public offices included member of the Connecticut governor's council (1784-1803), judge of the Windham County court, and judge of probate (1775-1809).

WILLIAMSBURG   Williamsburg was founded as Middle Plantation in 1633. The site of the College of William and Mary (1693), the town became the Virginia capital in 1699 at which time it was renamed to honor King William III. In the early 18th century Governor Francis Nicholson planned the city on baroque principles, and Governor Alexander Spotswood designed the Governor's Palace and other structures in the same tradition, setting a model for the grand country houses of the later 18th century. Designated a city in 1722, Williamsburg attained a population of almost 2,000, which swelled to over 5,000 during legislative and judicial "Publick Times." America's first mental hospital opened there in 1733. The capital moved to Richmond in 1780.

WILLIAMSON, ANDREW (?1730-86)   A military leader, popularly known as "Arnold of Carolina," Williamson was born in Scotland and raised on the Carolina frontier. In 1761 he served as a lieutenant in the South Carolina regiment during a campaign against the Cherokee and in 1765 settled down as farmer and landowner. With the outbreak of the Revolution, Williamson was elected to the provincial congress and as a brigadier general of the South Carolina militia saw action in Robert Howe's 1778 Florida expedition. Accused of treason for failing to defend Charleston in 1780, he defected to the British. After the war, he was cleared of the charge of treason and allowed to remain in South Carolina.

WILLIAMSON, HUGH (1735-1819)   A scientist, businessman, and political leader, Williamson was born in West Nottingham, Pennsylvania, and educated at the College of Philadelphia (later the University of Pennsylvania). After graduation in 1757, he briefly studied theology in Connecticut but soon shifted to medicine. In 1761 he was appointed professor of mathematics at the College of Philadelphia; he left that post in 1764 to gain his medical degree at the University of Utrecht in the Netherlands. Williamson returned to Philadelphia to establish a medical practice, but poor health forced him to enter private business. He nonetheless maintained a strong personal interest in science, was a close colleague of Benjamin Franklin, and was elected to the American Philosophical Society (1768).

At the outbreak of the Revolution, Williamson moved to Edenton, North Carolina, where he carried on trade with the West Indies. Volunteering his medical expertise to the North Carolina militia, he was appointed surgeon general and saw action in the Battle of Camden. After the war, Williamson served in the North Carolina House of Commons (1782), the

Continental Congress (1782-85, 1787, 1788), was a delegate to the Constitutional Convention (1787), and supported the ratification of the U.S. Constitution in 1788. After a term in the U.S. Congress (1789-93), he retired to New York City to devote himself to scientific work.

WILLING, THOMAS (1731-1821)   A financier and political leader, born in Philadelphia, Willing was educated in England and returned to America in 1747 to join the family firm. He later established his own concern with Robert Morris in 1754. Entering public life, Willing was appointed to the Philadelphia Common Council in 1757 and became mayor of the city in 1763. Elected to the Continental Congress in 1775, he voted against independence, fearing an American military defeat. During the Revolution, Willing was an active fundraiser for the Continental Army. In 1781 he was named president of the Bank of North America and later advised the U.S. government on fiscal affairs.

See also Morris, Robert.

WILSON, JAMES (1742-98)   Wilson's distinguished career as scholar, lawyer, statesman, and judge began in Scotland, where he was born and received a university education. In 1765 he came to Pennsylvania and practiced law. Involved in patriot activity, Wilson published a pamphlet in 1774 that argued that Parliament had no power over the colonies; they owed allegiance only to the Crown (*Considerations on the Nature and the Extent of the Legislative Authority of the British Parliament*). In 1775 he was elected to a first term in the Continental Congress; he served actively until 1777 and was reelected to serve in 1785-87. Although initially cautious, Wilson voted for independence and signed the Declaration of Independence. His image as a conservative "aristocrat" was enhanced in the late 1770s by his legal defense of accused traitors, his association with the social elite of Philadelphia, and his ambitious business activities.

During these years Wilson developed the opinions about American government that guided his actions during the constitution-making of the late 1780s. In Congress he argued that the national government should have greater powers and that representation there should be by population. In Pennsylvania he opposed the unicameral constitution of 1776 as dangerously unbalanced in favor of the legislative branch. A leader of the Constitutional Convention of 1787, Wilson argued for a vigorous and balanced national government grounded on the principle of popular sovereignty. He led the campaign for adoption of the Constitution in the Pennsylvania convention (1787) and invoked the same ideas while working for revision of the state constitution in 1789-90. Wilson was appointed a justice of the U.S. Supreme Court in 1789 and served until his death, but his later career was clouded by business failures.

Bibliography: Smith, Charles Page, *James Wilson, Founding Father: 1742-1798* (Univ. of North Carolina Press, 1956).

Douglas M. Arnold
The Papers of Benjamin Franklin

WINSLOW, EDWARD (1595-1655)   An author and administrator, Winslow was a leader of the 1620 Plymouth settlement and a chief negotiator with the Massasoit Indians. His 1624 *Good News from New England: or A true Relation of things very remarkable at the Plantation of Plimoth* was the first publication about the colony. As an "undertaker," he assumed the colony's debts in exchange for trading privileges, and his explorations of the eastern coast fostered Plymouth's commerce. In 1629 he became the colony's agent, procuring land from the Council for New England in 1630 and defending the colony in the Privy Council in 1633 and again in 1646. He held leadership positions in the colony from 1624 to 1645, including that of governor (1633, 1636, 1644), and was an organizer of the New England Confederation. After 1645 he stayed primarily in England, where he was a founder (1649) of the Society for the Propagation of the Gospel and served Oliver Cromwell.

See also New England Confederation; Plymouth Society for the Propagation of the Gospel.

WINSLOW, JOHN (1703-74)   A colonial military officer, born in Marshfield, Massachusetts, Winslow received no formal schooling but joined the militia and served in a variety of public offices in Plymouth County during his early adult years. In 1740 he was appointed captain of the Boston militia company that accompanied the British expedition to the West Indies, and in the following year he saw action at Cartagena with Gooch's American regiment at the end of the War of Jenkin's Ear.

Winslow returned to Massachusetts in 1751 to serve briefly in the General Court (1751-53). In 1754, promoted to the rank of major general, he was placed in command of a Massachusetts expedition up the Kennebec River that gained the alliance of the local Indians and founded the forts of Western (later to become Augusta) and Halifax. In 1755, Winslow led a New England battalion against the French on the Chignecto Isthmus of Nova Scotia and later directed the deportation of the French settlers from Acadia. Massachusetts Governor William Shirley appointed him commander of the colony's contingent in the unsuccessful Crown Point Expedition in 1756. Winslow resigned from active ser-

vice in the militia in 1757 and was later elected again to the General Court (1757-58, 1761-65).

WINSLOW, JOSIAH (c.1629-80)   The first American-born governor of Plymouth Colony, Winslow was born at Plymouth and moved at an early age with his family to nearby Marshfield. After briefly attending Harvard College, he visited England with his father in 1651 and returned to assume command of the militia at Marshfield in the following year. Winslow's political career began with his appointment in 1658 as Plymouth commissioner for the United Colonies of New England, a position he maintained until 1672. His military reputation was unrivaled in the colony, and in 1659 he was named commander in chief of Plymouth, succeeding Miles Standish.

The most serious challenge facing Winslow was keeping the peace with the nearby Wampanoag Indians, and he accomplished this at least temporarily in 1662 by capturing and holding hostage Alexander, son of the Wampanoag chief Massasoit. In 1672, Winslow was one of the signers of the Articles of Confederation of the New England Colonies and was appointed governor of New Plymouth in 1673. During King Philip's War (1675-76) he was commander in chief of the forces of the United Colonies and supervised the virtual destruction of the Narragansett people. Winslow remained active in public life up to the time of his death.

WINTHROP, FITZ-JOHN (1638-1707)   Colonial military and political leader, he was the son of John Winthrop, the first governor of Connecticut Colony, and grandson of John Winthrop, the first governor of Massachusetts Bay Colony. Fitz-John Winthrop was born in Ipswich, Massachusetts, and moved with his family to Connecticut at the age of 10. After entering Harvard College, Winthrop left for England to serve with the Parliamentary Army during the English Civil War. Following active service in Scotland, he remained in England after the Restoration and was named a Fellow of the Royal Society.

Winthrop returned to Connecticut in 1663, taking up residence in New London and later representing that town (1671, 1678) in the General Assembly. Appointed chief military officer of New London County in 1672, he fought against the Dutch at Southold, Long Island, in 1673 and against the Narragansett in King Philip's War (1675-76). In 1676, with the death of his father, Winthrop returned to Boston and served on the governor's council (1676-88) and was named commander of the New England expedition against Canada in 1690. The failure of that mission damaged his reputation, but after being ultimately acquitted of all charges against him he served as governor of Connecticut from 1698 until his death.

WINTHROP, JOHN (1588-1649)   The first governor of Massachusetts Bay Colony, Winthrop was born in Suffolk, England, and was educated at Cambridge University. He practiced law (1613-29) in London. Winthrop sailed (1630) with the Puritans as leader and governor of the new Massachusetts Bay Colony. He was elected governor each year until 1633. In 1634, amid dissension over the extent of the governor's authority, he was replaced by deputy governor Thomas Dudley. Winthrop continued to exert leadership over the colony and was elected to the governorship for several other terms (1637-40, 1642-44, 1646-49).

Winthrop governed the colony with a mix of politics and religion. Not believing in complete democracy, he felt that officials, once elected, should govern according to their personal philosophy. His involvement in the Antinomian Controversy resulted in a law (1637) passed to prevent followers of Anne Hutchinson from settling in Massachusetts. He was instrumental in the formation of the

John Winthrop, the first governor of Massachusetts Bay Colony, effectively led the colony from 1630 until his death in 1649. *(Library of Congress)*

United Colonies (1645), a confederation of New England colonies for military purposes, and he served as its first president. He kept a journal that contains valuable information about the early years of the Massachusetts Bay Colony.

See also Massachusetts Bay Company; Puritans.

WINTHROP, JOHN (1606-76)   A colonial governor, he was born in England, educated in Ireland, and practiced law in London before joining the Royal Navy. The son of John Winthrop, governor of the Massachusetts colony, he came to America in 1631 and in 1632 helped to found Ipswich, Massachusetts. He planned the construction of Fort Saybrook at the mouth of the Connecticut River and was made its governor in 1636. Winthrop promoted business in both the Saybrook and Massachusetts colonies. By 1650 he had become a freeman in Connecticut. He moved to New Haven and, in 1657, was elected governor of Connecticut, a position he held (except for one year) until his death.

WINTHROP, JOHN (1714-78)   Having early shown a proclivity for science, Winthrop went on to become one of the most eminent American scientists of his time. After distinguishing himself as a student at Harvard College, from which he graduated in 1735, he was appointed Hollis Professor of Science at the young age of 23. As an educator he was known for his experiments with electricity and magnetism and for introducing the study of fluxion, the basis for modern calculus. In the wider scholarly world he was renowned for his observations on sunspots, comets, and earthquakes. He was made a Fellow of the Royal Society of London in recognition of his 1761 expedition to Newfoundland to observe the transit of Venus and of the many articles he contributed to the society's *Philosophical Transactions.* He received law degrees from both Harvard and the University of Edinburgh.

Winthrop was progressive in religion and politics as well. Attacking traditional notions of the relation of God to creation, he maintained that physical phenomena were the result of natural causes. Reverence for God, he believed, should arise not from fear of God's displeasure but from contemplation of the sublime complexity of the universe. Also, he assisted the Reverend Charles Chauncy of Boston in the composition of religious treatises positing the salvation of all men. Although politically naive, he was an early and strident supporter of American independence, serving during the Revolutionary War in several administrative capacities.

Kenneth P. Minkema
University of Connecticut

WISE, JOHN (1652-1725)   A Congregational leader and writer, Wise was born in Roxbury, Massachusetts, and graduated from Harvard in 1673. After ordination as a Congregational minister, he preached briefly at Branford, Connecticut, refusing an offer to become its resident minister. During King Philip's War (1675-76), Wise served as chaplain of the colonial forces in their expedition against the Narragansett.

In 1680 he accepted appointment as minister of the Congregational church in Ipswich, Massachusetts, and in that position became one of the most outspoken opponents of Governor Edmund Andros. Wise led the public protests against the imposition of Andros's 1687 tax and was subsequently arrested and stripped of his ministerial post at the governor's insistence. Wise's refusal to accept this punishment and his protracted legal battles ultimately resulted in a reversal of his conviction, his reinstatement in the clergy, and spurred the recall of Governor Andros. Wise later served as chaplain for the Massachusetts troops in the 1690 expedition to Quebec. A prolific writer and pamphleteer, Wise gained a reputation as a champion of religious and political freedom. Several of his works were reprinted in 1772 to aid the Revolutionary cause.

See also Andros, Edmund.

WISTAR, CASPAR (1696-1752)   A glass manufacturer, industrialist, and colonial leader, born near Heidelberg, Germany, Wistar immigrated to Philadelphia in 1717. Having no formal education and no vocational training, he initially hired himself out for day labor until he had saved enough money to open his own business, a small workshop for manufacturing brass buttons.

In 1725, Wistar joined the Quakers and gradually became involved in the glassmaking industry. In 1738 he purchased a tract of land at Allowaystown in nearby Salem County, New Jersey, on which he planned to establish a center for the manufacture of glass. He subsequently built the main structures and gained the services of a staff of Belgian glassmakers, whom he persuaded to immigrate to America in 1740. An important inducement was Wistar's visionary plan for the cooperative ownership of the glassworks; the employees were to be guaranteed a one-third share in all profits. In the following years, German and Portuguese glassmakers joined the staff and were settled in the adjacent workers' community, called "Wistarberg." By the middle of the 18th century, "Wistar glass" was highly regarded throughout the American colonies. The artisans of Wistarberg laid the groundwork for the later American glassmaking industry.

WITCHCRAFT   Witchcraft beliefs were widely held in early America. They were common among Indians who comprised the native populations, among recently arrived

Interest in witchcraft and the Salem trials resulted in public meetings on the subject in many towns, including Boston. *(Library of Congress)*

European immigrants, and among Africans who were brought to the colonies against their will. The content of these beliefs varied from group to group and even within groups, and some communities were much more deeply influenced by them than were others. They had their greatest impact among the English settlers in New

England, whose fear of witchcraft was so great in the middle and late 17th century that they prosecuted scores of their neighbors for this crime and hanged at least 36 of them. Most of New England's presumed witches were women.

New England Witchcraft.   New Englanders conceived of witchcraft in many ways, but they most often described it as the supernatural power to harm. According to Puritan belief, witches signed a contract, or covenant, with Satan, in which they agreed to serve him and he in turn agreed to give them the power to injure or kill their neighbors and destroy their neighbors' property. Neither the ministers who wrote about witchcraft nor the accusers who identified the community's witches said very much about why women were more likely than men to practice witchcraft, but New Englanders clearly believed this to be the case: more than three-quarters of the accused were women, and women were found among convicted and executed witches in even higher proportions. Accused males tended to be either husbands or sons of women who were already suspected of being witches. Daughters and granddaughters were also likely suspects.

Although in some cultures individuals have been known to practice witchcraft, the grounds for assuming that colonial New England women did so are slender. Women sometimes confessed to being witches, but usually under duress. The other evidence for the validity of accusations comes from accusers, but their testimony that certain women cast spells or put curses on them can hardly be taken at face value. Accusations usually grew out of quarrels between neighbors, with an angry and resentful accuser attributing some personal misfortune to the anger and resentment of the accused. For these reasons, explanations for why women were the main targets of witchcraft accusations and prosecutions have focused on the shared characteristics of witches and their relationships with other members of their communities.

Witches were generally older women, usually beyond their childbearing years. Most of them were married, but widows, spinsters, and other women alone may have been overrepresented among the accused, given that there were many fewer women alone than married women in the adult population. Witches also shared an unusual position in New England's social order in that most of them did not have brothers or sons; with no legitimate heirs in their immediate families, these women were potential or actual inheritors of substantially larger portions of their fathers' or husbands' estates than were women in families with male heirs. The existence of these and other, less extensive patterns in the lives of suspected witches suggests that the accusations can be attributed to a widespread fear of particular women in colonial New England.

That fear was enduring as well as pervasive. Although some years witnessed only occasional accusations and no prosecutions, witchcraft suspicion was a regular feature of New England's social landscape from the late 1640s until the early 18th century. The best-known and most devastating episode was the 1692-93 outbreak in Salem, Massachusetts, during which some of the established patterns of accusation were less visible, and individuals who at other times would have escaped prosecution (prominent men and women, for instance) found themselves publicly denounced as agents of Satan. Conviction and execution of some of these "unlikely" witches led to the demise not only of witchcraft trials in New England but of official Puritan support for witchcraft beliefs. Once that had happened, witchcraft no longer played a significant role in New England's history.

Bibliography: Boyer, Paul and Nissenbaum, Stephen, *Salem Possessed: The Social Origins of Witchcraft* (Harvard Univ. Press, 1974); Demos, John, *Entertaining Satan: Witchcraft and the Culture of Early New England* (Oxford Univ. Press, 1982); Karlsen, Carol F., *The Devil in the Shape of a Woman: Witchcraft in Colonial New England* (Norton, 1987).

Carol F. Karlsen
University of Michigan

WITHERSPOON, JOHN (1723-94)   A Presbyterian minister and political activist, he was born in Scotland and, after earning his divinity degree in 1743, was an outspoken clergyman, especially regarding popular rights. He came to America in 1768 to assume the presidency of the College of New Jersey (now Princeton University), a post he held until 1794. During this time he unified the American Presbyterian Church and advocated a "common sense" education philosophy. As a delegate to the 1776 Continental Congress, he signed the Declaration of Independence and continued to serve in Congress until 1782. He was at various times in the New Jersey legislature.

WOLCOTT, OLIVER (1726-97)   A political and military leader, Wolcott was born in Windsor, Connecticut, and graduated from Yale in 1767. After participating in Governor Clinton's 1767 expedition to Canada, he settled in Litchfield, Connecticut, where he served as sheriff, deputy in the provincial assembly, judge of probate (1772-81), and judge of the county court (1774-78). In 1774 he was appointed colonel of the Connecticut militia and commissary-general of the Continental Army in the following year; the Continental Congress also appointed him one of its commissioners for Indian affairs. In that position Wolcott arbitrated several important territorial disputes, among them the conflicting claims of Connecticut and Pennsylvania in the Wyoming Valley and the New York-Vermont boundary dispute.

Wolcott was a member of the Continental Congress from 1775 to 1783 and was one of the signers of the Declaration of Independence. Promoted to the rank of brigadier general in 1776, he saw action in the Hudson Valley against General Burgoyne and in 1779, as a major general, defended the Connecticut coast against the raids of former New York governor William Tryon. After the war, Wolcott continued to advise the government on Indian affairs and later served as governor of Connecticut (1796-97).

See also Wyoming Valley Violence.

WOLFE, JAMES (1727-59) A British military officer, Wolfe was born in Kent, England, and educated at the military school at Greenwich. He entered active service in 1741 as a second lieutenant with the 44th Foot Regiment and his early military postings were varied. After active service on the Continent during the War of the Austrian Succession, he was stationed in the Netherlands, in Scotland, in Ireland, and in various English garrisons.

In 1758, during the French and Indian War, Wolfe was dispatched to North America, where as a brigadier general commanding a division he served under Lord Amherst in the successful siege of Louisburg. Wolfe, returned to England and promoted to the rank of major general, in 1759 was asked by William Pitt to lead a new expedition to Canada. Landing near Quebec in June with a fleet and a force of approximately 8,000 men, Wolfe was initially repulsed by the French defenders under the Marquis de Montcalm but subsequently decided on a daring surprise attack on the Quebec citadel. Under cover of darkness 5,000 of his troops were lowered by ropes down the cliff above the city and quickly overran its defenses. Although mortally wounded in the fighting at Quebec, Wolfe by this victory played an important role in the British conquest of Canada.

See also French and Indian War; Montcalm, Marquis de.

WOMEN An older interpretation of the history of women in the colonies suggests that their status was higher in America than in Britain because of a combination of several factors, including their relative scarcity, their importance to primitive economic enterprise, and the resulting fluidity of gender roles. More recent historical work, however, has revealed that the impact of the imbalanced sex ratio of the earliest settlements tended to lower the age at marriage, thereby increasing the number of childbearing years for the average women, that the frontier conditions of farming imposed a burden of unrelenting toil on wives, and that gender roles were possibly more rigid in the colonies than back home. This was, in short, no "golden age" for women, and improvements in women's lives tended to come at the concluding moments of the colonial period.

The overwhelming fact of colonial women's lives was an extraordinarily high birth rate. Today there are about 14 live births for every 1000 persons in the population, but before 1800 the birth rate stood at about 55, a burden nearly four times greater. A woman who married in her early twenties could expect to bear her first child within a year or two of her wedding and, if the marriage was uninterrupted by the death of either spouse, spend most of her next twenty years raising from six to eight children. Death usually claimed one of the partners before the last child reached majority. Women were thus preoccupied with children. Moreover, the household was the workplace. Better than 9 in 10 of all colonial families practiced farming, and women were responsible for the production and preparation of nearly all the family's foodstuffs as well as of the fiber from which they made the family's clothing. Only the wealthiest of women, with numerous servants, could escape these burdens of physical labor.

Women were largely excluded from the public world of colonial society. As children, girls were generally excluded from publicly supported schools, and studies of literacy suggest that even in New England, the most educated section of the colonies, fewer than half the women could sign their names. Educated and literate women such as the poet Anne Bradstreet and the Indian-captive Mary Rowlandson, whose narrative was the first best seller in American history, published their works anonymously. More generally, married women could neither make contracts nor own property; they could neither vote nor hold office. They were, in short, largely dependent upon their husbands for civil protection. In the words of the common law, as summarized by English jurist William Blackwell in 1765: "The very being or legal existence of the woman is suspended during the marriage, or at least is incorporated and consolidated into that of the husband; under whose wing, protection, and cover, she performs every thing." The only exception to this doctrine of "coverture" existed in special covenants and marriage settlements, but these were available in practice only to the wealthy, who wished to protect the property that might be inherited by their daughters.

These realities of childbearing, work, and legal discrimination were reinforced by a comprehensive ideology of women's subordination. Women were generally considered to be weak and unintelligent and were counseled to be passive and silent; "a true wive," John Winthrop declared in 1645, "accounts her subjection her honor and

WOMEN: TOPIC GUIDE

GENERAL

Abortion
Bundling
Casket Girls
Contraception
Daughters of Liberty
Demography, Historical
Divorce
Dress

Edenton Ladies Tea Party
Household Industries
Population
Social Welfare
Witchcraft
Women, Legal Status of
    Common Law

BIOGRAPHIES

Adams, Abigail
Alden, Priscilla
Alexander, Mary Spratt Provoost
Berkeley, Lady Frances
Bosomworth, Mary Musgrove
Bradford, Cornelia Smith
Bradstreet, Anne Dudley
Brent, Margaret
Burr, Esther Edwards
Butterworth, Mary Peck
Cofitachique, Lady of
Colden, Jane
Corbin, Margaret Cochran
Dare, Virginia
Darragh, Lydia Barrington
Drinker, Elizabeth Sandwith
Duston, Hannah
Dyer, Mary
Edwards, Sarah Pierpont
Estaugh, Elizabeth Haddon
Fisher, Mary
Frankland, Agnes Surriage
Franklin, Ann Smith
Franklin, Deborah Read
Goddard, Sarah Updike
Hallam, Lewis
Hart, Nancy
Heck, Barbara Ruckle
Hume, Sophia Wigington
Hutchinson, Anne Marbury

Jemison, Mary
Johnston, Henrietta
Knight, Sarah Kemble
Lee, Mother Ann
Lennox, Charlotte Ramsey
Logan, Martha Daniell
Masters, Sybilla
McCrea, Jane
Mecom, Jane Franklin
Montour, Madame
Moody, Lady Deborah
Nurse, Rebecca
Osborn, Sarah Haggar
Pinckney, Elizabeth Lucas
Pocahontas
Ramsay, Martha Laurens
Ross, Betsy
Rowlandson, Mary
Sampson, Deborah
Starbuck, Mary Coffyn
Tekakwitha, Catherine
Turell, Jane Coleman
Van Rensselaer, Maria Van Cortlandt
Ward, Nancy
Warren, Mercy Otis
Washington, Martha Custis
Wheatley, Phillis
Wilkinson, Jemima
Wright, Patience Lovell
Zane, Elizabeth

freedom." One of the worst offenses was a woman's rejection of this patriarchal system. Anne Hutchinson, one such rebel, "a woman of fierce and haughty carriage" according to Winthrop, was expelled from Massachusetts Bay Colony for her sin. The Quaker evangelist Mary Dyer was another; she repeatedly returned to preach after being banned from Boston and New Haven, finally being executed by the Puritans for her effrontery. Perhaps the most remarkable aspect of this ideology of subordination was the extent to which women accepted it themselves; one

historian finds in women's letters and documents of the early 18th century habitual reference to themselves as "weaker vessels" and "helpless," despite their ability to raise children and crops in the wilderness.

For servant and slave women subordination was even more extreme. About a third of colonial households included servants, and about a third of those servants were women; one historian estimates that half of the women colonists arrived under terms of indenture. The available record suggests that female servants were subject not only to hard physical labor but frequent sexual abuse; "bastards" born to servant women were themselves subject to indentures for the term of their childhoods. It has been argued that gender roles among black slave women were less rigid than among whites, but only because they were expected to work in the fields alongside their men. Moreover, masters refused to recognize slave marriage and encouraged promiscuous behavior in order to maximize the birth rate; slave women, on average, each bore eight to ten children, an average higher than that of their white sisters.

The church offered one important avenue of social participation outside the household. While the Puritans attempted to limit the participation of outspoken women, the Society of Friends (Quakers) provided an alternative model where preaching and prophesying were open to them. The Great Awakening of the second quarter of the 18th century greatly expanded women's participation within American religion, and some women outside the Quakers assumed leadership roles in American society for the first time. Sarah Osborn of Newport, Rhode Island, held weekly religious meetings in her home for hundreds during the 1750s; "Mother" Ann Lee of the Shakers emigrated to the colonies in the 1770s, and the 1780s saw the revivalist preaching of Jemima Wilkinson.

In many ways the period of the Revolution was a turning point for women just as it was a turning point for the country as a whole. Although traditional roles remained intact, many questions were raised about them during this period of turmoil. As men marched off to war, women were placed in positions of management of family farms and businesses. Especially in the campaigns for nonimportation and greater reliance upon domestic production, women played an expanded leadership role. Groups such as the Ladies Association of Philadelphia were important as fundraisers for the patriot cause. Some women, such as Deborah Sampson, even disguised themselves as men, enlisted, and fought with the rebel forces.

From a legal and political point of view, the Revolution changed little in women's relation to society. But it did seem to play a role in changing many women's expectations. Abigail Adams's famous plea to her husband, John, to "remember the ladies" in his work in Philadelphia was directed less to the shape of the new republic than to the structure of family life. "Do not put such unlimited powers into the hands of the husbands," she wrote in a letter, for "all men would be tyrants if they could." Adams had in mind a new companionate ideal of marriage that contrasted with the older notions of patriarchal hierarchy. This new ideal took root among the affluent merchant and planter classes of the late 18th century and was very much tied to the liberation of wealthy women from domestic labor. But through the writings of women such as Judith Sargent Murray, who promoted marriages of "mutual esteem,

mutual friendship, mutual confidence," these ideas were disseminated widely within urban society and probably to commercial farm families as well.

Perhaps the most enduring change outside the family was in the area of education. During the 1780s and 1790s many "female academies" were founded in America; typical was the Philadelphia Young Ladies Academy founded in 1787. In his address at the opening of this institution, Benjamin Rush proposed that education for women should prepare them to fulfill new roles as companionate wives; moreover, Rush argued that women had a new civic role to play by educating their sons in republican virtue and values. This concept of "Republican Motherhood" was an important legacy of the Revolution in women's lives, although it most directly affected middle- and upper-class women and had little impact on the poor.

There were other ways, however, in which the legacy of independence worked for change in the lives of ordinary women. Social historians have discovered that in the late 18th century premarital conception increased by more than 30 percent; other studies have found a greater variation in the marital choices of daughters, who tended to marry out of their birth order and to select husbands whose economic status differed from that of their parents, suggesting the diminishing power of parental control. With the increase in women's education, and the greater number of women's religious and charity associations, these trends were auguries of social changes that would become movements in the 19th century.

Bibliography: Koehler, Lyle, *A Search for Power: The "Weaker Sex" in Seventeenth-Century New England* (Univ. of Illinois Press, 1980); Norton, Mary Beth, *Liberty's Daughters: The Revolutionary Experience of American Women, 1750-1800* (Little, Brown, 1980); Smith, Daniel Blake, *Inside the Great House: Planter Family Life in Eighteenth-Century Chesapeake Society* (Cornell Univ. Press, 1980); Ulrich, Laurel Thatcher, *Good Wives: Image and Reality in the Lives of Women in Northern New England, 1650-1750* (Knopf, 1982); Woloch, Nancy, *Women and the American Experience* (Knopf, 1984).

John Mack Faragher
Mount Holyoke College

WOMEN, LEGAL STATUS OF   Under the English system of common law adopted in the colonies, single women possessed the same rights and liabilities as men, although not the political rights (the vote, the right to public office) associated with property ownership. After marriage, men were responsible for the economic support of their wives, and women's property rights diminished. *Femes coverts* did not own personal property and lost managerial rights over real property to their husbands, while retaining title. They could not make contracts, wills, sue in their own names, act as legal guardians, or manage estates. While serving as the designated agents of their husbands, women could make certain kinds of business agreements, and with a power of attorney they could act for the family in most respects. With their husbands' consent, women could be *feme sole* traders or make wills of personalty.

During widowhood, women received support from their husbands' estates in the form of a one-third interest in realty, known as dower. Separate estates, although rare in the colonies, gave married women the right to own and control property independently of their husbands. Executed in the colonial period as trusts, separate estates were administered under equity law, a legal system that complemented the more dominant system of common law.

Under criminal law women generally received the same treatment as men, although in theory wives who committed noncapital crimes in the presence of their husbands or with their knowledge and consent were said to be acting under coercion and were not held responsible in the courts. In practice, this theory was not always applied. During pregnancy, women were not executed for capital crimes.

Diversity existed in the colonies on many issues concerning women's legal status, stemming from economic and ideological interests. Dissenters from the Church of England, in particular, acted to reform English law on conveyancing, divorce, and inheritance, while royal and proprietary colonies generally followed English precedent.

Bibliography: Salmon, Marylynn, *Women and the Law of Property in Early America* (Univ. of North Carolina Press, 1986).

Marylynn Salmon
University of Maryland, Baltimore County

WOOD, ABRAHAM (flourished 1638-80) An explorer and colonial official, Wood emigrated to Virginia sometime before 1638 and became one of the greatest landowners and Indian traders in Virginia. Beginning in 1646 he maintained the garrison at Fort Henry, Virginia, eventually rising to the rank of major general. In 1650 he accompanied Edward Bland on an exploration of the interior of Virginia. Sometime within the next decade he may have traveled to the Ohio and Mississippi rivers, but it remains a matter of dispute whether these trips were actually made. He sponsored a series of explorations, however, which are the best documented of the 17th century: in 1671 the first recorded expedition to cross the Appalachian mountains, that of Thomas Batts and Robert Fallam; and in 1673 the expedition of James Needham and Gabriel Arthur to the interior Cherokee.

See also Batts, Thomas; Bland, Edward; Needham, James.

WOOD, WILLIAM (flourished 1629-35) The author William Wood may have come to Massachusetts Bay Colony from Lincolnshire, England, as he dedicated his book, *New Englands Prospect*, to a Lincolnshire aristocrat. Wood settled in Lynn, Massachusetts, in 1629 and became a freeman in 1631. He left the colony in 1633, and his subsequent activities are not certain, although he may have returned to New England. Wood's book describing the New England settlements and the Indians had three contemporary editions, 1634, 1635, and 1639, followed by a 1764 Boston edition. Its view of colonial life was so favorable that the General Court of Massachusetts Bay thanked Wood in their letters to the colony's supporters.

WOODMASON, CHARLES (c.1720-post 1776) Settler, Anglican cleric, and vivid chronicler of life on the Carolina frontier, Woodmason, English by birth, left wife and family in 1752 to emigrate to South Carolina, where he acquired land and slaves and held various local offices. After 1762 he lived in Charleston, where he was a merchant and held town offices, including that of stamp tax collector, which made him the focus of popular outrage. Stung by this rejection, he applied for a position as itinerant Anglican minister to the backcountry settlers. After ordination in England in 1765, he moved to St. Mark's Parish, where he spent the next seven years battling frontier "Heathens, Arians, and Hereticks." His journals and sermons from that period provide a classic glimpse of frontier life. A supporter of the Regulator Movement, he authored the "Remonstrance" of 1767 and produced a stream of petitions and protests to the authorities. In 1772 he left the frontier to take a position in Virginia, then moved to Maryland. A Loyalist, he left for England in 1774 and died sometime after 1776.

See also Regulators.

WOODWARD, HENRY (c.1646-86) A colonist, surgeon, and Indian trader and the first English settler in South Carolina, Woodward was born in Barbados and came to North America in 1664, settling near Cape

Fear. He explored Port Royal in 1666. Captured by the Spanish, he was imprisoned at St. Augustine, Florida, but escaped to become an interpreter and Indian agent. In 1674 he headed the colony's program to expand trade with the interior tribes, forging an alliance with the Savannah River Westo. Over the next decade he helped to build the colony's trade in deerskins with the Lower Creek.

WOOL ACT (1699)   This act of Parliament was one of the first of a series of measures designed to protect Britain's industrial economy through mercantilist trade sanctions. Influenced by the rising support for mercantilism that resulted in the passage of the first of the Navigation Acts in 1696, Parliament passed the Wool Act as a response to the economic threat posed by Irish and American sheepowners. By the act, wool produced in Ireland or in the American colonies could be sold only in England; export or intercolonial wool trade was forbidden. The Wool Act served as the model for the Enumerated Articles Act of 1705.

See also Navigation Acts.

WOOLMAN, JOHN (1720-72)   Few did more to lay the spiritual foundation for the abolition movement than did John Woolman. Born at Rancocas, New Jersey, on October 19, 1720, of Quaker parents, and a product of their way of life, he was thoughtful, compassionate, and profoundly religious. Skilled in many professions, Woolman worked as a tailor.

Woolman's lifelong campaign against slavery began when his employer, a storekeeper, sold a black woman and ordered him to prepare the bill of sale while the customer waited. Woolman was uneasy but reluctantly wrote it, informing the storekeeper and the purchaser, a fellow Quaker, that he "Believed slave-keeping to be a practice inconsistent with Christianity." Later he refused to take part in such activities.

In 1743, Woolman embarked on a series of missionary travels. For 30 years he traveled on foot throughout America and appealed to the consciences of slave owners everywhere. Woolman believed both the owner and the slave suffered acutely from the system, stating, "For while the life of one is made grevous by the Rigour of another, it entails Misery on both." Woolman abstained from wearing dyed clothing, consuming sugar, or using any product connected with slavery. He published his ideas in *Some Considerations on the Keeping of Negroes* (1754). As a result of his inspired efforts, the Quakers declared

slaveholding a disownable offense. His ideas influenced Benjamin Franklin, Benjamin Rush, and Anthony Benezet, and led to Pennsylvania's abolition law of 1780.

Woolman also worked for the benefit of the poor, advocated better treatment of Indians, and preached against war. He published his views on the poor in *A Plea for the Poor* (1763). In 1772 Woolman contracted smallpox while on a mission to England and died. He is best remembered for expressing his views with sympathy, love, and sincerity, without provoking bitterness. Woolman's *Journal* was published posthumously in 1774.

Bibliography: Moulton, Phillips P., ed., *The Journal and Major Essays of John Woolman* (Oxford Univ. Press, 1971); Whitney, Janet, *John Woolman: American Quaker* (Little, Brown, 1942).

Rodger C. Henderson
Pennsylvania State University

WOOSTER, DAVID (1711-77)   A military leader, born in Stratford, Connecticut, Wooster graduated from Yale in 1738 and served in the 1745 Louisburg campaign as a captain of the Connecticut militia. Although Wooster later left the army to become a merchant in New Haven, he served in the French and Indian War as a colonel of the militia and in 1763 was appointed collector of customs at New Haven. At the outbreak of the Revolutionary War, he was named a brigadier general of the Continental Army. His poor leadership during the invasion of Canada in 1776 resulted in his recall by Congress. As a major general of the Connecticut militia, he fell in battle in 1777 during William Tryon's Connecticut raid.

WRIGHT, PATIENCE LOVELL (1725-86)   Sculptor in wax and a celebrity, Wright was born to a strict Quaker family in Bordentown, New Jersey, but fled her restrictive background and went to Philadelphia. There she married Joseph Wright, a cooper, in 1748. When her husband died in 1769, Patience used her talent as a modeler in wax to create a traveling wax museum. The unusual exhibit featured statues of familiar, contemporary personages, and it was very successfully received. Fire destroyed much of the exhibit in New York and Wright decided to move to London. She arrived in 1772, armed with many letters of reference from her famous subjects, and her friend Benjamin Franklin introduced her to London society. Because of her talent as well as her enormous force of personality— her conversation was profane, far-ranging, and never dull—Wright quickly became very well known. The King and Queen received her, and soon she was giving them advice and addressing them as "George" and "Charlotte." A fierce patriot, it is said that she passed on war information she picked up in the company of London society, perhaps by concealing it in wax sculptures sent home. She made plans to return home in 1786 but died in a fall in London.

WYATT, SIR FRANCIS (1588-1644) Governor of Virginia, Sir Francis Wyatt came from a distinguished family that included the poet Thomas Wyatt. He was born in Kent, England, and his association with his wife's uncle, Sir Edwin Sandys, brought him the governorship of the troubled Virginia Company as George Yeardley's replacement in 1621. He dealt well with the Indian massacre of 1622 but could not prevent the company's dissolution in 1624. Appointed as the first royal governor, he called the "convention" assembly in 1625 to petition for help and to keep the "liberty of generall Assemblie." He left for England in 1626 but was governor again from 1639 to 1641.

WYOMING VALLEY VIOLENCE A fertile, 25-mile stretch along the Susquehanna River, in what is now Pennsylvania, the Wyoming Valley was the scene of bloody territorial disputes. First extensively settled by Connecticut farmers under a grant by the Susquehanna Company, it was also claimed by the colony of Pennsylvania. In 1774, to strengthen its legal authority, the Connecticut assembly chartered the township of Westmoreland there and in the following year prohibited further immigration. New settlers, however, arrived from the Hudson Valley, and their Loyalist sentiments immediately aroused hostility. Some of the newcomers were arrested and sent to prison in Connecticut, providing a reason for the British colonel John Butler, stationed in Niagara, to come to the Loyalist settlers' aid. In July 1778, Butler's force of Loyalists and Iroquois overran the valley, destroying houses and livestock and leaving only about 60 of the settlers alive. This shocking massacre discouraged further British-Iroquois operations and led to the campaign of General John Sullivan against the Iroquois. Connecticut settlers returned to the Wyoming Valley in 1779 and, although territorial jurisdiction was given to Pennsylvania in 1782, the Compromise Act of 1799 confirmed individual Connecticut settlers' claims.

See also Sullivan, John.

WYTHE, GEORGE (1726-1806) A lawyer and statesman, he was born in Virginia and studied law. Upon inheriting his father's estate in Williamsburg, he was elected to the House of Burgesses in 1754-55 and again from 1758 to 1761, when he represented the College of William and Mary. With war threatening, he went to Congress in 1775, where he signed the Declaration of Independence. He worked closely with Thomas Jefferson and others on the revision of Virginia's laws and, by 1778, he was a judge on the Virginia high court. In 1779 he held the first chair of law in America, at William and Mary. He served on the 1788 Virginia convention that ratified the Constitution.

Y

YALE, ELIHU (1649-1721) Merchant and benefactor of Yale College, Elihu Yale was born in Boston and educated in England. From 1671 to 1692 he rose through the ranks of the East India Company in Madras, India, and became governor and president at Fort St. George. A dispute with the company led to a fine, but he nevertheless retired to England a wealthy man from his trading ventures. He was a generous donor to schools, churches, and missionary societies, and in 1718 he gave the Collegiate School in Connecticut bales of cloth that the college sold for 562 pounds and 12 shillings. The trustees, in gratitude, renamed the college (today Yale University) after him.

YALE UNIVERSITY Founded in 1701 as the "Collegiate School within his Majesties Colony of Connecticot," Yale was created by 10 ministers who all brought books to the parsonage of Reverend Samuel Russel in Branford, Connecticut. The first Rector, Abraham Pierson, held classes in his home in Killingworth. In 1707 the college was relocated to Saybrook and in 1716 to its present site in New Haven. The college received its name from its benefactor, Elihu Yale, who in 1718 sent a gift of 9 bales of East India goods, which the college sold for 562 pounds and 12 shillings to pay for books and buildings. In 1731 a second benefactor, George Berkeley, donated books and his Rhode Island farm.

YAMASSEE WAR (1715-16) A conflict between South Carolina colonists and local Indian peoples, it resulted in the expansion of English colonization southward. The Yamassee were originally settled in Florida, but a campaign of enslavement by the Spanish in the late 17th century forced them to seek shelter in South Carolina. There, too, they eventually came into conflict with European colonists.

Open hostilities began on March 15, 1715, with a surprise attack by the Yamassee (reportedly instigated by their old enemies the Spanish) on the English settlement at Port Royal, during which 90 colonists were killed. This attack was followed by the raids of Yamassee bands on isolated plantations throughout the colony. The Yamassee gained many allies among the surrounding Indian peoples, and the colonists simultaneously received support from New England, Virginia, and North Carolina. By late 1715 the tide had turned, with a decisive battle at Salkechuh on the Combahee River between the Yamassee and the South Carolina militia, after which the Yamassee fled across the Savannah River into Florida. In the following year a peace treaty was officially signed, but the removal of the Yamassee opened the way for the colonization of Georgia.

YANKEE DOODLE A song popular among the patriot troops of the Revolutionary War, it apparently originated in England in the mid-18th century, was introduced in North America by British troops during the French and Indian War or the early phase of the Revolution in derision of the American soldiers, but was picked up by the intended victims in celebration. The earliest manuscript lyric dates from 1775, and the earliest printed version from 1778, although the music and lyrics were not published in the United States before 1794. The term "yankee," possibly derived from the Hudson Dutch "jankee," or "little John," was being pejoratively applied by the English to New Englanders, particularly sailors, by the early 18th century. The term was given wide currency by the popularity of the song. Royall Tyler's 1787 play "The Contrast" combined the Yankee with his homespun character Jonathan to first suggest the traits of cynical wit, caution, and shrewdness in business that have since become conventional.

See also Jonathan.

YANKEE-PENNAMITE WARS (1769-72, 1775, 1784) A series of conflicts between Connecticut and Pennsylvania settlers in the Wyoming Valley of Pennsylvania. The origin of the conflict lay in the 1754 purchase of territory from the Iroquois Confederacy by the Susquehanna Land Company of Connecticut. The first Connecticut settlers, who arrived in 1762, were driven out by local Indians the following year.

In the late 1760s settlers from Pennsylvania began to arrive in the area, and in 1769 they drove out a new contingent of Connecticut colonists. This led to a counterattack and occupation of the valley in 1770 by the Connecticut or "Yankee" faction, and by 1772 the Yankee claims seemed secure. In 1775, however, the sheriff of nearby Northumberland County in Pennsylvania led a "Pennamite" militia force into the valley. The conflict subsided during the Revolution, but following the 1782 decision of a boundary commission that the

At the surrender at Yorktown, the British forces marched between files of victorious Americans. *(Library of Congress*

land belonged to Pennsylvania, renewed fighting began and the Yankee settlers were forcibly evicted in 1784. The conflict was finally resolved with the Compromise Act of 1799, which compensated Pennsylvania for lost land and confirmed the rights of the Yankees to remain.

See also Wyoming Valley Violence.

YEARDLEY, SIR GEORGE (c.1587-1627) Governor of Virginia, Sir George Yeardley served with Thomas Gates in Holland and sailed with him to Virginia in 1609. After Thomas Dale left in 1616, Yeardley was acting governor until 1617 and governor in 1618. He ended martial law and held the first representative assembly, but he did not succeed in fulfilling the company's commercial plans for the ill-equipped settlers. He quit his

post in 1621 but still managed his investment in the 80,0000-acre Southampton Hundred. He carried the petitions from the 1625 "convention" assembly to England, where he outlined the conditions in Virginia. He was reappointed governor in 1626, serving until his death.

YORKTOWN, SURRENDER AT (1781) The British surrender at Yorktown, Virginia, followed a campaign that trapped the British on the Yorktown peninsula. Hemmed in by the French fleet and the American-French ground forces, the British commander in the South, Lord Cornwallis, surrendered to the Franco-American army under George Washington and the Comte de Rochambeau on October 19, 1781. The British marched to Surrender Field between two lines of victorious soldiers. Pleading illness, Cornwallis sent his second in command, Brigadier General Charles O'Hara. When O'Hara attempted to surrender to Rochambeau, the latter waved him to Washington, who indicated that his second in command, Major General Benjamin Lincoln, whom the British had defeated at Charleston, would accept the surrender.

See also Revolutionary War Battles.

Bibliography: Freeman, Douglas Southall, *George Washington*, vol. 5: *Victory with the Aid of France* (1952; reprint Kelley, 1975).

YOUNGS, JOHN (1623-98)   A colonial soldier and official, Youngs was born in Southwold, England, and came with his parents in 1637 to Salem, Massachusetts, going from there to Long Island in 1640. Appointed deputy from Southold, Long Island, to New Haven Colony in 1660, he petitioned in 1662, after Connecticut had been consolidated, for the union of Long Island and Connecticut. In 1664 he helped capture New Amsterdam from the Dutch, and in 1665 he represented Southold when the Duke of York united Long Island, Staten Island, and Westchester. After the Dutch retook New York, Youngs gave Southold to Connecticut, but in 1676, after the final defeat of the Dutch, Youngs acknowledged the Duke of York. He was instrumental in organizing New York's first representative assembly in 1683 and set the boundary between New York and Connecticut. From 1686 to 1698 he served on the New York governor's council.

YUMA   The area around the junction of the Colorado and Gila rivers, the site of the settlement of Yuma, was occupied by Yuma Indians when Hernando de Alarcón sailed up the Colorado in 1540 in a vain attempt to link up with the expedition of Francisco Vasquez de Coronado. The Spanish took little interest in the area until the 1770s, when Juan Bautista de Anza established an overland route from Arizona to Monterey, California. In 1779 two settlements were founded, but the Spaniards soon alienated the Indians by appropriating their cultivated land and food stores. On July 17, 1781, the Yuma struck back, destroying the Spanish settlements and killing 55 inhabitants, among them Fernando Rivera y Moncada and Francisco Garces. The Spanish then abandoned the area.

See also Alarcón, Hernando de.

Z

ZANE, ELIZABETH (?1766-1831?) A frontier heroine, Zane is said to have saved the fort at what is now Wheeling, West Virginia, from one of the last Indian attacks of the Revolutionary War by replenishing the defenders' supply of gunpowder. In September 1782, on her way to her brother's house, she was able to dart across the firing line of the astonished Indians, who ceased shooting, exclaiming, "Squaw! squaw!" She filled a tablecloth with gunpowder and made a run for the fort. This time the Indians opened fire, but she managed to reach the gate of the fort. With the powder she delivered, the group inside was able to neutralize the Indians until help came. Not all historians confirm this legend.

ZEISBERGER, DAVID (1721-1808) A Moravian missionary, born in Zauchtenthal, Moravia, Zeisberger was educated at Herrnhut, Saxony. After leaving school, he was indentured to a merchant in Herndyk, Holland, later making his way to England. There Zeisberger met Count Nicolaus Zinzendorf and gained the permission of Governor James Oglethorpe to join the Moravian colony at Savannah, Georgia. Zeisberger soon left Georgia, migrating in 1739 to Pennsylvania to undertake missionary work among the Indians on behalf of the Moravian Brethren.

His first great success came in 1745 when he was invited by Iroquois chief Hendrick to live in his village and learn the Onandaga language. For the next 18 years Zeisberger lived and preached among the Iroquois, but in 1763 he turned his attention to the neighboring Delaware, helping to establish the village of Friedenshütten in the Wyoming Valley. His later years were spent in Ohio, where he helped found several new villages, Gnadenhütten among them. The American Revolution, however, disrupted his work. In 1781 he was arrested by the British and brought to Detroit on suspicion of spying, and in the following year the Gnadenhütten Massacre resulted in the death or exile of many of his Indian converts.

ZENGER, JOHN PETER (1697-1746) A colonial printer and journalist, Zenger was born in Germany and emigrated with his family in 1710 to New York, where he was apprenticed to the printer William Bradford. In 1725 he entered a partnership with Bradford, but by 1726, Zenger had his own business. In 1730 he printed the first arithmetic text in the colony, Peter Venema's *Arithmetica*. In 1734 he was arrested and in 1735 went to trial for libel because he printed antigovernment articles in his newspaper, the *New-York Weekly Journal*. Zenger was defended by Andrew Hamilton, who convinced the jury that criticism was not libel. The Zenger case is considered the first victory for freedom of the press in the colonies. He subsequently became the public printer for New York (1737) and New Jersey (1738).

INDEX

Bold numbers indicate main essays

A

Abenaki Indians 222, 291, 352
    Casco Treaties **63-64**
    and Revolutionary War 205
Abigail (ship) 129
Abolition movement 463
Abortion **1**
Abraham, Plains of **1**, 148, 277
Academy and Charitable School 15
Acadia 57, 149, 153, 165, 252
Acculturation 155-156
Act Concerning Religion—*See also*
    Toleration Act
Act of Naturalization 176
Act of Union 107, 176
Acts of Trade **1-2**, 81, 275, 382
Adair, James **2**
Adams, Abigail **2-3**, 429, 461
Adams, John **3**, 83, 103, 234, 260,
    385, 429
    and the Boston Massacre 43
    and the Staten Island Peace Con-
      ference **410**
    Treaty of Paris (1783) 317-318
Adams, Samuel **3**, 82-83, 261, 361,
    399
Adams-Onis Treaty 406
Adobe **4**
Adoption
    by Indians 204
Africa **4**
    Slave trade with 376
    and Triangular trade 377, 425
African-Indian Contact 4
African Slavery in America (Paine)
    316
Afro-Americans
    Culture of 394
    and Free blacks **146**
    and Plantation System **333**
    and Revolutionary War **5**, 22
    and Slavery 391, **392-395**
Age of Reason (Paine) 236, 316
Agriculture **6-9**
    Corn 7, **93**, 206, 299
    and Household Industries **192-
      193**
    Indigo **210**, 331, 333
    of Latin American Indians 206
    New World crops **299**
    Plantation System 4, **333**, 391-
      392
    Potatoes 299, **338-339**
    Self-sufficient and market farm-
      ing **386-387**
    of South Carolina 401
    Tobacco 7-8, 318-319, **421**, 435-
      436
    Wheat **448**
Aguayo, Josef de Azlor y Virto de
    Vera, Marquis de 9, 383
Aix-La-Chapelle, Treaty of 49, 147,
    223, 242-243
Alabama
    Indians of 96
Alamance, Battle of 9, 355
Alarcon, Hernando de **9**, 94, 111, 467
Alarcon, Martin de 383

Alaska
    Indians of 309-310
    Russia in **9-11**, 344, 389
Albany, New York 11, 38, 140
Albany Congress **11**, 144
Albany Convention **11**
Albany Plan of Union 11
Albemarle Settlements **11-12**, 307
Albuquerque, New Mexico **12**
Alcohol
    Consumption of **12**, 155, 416
Alden, John **12**, 409
Alden, Priscilla **12-13**, 409
Alden, Timothy 12
Aleut Revolt 9, **13**
Aleuts 9, **13**, 70
Alexander, James **13**
Alexander, Mary Spratt Provoost **13**
Alexander, William **13-14**, 240
Algonquin Indians 4, **14-15**, 207,
    340, 412
Alison, Francis **15**, 108
Allan, John **16**
Allen, Ethan **15-16**, 25-26, 178, 421,
    433
Allen, Ira 178
Allen, John 184
Allen, William **16**
Allerton, Isaac **16**, 282
Alliance (ship) 33
Allouez, Claude Jean **16**, 273
Alvarado, Pedro de 304
Amadas, Philip 307, 352
America, naming of **16**, 433
American Academy of Arts and
    Sciences 44
American Company (theater com-
    pany) 172, 419
American Crisis (Paine) 316
American Magazine 171
American Philosophical Society
    144, 159, 188, 329, 372-373, 385,
    454
      Benjamin Franklin and 15, 17,
      19, 41
American Revenue Act 417
American Revolution—*See Revolu-
    tionary War*
American Society 17
America (ship) 220
Amherst, Jeffrey 1, **17**, 148, 315,
    335, 346, 377, 421
Amish 267, 324
Amman, Jakob 267
Amundsen, Roald 311
Anabaptists 267
Andre, John **17**, 26, 303
Andros, Edmund **17**, 39, 55, 61, 67,
    81, 116, 118, 130, 170, 260, 457
Androscoggin River 423
Anglicanism **19-20**, 174, **356**, 357,
    359-360, 399
Anglo-Dutch Wars **20-21**, 297, 411
Anglo-Spanish War **21**
Annapolis, Maryland **21**
Annapolis Convention 21, 182
Anne (Queen of England) 276
Antinomian Controversy 76, 198,
    456
Antinomianism **21**, 198, 369
Antiproprietary party 119
Anti-Rent War 319

Antislavery **21-22**, **391-392**
Anza, Juan Baptista de **23**, 160, 277,
    467
Apache Indians 12, **23**, 35
Apalachee Indians 207, 286, 387
Appalachian Mountains **23**, 34
    Fall Line **137**
Appamatuck Indians 339
Appeal to the Public, An (Chandler)
    356
Aptheker, Herbert 391
Aranbega—*See Norumbega*
Arapaho Indians 177
Arawak Indians **23-24**
Arcadie 433
Architecture **24-25**, 184, 288, 397
    of Kaskaskia 221
Argall, Samuel **25**, 106, 338
Arikara Indians 176-177
Aristarchus (slave) 65
Arizona
    Indians of 345, 427
    Tucson **427**
Arkansas Post **25**
Ark (ship) 254
Armstrong, John **25**, 288
Arnold, Benedict 17, **25-26**, 88, 296,
    303, 362, 364, 437
Arnold of Carolina—*See Williamson,
    Andrew*
Art **26**; *See also Crafts; specific art-
    ist*
Arthur, Gabriel 134, 288, 462
Articles of Confederation **26-27**, 31,
    82, 84, 90, 108, 112, 169, 204, 257
Articles of Surrender 122
Asbury, Francis **27-28**, 269
Ashe, John Baptist **28**, 167
Asiento **28**, 49
Assiniboine Indians 177, 186
Atahualpa 304, 332
Atkin, Edmund **28**
Atlantic Pilot (De Brahm) 102
Atondo, Isidor de 224
Attakullakulla, Chief 116, 315, 414,
    442
Attucks, Crispus 6, **28**, 43
Aubry, Charles Philippe 244
Auchmuty, Samuel 210
Audiencias **28**, 95
Augsburg, War of the League of 151,
    276, 442
Augusta, Congress of **28**
Augusta, Treaty of **29**
Aulnay, Charles Menou d' 149
Austrian Succession, War of the—
    See King George's War
Avila, Pedrarias de 332
Aviles, Pedro Menendez de 166,
    266-267
Awashonks 71
Ayllon, Lucas Vasquez de **29**, 59,
    115, 246, 306, 391
Aztec Indians 206, 277-278, 419

B

Backus, Isaac 30, 33
Bacon, Nathaniel 30, 37, 414, 435
Bacon's Rebellion 8, **30-31**, 37, 137,
    307, 319, 414
    and Deference **105**

Baffin, William **31**, 310
Baffin Island 306
Bahamas 82
Baker, Samuel 106
Baker, William 106
Balboa, Vasco Nunez de **31**, 332
Baltimore, Lord of—*See Calvert,
    Cecilius*
Baltimore, Maryland **31**
Bancroft, Edward 101
Banister, John **31**, 384
Bank of Massachusetts 32
Bank of New York 32
Bank of North America 32, **32**, 190,
    454
Banks and banking **31-32**; *See also
    specific bank*
    Massachusetts Land Bank 262
Banneker, Benjamin 32, 396
Bannock Indians 175
Baptists **32-33**, 174-175, 234, 356-
    357, 359-360
Barbastro, Luis Cancer de 115
Bard, John 33
Barlow, Arthur 307
Barlow, Joel 88
Barnwell, John 307, 428
Barre, Isaac 33, 367
Barry, John 33
Bartlett, Josiah 33
Barton, Thomas 357
Bartram, John 33, 240, 325, 329
Bartram, William 33, 384
Bashmakov, Pyotr 9, **34**, 134
Batchellor, Stephen 291
Batts, Thomas 34, 134, 462
Bayard, John Bubenheim 34
Bayard, Judith 411
Bay of San Pedro 242
Bay of Smokes 242
Bay Psalm Book 18, **34**, 284, 342
Beachy Head, Battle of 49
Bear River Indians 428
Beaufort, South Carolina 34
Beaumarchais, Pierre Augustine
    Caron de **34**
Beaver (ship) 43
Beaver Wars **35**, 158, 207, 211
Bedloe's Island 33
Beekman, Margaret 238
Beissel, Johann Conrad 285
Bell, Robert 35
Beltran, Bernaldino 131
Benavides, Alonso 35
Benezet, Anthony 21, 35
Bennington, Battle of 409
Bering, Vitus Jonassen 9, **35-36**, 70,
    311
Bering Straits Hypothesis **36-37**
Berkeley, George **37**, 396, 465
Berkeley, John 84, 289, 293, 400
Berkeley, Lady Frances **37**
Berkeley, William 30, **37**, 98, 400,
    414, 435
Bermuda Company 37, 438
Bethesda orphanage 450
Bettering House 398
Beverley, Robert **37-38**
Beverwyck **38**
Bienville, Jean-Baptists le Moyne,
    Sieur de **38**, 84, 275, 286, 298
Billing, George 293

in New England colonies 18, 330, 359
in New France 149, 272-273
in New Hampshire 85
in New Jersey 293
in New Netherland 297
in Pennsylvania 324, 328, 355, 359
in Rhode Island 32-33, 298, 359, 369
Separation of church and state 30
of Slaves 394
in Southern colonies 19, 359
in Spanish colonies 403, 405
Spanish Inquisition 210
and Toleration Act 355, **421-422**
Relly, James 284
Rensselaerswyck 11, 38, 319, **360**, 431
Repartimiento 129, 231, **360**
Reprisal (ship) 450
Republicanism **360-361**
Republican Party 326
Requerimiento **361**
Restraining Act, New England **289**
Revere, Paul 26, 235, 313, 341, **361**, 399, 412, 443
Revitalization movements **362**
Revolutionary War
Battles of 51, 88-89, 93-94, 160-161, 167, 178, 189, 193-194, 235, 260-261, 302-303, 308-309, **362-366**, 444, 466-467
Causes of **366-368**, 376-377, 423, 449
in Connecticut 88
Delaware in the 108
France in 362, 374
and Free blacks **146**
Georgia in 167
Indians in **204-205**, 209-210, 354
and Loyalists **244-245**
in Massachusetts 260-261, 362
New Hampshire in 292
New York City in 303, 364
New York in 302-303, 364-365
North Carolina in 308-309
Olive Branch Petition **314**
in Rhode Island 369-370
in South Carolina 365, 402
Spain in 362
Treaty of Paris (1783) **317-318**
Reynolds, John 166
Reynoso, Alonso de 368
Rhet, William 41
Rhode Island **368-370**
Gaspee incident 160
Governors of 96
Indians of 368-369
Newport **298**
as part of Dominion of New England 116
Primogeniture and entail in 342
Providence Plantation **344**
Religion in 32-33, 298, 359, 369
in Revolutionary War 369-370
and Roger Williams **453**
and Slavery 370
Rhode Island, Battle of 370
Rhode Island College 50, 78, 410
Ribault, Jean 166, 231, 338, **370-371**, 380

Rice **371**
Richelieau, Cardinal 149
Rights of Man (Paine) 316
Rio de la Plata 403
Rio Grande **371**
Rios, Domingo Teran de Los **371**
Rising, Johan 289, **371**
Rittenhouse, David 258, 325, 329, **371-373**, 385, 413
Ritter, Georg 173
Riu, Francisco 429
Rivera y Moncada, Fernando de 337, **373**, 383, 467
Riverways 274, 371, **423-424**; *See also specific river*
Rivington, James **373**
Roadways 99, 177, 338, **373-374**, 424-425, 451
Great Road of the Valley 177, 373
Great Trading and War Path 99, 177, 373, 451
Great Trail 373
Great Wagon Road 307
Old Spanish Trail **313-314**
Wilderness Road 41, 99, 177, 222, 373, 451
Roanoke Island 229
Roanoke River 424
Robertson, James **374**, 445
Roberval, Jean Francoise de la Rocque, Sieur de 62, **374**
Robinson, Beverley **374**
Robinson, Faith 426
Rochambeau, Jean Baptiste Donatien de Vimeur 366, 370, **374**, 466
Rockingham, Lord 367
Rodney, Caesar 108, **374-375**
Rogers, Robert 193, **375**
Roger's Rangers 346, 375
Rolfe, John 272, 334, 339, **375**, 421, 434, 450
Roman Catholic Church 31, 349, 356-357, 360, **375-376**; *See also Catholicism*
and Company of a Hundred Associates 196, **197**
and Indian conversions 16, 35, 57-58, 160, 173, 253, 264, 272-274, 312, 340, 352, 362, 418
Missions of 35, 42, 57-58, 109, 115-116, 140, 159, 172, 221, 230, 241, **272-274**, 312, 330, 340, 352, 387, 405, 407
and Toleration Act of Maryland 355, 422
Romney (ship) 236
Ross, Betsy **376**, 410
Ross, George **376**
Rowlandson, Joseph 376
Rowlandson, Mary 204, **376**, 459
Royal African Company **376**
Royal colony 344, **376-377**
Georgia 166-167
Royal Disallowance **377**
Rubi, Marques de 227, **377**
Ruggles, Timothy **377**
Rules and Regulations (Georgia) 167
Rum Act 166
Rum trade **377**, 425
Rupert's Land **377**
Rush, Benjamin 12-13, 17, 21, 265,

325-326, 329, **377-378**, 461
Russel, Samuel 465
Russia
Aleut Revolt 13
Explorations by 70, 134, 225
and League of Armed Neutrality **232**
Russian-American Company 9, 344, 389
Rutgers, Henry 378
Rutgers University 78, 122, **378**
Rutledge, Edward **378**, 410
Rutledge, John **378**
Ryswick, Treaty of 49, 224, 338, 349, **378-379**

S

Sabeata, Juan 241, 266
Sachems **380**
Sac Indians 142
Saco River 423
Sagadahoc Colony 172
Sagoyewatha 354
St. Andrews Society 398
St. Augustine 266-267, **380**, 407
St. Bartholomew's Day Massacre 195
St. Cecilia Society 285
St. Clair, Arthur 54, **380**, 421
St. Croix Settlement **380-381**
St. Denis, Louis Juchereau de 287, **381**
St. John, J. Hector 97
St. Lawrence River 133, 165, 176, 242, **381**, 423
and New France 149
and Northwest Passage 310
St. Leger, Barry 218, **381**
St. Louis 70, **381-382**
St. Mary's City **382**
St. Mary's River 423
Sainte Catherine (ship) 216
Salas, Juan 64
Salem, Massachusetts 84, 263, 289, 299, 311, **382**, 458
Salem, Peter 6
Salinan Indians 57
Salm (ship) 414
Saltonstall, Dudley **382**
Salutary neglect **382**
Sampson, Deborah **382-383**, 461
San Agustin (ship) 71
San Antonio 140, **383**, 405
Sanderson, Robert 26
San Diego, California 140, 337, 373, **383**
Sandwich Islands 92, 232
Sandys, Edwin 464
Sandys, George **383**
San Ildefonso, Treaty of 290
Sanitation 113-114
San Salvador 82
Santa Fe, New Mexico 140, **383**, 405
and Old Spanish Trail **313-314**
Roads and trails 373
and Roman Catholic Church 375
Santa Maria (ship) 82
Santee River 424
Santiago (ship) 186
San Xavier del Bac 272
Saratoga, Battle of 236, 341

Saratoga, New York 303
Sargent, Winthrop 284
Sarsi Indians 177
Sassacus 327, **383**, 429
Sassamon, John 268
Sault Sainte Marie **383**
Saunders, Richard 335
Saur, Christopher 325
Savannah, Georgia **383-384**
Savannah River 165, 424
Sawmills 271
Saybrook Platform 87
Sayle, William 67
Sayre, Stephen **384**
Scalping **384**
Scaticook Indians 442
Schools—*See Education*
Schuyler, Gertrude 430
Schuyler, Philip John 89, 278, 362, **384**, 430
Schuyler, Robert 278
Schwenkfelders 324
Science 43, 128, 220, 371-372, **384-385**, 456
Scioto Path 177
Scorpion (ship) 19
Seabury, Samuel **385-386**
Sea Captain's Club 398
Searle, James **386**
Sears, Isaac **386**
"Seasoning" 113
Second Hundred Years' War 48-49, 362
Segresser, Felipe **386**
Seigneurial system 151
Self-sufficient and market farming 193, **386-387**
Seminole Indians 4, **387**, 394
Senauki 422
Seneca Indians 105, 141, 169, 211, 224, 304, 332, 335, 354, 391
Separatists 17-18, 45
Serapis (ship) 220
Serra, Junipero 143, 242, 337, 373, 383
387
Serrano Indians 57
Seven Nations Confederacy 15
Seven Years' War—*See French and Indian War*
Sevier, John 145, 374, **387-388**, 445
Seville, Treaty of 21
Seward, William 9
Shackamaxon, Treaty of **388**, 416
Shakers 233, **388**
Shakespeare, William 161
Shasta Indians 57
Shawnee Indians 93, 141, 205, 207, 212, 324, 332, 335, 389
and French and Indian War 209
Lord Dunmore's War **241-242**
and Revolutionary War 209
Shays, Daniel 388
Shays' Rebellion 44, 88, 236, 261, 341, 355, **388**
Shelburne, William Petty 389
Shelby, Isaac **389**
Shelekhov, Gregor Ivanovich 9, 134, **389**
Shepard, Thomas 236
Sherman, Roger **389**, 1032
Shikellamy, Chief **389-390**

Other titles of interest